SECURITIES REGULATION: CASES AND ANALYSIS

by

STEPHEN J. CHOI
Professor of Law
New York University Law School

A.C. PRITCHARD
Professor of Law
University of Michigan Law School

FOUNDATION PRESS
NEW YORK, NEW YORK
2005

© 2005 By FOUNDATION PRESS

    395 Hudson Street
    New York, NY 10014
    Phone Toll Free 1–877–888–1330
    Fax (212) 367–6799
    fdpress.com

Printed in the United States of America

ISBN 1–58778–903–5

 TEXT IS PRINTED ON 10% POST CONSUMER RECYCLED PAPER

Stephen Choi

To Un Kyung, Una, Sehan, and Sejin.

Adam Pritchard

To Joan, Liza, and Ben.

*

PREFACE

The United States enjoys the largest and best policed capital markets in the world. Since the Great Depression, the Securities and Exchange Commission ("SEC") has overseen the regulation of much of the securities markets, enforcing and interpreting the federal securities laws. Over this time period, the securities markets have seen great technological changes. And with these changes have come corresponding additions, reforms, and only rarely, subtractions, from the securities laws. The reforms continue. Recently, Congress enacted the Sarbanes-Oxley Act of 2002 in response to the scandals at Enron, WorldCom and other large, publicly-held corporations. In 2005, the SEC reformed the "gun-jumping" rules that govern the public offering process.

Our approach in this first edition of *Securities Regulation: Cases and Analysis* is to provide enough material for a three or four credit hour basic class in securities regulation offered at virtually every law school. It is specifically not intended for more advanced classes in securities regulation. We have included only the topics covered in most basic classes, such as materiality, the definition of a security, public offerings, etc. Accordingly, some topics covered in other books, such as broker-dealer regulation and investment companies, are omitted. This allows us to produce a much shorter book than the average for the field without sacrificing depth of coverage for the topics that are included. Students and Professors will find additional material relating to the book at our website, http://www.choipritchard.com, including a Glossary of technical terms and suggested readings to go with each chapter.

Because securities regulation is constantly evolving, we start with the underlying business problem facing companies and investors. Each chapter begins with a brief essay laying out the economics of the subject of the chapter. Securities markets are all about money, so understanding the economic incentives of the various actors is essential to understanding the effects of the regulatory regime (and efforts to reform the regime). We have tried to present the economics in a way that appeals to common sense and intuition; we have scrupulously avoided bogging the book down with mathematical models and references to studies in finance journals. We also include in these discussions, and at various points throughout the book, insights from the field of behavioral law and economics.

The common sense approach is reinforced by organizing each chapter around a single "Motivating Hypothetical." The Motivating Hypothetical introduces a business, its principal officers, and a business problem or need. The scenario is chosen to be a typical situation that the students are likely to see in practice. We then present hypotheticals throughout the chapter that build on the Motivating Hypothetical. By relying on the Motivating Hypothetical throughout the chapter we avoid having to introduce a new set of facts for each of the hypotheticals. The hypotheticals challenge the students to apply the legal rules presented in the cases and materials and allow the professor to spend class time on a real-world problem, rather than simply going over the cases and statutes.

We also include questions in the introductory paragraphs that precede each of the cases. These questions are designed to focus the students on the main issue addressed by the case. We then include a series of questions after each of the cases to push the students to see the practical implications of the court's holding and reasoning. If you can answer the questions and hypotheticals, you are doing a good job with your reading. In addition to the hypotheticals and questions, we also include Notes that cover topics not found in the cases and other primary materials. Interspersing the Notes with the primary materials allows us to present important points in a logical order and a concise fashion.

We make extensive use of charts and tables to present the material in a way that crystallizes the most important points. Many areas in the securities laws, such as public offerings and resales, involve a number of statutes and regulations intersecting to create the operative legal regime. It is easy for students to get lost in the dense language of the statutes and regulations; it only becomes worse when the need arises to understand how the rules and regulations interact. Our graphic presentations help focus students on those interactions.

Finally, we present the material in a different order than is used in most books. Most books, after some introductory material, present the securities laws in their historical sequence, i.e., first covering the Securities Act of 1933 and then turning to the Exchange Act of 1934. We have reversed the usual order, presenting the Exchange Act first, and leaving the Securities Act for later in the book. Our rationale for presenting the Exchange Act first is that the law is more inclusive. The Exchange Act applies to all public companies (indeed, it defines what a public company is) and its antifraud provisions apply to all disclosures made by those companies and their affiliates. The individual chapters generally stand on their own, however, so professors who prefer the more traditional order can easily adapt the book to their needs.

STEPHEN J. CHOI
A.C. PRITCHARD

June, 2005

EDITORIAL NOTE AND ACKNOWLEDGMENTS

As with other casebooks, in our editing of the cases, we omit most footnotes and case and statute citations without indication. Footnote numbers in cases are as in the original, with no renumbering to take account of omitted footnotes.

We have many people to thank for helping with this book at various stages. We thank Dale Oesterle, Alan Palmiter, Eung Chil Park, Hillary Sale, and Bill Williams for their helpful comments on drafts of this book. We also thank the many law students who served as our "guinea pigs" with the draft version of the book. Their sacrifices have made for a better finished product. We also thank Dexter Eng, Meg Holzer, Alice Kim, Mario Mendolaro, Serena Palumbo, and Yaman Shukairy for their invaluable research and editorial assistance. Three others deserve special thanks for contributions above and beyond the call of duty. Sahar Kianfar was our tech wizard, designing both our PowerPoint slides and our website. Janis Proctor showed remarkable patience in word processing through multiple revisions. Un Kyung Park provided constant editorial revisions (particularly to Choi's sometimes uneven prose). Finally, Pritchard acknowledges the generous support of the Elkes Fund for Faculty Excellence in the Law, which allowed him the release time to complete this book.

We are grateful for permission to reprint copyrighted material from *Remarks of Milton Freeman, Conference on Codification of the Federal Securities Laws*, 22 Bus. Law. 793, 922 (1967). Copyright © 1967 by the American Bar Association. Reprinted with the permission of The Business Lawyer and the estate of Milton Freeman.

With any luck, we will be producing a second edition of this book in a few years. We would be delighted to hear from our fellow securities regulation professors with any criticisms or suggestions. We will do our best to make the second edition better for both students and professors. We hope you enjoy the book.

*

SUMMARY OF CONTENTS

*

TABLE OF CONTENTS

*

TABLE OF CASES

Principal cases are in bold type. Non-principal cases are in roman type. References are to Pages.

*

SECURITIES REGULATION: CASES AND ANALYSIS

*

CHAPTER 1

INTRODUCTION TO THE SECURITIES MARKETS AND SECURITIES REGULATION

MOTIVATING HYPOTHETICAL

Extreme Inc. manufactures extreme sports equipment in Jackson Hole, Wyoming. Marcel, Extreme's CEO, founded Extreme twenty years ago. Today, Extreme has $5 billion in common stock publicly traded on the New York Stock Exchange (NYSE). Extreme's common stock currently trades at a price of $20 per share. Analysts working for various investment banks distribute regular opinions on Extreme; on average, they rate Extreme's stock a "Buy." Jennifer, an individual investor residing in New York, is considering whether to use $10,000 she recently won in the state lottery to purchase Extreme shares through her broker, who will execute the transaction through the New York Stock Exchange.

I. THE BASICS

Congress enacted the federal securities laws in the 1930s in the midst of the Great Depression. Congress' goal was to protect investors who were considering putting capital into the country's financial markets from abuses by company insiders and market professionals. Those laws seek to protect investors by encouraging full disclosure and deterring fraud.

The federal securities laws regulate transactions involving financial instruments falling within the definition of a "security." The most prevalent types of securities include common stock, preferred stock, and bonds.

Securities transactions can be divided into two basic categories. In a "primary" transaction, a company (the "issuer") offers and sells its own securities to investors, taking the proceeds into the issuer's coffers. In a "secondary" transaction, one investor resells securities of the issuer to another investor. The issuer does not participate in the transaction and no money in a secondary transaction goes to the issuer. Instead, money transfers from the buying investor to the selling investor. If Jennifer purchases Extreme shares through a broker who executes the transaction on the NYSE, she will purchase the shares from another investor seeking to sell the securities.

In securities transactions, information is money. Those investors armed with an informational advantage (such as insiders of a company) are able to obtain systematically higher returns from their trades than un-informed investors. Marcel, the CEO of Extreme Inc., will have access to non-public information on Extreme's finances, strategic plans, and merger and acquisition opportunities. Left unregulated, Marcel could buy Extreme stock when the market undervalues the stock and sell stock when it is overvalued. Jennifer, the outside investor considering an Extreme invest-ment, however, suffers from a corresponding informational disadvantage. Any gains that Marcel makes from trading come dollar-for-dollar at the expense of investors like Jennifer.

Securities market analysts may help Jennifer partially overcome her informational disadvantage. Analysts, however, lack the same access to information as a corporate insider. Analysts also may not always provide the best advice. Sell-side analysts employed within a large brokerage firm may face pressure (as highlighted by the New York State Attorney General's investigation of Merrill Lynch in 2002) to provide overly optimistic ratings as a means of drumming up investment banking business for the brokerage firm. Can we really trust a "buy" rating?

The U.S. securities regime relies primarily on disclosure by those with an advantage in the markets, including, among others, insiders of corpora-tions. The two most important federal securities laws are the Securities Act of 1933 ("Securities Act"; practitioners sometimes call it the " '33 Act") and the Securities Exchange Act of 1934 ("Exchange Act"; practitioners sometimes call it the " '34 Act"). These statutes will be our main focus in this book. The Securities Act focuses on primary transactions by an issuing company selling securities to investors. The Exchange Act deals with secondary transactions between two investors in the marketplace; it also regulates securities market intermediaries, including broker-dealers and the securities exchanges. To assist in the protection of investors and the capital markets, Congress also established the Securities and Exchange Commission (SEC) when it enacted the Exchange Act. The SEC, an independent administrative agency, develops rules and regulations to inter-pret and implement the securities laws passed by Congress and enforces those statutes and regulations.

Before exploring the federal securities laws, we first outline the most common types of securities investments and the markets in which investors transact in these securities. We then ask why people invest in securities rather than other forms of saving. Finally, we focus on the valuation of securities. At the right price almost any investment becomes attractive to investors. What determines the price an investor is willing to pay for a particular investment? What information does an investor need to calculate this price?

II. TYPES OF SECURITIES

Where to invest? An investor can put money into a bank account. The investor could invest in real estate, making a bet that the price of land will rise. Alternatively, the investor may purchase publicly-traded stocks or bonds in the capital markets. Securities regulation covers only a subset of the available investment vehicles.

We leave the definition of "security" for purposes of federal securities regulation to a more detailed analysis in Chapter 3. Some investments, however, clearly fit the definition. The most common form of securities investments involves interests in a corporate entity. Corporations are legal entities created under state law. Most public corporations choose Delaware as their state of incorporation. Under Delaware corporate law, corporations have great flexibility in issuing different ownership interests in the corporation, including common stock, preferred stock and bonds.

How do these varying ownership interests differ? Ownership encompasses several different attributes, including rights to (1) cash flows, (2) assets in liquidation, and (3) voting power, which, among other things, allows shareholders to elect the corporate board of directors. The diverse forms of ownership interests in a corporation allow investors to obtain different "bundles" of these rights.

Corporations enjoy great latitude in altering the general packages of rights for the different classes of securities. Nonetheless, the three basic types of securities—common, preferred, and debt—have typical characteristics as summarized in the table below.

Type of Security	Cash Flow Rights	Liquidation Rights	Voting Rights
Common	Residual and discretionary dividend	Residual	Yes
Preferred	Fixed and discretionary dividend	Medium	Contingent (e.g., if dividend not paid for certain number of quarters)
Debt	Fixed and certain interest payment	Highest	None

A. COMMON STOCK

Common stock gives investors the greatest amount of voting control over the corporation. Common shareholders typically receive most, if not all, of the votes to elect the board of directors. Under state corporate law, the directors and officers of a corporation owe a fiduciary duty to the common stockholders and the corporation. That duty encompasses both a duty of care as well as a duty of loyalty in pursuing the best interests of the shareholders.

In contrast to their strong voting rights, common stockholders enjoy no fixed monetary claim on the cash flows of a corporation. Instead, common stock is "residual"—the owners of common stock receive a share of corporate profits only after the claims of all other ownership interests are satisfied (i.e., the claims of debt and preferred stockholders). Even then, corporations are not obliged to distribute money to their common stockholders. Distribution of assets to common stockholders is at the board of directors' discretion.

Corporations may distribute assets to shareholders either by issuing dividends or by repurchasing stock from the shareholders. (Less commonly, they can also distribute assets to shareholders in liquidation.) Dividends, if declared by the board, must be distributed pro rata among a given class of shares. Stock repurchases, however, may occur through private negotiation, open market transactions, or, if for a larger number of shares, through a repurchase tender offer. Of these types of repurchases, only tender offers must be pro rata.

Why would a board ever declare a dividend or repurchase shares? Under state corporate law, the board of directors owes fiduciary duties of loyalty and care to the common shareholders. Such duties provide a (weak) legal impetus for the board to declare a dividend if the corporation has no better use for the capital. Of course, dividends are not always in the best interests of the shareholders. Corporations with cash-intensive investment projects that will pay off handsomely in the future may choose not to pay dividends. Accordingly, the business judgment rule ordinarily protects a board's decision not to declare a dividend. The business judgment rule does not protect the board if the shareholders decide to express their displeasure with a lack of dividends by electing a new board of directors. But the directors and officers of a corporation can generally rely on the passivity of dispersed public shareholders to prevent the election of a new board; their positions are relatively secure.

Tax consequences also affect a firm's decision to pay dividends. Until recently, dividends paid out to individuals were taxed at ordinary income rates. Because publicly-traded corporations already pay taxes on income at the corporate tax rate, the tax on dividends represents a second tax on the same income. Corporations (with shareholders' tacit approval) would avoid the double tax by retaining earnings, eschewing dividend payments. In 2003, Congress lowered the maximum tax rate on dividends to 15% (down from the maximum ordinary income rate at the time of 38.6%). Prompted by the reduction in dividend taxes, Microsoft and other companies declared large dividends. In Microsoft's case, $32 billion in dividends was distributed in December, 2004. Personal income in the United States rose by 3.7% in the same month, a sharp jump attributable in large part to Microsoft's dividend.

Finally, common stock provides investors with the weakest claim on corporate assets in liquidation. Companies facing liquidation must typically pay out assets according to the absolute priority rule. Under the absolute priority rule, common stockholders come last among the holders of a corporation's securities. In a corporation, debt holders typically come first, receiving any assets in liquidation, up to the principal amount and unpaid interest, before common shareholders receive anything. (There is also a priority among debt holders, with creditors holding liens on specific assets, the "secured creditors," getting paid first.) Preferred shares, discussed below, typically come second. The absolute priority rule stipulates that only after the contracted-for claims of debt holders and preferred shareholders are satisfied will common shareholders receive anything in liquidation. The absolute priority rule, however, is not always followed. Particularly in Chapter 11 bankruptcy reorganizations, shareholders may bargain for claims on the corporation's assets that would otherwise go to pay more senior securities holders under the absolute priority rule. We leave a more detailed discussion of bankruptcy to a course in corporate reorganizations.

B. PREFERRED STOCK

Many corporations only have one class of equity securities: common stock. Some corporations, however, will issue another, more senior class of equity securities, generally referred to as "preferred" stock. State corporate law does not mandate or even specify the exact characteristics of preferred stock. Indeed, many corporations will call securities with characteristics similar to preferred stock by a different name (e.g., Class A common stock or some other variant).

Why do some corporations use preferred stock while others do not? Corporations typically issue preferred stock in two situations. First, relatively new (and non-publicly-traded) startup companies will often issue preferred stock to outside investors providing capital. During the late 1990s, many would-be entrepreneurs started companies to sell dog food, books, pharmaceuticals, and a whole host of other products and services over the Internet. At the time, many of these companies seemed promising but highly risky. Some companies were started in people's garages or bedrooms. The Internet provided the entrepreneurs with a vast new commercial space in which to compete. To compete effectively and grab market share quickly, the Internet startup companies needed large and quick infusions of capital. Although some entrepreneurs provided significant financial resources out of their own pockets, many did not have the millions of dollars necessary to expand a business rapidly enough to cover the national marketplace.

Outside investors provided a solution for the cash-strapped Internet entrepreneurs. For Internet startup companies, venture capital firms formed the primary source of initial outside money. Venture capital firms specialize in obtaining funds from other investors (which the venture capitalists typically pool into a particular venture fund) and re-investing such funds into mid- and late-stage (i.e., almost ready to go public) startup companies. Venture capital firms provide expertise in identifying promising startup companies. After an investment is made, venture capital firms also provide management advice as well as business contacts for the startup companies (with potential suppliers, customers, employees, etc.). In addition, venture capital firms often obtain seats on the boards of directors of the startup companies, sometimes even a majority position, to ensure some degree of control over the direction of the company.

Venture capital firms making an investment in a startup company often structure the investment as preferred stock. Investing in preferred stock gives a venture capital firm some reassurance that if the high-risk startup company performs poorly, the venture capital firm will have the ability to receive at least some of the money back before the entrepreneurs—who typically hold common stock—receive anything. In addition, preferred stock gives the venture capitalists some upside return, albeit not as great as common stock, if the startup does well. Much of the preferred stock issued to venture capital firms carries the right to convert into common stock (at a predetermined price) at the discretion of the preferred stockholder. Convertible preferred stock provides the venture capitalists with an even greater ability to share in the upside of the startup if it does an initial public offering (IPO).

A relatively recent type of preferred stock is the "participating preferred." Venture capital investors in pre-IPO companies often negotiate for participating preferred shares in return for their investment. Participating preferred shares allow holders the right to residual distributions as if they held an equivalent number of common shares. If common shareholders are paid a dividend of $10 per share then participating preferred shares also receive the same $10 per share. Unlike common, however, participating preferred holders are entitled to a preference over common shareholders in getting their initial investment back upon liquidation. For pre-IPO companies that succeed, participating preferred performs like common stock. For less successful companies, participating preferred operates more like debt, providing its holders some protection from the downside risk of the investment.

Preferred stock is also used by older, more established companies that need an infusion of cash. Warren Buffett of Omaha, Nebraska, one of the most successful investors of recent times, specializes in finding undervalued companies and making a relatively large investment in them, sometimes even purchasing the entire company. Buffett (through his investment vehicle Berkshire Hathaway) has purchased, among other companies, See's Candy, GEICO Insurance, and Dairy Queen. If Warren Buffett does not buy an entire company, he often takes a large position by investing in the preferred stock of the corporation. Investing in preferred stock provides Buffett with some reassurance of getting paid back his investment, at least before common stockholders receive money, while allowing Buffett to share in much of the upside if the company does well. Typically there is a reason why an established company needs an infusion of cash (i.e., the company is in trouble) and the reassurance provided by holding preferred rather than common stock is particularly valuable.

Companies in which Buffett has taken a preferred stock position include Gillette, USAir, and Salomon Brothers. Take the example of USAir (Buffett's admittedly worst investment decision). In 1989, Buffett injected $358 million into USAir in return for 9.25% of its preferred stock. Buffett hoped that the ownership of a "senior" security with a provision for dividends paid at 9.25% annually would protect him against the risks involved with investing in USAir at the time. Although the 9.25% dividend payment was not mandatory (but simply cumulated if not paid), Buffett wrote a penalty clause into the preferred stock purchase contract, providing for a penalty dividend (raising the dividend payment rate to between 13.25% and 14%) for any unpaid dividends. When USAir eventually ran into substantial financial difficulties in the early 1990s, Berkshire Hathaway was able to collect hundreds of millions of dollars in dividends over the time period as a result of its preferred stock investment.

Why is preferred stock "preferred"? First, consider the rights to a corporation's ongoing cash flows. Common stockholders have no absolute right to cash flows, instead depending on the discretion of the board of directors to declare a dividend or stock repurchase. Common stockholders, nonetheless, may rely on the board of directors (as obligated under the board's fiduciary duties to common stockholders) to at least consider the best interests of the common stockholders. Preferred stockholders, like holders of corporate debt such as bonds, generally enjoy no such open-ended fiduciary duty protection; they must look instead to their preferred stock contract to protect their rights. (Fiduciary duties may, however, fill in the interstices of these contractual rights.)

With respect to ongoing cash flows, preferred stock does not receive interest from the corporation, but instead is entitled to a "fixed" dividend payment. As with common stock, preferred stock gives corporations flexibility in determining the best use of scarce resources. Without the protection of fiduciary duties, preferred stock contracts typically will specify that the fixed dividend owed to preferred stockholders must be paid before common stockholders receive any dividends. Moreover, any unpaid preferred stock dividends cumulate over time and all arrearages must be paid before common shareholders receive any dividend. As with Berkshire Hathaway's preferred stock contract with USAir, the amount of the dividend may increase due to a penalty provision for missed dividend payments.

In liquidation, preferred stock comes before common stock. Preferred stock contracts typically specify that preferred stockholders receive any cumulated, unpaid dividends in addition to (at least in theory) a contracted-for share of any remaining assets before common stockholders receive any payment in liquidation. Unlike common stock, preferred stock generally does not enjoy voting rights. As with most other aspects of securities, however, corporations and investors may tailor different packages of rights to meet their needs. Usually, preferred stock contracts will provide that if dividends to the preferred stockholders are missed for a certain number of quarters (typically two or three), then preferred stockholders will receive some voting rights to elect the board of directors. Other preferred stock contracts may specify that the preferred stockholders have the power to elect some fraction of the board of directors (e.g., two directors out of seven).

Preferred stock may feature many other contractual provisions. Because these rights are negotiated between specific investors and corporations, preferred stocks vary greatly in their terms. Some preferred stock-holders enjoy conversion rights that allow them to convert their preferred shares into a specified number of common shares. Warren Buffett's preferred stock investment in USAir included such a conversion right into common stock. While the dividend for preferred shares is fixed and more certain than the dividend for common shares, the residual dividend interest of common shares may be more valuable under certain circumstances. For example, imagine that an Internet startup company has two classes of shares: common and preferred stock, with the preferred paying a fixed dividend of $1 per share. If the corporation earns $100 per share of common stock in net earnings per year (after the preferred shares are paid their dividends), the common stock has a much more valuable interest in the company. A conversion feature allows preferred stockholders to share in the greater financial interest by converting their preferred stock into common stock.

C. BONDS

Bonds are a loan by investors to the corporation. Bonds may take many different forms in the public capital markets, including notes (typically shorter-term debt of a maturity period less than ten years) and indentures (longer-term bonds). The initial investment an investor makes in a bond is known as the principal amount. Unlike equity, bonds have a fixed term and the principal invested is repaid at a specified maturity date. Corporations owe bondholders fixed and certain periodic interest payments until the maturity date of the bond.

Not all bonds pay periodic interest. Zero coupon bonds pay no interest. Instead, they are sold at a discount relative to the principal amount of the bond. At the end of the maturity, the bondholders receive the full principal amount. The value of the bonds grows from the initial, discounted purchase price to the end principal payment, thereby providing an implicit interest payment equal to the growth in value of the principal amount of the bond over time. Zero coupon bonds allow issuers to obtain capital by issuing bonds without having to meet yearly interest payments. Instead, the full amount of implicit interest—along with the principal invested—is due at the maturity date of the bond.

As a debt instrument, bonds provide investors with much greater financial security compared to equity investments (i.e., common and preferred stock). As noted above, bondholders enjoy priority over equity in the case of liquidation. Bonds may also vary in their priority position with respect to other debt of the same issuer. Corporations may issue "senior" bonds that receive priority in payments over junior bonds. Some bondholders may also obtain a security interest in a specific asset of the corporation, providing even greater security (up to the value of the encumbered asset) for the repayment of the debt.

In theory, bondholders must all receive their principal amount as well as any interest payments owed before equity receives even a penny in liquidation. In practice, the federal bankruptcy regime furnishes a mechanism for equity to be paid even if debt is not fully paid off, providing for a limited route around the absolute priority rule. Even if the absolute priority rule is followed, priority does not help bondholders if the company has few assets left to distribute. To avoid this unpleasant situation, bond holders turn to contract for protection. Bond covenants typically include a number of provisions to ensure that the corporation will maintain an adequate equity "cushion" providing for sufficient resources both to make the periodic interest payments and cover the principal owed on the bonds. Such provisions are all negotiated and may therefore vary across different bonds. Among such provisions are restrictions on the ability of the corporation to make dividends to its shareholders, sell specific assets, and exceed a specified debt-equity ratio.

HYPOTHETICAL ONE

Extreme, Inc. needs to raise more capital to expand its marketing efforts into Asia. Parachuting off the rapidly growing number of skyscrapers in Seoul, Jakarta, and other cities has become quite the rage. Marcel, the CEO of Extreme, proposes to issue a number of different securities. Put yourself in the shoes of Extreme's chief financial officer. What advice would you give Marcel on the pros and cons of issuing each of the following types of securities from the perspective of maximizing the value of Extreme for its present common stockholders?

1. *Debt.* Extreme will offer $500 million of debt securities paying an interest rate of 15% and maturing in ten years. The debt securities take priority over Extreme's common stock but their payment is not secured by any of Extreme's assets.

2. *Units of securities termed "Nadas."* The "Nada" units will provide no rights to ordinary dividends or interest, no rights to assets in liquidation, and no voting rights. All Nada unit holders, however, are entitled to an autographed picture of Marcel, the CEO of Extreme, once a year. In addition, Extreme will select, at random, one unit holder per year for the next ten years who will receive a special dividend of $10 million. Marcel hopes to offer the Nada at a price of $50 per unit (selling 10 million units to the public).

III. THE CAPITAL MARKET

Securities transactions can take place in a number of different venues. An individual owner of Extreme Inc. common stock may sell the securities through a negotiated transaction with her neighbor. To close the deal, the individual owner may transfer the stock certificates in Extreme to the neighbor in exchange for cash in a face-to-face transaction.

Individually negotiated deals of this sort are unusual; most securities transactions take place through organized markets with the assistance of professional securities market intermediaries (i.e., broker-dealers). What advantages do organized markets and professional intermediaries provide to investors seeking to purchase or sell securities?

Organized markets provide investors with liquidity and transparency. Without an organized marketplace, individual investors seeking to sell a security may spend a lot of time and money finding an investor willing to purchase the security. Even if the selling investor locates a potential purchaser, the seller has no assurance that he is receiving the best price for the securities. In an organized market, a selling investor can quickly find others seeking to purchase his securities. Intermediaries may also assist in creating liquidity, standing in to purchase or sell securities when other investors are unwilling to do so. Information on the trades (and offers) of other investors may also flow more easily in an organized market, providing transparency. With transparency, investors can determine the best available prices for their desired transactions.

As noted above, securities regulation divides securities market transactions into two basic types. First, corporations may sell their own securities into the marketplace, a primary market transaction. Second, investors may enter into a securities transaction with one another, a secondary market transaction.

A. PRIMARY MARKET TRANSACTIONS

Primary market transactions range from large multi-country offerings raising billions of dollars to smaller deals for a million dollars or less taking place solely in the United States. Companies typically turn to the capital markets when they need a large amount of money to finance a profitable business project. Extreme Inc., for example, requires additional funds to expand into the skyscraper parachuting market in Asia.

Large, well-established companies such as Microsoft and IBM often have a number of different sources of capital. Microsoft, for example, enjoys a significant amount of cash built up over the years from its highly profitable software business, although its massive dividend payout at the end of 2004 significantly cut into this cash reserve. Retained earnings eliminate the need to turn to the public capital markets to finance new lines of business. Companies with lesser cash flows such as Extreme must issue securities to the public capital markets if they need a large amount of funds to exploit growth opportunities.

Although issuers may sell securities directly to investors without the assistance of any securities market institutions, such offerings are rare (and typically are done as "rights" offerings to an issuer's pre-existing shareholders and not to the general public). Instead, issuers will employ a number of different intermediaries to assist in a large offering of securities. Many of the institutions are located on Wall Street and play a major role in both primary and secondary market transactions. Major Wall Street securities houses today include Goldman Sachs, Morgan Stanley, Merrill Lynch, and CS First Boston, among others. Commercial banks, including Citigroup and J.P. Morgan Chase, also play an increasingly important role in securities transactions. Although we discuss the public offering process more fully in Chapter 7, we briefly describe the different institutions below.

Underwriters. Many of the large Wall Street financial firms have investment banking divisions. Among other things, the investment banks assist issuers seeking to make a public offering of securities to investors. The investment banks provide advice and financial expertise, particularly for companies going public for the first time. In addition, the investment banks may play an underwriting role, taking on the financial risk that the offering will not sell to investors. In a firm commitment offering, for example, a syndicate of underwriters will purchase securities at a discount from the issuer. The underwriters then bear the full risk of being able to sell the offering to the public. The underwriters are compensated for this risk by the "spread," the difference between the discounted price they pay the issuer and the price paid by the investing public.

Attorneys. Attorneys are a ubiquitous feature in commercial transactions. (Good news for your career prospects!) For securities offerings, a specialized set of law firms routinely assists both issuers and investment banks in complying with the regulatory requirement for a public offering. These firms include Cravath, Swaine and Moore, Cleary Gottlieb, and Sullivan and Cromwell among other major New York City-based law firms. The attorneys for the issuer will typically take the lead role in drafting disclosures to be filed with the SEC.

Accounting Firms. The value of an investment is determined by the expected return from the investment into the future. That return depends on the financial performance of the business: more future profits for the business typically translate into greater returns for the investor. Past financial performance, however, can provide the investor with an important glimpse into a company's financial future. Companies with fast growth in sales may be more likely to experience future growth. Companies with declining profit margins and stagnant or declining sales, in contrast, may present a more bleak financial future for investors.

Despite the importance of past financial performance in determining the value of an investment, investors face a crucial risk in using historical financial information. Unscrupulous management may "cook the books" and falsify financial numbers. If sales grew to only $10 million for the prior quarter, a manager may make the company look better in the eyes of investors by changing this number to $20 million with a couple of keystrokes on her computer.

Things are rarely so simple. If investors realize the ease with which managers may falsify financial numbers, the investors will lose confidence in the reported numbers and demand a large discount before they buy shares from issuers. Audited financial statements provide one way that companies may help convince investors of the veracity of their financial disclosures. Accounting firms such as the "Big Four" of Deloitte Touche Tohmatsu, Ernst & Young, KPMG and PricewaterhouseCoopers, among others, provide such auditing services.

Public accounting firms rely in part on their longstanding reputations for honesty and accuracy to convince investors to accept audited financials as truthful. An accounting firm with a better reputation can better attract clients and charge higher fees. Thus, accounting firms have a strong incentive to maintain their reputations. Audits, however, are not foolproof. If the audit partner for a particular client cuts corners or succumbs to pressure from company management to provide falsified financials, investors will receive inaccurate information. The collapse of Arthur Andersen—formerly a "Big Five" accounting firm—was in large part due to the acquiescence of the lead Arthur Andersen partner in Enron's financial shenanigans. At the time of its collapse, Enron was the largest public company ever to file for bankruptcy. The subsequent criminal prosecution of Arthur Andersen for obstructing the SEC's investigation into the fall of Enron drew headlines for months. In response to Arthur Andersen's role in Enron, Congress enacted the Sarbanes–Oxley Act of 2002, which provided, among other things, for extensive reforms of the oversight of public company auditors in the United States (a topic we cover in Chapter 4).

Institutional Investors. Institutional investors are the dominant force in today's securities markets. Mutual funds aggregate the investment money of many smaller investors and reinvest the funds in securities. Mutual funds have two primary styles for allocating their investment dollars. Index funds reinvest the funds into a defined broad-based basket of securities. Vanguard's S & P 500 fund, for example, invests in a value-weighted basket of companies comprising the S & P list of America's 500 biggest companies. This casebook's authors are long-term investors in index mutual funds. Actively-managed funds, in contrast, research (at some cost) various investment opportunities to determine where best to put the investors' money. Although active management in theory may result in better investment opportunities, investors must pay for the privilege of active management, bearing much higher fund expenses on average than investors in index funds. The available research suggests that these greater fund expenses cause the average actively-managed fund to trail both the overall market and index funds (which generally aspire only to match the market). Other institutional investors include pension funds and insurance companies.

The presence of institutional investors in the primary offering market has two countervailing consequences for the regulation of public offerings. On the one hand, institutional investors are sophisticated investors who arguably require less protection. On the other hand, institutional investors may cut "sweetheart" deals for themselves with the issuers or underwriters. In the late 1990s, underwriters would commonly allocate a larger share of hot initial public offering stock to favored institutional investors. The favored investors, in turn, would promise to purchase stock in the after-market, driving up the price of the IPO stock (a practice known as "IPO laddering"). The institutional investors would then exit from the stock at a profit, leaving smaller retail investors holding the overpriced IPO stock. The SEC brought major enforcement actions against participants in the IPO laddering scandal, obtaining large settlements from several of the major investment banks. Such schemes suggest that ordinary small investors may need protection from the big players.

B.   SECONDARY MARKET TRANSACTIONS

The secondary market is closely linked to primary market transactions. Through an active secondary market, investors can resell securities both quickly and at a low cost, giving the investors liquidity. Investors also care about transacting in markets with good price transparency, in which the market price will reflect the best available price for a transaction in a particular security. Investors who can rely on a liquid and transparent secondary market in which to resell their securities will be more willing to purchase securities in the first place. Without the prospect of a strong secondary market, issuers face considerable difficulty in selling securities to investors, who will demand a substantial "illiquidity" discount.

Secondary market transactions between investors take place in several different venues. Some secondary market transactions occur through negotiated one-on-one transactions. Larger institutional investors in particular may engage in block transactions, selling and purchasing large numbers of shares in a particular company through a negotiated deal. Smaller investors will use brokers to execute their transactions. Among large brokerage firms dealing with individual investors are Merrill Lynch, Morgan Stanley, Charles Schwab, and E*TRADE FINANCIAL.

There are two common types of orders in the secondary markets. First, investors may make a "market" order, indicating the investor would like to purchase a specified number of shares in a company at the best available market price. Second, investors may place a "limit" order. An investor placing a limit order specifies both the number of shares as well as the limit price. Brokers are instructed not to execute the limit order until the market price reaches (or is better than) the specified limit price. Jennifer, for example, could specify that she would like to purchase 1,000 shares of Extreme at a price of $18 per share. Suppose the current market price of Extreme is $20 per share. Jennifer's order will not be executed until Extreme's price falls to $18 or lower.

When a broker receives a trade execution order from a customer, the broker may attempt to match a particular trade order with trade orders submitted by the brokers' other customers (matching a buy order with a corresponding sell order, for example). For orders where no internal match exists, the broker will then route the order to some trading forum to receive trade execution. The three primary forms of third-party maintained markets include (1) the organized securities exchanges, (2) Nasdaq, and (3) electronic communication networks (ECNs).

1.   SECURITIES EXCHANGES

Several organized securities exchanges operate in the United States. The most prominent of these markets is the New York Stock Exchange (NYSE). There are other securities exchanges, including the American Stock Exchange (AMEX), the Boston Stock Exchange, the Pacific Stock Exchange, and the Philadelphia Stock Exchange. Major stock exchanges outside the United States include the London Stock Exchange, the

Deutsche Bourse, and the Tokyo Stock Exchange. Increasingly, securities of large, multinational companies are traded in more than one securities market.

Organized securities exchanges have historically been characterized by the presence of a physical trading floor. Although investors typically cannot interact with others directly on the trading floor of an exchange, they may do so through brokers. Trades routed to the NYSE that are not completed by the NYSE's electronic order system end up in the hands of a broker working on the trading floor at the NYSE (known as a "floor broker") for execution. Over 800 brokers operate on the NYSE trading floor.

Floor brokers have several options in executing their customers' trades. The NYSE maintains twenty trading posts, each manned by a specialist. Specialist firms on the NYSE include LaBranche & Co. and Spear, Leeds & Kellogg (a unit of Goldman Sachs). A particular traded security is assigned one specialist and one trading post. Floor brokers interested in trading the security congregate around the trading post where they can obtain continuous information on the latest transaction price in the security. Floor brokers may execute trades with other brokers on the floor seeking to make the opposite transaction.

The specialist for a particular stock plays a central role in maintaining liquidity for that stock. Instead of executing an order themselves, floor brokers may employ the specialist as an agent. The specialist maintains a limit order book, listing various limit orders received from floor brokers, which consist of a desired quantity and price for the purchase or sale of a security. As the market price moves to a particular limit price, the specialist will assist in the execution of these limit orders, matching together customer orders. The specialist also maintains its own inventory of stock. When short-term imbalances result in insufficient trade volume to match opposing trades, the NYSE requires specialists to maintain liquidity by trading out of their own inventory. So the specialist must sell when other investors are unwilling to sell and must buy when other investors are unwilling to buy (after making appropriate adjustment in the price of the security).

The role of specialists has not been without controversy. In 2004, the NYSE and SEC reached settlements with many of the largest specialist firms on the NYSE for improper order handling. The NYSE and SEC had alleged, among other things, that the specialist firms were engaged in "interpositioning." Suppose Ricky wants to sell Extreme shares at $19 per share, so he puts in a limit order to sell 10,000 shares at $19 or higher. Jennifer, on the other hand, wants to purchase Extreme's shares at $20 per share, so she places a limit order to purchase 10,000 shares at $20 or lower. Matching the two investors will result in a profitable trade between the two—the trade would be executed somewhere between their desired transaction prices, say $19.50 per share. Rather than matching, a specialist could instead engage in the following two transactions, interpositioning itself between Ricky and Jennifer. First, the specialist could purchase 10,000 shares from Ricky at $19 per share for the specialist's own account. Second, the specialist could then quickly turn around and sell the 10,000 shares to

Jennifer at $20 per share. Doing so locks in a guaranteed profit of $1 per share for the specialist at the expense of both Ricky and Jennifer. The large specialist firms accused of interpositioning, including LaBranche & Co. and Spear, Leeds & Kellogg, settled with regulators for an aggregate $242 million. As is common with securities enforcement settlements (covered in Chapter 4), the firms settled without admitting or denying the allegations.

2. THE NASDAQ MARKET

Many securities transactions do not take place in a physical marketplace. Instead, the function of bringing together potential buyers and sellers occurs through electronic communications. The most important of the electronic markets is the Nasdaq market. The Nasdaq is actually three markets—the Nasdaq–NMS (for "National Market System"), Small Cap, and Bulletin Board. The three tiers differ in their listing requirements, with the NMS the most demanding.

Nasdaq encompasses an electronic network linking together dealers in a particular security. Such dealers, known as "market makers," hold themselves out as continuously willing to both purchase and sell a particular security—for their own account—at publicly-quoted prices. For example, a market maker may hold itself out as continuously willing to purchase a block of 100 shares of Extreme common stock at $19.90 per share (the bid price) and to sell 100 shares at $20.10 per share (the ask price). If Extreme's shares are in fact worth $20 per share, the market maker earns a return on the twenty cents bid-ask spread between the two prices as depicted below:

$20.10 (Ask Price)

  [20¢ bid-ask spread]

$19.90 (Bid Price)

Market makers do not know whether investors will accept the market makers' two-sided buy-sell quotation. If the market maker guesses wrong (e.g., sets the bid and ask prices too high), it may just get investors selling securities to the market maker (at the high price) but no investors buying. The bid-ask spread compensates the market maker for providing liquidity while bearing the risk that more informed investors in the market may take advantage of the market maker (e.g., by selling shares to the market maker when the market maker sets its bid price too high).

Several different market makers may quote prices for any one Nasdaq-listed security. Competition among these market makers helps to narrow the bid-ask spread, thereby reducing investors' trading costs. Unlike in a securities exchange, investors seeking to transact in a Nasdaq security typically deal (through their brokers) with a market maker instead of an investor seeking to make the opposite transaction. Imagine, for example, that four market makers deal in Extreme's shares: Goldman Sachs (GSCO), Merrill Lynch (MLCO), Morgan Stanley (MSCO), and Salomon Smith Barney (SBSH). A typical display of the available bid and ask quotes from the market makers for Extreme's shares on a Nasdaq Level II Workstation will look something like this:

Bid			**Offer**		
Dealer	Quantity	Price	Dealer	Quantity	Price
GSCO	20	19.90	MLCO	10	20.10
MSCO	10	19.86	MSCO	40	20.25
SBSH	30	19.72	GSCO	10	20.32
MLCO	10	19.51	SBSH	20	20.42

The Nasdaq Level II Workstation will also display the last transaction price as well as "inside" bid (i.e., the highest offer to purchase price) and ask prices (i.e., the lowest offer to sell price). A list of past transactions, prices and quantities is also provided to give traders a sense of the market's "direction" for the particular stock. The bid and ask prices and quantities displayed in the Workstation frequently change as market makers react to information about the company, its industry and the overall economy, as well as the flow of transactions. Although Goldman Sachs has the highest bid price in the above example, Morgan Stanley can easily occupy this position by increasing its bid price up to $19.95 (for example, in reaction to news that Extreme's sales are going better than expected).

The importance of the NYSE and Nasdaq for secondary transactions in the United State cannot be overstated. In 2001, the NYSE handled transactions amounting to 308 billion shares worth a total of $10.5 trillion. See NYSE Fact Book (located at http://www.nysedata.com/factbook/main.asp). While the NYSE was the largest market in terms of share and dollar volume for decades, the Nasdaq has recently exceeded the NYSE. In 2001, the Nasdaq handled transactions totaling 471 billion shares worth a total of $10.9 trillion. See Nasdaq Market Statistics (available at http://www.Nasdaq.com).

The NYSE remains the clear leader in terms of overall market valuation. In December 2001, NYSE listed companies had a total market valuation of $11.7 trillion while Nasdaq listed companies had a total market valuation of $2.9 trillion. See Nasdaq Market Statistics (available at http://www.Nasdaq.com). Both Nasdaq and the NYSE enjoy trading volumes far greater than AMEX or any other organized trading market in the United States.

The NYSE is not only the largest securities market in the United States in terms of market value, it also provides a good degree of the regulation governing securities transactions. Similarly, the National Association of Securities Dealers (NASD), a minority shareholder of Nasdaq, also acts as a self-regulatory organization (SRO). As SROs, the NYSE and NASD impose various requirements on listed companies. In addition to minimum capitalization requirements, the NYSE and NASD require that listed companies have a board of directors consisting of a majority of independent directors. The NYSE and NASD also provide active monitoring for securities law violations in their respective markets. Broker-dealers must be members of either the NYSE or the NASD and frequently belong to both. Membership subjects them to discipline by the SROs. The SEC plays an active role in overseeing NYSE and NASD regulation to ensure that these SROs are protecting investors.

3.   ELECTRONIC COMMUNICATION NETWORKS

New electronic markets have emerged to compete with the Nasdaq and NYSE, commonly referred to as electronic communication networks (ECNs). ECNs eliminate any third-party intermediary between potential buyers and sellers of a security, such as market makers in the Nasdaq market. Among major ECNs are Archipelago, Instinet, and INET.

Consider the operation of a typical ECN. An investor first places a limit order, indicating the price and quantity of the security in which the investor wishes to transact. Suppose Sarah wishes to purchase 100 shares of Extreme at $20 per share. Upon receiving Sarah's order, the ECN will scan all of its existing limit orders from investors until it finds an investor who desires to sell 100 shares of Extreme at $20 per share (or less) and matches the two investors, executing a trade. If more than one seller exists at the $20 per share price, then the seller with the lowest price (and, if tied on price, the earlier posted time) is matched with Sarah. If no such seller exists, then the ECN will record Sarah's order in a limit order book until a matching order is received. Sarah may also cancel her order at any time.

Some ECNs also maintain links with Nasdaq, publishing the highest offer to purchase (the bid price) and the lowest offer to sell (the ask price) received by the ECN in Nasdaq's Level II Workstation's display of existing bids and offers for a particular stock. Archipelago, for example, maintains such links with Nasdaq. You can view the limit orders within the Archipelago system for a particular security (e.g., Microsoft's ticker symbol is MSFT) by going to Archipelago's web site at www.tradearca.com.

IV.   INVESTMENT DECISIONS

Investors purchase securities for a variety of reasons. Some investors may buy the stock of a company because they like the company's products. An investor may buy Disney stock, for example, because he is a big fan of Tigger. Most investors, however, make investments in order to receive even more money in the future. An investor, for example, may use $100 to purchase the stock of a company only because she believes that the stock will return a total of $110 next year through a combination of dividends and capital appreciation.

How much should an investor pay for any given investment? In some cases, the answer is straightforward. Consider how much you would pay if someone offered you an investment that "returned" $10 today (e.g., they want to sell you a $10 bill). Most rational people would not pay more than $10 for the $10 bill. In a competitive marketplace, purchasers bidding against one another will drive up the price of the $10 bill to exactly $10.

This trivial example provides a useful starting point for considering identifying the information that investors want. Why is it so easy to value a $10 bill? The return from the investment is certain, $10. Also, the investor receives the $10 immediately. How do other investments differ from the $10 bill? Most investments are uncertain in their expected return and will pay off only in the future. Everyone knows that a $10 bill is worth $10. But what is the expected payoff from an investment in the common stock of Extreme Inc.?

Investors must make their best guess at the expected return from an investment into the future. How is an investor supposed to compare whether she should part with a certain amount of money today for an uncertain return of money sometime in the future? The most common financial technique to make such an investment decision is to reduce the expected return from an investment to its "present discount value" (PDV) in today's dollars. Investors may then compare an investment return's PDV with the required upfront investment to decide whether the investment is worthwhile. We begin our discussion of the valuation of securities by showing how to calculate the present discount value for an investment.

A.   PRESENT DISCOUNT VALUATION

Money tomorrow is worth less than the same dollar amount of money today. At the very least, an investor may take a dollar and simply put it into a bank savings account to generate more money in the future. One dollar today, when invested in a savings account at a simple interest rate of 2% per year, for example, will grow to $1.02 in a year's time.

1.   INTEREST

Why do banks pay a positive interest rate for the privilege of obtaining money today? First, people are impatient. Most people would rather consume the same quantity and quality of a particular good today than wait until the future, all other things being equal. In the extreme, consider whether you would rather have $1,000 today or $1,000 one hundred years from now. Part of our impatience is due to the risk that death poses for spending. You can't take it with you. Although some (but not all) care about future generations, most people appear to expect their descendants to fend for themselves.

Second, inflation can erode the purchasing power of cash. Cash, in and of itself, provides no direct value: What can you actually *do* with a $10 bill?

Instead, money is valuable because it serves as a common unit of exchange in a market-based economy. The U.S. Treasury can alter the amount of cash in the economy simply by printing more bills. Doubling the money supply, all other things being equal, simply halves the value of a dollar. Although a nominal $1 today will still be worth $1 tomorrow, the purchasing power of that $1 tomorrow will be less as the price of goods and services increases due to inflation.

Finally, a dollar in the hands of an investor today is certain. The investor can choose to spend the dollar or invest it. In contrast, a monetary return promised some time in the future presents the risk that the investor may not in fact receive the full (or any) return. Banks may fail (although FDIC insurance minimizes this risk for the average depositor). Companies may go bankrupt. Investors, therefore, must factor in the risk of failure in evaluating an investment. To induce investors to part with the sure thing represented by money today for the uncertain promise of money tomorrow, companies must compensate investors in the form of a higher promised return than they can expect from less risky investments. If an investor can put money into a relatively safe savings account with the expectation of receiving a 2% annual return, the same investor may choose to put the same amount of money into a risky corporate investment only if promised a 5% return.

2. PRESENT VALUE

Once we accept the proposition that money today is worth more than money tomorrow, we need to find a method to translate the value of money tomorrow into today's equivalent value.

How much would you pay today for the promise of a payment of $1.02 a year from now if the applicable interest rate were 2%? (Assume for now that the promise is risk-free.) If the interest rate is 2%, then an investor could put $1 into the bank today to receive $1.02 a year from now. Conversely, the promise of payment of $1.02 next year is worth at most $1 in today's dollars to an investor. Accordingly, $1 today is the equivalent of $1.02 next year. More generally, the PDV of any monetary value in the future is the amount of money the market would pay today to receive the future money.

Two components are needed to calculate the PDV for any particular investment. First, investors must come up with their best guess as to the value of the investment return in the future. Take, for example, an investor considering an investment of $10,000 into an oil well drilling project in return for 5% of the net profits. The investor must calculate her best guess as to the size of the net profits (e.g., $100,000 per year for the next five years) and then her return from the net profits (in this case, $5,000 per year, representing 5% of the net profits).

Second, the investor must discount the general time value of money as well as the risk inherent in the investment. If a bank promised a return of $5,000 per year for the next five years, the discount rate would likely reflect only the time value of money and not a great additional risk factor. On the other hand, an investment in an oil well drilling project is significantly more risky than an investment in a bank. The oil well may fail to generate any oil. Even if oil is found, the oil may be of low quality or quantity or difficult to extract. Or, the promoters of the oil well investment may take all the profits and fail to distribute them to investors, skipping town with all the money instead. So the discount rate needs to reflect these risks as well.

And now a bit of math (there won't be much, we promise): To formalize the expected monetary return, imagine that an investment will provide an expected return of d_0 immediately, d_1 in one year's time, and so on. Call the discount rate for a particular investment during a particular year r_x, where r_1 is the discount rate for the first year, r_2 is the discount rate for the second year, and so on.

We can combine the expected return and the discount rate into the following PDV formula:

$$PDV = d_0 + \frac{d_1}{1 + r_1} + \frac{d_2}{(1 + r_1)(1 + r_2)} + \frac{d_3}{(1 + r_1)(1 + r_2)(1 + r_3)} + \ldots$$

If we assume a constant discount rate r over time, then we get:

$$PDV = d_0 + \sum_t \frac{d_t}{(1 + r)^t}$$

HYPOTHETICAL TWO

Corporations not only issue securities; they may also invest corporate funds in securities and other investment vehicles. Suppose you are the chief financial officer of Extreme, Inc. Although Extreme will need a large amount of funds in a couple of years to finance an expansion into the Asian market, for now it just needs to find a good place to "park" its money. Suppose that Extreme has $10 million cash on hand today. Calculate the present discount value of the following options.

1. Marcel, Extreme's CEO, will take the $10 million and put it under his mattress at home. Two years from now, he will take the money out and return it to Extreme's corporate offices. Assume that Marcel's mattress is quite safe and that the yearly discount rate is 5%.

2. Extreme will invest the $10 million into the purchase of U.S. government bonds. The bonds will mature in two years' time. They provide two interest payments of $1 million each at the end of year one and year two, and then a final payment of $10 million at the end of year two. Assume that the relevant discount rate is 5% per year.

3. Extreme will purchase a "perpetuity" from the U.S. government with the $10 million. The perpetuity will provide $1 million every year indefinitely starting one year from now (but no terminal payment because the investment is perpetual). Assume that the relevant discount rate is 5% per year.

4. Extreme will purchase an "annuity" from the U.S. government with the $10 million. Annuities pay a specified amount of money every year (starting in one year) for a fixed period of time (there is no terminal payment). Suppose the U.S. government annuity will pay $3 million every year for the next four years. Assume that the relevant discount rate is 5% per year.

5. Extreme will use the $10 million to purchase bonds issued by Crafty Cartoons, a distributor of children's animated programs. The bonds pay no interest in years one and two (they are "zero-coupon" bonds). Instead, the bonds provide a lump sum payoff of $15 million at the end of year three.

B. WHAT RISKS MATTER

Most investors are risk averse and will avoid risks unless they receive compensation. Imagine that an investor is faced with two possible investments, each promising an expected return of $10,000 in a year's time. Let's call them "Safe" and "Risky." The Safe investment has little to no risk while the Risky investment is highly variable in its return. Imagine that each investment is priced at $9,000 in the market. If this were the case, all investors would choose the Safe over the Risky investment. Both result in an expected gain of $1,000 (the $10,000 return minus the cost of $9,000 to purchase the investment). Crucially, however, the Safe investment involves less risk than the Risky investment, thus making it more attractive to risk averse investors.

Obviously, this is not a sustainable equilibrium. As investors shift funds to purchase the Safe investment, the price of the investment will increase due to the greater demand. Correspondingly, the price of the Risky investment will decrease due to the lack of any demand. Suppose that equilibrium is reached when the price of the Safe investment is $9,500 and the price for the Risky investment is $8,000. At these prices, the Safe investment's high price results in a return of only 5.3% while the Risky investment's lower price generates a return of 25%, thereby compensating the investors in the Risky investment for the added risk.

Although uncertainties may affect almost all types of investments, not all risks are the same. Even risks of the same individual magnitude viewed in isolation may not affect the value of an investment in the same way. Investors are not necessarily passive when it comes to risk and may be able to reduce the risks they face. When such actions are relatively cheap and readily available, the market price may not reflect an additional discount for bearing those risks.

Diversification provides an important avenue for investors to reduce their risks in a low cost manner. The risks in certain investments may at least partially cancel out. Suppose we have two companies—Joe's Ice Cream Shop and Jane's Umbrella Store. Suppose that $100 invested in either Joe's or Jane's earns the following:

	Rain (50%)	Sunny (50%)
Joe's Ice Cream	$ 20	$200
Jane's Umbrella	$200	$ 20

An investor who puts $100 into Joe's Ice Cream can expect to earn $110 on average. But the $110 is not certain. When it rains, the return for the investment will only be $20. When it is sunny, however, the return is $200. Similarly, an investment of $100 into Jane's Umbrella will result in an average return of $110, although with a similar—*but not synchronized*—volatility.

How can a potential investor in Joe's or Jane's stock reduce the risk to which he is exposed? Imagine that the investor put $50 into both Joe's Ice Cream and Jane's Umbrella. The investor would then receive $110 when it rains ($10 from Joe, $100 from Jane) and $110 when it is sunny ($100 from Joe, $10 from Jane) from holding a portfolio of both companies.

In all three investment possibilities (all in Joe's, all in Jane's, and split 50–50 between the two companies), the *expected* return is $110. Only in the 50–50 portfolio investment, however, is the variability in the return zero. Whether it rains or shines, the investor will receive $110. Investors who construct a portfolio of companies that provide different return performance across varying states of the world reduce their risk from investing. Big payouts are eliminated, but so are small ones, and the investor sleeps better at night.

The category of risks that can be reduced through diversification of investments is known as "unsystematic risk." If a particular risk does not affect all companies in a similar manner, then companies that perform differently in response to that risk may be matched to reduce the investor's overall variability of returns. The weather affects ice cream and umbrella companies in different ways, giving rise to a diversification opportunity that allows the investor to construct a more stable portfolio of investments. Consequently, that investor will not insist upon a discount for the firm-specific risks of investing in Joe's Ice Cream or Jane's Umbrella.

Other risks cannot be so easily reduced through diversification. Such risks are known as systematic risks and affect all companies similarly, although not necessarily with the same magnitude. If the Federal Reserve raises interest rates, for example, that increase may have a generally negative effect on companies in the economy. Similarly, a sudden growth in the number of college graduates providing skilled labor may have a generally positive impact on companies. The stock market as a whole will reflect those trends.

Financial economists have formalized the relationship between the required return for a particular publicly traded security and the systematic risk the security poses for investors. In one well-known asset pricing model, the Capital Asset Pricing Model (CAPM), the return for a security is a function of both the risk-free rate (R_f) (e.g., the interest rate for U.S. government treasury bonds) and the relationship of the security's return performance to the return performance of the entire stock market (R_m). We can represent the CAPM equation for the discount rate as follows:

$$R = R_f + \text{beta}(R_m - R_f)$$

The relationship between a stock's performance and the market performance is measured by "beta." A low beta indicates that the particular stock does not move greatly with the movement of returns in the market as a whole. Conversely, a high beta represents a large movement of the particular stock's returns with the market returns. High betas indicate a great amount of systematic risk and correspondingly a high required discount rate for the returns. In 2004, the beta for Yahoo, Inc. was 3.228 (indicating a relatively large discount rate under the CAPM model). The beta for Coca-Cola Co., in contrast, was only 0.313 in 2004 (giving a much lower discount rate for returns in Coca-Cola Co. stock).

V.   WHO PROVIDES INFORMATION TO INVESTORS?

Investors attempting to calculate the present discounted value of a particular investment require a significant amount of information to determine both the expected return over time as well as the appropriate discount rate to apply to the return. How does an investor obtain this information?

Investors lacking the information necessary to value an investment are at a disadvantage in the capital markets. Corporations selling common stock to the public enjoy a large informational advantage over investors. Unsuspecting investors may purchase overvalued securities from unscrupulous issuers. In the secondary market, investors with more information (including corporate officers engaged in insider trading) will enjoy systematically greater returns at the expense of the uninformed investors in the market.

The primary goal of securities regulation in the United States is to reduce the informational disadvantage facing outside investors. In this Part we first consider whether private market actors may have an incentive to provide investment-related information voluntarily. Second, we examine the case for mandatory disclosure requirements despite the presence of private market incentives to provide information.

A.   THE INCENTIVE TO PROVIDE INFORMATION

Information is a valuable commodity in the capital markets. Suppose Jennifer learns that Extreme Inc.'s new extreme sports products are about to be favorably reviewed by *On the Edge* magazine. Jennifer can profitably purchase Extreme stock before the magazine hits the newsstand. After the public learns of the reviews, and Extreme's share price rises as a result, Jennifer can then unwind her position, selling the shares at a profit.

The value of a particular piece of information for securities trading depends on the number of potential traders with the specific information. Information that Microsoft manufactures Windows XP is important for investors, but this information is already well known to almost all investors. Consequently, as we discuss in more detail below, the information is already impounded into the stock market price of Microsoft's common stock, and as a result indirectly affects even those investors who lack the information. On the other hand, a corporate officer who knows that Microsoft is about to introduce a new version of windows—Windows XP II—before any public investor knows of this information can trade profitably in Microsoft's stock before the public announcement.

Why would anyone disseminate important and non-public investment information widely to the market? To put this in another way: Given that information is costly to generate and distribute, why would anyone research and then distribute the information widely, thereby reducing the trading advantage of holding the information? To answer these questions, it may be helpful to divide information in the financial markets into two categories: (a) information from inside the corporation (inside information) and (b) information useful in valuing the corporation that comes from outside the corporation (outside information).

Inside information encompasses all information known by anyone within a corporation that may affect the market price for the corporation's securities. Inside information includes information on the company's products, profitability, and management team, among other things.

Companies such as Extreme have an incentive to provide their firm-specific, inside information voluntarily to the marketplace. Imagine that an array of companies seeks to sell securities to investors through primary transactions. For now, assume only that antifraud liability applies to deter misrepresentations, but disclosure is not mandatory. Some of the companies are a better investment than others. Assume that all of the companies offering securities refuse to make disclosures to prospective investors. When an investor calls to ask a question about the offering, the companies all reply "no comment."

If you were an investor in such a situation, how much would you be willing to pay for the securities being offered by these companies? Unable to distinguish among companies, rational investors will pay the expected value approximating the average return for the group of companies. Paying greater than the average value will result in the investor systematically earning negative returns, not a stable situation in the capital markets. But not all companies are average. Some companies will provide a higher return than the average and some will provide a lower return.

Now consider the incentives of the managers of a higher value company seeking to offer securities to the market. If the managers remain silent with all the other companies, the higher value company will receive the average price for all companies. However, if the managers can make a credible (and low-cost) disclosure of their company's true value to investors, then the higher value company will receive substantially more money for its offering of securities. So long as antifraud liability lends credibility to a company's disclosures, the high value company will want to disclose its inside information to investors as part of its offering of securities. Once one company begins disclosing, investors, if rational, will reduce the value they assign to the companies that opt for silence. Among those companies that remain silent, those at the higher end of the valuation spectrum will then have added pressure to disclose their value to investors voluntarily, thereby increasing the amount of money investors would be willing to pay for the companies' securities.

Why might companies *not* disclose information voluntarily? First, companies may not plan on issuing securities to the market anytime soon. Although Extreme may want to convince investors that Extreme is a good investment when it is selling common stock, Extreme's managers may have fewer incentives to disclose when Extreme is not selling securities. A company, of course, may disclose in between offerings to foster a strong secondary market. Doing so may reduce the risk facing investors trading in the secondary market, thus reducing the costs of secondary market trading. This accrues to the benefit of the company if investors then pay more for any securities the issuer sells in primary offerings.

Second, antifraud liability may not provide sufficient credibility to disclosures. Antifraud liability does not work perfectly. Suits are sometimes brought even when no fraud has been committed; conversely, suits are sometimes not brought when fraud has occurred. For example, few private securities fraud class actions are brought against initial public issuers offering relatively small amounts of securities. Lower value companies may take advantage of imperfections in the antifraud regime to make disclosures misrepresenting themselves as high value firms. If fraud muddies the waters, investors will be unable to distinguish among different value companies based on their disclosures. As a result, high value companies will be unable to use disclosure to distinguish themselves from the low value companies. High value companies may, instead, choose to raise money outside of the capital markets. If high value companies exit the public capital markets, only the low value companies will be left offering securities. This process reduces the average value of companies left in the market, inducing more companies to exit the markets, a downward spiral commonly known as the "lemons" problem (a reference to the market for used cars).

Third, managers may profit more from a less than fully informed securities market. If the investing public knows less about an issuer's firm-specific information, managers may more easily engage in insider trading. We will see in Chapter 6 that the securities laws prohibit insider trading, but such prohibitions are imperfect. Regulators may fail to detect all forms of insider trading. A manager who uses a friend to trade securities in only small amounts may cruise under the radar screen of the SEC. The securities laws only prohibit trades involving a "material" informational advantage over the investing public. Managers can trade if their informational advantage does not rise to the level of materiality. If the definition of materiality (covered in Chapter 2) does not match up with potential profitability, insiders may be able to profit from their informational advantages.

Finally, the incentive of issuers to disclose voluntarily extends only to inside information. Outside information may also create informational disparities among investors. No company operates in a vacuum. The value of Extreme Inc., for example, depends on the plans of its competitors to introduce competing extreme sports products. Information on the upcoming snow conditions in mountain areas also will affect the value of Extreme's common stock. Similarly, information on whether regulators may impose greater safety regulations on the various extreme sports for which Extreme produces gear will affect Extreme's stock price.

The market provides a number of responses to these problems. These solutions, however, have their own problems. First, firms may turn to third parties to certify the information they disclose to the market. The reputation of the third party intermediaries may help establish of the veracity of disclosure. As discussed above, underwriters typically participate in firm commitment offerings, putting their reputation on the line (as well as their own financial capital) when they sell an offering. Audit firms also put their reputations on the line when they certify the financial statements of a firm.

High reputation underwriters and auditors earn substantial fees for their services. Firms pay this fee to "rent" the reputation of the intermediaries because they can demand a higher price when selling the firms' securities. Despite this interest in maintaining the value of a reputation for veracity, some intermediaries may sacrifice their reputation in return for a quick gain. The fall of Arthur Andersen as a major audit firm was due in large part to the questionable actions of the lead audit partner for Enron, resulting in short-term profits in the form of more Enron-related business.

Second, securities analysts provide investment information to the market, by researching both firm-specific and outside information. Buy-side analysts work for large institutional investors, providing investment analysis used in determining which investments the institutional investors should purchase or sell. Sell-side analysts, on the other hand, are employed by the large securities brokerage firms. Merrill Lynch, for example, employs many analysts covering a wide variety of industries and businesses. In addition to providing execution of order services, Merrill Lynch also sells investment advice to its brokerage customers. The advice is implicitly paid for as a portion of the broker's commission.

In the past, brokerage commissions were fixed by regulation, resulting in substantial brokerage profits. These profits were partially used to subsidize sell-side analyst research for investors. In 1975, however, brokerage commissions were deregulated, leading to intense competition. Commissions that used to run into the $100 range now run for as little as $9.95, or even lower, at some Internet brokerage sites. The sharp drop in commissions has cut into brokerage profits.

Although brokerage firms still employ substantial numbers of sell-side analysts, the funding for analysts has necessarily shifted to other sources. Many Wall Street brokerage firms turned to their growing investment banking businesses in the 1980s and 1990s to help subsidize analyst research. In return, the provision of analyst research on select companies to the marketplace became a selling point for the investment banking business. Investment banking partners would routinely tout the strength of their analysts in obtaining business from companies doing public offerings for the first time. A positive analyst report from a large Wall Street brokerage firm on a recently-public Internet startup company, for example, could help bolster the stock price of the startup.

The close connection between investment banking and analyst research within the large Wall Street firms created a conflict of interest for analysts. Although investment banks represented that their analysts' research provided accurate information for investors, the analysts were compensated based on the amount of investment banking business attributable to the analysts' efforts. In the early 2000s, this conflict of interest became public as the result of an investigation by Elliot Spitzer, the New York State Attorney General. Spitzer and the SEC eventually reached a settlement with ten Wall Street investment banks. The settlement provided for a $1.4 billion settlement fund in addition to various structural reforms separating investment banking from analyst research within the investment banks.

B. THE ARGUMENT FOR MANDATORY DISCLOSURE

Although issuers have incentives to disclose information voluntarily to the market, those incentives are not perfect. We have seen that (a) firms not intending to issue securities into the public market may not have great incentives to disclose voluntarily; (b) antifraud liability may not ensure the veracity of disclosures; (c) managers may have a self interest in restricting disclosures (e.g., to enhance their insider trading opportunities); and (d) such disclosures will not necessarily encompass information coming from outside the disclosing firm. Moreover, the intermediaries that help provide credibility to issuer disclosures, as well as the analysts that provide an independent source of information on firms, may face their own set of hurdles in remaining credible to the investing public.

Given the problems with voluntary disclosure, a system of mandatory disclosure may increase investor welfare. In addition, commentators have argued that a number of affirmative benefits may flow from a mandatory disclosure system. We briefly canvass some of these arguments below.

1. COORDINATION PROBLEMS

A coordination problem may exist among companies making disclosures to the market. Information on a particular company is more valuable if investors can use the information to compare the company against other possible investment opportunities. To the extent Extreme Inc. performs poorly compared with other sporting goods providers, investors will pay less for Extreme's shares.

Comparisons are more difficult if disclosures are not consistent. If one company defines annual revenue to include all sales made in the last fifteen months while another defines annual revenue as sales occurring in the last twelve months, then the two revenue numbers will not be comparable. Today, financial statements prepared in different countries present potential comparison problems for investors. German accounting principles, for example, permit companies to create reserves, allowing a company to shift profits from a good year to mask losses in a subsequent bad year. U.S. generally accepted accounting principles (U.S. GAAP), on the other hand, do not allow for such reserves. In addition, the U.S. securities regime does not force all companies with securities trading in U.S. markets to reconcile their accounting statements fully to U.S. GAAP. Instead, the U.S. securities regime allows foreign issuers to file with the U.S. SEC the same filings as they would in their home country together with a statement describing material differences between the regimes in the home country and the U.S.

The value of mandatory standardization can be exaggerated. Even if the government does not mandate one particular standard, the market may develop its own standard. Once a standard takes hold, investors will penalize issuers who fail to disclose according to the standard; non-conformity will be viewed as a signal that something is amiss with the issuer. The accounting industry, for example, develops standardized methods of accounting treatment. Financial accounting and reporting standards in the U.S. have long been primarily administered by the Financial Accounting Standards Board (FASB), a private entity.

2.   AGENCY COSTS

Disclosure plays a large role in controlling agency costs within large public corporations. With accurate disclosure on a company's financial performance, for example, outside investors can compare how well managers at a particular firm are performing relative to the managers of the firm's competitors. Of course, other factors may affect a firm's financial performance (including a poor economy, war, and other external factors). Nonetheless, a comparison with a firm's competitors controls for many such factors and provides a clearer glimpse into the quality of a firm's managers. Directors may then discipline (or terminate) managers who perform poorly over a repeated number of quarters.

Disclosure may also reveal the compensation, share ownership, and trading patterns of a firm's managers. Top executive officers may persuade the board of directors to award the officers exorbitant pay packages. Officers may trade on inside information. Once such information is disclosed, shareholders again will be better placed to decide which managers should be replaced (through the shareholders' power to elect the board of directors). Disclosure of egregious pay packages and instances of insider trading may assist the SEC and private plaintiffs' attorneys in filing lawsuits against the corporate officers. Corporate officers may also face public opprobrium once their misbehavior is revealed.

Managers intent on shirking their job responsibilities or siphoning corporate resources to themselves may not voluntarily choose to disclose information concerning firm performance, executive compensation and stock trading patterns. If investors cannot completely decipher the meaning of a firm's silence on such matters (e.g., other firms may choose not to disclose information on an executive's compensation for fear that competitors may initiate a bidding war for the executive's services), then managers will be able to remain silent without suffering a large share price discount.

The agency problem may be particularly acute in the context of initial public offerings. After an issuer raises funds from an initial public offering, those in control of the issuer have many potential avenues for mischief with the funds. Companies may use the funds to pay the executives high salaries, or purchase goods and services from parties related to those in control at disadvantageous terms for the issuer. The presence of a large amount of liquid funds makes the benefit to managers from engaging in such expropriation of private benefits of control both more rewarding and easier to execute. For more on agency costs in the context of initial public offerings and the role of mandatory disclosure in reducing such problems, see Paul G. Mahoney, *Mandatory Disclosure as a Solution to Agency Problems*, 62 U. Chi. L. Rev. 1047 (1995). In sum, agency costs may lead managers and promoters to disclose less information than is in the best interests of both investors and the issuer. Mandatory disclosure of items related to areas where managers may siphon value from investors (e.g., executive compensation and related-party transactions between an issuer and its managers or promoters) therefore may enhance shareholder welfare.

3.   POSITIVE EXTERNALITIES

A positive externality may occur when a company makes a firm-specific disclosure to the public marketplace. Third parties unconnected with the issuer may benefit from these disclosures in at least two ways.

First, more disclosures will provide more accurate securities prices. The information itself may help investors value the company's business prospects. Moreover, the disclosed information may help subsidize the efforts of analysts in the stock market to research other information (acting as the stepping stones to even more exhaustive research). The additional analyst-driven information may then further increase the accuracy of securities prices.

Second, firm-specific information on a particular issuer may prove useful to competitors and other third parties. An issuer will take into account the cost to itself of providing information. The issuer will not, however, value the benefit to third parties. Indeed, in some cases, the issuer will treat a third party benefit as an affirmative cost to itself. Suppose competitors receive disclosure from a particular issuer about its firm-specific research and development plans. Extreme may seek to put $10 million into researching a new line of extreme video game machines expecting big profits, but only if Extreme is the first mover into this new market niche. If competitors learn about Extreme's plans, however, the competitors will have time to put together their own extreme video game offerings, undermining Extreme's first mover advantage.

Because the issuer will either ignore or treat as a cost the benefits of disclosure to competitors and other third parties, the issuer will not fully internalize all the effects from its information disclosure decisions. We can perhaps justify mandatory disclosure as a means of increasing disclosure to levels that issuers would otherwise not voluntarily wish to make. For an extended discussion on interfirm externalities, see Merritt B. Fox, *Retaining Mandatory Securities Disclosure: Why Issuer Choice is Not Investor Empowerment*, 85 Va. L. Rev. 1335 (1999).

The issuer will not ignore the benefit of disclosure to all those who receive information. If investors value disclosed information, they will reward the issuer disclosing such information through a high stock market price. Nonetheless, issuers will fail to take into account the full positive effect of their disclosure on overall stock market price accuracy and on their competitors. At the margin, will the issuer's failure to take into account these positive externalities reduce the amount of disclosure? Possibly. On the other hand, whether a mandatory regulation regime will result in the right level of disclosure is also questionable. Will regulators be able to specify the level of disclosure that optimally accounts for improved price accuracy and benefits to competitors? Although issuers on their own may opt for too little disclosure, regulators may be inclined to require too much.

4. DUPLICATIVE INFORMATION RESEARCH

Information cannot be produced for free. Investors competing with one another will have an incentive to expend large resources to obtain an informational advantage over other traders in the capital markets. The winner of such an information race obtains large trading profits. Those who lose the race gain little or no trading profits—the market will have already reacted to the information embedded in the large trade orders previously placed by the winner.

The "winner-take-all" nature of research leads to excessive and duplicative investment in research. When advisors for a mutual fund attempt to predict the earnings for Extreme, this effort requires both time and money. An advisor may interview customers, suppliers, and other industry participants to get a sense of Extreme's earnings. The advisor will also obtain data on general industry trends and review as much information as possible specific to Extreme. From this information, the advisor will then spend long hours calculating future income streams. All this effort may gain a specific mutual fund a trading advantage before Extreme itself announces its earnings. In comparing the performance of two funds, the fund that obtains the information first may significantly enhance its relative performance. It may not matter to society, however, whether Fidelity or Vanguard learns about an issuer's earnings one hour ahead of the other fund. If the private gain to a fund from research exceeds the social benefit, individual funds may engage in excessive information research races.

For information inside the issuer (firm-specific information), the issuer can discourage such wasteful battles to win the informational race. Extreme represents the lowest-cost source of inside information on the value of Extreme's securities. Outside investors may attempt to recreate such information only at high cost. (How can outside investors learn about a corporation's internal business plans for the future? Corporate espionage?) Moreover, many outside investors may each attempt to do so, resulting in duplicative research costs as each investor reinvents the wheel. Extreme can undercut these incentives by simply disclosing its internal business plans publicly. Mandatory disclosure under the federal securities laws forces issuers to disclose much of their internal firm specific information, thereby reducing duplicative information research in the secondary market. For more on mandatory disclosure and wasteful information races, see John C. Coffee, *Market Failure and the Economic Case for a Mandatory Disclosure*, 70 Va. L. Rev. 717 (1984).

5.   COSTS OF MANDATORY DISCLOSURE

Notwithstanding these substantial arguments in favor of mandatory disclosure, its desirability is hardly a given. Regulators are not perfect. They make mistakes in gauging the correct level of mandatory disclosure. Behavioral biases, for example, may cause regulators at the SEC to ignore less visible (but nonetheless important) information in favor of more salient and recent information. Regulators may be excessively optimistic about their own abilities to provide solutions to problems in the financial markets. Tunnel vision may limit the ability of regulators to consider alternative regulatory solutions.

Perhaps more troubling than cognitive problems is the risk of agency capture. Regulators may come under the influence of wealthy and well-organized participants in the securities markets. A regulator considering her exit options after leaving the SEC may wish to establish a reputation for "reasonableness" with investment bankers, auditors, and Wall Street law firms. Even if regulators do not become captured by outside interests, the regulators may systematically select regulations designed to increase the authority and prestige of the SEC even at the expense of investor welfare. (Investors, after all, ultimately bear the cost of the regulatory regime.) As a monopolistic regulator in the United States, the SEC has little incentive to cater to the interests of investors. Even if SEC regulators make mistakes or are captured by industry participants, issuers and investors cannot opt for an alternative securities regulation regime. For more on the costs of regulatory error, see Stephen J. Choi and A.C. Pritchard, *Behavioral Economics and the SEC*, 56 Stan. L. Rev. 1 (2003).

C.   How Does Information Disclosure Matter?

A key assumption underlying the debate over mandatory disclosure is that investors actually pay attention to disclosures. If disclosures were simply irrelevant to the capital markets, then imposing mandatory disclosure would squander the valuable time and money of the issuer (and therefore indirectly the funds of its shareholders). The SEC has decided that investors are most interested in financial results, the management's biography, the composition of the board of directors, and the business and properties of the issuer.

Even if investors value such information, they must still obtain, read, and digest the information in order to make an informed investment decision. Moreover, information outside of an issuer's disclosures to the market may be important to the valuation of the issuer. Information on tensions in the Middle East, for example, may be useful in valuing an oil company's stock. Investors making their own investment analyses should also incorporate such outside information. The complexity of the decision can be overwhelming.

Not surprisingly, most individual investors simply don't try. Many a corporate annual report has ended up unread in the trash can. If small investors don't take advantage of the information provided through mandatory disclosure, what is the point? Perversely, such disclosures may give larger, more sophisticated investors (with enough money at stake to make research worthwhile) an informational advantage over the small investors who do not read the disclosures. Rather than reducing informational advantages in the capital markets, mandatory disclosure may increase them.

This paints too bleak a picture. Small investors may benefit from mandatory disclosure, even if they never glance at the unceasing stream of disclosure generated. Investors may: (1) obtain the information indirectly through the recommendations of various securities market intermediaries; and (2) benefit from the information indirectly if the information is incorporated into the stock market price for securities that trade in an "efficient market."

1.   FILTERING MECHANISMS

Investors who do not read disclosed information may nonetheless learn its content and implications indirectly through securities market intermediaries. Brokers, for example, hold themselves out as providing value to investors through their access to many sources of investment-related information. In theory, brokers will review the available research on a firm, reading the firm's mandatory disclosure filings as well as analyst reports on the firm. Brokers will then make recommendations to individual investor clients. Through the filtering mechanism of the broker, individual investors may learn indirectly about disclosed information.

Other intermediaries assist investors who cannot spare the time to read information disclosures. Mutual funds, for example, allow investors to "hire" professional money managers to allocate their investment funds. In an actively-managed mutual fund, a fund manager will research various securities in search of investment opportunities. As the fund grows larger, the fund manager can spread the cost of research across all the individual holders of the fund. Individuals with better things to do than read SEC filings can invest, with minimal effort, through a mutual fund while still benefitting from the expertise of the fund manager in picking profitable securities for investment.

Once again, however, agency costs muddy the waters. Agency problems are not unique to managers within a corporation. Brokers may not faithfully serve the interests of their investor clients. So-called "boiler room" brokers engage in cold calls to investors, touting "can't miss" investments. More often than not, investors who purchase such investments lose while the brokers receive hefty commissions. The SEC's website quotes one cold-calling broker as stating: "You'd hammer them. I always remember this one guy, I mean, I just stayed on the phone for almost an hour, and he finally bought." Your broker may not be your friend.

Similarly, fund managers may not always have the best interests of the fund investors in mind when doing research. And they certainly do not work for free. In a 2001 study of advisory fees in the mutual fund industry, John Freeman and Stewart Brown show that equity fund managers' fees were almost ten times greater than those of comparable pension fund managers. They write that this discrepancy "translates into equity mutual fund shareholders being overcharged to the tune of nearly $9 billion-plus annually." John P. Freeman and Stewart L. Brown, *Mutual Fund Advisory Fees: The Cost of Conflicts of Interest*, 26 J. Corp. L. 609 (2001). So your fund manager may not be your friend, either.

2.   THE EFFICIENT CAPITAL MARKET HYPOTHESIS

Despite the conflicts facing intermediaries, individual investors are not necessarily out of luck if they rely on a less than scrupulous broker or mutual fund manager. For firms whose securities are widely followed and actively traded, another mechanism may help ensure that even those investors who cannot be bothered with research are able to buy and sell securities at a price that reflects all of that information: efficient capital markets.

Financial economists developed the efficient capital markets hypothesis (ECMH) in the 1960s. The ECMH posits that the securities market price of an actively traded security will incorporate information related to the security. Three different versions of the ECMH align with the amount of information assumed to be incorporated into the stock market price: weak, semi-strong and strong.

a.   *Weak ECMH*

Under the weak version of the ECMH, the current market price of a security reflects the information found in all past prices for that security. If the weak version of the ECMH is true, investors cannot earn greater than normal returns by trading based on a security's past price patterns. Suppose we start with the assumption that a large drop in price is typically followed a week later by a large increase in price. The weak version of the ECMH postulates that such a systematic pattern cannot occur. Put another way, if the weak form of the ECMH is true, stock market prices follow a "random walk." Knowledge of past prices will not help investors predict whether a stock's price is headed lower or higher.

This result should not be surprising. Information on past price patterns for securities is both cheap and widely available. For example, see how long it takes you to find the common stock prices for Coca-Cola Inc. (ticker symbol KO) over the last year at one of the many websites devoted to financial information, such as www.finance.yahoo.com.

How does it work? Suppose that thousands of traders are armed with both (a) knowledge of the systematic stock market price pattern (e.g., that a large drop is always followed by a corresponding increase), and (b) information on a large price drop for a particular company's stock, such as KO. Assume that KO's stock price drops from $45 per share to $35 per share. Everyone knows that KO's stock price will jump back up by $10 in one week, so it will soon be trading at $45 per share again. But if KO's stock price is sure to increase by $10 in a week, an investor can lock in guaranteed profits by purchasing KO stock today at the lower $35 per share price. (This process is known in financial circles as "arbitrage.") Competition will quickly drive the price of KO to $45 (long before the week elapses), thereby eliminating the certain profit from trading in the stock of Coca-Cola.

b. Semi-strong ECMH

The semi-strong version of the ECMH hypothesis builds on the weak version, but it incorporates a broader range of information. Under the semi-strong hypothesis, the stock market price of an actively-traded company's stock will reflect all relevant *publicly* available information. Although not all publicly available information is as readily obtained as information on past stock prices, by definition this category of information is broadly available to the investing public. Information that Extreme Inc. is about to enter the sports drink market, for example, can give the holder of such information a large trading advantage in Extreme stock. But that advantage persists only as long as no other investors know of Extreme's imminent sports drink plans. Once the plans are made public, the possibility of profitable trades will have disappeared.

What is the mechanism here? If *all* investors learn of Extreme's plans simultaneously, the stock market price may simply adjust to reflect the news before any trading occurs. Even if only *some* investors learn of the plans, trades by those informed investors will quickly drive the price higher or lower, depending on the market's assessment of those plans. With increased demand for Extreme's stock (assuming the entry into the sports drink market is positive news), the stock market price of Extreme will rise, incorporating the new information. Increased demand signals to the rest of the market that some investors believe that Extreme is a good buy. Moreover, the signal is credible because the investors are putting their money on the line.

c. Strong ECMH

The strong version of the ECMH posits that the stock market price of a company incorporates all information, whether or not the information is available to the public. The mechanism? There is none—the available evidence contradicts the strong version of the ECMH. Insiders trading in their company's equity produce systematically higher returns. This outcome would be impossible if their informational advantages afforded them no trading advantages as the strong version of the ECMH posits. So it is generally agreed that the strong version of the ECMH is false. (If it were true, of course, most securities regulation would be pointless, we would not have written this book, and you would not be taking this course.)

d. Implications of ECMH

Among the three versions of the ECMH, the semi-strong version of the ECMH has had the greatest effect on securities regulation. In particular, securities regulators have been influenced by the notion that investors who do not obtain or read a particular piece of information on a company may nonetheless "indirectly" receive the information as the stock market price incorporates the information. For example, the SEC has allowed relatively large public issuers to "incorporate by reference" their prior SEC filings in public offering disclosures (discussed in Chapter 7). The presumption is that the market has already incorporated the information in those prior filings and the price of the offered securities will reflect it. Another prominent example is the Supreme Court's decision in *Basic v. Levinson*, 485 U.S. 224 (1988) (excerpted in Chapters 2 and 5), which relied in part on the notion that the capital market may incorporate disclosed information in the stock market price. The Court adopted the "fraud-on-the-market" theory, which presumes reliance even for investors who did not directly view or read a misstatement alleged to have affected a company's stock price. Defenses to the theory follow the limits of the ECMH identified by finance economists. Defendants may rebut the presumption with a showing that the market for a particular company's securities does not enjoy active trading or a substantial following of analysts. Markets without these features cannot be presumed to be informationally efficient.

Despite the influence of the semi-strong version of the ECMH on securities regulation, the theory remains controversial. Many argue that investors are frequently irrational in their investment decisions. This lack of rationality, in turn, may translate into stock market prices that do not accurately reflect all publicly available information. The most prominent version of this theory is called noise trading. Under this theory, a substantial segment of investors does not trade based on information and instead simply engages in random "noise" trades. Institutional investors, instead of arbitraging the noise away (leading to accurate securities prices), may attempt to "ride the wave" and trade with irrational trends in securities prices, hoping to cash out before the momentum fades.

More recently, both economists and legal academics have developed a growing appreciation of the fallibility of human decision making. Investors may be prone to over-optimism, placing too much weight on their ability to make good investment choices. Investors may also ignore less salient, but nonetheless important, information and pay excessive attention to recent and more salient information. Immediately following a large stock market scandal, investors may take an overly pessimistic view of stock investments, for example. Investors may display loss aversion, placing too much weight on avoiding the realization of a loss, leading the investors to hold on too long to losing investments instead of taking their losses to help reduce their taxes. Conversely, investors may take excessive risks with newly earned money (the so-called "house" money effect).

If investors do not price securities rationally, the possibility for irrational "bubbles" (essentially, enthusiasm for stocks not grounded in realistic prospects of profit) arises. In a bubble market, stock market prices are likely to stray far from the fundamental value of the shares, i.e., the stream of dividends and capital gains the shares are likely to produce. Many point to the sharp rise of stock market prices at the end of the 1990s, particularly for Internet-related companies, followed by the rapid deflation of these prices in the early 2000s, as evidence that the U.S. securities markets suffered from such a bubble.

The possibility of stock market bubbles requires us to refine what we mean by "efficient" capital markets. One meaning of efficiency is "fundamental" efficiency. A stock market is fundamentally efficient if the prices reflect the underlying present discounted value of the return investors may expect from purchasing a security. If investors reacted rationally to information and did not suffer from any behavioral biases, the stock market would be fundamentally efficient (at least in the semi-strong sense of the ECMH).

A conclusion that the stock market is fundamentally efficient furnishes a strong basis for normative arguments against the regulation of the securities markets. If investors incorporate all available public information into stock prices then issuers, assuming no agency costs, will internalize fully the choices they make that may affect investor welfare. For example, if issuers fail to adopt the corporate governance protections that investors expect, the issuers' stock market price will take a hit, making it difficult for the issuer to raise capital. An extreme version of this argument holds that securities regulation should follow the path of state corporate law and allow issuers to choose the regulatory regime to apply to transactions in the issuers' securities. If issuers choose a regime that poorly protects investors, investors will respond by appropriately discounting the price of the issuer's shares. Issuers seeking to offer securities will therefore consider both their own welfare and that of investors in choosing a securities regime. Putting these academic arguments to one side, fundamental efficiency seems difficult to square with the dramatic fluctuations we have seen in the stock market in recent years.

Even if we doubt the stock market's fundamental efficiency, the market may nonetheless be "informationally" efficient. Investors may generally have behavioral biases and other defects in processing information that lead to stock market bubbles and other forms of irrational pricing. But when new information regarding a security arrives in the market, the market may nonetheless quickly incorporate that information into the stock market. The level of stock prices may not reflect the true underlying value of companies; in an informationally efficient market the *relative* changes in stock prices may still reflect accurately the value of new information.

Suppose that Extreme Inc. puts out a false press release claiming that its upcoming revenues will far exceed analysts' expectations. Even if the market is not fundamentally efficient, the market may still react to the fraudulent press release. Moreover, once the fraud is revealed, the corresponding drop in the stock market price on the revelation date may provide a good proxy for the magnitude of the fraud. In determining both the materiality of the fraud (meaning how important the information is to the average investor, our topic in Chapter 2) and the amount of damages (reflecting the magnitude of the fraud, covered in Chapter 5), the reaction of the stock market may provide our best available measure if the market is informationally efficient.

VI. THE REGULATORY APPARATUS

We finish our introduction to the securities markets and their regulation with (a) a brief summary of the various components of the securities laws, (b) a discussion of the SEC's role in administering the securities laws, and (c) an overview of the role of self-regulatory organizations (including the NYSE and NASD) in regulating the securities markets.

A.   THE FEDERAL SECURITIES LAWS

Securities transactions in the United States are governed primarily by the federal securities laws. The federal securities laws comprise several pieces of legislation initially enacted during the Great Depression and amended over time. The federal securities laws include the:

- Securities Exchange Act of 1934
- Securities Act of 1933
- Investment Company Act of 1940
- Investment Advisers Act of 1940
- Trust Indenture Act of 1939
- Public Utility Holding Company Act of 1935
- Sarbanes–Oxley Act of 2002

1.   SECURITIES EXCHANGE ACT OF 1934

The Exchange Act primarily regulates secondary market transactions and the market professionals and institutions that facilitate such transactions. The Exchange Act's first line of protection for investors is disclosure, following a theme common throughout the securities laws. As covered in greater detail in Chapter 4, the Exchange Act imposes periodic reporting requirements for certain types of publicly traded companies, commonly referred to as "Exchange Act reporting issuers." Exchange Act reporting issuers must file annual Form 10–K reports and quarterly Form 10–Q reports with the SEC.

The Form 10–K and 10–Q disclosure forms include information relevant to investors, including a description of the issuer's business and properties; the directors and officers of the issuer; the ownership of the issuer; and past financial statements. Exchange Act reporting issuers must also file a Form 8–K for certain major events, such as bankruptcy or a change in control of the issuer. These disclosures must all be filed electronically, and the SEC makes these filings available to everyone through its EDGAR system on its website, www.sec.gov.

Disclosures alone may not assist investors in the secondary market if issuers and their officers commit fraud. To combat fraud, the Exchange Act provides for antifraud liability. By far the most important antifraud provision is Rule 10b–5, promulgated by the SEC under § 10(b) of the Exchange Act. Although Rule 10b–5 does not provide an explicit private cause of action for fraud, courts have developed a detailed antifraud doctrine under Rule 10b–5, prohibiting not only fraudulent disclosures (covered in Chapter 5), but also insider trading (in Chapter 6). Antifraud liability is not cost-free. An expansive Rule 10b–5 regime may encourage plaintiffs' attorneys to file suits after a large drop in a firm's stock price with only minimal evidence that the firm and its officers and directors fraudulently disclosed materially misleading information. Defendants may settle even non-meritorious claims to avoid the expense of defending such a suit and the distraction on management, among other reasons. In 1995, Congress responded to the fear of frivolous suits with the passage of the Private Securities Litigation Reform Act (also covered in Chapter 5).

Fraud is not the only danger lurking in the secondary markets. Some secondary market participants may attempt to manipulate securities prices. To address this concern, the Exchange Act contains anti-manipulation provisions. Prior to the enactment of the securities laws, Congress received extensive (but less than conclusive) testimony on the presence of manipulative trades in the securities markets before the stock market crash of 1929. According to the testimony, unscrupulous traders would routinely band together to form a "stock pool." Members of the pool would buy a particular stock, generating an upward momentum in the stock price. Once the stock price rose, pool members would cash out at a profit before the stock price came back down. Section 9 of the Exchange Act now prohibits such manipulation.

The Exchange Act regulates many of the professional intermediaries that operate in the securities markets. The Exchange Act requires brokers, national securities exchanges, and municipal securities dealers, among others, to register with the SEC. Registration subjects these entities to extensive regulation by the SEC (a topic for a more advanced course in securities regulation).

The Exchange Act also regulates shareholder voting by mandating disclosure in connection with the solicitation of proxies. Congress hoped to make managers more accountable to shareholders by requiring disclosure when shareholders were asked to vote. We take up this topic in Chapter 11. Finally, the Exchange Act regulates disclosure in connection with tender offers and the timing and process for such offers. We take up this topic in Chapter 12.

2.   SECURITIES ACT OF 1933

The Securities Act of 1933 focuses on primary market transactions. The Securities Act provides three approaches to regulating the primary market. First, the Securities Act requires issuers making a public offering to file mandatory disclosure documents containing information deemed important to investors. The two major disclosure documents are the registration statement and the prospectus, which repeats the information found in Part I of the registration statement. The registration statement and prospectus contain information on the issuer's business, properties, material legal proceedings, directors and officers, ownership, and financials. The SEC has rationalized the disclosure requirements imposed by the Securities Act (for public offerings) and those imposed by the Exchange Act (for periodic filings). Under the system of "integrated disclosure" the requirements are the same for both Acts. Information is also provided on the offering itself, including the number of shares offered and the price, the underwriters involved in the offering (and their fees and discounts), and the use of the proceeds from the offering. We cover this subject in Chapter 7.

Second, the Securities Act provides for an intricate public offering procedure, often referred to as the "gun-jumping" rules, designed both to ensure that the prospectus is distributed widely to investors and that the prospectus is sent to investors before they receive other (written) information. The prohibition on giving additional information to investors is often referred to as the "quiet period" of a public offering. This topic is also covered in Chapter 7.

Finally, the Securities Act imposes heightened antifraud liability for material misstatements (and omissions creating a "half truth") in public offering documents, the topic of Chapter 8. Issuers seeking to raise capital from the market may be tempted to commit fraud to boost the proceeds from the offering. Heightened antifraud liability is intended to counter this incentive to engage in fraud.

3.   INVESTMENT COMPANY ACT OF 1940 AND INVESTMENT ADVISERS ACT OF 1940

The Investment Company Act of 1940 and the Investment Advisers Act of 1940 regulate, among other things, mutual funds and their directors, managers, and advisors. The Investment Company Act requires that certain defined investment companies register with the SEC. Among other things, the Investment Company Act provides specific requirements governing the responsibilities of the fund's board of directors, the capital structure of the fund, and transactions between a fund and its insiders. In addition, the Investment Company Act regulates disclosures to fund investors, including mandatory disclosures on fund objectives, risks, and performance.

The Investment Advisers Act, in turn, imposes a number of requirements on certain investment advisers. Among other things, investment advisers must register with the SEC, avoid certain types of fee arrangements, and maintain specified books and records. The Investment Advisers Act also limits advertising by investment advisors. For example, investment advisers may not use testimonials in their advertisements. We leave topics arising under these laws to more advanced courses in securities regulation.

4.   TRUST INDENTURE ACT OF 1939

The Trust Indenture Act of 1939 regulates contractual terms relating to publicly issued debt securities, including bonds, notes, and debentures above a specified dollar amount (presently $10 million). The formal agreement between the issuer and the holders of public debt securities is known as a "trust indenture." The Act specifies that the trust indenture must, among other things, provide for the appointment of a trustee to represent the public bondholders as a group. The Act also provides for the independence of the trustee as well as standards governing the conduct of the trustee. This law is generally covered in courses on corporate finance.

5.   PUBLIC UTILITY HOLDING COMPANY ACT OF 1935

The Public Utility Holding Company Act of 1935 (PUHCA) regulates public utilities, including interstate electricity and natural gas holding companies. Among other things, the Act prevents regulated utilities from taking funds generated from a regulated business and using such funds to subsidize non-regulated side businesses. The SEC is charged with limiting the size of the regulated utilities and, in doing so, may regulate the rates of the utilities as well as the organization of utility holding companies and transactions among companies within the holding company structure. Although public utilities were the mainstay of the SEC's regulatory work in the agency's earliest days, today the Act is largely of historical significance, shot through with exceptions and exemptions. (The SEC has called for its repeal, and the SEC does not yield authority easily.) Accordingly, we do not spend any time on the PUHCA in this casebook.

6.   SARBANES–OXLEY ACT OF 2002

The Sarbanes–Oxley Act of 2002 represents Congress' most recent major legislation affecting the securities markets. Congress enacted the Sarbanes–Oxley Act in response to corporate scandals at Enron, WorldCom, Adelphia, Global Crossing, and Tyco, among other major publicly-held corporations, providing new regulation for almost all significant players in the capital markets. The law is a mélange of legislative reactions to the scandal du jour. Among other things, the Act establishes a new quasi-governmental Public Company Accounting Oversight Board to regulate accountants along the lines of the SROs. It also prohibits auditors from performing certain non-audit consulting services for reporting issuers and requires companies to have audit committees made up exclusively of independent directors to oversee the company's relationship with its outside accountants. The Act directs the SEC to promulgate new rules to encourage more objective securities market analysts (which the SEC has now done with Regulation AC). Attorneys for issuers are obligated under the Act to reveal evidence of securities law violations to the corporate board of directors. Corporate CEOs and CFOs face new certification requirements for the information contained in their Form 10–K and 10–Q filings, as well as on the internal control structure of their companies. Finally, the Act increases the fines and criminal penalties for white-collar crime. We cover the more notable features of the Sarbanes–Oxley Act in greater detail in Chapter 4.

B. THE SECURITIES AND EXCHANGE COMMISSION

Congress typically intervenes only sporadically in the securities market, stepping in with legislation such as the Sarbanes–Oxley Act only when there has been a crisis that captures legislators' attention. Instead, the task of monitoring the market, enforcing the securities laws, and developing new regulations is largely left with an administrative agency: the Securities and Exchange Commission.

The Securities and Exchange Commission was established by the Securities Exchange Act of 1934. At the top of the SEC is a commission consisting of five commissioners (one of whom is appointed chairman). Although the President appoints the commissioners, the Exchange Act requires that not more than three of the commissioners come from the same political party. Joseph Kennedy served as the SEC's first Chairman in 1934. One of Kennedy's successors was William O. Douglas, appointed the SEC Chairman in 1936, more familiar to you perhaps in his later role as an Associate Justice of the U.S. Supreme Court.

The SEC is charged with administering the federal securities laws. A regulatory staff serves in addition to the five commissioners. Headquartered in Washington, D.C., the SEC also has several regional offices, the largest of which is in New York. The SEC divides its staff into several different divisions, including:

- Corporation Finance
- Market Regulation
- Investment Management
- Enforcement

The Division of Corporation Finance handles information disclosure by issuers to investors, reviewing Exchange Act periodic filings (Forms 10–K,

10–Q, and 8–K) as well as disclosure filings relating to public offerings (e.g., the registration statement). Much of the Division of Corporation Finance's attention is focused on reviewing the registration statements of companies engaged in public offerings, particularly for IPO issuers. Corporation Finance attempts to review all registration statements of IPO issuers (but a much smaller fraction for more seasoned issuers), providing comments to the issuers on the preliminary registration statements. As part of its focus on disclosure, Corporation Finance frequently reviews and proposes changes to disclosure forms and rules for approval by the Commissioners of the SEC. This division also provides guidance to companies on complying with the rules and forms.

The Division of Market Regulation deals primarily with the regulation of the securities professionals associated with the public capital markets. As part of its function, Market Regulation regulates, among others, broker-dealers and the self-regulatory organizations (including the National Association of Securities Dealers and the NYSE). The rise of the Internet has posed a particular challenge for Market Regulation in determining the reach of what constitutes a broker-dealer. In the late 1990s, entrepreneurs established websites to help sell private placement offerings to investors. Through a series of no-action letters and an interpretive release, the Division of Market Regulation made clear that many operators of these websites were required to register as broker-dealers with the SEC, thus raising the level of regulation as well as costs of compliance. Broker-dealer registration is required if the website is in the business of effecting or inducing transactions in securities.

The Division of Investment Management is charged with regulating both investment companies and investment advisors. Investment Management regulates mutual funds like those offered by Vanguard and Fidelity. The mutual fund industry has long enjoyed its reputation as one of the "cleaner" sectors of the investment industry, a notable distinction in an industry that draws more than its fair share of sleazy operators. Recently, however, Investment Management has been confronted with a spate of scandals relating to late trading and other abuses within the mutual fund industry. Investors purchasing or redeeming a mutual fund share do so at the net asset value (NAV) of the share, calculated after the purchase or redeem order is made. The NAV is typically calculated at 4:00 PM for most funds. Thus, investors purchasing at 4:10 PM would receive the NAV calculated as of 4:00 PM on the next business day. Late trading allows favored investors to purchase (or redeem) a mutual fund's shares *after* 4:00 PM based on that day's NAV set at 4:00 PM (instead of the next day's NAV). Thus, if new information comes out after 4:00 PM affecting the prices of securities held by a particular mutual fund, a late trading investor may make an almost guaranteed profit, diluting the interests of all other holders of the fund.

The Division of Enforcement investigates securities law violations. The SEC may initiate enforcement actions in federal court or conduct administrative proceedings. In criminal cases, the SEC must make a referral to the

Justice Department for prosecution. (These topics are covered in greater detail in Chapter 4.) Many of the SEC enforcement actions result in a negotiated settlement. Working in conjunction with the New York State Attorney General, the SEC obtained a $1.4 billion settlement from ten of the major Wall Street investment banks in 2002. Under the terms of the settlement, over $800 million was earmarked for independent securities analyst research and investor restitution. The settlement also required that the investment banks separate their research analysts from their investment banking businesses, "including prohibiting analysts from receiving compensation for investment banking activities and prohibiting analysts' involvement in investment banking 'pitches' and 'roadshows.'" Furthermore, the research department's budget and analysts' compensation cannot be tied to revenues generated from investment banking.

In addition to these Divisions, the SEC has separate offices devoted to particular functions. Among the more important offices are the Office of the General Counsel, the Office of the Chief Accountant, the Office of Economic Analysis and the Office of Municipal Securities. The Office of General Counsel (widely known as the brain trust of the agency–at least when Pritchard worked there) provides legal advice to the Commissioners, drafts the opinions of the Commission in administrative proceedings, and represents the agency in the courts of appeals. The Office of the Chief Accountant provides guidance to public companies and their auditors on accounting, financial reporting, and auditing questions. Together with the Division of Corporation Finance and the newly created Public Company Accounting Oversight Board, the Office of the Chief Accountant also monitors the accounting profession. The Office of Economic Analysis provides the SEC with advice on economic and empirical issues, including cost-benefit analysis of proposed rules and regulations. The Office of Municipal Securities oversees the sale of securities by state and local governments, exercising most of its regulatory authority over the broker-dealers who sell the government securities.

The SEC and its staff have a variety of means by which to influence the capital markets. First, the SEC may engage in formal rulemaking. Corporate Finance, for example, is active in developing regulations focusing on securities offerings. Market Regulation directs its attention to rulemaking affecting institutions serving the secondary markets, including broker-dealers. The commissioners of the SEC have the ultimate authority to approve new regulations after the appropriate notice and comment period for public review.

Second, the SEC brings enforcement actions. The Division of Enforcement is charged with bringing civil enforcement actions for violations of the securities laws. Enforcement actions not only punish violators of the securities laws but also send a deterrent message to others in the securities market.

Third, the SEC's staff often will grant individuals and companies a "no-action letter." A no-action letter consists of a letter requesting that the SEC's staff take a position that if the conditions as detailed in the letter are met, the staff will then recommend that no enforcement action take place against the parties in the described transaction. The SEC's staff, in granting a no-action letter, will then write a responding letter detailing the staff's position on whether the facts specified in the original letter would warrant an enforcement action. No-action letters represent the opinion only of the SEC staff and not necessarily the view of the SEC's commissioners. Moreover, private litigants are not bound by a no-action letter and may bring suit in court based on the same fact pattern, although the court may defer to the interpretation in the no-action letter.

Finally, the SEC may influence both participants in the capital markets and the courts through its communications. Most important are the Commission's releases. Releases announce the Commission's enforcement actions, set forth the agency's interpretations of the law, propose rules and explain the rules adopted. Individual commissioners and division heads often will give speeches on their views on the capital markets and securities regulation. In addition, the SEC will on occasion file an amicus brief with a court adjudicating a private securities lawsuit. More informally, the SEC staff answers questions on the telephone.

C.   SELF–REGULATORY ORGANIZATIONS

The SEC is not the only regulator of the securities markets. Several quasi-private regulatory entities operate as an additional layer of investor protection. Among these entities are the National Association of Securities Dealers (NASD) and the national securities exchanges (including the NYSE). The SEC has the power to approve, disapprove or modify SRO rules as it "deems necessary or appropriate to insure the fair administration of the self-regulatory organization" under § 19 of the Exchange Act.

Established in 1939, the NASD is a private, non-profit, membership-based organization, composed of broker and securities dealer members. The NASD regulates both broker-dealers in the United States and the primary over-the-counter market in which they trade, the Nasdaq (in which the NASD maintains a minority equity ownership position), through its subsidiary, NASD Regulation Inc. Almost all brokers and dealers in the United States are members of the NASD. The Exchange Act requires that the NASD, as a self-regulatory organization, adopt rules "designed to prevent fraudulent and manipulative acts and practices, to promote just and equitable principles of trade ... and, in general, to protect investors and the public interest."

The NASD, among other things, imposes a suitability requirement on its brokers. NASD Rule 2310 provides that "[i]n recommending to a customer the purchase, sale or exchange of any security, a member shall have reasonable grounds for believing that the recommendation is suitable for such customer upon the basis of facts, if any, disclosed by such customer as to his other security holdings and as to his financial situation and needs." The NASD also brings enforcement actions against broker-dealers. In 2004, for example, the NASD imposed fines totaling $650,000 on brokerage firms for failing to install appropriate supervisory systems and controls designed to stop the late trading of mutual funds (as described above).

The NASD provides investors with a great deal of information on brokers. The NASD's "BrokerCheck" system (available at http://www.nasd.com) allows any investor to examine the background and past disciplinary history of brokers registered with the NASD. The NASD also maintains an active arbitration system for customers, brokers, and brokerage firms. Most brokerage agreements provide for mandatory arbitration in case of disputes. Common investor complaints against brokers include allegations that a broker sold unsuitable securities to the investor, that the broker "churned" the investor's account to generate unwarranted trading commissions for the broker, or that the broker failed to execute the customer's orders properly, resulting in a loss for the customer. Arbitration provides a low-cost and speedy method of resolving complaints against brokers and brokerage firms. However, some question whether arbitration sacrifices consistency and fairness in adjudication to obtain these benefits.

The Nasdaq and NYSE provide a number of requirements for companies that list for trading. Listed companies must meet minimum capitalization and asset requirements. Both the Nasdaq and NYSE also impose minimum corporate governance requirements. In 2003, the NASD and the NYSE promulgated new director independence rules. Listed companies must have a majority of "independent" directors. Moreover, listed companies must establish audit, executive compensation, and director nominating committees consisting entirely of independent directors. The concept of an independent director is defined narrowly. Independent directors are those directors with no material relationship with the company, including significant banking, commercial, consulting, legal, accounting, charitable, and familial relationships. The board of directors of a listed company on either Nasdaq or the NYSE is required to make an affirmative determination of the independence of individual directors and to disclose this determination in its annual proxy statement.

Another important quasi-governmental body is the new Public Company Accounting Oversight Board (PCAOB) created by Congress as part of the Sarbanes–Oxley Act of 2002. The PCAOB consists of a five-member board, only two of which members may have experience as certified public accountants. A non-profit, private entity, the PCAOB is authorized under the Sarbanes–Oxley Act to oversee the audit of public companies as well as to establish requirements for auditor independence. Public accounting firms are required to register with the PCAOB. The PCAOB may conduct investigations of public accounting firms and impose sanctions. The PCAOB is funded in part from a levy imposed on all Exchange Act reporting issuers. As with the other self-regulatory organizations, the PCAOB is subject to both oversight and enforcement authority by the SEC.

This Chapter has introduced the common types of securities investments and the major markets for securities transactions. We have also provided a glimpse into the motivations of investors. To understand the purpose of the securities laws and to assess their effectiveness, we first need to understand why investors invest and what information investors require to make informed decisions. Investors typically will part with their hard-earned money only if they expect to receive even more money back in the future. We have explained the present discount valuation method of determining the value of investments in today's dollars. The PDV formula is only as good as the information put into the formula. Investors require information on a company's businesses, assets, management, financials, and regulatory and competitive environment, among other things, to value accurately a company's expected cash flow and exposure to market risk. Finally, we have briefly summarized both the different components of the federal securities laws and the regulatory entities charged with enforcing and implementing those laws.

The rest of the casebook covers a number of topics important to understanding the federal securities regime governing both secondary market and primary market transactions. We make no claim to comprehensiveness in our coverage. Instead, we select topics that highlight the major motivations behind the securities laws and the assumptions about investor behavior embedded in those laws. Throughout the book, we emphasize the importance of disclosure as a means of reducing informational disparities in both the secondary and primary markets. Our goal here is to help you understand the basic approaches to securities regulation.

CHAPTER 2

MATERIALITY

Rules and Statutes

—*Regulation S–K, Items 303, 401, 403, 404, 406*

—*Rules 10b–5, 12b–20 of the Exchange Act*

MOTIVATING HYPOTHETICAL

Six Feet, Inc. is in the funeral business. It owns a chain of funeral homes across the U.S. and Canada. Its shares are listed on the NYSE. David is the Chairman of the Board and CEO. His younger brother, Nate, is the President and COO. Although the two have worked hard together to make Six Feet the "death services" powerhouse that it is today, they have not always agreed about business strategy. David thinks that Six Feet needs to merge with another company in the funeral business to continue its growth. Nate thinks that they should continue to grow Six Feet through internal expansion.

I. WHAT MATTERS TO INVESTORS?

We learned in Chapter 1 that information is the lifeblood of the securities markets. Current and complete information also plays a critical role in allowing shareholders to evaluate the performance of management and the board of directors. Consequently, disclosure is the focal point of federal securities regulation.

Notwithstanding the importance of information and disclosure to the decisions of investors, not all information will be equally relevant. The structure of the CEO's compensation package is likely to be important to most investors; the fact that the CEO enjoys fly-fishing in his spare time is not. Misleading statements regarding the compensation package are appropriately met by an SEC enforcement action and, potentially, a private class action; misleading statements about the CEO's hobbies are appropriately met by "Who cares?" Choices must be made in determining what information must be disclosed in the corporation's periodic filings and what false or omitted information will give rise to liability.

The concept of materiality is a common threshold used in many areas to determine what information is important enough to warrant regulation. Consider antifraud liability. Exchange Act Rule 10b–5 antifraud liability covers not only the disclosures filed with the SEC, but also voluntary disclosures such as press releases by the company and interviews provided by the CEO among other affirmative statements. The antifraud prohibition of Exchange Act Rule 10b–5 creates liability for both making "any untrue statement of a material fact" and omitting "to state a material fact necessary in order to make the statements made, in the light of the circumstances under which they were made, not misleading." So if a statement is made, there is always a duty to tell the truth, and to tell the whole truth. But whether there has been an affirmative misleading misstatement or an omission which creates a misleading impression, the plaintiff or the SEC must also show that misleading statement or omitted fact was material. If a person has made no statement at all, we ordinarily will not reach the question of materiality because there is no general duty to volunteer information. In other words, silence is golden. The exception to this golden rule, however, is that under insider trading doctrine, companies and their officers and directors have a duty to disclose all material facts before buying or selling the company's securities. Insider trading is a fraud of pure omission—the insider who trades while enjoying an informational advantage over the public is also liable under Rule 10b–5, but only if the insider's non-public information is material.

The concept of materiality extends beyond the realm of antifraud liability. The SEC has used its rulemaking powers to make a series of ex ante determinations of what information is important to investors, and should therefore be disclosed in various SEC filings, such as the annual Form 10–K and quarterly Form 10–Q. These SEC filing requirements are contained in Regulation S–K, the focal point of the SEC integrated disclosure system. For these disclosure items, most of the discretion has been removed from the issuer and its counsel: if an item is listed in Regulation S–K, it must be disclosed, whether or not it would independently be deemed material. The SEC has determined that investors will find the required information relevant most of the time. Moreover, as we discussed in Chapter 1, a consistent set of disclosure obligations allows investors to compare firms more easily.

Although there is no general duty to disclose all material information, materiality plays an important role in applying the Regulation S–K disclosure items. Some items in the laundry list of disclosures mandated by the SEC in Regulation S–K are required only if they are "material." Item 101(a) of Regulation S–K, for example, requires issuers to disclose information on the general development of their business over the past five years as well as information pertaining to earlier periods if "material to an understanding of the general development of the business." Moreover, Regulation S–K's disclosure items do not exhaust the list of mandatory disclosures. Exchange Act Rule 12b–20 requires:

> In addition to the information expressly required to be included in a statement or report, there shall be added such further material information, if any, as may be necessary to make the required statements, in the light of the circumstances under which they are made not misleading.

Rule 408 of the Securities Act expresses a similar prohibition of misleading "half truths."

What information crosses the materiality threshold? The Supreme Court provided the seminal formulation of materiality in *TSC Industries, Inc. v. Northway,* 426 U.S. 438 (1976). According to *TSC Industries,* information is material if there is a "substantial likelihood that the disclosure ... would have been viewed by the reasonable investor as having significantly altered the 'total mix' of information made available." Unfortunately, determining whether a particular morsel of information is material is often an uncertain process. Who is the reasonable investor? What information would the reasonable investor consider significant? What constitutes the total mix of information?

In this chapter, we canvass how courts determine whether specific types of information are material. We start with forward-looking information in Part II, dealing with future and necessarily contingent events. Then we discuss how materiality is applied to historical facts in Part III. In particular, is it possible to use numerical rules of thumb to ease the uncertainty in deciding whether a particular fact is material? In Part IV we discuss the possibility that a statement about a person's belief in a particular opinion or conclusory statement can qualify as a material "fact." In Part V we consider how the "total mix of information" may work to treat information as immaterial that would be material in isolation. Finally, we conclude with a discussion of materiality as applied to information that sheds light on managers' integrity. Even if information is important to investors, are there any countervailing reasons, such as privacy concerns, to not require disclosure?

II. FORWARD-LOOKING INFORMATION

The case below outlines the general standard of materiality under the securities laws. In addition, it provides guidance in applying that standard to "forward-looking" information, i.e., disclosures regarding events that may or may not come to pass. Investors are more interested in what a company is going to do in the future than what it has done in the past. A brighter future for a company translates in higher expected earnings and a correspondingly higher return from ownership of the company's shares. So insights into the company's future will be eagerly digested by the markets. What problems do companies and their counsel face in assessing the materiality of forward-looking information that are not present in assessing the materiality of historical facts?

Basic Inc. v. Levinson
485 U.S. 224 (1988).

■ JUSTICE BLACKMUN delivered the opinion of the Court.

This case requires us to apply the materiality requirement of § 10(b) of the Securities Exchange Act of 1934 and the Securities and Exchange

Commission's Rule 10b–5 in the context of preliminary corporate merger discussions. . . .

I

Prior to December 20, 1978, Basic Incorporated was a publicly traded company primarily engaged in the business of manufacturing chemical refractories for the steel industry. As early as 1965 or 1966, Combustion Engineering, Inc., a company producing mostly alumina-based refractories, expressed some interest in acquiring Basic . . . The "Strategic Plan," dated October 25, 1976, for Combustion's Industrial Products Group included the objective: "Acquire Basic Inc. $30 million."

Beginning in September 1976, Combustion representatives had meetings and telephone conversations with Basic officers and directors, including petitioners here, concerning the possibility of a merger. During 1977 and 1978, Basic made three public statements denying that it was engaged in merger negotiations.[4] On December 18, 1978, Basic asked the New York Stock Exchange to suspend trading in its shares and issued a release stating that it had been "approached" by another company concerning a merger. On December 19, Basic's board endorsed Combustion's offer of $46 per share for its common stock, and on the following day publicly announced its approval of Combustion's tender offer for all outstanding shares.

Respondents are former Basic shareholders who sold their stock after Basic's first public statement of October 21, 1977, and before the suspension of trading in December 1978. Respondents brought a class action against Basic and its directors, asserting that the defendants issued three false or misleading public statements and thereby were in violation of § 10(b) of the 1934 Act and of Rule 10b–5. Respondents alleged that they were injured by selling Basic shares at artificially depressed prices in a market affected by petitioners' misleading statements and in reliance thereon.

---

4. On October 21, 1977, after heavy trading and a new high in Basic stock, the following news item appeared in the Cleveland Plain Dealer: "[Basic] President Max Muller said the company knew no reason for the stock's activity and that no negotiations were under way with any company for a merger. He said Flintkote recently denied Wall Street rumors that it would make a tender offer of $25 a share for control of the Cleveland-based maker of refractories for the steel industry."

On September 25, 1978, in reply to an inquiry from the New York Stock Exchange, Basic issued a release concerning increased activity in its stock and stated that "management is unaware of any present or pending company development that would result in the abnormally heavy trading activity and price fluctuation in company shares that have been experienced in the past few days." On November 6, 1978, Basic issued to its shareholders a "Nine Months Report 1978." This Report stated: "With regard to the stock market activity in the Company's shares we remain unaware of any present or pending developments which would account for the high volume of trading and price fluctuations in recent months."

The District Court ... granted summary judgment for the defendants. It held that, as a matter of law, any misstatements were immaterial: there were no negotiations ongoing at the time of the first statement, and although negotiations were taking place when the second and third statements were issued, those negotiations were not "destined, with reasonable certainty, to become a merger agreement in principle."

The United States Court of Appeals for the Sixth Circuit ... reversed the District Court's summary judgment, and remanded the case. The court reasoned that while petitioners were under no general duty to disclose their discussions with Combustion, any statement the company voluntarily released could not be " 'so incomplete as to mislead.' " In the Court of Appeals' view, Basic's statements that no negotiations were taking place, and that it knew of no corporate developments to account for the heavy trading activity, were misleading. With respect to materiality, the court rejected the argument that preliminary merger discussions are immaterial as a matter of law, and held that "once a statement is made denying the existence of any discussions, even discussions that might not have been material in absence of the denial are material because they make the statement made untrue."

We granted certiorari, to resolve the split ... among the Courts of Appeals as to the standard of materiality applicable to preliminary merger discussions. ...

II

The 1934 Act was designed to protect investors against manipulation of stock prices. Underlying the adoption of extensive disclosure requirements was a legislative philosophy: "There cannot be honest markets without honest publicity. Manipulation and dishonest practices of the market place thrive upon mystery and secrecy." This Court "repeatedly has described the 'fundamental purpose' of the Act as implementing a 'philosophy of full disclosure.' "

The Court previously has addressed various positive and common-law requirements for a violation of § 10(b) or of Rule 10b–5. ... The Court also explicitly has defined a standard of materiality under the securities laws, see *TSC Industries, Inc. v. Northway, Inc.*, 426 U.S. 438 (1976), concluding in the proxy-solicitation context that "[a]n omitted fact is material if there is a substantial likelihood that a reasonable shareholder would consider it important in deciding how to vote." Acknowledging that certain information concerning corporate developments could well be of "dubious significance," the Court was careful not to set too low a standard of materiality; it was concerned that a minimal standard might bring an overabundance of information within its reach, and lead management "simply to bury the shareholders in an avalanche of trivial information—a result that is hardly conducive to informed decisionmaking." It further explained that to fulfill the materiality requirement "there must be a substantial likelihood that the disclosure of the omitted fact would have been viewed by the reasonable investor as having significantly altered the 'total mix' of information made available." We now expressly adopt the *TSC Industries* standard of materiality for the § 10(b) and Rule 10b–5 context.

III

The application of this materiality standard to preliminary merger discussions is not self-evident. Where the impact of the corporate development on the target's fortune is certain and clear, the *TSC Industries* materiality definition admits straightforward application. Where, on the other hand, the event is contingent or speculative in nature, it is difficult to ascertain whether the "reasonable investor" would have considered the omitted information significant at the time. Merger negotiations, because of the ever-present possibility that the contemplated transaction will not be effectuated, fall into the latter category.[9]

A

Petitioners urge upon us a Third Circuit test for resolving this difficulty. Under this approach, preliminary merger discussions do not become material until "agreement-in-principle" as to the price and structure of the transaction has been reached between the would-be merger partners. By definition, then, information concerning any negotiations not yet at the agreement-in-principle stage could be withheld or even misrepresented without a violation of Rule 10b–5.

Three rationales have been offered in support of the "agreement-in-principle" test. The first derives from the concern expressed in *TSC Industries* that an investor not be overwhelmed by excessively detailed and trivial information, and focuses on the substantial risk that preliminary merger discussions may collapse: because such discussions are inherently tentative, disclosure of their existence itself could mislead investors and foster false optimism. The other two justifications for the agreement-in-principle standard are based on management concerns: because the requirement of "agreement-in-principle" limits the scope of disclosure obligations, it helps preserve the confidentiality of merger discussions where earlier disclosure might prejudice the negotiations; and the test also provides a usable, bright-line rule for determining when disclosure must be made.

None of these policy-based rationales, however, purports to explain why drawing the line at agreement-in-principle reflects the significance of the information upon the investor's decision. The first rationale, and the only one connected to the concerns expressed in *TSC Industries*, stands soundly rejected, even by a Court of Appeals that otherwise has accepted the wisdom of the agreement-in-principle test. "It assumes that investors are nitwits, unable to appreciate—even when told—that mergers are risky propositions up until the closing." Disclosure, and not paternalistic withholding of accurate information, is the policy chosen and expressed by Congress. We have recognized time and again, a "fundamental purpose" of

---

9. We do not address here any other kinds of contingent or speculative information, such as earnings forecasts or projections.

the various Securities Acts, "was to substitute a philosophy of full disclosure for the philosophy of caveat emptor and thus to achieve a high standard of business ethics in the securities industry." The role of the materiality requirement is not to "attribute to investors a child-like simplicity, an inability to grasp the probabilistic significance of negotiations," but to filter out essentially useless information that a reasonable investor would not consider significant, even as part of a larger "mix" of factors to consider in making his investment decision.

The second rationale, the importance of secrecy during the early stages of merger discussions, also seems irrelevant to an assessment whether their existence is significant to the trading decision of a reasonable investor. To avoid a "bidding war" over its target, an acquiring firm often will insist that negotiations remain confidential, and at least one Court of Appeals has stated that "silence pending settlement of the price and structure of a deal is beneficial to most investors, most of the time."[11]

We need not ascertain, however, whether secrecy necessarily maximizes shareholder wealth—although we note that the proposition is at least disputed as a matter of theory and empirical research—for this case does not concern the timing of a disclosure; it concerns only its accuracy and completeness.[13] We face here the narrow question whether information concerning the existence and status of preliminary merger discussions is significant to the reasonable investor's trading decision. Arguments based on the premise that some disclosure would be "premature" in a sense are more properly considered under the rubric of an issuer's duty to disclose. The "secrecy" rationale is simply inapposite to the definition of materiality.

The final justification offered in support of the agreement-in-principle test seems to be directed solely at the comfort of corporate managers. A bright-line rule indeed is easier to follow than a standard that requires the exercise of judgment in the light of all the circumstances. But ease of application alone is not an excuse for ignoring the purposes of the Securities Acts and Congress' policy decisions. Any approach that designates a single fact or occurrence as always determinative of an inherently fact-specific finding such as materiality, must necessarily be overinclusive or underinclusive. In *TSC Industries* this Court explained: "The determination [of materiality] requires delicate assessments of the inferences a 'reasonable shareholder' would draw from a given set of facts and the significance of those inferences to him. . . ."

* * *

11. Reasoning backwards from a goal of economic efficiency, the Court of Appeals [for the Seventh Circuit] stated: "Rule 10b–5 is about fraud, after all, and it is not fraudulent to conduct business in a way that makes investors better off. . . ."

13. See *SEC v. Texas Gulf Sulphur Co.*, 401 F.2d 833, 862 (CA2 1968) (en banc)

("Rule 10b–5 is violated whenever assertions are made, as here, in a manner reasonably calculated to influence the investing public . . . if such assertions are false or misleading or are so incomplete as to mislead . . . "), cert. denied sub nom. *Coates v. SEC*, 394 U.S. 976 (1969).

We therefore find no valid justification for artificially excluding from the definition of materiality information concerning merger discussions, which would otherwise be considered significant to the trading decision of a reasonable investor, merely because agreement-in-principle as to price and structure has not yet been reached by the parties or their representatives.

B

The Sixth Circuit explicitly rejected the agreement-in-principle test, as we do today, but in its place adopted a rule that, if taken literally, would be equally insensitive, in our view, to the distinction between materiality and the other elements of an action under Rule 10b–5:

> When a company whose stock is publicly traded makes a statement, as Basic did, that 'no negotiations' are underway, and that the corporation knows of 'no reason for the stock's activity', and that 'management is unaware of any present or pending corporate development that would result in the abnormally heavy trading activity', information concerning ongoing acquisition discussions becomes material by virtue of the statement denying their existence. . . .

* * *

> In analyzing whether information regarding merger discussions is material such that it must be affirmatively disclosed to avoid a violation of Rule 10b–5, the discussions and their progress are the primary considerations. However, once a statement is made denying the existence of any discussions, even discussions that might not have been material in absence of the denial are material because they make the statement made untrue.

This approach, however, fails to recognize that, in order to prevail on a Rule 10b–5 claim, a plaintiff must show that the statements were misleading as to a material fact. It is not enough that a statement is false or incomplete, if the misrepresented fact is otherwise insignificant.

C

Even before this Court's decision in *TSC Industries*, the Second Circuit had explained the role of the materiality requirement of Rule 10b–5, with respect to contingent or speculative information or events, in a manner that gave that term meaning that is independent of the other provisions of the Rule. Under such circumstances, materiality "will depend at any given time upon a balancing of both the indicated probability that the event will occur and the anticipated magnitude of the event in light of the totality of the company activity." *SEC v. Texas Gulf Sulphur Co.*, 401 F.2d, at 849. . . .

In a subsequent decision, the late Judge Friendly, writing for a Second Circuit panel, applied the *Texas Gulf Sulphur* probability/magnitude approach in the specific context of preliminary merger negotiations. After acknowledging that materiality is something to be determined on the basis of the particular facts of each case, he stated:

Since a merger in which it is bought out is the most important event that can occur in a small corporation's life, to wit, its death, we think that inside information, as regards a merger of this sort, can become material at an earlier stage than would be the case as regards lesser transactions—and this even though the mortality rate of mergers in such formative stages is doubtless high. *SEC v. Geon Industries, Inc.,* 531 F.2d 39, 47–48 (1976).

We agree with that analysis.[16]

Whether merger discussions in any particular case are material therefore depends on the facts. Generally, in order to assess the probability that the event will occur, a factfinder will need to look to indicia of interest in the transaction at the highest corporate levels. Without attempting to catalog all such possible factors, we note by way of example that board resolutions, instructions to investment bankers, and actual negotiations between principals or their intermediaries may serve as indicia of interest. To assess the magnitude of the transaction to the issuer of the securities allegedly manipulated, a factfinder will need to consider such facts as the size of the two corporate entities and of the potential premiums over market value. No particular event or factor short of closing the transaction need be either necessary or sufficient by itself to render merger discussions material.[17]

As we clarify today, materiality depends on the significance the reasonable investor would place on the withheld or misrepresented information.[18]

---

16. The SEC in the present case endorses the highly fact-dependent probability/magnitude balancing approach of *Texas Gulf Sulphur.* It explains: "The *possibility* of a merger may have an immediate importance to investors in the company's securities even if no merger ultimately takes place." The SEC's insights are helpful, and we accord them due deference.

17. To be actionable, of course, a statement must also be misleading. Silence, absent a duty to disclose, is not misleading under Rule 10b–5. "No comment" statements are generally the functional equivalent of silence. See . . . New York Stock Exchange Listed Company Manual § 202.01 (premature public announcement may properly be delayed for valid business purpose and where adequate security can be maintained); American Stock Exchange Company Guide §§ 401–405 (similar provisions).

It has been suggested that, given current market practices, a "no comment" statement is tantamount to an admission that merger discussions are underway. See *Flamm v. Eberstadt,* 814 F.2d at 1178. That may well hold true to the extent that issuers adopt a policy of truthfully denying merger rumors when no discussions are underway, and of issuing "no comment" statements when they are in the midst of negotiations. There are, of course, other statement policies firms could adopt; we need not now advise issuers as to what kind of practice to follow, within the range permitted by law. Perhaps more importantly, we think that creating an exception to a regulatory scheme founded on a prodisclosure legislative philosophy, because complying with the regulation might be "bad for business," is a role for Congress, not this Court.

18. We find no authority in the statute, the legislative history, or our previous decisions for varying the standard of materiality depending on who brings the action or whether insiders are alleged to have profited.

We recognize that trading (and profit making) by insiders can serve as an indication of materiality. We are not prepared to agree, however, that "[i]n cases of the disclosure of inside information to a favored few, determination of materiality has a different aspect than when the issue is, for example, an inaccuracy in a publicly disseminated

The fact-specific inquiry we endorse here is consistent with the approach a number of courts have taken in assessing the materiality of merger negotiations. Because the standard of materiality we have adopted differs from that used by both courts below, we remand the case for reconsideration of the question whether a grant of summary judgment is appropriate on this record.

* * *

NOTES

1. *The reasonable shareholder.* The Supreme Court's invocation of the "reasonable shareholder" in its formulation of the materiality standard makes clear that the standard is an objective one—information relevant only to the idiosyncratic investor about a company does not define the company's disclosure obligations. The lower courts have generally held that issuers are not responsible for the subjective preferences of a particular investor.

Who determines what is material to the reasonable shareholder? The Supreme Court cautioned in *TSC Industries, Inc. v. Northway,* 426 U.S. 438, 450 (1976), that materiality is a mixed question of law and fact that should ordinarily be determined by the fact finder at trial. This caution is frequently ignored. Lower courts, anxious to dismiss what they perceive to be weak cases, have frequently concluded that no reasonable jury could conclude that the information misrepresented or omitted was material, thereby making dismissal or summary judgment appropriate.

2. *Forward-looking information.* Forward-looking information (often referred to as "soft" information) receives mixed treatment under the securities laws. On the one hand, the SEC has made clear that companies in the "quiet period" leading up to a public offering of securities disclose soft information only at their peril (as discussed in Chapter 7). Particularly disfavored are projections of future financial performance. The SEC's position assumes that investors are particularly vulnerable to over-optimistic forward-looking disclosures.

In contrast, other areas of the securities laws recognize the importance of forward-looking information to investors attempting to decide among different investment options. To induce companies to make such disclosures (and in response to the perceived risk of frivolous litigation targeting soft disclosures), Congress enacted a safe harbor for forward-looking statements as part of the Private Securities Litigation Reform Act of 1995 (covered in Chapter 5). As we come back to the issue of forward-looking information both in the context of the quiet period and the safe harbor, consider how you would balance the importance of such information to investors against the risk that because such information is inherently difficult to verify, investors are more easily lead astray.

press release." Devising two different standards of materiality, one for situations where insiders have traded in abrogation of their duty to disclose or abstain (or for that matter when any disclosure duty has been breached), and another covering affirmative misrepresentations by those under no duty to disclose (but under the ever-present duty not to mislead), would effectively collapse the materiality requirement into the analysis of defendant's disclosure duties.

QUESTIONS

1. Are shareholders better off if merger negotiations must be disclosed?

2. What could Basic have done to maintain the confidentiality of its merger negotiations with Combustion?

3. Is a judge or jury assessing the probability of an event after it has occurred likely to assign the same probability as the issuer and its counsel did when they were drafting the disclosure?

4. Was the potential merger with Basic necessarily material to Combustion shareholders?

5. Is the Court correct to focus on the informational needs of the "reasonable investor"? Aren't "unreasonable investors" substantially more likely to make poor investment choices?

HYPOTHETICAL ONE

David, the CEO of Six Feet, has had several conversations with Sarah, the CEO of Dearly Departed, Inc. (Six Feet's chief competitor with a similar market share), about the possibility of merging their two companies. So far their discussions have been relatively informal, but they have discussed a merger ratio for a possible stock-for-stock merger, with Six Feet to be the survivor of the merger. They have also agreed that David would be the Chairman of the Board of the merged company and Sarah the CEO and President. (Nate, the President of Six Feet, would be looking for work!)

David and Sarah have agreed on the important terms, but David is not sure that he wants to take the deal to Six Feet's board. David and Nate hold two of the three seats on Six Feet's board, with the remaining seat held by Federico. Federico, Six Feet's Vice-President for Death Services, is the creative spark behind Six Feet's growth—he came up with the idea of caskets bearing the logo of the deceased's favorite sports team—and also a substantial shareholder. Federico has been wary of taking on too much risk, but he also despises Nate and would be happy to see him go. David is uncertain which way Federico will vote if the merger is presented to the board. Moreover, Six Feet and Dearly Departed have very substantial shares of the funeral services market in a number of metropolitan areas and any merger between the two could very well draw the scrutiny of the antitrust authorities.

David is pondering all of these variables at the time he is interviewed by *The Eulogy*, a magazine devoted to the funeral business. In response to the reporter's question, "Does Six Feet have any acquisitions in the pipeline?" David says "We do not currently have any major acquisitions in mind, but Six Feet is always looking for opportunities to expand if they make business sense." Does David's response contain a material omission?

———————

The following case applies *Basic*'s probability times magnitude standard to a non-acquisition context. In addition, the case identifies an external source of evidence for determining whether a reasonable shareholder would consider the contested disclosure or omission material. The case, following a common approach taken in many courts, looks to whether the company's stock price has an abnormal reaction around the date at which a public announcement is made revealing the previously undisclosed fraud or omission. Finally, it discusses the relation between materiality determinations and disclosure items mandated by the SEC through rule-making (in Regulation S–K, for example). Does the court give appropriate weight to the determinations of the SEC?

Oran v. Stafford

226 F.3d 275 (3d Cir. 2000).

■ ALITO, CIRCUIT JUDGE.

Plaintiffs brought this securities class action against American Home Products Corporation and certain of its directors and officers after AHP, in response to reports of serious medical side effects, withdrew its prescription weight-loss drugs Pondimin and Redux from the market. Stockholder plaintiffs allege that AHP made material misrepresentations and omissions regarding the safety of the drugs while failing to disclose several studies linking the drugs to heart-valve damage. As a result, plaintiffs claim, they suffered substantial financial loss when AHP's stock prices dropped following public disclosure of the withheld information. . . .

I.

* * *

A.   The Heart Valve Reports

Defendant American Home Products Corporation . . . is engaged in the research, development, manufacture and marketing of prescription and over-the-counter medications. . . . Pondimin was marketed together with another drug, phentermine, in a combination popularly known as "fen-phen." Pondimin was approved by the Food and Drug Administration in 1973. Redux was recommended for approval by an FDA Advisory Committee in November 1995 and approved by the FDA in 1996.

In February 1994, AHP learned that a Belgian cardiologist had documented leaky heart valves in seven patients who had been taking diet pills containing Pondimin and Redux. By the time the FDA Advisory Committee voted to approve Redux in November 1995, AHP knew of at least 31 cases of heart valve abnormalities in European diet-pill users, but had informed the FDA about only eight of those cases. During the same time period, AHP also received hundreds of adverse reaction reports of patients displaying symptoms often associated with heart and lung problems. AHP represented to the FDA that these symptoms were reactions to the drugs and were not caused by any underlying heart condition.

In March 1997, AHP representatives met separately with cardiologists from the Mayo Clinic and MeritCare Health Systems, who informed AHP that they had documented heart-valve abnormalities in a total of 17 fen-phen users. Dr. Heidi Connolly, the Mayo cardiologist, informed AHP that she had never seen this type of valve damage except in patients with rare cancers or in those who had taken ergotamine, a migraine drug that, like Redux and Pondimin, affects the body's serotonin level. Although AHP continued to investigate the Mayo data throughout 1997, it did not immediately release the reports to the public.

The Mayo data, which by that time included 24 reports of heart-valve abnormalities in fen-phen users, was finally disclosed to the public on July 8, 1997. On that date, AHP, Mayo, MeritCare and the FDA each made a public announcement concerning the reports. The Mayo announcement noted that the information "raise[d] significant concern that this combination of appetite suppressants has important implications regarding valvular disease." AHP's announcement similarly stated that the company was investigating "the potential association of valvular heart disorders with the combination use of [fen-phen]." The Mayo, FDA, and AHP announcements, however, all emphasized that there was no conclusive evidence establishing a causal relationship between fen-phen and heart valve disorders and that further study was needed before such a link could be confirmed. Following these announcements, there was no decline in the New York Stock Exchange price of AHP common stock.

B.   The Withdrawal of Redux and Pondimin

On September 12, 1997, the FDA informed AHP of a survey showing that 92 of 291 fen-phen users had developed heart-valve abnormalities. The next business day, September 15, 1997, AHP announced that it was withdrawing Pondimin and Redux from the market. The same day, AHP issued a press release estimating total lost profits of 14 cents per share for 1997 and 1998 as a result of lost sales of the two drugs, as well as a one-time product withdrawal loss of $200 million to $300 million. On September 15, the day of the withdrawal announcement, the closing price of AHP common stock fell 3 11/16 points, to 73 1/4.

On September 16, 1997, a Wall Street Journal article reported that AHP "face[s] lawsuits, including one seeking class-action status, from people who claim to have been harmed by the drugs. American Home says it is likely it will face legal action." Nevertheless, AHP's stock rose slightly for the day. On September 17, 1997, articles in the Wall Street Journal and the New York Times reported that AHP had known about possible heart-valve abnormalities since at least March 1997, and that the company faced substantial personal injury liability exposure. That day, AHP stock suffered a 4 1/4 point decline, to close at 69 15/16.

C.   AHP's Public Statements During the Class Period.

Plaintiffs allege that from March 1, 1997, through September 16, 1997, AHP made material misrepresentations and omissions regarding the safety of Pondimin and Redux, as well as AHP's knowledge of the heart-valve reports. For example, on March 27, 1997, AHP issued its Annual Report, which contained a statement that "Redux, the first prescription weight-loss drug to be cleared by the FDA in more than 20 years, was one of the most successful drug launches ever." The report contained no reference to either the European or the Mayo data. On April 21, 1997, AHP issued a press release addressing newspaper reports of a death that had been mistakenly attributed to Redux by an FDA official. The press release noted that "[s]cientific evidence has shown Redux to be safe and effective when used as indicated." In addition, in various releases listing Redux and Pondimin's side effects, AHP omitted any mention of heart-valve damage.

Plaintiffs also contend that, following the public disclosure of the Mayo data on July 8, 1997, AHP issued further misleading statements that were designed to minimize the impact of that data. Although AHP's statements to the public discussed "a possible serious heart valve disorder" and "an unusual type of serious regurgitant valvular heart disease," AHP failed to disclose that it had been aware of the Mayo data since March 1997, and of the European data since early 1995. According to plaintiffs, this omission served to materially mislead investors as to AHP's potential exposure to damages from products liability litigation arising out of the two drugs.

* * *

II.

* * *

A.

To state a valid securities fraud claim under Rule 10b–5, a plaintiff must first establish that defendant, in connection with the purchase or sale of a security, "made a materially false or misleading statement or omitted to state a material fact necessary to make a statement not misleading." * * *

Plaintiffs maintain that they pled several material misrepresentations and omissions, namely: (1) that AHP failed to disclose the Mayo data prior to July 8, 1997, and issued misleading statements minimizing the import of that data following disclosure; (2) that AHP failed to disclose the European data and adverse reaction reports, even after the Mayo data became public; (3) that AHP misled investors by publicizing the fact of Redux's FDA approval without disclosing that it had withheld much of the European data from the FDA; and (4) that AHP failed to disclose when it had first learned about the European data, the adverse reaction reports, or the Mayo data. Before we address these alleged omissions and misrepresentations in detail, we briefly review this Circuit's explication of the materiality standard.

Material information is "information that would be important to a reasonable investor in making his or her investment decision." Generally, undisclosed information is considered material if "there is a substantial likelihood that the disclosure would have been viewed by the reasonable investor as having 'significantly altered the "total mix" of information' available to that investor."

In *Burlington*[, 114 F.3d 1410 (3d Cir.1997)], however, this Court fashioned a special rule for measuring materiality in the context of an efficient securities market. This rule was shaped by the basic economic insight that in an open and developed securities market like the New York Stock Exchange, the price of a company's stock is determined by all available material information regarding the company and its business. In such an efficient market, "information important to reasonable investors . . . is immediately incorporated into the stock price." As a result, when a stock is traded in an efficient market, the materiality of disclosed information may be measured post hoc by looking to the movement, in the period immediately following disclosure, of the price of the firm's stock. Because in an efficient market "the concept of materiality translates into information that alters the price of the firm's stock," if a company's disclosure of information has no effect on stock prices, "it follows that the information disclosed . . . was immaterial as a matter of law."

With these standards in mind, we turn to plaintiffs' specific allegations of material misrepresentation.

1. AHP first learned of the Mayo data suggesting a link between fenphen and heart-valve disorders in March 1997. It did not, however, release this data to the public until July 8, 1997. The District Court concluded that AHP's failure to disclose this data prior to July 8 was not a material omission, and we agree.

Because the Mayo data was actually disclosed on July 8, we apply *Burlington* and look to the movement in the price of AHP's stock following disclosure to determine if the information was material. As the District Court noted, the July 8 disclosure had no appreciable negative effect on the company's stock price; in fact, AHP's share price rose by $3.00 during the four days after the Mayo disclosure. Under *Burlington*'s market test, this price stability is dispositive of the question of materiality.

Plaintiffs counter, however, that this lack of adverse price movement may be traceable to defendant's own "spinning" of the Mayo data—which, plaintiffs maintain, itself constituted a material misrepresentation. Plaintiffs argue, in effect, that had AHP not deceptively downplayed the significance of the Mayo data through its sanguine and allegedly misleading statements, investors would have realized the import of the information, and share prices would have tumbled following the June 8 announcement.

We reject this argument, and agree with the District Court that AHP's so-called "spinning" of the Mayo data was not materially misleading. AHP, in its public statements, did characterize the Mayo data as "limited and therefore inconclusive," and emphasized that "additional scientific investigation must be conducted before any possible link can be confirmed." There is, however, nothing in these statements that could reasonably be characterized as inaccurate. The FDA's own June 8 press release confirmed that "[p]resently there is no conclusive evidence establishing a causal relationship between [Pondimin and Redux] and valvular heart disease." Mayo's public statement that same day was similarly ambivalent: "We believe these cases raise significant concern that this combination of appetite suppressants has important implications regarding valvular heart disease. But more comprehensive study is needed to confirm the associations."

These third-party statements support the District Court's conclusion that AHP's characterization of the Mayo data as "inconclusive" was neither false nor misleading. . . .

2. Plaintiffs next argue that AHP's statements regarding the Mayo data must be viewed in light of the company's failure to disclose the European data and the adverse reaction reports. In their view, had this data not been withheld, it would have corroborated the Mayo report and alerted investors to the possibility of a significant link between the two drugs and valvular heart disease. In particular, plaintiffs assert that AHP's statements characterizing the Mayo data as "inconclusive" became materially misleading in light of this additional withheld data.

Plaintiffs do not allege that the European data and adverse reaction reports, taken by themselves, established any statistically significant relationship between AHP's products and valvular heart disease. Nor does the Amended Complaint assert that the withheld data, even when viewed in conjunction with the Mayo report, could have demonstrated any medically conclusive link in light of the millions of prescriptions written for Pondimin and Redux. In fact, plaintiffs never clearly explain how the accumulation of additional anecdotal data, short of the point of statistical significance, would have added anything to the disclosures already made on July 8, 1997. Because the link between the two drugs and heart-valve disorders was never definitively established during the relevant period even after the withheld data is taken into account, AHP's failure to disclose this data cannot render its statements about the inconclusiveness of the relationship materially misleading.

AHP characterized the Mayo data as inconclusive. Had it simultaneously disclosed the European data and the adverse reaction reports, the aggregate of available information would nevertheless have led a reasonable investor to the same conclusion—that the relationship between the two drugs and heart valve disorders was still inconclusive. As the Second Circuit has noted, "[d]rug companies need not disclose isolated reports of illnesses suffered by users of their drugs until those reports provide statistically significant evidence that the ill effects may be caused by—rather than randomly associated with–use of the drugs and are sufficiently serious and frequent to affect future earnings." The withheld reports did not provide such statistically significant evidence. Therefore, we agree with the District Court that the disclosure of the European data and the adverse reaction reports would not have "significantly altered the 'total mix' of information" available to AHP's investors.

3. Plaintiffs next contend that they were materially misled about the FDA approval process for Redux. Although AHP had become aware of at least 31 cases of heart valve abnormalities in European diet-pill users by the time that the FDA Advisory Committee voted to approve Redux in 1995, the company informed the FDA of only eight of those reports. This

non-disclosure, plaintiffs contend, rendered materially misleading AHP's later statements about the approval process, which plaintiffs claim suggested that AHP had disclosed to the agency all available safety data.[4]

As an initial matter, we note that plaintiffs do not allege that AHP withheld any information that it was legally required to disclose to the FDA. Certainly, the simple failure to disclose the additional European cases—which, as we have explained above, fail to establish a statistically significant causal relationship—cannot by itself serve as a basis for securities fraud liability.

Plaintiffs, however, argue that AHP put the subject of FDA approval "in play" by publicizing the agency's determination that Redux was safe, and that once that subject was in play, AHP was required to disclose any material facts that would have tended to contradict its positive representations. Plaintiffs rely principally on *Shapiro v. UJB Financial Corp.*, 964 F.2d 272, 281 (3d Cir.1992), which dealt with a defendant's characterization of its financial management practices as "adequate." Finding that such a statement could, in some circumstances, be actionable, this Court reasoned that:

> if a defendant has not commented on the nature and quality of the management practices that it has used to reach a particular statement of loan loss reserves, earnings, assets, or net worth, it is not a violation of the securities laws to fail to characterize these practices as inadequate, meaningless, out of control, or ineffective. However, where a defendant affirmatively characterizes management practices as "adequate," "conservative," "cautious," and the like, the subject is "in play." For example, if a defendant represents that its lending practices are "conservative" and that its collateralization is "adequate," the securities laws are clearly implicated if it nevertheless intentionally or recklessly omits certain facts contradicting these representations. Likewise, if a defendant characterizes loan loss reserves as "adequate" or "solid" even though it knows they are inadequate or unstable, it exposes itself to possible liability for securities fraud. By addressing the quality of a particular management practice, a defendant declares the subject of its representation to be material to the reasonable shareholder, and thus is bound to speak truthfully.

We do not believe that AHP's statements regarding the FDA approval process were materially misleading under *Shapiro*. Unlike the defendant in *Shapiro*, AHP did not make any "affirmative characterization" that the FDA's approval was based on a complete review of every piece of relevant medical information. Rather, AHP made a simple (and accurate) factual assertion that the FDA had found that Redux had an "acceptable safety profile" following a "thorough review of more than 17 clinical trials."

---

4. For example, on August 19, 1997, AHP issued a press release stating that "[t]he FDA cleared Redux for marketing in April, 1996 following a thorough review of more than 17 clinical trials which indicated that, at the dose recommended for treatment of obesity, dexfenfluramine is an effective appetite suppressant with an acceptable safety profile."

Accordingly, we find that these statements did not constitute any material misrepresentation or omission.

4.   Finally, plaintiffs charge that AHP's failure to disclose the dates on which it first learned of the European data, adverse reaction reports, and Mayo data constituted a material omission. This information was material to investors, they assert, because of the light it would have cast on AHP's potential products liability exposure. According to the plaintiffs, the materiality of this undisclosed information was confirmed by the four-percent drop in share prices on September 17, the day that the New York Times and Wall Street Journal reported that AHP had known about possible heart-valve abnormalities since at least March 1997.

Under the rationale of *Burlington*, this share price activity does suggest that investors viewed this final category of undisclosed information as material.[5] This does not end our inquiry, however. Even non-disclosure of material information will not give rise to liability under Rule 10b–5 unless the defendant had an affirmative duty to disclose that information. "Silence, absent a duty to disclose, is not misleading under Rule 10b–5." Such a duty to disclose may arise when there is insider trading, a statute requiring disclosure, or an inaccurate, incomplete or misleading prior disclosure.

None of these circumstances were present here. Plaintiffs do not allege that there was any statute requiring disclosure of this information. Nor do they allege that AHP was trading in its own stock during the relevant period.

Plaintiffs argue, however, that AHP's prior disclosures regarding its potential liability—particularly its July 8 disclosure of the Mayo study— were incomplete and therefore misleading because they failed to mention when the company first became aware of the adverse heart-valve data. We cannot agree. As an initial matter, it is clear that until the FDA notified AHP on September 12 of its own data showing a link between the two drugs and heart-valve disorders, there was no statistically significant evidence establishing a serious health risk. Prior to that date, then, the threat of product liability exposure was purely speculative, and any evidence of when AHP first learned of the adverse Mayo and European data was immaterial as a matter of law.

* * *

5. The District Court pointed to an alternative explanation for this share price drop that it found more plausible: a delayed investor reaction to AHP's withdrawal of Pondimin and Redux two days earlier. While we agree that this is a reasonable explanation—more reasonable, perhaps, than that proffered by plaintiffs—we note that in deciding a motion to dismiss, a court must draw all reasonable inferences in favor of the nonmoving party. Here, there is nothing inherently implausible in the theory advanced by plaintiffs. Consequently, we believe that the District Court erred in adopting its own interpretation of the September 17 share price drop rather than accepting the theory put forward by plaintiffs. We believe, however, that this error was harmless because, as we explain below, plaintiffs have not pled any affirmative duty on AHP's part to disclose the disputed information.

In short, even assuming arguendo that the date on which AHP was put on notice of the adverse health data was material at the time the public learned of it, we hold that AHP was under no affirmative duty to disclose this information under federal securities law. Therefore, this omission cannot form the basis for liability.

B.

Plaintiffs next argue that AHP had an affirmative obligation to disclose the heart-valve data's effect on AHP's future prospects under SEC Regulation S–K, Item 303(a). S–K 303 requires a company to include in its SEC filings a discussion of "any known trends or uncertainties that have had or that the registrant reasonably expects will have a material favorable or unfavorable impact on net sales or revenues or income from continuing operations." Plaintiffs allege that by omitting material information concerning the link between its drugs and valvular heart disorder from its 1996 Form 10–K and Annual Report, and its 1997 First and Second Quarter Form 10–Qs, AHP breached its duty of disclosure under the regulation.

To succeed on this claim, however, plaintiffs must first establish either that S–K 303 creates an independent private right of action, or that the regulation imposes an affirmative duty of disclosure on AHP that, if violated, would constitute a material omission under Rule 10b–5. We address these possibilities in turn. . . .

Neither the language of the regulation nor the SEC's interpretative releases construing it suggest that it was intended to establish a private cause of action, and courts construing the provision have unanimously held that it does not do so.

Plaintiffs respond, however, that even if there is no independent private cause of action under SK–303, the regulation nevertheless creates a duty of disclosure that, if violated, constitutes a material omission under Section 10(b) of the Securities Exchange Act and Rule 10b–5. In evaluating this argument, we must examine whether the disclosure mandated by SK–303 is governed by standards consistent with those that the Supreme Court has imposed for private fraud actions under the federal securities laws.

The SEC, whose interpretation is entitled to considerable deference, has characterized a company's disclosure obligations under SK–303 as follows:

Where a trend, demand, commitment, event or uncertainty is known, management must make two assessments:

(1) Is the known trend, demand, commitment, event or uncertainty likely to come to fruition? If management determines that it is not reasonably likely to occur, no disclosure is required.

(2) If management cannot make that determination, it must evaluate objectively the consequences of the known trend, demand, commitment, event or uncertainty, on the assumption that it will come to fruition. Disclosure is then required unless management determines

that a material effect on the registrant's financial condition or results of operations is not reasonably likely to occur.

This test varies considerably from the general test for securities fraud materiality set out by the Supreme Court in *Basic Inc. v. Levinson*, which premised forward-looking disclosure "upon a balancing of both the indicated probability that the event will occur and the anticipated magnitude of the event in light of the totality of the company activity." As the SEC specifically noted, "[t]he probability/magnitude test for materiality approved by the Supreme Court in *Basic* ... is inapposite to Item 303 disclosure"; rather, SK–303's disclosure obligations extend considerably beyond those required by Rule 10b–5.

Because the materiality standards for Rule 10b–5 and SK–303 differ significantly, the "demonstration of a violation of the disclosure requirements of Item 303 does not lead inevitably to the conclusion that such disclosure would be required under Rule 10b–5. Such a duty to disclose must be separately shown."[9] We find this reasoning persuasive, and thus hold that a violation of SK–303's reporting requirements does not automatically give rise to a material omission under Rule 10b–5. Because plaintiffs have failed to plead any actionable misrepresentation or omission under that Rule, SK–303 cannot provide a basis for liability.

* * *

NOTES

The *Oran* court applied the probability times magnitude standard from *Basic* even though the forward-looking information it was assessing did not involve a merger or other acquisition. This is consistent with the practice of other lower courts; the Supreme Court has not revisited this question since it reserved the issue in *Basic*.

QUESTIONS

1. Do you agree that data that fail to rise to the level of "statistical significance" do not alter the total mix of information?

2. Should the lack of market movement in response to a disclosure establish the non-materiality of that disclosure? Conversely, should a significant market response be conclusive evidence of materiality?

3. The SEC concedes that items required to be disclosed under Item 303 extend beyond those required under the materiality standard of *Basic*. Why would the SEC mandate disclosure of items not likely to influence the reasonable investor? Conversely, if the SEC requires disclosure of particular information, should that be considered *per se* material for purposes of Rule 10b–5 and other antifraud provisions?

---

9. In *Steckman v. Hart Brewing, Inc.*, 143 F.3d 1293, 1296 (9th Cir. 1998), the Ninth Circuit held that allegations which state a claim under SK–303 also sufficiently state a claim under Sections 11 and 12(a)(2) of the Securities Act. The court carefully limited its holding, however, making clear that it did not extend to claims under Section 10(b) or Rule 10b–5. Accordingly, *Steckman* does not support plaintiffs' position here.

4. Discussions of materiality by courts inevitably overlap with discussions of whether there has been a misstatement and whether there is a duty to disclose. Materiality, however, is a distinct element of all the private causes of action for fraud under the securities laws. If a company has made a misstatement, why excuse it from liability if the misstatement was not material?

5. Did AHP have any plausible business reason for withholding the information regarding a possible link between fen-phen and heart-valve disorders for as long as it did? If so, is that justification relevant to a determination of materiality?

HYPOTHETICAL TWO

David, the CEO of Six Feet, is doing a webcast for analysts, institutional investors and others interested in Six Feet's growth prospects. David tells his audience that Six Feet should enjoy 10–15% growth in revenues for the foreseeable future, as the aging baby boomer population adds to its clientele. Six Feet's stock price jumps 10% during the webcast on heavy trading volume. What David fails to mention, however, is that Six Feet has been seeing a steady increase in the number of people opting for cremation, a service with much lower profit margins. Over the last three years, the number of cremations that Six Feet has performed has risen from 10% of its total business to 20%. The trend has been driven in part by the steadily rising prices for burial plots, but it is unclear whether this inflation in the price of cemetery space will continue. Has David made a material omission in his webcast remarks?

III.   HISTORICAL FACTS

Insight into future profits is what investors are most interested in, but some historical facts, such as accounting data on revenues and profits, may shed important light on a company's future course. However, even historical facts can be contested, particularly in the often murky area of accounting. In making materiality determinations, issuers, their counsel and their accountants crave certainty, which is frequently all too elusive. In the next case, the Second Circuit follows the SEC's lead in rejecting one very commonly used rule of thumb for materiality.

Ganino v. Citizens Utilities Company

228 F.3d 154 (2d Cir. 2000).

■ KATZMANN, CIRCUIT JUDGE.

The plaintiffs-appellants appeal from a final judgment . . . granting the defendants-appellees' motion to dismiss the Second Amended Complaint for failure to state a claim under Section[] 10(b) and Rule 10b–5. The district court held: (1) the misrepresentations regarding certain payments amounting to 1.7% of total annual revenue were immaterial as a matter of law; (2) the lack of share price movement following the release of corrective information was evidence of immateriality. . . . For the reasons that follow, we reverse in part, vacate in part, and remand with instructions.

I. BACKGROUND

A. Factual Background

* * *

Citizens is a publicly traded communications and public services company. As of 1995, Citizens had reported over fifty consecutive years of increased revenue, earnings, and earnings per share, a fact which it emphasized in its public comments. In 1995, however, Citizens would not receive approximately $38 million in revenue from Pacific Bell. In order to continue to report increased earnings, the Company had to find another source of revenue.

That replacement source was Hungarian Telephone & Cable Corporation, a U.S. company which provides telephone services in Hungary under telecommunications concessions from the Hungarian government. . . . Beginning in May 1995, HTCC and Citizens (through a wholly owned subsidiary of Citizens) entered into a series of agreements under which Citizens agreed in 1995 to make and/or guarantee loans to HTCC. In consideration for these loans and guarantees, Citizens received substantial fees, consisting primarily of HTCC stock and options. In addition, Citizens also provided management consulting services to HTCC.

1. Allegations of Material Misrepresentations

Although Citizens earned and received approximately $10.1 million in Financial Support Fees from HTCC in 1995, Citizens, according to the Complaint, fraudulently recognized this sum as 1996 first and second quarter income without proper disclosure. Because Citizens' 1995 [10–K] filed with the Securities and Exchange Commission stated that Citizens "ha[d] been compensated for . . . guarantees and financial support [to HTCC]," investors were allegedly misled into believing that the $10.1 million booked in 1996 was new income, unrelated to the 1995 HTCC loan and guarantee transactions.

a. May 7, 1996 Announcement of 1996 First Quarter Financial Results and First Quarter Form 10–Q

On May 7, 1996, Citizens publicly announced an after-tax net income of $38.9 million for the first quarter of 1996, up 15% from the corresponding period in 1995. These results were reflected in its 1996 first quarter financial statement. The defendants did not disclose that "as much as $6.9 million of the $38.9 million . . . was HTCC related income which was deceptively 'stored' by Citizens" until the first quarter of 1996. According to the Complaint, the defendants also concealed the fact that this $6.9 million made up most if not all of the reported 15% increase during the first quarter of 1996.

b. August 15, 1996 Press Release and 1996 Second Quarter Form 10–Q

On August 15, 1996, Citizens issued another press release announcing "record ... profits for the three-and six-month periods ended June 30, 1996," with the second quarter's net income of $46.3 million representing a 10% increase over the comparable period in the preceding year. Citizens attributed this growth to "continuous above-average growth in volume and profitability in each of its sectors, particularly telecommunications." These results were reflected in its 1996 second quarter financial report. The Complaint charges that the August 15, 1996 press release and the 1996 Second Quarter Form 10–Q both failed to disclose that "approximately $10 million of the $85.1 million of reported income for the six months ended June 30, 1996 was HTCC related income" which should have been recognized in 1995. The Complaint states that the defendants also concealed the fact that this approximately $10 million accounted for the full 10% increase in income for the first six months of 1996 over the comparable period in 1995.

* * *

On April 30, 1997, Citizens issued a press release announcing lower than expected earnings for the first quarter of 1997. These results were reflected in the Company's 1997 First Quarter Form 10–Q. Neither document attributed the drop in income to the decrease in HTCC Fees. Instead, according to the Complaint, the press release misleadingly focused on rising expenses. Beginning in or about May 1997, industry analysts began to report weaknesses in Citizens' earnings position. Their predictions were confirmed by Citizens in August 1997 with the filing of its 1997 Second Quarter Form 10–Q, which also disclosed that the reported income for the first two quarters of 1996 included material income from HTCC.

d. Other Misrepresentations

The defendants allegedly made other material misrepresentations. According to the Complaint, the defendants failed to disclose that the Fees were non-recurring income, in violation of a Generally Accepted Accounting Principle[4] that companies report "extraordinary, unusual or infrequently occurring events and transactions."

* * *

B. Procedural History

* * *

4. Generally Accepted Accounting Principles are the official standards adopted by the American Institute of Certified Public Accountants, a private professional association, through three successor groups it established: the Committee on Accounting Procedure, the Accounting Principles Board, and the Financial Accounting Standards Board. GAAP does not prescribe a fixed set of rules, but rather represents "the range of reasonable alternatives that management can use." The SEC treats the FASB's standards as authoritative.

The district court granted the defendants' motion to dismiss. Focusing on the issue of materiality, the court quoted a newspaper article which observed that " '[m]ost auditors—and their corporate clients—define materiality as any event or news that might affect a company's earnings, positively or negatively, by 3% to 10% . . . [it] has become standard practice in corporate America. Thus, if a particular charge or event doesn't meet the 3% to 10% level, companies feel they don't have to disclose it.' " Applying this 3% to 10% range, the court held that "the amount in issue here—1.7% of Citizens' revenues for the relevant time period, pursuant to GAAP—is immaterial as a matter of law." In addition, the court found that the lack of change in Citizens' stock price following the filing of the 1997 Second Quarter Form 10–Q on August 7, 1997, to be evidence of immateriality.

* * *

II. DISCUSSION

* * *

2. Materiality

At the pleading stage, a plaintiff satisfies the materiality requirement of Rule 10b–5 by alleging a statement or omission that a reasonable investor would have considered significant in making investment decisions. It is not sufficient to allege that the investor might have considered the misrepresentation or omission important. On the other hand, it is not necessary to assert that the investor would have acted differently if an accurate disclosure was made. An omitted fact may be immaterial if the information is trivial, or is "so basic that any investor could be expected to know it." Therefore, whether an alleged misrepresentation or omission is material necessarily depends on all relevant circumstances of the particular case.

Materiality is a mixed question of law and fact. We have held that, when presented with a Rule 12(b)(6) motion, "a complaint may not properly be dismissed . . . on the ground that the alleged misstatements or omissions are not material unless they are so obviously unimportant to a reasonable investor that reasonable minds could not differ on the question of their importance."

a. Numerical Benchmark

The district court held that the alleged misrepresentations of the HTCC Fees as having been received in 1996 were immaterial as a matter of law because the Fees amounted to only 1.7% of Citizens' 1996 total revenue. The plaintiffs and the SEC, as amicus curiae, contend that the court's exclusive reliance on a single numerical or percentage benchmark to determine materiality was error. Their position is supported by ample authority. In *Basic*, the Supreme Court expressly rejected the use of a numerical formula:

A bright-line rule indeed is easier to follow than a standard that requires the exercise of judgment in the light of all the circumstances. But ease of application alone is not an excuse for ignoring the purposes of the Securities Acts and Congress' policy decisions. Any approach that designates a single fact or occurrence as always determinative of an inherently fact-specific finding such as materiality, must necessarily be overinclusive or underinclusive.

* * *

Following *Basic*, we have consistently rejected a formulaic approach to assessing the materiality of an alleged misrepresentation. ...

With respect to financial statements, the SEC has commented that various "[q]ualitative factors may cause misstatements of quantitatively small amounts to be material." SEC Staff Accounting Bulletin No. 99 (representing interpretations and practices followed by the SEC's Division of Corporation Finance and the Office of the Chief Accountant in administering disclosure requirements of federal securities law). Of particular relevance to this action are the following:

- whether the misstatement masks a change in earnings or other trends

- whether the misstatement hides a failure to meet analysts' consensus expectations for the enterprise[.]

Unlike, for example, a rule promulgated by the SEC pursuant to its rulemaking authority, SAB No. 99 does not carry with it the force of law. Nonetheless, because SEC staff accounting bulletins "constitute a body of experience and informed judgment," and SAB No. 99 is thoroughly reasoned and consistent with existing law—its non-exhaustive list of factors is simply an application of the well-established *Basic* analysis to misrepresentations of financial results—we find it persuasive guidance for evaluating the materiality of an alleged misrepresentation.

* * *

d. This Complaint

Applying the foregoing principles to this action, we conclude that the Complaint alleged material misrepresentations in the 1996 First and Second Quarter Form 10–Qs and corresponding press releases, namely, the alleged misrepresentation of $10.1 million of Fees received in 1995 as 1996 income. The $6.9 million of 1995 Fees booked during the first quarter of 1996 equaled 17.7% of Citizens' reported after-tax net income ($38.9 million), and 11.7% of its pre-tax net income ($58.78 million) for that quarter. The $10.1 million reflected in the 1996 Second Quarter Form 10–Q amounted to 11.9% of after-tax net income ($85.15 million), and 8% of pre-tax net income ($126.62 million) for the first six months of 1996. We believe it is inappropriate to determine at this stage of the litigation that these substantial amounts, both in absolute terms and as percentages of total net income for the respective quarters, were immaterial as a matter of law.

Aside from the magnitude of the overstatements, the Complaint alleged that the defendants deceptively stored the Fees until 1996 in order to manage the Company's 1995 and 1996 income, and that they did so in order to conceal Citizens' failure to meet analysts' expectations and to sustain its 51–year earnings trend. The Complaint asserted that the $6.9 million of Fees reported in the First Quarter Form 10–Q accounted for "a substantial portion, if not all, of the increase in income for the first quarter 1996 compared to the first quarter of 1995[.]" Moreover, according to the Complaint, analysts' projections of Citizens' "income for the first six (6) months of 1996 were met and exceeded only as a result of th[e] additional HTCC-related income, and the increase in income for the first six months of 1996 compared to the first six months of 1995 was due entirely to the income recognized from HTCC." Viewed in this context, it cannot be said that no reasonable investor would have considered the misreporting of 1995 Fees as 1996 income to be significant or to have altered the total mix of information affecting their investment decisions. We therefore conclude that the Complaint alleged material misrepresentations. . . .

e.   Market Response

The defendants urge us to affirm the district court's decision based on the lack of movement in Citizens' stock price after it filed its 1997 Second Quarter Form 10–Q on August 7, 1997, which the court held was "significant evidence" that none of the alleged misstatements of income were material to the investing public. According to the Complaint, on that date Citizens first publicly acknowledged that the reported income for the first and second quarters of 1996 included substantial payments from HTCC. The plaintiffs challenge this evidence, noting that Citizens' stock price did experience a "precipitous drop" in May 1997, when reports of Citizens' poor earnings outlook first emerged.

The Complaint alleges only that earnings and earnings per share fell in May 1997, not price per share. However, drawing all reasonable inferences in favor of the non-moving party, as we must, we infer that Citizens' price per share dropped correspondingly in May 1997. In granting the defendants' motion to dismiss, the court did not draw this inference and did not appropriately resolve the disputed factual issue of whether the alleged misrepresentations adversely affected Citizens' share price during the Class Period. We therefore vacate the district court's decision to the extent it held that the steadiness of Citizens' stock price after August 7, 1997 proved that the misreporting of 1995 Fees as 1996 income was immaterial.

* * *

CONCLUSION

For the reasons explained above, the judgment of the district court dismissing the Complaint for failure to state a claim is hereby vacated. We reverse the district court's holding with respect to materiality. . . .

QUESTIONS

1. Why do you think that Citizens "emphasized in its public comments" that it "had reported over fifty consecutive years of increased revenue, earnings, and earnings per share"? Why is that relevant to the determination of materiality?

2. Does the fact that the company made the misrepresentation suggest that it must have been material? Why would the company bother to make the misstatement if it didn't think it would influence investors?

3. Why did the court reject the district court's holding that a 1.7% discrepancy in total revenues was immaterial as a matter of law?

4. Why did the court reverse the district court's finding of immateriality based on the lack of stock price reaction at the time of Citizens' August 1997 Form 10–Q filing?

HYPOTHETICAL THREE

Six Feet offers financing to families that have not set aside money to pay for the burial of their loved ones. These loans, for which Six Feet charges an interest rate well above the prime rate, have a substantial default rate. (It turns out people are less willing to pay several thousand dollars in debt after their loved one has been buried. What's Six Feet going to do, dig them up?) Accordingly, Six Feet set aside a "loan loss" reserve for the loans that turn out to be uncollectible (the loan loss reserve is disclosed in Six Feet's financial statements). The reserve is not large, amounting to 10–15% of the outstanding loans. The loans, however, make up a substantial business segment for Six Feet, generating between 35–40% of Six Feet's profits. Moreover, the reserves have been a useful resource of "smoothing" Six Feet's earnings—typically by plus or minus 2% per year. If it looks like Six Feet may fall short of Wall Street's forecasted earnings, Arthur—Six Feet's CFO—simply dips into the loan loss reserve, declaring the reserve to be greater than needed, and adding the excess reserve to that quarter's revenue. This financial flexibility has allowed Arthur and Six Feet to meet expectations for 23 consecutive quarters. Is Six Feet's loan loss reserve practice materially misleading?

IV.   OPINIONS

Are "just the facts, ma'am" relevant to the determination of materiality? The Supreme Court answers that immortal question in the following— somewhat less than immortal—opinion.

Virginia Bankshares, Inc. v. Sandberg

501 U.S. 1083 (1991).

■ JUSTICE SOUTER delivered the opinion of the Court.

Section 14(a) of the Securities Exchange Act of 1934 authorizes the Securities and Exchange Commission to adopt rules for the solicitation of proxies, and prohibits their violation. . . .

The questions before us are whether a statement couched in conclusory or qualitative terms purporting to explain directors' reasons for recommending certain corporate action can be materially misleading within the meaning of Rule 14a–9. ... We hold that knowingly false statements of reasons may be actionable even though conclusory in form. ...

I

In December 1986, First American Bankshares, Inc. (FABI), a bank holding company, began a "freeze-out" merger, in which the First American Bank of Virginia (Bank) eventually merged into Virginia Bankshares, Inc. (VBI), a wholly owned subsidiary of FABI. VBI owned 85% of the Bank's shares, the remaining 15% being in the hands of some 2,000 minority shareholders. FABI hired the investment banking firm of Keefe, Bruyette & Woods (KBW) to give an opinion on the appropriate price for shares of the minority holders, who would lose their interests in the Bank as a result of the merger. Based on market quotations and unverified information from FABI, KBW gave the Bank's executive committee an opinion that $42 a share would be a fair price for the minority stock. The executive committee approved the merger proposal at that price, and the full board followed suit.

Although Virginia law required only that such a merger proposal be submitted to a vote at a shareholders' meeting, and that the meeting be preceded by circulation of a statement of information to the shareholders, the directors nevertheless solicited proxies for voting on the proposal at the annual meeting set for April 21, 1987. In their solicitation, the directors urged the proposal's adoption and stated they had approved the plan because of its opportunity for the minority shareholders to achieve a "high" value, which they elsewhere described as a "fair" price, for their stock.

Although most minority shareholders gave the proxies requested, respondent Sandberg did not, and after approval of the merger she sought damages in the United States District Court for the Eastern District of Virginia from VBI, FABI, and the directors of the Bank. ... Sandberg alleged, among other things, that the directors had not believed that the price offered was high or that the terms of the merger were fair, but had recommended the merger only because they believed they had no alternative if they wished to remain on the board. ...

II

We consider first the actionability per se of statements of reasons, opinion, or belief. Because such a statement by definition purports to express what is consciously on the speaker's mind, we interpret the jury verdict as finding that the directors' statements of belief and opinion were made with knowledge that the directors did not hold the beliefs or opinions expressed, and we confine our discussion to statements so made. ... Shareholders know that directors usually have knowledge and expertness far exceeding the normal investor's resources, and the directors' perceived superiority is magnified even further by the common knowledge that state law customarily obliges them to exercise their judgment in the shareholders' interest. Naturally, then, the shareowner faced with a proxy request will think it important to know the directors' beliefs about the course they recommend and their specific reasons for urging the stockholders to embrace it.

But, assuming materiality, the question remains whether statements of reasons, opinions, or beliefs are statements "with respect to ... material fact[s]" so as to fall within the strictures of the Rule. Petitioners argue that we would invite wasteful litigation of amorphous issues outside the readily provable realm of fact if we were to recognize liability here on proof that the directors did not recommend the merger for the stated reason ....

Attacks on the truth of directors' statements of reasons or belief ... are factual in two senses: as statements that the directors do act for the reasons given or hold the belief stated and as statements about the subject matter of the reason or belief expressed. ... Reasons for directors' recommendations or statements of belief are ... characteristically matters of corporate record subject to documentation, to be supported or attacked by evidence of historical fact outside a plaintiff's control. Such evidence would include not only corporate minutes and other statements of the directors themselves, but circumstantial evidence bearing on the facts that would reasonably underlie the reasons claimed and the honesty of any statement that those reasons are the basis for a recommendation or other action, a point that becomes especially clear when the reasons or beliefs go to valuations in dollars and cents.

It is no answer to argue, as petitioners do, that the quoted statement on which liability was predicated did not express a reason in dollars and cents, but focused instead on the "indefinite and unverifiable" term, "high" value, much like the similar claim that the merger's terms were "fair" to shareholders. The objection ignores the fact that such conclusory terms in a commercial context are reasonably understood to rest on a factual basis that justifies them as accurate, the absence of which renders them misleading. Provable facts either furnish good reasons to make a conclusory commercial judgment, or they count against it, and expressions of such judgments can be uttered with knowledge of truth or falsity just like more definite statements, and defended or attacked through the orthodox evidentiary process that either substantiates their underlying justifications or tends to disprove their existence. ...In this case, whether $42 was "high," and the proposal "fair" to the minority shareholders, depended on whether provable facts about the Bank's assets, and about actual and potential levels of operation, substantiated a value that was above, below, or more or less at the $42 figure, when assessed in accordance with recognized methods of valuation.

Respondents adduced evidence for just such facts in proving that the statement was misleading about its subject matter and a false expression of the directors' reasons. Whereas the proxy statement described the $42 price as offering a premium above both book value and market price, the evidence indicated that a calculation of the book figure based on the appreciated value of the Bank's real estate holdings eliminated any such premium. The evidence on the significance of market price showed that KBW had conceded that the market was closed, thin, and dominated by FABI, facts omitted from the statement. There was, indeed, evidence of a "going concern" value for the Bank in excess of $60 per share of common stock, another fact never disclosed. However conclusory the directors' statement may have been, then, it was open to attack by garden-variety evidence, subject neither to a plaintiff's control nor ready manufacture, and there was no undue risk of open-ended liability or uncontrollable litigation in allowing respondents the opportunity for recovery on the allegation that it was misleading to call $42 "high."

* * *

The question arises, then, whether disbelief, or undisclosed belief or motivation, standing alone, should be a sufficient basis to sustain an action under § 14(a), absent proof by the sort of objective evidence described above that the statement also expressly or impliedly asserted something false or misleading about its subject matter. We think that proof of mere disbelief or belief undisclosed should not suffice for liability under § 14(a), and if nothing more had been required or proven in this case, we would reverse for that reason.

On the one hand, it would be rare to find a case with evidence solely of disbelief or undisclosed motivation without further proof that the statement was defective as to its subject matter. While we certainly would not hold a director's naked admission of disbelief incompetent evidence of a proxy statement's false or misleading character, such an unusual admission will not very often stand alone, and we do not substantially narrow the cause of action by requiring a plaintiff to demonstrate something false or misleading in what the statement expressly or impliedly declared about its subject.

On the other hand, to recognize liability on mere disbelief or undisclosed motive without any demonstration that the proxy statement was false or misleading about its subject would authorize § 14(a) litigation confined solely to what one skeptical court spoke of as the "impurities" of a director's "unclean heart." ... While it is true that the liability, if recognized, would rest on an actual, not hypothetical, psychological fact, the temptation to rest an otherwise nonexistent § 14(a) action on psychological enquiry alone would threaten ... strike suits and attrition by discovery. We therefore hold disbelief or undisclosed motivation, standing alone, insufficient to satisfy the element of fact that must be established under § 14(a).

C

Petitioners' fall-back position assumes the same relationship between a conclusory judgment and its underlying facts.... [P]etitioners argue that even if conclusory statements of reason or belief can be actionable under

§ 14(a), we should confine liability to instances where the proxy material fails to disclose the offending statement's factual basis. There would be no justification for holding the shareholders entitled to judicial relief, that is, when they were given evidence that a stated reason for a proxy recommendation was misleading and an opportunity to draw that conclusion themselves.

The answer to this argument rests on the difference between a merely misleading statement and one that is materially so. While a misleading statement will not always lose its deceptive edge simply by joinder with others that are true, the true statements may discredit the other one so obviously that the risk of real deception drops to nil. Since liability under § 14(a) must rest not only on deceptiveness but materiality as well (i.e., it has to be significant enough to be important to a reasonable investor deciding how to vote), petitioners are on perfectly firm ground insofar as they argue that publishing accurate facts in a proxy statement can render a misleading proposition too unimportant to ground liability.

But not every mixture with the true will neutralize the deceptive. If it would take a financial analyst to spot the tension between the one and the other, whatever is misleading will remain materially so, and liability should follow. The point of a proxy statement, after all, should be to inform, not to challenge the reader's critical wits. Only when the inconsistency would exhaust the misleading conclusion's capacity to influence the reasonable shareholder would a § 14(a) action fail on the element of materiality.

Suffice it to say that the evidence invoked by petitioners in the instant case fell short of compelling the jury to find the facial materiality of the misleading statement neutralized. The directors claim, for example, to have made an explanatory disclosure of further reasons for their recommendation when they said they would keep their seats following the merger, but they failed to mention what at least one of them admitted in testimony, that they would have had no expectation of doing so without supporting the proposal.[7] And although the proxy statement did speak factually about the merger price in describing it as higher than share prices in recent sales, it failed even to mention the closed market dominated by FABI. None of these disclosures that the directors point to was, then, anything more than a half-truth, and the record shows that another fact statement they invoke was arguably even worse. The claim that the merger price exceeded book value was controverted, as we have seen already, by evidence of a higher book value than the directors conceded, reflecting appreciation in the Bank's real estate portfolio. Finally, the solicitation omitted any mention of the Bank's value as a going concern at more than $60 a share, as against

---

7. Petitioners fail to dissuade us from recognizing the significance of omissions such as this by arguing that we effectively require them to accuse themselves of breach of fiduciary duty. Subjection to liability for misleading others does not raise a duty of self-accusation; it enforces a duty to refrain from misleading. We have no occasion to decide whether the directors were obligated to state the reasons for their support of the merger proposal here, but there can be no question that the statement they did make carried with it no option to deceive.

the merger price of $42. There was, in sum, no more of a compelling case for the statement's immateriality than for its accuracy.

* * *

■ JUSTICE SCALIA, concurring in part and concurring in the judgment.

I

As I understand the Court's opinion, the statement "In the opinion of the Directors, this is a high value for the shares" would produce liability if in fact it was not a high value and the directors knew that. It would not produce liability if in fact it was not a high value but the directors honestly believed otherwise. The statement "The Directors voted to accept the proposal because they believe it offers a high value" would not produce liability if in fact the directors' genuine motive was quite different—except that it would produce liability if the proposal in fact did not offer a high value and the Directors knew that.

I agree with all of this. However, not every sentence that has the word "opinion" in it, or that refers to motivation for directors' actions, leads us into this psychic thicket. Sometimes such a sentence actually represents facts as facts rather than opinions—and in that event no more need be done than apply the normal rules for § 14(a) liability. I think that is the situation here. In my view, the statement at issue in this case is most fairly read as affirming separately both the fact of the Directors' opinion and the accuracy of the facts upon which the opinion was assertedly based. It reads as follows:

> The Plan of Merger has been approved by the Board of Directors because it provides an opportunity for the Bank's public shareholders to achieve a high value for their shares.

Had it read "because in their estimation it provides an opportunity, etc.", it would have set forth nothing but an opinion. As written, however, it asserts both that the board of directors acted for a particular reason and that that reason is correct. This interpretation is made clear by what immediately follows: "The price to be paid is about 30% higher than the [last traded price immediately before announcement of the proposal]. . . . [T]he $42 per share that will be paid to public holders of the common stock represents a premium of approximately 26% over the book value. . . . [T]he bank earned $24,767,000 in the year ended December 31, 1986. . . ." These are all facts that support and that are obviously introduced for the purpose of supporting the factual truth of the "because" clause, i.e., that the proposal gives shareholders a "high value."

If the present case were to proceed, therefore, I think the normal § 14(a) principles governing misrepresentation of fact would apply.

* * *

NOTES

Although *Virginia Bankshares* makes clear that opinions—when offered—can be actionable, the law is also clear that motives need not be disclosed if the facts are fully disclosed and the motive is neither deceptive nor manipulative. *Vaughn v. Teledyne, Inc.*, 628 F.2d 1214, 1221 (9th Cir. 1980). On the other hand, conflicts of interest generally must be disclosed. *TSC Industries v. Northway*, 426 U.S. 438, 453–454 n. 15 (1976).

QUESTIONS

1. What are examples of "conclusory or qualitative" statements expressing an "opinion," "beliefs," or "reasons"?

2. What is the risk of "open-ended liability or uncontrollable litigation" to which the Court refers?

3. Why didn't the directors' conflict of interest and FABI's domination of the Bank render the opinions of its nominees on the Bank's board immaterial?

HYPOTHETICAL FOUR

David, the CEO and Chairman of Six Feet, has decided to proceed with the merger with Dearly Departed. He persuades Federico, one of the two other board members, to go along and the Six Feet board approves the merger 2–1, with Nate, the President and the other board member, dissenting. The proxy statement that Six Feet sends to its shareholders describes David and Federico's view that the merger is a "great deal" for Six Feet shareholders (and that David would be the Chairman of the combined company). Nate, however, has been bad-mouthing the deal in the press. Nate says that the company could have been sold for cash at a 50% premium to the current market price and that David and Federico only agreed to a "merger of equals" stock swap with Dearly Departed because David insisted on continuing as Chairman. Does Six Feet's proxy statement contain a material omission?

V. THE "TOTAL MIX"

Recall that in *Basic*, the Supreme Court quoted *TSC Industries, Inc. v. Northway, Inc.*, 426 U.S. 438 (1976), for the proposition that materiality requires "a substantial likelihood that the disclosure of the omitted fact would have been viewed by the reasonable investor as having significantly altered the 'total mix' of information made available." The "total mix" formulation has been an important basis upon which courts have dismissed suits that they perceive to be weak or non-meritorious. In the case below, the court applies one of the materiality doctrines that have grown out of the "total mix" language from *TSC Industries*: the "truth on the market" defense.

Longman v. Food Lion, Inc.

197 F.3d 675 (4th Cir. 1999).

■ NIEMEYER, CIRCUIT JUDGE:

On the day after ABC aired its "PrimeTime Live" television broadcast on November 5, 1992, detailing allegedly widespread unsanitary practices and labor law violations in grocery stores owned by Food Lion, Inc., the price of Food Lion's Class A stock fell approximately 11%, and the price of its Class B stock fell approximately 14%. A week later, stockholders David Longman, Jeffrey Feinman, and others who had purchased Food Lion stock during the 2–½–year period before the broadcast filed these two class actions against Food Lion, which were later consolidated, alleging securities fraud under § 10(b) of the Securities Exchange Act of 1934 and Rule 10b–5 promulgated thereunder. The plaintiffs alleged that Food Lion affirmatively misled the market and failed to disclose that its earnings during the 2–½–year period were artificially inflated due to its misrepresentations about and failure to disclose widespread violations of federal labor laws and pervasive, unsanitary food handling practices. They alleged that these violations and practices were attributable to Food Lion's "Effective Scheduling System," which required employees to perform certain duties within specified times at the risk of losing their jobs.

* * *

I

Food Lion is a publicly traded (over the counter) company with headquarters in Salisbury, North Carolina, that operates a chain of approximately 1,000 retail grocery stores in the southeastern part of the United States. During the relevant period, its earnings exceeded $200 million per year, and it employed about 60,000 persons.

As a management tool, Food Lion has employed a labor scheduling system, known as "Effective Scheduling," to assist department managers in scheduling their workforces based on the time that it should take an average employee to complete various tasks. While some stores have never met the goals set by the Effective Scheduling guidelines, others consistently have met those goals. In their complaints, plaintiffs alleged that the Effective Scheduling system established guidelines that were not attainable for many employees, thereby causing them to work "off the clock" without additional pay and to cut corners, including disregarding sanitary practices.

During the 2–½–year "Class Period" between May 7, 1990, when Food Lion issued its 1989 Annual report, and November 5, 1992, when the PrimeTime Live broadcast aired, plaintiffs purchased stock in Food Lion, allegedly relying on its rosy statements about its relationship with its employees and the cleanliness of its stores. Plaintiffs alleged that during this period, Food Lion "reported optimistically about its future" when, in fact, its profits and optimistic outlook were dependent on a system that required its employees to violate the labor laws and to pursue unsanitary methods, facts which Food Lion failed to report.

In its 1989 Annual Report, circulated on May 7, 1990, Food Lion stated that the Human Resources Department "continues to insure that Food Lion employees receive competitive wages and excellent benefits;" that although inflation led to higher costs, "[t]hese costs were recovered primarily through improved operating efficiencies and an increased average selling price per item;" and that "[w]e will continue to pay close attention to service levels and cleanliness in our stores and believe we will achieve high marks from customers in these areas." The report said nothing about any widespread labor or sanitary problems.

During the Class Period, Food Lion continued to face and to resist the efforts of the United Food and Commercial Workers Union to organize Food Lion workers. When the union called for a boycott of Food Lion, the company issued a press release on August 30, 1990, stating:

> How ironic it is on this Labor Day weekend for a union leader to call for the destruction of more than 45,000 jobs of Food Lion employees in retaliation for their desire to remain union free. Such blatant threats and arrogant disregard of true employee free choice is the kind of coercion of employees that totally desecrates the purpose and spirit of Labor Day.
>
> The fact is, Food Lion opens more than 100 stores each year and adds more than 5,000 employees each year. Food Lion could not do this without offering competitive wages and excellent benefits. On average, Food Lion receives three to four applications for every available job.

About a year later, on September 11, 1991, the UFCW announced that it had filed a lengthy complaint with the Department of Labor, accusing Food Lion of widespread labor violations in tacitly encouraging employees to work "off the clock" without pay. In its press release, the union stated:

> More than 37 percent of the after-tax profit of the nation's fastest-growing retail food chain, Food Lion, is derived from illegal off-the-clock work of employees.
>
> * * *
>
> Food Lion's profit is reported to exceed the industry average," the complaint [filed with the Department of Labor] states, "and its profit advantage is widely attributed to more efficient operations. With over one-third of its profit derived from illegal off-the-clock work, it is clear that Food Lion's profit advantage is unfairly obtained.
>
> * * *
>
> Food Lion could owe as much as $194 million in back wages. With liquidated damages allowed by law, its liability could be "as high as $388 million."

Food Lion responded with its own press release the same day:

> Food Lion has a very clear policy against working off the clock. Employees, including managers, who have violated this policy have received discipline up to and including discharge.
>
> This Complaint and news release by the UFCW union is simply one more example of the union's attempt to harass and coerce Food

Lion management into recognizing the union without regard to the sentiments of our employees.

Food Lion employees have repeatedly rejected the UFCW union despite union efforts for more than ten years.

* * *

As has been the case in all other attacks on Food Lion by this union, the company intends to defend itself vigorously in this matter.

On the following day, Food Lion issued another press release, stating:

The UFCW's most recent claims of illegal employment practices by Food Lion and its employees insult the hard work and integrity of all Food Lion employees. Those ingredients are the key to Food Lion's success and ability to bring customers extra low prices. It is not off the clock work by employees or other illegal employment practices as the UFCW-sponsored propaganda alleges.

* * *

Food Lion denies union claims of employee mistreatment, but the public doesn't have to accept the word of either the Company or the union. Let employees and the free marketplace decide that.

* * *

Nothing has been proven and nothing has been decided. Nevertheless, Food Lion is immediately commencing a detailed investigation of all the allegations in the Complaint and will take appropriate action.

* * *

Food Lion's 1991 Annual Report, circulated on June 1, 1992, referred to "continued and constant harassment of Food Lion by the United Food and Commercial Workers Union," but it also stated more positively, "We believe that Food Lion's Extra Low Prices and its clean and conveniently located stores are especially well suited to the demands of our customers." The report quoted a store manager as saying, "Food Lion also provides job security, good wages, good working conditions and some of the best benefits in the supermarket industry." The report also included an unattributed statement that "Food Lion is one of the best-managed high growth operators in the food retailing industry." This Annual Report, like the 1989 Annual Report, did not acknowledge any widespread labor violations or sanitation problems.

Finally, in July 1992, Food Lion filed a form 10–Q with the Securities and Exchange Commission which stated:

Management and legal counsel for the Company are currently investigating and evaluating the allegations contained in the [UFCW] Complaints. The ultimate liability, if any, which may result is not presently determinable; however, in the opinion of management, the Company has meritorious defenses to the allegations and the Company intends to defend the allegations vigorously and any liability will not have a material adverse effect on the financial condition or results of operations of the Company.

On August 3, 1993, approximately one year after this public filing (and several months after the close of the Class Period), the Department of Labor announced a settlement of the UFCW-instigated complaints against Food Lion, in which Food Lion agreed to pay $16.2 million, $8.1 million in 1993 and $8.1 million in 1994. The $16.2 million represented $13.2 million in back wages for current and former Food Lion employees and $3 million in penalties. The cost of the settlement to shareholders was 1.67 cents per share for each year, 1993 and 1994 (i.e., $8.1 million divided by the 484,000,000 shares outstanding). Experts retained by both the plaintiffs and the defendants agreed that the settlement was not material to Food Lion's earnings. Indeed, the expert for Food Lion stated that the settlement's effect on income was "de minimis."

On November 5, 1992, after all of the publicity about Food Lion's ongoing labor disputes but nine months before the Department of Labor settlement, ABC broadcast a PrimeTime Live episode about Food Lion stores, alleging widespread unsanitary practices and off-the-clock work by Food Lion employees. PrimeTime Live attributed these deficiencies to Food Lion's Effective Scheduling system. The broadcast included interviews with former and current Food Lion employees and a hidden camera investigation conducted by two ABC employees who obtained jobs at three Food Lion stores. The employees who were interviewed alleged various unsanitary business practices, including pulling meat out of a dumpster and selling it, bleaching fish and pork with Clorox "[t]o get the smell out" and then selling them, mixing rotten pork with other pork and selling it as fresh sausage, and cutting off the edge of a block of cheese that had been nibbled by rats so that the rest of the block could be sold. An employee stated that she used "fingernail polish remover to take the dates off" of products so that they could be sold after the manufacturer's date for sale had passed. . . .

Several employees described how they worked extra hours off the clock in order to be able to complete their assigned tasks. . . .

* * *

II

* * *

[A]t issue in this case [is] whether Food Lion made a false statement or omission of material fact. To establish this element, plaintiffs must point to a factual statement or omission—that is, one that is demonstrable as being true or false. Also, the statement must be false, or the omission must render public statements misleading. And finally, any statement or omission of fact must be material. Materiality is an objective concept, "involving the significance of an omitted or misrepresented fact to a reasonable investor." Thus, a fact stated or omitted is material if there is a substantial likelihood that a reasonable purchaser or seller of a security (1) would consider the fact important in deciding whether to buy or sell the security or (2) would have viewed the total mix of information made available to be significantly altered by disclosure of the fact.

These components—a factual statement or omission that is false or misleading and that is material—interact to provide a core requirement for a securities fraud claim. While opinion or puffery will often not be actionable, in particular contexts when it is both factual and material, it may be actionable. Thus, for example, a CEO's expression of "comfort" with a financial analyst's prediction of his company's future earnings was held not to be factual in that, as a future projection, it was not capable of being proved false. On the other hand, the Supreme Court has held that an opinion by board members to minority stockholders that the stock price of $42 for the purchase of their shares was a "high value" and represented a "fair" transaction could be both factual and material. See *Virginia Bankshares*, 501 U.S. at 1090–93. . . .

With these relevant principles in hand, we turn to the misstatements and omissions that plaintiffs in this case allege "caused" them to purchase Food Lion stock during the Class Period.

III

The essence of the plaintiffs' claim is that during the Class Period, Food Lion's earnings were "artificially inflated due to Food Lion's widespread violations of federal labor laws and pervasive unsanitary food-handling practices" and that Food Lion failed to disclose these facts and, indeed, publicly denied them. Plaintiffs contend that the true facts were "first disclosed to the public in credible fashion" when ABC News aired PrimeTime Live on November 5, 1992, presenting "an expose on Food Lion's labor and sanitation practices." . . .

A

Throughout the Class Period, Food Lion expressed, in public statements, substantial pride in the fact that its employees were well-paid and enjoyed good benefits. It claimed that it provided its employees with job security, good working conditions, and "some of the best benefits in the supermarket industry." Its Annual Reports for 1989 and 1991 and similar public statements expressed a belief that "Food Lion is one of the best-managed high growth operators in the food retailing industry."[2]

2. While not material to our holding, we note that we can find nothing in the record that would make these general statements by Food Lion, standing alone, actionable. First, these statements are immaterial puffery that is not actionable under the securities laws. Second, there is no evidence in the record that Food Lion employees were not well paid; that Food Lion did not have "some of the best benefits" in the industry; or that Food Lion was not well managed. Third, whether or not these statements are true, they do not bear on plaintiffs' claims that Food Lion forced its employees to work off the clock. Even if Food Lion's employees worked overtime without pay, they could still be well-paid compared to other employees in the industry.

Plaintiffs claim that these rosy statements about employee compensation and benefits masked Food Lion's real labor problems that were created by its Effective Scheduling system and by the UFCW's complaint filed with the Department of Labor charging Food Lion with wage/hour violations. Plaintiffs' contention focuses on the allegation that Food Lion knew about employees being forced to work off the clock and that, even though the practice was widespread, it failed to disclose it. Because such work provided productivity from employees without compensation, the plaintiffs' theory goes, the practice illegally and artificially inflated Food Lion's earnings.

In addition, plaintiffs contend that, to the extent that the practices were made public by the UFCW and others, Food Lion's response was deceptive in explicitly denying or giving the implicit impression that it did not have significant amounts of off-the-clock work. For example, Food Lion said in response to the UFCW's complaint that it "intends to defend itself vigorously in this matter;" that the company's success was based upon the "hard work and integrity of all Food Lion employees," rather than on any "illegal employment practices;" and that "UFCW sponsored claims of extensive wage/hour violations are simply untrue." . . . Plaintiffs also point to the fact that, during this same period, Food Lion omitted to admit that its profits were substantially dependent on this off-the-clock work.

Plaintiffs' securities fraud claim cannot succeed because, despite the fact that Food Lion denied the charges, the nature of the off-the-clock claims and the claims' risk to earnings were in fact well known to the market before the PrimeTime Live broadcast, and therefore Food Lion's omissions were not material. On September 11, 1991, for instance, more than a year before the PrimeTime Live broadcast, the UFCW publicly announced that it had filed a complaint with the Department of Labor, asserting that 183 people had claimed to have illegally worked off the clock, that "[m]ore than 37 percent of the after tax profit" of Food Lion was attributable to off the clock work, and that "Food Lion could owe as much as $194 million in back wages." The union warned that Food Lion's liability could be as high as $388 million based on claims for liquidated damages. Even as Food Lion denied the claims, however, it nevertheless promised to conduct an investigation of the allegations and take appropriate action. The market had a full opportunity to evaluate these claims and to reflect their risk in the market price for Food Lion stock. The PrimeTime Live broadcast added nothing to inform the market further. Rather, it simply repeated earlier charges through experiences of seven employees.

Because the market was thus informed of the union's charges before PrimeTime Live aired, what PrimeTime Live disclosed was not material. Indeed, even the much larger problem alleged more than a year earlier by the union was not material. Food Lion settled all of the claims made by the union with the Department of Labor for $16.2 million, $8.1 million payable in each of 1993 and 1994. During the same period, Food Lion's earnings exceeded $200 million per year. Experts on both sides agree that this settlement, reflecting a charge of less than two cents per share for each year, was not material to Food Lion's stock price. And consistent with this conclusion, Food Lion's share price did not drop following announcement of the Department of Labor settlement. . . .

B

We turn now to the second category of alleged misstatements and omissions by Food Lion—those which related to unsanitary practices. The plaintiffs have juxtaposed Food Lion's ongoing public statements about the cleanliness of its stores with the PrimeTime Live broadcast which revealed allegedly widespread unsanitary practices. In its 1989 Annual Report, Food Lion stated: "We will continue to pay close attention to service levels and cleanliness in our stores and believe we will achieve high marks from customers in these areas." Similarly, in its 1991 Annual Report, Food Lion stated: "We believe that Food Lion's Extra Low Prices and its clean and conveniently located stores are especially well suited to the demands of our customers."

On their face, these statements are the kind of puffery and generalizations that reasonable investors could not have relied upon when deciding whether to buy stock. . . .

Before considering the broadcast, the district court noted that, with a few exceptions, most of the broadcast was inadmissible hearsay. None of the people who spoke were under oath or subject to cross examination. In the absence of the evidence presented by the Prime–Time Live broadcast, or at least most of it, the district court was left with the affidavits of Food Lion which demonstrated that it had no corporate policy, written or unwritten, that would permit or encourage unsanitary food-handling practices. The court noted that Food Lion had "an audit staff in place who conducted surprise inspections of Food Lion stores to ensure that the stores complied with health and sanitation policies." And the court concluded that Food Lion's efforts were apparently sufficient to satisfy federal, state, and local inspections which revealed that Food Lion's record was "just as good, if not better, than its competitors' inspection reports."

But even considering the entire PrimeTime Live broadcast, the district court stated it "still does not present evidence of widespread unsanitary conditions of which Defendants knew." It noted that "with respect to the sanitary conditions at Food Lion's 1,000 stores, the [PrimeTime Live] broadcast is insufficient to draw any conclusions about Food Lion's operations as a whole." The court pointed out that the broadcast was filmed at only 3 of Food Lion's almost 1,000 stores and that out of 60,000 active employees and 40,000 former employees, PrimeTime Live interviewed a total of 70 current and former employees, 22 of whom had left the employ of Food Lion as much as 8 years before the Class Period. The district court concluded:

> [T]o the extent that there are any isolated instances of workplace errors, . . . not only is there not a substantial likelihood that the reasonable investor would consider the limited instances of workplace errors important in deciding whether to purchase Food Lion securities, but the Court also finds . . . that Defendants were taking steps to

remedy these isolated problems. As a result, the Court finds that to the extent that there is any omission by Defendants in their Annual and Quarterly Reports of isolated instances of workplace errors, this omission not only is not material as required by § 10b but also could not make any affirmative statements misleading in Defendants' Annual and Quarterly Reports.

We agree with the district court that, based on the record in this case, Food Lion was not required to make public statements about the existence of various sanitation problems that were revealed from time to time. These day-to-day conditions were not shown to be material to the price of Food Lion's stock. We also agree, as earlier noted, that the public statements that it did make were no more than soft, puffing statements about clean and conveniently located stores that no reasonable investor could rely upon in buying or selling Food Lion stock. Accordingly, we conclude that Food Lion did not defraud the market with false statements or omissions of material fact as required to maintain an action under § 10(b) of the Securities Exchange Act and Rule 10b–5 promulgated thereunder.

* * *

For the foregoing reasons, the judgment of the district court is AFFIRMED.

* * *

NOTES

The "truth on the market" defense applied in *Food Lion* is one variation on the "total mix" doctrine. Another variation developed by the lower courts is the "bespeaks caution" doctrine. Under the "bespeaks caution" doctrine, forward-looking statements are rendered immaterial as a matter of law if they are accompanied by disclosure of risks that may preclude the forward-looking projection from coming to fruition. See, e.g., *Kaufman v. Trump's Castle Funding*, 7 F.3d 357 (3d Cir. 1993). The doctrine has been codified and expanded by Congress as a "safe harbor" for forward-looking statements, part of the Private Securities Litigation Reform Act. We discuss the forward-looking safe harbor in Chapter 5.

QUESTIONS

1. Why did the court hold that the disclosure of the Department of Labor settlement with Food Lion over the "off-the-clock" labor practices was not material?

2. Why did the court hold that the unsanitary practices of Food Lion grocery stores were not material?

3. What is "puffery"? How does it differ from an "opinion"?

HYPOTHETICAL FIVE

Six Feet has been having some problems with its employees, who are dissatisfied with what they see as low pay and depressing working conditions.

The United Bereavement Workers of America has been attempting to organize the Six Feet employees. The Union and its allies in the environmental movement have been publicizing the dangers of the embalming fluid used by Six Feet, a chemical developed by Federico, Six Feet's Vice-President of Death Services. Federico believes that the embalming fluid gives the corpses "a fresher, more lifelike" appearance.

Ruth, the Vice-President for Human Resources at Six Feet, issues a press release disputing the Union's claims that the embalming fluid is dangerous and stating that "Six Feet has no higher priority than the safety of its employees." Three months later, OSHA imposes a $1 million fine on Six Feet for unsafe labor conditions and bars Six Feet from any further use of Federico's embalming fluid. (OSHA reveals that Federico did no testing whatsoever to evaluate the safety of the embalming fluid.) OSHA's action fuels the frustration of Six Feet's employees, who vote to recognize the Union as their bargaining agent. The Union, after staging a costly three week strike (the bodies were piling up), manages to extract a 20% increase in wages for the Six Feet employees. Was Ruth's press release materially misleading?

VI. MANAGEMENT INTEGRITY

One of the fundamental premises behind Congress's adoption of the Exchange Act was that full disclosure would make management and directors more accountable to shareholders. "Sunlight," according to that apostle of disclosure Louis Brandeis, "is said to be the best of disinfectants: electric light the most efficient policeman." Louis D. Brandeis, *Other People's Money* 92 (1913). Following this philosophy, the SEC includes a series of items in Regulation S–K (Subpart 400) relating to the competence and integrity of management. Item 401 of Regulation S–K provides for biographical information on directors and officers, including business experience for the past five years. Item 402 requires disclosure of executive compensation (including stock options). Item 404 details disclosures for transactions between the issuer and certain related parties, including family members of any director or officer.

As you read the section below, consider whether the SEC is concerned only with accountability to shareholders in mandating these disclosures or if it has other policy objectives in mind. Keep in mind that the SEC's mandatory disclosure items are just the beginning, as additional disclosure may be necessary to avoid creating a misleading omission. Consider what statements were rendered misleading by the facts that were omitted from the filings in the case below.

In The Matter of Franchard Corporation

42 S.E.C. 163 (1964).

■ CARY, CHAIRMAN.

These are consolidated proceedings pursuant to Sections 8(c) and 8(d) of the Securities Act of 1933 to determine whether a stop order should issue suspending the effectiveness of three registration statements filed by Franchard Corporation, formerly Glickman Corporation and whether certain post-effective amendments filed by the registrant should be declared effective. These proceedings raise important issues as to the disclosures to be required in a registration statement concerning (1) the use of substantial amounts of a company's funds for the personal benefit of its controlling person on whose business reputation public offerings of its securities were largely predicated; (2) the pledge by a dominant stockholder of his control stock; (3) the adequacy of performance of a board of directors. . . . In essence, we are concerned here with the role that can and should be performed by the disclosure requirements of the Securities Act in assisting investors to evaluate management. . . .

I. FACTS

A. BACKGROUND

Louis J. Glickman has for many years been a large-scale real estate developer, operator and investor. From 1954, to 1960, he acquired control of real estate in this country and in Canada by means of "syndication" arrangements. These arrangements involved the acquisition by Glickman, through purchase, contract or option, of an interest in real estate; the organization of a legal entity, usually a limited partnership but in some instances a corporation, in which Glickman retained a controlling position, and in which interests were sold to the public for cash; and the acquisition by this entity of the property interest in question. Glickman conducted some of these syndication activities and certain other phases of his real estate business through a number of wholly owned corporations, the most important of which was Glickman Corporation of Nevada, now known as Venada Corporation.

In May of 1960, Glickman caused registrant to be formed in order to group under one entity most of the publicly owned corporations and limited partnerships under his control. . . . Registrant's stock was divided into two classes, Class A common and Class B common, with the B stockholders given the right to elect 2/3 of registrant's directors until 1971, when all outstanding B shares become A shares. Glickman established control of registrant by acquiring 450,000 of its 660,000 authorized B shares for $1 per share. He exercised a dominant role in the management of registrant's affairs as president at the time of its formation and later as its first chairman of the board.

The first of the three registration statements here involved ('1960 filing') became effective on October 12, 1960. . . . [The October 12, 1960 offering involved both Class A and B shares. The registrant then issued Class A shares through two additional registration statements that became effective on October 2, 1961 and then on December 1, 1961.]

B. GLICKMAN'S WITHDRAWALS AND PLEDGES

Registrant's 1960 prospectus stated that Glickman had from time to time advanced substantial sums to the partnerships and corporations that were about to become subsidiaries of the registrant. It also said that he had advanced $211,000 to the registrant for the purpose of defraying its organization and registration costs and that this advance would be repaid without interest out of the proceeds of the public offering. On October 14, 1960—two days after the effective date of registrant's 1960 filing—Glickman began secretly to transfer funds from the registrant to Venada, his wholly owned corporation. Within 2 months the aggregate amount of these transfers amounted to $296,329. By October 2, 1961, the effective date of registrant's first 1961 filing, Glickman had made 45 withdrawals which amounted in the aggregate to $2,372,511.[8] Neither the 1961 prospectuses nor any of the effective amendments to the 1960 filing referred to these transactions.

All of registrant's prospectuses stated that Glickman owned most of its B as well as a substantial block of its A stock. On the effective date of the 1960 filing Glickman's shares were unencumbered. In the following month, however, he began to pledge his shares of finance his personal real estate ventures. By August 31, 1961, all of Glickman's B and much of his A stock had been pledged to banks, finance companies, and private individuals. On the effective dates of the two 1961 filings the loans secured by these pledges aggregated about $4,250,000. The effective interest rates on these loans ran as high as 24 percent annually. Glickman retained the right to vote the pledged shares in the absence of a default on the loans. The two 1961 filings made no mention of Glickman's pledges or the loans they secured.

C.   ACTION OF THE BOARD OF DIRECTORS

In May 1962, the accountants who had audited the financial statements in registrant's 1960 and 1961 filings informed its directors that Glickman had from time to time diverted funds from the registrant's treasury to Venada. The directors then met with Glickman, who assured them that the withdrawals had been without wrongful intent and would not recur. Glickman agreed to repay all of the then known unauthorized withdrawals with interest at the rate of 6 percent. Registrant's directors soon discovered that Glickman had made other withdrawals, and they retained former United States District Court Judge Simon H. Rifkind to determine Glickman's liability to registrant. Glickman agreed to be bound by Judge Rifkind's determination and was continued in office.

In a report submitted on August 20, 1962, Judge Rifkind found that Glickman had on many occasions withdrawn substantial sums from regis-

---

8. In most instances the amounts were returned relatively soon but were followed by fresh withdrawals. The amounts owed registrant by Glickman often exceeded $1 million and on one occasion were close to $1,500,000. The withdrawals by Glickman were accomplished by transfers of funds from registrant and its subsidiaries directly to Venada and expenditures by registrant and its subsidiaries for Venada's benefit. During this period, registrant and its subsidiaries had a number of relationships with Venada which regularly required them to make payments directly to it or on its behalf. The interspersal of Glickman's unauthorized withdrawals among a large number of usual and proper disbursements on the books of registrant and its subsidiaries facilitated concealment of his activities.

trant; that Bernard Mann, who was registrant's as well as Venada's treasurer but not a member of registrant's board of directors, was the only one of registrant's officers who had known of the withdrawals and had collaborated with Glickman in effecting them; that registrant's inadequate administrative procedures had to some extent facilitated Glickman's wrong-doing; and that all of the withdrawals had been made good with 6 percent interest. Judge Rifkind also found that 6 percent was an inadequate interest rate because Glickman and Venada had been borrowing at appreciably higher interest rates from commercial finance companies and others.

On November 30, 1962, registrant's directors learned that Glickman had continued to make unauthorized withdrawals after he had promised to desist from so doing and after the issuance of the Rifkind report, that Glickman and his wife had pledged all of their shares of the registrant's stock, and that Glickman and Venada were in financial straits. Glickman and Mann thereupon resigned from all of their posts with the registrant, and Glickman sold all his B stock and some of his Class A stock to a small group of investors. Monthly cash distributions to A stockholders, which registrant had made every month since its inception, were discontinued in January 1963, and registrant changed its name from Glickman Corporation to Franchard Corporation.

II.   ALLEGED DEFICIENCIES—ACTIVITIES OF MANAGEMENT

A.   GLICKMAN'S WITHDRAWALS OF REGISTRANT'S FUNDS AND PLEDGES OF HIS SHARES

Of cardinal importance in any business is the quality of its management. Disclosures relevant to an evaluation of management are particularly pertinent where, as in this case, securities are sold largely on the personal reputation of a company's controlling person. The disclosures in these respects were materially deficient. The 1960 prospectus failed to reveal that Glickman intended to use substantial amounts of registrant's funds for the benefit of Venada, and the 1961 prospectuses made no reference to Glickman's continual diversion of substantial sums from the registrant. Glickman's pledges were not discussed in either the effective amendments to the 1960 filings or in the two 1961 filings.

In our view, these disclosures were highly material to an evaluation of the competence and reliability of registrant's management—in large measure, Glickman. In many respects, the development of disclosure standards adequate for informed appraisal of management's ability and integrity is a difficult task. How do you tell a 'good' business manager from a 'bad' one in a piece of paper? Managerial talent consists of personal attributes, essentially subjective in nature, that frequently defy meaningful analysis through the impersonal medium of a prospectus. Direct statements of opinion as to management's ability, which are not susceptible to objective verification, may well create an unwarranted appearance of reliability if placed in a prospectus. The integrity of management—its willingness to place its duty to public shareholders over personal interest—is an equally elusive factor for the application of disclosure standards.

Evaluation of the quality of management—to whatever extent it is possible—is an essential ingredient of informed investment decision. A need so important cannot be ignored, and in a variety of ways the disclosure requirements of the Securities Act furnish factual information to fill this need. Appraisals of competency begin with information concerning management's past business experience, which is elicited by requirements that a prospectus state the offices and positions held with the issuer by each executive officer within the last 5 years. With respect to established companies, management's past performance, as shown by comprehensive financial and other disclosures concerning the issuer's operations, furnish a guide to its future business performance. To permit judgments whether the corporation's affairs are likely to be conducted in the interest of public shareholders, the registration requirements elicit information as to the interests of insiders which may conflict with their duty of loyalty to the corporation. Disclosures are also required with respect to the remuneration and other benefits paid or proposed to be paid to management as well as material transactions between the corporation and its officers, directors, holders of more than 10 percent of its stock, and their associates.

Glickman's withdrawals were material transactions between registrant and its management, and the registration forms on which registrant's filings were made called for their disclosure. Registrant's argument that the withdrawals were not material because Glickman's undisclosed indebtedness to registrant never exceeded 1.5 percent of the gross book value of registrant's assets not only minimizes the substantial amounts of the withdrawals in relation to the stockholders' equity and the company's cash flow, but ignores the significance to prospective investors of information concerning Glickman's managerial ability and personal integrity. Registrant as such had no operating history. It concedes that the initial public offering in 1960 was made primarily, if not solely, on Glickman's name and reputation as a successful real estate investor and operator, and it is equally clear that the 1961 offerings were also predicated on his reputation. All of the prospectuses spoke of Glickman's many years of experience "in the creation and development of real estate investment opportunities' as an investor in real property for his own account." The prospectuses also made it clear that Glickman would dominate and control registrant's operations, and prospective investors in registrant's securities were, in effect, being offered an opportunity to "buy" Glickman management of real estate investments.

A description of Glickman's activities was important on several grounds. First, publication of the facts pertaining to Glickman's withdrawals of substantial funds and of his pledges of his control stock would have clearly indicated his strained financial position and his urgent need for cash in his personal real estate ventures. In the context here, these facts were as material to an evaluation of Glickman's business ability as financial statements of an established company would be to an evaluation of its management's past performance.

Second, disclosure of Glickman's continual diversion of registrant's funds to the use of Venada, his wholly owned corporation, was also germane to an evaluation of the integrity of his management. This quality is always a material factor. In the circumstances of this case the need for disclosure in this area is obvious and compelling. We have spoken of Glickman's dominance. Moreover, Venada was registrant's most important tenant and Glickman would constantly be dealing with himself on behalf of registrant in the context of pressures created by his personal strained financial condition. Even aside from the issues relating to Glickman's character, publication of the fact that he was diverting funds to Venada to bolster that company's weak financial condition was important in evaluating registrant's own operations.

Third, Glickman's need for cash as indicated by withdrawals from registrant and his substantial borrowings and pledges of registrant's shares gave him a powerful and direct motive to cause registrant to pursue policies which would permit high distribution rates and maintain a high price for registrant's A shares. The higher that price, the greater his borrowing power; a decline in that price, on the other hand, would lead to the defaults and the consequent loss of control that eventually came to pass. Since prices of cash flow real estate stocks were directly responsive to changes in cash distribution policies, and since, in any event, Glickman needed to derive as much cash as possible from registrant's operations, his financial involvements gave him a peculiarly strong personal interest in setting registrant's current cash distribution rate at the highest possible level and to overlook or to minimize the long-term impact on registrant of an unduly generous distribution policy. Investors were entitled to be apprised of these facts and such potential conflicts of interest.

Finally, the possibility of a change of control was also important to prospective investors. As we have noted, registrant's public offerings were largely predicated on Glickman's reputation as a successful real estate investor and operator. Disclosure of Glickman's secured loans, the relatively high interest rates that they bore, the secondary sources from which lenders could declare defaults would have alerted investors to the possibility of a change in the control and management of registrant and apprised them of the possible nature of any such change. . . .

We . . . cannot agree with registrant's contention that disclosure of Glickman's borrowings and pledges of registrant's stock would have been an 'unwarranted revelation' of Glickman's personal affairs. An insider of a corporation that is asking the public for funds must, in return, relinquish various areas of privacy with respect to his financial affairs which impinge significantly upon the affairs of the company. That determination was made by the Congress over 30 years ago when it expressly provided in the Securities Act for disclosure of such matters as remuneration of insiders and the extent of their shareholdings in and the nature of their other material transactions with the company.

With respect to disclosure of pledged shares, registrant is not aided by pointing out that our registration forms under the Securities Act and the reports required under the Securities Exchange Act do not call for disclosure of encumbrances on a controlling stockholder's shares, and that proposals to require such disclosures in reports filed with us under the Securities Exchange Act have not been adopted.* The fact that such disclosures are not required of all issuers and their controlling persons in all cases does not negate their materiality in specific cases. The registration forms promulgated by us are guides intended to assist registrants in discharging their statutory duty of full disclosure. They are not and cannot possibly be exhaustive enumerations of each and every item material to investors in the particular circumstances relevant to a specific offering. The kaleidoscopic variety of economic life precludes any attempt at such an enumeration. The preparation of a registration statement is not satisfied, as registrant's position suggests, by a mechanical process of responding narrowly to the specific items of the applicable registration form. On the contrary, Rule 408 under the Securities Act makes clear to prospective registrants that: "In addition to the information expressly required to be included in a registration statement, there shall be added such further material information, if any, as may be necessary to make the required statements in the light of the circumstances under which they were made, not misleading."

B. ACTIVITIES OF REGISTRANT'S DIRECTORS

Another issue raised in these proceedings concerns the disclosure to be required in a prospectus regarding the adequacy of performance of managerial functions by registrant's board of directors. The Division urges that the prospectuses, by identifying the members of the board of directors, impliedly represented that they would provide oversight and direction to registrant's officers. In fact, the Division argues, the board was a nullity because the directors consistently agreed to Glickman's proposals, derived their information as to the current state of registrant's finances from Glickman's sporadic oral reports, and permitted him to fix each officer's area of responsibility.

It was obvious, however, that Glickman would exercise the dominant role in managing registrant's operations and the prospectuses contained no affirmative representations concerning the participation of the directors in registrant's affairs. Moreover, the board met regularly and received information as to registrant's affairs from Glickman and in connection with the preparation of registrant's registration statements, post-effective amendments, and periodic reports filed with us. It is clear we are not presented with a picture of total abdication of directorial responsibilities. Thus, the question posed by the Division must be whether the prospectuses were deficient in not disclosing that the directors, in overseeing the operations of the company, failed to exercise the degree of diligence which the Division believes was required of them under the circumstances in the context of the day-to-day operations of the company. We find no deficiencies in this area.

* [Editors' note: Such disclosure is now required by Regulation S–K, Item 403(c).]

This is an issue raising fundamental considerations as to the functions of the disclosure requirements of the Securities Act. The civil liability provisions of Section 11 do establish for directors a standard of due diligence in the preparation of a registration statement—a Federal rule of directors' responsibility with respect to the completeness and accuracy of the document used in the public distribution of securities. The Act does not purport, however, to define Federal standards of directors' responsibility in the ordinary operations of business enterprises and nowhere empowers us to formulate administratively such regulatory standards.[36] The diligence required of registrant's directors in overseeing its affairs is to be evaluated in the light of the standards established by State statutory and common law.

In our view, the application of these standards on a routine basis in the processing of registration statements would be basically incompatible with the philosophy and administration of the disclosure requirements of the Securities Act. Outright fraud or reckless indifference by directors might be readily identifiable and universally condemned. But activity short of that, which give rise to legal restraints and liabilities, invokes significant uncertainty. And for various reasons, including the complexity and diversity of business activities, the courts have exhibited a marked reluctance to interfere with good faith business judgments. The general principles reflected in statutory commandments or evolved from decisions in particular cases, while, perhaps readily articulated, furnish vague guidance for judgment in many situations. The courts are required to formulate and apply standards of directorial responsibility on the basis of a judicially developed record in the particular case in order to establish rights and liabilities in that case. ... To generally require information in Securities Act prospectuses as to whether directors have performed their duties in accordance with the standards of responsibility required of them under State law would stretch disclosure beyond the limitations contemplated by the statutory scheme and necessitated by considerations of administrative practicality.

To be sure, we have required disclosures concerning particular transactions which have raised questions of noncompliance with State or Federal law governing business conduct. We have also required disclosures concerning directors' performance in situations involving a virtual abdication of

---

36. The deterrent effect of disclosures required by the Securities Act and other provisions of the Federal securities laws do, of course, have an impact on standards of conduct for directors. As Mr. Justice Frankfurter, a major architect of the Securities Act, stated in describing the impact of the Act: "The existence of bonuses, of excessive commissions and salaries, of preferential lists and the like, may all be open secrets among the knowing, but the knowing are few. There is a shrinking quality to such transactions; to force knowledge of them into the open is largely to restrain their happening. Many practices safely pursued in private lose their justification in public. Thus social standards newly defined gradually establish themselves as new business habits."

Moreover, representations in prospectuses or documents filed with us may also create obligations that a corporation and its directors must fulfill and thus affect management's level of performance. * * *

responsibility or where the prospectus has made affirmative representations by which their performance could be tested. And these cases may not exhaust the areas where disclosure might be necessary as to activities of directors which do not comply with applicable standards. But the disclosures sought here by the staff would require evaluation of the entire conduct of a board of directors in the context of the whole business operations of a company in the light of diverse and uncertain standards. In our view, this is a function which the disclosure requirements of the Securities Act cannot effectively discharge. It would either result in self-serving generalities of little value to investors or grave uncertainties both on the part of those who must enforce and those who must comply with that Act.

* * *

NOTES

Item 404 of Regulation S–K now requires disclosure of transactions in excess of $60,000 between the issuer and directors, officers, 5% stockholders and the family members of any of those classes. The Item is written to sweep in corporations or other entities in which those individuals have a "material" interest (defined as greater than 10% of the equity of that entity).

Still more restrictive is § 402 of the Sarbanes–Oxley Act, which now prohibits loans by public companies to their executive officers and directors. In addition, § 406 of the Sarbanes–Oxley Act (implemented by the SEC in Item 406 of Regulation S–K) requires disclosure of whether the company has a code of ethics for its CEO, CFO, and controller. If the company does not have such a code of ethics, it is required to explain why not.

QUESTIONS

1. How can Glickman's withdrawals, which accounted for less than 1.5% of the gross book value of the Registrant, be material?

2. At the time of the *Franchard* case, "encumbrances on a controlling stockholder's shares" was not an enumerated item required to be disclosed. What basis does the SEC have for concluding that the Registrant nonetheless should have disclosed it?

3. What if Glickman had a heart condition that made him more likely than the average CEO to die or become disabled? Should this be a required disclosure in the registration statement pursuant to Rule 408 of the Securities Act?

4. Did the SEC let the Franchard directors off too lightly? Aren't the disclosures relating to the performance of directors of vital importance to investors?

HYPOTHETICAL SIX

Six Feet rents a number of funeral homes from Keith, David's former partner, who has custody of their adopted daughter, Taylor. David (the CEO and Chairman of the Board) believes that because the rentals are at a fair market price, the lease agreements with Keith are not material. Does Six Feet need to disclose the lease agreements with Keith?

As *Franchard* makes clear, the securities laws will frequently require disclosure of facts that will at least make management uncomfortable. Do the securities laws require disclosure of facts that could lead to consequences significantly more painful?

SEC v. Fehn

97 F.3d 1276 (9th Cir. 1996).

■ MICHAEL DALY HAWKINS, CIRCUIT JUDGE.

* * *

FACTUAL AND PROCEDURAL BACKGROUND

I.   The Initial Public Offering by CTI Technical, Inc.

CTI Technical, Inc. was incorporated in Nevada in January 1987 by its promoter, Las Vegas resident Edwin "Bud" Wheeler. Although Wheeler directed CTI's operations from the date of its incorporation, his status as company president and chief executive officer was not disclosed publicly until August 1988. In June 1987, seeking to raise capital to acquire other businesses, CTI conducted a $200,000 "blind pool" initial public offering of securities.

The CTI offering was tainted by violations of state and federal securities laws. First, CTI violated state blue sky laws by failing to register its securities with the states in which those securities were sold. Second, although CTI filed a Form S–18 registration statement with the SEC, it violated the Securities Act of 1933 and SEC regulations by failing to disclose that Wheeler was the promoter of the company and controlled its nominal directors. Finally, Wheeler and Stoneridge Securities, Inc., underwriter for the IPO, attempted to defraud investors by manipulating the price of the securities in aftermarket trading. [Eds.–The violations relating to the 1987 IPO are referred to as the "earlier securities law violations" below].

* * *

B.   Whether Fehn Aided and Abetted Violations of Sections 10(b) and 15(d) of the Securities Exchange Act and Related Regulations

[Eds.—Fehn was a California attorney retained to represent CTI, Wheeler, CTI's underwriter, and various CTI officers and directors in connection with CTI's public offering of securities under the Securities Act and CTI's compliance with reporting and disclosure requirements under the Exchange Act. The SEC brought a complaint against Fehn for aiding and abetting violations of the securities laws in connection with the wrongdoings by CTI in meeting its Exchange Act periodic reporting requirements. For Fehn to be liable for aiding and abetting, which is only available in an SEC enforcement action, there must be a primary violation by CTI.]

Fehn[] ... contends that the district court erred in finding primary violations of Sections 10(b) and 15(d) of the Securities Exchange Act, insisting that these provisions and their implementing regulations did not require disclosure of Wheeler's role as promoter, or of the contingent liabilities stemming from CTI's and Wheeler's earlier securities law violations. In the alternative, he contends that such a disclosure requirement was trumped by Wheeler's Fifth Amendment privilege against self-incrimination. ...

Fehn insists that the securities laws impose no duty to disclose, in a quarterly Form 10–Q, a failure to identify a company's promoter at the time of an initial public offering or the existence of prior securities law violations.

We disagree. Read against the backdrop of events in this case, these provisions required CTI and Wheeler to describe correctly Wheeler's role at CTI and to disclose the contingent liabilities stemming from earlier securities law violations.

In considering whether disclosure of Wheeler's role as promoter was necessary, we first note that Item 15(d) of Form S–18, the form for submitting registration statements to the SEC, requires companies registering securities to identify their promoter in the registration statement. When CTI submitted its Form S–18 to the SEC, however, it plainly failed to disclose that Wheeler was promoter of the company. That deficient registration statement was subsequently disseminated to investors, prospective investors, and the general public. We next note that the Form 10–Q's CTI submitted to the SEC in late 1988, at Fehn's direction and pursuant to Rule 15d–3, represented that Wheeler had only recently become president and CEO of CTI, when, in fact, he had been its promoter and had directed its activities since its incorporation in January 1987.

These statements in the Form 10–Q's were not only misleading in their own right, but, read in conjunction with CTI's deficient Form S–18, compounded the misinformation about Wheeler's role at CTI. First, because these statements about Wheeler's role were objectively untrue and, in our view, material, the Form 10–Q's contained an "untrue statement of a material fact" in violation of Rule 10b–5. Second, the statements characterizing Wheeler's role were further misleading when read in conjunction with CTI's earlier Form S–18. Because the Form S–18 had previously failed to identify Wheeler as CTI's promoter, the Form 10–Q's representation that Wheeler had only recently joined the company further clouded the identity of the promoter because it suggested Wheeler was not CTI's promoter. Rule 12b–20 requires the disclosure of "further material information, if any, as may be necessary to make the required statements, in the light of the circumstances under which they are made not misleading." Rule 12b–20's reference to "required statements" encompasses Form S–18, since item 15(d) of Form S–18 mandates disclosure of the issuer's promoter. In this case, Rule 12b–20 required disclosure of Wheeler's true relationship with CTI, because that disclosure was "further material information . . . necessary" to make Form S–18 "not misleading."

We next consider whether it was necessary to disclose the contingent liabilities stemming from CTI's and Wheeler's earlier securities law violations. We first note that the Form 10–Q's contained required financial information supplied by CTI's accountants and reviewed by Fehn. That information did not reflect, however, the considerable exposure CTI faced in light of potential private lawsuits arising out of the same set of facts that had led to the 1988 SEC investigation against CTI and Wheeler, the 1989 complaint and injunction against CTI, and Wheeler's conviction. As such, the Form 10–Q's violated the provisions of Rules 10b–5 and 12b–20, which require the disclosure of information where it is "necessary" to make other statements "not misleading."

Fehn contends that the earlier securities law violations did not have to be disclosed because they "did not create any material, contingent financial liabilities." For this proposition, he relies on the Financial Accounting Standards Board's Financial Accounting Standard Number 5 which covers "accounting for contingencies." We reject Fehn's argument for two reasons. First, we note that the standard set forth in FASB 5 requires that "disclosure of the contingency shall be made when there is at least a reasonable possibility that a loss . . . may have been incurred." Indeed, FASB 5 specifically covers contingent liability stemming from private litigation . . .

A more important flaw in Fehn's argument, however, is that it contravenes the securities-law standard for determining the materiality of a corporate event that has not yet occurred. In evaluating the materiality of an event that is "contingent or speculative in nature," *Basic* provides that "materiality 'will depend at any given time upon a balancing of both the indicated probability that the event will occur and the anticipated magnitude of the event in light of the totality of the company activity.' " *Basic*, 485 U.S. at 238. This standard requires an issuer to weigh the likelihood of a potential event and the magnitude of that potential event in determining the materiality of an omission. Applying this standard here, we conclude that the omissions in this case were material. Although CTI's liabilities were not inevitable, but instead were contingent, they represented a potentially large financial loss for CTI.

* * *

As an alternate defense to CTI's failure to disclose potential liabilities arising from earlier securities law violations, Fehn argues that such a disclosure, even if required under the securities laws, would have violated Wheeler's Fifth Amendment privilege against self-incrimination.

We disagree. As the Supreme Court long ago explained, "[w]henever [a court] is confronted with the question of a compelled disclosure that has an incriminating potential," the "[t]ension between the State's demand for disclosures and the protection of the right against self-incrimination" must be resolved by "balancing the public need on the one hand, and the individual claim to constitutional protections on the other."

A key principle guiding this balancing analysis is that "the mere possibility of incrimination is insufficient to defeat the strong policies in favor of [] disclosure." To invoke the privilege against self-incrimination, a claimant must show "that the compelled disclosures will themselves confront the claimant with 'substantial hazards of self-incrimination.'" A corollary to this principle is that "the Fifth Amendment privilege may not be invoked to resist compliance with a regulatory regime constructed to effect the State's public purposes unrelated to the enforcement of its criminal laws."

In determining whether a compelled disclosure threatens self-incrimination, several factors are to be considered: (1) whether the disclosure requirement targets a " 'highly selective group inherently suspect of criminal activities,' " rather than the public generally; (2) whether the requirement involves " 'an area permeated with criminal statutes,' " rather than " 'an essentially noncriminal and regulatory area of inquiry,' "; and (3) whether compliance would compel disclosure of information that "would surely prove a significant 'link in a chain' of evidence tending to establish [] guilt,'', rather than disclosing "no inherently illegal activity."

* * *

The disclosure requirements contained in Sections 10(b) and 15(d) of the Securities Exchange Act and related regulations do not target a "highly selective group inherently suspect of criminal activities," nor do they regulate an activity that is "permeated with criminal statutes." Although disclosure might have revealed past criminal violations in this case, the disclosure requirement does not, in general, mandate revelation of "inherently illegal activity." We therefore conclude that the disclosure requirements in this case did not violate Wheeler's Fifth Amendment privilege against self-incrimination.

* * *

NOTES

Fehn represents the usual judicial response to claims that the Fifth Amendment shields an individual from disclosure requirements. A notable exception to the cases requiring disclosure is *United States v. Matthews*, 787 F.2d 38 (2d Cir. 1986), which held that the omission of the fact that the defendant had been informed by the U.S. Attorney that he was likely to be indicted was not grounds for a criminal prosecution for failure to disclose that fact. It is less clear that a civil enforcement action by the SEC also would have failed.

If the criminal investigation has led to a formal indictment, disclosure is specifically required under Item 401(f)(2) of Regulation S–K. Other forms of wrongdoing have also been required to be disclosed. For example, Item 401(f)(5) of Regulation S–K requires disclosure if an officer or director has been found by a court or by the SEC to have violated the securities laws. Disclosure is also required if the officer or director filed for bankruptcy, or if he served as an executive officer of a company that filed for bankruptcy.

Note also that Item 401 limits disclosure of criminal cases and adjudications to only those occurring during the previous five years. Earlier offenses are not addressed by the regulation. The mere fact that Item 401 does not specifically require the disclosure of earlier offenses, however, does not end the inquiry. Instead, the issuer (and other disclosing parties) must independently determine whether any earlier offenses are material for investors to obtain a complete understanding of any disclosed information, including information on criminal cases and adjudications within the previous five years as well as any statements on the qualifications of the officers and directors. (See Rule 408 of the Securities Act and Rule 12b–20 of the Exchange Act.)

Item 401 does not require that unadjudicated civil cases against officers or directors be disclosed. Disclosure may still be required, however, if a civil lawsuit or criminal investigation substantially reflects on management integrity. Unadjudicated wrongdoing (even of a criminal nature) is generally held not to be material. Disclosure of wrongdoing may be required, however, if the issuer is proclaiming its faithfulness in obeying the law. Another important exception to the presumption of immateriality occurs when the wrongdoing involves self-dealing by the officer or director. For example, in a proxy case involving undisclosed bribes to foreign officials, the Ninth Circuit drew

> a sharp distinction ... between allegations of director misconduct involving a breach of trust or self-dealing—the nondisclosure of which is presumptively material—and allegations of simple breach of fiduciary duty/ waste of corporate management—the nondisclosure of which is never material for § 14(a) purposes ... the distinction between "mere" bribes and bribes coupled with kickbacks to the directors makes a great deal of sense, indeed it is fundamental to a meaningful concept of materiality under § 14(a) and the preservation of state corporate law.

Gaines v. Haughton, 645 F.2d 761, 776–778 (9th Cir. 1981).

Lawsuits involving a wrongful benefit to a director or officer may be required to be disclosed as omissions of a material fact, even if they have not yet been adjudicated. Even then, the suit may not be required to be disclosed if the allegations made do not substantially undercut the directors' or officers' fitness to serve. *See, e.g., GAF Corp. v. Heyman*, 724 F.2d 727 (2d Cir. 1983) (disclosure of pending suit for breach of fiduciary duty in managing family trust not required in context of proxy fight in which the family member who filed suit was supporting the insurgent in the proxy fight). If disclosure of a pending lawsuit is required, disclosure of the basic facts will suffice; it is not necessary to concede the merits of the pending claim.

QUESTIONS

1. Is it realistic to expect company officers to disclose facts that could lead to their indictment? Is disclosure the real goal?

2. Can we apply the reasoning of *Fehn* to other forms of illegal activities? What if Fehn and the other officers of CTI were importing illegal drugs into the

United States (as of yet undetected by the DEA)? Would they have to disclose this information in their Form 10–K or face Rule 10b–5 antifraud liability?

HYPOTHETICAL SEVEN

David and Nate, the CEO and President of Six Feet respectively, have a little sister, Claire. Claire is ostensibly an employee of Six Feet, drawing a salary of $50,000 per year as David's executive assistant, but she is rarely, if ever, seen at Six Feet's headquarters. David keeps her on the payroll so that she can be covered by Six Feet's health plan. Claire's recurring trips to rehab for her drug problem are tremendously expensive, but Six Feet has remarkably generous mental health benefits included in its employee health plan. Does Six Feet need to disclose Claire's employment arrangement?

CHAPTER 3

THE DEFINITION OF A "SECURITY"

Rules and Statutes

—*Sections 2(a)(1), 2(a)(3), 3(a)(3) of the Securities Act*

—*Sections 3(a)(10), 3(a)(14), 27 and 29 of the Exchange Act*

MOTIVATING HYPOTHETICAL

HiWiFi makes wireless routers with an extraordinary range—they transmit up to triple the range of those produced by the competition. HiWiFi is still closely held—the majority of its shares are owned by Joan, who is also the CEO. The other shares are owned by Joan's sister, Kristine, who serves as the Chief Technology Officer. Joan and Kristine believe that HiWiFi is poised for explosive growth given its technological edge over the competition.

I. DO THE SECURITIES LAWS APPLY?

A threshold question to the application of the securities laws: Is this a security? Not surprisingly, the securities laws only apply if the instrument in question is a security. (Or purports to be—the federal securities laws cover forged or nonexistent securities if, as represented by the fraudster, they fall within the statutory definition.)

The presence of a "security" in a transaction leads to a number of regulatory consequences under the Securities Exchange Act of 1934. The most significant of these is the application of the "catch-all" antifraud Rule 10b–5 (which we will cover in detail in Chapter 5). If Rule 10b–5 applies, contractual limits on remedies are likely to be ineffective because § 29(a) of the '34 Act voids agreements to waive compliance with any rule under the Exchange Act. Other consequences for private litigation include federal jurisdiction and nationwide service of process. Exchange Act § 27. The presence of a security also brings with it the monitoring and enforcement of the SEC and possible criminal sanctions for violations of the securities laws (covered in Chapter 4). Scam artists peddling a security risk the might of the long arm of the federal law.

The presence of a security also triggers the provisions of the Securities Act of 1933. Anyone selling a security to the public must comply with the registration, prospectus delivery and "gun-jumping" rules imposed by § 5 of that Act (the subject of Chapter 7). The public offering of a security triggers the antifraud rules of §§ 11 and 12(a)(2) (covered in Chapter 8), which are considerably more generous to plaintiffs than Rule 10b–5 or common law fraud. Parties seeking to avoid the burdens imposed on public offerings under the '33 Act must structure their sale of securities to be eligible for complicated, and sometimes arcane, offering exemptions (the focus of Chapter 9).

A policy question lurks in asking whether the instrument in question is a "security": *Should* the securities laws apply to the transaction in question? Why do we apply securities regulations only to certain transactions? Home purchases, for example, are not covered by the securities laws, even though they are the most substantial investment that most people make. Your savings account at the local bank, another large repository of investment dollars, is not a security. How does a "security" differ from these other investments? Because securities regulation applies only to transactions in securities, the question of "what is a security" is in many ways the same as asking "should we apply securities regulation here?"

For the Congress that adopted the '33 and '34 Acts, the importance of the securities markets to the national economy was the paramount justification for federal regulation. The recent experience of the stock market crash of October 1929 and the popular association of that crash with the ensuing Great Depression were reason enough to treat securities differently from other investments. Other justifications, however, were also important. Foremost among these was the perception that state regulation, commonly referred to as "Blue Sky" regulation, had failed to protect investors from abuses by stock promoters, insiders and market professionals. This was not because the Blue Sky laws were poorly drafted, but because it was difficult for Midwestern states (whose investors were allegedly being defrauded) to exercise jurisdiction over those cheats back East. Worse yet, the regulators in New York (even though armed with the powerful Martin Act) did little to root out the bad apples.

Those rationales for federal regulation of securities are primarily historical. What theories justify the federal regulation of "securities" in today's market? As discussed in Chapter 1, securities markets are notable for their pervasive problem of information asymmetry. Company insiders and market professionals will inevitably be better able to value a security than will outside investors. If the insiders and professionals are free to exploit that informational advantage, outsiders will be reluctant to participate in the market.

Compare the investment in a share of common stock with the purchase of a half pint of peanut butter and chocolate chunk ice cream. The typical small investor will purchase 100 shares of common stock at a price of, say, $20 per share. That $2,000 may be a substantial portion of the investor's wealth. Disappointment in the investment will not be immediately apparent: The investor will learn of the company's shortcomings only in the long run when it fails to produce the expected profits, and she may not be sufficiently diversified to overcome the damage to her portfolio. To a small investor with almost all her "eggs" in one stock basket, a drop in the value of the stock value will impose real financial hardship. The price of the half pint of ice cream, by contrast, is likely to be a small expenditure for the individual. Only those who like peanut butter and chocolate will purchase at all, and disappointment in the ice cream will be apparent immediately upon tasting. Moreover, that disappointment can be remedied easily in the future by choosing another brand or another flavor, or even switching to pudding or frozen yogurt, until the individual has found a sweet treat that suits her.

Companies, in theory, could help reduce the problem of information asymmetry facing investors by volunteering disclosure, but we saw the limits of that solution in Chapter 1. And investors would face enormous collective action problems in coordinating their demands for disclosure. Moreover, lurking in the background is the suspicion that many (most?) investors are driven by irrational whimsy and infectious greed. "Greed is good"* sometimes; more often, it may lead investors to chase after phantom high returns without pausing to consider the risks behind speculative investments. Left unregulated, the markets may lead to bubbles of the sort that led to the crash of 1929 and the precipitous decline of the Nasdaq index following the Internet stock fueled run-up in the late 1990s. Regulation of securities, in theory, helps reduce the risk to the investor. Perhaps regulation helps keep such investor frenzies in check, thereby also potentially avoiding their disruptive effects on the overall economy.

All of these reasons counsel in favor of a broad interpretation of the definition of "security" in the securities laws. Congress certainly encouraged a broad reading by enumerating virtually identical definitions in § 2(a)(1) of the Securities Act and § 3(a)(10) of the Exchange Act including long lists of instruments ("stocks," "bonds," "fractional undivided interest in oil, gas, or other mineral right," etc.). The definitions sweep even more broadly, however, with their "catch-all" provisions to cover newly-devised instruments of investment (most notably, as we shall see in the cases that follow, "investment contracts"). "Investment contract" sweeps broadly to allow the SEC to go after the latest investment scam, no matter how cleverly disguised. The Supreme Court validated that expansive scope, deciding five cases implicating the definition of a security in the 40 years after the enactment of the '33 and '34 Acts; each time, the Court concluded that the instrument in question was a security. That expansive approach ended when Lewis F. Powell, Jr. joined the Court in 1972—the court rejected a broad reading of "security" in three of the four security definition cases decided during Powell's fifteen-year tenure. What turns on the breadth of the definition of a "security"?

HYPOTHETICAL ONE

Joan, the CEO of HiWiFi, seeks to hire a network engineer to help in designing HiWiFi's new extreme range product offerings for the upcoming holiday season. Chris, a recent college graduate, is interested in the position.

---

* Gordon Gecko famously spoke this phrase in the movie "Wall Street" (1987).

Because HiWiFi is short of cash, Joan wants to pay Chris with several different forms of compensation. Consider whether any of the following transactions should receive the protection of the federal securities laws.

1. Joan pays Chris with precious gems. Joan tells Chris that for every month he works at HiWiFi, he will earn a two-carat diamond. After one year, Chris takes the diamonds to a jeweler for appraisal and discovers that they are really Cubic Zirconia.

2. Joan pays Chris with common stock in HiWiFi. She tells Chris that the stock is quite valuable because HiWiFi is a "can't miss company." Unfortunately, HiWiFi's stock drops in value over the next year.

II.   "INVESTMENT CONTRACT"

The Supreme Court's earliest cases addressing the definition of a security involved the definition's "catch-all" provision, "investment contract." The case below sets forth the test (now known as the *Howey* test) for determining whether an instrument is an "investment contract."

SEC v. W. J. Howey Co.

328 U.S. 293 (1946).

■ MR. JUSTICE MURPHY delivered the opinion of the Court.

This case involves the application of § 2(1) of the Securities Act of 1933 to an offering of units of a citrus grove development coupled with a contract for cultivating, marketing and remitting the net proceeds to the investor.

The Securities and Exchange Commission instituted this action to restrain the respondents from using the mails and instrumentalities of interstate commerce in the offer and sale of unregistered and nonexempt securities in violation of § 5(a) of the Act. . . .

The respondents, W. J. Howey Company and Howey-in-the-Hills Service, are Florida corporations under direct common control and management. The Howey Company owns large tracts of citrus acreage in Lake County, Florida. During the past several years it has planted about 500 acres annually, keeping half of the groves itself and offering the other half to the public "to help us finance additional development." Howey-in-the-Hills Service, Inc., is a service company engaged in cultivating and developing many of these groves, including the harvesting and marketing of the crops.

Each prospective customer is offered both a land sales contract and a service contract, after having been told that it is not feasible to invest in a grove unless service arrangements are made. While the purchaser is free to make arrangements with other service companies, the superiority of Howey-in-the-Hills Service, Inc., is stressed. Indeed, 85% of the acreage sold during the 3–year period ending May 31, 1943, was covered by service contracts with Howey-in-the-Hills Service, Inc.

The land sales contract with the Howey Company provides for a uniform purchase price per acre or fraction thereof, varying in amount only in accordance with the number of years the particular plot has been planted with citrus trees. Upon full payment of the purchase price the land is conveyed to the purchaser by warranty deed. Purchases are usually made in narrow strips of land arranged so that an acre consists of a row of 48 trees. During the period between February 1, 1941, and May 31, 1943, 31 of the 42 persons making purchases bought less than 5 acres each. The average holding of these 31 persons was 1.33 acres and sales of as little as 0.65, 0.7 and 0.73 of an acre were made. These tracts are not separately fenced and the sole indication of several ownership is found in small land marks intelligible only through a plat book record.

The service contract, generally of a 10–year duration without option of cancellation, gives Howey-in-the-Hills Service, Inc., a leasehold interest and "full and complete" possession of the acreage. For a specified fee plus the cost of labor and materials, the company is given full discretion and authority over the cultivation of the groves and the harvest and marketing of the crops. The company is well established in the citrus business and maintains a large force of skilled personnel and a great deal of equipment, including 75 tractors, sprayer wagons, fertilizer trucks and the like. Without the consent of the company, the land owner or purchaser has no right of entry to market the crop; thus there is ordinarily no right to specific fruit. The company is accountable only for an allocation of the net profits based upon a check made at the time of picking. All the produce is pooled by the respondent companies, which do business under their own names.

The purchasers for the most part are non-residents of Florida. They are predominantly business and professional people who lack the knowledge, skill and equipment necessary for the care and cultivation of citrus trees. They are attracted by the expectation of substantial profits. ... Many of these purchasers are patrons of a resort hotel owned and operated by the Howey Company in a scenic section adjacent to the groves. The hotel's advertising mentions the fine groves in the vicinity and the attention of the patrons is drawn to the groves as they are being escorted about the surrounding countryside. They are told that the groves are for sale; if they indicate an interest in the matter they are then given a sales talk.

* * *

Section 2[a](1) of the Act defines the term "security" to include the commonly known documents traded for speculation or investment. This definition also includes "securities" of a more variable character, designated by such descriptive terms as "certificate of interest or participation in any profit-sharing agreement," "investment contract" and "in general, any interest or instrument commonly known as a 'security.'" The legal issue in this case turns upon a determination of whether, under the circumstances, the land sales contract, the warranty deed and the service contract together constitute an "investment contract" within the meaning of § 2[a](1). An affirmative answer brings into operation the registration requirements of § 5(a). . . . The lower courts, in reaching a negative answer to this problem, treated the contracts and deeds as separate transactions involving no more than an ordinary real estate sale and an agreement by the seller to manage the property for the buyer.

The term "investment contract" is undefined by the Securities Act or by relevant legislative reports. But the term was common in many state "blue sky" laws in existence prior to the adoption of the federal statute and, although the term was also undefined by the state laws, it had been broadly construed by state courts so as to afford the investing public a full measure of protection. Form was disregarded for substance and emphasis was placed upon economic reality. An investment contract thus came to mean a contract or scheme for "the placing of capital or laying out of money in a way intended to secure income or profit from its employment." This definition was uniformly applied by state courts to a variety of situations where individuals were led to invest money in a common enterprise with the expectation that they would earn a profit solely through the efforts of the promoter or of some one other than themselves.

By including an investment contract within the scope of § 2[a](1) of the Securities Act, Congress was using a term the meaning of which had been crystallized by this prior judicial interpretation. It is therefore reasonable to attach that meaning to the term as used by Congress, especially since such a definition is consistent with the statutory aims. In other words, an investment contract for purposes of the Securities Act means a contract, transaction or scheme whereby a person invests his money in a common enterprise and is led to expect profits solely from the efforts of the promoter or a third party, it being immaterial whether the shares in the enterprise are evidenced by formal certificates or by nominal interests in the physical assets employed in the enterprise. . . . It permits the fulfillment of the statutory purpose of compelling full and fair disclosure relative to the issuance of "the many types of instruments that in our commercial world fall within the ordinary concept of a security." It embodies a flexible rather than a static principle, one that is capable of adaptation to meet the countless and variable schemes devised by those who seek the use of the money of others on the promise of profits.

The transactions in this case clearly involve investment contracts as so defined. The respondent companies are offering something more than fee simple interests in land, something different from a farm or orchard coupled with management services. They are offering an opportunity to contribute money and to share in the profits of a large citrus fruit enterprise managed and partly owned by respondents. They are offering this opportunity to persons who reside in distant localities and who lack the equipment and experience requisite to the cultivation, harvesting and marketing of the citrus products. Such persons have no desire to occupy the land or to develop it themselves; they are attracted solely by the prospects of a return on their investment. Indeed, individual development of the plots of land that are offered and sold would seldom be economically feasible due to their small size. Such tracts gain utility as citrus groves only when cultivated and developed as component parts of a larger area. A common enterprise managed by respondents or third parties with adequate personnel and equipment is therefore essential if the investors are to achieve their paramount aim of a return on their investments. Their respective shares in this enterprise are evidenced by land sales contracts and warranty deeds, which serve as a convenient method of determining the investors' allocable shares of the profits. The resulting transfer of rights in land is purely incidental.

Thus all the elements of a profit-seeking business venture are present here. The investors provide the capital and share in the earnings and profits; the promoters manage, control and operate the enterprise. It follows that the arrangements whereby the investors' interests are made manifest involve investment contracts, regardless of the legal terminology in which such contracts are clothed. The investment contracts in this instance take the form of land sales contracts, warranty deeds and service contracts which respondents offer to prospective investors. And respondents' failure to abide by the statutory and administrative rules in making such offerings, even though the failure result from a bona fide mistake as to the law, cannot be sanctioned under the Act.

This conclusion is unaffected by the fact that some purchasers choose not to accept the full offer of an investment contract by declining to enter into a service contract with the respondents. The Securities Act prohibits the offer as well as the sale of unregistered, non-exempt securities. Hence it is enough that the respondents merely offer the essential ingredients of an investment contract.

We reject the suggestion of the Circuit Court of Appeals that an investment contract is necessarily missing where the enterprise is not speculative or promotional in character and where the tangible interest which is sold has intrinsic value independent of the success of the enterprise as a whole. The test is whether the scheme involves an investment of money in a common enterprise with profits to come solely from the efforts of others. If that test be satisfied, it is immaterial whether the enterprise is speculative or non-speculative or whether there is a sale of property with or without intrinsic value. The statutory policy of affording broad protection to investors is not to be thwarted by unrealistic and irrelevant formulae.

* * *

NOTES

1. *The* Howey *test.* The *Howey* test introduced here requires "a contract, transaction or scheme" and four additional elements:

1. a person invests his money
2. in a common enterprise and
3. is led to expect profits

4.   solely from the efforts of the promoter or a third party.

Each of these elements has received a substantial gloss in subsequent cases, as we shall see below. In considering these four elements, keep in mind that each must be satisfied before a court will conclude that the instrument in question is a security.

QUESTIONS

1.   Would the offer and sale of tracts of the orange grove–without the additional offering of the service agreement—have been a security?

2.   What if the service agreement was offered by an unaffiliated company? Would the service agreement standing alone be a security? Put another way, would you be purchasing a security if you hired someone to tend the orange trees in your backyard in exchange for a percentage of the profits from the sale of the oranges produced there?

3.   Does it matter that the service contracts were ''optional''?

4.   What if the purchasers were not out-of-state tourists but instead retired and wealthy citrus tree company executives who understood the economics of the citrus fruit industry? Would this change the outcome in *Howey* (assuming everything else is the same)?

5.   Is the regulation of the sale of orange groves by the Howey Company what Congress had in mind when it enacted the securities laws? Or does *Howey* simply divert the SEC's attention away from the primary capital markets toward less important, esoteric transactions?

HYPOTHETICAL TWO

Suppose that Joan, the CEO of HiWiFi, decides that she wants to raise capital from the public capital market. She does not, however, like the prospect of federal securities regulation. Imagine, moreover, that *Howey* had come out the other way and the Supreme Court chose not to treat the offer of strips of land coupled with service contracts as investment contracts unless specifically labeled ''investment contracts.'' After consulting with her attorneys, Joan decides to sell ''Special, Transferable Ownership Certificate Koupons'' or ''S.T.O.C.K.'' Each S.T.O.C.K. unit consists of ownership of a thin strip of HiWiFi's main manufacturing plant and an obligatory service contract giving HiWiFi the exclusive right to utilize the strip of the factory. All profits are pooled and distributed pro rata to the S.T.O.C.K. holders. If the S.T.O.C.K. units are not investment contracts (and are not otherwise securities), what mischief is possible?

A.   ''A PERSON INVESTS HIS MONEY''

The case below addresses the question of what constitutes an ''investment'' for purposes of the *Howey* test. Note that Justice Powell authored this opinion for the Court. Is the employment relationship at issue one that requires federal regulation? Are the securities laws well tailored to regulate that relationship?

International Brotherhood of Teamsters v. Daniel

439 U.S. 551 (1979).

■ MR. JUSTICE POWELL delivered the opinion of the Court.

This case presents the question whether a noncontributory, compulsory pension plan constitutes a "security" within the meaning of the Securities Act of 1933 and the Securities Exchange Act of 1934.

I

In 1954 multi-employer collective bargaining between Local 705 of the International Brotherhood of Teamsters, Chauffeurs, Warehousemen, and Helpers of America and Chicago trucking firms produced a pension plan for employees represented by the Local. The plan was compulsory and noncontributory. Employees had no choice as to participation in the plan, and did not have the option of demanding that the employer's contribution be paid directly to them as a substitute for pension eligibility. The employees paid nothing to the plan themselves....

At the time respondent brought suit, employers contributed $21.50 per employee man-week and pension payments ranged from $425 to $525 a month depending on age at retirement. In order to receive a pension an employee was required to have 20 years of continuous service, including time worked before the start of the plan.

The meaning of "continuous service" is at the center of this dispute. Respondent began working as a truck driver in the Chicago area in 1950, and joined Local 705 the following year. When the plan first went into effect, respondent automatically received 5 years' credit toward the 20–year service requirement because of his earlier work experience. He retired in 1973 and applied to the plan's administrator for a pension. The administrator determined that respondent was ineligible because of a break in service between December 1960 and July 1961.[4] Respondent appealed the decision to the trustees, who affirmed. Respondent then asked the trustees to waive the continuous-service rule as it applied to him. After the trustees refused to waive the rule, respondent brought suit in federal court against the International Union (Teamsters), Local 705 (Local), and Louis Peick, a trustee of the Fund.

Respondent's complaint alleged that the Teamsters, the Local, and Peick misrepresented and omitted to state material facts with respect to the value of a covered employee's interest in the pension plan. Count I of the complaint charged that these misstatements and omissions constituted a fraud in connection with the sale of a security in violation of § 10(b) of the Securities Exchange Act of 1934 and the Securities and Exchange Commission's Rule 10b–5. ... Other counts alleged violations of various labor law and common-law duties. ...

---

4. Respondent was laid off from December 1960 until April 1961. In addition, no contributions were paid on his behalf between April and July 1961, because of embezzlement by his employer's bookkeeper. During this 7–month period respondent could have preserved his eligibility by making the contributions himself, but he failed to do so.

The petitioners moved to dismiss the first two counts of the complaint on the ground that respondent had no cause of action under the Securities Acts. The District Court denied the motion. It held that respondent's interest in the Pension Fund constituted a security within the meaning of § 2[a](1) of the Securities Act, and § 3(a)(10) of the Securities Exchange Act, because the plan created an "investment contract" as that term had been interpreted in *SEC v. W. J. Howey Co.*, 328 U.S. 293 (1946). ...

The order denying the motion to dismiss was certified for appeal ... and the Court of Appeals for the Seventh Circuit affirmed. Relying on its perception of the economic realities of pension plans and various actions of Congress and the SEC with respect to such plans, the court ruled that respondent's interest in the Pension Fund was a "security." According to the court, a "sale" took place either when respondent ratified a collective-bargaining agreement embodying the Fund or when he accepted or retained covered employment instead of seeking other work. The court did not believe the subsequent enactment of the Employee Retirement Income Security Act of 1974 affected the application of the Securities Acts to pension plans, as the requirements and purposes of ERISA were perceived to be different from those of the Securities Acts.[10] We granted certiorari and now reverse.

II

"The starting point in every case involving construction of a statute is the language itself." In spite of the substantial use of employee pension plans at the time they were enacted, neither § 2[a](1) of the Securities Act nor § 3(a)(10) of the Securities Exchange Act, which defines the term "security" in considerable detail and with numerous examples, refers to pension plans of any type. Acknowledging this omission in the statutes, respondent contends that an employee's interest in a pension plan is an "investment contract," an instrument which is included in the statutory definitions of a security.

To determine whether a particular financial relationship constitutes an investment contract, "[t]he test is whether the scheme involves an investment of money in a common enterprise with profits to come solely from the efforts of others." This test is to be applied in light of "the substance—the economic realities of the transaction—rather than the names that may have been employed by the parties." Looking separately at each element of the *Howey* test, it is apparent that an employee's participation in a noncontributory, compulsory pension plan such as the Teamsters' does not comport with the commonly held understanding of an investment contract.

A. Investment of Money

An employee who participates in a noncontributory, compulsory pension plan by definition makes no payment into the pension fund. He only

10. Respondent did not have any cause of action under ERISA itself, as that Act took effect after he had retired.

accepts employment, one of the conditions of which is eligibility for a possible benefit on retirement. Respondent contends, however, that he has "invested" in the Pension Fund by permitting part of his compensation from his employer to take the form of a deferred pension benefit. By allowing his employer to pay money into the Fund, and by contributing his labor to his employer in return for these payments, respondent asserts he has made the kind of investment which the Securities Acts were intended to regulate.

In order to determine whether respondent invested in the Fund by accepting and remaining in covered employment, it is necessary to look at the entire transaction through which he obtained a chance to receive pension benefits. In every decision of this Court recognizing the presence of a "security" under the Securities Acts, the person found to have been an investor chose to give up a specific consideration in return for a separable financial interest with the characteristics of a security. In every case the purchaser gave up some tangible and definable consideration in return for an interest that had substantially the characteristics of a security.

In a pension plan such as this one, by contrast, the purported investment is a relatively insignificant part of an employee's total and indivisible compensation package. No portion of an employee's compensation other than the potential pension benefits has any of the characteristics of a security, yet these noninvestment interests cannot be segregated from the possible pension benefits. Only in the most abstract sense may it be said that an employee "exchanges" some portion of his labor in return for these possible benefits.[12] He surrenders his labor as a whole, and in return receives a compensation package that is substantially devoid of aspects resembling a security. His decision to accept and retain covered employment may have only an attenuated relationship, if any, to perceived investment possibilities of a future pension. Looking at the economic realities, it seems clear that an employee is selling his labor primarily to obtain a livelihood, not making an investment.

Respondent also argues that employer contributions on his behalf constituted his investment into the Fund. But it is inaccurate to describe these payments as having been "on behalf" of any employee. The trust agreement used employee man-weeks as a convenient way to measure an employer's overall obligation to the Fund, not as a means of measuring the employer's obligation to any particular employee. Indeed, there was no fixed relationship between contributions to the Fund and an employee's potential benefits. A pension plan with "defined benefits," such as the Local's, does not tie a qualifying employee's benefits to the time he has worked. One who has engaged in covered employment for 20 years will receive the same benefits as a person who has worked for 40, even though the latter has worked twice as long and induced a substantially larger

---

12. This is not to say that a person's "investment," in order to meet the definition of an investment contract, must take the form of cash only, rather than of goods and services.

employer contribution. Again, it ignores the economic realities to equate employer contributions with an investment by the employee.

B. Expectation of Profits From a Common Enterprise

[The Court concluded that this element was lacking as well because most] of its income comes from employer contributions, a source in no way dependent on the efforts of the Fund's managers. . . . Not only does the greater share of a pension plan's income ordinarily come from new contributions, but unlike most entrepreneurs who manage other people's money, a plan usually can count on increased employer contributions, over which the plan itself has no control, to cover shortfalls in earnings.

* * *

IV

If any further evidence were needed to demonstrate that pension plans of the type involved are not subject to the Securities Acts, the enactment of ERISA in 1974 would put the matter to rest. Unlike the Securities Acts, ERISA deals expressly and in detail with pension plans. ERISA requires pension plans to disclose specified information to employees in a specified manner in contrast to the indefinite and uncertain disclosure obligations imposed by the antifraud provisions of the Securities Acts. Further, ERISA regulates the substantive terms of pension plans, setting standards for plan funding and limits on the eligibility requirements an employee must meet. For example, with respect to the underlying issue in this case—whether respondent served long enough to receive a pension—§ 203(a) of ERISA, now sets the minimum level of benefits an employee must receive after accruing specified years of service, and § 203(b), governs continuous-service requirements. Thus, if respondent had retired after § 1053 took effect, the Fund would have been required to pay him at least a partial pension. The Securities Acts, on the other hand, do not purport to set the substantive terms of financial transactions.

The existence of this comprehensive legislation governing the use and terms of employee pension plans severely undercuts all arguments for extending the Securities Acts to noncontributory, compulsory pension plans. Congress believed that it was filling a regulatory void when it enacted ERISA, a belief which the SEC actively encouraged. Not only is the extension of the Securities Acts by the court below unsupported by the language and history of those Acts, but in light of ERISA it serves no general purpose. Whatever benefits employees might derive from the effect of the Securities Acts are now provided in more definite form through ERISA.

V

We hold that the Securities Acts do not apply to a noncontributory, compulsory pension plan. . . .

NOTES

1. *Alternative regulatory schemes.* Both § 2(a)(1) of the Securities Act and § 3(a)(10) of the Exchange Act provide that the definition for a "security" applies "unless the context otherwise requires." In *Daniel*, the presence of an alternative federal regulatory scheme protecting investors, in this case ERISA, appears to have influenced the Court in reaching its conclusion that the pension plan was not an investment contract. Part of the Court's rationale turned on the fact that Congress believed ERISA filled a "regulatory void," implying that the securities laws did not already cover pension plans. Another part of the Court's rationale focused on the lack of need for the securities laws because ERISA already protects the interests of employees in a pension fund "in more definite form."

The Court emphasized the importance of an alternative regulatory scheme more strongly in *Marine Bank v. Weaver*, 455 U.S. 551 (1982), where it concluded that a certificate of deposit was not a security. The *Marine Bank* Court had this to say about federal banking regulation:

> This certificate of deposit was issued by a federally regulated bank which is subject to the comprehensive set of regulations governing the banking industry. Deposits in federally regulated banks are protected by the reserve, reporting, and inspection requirements of the federal banking law. ...In addition, deposits are insured by the Federal Deposit Insurance Corporation. Since its formation in 1933, nearly all depositors in failing banks insured by the FDIC have received payment in full, even payment for the portions of their deposits above the amount insured. ...

455 U.S. at 557. The presence of an alternative *federal* regulatory regime that fully protects investors strongly influenced the *Marine Bank* Court. Subsequent lower court opinions, however, have concluded that *state* regulation carries little weight in the *Howey* test.

2. *Other pension schemes.* The pension scheme in *Daniel* was deemed not to be a security because it was mandatory and non-contributory. What about benefit plans that are voluntary and require employee contributions? The SEC takes the position that plans of this sort are securities. Sec. Act. Rel. 6281 (1981). Securities Act § 3(a)(2), however, generally exempts such plans from the registration requirements. And what about plans in between these two poles (voluntary/non-contributory and mandatory/contributory)? The SEC considers these plans not to be securities. Sec. Act. Rel. 6188 (1980).

QUESTIONS

1. Is there any way to view an employee as making a "choice" with respect to a compulsory, noncontributory pension plan?

2. Why does the presence of an alternative federal regulatory scheme influence the determination of whether there is a security?

3. What sorts of consideration count as an "investment" for purposes of the *Howey* test? Must the investor part with cash?

HYPOTHETICAL THREE

HiWiFi awards its employees "profit participation units." The value of the unit is tied to the company's net earnings, with 25% of earnings paid out annually to the holders of the units (pro rata based on the number of units held). The employees' entitlement to their share of the units vests by 10% per year, reaching full vesting in year ten of employment. HiWiFi gives its employees the option of taking cash in lieu of the units, but the value of the cash is approximately 50% of the expected present discounted value of the profit participation units. Are the profit participation units securities?

B.   "[I]N A COMMON ENTERPRISE"

The *Howey* Court did not define, for purposes of a "common enterprise," with whom the investor must have an interest in "common." Other investors? The promoter or managers of the enterprise? The following case outlines the divergent positions taken by the lower courts on the issue of commonality.

SEC v. SG Ltd.

265 F.3d 42 (1st Cir. 2001).

■ SELYA, CIRCUIT JUDGE.

These appeals . . . require us to determine whether virtual shares in an enterprise existing only in cyberspace fall within the purview of the federal securities laws. SG Ltd., a Dominican corporation, and its affiliate, SG Trading Ltd. asseverate that the virtual shares were part of a fantasy investment game created for the personal entertainment of Internet users, and therefore, that those shares do not implicate the federal securities laws. The Securities and Exchange Commission, plaintiff below and appellant here, counters that substance ought to prevail over form, and that merely labeling a website as a game should not negate the applicability of the securities laws.

I.   BACKGROUND

The underlying litigation was spawned by SG's operation of a "Stock-Generation" website offering on-line denizens an opportunity to purchase shares in eleven different "virtual companies" listed on the website's "virtual stock exchange." SG arbitrarily set the purchase and sale prices of each of these imaginary companies in biweekly "rounds," and guaranteed that investors could buy or sell any quantity of shares at posted prices. SG placed no upper limit on the amount of funds that an investor could squirrel away in its virtual offerings.

The SEC's complaint focused on shares in a particular virtual enterprise referred to by SG as the "privileged company," and so do we. SG advised potential purchasers to pay "particular attention" to shares in the privileged company and boasted that investing in those shares was a "game without any risk." To this end, its website announced that the privileged company's shares would unfailingly appreciate, boldly proclaiming that "[t]he share price of [the privileged company] is supported by the owners of SG, this is why its value constantly rises; on average at a rate of 10% monthly (this is approximately 215% annually)." To add plausibility to this representation and to allay anxiety about future pricing, SG published prices of the privileged company's shares one month in advance.

While SG conceded that a decline in the share price was theoretically possible, it assured prospective participants that "under the rules governing the fall in prices, [the share price for the privileged company] cannot fall by more than 5% in a round." To bolster this claim, it vouchsafed that shares in the privileged company were supported by several distinct revenue streams. According to SG's representations, capital inflow from new participants provided liquidity for existing participants who might choose to sell their virtual shareholdings. As a backstop, SG pledged to allocate an indeterminate portion of the profits derived from its website operations to a special reserve fund designed to maintain the price of the privileged company's shares. SG asserted that these profits emanated from four sources: (1) the collection of a 1.5% commission on each transaction conducted on its virtual stock exchange; (2) the bid-ask spread on the virtual shares; (3) the "skillful manipulation" of the share prices of eight particular imaginary companies, not including the privileged company, listed on the virtual stock exchange; and (4) SG's right to sell shares of three other virtual companies (including the privileged company). As a further hedge against adversity, SG alluded to the availability of auxiliary stabilization funds which could be tapped to ensure the continued operation of its virtual stock exchange.

SG's website contained lists of purported "big winners," an Internet bulletin board featuring testimonials from supposedly satisfied participants, and descriptions of incentive programs that held out the prospect of rewards for such activities as the referral of new participants (e.g., SG's representation that it would pay "20, 25 or 30% of the referred player's highest of the first three payments") and the establishment of affiliate websites.

At least 800 United States domiciliaries, paying real cash, purchased virtual shares in the virtual companies listed on the defendants' virtual stock exchange. In the fall of 1999, over $4,700,000 in participants' funds was deposited into a Latvian bank account in the name of SG Trading Ltd. The following spring, more than $2,700,000 was deposited in Estonian bank accounts standing in the names of SG Ltd. and SG Perfect Ltd., respectively.

In late 1999, participants began to experience difficulties in redeeming their virtual shares. On March 20, 2000, these difficulties crested; SG unilaterally suspended all pending requests to withdraw funds and sharply reduced participants' account balances in all companies except the privileged company. Two weeks later, SG peremptorily announced a reverse stock split, which caused the share prices of all companies listed on the virtual stock exchange, including the privileged company, to plummet to 1/10,000 of their previous values. At about the same time, SG stopped responding to participant requests for the return of funds, yet continued to solicit new participants through its website.

The SEC undertook an investigation into SG's activities, which culminated in the filing of a civil action in federal district court. The SEC's complaint alleged, in substance, that SG's operations constituted a fraudulent scheme in violation of the registration and antifraud provisions of the federal securities laws. The SEC sought injunctive relief, disgorgement, and civil penalties.

These appeals hinge on whether the district court erred in ruling that transactions in the privileged company's shares did not constitute transactions in securities. In the pages that follow, we explore the makeup of that particular type of security known as an investment contract; examine the district court's rationale; and apply the tripartite "investment contract" test to the facts as alleged. . . .

II. THE LEGAL LANDSCAPE

These appeals turn on whether the SEC alleged facts which, if proven, would bring this case within the jurisdictional ambit of the federal securities laws. Consequently, we focus on the type of security that the SEC alleges is apposite here: investment contracts.

A.   Investment Contracts

The applicable regulatory regime rests on two complementary pillars: the Securities Act of 1933 and the Securities Exchange Act of 1934. These statutes employ nearly identical definitions of the term "security." Congress intended these sweeping definitions . . . to encompass a wide array of financial instruments, ranging from well-established investment vehicles (e.g., stocks and bonds) to much more arcane arrangements. Included in this array is the elusive, essentially protean, concept of an investment contract.

Judicial efforts to delineate what is—and what is not—an investment contract are grounded in the seminal case of *SEC v. W.J. Howey Co.*, 328 U.S. 293 (1946).

* * *

The *Howey* test has proven to be versatile in practice. Over time, courts have classified as investment contracts a kaleidoscopic assortment of pecuniary arrangements that defy categorization in conventional financial terms, yet nonetheless satisfy the *Howey* Court's three criteria. See, e.g., *Teague v. Bakker*, 35 F.3d 978, 981, 990 (4th Cir.1994) (purchase of life partnership in evangelical community); *Long v. Shultz Cattle Co.*, 881 F.2d 129, 132 (5th Cir.1989) (cattle-feeding and consulting agreement); *Miller v. Cent. Chinchilla Group*, 494 F.2d 414, 415, 418 (8th Cir.1974) (chinchilla breeding and resale arrangement).

B.   The District Court's Rationale.

We pause at this juncture to address the district court's rationale. Relying upon a dictum from *Howey* discussing "the many types of instruments that in our commercial world fall within the ordinary concept of a security," the district court drew a distinction between what it termed "commercial dealings" and what it termed "games." Characterizing purchases of the privileged company's shares as a "clearly marked and defined game," the court concluded that since that activity was not part of the commercial world, it fell beyond the jurisdictional reach of the federal securities laws. In so ruling, the court differentiated SG's operations from a classic Ponzi or pyramid scheme on the ground that those types of chicanery involved commercial dealings within a business context.

We do not gainsay the obvious correctness of the district court's observation that investment contracts lie within the commercial world. Contrary to the district court's view, however, this locution does not translate into a dichotomy between business dealings, on the one hand, and games, on the other hand, as a failsafe way for determining whether a particular financial arrangement should (or should not) be characterized as an investment contract. *Howey* remains the touchstone for ascertaining whether an investment contract exists—and the test that it prescribes must be administered without regard to nomenclature. Cf. William Shakespeare, Romeo & Juliet, act 2, sc. 2 (circa 1597) ("A rose by any other name would smell as sweet."). As long as the three-pronged *Howey* test is satisfied, the instrument must be classified as an investment contract. Once that has occurred, "it is immaterial whether the enterprise is speculative or nonspeculative or whether there is a sale of property with or without intrinsic value." It is equally immaterial whether the promoter depicts the enterprise as a serious commercial venture or dubs it a game.

* * *

III.   ADMINISTERING THE TRIPARTITE TEST

What remains is to analyze whether purchases of the privileged company's shares constitute investment contracts. We turn to that task, taking the three *Howey* criteria in sequence.

A.   Investment of Money

The first component of the *Howey* test focuses on the investment of money. The determining factor is whether an investor "chose to give up a specific consideration in return for a separable financial interest with the characteristics of a security." We conclude that the SEC's complaint sufficiently alleges the existence of this factor.

To be sure, SG disputes the point. It argues that the individuals who purchased shares in the privileged company were not so much investing money in return for rights in the virtual shares as paying for an entertainment commodity (the opportunity to play the StockGeneration game). This argument suggests that an interesting factual issue may await resolution—whether participants were motivated primarily by a perceived investment opportunity or by the visceral excitement of playing a game. Nevertheless, this case comes to us following a dismissal under Rule 12(b)(6), and the SEC's complaint memorializes, inter alia, SG's representation that participants could "firmly expect a 10% profit monthly" on purchases of the privileged company's shares. That representation plainly supports the SEC's legal claim that participants who invested substantial amounts of money in exchange for virtual shares in the privileged company likely did so in anticipation of investment gains. Given the procedural posture of the case, no more is exigible to fulfill the first part of the *Howey* test.

B.   Common Enterprise

The second component of the *Howey* test involves the existence of a common enterprise. Before diving headlong into the sea of facts, we must dispel the miasma that surrounds the appropriate legal standard.

1.   The Legal Standard. Courts are in some disarray as to the legal rules associated with the ascertainment of a common enterprise. Many courts require a showing of horizontal commonality—a type of commonality that involves the pooling of assets from multiple investors so that all share in the profits and risks of the enterprise. Other courts have modeled the concept of common enterprise around fact patterns in which an investor's fortunes are tied to the promoter's success rather than to the fortunes of his or her fellow investors. This doctrine, known as vertical commonality, has two variants. Broad vertical commonality requires that the well-being of all investors be dependent upon the promoter's expertise. In contrast, narrow vertical commonality requires that the investors' fortunes be "interwoven with and dependent upon the efforts and success of those seeking the investment or of third parties."

Courts also differ in the steadfastness of their allegiance to a single standard of commonality. Two courts of appeals recognize only horizontal commonality. Two others adhere exclusively to broad vertical commonality.[1] The Ninth Circuit recognizes both horizontal commonality and narrow vertical commonality. To complicate matters further, four courts of appeals have accepted horizontal commonality, but have not yet ruled on whether they also will accept some form of vertical commonality. At least one of these courts, however, has explicitly rejected broad vertical commonality.

Thus far, neither the Supreme Court nor this court has authoritatively determined what type of commonality must be present to satisfy the common enterprise element.

The case at bar requires us to take a position on the common enterprise component of the *Howey* test. We hold that a showing of horizontal commonality—the pooling of assets from multiple investors in such a manner that all share in the profits and risks of the enterprise— satisfies the test. This holding flows naturally from the facts of *Howey*, in which the promoter commingled fruit from the investors' groves and allocated net profits based upon the production from each tract. Adopting this rule also aligns us with the majority view. . . . Last, but surely not least, the horizontal commonality standard places easily ascertainable and pre-

---

1.   We note that broad vertical commonality is an expansive concept which typically overspreads other types of commonality.

dictable limits on the types of financial instruments that will qualify as securities.

2. Applying the Standard. Here, the pooling element of horizontal commonality jumps off the screen. The defendants' website stated that: "The players' money is accumulated on the SG current account and is not invested anywhere, because no investment, not even the most profitable one, could possibly fully compensate for the lack of sufficiency in settling accounts with players, which lack would otherwise be more likely." Thus, as the SEC's complaint suggests, SG unambiguously represented to its clientele that participants' funds were pooled in a single account used to settle participants' on-line transactions. Therefore, pooling is established.

Of course, horizontal commonality requires more than pooling alone; it also requires that investors share in the profits and risks of the enterprise. The SEC maintains that two separate elements of SG's operations embody the necessary sharing. First, it asserts that SG was running a Ponzi or pyramid scheme dependent upon a continuous influx of new money to remain in operation,[3] and argues that such arrangements inherently involve the sharing of profit and risk among investors. Second, the SEC construes SG's promise to divert a portion of its profits from website operations to support the privileged company's shares as a bond that ties together the collective fortunes of those who have purchased the shares. While we analyze each of these theories, we note that any one of them suffices to support a finding of commonality.

We endorse the SEC's suggestion that Ponzi schemes typically satisfy the horizontal commonality standard. . . .

SG's flat 10% guaranteed return applied to all privileged company shares, expected returns were dependent upon the number of shares held, the economic assurances were based on the promoter's ability to keep the ball rolling, the investment was proclaimed to be free from risk, and participants were promised that their principal would be repaid in full upon demand. . . . we think that these facts suffice to make out horizontal commonality.

In all events, SG's promise to pay referral fees to existing participants who induced others to patronize the virtual exchange provides an alternative basis for finding horizontal commonality. The SEC argues convincingly that this shows the existence of a pyramid scheme sufficient to satisfy the horizontal commonality standard.

* * *

3. While the terms "Ponzi" and "pyramid" often are used interchangeably to describe financial arrangements which rob Peter to pay Paul, the two differ slightly. In Ponzi schemes—name after a notorious Boston swindler, Charles Ponzi, who parlayed an initial stake of $150 into a fortune by means of an elaborate scheme featuring promissory notes yielding interest at annual rates of up to 50%—money tendered by later investors is used to pay off earlier investors. In contrast, pyramid schemes incorporate a recruiting element; they are marketing arrangements in which participants are rewarded financially based upon their ability to induce others to participate. The SEC alleges that SG's operations aptly can be characterized under either appellation.

StockGeneration participants who recruited new participants were promised bonuses worth 20%–30% of the recruit's payments. Taking as true the SEC's plausible allegation that the sine qua non of SG's operations was the continued net inflow of funds, the investment pool supporting the referral bonus payments was entirely dependent upon the infusion of fresh capital. Since all participants shared in the profits and risks under this pyramidal structure, it furnishes the sharing necessary to warrant a finding of horizontal commonality.

We will not paint the lily. We conclude, without serious question, that the arrangement described in the SEC's complaint fairly can be characterized as either a Ponzi or pyramid scheme, and that it provides the requisite profit-and-risk sharing to support a finding of horizontal commonality. Taking as true the SEC's allegation that SG's ability to fulfill its pecuniary guarantees was fully predicated upon the net inflow of new money, the fortunes of the participants were inextricably intertwined. As long as the privileged company continued to receive net capital infusions, existing shareholders could dip into the well of funds to draw out their profits or collect their commissions. But all of them shared the risk that new participants would not emerge, cash flow would dry up, and the underlying pool would empty.

SG's most perfervid argument against a finding of horizontal commonality consists of a denial that its operations comprise a Ponzi or pyramid scheme. It says that any such scheme requires a material misrepresentation of fact and some element of fraud or deception, and adds that those additional features are lacking here; to the contrary, the rules of StockGeneration were fully and accurately disclosed to all participants. We do not gainsay that considerable disclosure occurred. SG emphasized that new participants constituted the sole source of all financial income for its StockGeneration website.[4] Indeed, in describing the structure and mechanism of its virtual stock exchange, SG drew a colorful analogy between the privileged company's shares and an enormous card table with a mountain of money. According to SG, thousands of participants continuously threw money onto the table by purchasing shares in the privileged company, while other participants simultaneously sold their shares back to the exchange to retrieve their winnings from the table. SG remarked that the system would remain stable so long as the size of the mountain either remained constant or continued to grow.

Despite the fact that SG was relatively candid in pointing out the fragile structure of the venture, its argument lacks force. Even if we assume, for argument's sake, that misrepresentations of fact and badges of fraud are necessary for the existence of a Ponzi or pyramid scheme, the SEC's complaint contains allegations sufficient, as a matter of pleading, to establish both elements. First, the complaint alleges that SG materially

---

4. SG specifically addressed this issue on its website, declaring that: "New players: that is the only source of all financial income to any game. It does not and cannot have other sources of income. Otherwise, the game becomes unprofitable and therefore simply pointless."

misrepresented the nature of the enterprise by concealing the fact that the supply of new participants inevitably would be exhausted, causing the scheme to implode and all existing participants to lose their money.[5] Second, the SEC's complaint plausibly characterized SG's flat guarantee of a 10% monthly return on the privileged company's shares and its assurances that it would support those shares as material misrepresentations of fact. Third, the SEC alleged that SG deceived participants by failing to disclose its intent to keep investor money for itself.

For present purposes, it is enough that the SEC's allegations, taken as true, satisfy the common enterprise component of the *Howey* test.[6]

C. Expectation of Profits Solely From the Efforts of Others

[The court concluded that investors were led to expect profits from the efforts of the promoters of the website].

IV. CONCLUSION

We need go no further. Giving due weight to the economic realities of the situation, we hold that the SEC has alleged a set of facts which, if proven, satisfy the three-part *Howey* test and support its assertion that the opportunity to invest in the shares of the privileged company, described on SG's website, constituted an invitation to enter into an investment contract within the jurisdictional reach of the federal securities laws.

* * *

QUESTIONS

1. Do you think StockGeneration was a game or an investment? Does it matter what the participants in StockGeneration thought? Were the participants deceived?

2. Which formulation of commonality do you think best serves the purposes of the securities laws?

5. As the SEC points out, SG specifically represented on its website that SG was not a pyramid scheme that would "collapse inevitably as soon as the inflow of new players stops." It went on to state:

> This is not a pyramid. The similarities are purely superficial here. A whale might look like a fish, but there are millions of years of evolution between the two. The main fundamental difference is the lack of critical points in time, namely those of mass payments. By manipulating profit, an optimal way of spreading them in time is successfully found.

6. If more were needed—and we doubt that it is—SG's promise to divert a portion of profits from website operations to support share prices if the need arose also warrants a finding of horizontal commonality. Through this arrangement, SG provided participants with the opportunity to share income derived from website operations on a pro rata basis. The SEC's complaint notes these facts and alleges in substance that a percentage of participants' funds were pooled; that participants were told of their entitlement to support from this monetary pool; and that they collectively stood to gain or lose (depending on whether they received the guaranteed return on their shares). In and of themselves, these averred facts boost the SEC across the legal threshold for horizontal commonality.

3.   How does broad vertical commonality differ from the prong requiring "the efforts of the promoter or a third party"?

4.   Each investor in StockGeneration had the opportunity to earn referral fees for bringing in new recruits (of up to "20%–30% of the recruit's payments"). Do referral fees fit within the court's definition of commonality?

HYPOTHETICAL FOUR

Kristine, the Chief Technology Officer of HiWiFi, has an idea for financing HiWiFi's growth while giving its distributors incentives at the same time. Although HiWiFi sells many of its routers through its website, it also sells them through a commission arrangement with coffee shops. The coffee shops use the router to provide Internet access to their customers. When the customers note the long range provided by HiWiFi's signal, the coffee shops try to sell the customers a HiWiFi router. Kristine thinks the coffee shops would promote the router more aggressively if they were given exclusive rights to use and sell the router in their area. She proposes selling "distribution shares" to the coffee shops, giving them both the exclusive right to sell routers in their area and a higher percentage of the profits from the routers that the coffee shop sells. The money HiWiFi raises from selling the distribution shares will be used for an international advertising campaign promoting the availability of the HiWiFi router signal "in the world's most exclusive coffee shops." Are the distribution shares a security?

C.   "[I]S LED TO EXPECT PROFITS"

The third element of the *Howey* test has important implications for the test as a whole. The notion that investors are "led" suggests that the actions of the promoter that induce the investor to part with his or her money will be a crucial part of the inquiry. Such an approach lends itself to the application of an objective standard: What are the reasonable expectations of the individuals to whom the instrument is offered? Do you think the purchasers of the "stock" in the case below could have reasonably expected the federal securities laws would apply to their investments?

United Housing Foundation, Inc. v. Forman

421 U.S. 837 (1975).

■ MR. JUSTICE POWELL delivered the opinion of the Court.

The issue in these cases is whether shares of stock entitling a purchaser to lease an apartment in Co-op City, a state subsidized and supervised nonprofit housing cooperative, are "securities" within the purview of the Securities Act of 1933 and the Securities Exchange Act of 1934.

Co-op City is a massive housing cooperative in New York City. Built between 1965 and 1971, it presently houses approximately 50,000 people on a 200–acre site containing 35 high-rise buildings and 236 town houses. The project was organized, financed, and constructed under the New York State Private Housing Finance Law ... enacted to ameliorate a perceived crisis in the availability of decent low-income urban housing. In order to encourage private developers to build low-cost cooperative housing, New York provides them with large long-term, low-interest mortgage loans and substantial tax exemptions. ... The developer ... must agree to operate the facility "on a nonprofit basis," and he may lease apartments only to people whose incomes fall below a certain level and who have been approved by the State.

The United Housing Foundation, a nonprofit membership corporation established for the purpose of "aiding and encouraging" the creation of "adequate, safe and sanitary housing accommodations for wage earners and other persons of low or moderate income," was responsible for initiating and sponsoring the development of Co-op City. ... UHF organized the Riverbay Corporation to own and operate the land and buildings constituting Co-op City. Riverbay, a nonprofit cooperative housing corporation, issued the stock that is the subject of this litigation. ...

To acquire an apartment in Co-op City an eligible prospective purchaser must buy 18 shares of stock in Riverbay for each room desired. The cost per share is $25, making the total cost $450 per room, or $1,800 for a four-room apartment. The sole purpose of acquiring these shares is to enable the purchaser to occupy an apartment in Co-op City; in effect, their purchase is a recoverable deposit on an apartment. The shares are explicitly tied to the apartment: they cannot be transferred to a nontenant; nor can they be pledged or encumbered; and they descend, along with the apartment, only to a surviving spouse. No voting rights attach to the shares as such: participation in the affairs of the cooperative appertains to the apartment, with the residents of each apartment being entitled to one vote irrespective of the number of shares owned.

Any tenant who wants to terminate his occupancy, or who is forced to move out, must offer his stock to Riverbay at its initial selling price of $25 per share. ...

In May 1965, subsequent to the completion of the initial planning, Riverbay circulated an Information Bulletin seeking to attract tenants for what would someday be apartments in Co-op City. After describing the nature and advantages of cooperative housing generally and of Co-op City in particular, the Bulletin informed prospective tenants that the total estimated cost of the project, based largely on an anticipated construction contract with [its contractor], was $283,695,550. Only a fraction of this sum, $32,795,550, was to be raised by the sale of shares to tenants. The remaining $250,900,000 was to be financed by a 40–year low-interest mortgage loan from the New York Private Housing Finance Agency. After construction of the project the mortgage payments and current operating expenses would be met by monthly rental charges paid by the tenants. While these rental charges were to vary, depending on the size, nature, and location of an apartment, the 1965 Bulletin estimated that the "average" monthly cost would be $23.02 per room, or $92.08 for a four-room apartment.

Several times during the construction of Co-op City, Riverbay, with the approval of the State Housing Commissioner, revised its contract with [its contractor] to allow for increased construction costs. In addition, Riverbay incurred other expenses that had not been reflected in the 1965 Bulletin. To meet these increased expenditures, Riverbay, with the Commissioner's approval, repeatedly secured increased mortgage loans from the State Housing Agency. Ultimately the construction loan was $125 million more than the figure estimated in the 1965 Bulletin. As a result, while the initial purchasing price remained at $450 per room, the average monthly rental charges increased periodically, reaching a figure of $39.68 per room as of July 1974.

These increases in the rental charges precipitated the present lawsuit. Respondents, 57 residents of Co-op City, sued in federal court on behalf of all 15,372 apartment owners, . . . seeking upwards of $30 million in damages, forced rental reductions, and other "appropriate" relief. . . . The heart of respondents' claim was that the 1965 Co-op City Information Bulletin falsely represented that [the contractor] would bear all subsequent cost increases due to factors such as inflation. Respondents further alleged that they were misled in their purchases of shares since the Information Bulletin failed to disclose several critical facts. On these bases, respondents asserted two claims under the fraud provisions of the federal Securities Act § 17(a); the Securities Exchange Act § 10(b) and Rule 10b–5. . . .

Petitioners, while denying the substance of these allegations, moved to dismiss the complaint on the ground that federal jurisdiction was lacking. They maintained that shares of stock in Riverbay were not "securities" within the definitional sections of the federal Securities Acts. . . .

The District Court granted the motion to dismiss. . . .

The Court of Appeals for the Second Circuit reversed. It rested its decision on two alternative grounds. First, the court held that since the shares purchased were called "stock" the Securities Acts, which explicitly include "stock" in their definitional sections, were literally applicable. Second, the Court of Appeals concluded that the transaction was an investment contract within the meaning of the Acts and as defined by *Howey*, since there was an expectation of profits from three sources: (i) rental reductions resulting from the income produced by the commercial facilities established for the use of tenants at Co-op City; (ii) tax deductions for the portion of the monthly rental charges allocable to interest payments on the mortgage; and (iii) savings based on the fact that apartments at Co-op City cost substantially less than comparable nonsubsidized housing. . . .

In providing [the definition of a security under § 2(a)(1) of the Securities Act] Congress did not attempt to articulate the relevant economic criteria for distinguishing "securities" from "non-securities," rather, it sought to define "the term 'security' in sufficiently broad and general terms so as to include within that definition the many types of instruments that in our commercial world fall within the ordinary concept of a security." The task has fallen to the Securities and Exchange Commission, the body charged with administering the Securities Acts, and ultimately to the federal courts to decide which of the myriad financial transactions in our society come within the coverage of these statutes.

In making this determination in the present case we do not write on a clean slate. Well-settled principles enunciated by this Court establish that the shares purchased by respondents do not represent any of the "countless and variable schemes devised by those who seek the use of the money of others on the promise of profits," and therefore do not fall within "the ordinary concept of a security."

We reject at the outset any suggestion that the present transaction, evidenced by the sale of shares called "stock,"[13] must be considered a security transaction simply because the statutory definition of a security includes the words "any . . . stock." Rather we adhere to the basic principle that has guided all of the Court's decisions in this area: "(I)n searching for the meaning and scope of the word "security" in the Act(s), form should be disregarded for substance and the emphasis should be on economic reality."

The primary purpose of the Acts of 1933 and 1934 was to eliminate serious abuses in a largely unregulated securities market. The focus of the Acts is on the capital market of the enterprise system: the sale of securities to raise capital for profit-making purposes, the exchanges on which securities are traded, and the need for regulation to prevent fraud and to protect the interest of investors. Because securities transactions are economic in character Congress intended the application of these statutes to turn on the economic realities underlying a transaction, and not on the name appended thereto. . . .

* * *

In holding that the name given to an instrument is not dispositive, we do not suggest that the name is wholly irrelevant to the decision whether it is a security. There may be occasions when the use of a traditional name such as "stocks" or "bonds" will lead a purchaser justifiably to assume that the federal securities laws apply. This would clearly be the case when the underlying transaction embodies some of the significant characteristics typically associated with the named instrument.

In the present case respondents do not contend, nor could they, that they were misled by use of the word "stock" into believing that the federal securities laws governed their purchase. Common sense suggests that people who intend to acquire only a residential apartment in a state-subsidized cooperative, for their personal use, are not likely to believe that in reality they are purchasing investment securities simply because the transaction is evidenced by something called a share of stock. These shares have none of the characteristics "that in our commercial world fall within the ordinary concept of a security." Despite their name, they lack . . . the most common feature of stock: the right to receive "dividends contingent

---

13. While the record does not indicate precisely why the term "stock" was used for the instant transaction, it appears that this form is generally used as a matter of tradition and convenience.

upon an apportionment of profits." Nor do they possess the other characteristics traditionally associated with stock: they are not negotiable; they cannot be pledged or hypothecated; they confer no voting rights in proportion to the number of shares owned; and they cannot appreciate in value. In short, the inducement to purchase was solely to acquire subsidized low-cost living space; it was not to invest for profit.

The Court of Appeals, as an alternative ground for its decision, concluded that a share in Riverbay was also an "investment contract" as defined by the Securities Acts. Respondents further argue that in any event what they agreed to purchase is "commonly known as a 'security' " within the meaning of these laws. In considering these claims we again must examine the substance—the economic realities of the transaction—rather than the names that may have been employed by the parties. We perceive no distinction, for present purposes, between an "investment contract" and an "instrument commonly known as a 'security.' " In either case, the basic test for distinguishing the transaction from other commercial dealings is "whether the scheme involves an investment of money in a common enterprise with profits to come solely from the efforts of others." *Howey*, 328 U.S. at 301.[16]

This test, in shorthand form, embodies the essential attributes that run through all of the Court's decisions defining a security. The touchstone is the presence of an investment in a common venture premised on a reasonable expectation of profits to be derived from the entrepreneurial or managerial efforts of others. By profits, the Court has meant either capital appreciation resulting from the development of the initial investment . . . or a participation in earnings resulting from the use of investors' funds. . . . In such cases the investor is "attracted solely by the prospects of a return" on his investment. By contrast, when a purchaser is motivated by a desire to use or consume the item purchased—"to occupy the land or to develop it themselves," as the *Howey* Court put it—the securities laws do not apply.

In the present case there can be no doubt that investors were attracted solely by the prospect of acquiring a place to live, and not by financial returns on their investments.

* * *

Nowhere does the Bulletin seek to attract investors by the prospect of profits resulting from the efforts of the promoters or third parties. On the contrary, the Bulletin repeatedly emphasizes the "nonprofit" nature of the endeavor. It explains that if rental charges exceed expenses the difference will be returned as a rebate, not invested for profit. It also informs

---

16. This test speaks in terms of "profits to come solely from the efforts of others." Although the issue is not presented in this case, we note that the Court of Appeals for the Ninth Circuit has held that "the word 'solely' should not be read as a strict or literal limitation on the definition of an investment contract, but rather must be construed realistically, so as to include within the definition those schemes which involve in substance, if not form, securities." We express no view, however, as to the holding of this case.

purchasers that they will be unable to resell their apartments at a profit since the apartment must first be offered back to Riverbay "at the price . . . paid for it." In short, neither of the kinds of profits traditionally associated with securities was offered to respondents.

The Court of Appeals recognized that there must be an expectation of profits for these shares to be securities, and conceded that there is "no possible profit on a resale of (this) stock." The court correctly noted, however, that profit may be derived from the income yielded by an investment as well as from capital appreciation, and then proceeded to find "an expectation of "income" in at least three ways." Two of these supposed sources of income or profits may be disposed of summarily. We turn first to the Court of Appeals' reliance on the deductibility for tax purposes of the portion of the monthly rental charge applied to interest on the mortgage. We know of no basis in law for the view that the payment of interest, with its consequent deductibility for tax purposes, constitutes income or profits. These tax benefits are nothing more than that which is available to any homeowner who pays interest on his mortgage.[20]

The Court of Appeals also found support for its concept of profits in the fact that Co-op City offered space at a cost substantially below the going rental charges for comparable housing. Again, this is an inappropriate theory of "profits" that we cannot accept. The low rent derives from the substantial financial subsidies provided by the State of New York. This benefit cannot be liquidated into cash; nor does it result from the managerial efforts of others. In a real sense, it no more embodies the attributes of income or profits than do welfare benefits, food stamps, or other government subsidies.

The final source of profit relied on by the Court of Appeals was the possibility of net income derived from the leasing by Co-op City of commercial facilities, professional offices and parking spaces, and its operation of community washing machines. The income, if any, from these conveniences, all located within the common areas of the housing project, is to be used to reduce tenant rental costs. Conceptually, one might readily agree that net income from the leasing of commercial and professional facilities is the kind of profit traditionally associated with a security investment.[21] But in the present case this income—if indeed there is any is far too speculative and insubstantial to bring the entire transaction within the Securities Acts.

20. Even if these tax deductions were considered profits, they would not be the type associated with a security investment since they do not result from the managerial efforts of others.

21. The 'income' derived from the rental of parking spaces and the operation of washing machines clearly was not profit for respondents since these facilities were provided exclusively for the use of tenants. Thus, when the income collected from the use of these facilities exceeds the cost of their operation the tenants simply receive the return of the initial overcharge in the form of a rent rebate. Indeed, it could be argued that the 'income' from the commercial and professional facilities is also, in effect, a rebate on the cost of goods and services purchased at these facilities since it appears likely that they are patronized almost exclusively by Co-op City residents.

Initially we note that the prospect of such income as a means of offsetting rental costs is never mentioned in the Information Bulletin. Thus it is clear that investors were not attracted to Co-op City by the offer of these potential rental reductions. Moreover, nothing in the record suggests that the facilities in fact return a profit in the sense that the leasing fees are greater than the actual cost to Co-op City of the space rented. The short of the matter is that the stores and services in question were established not as a means of returning profits to tenants, but for the purpose of making essential services available for the residents of this enormous complex. . . . Undoubtedly they make Co-op City a more attractive housing opportunity, but the possibility of some rental reduction is not an "expectation of profit" in the sense found necessary in *Howey*.

There is no doubt that purchasers in this housing cooperative sought to obtain a decent home at an attractive price. But that type of economic interest characterizes every form of commercial dealing. What distinguishes a security transaction—and what is absent here—is an investment where one parts with his money in the hope of receiving profits from the efforts of others, and not where he purchases a commodity for personal consumption or living quarters for personal use.

In holding that there is no federal jurisdiction, we do not address the merits of respondents' allegations of fraud. . . . We decide only that the type of transaction before us, in which the purchasers were interested in acquiring housing rather than making an investment for profit, is not within the scope of the federal securities laws.

* * *

NOTES

1. *Real estate as a "security."* Other interests in real estate have posed difficult questions for courts grappling with the definition of investment contract. The easy case at one end of the spectrum is the purchase of land in fee simple, even if promoted as a speculative investment: any profits expected would not come "from the efforts of others." The easy case at the other end is the syndication of an office building or apartment complex. A typical syndication transaction involves a promoter selling limited partnership interests to investors. The limited partnership then purchases the office building or apartment complex. The promoter, who takes the position of general partner, often manages the real estate, paying out a portion of the rent to the limited partners over time. The limited partnership interests typically sold in such transactions clearly fall within the definition of investment contract.

More difficult questions are raised, however, by real estate interests between the two extremes. Consider a condominium in a resort community which the owners occupy for a portion of the year and rent out, with the assistance of the manager of the complex, for the rest of the year. The SEC takes the position that such an arrangement may constitute a security under the following circumstances:

    1.   The condominiums, with any rental arrangement or other similar service, are offered and sold with emphasis on the economic benefits to the purchaser to be derived from the managerial efforts of the promot-

er, or a third party designated or arranged for by the promoter, from rental of the units;

2. The offering of participation in a rental pool arrangement; and

3. The offering of a rental or similar arrangement whereby the purchaser must hold his unit available for rental for any part of the year, must use an exclusive rental agent, or is otherwise materially restricted in his occupancy or rental of his unit.

Sec. Act Rel. 5347 (1973). This guidance provided by the SEC acts as a checklist of arrangements to avoid if the developer wants to escape the complications of the federal securities laws. Should the SEC provide more guidance to investors and promoters on the somewhat murky question of what is a security?

QUESTIONS

1. Does a Co-op share or a share of IBM better fit the traditional characteristics of "stock"? Does all stock have the same characteristics?

2. Why does the Court also find that the Co-op shares are not investment contracts?

3. *Forman* hints at one unified approach to the definition of a security focusing on the economic realities. Should courts use the *Howey* test to determine whether the stock of particular companies counts as a security?

4. Was it a mistake to label the instrument at issue in *Forman* "stock"? What would have happened in future projects of this type if the Court had held that anything labeled "stock" fell within the definition of a security?

5. Would eliminating the anti-waiver provision in § 29(a) of the Exchange Act reduce the temptation to interpret narrowly the definition of security? What problems would eliminating § 29(a) create?

The next case addresses the question of what form the profits must take. The Court in *Forman* stated that: "By profits, the Court has meant either capital appreciation resulting from the development of the initial investment ... or a participation in earnings resulting from the use of investors' funds." What about investments that provide a fixed return and no participation in earnings, such as debt? Despite the language in *Forman*, the Court has taken a broad view on this issue.

SEC v. Edwards

540 U.S. 389 (2004).

■ JUSTICE O'CONNOR delivered the opinion of the Court.

"Opportunity doesn't always knock ... sometimes it rings." And sometimes it hangs up. So it did for the 10,000 people who invested a total of $300 million in the payphone sale-and-leaseback arrangements touted by respondent under that slogan. The Securities and Exchange Commission argues that the arrangements were investment contracts, and thus were subject to regulation under the federal securities laws. In this case, we must decide whether a moneymaking scheme is excluded from the term "investment contract" simply because the scheme offered a contractual entitlement to a fixed, rather than a variable, return.

I

Respondent Charles Edwards was the chairman, chief executive officer, and sole shareholder of ETS Payphones, Inc. ETS ... sold payphones to the public via independent distributors. The payphones were offered packaged with a site lease, a 5–year leaseback and management agreement, and a buyback agreement. All but a tiny fraction of purchasers chose this package, although other management options were offered. The purchase price for the payphone packages was approximately $7,000. Under the leaseback and management agreement, purchasers received $82 per month, a 14% annual return. Purchasers were not involved in the day-to-day operation of the payphones they owned. ETS selected the site for the phone, installed the equipment, arranged for connection and long-distance service, collected coin revenues, and maintained and repaired the phones. Under the buyback agreement, ETS promised to refund the full purchase price of the package at the end of the lease or within 180 days of a purchaser's request.

In its marketing materials and on its website, ETS trumpeted the "incomparable pay phone" as "an exciting business opportunity," in which recent deregulation had "open[ed] the door for profits for individual pay phone owners and operators." According to ETS, "[v]ery few business opportunities can offer the potential for ongoing revenue generation that is available in today's pay telephone industry."

The payphones did not generate enough revenue for ETS to make the payments required by the leaseback agreements, so the company depended on funds from new investors to meet its obligations. In September 2000, ETS filed for bankruptcy protection. The SEC brought this civil enforcement action the same month. It alleged that respondent and ETS had violated the registration requirements of §§ 5(a) and (c) of the Securities Act of 1933, the antifraud provisions of both § 17(a) of the Securities Act of 1933, and § 10(b) of the Securities Exchange Act of 1934. The Court of Appeals ... held that respondent's scheme was not an investment contract, on two grounds. First, it read this Court's opinions to require that an investment contract offer either capital appreciation or a participation in the earnings of the enterprise, and thus to exclude schemes, such as respondent's, offering a fixed rate of return. Second, it held that our opinions' requirement that the return on the investment be "derived solely from the efforts of others" was not satisfied when the purchasers had a contractual entitlement to the return. We conclude that it erred on both grounds.

II

"Congress' purpose in enacting the securities laws was to regulate *investments*, in whatever form they are made and by whatever name they are called." To that end, it enacted a broad definition of "security," sufficient "to encompass virtually any instrument that might be sold as an investment." Section 2(a)(1) of the 1933 Act, and § 3(a)(10) of the 1934 Act in slightly different formulations which we have treated as essentially identical in meaning, define "security" to include "any note, stock, treasury stock, security future, bond, debenture, . . . investment contract, . . . [or any] instrument commonly known as a 'security'." "Investment contract" is not itself defined.

The test for whether a particular scheme is an investment contract was established in our decision in *SEC v. W.J. Howey Co.*, 328 U.S. 293 (1946). We look to "whether the scheme involves an investment of money in a common enterprise with profits to come solely from the efforts of others." . . .

In reaching that result, we first observed that when Congress included "investment contract" in the definition of security, it "was using a term the meaning of which had been crystallized" by the state courts' interpretation of their " 'blue sky' " laws. The state courts had defined an investment contract as "a contract or scheme for 'the placing of capital or laying out of money in a way intended to secure income or profit from its employment,' " and had "uniformly applied" that definition to "a variety of situations where individuals were led to invest money in a common enterprise with the expectation that they would earn a profit solely through the efforts of the promoter or [a third party]." Thus, when we held that "profits" must "come solely from the efforts of others," we were speaking of the profits that investors seek on their investment, not the profits of the scheme in which they invest. We used "profits" in the sense of income or return, to include, for example, dividends, other periodic payments, or the increased value of the investment.

There is no reason to distinguish between promises of fixed returns and promises of variable returns for purposes of the test, so understood. In both cases, the investing public is attracted by representations of investment income, as purchasers were in this case by ETS' invitation to " 'watch the profits add up.' " Moreover, investments pitched as low-risk (such as those offering a "guaranteed" fixed return) are particularly attractive to individuals more vulnerable to investment fraud, including older and less sophisticated investors. Under the reading respondent advances, unscrupulous marketers of investments could evade the securities laws by picking a rate of return to promise. We will not read into the securities laws a limitation not compelled by the language that would so undermine the laws' purposes.

Respondent protests that including investment schemes promising a fixed return among investment contracts conflicts with our precedent. We disagree. No distinction between fixed and variable returns was drawn in the blue sky law cases that the *Howey* Court used, in formulating the test, as its evidence of Congress' understanding of the term. Indeed, two of those cases involved an investment contract in which a fixed return was promised.

None of our post-*Howey* decisions is to the contrary. . . .

The Eleventh Circuit's perfunctory alternative holding, that respondent's scheme falls outside the definition because purchasers had a contractual entitlement to a return, is incorrect and inconsistent with our precedent. We are considering investment contracts. The fact that investors have bargained for a return on their investment does not mean that the return is not also expected to come solely from the efforts of others. . . .

We hold that an investment scheme promising a fixed rate of return can be an "investment contract" and thus a "security" subject to the federal securities laws.

*   *   *

QUESTIONS

1. Was the Court's conclusion that a guaranteed return did not exclude a financial instrument from the definition of a security consistent with the emphasis on risk reduction in *Daniel* and *Marine Bank*?

HYPOTHETICAL FIVE

Joan and Kristine are sisters and the top officers of HiWiFi. Their parents, Leonard and Delores, each invested $100,000 to help get HiWiFi off the ground. The terms of the investments are exceptionally generous. HiWiFi is not obliged to pay any dividends or interest on the investment for the first five years. After five years, interest must be paid on the investment at the prime rate plus 1%, but only if there are net earnings from which to pay the interest. The investments are not for a definite term, but Leonard and Delores can each demand repayment of their principal after twenty years. Realistically speaking, Leonard and Delores (both well into their retirement years) are unlikely to be around to demand repayment. The investments are really a form of estate planning.

After making the investment, however, Leonard becomes fed up with the spam in his email inbox offering a variety of pornography and decides he does not want any part of "this decadent Internet thing." Nor does he want his daughters involved. Leonard demands repayment of his $100,000, but Joan and Kristine refuse. Leonard now says that Joan and Kristine defrauded him by failing to disclose all of the smut on the Internet and he has filed suit against HiWiFi under Rule 10b–5. (Delores would not dream of suing her daughters.) Did HiWiFi sell Leonard a security?

D.   "[S]OLELY FROM THE EFFORTS OF THE PROMOTER OR A THIRD PARTY"

The fourth element of the *Howey* test for an investment contract is whether the scheme generates returns "solely from the efforts of the promoter or a third party." In the case of out-of-state tourists purchasing strips of citrus fruit land and corresponding service contracts prohibiting the tourists from even entering the property, the profits derived from the investment are entirely due to the efforts of the operators of the service company (the promoter).

But what about cases where the investors contribute a modicum of effort? The investors in *Howey*, for example, could have contributed not only cash for their investment, but also one day's worth of labor, during which they would get the opportunity to pick oranges for the service company. The profits no longer stem "solely" from the efforts of others. Does this minimal effort from the investors remove the scheme from the definition of *Howey*?

The fourth element of the *Howey* test has been particularly critical in determining whether an investment contract is present in two common arrangements: partnerships and franchises. These arrangements share the common feature that their investors will frequently be involved in the management of the enterprise. However, the level of control can vary considerably within these broad categories, making generalizations difficult.

Consider a franchise relationship. Many retail businesses, eager to replicate what works in one location, seek to duplicate that success in other locales. A pizza restaurant may produce especially tasty pepperoni pizza and have a certain "look" that attracts many customers. The corporate owner of the pizza restaurant, rather than opening up new restaurants itself, may seek others to open new restaurants. Acting as a franchisor, the corporate owner may divide up various areas into distinct geographical regions. The franchisor will then sell the right to establish a new restaurant in a particular region to a prospective franchisee for a fee, typically in the tens of thousands of dollars, as well as an ongoing royalty payment based on the restaurant's profits. What happens next depends on the particular franchise relationship. The franchisee typically must invest money to lease a location, build a restaurant, and get the business going. The franchisor, in turn, will spend money on national advertising campaigns and ensure that the various franchises maintain consistent product quality and restaurant appearance. Although the franchisee typically has day-to-day control over operations at the franchisee's specific restaurant, the degree of control can vary considerably. If the franchisee invests considerable capital and enjoys only limited control (i.e., the pizza franchisor sets the prices, hours, and provides detailed instructions for hiring employees, the decor of the restaurant and so on), is the franchise agreement a security?

One reasonably clear rule in this area is that limited partnership interests are presumed to be securities unless limited partners exercise effective control over the enterprise. The case below applies the fourth element to a general partnership. Note that the author of the opinion is Justice Powell, sitting by designation on the Fourth Circuit after his retirement from the Supreme Court.

Rivanna Trawlers Unlimited v. Thompson Trawlers, Inc.

840 F.2d 236 (4th Cir. 1988).

■ POWELL, ASSOCIATE JUSTICE.

The dispositive issue presented in this case is whether the district court correctly concluded that appellants' general partnership interests in

Rivanna Trawlers Unlimited are not securities within the meaning of the federal securities laws. We hold that these interests are not securities, and affirm.

The appellate record indicates that the Virginia general partnership, Rivanna Trawlers Unlimited, was formed in August 1982 when twenty-three parties executed an agreement for the purpose of forming a general partnership, "which will acquire, own, lease and operate multi-purpose fishing vessels and otherwise engage in the commercial fishing business. ..." ... On August 30, 1982 RTU purchased four fishing boats and entered into several agreements for their management and maintenance with Thompson Management, Inc. By the spring of 1983 the partners were expressing concern over the partnership's operations and they were considering management alternatives. Operation of the fishing boats had not been meeting the partners' financial expectations. The partners subsequently replaced RTU's external managers twice and removed RTU's original managing partner Walter B. Salley, Sr. ... and replaced him with a managing partnership committee.

In August 1984 RTU and a number of its partners filed a complaint against Thompson Trawlers, Inc., Thompson Management, Inc. and various other companies and individuals. ... These plaintiffs alleged that their interests in the general partnership were "investment contracts" as defined in the federal securities laws, and that appellees had violated these laws. ...

I

* * *

B

We address first appellants' claim that their interests in the RTU partnership were investment contracts, and therefore were securities within the meaning of the federal securities laws. The Supreme Court has defined an investment contract as "a contract, transaction or scheme whereby a person invests his money in a common enterprise and is led to expect profits solely from the efforts of the promoter or a third party. ..." The critical issue on this appeal is whether appellants' general partnership interests in RTU meet the third prong of the *Howey* test—that is, the expectation of profits derived solely from the efforts of others.[4] General partnerships ordinarily are not considered investment contracts because they grant partners—the investors—control over significant decisions of

---

4. In *SEC v. Glenn W. Turner Enters.*, 474 F.2d 476, 482 (9th Cir. 1973) the Ninth Circuit held that the term "solely" should not be given a literal construction. A more liberal interpretation of the term solely, as used in *Howey*, has been adopted by eight additional circuits. In light of the Supreme Court's statements that economic reality is to govern over form in determining what is a "security," we agree that the term solely—used in *Howey*—must not be given a literal construction in all circumstances.

the enterprise. In *Williamson v. Tucker*, 645 F.2d 404, 422 (5th Cir. 1981), a leading case, the Fifth Circuit identified a narrow exception to the strong presumption that a general partnership is not a security. The court stated that:

> ... a partnership can be an investment contract only when the partners are so dependent on a particular manager that they cannot replace him or otherwise exercise ultimate control.

Only when this degree of dependence by the partners exists is there an investment contract. Moreover, the court emphasized that "[t]he delegation of rights and duties—standing alone—does not give rise to the sort of dependence on others which underlies the third prong of the *Howey* test." In other words, the mere choice by a partner to remain passive is not sufficient to create a security interest. The critical inquiry is, "whether the powers possessed by the [general partners] in the [partnership agreement] were so significant that, regardless of the degree to which such powers were exercised, the investments could not have been premised on a reasonable expectation of profits to be derived from the management efforts of others."

We agree with the Fifth Circuit, as well as the other circuits that appear to have embraced the *Williamson* reasoning, that only under certain limited circumstances can an investor's general partnership interest be characterized as an investment contract. A court must examine the partnership agreement and circumstances of a particular partnership to determine the reality of the contractual rights of the general partners. When, however, a partnership agreement allocates powers to the general partners that are specific and unambiguous, and when those powers are sufficient to allow the general partners to exercise ultimate control, as a majority, over the partnership and its business, then the presumption that the general partnership is not a security can only be rebutted by evidence that it is not possible for the partners to exercise those powers.[7] As the district court stated, "[e]ven when general partners do not individually have decisive control over major decisions, they do have the sort of influence which generally provides them with access to important information and protection against a dependence on others." In a case of this kind, it also is important to bear in mind that Congress, in enacting the securities laws, did not intend to provide a federal remedy for all common law fraud.

C

The RTU Partnership Agreement confers broad authority on the partners to manage and control the business. It provides that the partner-

---

7. If and to the extent that *Williamson* and other cases may be read to require a court to look to the actual knowledge and business expertise of each partner in order to assess his or her individual ability intelligently to exercise the power of a general partner, we do not agree. Such an inquiry would undercut the strong presumption that an interest in a general partnership is not a security. It also would unduly broaden the scope of the Supreme Court's instruction that courts must examine the economic reality of partnership interests. We note that no such specific argument is made in this case. Appellants' complaint and briefs properly speak only in terms of the rights and authority of the partners as a group.

ship can be dissolved by a concurrence of 60% in interest of the partners. It also states that, "[c]oncurrence of sixty percent (60%) in interest of the partners should be required with respect to policy and management decisions on [sic] the partnership business. ..." Policy and management decisions include: (i) the power to sell and convey, lease, mortgage, or encumber partnership assets; (ii) the power to borrow or lend sums on behalf of the partnership when in excess of $5000; (iii) the power to hire agents to manage or operate the business of the partnership; (iv) and the power to appoint a successor to the managing partner named in the agreement. Moreover, at all times, each partner has reasonable access to the partnership's books of account and has the right to demand an audit of the partnership. Unanimous consent of the partners is required to transfer legal ownership of partnership interests, and additional partners can be added only with the unanimous consent of the partners. Finally, unanimous consent of the partnership also is required to distribute profits other than in proportion to the partners' respective interests.

As the district court found, the express powers granted to the partners are sufficient, on their face, to give them the authority to manage their investments. Normally, such authority renders unnecessary the protection of the federal securities laws. ... "[A]n investor who has the ability to control the profitability of his investment, either by his own efforts or by majority vote in group ventures, is not dependent upon the managerial skills of others." In this case, the partners not only had the authority under the agreement to manage the business, they exercised this authority and demonstrated that they were not dependent on the irreplaceable skills of others. Members of the partnership negotiated with external management groups, inspected the boats on behalf of the partnership, and reviewed partnership insurance material and financial information. Significantly, on two separate occasions the external managers were replaced. Moreover, as previously mentioned, by vote of the partners, one of the promoters, Walter Salley, Sr., was removed as managing partner of RTU and replaced with a management committee of partners. ...

The real gravamen of appellants' complaint lies in common law fraud. As previously mentioned, the securities laws were not intended to be a substitute for state fraud actions. We affirm the district court's finding that appellants' partnership interests are not securities within the meaning of the Securities Act of 1933 or the Securities and Exchange Act of 1934.

* * *

NOTES

1. *"Solely."* As Justice Powell notes in *Rivanna Trawlers*, the lower courts have generally read the word "solely" out of the fourth element of the *Howey* standard. The cases that prompted this liberal reading involved ostensible franchise arrangements in which the investors were provided financial incentives to recruit other investors to participate in pyramid schemes. As the Ninth Circuit explained:

Adherence to [a literal] interpretation could result in a mechanical, unduly restrictive view of what is and what is not an investment contract. It could be easy to evade by adding a requirement that the buyer contribute a modicum of effort. Thus the fact that the investors here were required to exert some efforts if a return were to be achieved should not automatically preclude a finding that the Plan or Adventure is an investment contract. To do so would not serve the purpose of the legislation. Rather we adopt a more realistic test, whether the efforts made by those other than the investor are the undeniably significant ones, those essential managerial efforts which affect the failure or success of the enterprise.

SEC v. Glenn W. Turner Enterprises, Inc., 474 F.2d 476, 482 (9th Cir. 1973).

Franchise arrangements typically require effort on the part of the franchisee. The question becomes whether the franchisee's efforts "are the undeniably significant ones" in determining whether the business will be a success. Merely labeling an essentially passive investment a franchise will not avoid the definition of "security"; courts will look through to the "economic reality" of the transaction.

2. *Timing of the efforts of others.* An interesting timing question is lurking in "the efforts of others" prong. Does it make a difference if the promoter's significant efforts were all contributed before the sale of the investment? According to the D.C. Circuit, it does. In *SEC v. Life Partners, Inc.,* 87 F.3d 536 (D.C. Cir. 1996), the court addressed whether a "viatical settlement" (essentially the purchase of the anticipated proceeds from the life insurance policy of a terminally ill individual) met the definition of "security." The court held that it did not, reasoning that the efforts of the promoter in locating the insureds and pooling the funds of the purchasers to buy the policies all occurred *before* the actual investment. After the investment was made, the return on the investment depended exclusively on the life span of the insured—a matter beyond the promoter's control. The D.C. Circuit had this to say about the importance of timing:

> If the investor's profits depend [after the time of sale] predominantly upon the promoter's efforts, then the investor may benefit from the disclosure and other requirements of the federal securities laws. But if the value of the promoter's efforts has already been impounded into the promoter's fees or into the purchase price of the investment, and if neither the promoter nor anyone else is expected to make further efforts that will affect the outcome of the investment, then the need for federal securities regulation is greatly diminished.

87 F.3d at 547. Because the promoter's post-investment efforts were "ministerial," the *Life Partners* court concluded that the investment was not a security.

QUESTIONS

1. Why does Justice Powell think that the "mere choice by a partner to remain passive is not sufficient to create a security interest"?

2. Would a lack of actual knowledge or business expertise on the part of the partners be enough to show that it is not possible for the partners to exercise their contractual powers of control?

HYPOTHETICAL SIX

HiWiFi has decided to move into the retail business on its own to sell its long range wireless gear. Rather than purchase and operate its own stores, HiWiFi decides to set up retail distribution through franchise agreements with third parties, charging them $100,000 each for the right to open a store in a particular geographic territory. Doing so allows HiWiFi to develop a retail presence without having to expend much of its own capital. Nonetheless, to maintain quality and uniformity across its many planned "HiWiFi Outlet" stores, the company intends to have each franchisee sign a detailed contract specifying the layout of each store, the type of advertising, the placement of products, the price of the products, the training of employees, and store hours. Franchisees are responsible for all costs of running their stores. In addition, franchisees must pay HiWiFi 10% of their net profits. Is HiWiFi's franchise agreement an investment contract?

III. "STOCK"

The *Howey* test for an investment contract requires courts to perform an in-depth inquiry into the substance of a transaction to determine if a security is present. Recall, however, that "investment contract" is only one item in the long laundry list of instruments defined as securities. The following cases address the relation between the *Howey* test for investment contract and other items on that list, in this case "stock."

Landreth Timber Company v. Landreth

471 U.S. 681 (1985).

■ JUSTICE POWELL delivered the opinion of the Court.

This case presents the question whether the sale of all of the stock of a company is a securities transaction subject to the antifraud provisions of the federal securities laws.

I

Respondents Ivan K. Landreth and his sons owned all of the outstanding stock of a lumber business they operated in Tonasket, Washington. The Landreth family offered their stock for sale through both Washington and out-of-state brokers. Before a purchaser was found, the company's sawmill was heavily damaged by fire. Despite the fire, the brokers continued to offer the stock for sale. Potential purchasers were advised of the damage, but were told that the mill would be completely rebuilt and modernized.

Samuel Dennis, a Massachusetts tax attorney, received a letter offering the stock for sale. On the basis of the letter's representations concerning the rebuilding plans, the predicted productivity of the mill, existing contracts, and expected profits, Dennis became interested in acquiring the stock. He talked to John Bolten, a former client who had retired to Florida, about joining him in investigating the offer. After having an audit and an inspection of the mill conducted, a stock purchase agreement was negotiated, with Dennis the purchaser of all of the common stock in the lumber company. Ivan Landreth agreed to stay on as a consultant for some time to help with the daily operations of the mill. Pursuant to the terms of the stock purchase agreement, Dennis assigned the stock he purchased to B & D Co., a corporation formed for the sole purpose of acquiring the lumber company stock. B & D then merged with the lumber company, forming petitioner Landreth Timber Co. Dennis and Bolten then acquired all of petitioner's Class A stock, representing 85% of the equity, and six other investors together owned the Class B stock, representing the remaining 15% of the equity.

After the acquisition was completed, the mill did not live up to the purchasers' expectations. Rebuilding costs exceeded earlier estimates, and new components turned out to be incompatible with existing equipment. Eventually, petitioner sold the mill at a loss and went into receivership. Petitioner then filed this suit seeking rescission of the sale of stock and $2,500,000 in damages, alleging that respondents had widely offered and then sold their stock without registering it as required by the Securities Act of 1933. Petitioner also alleged that respondents had negligently or intentionally made misrepresentations and had failed to state material facts as to the worth and prospects of the lumber company, all in violation of the Securities Exchange Act of 1934.

Respondents moved for summary judgment on the ground that the transaction was not covered by the Acts because under the so-called "sale of business" doctrine, petitioner had not purchased a "security" within the meaning of those Acts. . . .

II

* * *

As we have observed in the past, [the definition of a security under Section 2(a)(1) of the '33 Act] is quite broad and includes both instruments whose names alone carry well-settled meaning, as well as instruments of "more variable character [that] were necessarily designated by more descriptive terms," such as "investment contract" and "instrument commonly known as a 'security.'" The face of the definition shows that "stock" is considered to be a "security" within the meaning of the Acts. As we observed in *United Housing Foundation, Inc. v. Forman*, most instruments bearing such a traditional title are likely to be covered by the definition.

As we also recognized in *Forman*, the fact that instruments bear the label "stock" is not of itself sufficient to invoke the coverage of the Acts. Rather, we concluded that we must also determine whether those instruments possess "some of the significant characteristics typically associated with" stock, recognizing that when an instrument is both called "stock" and bears stock's usual characteristics, "a purchaser justifiably [may] assume that the federal securities laws apply." We identified those characteristics usually associated with common stock as (i) the right to receive dividends contingent upon an apportionment of profits; (ii) negotiability; (iii) the ability to be pledged or hypothecated; (iv) the conferring of voting rights in proportion to the number of shares owned; and (v) the capacity to appreciate in value.[2]

Under the facts of *Forman*, we concluded that the instruments at issue there were not "securities" within the meaning of the Acts. . . .

In contrast, it is undisputed that the stock involved here possesses all of the characteristics we identified in *Forman* as traditionally associated with common stock. Indeed, the District Court so found. Moreover, unlike in *Forman*, the context of the transaction involved here—the sale of stock in a corporation—is typical of the kind of context to which the Acts normally apply. It is thus much more likely here than in *Forman* that an investor would believe he was covered by the federal securities laws. Under the circumstances of this case, the plain meaning of the statutory definition mandates that the stock be treated as "securities" subject to the coverage of the Acts.

Reading the securities laws to apply to the sale of stock at issue here comports with Congress' remedial purpose in enacting the legislation to protect investors by "compelling full and fair disclosure relative to the issuance of 'the many types of instruments that in our commercial world fall within the ordinary concept of a security.' " Although we recognize that Congress did not intend to provide a comprehensive federal remedy for all fraud, we think it would improperly narrow Congress' broad definition of "security" to hold that the traditional stock at issue here falls outside the Acts' coverage.

III

Under other circumstances, we might consider the statutory analysis outlined above to be a sufficient answer compelling judgment for petitioner. Respondents urge, however, that language in our previous opinions, including *Forman*, requires that we look beyond the label "stock" and the characteristics of the instruments involved to determine whether application of the Acts is mandated by the economic substance of the transaction. . . .

A

It is fair to say that our cases have not been entirely clear on the proper method of analysis for determining when an instrument is a "security." This Court has decided a number of cases in which it looked to the economic substance of the transaction, rather than just to its form, to determine whether the Acts applied. . . .

---

2. Although we did not so specify in *Forman*, we wish to make clear here that these characteristics are those usually associated with common stock, the kind of stock often at issue in cases involving the sale of a business. Various types of preferred stock may have different characteristics and still be covered by the Acts.

This so-called "*Howey* test" formed the basis for the second part of our decision in *Forman*, on which respondents primarily rely. As discussed above, the first part of our decision in *Forman* concluded that the instruments at issue, while they bore the traditional label "stock," were not "securities" because they possessed none of the usual characteristics of stock. We then went on to address the argument that the instruments were "investment contracts." Applying the *Howey* test, we concluded that the instruments likewise were not "securities" by virtue of being "investment contracts" because the economic realities of the transaction showed that the purchasers had parted with their money not for the purpose of reaping profits from the efforts of others, but for the purpose of purchasing a commodity for personal consumption.

Respondents contend that *Forman* and the cases on which it was based require us to reject the view that the shares of stock at issue here may be considered "securities" because of their name and characteristics. Instead, they argue that our cases require us in every instance to look to the economic substance of the transaction to determine whether the *Howey* test has been met. According to respondents, it is clear that petitioner sought not to earn profits from the efforts of others, but to buy a company that it could manage and control. Petitioner was not a passive investor of the kind Congress intended the Acts to protect, but an active entrepreneur, who sought to "use or consume" the business purchased just as the purchasers in *Forman* sought to use the apartments they acquired after purchasing shares of stock. Thus, respondents urge that the Acts do not apply.

We disagree with respondents' interpretation of our cases. First, it is important to understand the contexts within which these cases were decided. All of the cases on which respondents rely involved unusual instruments not easily characterized as "securities." Thus, if the Acts were to apply in those cases at all, it would have to have been because the economic reality underlying the transactions indicated that the instruments were actually of a type that falls within the usual concept of a security. In the case at bar, in contrast, the instrument involved is traditional stock, plainly within the statutory definition. There is no need here, as there was in the prior cases, to look beyond the characteristics of the instrument to determine whether the Acts apply.

Contrary to respondents' implication, the Court has never foreclosed the possibility that stock could be found to be a "security" simply because it is what it purports to be. ... Nor does *Forman* require a different result. Respondents are correct that in *Forman* we eschewed a "literal" approach that would invoke the Acts' coverage simply because the instrument carried the label "stock." *Forman* does not, however, eliminate the Court's ability to hold that an instrument is covered when its characteristics bear out the label.

Second, we would note that the *Howey* economic reality test was designed to determine whether a particular instrument is an "investment contract," not whether it fits within any of the examples listed in the statutory definition of "security." ... Moreover, applying the *Howey* test to traditional stock and all other types of instruments listed in the statutory definition would make the Acts' enumeration of many types of instruments superfluous.

Finally, we cannot agree with respondents that the Acts were intended to cover only "passive investors" and not privately negotiated transactions involving the transfer of control to "entrepreneurs." The 1934 Act contains several provisions specifically governing tender offers, disclosure of transactions by corporate officers and principal stockholders, and the recovery of short-swing profits gained by such persons. See, e.g., 1934 Act, §§ 14, 16. Eliminating from the definition of "security" instruments involved in transactions where control passed to the purchaser would contravene the purposes of these provisions. Furthermore, although § 4(2) of the 1933 Act exempts transactions not involving any public offering from the Act's registration provisions, there is no comparable exemption from the anti-fraud provisions. Thus, the structure and language of the Acts refute respondents' position.

* * *

IV

We also perceive strong policy reasons for not employing the sale of business doctrine under the circumstances of this case. By respondents' own admission, application of the doctrine depends in each case on whether control has passed to the purchaser. It may be argued that on the facts of this case, the doctrine is easily applied, since the transfer of 100% of a corporation's stock normally transfers control. We think even that assertion is open to some question, however, as Dennis and Bolten had no intention of running the sawmill themselves. Ivan Landreth apparently stayed on to manage the daily affairs of the business. Some commentators who support the sale of business doctrine believe that a purchaser who has the ability to exert control but chooses not to do so may deserve the Acts' protection if he is simply a passive investor not engaged in the daily management of the business. In this case, the District Court was required to undertake extensive fact-finding, and even requested supplemental facts and memoranda on the issue of control, before it was able to decide the case.

More importantly, however, if applied to this case, the sale of business doctrine would also have to be applied to cases in which less than 100% of a company's stock was sold. This inevitably would lead to difficult questions of line-drawing. The Acts' coverage would in every case depend not only on the percentage of stock transferred, but also on such factors as the number of purchasers and what provisions for voting and veto rights were agreed upon by the parties. As we explain more fully in *Gould v. Ruefenacht*, 471 U.S. 701, 704–706 (1985), decided today as a companion to this case, coverage by the Acts would in most cases be unknown and unknowable to the parties at the time the stock was sold. These uncertainties attending the applicability of the Acts would hardly be in the best interests of either party to a transaction. Respondents argue that adopting petitioner's approach will increase the workload of the federal courts by converting state and common-law fraud claims into federal claims. We find more daunting, however, the prospect that parties to a transaction may never know whether they are covered by the Acts until they engage in extended discovery and litigation over a concept as often elusive as the passage of control.

V

In sum, we conclude that the stock at issue here is a "security" within the definition of the Acts, and that the sale of business doctrine does not apply. . . .

NOTES

1. *Limited liability companies.* Limited liability companies (LLCs) are an important new alternative to corporations and partnerships as an organizational form. LLCs are attractive to individuals starting a business because they combine the limited liability of the corporation with the tax advantages of the partnership's "pass through" tax treatment.

Are LLC interests securities? As a recent innovation, LLC interests are not found in the statutory definition list, so courts have turned to the investment contract analysis to answer the question. The closest available analogy is the dividing line between general and limited partnerships, with "member-managed" LLCs likely to be aligned with general partnerships and "manager-managed" LLCs lining up with limited partnerships.

QUESTIONS

1. How does the *Landreth* Court (Powell, J.) distinguish *Forman* (Powell, J.)?

2. What does the Court say about whether the economic realities should drive all determinations of what instruments are securities? Is there one unified test for the definition of a security?

3. How could the parties have avoided the application of the securities laws to the sale of Landreth Timber?

HYPOTHETICAL SEVEN

Joan and Kristine, the CEO and Chief Technology Officer respectively of HiWiFi, have attracted a potential investor for HiWiFi. Interplanetary Investments is a venture capital fund that thinks HiWiFi has a bright future and is anxious to invest. Interplanetary, however, wants substantial control over HiWiFi while it is getting established because it believes Joan and Kristine need a strong guiding hand. In exchange for Interplanetary's investment of $20 million, HiWiFi and Interplanetary agree to the following terms: (1) Interplanetary will receive the right to name three out of five HiWiFi directors (Joan and Kristine will hold the other two seats); (2) the Chairman must be an Interplanetary nominee; (3) Interplanetary will have the right to replace Joan and Kristine as officers of the company; (4) Interplanetary will have the right to veto any merger, sale of a majority of HiWiFi's equity, or sale of substantially all of HiWiFi's assets; (5) Interplanetary will have the right to convert its interest into common stock if HiWiFi should make an initial public offering; and (6) Interplanetary will be entitled to an annual payment of $2 million, beginning three years after the agreement's inception. If the interest is labeled "preferred stock," has Interplanetary purchased a security? What if it is labeled an "investment agreement"?

IV. "NOTE"

The one financial instrument more ubiquitous than "stock" is the "note." Indeed, "note" precedes "stock" in the definitions of a security contained in § 2(a)(1) of the '33 Act and § 3(a)(10) of the '34 Act. After *Landreth* ruled that all investments labeled as stock that bear out the characteristics of stock are securities, a fair question to ask was whether the same applied for notes. Are all notes that bear out the characteristics of a note (i.e., a specified interest rate, principal amount, and maturity term) also securities? Tens of thousands of notes are issued each day. As the next case makes clear, only a fraction of them are securities.

Reves v. Ernst & Young

494 U.S. 56 (1990).

■ JUSTICE MARSHALL delivered the opinion of the Court.

This case presents the question whether certain demand notes issued by the Farmers Cooperative of Arkansas and Oklahoma are "securities" within the meaning of § 3(a)(10) of the Securities Exchange Act of 1934. We conclude that they are.

I

The Co–Op is an agricultural cooperative that, at the time relevant here, had approximately 23,000 members. In order to raise money to support its general business operations, the Co–Op sold promissory notes payable on demand by the holder. Although the notes were uncollateralized and uninsured, they paid a variable rate of interest that was adjusted monthly to keep it higher than the rate paid by local financial institutions. The Co–Op offered the notes to both members and nonmembers, marketing the scheme as an "Investment Program." Advertisements for the notes, which appeared in each Co–Op newsletter, read in part: "YOUR CO–OP has more than $11,000,000 in assets to stand behind your investments. The Investment is not Federal [sic] insured but it is . . . Safe . . . Secure . . . and available when you need it." Despite these assurances, the Co–Op filed for bankruptcy in 1984. At the time of the filing, over 1,600 people held notes worth a total of $10 million.

After the Co–Op filed for bankruptcy, petitioners, a class of holders of the notes filed suit against Arthur Young & Co., the firm that had audited the Co–Op's financial statements (and the predecessor to respondent Ernst

& Young). Petitioners alleged, inter alia, that Arthur Young had intentionally failed to follow generally accepted accounting principles in its audit, specifically with respect to the valuation of one of the Co–Op's major assets, a gasohol plant. Petitioners claimed that Arthur Young violated these principles in an effort to inflate the assets and net worth of the Co–Op. Petitioners maintained that, had Arthur Young properly treated the plant in its audits, they would not have purchased demand notes because the Co–Op's insolvency would have been apparent. On the basis of these allegations, petitioners claimed that Arthur Young had violated the antifraud provisions of the 1934 Act as well as Arkansas' securities laws.

II

A

This case requires us to decide whether the note issued by the Co–Op is a "security" within the meaning of the 1934 Act. . . .

The fundamental purpose undergirding the Securities Acts is "to eliminate serious abuses in a largely unregulated securities market." In defining the scope of the market that it wished to regulate, Congress painted with a broad brush. . . . Congress . . . did not attempt precisely to cabin the scope of the Securities Acts. Rather, it enacted a definition of "security" sufficiently broad to encompass virtually any instrument that might be sold as an investment.

Congress did not, however, "intend to provide a broad federal remedy for all fraud." Accordingly, "[t]he task has fallen to the Securities and Exchange Commission, the body charged with administering the Securities Acts, and ultimately to the federal courts to decide which of the myriad financial transactions in our society come within the coverage of these statutes." In discharging our duty, we are not bound by legal formalisms, but instead take account of the economics of the transaction under investigation. Congress' purpose in enacting the securities laws was to regulate investments, in whatever form they are made and by whatever name they are called.

A commitment to an examination of the economic realities of a transaction does not necessarily entail a case-by-case analysis of every instrument, however. Some instruments are obviously within the class Congress intended to regulate because they are by their nature investments. In *Landreth Timber Co. v. Landreth*, 471 U.S. 681 (1985), we held that an instrument bearing the name "stock" that, among other things, is negotiable, offers the possibility of capital appreciation, and carries the right to dividends contingent on the profits of a business enterprise is plainly within the class of instruments Congress intended the securities laws to cover. *Landreth Timber* does not signify a lack of concern with economic reality; rather, it signals a recognition that stock is, as a practical matter, always an investment if it has the economic characteristics traditionally associated with stock. Even if sparse exceptions to this generalization can be found, the public perception of common stock as the paradigm of a security suggests that stock, in whatever context it is sold, should be treated as within the ambit of the Acts.

We made clear in *Landreth Timber* that stock was a special case, explicitly limiting our holding to that sort of instrument. Although we refused finally to rule out a similar per se rule for notes, we intimated that such a rule would be unjustified. Unlike "stock," we said, " 'note' may now be viewed as a relatively broad term that encompasses instruments with widely varying characteristics, depending on whether issued in a consumer context, as commercial paper, or in some other investment context." While common stock is the quintessence of a security, and investors therefore justifiably assume that a sale of stock is covered by the Securities Acts, the same simply cannot be said of notes, which are used in a variety of settings, not all of which involve investments. Thus, the phrase "any note" should not be interpreted to mean literally "any note," but must be understood against the backdrop of what Congress was attempting to accomplish in enacting the Securities Acts.[2]

Because the *Landreth Timber* formula cannot sensibly be applied to notes, some other principle must be developed to define the term "note." A majority of the Courts of Appeals that have considered the issue have adopted, in varying forms, "investment versus commercial" approaches that distinguish, on the basis of all of the circumstances surrounding the transactions, notes issued in an investment context (which are "securities") from notes issued in a commercial or consumer context (which are not).

The Second Circuit's "family resemblance" approach begins with a presumption that any note with a term of more than nine months is a "security." Recognizing that not all notes are securities, however, the Second Circuit has also devised a list of notes that it has decided are obviously not securities. Accordingly, the "family resemblance" test permits an issuer to rebut the presumption that a note is a security if it can show that the note in question "bear[s] a strong family resemblance" to an item on the judicially crafted list of exceptions, or convinces the court to add a new instrument to the list.

In contrast, the Eighth and District of Columbia Circuits apply the test we created in *SEC v. W.J. Howey Co.*, 328 U.S. 293, (1946), to determine whether an instrument is an "investment contract" to the determination whether an instrument is a "note."

2. An approach founded on economic reality rather than on a set of per se rules is subject to the criticism that whether a particular note is a "security" may not be entirely clear at the time it is issued. Such an approach has the corresponding advantage, though, of permitting the SEC and the courts sufficient flexibility to ensure that those who market investments are not able to escape the coverage of the Securities Acts by creating new instruments that would not be covered by a more determinate definition. One could question whether, at the expense of the goal of clarity, Congress overvalued the goal of avoiding manipulation by the clever and dishonest. If Congress erred, however, it is for that body, and not this Court, to correct its mistake.

We reject the approaches of those courts that have applied the *Howey* test to notes; *Howey* provides a mechanism for determining whether an instrument is an "investment contract." The demand notes here may well not be "investment contracts," but that does not mean they are not "notes." To hold that a "note" is not a "security" unless it meets a test designed for an entirely different variety of instrument "would make the Acts' enumeration of many types of instruments superfluous," and would be inconsistent with Congress' intent to regulate the entire body of instruments sold as investments.

The other two contenders—the "family resemblance" and "investment versus commercial" tests—are really two ways of formulating the same general approach. Because we think the "family resemblance" test provides a more promising framework for analysis, however, we adopt it. The test begins with the language of the statute because the Securities Acts define "security" to include "any note," we begin with a presumption that every note is a security.[3] We nonetheless recognize that this presumption cannot be irrebuttable. As we have said, Congress was concerned with regulating the investment market, not with creating a general federal cause of action for fraud. In an attempt to give more content to that dividing line, the Second Circuit has identified a list of instruments commonly denominated "notes" that nonetheless fall without the "security" category (types of notes that are not "securities" include "the note delivered in consumer financing, the note secured by a mortgage on a home, the short-term note secured by a lien on a small business or some of its assets, the note evidencing a 'character' loan to a bank customer, short-term notes secured by an assignment of accounts receivable, or a note which simply formalizes an open-account debt incurred in the ordinary course of business (particularly if, as in the case of the customer of a broker, it is collateralized)") [and] ("notes evidencing loans by commercial banks for current operations").

We agree that the items identified by the Second Circuit are not properly viewed as "securities." More guidance, though, is needed. It is impossible to make any meaningful inquiry into whether an instrument bears a "resemblance" to one of the instruments identified by the Second Circuit without specifying what it is about those instruments that makes them non-"securities." Moreover, as the Second Circuit itself has noted, its list is "not graven in stone," and is therefore capable of expansion. Thus, some standards must be developed for determining when an item should be added to the list.

---

3. The Second Circuit's version of the family resemblance test provided that only notes with a term of more than nine months are presumed to be "securities." No presumption of any kind attached to notes of less than nine months' duration. The Second Circuit's refusal to extend the presumption to all notes was apparently founded on its interpretation of the statutory exception for notes with a maturity of nine months or less. Because we do not reach the question of how to interpret that exception, we likewise express no view on how that exception might affect the presumption that a note is a "security."

An examination of the list itself makes clear what those standards should be. In creating its list, the Second Circuit was applying the same factors that this Court has held apply in deciding whether a transaction involves a "security." First, we examine the transaction to assess the motivations that would prompt a reasonable seller and buyer to enter into it. If the seller's purpose is to raise money for the general use of a business enterprise or to finance substantial investments and the buyer is interested primarily in the profit the note is expected to generate, the instrument is likely to be a "security." If the note is exchanged to facilitate the purchase and sale of a minor asset or consumer good, to correct for the seller's cash-flow difficulties, or to advance some other commercial or consumer purpose, on the other hand, the note is less sensibly described as a "security." Second, we examine the "plan of distribution" of the instrument to determine whether it is an instrument in which there is "common trading for speculation or investment." Third, we examine the reasonable expectations of the investing public: The Court will consider instruments to be "securities" on the basis of such public expectations, even where an economic analysis of the circumstances of the particular transaction might suggest that the instruments are not "securities" as used in that transaction. Finally, we examine whether some factor such as the existence of another regulatory scheme significantly reduces the risk of the instrument, thereby rendering application of the Securities Acts unnecessary.

We conclude, then, that in determining whether an instrument denominated a "note" is a "security," courts are to apply the version of the "family resemblance" test that we have articulated here: A note is presumed to be a "security," and that presumption may be rebutted only by a showing that the note bears a strong resemblance (in terms of the four factors we have identified) to one of the enumerated categories of instrument. If an instrument is not sufficiently similar to an item on the list, the decision whether another category should be added is to be made by examining the same factors.

B

Applying the family resemblance approach to this case, we have little difficulty in concluding that the notes at issue here are "securities." Ernst & Young admits that "a demand note does not closely resemble any of the Second Circuit's family resemblance examples." Nor does an examination of the four factors we have identified as being relevant to our inquiry suggest that the demand notes here are not "securities" despite their lack of similarity to any of the enumerated categories. The Co–Op sold the notes in an effort to raise capital for its general business operations, and purchasers bought them in order to earn a profit in the form of interest.[4] Indeed, one of the primary inducements offered purchasers was an interest rate constantly revised to keep it slightly above the rate paid by local banks and savings and loans. From both sides, then, the transaction is most

---

4. We emphasize that by "profit" in the context of notes, we mean "a valuable return on an investment," which undoubtedly includes interest. . . .

naturally conceived as an investment in a business enterprise rather than as a purely commercial or consumer transaction.

As to the plan of distribution, the Co–Op offered the notes over an extended period to its 23,000 members, as well as to nonmembers, and more than 1,600 people held notes when the Co–Op filed for bankruptcy. To be sure, the notes were not traded on an exchange. They were, however, offered and sold to a broad segment of the public, and that is all we have held to be necessary to establish the requisite "common trading" in an instrument.

The third factor—the public's reasonable perceptions—also supports a finding that the notes in this case are "securities." We have consistently identified the fundamental essence of a "security" to be its character as an "investment." The advertisements for the notes here characterized them as "investments," and there were no countervailing factors that would have led a reasonable person to question this characterization. In these circumstances, it would be reasonable for a prospective purchaser to take the Co–Op at its word.

Finally, we find no risk-reducing factor to suggest that these instruments are not in fact securities. The notes are uncollateralized and uninsured. Moreover, ... the notes here would escape federal regulation entirely if the Acts were held not to apply.

The court below found that "[t]he demand nature of the notes is very uncharacteristic of a security," on the theory that the virtually instant liquidity associated with demand notes is inconsistent with the risk ordinarily associated with "securities." This argument is unpersuasive. Common stock traded on a national exchange is the paradigm of a security, and it is as readily convertible into cash as is a demand note. The same is true of publicly traded corporate bonds, debentures, and any number of other instruments that are plainly within the purview of the Acts. The demand feature of a note does permit a holder to eliminate risk quickly by making a demand, but just as with publicly traded stock, the liquidity of the instrument does not eliminate risk altogether. Indeed, publicly traded stock is even more readily liquid than are demand notes, in that a demand only eliminates risk when, and if, payment is made, whereas the sale of a share of stock through a national exchange and the receipt of the proceeds usually occur simultaneously.

We therefore hold that the notes at issue here are within the term "note" in § 3(a)(10).

III

Relying on the exception in the statute for "any note ... which has a maturity at the time of issuance of not exceeding nine months," § 3(a)(10), respondent contends that the notes here are not "securities," even if they would otherwise qualify. Respondent cites Arkansas cases standing for the proposition that, in the context of the state statute of limitations, "[a] note payable on demand is due immediately." Respondent concludes from this rule that the "maturity" of a demand note within the meaning of § 3(a)(10) is immediate, which is, of course, less than nine months. Respondent therefore contends that the notes fall within the plain words of the exclusion and are thus not "securities."

Petitioners counter that the "plain words" of the exclusion should not govern. Petitioners cite the legislative history of a similar provision of the 1933 Act, § 3(a)(3), for the proposition that the purpose of the exclusion is to except from the coverage of the Acts only commercial paper—short-term, high quality instruments issued to fund current operations and sold only to highly sophisticated investors. Petitioners also emphasize that this Court has repeatedly held that the plain words of the definition of a "security" are not dispositive, and that we consider the economic reality of the transaction to determine whether Congress intended the Securities Acts to apply. Petitioners therefore argue, with some force, that reading the exception for short-term notes to exclude from the Acts' coverage investment notes of less than nine months' duration would be inconsistent with Congress' evident desire to permit the SEC and the courts flexibility to ensure that the Acts are not manipulated to investors' detriment. If petitioners are correct that the exclusion is intended to cover only commercial paper, these notes, which were sold in a large scale offering to unsophisticated members of the public, plainly should not fall within the exclusion.

We need not decide, however, whether petitioners' interpretation of the exception is correct, for we conclude that even if we give literal effect to the exception, the notes do not fall within its terms.

Respondent's contention that the demand notes fall within the "plain words" of the statute rests entirely upon the premise that Arkansas' statute of limitations for suits to collect demand notes is determinative of the "maturity" of the notes, as that term is used in the federal Securities Acts. The "maturity" of the notes, however, is a question of federal law. To regard States' statutes of limitations law as controlling the scope of the Securities Acts would be to hold that a particular instrument is a "security" under the 1934 Act in some States, but that the same instrument is not a "security" in others. We are unpersuaded that Congress intended the Securities Acts to apply differently to the same transactions depending on the accident of which State's law happens to apply.

* * *

Neither the law of Arkansas nor that of any other State provides an answer to the federal question, and as a matter of federal law, the words of the statute are far from "plain" with regard to whether demand notes fall within the exclusion. If it is plausible to regard a demand note as having an immediate maturity because demand could be made immediately, it is also plausible to regard the maturity of a demand note as being in excess of nine months because demand could be made many years or decades into the future. Given this ambiguity, the exclusion must be interpreted in accordance with its purpose. As we have said, we will assume for argument's sake that petitioners are incorrect in their view that the exclusion is intended to exempt only commercial paper. Respondent presents no competing view to explain why Congress would have enacted respondent's version of the exclusion, however, and the only theory that we can imagine that would support respondent's interpretation is that Congress intended to create a bright-line rule exempting from the 1934 Act's coverage all notes of less than nine months' duration, because short-term notes are, as a general rule, sufficiently safe that the Securities Acts need not apply. As we have said, however, demand notes do not necessarily have short terms. In light of Congress' broader purpose in the Acts of ensuring that investments of all descriptions be regulated to prevent fraud and abuse, we interpret the exception not to cover the demand notes at issue here. Although the result might be different if the design of the transaction suggested that both parties contemplated that demand would be made within the statutory period, that is not the case before us.

IV

For the foregoing reasons, we conclude that the demand notes at issue here fall under the "note" category of instruments that are "securities" under the 1933 and 1934 Acts. We also conclude that, even under respondent's preferred approach to § 3(a)(10)'s exclusion for short-term notes, these demand notes do not fall within the exclusion. . . .

■ CHIEF JUSTICE REHNQUIST, with whom JUSTICE WHITE, JUSTICE O'CONNOR, and JUSTICE SCALIA join, concurring in part and dissenting in part.

I join Part II of the Court's opinion, but dissent from Part III and the statements of the Court's judgment in Parts I and IV. In Part III, the Court holds that these notes were not covered by the statutory exemption for "any note . . . which has a maturity at the time of issuance of not exceeding nine months." Treating demand notes as if they were a recent development in the law of negotiable instruments, the Court says "if it is plausible to regard a demand note as having an immediate maturity because demand could be made immediately, it is also plausible to regard the maturity of a demand note as being in excess of nine months because demand could be made many years or decades into the future. Given this ambiguity, the exclusion must be interpreted in accordance with its purpose."

But the terms "note" and "maturity" did not spring full blown from the head of Congress in 1934. Neither are demand notes of recent vintage. "Note" and "maturity" have been terms of art in the legal profession for centuries, and a body of law concerning the characteristics of demand notes, including their maturity, was in existence at the time Congress passed the 1934 Act.

In construing any terms whose meanings are less than plain, we depend on the common understanding of those terms at the time of the statute's creation. Contemporaneous editions of legal dictionaries defined "maturity" as "[t]he time when a . . . note becomes due." Pursuant to the dominant consensus in the case law, instruments payable on demand were considered immediately "due" such that an action could be brought at any time without any other demand than the suit. . . .

Petitioners . . . rely, virtually exclusively, on the legislative history of § 3(a)(3) of the 1933 Act for the proposition that the term "any note" in the exemption in § 3(a)(10) of the 1934 Act encompass only notes having the character of short-term "commercial paper" exchanged among sophisticated traders. I am not altogether convinced that the legislative history of § 3(a)(3) supports that interpretation even with respect to the term "any note" in the exemption in § 3(a)(3), and to bodily transpose that legislative history to another statute has little to commend it as a method of statutory construction.

The legislative history of the 1934 Act—under which this case arises— contains nothing which would support a restrictive reading of the exemption in question. . . . Although I do not doubt that both the 1933 and 1934 Act exemptions encompass short-term commercial paper, the expansive language in the statutory provisions is strong evidence that, in the end, Congress meant for commercial paper merely to be a subset of a larger class of exempted short-term instruments.

The plausibility of imputing a restrictive reading to § 3(a)(10) from the legislative history of § 3(a)(3) is further weakened by the imperfect analogy between the two provisions in terms of both phraseology and nature. Section 3(a)(10) lacks the cryptic phrase in § 3(a)(3) which qualifies the class of instruments eligible for exemption as those arising "out of . . . current transaction[s] or the proceeds of which have been or are to be used for current transactions. . . ." While that passage somehow may strengthen an argument for limiting the exemption in § 3(a)(3) to commercial paper, its absence in § 3(a)(10) conversely militates against placing the same limitation thereon.

The exemption in § 3(a)(3) excepts the short-term instruments it covers solely from the registration requirements of the 1933 Act. The same instruments are not exempted from the 1933 Act's antifraud provisions. By contrast, the exemption in § 3(a)(10) of the 1934 Act exempts instruments encompassed thereunder from the entirety of the coverage of the 1934 Act including, conspicuously, the Act's antifraud provisions.

* * *

In sum, there is no justification for looking beyond the plain terms of § 3(a)(10), save for ascertaining the meaning of "maturity" with respect to demand notes. That inquiry reveals that the Co–Op's demand notes come within the purview of the section's exemption for short-term securities. . . .

NOTES

1. *The "family resemblance" test.* In contrast to the *Howey* test, the *Reves* "family resemblance" test for notes is a multi-factor balancing test, so an instrument need not satisfy each of the factors to be deemed a security. The open-ended nature of the test means that claims based on novel debt instruments will be difficult to resolve as a matter of law. In addition, counsel advising clients will not be able to offer as much certainty as their clients might like.

QUESTIONS

1. Do you agree with the Court that stocks are a "special case"? Are notes a "special case"?

2. What is the difference between the *Howey* and *Reves* tests?

3. Are the Coop Demand notes investment contracts under *Howey?* Why not just use *Howey* to determine whether a note is a security?

4. Why are loans made for commercial rather than general business purposes not securities?

5. Under the majority's interpretation, would a note payable in six months, renewable at the discretion of the creditor for an additional twelve months, be a security?

HYPOTHETICAL EIGHT

HiWiFi has devised another scheme to raise capital to finance its growth. Kristine, the Chief Technology Officer, has identified a group of twenty insurance companies interested in lending money to HiWiFi. The consortium agrees to lend $100 million to build a new factory in Thailand to expand the production of the routers. The loan will be repaid over a twenty-year term and will be secured by a mortgage on the factory. The interest rate is floating at prime + 5%. The loan agreement explicitly authorizes the insurance companies to transfer their interests in the loan agreement to other institutional investors. (The insurance companies may need to do this if they face liquidity problems arising from a greater-than-expected level of claims, e.g., a hurricane.) Finally, the loan agreement gives the insurance companies an option to purchase stock in HiWiFi at a fixed price after the first five years of the term of the loan in exchange for a reduction in the interest rate. Is the loan agreement a security?

CHAPTER 4

DISCLOSURE AND ACCURACY

Rules and Statutes

—*Sections 17(a), 24 of the Securities Act*

—*Sections 4C, 10A, 12(a), 12(b), 12(g)(1), 12(g)(4), 12(g)(5), 12(j), 12(k), 13(a), 13(b), 13(c), 13(g), 13(i), 13(j), 13(k), 13(l), 15(c)(4), 15(d), 21, 21B, 21C, 23(a), 25, 32, 36 of the Exchange Act*

—*Rules 10A–1, 10A–2, 10A–3, 10b–9, 12b–20, 12g–1, 12g–4, 12g5–1, 12h–3, 13a–1, 13a–11, 13a–13, 13a–14, 13a–15, 13b2–1, 13b2–2, 14a–3, 15c2–11, 15d–3, 15d–14, 15d–15 of the Exchange Act*

—*Regulation FD, Regulation G, Regulation S–K*

—*Forms 8–K, 10, 10–K, 10–Q, 20–F*

—*Sarbanes–Oxley Act, Sections 304, 404, 408*

—*SEC Rules of Practice 102(e), 205*

—*18 U.S.C. §§ 1348, 1349, 1350, 18 U.S.C. § 1514A*

MOTIVATING HYPOTHETICAL

Mouthwatering, Inc. makes barbeque sauce for ribs. Mouthwatering has been a public company trading on the Nasdaq–Small Cap since its IPO eight years ago. Those eight years have seen steady growth for Mouthwatering as it has established its brand and the stock price has risen accordingly; it now has approximately 5,000 shareholders and a market capitalization of $100 million. This period of steady growth for the company has required that all of the firm's profits be ploughed back into the company to finance its expansion. Adam, the founder, CEO and Chairman of the board of Mouthwatering is ready to cash in his controlling block of shares. Building the company has left him exhausted and he is ready to take a couple years off to work in his garden. Besides, Mouthwatering really needs to affiliate itself with a major food company to access the national and international distribution channels necessary to sustain Mouthwatering's growth. Adam thinks the best way for him to sell his shares and for Mouthwatering to find a distribution partner is to sell the company to one of the major international food producers. Adam is anxious, however, to get as much as possible for his shares just in case he decides he likes retirement.

I. MANDATORY DISCLOSURE AND ACCURACY

Recall from Chapter 1 the arguments favoring mandatory disclosure: (1) it facilitates comparable disclosures by different companies; (2) it helps reduce agency costs within the firm; (3) it helps overcome an externality problem for firms disclosing information; and (4) it reduces duplicative research by professional investors and analysts. These arguments suggest that mandatory disclosure may be necessary to bring disclosure to its socially optimal level. Congress adopted mandatory disclosure for companies with securities listed on a national securities exchange as part of the Exchange Act in 1934. Congress's chief aim was to combat what it saw as abuses by insiders in the decade leading up to the market crash of October 1929. In 1964, Congress extended mandatory disclosure to certain companies traded in the over-the-counter market.

To be "mandatory," mandatory disclosure requires that someone decide what information must be disclosed. Congress has left the specifics of mandatory disclosure to the SEC. The SEC's authority over disclosure is one source of potential weakness of mandatory disclosure. Just as one can have doubts that markets will produce the optimal level of disclosure, one can doubt the ability of the SEC to determine that optimal level. The SEC tends to see disclosure as the solution for every ailment that plagues the corporate world. Every scandal is met with a new disclosure requirement; seldom does the SEC discard outdated disclosure requirements. For example, amidst considerable political fretting over "excessive" salaries in the early 1990s, the SEC required more extensive disclosure of the salaries of the top five executives of each publicly-held company. Rather than a decline in salaries, the increased disclosure correlated with an upward spiral in executive compensation as compensation consultants have pushed boards to hire above average executives at above average salaries. The result has been a "Lake Woebegone" effect, with all executives wanting to be paid at above the average scale. But the SEC was seen as "doing something." As you read the materials below, consider whether you regard mandatory disclosure as socially useful or just "doing something" about the crisis du jour.

The mandatory disclosure requirements of the Exchange Act are triggered when a firm becomes a "public company." We begin the chapter by answering the question, "What is a public company?" We turn then to these questions: When must a public company disclose? What must be disclosed? And to whom?

Making disclosure mandatory is one thing; making it truthful is quite another. Disclosure will do investors little good if it does not reflect reality. The agency cost problems that interfere with voluntary disclosure, however, may also lead managers to be less than truthful with disclosure, even if it is made mandatory. In response, the Exchange Act provides a wide variety of measures to promote accuracy by enhancing firms' corporate governance and internal controls, topics that we cover in this chapter.

The Exchange Act also imposes penalties for inaccuracy. In the final section of the chapter, we look at the wide range of civil enforcement tools available to the SEC. (The SEC has analogous enforcement authority under the Securities Act, but for ease of exposition we will focus solely on the Exchange Act's enforcement authority here. We leave the private enforcement of the securities laws to our discussion of Rule 10b–5 in Chapter 5 and the Securities Act liability provisions in Chapter 8.) We also touch upon the criminal enforcement authority wielded by the Justice Department and the issues raised by the interaction between the SEC's civil enforcement authority and the Justice Department's criminal authority.

II.   WHAT IS A "PUBLIC COMPANY?"

The overwhelming majority of companies in the United States are "private" companies. Private companies are closely held by their managers and a small circle of friends and family. These investments are based, in large part, on the investors' trust in the character of the managers. That trust is based on long-standing personal relationships. Trust of this sort will be harder to come by for firms whose capital needs require them to cast a wider net in search of investors. When the firm is first seeking outside equity investment, it is likely to come from a relatively small number of venture capitalists who will subject the firm and its managers to a thorough vetting before investing. The venture capitalists will also insist on carefully detailed contracts that give them substantial control over the enterprise.

Personal relationships and contractual protections are not a practical means of reassuring investors in a more broadly-held enterprise. The individual investor—one of perhaps thousands of investors—faces a daunting collective action problem in holding managers accountable. State corporate law helps answer the problem of creating the trust necessary to encourage investment by establishing a board of directors to protect shareholder interests and imposing an array of fiduciary duties that directors and managers owe to shareholders. But even with the mechanism of the derivative suit under corporate law to help ameliorate the collective action problem in enforcing these duties, the individual shareholder still faces a problem of information asymmetry. She simply may not have the information needed to assess whether the managers and directors are living up to the standards imposed on them by state corporate law. The cost of negotiating with management to obtain such information likely outweighs the increase in value of the shares in the individual shareholder's possession, even when the benefit to all the outstanding shares exceeds such costs. A primary purpose of the federal securities laws is to provide this information to investors in companies with broadly dispersed ownership.

A. PUBLIC COMPANY STATUS

Congress first defined the concept of "public" companies rather narrowly. Section 12(a), part of the original Exchange Act as it was adopted in 1934, prohibits broker-dealers from effecting transactions over a national securities exchange "unless a registration is effective" for that security. To accommodate constitutional concerns of the New Deal era, Congress (with a few minor exceptions) did not extend the prohibition to transactions not involving a broker-dealer. The process for registration is set forth in § 12(b) and the SEC has provided Form 10 as the basic form for registration. (Form 10-SB is for small business issuers and Form 20-F is for foreign private issuers.)

[handwritten margin note: See. 12(a)]

[handwritten margin note: Registration 12(b) + form 10 form 20 - foreign private issuers]

Congress broadened the category of public companies in 1936 when it added § 15(d). That section requires companies registering securities for a sale in a public offering under the Securities Act to comply thereafter with the periodic disclosure requirements of the Exchange Act at least until the next fiscal year after the effective registration date. Section 15(d) registrants are not required, however, to comply with the Exchange Act's requirements for proxy solicitations and tender offers under § 14 (covered in Chapters 11 and 12), nor are their insiders subject to the reporting of stock trades and short-swing profits rules imposed by § 16 (covered in Chapter 6).

[handwritten margin note: 15 (d]

The next big expansion came in 1964, when Congress adopted § 12(g) of the Exchange Act. The constitutional concerns of the New Deal were by that time of purely historical interest. Section 12(g) accordingly omits any reliance on broker-dealers as a jurisdictional hook. Instead, it requires all issuers having a nexus to interstate commerce to register with the SEC if they have more than a minimum level of assets and a minimum number of holders of their equity securities. This provision roped in many companies whose stock traded widely in the over-the-counter market but which had not listed on a national securities exchange or completed a public offering under the Securities Act. Thus, the 1964 amendment closed a loophole strongly disliked by both the exchanges and the SEC. The minimums set by § 12(g) are subject to revision by the SEC; they are currently set by Rule 12g-1 at $10 million in total assets and 500 shareholders. The addition of § 12(g) means that § 15(d) today does relatively little work, as few companies doing a public offering of their equity will end up with fewer than 500 shareholders after the offering. Section 15(d) does, however, continue to capture firms that offer *debt* to the public while holding their equity closely.

[handwritten margin note: 12 (g)]

[handwritten margin note: 10 mll. in assets + 500 Shs]

The minimum levels set by Rule 12g-1 are measured as of the last day of the issuer's fiscal year, so companies wishing to avoid the status of being a public company may seek to sell assets or buy out some of their shareholders in order to avoid triggering § 12(g). (Combining the holdings of multiple owners in a trust or similar vehicle will not work—Rule 12g5-1(b)(3) directs issuers to count beneficial, rather than legal, owners, if the form of ownership is being used to circumvent the registration requirements.) The 500 shareholder limit may be a particular concern for growing companies that use stock options as compensation to attract employees. If

[handwritten margin note: → can sell assets]

the number of employees receiving options grows too large, the company may find itself "going public" before it is ready to do an IPO. This occasionally creates a problem for companies in the high-tech sector that are heavily dependent upon option-based compensation. For those companies anxious to expose themselves to SEC requirements (a very small set, indeed, but the Nasdaq now requires reporting status for issuers wishing to be quoted even in its lowest tier "Bulletin Board"), § 12(g) allows companies to register voluntarily even if the statutory minimums are not satisfied.

B.   ESCAPING PUBLIC COMPANY STATUS

A more common phenomenon is companies seeking to avoid the exposure and expense of public status, i.e., "going dark." Escaping public company status, however, is not easy. Consider H.J. Heinz, Inc., a company listed on the NYSE (ticker: HNZ), a national securities exchange. To avoid status as a public company, Heinz may attempt to delist from the NYSE, incurring the corresponding drop in liquidity from leaving the NYSE. Even with delisting, Heinz nonetheless still faces public company status pursuant to § 12(g) due to its substantial assets and dispersed group of shareholders. Under Rule 12g–4, an issuer may terminate registration as a public company only if it certifies to the SEC that it has fewer than 300 shareholders of record. Alternatively, the issuer may show that it has fewer than 500 shareholders and less than $10 million in total assets on the last day of each of its prior three fiscal years. For a company such as Heinz with thousands of shareholders of record, reducing that number below the requisite minimum is simply not feasible. Heinz can only avoid public company status through a "going private transaction" under which Heinz buys back a considerable portion of its publicly-held shares, which would be an overwhelming expense.

Avoiding public company status is more likely for recently-public issuers qualifying as a public company solely under § 15(d). To terminate their public company status, issuers required to file under § 15(d) must show that the company has fewer than 300 shareholders of record (and may do so only after the fiscal year during which the registered public offering became effective).

The table below summarizes the three categories of public companies, which we will refer to collectively as "Exchange Act reporting companies," a commonly used term of art, as well as the process for terminating public company status.

Section	Trigger	Requirements	Termination
§ 12(a)	Exchange listing	- Periodic filings - Proxy rules + annual report - Tender offer rules - Insider stock transactions (§ 16)	Delisting & either (a) < 300 shareholders or (b) < 500 shareholders + < $10 m. in assets for 3 years

§ 12(g)	> 500 shareholders + > $10 m. in assets	- Periodic filings - Proxy rules + annual report - Tender offer rules - Insider stock transactions (§ 16)	Either (a) < 300 shareholders or (b) < 500 shareholders + < $10 m. in assets for 3 years
§ 15(d)	Registered public offering	- Periodic filings	< 300 shareholders + No earlier than next fiscal year after offering

HYPOTHETICAL ONE

Mouthwatering has a subsidiary, Ribs2U.com, which sells frozen slabs of ribs over the Internet. Mouthwatering sold 20% of Ribs2U.com's stock in a series of private placements five years ago at the height of the Internet craze. More recently, however, Ribs2U.com has struggled as fears of mad cow disease have dampened the demand for beef ribs. Ribs2U.com has had to downsize substantially in the face of this decline in demand. Currently, the subsidiary has 600 minority shareholders of record and $13 million in assets. Adam would like to avoid the cost of maintaining Ribs2U.com as a public company. Ribs2U.com packs the ribs for shipping in a warehouse that it owns that has been appraised at $4 million. Adam proposes that Ribs2U.com sell the warehouse to Mouthwatering, which will then lease the warehouse back to Ribs2U.com. Ribs2U.com would use the proceeds of the sale to buy back the shares of approximately 125 of its shareholders. Will Adam's plan to take Ribs2U.com private work?

III.   WHEN MUST A PUBLIC COMPANY DISCLOSE, AND TO WHOM?

The SEC, acting pursuant to authority conferred by Exchange Act § 13(a), requires three principal disclosure documents from public companies: Form 8–K, filed on the occurrence of specified events deemed to be of particular importance to investors; Form 10–K, filed annually; and Form 10–Q, filed quarterly.

The items required to be disclosed on these forms are drawn from the SEC's streamlined integrated disclosure system, which provides a consistent set of disclosure requirements for both the Securities and Exchange Acts. Those requirements are found in Regulation S–K (non-financial statement information) and Regulation S–X (financial statements). The different information disclosure forms contained in the securities laws then refer to specific portions of Regulations S–K and S–X. Not only do Forms 8–K, 10–K, and 10–Q reference Regulations S–K and S–X, the registration statements—Forms S–1 and S–3—for companies engaged in a public offering (as discussed in Chapter 7) also draw from the same Regulations.

For example, consider the biographical information on the top management and directors of an issuer. Item 11(k) of Form S–1 requires the issuer to disclose information relating to its executive officers and directors. Rather than specify the required information, Item 11(k) simply references the information contained in Item 401 of Regulation S–K. Likewise, Item 10 of the annual Form 10–K filing for the Exchange Act also requires disclosure on the issuer's executive officers and directors. Item 10 references the same information contained in Item 401 of Regulation S–K (among other provisions). At least for company-related information, the integrated disclosure system produces *identical* disclosure items across these different forms.

What justifies the integrated disclosure system? As we discussed earlier in Chapter 2 (Materiality), investors require similar information when deciding to make an investment regardless of the type of transaction. Investors buying a share of Microsoft in the secondary market need to know information about Microsoft's future plans and prospects, as well as information on its management, regulatory environment, and past financials, just as much as investors who are purchasing shares directly from Microsoft in a seasoned offering. The integrated disclosure system provides a common set of desired investment-related information.

A. FORM 8–K

In § 409 of the Sarbanes–Oxley Act, Congress gave the SEC authority to require Exchange Act reporting companies to disclose "on a rapid and current basis" material information regarding changes in a company's financial condition or operations. The 8–K, or "current" report, comes closest to requiring "real-time" disclosure; items required by Form 8–K must be made within four business days of the specified event.

The SEC has sorted events requiring current disclosure into the following sections:

1. Registrant's Business & Operations	• Entry into, a material amendment to, or termination of a "material definitive agreement," defined as contracts *outside* the ordinary course of business. • Filing of bankruptcy or receivership.
2. Financial Information	• Completion of the acquisition or disposition of assets constituting more than 10% of the registrant's total assets. • Results of operations and financial condition (if they are disclosed by press release before the filing of the 10–Q or 10–K). • Creation or triggering of an off-balance sheet arrangement. • Costs associated with exit or disposal activities, including termination benefits for employees, contract termination costs and other associated costs.

	• Material impairments to assets such as goodwill.
3. Securities & Trading Markets	• Receipt of a notice of delisting or a transfer of listing. • Unregistered sale of equity securities. • Material modifications to the rights of security holders.
4. Matters Related to Accountants & Financial Statements	• Changes in the company's outside auditor (and the reasons for the change). • Notice that previously issued financial statements or audit reports should no longer be relied upon.
5. Corporate Governance & Management	• A change in control of the registrant. • Departure or election/appointment of directors and principal officers. • Amendments to the articles of incorporation or bylaws. • Changes in the company's fiscal year. • Temporary suspension of trading under employee benefit plans. • Amendment to the registrant's code of ethics or the waiver of the requirements of that code.
6.	• Reserved for later use.
7. Regulation FD	• Any disclosure required to comply with Regulation FD (discussed below).
8. Other Events	• Anything that the issuer, at its option, thinks would be of interest to its security holders.
9. Financial Statements & Exhibits	• For businesses acquired by the registrant.

A few things to note about the Form 8–K disclosure requirements. Under § 1 of Form 8–K, only "material definitive agreements" need to be disclosed. Letters of intent for mergers or acquisitions, which generally would meet the definition of materiality under *Basic v. Levinson* (excerpted in Chapter 2), only need to be disclosed if they impose enforceable obligations. Public companies may use the Form 8–K to satisfy filing obligations arising from business combinations, such as the disclosure requirements imposed on tender offers under § 14 of the Exchange Act (discussed in Chapter 12). *[handwritten margin note: material definitive agreements need to be disclosed]*

The disclosure of off-balance sheet arrangements required by § 2 of Form 8–K is an attempt to police the type of financial maneuverings that led to the downfall of Enron (a principal impetus for the passage of the Sarbanes–Oxley Act in 2002). The provision was adopted in response to Enron's creative efforts to shift underperforming assets and debt off its balance sheet, thereby improving how the public viewed Enron's financial health. In a typical off-balance sheet transaction, Enron would sell an underperforming asset to a "special purpose entity" partly owned by Enron, secretly promising to buy back the assets at a profit later in time. The promise to buy back the assets at a higher price meant that the sales in reality were loans to Enron. Any debt the special purposes entities incurred was also kept off of Enron's books, despite the close connection between Enron and the entities.

The requirement that "Material Impairments" of assets be disclosed under § 2 is likely to apply when a company determines that goodwill (the intangible value of a company's reputation and business contacts) put on its books in connection with an acquisition can no longer be valued at its acquisition value. Such a disclosure can be an embarrassing admission by management that the acquisition may not have worked out as hoped, hence the drop in goodwill value.

The disclosures required by § 3 relate directly to the interests of shareholders. The delisting or change in listing of a company's stock may signal lower liquidity for that stock in the future. The sale of unregistered securities generally results in the dilution of the interests of current stockholders. Finally, a change in the rights of security holders affects their interests directly, often in a negative manner.

Section 4 reflects similarly bad news for securities holders. A change in the company's outside auditor may simply reflect an effort to save money, but it also may represent a disagreement with the auditors over appropriate accounting practices. Companies changing their accountants are required to disclose not only the fact of the change, but also any disagreements they may have had with their former accountants prior to the change. Worse still for a company is a restatement of prior financial results, or a determination that results will need to be restated. Companies making disclosures of this sort typically suffer an immediate loss of credibility in the markets, not to mention a large stock price drop.

Noteworthy in § 5 is the disclosure requirements relating to the company's code of ethics. The Exchange Act does not require companies to have a code of ethics ("You can't legislate morality!"), but it does attempt to shame companies into adopting one (and sticking to it) by requiring disclosure of any such code, or an explanation of why there is none, and any waivers from that code. Form 8–K's emphasis on a company's code of ethics flows from § 406 of the Sarbanes–Oxley Act. Enron, for example, did have a code of ethics prohibiting its top officers from serving as the general partner for outside limited partnerships due to the resulting conflicts of interest. The Enron board twice waived these requirements for Andrew Fastow, the CFO of Enron, without disclosing the waivers to the public.

In the SEC's ideal world, companies would make *all* of their disclosures through filings with the SEC, perhaps with an accompanying press release put out through the newswires. The agency has not yet achieved this dream, but § 8 of Form 8–K authorizes a company, at its option, to use the form to disclose anything that the company considers relevant to its security holders. Disclosure through the Form 8–K ensures broad dissemination via the EDGAR website. Unlike the mandatory items, there is no time requirement specified for optional disclosures under § 8.

HYPOTHETICAL TWO

Relations with Mouthwatering's outside auditors, Apple & Tree, have gotten a bit rocky. Eve, Mouthwatering's CFO, has been feeling the heat from Adam over the company's earnings. Adam wants to show a consistent pattern of growth in earnings per share to justify a high price for the company in any acquisition. Unfortunately, the fundamentals of the business have not kept pace recently with Wall Street's expectations.

Eve was able to meet last quarter's numbers only by making a side deal with the Viper's Den, a restaurant chain that features Mouthwatering's sauce on many of its menu items. The Viper's Den agreed to purchase a huge quantity of sauce to sell to its customers on a retail basis. Eve's side deal with Viper, however, allows Viper to return any sauce it hasn't sold after six months if sales do not meet expectations. Despite this contingency, Eve booked all of the expected profits from the sale as part of last quarter's earnings without setting aside a sales return allowance.

Apple & Tree is now conducting the company's annual audit and it says that booking the revenues from Viper last quarter was not consistent with U.S. generally accepted accounting principles. Moreover, Apple & Tree says it will resign and go to the SEC if Mouthwatering does not restate last quarter's revenues to conform to the auditor's interpretation of GAAP. Mouthwatering's board makes it clear that it intends to fire Eve, but she resigns before they get the chance. Does Mouthwatering need to file a Form 8–K?

B.   FORMS 10–K AND 10–Q

The SEC requires the most extensive disclosure on Form 10–K, which like other disclosure requirements in the securities laws, draws its specific requirements from the integrated disclosure of Regulation S–K (Items 101–103, 201, 301–305, 401–404, 601 and 701). Many of these items track our discussion in Chapter 2 on what information investors would desire in making an investment decision. These information items include, among others, information on a registrant's:

- Business
- Properties
- Legal Proceedings
- Market for Common Stock
- Management Discussion and Analysis of Financial Condition and Results of Operation (MD & A)
- Directors and Officers

- Executive Compensation
- Security Ownership of Certain Beneficial Owners and Management
- Certain Relationships and Related Transactions
- Principal Accounting Fees and Services

Issuers are also required to disclose the outcome of any matters submitted to a vote of their shareholders. In addition, issuers are encouraged to combine their Form 10–K, which is filed with the SEC, with the annual report that they are required to send to their shareholders under Rule 14a–3 (setting forth information those engaged in a proxy solicitation must furnish to shareholders). Recall that not all Exchange Act reporting issuers are subject to the proxy solicitation requirements of § 14. Although §§ 12(b) and 12(g) reporting issuers are subject to those rules, § 15(d) issuers are not.

Foreign private issuers with securities trading on an exchange or the Nasdaq use Form 20–F instead of Form 10–K. Since 1999, the disclosure requirements of Form 20–F closely follow the international disclosure standards promulgated by the International Organization of Securities Commissions (IOSCO). Form 20–F does not directly reference Regulation S–K, but many of the non-financial disclosure items of Form 20–F track the parallel non-financial disclosure items of Form 10–K. For financial information, companies using Form 20–F may either provide information following U.S. generally accepted accounting principles (U.S. GAAP) or provide information pursuant to another "comprehensive body of accounting principles" and provide a reconciliation to U.S. GAAP.

Probably the largest expense imposed by the periodic filing requirements on public companies is the audited financial statements that must be filed with the Form 10–K. The financial data required to be disclosed is specified in Regulation S–X. We discuss later in the chapter the mechanism imposed by the Exchange Act to ensure the integrity of the audit required by Regulation S–X. The financial disclosures are supplemented by Regulation S–K Item 303, the Management Discussion and Analysis (MD & A) section. Item 303 requires a narrative discussion of the issuer's "financial condition, changes in financial condition and results of operations."

The MD & A discussion goes beyond a mere explanation of the historical data provided in the financial statements and how the reporting period differed from prior periods. Companies are also required to disclose "known trends or uncertainties" that the issuer "reasonably expects" to affect the firms' liquidity, capital resources, net sales, revenues or income in the future. Although this requirement to predict the future makes managers and their legal counsel nervous, some wiggle room is left by the qualifiers that the "trends or uncertainties" be "known" and they must be "reasonably" expected to have an impact. Nonetheless, this forward-looking requirement leaves substantial room for second-guessing if a potential adverse development not disclosed by the issuer actually comes to pass. Companies may worry in particular about a private antifraud suit based on a previous forward-looking statement that has not borne out. Some comfort

is provided by the forward-looking safe harbor of Exchange Act § 21E (discussed in Chapter 5) affording protection against private liability.

A recent addition to Regulation S–K Item 303 is subsection (a)(4), which requires the disclosure of "Off balance sheet arrangements." As discussed above, Enron involved, among other things, the creation of limited partnership entities through which Enron was effectively able to shift debt off its balance sheet (but not the economic burden associated with the debt) and on to the books of the limited partnerships. Enron creatively used the latitude provided within GAAP to disguise its real financial exposure arising from the transactions. Item 303(a)(4) closes that loophole in GAAP by requiring supplementary disclosure of guarantees and contingent obligations if they are "reasonably likely" to affect the registrant's financial situation.

The quarterly Form 10–Q imposes a lighter burden than the annual Form 10–K. Most notably, the financial statements required to be disclosed with the Form 10–Q need not be audited, although they must comply with GAAP standards. Foreign issuers are not required to file quarterly reports.

no audit Req

Both Forms 10–K and 10–Q must be certified by the chief executive officer and chief financial officer of the registrant. Section 302 of the Sarbanes–Oxley Act (as implemented in Rules 13a–14(a) and 15d–14(a) of the Exchange Act) requires that these officers personally certify that:

- They have reviewed the report;
- Based on the officer's knowledge, the report does not contain material misstatements or omissions;
- Based on the officer's knowledge, the financial statements "fairly present in all material respects" the issuer's results and financial condition;
- They are responsible for establishing and maintaining internal control and have:
    —Designed those controls so that material information is made known to them,
    —Evaluated the effectiveness of those controls within 90 days of the report, and
    —Presented the conclusion of their evaluation in the report;
- They have disclosed to the company's auditors and audit committee any weaknesses in those internal controls and any fraud by persons who have a significant role in the issuer's internal controls;
- Any changes to internal controls made subsequent to the evaluation are disclosed in the report.

This certification requirement does two things. First, it focuses the CEO and the CFO on the need for accuracy in reporting. These officers are unlikely to skimp on resources for financial reporting if they have to sign off on the results. Second, it reduces the ability of the CEO and CFO to claim ignorance of misstatements or omissions in the periodic reports.

focus attention

→ no claim of ignorance

Furthermore, if they certify that the report contains no misstatements or omissions, they have made an additional misstatement in certifying that the report does not contain a misstatement or omission. As a result, the certification requirement may make it difficult for the CEO and CFO to evade personal liability in a private antifraud action.

Note that prior to Sarbanes–Oxley, Form 10–K already required the signatures of the CEO and CFO and Form 10–Q required the signature of the CFO. The CEO and CFO arguably may face both private antifraud liability (under Rule 10b–5 as discussed in Chapter 5) and an SEC enforcement action for material misstatements or half-truths in the Form 10–K or 10–Q based on their signing off on these documents. What additional deterrence do the certification requirements imposed under Sarbanes–Oxley provide?

Consider this question in the context of *W.R. Grace*, a pre-Sarbanes–Oxley case involving an investigation by the SEC under § 21(a) of the Exchange Act. As we discuss later in the chapter, the SEC enjoys a number of administrative proceedings with which to pursue those who violate the Exchange Act and the SEC's rules and regulations under the Act. An investigation pursuant to § 21(a) represents one of the SEC's more informal and least threatening means of enforcing the securities laws, resulting in no penalties, constraints on future actions, or formal censure. Instead, the SEC issues a public report detailing violations of the securities laws.

In the Matter of W. R. Grace & Co.

Exchange Act Release No. 39157 (1997).

The staff of the Division of Enforcement has conducted an investigation into whether W. R. Grace & Co. ("WRG") violated certain provisions of the federal securities laws and whether certain former officers and directors of WRG contributed to any such violations. . . .

In the Administrative Order against WRG, the Commission found that WRG, in its 1992 annual report on Form 10–K and its 1993 proxy statement, did not fully disclose the substantial retirement benefits it had agreed to provide J. Peter Grace, Jr., effective at his retirement as chief executive officer on December 31, 1992. . . . As a result, WRG violated Sections 13(a) and 14(a) of the Exchange Act and Rules 13a–1, 14a–3 and 14a–9 thereunder.

The Commission is issuing this Report of Investigation [under § 21(a)] to emphasize the affirmative responsibilities of corporate officers and directors to ensure that the shareholders whom they serve receive accurate and complete disclosure of information required by the proxy solicitation and periodic reporting provisions of the federal securities laws. Officers and directors who review, approve, or sign their company's proxy statements or periodic reports must take steps to ensure the accuracy and completeness of the statements contained therein, especially as they concern those matters within their particular knowledge or expertise. To fulfill this responsibility, officers and directors must be vigilant in exercising their authority throughout the disclosure process.

In this case, both Grace, Jr., then the chairman of WRG's board of directors, and J. P. Bolduc, then WRG's chief executive officer and a member of WRG's board of directors, knew of Grace, Jr.'s substantial retirement benefits.... Eben Pyne, a non-management member of the board, also was aware of Grace, Jr.'s benefits.... [T]hese officers and directors reviewed all or portions of the relevant documents, and all but Pyne signed the relevant reports. Although the record does not demonstrate that Bolduc, [and] Pyne acted in bad faith, the Commission concludes that they did not fulfill their obligations under the federal securities laws. Bolduc [and] Pyne, each assumed, without taking the steps necessary to confirm their assumptions, that WRG's procedures would produce drafts of disclosure documents describing all matters that required disclosure.[5] Each also assumed, without taking steps necessary to confirm their assumptions, that other corporate officers, including counsel, had conducted full and informed reviews of the drafts. Bolduc [and] Pyne each had a responsibility to go beyond the established procedures to inquire into the reasons for non-disclosure of information of which they were aware.

* * *

III.   Grace, Jr., Bolduc, and Pyne Failed to Take Steps to Ensure that Grace, Jr.'s Retirement Benefits were Fully Disclosed.

During the latter part of 1992, Grace, Jr.'s health was deteriorating. Pursuant to delegated authority from WRG's board of directors, WRG's Compensation, Employee Benefits and Stock Incentive Committee entered into negotiations with Grace, Jr., which resulted in his retirement from WRG as its chief executive officer, effective on December 31, 1992. Pyne, then chairman of the Compensation Committee, met several times with Grace, Jr. during November and December 1992. The negotiations resulted in an agreement in principle with respect to Grace, Jr.'s proposed retirement benefits. Among the provisions of this agreement in principle was an understanding that Grace, Jr. would continue to receive in retirement various substantial perquisites which he had received while chief executive officer. On December 7, 1992, WRG's board of directors approved Grace, Jr.'s proposed retirement benefits.

Subsequently, Grace, Jr. and Pyne, on behalf of WRG, executed a letter agreement dated December 21, 1992, which reflected the terms of this agreement in principle.[8] ... Pursuant to this provision of the Retirement

---

5. Indeed, this matter demonstrates that corporate disclosure mechanisms cannot compensate for the failures of individuals. WRG's procedures failed because, among other reasons, Grace, Jr. did not disclose some of his retirement benefits ... in questionnaires which WRG distributed to officers and directors to gather information for disclosure in WRG's proxy statements and periodic reports.

8. Bolduc and Pyne each assert that they assumed that this letter agreement, because it was drafted by WRG's legal counsel, would receive full consideration in WRG's disclosure process.

Agreement, Grace, Jr. received the following benefits, among others, from WRG in 1993: (a) continued use of a Company-owned and maintained apartment with a market value estimated by WRG to be in excess of $3 million, with services of a cook, who was a WRG employee; (b) use of a company limousine and driver on a 24 hour basis; (c) the services of full-time secretaries and administrative assistants; (d) the use of corporate aircraft for personal and business travel; (e) home nursing services; and (f) security services.

While there was general knowledge within management that Grace, Jr.'s Retirement Agreement provided for the continuation of benefits that he had received before retirement, specific information about Grace, Jr.'s benefits was not generally available to WRG's management. Only non-management directors were involved in the negotiation or approval of Grace, Jr.'s retirement benefits.... However, Grace, Jr. and Pyne met with Bolduc in December 1992 to discuss Grace, Jr.'s retirement benefits after the negotiations over these benefits were completed. At that time, Bolduc became aware of each of the "other benefits" that WRG was providing to Grace, Jr.

The Company provided Grace, Jr. with directors' and officers' questionnaires in the course of preparing its 1992 Form 10–K and 1993 proxy statement and its 1993 Form 10–K and 1994 proxy statement. These questionnaires contained questions asking whether Grace, Jr. received certain benefits from the Company during the preceding year, including, among other things, use of Company property, including apartments; housing and other living expenses (including domestic service) provided at his principal and/or vacation residence; and other perquisites. Grace, Jr. incorrectly responded "no" to these questions.

The final version of WRG's 1993 proxy statement contained language discussing Grace, Jr.'s Retirement Agreement, including a statement that Grace, Jr. would receive "certain other benefits." WRG filed the Retirement Agreement as an exhibit to its 1992 Form 10–K, but did not further describe Grace, Jr.'s "other benefits," nor did WRG disclose the costs of providing them in any of its proxy statements or periodic reports filed with the Commission before 1995.[10]

Because WRG's senior management was excluded from the negotiation and approval of Grace, Jr.'s retirement benefits, WRG's disclosure counsel made arrangements for Pyne to review the executive compensation section of WRG's draft 1993 proxy statement, and Pyne did so. Bolduc, in his capacity as WRG's CEO, reviewed drafts of WRG's 1993 proxy statement and signed WRG's 1992 Form 10–K, which incorporated the proxy statement's section on executive compensation by reference. Grace, Jr., in his capacity as chairman, also signed the 1992 Form 10–K. Although Grace,

10. After information concerning Grace, Jr.'s "other benefits" became public, WRG disclosed in its 1995 proxy statement that the benefits provided to Grace, Jr. pursuant to the "other benefits" provision cost the Company $3,601,500 in fiscal year 1993, of which approximately $2,700,000 was attributable to Grace, Jr.'s having access to corporate aircraft.

Jr., Bolduc, and Pyne knew about the "other benefits" WRG had agreed to provide Grace, Jr. upon his retirement, they did not question the absence of information about these "other benefits" in WRG's disclosure of Grace, Jr.'s retirement benefits. Even if Bolduc and Pyne, as each asserted, assumed that WRG's legal counsel (whose office had participated in drafting the Retirement Agreement) had considered the adequacy of the disclosure concerning Grace, Jr.'s benefits, they should not have relied upon that assumption. They should have raised the issue of disclosure of Grace, Jr.'s "other benefits," for example, by discussing the issue specifically with disclosure counsel, telling counsel exactly what they knew about the benefits, and asking specifically whether the benefits should be disclosed.[11] As a result, WRG's 1992 Form 10–K and 1993 proxy statement failed to disclose specific information about the "other benefits."

* * *

V.   CONCLUSION

Serving as an officer or director of a public company is a privilege which carries with it substantial obligations. If an officer or director knows or should know that his or her company's statements concerning particular issues are inadequate or incomplete, he or she has an obligation to correct that failure. An officer or director may rely upon the company's procedures for determining what disclosure is required only if he or she has a reasonable basis for believing that those procedures have resulted in full consideration of those issues.[16]

Grace, Jr., Bolduc [and] Pyne . . . did not fulfill their obligations under the federal securities laws. Grace, Jr., Bolduc, and Pyne knew or should have known that Grace, Jr.'s retirement benefits were not fully disclosed in drafts of WRG's 1993 proxy statement and 1992 Form 10–K. . . . As noted, Grace, Jr. failed to identify information relating to [this issue] in his D & O questionnaires. Grace, Jr., Bolduc, [and] Pyne, given their positions as directors or senior officers and their particular knowledge of these transactions, should have inquired as to whether the securities laws required disclosure of this information. This inquiry could have included seeking the specific and fully informed advice of counsel. If they were not reasonably satisfied as to the answers they received, they should have insisted that the documents be corrected before they were filed with the Commission.[17]

WRG's violations resulted, in part, from its corporate culture, which reflected Grace, Jr.'s substantial influence over the Company.[18] Given this

---

11. This might have established that counsel was not in fact fully informed about these benefits or that Grace, Jr. had incorrectly filled out his D & O questionnaires regarding these benefits.

16. Procedures or mechanisms established to identify and address disclosure issues are effective only if individuals in positions to affect the disclosure process are vigilant in exercising their responsibilities.

17. Bolduc [and] Pyne . . . would each bear this responsibility even if, as each asserted, each assumed that WRG's internal mechanisms for preparing the relevant disclosure documents, including review of counsel, would address these issues.

18. There is some evidence that Bolduc recognized that Grace, Jr. exercised a degree of influence over WRG which was inappropri-

circumstance, Bolduc [and] Pyne . . . should have been more attentive to issues concerning disclosure of information relating to Grace, Jr. . . . Bolduc [and] Pyne . . . did not adequately follow through on fostering accurate and complete disclosure, which should have been their touchstone as members of WRG's board of directors or as officers of WRG.

Since Grace, Jr.'s death, WRG has substantially revised the composition of its board of directors. Because of the unique circumstances presented here (including the death of Grace, Jr.), the Commission has determined not to issue cease-and-desist orders or take other action against Bolduc [and] Pyne . . . in this matter. However, the Commission remains resolved to take enforcement action, where appropriate, against individual directors and officers who have violated or caused violations of the federal securities laws.

DISSENT OF COMMISSIONER STEVEN M.H. WALLMAN

The Section 21(a) report In the Matter of W.R. Grace & Co articulates a certain legal standard, and then applies that standard to these facts. I take issue with that standard specifically to the extent it suggests that officers and directors must ensure the accuracy and completeness of company disclosures. Moreover, I do not agree that, when the appropriate legal standard is applied to the particular facts of this case as described in the Report itself, there has been a violation of law on the part of the . . . individuals cited.

Certain of the disclosures of W.R. Grace & Co. relating to perquisites . . . were not in compliance with applicable requirements. The Company has consented to the issuance of a cease and desist order with respect to these matters.

As for individual liability, the record suggests that were J. Peter Grace, Jr. still alive, further examination as to whether he was a cause of the Company's improper disclosures would be in order. But in attempting to find other individuals who were responsible for the Company's conduct, I disagree with the Commission's conclusion that, on this record, J.P. Bolduc [and] Eben Pyne . . . failed to fulfill their obligations under the federal securities laws.[20] To conclude otherwise is to impose strict liability for such a disclosure failure—which simply is not the law.

In this case, as stated in the Report, Grace, Jr. exerted an unusual amount of control over the Company. But the Company also had policies and procedures in place designed to satisfy the Company's disclosure obligations. The Company prepared and distributed appropriate director and officer questionnaires requesting information concerning, specifically, the receipt of perquisites and other benefits. . . . The Company also sur-

---

ate for a public corporation and attempted to limit that influence.

20. I understand that Grace, Jr. received compensation and perquisites that many believe were inappropriate, and that many believe the board or others in management should have taken action to reduce those benefits. But we at the Commission do not administer the corporate law, which is the proper venue for those complaints.

veyed the chief financial officers of the Company's operating units for the same information. Draft documents were circulated among senior management (including Bolduc) and members of the board for their review and comment. A substantial number of people were involved in the creation or review of the relevant disclosure documents. From the record, there do not appear to have been any red flags or warnings to indicate that this system—which included the employment of respected and competent securities counsel—was breaking down, or was inadequate to produce documents that would comply with the federal securities laws. Yet, even though appropriate procedures were in place, and followed, insufficient disclosures were made. . . .

Whether disclosure of certain matters is required under the federal securities laws is a legal (or mixed legal and factual) determination that ultimately has to be made by counsel after being informed of the relevant facts. Bolduc [and] Pyne . . . were aware of the documents relevant to the . . . questioned disclosures at issue in this case: the retirement agreement with Grace, Jr. . . . The existence of these documents also was known to various attorneys in the [WRG] Office of Legal Counsel [OLC]—the office whose job it was to prepare disclosure in accordance with legal requirements, and the same office that drafted these documents. . . .

* * *

The two questioned disclosures in this case both turn on fine line legal interpretations. Bolduc [and] Pyne . . . were not lawyers; they were not versed in SEC line item disclosure requirements; they were not possibly capable of making the fine judgment calls on whether disclosure of the items at issue here was sufficient or warranted. These decisions were the domain of counsel. Bolduc [and] Pyne were not in a position to second-guess this type of disclosure and had every right to rely on a system designed to produce appropriate disclosure. If there were any attorneys in OLC who were unsure, or unaware, of the significance, or specifics, of the terms of . . . the retirement agreement . . . and clarification was needed to make a determination of what the law required in terms of disclosure, then it was the responsibility of those attorneys to ask the appropriate questions.

The issue then is simple: did legal counsel have the necessary facts to do the job that was required—and if not, did these . . . individuals know (or, perhaps, should these . . . individuals have known) that counsel did not have the necessary facts.

It is clear that disclosure counsel in particular was well aware of the facts regarding Grace, Jr.'s retirement package since he was supplied with an actual copy of the retirement agreement—an agreement filed publicly as an exhibit to the Company's Form 10–K. The agreement specifically provided that:

> All other benefits and arrangements currently provided [Grace, Jr.] as chief executive officer (including, but not limited to, the use of office space and corporate aircraft) will continue to be provided to [him].

There was no change in the benefits being granted Grace, Jr. from previous years—what he received as CEO he was to continue to receive in retirement. Disclosure counsel, knowing these facts, then apparently made the determination that the description of these continued benefits as certain other benefits was adequate disclosure under Item 402(h) of Regulation S–K, and presented drafts with that disclosure to Bolduc and Pyne.

Bolduc and Pyne knew that disclosure counsel had reviewed this certain other benefits language and the retirement agreement and appeared to be in possession of all relevant facts, including that Grace, Jr. was now retired. Bolduc and Pyne relied on disclosure counsel to make the legal determination as to what the law required regarding disclosure of the retirement agreement, including the level of detail regarding disclosure of any specific terms or conditions. Given the plain language of both the disclosure and the relevant portion of the retirement agreement, I fail to see where the red flag exists that would require non-lawyers to question the explicit determinations of their disclosure counsel as to the level of disclosure detail.

Moreover, details regarding the benefits in question—all of which Grace, Jr. had been receiving while he was still Chief Executive Officer— were not disclosed in previous filings with the Commission made prior to his retirement. I would venture to say that many securities lawyers would not know that the Company's summary disclosure of these very same benefits in a later filing would somehow now be inadequate because of Grace, Jr.'s retirement and change in status from executive officer and director to non-employee director/consultant. In fact, I would suspect that most securities lawyers would believe that less, not more, disclosure would be required upon such a change. It is simply not the law to require non-securities law experts to guess at the legal significance from a federal securities law disclosure standpoint of such a change in status and, therefore, be required to question the articulated judgment of their disclosure counsel and the resultant level of disclosure.

* * *

If the facts were different, it might be possible to conclude that these . . . individuals knew or had reason to know that the process had not worked appropriately, and there then might be reason to impose upon them a duty of inquiry that might rise to the level of querying and second-guessing counsel's judgments and disclosures. Examples might include knowing that Grace, Jr. had intentionally or otherwise not completed his questionnaire properly, or the presence of past mistakes or omissions in the Company's disclosure documents that would have alerted them to the fact that their disclosure process was failing. But those are not the facts of this record or as stated in the Report.

The Commission is understandably wary about pursuing lawyers for their legal judgments. I share that wariness and believe that when professionals—whether lawyers, accountants or others—are acting in their capacity as such they must be given the opportunity to exercise their professional judgment without fear that a mistake, no matter how innocent—or difference of judgment with the Commission—will result in their being viewed as having violated the federal securities laws. We need to recognize that in those circumstances where such judgments are made, there simply may be no person that will be individually liable. Holding the client liable for not questioning the legal judgment of counsel is not the answer.

If the Commission believes it has a case against these . . . individuals, then it should have brought it. The record, however, did not support any such case. There is a well-known maxim: bad facts make bad law. Here, we have bad circumstances. The Report is only a Section 21(a) report—negotiated by the parties in lieu of any further or other action of the Commission. It puts this matter to rest for these individuals.

There is no appeal and no court ruling on the law. My hope is that the Report will be limited to the very specific facts of this very specific case, and go no further.

I respectfully dissent.

QUESTIONS

1. Why do you think the SEC did not impose a more stringent sanction on Bolduc, the CEO of WRG, and Pyne, an outside director? Why did Bolduc and Pyne consent to the entry of the order? Why was the company treated more harshly than the individuals?

2. How would the certification requirement for periodic filings under Rules 13a–14 and 15d–14(a) change Bolduc's thinking regarding the disclosure questions faced in this case?

3. Should an outside director like Pyne be responsible for mistakes in the company's disclosure?

4. Should it matter that Grace Jr. "dominated" the company? If so, how?

5. Commissioner Wallman is troubled by what he sees as the SEC second-guessing Bolduc and Pyne for relying on the company's lawyers to determine the company's disclosure. Do you share his concern? Should the advice of counsel be a defense to an SEC enforcement action?

HYPOTHETICAL THREE

Mouthwatering's subsidiary, Ribs2U.com (in the business of supplying frozen slabs of ribs over the Internet), has struggled recently due to worries over mad cow disease. Things may be looking up for Ribs2U.com, however, in pork ribs. Iowa is expecting a bumper crop of corn this fall, which means that pork prices should drop this winter and Ribs2U.com should shift from loss to profit. Adam, the CEO of Mouthwatering, has been keeping track of the decline in the price of corn futures and he expects that RibsU.com could contribute 10% of Mouthwatering's profits next quarter if corn and pork prices decline as expected. Mouthwatering's most recent 10–K, however, makes no mention of the likely drop in pork prices in the MD & A section of its filing. Adam reasons that you cannot count on the weather, so the expected decline in pork prices may not come about. Has Mouthwatering violated § 13(a) by failing to discuss the effects of Iowa's fine summer weather on Ribs2U.com's profits?

C.   THE PROBLEM OF SELECTIVE DISCLOSURE

The question of who has access to SEC filings is an easy one—thanks to the SEC's EDGAR system, anyone with access to the Web can review any Form 10–K, 10–Q or 8–K the same day it is filed. Curious readers may access the EDGAR system at www.sec.gov. Companies are now required to make these filings electronically with the SEC and they are automatically posted to the EDGAR website. But companies do not communicate with the investing public solely through filings mandated by the SEC. For most public companies, voluntary disclosures, such as press releases, analyst conferences, and investor relations personnel's responses to questions, are an equally important means of spreading news about the company. For example, most public companies will not wait for the filing of their Form 10–Q to announce their earnings for the prior quarter. Instead, the first public disclosure of that information (and the disclosure that the securities markets will respond to) will be in the form of a press release announcing the quarterly earnings followed shortly thereafter by the filing of a Form 8–K with the SEC.

Voluntary disclosures of this sort, in contrast to the mandatory disclosures required by Forms 10–K, 10–Q, and 8–K, are regulated less heavily by the SEC, although they may be considered just as material by the markets. The antifraud Rule 10b–5 still applies to voluntary disclosures by companies, but the form and content of such disclosures are otherwise unregulated. The SEC became concerned in the late 1990s that companies were sometimes using communications less broadly available than the press release to convey information to investors. As a result, some investors were receiving material information sooner than others. Further, the SEC was concerned that companies were currying favor with market analysts by favoring them with information not available to other investors, which may have induced the analysts to be less than objective in their opinions. Regulation FD, discussed in the release below, was the SEC's response to the problem of selective disclosure.

Touted as bolstering the integrity of the capital markets, Regulation FD covers domestic Exchange Act reporting companies (foreign issuers are exempt) and those working on the behalf of such companies ("company sources"). A company source that discloses non-public material information to certain delineated groups of "covered" persons, including broker-dealers, investment advisors, investment companies, or any investor in the company that is reasonably expected to trade on the information, must also disclose the information to the public market. If the selective disclosure is intentional, then the company must disclose the information simultaneously to the entire market. If non-intentional, then the company must disclose the information to the market within 24 hours of the selective disclosure or by the time trading commences on the New York Stock Exchange, whichever is sooner. In promulgating Regulation FD, the SEC specifically excluded private liability for violations.

The SEC has a variety of enforcement proceedings at its disposal to enforce Regulation FD. Among the various SEC administrative proceedings we canvass later in the chapter is the cease-and-desist proceeding under § 21C of the Exchange Act. In a § 21C proceeding against a person directly committing a securities law violation, the SEC bears only the burden of showing that a person "is violating, has violated, or is about to violate" the Exchange Act. Moreover, the proceeding initially takes place before an SEC Administrative Law Judge, with review by the Commission and then eventually a federal court of appeals.

In the Matter of Siebel Systems, Inc.

Exchange Act Release No. 46896 (2002).

I.   The Securities and Exchange Commission deems it appropriate that public administrative proceedings be, and hereby are, instituted pursuant to Section 21C of the Securities Exchange Act of 1934 against Siebel Systems, Inc.

II.   In anticipation of the institution of these proceedings, Respondent has submitted an Offer of Settlement which the Commission has determined to accept. Solely for the purpose of these proceedings and any other proceedings brought by or on behalf of the Commission, or to which the Commission is a party, and without admitting or denying the findings herein, except as to the Commission's jurisdiction over it and the subject matter of these proceedings, which Respondent admits, Respondent consents to the entry of this Order . . . .

III.   Facts

Regulation FD . . . prohibits issuers from selectively disclosing material, nonpublic information to certain persons–securities analysts, broker-dealers, investment advisers and institutional investors–before disclosing the same information to the public. On November 5, 2001, the Company's Chief Executive Officer disclosed material, nonpublic information to persons outside the Company at an invitation-only technology conference hosted by Goldman Sachs & Co. in California.

* * *

On October 17, 2001, the Company reported its third quarter 2001 results. During the third quarter, Respondent's sales and earnings had declined compared to the third quarter of 2000. The Company also missed certain analysts' earnings expectations. In a public conference call to announce the Company's third quarter results, the Company's CEO stated:

> Since September 11, we have faced an . . . environment for information technology that has been as difficult as any in the history of the information technology industry. Things have been tough. We think

that they will continue to be quite tough in the short term. We have an exceptionally soft market for information technology.... Spending for tech products and services continues to slide. We expect things will be quite tough through the remainder of the year.

After the earnings became public, Respondent's stock price declined 19% to $17.38. In the three weeks following the conference call, Respondent and Goldman Sachs discussed Respondent's participation in the Technology Conference. The format of the conference would be a "fireside chat"—an informal question and answer session in which the Company's CEO would respond to questions initially from the Goldman Sachs analyst who organized the conference and then from the audience....

On November 1, 2001, Goldman Sachs provided Respondent with an advance list of the attendees for the Technology Conference. The Company's IR Director sent an electronic mail message attaching the attendee list and logistical information to the Company's CEO and its Chief Financial Officer. The list of nearly 200 attendees included broker-dealers, investment advisers, investment companies and institutional shareholders, including the largest institutional holder of Respondent's stock....

* * *

Respondent's stock closed at $17.29 per share on November 2, 2001. Later that evening, Respondent's IR Director, who was responsible for coordinating the Company's participation at the Technology Conference, transmitted talking points to the Company's CEO for him to use at the conference. The talking points contained information about, among other things, the Company's general financial condition, its management team, its position in the CRM market, product information and market opportunity, all of which was public information. The IR Director prepared the talking points to help ensure that no material, nonpublic information was disclosed at the Technology Conference.

* * *

By virtue of his position at the Company, Respondent's CEO had access to information concerning, among other things, the Company's sales pipeline, deal closure rate, trends in its revenues and performance in comparison to prior periods and to projections for both the current period and future periods. Such information reflected that the Company's projected license revenue in the fourth quarter of 2001 was trending upwards and would exceed the license revenue that the Company reported in its third quarter results three weeks earlier. At the time he entered the conference, Respondent's CEO was aware of material, nonpublic information concerning what the Company was observing in its sales pipeline and reflecting a positive trend in the transactions that the Company was completing and expected to complete with its customers.

At 10:00 a.m. on November 5, 2001, Respondent's CEO appeared at the Technology Conference. After a brief introduction, the moderator engaged him in the following discussion:

Moderator: ... the software that you sell gives you a good window into sales pipelines[3] ... you've been pretty good in seeing what's going on in the overall economy and what that means for the software sector. I wonder if you could give us an update of what you're seeing after September, maybe how the economy is looking and how the software business is looking during the month of October. Are customers still paralyzed or are we getting back to normalcy?

A: ... [T]he business decisions appear to be quite normal right now, and so we're pretty optimistic about what we're seeing at this time. People are engaging ... people are engaging in software evaluations, ... software selection, ... vendor negotiations, procurement, installations, ... contracts are getting signed, ... they're expanding their existing previous appointments, so right now it appears we're seeing a return to normal behavior in IT buying patterns.

Q: Would you, how would you characterize the sort of sales activity levels and linearity throughout ... the quarter?

A: I think the linearity of this Q4 will be about what we saw in Q4 of the previous two years. It was, the behavior of the market appears normal....

* * *

Q: I think there were a lot of concerns that Q4 the bottom could just fall out, that the business we saw in September was just a hint of what we're going to see this quarter. It sounds like from what you're saying that business is getting back more to normal. Before September 11th that the bottom is not, does not appear to be falling out.

A: I think that was a legitimate concern, and I shared that concern, and I think I communicated that concern quite clearly in our [third quarter] conference call. I mean if we had seen continued geo-political dislocation, it could have been a nightmare out there in Q4. The good news is we're not seeing that. So, that's, that is a relief for everybody.

These disclosures were based on nonpublic information that was internal to and reflected trends in the Company's business and were a departure from the talking points that the IR Director had prepared.

The Company did not simultaneously disclose the statements that were made by its CEO at the Technology Conference. There was no web-cast of the conference and the Company neither issued a press release nor filed any disclosure on Form 8–K with the Commission concerning its CEO's remarks at the conference.

---

3.   The Company uses its own software to track the status of pending sales by its sales force and to forecast trends in the market for its software. See Carleen Hawn, The Man Who Sees Around Corners, Forbes, January 21, 2002 at 72, 73–74 ("In November and December [2001] Siebel reps hit clients with 'far more product evaluations, demonstrations and visits than in the entire third quarter, and the rate of deal closings was much greater.' All of which, of course, was meticulously tracked by his software. Better yet, [the Company's CEO] says, Siebel is a good leading indicator for the rest of tech.")

Although analyst conferences attended by Respondent's management are normally broadcast to the public, the IR Director, and therefore, the Company, knew that the Technology Conference would not be web-cast. On October 11, 2001, Goldman Sachs informed the assistant to the Company's IR Director that the Technology Conference would not be broadcast over the World Wide Web. On November 1, 2001, the Company's IR Director requested her assistant to obtain the links to the web-cast. The IR Director's assistant then informed her that the Technology Conference would not be web-cast. Although the IR Director communicated with the Company's CEO shortly before the Technology Conference began, she did not provide this information to him.

At 10:00 a.m., when its CEO began speaking at the Technology Conference, the Company's stock was trading at $18.98 per share. Although he spoke for roughly forty minutes, the Company's CEO made the disclosures identified above within the first ten minutes of his presentation. Towards the end of his remarks, the Company's stock had increased to $19.81 per share. Trading volume during the period of his presentation was heavy, with over 4.6 million shares traded.

Following the disclosures, Respondent's stock price continued to rise. By 1:00 p.m., when the first reports about the comments by the Company's CEO began to appear in the media, Respondent's stock had increased to $20.15 per share or roughly 16.5% higher than the prior day's close. Trading volume for the day exceeded 33 million shares, roughly double the normal daily volume. Certain attendees at the conference either traded Respondent's stock or communicated information to others who traded or were in a position to trade while in possession of the information. For example, one of the attendees purchased 5,000 shares at 10:30 a.m. and an additional 10,000 shares at 11:05 a.m. Another attendee purchased 5,000 shares at 10:53 a.m. and an additional 120,000 additional shares at 11:27 a.m. Similarly, a Goldman Sachs employee attending the conference sent electronic messages to Goldman Sachs' internal message board. In these messages, the Goldman Sachs employee reported the "return to normalcy" and "Q4 linearity" comments made by the Company's CEO at the conference. Goldman Sachs' sales and trading desks had access to these messages, and was the most active firm trading Respondent's stock that day.

IV.   Legal discussion

The Commission adopted Regulation FD to level the playing field for all investors with respect to the disclosure of material, nonpublic information by issuers or persons acting on their behalf. Prior to Regulation FD, small investors were often disadvantaged because they did not have equal access to such information at the same time as large institutional investors and other securities industry professionals. This disparity in access stemmed from the long held view by some that, when it came to the disclosure of material, nonpublic information, certain select investors were entitled to earlier and better access than others. The Commission rejected this notion when it adopted Regulation FD and expressed its view that all investors or potential investors should have equal access to the same information at the same time, regardless of status. In adopting Regulation FD, the Commission recognized that "selective disclosure leads to a loss of investor confidence in the integrity of our capital markets." Regulation FD is designed to level the playing field and bolster investor confidence by prohibiting issuers from disclosing material, nonpublic information to a few selected persons prior to public disclosure. Under Regulation FD, an issuer disclosing material, nonpublic information to a few selected persons must simultaneously disclose that information to the public.

In this case, Respondent failed simultaneously to disclose to the public the material, nonpublic information that its CEO disclosed to attendees at the invitation-only Technology Conference. Respondent's selective disclosures benefited those investors at the conference who "were privy to the information beforehand [and] were able to make a profit or avoid a loss" and disadvantaged "those who were kept in the dark." As set forth below, Respondent violated Regulation FD.

A.   Regulation FD

Regulation FD prohibits an issuer, or persons acting on its behalf,[8] from selectively disclosing material, nonpublic information to certain persons outside the issuer. Regulation FD identifies those persons outside the issuer as: (1) broker-dealers and their associated persons; (2) investment advisers, certain institutional investment managers, and their associated persons; (3) investment companies, hedge funds, and their affiliated persons; and (4) any holder of the issuer's securities under circumstances where it is reasonably foreseeable that such a person would purchase or sell securities on the basis of the information.

Regulation FD distinguishes between "intentional" selective disclosures and "non-intentional" selective disclosures. A selective disclosure is "intentional" when the person making the disclosure knows, or is reckless in not knowing, that the information being communicated is both "material" and "nonpublic."[10] Information is material if there is a substantial likelihood that a reasonable investor would consider the information important in making an investment decision or if the information would significantly alter the total mix of available information. Information is nonpublic if it has not been disseminated in a manner making it available to investors generally. An issuer who fails to comply with Regulation FD is subject to a

---

8. Rule 101(c) of Regulation FD defines a "person acting on an issuer's behalf" as, in part, senior officials of the issuer or any other officer, employee, or agent of the issuer who regularly communicates with securities market professionals or the issuer's security holders. In addition, Rule 101(f) defines "senior official" as any "director, executive officer . . . investor relations or public relations officer, or other person with similar functions."

10. A disclosure is "non-intentional" when the person making the disclosure does not have that mental state. In its Adopting Release, the Commission observed that "in the case of a selective disclosure attributable to a mistaken determination of materiality, liability will arise only if no reasonable person under the circumstances would have made the same determination."

Commission enforcement action for violations of Sections 13(a) or 15(d) of the Exchange Act and Regulation FD.

B.   Respondent Violated Section 13(a) of the Exchange Act and Regulation FD

The attendees of the Technology Conference were "person[s] outside the issuer" set forth in Regulation FD. Prior to the Technology Conference, Goldman provided the Company's IR staff with the list of the persons who were expected to attend the conference. The Company's IR Director sent the Company's CEO an electronic mail message attaching this list. The list of attendees included broker-dealers, investment advisers, investment companies and institutional shareholders, including the largest institutional holder of Respondent's stock. The IR Director also knew that at least one investor was considering whether to convert a short position in the Company's stock into a long position, and that this investor was listed as an attendee on the attachment that the IR Director included in the e-mail to the Company's CEO. Thus, the Company knew going into the conference that it would be attended by persons outside the issuer covered under Regulation FD, including holders of its securities, "under circumstances in which it [was] reasonably foreseeable" that such persons would "purchase or sell the [Company's] securities on the basis of the information" provided at the conference.

The disclosure by Respondent's CEO that the Company was "pretty optimistic" because it was witnessing "a return to normal behavior in IT buying patterns" and that "the linearity of this Q4 will be about what we saw in Q4 of the previous two years" constituted material, nonpublic information. When the Company's CEO made these statements, he was speaking about what the Company was observing in its sales pipeline. He was answering a question posed by the moderator in which the moderator referenced Respondent's use of its own software to track its "sales pipelines." Thus, the disclosures were based on nonpublic information that was internal to and reflected trends in the Company's business. A reasonable investor would have considered this information important in making an investment decision regarding the Company's stock. The information was also material because it significantly altered the total mix of available information. The information disclosed at the Technology Conference sharply contrasted with statements made by Respondent's CEO on October 17, 2001, when he explained the Company's third quarter 2001 results in the conference call. His message to the public at that time was that the Company was facing "an exceptionally soft market for information technology" and that things would remain "quite tough" for the rest of the year.

* * *

Certain attendees at the conference who received this information recognized that the Company's CEO was communicating new information about the Company's business because immediately following his disclosures, they purchased Respondent's stock or communicated this information to others who traded.

Respondent's disclosures were intentional within the meaning of Regulation FD. A disclosure is intentional when the person making the disclosure knows or is reckless in not knowing that the information he is disclosing is both material and nonpublic. Respondent's CEO knew that his "return to normalcy" and "Q4 linearity" comments were based on internal information concerning what the Company was observing in its sales pipeline and reflecting a positive trend in the transactions that the Company was completing and expected to complete with its customers. He was aware that this information was both material and nonpublic. The IR Director knew that the Technology Conference was not being web-cast or otherwise disseminated to the public but failed to provide this information to the Company's CEO before he made his statements. In the circumstances of this case, the Company knew or was reckless in not knowing that it was selectively disclosing material nonpublic information at the Technology Conference—amounting to an "intentional" selective disclosure within the meaning of Regulation FD.

V.   Based on the foregoing, the Commission finds that Respondent violated Section 13(a) of the Exchange Act and Regulation FD.

ACCORDINGLY, IT IS HEREBY ORDERED, pursuant to Section 21C of the Exchange Act, that Respondent cease and desist from committing or causing any violations and any future violations of Section 13(a) of the Exchange Act and Regulation FD.

Once the SEC obtains a cease-and-desist order, as in *Siebel Systems*, the SEC may then seek further sanctions if the party against whom the order is issued subsequently violates the order. The *Siebel* litigation release below that followed the *Siebel* § 21C proceeding involves that scenario.

Siebel Systems, Inc., Kenneth A. Goldman and Mark D. Hanson

Litigation Release No. 18766 (2004).

The Securities and Exchange Commission today filed a civil action against Siebel Systems, Inc., charging that Siebel violated Regulation FD and a Commission cease-and-desist order. Two senior Siebel executives, Kenneth A. Goldman, the company's chief financial officer, and Mark D. Hanson, a current senior officer and the company's former Investor Relations Director, are charged with aiding and abetting Siebel's violations.

* * *

Regulation FD prohibits issuers from selectively disclosing material nonpublic information to certain persons–securities analysts, broker-dealers, investment advisers and institutional investors–before disclosing the same information to the public. In November 2002, the Commission issued an order finding that Siebel violated Regulation FD and requiring Siebel to cease and desist from committing or causing any future violations. Siebel settled that matter without admitting or denying the Commission's findings. As part of the settlement, Siebel also agreed to pay a $250,000 civil penalty.

The Commission's Complaint alleges that, six months after the cease-and-desist order was issued, Goldman disclosed material nonpublic information during two private events he attended with Hanson in New York on April 30, 2003, a "one-on-one" meeting with an institutional investor and an invitation-only dinner hosted by Morgan Stanley. The Commission charges that, at both the meeting and the dinner, Goldman made positive comments about the Company's business activity levels and transaction pipeline that materially contrasted with negative public statements Siebel made about its business in the preceding several weeks. According to the Complaint, based on Goldman's comments in the April 30 meeting, an institutional investor converted its 108,200 share short position in Siebel stock into a 114,200 share long position–a net change of 222,400 shares. On May 1, 2003, the day following the private meetings, the company's stock price closed approximately 8% higher than the prior day's close, and the trading volume was nearly twice the average daily volume for the preceding year.

The Commission alleges that Hanson, who had been put in charge of Siebel's Regulation FD compliance, failed to prevent the selective disclosures, and that both Hanson and Goldman failed to cause Siebel to make a public disclosure the next day. Finally, the Complaint alleges that Siebel failed to maintain disclosure controls and procedures designed to ensure the proper handling of information that is required to be disclosed in reports filed or submitted under the Exchange Act and to ensure that management has the information it needs to make timely disclosure decisions.

The Commission's Complaint charges Siebel with violating, and Goldman and Hanson with aiding and abetting Siebel's violations of, the Commission's cease-and-desist order, Section 13(a) of the Securities Exchange Act of 1934 and Regulation FD thereunder by making an intentional selective disclosure of material nonpublic information or, alternatively, a non-intentional selective disclosure. The Commission's Complaint also charges Siebel with violating Section 13(a) and Rule 13a–15 thereunder for its failure to maintain adequate disclosure controls and procedures. The Commission is seeking an order commanding Siebel to comply with the Commission's cease-and-desist order, permanent injunctions and civil penalties against all defendants, and other equitable relief to ensure that Siebel adopts adequate Regulation FD compliance policies and practices and that it maintains adequate disclosure controls and procedures.

NOTES

1. *Regulation FD.* Three features of Regulation FD bear emphasizing. First, the prohibition against selective disclosure is imposed on the *issuer* pursuant to

§ 13(a)'s reporting obligations for public companies. The officer of the company who actually makes the selective disclosure is a "cause" or an "aider and abettor" of the violation by the company and therefore subject to enforcement action as well. Neither the issuer nor the officer has violated the antifraud provisions of the Exchange Act. Second, only selective disclosures to "covered persons" are forbidden: broker-dealers, investment advisers, investment companies, and holders of the issuer's securities (if it is "reasonably foreseeable" that the holder will trade on the information). This limitation was intended to exclude answers to questions posed by journalists from the reach of Regulation FD. Also expressly excluded from the ban are persons owing "a duty of trust or confidence to the issuer (such as attorney, investment banker, or accountant)," persons who agree to maintain the information in confidence, and credit rating agencies. Communications made in connection with an offering registered under the Securities Act are also excluded, so Regulation FD will not interfere with the traditional public offering "road show" (discussed in Chapter 7). Third, inadvertent selective disclosures can be corrected by "promptly" filing a Form 8–K with the disclosed information. A press release, if "reasonably designed to provide broad, non-exclusionary distribution of the information to the public," will also suffice.

2. *Regulation G.* Another rule relating to voluntary disclosures is Regulation G. Under Regulation G, if public disclosure of any material information includes a non-GAAP financial measure, such as pro forma financials, the registrant must include, in the same disclosure or release: a presentation of the most directly comparable GAAP financial measure and a reconciliation of the disclosed non-GAAP financial measure to the most directly comparable GAAP financial measure. The reconciliation must be quantitative for historic measures and, to the extent possible without unreasonable efforts, for prospective measures. If the prospective GAAP financial measure is not calculable due to unavailable information, the registrant must identify the missing information and disclose its probable significance. Regulation G also cautions that a non-GAAP financial measure, taken together with the accompanying information, may not misstate a material fact or omit to state a material fact necessary to make the presentation of the non-GAAP financial measure not misleading, in light of the circumstances under which it is presented.

QUESTIONS

1. Why was the Goldman Sachs Technology Conference considered "non-public"?

2. Did investors other than the attendees at the Technology Conference benefit from the CEO's selective disclosures in any way? Are investors better off if the CEO does not speak?

3. Is there anything that Siebel could have done (after the CEO discloses at the Goldman Sachs Conference) to avoid the first enforcement action?

4. Did the participants who traded in Siebel stock while attending the technology conference do anything wrong?

5. What procedures could Siebel have adopted to prevent the Regulation FD violation in the second case?

HYPOTHETICAL FOUR

Eve, Mouthwatering's Chief Financial Officer, has caused Mouthwatering to overstate its revenues from the Viper's Den. Mouthwatering's auditor, Apple & Tree, had discovered the overstated revenues and demanded that Mouthwatering restate its past financial statements to correct the overstatement. Eve resigned right before the board of directors would have fired her for her role in overstating the revenues. On the day that Eve resigned, Mouthwatering issued a press release after the market closed announcing that she had resigned for "personal reasons." The press release made no mention of Apple & Tree's demand that Mouthwatering restate its revenues. That same evening Adam drowned his sorrows at the local watering hole, the Paradise Lounge. "That Eve," moaned Adam to the bartender, "has ruined everything. I was going to hit a big payday when we sold Mouthwatering to a big food conglomerate, but who will buy the company if we have to restate our earnings?" The bartender, Snake, responded "Live and learn," as he drew Adam another beer. After serving Adam, Snake went to the backroom, called his broker and told him that he wanted to sell short 10,000 shares of Mouthwatering stock. "Thanks for the tip" says Snake after Adam leaves an extra $20 on the bar. Has Mouthwatering violated Regulation FD?

IV.   ACCURACY OF DISCLOSURE

A.   BOOKS AND RECORDS

The Exchange Act encourages accurate disclosure through both internal and external mechanisms. As we will see in Chapter 5, antifraud liability deters company officials from providing materially inaccurate disclosures. The specter of antifraud liability is bolstered by numerous other mechanisms that encourage accurate disclosures.

Most directly, the Exchange Act requires that the company "make and keep books, records, and accounts, which, in reasonable detail, accurately and fairly reflect the transactions and dispositions of the assets of the issuer." Section 13(b)(2)(A). In adopting this provision in 1975 as part of the Foreign Corrupt Practices Act, Congress drew a connection between the company's *external* disclosures regarding its financial situation and the accuracy of the company's *internal* information.

Three things are noteworthy about this requirement that the company maintain accurate books and records. First, the provision imposes strict liability—there is no knowledge, or even negligence, requirement. Inaccuracies are actionable, regardless of the company's knowledge of them. Second, there is no "materiality" qualifier—any inaccuracy, no matter how trivial, is potentially actionable. Third, (and this likely follows from the first two points), Congress provided no private right of action to enforce § 13(b)(2) and the courts have not implied one. Only the SEC (and in extreme cases, the Justice Department) can enforce the provision. As discussed later in the chapter, the SEC can bring an administrative proceeding for violations of §§ 12, 13, 14, and 15(d) of the Exchange Act pursuant to § 15(c)(4). In the

Tonka case below, the SEC used its powers under § 15(c)(4) to bring an action for a violation of § 13(b).

Taking a "belt and suspenders" approach, Congress not only requires that companies produce the *outcome* of accurate books and records, it also mandates procedures designed to produce accurate books and records. Exchange Act § 13(b)(2)(B). The issuer in the *Tonka* below failed to meet this procedural standard.

In the Matter of Tonka Corporation
Accounting and Auditing Release No. 73 (1985).

The Commission deems it appropriate and in the public interest that proceedings pursuant to Section 15(c)(4) of the Securities and Exchange Act of 1934, be, and they hereby are, instituted with respect to Tonka Corporation. These proceedings are instituted to determine whether Tonka failed to devise and maintain a system of internal accounting controls sufficient to provide reasonable assurances that transactions were executed in accordance with management's general or specific authorization and that access to assets was permitted only in accordance with management's general or specific authorization as required by Section 13(b)(2)(B) of the Exchange Act.

* * *

This administrative proceeding involves a fraudulent scheme whereby approximately $2,000,000 of corporate funds of Tonka Corporation were misappropriated by Tonka's former chief financial officer and treasurer, L. Martin LeBus. LeBus was assisted in this scheme by D. Douglas Titus and James H. Peters, officers of Winchester Industries, Inc., a privately held company which LeBus controlled, and by a personal friend, Galley W. Smith, III. LeBus abused his powers as chief financial officer of Tonka by funneling corporate funds into Winchester, a shell corporation, under the guise of a legitimate corporate investment. The inadequacy of Tonka's internal controls with respect to its investments facilitated LeBus' ability to perpetrate his fraud.

* * *

In May 1981, LeBus began his employment at Tonka as the company's chief financial officer and treasurer. LeBus' responsibilities included establishing and maintaining banking relationships, negotiating short-term and long-term financing, implementing an effective cash management system and managing Tonka's legal, tax and accounting staffs. . . . Tonka's investments prior to 1981 consisted mainly of short-term liquid investments such as certificates of deposits and commercial paper. . . .

At a December 9, 1981 board meeting, Tonka's board of directors adopted a resolution authorizing LeBus, as chief financial officer, to enter into investment opportunities on behalf of Tonka. LeBus was authorized by the board to invest up to $10,000,000 without prior authorization from

Tonka's chief executive officer or the board of directors. The scope of LeBus' investment authority was defined by Tonka's short-term investment policy which was reflected in the November 10, 1981 memorandum sent to LeBus from Tonka's assistant treasurer. Permissible investments . . . were short-term, liquid investments such as commercial paper, certificates of deposit, T–Bills, municipal bonds and money market funds.

At a March 29, 1982 board meeting, LeBus recommended to the board of directors that it authorize management, specifically LeBus, to invest in a professionally managed corporate cash management fund. LeBus presented the board with a prospectus that had been distributed by a well-known national brokerage firm as well as a written proposal which recommended that he be given authority to invest $1,000,000 in a recently-established cash management fund in order to take advantage of its high yield and 85% federal corporate dividend tax exemption. In addition, LeBus requested that he be given authority to invest in similar investment vehicles if the new cash management fund continued to show strong performance. There apparently was no discussion as to what period of time would be used to judge the performance of the cash management fund investment. LeBus informed management that the cash management fund would be a registered investment company and would make investments only in public companies. The board authorized the proposal based on LeBus' representations and the information before it.

D.   Purchase of Winchester Preferred Stock and LeBus' Misappropriation

* * *

[LeBus ordered a series of purchases of Winchester preferred stock on behalf of Tonka on April 12, 1982, May 12, 1982, and January 1983. The shares of Winchester were not registered and not freely transferable. LeBus had incorporated Winchester in 1973 and was at all times in control of Winchester, a shell corporation with no assets prior to the investment by Tonka. LeBus never disclosed his relationship with Winchester despite a conflict of interest policy at Tonka that prohibited employees from doing business in companies over which the employee had substantial influence. No offering circular for Winchester or other information was requested or received by anyone at Tonka.]

LeBus directed a scheme to funnel Tonka corporate funds to Winchester in order to misappropriate Tonka corporate funds for his own benefit. LeBus and his associates, Titus, Peters and Smith, utilized some of the funds received from Tonka as direct cash payments and to repay certain loans. In other instances, LeBus and his associates made investments in various enterprises which they intended to parlay into monetary gain.

For about a year from the date of Tonka's initial Winchester investment, LeBus used the funds Tonka had invested in Winchester to invest in securities and write covered call options. All earnings from the securities investments and option sales were directed to LeBus and his associates and not to Tonka. In addition, LeBus and his associates received cash payments and loans from Winchester through the use of the funds Tonka had invested.

Winchester, at LeBus' direction, also went outside the stock market for investments in 1982 and 1983 and purchased two air freight companies as well as investing in a public company in the hopes of taking control of the company in order to take advantage of the substantial net operating loss carry forward by selling the company. Tonka received no benefit from such investments. Eventually, Tonka wrote-off its investment in Winchester in early 1984 in its 1983 Annual Report on Form 10–K when an internal inquiry by Tonka led to the determination that the investment was worthless. Later in 1984, Tonka received a $1.7 million reimbursement from its insurers for losses associated with its investment in Winchester.

E.   Tonka's Review of the Investment

During the preparation of financial statements for Tonka's second quarter 1982 Quarterly Report on Form 10–Q, it was necessary to value Tonka's investment in Winchester preferred stock. Around June or July 1982 a member of Tonka's corporate accounting department contacted Tonka's controller, who was in part responsible for the company's internal control function, to inform him that he could not find a listing for Winchester preferred stock in the Wall Street Journal. Previously, LeBus had informed Tonka's controller that the board of directors had authorized him to invest in the cash management fund and similar type investment vehicles and explained the concept of the cash management fund investment to the controller. LeBus was the only Tonka management employee who provided Tonka's controller with any information as to what the board authorized him to invest in on behalf of Tonka. According to Tonka's controller, sometime in the spring of 1982, he read an article on the cash management fund and was familiar with the concept behind the investment vehicle.

As a result of Tonka's corporate staff accountant's inquiry, Tonka's controller contacted LeBus and questioned him about the market value of Tonka's investment. LeBus told Tonka's controller that the Winchester preferred stock was redeemable at par (face) value with thirty days notice. This was a false statement. Tonka's controller conducted no further inquiry, such as requesting a prospectus from Winchester or requesting information concerning the redeemability of the shares. In fact, no prospectus then existed for Winchester, the stock was restricted and the Winchester certificates made no reference to being redeemable at par value with 30 days notice.

In November 1982, a Tonka staff accountant attempted to ascertain the market value of Tonka's short-term investment portfolio pursuant to the preparation of a budget plan the company was compiling for its 1983 fiscal year. Tonka's corporate staff accountant contacted the registered representative for Tonka's brokerage account in Jackson, Mississippi and was informed for the first time that the Winchester securities were purchased pursuant to a private placement and that the registered representative had no idea of the market value of the securities. Since the Winchester investment was purchased pursuant to a private placement, it consisted of restricted stock that was not freely transferable, and since LeBus' statement that the stock was redeemable at par was false, the Winchester stock was not liquid as Tonka expected it to be. The accountant informed Tonka's controller of his conversation with the registered representative. Tonka's controller then contacted LeBus and was once again assured that the Winchester preferred stock was redeemable at par value with thirty days notice. Once again Tonka's controller did not conduct any independent inquiry and relied solely on LeBus' representations, as chief financial officer, as to the value of the Winchester securities. No one at Tonka had ever seen the Winchester certificates or any information about Winchester....

As noted above, in January 1983, LeBus directed Tonka's controller to wire transfer an additional $1,000,000 to Winchester. Tonka's controller implemented LeBus' request without question and wired $1,000,000 to a Winchester bank account with a bank in St. Paul, Minnesota. LeBus told Tonka's controller at the time of the January 1983 investment that the investment in Winchester had been a good one and that it would continue to bring the company a high yield. Tonka's controller did not request any information or ask any questions about the investment.

F.   Tonka's Discovery of LeBus' Association with Winchester

Beginning in July 1982 through October 1983, Tonka received what it believed to be quarterly dividends from Winchester. The dividend checks were accompanied by a cover letter signed by either Titus or Peters which informed Tonka that the check Tonka received from Winchester represented the company's earned quarterly dividend on its investment in Winchester. However, the money Tonka received from Winchester was actually a return of part of the $2,000,000 that it had invested in the company.

In October 1983, Winchester missed a dividend payment to Tonka. The same Tonka corporate staff accountant who previously had sought to ascertain a market value for the Winchester investment informed Tonka's corporate accountant who in turn contacted LeBus and informed him of the problem. LeBus told Tonka's corporate accountant that he would take care of the matter. LeBus, shortly thereafter, told Tonka's corporate accountant that he had contacted the company and he had been assured that Winchester would pay the dividend by selling some of its securities holdings. LeBus also later informed Tonka's corporate accountant that he had instructed Winchester not to pay the dividend because Tonka was in the process of selling its holdings in Winchester and the withheld dividend would enhance the price at which the company could sell its Winchester stock. Tonka's corporate accountant was satisfied with LeBus' explanation and made no further inquiry into the matter.

When Tonka missed a second dividend payment from Winchester in late January 1984, the general counsel commenced an inquiry into Tonka's Winchester investment and discovered some correspondence which listed

Titus as an officer of Winchester. Tonka's general counsel, who remembered that Titus had represented LeBus in a house closing, became suspicious and contacted Tonka's chief executive officer. Shortly thereafter, Tonka's chief executive officer contacted LeBus and asked him if he had any association with Winchester. LeBus denied any such association and assured him that the investment was good. Tonka's general counsel and Tonka's controller continued to investigate the Winchester investment. LeBus attempted to cover-up his relationship with Winchester at this time by telling Tonka's controller that Tonka did not have to worry about the investment because it was sound and that any investigations by Tonka's controller into the matter would open "a can of worms."

In February 1984, Tonka retained an outside law firm to help with its inquiry into the Winchester investment.... Tonka's general counsel requested the articles of incorporation for Winchester and discovered that LeBus was the incorporator of Winchester. Finally, a few days later, after he learned that Tonka and the law firm would be reviewing documents at Winchester, LeBus admitted his misconduct and stated that the documents at Winchester would show that he was associated with the company and had received loans from Winchester. Thereafter, LeBus was discharged at a special meeting of Tonka's board of directors on Sunday, February 19, 1984, and the company publicly disclosed the improper investment on the next day. The company on its own initiative conducted an investigation through its audit committee with the assistance of outside counsel, immediately following the discovery of the misappropriation, and in early May 1984, adopted certain additional measures to strengthen its internal controls.

II.   OPINION

A.   Tonka's Internal Controls

Although Tonka discovered the fraud and took measures to strengthen its investment controls, Tonka's previous internal controls were not adequate to prevent and detect LeBus' fraud in a timely manner. LeBus' scheme succeeded because, in effect, LeBus, as the chief financial officer, was the only check on the exercise of the investment authority that the Board had conferred upon him. There was no procedure to check or monitor the investment or its performance. No one requested or received any financial information concerning Winchester even in the course of attempting to ascertain a market value for the Winchester stock.

* * *

Tonka's controller did not question LeBus about the lack of information available for Winchester or consult other Tonka management concerning the investment. There were no formal systems or procedures in place to provide a vehicle for such a challenge.

In October 1983, Winchester missed its first dividend payment to Tonka. Tonka's corporate accountant was satisfied with LeBus' representation that he instructed Winchester not to pay the dividend because Tonka was in the process of selling the stock. It was not until Winchester's second missed dividend payment, in January 1984, that Tonka made an inquiry into the Winchester investment. Once Tonka made an independent inquiry into the nature of the Winchester investment, it quickly discovered that LeBus had misappropriated Tonka funds. Tonka thereafter adopted procedures to strengthen its control of the use of corporate funds.

B.   Section 13(b)(2)(B) of the Exchange Act

During the period 1982 through at least January 1984, Tonka failed to devise and maintain a system of internal accounting controls with respect to its investments sufficient to provide reasonable assurances that among other things:

1. transactions were executed in accordance with management's general or specific authorization; and

2. access to assets was permitted only in accordance with management's general or specific authorization as required by Section 13(b)(2)(B) of the Exchange Act.

LeBus' diversion of corporate funds to a sham corporation which he controlled and the use of those funds to his own benefits and that of his associates for non-corporate purposes demonstrates the inadequacies in Tonka's internal accounting system, which failed to prevent or to detect the fraud for almost two years despite the existence of questionable circumstances.

The books and records provisions of the Foreign Corrupt Practices Act were designed, among other things, to insure that issuers would devise and maintain a system of internal accounting controls sufficient to provide reasonable assurances that assets are properly accounted for and used according to management's authorization. The Commission has noted that an issuer need not always select the best or the most effective control measures as long as the one selected is reasonable under the circumstances. However, Tonka's internal controls were not reasonably adequate to assure the proper use of Tonka's assets, because while LeBus was given authority to invest up to $10,000,000 of Tonka funds, there was no system to check on whether the chief financial officer was abusing the investment authority conferred upon him, and Tonka personnel relied entirely on LeBus' representations.

LeBus, as treasurer and chief financial officer, received authorization to make investments of up to $10,000,000, without prior approval. Although such authority may not be unusual for a chief financial officer, LeBus controlled the function of selecting depositories for Tonka funds as well as purchasing, exchanging, selling and transferring Tonka investment securities. There was no regular internal accounting procedure at Tonka to [do] periodic reviews of investments to determine whether investments had been made pursuant to management authorization or were in accordance with established investment guidelines. During the two-year period of

LeBus' fraud, no one at Tonka requested or reviewed financial statements concerning Winchester.

* * *

Tonka's failure to have any type of independent review facilitated his ability to enter into investments which were not in accordance with management authority and permitted LeBus to apply corporate funds in a manner inconsistent with management authorization in violation of Section 13(b)(2)(B). In May 1984, Tonka implemented new controls as a result of LeBus' misappropriation of corporate funds. Tonka's internal auditor now reviews investments on a quarterly basis to test whether they are in compliance with management authorization and summarizes his tests in a quarterly report to the board. In addition, the corporate accounting department determines whether investments are in accordance with investment guidelines at the time it books the investment. Tonka's chief executive officer must approve investments over $1,000,000 in a single issuer. Had any of these new controls been in place in 1982, LeBus would not have as easily had the opportunity to misappropriate the $2,000,000 of Tonka corporate funds.

The existence of reasonably adequate internal controls are essential to enhance accountability for corporate assets. Section 13(b)(2)(B) is designed, among other things, to ensure that corporations will account for their funds properly and to ensure that checks are maintained on how corporate funds are spent. In order to maintain accountability for the disposition of its assets, a business must attempt to make it difficult for its assets to be misappropriated.

The Commission has emphasized the need for issuers to maintain reasonably adequate internal controls. The Commission has brought several actions against issuers for inadequate internal controls which resulted in misappropriation or misuse of corporate assets. Although Tonka substantially recovered its loss from its insurers, misappropriations by executive officers emphasize the necessity of the Commission to scrutinize the reasonableness of issuers' internal controls to ensure compliance with Section 13(b)(2)(B).[7]

III. FINDINGS

Based on the foregoing, the Commission finds that:

Tonka violated Section 13(b)(2)(B) of the Exchange Act, in that it failed to devise and maintain a system of internal accounting controls with respect to corporate investments sufficient to provide reasonable assurances that transactions were executed in accordance with management's general or specific authorization and that access to assets was permitted only in accordance with management' general or specific authorization.

---

7. In addition to the misappropriation of Tonka corporate funds, LeBus submitted false conflict of interest questionnaires to Tonka in connection with preparation of its 1982 and 1983 proxy materials.

IV. TONKA'S OFFER OF SETTLEMENT

Tonka has submitted an Offer of Settlement in which, solely for the purpose of this proceeding ... and without admitting or denying the Facts, Opinion or Findings herein, it consents to the issuance of this Order.

In the Offer of Settlement, Tonka represents and undertakes that:

1. It has in place internal controls with respect to corporate investments designed to comply with Section 13(b)(2)(B) of the Exchange Act;

2. It will maintain the internal controls referred to in paragraph 1 above or such other internal controls with respect to corporate investments which Tonka's audit committee may adopt from time to time; and

3. It will, within ten (10) days of the end of the month during which the Commission initiates these proceedings and issues the ORDER in this matter, attach a copy of the ORDER as an exhibit to a Current Report on Form 8–K to be filed with the Commission.

V. ORDER

In view of the foregoing, the Commission deems it appropriate and in the public interest to accept the Offer of Settlement of Tonka and, accordingly, IT IS HEREBY ORDERED that Tonka:

(1) Comply with Section 13(b)(2)(B) of the Exchange Act; and

(2) Comply with the undertakings set forth in its Offer of Settlement.

NOTES

1. *Accurate books and records.* The Exchange Act § 13(b)(2) requirement of accurate books and records is bolstered by § 13(b)(5), which states that "No person shall knowingly circumvent or knowingly fail to implement a system of internal accounting controls or knowingly falsify any book, record or account described in [§ 13(b)(2)]." What does § 13(b)(5)'s focus on knowing violations add to deterrence? Section 13(b)(4) makes clear that criminal penalties may apply for violations of § 13(b)(2)'s requirement of accurate books and records only if the violator has also run afoul of § 13(b)(5).

2. *Sarbanes–Oxley and internal controls.* Additional mechanisms for ensuring accuracy of books and records were added by the Sarbanes–Oxley Act. Recall that CEOs and CFOs are now required under § 302 of Sarbanes–Oxley (as implemented in Exchange Act Rule 13a–14) to certify that they have reviewed the company's internal controls on a regular basis. Another provision added by Sarbanes–Oxley intended to make officers think hard about the accuracy of company's financial statements is § 304. That section requires CEOs and CFOs to return bonus and other incentive compensation to the company for any period that the company is required to restate its financial results as a result of "misconduct." "Misconduct" is not defined, nor is it limited to misconduct by the CEO and CFO.

Section 404 of the Sarbanes–Oxley Act adds to the CEO/CFO certification requirement of § 302. Under § 404, managers must include a statement in the company's annual report on the manager's responsibility for the company's internal controls for financial reporting and provide an assessment of those controls. Section 404 also requires that "each registered public accounting firm that prepares or issues the audit report for the issuer" shall attest to the management's assessment of the firm's system of internal controls for financial reporting. Auditors are now required to not only certify the integrity of their client's financial statements, but also assess the mechanisms that their corporate clients have adopted to generate the financial information that goes into those statements.

QUESTIONS

1. Why is Tonka being sanctioned here? Isn't the company the victim of LeBus's theft?

2. Did Tonka violate § 13(b)(2)(A)?

3. Do we need a legal rule instructing companies to not let their employees steal? Does § 13(b)(2) serve some additional purpose?

4. What more could Tonka's employees have done to uncover LeBus's wrongdoings sooner than they did?

5. Tonka beefed up its internal controls in response to LeBus's misappropriation. Why didn't Tonka's insurers require Tonka to adopt those internal controls when it took out the policy that reimbursed Tonka for LeBus's misappropriation?

HYPOTHETICAL FIVE

The troubles for Adam, the CEO of Mouthwatering, have gone from bad to worse. Recall that Eve, the former CFO of Mouthwatering, engineered a transaction with the Viper's Den that overstated Mouthwatering's revenues. Mouthwatering's audit committee has been investigating the transaction with the Viper's Den. In the course of its investigation, the audit committee has found more mischief by Eve. It turns out that to get a shipment of cayenne pepper (a key ingredient in Mouthwatering's barbeque sauce) delivered on time, Eve paid $75,000 to a customs official in French Guiana. Needless to say, the payment does not show up in Mouthwatering's financial statements. Nor does the $500,000 slush fund from which Eve got the money for the bribe. Adam delegates all that "money stuff" to Eve and had no idea that there was a slush fund. Have any provisions of § 13(b) been violated? If so, by whom? Is § 304 of the Sarbanes–Oxley Act implicated by the bribe or the contract with the Viper's Den?

B.   THE INDEPENDENT AUDITOR

The SEC requires that the financial statements filed with the Form 10–K be audited by an independent accounting firm. See Exchange Act Rule 13a–1. Virtually all large public companies employ as their auditors one of the "Big Four" accounting firms: Deloitte Touche Tohmatsu, Ernst & Young, KPMG and PricewaterhouseCoopers. The demise of the fifth member of the "Big Five"—Arthur Andersen—as a result of its involvement in the accounting fraud at Enron, led to the inclusion of an elaborate set of requirements for auditors in the Sarbanes–Oxley Act.

The SEC enjoys several avenues to discipline public company auditors. Because the audit firms certify the financial statements to the SEC, they subject themselves to discipline by the SEC under the agency's rules of practice (Rule 102(e)). As part of the Sarbanes–Oxley Act, Congress codified the SEC's authority under Rule 102(e) to discipline accountants in § 4C of the Exchange Act. Accountants may be barred from practicing before the SEC if they are found:

Bar of auditors

1. ↓ no qualification

2. Lack of integrity and unethical conduct

3. willful violation

Improper prof. conduct
Negligent conduct

(i)   Not to possess the requisite qualifications to represent others;

(ii) To be lacking in character or integrity or to have engaged in unethical or improper professional conduct; or

(iii) To have willfully violated, or willfully aided and abetted the violation of any provision of the Federal securities laws or the rules and regulations thereunder.

Exchange Act § 4C. Section 4C goes on to define "improper professional conduct" as "intentional or knowing conduct, including reckless conduct, that results in a violation of applicable professional standards" as well as negligent conduct in the form of either "a single instance of highly unreasonable conduct" or "repeated instances of unreasonable conduct." Notably, "practice" before the SEC is defined to include not only appearances in administrative proceedings before the SEC, but also the provision of advice to companies regarding documents that will be filed with the SEC. SEC Rule of Practice 205.2.

The provision most directly traceable to Arthur Andersen's demise is 18 U.S.C. § 1520, which makes it a criminal offense, with up to ten years of jail time, to destroy corporate audit records. Perhaps of the greatest long-run importance, however, is a new quasi-governmental regulator for auditors of public companies created under the Sarbanes–Oxley Act, the Public Company Accounting Oversight Board (generally known by its acronym PCAOB, or more fun, but less linear, the "Peekaboo"). A non-profit corporation, the PCAOB is responsible for setting standards for audits as well as the supervision and discipline of public accountants. The PCAOB operates under the oversight of the SEC.

Regulation of the auditing function also extends to the issuer's corporate governance. Under § 10A(m) of the Exchange Act, also a product of the Sarbanes–Oxley Act, the retention, compensation and oversight of the company's external auditor must be entrusted to an audit committee of the board of directors. The audit committee also has the authority to hire its own advisors (typically legal counsel) at the company's expense. The auditors must report to the audit committee "critical accounting policies and practices," alternative treatments of financial information discussed with management and any other "material written communications" between the auditor and management. The audit committee is also responsible for approving any non-audit services (now strictly limited, as discussed below) provided by the company's auditor. Finally, the audit committee is charged with establishing procedures for dealing with complaints relating to auditing and internal controls. "Whistleblowers" who make such complaints are protected from retaliation by both civil and criminal sanctions against those who retaliate.

The audit committee must be made up exclusively of independent directors, meaning that the only compensation the director can receive from the company is the director's fee—no consulting or other employment arrangements are permitted. The SEC has bolstered this independence requirement with a disclosure requirement, Regulation S–K Item 309, relating to the expertise of the audit committee. Item 309 requires the company to disclose whether any member of the audit committee qualifies as a "financial expert," which requires either experience as an accountant or an accounting officer, or experience supervising an accounting officer or overseeing public accountants. Listing requirements for the NYSE and Nasdaq require financial literacy for *all* audit committee members. Both the NYSE and Nasdaq also require that a majority of the board of directors of listed companies meet their respective independence standards.

In addition to creating a new regulatory and oversight apparatus, Congress also imposed new responsibilities on auditors. Auditors must adopt procedures to detect "illegal acts that would have a direct and material effect" on financial statements and identify material related party transactions (§ 10A(a)(1)). Auditors are also required to evaluate the ability of the client to continue as a going concern through its next fiscal year. These duties were added to existing responsibilities to report illegal acts to management and the audit committee or entire board of directors (§ 10A(b)). A board of directors receiving such a report must notify the SEC; if it fails to do so, the audit firm must provide notice to the SEC itself. (A similar "whistleblowing" requirement, minus the requirement of a report to the SEC, is imposed on lawyers by Rule 205.3 of the SEC's Rules of Practice, discussed below.) Finally, Exchange Act Rule 13b2–2 prohibits officers and directors of the issuer from misleading the auditor in connection with any filing to be made with the SEC.

Congress also mandated a more stringent definition of auditor independence. Congress worried that the lure of lucrative contracts for other services would lead auditors to knuckle under to management pressure, thereby compromising the integrity of the audit. Consequently, auditors are now banned from providing a broad array of services to their audit clients, including: bookkeeping, designing financial systems, appraisal and valuation services, actuarial services, internal auditing functions, management and human resources services, investment services and legal services. Auditors may still provide, among other things, tax planning advice to their clients so long as they obtain prior approval from the audit committee. The PCAOB is authorized to ban the provision of other services as well. Audit firms are also required by § 10A(j) to rotate the partner in charge of the audit for each client at least once every five years. Too familiar a relationship between the partner and company executives can compromise independence. In the same vein, § 10A(*l*) bans audit firms from auditing companies whose CEOs, CFOs, or controllers were employed by the audit firm and that employee participated in the audit of the company during the prior year.

HYPOTHETICAL SIX

Apple & Tree, the accounting firm for Mouthwatering, is worried about a possible blight to its reputation from all the financial shenanigans at Mouthwatering involving Eve, the former CFO. Apple & Tree recently got a call from the SEC's Division of Enforcement. One of Apple & Tree's junior accountants for the Mouthwatering engagement, Seth, has been talking to the government. Seth has told the Enforcement Division that he came across a bank statement from EdenBank for a $500,000 account when he was working on the Mouthwatering audit. When he asked Eve about the account and why it did not appear on Mouthwatering's balance sheet, Eve told him not to worry about it, that it was a "temporary" account, and that it would soon be consolidated with Mouthwatering's primary account. Seth was worried, however, and raised it with the partner in charge of the Mouthwatering audit, John Apple. John raised the issue with Adam, who told him "not to worry about it because Eve always gets the money stuff sorted out before the time we need to file." John then told Seth that if Eve told him that it would be taken care of, it would be taken care of, and that he should not be harassing the CFO of such an important client. Apple & Tree signed off on the audit without qualification and Adam and Eve both certified the 10–K with financial statements that did not reflect the $500,000 account. The Enforcement Division says that it is now considering action against Apple & Tree and John Apple. Does Apple & Tree have a problem?

C.   THE ROLE OF LAWYERS IN ENFORCING THE SECURITIES LAWS

Lawyers, like accountants, are subject to censure and suspension under the SEC's Rule of Practice contained in Rule 102(e) as codified largely in Section 4C of the Exchange Act. As with accountants, "practice" before the SEC includes not only appearances in administrative proceedings before the SEC, but also the provision of advice to companies regarding documents that will be filed with the SEC. SEC Rule of Practice 205.2. Thus, legal advice to a registrant that the SEC subsequently determines to have been incorrect can be potentially career ending for the securities lawyer. Few companies would be willing to hire a corporate lawyer who cannot provide advice on SEC filings. That possibility no doubt deters many lawyers from offering advice that pushes the boundaries of the law.

This draconian authority under Rule 102(e) has been used exceedingly sparingly; as a matter of policy the SEC has not used its administrative authority to suspend lawyers before a court has made a finding of wrongdoing by the lawyer. The most common basis for excluding a lawyer from practice before the SEC has been a prior disbarment by state bar authorities. Lawyers can also, however, be found to be the "cause" of the violation of § 13(a) by a public company, thereby exposing the lawyer to an injunction or a cease and desist order. Such a finding is hardly likely to enhance a corporate lawyer's career prospects.

The "whistleblowing" obligations of lawyers are (for now) somewhat less stringent than those imposed on accountants. Section 307 of Sarbanes–Oxley required the SEC to establish rules "setting forth minimum standards of professional conduct for attorneys appearing and practicing before the Commission in any way in the representation of issuers." The SEC responded with Rule of Practice 205. Lawyers are required to report material violations of state or federal securities law and material breaches of fiduciary duty to the company's chief legal officer (i.e., the company's general counsel) or to both the chief legal officer and the chief executive officer. SEC Rule of Practice 205.3(b)(1). The chief legal officer is then required to investigate the matter and cause the company to take an appropriate response if he or she determines that there has been a material violation. The chief legal officer is required to report back to the lawyer initiating the investigation. Rule 205.3(b)(2). If the lawyer believes that the company's response is insufficient, the lawyer must report the problem to the company's audit committee, any other board committee consisting solely of independent directors, the entire board, or a "qualified legal compliance committee," if the issuer has established one. Rule 205.3(b)(3), (c). The "qualified legal compliance committee" must have at least one member of the audit committee and two or more independent directors. The lawyer *may* reveal confidential information to the SEC without the issuer's consent to "prevent the issuer from committing a material violation that is likely to cause substantial injury to the financial interest or property of the issuer or investors" or to rectify the consequences of such violation that has already occurred, if the attorney's services were used to facilitate the violation. The lawyer may also disclose to the SEC to prevent the issuer from committing perjury in a SEC investigation or enforcement action or perpetrating a fraud on the SEC. Rule 205.3(d).

QUESTIONS

1. What are the implications of the observation by an SEC Commissioner that "in securities matters (other than those where advocacy is clearly proper) the attorney will have to function in a manner more akin to that of the auditors than to that of the advocate"? Sommer, *The Emerging Responsibilities of the Securities Lawyer*, 1973–1974 Fed. Sec. L. Rep. (CCH) ¶ 79,61 at 83,689, 83,690 (1974).

2. Who is the securities lawyer's client? Management? The board of directors? Current shareholders? Prospective shareholders? The company?

3. Is the SEC the appropriate authority to supervise the conduct of lawyers? Is this role consistent with the agency's enforcement obligations?

HYPOTHETICAL SEVEN

Isaac is a partner at the law firm of Cain & Abel, the outside counsel for Mouthwatering on a number of transactions. In drafting the Form 10–K for Mouthwatering, Isaac discovers that right before her departure, Eve (the former CFO) withdrew $10 million from Mouthwatering's corporate bank account and spent the entire amount on a fun-filled night in Las Vegas. Isaac reports the matter to Jacob, Mouthwatering's general counsel. Jacob thanks Isaac and tells him that the company knows about the theft but wants to keep things "quiet" in the upcoming Form 10–K to give the company a chance to "make up" the $10 million deficit before the markets find out. Jacob tells Isaac specifically not to report this information to Mouthwatering's audit committee but to keep the information to himself. Jacob concludes by telling Isaac: "Mouthwatering is one of Cain & Abel's best clients; I'm sure you want to keep it that way."

V.   ENFORCEMENT ISSUES

We have seen some of the administrative proceedings available to the SEC in the course of examining the Exchange Act's disclosure requirements. The remainder of the chapter focuses on issues arising from government enforcement of securities violations. The SEC exercises civil authority, which it can exercise both in its own administrative proceedings and in actions brought in federal district court. As you will see in the materials below, the SEC has very broad investigative and subpoena power and a range of sanctions available to it.

The Justice Department prosecutes criminal violations of the securities laws. The relationship between the SEC and Justice is ordinarily cooperative, with most criminal prosecutions for securities law violations arising from referrals by the SEC. The availability of both civil and criminal sanctions, however, can raise serious issues for the target of the investigation.

A.   ADMINISTRATIVE PROCEEDINGS

The SEC has a range of internal administrative proceedings available to it to address violations of the securities laws. Those proceedings carry with them a diverse range of sanctions. The table below summarizes the principal proceedings available under the Exchange Act for violations relating to disclosure by public companies and the sanctions available in each.

Section	Proceeding	Sanctions
21C	Cease-and-desist	- Temporary orders - Cease-and-desist-order from violating securities laws - Disgorgement - Officer and Director bar from public companies
15(c)(4)	Disclosure violations	- Order to stop disclosure violations

21(a)	Report of investigation	- Public announcement of violation of securities laws
12(j) & (k)	Trading suspensions	- Halt trading for ten days or indefinitely

1. SECTION 21C

Section 21C of the Exchange Act, and its counterpart § 8A of the Securities Act, give the SEC considerable flexibility (as seen in the *Siebel Systems* case) to impose a cease and desist order on any person who is "violating, has violated, or is about to violate any provision" of the Exchange Act or any SEC rule or regulation promulgated under the Act. Despite the array of alternate enforcement proceedings, the SEC relies primarily on cease and desist proceedings under § 21C to enforce the securities laws.

Although defendants are entitled to notice and an administrative hearing, the SEC does not have to endure the delay of going through the courts to obtain the initial cease and desist order. The SEC's Division of Enforcement can proceed in an administrative proceeding, initially before an SEC Administrative Law Judge, with review by the Commission itself (and subsequent review in the courts of appeals, discussed below). The federal rules of civil procedure do not apply in SEC administrative hearings; instead, the proceedings are governed by the agency's more flexible rules of practice.

In a § 21C proceeding against a person directly committing a securities law violation, the Division only needs to show that a person "is violating, has violated, or is about to violate" the Exchange Act. For "other persons" who contribute to the violation, the SEC must show that the "other person . . . is, was, or would be a cause of the violation, due to an act or omission the person knew or should have known would contribute to such violation." The cease and desist order may simply order the wrongdoer to "cease committing or causing such violation." If the SEC also seeks to order the wrongdoer to cease and desist from engaging in "any future violation of the same provision," the SEC may need to show a likelihood of future violation (as discussed below in the *KPMG* case).

Despite the minimal burden imposed on the SEC to make its case (and the home court advantage), the cease-and-desist proceeding nonetheless makes significant sanctions available to the SEC. The order that the respondent "cease and desist" from violating the securities laws is backed by the threat of civil penalties and an injunction in court if the subject of the order fails to comply (the object of the subsequent suit brought by the SEC in *Siebel Systems*). In addition, the SEC has the power in a § 21C proceeding to order the disgorgement of funds procured as a result of the violation. Section 21C(e). And accountants who have "willfully" violated the "whistleblowing" obligation of § 10A(b) to report illegal acts to management and the audit committee or entire board of directors are also subject to civil penalties in a § 21C proceeding. Section 10A(d). Section 21B sets forth the applicable penalties in three tiers ranging from $5,000 to $500,000. Finally, if the SEC determines that the respondent has violated § 10(b)'s antifraud prohibition, it can use a § 21C proceeding to bar that person from serving as an officer or director of a public company if it also determines that "the conduct of that person demonstrates unfitness to serve as an officer or director." Section 21C(f).

The SEC has the power to issue temporary orders requiring the respondent in the proceeding to stop the violation and to prevent the dissipation of assets pending the outcome of a § 21C proceeding. Section 21C(c). The SEC can issue temporary cease and desist orders if the agency determines that the violation is "likely to result in significant dissipation or conversion of assets, significant harm to investors, or substantial harm to the public interest." The temporary order requires notice to the respondent and a hearing before the Commission, unless the Commission determines that "notice and hearing prior to entry [of the temporary order] would be impracticable or contrary to the public interest." This authority allows the SEC to move quickly if it has concerns that a respondent may try to hide assets before the proceeding can be concluded.

QUESTIONS

1. What is disgorgement? How does it differ from damages and civil penalties?

2. What benefit does the SEC gain from first obtaining a § 21C cease and desist order instead of going directly to court?

3. How often will the SEC determine that a person it has found guilty of fraud under § 10(b) is nonetheless *fit* to serve as an officer or director?

2.   SECTION 15(c)(4)

Section 15(c)(4) allows for an SEC administrative proceeding for violations of §§ 12, 13, 14, and 15(d) of the Exchange Act, covering, among other things, the periodic disclosure requirements for public companies and the proxy solicitation requirements (covered in Chapter 11). The SEC may use § 15(c)(4) to bring an action against both the person or issuer who may have violated one of those provisions, as well as "any person who was a cause of the failure to comply." This authority allows the SEC to sanction not only the employees of the issuer (including its officers and directors), but also outside accountants and lawyers if they are the "cause" of a misleading or late filing. The power to sanction individuals gives the SEC substantial negotiating leverage, as officers and directors may be quite happy to agree to settlements sanctioning the issuer if they can escape being named in the order as individual violators.

The § 15(c)(4) proceeding is somewhat limited, however, when compared with the cease-and-desist proceeding available to the SEC under § 21C. (Congress adopted § 21C as an amendment to the Exchange Act long after § 15(c)(4) was adopted.) The SEC must go to court if a respondent violates a § 15(c)(4) order to obtain a court order compelling obedience. Only if the respondent violates the court order is the more serious sanction of contempt available. By contrast, the SEC can immediately seek civil penalties in court if the terms of a cease-and-desist order are violated. Moreover, the § 15(c)(4) proceeding does not afford the disgorgement remedy and officer and director bar provided by the § 21C proceeding. The SEC has held that § 15(c)(4), unlike § 21C, does not give the SEC the power to impose compliance orders dealing with future violations. See *In Re Kern*, 50 S.E.C. 596, 598 (1991).

QUESTIONS

1. Given the availability of a § 21C cease-and-desist proceeding, why would the SEC ever use a § 15(c)(4) proceeding to pursue a violation of §§ 12, 13, 14, and 15(d) of the Exchange Act?

3. SECTION 21(a)

Section 21(a) gives the SEC broad authority to investigate any person who may have violated (or is about to violate) the Exchange Act or the rules of one of the self-regulatory organizations (SROs), such as the NYSE, or to secure information "to serve as a basis for recommending further legislation concerning the matters to which this title relates." The report authorized by § 21(a) can be used to publicize violations or to outline problems that may require additional legislation or regulation. It also can be used, however, to publicize violations of the law in cases where the SEC determines that further sanctions are not warranted. The § 21(a) report issued by the SEC in *W.R. Grace* above is the least stringent sanction available to the SEC–no penalties, no constraints on future action, not even a formal censure. As used in this setting, a § 21(a) report amounts to little more than a public scolding by the Commission. Occasionally, however, respondents agree to governance reforms as part of an agreed-upon § 21(a) report.

4. SECTIONS 12(j) & 12(k)

The SEC can take direct steps to limit the harm caused to investors by misstatements or selective disclosures. Section 12(k) allows the SEC to suspend trading in any security for up to ten days if the agency determines "that the public interest and the protection of investors so require." The SEC is authorized to halt trading for longer periods under § 12(j), but that provision requires the SEC to provide notice and a hearing to the issuer before trading can be halted. An attempt by the SEC to circumvent the notice and hearing requirements of § 12(j) by issuing repeated ten-day suspensions under § 12(k) was rebuffed by the Supreme Court in *SEC v. Sloan*, 436 U.S. 103 (1978). The SEC has bootstrapped the effectiveness of § 12(k), however, by promulgating Rule 15c2–11, which prohibits broker-dealers from initiating or resuming trading in a public company if it does not have current information on that company. The SEC has used § 12(k) to suspend trading in "shell" companies (firms with few or no assets or operations) that have not filed their periodic reports. After the ten-day suspension, Rule 15c2–11 steps in to stop broker-dealers from *resuming* trades in the securities of companies with inadequate current information. Thus, through creative rulemaking the SEC has replaced a portion of the authority it lost in *Sloan*.

B. INVESTIGATIONS AND STRATEGY

The sources that prompt SEC investigations are varied—review of company filings, market surveillance done by the SEC and the SROs, complaints from investors ("short" sellers—hoping to drive down the price of a security—are a common source), "whistleblowing" by current and former employees of public companies, reading the *Wall Street Journal* and other business oriented media, referrals from other government agencies and the SROs, and occasionally, tips from disgruntled ex-spouses. (Free advice from the authors: it's not a good idea to tell your spouse or partner about your insider trading shortly before dumping him or her.) Most SEC investigations begin with a preliminary, or informal, inquiry by the staff of the Division of Enforcement. The policy of the SEC is ordinarily to keep such preliminary investigations confidential. Moreover, even the targets of the inquiry do not have the right to be notified. Subjects of the investigation are likely to learn about the inquiry soon enough, however, as the Enforcement staff will be seeking voluntary cooperation (generally informal interviews and document requests) from both the targets of the investigation and others who may have relevant information. Therefore, it is not unusual to see companies disclose investigations in press releases or in a periodic filing.

Many investigations never get beyond the informal stage, either because the staff determines that no violations of the securities laws have occurred or because the target of investigation cooperates and eventually agrees to the entry of an order in either an administrative proceeding (a "consent order" under either § 21C, as we saw in the first *Siebel Systems* case, or § 15(c)(4), as in *Tonka*) or an injunctive action in district court (a "consent decree"). Both the initiation and settlement of administrative proceedings and court actions require Commission approval.

If the staff and the target of the investigation cannot agree on an appropriate resolution of the matter, the target will ordinarily be allowed to present his side of the case to the Commissioners in the form of a "Wells submission." A "Wells submission" is an opportunity to explain why the violation alleged by the staff was inadvertent or not in bad faith, or that the staff has incorrectly interpreted the requirements of the law. The overwhelming majority of investigations are settled, as targets are eager to avoid: (1) the continuing harm to their reputation from having their misconduct aired in litigation with the SEC; (2) the enormous expense of litigating against the resources of the federal government; (3) a referral to the Department of Justice for possible criminal prosecution; and (4) the ruinous potential private liability that could come from the collateral estoppel effect of an adverse judgment. Plaintiffs' attorneys are likely to "piggyback" on an SEC victory with a securities fraud class action. As you have seen above, consent orders and consent decrees routinely contain a stipulation that the subject of the order or decree is not admitting to the wrongdoing, so the target is free to relitigate the facts in any private action. A standard clause in SEC settlement agreements, however, makes it a term of the agreement that the settling party will not deny publicly any allegation in the SEC's complaint. A public denial of wrongdoing will likely provoke a motion by the SEC to vacate the settlement (followed by a prompt retraction of the denial by the settling party).

The case below outlines what the SEC expects from the targets of its investigations. It is followed by a press release explaining the consequences of a failure to cooperate. How likely is it that a corporation will choose to contest SEC charges?

Report of Investigation Pursuant to Section 21(A) of the Securities Exchange Act of 1934 and Commission Statement on the Relationship of Cooperation to Agency Enforcement Decisions

Exchange Act Release No. 44969 (2001).

Today, we commence and settle a cease-and-desist proceeding against Gisela de Leon–Meredith, former controller of a public company's subsidiary. Our order finds that Meredith caused the parent company's books and records to be inaccurate and its periodic reports misstated, and then covered up those facts.

We are not taking action against the parent company, given the nature of the conduct and the company's responses. Within a week of learning about the apparent misconduct, the company's internal auditors had conducted a preliminary review and had advised company management who, in turn, advised the Board's audit committee, that Meredith had caused the company's books and records to be inaccurate and its financial reports to be misstated. The full Board was advised and authorized the company to hire an outside law firm to conduct a thorough inquiry. Four days later, Meredith was dismissed, as were two other employees who, in the company's view, had inadequately supervised Meredith; a day later, the company disclosed publicly and to us that its financial statements would be restated. The price of the company's shares did not decline after the announcement or after the restatement was published. The company pledged and gave complete cooperation to our staff. It provided the staff with all information relevant to the underlying violations. Among other things, the company produced the details of its internal investigation, including notes and transcripts of interviews of Meredith and others; and it did not invoke the attorney-client privilege, work product protection or other privileges or protections with respect to any facts uncovered in the investigation.

The company also strengthened its financial reporting processes to address Meredith's conduct—developing a detailed closing process for the subsidiary's accounting personnel, consolidating subsidiary accounting functions under a parent company CPA, hiring three new CPAs for the accounting department responsible for preparing the subsidiary's financial statements, redesigning the subsidiary's minimum annual audit require-ments, and requiring the parent company's controller to interview and approve all senior accounting personnel in its subsidiaries' reporting pro-cesses.

Our willingness to credit such behavior in deciding whether and how to take enforcement action benefits investors as well as our enforcement program. When businesses seek out, self-report and rectify illegal conduct, and otherwise cooperate with Commission staff, large expenditures of government and shareholder resources can be avoided and investors can benefit more promptly. . . .

[T]he paramount issue in every enforcement judgment is, and must be, what best protects investors. There is no single, or constant, answer to that question. Self-policing, self-reporting, remediation and cooperation with law enforcement authorities, among other things, are unquestionably impor-tant in promoting investors' best interests. But, so too are vigorous enforcement and the imposition of appropriate sanctions where the law has been violated. Indeed, there may be circumstances where conduct is so egregious, and harm so great, that no amount of cooperation or other mitigating conduct can justify a decision not to bring any enforcement action at all. In the end, no set of criteria can, or should, be strictly applied in every situation to which they may be applicable.

* * *

In brief form, we set forth below some of the criteria we will consider in determining whether, and how much, to credit self-policing, self-report-ing, remediation and cooperation–from the extraordinary step of taking no enforcement action to bringing reduced charges, seeking lighter sanctions, or including mitigating language in documents we use to announce and resolve enforcement actions.

1. What is the nature of the misconduct involved? Did it result from inadvertence, honest mistake, simple negligence, reckless or deliberate indifference to indicia of wrongful conduct, willful misconduct or una-dorned venality? Were the company's auditors misled?

2. How did the misconduct arise? Is it the result of pressure placed on employees to achieve specific results, or a tone of lawlessness set by those in control of the company? What compliance procedures were in place to prevent the misconduct now uncovered? Why did those procedures fail to stop or inhibit the wrongful conduct?

3. Where in the organization did the misconduct occur? How high up in the chain of command was knowledge of, or participation in, the misconduct? Did senior personnel participate in, or turn a blind eye toward,

obvious indicia of misconduct? How systemic was the behavior? Is it symptomatic of the way the entity does business, or was it isolated?

4.   How long did the misconduct last? Was it a one-quarter, or one-time, event, or did it last several years? In the case of a public company, did the misconduct occur before the company went public? Did it facilitate the company's ability to go public?

5.   How much harm has the misconduct inflicted upon investors and other corporate constituencies? Did the share price of the company's stock drop significantly upon its discovery and disclosure?

6.   How was the misconduct detected and who uncovered it?

7.   How long after discovery of the misconduct did it take to implement an effective response?

8.   What steps did the company take upon learning of the misconduct? Did the company immediately stop the misconduct? Are persons responsible for any misconduct still with the company? If so, are they still in the same positions? Did the company promptly, completely and effectively disclose the existence of the misconduct to the public, to regulators and to self-regulators? Did the company cooperate completely with appropriate regulatory and law enforcement bodies? Did the company identify what additional related misconduct is likely to have occurred? Did the company take steps to identify the extent of damage to investors and other corporate constituencies? Did the company appropriately recompense those adversely affected by the conduct?

9.   What processes did the company follow to resolve many of these issues and ferret out necessary information? Were the Audit Committee and the Board of Directors fully informed? If so, when?

10.   Did the company commit to learn the truth, fully and expeditiously? Did it do a thorough review of the nature, extent, origins and consequences of the conduct and related behavior? Did management, the Board or committees consisting solely of outside directors oversee the review? Did company employees or outside persons perform the review? If outside persons, had they done other work for the company? Where the review was conducted by outside counsel, had management previously engaged such counsel? Were scope limitations placed on the review? If so, what were they?

11.   Did the company promptly make available to our staff the results of its review and provide sufficient documentation reflecting its response to the situation? Did the company identify possible violative conduct and evidence with sufficient precision to facilitate prompt enforcement actions against those who violated the law? Did the company produce a thorough and probing written report detailing the findings of its review? Did the company voluntarily disclose information our staff did not directly request and otherwise might not have uncovered? Did the company ask its employees to cooperate with our staff and make all reasonable efforts to secure such cooperation?

12.   What assurances are there that the conduct is unlikely to recur? Did the company adopt and ensure enforcement of new and more effective internal controls and procedures designed to prevent a recurrence of the misconduct? Did the company provide our staff with sufficient information for it to evaluate the company's measures to correct the situation and ensure that the conduct does not recur?

13.   Is the company the same company in which the misconduct occurred, or has it changed through a merger or bankruptcy reorganization?

We hope that this Report of Investigation and Commission Statement will further encourage self-policing efforts and will promote more self-reporting, remediation and cooperation with the Commission staff. We welcome the constructive input of all interested persons. We urge those who have contributions to make to direct them to our Division of Enforcement. The public can be confident that all such communications will be fairly evaluated not only by our staff, but also by us. We continue to reassess our enforcement approaches with the aim of maximizing the benefits of our program to investors and the marketplace.

QUESTIONS

1.   Should the SEC factor a defendant's decision to assert the attorney-client privilege in determining the appropriate level of sanctions?

2.   Why is the period of time over which the misconduct occurred relevant in determining the appropriate sanction?

3.   Is the drop in the company's share price upon disclosure of the wrongdoing a relevant consideration in determining the appropriate level of sanctions?

Lucent Settles SEC Enforcement Action Charging the Company with $1.1 Billion Accounting Fraud

Press Release 2004–67.

Washington, D.C., May 17, 2004—The Securities and Exchange Commission today charged Lucent Technologies Inc. with securities fraud, and violations of the reporting, books and records and internal control provisions of the federal securities laws. The SEC also charged nine current and former Lucent officers, executives and employees, and one former Winstar Communications Inc. officer with securities fraud and aiding and abetting Lucent's violations of the federal securities laws. The SEC's complaint alleges that Lucent fraudulently and improperly recognized approximately $1.148 billion of revenue and $470 million in pre-tax income during its fiscal year 2000.

Lucent and three of the former Lucent employees agreed to settle the case without admitting or denying the allegations. As part of the settlement, Lucent agreed to pay a $25 million penalty for its lack of cooperation.

"Companies whose actions delay, hinder or undermine SEC investigations will not succeed," said Paul Berger, Associate Director of Enforcement. "Stiff sanctions and exposure of their conduct will serve as a reminder to companies that only genuine cooperation serves the best interests of investors."

The SEC's complaint alleges that Lucent's violations of generally accepted accounting principles (GAAP) were due to the fraudulent and reckless actions of the defendants and deficient internal controls that led to numerous accounting errors by others. In their drive to realize revenue, meet internal sales targets and/or obtain sales bonuses, the complaint alleges, defendants . . . improperly granted, and/or failed to disclose, various side agreements, credits and other incentives to induce Lucent's customers to purchase the company's products. These extra-contractual commitments were made in at least ten transactions in fiscal 2000, and Lucent violated GAAP by recognizing revenue on these transactions both in circumstances: (a) where it could not be recognized under GAAP; and (b) by recording the revenue earlier than was permitted under GAAP.

In carrying out their fraudulent conduct, according to the complaint, these Lucent officers, executives and employees violated and circumvented Lucent's internal accounting controls, falsified documents, hid side agreements with customers, failed to inform personnel in Lucent's corporate finance and accounting structure of the existence of the extra-contractual commitments or, in some instances, took steps to affirmatively mislead them.

* * *

Lucent's Lack of Cooperation

Lucent's penalty for its failure to cooperate is based on the following conduct.

Throughout the investigation, Lucent provided incomplete document production, producing key documents after the testimony of relevant witnesses, and failed to ensure that a relevant document was preserved and produced pursuant to a subpoena. As a result, the staff's ability to conduct an efficient and comprehensive investigation was impeded.

After reaching an agreement in principle with the staff to settle the case, Lucent's former Chairman/CEO and outside counsel agreed to an interview with Fortune magazine. During the interview, Lucent's counsel characterized Lucent's fraudulent booking of the $125 million software pool agreement between Lucent and Winstar as a "failure of communication," thus denying that an accounting fraud had occurred. Lucent's statements were made after Lucent had agreed in principle to settle this case without admitting or denying the allegations concerning, among other things, the Winstar transaction. Lucent's public statements undermined both the spirit and letter of its agreement in principle with the staff.

After reaching an agreement in principle with the staff to settle the case, and without being required to do so by state law or its corporate charter, Lucent expanded the scope of employees that could be indemnified against the consequences of this SEC enforcement action. Such conduct is contrary to the public interest.

Lucent also failed over a period of time to provide timely and full disclosure to the staff on a key issue concerning indemnification of employees. Failure to provide accurate and complete disclosure to the staff undermines the integrity of SEC investigations.

* * *

QUESTIONS

1. How should Lucent have responded to the news that it was under SEC investigation?

2. What provision of § 21(a) of the Exchange Act, granting the SEC authority to conduct investigations, authorizes penalties for non-cooperation?

3. Should the SEC sanction companies more severely for agreeing to indemnify their employees for costs relating to an SEC investigation?

HYPOTHETICAL EIGHT

Adam, the CEO of Mouthwatering, calls you, having just received a phone call from a staff attorney at the SEC's Division of Enforcement. The enforcement attorney told him that they would like to talk to him informally about an unusual trading pattern in Mouthwatering's stock before the firm announced the resignation of Eve, the CFO of Mouthwatering. (Mouthwatering's press release said that Eve had left for "personal reasons," but the stock price nonetheless took a big hit.) Adam is in a panic; he doesn't want an investigation to jeopardize the potential sale of Mouthwatering. He asks you how to make this problem go away quickly and easily. What advice do you give him?

C. SUBPOENAS

As noted above, most investigations are concluded by a settlement after the staff's informal investigation. If the target refuses to cooperate with the staff's informal investigation, the Enforcement staff must seek the Commission's approval of a formal investigation (also ordinarily non-public). Section 21(a) of the Exchange Act authorizes the SEC to "in its discretion, make such investigations as it deems necessary to determine whether any person has violated, is violating, or is about to violate any provision of this title, the rules or regulations thereunder, [the rules and regulations of SROs], and may require or permit any person to file with it a statement in writing, under oath or otherwise as the Commission shall determine, as to all the facts and circumstances concerning the matter to be investigated." Once the Commission votes to begin a formal investigation under § 21(a), the Enforcement staff has the power to issues subpoenas under § 21(b), which carries with it the power to subpoena documents and testimony.

Although the SEC has the power to issue subpoenas, it must go to district court to get an order mandating compliance if the recipient of the subpoena refuses to comply voluntarily. Exchange Act § 21(c). A judicial order to comply with a subpoena is backed up by the court's power of contempt. Under the interpretation of § 21(c) in the case below, what would an impermissible use of the SEC's subpoena power look like?

RNR Enterprises, Inc. v. SEC

122 F.3d 93 (2d Cir. 1997).

■ JACOBS, CIRCUIT JUDGE.

Respondent-appellant Richard K. Wells challenges the enforceability of an administrative subpoena served on him and a company he controls pursuant to a Formal Order of the SEC that opened an investigation into a particular industry, but did not name either Wells or his company.

In July 1996, the SEC moved in the Southern District of New York for an order enforcing previously issued subpoenas against Wells; Robert J. Carlo; and RNR Enterprises, Inc. A subpoena *ad testificandum* . . . directed that Wells appear to give testimony in the Matter of Certain Sales of Unregistered Securities of Telecommunications Technology Ventures, an investigation "pursuant to a formal order issued by the Securities and Exchange Commission under the authority of Section 20(a) of the Securities Act of 1933 and Section 21(a) of the Securities Exchange Act of 1934."

The Formal Order identified in the subpoena was issued by the SEC in July 1994. In relevant part, the Formal Order recited that information known to the SEC tended to show the following things:

- that there had been possible violations of federal securities laws in connection with the offering and sale of securities in "ventures that acquire licenses for, or develop or operate transmission facilities of, or otherwise concern, Specialized Mobile Radio . . . and similar telecommunications technologies that are subject to licensing by the United States Federal Communications Commission."

- specifically, that from 1988 to the present, certain persons had offered such "Telecommunications Technology Securities" without filing the requisite registration statements with the SEC; obtained money or property by means of untrue statements or misleading omissions of material fact, made in connection with the offer, purchase or sale of such securities; or effected transactions in such securities without first registering as brokers or dealers.

The Formal Order directed that "a private investigation be conducted to determine whether any persons have engaged, are engaged, or are about to engage, in any of the [alleged] acts, practices, or courses of business, or in any acts, practices, or courses of business of similar purport or object," and it authorized two designated SEC officers to (among other things) "subpoena witnesses and compel their attendance" for the purposes of the investigation. . . .

In support of its enforcement motion, the SEC filed a declaration written by an SEC attorney, which:

- identified Wells as the Chairman and Chief Executive Officer of RNR;

- described the business of RNR as the acquisition and development of "specialized mobile radio properties";

- recited the determination by Commission staff "that Respondents might have information relevant to the Investigation";

- represented that the subpoenas sought "testimony that will assist the Commission in determining whether there have been violations of the federal securities laws as described in the Formal Order," specifically, that the SEC needed the testimony of all three respondents in order to obtain information concerning RNR's 1995 offering of $5 million of unregistered securities to the public;

- and reported that Wells had appeared and answered some of the SEC's initial questions, but stopped answering questions on the advice of counsel, and later refused to appear and testify.

* * *

II

The courts' role in a proceeding to enforce an administrative subpoena is extremely limited. To win judicial enforcement of an administrative subpoena, the SEC must show [1] that the investigation will be conducted pursuant to a legitimate purpose, [2] that the inquiry may be relevant to the purpose, [3] that the information sought is not already within the Commissioner's possession, and [4] that the administrative steps required have been followed.

[A] governmental investigation into corporate matters may be of such a sweeping nature and so unrelated to the matter properly under inquiry as to exceed the investigatory power. However, it is sufficient if the inquiry is within the authority of the agency, the demand is not too indefinite and the information sought is reasonably relevant. The respondent opposing enforcement must shoulder the burden of showing that the subpoena is unreasonable or was issued in bad faith or for an improper purpose, or that compliance would be unnecessarily burdensome.

Construing his arguments liberally, Wells challenges the legitimacy of the investigation, the relevance of his testimony to it, and the SEC's good faith, and asserts violations of due process and the APA. His claims are without merit.

The Formal Order indicates that it was issued because the SEC had information suggesting that securities laws had been violated in connection with the offering and sale of "Telecommunications Technology Securities." The Formal Order reflects a legitimate investigatory purpose.

Moreover, the information sought by the subpoena is relevant to that investigation. We defer to the agency's appraisal of relevancy, which must be accepted so long as it is not obviously wrong. . . . We measure the relevance of the sought-after information against the general purposes of the agency's investigation, which necessarily presupposes an inquiry into the permissible range of investigation under the statute. An affidavit from a governmental official is sufficient to establish a prima facie showing that these requirements have been met.

The Formal Order does not name Wells or RNR, but it does describe companies of a specific and discrete type—a category that includes RNR— and specifies as one reason for the investigation the possible offerings by such companies of unregistered securities. The SEC's allegations concerning RNR's Offering confirm that an inquiry into the offering is within the scope of the Formal Order. Wells has not carried his burden of showing that the subpoena was unreasonable. Although Wells describes in a conclusory fashion the alleged improprieties by SEC personnel, he has altogether failed to demonstrate that the subpoena was sought in bad faith.

Wells contends that his due process rights were violated because the Formal Order (i) did not name RNR, (ii) predated the establishment of RNR and (iii) improperly "encompasses an entire industry." These arguments notwithstanding, the procedures followed by the SEC in Wells's case are authorized. The statute and regulations do not preclude an industry-wide administrative investigation of possible securities law violations where, as set forth in the Formal Order, information before the SEC shows that violations of federal securities laws may have occurred on an industry-wide basis. Nor do they require that the order authorizing the investigation target by name a specific company or person suspected of violating securities laws. The SEC often undertakes investigations into suspicious securities transactions without any knowledge of which of the parties involved may have violated the law. Additionally, there is no requirement that the scope of the investigation be limited to companies that existed before the Formal Order was issued where (as here) the Formal Order expressly provided that the investigation would encompass persons who "are about to engage" in the alleged acts, and the Order remained in effect at the time the subpoenas were issued.

Moreover, [d]ue process does not require notice, either actual or constructive, of an administrative investigation into possible violations of the securities laws. . . .

As we have discussed, the investigation authorized by the Formal Order in this case is within the SEC's authority; the inquiry into possible securities violations related to the Offering falls within the scope of the Formal Order; the information sought by the subpoena served on Wells is relevant to the purpose of the investigation authorized by the Formal Order; and Wells has not shown that the subpoena was unreasonable or issued in bad faith. Neither the securities laws nor the Constitution impose a distinct requirement that, before issuing the subpoena, the SEC issue a Formal Order authorizing by name an investigation of RNR or Wells.

* * *

QUESTIONS

1.   Is it reasonable of the SEC to investigate an entire industry for possible violations of the securities laws? Is it likely to be a good use of enforcement resources?

2.   Should the SEC be required to show probable cause that a violation of the securities laws has occurred in order to have its subpoenas enforced, something not currently required under § 21 of the Exchange Act?

3.   Does the ability of the target of a SEC administrative subpoena to challenge the enforceability of the subpoena in court for bad faith or an improper purpose on the part of the SEC afford much protection to the target?

The following case raises the issue of overlapping SEC and Justice Department investigations. It is not unusual for the SEC to be investigating at the same time as a grand jury is considering a possible indictment. Testimony from an SEC investigation can be used against the witness, not only in the SEC proceeding, but also in a criminal case or in private litigation, such as a class action (the testimony may be obtainable under the Freedom of Information Act after the SEC has concluded its investigation if the witness does not seek confidential treatment). Private parties cannot directly free ride on the SEC's investigative efforts—§ 21(g) of the Exchange Act requires SEC permission for any private action to be consolidated with an SEC injunctive action and such permission will rarely be granted.

SEC administrative proceedings are civil rather than criminal, so the rights afforded criminal defendants do not apply, but witnesses are afforded some protections by the SEC's Rules of Practice. Witnesses giving testimony under oath as part of a formal investigation may be accompanied by counsel (and witnesses cannot be compelled to testify at all in an informal investigation). Moreover, the Fifth Amendment privilege against self-incrimination can be asserted in response to inquiries by the SEC. If a witness invokes his Fifth Amendment right, however, an adverse inference can be drawn against him in the SEC proceeding (but not in any parallel criminal action). In addition, the Fifth Amendment does not protect an individual from having to disclose records that belong to the corporation, even if those records would tend to incriminate the individual. Nor does the Fifth Amendment give the target of an investigation the right to block subpoenas directed to third parties (or even be notified of those subpoenas). See *SEC v. O'Brien*, 467 U.S. 735 (1984). As you read the following case, consider whether cooperation between the SEC and the Justice Department poses risks for the rights of the targets of their investigations.

SEC v. Dresser Industries, Inc.

628 F.2d 1368 (D.C. Cir. 1980).

■ WRIGHT, CHIEF JUDGE.

Dresser Industries, Inc. appeals from a decision of the District Court requiring obedience to a subpoena *duces tecum* issued by the Securities and

Exchange Commission on April 21, 1978, and denying Dresser's motion to quash the subpoena. The subpoena was issued in connection with an SEC investigation into Dresser's use of corporate funds to make what are euphemistically called "questionable foreign payments," and into the adequacy of Dresser's disclosures of such payments under the securities laws.

The principal issue facing this en banc court is whether Dresser is entitled to special protection against this SEC subpoena because of a parallel investigation into the same questionable foreign payments now being conducted by a federal grand jury under the guidance of the United States Department of Justice. Dresser argues principally that the SEC subpoena abuses the civil discovery process of the SEC for the purpose of criminal discovery and infringes the role of the grand jury in independently investigating allegations of criminal wrongdoing. . . .

I. BACKGROUND

A. *Origin of the Investigations*

Illegal and questionable corporate payments surfaced as a major public problem in late 1973, when several major scandals implicated prominent American corporations in improper use of corporate funds to influence government officials in the United States and foreign countries. . . . SEC investigation revealed that many corporate officials were falsifying financial records to shield questionable foreign and domestic payments from exposure to the public and even, in many cases, to corporate directors and accountants.

* * *

[T]he problem of questionable foreign payments proved so widespread that the SEC devised a "Voluntary Disclosure Program" to encourage corporations to conduct investigations of their past conduct and make appropriate disclosures without direct SEC coercion. Participation in the Voluntary Disclosure Program would not insulate a corporation from an SEC enforcement action, but the Commission would be less likely to exercise its discretion to initiate enforcement actions against participants. The most important elements of the Voluntary Disclosure Program were (1) an independent committee of the corporation would conduct a thorough investigation into questionable foreign and domestic payments made by the corporation; (2) the committee would disclose the results of this investigation to the board of directors in full; (3) the corporation would disclose the substance of the report to the public and the SEC on Form 8–K; and (4) the corporation would issue a policy statement prohibiting future questionable and illegal payments and maintenance of false or incomplete records in connection with them. Except in "egregious cases" the SEC would not require that public disclosures include specific names, dates, and places. Rather, the disclosures might be "generic" in form. Thus companies participating in the Voluntary Disclosure Program would ordinarily be spared the consequences to their employees, property, and business that might result from public disclosure of specific instances of foreign bribery or kickbacks. However, companies participating in the Voluntary Disclosure Program had to agree to grant SEC requests for access to the final report and to the unexpurgated underlying documentations.

B. *The Dresser Investigations*

On January 27, 1976 an attorney and other representatives of Dresser met with members of the SEC staff to discuss a proposed filing. At the meeting Dresser agreed to conduct an internal inquiry into questionable foreign payments, in accordance with the terms of the Voluntary Disclosure Program. The next day Dresser submitted a Form 8–K describing, in generic terms, one questionable foreign payment. On November 11, 1976 Dresser filed a second Form 8 K reporting the results of the internal investigation. On February 10, 1977 the company supplemented this report with a third Form 8–K concerning a questionable payment not reported in the earlier reports. The reports concerned Dresser's foreign activities after November 1, 1973. All disclosures were in generic, not specific, terms.

As part of its general monitoring program the SEC staff requested access to the documents underlying Dresser's report. On July 15, 1977 Dresser refused to grant such access. The company argued that allowing the staff to make notes or copies might subject its documents to public disclosure through the Freedom of Information Act. Dresser stated that such disclosure could endanger certain of its employees working abroad. During the ensuing discussions with the staff Dresser attempted to impose conditions of confidentiality upon any SEC examination of its documents, but the staff did not agree. Instead, it issued a recommendation to the Commission for a formal order of investigation in the Dresser case. This recommendation was predicated on the staff's conclusions that Dresser:

1. may have used corporate funds for non-corporate purposes;

2. may have made false and misleading statements concerning the existence of and circumstances surrounding material obligations of Dresser to certain foreign governments and to other entities; and

3. may have made false entries and caused false entries to be made upon the books and records of Dresser, and its affiliates and subsidiaries with respect to, among other things, payments to foreign government officials.

Moreover, the staff reported that Dresser's proxy soliciting materials, reports, and statements may have been misleading with respect to the potential risks involved in its conduct of business through questionable foreign payments, and may have included false statements in connection with such payments. Dresser vigorously opposed issuance of an order of investigation.

Meanwhile, the Department of Justice had established a task force on transnational payments to investigate possible criminal violations arising from illegal foreign payments. Two SEC attorneys participated in the task force. In the summer of 1977 the Justice task force requested access to SEC files on the approximately 400 companies, including Dresser, that had participated in the Voluntary Disclosure Program. Pursuant to Commission authorization the SEC staff transmitted all such files to the Justice task force in August 1977. After its preliminary investigation of the Form 8–K's submitted by Dresser under the Voluntary Disclosure Program, Justice presented Dresser's case to a grand jury in the District of Columbia on January 25, 1978.... [T]he District of Columbia grand jury subpoenaed Dresser's documents on April 21, 1978. At roughly the same time the SEC issued a formal order of private investigation, authorizing the staff to subpoena the documents and to obtain other relevant evidence. Pursuant to that order the staff issued a subpoena *duces tecum*, returnable on May 4, 1978. This subpoena covered substantially the same documents and materials subpoenaed by the grand jury, and more. Dresser did not respond to the subpoena.... On June 30, 1978, the District Court issued a memorandum opinion and order rejecting all of Dresser's objections to the SEC subpoena and requiring Dresser to comply with the subpoena within ten days after notice from the SEC.... This appeal followed.

* * *

II. GENERAL PRINCIPLES

A. *Parallel Investigations*

The civil and regulatory laws of the United States frequently overlap with the criminal laws, creating the possibility of parallel civil and criminal proceedings, either successive or simultaneous. In the absence of substantial prejudice to the rights of the parties involved, such parallel proceedings are unobjectionable under our jurisprudence.

The Constitution, therefore, does not ordinarily require a stay of civil proceedings pending the outcome of criminal proceedings. Nevertheless, a court may decide in its discretion to stay civil proceedings, postpone civil discovery, or impose protective orders and conditions "when the interests of justice seem ( ) to require such action, sometimes at the request of the prosecution, ... sometimes at the request of the defense." The court must make such determinations in the light of the particular circumstances of the case. Other than where there is specific evidence of agency bad faith or malicious governmental tactics, the strongest case for deferring civil proceedings until after completion of criminal proceedings is where a party under indictment for a serious offense is required to defend a civil or administrative action involving the same matter. The noncriminal proceeding, if not deferred, might undermine the party's Fifth Amendment privilege against self-incrimination, expand rights of criminal discovery beyond the limits of Federal Rule of Criminal Procedure 16(b), expose the basis of the defense to the prosecution in advance of criminal trial, or otherwise prejudice the case. If delay of the noncriminal proceeding would not seriously injure the public interest, a court may be justified in deferring it.... In some such cases, however, the courts may adequately protect the government and the private party by merely deferring civil discovery or entering an appropriate protective order. The case at bar is a far weaker one for staying the administrative investigation. No indictment has been returned; no Fifth Amendment privilege is threatened; Rule 16(b) has not come into effect; and the SEC subpoena does not require Dresser to reveal the basis for its defense.

B. *SEC Investigations*

The case at bar concerns enforcement of the securities laws of the United States, especially the Securities Act of 1933, and the Securities Exchange Act of 1934. These statutes explicitly empower the SEC to investigate possible infractions of the securities laws with a view to both civil and criminal enforcement, and to transmit the fruits of its investigations to Justice in the event of potential criminal proceedings. . . . Under the . . . '34 Act the SEC may "transmit such evidence as may be available concerning such acts or practices . . . to the Attorney General, who may, in his discretion, institute the necessary criminal proceedings under this chapter." The '33 Act is to similar effect.

Effective enforcement of the securities laws requires that the SEC and Justice be able to investigate possible violations simultaneously. . . . If the SEC suspects that a company has violated the securities laws, it must be able to respond quickly: it must be able to obtain relevant information concerning the alleged violation and to seek prompt judicial redress if necessary. Similarly, Justice must act quickly if it suspects that the laws have been broken. Grand jury investigations take time, as do criminal prosecutions. If Justice moves too slowly the statute of limitations may run, witnesses may die or move away, memories may fade, or enforcement resources may be diverted. The SEC cannot always wait for Justice to complete the criminal proceedings if it is to obtain the necessary prompt civil remedy; neither can Justice always await the conclusion of the civil proceeding without endangering its criminal case. Thus we should not block parallel investigations by these agencies in the absence of "special circumstances" in which the nature of the proceedings demonstrably prejudices substantial rights of the investigated party or of the government.

* * *

The investigation of Dresser based as it was on the staff's conclusion that Dresser may have engaged in conduct seriously contravening the securities laws falls squarely within the Commission's explicit investigatory authority. . . . Since the validity of summonses or subpoenas "depend(s) ultimately on whether they were among those authorized by Congress," we conclude that this subpoena is enforceable. . . .

Fulfillment of the SEC's civil enforcement responsibilities requires this conclusion . . . [T]he SEC must often act quickly, lest the false or incomplete statements of corporations mislead investors and infect the markets. Thus the Commission must be able to investigate possible securities infractions and undertake civil enforcement actions even after Justice has begun a criminal investigation. For the SEC to stay its hand might well defeat its purpose.

* * *

No one would suggest that the grand jurors, unassisted by accountants, lawyers, or others schooled in the arcana of corporate financial accounting, could sift through the masses of Dresser's corporate documents and arrive at a coherent picture of the company's foreign payments and disclosure practices. In this area, as in many areas of great complexity, the grand jurors are assisted guided and influenced, in fact not only by the United States Attorneys assigned to the investigation, but also by experts provided by the federal regulatory agencies with experience in the particular subject areas. This expert assistance is permitted under Rule 6(e), and it promotes the efficiency and rationality of the criminal investigative process. In this case two SEC agents have been assigned to Justice's task force on transnational payments to assist in the investigation of companies possibly involved in illegal foreign payments. There can be little doubt that the grand jury's deliberations will be influenced by the work of these SEC agents. Any additional influence that might arise as a result of enforcement of the SEC subpoena and transmittal of documents to Justice thereafter is likely to be inconsequential.

We conclude that the danger that enforcement of this subpoena might infringe the role of the grand jury is too speculative and remote at this point to justify so extreme an action as denying enforcement of this subpoena.

In essence, Dresser has launched this attack on the parallel SEC and Justice proceedings in order to obtain protection against the bare SEC proceeding, which it fears will result in public disclosure of sensitive corporate documents. The prejudice Dresser claims it will suffer from the parallel nature of the proceedings is speculative and undefined if indeed Dresser would suffer any prejudice from it at all. Any entitlement to confidential treatment of its documents must arise under the laws pertaining to the SEC; the fortuity of a parallel grand jury investigation cannot expand Dresser's rights in this SEC enforcement action. . . .

IV. COOPERATION BETWEEN SEC AND JUSTICE

Congress understands and approves of the "close working relationship" between the agencies in their investigative capacities. . . . Congress manifestly did not intend that the SEC be forbidden to share information with Justice at this stage of the investigation. . . . In view of Congress' concern that the agencies share information "at the earliest stage of any investigation in order to insure that the evidence needed for a criminal prosecution does not become stale," and that the agencies avoid "a costly duplication of effort," it would be unreasonable to prevent a sharing of information at this point in the investigation. . . . Where the agency has a legitimate noncriminal purpose for the investigation, it acts in good faith even if it might use the information gained in the investigation for criminal enforcement purposes as well. In the present case the SEC plainly has a legitimate noncriminal purpose for its investigation of Dresser. It follows that the investigation is in good faith, in the absence of complicating factors. There is, therefore, no reason to impose a protective order [barring the SEC from sharing information with Justice.]

* * *

Allowing early participation in the case by the United States Attorney minimizes statute of limitations problems. The more time a United States Attorney has, the easier it is for him to become familiar with the complex facts of a securities fraud case, to prepare the case, and to present it to a grand jury before expiration of the applicable statute of limitations. Earlier initiation of criminal proceedings moreover is consistent with a defendant's right to a speedy trial.... On the other side of the balance, the ... concern for preserving the limitations on criminal discovery is largely irrelevant at this stage of the proceedings.... Thus this would be an inappropriate situation to impose a "prophylactic" rule against cooperation between the agencies. We believe the courts can prevent any injustice that may arise in the particular circumstances of parallel investigations in the future.

V. OTHER ISSUES

* * *

Dresser argues that the District Court erred in granting judgment for the SEC without permitting Dresser to conduct discovery into the propriety of the SEC investigation. Although the precise nature of Dresser's desired discovery is not clear, the company apparently would investigate: (1) the SEC criminal referral and the concurrent criminal investigation, with a view to the possibility that the SEC has proceeded in bad faith; (2) the ethical propriety of SEC agents' participation in the criminal investigation; (3) the existence of an SEC commitment of confidentiality; and (4) the basis for the SEC staff's decision to request a formal investigation of Dresser.

We recognize that discovery may be available in some subpoena enforcement proceedings where the circumstances indicate that further information is necessary for the courts to discharge their duty.... However, district courts must be cautious in granting such discovery rights, lest they transform subpoena enforcement proceedings into exhaustive inquisitions into the practices of the regulatory agencies. Discovery should be permitted only where the respondent is able to distinguish himself from "the class of the ordinary (respondent)," by citing special circumstances that raise doubts about the agency's good faith. Even then, district courts must limit discovery to the minimum necessary in the interests of justice by requiring specific interrogatories or affidavits rather than "full-dress discovery and trial."

We conclude that the District Court acted within its discretion in denying Dresser discovery in this case, and that it properly granted judgment to the SEC on the record before it.... Dresser's suggestion that the order of investigation is improper because there was no "likelihood that a violation has been or is about to be committed," does not distinguish Dresser from any other recalcitrant subpoena respondent. At this stage of the investigation neither this court nor the SEC could know whether Dresser has violated the law. The Commission's discretion concerning which potential violators to investigate is, while not unbounded, extremely broad. Dresser has suggested no improper motive for the SEC investigation, Dresser's bare protestations of innocence do not suffice to call the SEC's bona fides into question.

* * *

NOTES

1. *Parallel proceedings.* The usual pattern when the Justice Department has decided to prosecute someone for a securities violation is a coordinated announcement of the criminal indictment and the SEC's enforcement action. The SEC—as a matter of discretion and with the consent of the court—will then typically stay its action until the criminal case has been resolved. If the defendant is convicted, collateral estoppel provides the SEC with an easy case. If the defendant is acquitted, the SEC gets another bite at the apple with the lower preponderance of the evidence standard for civil cases.

2. *Subpoena enforcement.* Enforcement of SEC subpoenas will be denied if the target of the subpoena can demonstrate that the agency is investigating in "bad faith." For a rare example of a target successfully challenging the enforcement of an SEC subpoena, see *SEC v. Wheeling–Pittsburgh Steel Corp.*, 648 F.2d 118 (3d Cir. 1981) (en banc), in which the target of the investigation alleged that the SEC's investigation was prompted by pressure from an influential Senator. Under the circumstances, the appellate court held that the target was entitled to discovery on the issue of the agency's purpose in bringing the investigation.

3. *The Foreign Corrupt Practices Act.* The mid–1970s scandal over bribes paid by U.S. companies to foreign officials led Congress to adopt § 13(b)(2) of the Exchange Act, requiring accurate books and records. Few companies were disclosing the existence of slush funds to pay bribes on their balance sheets. It also led Congress to prohibit directly the payment of bribes in § 30A of the Exchange Act. The latter provision sits rather oddly in the securities laws, as it has no apparent connection to the protection of investors or the regulation of the securities markets. Nonetheless, the SEC is charged with civil enforcement of the provision. (The Justice Department, of course, enforces criminal violations of the law.)

QUESTIONS

1. *Dresser* describes the SEC's efforts in the 1970s to push firms toward adopting internal corporate procedures for "investigation, disclosure, and prevention of illegal corporate payments." Eventually the SEC devised a "Voluntary Disclosure Program" to encourage corporations to conduct investigations of their past conduct and make appropriate disclosures without direct SEC coercion. Are changes in a company's corporate governance an appropriate area for SEC enforcement and use of the court's equitable powers? Does it infringe on state corporate law? Shareholder democracy?

2. What would be the advantages and disadvantages of consolidating criminal and civil enforcement in one agency?

3. Why does the SEC insist on seeing the documents underlying a corporation's internal investigation of wrongdoing?

4. Why is the court concerned that granting a defendant discovery rights could "transform subpoena enforcement into exhaustive inquisitions into the practices of the regulatory agencies"? Doesn't the public have the right to know how the SEC conducts its investigations?

HYPOTHETICAL NINE

Recall that Eve, the former CFO of Mouthwatering, resigned after the board discovered the overstated revenues from Eve's dealings with the Viper's Den. The SEC has subpoenaed Adam's (the CEO of Mouthwatering) email records. Adam is worried about handing over an email that he sent to Eve telling her to "do whatever you have to do to find another $400,000 in revenues" shortly before she booked the contract with the Viper's Den. Does Adam have to turn over his email?

D.   JUDICIAL REVIEW OF ADMINISTRATIVE REMEDIES

SEC orders arising from the agency's administrative proceedings are subject to review either in the court of appeals for the circuit in which the "person aggrieved by a final order of the Commission . . . resides or has his principal place of business, or for the District of Columbia Circuit." Exchange Act § 25(a)(1). Thus, litigants challenging the SEC have a limited choice of fora in which to do so. The D.C. Circuit has delivered a number of key losses for the SEC on points of administrative law, so it is a popular choice for litigants challenging the agency's decisions. Whatever the forum, the SEC enjoys the presumption that its factual findings are correct: "The findings of the Commission as to the facts, if supported by substantial evidence are conclusive." Exchange Act § 25(a)(4). And the agency's interpretation of the law will ordinarily be afforded deference under *Chevron U.S.A. Inc. v. Natural Res. Def. Council*, 467 U.S. 837 (1984), so challenges to SEC action face an uphill battle.

The *KPMG* case below addresses the standards for judicial review of the SEC's administrative actions. It involves a rather nuanced application of the principle that the auditor must be "independent" of the company. The American Institute of Certified Public Accountants (AICPA), the national professional organization for certified public accountants, promulgates a Code of Professional Conduct to govern accountants. Section 302 of the Code provides, in part, that:

A member in public practice shall not

(1) Perform for a contingent fee any professional services for, or receive such a fee from a client for whom the member or the member's firm performs,

    (a) an audit or review of a financial statement. . . .

The *KPMG* opinion also addresses the appropriate standard for cease-and-desist orders under § 21C. Are enforcement proceedings the appropriate means for regulating the accounting profession? Should respondents be afforded greater procedural protections?

KPMG, LLP v. SEC

289 F.3d 109 (D.C. Cir. 2002).

■ ROGERS, CIRCUIT JUDGE.

KPMG, LLP challenges a cease-and-desist order entered by the Securities and Exchange Commission, pursuant to Section 21C(a) of the Securities Exchange Act, on the basis of several violations of the securities laws and regulations. KPMG principally contends that the Commission lacks authority to turn the ancillary authority provided by Section 21C into an independent basis to sanction accountants, failed to give fair notice of its novel interpretation of Rule 302 of the Code of Professional Conduct of the American Institute of Certified Public Accountants ("AICPA"), and adopted an improper presumption in concluding there was a sufficient risk of future violations warranting a cease-and-desist remedy. KPMG also contends that the cease-and-desist order is overbroad and vague. We hold that although KPMG did not have fair notice of the Commission's interpretation of AICPA Rule 302, the Commission properly could use a negligence standard to enforce violations of the Exchange Act and Commission rules under Section 21C. . . .

I.

The Commission issued the cease-and-desist order following an evidentiary hearing that commenced, based on allegations by the Division of Enforcement and the Office of the Chief Accountant, with the issuance on December 4, 1997, of an order instituting a proceeding under Commission Rule of Practice 102(e) and Section 21C of the Exchange Act. . . .

[KPMG lent money to the four founding principals of BayMark, a financial and business consulting firm, and granted BayMark and its subsidiaries, including KPMG BayMark Strategies, the rights to use the "KPMG" name in return for a royalty fee of five percent of BayMark's quarterly consolidated fee income. The SEC Office of the Chief Accountant (OCA), upon becoming aware of KPMG's arrangement with BayMark, warned KPMG against having BayMark provide consulting services to KPMG's audit clients.]

Notwithstanding this warning, on November 3, 1995, Strategies entered into an agreement with PORTA—a long-standing KPMG audit client facing financial difficulties—to provide "turnaround services" and assist it with financing. Leonard Sturm, KPMG's engagement partner for PORTA's 1994 audit, had introduced PORTA to BayMark. Under the agreement between PORTA and Strategies, one of BayMark's founding principals, Edward Olson, would be Chief Operating Officer of PORTA and Strategies would receive a management fee of $250,000 and a "success fee" based on a percentage of PORTA's earnings, disposed inventory, and restructured debt. On November 9, 1995, PORTA's Board of Directors elected Olson president and Chief Operating Officer of the company.

Sturm became aware that PORTA was engaging BayMark and contacted [KPMG's Department of Professional Practice, "DPP"] to determine whether it was okay for BayMark to provide services to an audit client. [Chris Trattou, a KPMG senior manager] indicated that it was okay and that the Commission had no objection to it. Once Sturm learned that Olson was an officer of PORTA, he inquired again as to whether there were any independence concerns with the audit. Trattou discussed the matter with Michael Conway, the partner in charge of the DPP; they disagreed as to the propriety of the arrangement, with Conway . . . expressing concern.

After several meetings in December 1995 between Conway . . . and OCA staff, OCA staff indicated that in order to resolve its independence concerns, KPMG would need to drop the KPMG initials from the BayMark parties' names, eliminate the royalty fee arrangement, and bring about the repayment of the $400,000 in loans made to the BayMark principals. Conway agreed to undertake negotiations with BayMark to make these changes. Although Conway alerted OCA staff to the existence of six dual engagements where KPMG was the auditor of record and BayMark had contracts with those clients, Conway did not inform OCA staff of the detailed entanglements involved with PORTA, i.e., the outstanding loan to Olson, Olson's status as an officer of PORTA and a principal of BayMark, and the success fee arrangement.

The evidence also showed that sometime before December 27, 1995, Trattou called Sturm with an answer to Sturm's earlier independence inquiries. Trattou indicated that the Commission was aware of the PORTA situation and that the KPMG audit of PORTA could proceed. On December 27, 1995, PORTA signed KPMG's engagement letter to conduct its 1995 audit. When OCA staff discovered the PORTA audit, it informed Conway that KPMG was not independent from PORTA because none of the structural changes to the BayMark strategic alliance had been implemented and a loan was outstanding to Olson who was part of PORTA's management. By letter of June 21, 1996, OCA advised PORTA that KPMG's independence had been compromised and that PORTA's audited financial statements included in its 1995 annual report would be considered unaudited and not in compliance with federal securities laws.

* * *

The Commission . . . concluded, on the basis of KPMG's debtor/creditor relationship with Olson and its right to share in Strategies' "success" fee, that KPMG's independence was impaired under [generally accepted accounting standards]. Noting that KPMG admitted that the loan to Olson impaired its independence under GAAS, the Commission characterized the violation as a "serious" mistake that arose from KPMG's failure to exercise ordinary care to maintain its independence. Further, the Commission interpreted AICPA Rule 302 to "flatly prohibit[] an auditor from 'per-for[ming] for a contingent fee any professional services for, or receiv[ing] such a fee' from a client," and found that KPMG violated Rule 302 by receiving such a fee. The Commission concluded that "these relationships, whether considered individually or collectively, impaired [KPMG's] independence." Because of these impairments, the Commission concluded that KPMG violated Rule 2–02(b)(1) of Regulation S–X, which requires that the accountant's report "state whether the audit was made in accordance with generally accepted auditing standards." In addition, the Commission concluded that PORTA violated Section 13(a) of the Exchange Act, and Rule 13a–1, which requires issuers to file reports certified by independent public accountants. The Commission repeated that each of the two impairments (the debtor/creditor relationship and the contingency fee arrangement) "considered on its own, compromised [KPMG's] independence and each is sufficient, on its own, to support our finding of violations of Section 13(a) and Rule 13a–1," and "[s]imilarly, each impairment is sufficient, standing alone, to compromise independence under GAAS and to support our finding of violation of Rule2–02(b)(1)."

Turning to the question of the appropriate sanctions for the violations, the Commission concluded that under Section 21C it could issue a cease-and-desist order for negligent conduct that causes a primary violation of the securities laws and regulations, and that KPMG had acted negligently in determining that it was independent from PORTA. As a result, the Commission issued a cease-and-desist order to KPMG because it acted negligently, which resulted in its primary violation of Rule 2–02(b) of Regulation S–X, and in its being a cause of PORTA's violations of Section 13(a) of the Exchange Act, and Rule 13a–1. The Commission denied KPMG's motion for reconsideration and KPMG appealed to the court.

In Part II, we address KPMG's challenges to the determinations underlying the Commission's decision to issue a cease-and-desist order. In Part III, we address KPMG's challenges to the cease-and-desist order.

II.

KPMG contends that ... it lacked fair notice of the Commission's interpretation of AICPA Rule 302 prohibiting the receipt of contingent fees.... KPMG also contends that negligence is an impermissible basis for a cease-and-desist order against accountants who cause a violation of securities laws or regulations....

A.

* * *

[The SEC's interpretation of AICPA Rule 302 was at odds with AICPA's interpretation. AICPA rejected the SEC's interpretation of Rule 302 because "BayMark was not an accounting firm, and thus not a 'member in public practice,' and because the royalty BayMark was committed to pay KPMG was not linked to the attainment of any 'specified finding or result' and its amount was not 'dependent upon the finding or result' of any professional or other service." The Court reasoned that, at the very least, KPMG lacked any notice of the SEC's novel interpretation of Rule 302. Thus, as a matter of due process, the Court held "that the Commission erred in finding that KPMG had violated AICPA Rule 302 as a result of its arrangement with BayMark and BayMark's arrangement with PORTA."]

* * *

C.

KPMG also challenges the propriety of a negligence standard under Section 21C.... KPMG's contention that the Commission cannot use Section 21C "to bootstrap" its authority to regulate accountants fails on several grounds. First, Rule 102(e) provides that the Commission may sanction accountants in a particular manner. The rule provided at the time of the administrative proceeding that the Commission could "deny, temporarily or permanently, the privilege of appearing or practicing before it" to any accountant who had "engaged in unethical or improper professional conduct" or "willfully violated ... any provision of the Federal securities laws." No such barring order was entered here, and there is nothing in the rule itself to indicate that it is the exclusive means for addressing accountants' conduct. KPMG's contention that the Commission viewed Rule 102(e) to be the exclusive basis for disciplinary actions against accountants is an overstatement....

Second, the premise of KPMG's view that the Commission's invocation of Section 21C is no more than a way to circumvent the scienter requirement of Rule 102(e) is flawed. There is no support for the position that the culpability standards governing Rule 102(e) proceedings can be applied with equal force in Section 21C proceedings. The nature of the two proceedings is different. As the Commission points out, "one is a professional disciplinary proceeding designed to protect the integrity of the Commission's process while the other is a law enforcement proceeding," each involving "fundamentally different remedies.... "

* * *

Moreover, the Commission was virtually compelled by Congress' choice of language in enacting Section 21C to interpret the phrase "an act or omission the person knew or should have known would contribute to such violation" as setting a negligence standard. KPMG contends that the court should give no deference to the Commission's interpretation of Section 21C as regulating accounting negligence as it is an unexplained and unsupportable usurpation of authority. Yet the plain language of Section 21C invokes, as the Commission stated, "classic negligence language."

* * *

III.

KPMG challenges the cease-and-desist order as improper on a variety of grounds, only one of which we conclude has apparent merit....

* * *

The Commission's cease-and-desist order required that KPMG cease and desist from committing present or future violations of Rule 2–02(b) of Regulation S–X, or being the cause of any present or future violation of Section 13(a) of the Exchange Act or Rule 13a–1 thereunder due to an act or omission that KPMG knows or should know will contribute to such violation, by having any transactions, interests or relationships that would impair its independence under Rule 2–01 of Regulation S–X or under GAAS. In addressing KPMG's challenges to the order, our review of the Commission's choice of a sanction is limited by both the Administrative Procedure Act and Supreme Court precedent. The APA limits our inquiry to whether the Commission's sanction was "arbitrary, capricious, an abuse of discretion, or otherwise not in accordance with law." The Supreme Court has long instructed that the Commission's choice of sanction shall not be disturbed by the court unless the sanction is either "unwarranted in law or is without justification in fact."

A.

KPMG contends that the cease-and-desist order is overbroad because it bears no reasonable relation to the violations found. KPMG also contends that the order is unduly vague because by prohibiting all relationships that violate GAAS, the order incorporates broad, open-ended standards that require interpretation and exposes KPMG to the possibility of punishment for making good-faith but incorrect judgments about compliance. Neither contention is persuasive.

Section 21C authorizes the entry of a cease-and-desist order to prohibit "any future violation of the same provision" found to have been violated in the instant case. The provisions at issue are Rule 2–02(b) of Regulation S–X, Section 13(a) of the Exchange Act, and Rule 13a–1 promulgated thereunder. There is, consequently, no "sweeping order to obey the law" as KPMG contends, because the terms of the order are limited to these provisions. Further, the Commission stated that the order "extends only to violative acts 'the threat of which in the future is indicated because of their similarity or relation to those [past] unlawful acts.'" The order thus extends only to a subset of the violations comprehended by the rules and statutory provisions involved, namely those that are independence related. By concluding that the seriousness of KPMG's misconduct, combined with the flaws in its mode of assessing independence, created a serious risk of future independence-impairing relationships beyond the two circumstances at issue, the Commission justified an order aimed at preventing violations flowing from a broader array of independence impairments than the precise ones found. In so doing, it cannot be said that the order has "no reasonable relation to the unlawful practices found to exist."

* * *

Neither is there any requirement on the part of the Commission to tailor its order more narrowly to specific types of violations of the provisions involved. The "any future violation" language in Section 21C makes this clear and the "reasonable relationship" requirement does not impose such a limit. As the Supreme Court observed in *FTC v. Ruberoid Co.*, 343 U.S. 470, 72 (1952), cease-and-desist authority is "not limited to prohibiting the illegal practice in the precise form in which it is found to have existed in the past. If the Commission is to attain the objectives Congress envisioned, it cannot be required to confine its road block to the narrow lane the transgressor has traveled; it must be allowed effectively to close all roads to the prohibited goal, so that its order may not be by-passed with impunity." What KPMG would appear to suggest is required—namely an order so narrow that in the absence of copy-cat violations there would be no possibility of a violation of the order—ignores the expansive language used by Congress....

KPMG's challenge to the cease-and-desist order on vagueness grounds is similarly without merit. KPMG contends that because GAAS standards are "vague and open-ended" the Commission could not properly enjoin compliance with broad prohibitions that require subjective interpretation and complex judgments over which reasonable professionals may disagree. This court has observed ... that cease-and-desist orders should be "sufficiently clear and precise to avoid raising serious questions as to their meaning and application." KPMG nevertheless fails to show that such serious questions will necessarily arise to its detriment.

Section 21C allows for the order to enjoin the "causing [of] such violation and any future violation of the same provision, rule, or regulation." That is all the order did; it ordered KPMG to "cease and desist from committing any violation or future violation of Rule 2–02(b) of Regulation S–X, or from being a cause of any violation or future violation of Section 13(a) of the Securities Exchange Act of 1934 or Rule 13a–1 thereunder." The order merely tracks the statutory language and inserts the relevant provisions. Further, although GAAS may be a complex scheme and reasonable professionals may differ as to its application to discrete sets of facts, it is not a set of indefinite and open-ended standards subject to the whims of the Commission. Rather, as with most provisions of the law, there are broad areas of clarity an instances closer to the line where there will be some doubt. The rule, as amended, effective February 2001, includes examples of when independence will be found lacking, and while nonexclusive, the examples nonetheless inform the general standard.... If KPMG has a disagreement with the Commission as to its interpretation of a GAAS standard, it will have the opportunity to make the case for its interpretation in any contempt proceeding the Commission may institute to adjudicate an alleged violation of the order.

B.

More problematic, however, is KPMG's contention that in entering the cease-and-desist order, the Commission created an improper presumption that a past violation is sufficient evidence of "some risk" of future violation, and applied it in an arbitrary and capricious manner whereby it is, "in essence, irrebutable," ignoring KPMG's evidence of serious remediation and the ALJ's finding there was no future threat of harm. In seeking reconsideration by the Commission, KPMG argued that the Commission had failed to comply with the standard that it had established for issuance of a cease-and-desist order–namely some likelihood of future violation based on proof of some continuing or threatened conduct by KPMG creating an increased likelihood of future violations–and that there was no such evidence. The plain language of Section 21C, as well as the legislative history, undermine KPMG's contention that the Commission erred in proceeding on the basis of a lower risk of future violation than is required for an injunction. However, the precise manner in which the standard is met is unclear from the Commission's analysis on reconsideration.

In its original opinion, the Commission acknowledged that:

> in imposing sanctions, we traditionally have balanced a variety of mitigating and aggravating circumstances, such as the harm caused by the violations, the seriousness of the violations, the extent of the wrongdoer's unjust enrichment, and the wrongdoer's disciplinary record. The questions this case poses are whether, as a matter of either statutory command or in the exercise of our broad discretion, we will require some showing of likelihood of future violations before issuing a cease-and-desist order, and how that showing may be made.

The Commission had stated that a single violation sufficed to show the necessary likelihood. On reconsideration, the Commission explained that, consistent with the history leading up to the enactment of Section 21C, it had applied a standard for showing a risk of future violations that was significantly less than that required for an injunction. To the Commission, "although 'some risk' of future violations is necessary, it need not be very great to warrant issuing a cease-and-desist order and that in the ordinary case and absent evidence to the contrary, a finding of past violation raises a sufficient risk of future violation." Disclaiming that issuance of a cease-and-desist order is "automatic" on a finding of past violation, the Commission stated that "[a]long with the risk of future violations, we will continue to consider our traditional factors in determining whether a cease-and-desist order is an appropriate sanction based on the entire record."

The Commission proceeded to reject KPMG's argument that the violative conduct was isolated, inadvertent, and unconnected to any ongoing conduct or engagement. Rather, the Commission explained, that although "the isolated nature of the violations tended to counsel against relief ... we did not, and do not, consider the lack of care at senior levels that attended the independence determinations in this case to have been merely inadvertent or to be 'unconnected' to any ongoing conduct or engagement." The risk of future violations arises here, the Commission explained, "from the manifestly inadequate level of scrutiny given to independence issues and [KPMG's] consistent failure to recognize the seriousness of this misconduct." The Commission then noted that the loan to Olson, an officer of a registrant, was, in the words of a witness, "an absolute blatant out-and-out violation" of GAAS.

* * *

IV.

Accordingly, because KPMG lacked fair notice of the Commission's interpretation of AICPA Rule 302, we reverse the Commission's finding that the "success" fee/royalty arrangement violated that rule.... We affirm the Commission's determination that negligence is an appropriate basis for violations underlying a Section 21C cease-and-desist order, and reject KPMG's contentions that the order is overbroad and vague....

QUESTIONS

1. Do you agree that a negligence standard is a sufficient basis for the entry of a cease-and-desist order against "other persons" who "contribute to such violation" under § 21C?

2. Why wasn't the SEC's cease-and-desist order against KPMG void for overbreadth?

3. Why wasn't the SEC's cease-and-desist order against KPMG void for vagueness?

4. Is it sufficient that under the cease-and-desist order KPMG can dispute the SEC's interpretation of law in a contempt proceeding?

HYPOTHETICAL TEN

Apple & Tree is the accounting firm for Mouthwatering. Eve, the former CFO of Mouthwatering had maintained a secret slush fund of $500,000 from which she paid bribes to foreign officials. Seth, a junior accountant at Apple & Tree, earlier spilled the beans to the SEC on the audit partner at Apple & Tree for Mouthwatering, John Apple, for ignoring Eve's slush fund in the course of the audit. What sanctions can the SEC apply to John Apple and Apple & Tree in a § 21C proceeding?

E.   JUDICIAL REMEDIES

For more serious violations of the securities laws, the SEC is likely to seek relief in federal district court. The SEC has a broader range of sanctions available to it in court than it does in an administrative cease and desist proceeding. These sanctions include court injunctions against future violations, corporate governance reforms, disgorgement and civil penalties. In an extreme case, the SEC has even succeeded in having a new board of directors appointed by the court. See *International Controls Corp. v. Vesco*, 490 F.2d 1334 (2d Cir. 1974) (approving appointment of interim board of directors). Although § 21C provides for disgorgement from auditors who violate their whistleblowing duties, the SEC may seek disgorgement more generally from any defendant under a court's equitable powers.

1.   INJUNCTIONS

Section 21(d)(1) of the Exchange Act and its counterpart, § 20(b) of the Securities Act, authorize the SEC to file an action in the appropriate district court to enjoin violations of the securities laws, regulations thereunder, and the rules of the SROs. The SEC does not need to show irreparable injury or the inadequacy of other remedies in order to obtain an injunction. The *Aaron* case below addresses the question of the state of mind that the SEC must show when it seeks to halt the fraudulent sale of securities. *Aaron* involves the SEC's motion for an injunction based on violations of the antifraud provisions found in § 17(a) of the Securities Act and Rule 10b–5 and § 10(b) of the Exchange Act.

Aaron v. SEC

446 U.S. 680 (1980).

■ Mr. Justice Stewart delivered the opinion of the Court.

The issue in this case is whether the Securities and Exchange Commission is required to establish scienter as an element of a civil enforcement action to enjoin violations of Section 17(a) of the Securities Act of 1933, Section 10(b) of the Securities Exchange Act of 1934, and Commission Rule 10b–5 promulgated under that section of the 1934 Act.

I

When the events giving rise to this enforcement proceeding occurred, the petitioner was a managerial employee at E. L. Aaron & Co., a registered broker-dealer with its principal office in New York City. Among other responsibilities at the firm, the petitioner was charged with supervising the sales made by its registered representatives and maintaining the so-called "due diligence" files for those securities in which the firm served as a market maker. One such security was the common stock of Lawn–A–Mat Chemical & Equipment Corp., a company engaged in the business of selling lawn-care franchises and supplying its franchisees with products and equipment.

Between November 1974 and September 1975, two registered representatives of the firm, Norman Schreiber and Donald Cainson, conducted a sales campaign in which they repeatedly made false and misleading statements in an effort to solicit orders for the purchase of Lawn–A–Mat common stock. . . .

Upon receiving several complaints from prospective investors, an officer of Lawn–A–Mat informed Schreiber and Cainson that their statements were false and misleading and requested them to cease making such statements. This request went unheeded. Thereafter, Milton Kean, an attorney representing Lawn–A–Mat, communicated with the petitioner twice by telephone. In these conversations, Kean informed the petitioner that Schreiber and Cainson were making false and misleading statements and described the substance of what they were saying. The petitioner, in addition to being so informed by Kean, had reason to know that the statements were false, since he knew that the reports in Lawn–A–Mat's due diligence file indicated a deteriorating financial condition and revealed no plans for manufacturing a new car and tractor. Although assuring Kean that the misrepresentations would cease, the petitioner took no affirmative steps to prevent their recurrence. The petitioner's only response to the telephone calls was to inform Cainson of Kean's complaint and to direct him to communicate with Kean. Otherwise, the petitioner did nothing to prevent the two registered representatives under his direct supervision from continuing to make false and misleading statements in promoting Lawn–A–Mat common stock.

In February 1976, the Commission filed a complaint in the District Court for the Southern District of New York against the petitioner and seven other defendants in connection with the offer and sale of Lawn–A–Mat common stock. In seeking preliminary and final injunctive relief pursuant to § 20(b) of the 1933 Act and § 21(d) of the 1934 Act, the Commission alleged that the petitioner had violated and aided and abetted violations of three provisions—§ 17(a) of the 1933 Act, § 10(b) of the 1934 Act, and Commission Rule 10b–5 promulgated under that section of the 1934 Act.

The gravamen of the charges against the petitioner was that he knew or had reason to know that the employees under his supervision were engaged in fraudulent practices, but failed to take adequate steps to prevent those practices from continuing.

* * *

We granted certiorari to resolve the conflict in the federal courts as to whether the Commission is required to establish scienter—an intent on the part of the defendant to deceive, manipulate, or defraud[5]—as an element of a Commission enforcement action to enjoin violations of § 17(a), § 10(b), and Rule 10b–5.

II

The two substantive statutory provisions at issue here are § 17(a) of the 1933 Act, and § 10(b) of the 1934 Act. . . .

The civil enforcement mechanism for these provisions consists of both express and implied remedies. One express remedy is a suit by the Commission for injunctive relief. Section 20(b) of the 1933 Act provides:

> Whenever it shall appear to the Commission that any person is engaged or about to engage in any acts or practices which constitute or will constitute a violation of the provisions of this subchapter, or of any rule or regulation prescribed under authority thereof, it may in its discretion, bring an action in any district court of the United States . . . to enjoin such acts or practices, and upon a proper showing a permanent or temporary injunction or restraining order shall be granted without bond.

---

5. The term "scienter" is used throughout this opinion, as it was in *Ernst & Ernst v. Hochfelder*, 425 U.S. 185, 194, n. 12, to refer to "a mental state embracing intent to deceive, manipulate, or defraud." We have no occasion here to address the question, reserved in *Hochfelder*, whether, under some circumstances, scienter may also include reckless behavior.

Similarly, § 21(d) of the 1934 Act authorizes the Commission to seek injunctive relief whenever it appears that a person "is engaged or is about to engage in acts or practices [constituting]" a violation of the 1934 Act, or regulations promulgated thereto, and requires a district court "upon a proper showing" to grant injunctive relief. . . .

The issue here is whether the Commission in seeking injunctive relief either under § 20(b) for violations of § 17(a), or under § 21(d) for violations of § 10(b) or Rule 10b–5, is required to establish scienter. Resolution of that issue could depend upon (1) the substantive provisions of § 17(a), § 10(b), and Rule 10b–5, or (2) the statutory provisions authorizing injunctive relief "upon a proper showing," § 20(b) and § 21(d). We turn to an examination of each to determine the extent to which they may require proof of scienter.

[The court held that scienter is a necessary element of a violation of § 10(b) and Rule 10b–5 based on its prior holding in *Ernst & Ernst v. Hochfelder*, excerpted in Chapter 5. In contrast, while the Court found that the language of § 17(a) requires scienter, the Court held that scienter was not required under either § 17(a)(2) or § 17(a)(3).]

* * *

There remains to be determined whether the provisions authorizing injunctive relief, § 20(b) of the 1933 Act and § 21(d) of the 1934 Act, modify the substantive provisions at issue in this case so far as scienter is concerned.

The language and legislative history of § 20(b) and § 21(d) both indicate that Congress intended neither to add to nor to detract from the requisite showing of scienter under the substantive provisions at issue. Sections 20(b) and 21(d) provide that the Commission may seek injunctive relief whenever it appears that a person "is engaged or [is] about to engage in any acts or practices" constituting a violation of the 1933 or 1934 Acts or regulations promulgated thereunder and that, "upon a proper showing," a district court shall grant the injunction. The elements of "a proper showing" thus include, at a minimum, proof that a person is engaged in or is about to engage in a substantive violation of either one of the Acts or of the regulations promulgated thereunder. Accordingly, when scienter is an element of the substantive violation sought to be enjoined, it must be proved before an injunction may issue. But with respect to those provisions such as § 17(a)(2) and § 17(a)(3), which may be violated even in the absence of scienter, nothing on the face of § 20(b) or § 21(d) purports to impose an independent requirement of scienter. And there is nothing in the legislative history of either provision to suggest a contrary legislative intent.

This is not to say, however, that scienter has no bearing at all on whether a district court should enjoin a person violating or about to violate § 17(a)(2) or § 17(a)(3). In cases where the Commission is seeking to enjoin a person "about to engage in any acts or practices which . . . will constitute" a violation of those provisions, the Commission must establish a sufficient evidentiary predicate to show that such future violation may occur. An important factor in this regard is the degree of intentional wrongdoing evident in a defendant's past conduct. Moreover, as the Commission recognizes, a district court may consider scienter or lack of it as one of the aggravating or mitigating factors to be taken into account in exercising its equitable discretion in deciding whether or not to grant injunctive relief. And the proper exercise of equitable discretion is necessary to ensure a "nice adjustment and reconciliation between the public interest and private needs."

III

For the reasons stated in this opinion, we hold that the Commission is required to establish scienter as an element of a civil enforcement action to enjoin violations of § 17(a)(1) of the 1933 Act, § 10(b) of the 1934 Act, and Rule 10b–5 promulgated under that section of the 1934 Act. We further hold that the Commission need not establish scienter as an element of an action to enjoin violations of § 17(a)(2) and § 17(a)(3) of the 1933 Act. . . .

NOTES

1. *Section 17(a).* Section 17(a) is one of the few provisions of the Securities Act that applies to aftermarket sales of securities, as well as their distribution from issuers and their affiliates. The Court's opinion in *Aaron*, allowing the SEC to get an injunction for negligent conduct under §§ 17(a)(2) & (a)(3), has made § 17 a mainstay of SEC enforcement actions. Section 17 applies only to any person engaged in the "offer and sale of any security." Purchasers do not face liability under § 17. Thus, the SEC only needs to resort to Exchange Act § 10(b) and Rule 10b–5 when the defendant has committed fraud in the *purchase* of securities (a considerably less common phenomenon). Private plaintiffs have not been so fortunate, as most courts have held that § 17 does not create a private cause of action, leaving private plaintiffs to the more difficult Rule 10b–5 cause of action (discussed in Chapter 5).

2. *Collateral consequences.* The most important collateral consequence of an injunction is the reputational hit that the defendant will take when the injunction is announced. The SEC prolongs this effect on one's reputation by requiring disclosure an injunction against violating the securities laws entered within the last five years under Regulation S–K Item 401, which is incorporated by reference into a variety of required SEC filings. SEC cease-and-desist orders also must be disclosed. An injunction also triggers a variety of "bad boy" disqualifiers for certain non-registered offerings. Rule 262 of the Securities Act, for example, precludes an issuer from making a Regulation A offering if the issuer was subject within the prior five years to an injunction against, among other things, "making of any false filing with the Commission."

QUESTIONS

1. What state of mind must the SEC show to get an injunction for violations of substantive provisions that impose strict liability, such as § 5 of the Securities Act?

2. Is there a policy basis for distinguishing fraud in the purchase of securities (which requires scienter under Rule 10b–5 of the Exchange Act) from fraud in the sale of securities (which does not require scienter under §§ 17(a)(2) and (3) of the Securities Act)?

3. Why would Congress specify varying requirements for state of mind in the different provisions of § 17?

2. OTHER CIVIL REMEDIES

The other remedies available to the SEC in court go well beyond an injunction against future violations. The agency can also seek disgorgement of any ill-gotten gains from the defendant and a range of civil penalties. In addition, it can seek to bar a defendant from serving as an officer or director of a public company. The next two cases address the standards for awarding the various forms of relief available to the SEC.

Sargent deals with Rule 14e–3, promulgated under § 14(e) of the Exchange Act (discussed more fully in Chapter 6). Rule 14e–3 prohibits trades based on material, nonpublic information pertaining to a tender offer if the trading party knows or should know that the information derives from either the acquirer or target company or someone working on behalf of either entity. At issue in the *Sargent* case is the heightened civil penalties for insider trading violations that Congress enacted in the Insider Trading and Securities Fraud Enforcement Act of 1988.

SEC v. Sargent

329 F.3d 34 (1st Cir. 2003).

■ Torruella, Circuit Judge.

Defendant-appellee Dennis J. Shepard illegally shared confidential information regarding an upcoming tender offer with defendant-appellee Michael G. Sargent, who profited by using the information to trade in the target's stock. Sargent recommended the target's stock to co-defendant Robert Scharn, who also realized profits on the trades. In a civil enforcement action brought by plaintiff-appellant Securities and Exchange Commission against Shepard and Sargent, a jury found the defendants liable for violating Section 14(e) of the Securities Exchange Act, and Rule 14e–3 thereunder. As a remedy, the district court disgorged the defendants of the illicit profits. The SEC appeals the district court's denial of injunctive relief . . . and civil penalties. After careful review, we affirm.

I. Facts

In 1994, Purolator Products, a publicly held manufacturer of automotive parts, was the target of acquisition efforts by Mark IV Industries, Incorporated. Defendant Shepard and J. Anthony Aldrich (against whom the Commission did not file a complaint) were the sole shareholders of a consulting firm. Aldrich, a member of the board of directors for the target, had nonpublic information that Purolator and Mark IV were involved in negotiations regarding Mark IV's acquisition proposal. In July 1994, Aldrich shared the information with Shepard. Shepard agreed not to disclose the information and indicated that he understood his obligation to maintain its confidentiality.

On Saturday, September 10, 1994, Shepard told Sargent, his friend and dentist, that Aldrich was on the Purolator board and he stated, "I am aware of a company right now that is probably going to be bought," but "even if I had the money I can't buy stock in this company because I am too close to the situation." The following Monday, Sargent contacted his broker and asked him to do some research on Purolator. Sargent thereafter purchased a total of 20,400 shares of Purolator. Sargent also notified his close friend Scharn of his purchases in Purolator. Scharn then purchased 5,000 shares of Purolator. Within a few days of the tender offer announcement, Sargent sold all of his Purolator stock at a profit of $141,768. Scharn sold his shares at a profit of $33,100.

The SEC filed the current action in March 1996, charging Shepard, Sargent, Scharn, and a fourth defendant with tipping and/or trading in violation of Exchange Act Section 10(b), Rule 10b–5, Section 14(e), and Rule 14e–3 and seeking injunctive relief, disgorgement, prejudgment interest, and civil penalties. The . . . jury found Shepard and Sargent liable for violations of Section 14(e) and Rule 14e–3 but did not find them liable for violations of Section 10(b) and Rule 10b–5. The jury found Scharn not liable on all counts.

On March 27, 2002, the district court issued an amended final judgment ordering Sargent and Shepard jointly and severally liable for disgorgement of Sargent's and Scharn's trading profits, a total of $174,868. The court declined to enter an injunction against future violations. The court also refused to order the defendants to pay prejudgment interest on the disgorgement amount and to assess penalties pursuant to the Insider Trading and Securities Fraud Enforcement Act of 1988, codified in Section 21A(a) of the Exchange Act. This appeal of the district court's denial of an injunction, interest, and penalties followed.

* * *

The SEC argues that the district court relied on an erroneous legal standard in refusing to grant an injunction against future violations of securities laws. The agency claims that the court believed that defendants must pose a "relatively imminent" threat of recidivism in order to justify permanent injunctive relief. We disagree, finding instead that the district court reached the proper conclusion under the correct standard.

The Securities and Exchange Act permits the SEC to seek an injunction in federal district court to prevent violations of securities laws. Section 21(d). Such an injunction is appropriate where there is, "at a minimum, proof that a person is engaged in or is about to engage in a substantive violation of either one of the Acts or of the regulations promulgated thereunder." This court has upheld issuance of injunctions in cases where future violations were likely. . . .

The reasonable likelihood of future violations is typically assessed by looking at several factors, none of which is determinative. Courts consider, among other things, the nature of the violation, including its egregiousness and its isolated or repeated nature, as well as whether the defendants will, owing to their occupation, be in a position to violate again. The courts also take into account whether the defendants have recognized the wrongfulness of their conduct.

Under these factors, the district court acted within its discretion in denying an injunction with respect to Shepard. Shepard disclosed confidential information to Sargent, but this was a first-time violation. As the SEC admits, Shepard's violation was not an egregious one, particularly where he neither traded on the information himself nor derived any direct personal profit. Further, his current position as president of a web-casting company does not put him in a position where future violations are likely. We therefore affirm the denial of an injunction against Shepard.

With respect to Sargent, there was also no abuse of discretion on the part of the district court in denying an injunction. Sargent's violation was isolated and unsophisticated: he simply put two and two together and, based on a casual conversation, invested in one company without attempting to conceal his trades. Sargent is unlikely to be privy to insider information either through his occupation as a dentist or because of his wife's position as a consultant. Further, Sargent's acceptance of the jury verdict without further appeal is sufficient acknowledgment of the wrongfulness of his conduct. The district court's denial of an injunction against Sargent is affirmed.

* * *

V. Civil Penalties

Finally, the SEC seeks reversal of the denial of Congressionally-provided civil penalties, which can amount to a maximum of three times the illicit profits realized (or losses avoided), and are intended to "penalize [the] defendant for ... illegal conduct." In evaluating whether or not to assess civil penalties, a court may take seven factors into account, such as: (1) the egregiousness of the violations; (2) the isolated or repeated nature of the violations; (3) the defendant's financial worth; (4) whether the defendant concealed his trading; (5) what other penalties arise as the result of the defendant's conduct; and (6) whether the defendant is employed in the securities industry.

Applying these factors, we find no reason to reverse the district court with regard to civil penalties for Shepard. Shepard's violations consisted of a one-time tip to Sargent, and, as stated above, he did not personally realize any trades or direct profit. He, therefore, is left $174,868 worse off than he was prior to the activity for which he is liable. Further, he is not directly involved in the securities business, and he cooperated with and responded honestly to authorities. Finally, Shepard's financial net worth is not so high as to require civil penalties.

Applying the ... factors to Sargent, we also find that the district court acted within its discretion in refusing to assess civil penalties. Sargent was an outsider who made no efforts to conceal his isolated transaction, which involved trading in the same stock during a short period of time and, as discussed in part III above, was not an egregious violation of securities laws. He is not employed in the securities industry. While he may have a high net worth, that factor alone does not merit reversal of the district court's denial of civil penalties. Further, Sargent was criminally convicted for his actions, and the sanction imposed in the criminal case—a year's probation and a $5,000 fine–also tempers the need for an additional monetary penalty.

* * *

QUESTIONS

1. The SEC argued that the lower court inappropriately applied a "relatively imminent threat" test to determine whether to grant the SEC an injunction. The First Circuit said that an injunction is appropriate "where future violations were likely." How do the two tests differ?

2. The First Circuit's test for the application of a securities law injunction focuses on the possibility of future misconduct. Does this focus undermine any purpose of the securities laws?

3. Why should the application of civil penalties turn on net worth? We don't apply a financial net worth test to determine the appropriate fine for a speeding ticket. How do securities violations differ?

SEC v. First Pac. Bancorp
142 F.3d 1186 (9th Cir. 1998).

■ FERNANDEZ, CIRCUIT JUDGE.

The Securities and Exchange Commission brought a civil enforcement action against Leonard S. Sands, First Pacific Bancorp, and PacVen Inc. for violations of the antifraud, filing and disclosure provisions of the federal securities laws. The district court granted partial summary judgment in favor of the SEC on three of its claims. After a bench trial, the court ruled in favor of the SEC on all of its remaining claims. Sands, Bancorp and PacVen appeal the district court's grant of partial summary judgment. They also appeal the court's final judgment, which permanently enjoins them from future violations of the securities laws, orders them to disgorge $688,000 plus pre-judgment interest, and permanently bars Sands from acting as an officer or director of a public company. We affirm.

BACKGROUND

Sands was the chairman of the board, chief executive officer and corporate counsel of Bancorp, a Delaware corporation organized as a bank holding company, and owned 54% of its common stock. Sands was also the chairman of the board and corporate counsel of First Pacific Bank, Inc.

(Bank), the wholly owned subsidiary of Bancorp and its major asset. In addition, Sands was the president and the CEO of PacVen, a Nevada "blank check," also known as "shell," corporation formed for the purpose of merging with or acquiring other companies.

Beginning in the early 1980s, state and federal regulators repeatedly rated the Bank "unsatisfactory" because of its inadequate capital, earnings and liquidity, and because of its increasing amounts of classified assets and past due loans. In the late 1980s, Bancorp and Sands engaged in several financial transactions designed to raise additional capital for the failing Bank. They committed various securities law violations in the process.

The transaction which underlies most of the issues in this appeal was the Bancorp's 1987 public offering of securities. In April of 1987, it commenced a "mini-max" public offering with the intention of down-streaming its proceeds to the financially troubled Bank. Under the terms of the offering, Bancorp was required to sell a minimum of 750 "units," at $2,000 each, on an all-or-nothing basis by August 12, 1987. The underwriter later extended the deadline to October 10, 1987. If all 750 units were not sold by the deadline, the offering was to be cancelled and the funds were to be returned to the investors. . . .

On October 9, 1987, $1,688,000 was forwarded to the escrow agent for investment in the Bancorp offering, but of those funds, $1,000,000 was in the form of a check. . . . That check was later returned unpaid. Also, $500,000 had been raised in a public offering by PacVen in July of 1987, and was fraudulently diverted by Sands into the Bancorp offering. Thus, Bancorp only succeeded in raising $688,000 by the deadline, and only $188,000 of the funds came from bona fide investors.

However, Sands and Bancorp did not return the funds to the investors as they had promised in the Prospectus, but instead continued with the offering. On December 30, 1987, the date the offering was scheduled to close, Sands purchased 500 of the Bancorp units, paying $1,000,000 of his own funds. That purchase brought the total amount to $1,688,000. The offering was then closed and the proceeds were delivered to the Bank.

Among other things, the SEC sought to have Sands, Bancorp and PacVen disgorge the $688,000 raised in the Bancorp offering from outside investors, and to have Sands barred from serving as an officer or director of publicly held companies in the future. The district court granted both forms of relief and this appeal ensued.

* * *

A. DISGORGEMENT

Sands and Bancorp object to the district court's grant of summary judgment against them on the SEC's claim that their handling of the Bancorp offering constituted securities fraud. Sands also claims that even if the summary judgment were proper, he should not have been ordered to disgorge $688,000. . . .

(1) The summary judgment

* * *

Rule 10b–9 expressly provides that funds invested in the mini-max offering must be promptly refunded to the investors unless "(i) a specified number of units of the security are sold at a specified price within a specified time, and (ii) the total amount due to the seller is received by him by a specified date." Thus, Bancorp had to receive "the total amount due" to it, i.e. $1,500,000, by the October 10 deadline. A check is merely a "promise to pay." As this case vividly demonstrates, the receipt of a "promise to pay" $1,000,000 is not equivalent to the receipt of the actual "amount due" because the check may fail to clear.

* * *

Sands' main contention, however, is that he had "bona fide" intentions at the time of his investment in the offering, and he did not, therefore, act with the requisite scienter. This argument goes very wide of the mark. The fact that Sands made a real investment is not determinative because that investment occurred after the Bancorp offering had already failed to satisfy the minimum requirement. If he wanted to invest, fine. But the other investors' funds should have been returned to them.

In a mini-max offering, scienter is shown by a defendant's knowledge of the minimum requirement, and that the funds were retained even though the minimum amount was not raised.

* * *

When the $1,000,000 check ... was returned unpaid, Sands knew that Bancorp had failed to raise $1,500,000 as was required by the terms of the offering. But instead of refunding $688,000 to the investors, Sands retained those funds and proceeded to close the offering by investing $1,000,000 of his own money. That itself was fraudulent. . . . Thus, regardless of his long term intentions at the time of the investment, the knowing retention of the monies that others invested into Bancorp's failed offering satisfied the scienter requirement, and the district court did not err in granting summary judgment on that issue.

(2) The disgorgement order against Sands

The district court has broad equity powers to order the disgorgement of "ill-gotten gains" obtained through the violation of the securities laws. Disgorgement is designed to deprive a wrongdoer of unjust enrichment, and to deter others from violating securities laws by making violations unprofitable. Further, where two or more individuals or entities collaborate or have a close relationship in engaging in the violations of the securities laws, they have been held jointly and severally liable for the disgorgement of illegally obtained proceeds. Sands played the principal role in the fraudulent activities in connection with the Bancorp offering. He fraudulently diverted $500,000 from PacVen and later invested his own funds in order to close an offering that had already failed to meet the minimum requirement. As the chairman of the board, the CEO and the majority shareholder of Bancorp, and as the president and the CEO of PacVen, Sands clearly enjoyed a "close relationship" with those corporate codefendants. It was appropriate to hold Sands and his corporate codefendants jointly and severally liable for their jointly undertaken violations of the securities laws.

Sands argues that he should not have been ordered to disgorge the proceeds of the offering because he received no personal financial benefit as a result of that offering. We reject the argument. The infusion of capital from the Bancorp offering put off a bank failure and enabled the Bank to remain in operation for two and a half more years. During that time, Sands engaged in what the district court's findings characterized as "milking the asset," by paying himself hundreds of thousands of dollars in salaries, commissions, and consulting, management and legal fees.... The FDIC inspector found that Sands was paying himself excessive compensation, which amounted to two or three times what a CEO of a comparable, well-managed institution would receive.... Thus, Sands received substantial personal benefit from the infusion of the illegally obtained proceeds from the Bancorp offering into the failing Bank, which justified the district court's order directing Sands to disgorge those proceeds.[6]

* * *

B. OFFICER AND DIRECTOR BAR

Sands earnestly argues that he should not have been "permanently and unconditionally prohibited from acting as an officer or director of any issuer required to file reports pursuant to Sections 12(b), 12(g) or 15(d) of the Securities Exchange Act of 1934." We have listened carefully to his monody, but we agree with the district court that protection of the public justifies the bar....

The district court has broad equitable powers to fashion appropriate relief for violations of the federal securities laws, which include the power to order an officer and director bar. In addition to the court's inherent equitable powers, the Securities Enforcement Remedies and Penny Stock Reform Act of 1990 authorizes the court to order an officer and director bar "if the person's conduct demonstrates substantial unfitness to serve as an officer or director." § 21(d)(2). In determining whether to order the bar, a court may consider: "(1) the 'egregiousness' of the underlying securities law violation; (2) the defendant's 'repeat offender' status; (3) the defendant's 'role' or position when he engaged in the fraud; (4) the defendant's

---

6. The district court was not required to trace every dollar of the offering proceeds fraudulently retained by Sands. The amount he was ordered to disgorge had to be only "a reasonable approximation of profits causally connected to the violation." Nor does the fact that Sands' scheme ultimately failed and he lost a $1,000,000 of his own funds release him from his obligations toward the defraud-ed investors. As Judge Friendly once stated in a securities manipulation case, there is "no reason why, in determining how much should be disgorged in a case where defendants have manipulated securities so as to mulct the public, the court must give them credit for the fact that they had not succeeded in unloading all their purchases at the time when the scheme collapsed."

degree of scienter; (5) the defendant's economic stake in the violation; and (6) the likelihood that misconduct will recur."

The district court considered those factors, and found that Sands' "securities violations are egregious; he caused the collapse of a federally insured bank; he attempted to stymie banking regulators from doing their jobs; he is a recidivist; and the fraudulent conduct he committed occurred while serving in a corporate or fiduciary capacity." The district court also found that Sands had a high level of scienter, that he engaged in ongoing and recurrent violations, that he had failed to assume any responsibility for his violations of law, that he utterly failed to recognize the wrongful nature of his conduct, and that there was a strong likelihood of future violations. We see no error in those detailed findings.... We think we need only briefly comment on his audacious argument that the officer and director bar is against the public interest because it will interfere with his active involvement in charitable activities. Perhaps he is right that charities will not want to place him in positions of high visibility and prestige. If so, and if Sands does have a genuine interest in doing charitable works, we are certain that he can continue his charitable involvement in a less prestigious, but just as worthy, capacity. We touch on this argument because it underscores the purblindness of Sands and the perspicacity of the district court.

CONCLUSION

Sands, a sophisticated businessman and a lawyer, has engaged in numerous activities in violation of the securities laws and basic notions of right and wrong. He perpetuated a number of frauds upon investors and regulators. We need not sort out whether his principles are just plain wrong, or whether he is afflicted with akrasia, or whether there is some other explanation for his actions. What is clear is that he, along with Bancorp and PacVen, must disgorge the amounts that the unwitting investors were relieved of. Equally clear, the district court properly barred him from assuming a position from which he could inflict similar wrongs in the future.

AFFIRMED

NOTES

1. *Remedies.* The SEC's enforcement arsenal has been supplemented by the Sarbanes–Oxley Act. Exchange Act § 21C(c) allows the SEC to ask a court to temporarily freeze assets to prevent a company from making "extraordinary payments" to its officers and directors. This adds to the SEC's authority under § 21(d) to seek preliminary injunctive relief against persons who may be violating or about to violate the federal securities laws. The SEC can also seek to bar a person from participating in future penny stock offerings if their misconduct involved a penny stock offering (an investment sector well known for its serial fraudsters). Section 21(d)(6). The standard for the SEC to seek a directors and officers bar was changed from "substantial unfitness" to simply "unfitness." Finally, § 21(d)(5) authorizes the SEC to "seek, and Federal court may grant, any equitable relief that may be appropriate or necessary for the benefit of investors." This affirms the longstanding practice of the courts, which have repeatedly held that their inherent equitable powers enable them to fashion appropriate remedies.

In addition to the remedies outlined here, the SEC has a whole pantheon of remedies available for use against investment professionals, such as broker-dealers, investment companies and investment advisors. Most of these remedies are available in both administrative and court proceedings.

2. *Disgorgement.* The SEC has traditionally attempted to restore ill-gotten gains to defrauded investors when possible. If it is not possible to identify the victims, the money goes to the U.S. Treasury. That practice has been validated and expanded by the "Fair Funds for Investors" provision of the Sarbanes–Oxley Act, which makes providing relief to investors a priority—both disgorgement and civil penalties (which were previously paid to the Treasury) are now to be committed to investor compensation. Plaintiffs' attorneys are not a priority, however—§ 21(d)(4) prohibits the payment of disgorged funds "as payment for attorneys fees or expenses incurred by private parties seeking distribution of the disgorged funds."

Measuring the amount to be disgorged can sometimes be difficult. The SEC must show that "its disgorgement figure reasonably approximates the amount of unjust enrichment," but a showing of "actual profits on the tainted transactions at least presumptively" satisfies the government's burden, at which point the burden shifts to the defendant to show why his actual profits are not equivalent to his unjust enrichment. *SEC v. First City Financial Corp.*, 890 F.2d 1215, 1232 (D.C. Cir. 1989). This measurement issue creates the possibility for dueling econometric experts.

Disgorgement orders also stick with defendants—they are not dischargeable in bankruptcy if the violation involved fraudulently obtaining money. *SEC v. Bilzerian*, 153 F.3d 1278 (11th Cir. 1998).

QUESTIONS

1. As an investor, why would you care whether a public offering is conducted on a "mini-max" basis?

2. What is "akrasia"?

3. Is investor compensation the best use of the money recovered by the SEC?

4. How should a court determine whether an equitable remedy sought by the SEC is "appropriate or necessary for the benefit of investors"?

HYPOTHETICAL ELEVEN

The Story Thus Far: Mouthwatering has a number of problems that may (or may not) get it, its officers, and its auditors into trouble with the SEC:

- Eve's booking of the revenues from the Viper's Den contract without establishing a corresponding reserve for possible returns.

- The failure to disclose the expected increase in profits at the Ribs2U.com subsidiary.

- Mouthwatering's press release stating that Eve had resigned for "personal reasons."

- Adam's disclosure of the potential restatement to Snake, Adam's bartender.

- Eve's payment of the $50,000 bribe to the customs official and the secret slush fund from which she paid the bribe.

- Mouthwatering's audited financial statements, filed with its 10–K, show neither the bribe nor the slush fund. Adam, Eve, and Apple & Tree all certified the financial statements.

The SEC has now brought an action in district court, naming Mouthwatering, Adam, and Eve as defendants. What remedies are appropriate? And which defendants should be liable for those remedies?

F.   Criminal Enforcement

Criminal sanctions are an essential component of the enforcement of the securities laws. For the hard-core fraudster, only the threat of hard time will deter misconduct, particularly in light of the enormous pecuniary rewards from committing fraud. The threat of jail time is also important in dissuading the financial controller of a public company, who is under pressure from the CEO to meet Wall Street's earning expectations for the company. In the absence of jail time as a deterrent, a financial controller may, for example, attempt to reclassify a current expense as a capital investment, thereby shifting the accounting cost of the expense into future years, in order to raise current earnings. Doing so will solidify the controller's standing with the CEO and increase the share price at least temporarily, raising the value of the controller's stock options. The fraud may go undetected, leaving the controller to enjoy the profits from his exercised options. If the fraud is uncovered, civil penalties may not provide a large deterrent once they are discounted by the low probability of detection. Criminal sanctions substantially raised the expected cost of securities law violations.

Section 21(d) of the Exchange Act authorizes the SEC to refer criminal violations of the securities laws to the U.S. Attorney General for prosecution. Section 32(a) of the Exchange Act makes it a criminal offense to "willfully violate[] any provision [of the Exchange Act] or any rule or regulation thereunder" or to "willfully and knowingly make[], or cause[] to be made, any statement in any application, report, or document required to be filed under [the Exchange Act] ... which statement was false or misleading with respect to any material fact." Stiff penalties await those convicted: up to $5,000,000 in fines and twenty years' imprisonment for natural persons, and $25,000,000 in fines for corporations. A defendant can avoid imprisonment (but not fines), however, "if he proves that he had no knowledge of such rule or regulation." What do "willfully" and "knowingly" mean in this context? How do they differ?

United States v. Dixon

536 F.2d 1388 (2d Cir. 1976).

■ FRIENDLY, CIRCUIT JUDGE.

I.

Appellant Lloyd Dixon, Jr., was the president of AVM Corporation of Jamestown, New York, a manufacturer of voting machines ... subject to the proxy and reporting requirements of the Securities Exchange Act of 1934....

Acting under [the authority granted under Section 14(a) of the Exchange Act] the Securities and Exchange Commission has long provided that no solicitation of proxies may be made unless each person solicited is or has been "furnished with a written proxy statement containing the information specified in Schedule 14A." Item 7e of Schedule 14A provides in pertinent part:

... State as to each of the following persons who was indebted to the issuer or its subsidiaries at any time since the beginning of the last fiscal year of the issuer, (i) the largest aggregate amount of indebtedness outstanding at any time during such period, (ii) the nature of the indebtedness and of the transaction in which it was incurred, (iii) the amount thereof outstanding as of the latest practicable date, and (iv) the rate of interest paid or charged thereon:

(1) Each director or officer of the issuer;

(2) Each nominee for election as a director; and,

(3) Each associate of any such director, officer or nominee.

Instructions.

1. Include the name of each person whose indebtedness is described and the nature of the relationship by reason of which the information is required to be given.

2. This paragraph does not apply to any person whose aggregate indebtedness did not exceed $10,000 or 1 percent of the issuer's total assets, whichever is less, at any time during the period specified....

The other set of provisions requires the filing of reports with the SEC. The basic requirements are laid down in § 13, with the SEC having power to fill in the details. Acting under this authority the SEC has required the filing of an annual report, commonly known as a 10–K report. One item required in such reports is as follows:

Schedule II Amounts receivable from underwriters, promoters, directors, officers, employees, and principal holders (other than affiliates) of equity securities of the person and its affiliates. The schedule prescribed by § 210.12–03 shall be filed with respect to each person among the underwriters, promoters, directors, officers, employees, and principal holders (other than affiliates) of equity securities of the person and its affiliates, from whom an aggregate indebtedness of more than $20,000 or 1 percent of total assets, whichever is less, is owed, or at any time during the period for which related income statements are required to be filed, was owed. . . .

* * *

The instant indictment . . . contained six counts. Count II charged that Dixon "did knowingly, willfully and unlawfully" solicit proxies in violation of the SEC's Rule quoted above [in Schedule 14A], as the proxy statement did not disclose loans to Dixon during the fiscal year ended December 31, 1970, and he was not within the exemption provided for borrowers whose loans at no time exceeded $10,000. Count VI charged that Dixon and the AVM Corporation "unlawfully, willfully and knowingly" violated § 13 of the Securities Exchange Act by filing a 10–K report for 1970 which omitted to include a Schedule II although such inclusion was required to reflect any loans to insiders which, like Dixon's, amounted to more than $20,000 at any time during the year. . . .

A jury returned a verdict of guilty on all counts. The judge sentenced Dixon to one year's imprisonment on each count, the sentence to be served concurrently, and substantial fines.

II.

The Government presented its case through two witnesses, William Lewis and Robert M. Entwisle, who were respectively AVM's secretary-treasurer and its general counsel at the time here in question. Lewis testified under a grant of immunity.

The proof left no doubt that the highest aggregate balance of loans to Dixon during 1970 substantially exceeded the $20,000 exemption from the 10–K Schedule II filing and the $10,000 exemption from the proxy statement disclosure. His loans from AVM were channeled through two accounts, #[2510–00] and #2512–02. . . . [The court provided a list of transactions involving both accounts during 1970 in which Dixon increased his debt.]

[B]y November 30 the confirmation statement reflecting these loans and signed by him to be sent to Ernst & Ernst, the accounting firm doing the AVM annual audit, showed a total debt of $67,868.08 for both accounts. Dixon stipulated that at least $65,368.08 was personal debt.

In December 1970, Dixon initiated a number of transactions which gave the appearance that he had retired a large portion of his debt. He instructed Lewis to transfer $9,000 to Dixon's father's account, the elder Dixon being at that time Chairman of the Board of AVM. This transaction had the effect of canceling the February and May debits of $5,000 and $4,000 from the #2510–00 account. Dixon paid AVM $30,000, which he had borrowed from a Jamestown bank, to be applied to the #2510–00 account. He then had Lewis take an advance of $5,000 on Lewis' account and apply the money to the #2510–00 debt. Finally, Dixon retired the #2512–02 account and paid an additional $700 on the #2510–00 account. He thus reduced his total indebtedness to $19,100 as of December 31, 1970. Dixon stipulated that $14,600 of this constituted loans used for personal purposes.

As was his practice, Dixon renewed his AVM loans after January 1 and used the monies to pay off the loans from the bank and Lewis by which he had reduced his AVM accounts prior to the year's end. Thus on February 1, 1971 he took a fresh $30,000 advance, debited to the #2510–00 account, and on February 22 used the account to obtain $5,000 with which to repay Lewis. A $300 advance at the end of the month brought the #2510–00 total back up to $54,400.

The evidence thus established that the proxy statement sent out March 19, 1971 and the 10–K report filed on March 25, 1971 did not contain the information on Dixon's indebtedness that was required. Dixon's principal defense was that he thought the "SEC rules" provided for a $20,000 exemption, determined on the basis of year-end indebtedness, rather than by the highest aggregate balance during the year. Since Dixon's year-end balance still exceeded the $10,000 exemption in the proxy rules, it seems, although the record and briefs are not altogether clear on this, that the defense encompassed an assertion that Dixon thought a $20,000 year-end balance was the test for exemption from both rules. A principal reason for the lack of clarity was that Dixon, exercising his constitutional privilege, did not take the stand; instead his counsel sought to elicit the evidence of Dixon's state of mind by cross-examining Lewis and Entwisle.

* * *

III.

We shall deal first with Dixon's convictions on the two counts, II and VI, of violating the Securities Exchange Act. The failure to include a statement of Dixon's indebtedness in the proxy statement and a Schedule II in the 10–K report were clear violations of "any provision of this chapter, or any rule or regulation thereunder the violation of which is made unlawful or the observance of which is required under the terms of this chapter," the language of the first clause of § 32(a). The principal questions before us are whether Dixon was shown to have had the state of mind required for a conviction and whether the jury was properly charged.

In *United States v. Peltz*, 433 F.2d 48, 54–55 (2nd Cir. 1970), we pointed out that in regard to violations of the statute or applicable rules or regulations, § 32(a) requires only willfulness; that the "willfully and knowingly" language occurs only in the second clause of § 32(a) relating to false or misleading statements in various papers required to be filed; that the final proviso that "no person shall be subject to imprisonment under this section for the violation of any rule or regulation if he proves that he had no knowledge of such rule or regulation" shows that "A person can willfully violate an SEC rule even if he does not know [of] its existence"; and that whatever may be true in other contexts, "willfully" thus has a more restricted meaning in § 32(a). However, since the term must have some meaning, we held ... the prosecution need only establish "a realization on the defendant's part that he was doing a wrongful act"; it is necessary, we added, only that the act be "wrongful under the securities laws and that the knowingly wrongful act involve a significant risk of effecting the violation. . . . "

Dixon does not deny his knowledge that there were SEC rules requiring the reporting of loans to officers, of which there clearly was sufficient evidence; his contention is that he was incorrectly informed of their content. As the sentencing minutes show, Chief Judge Curtin believed Dixon knew that the exemptive provisions of those rules were not satisfied by a sufficiently low balance at year-end, however high the figure had previously been. Dixon contends the evidence of the latter was not sufficient to convince a reasonable juror beyond a reasonable doubt. Both the factual issue and the question of the effect of a decision on it favorable to Dixon may be close ones, but we need not resolve them. We do not have here the case of a defendant manifesting an honest belief that he was complying with the law. Dixon did a "wrongful act," in the sense of our decision in *Peltz*, when he caused the corporate books to show, as of December 31, 1970, debts of his father and of Lewis which in fact were his own. True, Dixon may have thought his year-end thimblerig would provide escape from a rule different from the one that existed. But such acts are wrongful "under the Securities Acts" if they lead, as here, to the very violations that would have been prevented if the defendant had acted with the aim of scrupulously obeying the rules (which would have necessarily involved correctly ascertaining them) rather than of avoiding them. Such an intention to deceive is enough to meet the modest requirements of the first clause of § 32(a) when violations occur.

* * *

NOTES

1. *Sarbanes–Oxley criminal offenses.* Apparently not satisfied with the criminal penalties provided by § 32(a) for violations of the general antifraud provision in § 10(b) of the Exchange Act, Congress added a separate securities fraud offense to the federal criminal code as part of the Sarbanes–Oxley Act:

Whoever knowingly executes, or attempts to execute, a scheme or artifice—

(1) to defraud any person in connection with any security of [a reporting company]; or

(2) to obtain, by means of false or fraudulent pretenses, representations, or promises, any money or property in connection with the purchase or sale of any security of [a reporting company];

shall be fined under this title, or imprisoned not more than 25 years, or both.

18 U.S.C. § 1348. Another new criminal offense makes attempts and conspiracies punishable to the same extent as the underlying crime. 18 U.S.C. § 1349. A final provision requires certification of financial statements by CEOs and CFOs that "the periodic report containing the financial statements fully complies with the requirements of section 13(a) or 15(d) of the Securities Exchange Act . . . and that information contained in the periodic report fairly presents, in all

material respects, the financial condition and results of operations of the issuer." Violators of the certification provisions "knowing that the periodic report accompanying the statement does not comport with all the requirements set forth in this section shall be fined not more than $1,000,000 or imprisoned not more than 10 years, or both." More serious sanctions of a $5,000,000 fine and/or 20 years in prison are available for a defendant who "willfully certifies any statement ... knowing that the periodic report accompanying the statement does not comport with all the requirements set forth in this section." 18 U.S.C. § 1350.

QUESTIONS

1. What is the difference between "willfully" and "knowingly"?

2. The court treats the counts against Dixon as falling under the first clause of § 32(a). The court therefore requires only that Dixon acted "willfully." Do you agree that failure to file the appropriate information under Schedule 14A or Form 10–K falls under the first clause of § 32(a)? Why isn't silence a misleading statement (i.e., telling the market that no major debts are owed by Dixon to AVM)? Why does § 32(a) distinguish affirmative fraudulent statements from other types of securities law violations?

3. Assuming that the counts against Dixon fall under the first clause of § 32(a), is the court correct to ignore whether Dixon "knowingly" failed to file the appropriate information under Schedule 14A and Form 10–K? What if Dixon is able to prove that "he had no knowledge of such rule or regulation"? What result if Dixon had complied with his imagined rule (true indebtedness measured at the end of the year only) and just had taken out a bank loan to pay down indebtedness briefly?

4. Some courts have held that "willfully" for § 32(a) includes "reckless" behavior. See *United States v. DeSantis*, 134 F.3d 760, 764 (6th Cir. 1998). Is this interpretation consistent with *Dixon*?

5. How do the criminal penalties under 18 U.S.C. § 1348 for fraud differ from penalties for criminal violations of the general antifraud provision in § 10(b) under § 32(a) of the Exchange Act?

6. How do the criminal penalties under 18 U.S.C. § 1350 for violation of § 302 of the Sarbanes–Oxley Act differ from penalties for criminal violations of Rule 13a–14 under § 32(a) of the Exchange Act?

CHAPTER 5

RULE 10b–5 ANTIFRAUD

Rules and Statutes
—*Sections 9, 10(b), 18, 20(a), 21D, 21E, 27, 28 and 29 of the Exchange Act*
—*Rule 10b–5 of the Exchange Act*

MOTIVATING HYPOTHETICAL

DigitalBase, Inc. is a leading provider of computer database systems, with annual revenues of over $3 billion. Its shares are traded on the Nasdaq/NMS. After many years of outstanding growth, DigitalBase's revenues and profits have leveled off. It has now been several years since DigitalBase's last major product introduction. DigitalBase's CEO, Hillary, has pinned DigitalBase's hopes for future growth on developing a technological innovation, the GigaBase, which DigitalBase's research scientists believe will be able to hold several times more information than existing databases. The problem is that manufacturing the GigaBase currently requires such exacting tolerances that it cannot be produced in commercial quantities at a competitive price. DigitalBase's manufacturing engineers have been working for over a year now to develop a cost-effective manufacturing process, but so far without success. Privately, DigitalBase's chief technology officer has told Hillary that he believes the odds of manufacturing the GigaBase in commercial quantities are about 50/50.

Publicly, Hillary has been relentlessly upbeat about the GigaBase. She introduced the GigaBase a year ago with the promise that it would double DigitalBase's profits within two years. In conference calls with investment analysts since then, Hillary has repeatedly assured the analysts that progress on the GigaBase was "on schedule." Now, however, DigitalBase's chief technology officer has told Hillary that the GigaBase cannot be brought to market for at least two years, if ever. DigitalBase (reluctantly) discloses this news in its next Form 10–Q filing. DigitalBase's stock price tanks when the news is released, going from $25 per share to $15 per share in heavy trading.

I. THE ECONOMICS OF SECURITIES FRAUD AND PRIVATE RIGHTS OF ACTION

Talk is cheap. This platitude is particularly true when false talk does not lead to sanctions against the speaker. The disclosure regime imposed by the federal securities laws would provide little useful information to investors if false statements by companies and their affiliates were not punished. In the worst case scenario, a failure to sanction officers who make false statements about their companies would quickly lead to the familiar downward spiral of the "lemons effect" that we covered in Chapter 1. Truthful issuers would be driven from the market by lying issuers, leading investors to ratchet downward what they are willing to pay for the stock of the remaining, more fraudulent, pool of firms. As the price discount investors demand of all firms increases, even greater pressure is placed on any lingering truthful firms to either exit or engage in fraud themselves, eventually leading to a collapse of the market altogether. The U.S. securities regime responds to the problem of false talk with antifraud liability.

Fraud affects the functioning of securities markets in a number of ways. Most conspicuously, fraud may influence how investors direct their capital. Firms that issue securities tend to disclose more information about their businesses in an effort to attract investors. If those disclosures are fraudulent, investors will pay an inflated price for those securities and companies will invest in projects that are not cost-justified. Fraud may also allow companies to retain money or other resources that would be better deployed elsewhere. Managers who fraudulently inflate their company's stock price may be able to invest in ill-advised empire building instead of paying cash flows as dividends to shareholders. Alternatively, managers may use fraud to keep the firm in business longer than justified when its assets should be redirected through the bankruptcy process. We can expect that investors will factor these costs into securities prices by discounting the amount that they are willing to pay for securities to reflect the risk of fraud. Therefore, if capital markets are infected by fraud, publicly-traded firms will face a higher cost of capital.

Misrepresentations by corporate managers also hurt the shareholders' ability to monitor the firm's performance and, more specifically, to evaluate the job the firm's managers are doing. Insofar as fraud insulates managers from scrutiny, it also may distort the market for corporate control. Poor managers may be able to discourage hostile acquirors by creating the illusion of strong performance. Managers may also have an incentive to distort prices in order to bolster their own compensation, either in the form of stock options or bonuses that are tied to the company's share price. Thus, deterring corporate misrepresentations can help make managers more accountable to shareholders.

The U.S. scheme of securities regulation deploys a variety of counter-measures to discourage fraud. Financial statements are audited by accounting firms, who are, in effect, "renting" their reputations to the firms that they audit. *[handwritten: rental of reputation by ind. auditors]* The work of the accountants is overseen by audit committees of outside directors, who also provide independent oversight of company disclosures. Rating agencies assess companies' creditworthiness. Analysts rate the credibility and completeness of company disclosures. In addition to these market mechanisms, we saw in Chapter 4 that SEC enforcement actions and criminal prosecution of defrauders by the Justice Department and state prosecutors further deter fraud.

The principal focus of this chapter, private rights of action, promises additional deterrence. In fact, the SEC considers private rights of actions a "necessary supplement" to its own efforts in policing fraud. Rule 10b–5, promulgated under § 10(b) of the Exchange Act, represents the most widely used securities antifraud provision for private plaintiffs. We begin with a discussion of the implied private cause of action under Rule 10b–5.

A. THE RULE 10b–5 PRIVATE CAUSE OF ACTION

The central focus of this chapter is Rule 10b–5 of the Exchange Act, the "catch-all" antifraud provision for the federal securities laws. The following excerpt explains how the rule was drafted and the relatively modest scope that was anticipated for the rule at its birth.

> It was one day in the year 1943, I believe. I was sitting in my office in the S.E.C. building in Philadelphia and I received a call from Jim Treanor who was then the Director of the Trading and Exchange Division. He said, 'I have just been on the telephone with Paul Rowen,' who was then the S.E.C. Regional Administrator in Boston, 'and he has told me about the president of some company in Boston who is going around buying up the stock of his company from his own shareholders at $4.00 a share, and he has been telling them that the company is doing very badly, whereas, in fact, the earnings are going to be quadrupled and will be $2.00 a share for this coming year. Is there anything we can do about it?' So he came upstairs and I called in my secretary and I looked at Section 10(b) and I looked at Section 17, and I put them together, and the only discussion we had there was where 'in connection with the purchase or sale' should be, and we decided it should be at the end.

> We called the Commission and we got on the calendar, and I don't remember whether we got there that morning or after lunch. We passed a piece of paper around to all the commissioners. All the commissioners read the rule and they tossed it on the table, indicating approval. Nobody said anything except Sumner Pike who said, 'Well,' he said, 'we are against fraud, aren't we?' That is how it happened.

Remarks of Milton Freeman, *Conference on Codification of the Federal Securities Laws*, 22 Bus. Law. 793, 922 (1967). From this rather mundane beginning, an elaborate common law of securities fraud has been created, largely by the courts, albeit with considerable encouragement from the SEC.

Although broad in its scope, Rule 10b–5 of the Exchange Act does not explicitly provide a private cause of action for those injured in connection with the purchase or sale of securities. Other antifraud provisions, such as §§ 11 and 12 of the Securities Act, which we will cover in Chapter 8, do provide explicitly for private liability. Within the Exchange Act itself, §§ 9(e) and 18 provide explicit causes of action for investors who have been harmed by securities fraud. Despite the lack of any language providing for a private cause of action in Rule 10b–5, in 1946 a federal district court

Implied Private cause of action

recognized an implied private cause of action. See *Kardon v. National Gypsum Co.*, 69 F. Supp. 512 (E.D. Pa. 1946). Because the private cause of action under Rule 10b–5 is judicially implied, much of the doctrine surrounding Rule 10b–5 has developed through case law. As then–Justice Rehnquist in 1975 opined about Rule 10b–5: "[W]e deal with a judicial oak which has grown from little more than a legislative acorn." *Blue Chip Stamps, et al. v. Manor Drug Stores*, 421 U.S. 723 (1975). The existence of that cause of action was subsequently acknowledged by the Supreme Court as "beyond peradventure." *Herman & MacLean v. Huddleston*, 459 U.S. 375 (1983).

The question that lingered much longer in the courts was the relation of the Rule 10b–5 implied private cause of action to private causes of action explicitly provided for by Congress in the Securities Act and the Exchange Act. The following case addresses the relation between Rule 10b–5 and § 11 of the Securities Act. Can a plaintiff bring suit under both?

Herman & MacLean v. Huddleston et al.

459 U.S. 375 (1983). *Availability express §11 cause of action, doesn't preclude implied see. 10(B) liab. [fraud in Reg.St].*

■ JUSTICE MARSHALL delivered the opinion of the Court.

These consolidated cases raise [the question] whether purchasers of *Issue* registered securities who allege they were defrauded by misrepresentations in a registration statement may maintain an action under § 10(b) notwithstanding the express remedy for misstatements and omissions in registration statements provided by § 11 of the Securities Act of 1933. . . .

I.

In 1969 Texas International Speedway, Inc. (TIS), filed a registration statement and prospectus with the Securities and Exchange Commission offering a total of $4,398,900 in securities to the public. The proceeds of the sale were to be used to finance the construction of an automobile speedway. The entire issue was sold on the offering date, October 30, 1969. TIS did not meet with success, however, and the corporation filed a petition for bankruptcy on November 30, 1970.

Allegation of fraud in registration statement (incl. misrepresent. of costs incurred in building speedway)

In 1972 plaintiffs Huddleston and Bradley instituted a class action in the United States District Court for the Southern District of Texas on behalf of themselves and other purchasers of TIS securities. The complaint alleged violations of § 10(b) of the 1934 Act and SEC Rule 10b–5 promulgated thereunder. Plaintiffs sued most of the participants in the offering, including the accounting firm, Herman & MacLean. . . . Plaintiffs claimed that the defendants had engaged in a fraudulent scheme to misrepresent or conceal material facts regarding the financial condition of TIS, including the costs incurred in building the speedway. . . .

After the jury rendered a verdict in favor of the plaintiffs on the submitted issues, the judge concluded that Herman & MacLean and others had violated § 10(b) and Rule 10b–5 by making fraudulent misrepresentations in the TIS registration statement. . . .

On appeal, the United States Court of Appeals for the Fifth Circuit held that a cause of action may be maintained under § 10(b) of the 1934 Act for fraudulent misrepresentations and omissions even when that conduct might also be actionable under § 11 of the 1933 Act. . . .

We granted certiorari to consider whether an implied cause of action under § 10(b) of the 1934 Act will lie for conduct subject to an express civil remedy under the 1933 Act. . . . We now affirm the Court of Appeals' holding that plaintiffs could maintain an action under § 10(b) of the 1934 Act. . . .

II.

The Securities Act of 1933 and the 1934 Act "constitute interrelated components of the federal regulatory scheme governing transactions in securities." The Acts created several express private rights of action, one of which is contained in § 11 of the 1933 Act. In addition to the private actions created explicitly by the 1933 and 1934 Acts, federal courts have implied private remedies under other provisions of the two laws. Most significantly for present purposes, a private right of action under § 10(b) of the 1934 Act and Rule 10b–5 has been consistently recognized for more than 35 years. The existence of this implied remedy is simply beyond peradventure.

The issue in this case is whether a party should be barred from invoking this established remedy for fraud because the allegedly fraudulent conduct would apparently also provide the basis for a damages action under § 11 of the 1933 Act. The resolution of this issue turns on the fact that the two provisions involve distinct causes of action and were intended to address different types of wrongdoing.

Section 11 of the 1933 Act allows purchasers of a registered security to sue certain enumerated parties in a registered offering when false or misleading information is included in a registration statement. The section was designed to assure compliance with the disclosure provisions of the Act by imposing a stringent standard of liability on the parties who play a direct role in a registered offering. If a plaintiff purchased a security issued pursuant to a registration statement, he need only show a material misstatement or omission to establish his prima facie case. Liability against the issuer of a security is virtually absolute, even for innocent misstatements. Other defendants bear the burden of demonstrating due diligence.

Although limited in scope, § 11 places a relatively minimal burden on a plaintiff. In contrast, § 10(b) is a "catchall" antifraud provision, but it requires a plaintiff to carry a heavier burden to establish a cause of action. While a § 11 action must be brought by a purchaser of a registered security, must be based on misstatements or omissions in a registration statement, and can only be brought against certain parties, a § 10(b) action can be brought by a purchaser or seller of "*any* security" against "*any* person" who has used "*any* manipulative or deceptive device or contrivance" in connection with the purchase or sale of a security. However, a § 10(b) plaintiff carries a heavier burden than a § 11 plaintiff. Most significantly, he must prove that the defendant acted with scienter, *i.e.*, with intent to deceive, manipulate, or defraud.

Since § 11 and § 10(b) address different types of wrongdoing, we see no reason to carve out an exception to § 10(b) for fraud occurring in a registration statement just because the same conduct may also be actionable under § 11. Exempting such conduct from liability under § 10(b) would conflict with the basic purpose of the 1933 Act: to provide greater protection to purchasers of registered securities. It would be anomalous indeed if the special protection afforded to purchasers in a registered offering by the 1933 Act were deemed to deprive such purchasers of the protections against manipulation and deception that § 10(b) makes available to all persons who deal in securities. . . .

This cumulative construction of the remedies under the 1933 and 1934 Acts is also supported by the fact that, when Congress comprehensively revised the securities laws in 1975, a consistent line of judicial decisions had permitted plaintiffs to sue under § 10(b) regardless of the availability of express remedies. In 1975 Congress enacted the most substantial and significant revision of this country's Federal securities laws since the passage of the Securities Exchange Act in 1934. When Congress acted, federal courts had consistently and routinely permitted a plaintiff to proceed under § 10(b) even where express remedies under § 11 or other provisions were available. In light of this well-established judicial interpretation, Congress' decision to leave § 10(b) intact suggests that Congress ratified the cumulative nature of the § 10(b) action.

A cumulative construction of the securities laws also furthers their broad remedial purposes. In enacting the 1934 Act, Congress stated that its purpose was "to impose requirements necessary to make [securities] regulation and control reasonably complete and effective." In furtherance of that objective, § 10(b) makes it unlawful to use "*any* manipulative or deceptive device or contrivance" in connection with the purchase or sale of any security. The effectiveness of the broad proscription against fraud in § 10(b) would be undermined if its scope were restricted by the existence of an express remedy under § 11. Yet we have repeatedly recognized that securities laws combating fraud should be construed "not technically and restrictively, but flexibly to effectuate [their] remedial purposes." We therefore reject an interpretation of the securities laws that displaces an action under § 10(b).

Accordingly, we hold that the availability of an express remedy under § 11 of the 1933 Act does not preclude defrauded purchasers of registered securities from maintaining an action under § 10(b) of the 1934 Act.

* * *

NOTES

1. *Significance of* Herman & MacLean. The most important effect of the *Herman & Maclean* decision is to relegate the private right of action provided for in § 18 of the Exchange Act (misstatements in filings with the SEC) to the dustbin of history. Section 18's explicit cause of action is more onerous to plead and prove than is the Rule 10b–5 cause of action. As a result, plaintiffs have little reason to use it. Sections 11 and 12 of the Securities Act, however, continue to play an important role in securities fraud litigation in the context of public offerings as discussed in Chapter 8.

2. *Section 9*. Section 9 of the Exchange Act prohibits manipulative acts on national securities exchanges. Section 9 completely bans manipulative activities that are fraudulent, but allows, within regulated limits, certain activities that, despite being susceptible to manipulation, may be important to the efficient functioning of securities markets. For example, stabilization efforts by an underwriter in the context of a public offering (covered in Chapter 7) are regulated rather than banned. Generally, § 9 prohibits wash sales, matched orders, manipulative transactions, touting, tipster sheets, and other misrepresentations.

Traders engaged in a wash sale or matched orders, for example, essentially sell securities to themselves, creating an artificial impression of elevated trading volume. As both the buyer and the seller in a transaction, a trader in a wash sale or matched order can progressively raise the price in the transactions in the hopes of influencing the overall market price. Section 9(a)(1) prohibits wash sales and matched orders effected for "the purpose of creating a false or misleading appearance of active trading in any security registered on a national securities exchange, or a false or misleading appearance with respect to the market for any such security...." For liability to attach, the wash sale or matched order must have been done with scienter for the purpose of creating a false or misleading appearance of active trading.

Section 9 also regulates stabilization tactics, options, and practices affecting secondary market volatility. Section 9(a)(2) prohibits manipulative activity on national securities exchanges. In enacting § 9(a)(2), Congress intended to ban tactics used to falsely create an appearance of genuine demand in a security. There are three separate elements to a cause of action under § 9(a)(2):

- Engaging in a series of transactions in any security registered on a national exchange creating actual or apparent active trading in such security, or raising or depressing the price of such security

- Carrying out these transactions with scienter

- Transacting for the purpose of inducing the purchase or sale of such security by others.

These elements have been interpreted broadly. For example, a "series of transactions" can include bids, purchases, sales, and short sales. Courts have held that as few as three transactions constitute a "series of transactions."

Unlike the majority of federal securities laws, § 9 explicitly provides both for SEC enforcement and a private right of action. Under § 9(e), the plaintiff class is limited to those who bought or sold securities on a national securities exchange at a price that was affected by market manipulation. Damages are measured by the change in price affected by the market manipulation.

3. _Overlap with state law causes of action._ The Exchange Act contains a "saving clause," § 28(a), preserving state causes of action against preemption. Congress made a significant incursion into state law remedies in 1998, however, when it passed the Securities Litigation Uniform Standards Act, codified in Exchange Act § 28(f), which preempts "covered class action[s]" under state law. The provision preempts class actions under state law involving the securities of issuers listed on one of the national exchanges or Nasdaq–NMS. The Act excludes from preemption, however, derivative actions under state corporate law. Fraud claims based on purchases by the issuer of its own securities or recommendations by the company's board concerning mergers and tenders offers are also excluded from preemption. Claims of this sort are routinely litigated in state corporate law actions.

QUESTIONS

1. The Court tells us that § 11 and Rule 10b–5 "address different types of wrongdoing." What are these different types?

2. What effect is the implication of a private cause of action under Rule 10b–5 likely to have on judicial interpretations of the explicit causes of action provided in §§ 11 and 12 of the Securities Act and §§ 9 and 18 of the Exchange Act? Conversely, what effect do the explicit causes of action have on interpretation of the private cause of action under Rule 10b–5?

3. Given the relatively low requirements for a plaintiff to pursue a Securities Act § 11 claim, why would a plaintiff also seek to bring an action under Rule 10b–5 for the same misstatement in a registration statement?

B.   THE CLASS ACTION MECHANISM

Securities transactions come in many varieties. The founders of a corporation may put seed money into the corporation in return for the initial capital stock. As the corporation grows larger, it may seek to issue securities to a small number of relatively wealthy, sophisticated investors (human and institutional) through a private placement. When a company (or its officers) commits fraud against a small number of investors, each investor may attempt to pursue a Rule 10b–5 or other available securities antifraud action individually.

Eventually, a growing corporation may seek to tap the public capital markets through a broad public offering to hundreds, if not thousands, of investors. Once a company's securities are public, investors may buy and sell that security thousands of times every day. If a public corporation commits fraud either in a public offering or through a misleading statement (or omission) that affects secondary market trading, an individual still has a private cause of action. Such an action, however, will generally not be cost justified. Filing and pursuing a securities fraud action takes a considerable amount of time and money. For any one investor among potentially thousands who are defrauded, the benefit of pursuing a fraud action individually (based on the small number of shares the one investor purchased) is typically far outweighed by the high fixed costs of the lawsuit.

[handwritten margin notes: 10b-5 action — class action — or individually — the only economically feasible action for dispersed shs.]

Defrauded public investors may turn instead to a class action in order to aggregate their common interests in a federal securities fraud lawsuit. In the typical securities fraud class action, the plaintiffs' attorney represents hundreds or thousands of investors who have purchased securities during the time that a misrepresentation was distorting the price of those securities. For fraud that affects the shares of a large public company, a class action may be the only economically feasible means for dispersed investors to pursue a legal remedy. Each of the individual investors may have a very small claim, but the aggregation of those claims can potentially sum to hundreds of millions of dollars.

HYPOTHETICAL ONE

Recall that Hillary, the CEO of DigitalBase, promised that the new GigaBase product line would "double" DigitalBase's profits within two years. Moreover, she reassured analysts that progress on GigaBase was "on schedule." It turns out that the release of GigaBase in fact will be delayed for at least two years (if not more). After the delay in GigaBase is revealed to the market, DigitalBase's stock price plummeted from $25 to $15 per share.

Assume that Hillary owns 40% of the outstanding voting common stock (for a total of 40 million shares). Assume that the other 60% of the stock is held by over 2000 outside investors, none of whom owns individually more than 0.1% of the stock.

1. Put yourself in the shoes of a plaintiffs' attorney. Should you file a class action against DigitalBase and Hillary based on her statements concerning GigaBase? What other information might you find useful with respect to GigaBase and Hillary to decide whether the action would be economically worthwhile?

2. Suppose you learn that DigitalBase and Hillary have a directors and officers liability insurance policy covering securities fraud actions. How does this affect your decision whether to file suit over the GigaBase disclosures?

C.   SORTING THE GOOD FROM THE BAD

As you will see in the cases that follow, the courts and Congress have worried that securities fraud class actions may fall short of optimal deterrence. Distinguishing fraud from mere business reversals is difficult. The external observer may not know whether a drop in a company's stock price is due to a prior intentional misstatement about its prospects—i.e., fraud—or a result of risky business decisions that did not pan out—i.e., misjudgment or bad luck. If unable to distinguish between the two, plaintiffs' lawyers must rely on limited, publicly available indicia (e.g., SEC filings and press releases from the company, evidence of insider trading by the managers allegedly responsible for the fraud) when deciding whom to sue. Thus, a substantial drop in stock price following news that contradicts a previous optimistic statement may be sufficient to provoke a lawsuit.

That leaves courts with the difficult task of sorting out the cases with potential merit from those with little or no merit (often referred to as "strike suits"). Courts and jurors, with hindsight, may have difficulty distinguishing knowingly false statements from unfortunate business decisions.

If plaintiffs can withstand a motion to dismiss, defendants generally will find settlement cheaper than litigating to a jury verdict, even if the defendants believe that a jury probably would decide in their favor. Fewer than one securities fraud class action per year goes to trial. Any case plausible enough to get past a judge may be worth settling if only to avoid the costs of discovery and attorneys' fees, which can be enormous in these cases. Securities fraud class actions are expensive to defend because the focus of litigation will often be scienter, that is, how much the defendants knew, and when they knew it. The most helpful source for uncovering those facts will be the documents in the company's possession. Producing all documents relevant to the knowledge of senior executives over many months or even years can be a massive undertaking for a corporate defendant. Having produced the documents, the company can then anticipate a long series of depositions, as the plaintiffs' counsel seeks to determine whether the executives' recollections square with the documents. Furthermore, the cost in lost productivity may dwarf the expense of attorneys' fees and other direct litigation costs. Beyond the cost in executives' time, the mere existence of the class action may disrupt relationships with suppliers and customers, who will be understandably leery of dealing with a business accused of fraud.

Putting to one side the costs of litigation, the enormous potential damages also make settlement an attractive option for the company, even when it thinks it has a good prospect of prevailing at trial. The math is straightforward: A 10% chance of a $250 million judgment means that a settlement for $24.9 million makes sense. The combination of the cost of litigating securities class actions and the potential for enormous judgments means that even weak cases may produce a settlement if they are not dismissed before trial. If both weak and strong cases lead to settlements, the deterrent effect of class actions is diluted because innocent and wrongful conduct both lead to sanctions. Moreover, plaintiffs' attorneys that realize the large incentive on the part of companies and their officers to settle even weak cases will respond with the filing of an even greater number of strike suits.

These weaknesses in the system have led the courts and Congress, which enacted the Private Securities Litigation Reform Act of 1995 (PSLRA), to impose limits on securities fraud class actions in recent years. Among other things the PSLRA:

- imposes a rebuttable presumption that the lead plaintiff in a class action is the shareholder with the largest financial interest in the class action litigation
- requires that plaintiffs plead with particularity facts leading to a strong inference of scienter
- imposes a stay on discovery until after the motion to dismiss
- provides a safe harbor for forward-looking statements

- limits the liability of defendants not engaged in intentional fraud to their proportionate share of the harm caused

Significantly, the empirical evidence indicates that the PSLRA has not diminished the number of lawsuits. This may be because the PSLRA did not change the measure of damages in most securities fraud cases. We will see in the damages section that this measure, an "out-of-pocket" measure designed primarily to compensate investors, creates potentially ruinous consequences for corporations and their officers exposed to antifraud liability, particularly in the context of fraud affecting the secondary market.

As you go through the materials in this chapter on Rule 10b–5 liability, consider how the PSLRA has affected (if at all) the ability of both plaintiffs filing a meritorious securities action claim as well as plaintiffs pursuing a more frivolous claim in hope of obtaining settlement from defendants.

QUESTIONS

1. Given the possibility that large damages may attract plaintiffs' attorneys to file non-meritorious suits, why do you think that Congress did not change the damages formula for Rule 10b–5 actions when it adopted the Private Securities Litigation Reform Act?

2. Are there are any alternatives to private causes of action for deterring fraud? What are the benefits and costs of those alternatives?

3. Who was harmed and who benefited from the misrepresentations made by Hillary and DigitalBase? Should all of them have the ability to bring a private cause of action under Rule 10b–5?

II.   WHO CAN SUE UNDER RULE 10b–5?

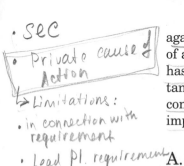

A threshold question under Rule 10b–5 is who can bring a lawsuit against individuals and entities that have violated the rule. The implication of a private cause of action raises the question of who else, besides the SEC, has standing to enforce the rule. Two aspects of Rule 10b–5 place important limits on who can sue under Rule 10b–5. The first is the rule's "in connection with" requirement. The second is the lead plaintiff provision imposed by the PSLRA.

A.   THE "IN CONNECTION WITH" REQUIREMENT

The question of who can sue for violations of Rule 10b–5 turns mainly on the courts' interpretation of the clause requiring that the fraud be "in connection with the purchase or sale of any security." The following two cases address limitations on standing to bring suit based on this language. The first answers the question of whether a plaintiff must have actually purchased or sold to recover.

Blue Chip Stamps, et al. v. Manor Drug Stores

421 U.S. 723 (1975).

■ JUSTICE REHNQUIST delivered the opinion of the Court.

This case requires us to consider whether the offerees of a stock offering, made pursuant to an antitrust consent decree and registered under the Securities Act of 1933, may maintain a private cause of action for money damages where they allege that the offeror has violated the provisions of Rule 10b–5 of the Securities and Exchange Commission, but where they have neither purchased nor sold any of the offered shares.

I

In 1963 the United States filed a civil antitrust action against Blue Chip Stamp Co. (Old Blue Chip), a company in the business of providing trading stamps to retailers, and nine retailers who owned 90% of its shares. In 1967 the action was terminated by the entry of a consent decree. The decree contemplated a plan of reorganization whereby Old Blue Chip was to be merged into a newly formed corporation, Blue Chip Stamps (New Blue Chip). The holdings of the majority shareholders of Old Blue Chip were to be reduced, and New Blue Chip, one of the petitioners here, was required under the plan to offer a substantial number of its shares of common stock to retailers who had used the stamp service in the past but who were not shareholders in the old company. Under the terms of the plan, the offering to nonshareholder users was to be proportional to past stamp usage and the shares were to be offered in units consisting of common stock and debentures.

The reorganization plan was carried out, the offering was registered with the SEC as required by the 1933 Act, and a prospectus was distributed to all offerees as required by § 5 of that Act. Somewhat more than 50% of the offered units were actually purchased. In 1970, two years after the offering, respondent, a former user of the stamp service and therefore an offeree of the 1968 offering, filed this suit. . . .

Respondent's complaint alleged, *inter alia,* that the prospectus prepared and distributed by Blue Chip in connection with the offering was materially misleading in its overly pessimistic appraisal of Blue Chip's status and future prospects. It alleged that Blue Chip intentionally made the prospectus overly pessimistic in order to discourage respondent and other members of the allegedly large class whom it represents from accepting what was intended to be a bargain offer, so that the rejected shares might later be offered to the public at a higher price. The complaint alleged that class members because of and in reliance on the false and misleading prospectus failed to purchase the offered units. . . .

The only portion of the litigation thus initiated which is before us is whether respondent may base its action on Rule 10b–5 of the Securities and Exchange Commission without having either bought or sold the securities described in the allegedly misleading prospectus. . . .

Section 10(b) of the 1934 Act does not by its terms provide an express civil remedy for its violation. Nor does the history of this provision provide any indication that Congress considered the problem of private suits under it at the time of its passage. Similarly there is no indication that the Commission in adopting Rule 10b–5 considered the question of private civil remedies under this provision.

Despite the contrast between the provisions of Rule 10b–5 and the numerous carefully drawn express civil remedies provided in the Acts of both 1933 and 1934, it was held in 1946 by the United States District Court for the Eastern District of Pennsylvania that there was an implied private right of action under the Rule. *Kardon v. National Gypsum Co.,* 69 F.Supp. 512. . . . Within a few years after the seminal *Kardon* decision, the Court of Appeals for the Second Circuit concluded that the plaintiff class for purposes of a private damage action under § 10(b) and Rule 10b–5 was limited to actual purchasers and sellers of securities. *Birnbaum v. Newport Steel Corp.,* 193 F.2d 461. . . . For the reasons hereinafter stated, we are of the opinion that *Birnbaum* was rightly decided, and that it bars respondent from maintaining this suit under Rule 10b–5.

* * *

III

The panel which decided *Birnbaum* [concluded that s]ince both § 10(b) and Rule 10b–5 proscribed only fraud "in connection with the purchase or sale" of securities, and since the history of § 10(b) revealed no congressional intention to extend a private civil remedy for money damages to other than defrauded purchasers or sellers of securities, in contrast to the express civil remedy provided by § 16(b) of the 1934 Act, the court concluded that the plaintiff class in a Rule 10b–5 action was limited to actual purchasers and sellers. . . .

In 1957 and again in 1959, the Securities and Exchange Commission sought from Congress amendment of § 10(b) to change its wording from "in connection with the purchase or sale of any security" to "in connection with the purchase or sale of, or any attempt to purchase or sell, any security." In the words of a memorandum submitted by the Commission to a congressional committee, the purpose of the proposed change was "to make section 10(b) also applicable to manipulative activities in connection with any attempt to purchase or sell any security." Opposition to the amendment was based on fears of the extension of civil liability under § 10(b) that it would cause. Neither change was adopted by Congress.

The longstanding acceptance by the courts, coupled with Congress' failure to reject *Birnbaum*'s reasonable interpretation of the wording of § 10(b), wording which is directed toward injury suffered "in connection with the purchase or sale" of securities, argues significantly in favor of acceptance of the *Birnbaum* rule by this Court.

Available evidence from the texts of the 1933 and 1934 Acts as to the congressional scheme in this regard, though not conclusive, supports the result reached by the *Birnbaum* court. The wording of § 10(b) directed at fraud "in connection with the purchase or sale" of securities stands in contrast with the parallel antifraud provision of the 1933 Act, § 17(a), reaching fraud "in the offer or sale" of securities. When Congress wished to provide a remedy to those who neither purchase nor sell securities, it had little trouble in doing so expressly. . . .

While the damages suffered by purchasers and sellers pursuing a § 10(b) cause of action may on occasion be difficult to ascertain, in the main such purchasers and sellers at least seek to base recovery on a demonstrable number of shares traded. In contrast, a putative plaintiff, who neither purchases nor sells securities but sues instead for intangible economic injury such as loss of a noncontractual opportunity to buy or sell, is more likely to be seeking a largely conjectural and speculative recovery in which the number of shares involved will depend on the plaintiff's subjective hypothesis. . . .

The principal express nonderivative private civil remedies, created by Congress contemporaneously with the passage of § 10(b), for violations of various provisions of the 1933 and 1934 Acts are by their terms expressly limited to purchasers or sellers of securities. Thus § 11(a) of the 1933 Act confines the cause of action it grants to "any person acquiring such security" while the remedy granted by § 12 of that Act is limited to the "person purchasing such security." . . .

Having said all this, we would by no means be understood as suggesting that we are able to divine from the language of § 10(b) the express "intent of Congress" as to the contours of a private cause of action under Rule 10b–5. When we deal with private actions under Rule 10b–5, we deal with a judicial oak which has grown from little more than a legislative acorn. Such growth may be quite consistent with the congressional enactment and with the role of the federal judiciary in interpreting it, but it would be disingenuous to suggest that either Congress in 1934 or the Securities and Exchange Commission in 1942 foreordained the present state of the law with respect to Rule 10b–5. It is therefore proper that we consider, in addition to the factors already discussed, what may be described as policy considerations when we come to flesh out the portions of the law with respect to which neither the congressional enactment nor the administrative regulations offer conclusive guidance.

Three principal classes of potential plaintiffs are presently barred by the *Birnbaum* rule. First are potential purchasers of shares, either in a new offering or on the Nation's post-distribution trading markets, who allege that they decided not to purchase because of an unduly gloomy representation or the omission of favorable material which made the issuer appear to be a less favorable investment vehicle than it actually was. Second are actual shareholders in the issuer who allege that they decided not to sell their shares because of unduly rosy representation or a failure to disclose unfavorable material. Third are shareholders, creditors, and perhaps others related to an issuer who suffered loss in the value of their investment due to corporate or insider activities in connection with the purchase or sale of securities which violate Rule 10b–5. It has been held that shareholder members of the second and third of these classes may frequently be able to circumvent the *Birnbaum* limitation through bringing a derivative action on behalf of the corporate issuer if the latter is itself a purchaser or seller of securities. But the first of these classes, of which respondent is a member, cannot claim the benefit of such a rule.

A great majority of the many commentators on the issue before us have taken the view that the *Birnbaum* limitation on the plaintiff class in a Rule 10b–5 action for damages is an arbitrary restriction which unreasonably prevents some deserving plaintiffs from recovering damages which have in fact been caused by violations of Rule 10b–5. The Securities and Exchange Commission has filed an amicus brief in this case espousing that same view. We have no doubt that this is indeed a disadvantage of the *Birnbaum* rule, and if it had no countervailing advantages it would be undesirable as a matter of policy, however much it might be supported by precedent and legislative history. But we are of the opinion that there are countervailing advantages to the *Birnbaum* rule, purely as a matter of policy, although those advantages are more difficult to articulate than is the disadvantage.

There has been widespread recognition that litigation under Rule 10b–5 presents a danger of vexatiousness different in degree and in kind from that which accompanies litigation in general. . . .

[I]n the field of federal securities laws governing disclosure of information even a complaint which by objective standards may have very little chance of success at trial has a settlement value to the plaintiff out of any proportion to its prospect of success at trial so long as he may prevent the suit from being resolved against him by dismissal or summary judgment. The very pendency of the lawsuit may frustrate or delay normal business activity of the defendant which is totally unrelated to the lawsuit.

* * *

The potential for possible abuse of the liberal discovery provisions of the Federal Rules of Civil Procedure may likewise exist in this type of case to a greater extent than they do in other litigation. The prospect of extensive deposition of the defendant's officers and associates and the concomitant opportunity for extensive discovery of business documents is a common occurrence in this and similar types of litigation. To the extent that this process eventually produces relevant evidence which is useful in determining the merits of the claims asserted by the parties, it bears the imprimatur of those Rules and of the many cases liberally interpreting them. But to the extent that it permits a plaintiff with a largely groundless claim to simply take up the time of a number of other people, with the right to do so representing an *in terrorem* increment of the settlement value, rather than a reasonably founded hope that the process will reveal relevant evidence, it is a social cost rather than a benefit. Yet to broadly expand the class of plaintiffs who may sue under Rule 10b–5 would appear to encourage the least appealing aspect of the use of the discovery rules.

Without the *Birnbaum* rule, an action under Rule 10b–5 will turn largely on which oral version of a series of occurrences the jury may decide to credit, and therefore no matter how improbable the allegations of the plaintiff, the case will be virtually impossible to dispose of prior to trial other than by settlement. . . .

The *Birnbaum* rule, on the other hand, permits exclusion prior to trial of those plaintiffs who were not themselves purchasers or sellers of the stock in question. The fact of purchase of stock and the fact of sale of stock are generally matters which are verifiable by documentation, and do not depend upon oral recollection, so that failure to qualify under the *Birnbaum* rule is a matter that can normally be established by the defendant either on a motion to dismiss or on a motion for summary judgment.

Obviously there is no general legal principle that courts in fashioning substantive law should do so in a manner which makes it easier, rather than more difficult, for a defendant to obtain a summary judgment. But in this type of litigation, where the mere existence of an unresolved lawsuit has settlement value to the plaintiff not only because of the possibility that he may prevail on the merits, an entirely legitimate component of settlement value, but because of the threat of extensive discovery and disruption of normal business activities which may accompany a lawsuit which is groundless in any event, but cannot be proved so before trial, such a factor is not to be totally dismissed. The *Birnbaum* rule undoubtedly excludes plaintiffs who have in fact been damaged by violations of Rule 10b–5, and to that extent it is undesirable. But it also separates in a readily demonstrable manner the group of plaintiffs who actually purchased or actually sold, and whose version of the facts is therefore more likely to be believed by the trier of fact, from the vastly larger world of potential plaintiffs who might successfully allege a claim but could seldom succeed in proving it. And this fact is one of its advantages.

[I]n the absence of the *Birnbaum* rule, it would be sufficient for a plaintiff to prove that he had failed to purchase or sell stock by reason of a defendant's violation of Rule 10b–5. . . . Plaintiff's proof would not be that he purchased or sold stock, a fact which would be capable of documentary verification in most situations, but instead that he decided *not* to purchase or sell stock. Plaintiff's entire testimony could be dependent upon uncorroborated oral evidence of many of the crucial elements of his claim, and still be sufficient to go to the jury. The jury would not even have the benefit of weighing the plaintiff's version against the defendant's version, since the elements to which the plaintiff would testify would be in many cases totally unknown and unknowable to the defendant. . . . The virtue of the *Birnbaum* rule, simply stated, in this situation, is that it limits the class of plaintiffs to those who have at least dealt in the security to which the prospectus, representation, or omission relates. And their dealing in the security, whether by way of purchase or sale, will generally be an objectively demonstrable fact in an area of the law otherwise very much dependent upon oral testimony. In the absence of the *Birnbaum* doctrine, bystanders to the securities marketing process could await developments on the sidelines without risk, claiming that inaccuracies in disclosure caused nonselling in a falling market and that unduly pessimistic predictions by the issuer followed by a rising market caused them to allow retrospectively golden opportunities to pass.

* * *

Thus we conclude that what may be called considerations of policy, which we are free to weigh in deciding this case, are by no means entirely on one side of the scale. Taken together with the precedential support for the *Birnbaum* rule over a period of more than 20 years, and the consistency of that rule with what we can glean from the intent of Congress, they lead us to conclude that it is a sound rule and should be followed.

* * *

NOTES

1. *The standing of the SEC.* Neither the SEC nor the Justice Department need to be a purchaser or seller to bring suit for violations of Rule 10b–5. *See SEC v. National Securities, Inc.*, 393 U.S. 453, 467 n. 9 (1969).

2. *Injunctive relief.* Lower courts have disagreed after *Blue Chip* on the question of whether a plaintiff must be a purchaser or seller in order to seek injunctive relief. *Compare Tully v. Mott Supermarkets, Inc.*, 540 F.2d 187, 194 (3d Cir. 1976) (allowing standing) *with Cowin v. Bresler*, 741 F.2d 410, 424–425 (D.C. Cir. 1984) (rejecting standing).

3. *Derivative actions.* Shareholders who have neither bought nor sold can bring a derivative action on behalf of the corporation if the corporation has purchased or sold securities. *See, e.g., Smith v. Ayres*, 845 F.2d 1360 (5th Cir. 1988).

4. *"Forced sellers."* The courts of appeals have also recognized standing for shareholders who have been fraudulently induced to give up their shares, for example, in a merger or liquidation. *See, e.g., Alley v. Miramon*, 614 F.2d 1372 (5th Cir. 1980).

QUESTIONS

1. What categories of investors are harmed by fraud even though they do not engage in a securities transaction?

2. The Court emphasizes that without the *Birnbaum* rule "[p]laintiff's entire testimony could be dependent upon uncorroborated oral evidence of many of the crucial elements of his claim, and still be sufficient to go to the jury." Does it follow that this will encourage vexatious litigation?

3. Does eliminating non-purchasers and sellers from Rule 10b–5 actions solve the vexatious litigation problem?

HYPOTHETICAL TWO

Jesse is an avid follower of DigitalBase. Five years ago, he purchased 10,000 shares of DigitalBase at $5 per share in the hopes of large capital appreciation. At the time of Hillary's optimistic statements on the future of the GigaBase product line less than a year ago, Jesse had been planning to sell his shares at the current market price of $25 per share (to finance the renovation of his house). Hillary's optimistic statements, however, convinced Jesse to hold on to his 10,000 shares.

1. After the public revelation of significant delays in GigaBase, Jesse's stock now is worth only $15 per share. Does Jesse have standing to file suit under Rule 10b–5 against DigitalBase and Hillary?

2. Suppose in addition to holding on to his 10,000 shares, Jesse also decided to increase his DigitalBase investment by an additional 100 shares at $25 per share at the time of Hillary's optimistic statements. Does Jesse have standing to file suit under Rule 10b–5 against DigitalBase and Hillary?

The next case addresses how close the connection must be between the fraud and the requisite purchase or sale of security. Does theft, if it involves a security, always give rise to a Rule 10b–5 claim?

SEC v. Zandford

535 U.S. 813 (2002).

■ JUSTICE STEVENS delivered the opinion of the Court.

The Securities and Exchange Commission (SEC) filed a civil complaint alleging that a stockbroker violated both § 10(b) of the Securities Exchange Act of 1934 and the SEC's Rule 10b–5, by selling his customer's securities and using the proceeds for his own benefit without the customer's knowledge or consent. The question presented is whether the alleged fraudulent conduct was "in connection with the purchase or sale of any security" within the meaning of the statute and the rule.

I

Between 1987 and 1991, respondent was employed as a securities broker in the Maryland branch of a New York brokerage firm. In 1987, he persuaded William Wood, an elderly man in poor health, to open a joint investment account for himself and his mentally retarded daughter. According to the SEC's complaint, the "stated investment objectives for the account were 'safety of principal and income.'" The Woods granted respondent discretion to manage their account and a general power of attorney to engage in securities transactions for their benefit without prior approval. Relying on respondent's promise to "conservatively invest" their money, the Woods entrusted him with $419,255. Before Mr. Wood's death in 1991, all of that money was gone.

In 1991, the National Association of Securities Dealers (NASD) conducted a routine examination of respondent's firm and discovered that on over 25 separate occasions, money had been transferred from the Woods' account to accounts controlled by respondent. In due course, respondent was indicted in the United States District Court for the District of Maryland on 13 counts of wire fraud. The . . . count alleged that respondent sold securities in the Woods' account and then made personal use of the proceeds. . . . Each of the other counts alleged that he made wire transfers between Maryland and New York that enabled him to withdraw specified sums from the Woods' accounts. Some of those transfers involved respondent writing checks to himself from a mutual fund account held by the Woods, which required liquidating securities in order to redeem the checks. Respondent was convicted . . . , sentenced to prison for 52 months, and ordered to pay $10,800 in restitution.

After respondent was indicted, the SEC filed a civil complaint in the same District Court alleging that respondent violated § 10(b) and Rule 10b–5 by engaging in a scheme to defraud the Woods and by misappropriating approximately $343,000 of the Woods' securities without their knowledge or consent. [The district court entered summary judgment against respondent. The Fourth Circuit reversed.]

The [Fourth Circuit] held that the civil complaint did not sufficiently allege the necessary connection because the sales of the Woods' securities were merely incidental to a fraud that "lay in absconding with the proceeds" of sales that were conducted in "a routine and customary fashion." . . . Respondent's "scheme was simply to steal the Woods' assets" rather than to engage "in manipulation of a particular security." Ultimately, the court refused "to stretch the language of the securities fraud provisions to encompass every conversion or theft that happens to involve securities." Adopting what amounts to a "fraud on the market" theory of the statute's coverage, the court held that without some "relationship to market integrity or investor understanding," there is no violation of § 10(b).

We granted the SEC's petition for a writ of certiorari, to review the Court of Appeals' construction of the phrase "in connection with the purchase or sale of any security." . . .

[W]e have explained that [§ 10(b)] should be "construed 'not technically and restrictively, but flexibly to effectuate its remedial purposes.' " In its role enforcing the Act, the SEC has consistently adopted a broad reading of the phrase "in connection with the purchase or sale of any security." It has maintained that a broker who accepts payment for securities that he never intends to deliver, or who sells customer securities with intent to misappropriate the proceeds, violates § 10(b) and Rule 10b–5. This interpretation of the ambiguous text of § 10(b), in the context of formal adjudication, is entitled to deference if it is reasonable. . . . While the statute must not be construed so broadly as to convert every common-law fraud that happens to involve securities into a violation of § 10(b), neither the SEC nor this Court has ever held that there must be a misrepresentation about the value of a particular security in order to run afoul of the Act.

The SEC claims respondent engaged in a fraudulent scheme in which he made sales of his customer's securities for his own benefit. Respondent submits that the sales themselves were perfectly lawful and that the subsequent misappropriation of the proceeds, though fraudulent, is not properly viewed as having the requisite connection with the sales; in his view, the alleged scheme is not materially different from a simple theft of cash or securities in an investment account. We disagree.

According to the complaint, respondent "engaged in a scheme to defraud" the Woods beginning in 1988, shortly after they opened their account, and that scheme continued throughout the 2–year period during which respondent made a series of transactions that enabled him to convert the proceeds of the sales of the Woods' securities to his own use. The securities sales and respondent's fraudulent practices were not independent events. This is not a case in which, after a lawful transaction had been consummated, a broker decided to steal the proceeds and did so. Nor is it a case in which a thief simply invested the proceeds of a routine conversion in the stock market. Rather, respondent's fraud coincided with the sales themselves.

Taking the allegations in the complaint as true, each sale was made to further respondent's fraudulent scheme; each was deceptive because it was neither authorized by, nor disclosed to, the Woods. With regard to the sales of shares in the Woods' mutual fund, respondent initiated these transactions by writing a check to himself from that account, knowing that redeeming the check would require the sale of securities. Indeed, each time respondent "exercised his power of disposition for his own benefit," that conduct, "without more," was a fraud. In the aggregate, the sales are properly viewed as a "course of business" that operated as a fraud or deceit on a stockbroker's customer. . . .

The benefit of a discretionary account is that it enables individuals, like the Woods, who lack the time, capacity, or know-how to supervise investment decisions, to delegate authority to a broker who will make decisions in their best interests without prior approval. If such individuals cannot rely on a broker to exercise that discretion for their benefit, then the account loses its added value. Moreover, any distinction between omissions and misrepresentations is illusory in the context of a broker who has a fiduciary duty to her clients. . . .

In *United States v. O'Hagan*, 521 U.S. 642 (1997), we held that the defendant had committed fraud "in connection with" a securities transaction when he used misappropriated confidential information for trading purposes. We reasoned that "the fiduciary's fraud is consummated, not when the fiduciary gains the confidential information, but when, without disclosure to his principal, he uses the information to purchase or sell securities. The securities transaction and the breach of duty thus coincide. This is so even though the person or entity defrauded is not the other party to the trade, but is, instead, the source of the nonpublic information." The Court of Appeals distinguished *O'Hagan* by reading it to require that the misappropriated information or assets not have independent value to the client outside the securities market. We do not read *O'Hagan* as so limited. In the chief passage cited by the Court of Appeals for this proposition, we discussed the Government's position that "the misappropriation theory would not . . . apply to a case in which a person defrauded a bank into giving him a loan or embezzled cash from another, and then used the proceeds of the misdeed to purchase securities," because in that situation "the proceeds would have value to the malefactor apart from their use in a securities transaction, and the fraud would be complete as soon as the money was obtained." Even if this passage could be read to introduce a new requirement into § 10(b), it would not affect our analysis of this case, because the Woods' securities did not have value for respondent apart from their use in a securities transaction and the fraud was not complete before the sale of securities occurred.

[T]he SEC complaint describes a fraudulent scheme in which the securities transactions and breaches of fiduciary duty coincide. Those breaches were therefore "in connection with" securities sales within the meaning of § 10(b).[4] Accordingly, the judgment of the Court of Appeals is reversed, and the case is remanded for further proceedings consistent with this opinion.

NOTES

1. *Privity.* The broad interpretation of the "in connection with" requirement in *Zandford* supports the generally expansive reading of that phrase in the lower courts. Courts have consistently rejected the argument that the "in connection with" requirement requires contractual privity between the plaintiff and the defendant. *See, e.g., SEC v. Texas Gulf Sulphur*, 401 F.2d 833, 858–861 (2d Cir. 1968) ("Rule 10b–5 is violated whenever assertions are made, as here, in a manner reasonably calculated to influence the investing public, e.g., by means of the financial media, if such assertions are false and misleading or are so incomplete as to mislead."). This conclusion's most important implications concern corporate issuers and officers, who are frequently named as defendants in Rule 10b–5 actions by plaintiffs alleging that their trades in the secondary markets were influenced by misrepresentations made by the corporate issuers and officers. This interpretation of the "in connection with" requirement extends to statements made that affect the stock price of other companies as well. *See Semerenko v. Cendant Corp.*, 223 F.3d 165 (3d Cir. 2000) (misstatements that affected the value of prospective merger partner are actionable). But see *Ontario Public Service Employees Union Pension Trust Fund v. Nortel Networks Corp.*, 369 F.3d 27 (2d Cir. 2004) (plaintiffs lacked standing to pursue claims against company that had a business relationship with issuer whose securities they purchased).

QUESTIONS

1. Suppose the broker in *SEC v. Zandford* decides to sell his year-old Porsche. The broker tells the buyer that the Porsche is in "great" condition and says: "The reason for the car's great condition is that I'm a securities broker and use

---

4. Contrary to the Court of Appeals' prediction, our analysis does not transform every breach of fiduciary duty into a federal securities violation. If, for example, a broker embezzles cash from a client's account or takes advantage of the fiduciary relationship to induce his client into a fraudulent real estate transaction, then the fraud would not include the requisite connection to a purchase or sale of securities. Likewise if the broker told his client he was stealing the client's assets, that breach of fiduciary duty might be in connection with a sale of securities, but it would not involve a deceptive device or fraud.

it only to drive back and forth to my office.'' In reality, the broker took the car out for racing every weekend. Shortly after the sale, the Porsche breaks down. Can the purchaser sue the broker under Rule 10b–5?

2. Suppose a con artist fraudulently convinces an elderly couple to purchase a piece of the Brooklyn Bridge with the couple's life savings (of $1 million in cash). The con artist then uses the money to buy shares of IBM. Does the elderly couple have a Rule 10b–5 cause of action against the con artist?

3. Suppose the broker persuades an elderly client to transfer $1 million worth of securities to a brokerage account with the broker's firm. The client instructs the broker to sell the portfolio and hold the cash until the client decides on a new investment strategy. Broker sells the securities as instructed, but then runs into financial difficulties and decides to misappropriate the proceeds from the sales. Does the client have a Rule 10b–5 action against the broker?

HYPOTHETICAL THREE

1. Hillary, the CEO of DigitalBase, gives an interview to a reporter from *Digital Weekly*, a magazine widely read by computer types. The magazine's central purpose is to keep its readers abreast of the latest developments in the technology sector. In excerpts from the interview published in the magazine, Hillary is quoted as saying that "The GigaBase is going to revolutionize information technology. Our customers will be able to store more information and access it more quickly than they ever dreamed possible." After reading this interview, Jill, an outside investor, decides against selling her shares. She instead borrows money to pay the law school tuition bill that has recently come due. Can Jill sue under Rule 10b–5?

2. Suppose Technology Workers of America is negotiating a labor contract with DigitalBase. The union threatens to strike causing the stock price to drop. In fact the threat was a bluff—the union never had any intention of striking. Should shareholders who sold their stock in response to the strike threat (or the SEC) be able to sue the union under Rule 10b–5?

B. The Lead Plaintiff in a Class Action

At least as important as the question of who can sue for violations of Rule 10b–5 is the question of who will represent the victims of securities fraud. In class actions, the hundreds or thousands of members of the plaintiff class cannot all play a role in the controlling the litigation. Instead, the litigation is supposed to be controlled by the "lead plaintiff" under a provision that Congress added to the securities laws as part of the PSLRA. The Third Circuit discusses the application of that provision in the case below. How does the court determine who should represent the class? And how should the court determine how much the attorney for the class will be paid?

In Re Cendant Corp. Litigation

264 F.3d 201 (3d Cir. 2001).

■ Becker, Chief Judge.

* * *

[Cendant Corporation was formed in 1997 through the merger of CUC International, Inc. and HFS Inc. Cendant's businesses included Avis, Century 21, and the Ramada and Howard Johnson hotel franchise chains. During April and July 1998, Cendant made a series of public statements announcing the restatement of several years worth of its financial statements. Cendant's stock fell from $35–5/8 in mid-April, 1998 prior to its first restatement announcement to $15–11/16 per share after the last announcement in July. Subsequent to the large stock drops, a number of securities fraud class action lawsuits were filed on behalf of investors who purchased CUC or Cendant stock during 1997.

The lawsuits named as defendants Cendant, its officers and directors, and other parties—including Ernst & Young, which had acted as CUC's independent public accountant from 1983 until the time of the creation of Cendant. By order of the Judicial Panel on Multidistrict Litigation, all cases relating to Cendant's accounting irregularities were transferred to the United States District Court for the District of New Jersey. On May 29, 1998, the District Court consolidated all of them. The District Court then proceeded to appoint as lead plaintiff a consortium of the three largest publicly-managed pension funds in the United States: the California Public Employees' Retirement System (CalPERS), the New York City Pension Funds (NYCPF), and the New York State Common Retirement Fund (NYSCRF) (collectively the "CalPERS Group"). The District Court also held an auction to determine the lead counsel for the plaintiffs' class action. Under the terms of the auction, candidates for lead counsel were asked to submit a bid based on the attorneys fees they were willing to accept. The District Court gave the CalPERS Group's chosen counsel the option to match what the court determined to be the lowest qualified bid.]

* * *

These are consolidated appeals from the District Court's approval of a $3.2 billion settlement of a securities fraud class action brought against Cendant Corporation and its auditors, Ernst & Young, and the Court's award of $262 million in fees to counsel for the plaintiff class. Both the settlement and the fee award are challenged in these appeals. The enormous size of both the settlement and the fee award presages a new generation of "mega cases" that will test our previously developed jurisprudence.

[The appellate court then reviewed (a) the selection of the lead plaintiff for the class action under the PSLRA, (b) the selection of the lead counsel for the class, and (c) the determination of attorney fees for the lead counsel.]

* * *

Throenle [a member of the plaintiff class] . . . argues that the members of the CalPERS Group were too conflicted to serve adequately in that capacity because they continued to hold huge amounts of Cendant stock during the Settlement negotiations. . . . Throenle's argument is based on the general assertion that a lead plaintiff who retains a substantial investment in a defendant corporation cannot adequately represent a class in a lawsuit against that corporation because this lead plaintiff will naturally be conflicted between trying to get maximum recovery for the class and trying to protect its ongoing investment in the corporation, e.g., by settling cheap or by securing corporate governance changes in lieu of cash, both of which are alleged here. . . .

Throenle's thesis is attractive. The problem with it is that Congress seems to have rejected it when it enacted the lead plaintiff provisions of the PSLRA. The Reform Act establishes a presumption that the class member "most capable of adequately representing the interests of class members" is the shareholder with the largest financial stake in the recovery sought by the class. The plaintiff with the largest stake in a given securities class action will almost invariably be a large institutional investor, and the PSLRA's legislative history expressly states that Congress anticipated and intended that such investors would serve as lead plaintiffs. We presume that Congress was aware that an institutional investor with enormous stakes in a company is highly unlikely to divest all of its holdings in that company, even after a securities class action is filed in which it is a class member.

By establishing a preference in favor of having such investors serve as lead plaintiffs, Congress must have thought that the situation present here does not inherently create an unacceptable conflict of interest. For this reason, the simple fact that the institutional investors . . . retained Cendant stock while the Settlement was negotiated is not nearly enough, standing alone, to support Throenle's claim that Lead Plaintiff was so conflicted that the Settlement should be overturned.[25]

* * *

The Reform Act establishes a two-step process for appointing a lead plaintiff: the court first identifies the presumptive lead plaintiff, and then determines whether any member of the putative class has rebutted the presumption. We begin by describing the manner in which courts charged with appointing a lead plaintiff should proceed under the PSLRA. We then measure the actions taken by the District Court against these standards.

1. Legal Standards

a. Identifying the Presumptive Lead Plaintiff

* * *

25. . . . In economic terms, the potential conflict may be demonstrated as follows. The motivation of a rational Sell Plaintiff is simple: he wants to secure the largest possible recovery. The rational Hold Plaintiff, however, is in a more complicated situation; her goal is to reach a settlement that will maximize the combined value of her share of the settlement and the stock that she continues to hold in the defendant firm. Consequently, though a rational Sell Plaintiff would be perfectly willing to push the defendant firm one dollar short of declaring bankruptcy, a rational Hold Plaintiff rarely would be so willing because the increased value of her share of the settlement fund would almost certainly be offset by a corresponding decrease in the value of her stock. Thus, there will often be a significant conflict between the interests of Sell Plaintiffs and Hold Plaintiffs, particularly in cases where the class's expected damages are very large. . . .

The section of the PSLRA that governs the appointment of the lead plaintiff is captioned "Rebuttable Presumption." The first subsection, captioned "in general," provides that "the court shall adopt a presumption that the most adequate plaintiff ... is the person or group of persons that": (1) filed the complaint or made a motion to serve as the lead plaintiff; (2) "in the determination of the court, has the largest financial interest in the relief sought by the class;" and (3) "otherwise satisfies the requirements of Rule 23 of the Federal Rules of Civil Procedure." The next subsection, captioned "rebuttal evidence," declares that the presumption established by the previous subsection "may be rebutted only upon proof by a member of the purported plaintiff class that the presumptively most adequate plaintiff—(aa) will not fairly and adequately protect the interests of the class; or (bb) is subject to unique defenses that render such plaintiff incapable of adequately representing the class."

* * *

The overall structure and legislative history of the statute suggest that in appointing a lead plaintiff a district court should engage in the following analysis. The initial inquiry (i.e., the determination of whether the movant with the largest interest in the case "otherwise satisfies" Rule 23) should be confined to determining whether the movant has made a prima facie showing of typicality and adequacy. The initial clause of the statute, which governs triggering the presumption, refers to determinations made by "the court," but the second, which deals with rebutting it, speaks of "proof by a member of the purported plaintiff class." This phrasing suggests that the threshold determination of whether the movant with the largest financial losses satisfies the typicality and adequacy requirements should be a product of the court's independent judgment, and that arguments by members of the purported plaintiff class as to why it does not should be considered only in the context of assessing whether the presumption has been rebutted. . . .

* * *

When making these determinations, courts should apply traditional Rule 23 principles. Thus, in inquiring whether the movant has preliminarily satisfied the typicality requirement, they should consider whether the circumstances of the movant with the largest losses "are markedly different or the legal theory upon which the claims [of that movant] are based differ[] from that upon which the claims of other class members will perforce be based."

In assessing whether the movant satisfies Rule 23's adequacy requirement, courts should consider whether it "has the ability and incentive to represent the claims of the class vigorously, [whether it] has obtained adequate counsel, and [whether] there is [a] conflict between [the movant's] claims and those asserted on behalf of the class." . . .

Because one of a lead plaintiff's most important functions is to "select and retain" lead counsel, one of the best ways for a court to ensure that it will fairly and adequately represent the interests of the class is to inquire whether the movant has demonstrated a willingness and ability to select competent class counsel and to negotiate a reasonable retainer agreement with that counsel. Thus, a court might conclude that the movant with the largest losses could not surmount the threshold adequacy inquiry if it lacked legal experience or sophistication, intended to select as lead counsel a firm that was plainly incapable of undertaking the representation, or had negotiated a clearly unreasonable fee agreement with its chosen counsel. We stress, however, that the question at this stage is not whether the court would "approve" that movant's choice of counsel or the terms of its retainer agreement or whether another movant may have chosen better lawyers or negotiated a better fee agreement; rather, the question is whether the choices made by the movant with the largest losses are so deficient as to demonstrate that it will not fairly and adequately represent the interests of the class, thus disqualifying it from serving as lead plaintiff at all. . . .

The PSLRA explicitly permits a "group of persons" to serve as lead plaintiff. But the goal of the Reform Act's lead plaintiff provision is to locate a person or entity whose sophistication and interest in the litigation are sufficient to permit that person or entity to function as an active agent for the class, and a group is not entitled to presumptive lead plaintiff status unless it "otherwise satisfies" Rule 23, which in turn requires that it be able to "fairly and adequately protect the interests of the class." If the court determines that the way in which a group seeking to become lead plaintiff was formed or the manner in which it is constituted would preclude it from fulfilling the tasks assigned to a lead plaintiff, the court should disqualify that movant on the grounds that it will not fairly and adequately represent the interests of the class. . . .

If, for example, a court were to determine that the movant "group" with the largest losses had been created by the efforts of lawyers hoping to ensure their eventual appointment as lead counsel, it could well conclude, based on this history, that the members of that "group" could not be counted on to monitor counsel in a sufficient manner.

Courts must also inquire whether a movant group is too large to represent the class in an adequate manner. At some point, a group becomes too large for its members to operate effectively as a single unit. When that happens, the PSLRA's goal of having an engaged lead plaintiff actively supervise the conduct of the litigation and the actions of class counsel will be impossible to achieve, and the court should conclude that such a movant does not satisfy the adequacy requirement.

Like many of the district courts that have considered this question, we do not establish a hard-and-fast rule; instead, we note only that a kind of "rule of reason prevails." We do, however, agree with the Securities and Exchange Commission that courts should generally presume that groups with more than five members are too large to work effectively.

* * *

b. *Determining Whether the Presumption Has Been Rebutted*

Once a presumptive lead plaintiff is located, the court should then turn to the question whether the presumption has been rebutted. The Reform Act is quite specific on this point, providing that the presumption "may be rebutted only upon proof by a member of the purported plaintiff class that the presumptively most adequate plaintiff—(aa) will not fairly and adequately protect the interests of the class; or (bb) is subject to unique defenses that render such plaintiff incapable of adequately representing the class." This language makes two things clear. First, only class members may seek to rebut the presumption, and the court should not permit or consider any arguments by defendants or non-class members. Second, once the presumption is triggered, the question is not whether another movant might do a better job of protecting the interests of the class than the presumptive lead plaintiff; instead, the question is whether anyone can prove that the presumptive lead plaintiff will not do a "fair[] and adequate[]" job. We do not suggest that this is a low standard, but merely stress that the inquiry is not a relative one. . . .

2. **Application of the Standards Here**

Under these standards, we believe that the District Court correctly identified the CalPERS Group as the presumptively most adequate plaintiff. The Group filed a motion to serve as lead plaintiff, and no party has questioned that of all the movants it has the largest financial interest in the relief sought by the Class. The District Court expressly found that the CalPERS Group satisfied Rule 23(a)'s typicality requirement. Although we have expressed concerns about certain potential conflicts of interest that might have undermined the CalPERS Group's position, we have concluded that they do not carry the day.

The District Court also found no obvious reason to doubt that a group composed of the three largest pension funds in the United States could adequately protect the class's interests. The CalPERS Group's members are legally sophisticated entities, their chosen counsel are well-qualified, and the Retainer Agreement that they negotiated was not plainly unreasonable. Moreover, although it is a group, there is no indication that the CalPERS Group was artificially created by its lawyers, and the fact that it contains three members offers no obvious reason to doubt that its members could operate effectively as a single unit. We therefore find no abuse of discretion in the District Court's determination that the CalPERS Group was the presumptive lead plaintiff.

We also conclude that the District Court was correct in holding that the CalPERS Group's presumptive lead plaintiff status had not been rebutted. Appellant Aboff and Douglas Wilson (who is not before us on appeal) offered three reasons why the statutory presumption in favor of the CalPERS Group had been rebutted. First, Aboff and Wilson represented that "they had negotiated a reduced fee schedule with their attorneys." As we stressed above, the question at this stage is not whether Aboff and Wilson would have done a better job of securing high-quality, low-cost counsel than the CalPERS Group; the question is whether the former have put forward "proof" that the latter would "not fairly and adequately represent the class." Had Aboff and Wilson shown that: (1) their fee agreement was substantially lower than that negotiated by the CalPERS Group; (2) their chosen counsel were as qualified or more qualified than those chosen by the presumptive lead plaintiff; and (3) the CalPERS Group had no adequate explanation for why it made the choice that it did, then the presumption may have been rebutted. But this would only happen if the facts suggested that the CalPERS Group had performed inadequately in an objective sense. But Aboff and Wilson did not make this showing simply by alleging that they negotiated a lower fee; hence we hold that the District Court did not abuse its discretion in rejecting this argument.

Aboff and Wilson's second contention was that the presumption had been rebutted because "considerations other than the interests of the class might have influenced the CalPERS group when it retained its attorneys." Specifically, they alleged that "counsel for the CalPERS group had made substantial contributions to the campaign of the New York State Comptroller, who, as sole trustee of the NYSCRF [a member of the CalPERS Group], has substantial influence over the decisions of the fund," and they argued that this "created an appearance of impropriety because the contributions may have played a role in the selection of the group's counsel—a practice known as 'pay-to-play.'" We likewise find no abuse of discretion in the District Court's decision to reject this argument.

Lest we be misunderstood, we observe that actual proof of pay-to-play would constitute strong (and, quite probably, dispositive) evidence that the presumption had been rebutted. A movant that was willing to base its choice of class counsel on political contributions instead of professional considerations would, it seems to us, have quite clearly demonstrated that it would "not fairly and adequately protect the interests of the class." . . .

The problem for Aboff and Wilson is that the District Court expressly found that they had not provided evidence in support of their pay-to-play allegations, and we have no basis upon which to disagree. When pressed by the District Court, Aboff and Wilson admitted that they had no evidence that the contributions, themselves legal, had influenced the CalPERS Group's selection process. Allegations of impropriety are not proof of wrongdoing. If they were, then any class member (or lawyer seeking to be appointed lead counsel) could disable any presumptive lead plaintiff by making unsupported allegations of impropriety. We therefore hold that the District Court did not abuse its discretion in rejecting Aboff and Wilson's pay-to-play arguments.

* * *

c. *The Auction*

We turn now to NYCPF's objection to the District Court's decision to employ an auction to select lead counsel. . . .

3.   Does the Reform Act Ever Permit an Auction?

The statutory section most directly on point provides that "the most adequate plaintiff shall, subject to the approval of the court, select and retain counsel to represent the class." This language makes two things clear. First, the lead plaintiff's right to select and retain counsel is not absolute—the court retains the power and the duty to supervise counsel selection and counsel retention. But second, and just as importantly, the power to "select and retain" lead counsel belongs, at least in the first instance, to the lead plaintiff, and the court's role is confined to deciding whether to "approve" that choice. Because a court-ordered auction involves the court rather than the lead plaintiff choosing lead counsel and determining the financial terms of its retention, this latter determination strongly implies that an auction is not generally permissible in a Reform Act case, at least as a matter of first resort.

This conclusion gains support when we examine the overall structure of the PSLRA's lead plaintiff section. The Reform Act contains detailed procedures for choosing the lead plaintiff, indicating that Congress attached great importance to ensuring that the right person or group is selected. The only powers expressly given to the lead plaintiff, however, are to "select and retain" counsel. If those powers are seriously limited, it would seem odd for Congress to have established such a specific means for choosing the lead plaintiff. But if the powers to "select and retain" lead counsel carry a great deal of discretion and responsibility, it makes perfect sense that Congress attached great significance to the identity of the person or group that would be making those choices.

* * *

[W]e think that the Reform Act evidences a strong presumption in favor of approving a properly-selected lead plaintiff's decisions as to counsel selection and counsel retention. When a properly-appointed lead plaintiff asks the court to approve its choice of lead counsel and of a retainer agreement, the question is not whether the court believes that the lead plaintiff could have made a better choice or gotten a better deal. Such a standard would eviscerate the Reform Act's underlying assumption that, at least in the typical case, a properly-selected lead plaintiff is likely to do as good or better job than the court at these tasks. Because of this, we think that the court's inquiry is appropriately limited to whether the lead plaintiff's selection and agreement with counsel are reasonable on their own terms.

In making this determination, courts should consider: (1) the quantum of legal experience and sophistication possessed by the lead plaintiff; (2) the manner in which the lead plaintiff chose what law firms to consider; (3) the process by which the lead plaintiff selected its final choice; (4) the qualifications and experience of counsel selected by the lead plaintiff; and (5) the evidence that the retainer agreement negotiated by the lead plaintiff was (or was not) the product of serious negotiations between the lead plaintiff and the prospective lead counsel.

* * *

Although we think ... that an auction is impermissible in most Reform Act cases, we do not rule out the possibility that it could be validly used. If the court determines that the lead plaintiff's initial choice of counsel or negotiation of a retainer agreement is inadequate, it should clearly state why (for both the benefit of the lead plaintiff and for the record) and should direct the lead plaintiff to undertake an acceptable selection process. If the lead plaintiff's response demonstrates that it is unwilling or unable to do so, then the court will, of necessity, be required to take a more active role.

4. Was the Auction in this Case Permissible?

We now analyze whether ... the District Court's decision to conduct an auction was justified.... The District Court gave several reasons for holding an auction. First, it noted that the PSLRA makes Lead Plaintiff's decision "subject to the approval of the court." The court stressed that "given the opportunity, absent class members would try to secure the most qualified representation at the lowest cost," and then observed that, at the end of the case, it would be required to ensure that the "total attorneys's fees and expenses" that it awarded to lead counsel did "not exceed a reasonable percentage of the amount of any damages and prejudgment interest actually paid to the class." The court concluded that holding an auction would aid it in making this determination and in protecting the class's interests because it would simulate the market, thus providing a "benchmark of reasonableness." Second, the District Court stated that holding an auction would have the "salutary" effect of "removing any speculative doubt" about Aboff and Wilson's pay-to-play allegations.

These reasons are not sufficient justification for holding an auction. The first (i.e., a generalized desire to hold down costs by "simulating" the market) would apply in every case, and thus cannot be enough to justify a procedure that we have concluded may only be used rarely. Further, there is no need to "simulate" the market in cases where a properly-selected lead plaintiff conducts a good-faith counsel selection process because in such cases—at least under the theory supporting the PSLRA—the fee agreed to by the lead plaintiff is the market fee.

Nor do we think that the laudable desire to dispel mere allegations of impropriety as to one member of the CalPERS Group is enough to justify holding an auction. Were it sufficient, then any disgruntled class member (or lawyer seeking to be appointed lead counsel) could disable the lead plaintiff from exercising its statutorily-conferred power by making unsupported allegations of impropriety.

* * *

For the foregoing reasons, we hold that the District Court abused its discretion by conducting an auction because its decision to do so was founded upon an erroneous understanding of the legal standards under-girding the propriety of conducting an auction under the PSLRA. With regard to counsel selection, however, this error was harmless because the counsel selected via the auction process were the same as those whom the Lead Plaintiff sought to have appointed in the first place.

* * *

The Reform Act confers on the lead plaintiff the power to "retain" lead counsel, but it also requires that the court ensure that the "total attorneys' fees and expenses awarded ... to counsel for the plaintiff class ... not exceed a reasonable percentage of the amount of any damages and prejudg-ment interest actually paid to the class." This latter provision makes clear that the court has an independent obligation to ensure the reasonableness of any fee request. The issue is the scope of this obligation.

Federal Rule of Civil Procedure 23(e) provides that no class action "shall ... be dismissed or compromised without the approval of the court," but the detailed standards set forth for reviewing attorneys fees in this Court's earlier cases are not contained in any statute or rule. Rather, they were developed because of recognition that in the class action context there is no way for "the class" to select, retain, or monitor its lawyers in the way that an individual client would, and because of doubts that a typical lead plaintiff in the non-PSLRA context is a terribly good agent for the class. In the ordinary case, the court is the only disinterested agent capable of protecting the class from its lawyers and its primary means of doing so is by scrutinizing the lawyers' proposed fee....

The Reform Act shifts the underpinnings of our class action attorneys fees jurisprudence in the securities area. As a preliminary matter, the PSLRA sets out a detailed procedure for choosing lead plaintiffs, the whole point of this process being to locate a lead plaintiff that will be an effective agent for the class. The properly-selected lead plaintiff is then charged with selecting and retaining lead counsel (subject to court approval). This regime is far different from the traditional case in which counsel is often "select-ed" and "retained" based on the fact that it filed the first suit. Conse-quently, courts have far more reason at the outset to think that counsel selection and retention were done in the best interests of the class in a typical Reform Act case than they do in other class action contexts, at least when the procedures of counsel selection employed by the lead plaintiff were adequate....

We therefore believe that, under the PSLRA, courts should accord a presumption of reasonableness to any fee request submitted pursuant to a retainer agreement that was entered into between a properly-selected lead plaintiff and a properly-selected lead counsel. This presumption will ensure that the lead plaintiff, not the court, functions as the class's primary agent vis-à-vis its lawyers. Further, by rendering ex ante fee agreements more reliable, it will assist those agreements in aligning the interests of the class and its lawyers during the pendency of the litigation.

Saying that there is a presumption necessarily assumes that it can be overcome in some cases, however. First, the presumption of reasonableness would likely be abrogated entirely were the court to find that the assumptions underlying the original retainer agreement had been materially altered by significant and unusual factual and/or legal developments that could not reasonably have been foreseen at the time of the original agreement. . . .

We stress, however, that not just any factual or legal development would suffice to justify a court's decision that the presumption of reasonableness had been rebutted on grounds of changed circumstances. Uncertainties are part of any ex ante negotiation and it should be presumed that the lead plaintiff and the lead counsel took the possibility of uncertainty into account in negotiating their agreement. Thus, only unusual and unforeseeable changes, i.e., those that could not have been adequately taken into account in the negotiations, could justify a court's decision to find the presumption abrogated.

Even if the presumption of reasonableness is not undermined by changed circumstances, however, courts must still consider whether it has been rebutted. As we have noted above, there is an arguable tension between the presumption of reasonableness accorded the arrangement between the Lead Plaintiff and properly selected counsel and the duty imposed on the Court by the Reform Act, to insure "that total attorneys' fees and expenses awarded by the court to counsel for the plaintiff class shall not exceed a reasonable percentage of the amount of any damages and prejudgment interest actually paid to the class." We resolve this tension by holding that the presumption may be rebutted by a prima facie showing that the (properly submitted) retained agreement fee is clearly excessive. In terms of the policy of the Reform Act, we do not believe that candidates for lead plaintiff designation will be deterred by the understanding that their retainer fee arrangement with Lead Counsel will be subject to judicial review for clear excessiveness.

* * *

Although the foregoing discussion suggests that, in view of a presumption, whatever fee is re-submitted by Lead Counsel pursuant to the Retainer Agreement on remand has a "leg up" for approval, we cannot blind ourselves to the reality that both the fee award of $262 million under the auction and (potentially up to) $187 million under the Retainer Agreement are staggering in their size, and, on the basis of the evidence in the record, may represent compensation at an astonishing hourly rate (as well as an extraordinarily high lodestar "multiplier"). Objectors contend that the lodestar figure is approximately $8,000,000, which would mean that the multiplier would be 45.75 if lead counsel were to receive the court awarded fee, and approximately 24 if it were to receive the negotiated fee. Lead counsel counter that the $8,000,000 figure was preliminary and that the final figure will be much higher, from 50% to 100%. Even so, the multiplier would still be extremely high.

At all events, this was a simple case in terms of liability with respect to Cendant, and the case was settled at a very early stage, after little formal discovery. Thus the possibility of rebuttal of the presumption of reasonableness must be seriously considered by the District Court on remand. . . .

* * *

NOTES

1. Cendant. The *Cendant* case is not typical of securities fraud class actions in at least two ways. The first is the size of the settlement, the largest ever paid by an issuer in a securities fraud class action. Settlements of $10 to $20 million are much more typical. The second is the percentage of recovery awarded to the plaintiffs' attorneys. Typical awards are in the 25% to 33% range (although much smaller in magnitude in the case of a smaller recovery for the class).

2. *Limits on plaintiffs.* The PSLRA imposes, in addition to the lead plaintiff provision discussed in *Cendant*, two additional limits on who can be a plaintiff in a securities fraud class action.

     a. A person may be a lead plaintiff in no more than five securities fraud class actions during any three-year period. This limit can be exceeded with the permission of the court (thus affording an out to institutional investors who may wish to be active in this area);

     b. The per-share recovery of the lead plaintiff cannot be greater than that of any other member of the class, although "reasonable costs and expenses" can be awarded.

Why might the latter provision discourage an investor from seeking the role of lead plaintiff?

3. *Court determination of reasonable attorneys' fees.* Courts typically follow two methods of determining reasonable attorneys' fees in securities class actions. First, courts apply the "lodestar" approach. Under the lodestar approach, courts first calculate a base attorney fee amount based on (1) the number of hours the attorneys reasonably expended on the matter and (2) the reasonable hourly market rate for attorneys with similar background and experience. Courts then apply a multiplier to this base amount, taking into account the riskiness of the litigation (i.e., the possibility that the plaintiffs' attorneys will receive nothing if there is no recovery for the class), the complexity of the case, as well as how well the attorneys performed for the class among other factors. Second, courts may instead award attorneys a percentage of the funds recovered for the class. Under a percentage approach, if the class receives no monetary recovery, the plaintiffs' attorneys also receive nothing. Even for courts that continue to follow the lodestar approach, the PSLRA places a percentage-of-the-recovery cap on the amount of damages. Under § 21D(a)(6), the attorney fees "shall not exceed a reasonable percentage of the amount of any damages and prejudgment interest actually paid to the class." Regardless of whether lodestar or a percentage-of-recovery approach is used by a court to determine the reasonableness of an attorney fee award, most fee awards typically range from 20% to 33% of the settlement amount.

Those interested in reading actual securities class action settlement notices, including the plaintiffs' attorneys' fee requests, may look at www.gilardi.com. Gilardi & Company is a large class action notice and claims administrator.

QUESTIONS

1. Prior to the PSLRA, it was not uncommon for investors with a relatively small stake to serve as the lead plaintiff for a private securities fraud class action. Often, such lead plaintiffs had prior relationships with the law firm. Who is in charge of the litigation in such a relationship?

2. Courts select the lead plaintiff—from among those investors who volunteer to fill the role—based on the investors' financial stake in the litigation. How should a court determine who has the greatest financial stake in a securities fraud class action?

3. Why might an institutional investor with a large stake in the outcome of a securities class action *not* seek the lead plaintiff position?

4. What role does the court play in reviewing attorneys' fees once a lead plaintiff has been selected under the PSLRA? If the lead plaintiff's deal with its attorneys represents the "market," what additional protection does judicial review produce?

III. ELEMENTS OF THE CAUSE OF ACTION

The elements of the Rule 10b–5 cause of action are similar to those required for common law fraud. Plaintiffs bear the burden of showing, (1) a material misstatement, (2) scienter, (3) reliance, and (4) loss causation. In this section, we cover each of these elements. As you learn about each of these requirements, consider how the PSLRA has affected the ability of private plaintiffs and their attorneys to plead and prove these elements.

Timing matters. It does a private plaintiff little good if enough information to prove scienter can be found through discovery, if the lawsuit is dismissed prior to discovery because the plaintiff cannot plead with particularity facts demonstrating scienter.

As you read the materials, note the "instrumentality of interstate commerce" requirement of Rule 10b–5. When would a securities transactions today not involve the use of an instrumentality of interstate commerce? Also keep in mind that the statute of limitations for fraud actions under the Exchange Act is the earlier of "(1) 2 years after the discovery of the facts constituting the violation; or (2) 5 years after such violation." 28 U.S.C. § 1658(b). The five-year limit is a statute of repose, which means that it is inconsistent with equitable doctrines such as tolling—five years means five years. See *Lampf, Pleva, Lipkind, Prupis & Petigrow v. Gilbertson*, 501 U.S. 350 (1991) (interpreting predecessor statute). The two-year limit, however, does not begin to run until plaintiffs are on "inquiry notice" of the fraud. Inquiry notice means the time at which the plaintiff knew or should have known the facts giving rise to his claim. *Law v. Medco Research, Inc.*, 113 F.3d 781 (7th Cir. 1997).

A. MISSTATEMENT OF A MATERIAL FACT

We discussed the concept of materiality in Chapter 2. Rule 10b–5 makes unlawful the use of an untrue statement concerning a material fact or an omission that, in light of the circumstances, makes other statements misleading.

1. DECEPTION

The requirement that the plaintiff prove a misstatement of material fact plays an important role both in limiting the type of conduct that can be actionable under Rule 10b–5, as well as the range of potential defendants, as the cases below illustrate. Rule 10b–5 also prohibits "any device, scheme, or artifice to defraud" as well as "any act, practice, or course of business which operates or would operate as a fraud or deceit upon any person." How do these parallel prohibitions interact with the prohibition on misstatements of a material fact? As you read *Santa Fe*, consider whether you think the plaintiffs were defrauded.

Santa Fe Industries, Inc., et al. v. Green et al.

430 U.S. 462 (1977).

■ Justice White delivered the opinion of the Court.

The issue in this case involves the reach and coverage of § 10(b) of the Securities Exchange Act of 1934 and Rule 10b–5 thereunder in the context of a Delaware short-form merger transaction used by the majority stockholder of a corporation to eliminate the minority interest.

I

In 1936, petitioner Santa Fe Industries, Inc., acquired control of 60% of the stock of Kirby Lumber Corp., a Delaware corporation. Through a series of purchases over the succeeding years, Santa Fe increased its control of Kirby's stock to 95%.... In 1974, wishing to acquire 100% ownership of Kirby, Santa Fe availed itself of § 253 of the Delaware Corporation Law, known as the "short-form merger" statute. Section 253 permits a parent corporation owning at least 90% of the stock of a subsidiary to merge with that subsidiary, upon approval by the parent's board of directors, and to make payment in cash for the shares of the minority stockholders. The statute does not require the consent of, or advance notice to, the minority stockholders. However, notice of the merger must be given within 10 days after its effective date, and any stockholder who is dissatisfied with the terms of the merger may petition the Delaware Court of Chancery for a decree ordering the surviving corporation to pay him the fair value of his shares, as determined by a court-appointed appraiser subject to review by the court.

Santa Fe obtained independent appraisals of the physical assets of Kirby—land, timber, buildings, and machinery—and of Kirby's oil, gas, and mineral interests. These appraisals, together with other financial information, were submitted to Morgan Stanley & Co., an investment banking firm retained to appraise the fair market value of Kirby stock. Kirby's physical assets were appraised at $320 million (amounting to $640 for each of the

500,000 shares); Kirby's stock was valued by Morgan Stanley at $125 per share. Under the terms of the merger, minority stockholders were offered $150 per share.

The provisions of the short-form merger statute were fully complied with. The minority stockholders of Kirby were notified the day after the merger became effective and were advised of their right to obtain an appraisal in Delaware court if dissatisfied with the offer of $150 per share. They also received an information statement containing, in addition to the relevant financial data about Kirby, the appraisals of the value of Kirby's assets and the Morgan Stanley appraisal concluding that the fair market value of the stock was $125 per share.

Respondents, minority stockholders of Kirby, objected to the terms of the merger, but did not pursue their appraisal remedy in the Delaware Court of Chancery. Instead, they brought this action in federal court on behalf of the corporation and other minority stockholders, seeking to set aside the merger or to recover what they claimed to be the fair value of their shares. The amended complaint asserted that, based on the fair market value of Kirby's physical assets as revealed by the appraisal included in the information statement sent to minority shareholders, Kirby's stock was worth at least $772 per share. The complaint alleged further that ... the purpose of the merger was to appropriate the difference between the "conceded pro rata value of the physical assets," and the offer of $150 per share—to "freez[e] out the minority stockholders at a wholly inadequate price," and that Santa Fe, knowing the appraised value of the physical assets, obtained a "fraudulent appraisal" of the stock from Morgan Stanley and offered $25 above that appraisal "in order to lull the minority stockholders into erroneously believing that [Santa Fe was] generous." This course of conduct was alleged to be "a violation of Rule 10b–5 because defendants employed a 'device, scheme, or artifice to defraud' and engaged in an 'act, practice or course of business which operates or would operate as a fraud or deceit upon any person, in connection with the purchase or sale of any security.' " ...

The District Court dismissed the complaint for failure to state a claim upon which relief could be granted. ...

A divided Court of Appeals for the Second Circuit reversed. It first agreed [with the district court] that there was a double aspect to the case: first, the claim that gross undervaluation of the minority stock itself violated Rule 10b–5; and second, that "without any misrepresentation or failure to disclose relevant facts, the merger itself constitutes a violation of Rule 10b–5" because it was accomplished without any corporate purpose and without prior notice to the minority stockholders. As to the first aspect of the case, the Court of Appeals did not disturb the District Court's conclusion that the complaint did not allege a material misrepresentation or nondisclosure with respect to the value of the stock; and the court declined to rule that a claim of gross undervaluation itself would suffice to make out a Rule 10b–5 case. With respect to the second aspect of the case, however, the court fundamentally disagreed with the District Court as to the reach and coverage of Rule 10b–5. The Court of Appeals' view was that, although the Rule plainly reached material misrepresentations and nondisclosures in connection with the purchase or sale of securities, neither misrepresentation nor nondisclosure was a necessary element of a Rule 10b–5 action; the Rule reached "breaches of fiduciary duty by a majority against minority shareholders without any charge of misrepresentation or lack of disclosure." . . .

We granted the petition for certiorari challenging this holding because of the importance of the issue involved to the administration of the federal securities laws. We reverse.

II

* * *

The Court of Appeals' approach to the interpretation of Rule 10b–5 is inconsistent with that taken by the Court last Term in *Ernst & Ernst v. Hochfelder*, 425 U.S. 185 (1976).

Ernst & Ernst makes clear that in deciding whether a complaint states a cause of action for "fraud" under Rule 10b–5, "we turn first to the language of § 10(b), for '[t]he starting point in every case involving construction of a statute is the language itself.' " In holding that a cause of action under Rule 10b–5 does not lie for mere negligence, the Court began with the principle that "[a]scertainment of congressional intent with respect to the standard of liability created by a particular section of the [1933 and 1934] Acts must . . . rest primarily on the language of that section," 425 U.S., at 200, and then focused on the statutory language of § 10(b)— "[t]he words 'manipulative or deceptive' used in conjunction with 'device or contrivance.' " The same language and the same principle apply to this case.

To the extent that the Court of Appeals would rely on the use of the term "fraud" in Rule 10b–5 to bring within the ambit of the Rule all breaches of fiduciary duty in connection with a securities transaction, its interpretation would, like the interpretation rejected by the Court in *Ernst & Ernst*, "add a gloss to the operative language of the statute quite different from its commonly accepted meaning." . . .

The language of § 10(b) gives no indication that Congress meant to prohibit any conduct not involving manipulation or deception. Nor have we been cited to any evidence in the legislative history that would support a departure from the language of the statute. "When a statute speaks so specifically in terms of manipulation and deception, . . . and when its history reflects no more expansive intent, we are quite unwilling to extend the scope of the statute. . . . " Thus the claim of fraud and fiduciary breach in this complaint states a cause of action under any part of Rule 10b–5 only if the conduct alleged can be fairly viewed as "manipulative or deceptive" within the meaning of the statute.

III

It is our judgment that the transaction, if carried out as alleged in the complaint, was neither deceptive nor manipulative and therefore did not violate either § 10(b) of the Act or Rule 10b–5.

As we have indicated, the case comes to us on the premise that the complaint failed to allege a material misrepresentation or material failure to disclose. The finding of the District Court, undisturbed by the Court of Appeals, was that there was no "omission" or "misstatement" in the information statement accompanying the notice of merger. On the basis of the information provided, minority shareholders could either accept the price offered or reject it and seek an appraisal in the Delaware Court of Chancery. Their choice was fairly presented, and they were furnished with all relevant information on which to base their decision....

IV

The language of the statute is, we think, "sufficiently clear in its context" to be dispositive here, but even if it were not, there are additional considerations that weigh heavily against permitting a cause of action under Rule 10b–5 for the breach of corporate fiduciary duty alleged in this complaint. Congress did not expressly provide a private cause of action for violations of § 10(b). Although we have recognized an implied cause of action under that section in some circumstances, we have also recognized that a private cause of action under the antifraud provisions of the Securities Exchange Act should not be implied where it is "unnecessary to ensure the fulfillment of Congress' purposes" in adopting the Act. As we noted earlier, the Court repeatedly has described the "fundamental purpose" of the Act as implementing a "philosophy of full disclosure"; once full and fair disclosure has occurred, the fairness of the terms of the transaction is at most a tangential concern of the statute....

A second factor in determining whether Congress intended to create a federal cause of action in these circumstances is "whether 'the cause of action [is] one traditionally relegated to state law....'" The Delaware Legislature has supplied minority shareholders with a cause of action in the Delaware Court of Chancery to recover the fair value of shares allegedly undervalued in a short-form merger. Of course, the existence of a particular state-law remedy is not dispositive of the question whether Congress meant to provide a similar federal remedy, but ... we conclude that "it is entirely appropriate in this instance to relegate respondent and others in his situation to whatever remedy is created by state law."

The reasoning behind a holding that the complaint in this case alleged fraud under Rule 10b–5 could not be easily contained. It is difficult to imagine how a court could distinguish, for purposes of Rule 10b–5 fraud, between a majority stockholder's use of a short-form merger to eliminate the minority at an unfair price and the use of some other device, such as a long-form merger, tender offer, or liquidation, to achieve the same result; or indeed how a court could distinguish the alleged abuses in these going private transactions from other types of fiduciary self-dealing involving transactions in securities. The result would be to bring within the Rule a wide variety of corporate conduct traditionally left to state regulation. In addition to posing a "danger of vexatious litigation which could result from a widely expanded class of plaintiffs under Rule 10b–5," this extension of the federal securities laws would overlap and quite possibly interfere with state corporate law. Federal courts applying a "federal fiduciary principle" under Rule 10b–5 could be expected to depart from state fiduciary standards at least to the extent necessary to ensure uniformity within the federal system. Absent a clear indication of congressional intent, we are reluctant to federalize the substantial portion of the law of corporations that deals with transactions in securities, particularly where established state policies of corporate regulation would be overridden. "Corporations are creatures of state law, and investors commit their funds to corporate directors on the understanding that, except where federal law *expressly* requires certain responsibilities of directors with respect to stockholders, state law will govern the internal affairs of the corporation."

We thus adhere to the position that "Congress by § 10(b) did not seek to regulate transactions which constitute no more than internal corporate mismanagement." There may well be a need for uniform federal fiduciary standards to govern mergers such as that challenged in this complaint. But those standards should not be supplied by judicial extension of § 10(b) and Rule 10b–5 to "cover the corporate universe."

The judgment of the Court of Appeals is reversed, and the case is remanded for further proceedings consistent with this opinion.

NOTES

1. *State remedies.* Lower courts have found some room to evade *Santa Fe's* warning against interfering with state corporate law by permitting Rule 10b–5 actions in cases in which plaintiffs allege that they have lost their state law remedies, such as injunctive relief or appraisal, as the result of a misrepresentation by the defendants. *Goldberg v. Meridor*, 567 F.2d 209 (2d Cir. 1977).

2. *Oral misstatements.* *Santa Fe's* requirement of deception for Rule 10b–5 liability can be satisfied by both oral and written statements. *Wharf (Holdings) Limited v. United International Holdings*, 532 U.S. 588 (2001). *Wharf (Holdings)* also makes clear that the secret intention not to honor a promise is an actionable misstatement if the defendant had the secret intention at the time the promise was made.

QUESTIONS

1. Is the Court's discussion of the intersection of state corporate law and federal securities law essential to its holding?

2. Does the Court's holding in *Santa Fe* mean that no breach of fiduciary duty can ever be a violation of Rule 10b–5?

3. Can there be deception even if there is no misstatement or omission? Does manipulation require a misstatement or omission?

2. THE DUTY TO UPDATE AND THE DUTY TO CORRECT

The next case addresses the question of whether a misstatement has to be false at the time it was made in order to state a cause of action. What if the statement was true when made, but, after some time passes, becomes false? Do corporations have a duty to update? Have the lower courts been true to the holding of *Santa Fe*?

Gallagher v. Abbott Laboratories

269 F.3d 806 (7th Cir. 2001).

■ EASTERBROOK, CIRCUIT JUDGE.

Year after year the Food and Drug Administration inspected the Diagnostic Division of Abbott Laboratories, found deficiencies in manufacturing quality control, and issued warnings. The Division made efforts to do better, never to the FDA's satisfaction, but until 1999 the FDA was willing to accept Abbott's promises and remedial steps. On March 17, 1999, the FDA sent Abbott another letter demanding compliance with all regulatory requirements and threatening severe consequences. This could have been read as more saber rattling—Bloomberg News revealed the letter to the financial world in June, and Abbott's stock price did not even quiver—but later developments show that it was more ominous. By September 1999 the FDA was insisting on substantial penalties plus changes in Abbott's methods of doing business. On September 29, 1999, after the markets had closed, Abbott issued a press release describing the FDA's position, asserting that Abbott was in "substantial" compliance with federal regulations, and revealing that the parties were engaged in settlement talks. Abbott's stock fell more than 6%, from $40 to $37.50, the next business day. On November 2, 1999, Abbott and the FDA resolved their differences, and a court entered a consent decree requiring Abbott to remove 125 diagnostic products from the market until it had improved its quality control and to pay a $100 million civil fine. Abbott took an accounting charge of $168 million to cover the fine and worthless inventory. The next business day Abbott's stock slumped $3.50, which together with the earlier drop implied that shareholders saw the episode as costing Abbott (in cash plus future compliance costs and lost sales) more than $5 billion. . . .

Plaintiffs in these class actions under § 10(b) of the Securities Exchange Act of 1934, and the SEC's Rule 10b–5, contend that Abbott committed fraud by deferring public revelation. . . . What sinks plaintiffs' position is their inability to identify any false statement—or for that matter any truthful statement made misleading by the omission of news about the FDA's demands.

Much of plaintiffs' argument reads as if firms have an absolute duty to disclose all information material to stock prices as soon as news comes into their possession. Yet that is not the way the securities laws work. We do not have a system of continuous disclosure. Instead firms are entitled to keep silent (about good news as well as bad news) unless positive law creates a duty to disclose. Until the Securities Act of 1933 there was no federal regulation of corporate disclosure. The 1933 Act requires firms to reveal information only when they issue securities, and the duty is owed only to persons who buy from the issuer or an underwriter distributing on its behalf; every other transaction is exempt under § 4. Section 13 of the Securities Exchange Act of 1934 adds that the SEC may require issuers to file annual and other periodic reports—with the emphasis on *periodic* rather than continuous. Section 13 and the implementing regulations contemplate that these reports will be snapshots of the corporation's status on or near the filing date, with updates due not when something "material" happens, but on the next prescribed filing date.

Regulations implementing § 13 require a comprehensive annual filing, the Form 10–K report, and less extensive quarterly supplements on Form 10–Q. The supplements need not bring up to date everything contained in the annual 10–K report; counsel for the plaintiff classes conceded at oral argument that nothing in Regulation S–K (the SEC's list of required disclosures) requires either an updating of Form 10–K reports more often than annually, or a disclosure in a quarterly Form 10–Q report of information about the firm's regulatory problems. The regulations that provide for disclosures on Form 10–Q tell us *which* items in the annual report must be updated (a subset of the full list), and how often (quarterly).

Many proposals have been made to do things differently—to junk this combination of sale-based disclosure with periodic follow-up and replace it with a system under which *issuers* rather than *securities* are registered and disclosure must be continuous. Regulation S–K goes some distance in this direction by defining identical items of disclosure for registration of stock and issuers' subsequent reports, and by authorizing the largest issuers to use their annual 10–K reports as the kernels of registration statements for new securities. But Regulation S–K does not replace periodic with continuous disclosure, and the more ambitious proposals to do this have not been adopted. . . .

Whatever may be said for and against these proposals, they must be understood as projects for legislation (and to a limited extent for the use of the SEC's rulemaking powers); judges have no authority to scoop the political branches and adopt continuous disclosure under the banner of Rule 10b–5. *Especially* not under that banner, for Rule 10b–5 condemns only fraud, and a corporation does not commit fraud by standing on its rights under a periodic-disclosure system. The Supreme Court has insisted that this judicially created right of action be used only to implement, and not to alter, the rules found in the text of the 1933 and 1934 Acts.

Trying to locate some statement that was either false or materially misleading because it did not mention the FDA's position, plaintiffs pointed in the district court to several reports filed or statements made by Abbott before November 2, 1999. [Among others, the court focused on Abbott's Form 10–K annual report for 1998 filed in March 1999.]

Plaintiffs rely principally on Item 303(a)(3)(ii) of Regulation S–K, which provides that registration statements and annual 10–K reports must reveal

> any known trends or uncertainties that have had or that the registrant reasonably expects will have a material favorable or unfavorable impact on net sales or revenues or income from continuing operations.

The FDA's letter, and its negotiating demands, are within this description, according to the plaintiff classes. We shall assume that this is so. The 10–K report did state that Abbott is "subject to comprehensive government regulation" and that "government regulatory actions can result in ... sanctions." Plaintiffs say that this is too general in light of the FDA's letter and Abbott's continuing inability to satisfy the FDA's demands. Again we shall assume that plaintiffs are right. But there is a fundamental problem: The 10–K report was filed on March 9, 1999, and the FDA's letter is dated March 17, eight days later. Unless Abbott had a time machine, it could not have described on March 9 a letter that had yet to be written.

Attempting to surmount this temporal problem, plaintiffs insist that Abbott had a "duty to correct" the 10–K report. Yet a statement may be "corrected" only if it was incorrect when made, and nothing said as of March 9 was incorrect. In order to maintain the difference between periodic-disclosure and continuous-disclosure systems, it is essential to draw a sharp line between duties to correct and duties to update.... If, for example, the 10–K report had said that Abbott's net income for 1998 was $500 million, and the actual income was $400 million, Abbott would have had to fix the error. But if the 10–K report had projected a net income of $125 million for the first quarter of 1999, and accountants determined in May that the actual profit was only $100 million, there would have been nothing to correct; a projection is not rendered false when the world turns out otherwise. Amending the 10–K report to show the results for 1999 as they came in—or to supply a running narrative of the dispute between Abbott and the FDA—would *update* the report, not *correct* it to show Abbott's actual condition as of March 9.

Updating documents has its place in securities law. A registration statement and prospectus for a new issue of securities must be accurate when it is used to sell stock, and not just when it is filed. Material changes in a company's position thus must be reflected in a registration statement promptly. But this does not imply changes in a 10–K annual report, even when that report is used ... as the principal disclosure document. Instead of changing the 10–K report weekly or monthly, the issuer must file and distribute an addendum to that document bringing matters up to date. Anyway ... Abbott did not sell any stock to the class members during the period from March 17 to November 2, 1999....

* * *

NOTES

1. *The duty to correct and the duty to update.* Every circuit to address the question has held that issuers have a duty to correct prior misstatements, even if the statements were believed to be true when made. Courts also agree that issuers do not have a duty to correct misstatements made by third parties, unless the issuer has somehow "entangled" itself with the statements by affirming them. The duty to update prior projections, however, has spawned considerably greater disagreement. The circuits range in their positions from the Seventh Circuit's outright rejection of the duty to update to the Second Circuit's cautious acceptance of the duty to update under certain circumstances. See, e.g., *In re Time Warner Inc. Sec. Litig.*, 9 F.3d 259 (2d Cir. 1993) (holding that a duty to update arises when "a corporation is pursuing a specific business goal and announces that goal as well as an intended approach for reaching it, it may come under an obligation to disclose other approaches to reaching the goal when those approaches are under active and serious consideration.").

2.   *Real time disclosure.* Congress called for "Real Time Issuer Disclosures" in § 409 of the Sarbanes–Oxley Act of 2002. The section provides:

> Each issuer reporting under section 13(a) or 15(d) shall disclose to the public on a rapid and current basis such additional information concerning material changes in the financial condition or operations of the issuer, in plain English, which may include trend and qualitative information and graphic presentations, as the Commission determines, by rule, is necessary or useful for the protection of investors and in the public interest.

The SEC has used its authority under § 409 to expand the episodic filing requirements under Form 8–K for Exchange Act reporting issuers. Falling short of a system of continuous disclosure, the SEC both expanded the types of events that require a Form 8–K filing and shortened the deadline for most items down to four days from the date of the event that triggers the Form 8–K filing requirement.

QUESTIONS

1.   Would investors be better off if companies such as Abbott Laboratories did have a duty to update the disclosures in their previously filed Form 10–K?

2.   Should the issuer's duty to correct extend to misstatements made by third parties?

3.   FORWARD–LOOKING STATEMENTS

Rule 10b–5, like other liability provisions of the securities laws, requires that statements be material before they are actionable. The general rule is the same as the materiality standard we discussed in Chapter 2: Would the information be important to a reasonable investor in deciding whether to purchase or sell the security? Congress adopted a special standard, however, for "forward-looking" statements as part of the PSLRA in § 21E of the Exchange Act (and its counterpart, § 27A of the Securities Act). The following case applies that standard.

Asher v. Baxter International Inc.

377 F.3d 727 (7th Cir. 2004).

■ EASTERBROOK, CIRCUIT JUDGE.

Baxter International, a manufacturer of medical products, released its second-quarter financial results for 2002 on July 18 of that year. Sales and profits did not match analysts' expectations. Shares swiftly fell from $43 to $32. This litigation followed; plaintiffs contend that the $43 price was the result of materially misleading projections on November 5, 2001, projections that Baxter reiterated until the bad news came out on July 18, 2002. Plaintiffs want to represent a class of all investors who purchased during that time ... in the open market.... [T]he district court dismissed the complaint for failure to state a claim on which relief may be granted. The court did not doubt that the allegations ordinarily would defeat a motion under Fed.R.Civ.P. 12(b)(6). Still, it held, Baxter's forecasts come within the safe harbor created by the Private Securities Litigation Reform Act of 1995. The PSLRA creates rules that judges must enforce at the outset of the litigation; plaintiffs do not question the statute's application before discovery but do dispute the district court's substantive decision.

Baxter's projection, repeated many times (sometimes in documents filed with the SEC, sometimes in press releases, sometimes in executives' oral statements), was that during 2002 the business would yield revenue growth in the "low teens" compared with the prior year, earnings-per-share growth in the "mid teens," and "operational cash flow of at least $500 million." Baxter often referred to these forecasts as "our 2002 full-year commitments," which is a strange locution. No firm can make "commitments" about the future—Baxter can't compel its customers to buy more of its products—unless it plans to engage in accounting shenanigans to make the numbers come out right no matter what happens to the business. But nothing turns on the word; the district court took these "commitments" as "forward-looking statements," and plaintiffs do not quarrel with that understanding. What they do say is that the projections were too rosy, and that Baxter knew it. That charges the defendants with stupidity as much as with knavery, for the truth was bound to come out quickly, but the securities laws forbid foolish frauds along with clever ones.

According to the complaint, Baxter's projections were materially false because: (1) its Renal Division had not met its internal budgets in years; ... (5) sales of that division's IGIV immunoglobin products had fallen short of internal predictions; and (6) in March 2002 the BioScience Division had experienced a sterility failure in the manufacture of a major product, resulting in the destruction of multiple lots and a loss exceeding $10 million....

The statutory safe harbor forecloses liability if a forward-looking statement "is accompanied by meaningful cautionary statements identifying important factors that could cause actual results to differ materially from those in the forward-looking statement." The fundamental problem is that the statutory requirement of "meaningful cautionary statements" is not itself meaningful. What must the firm say? Unless it is possible to give a concrete and reliable answer, the harbor is not "safe"; yet a word such as "meaningful" resists a concrete rendition and thus makes administration of the safe harbor difficult if not impossible. It rules out a caution such as:

"This is a forward-looking statement: caveat emptor." But it does not rule in any particular caution, which always may be challenged as not sufficiently "meaningful" or not pinning down the "important factors that could cause actual results to differ materially"—for if it had identified all of those factors, it would not be possible to describe the forward-looking statement itself as materially misleading. A safe harbor matters only when the firm's disclosures (including the accompanying cautionary statements) are false or misleadingly incomplete; yet whenever that condition is satisfied, one can complain that the cautionary statement must have been inadequate. The safe harbor loses its function. Yet it would be unsound to read the statute so that the safe harbor never works; then one might as well treat § 21E as defunct.

Baxter provided a number of cautionary statements throughout the class period. This one, from its 2001 Form 10–K filing—a document to which many of the firm's press releases and other statements referred—is the best illustration:

> Statements throughout this report that are not historical facts are forward-looking statements. These statements are based on the company's current expectations and involve numerous risks and uncertainties. Some of these risks and uncertainties are factors that affect all international businesses, while some are specific to the company and the health care arenas in which it operates.
>
> Many factors could affect the company's actual results, causing results to differ materially, from those expressed in any such forward-looking statements. These factors include, but are not limited to, interest rates; technological advances in the medical field; economic conditions; demand and market acceptance risks for new and existing products, technologies and health care services; the impact of competitive products and pricing; manufacturing capacity; new plant start-ups; global regulatory, trade and tax policies; regulatory, legal or other developments relating to the company's Series A, AF, and AX dialyzers; continued price competition; product development risks, including technological difficulties; ability to enforce patents; actions of regulatory bodies and other government authorities; reimbursement policies of government agencies; commercialization factors; results of product testing; and other factors described elsewhere in this report or in the company's other filings with the Securities and Exchange Commission. Additionally, as discussed in Item 3—"Legal Proceedings," upon the resolution of certain legal matters, the company may incur charges in excess of presently established reserves. Any such change could have a material adverse effect on the company's results of operations or cash flows in the period in which it is recorded.

* * *

> The company believes that its expectations with respect to forward-looking statements are based upon reasonable assumptions within the bounds of its knowledge of its business operations, but there can

be no assurance that the actual results or performance of the company will conform to any future results or performance expressed or implied by such forward-looking statements.

The district court concluded that these are "meaningful cautionary statements identifying important factors that could cause actual results to differ materially from those in the forward-looking statement." They deal with Baxter's business specifically, mentioning risks and product lines. Plaintiffs offer two responses. First they contend that the cautionary statements did not cover any of the six matters that (in plaintiffs' view) Baxter had withheld. That can't be dispositive; otherwise the statute would demand prescience. As long as the firm reveals the principal risks, the fact that some other event caused problems cannot be dispositive. Indeed, an unexpected turn of events cannot demonstrate a securities problem at all, as there cannot be "fraud by hindsight." The other response is that the cautionary statement did not follow the firm's fortunes: plants closed but the cautionary statement remained the same; sterilization failures occurred but the cautionary statement remained the same; and bad news that (plaintiffs contend) Baxter well knew in November 2001 did not cast even a shadow in the cautionary statement.

Before considering whether plaintiffs' objections defeat the safe harbor, we ask whether the cautionary statements have any bearing on Baxter's potential liability for statements in its press releases, and those its managers made orally. The press releases referred to, but did not repeat verbatim, the cautionary statements in the Form 10–K and other documents filed with the Securities and Exchange Commission. The oral statements did not do even that much. Plaintiffs say that this is fatal, because § 21E(c)(1)(A)(i) provides a safe harbor only if a written statement is "accompanied by" the meaningful caution; a statement published elsewhere differs from one that accompanies the press release. As for the oral statements: § 21E(c)(2)(A)(ii), a special rule for oral statements, provides a safe harbor only if the statement includes "that the actual results could differ materially from those projected in the forward-looking statement" and in addition:

> (i) the oral forward-looking statement is accompanied by an oral statement that additional information concerning factors that could cause actual results to differ materially from those in the forward-looking statement is contained in a readily available written document, or portion thereof;

> (ii) the accompanying oral statement referred to in clause (i) identifies the document, or portion thereof, that contains the additional information about those factors relating to the forward-looking statement; and

> (iii) the information contained in that written document is a cautionary statement that satisfies the standard established in paragraph (1)(A).

§ 21E (c)(2)(B). When speaking with analysts Baxter's executives did not provide them with all of this information, such as directions to look in the

10–K report for the full cautionary statement. It follows, plaintiffs maintain, that this suit must proceed with respect to the press releases and oral statements even if the cautionary language filed with the SEC in registration statements and other documents meets the statutory standard.

If this were a traditional securities suit—if, in other words, an investor claimed to have read or heard the statement and, not having access to the truth, relied to his detriment on the falsehood—then plaintiffs' argument would be correct. But this is not a traditional securities claim. It is a fraud-on-the-market claim. None of the plaintiffs asserts that he read any of Baxter's press releases or listened to an executive's oral statement. Instead the theory is that other people (professional traders, mutual fund managers, securities analysts) did the reading, and that they made trades or recommendations that influenced the price. In an efficient capital market, all information known to the public affects the price and thus affects every investor. *Basic Inc. v. Levinson*, 485 U.S. 224, 241–47 (1988), holds that reliance on the accuracy of the price can substitute for reliance on the accuracy of particular written or oral statements, when the statements affect the price–as they do for large and well-followed firms such as Baxter, for which there is a liquid public market. This works only to the extent that markets efficiently reflect (and thus convey to investors the economic equivalent of) all public information.

When markets are informationally efficient, it is impossible to segment information as plaintiffs propose. They ask us to say that they received (through the price) the false oral statements but not the cautionary disclosures. That can't be; only if the market is inefficient is partial transmission likely, and if the market for Baxter's stock is inefficient then this suit collapses because a fraud-on-the-market claim won't fly. An investor who invokes the fraud-on-the-market theory must acknowledge that all public information is reflected in the price, just as the Supreme Court said in *Basic*. Thus if the truth or the nature of a business risk is widely known, an incorrect statement can have no deleterious effect, and if a cautionary statement has been widely disseminated, that news too affects the price just as if that statement had been handed to each investor. If the executives' oral statements came to plaintiffs through professional traders (or analysts) and hence the price, then the cautions reached plaintiffs via the same route; market professionals are savvy enough to discount projections appropriately. Then § 21E(c)(2)(B) has been satisfied for the oral statements (and so too § 21E(c)(A)(i) for the press releases). And if the cautions did not affect the price, then the market must be inefficient and the suit fails for that reason. So we take the claim as the pleadings framed it: the market for Baxter's stock is efficient, which means that Baxter's cautionary language must be treated as if attached to every one of its oral and written statements. That leaves the question whether these statements satisfy the statutory requirement that they adequately "identify [] important factors that could cause actual results to differ materially from those in the forward-looking statement."

The parties agree on two propositions, each with support in decisions of other circuits. First, "boilerplate" warnings won't do; cautions must be tailored to the risks that accompany the particular projections. Second, the cautions need not identify what actually goes wrong and causes the projections to be inaccurate; prevision is not required. Unfortunately, these principles don't decide any concrete case—for that matter, the statutory language itself does not decide any concrete case....

Plaintiffs say that Baxter's cautions were boilerplate, but they aren't. Statements along the lines of "all businesses are risky" or "the future lies ahead" come to nothing other than caveat emptor (which isn't enough); these statements, by contrast, at least included Baxter-specific information and highlighted some parts of the business that might cause problems. For its part, Baxter says that mentioning these business segments demonstrates that the caution is sufficient; but this also is wrong, because then any issuer could list its lines of business, say "we could have problems in any of these," and avoid liability for statements implying that no such problems were on the horizon even if the management well knew that a precipice was in sight.

What investors would like to have is a full disclosure of the assumptions and calculations behind the projections; then they could apply their own discount factors ... however, this is not a sensible requirement. Many of the assumptions and calculations would be more useful to a firm's rivals than to its investors. Suppose, for example, that Baxter had revealed its sterility failure in the BioSciences Division, the steps it had taken to restore production, and the costs and prospects of each. Rivals could have used that information to avoid costs and hazards that had befallen Baxter, or to find solutions more quickly, and as Baxter could not have charged the rivals for this information they would have been able to undercut Baxter's price in future transactions. Baxter's shareholders would have been worse off....

Another form a helpful caution might take would be the disclosure of confidence intervals. After saying that it expected growth in the low teens, Baxter might have added that events could deviate 5% in either direction (so the real projection was that growth would fall someplace between 8% and 18%); disclosure of the probability that growth will be under 10% (or over 16%) would have done much to avoid the hit stock prices took when the results for the first half of 2002 proved to be unexpectedly low. Baxter surely had developed internally some estimate of likely variance. Revealing the mean, median, and standard deviation of these internal estimates, and pinpointing the principal matters that could cause results to differ from the more likely outcome, could help to generate an accurate price for the stock....

Whether or not Baxter could have made the cautions more helpful by disclosing assumptions, methods, or confidence intervals, none of these is required. The PSLRA does not require the most helpful caution; it is enough to "identify[] important factors that could cause actual results to differ materially from those in the forward-looking statement." This means that it is enough to point to the principal contingencies that could cause actual results to depart from the projection. The statute calls for issuers to reveal the "important factors" but not to attach probabilities to each potential bad outcome, or to reveal in detail what could go wrong; as we have said, that level of detail might hurt investors (by helping rivals) even as it improved the accuracy of stock prices. (Requiring cautions to contain elaborate detail also would defeat the goal of facilitating projections, by turning each into a form of registration statement. Undue complexity would lead issuers to shut up, and stock prices could become even less accurate. Incomplete information usually is better than none, because market professionals know other tidbits that put the news in context.) Moreover, "[i]f enterprises cannot make predictions about themselves, then securities analysts, newspaper columnists, and charlatans have protected turf. There will be predictions aplenty outside the domain of the securities acts, predictions by persons whose access to information is not as good as the issuer's. When the issuer adds its information and analysis to that assembled by outsiders, the collective assessment will be more accurate even though a given projection will be off the mark."

Yet Baxter's chosen language may fall short. There is no reason to think—at least, no reason that a court can accept at the pleading stage, before plaintiffs have access to discovery—that the items mentioned in Baxter's cautionary language were those thought at the time to be the (or any of the) "important" sources of variance. The problem is not that what actually happened went unmentioned; issuers need not anticipate all sources of deviations from expectations. Rather, the problem is that there is no reason (on this record) to conclude that Baxter mentioned those sources of variance that (at the time of the projection) were the principal or important risks. For all we can tell, the major risks Baxter knew that it faced when it made its forecasts were exactly those that, according to the complaint, came to pass, yet the cautionary statement mentioned none of them. Moreover, the cautionary language remained fixed even as the risks changed. When the sterility failure occurred in spring 2002, Baxter left both its forecasts and cautions as is. When Baxter closed the plants that (according to the complaint) were its least-cost sources of production, the forecasts and cautions continued without amendment. This raises the possibility—no greater confidence is possible before discovery—that Baxter knew of important variables that would affect its forecasts, but omitted them from the cautionary language in order to depict the projections as more certain than internal estimates at the time warranted. Thus this complaint could not be dismissed under the safe harbor, though we cannot exclude the possibility that if after discovery Baxter establishes that the cautions did reveal what were, ex ante, the major risks, the safe harbor may yet carry the day.

Baxter urges us to affirm the judgment immediately, contending that the full truth had reached the market despite any shortcomings in its cautionary statements. If this is so, however, it is hard to understand the sharp drop in the price of its stock. A "truth-on-the-market" defense is available in principle, . . . but not at the pleading stage.

* * *

NOTES

1. *Bespeaks caution.* The PSLRA's forward-looking safe harbor is a codification and expansion of the judicially developed "bespeaks caution" doctrine. Under that doctrine:

> [W]hen an offering document's forecasts, opinions or projections are accompanied by meaningful cautionary statements, the forward-looking statements will not form the basis for a securities fraud claim if those statements did not affect the "total mix" of information the document provided investors. In other words, cautionary language, if sufficient, renders the alleged omissions or misrepresentations immaterial as a matter of law.

Kaufman v. Trump's Castle Funding, 7 F.3d 357, 371–372 (3d Cir. 1993). Like the PSLRA's forward-looking safe harbor, the bespeaks caution doctrine only protects prospective statements, not historical facts. And also like the safe harbor, vague or boilerplate warnings will not be sufficient to protect statements from liability. Unlike the safe harbor, however, the bespeaks caution doctrine does not insulate knowingly false statements. The other important difference, is that the bespeaks caution doctrine, unlike the PSLRA safe harbor, applies to statements made in connection with tender offers and initial public offerings.

QUESTIONS

1. Does the forward-looking safe harbor make it hazardous to rely on forward-looking statements? Should investors be assumed to know this?

2. Are issuers better off with the safe harbor for forward-looking statements? If the safe harbor is such an attractive shelter, why not extend the same protection to all voluntary statements?

3. Why did the court conclude that it could not apply the safe harbor on a motion to dismiss?

4. Given the purpose of the PSLRA to reduce frivolous litigation, how effective is the forward-looking statement safe harbor in achieving this goal if defendants find it difficult to use the safe harbor to obtain a dismissal?

HYPOTHETICAL FOUR

Could Hillary, the CEO of DigitalBase, put out a press release containing earnings projection for DigitalBase covering the next five years so long as she includes "meaningful cautionary language" with the release and states that she is taking advantage of § 27A of the Securities Act and § 21E of the Exchange Act? Consider the following situations.

1. *Scenario One*: DigitalBase is in the middle of going through the registration process for its initial public offering.

2. *Scenario Two*: DigitalBase is late in the filing of its most recent Form 10–K.

3. *Scenario Three*: DigitalBase is not required to file reports under § 13(a) or § 15(d) of the Exchange Act.

4. *Scenario Four*: Hillbert Securities provides an outside review of DigitalBase that includes similar earnings projections covering the next five years. What result for Hillbert under § 27A and § 21E if Hillbert is not connected in any way to DigitalBase?

B.   SCIENTER

Ernst & Ernst v. Hochfelder

425 U.S. 185 (1976).

■ JUSTICE POWELL delivered the opinion of the Court.

The issue in this case is whether an action for civil damages may lie under § 10(b) of the Securities Exchange Act of 1934 (1934 Act), and Securities and Exchange Commission Rule 10b–5, in the absence of an allegation of intent to deceive, manipulate, or defraud on the part of the defendant.

I

* * *

[Nay, the president of a brokerage firm, perpetrated a fraud for many years, robbing investors of their money. Nay established a rule at his brokerage firm under which only he could open mail addressed to him. This "mail rule" allowed Nay to purloin the investor funds without anyone finding out about the transfers within the brokerage firm. Ernst & Ernst was the auditor for the brokerage firm. Plaintiffs alleged that Ernst & Ernst was negligent in failing to audit the brokerage firm properly and brought a private antifraud suit under § 10(b) and Rule 10b–5.]

Respondents contended that if Ernst & Ernst had conducted a proper audit, it would have discovered this "mail rule." The existence of the rule then would have been disclosed in reports to the Exchange and to the Commission by Ernst & Ernst as an irregular procedure that prevented an effective audit. This would have led to an investigation of Nay that would have revealed the fraudulent scheme. Respondents specifically disclaimed the existence of fraud or intentional misconduct on the part of Ernst & Ernst.

* * *

We granted certiorari to resolve the question whether a private cause of action for damages will lie under § 10(b) and Rule 10b–5 in the absence of any allegation of "scienter"—intent to deceive, manipulate, or defraud.[12] We conclude that it will not and therefore we reverse.

---

12. ... In this opinion the term "scienter" refers to a mental state embracing intent to deceive, manipulate, or defraud. In certain areas of the law recklessness is con-

II

* * *

A

Section 10(b) makes unlawful the use or employment of "any manipulative or deceptive device or contrivance" in contravention of Commission rules. The words "manipulative or deceptive" used in conjunction with "device or contrivance" strongly suggest that § 10(b) was intended to proscribe knowing or intentional misconduct.

In its *amicus curiae* brief, however, the Commission contends that nothing in the language "manipulative or deceptive device or contrivance" limits its operation to knowing or intentional practices. In support of its view, the Commission cites the overall congressional purpose in the 1933 and 1934 Acts to protect investors against false and deceptive practices that might injure them. The Commission then reasons that since the "effect" upon investors of given conduct is the same regardless of whether the conduct is negligent or intentional, Congress must have intended to bar all such practices and not just those done knowingly or intentionally. The logic of this effect-oriented approach would impose liability for wholly faultless conduct where such conduct results in harm to investors, a result the Commission would be unlikely to support. But apart from where its logic might lead, the Commission would add a gloss to the operative language of the statute quite different from its commonly accepted meaning. The argument simply ignores the use of the words "manipulative," "device," and "contrivance"—terms that make unmistakable a congressional intent to proscribe a type of conduct quite different from negligence. Use of the word "manipulative" is especially significant. It is and was virtually a term of art when used in connection with securities markets. It connotes intentional or willful conduct designed to deceive or defraud investors by controlling or artificially affecting the price of securities.

* * *

B

* * *

Neither the intended scope of § 10(b) nor the reasons for the changes in its operative language are revealed explicitly in the legislative history of the 1934 Act, which deals primarily with other aspects of the legislation. There is no indication, however, that § 10 (b) was intended to proscribe conduct not involving scienter. . . .

---

sidered to be a form of intentional conduct for purposes of imposing liability for some act. We need not address here the question whether, in some circumstances, reckless behavior is sufficient for civil liability under § 10(b) and Rule 10b–5. * * *

C

* * *

In each instance that Congress created express civil liability in favor of purchasers or sellers of securities it clearly specified whether recovery was to be premised on knowing or intentional conduct, negligence, or entirely innocent mistake. For example, § 11 of the 1933 Act unambiguously creates a private action for damages when a registration statement includes untrue statements of material facts or fails to state material facts necessary to make the statements therein not misleading. Within the limits specified by § 11(e), the issuer of the securities is held absolutely liable for any damages resulting from such misstatement or omission. But experts such as accountants who have prepared portions of the registration statement are accorded a "due diligence" defense. In effect, this is a negligence standard. An expert may avoid civil liability with respect to the portions of the registration statement for which he was responsible by showing that "after reasonable investigation" he had "reasonable ground[s] to believe" that the statements for which he was responsible were true and there was no omission of a material fact. The express recognition of a cause of action premised on negligent behavior in § 11 stands in sharp contrast to the language of § 10(b), and significantly undercuts the Commission's argument.

We also consider it significant that each of the express civil remedies in the 1933 Act allowing recovery for negligent conduct is subject to significant procedural restrictions not applicable under § 10(b). Section 11(e) of the 1933 Act, for example, authorizes the court to require a plaintiff bringing a suit under § 11, § 12 (2), or § 15 thereof to post a bond for costs, including attorneys' fees, and in specified circumstances to assess costs at the conclusion of the litigation.... These restrictions, significantly, were imposed by amendments to the 1933 Act adopted as part of the 1934 Act.... We think these procedural limitations indicate that the judicially created private damages remedy under § 10(b)—which has no comparable restrictions—cannot be extended, consistently with the intent of Congress, to actions premised on negligent wrongdoing. Such extension would allow causes of action covered by §§ 11, 12(2), and 15 to be brought instead under § 10(b) and thereby nullify the effectiveness of the carefully drawn procedural restrictions on these express actions. We would be unwilling to bring about this result absent substantial support in the legislative history, and there is none.

We have addressed, to this point, primarily the language and history of § 10(b). The Commission contends, however, that subsections (b) and (c) of Rule 10b–5 are cast in language which—if standing alone—could encompass both intentional and negligent behavior. These subsections respectively provide that it is unlawful "[t]o make any untrue statement of a material fact or to omit to state a material fact necessary in order to make the statements made, in the light of the circumstances under which they were made, not misleading ... " and "[t]o engage in any act, practice, or course of business which operates or would operate as a fraud or deceit upon any person.... " Viewed in isolation the language of subsection (b), and arguably that of subsection (c), could be read as proscribing, respectively, any type of material misstatement or omission, and any course of conduct, that has the effect of defrauding investors, whether the wrongdoing was intentional or not.

We note first that such a reading cannot be harmonized with the administrative history of the Rule, a history making clear that when the Commission adopted the Rule it was intended to apply only to activities that involved scienter. More importantly, Rule 10b–5 was adopted pursuant to authority granted the Commission under § 10(b). The rulemaking power granted to an administrative agency charged with the administration of a federal statute is not the power to make law. Rather, it is " 'the power to adopt regulations to carry into effect the will of Congress as expressed by the statute.' " Thus, despite the broad view of the Rule advanced by the Commission in this case, its scope cannot exceed the power granted the Commission by Congress under § 10(b). For the reasons stated above, we think the Commission's original interpretation of Rule 10b–5 was compelled by the language and history of § 10(b) and related sections of the Acts. When a statute speaks so specifically in terms of manipulation and deception, and of implementing devices and contrivances—the commonly understood terminology of intentional wrongdoing—and when its history reflects no more expansive intent, we are quite unwilling to extend the scope of the statute to negligent conduct.[33]

* * *

QUESTIONS

1. Why does Justice Powell say that the logic of the SEC's approach "would impose liability for wholly faultless conduct where such conduct results in harm to investors, a result the Commission would be unlikely to support"?

2. Does recklessness count as "intent to deceive, manipulate, or defraud"? If the defendant truly had no motive to deceive, should recklessness count as scienter?

---

33. As we find the language and history of § 10(b) dispositive of the appropriate standard of liability, there is no occasion to examine the additional considerations of "policy," set forth by the parties, that may have influenced the lawmakers in their formulation of the statute. We do note that the standard urged by respondents would significantly broaden the class of plaintiffs who may seek to impose liability upon accountants and other experts who perform services or express opinions with respect to matters under the Acts....

This case, on its facts, illustrates the extreme reach of the standard urged by respondents. As investors in transactions initiated by Nay, not First Securities, they were not foreseeable users of the financial statements prepared by Ernst & Ernst. Respondents conceded that they did not rely on either these financial statements or Ernst & Ernst's certificates of opinion. The class of persons eligible to benefit from such a standard, though small in this case, could be numbered in the thousands in other cases. Acceptance of respondents' view would extend to new frontiers the "hazards" of rendering expert advice under the Acts, raising serious policy questions not yet addressed by Congress.

3. The Court notes that in a § 11 action for a material misstatement (or omission where there is a duty to disclose) involving a public offering registration statement, Ernst & Ernst could escape liability by meeting its "due diligence" defense. To meet the due diligence defense, Ernst & Ernst must show that it performed its duties without negligence. Why should negligence on the part of Ernst & Ernst lead to § 11 liability but not Rule 10b–5 liability?

HYPOTHETICAL FIVE

Shortly after DigitalBase discloses the problems with GigaBase, its auditor, Arthur & Young, demands that it restate its revenues for the last year. It turns out that the DigitalBase sales staff for the western U.S.—under heavy pressure from Hillary, the CEO, to maintain market share until the GigaBase comes on line—has been providing some of the distributors who sell DigitalBase's product with secret side agreements allowing the distributors to return the product if it goes unsold. DigitalBase has been booking the revenue and profit from these sales as final despite the right of return, but Arthur & Young has now stumbled across the side agreements and insists that DigitalBase restate $250 million in revenues.

When DigitalBase issues the press release announcing the restatement, its stock price drops from $15 to $10. Assume that (before the revelation of the misleading revenue recognition practices) Arthur & Young issues a statement that it has reviewed DigitalBase's financials for the past year and has certified that they conform to generally accepted accounting principles. We know now that DigitalBase has in fact been overstating its sales. In conducting its review of DigitalBase, it is shown at trial that Randall, the lead partner from Arthur & Young, did not follow the industry-accepted practice of spot checking contracts with customers. If Randall had done so, it is likely that he would have uncovered the side agreements. Can Arthur & Young be held liable under Rule 10b–5?

In footnote twelve of the *Ernst & Ernst* opinion, Justice Powell reserved the question of whether "recklessness," as opposed to knowingly making a misstatement, would satisfy the scienter requirement. The Court has not returned to this question, but every circuit court that has addressed the question has concluded that recklessness satisfies Rule 10b–5's scienter standard. Congress flirted with codifying a scienter standard when it was drafting the PSLRA, but it instead simply adopted the pleading standard discussed in the case below.

The next case also addresses the question of how much evidence the plaintiff must put forward regarding the defendant's state of mind in order to withstand a motion to dismiss. For Rule 10b–5 (and other private claims under the Exchange Act), the PSLRA requires that complaints plead with particularity facts giving rise to a "strong inference" that the defendants had the requisite "state of mind," as codified in § 21D(b)(2) of the Exchange Act. Discovery, moreover, is stayed until after the motion to dismiss (§ 21D(b)(3)(B)), making it difficult for plaintiffs to uncover facts to meet the pleading with particularity requirement and thereby avoid dismissal. What sort of facts must a plaintiff offer to meet this heightened pleading requirement?

Florida State Bd. of Admin. v. Green Tree Fin. Corp.

270 F.3d 645 (8th Cir. 2001).

■ GIBSON, CIRCUIT JUDGE.

In this case we must assess the sufficiency of three complaints under the new pleading standards made applicable to securities fraud cases by the Private Securities Litigation Reform Act of 1995. [Plaintiffs] have each brought Rule 10b–5 actions against Green Tree Financial Corporation, its CEO, Lawrence Coss, and other executives, on the theory that they fraudulently overstated Green Tree's financial value. The investors allege that they bought securities in a market affected by this fraud and that when the true facts came to light, Green Tree's stock price tumbled and they lost their money.

* * *

For the purpose of a motion to dismiss, we take the facts from the complaints. Green Tree is a financial services corporation that originally specialized in lending money on house trailers, referred to as "manufactured housing," although it later diversified into other kinds of lending. Because manufactured housing loans are classified as "sub-prime," the interest rates are very high—as much as 200 to 400 basis points (two to four percentage points) above residential mortgage rates. Green Tree rose to prominence by pioneering the securitization of manufactured housing loans, which means that it pooled large numbers of these loans and put them into a trust, which sold securities for which the loans served as collateral. The securities entitled the purchaser to fixed interest and principal payments under the loans. Importantly, Green Tree did not relinquish all rights under the securitized loans; instead, it retained the right to keep a portion of the loan payments and it retained the obligation to service the loans. Green Tree's profit was therefore the spread between the interest it charged the borrowers and the interest it promised the instrument-holders, minus Green Tree's costs of servicing the loans. However, Green Tree retained the risk of losses from loan defaults, as well as the risk that borrowers would prepay their loans before incurring interest charges, so that the expected interest would never materialize. By absorbing these risks, Green Tree could take high-interest-rate manufactured-housing loans and turn them into low-interest-rate securities, thereby creating the profitable spreads that fueled Green Tree's growth.

As it securitized each loan pool, Green Tree booked a current gain on the transaction, even though the expected profits would not actually come into its coffers until much later and even though the amount of those profits would fluctuate with Green Tree's success in collecting the loan payments. This "gain-on-sale revenue" was the force that drove Green Tree's reported earnings during the periods covered by the complaints.

Gain-on-sale receivables made up 63.8% of the net revenue that Green Tree originally reported for 1996. In addition to the income, Green Tree also recorded the present value of the securitizations as balance sheet assets called "Excess Servicing Rights Receivable" or "Interest Only Securities." In 1996 "Excess Servicing Rights Receivable" was the greatest single asset on Green Tree's balance sheet.

In order to estimate the present value of the securitizations, Green Tree had to assume three things: (1) the discount rate (reflecting the lesser value of a dollar to be paid in the future than a dollar paid today); (2) the loan default rate; and (3) the loan prepayment rate. The numbers chosen for these assumptions played a crucial role in deciding the amount Green Tree would report as earnings on the securitizations and as the value of the Excess Servicing Rights Receivable. Choosing a figure for prepayment rate was especially difficult because if interest rates fell substantially or if other lenders competed aggressively, borrowers would be likely to refinance in large numbers. If that happened, the loans and consequently, the expected profit on them, would simply disappear. A discrepancy between assumed prepayment rates and actual prepayment experience could have a serious effect on Green Tree's earnings and balance sheet.

The crux of this suit is the investors' allegation that Green Tree used "unrealistic and unreasonable" assumptions in its gain-on-sale accounting, thus overvaluing its assets and overstating its earnings. In particular, the investors allege that the actual prepayment experience from 1995 to 1997 varied so much from the prepayment rate Green Tree assumed in its gain-on-sale accounting for 1994 and 1995 securitizations that Green Tree's financials and other publicly filed reports during the 1995–1997 period were materially false. The investors concede that Green Tree publicly disclosed its actual prepayment experience. However, they allege the defendants refused to disclose what prepayment assumptions Green Tree had used in its gain-on-sale accounting and that this constituted omission of a material fact necessary to prevent its financial reports from being misleading. Green Tree stated in its public filings with the SEC that its management regularly reevaluated Green Tree's prepayment assumptions in light of actual experience. According to the complaints, the defendants either knew that the discrepancy between the actual prepayment experience and the assumed rates rendered the financials materially false, or alternatively, recklessly disregarded this fact.

In any event, Green Tree's assumptions about prepayment rates turned out to be seriously inadequate. [In November 1997, Green Tree increased its prepayment reserve to cover the decline in its loan pools due to higher than expected prepayment rates. Green Tree's stock price plummeted as a result. After the first increase in reserves, Green Tree's CEO told investors that "I don't see any set of circumstances that would cause us to [write down the 1994–1995 securitization loan pools] again." Green Tree then proceeded to increase its reserves again in January 1998 while also restating its prior 1996 earnings downward by $200 million. Conseco, Inc. eventually acquired Green Tree and took charges totaling $350 million to write down the carrying value of the loan pools, reflecting adjustment to assumptions for prepayment rates, discount rates, and default rates.]

The investors allege that several motives prompted the defendants to spread misleading financial information through the market. First, they allege that the compensation of defendant Coss and other Green Tree executives was tied to Green Tree's financial results, which made the defendants want to maximize Green Tree's reported earnings. In particular, CEO Coss had a remarkable contract awarding him 2.5% of Green Tree's pre-tax income (minus other executives' bonuses). Coss's contract was to expire December 31, 1996. Accordingly, it was in Coss's personal interest to report as much income as possible before the expiration of his lucrative contract. Other motives alleged are: (1) the defendants' desire to maintain a high corporate credit rating to maximize the selling price of the loan pools; and (2) Green Tree's need to demonstrate exemplary financial results in order to fend off a pending derivative suit alleging that the company wasted corporate assets by paying excessive executive compensation.

* * *

III.

* * *

Our Circuit ruled before enactment of the Reform Act that recklessness satisfied the Rule 10b–5 scienter requirement, and the defendants do not contend that the Reform Act changed the substantive nature of the scienter requirement.[7] Our Circuit has adopted a definition of recklessness

> limited to those highly unreasonable omissions or misrepresentations that involve not merely simple or even inexcusable negligence, but an extreme departure from the standards of ordinary care, and that present a danger of misleading buyers or sellers which is either known to the defendant or is so obvious that the defendant must have been aware of it.

The question before us is whether the facts pleaded in the complaints adequately plead scienter. At the outset we must determine what pleading standard the investors have to satisfy. Complaints brought under Rule 10b–5 and section 10(b) are governed by special pleading rules unique to securities cases, which Congress adopted in the Private Securities Litigation Reform Act of 1995 as part of its attempt to curb abuses of securities

---

7. There is now substantial agreement among the Circuits that have considered the question that 21D(b)(2) was not intended to alter the substantive standard for scienter. In *In re Silicon Graphics Inc. Sec. Litig.*, 183 F.3d 970, 977 (9th Cir. 1999), the Ninth Circuit stated that the Reform Act adopted a heightened substantive standard for scienter, that of "deliberate recklessness," which "re-flects some degree of intentional or conscious misconduct." In a later case, however, the Ninth Circuit limited Silicon Graphics' holding to a pleading requirement, stating that "the [Reform Act] did not alter the substantive requirements for scienter under § 10(b)." Howard v. Everex Sys., Inc., 228 F.3d 1057, 1064 (9th Cir. 2000).

fraud litigation. In the Reform Act, Congress enacted two heightened pleading requirements for securities fraud cases. The first requires that the complaint specify each false statement or misleading omission and explain why the omission was misleading. Exchange Act § 21D(b)(1). The second requires that the complaint state "with particularity" facts giving rise to a "strong inference" that the defendant acted with the scienter required for the cause of action. Exchange Act § 21D(b)(2).

There is disagreement in the various circuits about the meaning of the strong-inference-of-scienter pleading standard. Our circuit has not yet decided the question. . . . The investors contend that to establish a strong inference of scienter, they have only to plead either (1) facts showing the defendants had the motive and opportunity to commit fraud or (2) facts constituting strong circumstantial evidence of scienter. The defendants contend that a complaint cannot survive under the Reform Act based on allegations showing motive and opportunity alone. Additionally, the defendants contend that the investors have not pleaded facts showing motive and opportunity, or any other theory adequate to raise a strong inference of scienter.

* * *

The strong inference standard has its genesis in case law antedating the Reform Act. Since its adoption in 1937, Federal Rule of Civil Procedure 9(b) has imposed a special pleading standard for fraud: "In all averments of fraud or mistake, the circumstances constituting fraud or mistake shall be stated with particularity. Malice, intent, knowledge, and other condition of mind of a person may be averred generally." Even though Rule 9(b) said that state of mind could be averred generally (rather than with particularity), some circuits began to apply a special standard in securities cases, requiring pleading of facts that would indicate scienter, rather than the mere conclusion that the defendant acted with scienter.

In particular, the Second Circuit began to require plaintiffs in fraud cases to plead facts that "give rise to a 'strong inference' that the defendants possessed the requisite fraudulent intent." In *Beck*, Judge Newman elaborated in a discussion that became the black-letter law of the Second Circuit:

> A common method for establishing a strong inference of scienter is to allege facts showing a motive for committing fraud and a clear opportunity for doing so. Where motive is not apparent, it is still possible to plead scienter by identifying circumstances indicating conscious behavior by the defendant, though the strength of the circumstantial allegations must be correspondingly greater.

* * *

The rule that pleading motive and opportunity alone would give rise to a strong inference of scienter was remarkable for two reasons. First, having the motive and opportunity to do wrong are certainly not the same as having the intent to do it. The rule, taken literally, presumes that anyone who has the chance to profit by wrongdoing is likely to do so. This is a large leap.

The second remarkable thing about the assertion that pleading motive and opportunity alone gives rise to a strong inference of fraud is the size of the breach it would leave in a pleading standard that was said to be stringent and tough. Nearly every highly ranked executive of a company could be said to have the motive and the opportunity to profit by misstatements. "Greed is a ubiquitous motive, and corporate insiders and upper management always have the opportunity to lie and manipulate."

Apparently because of the potentially wide applicability of "motive and opportunity," the Second Circuit soon retreated from a literal application of the rule. "Motive and opportunity" evolved into a term of art, meaning something far narrower than what it appears to mean.... [A]llegations of commonly held motives, even powerful ones such as the desire to stay CEO of a company, would not supply scienter under Rule 9(b)....

Nor would it constitute a pleading of "motive" to allege that the defendant wanted to maintain his or her company's profitability or credit rating, either for its own sake or to increase thereby the defendant's own compensation.... Instead, the Second Circuit came to interpret "motive and opportunity" as requiring allegations that the "defendants benefited in some concrete and personal way from the purported fraud," with the prototypic case being insider trading. Yet, the difference between a case in which the defendant allegedly lied to increase his or her performance-driven compensation and one in which he or she allegedly lied to profit from insider trading is not so much a difference in the type of motive as a difference in the evidence that the defendant intended to capitalize on the opportunity. In either case, the defendant stands to make money (how much money depends entirely on the facts of the cases). But in the insider trading case, trading at a particular time is circumstantial evidence that the insider knew the best time to trade because he or she had inside information not shared by the public. This in turn is circumstantial evidence that he or she kept the information from the public in order to trade on the unfair advantage. In contrast, in the executive compensation case, there is no tell-tale action (other than the false statement) to suggest guilty knowledge or purpose.

* * *

The Circuits that have interpreted the Reform Act have fallen into (at least) three camps. The Ninth Circuit ... raised the pleading standard to a level beyond that in the Second Circuit.

At the other end of the spectrum, the Second and Third Circuits have held that in using the "strong inference" language, the Reform Act adopted a pleading standard "approximately equal in stringency to that of the Second Circuit," including the motive-and-opportunity formulation. The Second Circuit qualified its conclusion by stating that "Congress's failure to include language about motive and opportunity suggests that we need not be wedded to these concepts in articulating the prevailing standard," but that courts should nevertheless be guided by the motive-and-opportunity cases. The Second and Third Circuits also agree that the Reform Act's additional requirement that facts pertaining to scienter be pleaded "with particularity" represents a "heightening of the [pleading] standard."

Occupying the middle ground, the First, Fifth, Sixth, Tenth, and Eleventh Circuits have held that the primary effect of the Reform Act is to require a pleading to state facts giving rise to a "strong inference of scienter." Allegations of motive and opportunity may or may not rise to that level in a particular case. "While it is true that motive and opportunity are not substitutes for a showing of recklessness, they can be catalysts to fraud and so serve as external markers to the required state of mind.... 'Motive' and 'opportunity' are simply recurring patterns of evidence."

Putting aside the Ninth Circuit standard ... the split in the other Circuits is more apparent than real. As we discussed above, the Second Circuit has dramatically constricted the types of "motive and opportunity" that it will recognize as sufficient to plead scienter. It will not allow plaintiffs to proceed based on widely held motives such as "(1) the desire to maintain a high corporate credit rating or otherwise sustain 'the appearance of corporate profitability, or of the success of an investment, [or] (2) the desire to maintain a high stock price in order to increase executive compensation or prolong the benefits of holding corporate office.'" Even complaints based on insider trading must allege more than that the defendant benefited from trading because of a false statement or misleading omission; the insider trades have to be "unusual," either in the amount of profit made, the amount of stock traded, the portion of stockholdings sold, or the number of insiders involved, before they will give rise to the required inference of scienter. This is the same kind of inquiry undertaken by courts that do not adhere to the motive-and-opportunity formulation. The search in the Second Circuit line of cases, as well as in the other circuits, is for facts that give a strong reason to believe that there was reckless or intentional wrongdoing. Taken as a whole, the cases simply do not substantiate the fear that courts applying the motive-and-opportunity formulation will permit pleadings to go forward without facts strongly suggesting wrongdoing....

Therefore, we can say three things about motive and opportunity allegations. First, motive and opportunity are generally relevant to a fraud case, and a showing of unusual or heightened motive will often form an important part of a complaint that meets the Reform Act standard. Second, in some cases the same circumstantial allegations that establish motive and opportunity also give additional reason to believe the defendant's misrepresentation was knowing or reckless. For instance, in insider trading cases, the timing of trades shows motive and opportunity, but it may also provide additional circumstantial evidence that the defendant knew of an advantage. Such allegations may meet the Reform Act standard, but if so it is because they give rise to a strong inference of scienter, not merely because they establish motive and opportunity. Third, when the complaint does not show motive and opportunity of any sort—either the unusual, heightened motive highlighted in the Second Circuit cases, or even an everyday motive such as keeping one's job—then other allegations tending to show scienter would have to be particularly strong in order to meet the Reform Act standard.

IV.

This case was decided under both the Federal Rules of Civil Procedure and the Reform Act. The Reform Act modifies the ordinary Rule 12(b)(6) dismissal mechanism in two limited ways. First, whereas under Rule 12(b)(6), we must assume all factual allegations in the complaint are true, under the Reform Act, we disregard "catch-all" or "blanket" assertions that do not live up to the particularity requirements of the statute.

Second, under Fed. R. Civ. P. 12(b)(6), the plaintiff is entitled to all reasonable inferences that may be drawn from the allegations of the complaint. However, under the Reform Act, a securities fraud case cannot survive unless its allegations collectively add up to a strong inference of the required state of mind.

* * *

V.

* * *

Even in the Second Circuit, pleading that a defendant's compensation depends on corporate value or earnings does not, by itself, establish motive to fraudulently misrepresent corporate value or earnings. Here, the investors allege that Coss's arrangement established a legally significant motive because the amount of his compensation was based on a percentage of Green Tree's pre-tax earnings, and his contract was set to expire at the end of 1996, making it urgent for Coss to maximize Green Tree's earnings for that year. Green Tree originally booked earnings for 1996 that allowed Coss to earn $102 million. Roughly a year later, Green Tree found it necessary to revise its 1996 earnings retrospectively.

We conclude that the magnitude of Coss's compensation package, together with the timing coincidence of an overstatement of earnings at just the right time to benefit Coss, provides an unusual, heightened showing of motive to commit fraud. The motive and opportunity allegations regarding Coss are therefore an important part of a circumstantial case against him and consequently, against Green Tree, which was subject to Coss's control.

The defendants contend that Coss's compensation is irrelevant because Coss wound up giving back a proportional amount of his 1996 compensation after the 1996 earnings were restated in January 1998. But Coss did not necessarily know at the time of the alleged misrepresentations and omissions that it would turn out that way. He could have acted recklessly to pile up earnings before his contract ran out, gambling that he would get away with it. The ultimate profitability of a course of conduct is not conclusive of intent. Just as we cannot countenance pleading fraud by hindsight, neither can we infer innocence by hindsight because the alleged misdeeds did not pay off. . . .

[T]he allegations provide powerful support for the idea that defendants hoped that the prepayment problem would come out in the wash—why else would they have waited until 1998 to reveal and remedy the problem? The complaints plead that defendants knew their assumed prepayment rate and they knew their actual rates as those rates were unfolding. This amounts to knowledge of the prepayment discrepancy. . . . The investors allege that the defendants knew facts that showed the assumptions were materially inadequate, but the defendants recklessly attempted to sweep the problem under the rug hoping a change in the economy would ameliorate the problem. We cannot conclude that this is a case in which the motive theory is too irrational to add to the weight of other circumstantial allegations, and we therefore must disagree with the district court's determination to the contrary.

* * *

The other executives besides Coss object that they did not share Coss's lucrative employment contract and that it is not plausible that they would commit fraud to enrich someone else. The compensation allegations against the other executives are obviously weaker evidence of motive than those against Coss and Green Tree. The investors did not plead that the other executives had incentive contracts that were about to expire or that their compensation was comparable to Coss's. Potts was alleged to have received a bonus of $1.25 million in 1996 and Richard Evans $350,000. [Plaintiffs] argue, "The primary motive was to enrich Coss, and along the way a trickle down effect would be felt in the bonuses of the other executives." This falls short of alleging the "concrete and personal" benefit that would add significantly to the allegations against the other executives.

The investors also allege that the defendants were motivated by the desire to maintain a high credit rating for Green Tree so that its securitizations would continue to sell at good prices. The desire to maintain a high credit rating is universally held among corporations and their executives and consequently does not contribute significantly to an inference of scienter.

The investors claim that defendants were motivated during the class period to show exemplary performance by Green Tree to enhance their defense of a derivative suit for corporate waste that was not filed until January 23, 1997, a year and a half into the class period alleged by the stockholders' and option traders' classes. The investors seem to concede that defense of a non-existent suit cannot supply a motive for the first year and a half of the alleged misrepresentation. Moreover, the defendants made their November 1997 and January 1998 revelations while the state suit was pending. While the pendency of a derivative suit could supply an important motive in some circumstances, we cannot say that it automatically satisfies the scienter requirement. The inference to be drawn depends on the facts of the case, and the timing issues in this case undermine the notion that the derivative suit played an important role in the events at issue.

[Plaintiffs] also argue that the defendants were motivated to overstate Green Tree's financial results in order to make it more attractive to a potential buyer.... The district court said that ... it would have been too implausible to suggest that Green Tree hoped a buyer would purchase the company without performing its own examination of Green Tree's financial status. Another problem with the theory is that the only merger on the horizon was the merger with Conseco, Inc., a transaction announced April 7, 1998—months after the November 1997 and January 1998 revelations.

This is too thin a reed on which to hang an inference of scienter existing during the class period. While this is not the kind of case in which the facts showing motive and opportunity alone create a strong inference of scienter, nevertheless, Coss's extraordinary compensation package, on the very eve of expiring, created a powerful incentive to see to it that Green Tree made plenty of money before his contract expired. For Coss and for Green Tree, this factor is an important part of the overall picture of scienter. It appears that the investors' motive allegations against the other executives are basically derivative from their case against Coss. They argue that "Coss was the dominant force at Green Tree" and that the Green Tree board of directors lacked independence from Coss. Although these contentions do not amount to a showing of an unusual, heightened motive for the other executives, they at least paint a rational and plausible picture of why the executives would have gone along with the alleged fraud. Thus, if the motive allegations do not add much to the investors' claims against the other executives, neither is there an utter lack of rational motive, which would require the investors to make a stronger circumstantial case than would otherwise be necessary.

VI.

In addition to the motive-and-opportunity allegations, the complaints contain other facts that give rise to a strong inference of fraud. In broad outline, the investors pleaded with particularity that defendants knew the prepayment assumptions on which their gain-on-sale accounting for the 1994 and 1995 pools were based, they knew that actual experience in 1995, 1996 and the first three quarters of 1997 deviated from those premises greatly, and they issued financials that did not take account of the disparity between the assumptions and actual experience.... There is no dispute that the prepayment problem led to Green Tree's $390 million write-down in January 1998.

One of the classic fact patterns giving rise to a strong inference of scienter is that defendants published statements when they knew facts or had access to information suggesting that their public statements were materially inaccurate. Here, the investors alleged that defendants published statements with knowledge of facts indicating crucial information in the statements was based on discredited assumptions. These allegations give rise to a strong inference of scienter. Additionally, the sheer size of the

$390 million write-down adds to the inference that the defendants must have been aware the problem was brewing.

The defendants respond that this is too simplistic a view of a case involving sophisticated financial transactions in which the accounting decisions were difficult and even very large mistakes could fall within the realm of good faith.... Undoubtedly, the accounting issues are complex; whether they were handled within the parameters of good faith decision-making or whether the decisions amounted to recklessness will surely be the focus of any trial of this case. We will not prejudge that issue. But neither the district court, nor we, can conduct a battle of experts on a motion to dismiss. Rather, we must assume the truth of the allegations pleaded with particularity in the complaint. The strong-inference pleading standard does not license us to resolve disputed facts at this stage of the case....

The investors have pleaded that during the various class periods, the defendants had in their possession facts that rendered their financial results materially false when they published them. Additionally, the investors have pleaded facts giving Coss, the dominant force within Green Tree, a substantial and urgent reason to delay owning up to the prepayment problem. Although the defendants other than Green Tree and Coss had less of a personal interest in putting off the hour of reckoning, the investors' theory that the others were subject to domination by Coss fits within a highly plausible theory of fraud. While the defendants have many good arguments explaining how and why they thought their statements proper, none of these arguments saps the investors' allegations of their force at this procedural stage. The facts pleaded with particularity add up to a strong inference of scienter, thus meeting the Reform Act standard.

* * *

NOTES

1. *The discovery stay.* Difficulties faced by plaintiffs in pleading the requisite "strong inference" of scienter are exacerbated by the PSLRA's discovery stay. Exchange Act § 21D(b)(3)(B). The discovery stay precludes discovery "unless the court finds upon the motion of any party that particularized discovery is necessary to preserve evidence or to prevent undue prejudice to that party." As a result, plaintiffs do not have access to the company's documents to search for the evidence that might support allegations of scienter.

2. *Mandatory sanctions inquiry.* Adding teeth to the pleading requirement is Exchange Act § 21D(c), which requires courts to make specific findings regarding compliance with Fed. R. Civ. P. 11 upon final adjudication. Sanctions for violating Rule 11 are mandatory, with a presumption created in favor of awarding attorneys' fees and costs to the prevailing party. So a complaint that lacked a factual basis could well lead to substantial sanctions. The provision appears to have been implemented only sporadically, however, despite its supposedly mandatory nature.

QUESTIONS

1. Are motive and opportunity alone enough to show scienter in the Second Circuit (pre-PSLRA)?

2. How did the PSLRA alter the Second Circuit test?

3. What did the court find persuasive here with respect to strong inference?

4. As a plaintiff's attorney, where would you look for evidence to plead scienter?

HYPOTHETICAL SIX

The plaintiffs allege the following facts in their complaint against Digital-Base and Hillary, the CEO. Hillary sold 500,000 shares of stock during the class period for proceeds of $12.5 million. In addition, the financial press reported that DigitalBase was actively seeking potential merger partners in the network services sector during the class period. The plaintiffs also allege that Hillary received weekly memoranda from DigitalBase's chief technology officer updating her on the progress of the GigaBase. The plaintiffs allege (in somewhat vague terms) that these memoranda repeatedly advised Hillary of the problems with the development of the GigaBase. The plaintiffs also allege that Hillary knew that DigitalBase's existing products were generally inferior to those offered at the time by its competitors, so she must have known that DigitalBase could not be maintaining its sales levels without providing inducements. DigitalBase and Hillary file a motion to dismiss the complaint. Have the plaintiffs adequately pleaded scienter?

C.   RELIANCE

The SEC need not prove reliance, that is, it need not show that it (or any actual investor) relied on a misstatement in making an investment decision. By contrast, private plaintiffs must prove reliance. This requirement is sometimes called "transaction causation" in recognition of the Supreme Court's rather flexible interpretation of the reliance requirement. Did the plaintiffs rely in the following case?

Affiliated Ute Citizens of Utah v. United States

406 U.S. 128 (1972).

■ JUSTICE BLACKMUN delivered the opinion of the Court.

* * *

Ute Development Corporation [UDC] was incorporated in 1958 with the stated purpose "to manage jointly with the Tribal Business Committee of the full-blood members of the Ute Indian Tribe ... all unadjudicated or unliquidated claims against the United States, all gas, oil, and mineral rights of every kind, and all other assets not susceptible to equitable and practicable distribution to which the mixed-blood members of the said tribe ... are now, or may hereafter become entitled ... and to receive the proceeds therefrom and to distribute the same to the stockholders of this corporation...."

[UDC proceeded to issue shares of its capital stock to mixed-blood members of the Ute Indian Tribe. UDC made an agreement with First

Security Bank of Utah (the bank) for the bank to serve as the stock transfer agent for the UDC shares, the bank to hold the stock certificates and issue receipts to the shareholders. UDC's articles provided that for the time period relevant to the case, mixed-blood shareholders seeking to sell their UDC stock must first offer the stock to other members of the Ute tribe. Only if the offer was not accepted by any member of the tribe could the stock be then sold to a nonmember at a price no lower than that offered to the members.]

* * *

In February 1965 Anita R. Reyos and 84 other mixed-bloods sued the bank, two of the bank's employee-officers, John B. Gale and Verl Haslem charging violations of the Securities Exchange Act of 1934 and of Rule 10b–5 of the Securities and Exchange Commission. . . . These plaintiffs had sold UDC shares to various nonmembers including the defendants Gale and Haslem.

* * *

Defendants Gale and Haslem were the bank's assistant managers at Roosevelt. They were also notaries public. . . . During 1963 and 1964 mixed-bloods sold 1,387 shares of UDC stock. All were sold to nonmembers of the tribe. Haslem purchased 50 of these himself and Gale purchased 63. . . . They paid cash for the shares they purchased. . . . In 1964 and 1965 UDC stock was sold by mixed-bloods at prices ranging from $300 to $700 per share. Shares were being transferred between whites, however, at prices from $500 to $700 per share.

Gale and Haslem possessed standing orders from non-Indian buyers. About seven of these were from outside the State. Some of the prospective purchasers maintained deposits at the bank for the purpose of ready consummation of any transaction.

The two men received various commissions and gratuities for their services in facilitating the transfer of UDC stock from mixed-bloods to non-Indians. Gale supplied some funds as sales advances to the mixed-blood sellers. He and Haslem solicited contracts for open purchases of UDC stock and did so on bank premises and during business hours.

The District Court concluded . . . as to Gale and Haslem: The two men had devised a plan or scheme to acquire, for themselves and others, shares in UDC from mixed-bloods. In violation of their duty to make a fair disclosure, they succeeded in acquiring shares from mixed-bloods for less than fair value. As to the bank: It was put upon notice of the improper activities of its employees, Gale and Haslem, knowingly created the apparent authority on their part, and was responsible for their conduct. Its liability was joint and several with that of Gale and Haslem.

* * *

[The Court ruled that Gale, Haslem, and the bank owed a duty of disclosure to the members of the tribe selling their shares to non-Indians because their activities to encourage a market in the UDC stock among non-Indians went beyond their function as the mere transfer agent. The bank also acknowledged its duty to the tribe members in transferring their shares.]

Clearly, the Court of Appeals was right to the extent that it held that the two employees had violated Rule 10b–5; in the instances specified in that holding the record reveals a misstatement of a material fact, within the proscription of Rule 10b–5 (2), namely, that the prevailing market price of the UDC shares was the figure at which their purchases were made.

We conclude, however, that the Court of Appeals erred when it held that there was no violation of the Rule unless the record disclosed evidence of reliance on material fact misrepresentations by Gale and Haslem. We do not read Rule 10b–5 so restrictively. To be sure, the second subparagraph of the rule specifies the making of an untrue statement of a material fact and the omission to state a material fact. The first and third subparagraphs are not so restricted. These defendants' activities, outlined above, disclose, within the very language of one or the other of those subparagraphs, a "course of business" or a "device, scheme, or artifice" that operated as a fraud upon the Indian sellers. This is so because the defendants devised a plan and induced the mixed-blood holders of UDC stock to dispose of their shares without disclosing to them material facts that reasonably could have been expected to influence their decisions to sell. The individual defendants, in a distinct sense, were market makers, not only for their personal purchases constituting 8 1/3% of the sales, but for the other sales their activities produced. This being so, they possessed the affirmative duty under the Rule to disclose this fact to the mixed-blood sellers. It is no answer to urge that, as to some of the petitioners, these defendants may have made no positive representation or recommendation. The defendants may not stand mute while they facilitate the mixed-bloods' sales to those seeking to profit in the non-Indian market the defendants had developed and encouraged and with which they were fully familiar. The sellers had the right to know that the defendants were in a position to gain financially from their sales and that their shares were selling for a higher price in that market.

Under the circumstances of this case, involving primarily a failure to disclose, positive proof of reliance is not a prerequisite to recovery. All that is necessary is that the facts withheld be material in the sense that a reasonable investor might have considered them important in the making of this decision. This obligation to disclose and this withholding of a material fact establish the requisite element of causation in fact.

Gale and Haslem engaged in more than ministerial functions. Their acts were clearly within the reach of Rule 10b–5. And they were acts performed when they were obligated to act on behalf of the mixed-blood sellers.... The liability of the bank, of course, is coextensive with that of Gale and Haslem.

* * *

QUESTIONS

1. If the plaintiffs in a fraud by omission case had to show reliance, how could they do so?

2. Suppose that Jane, a "mixed-blood" Ute, has a time-sensitive debt that must be paid immediately. In order to pay her debts, she plans on selling 100 UDC shares to Gale and Haslem at the price of $300 per share. Assume that due to time constraints, she is simply unable to find another purchaser other than Gale and Haslem. Later, Jane learns that UDC shares are reselling among non-members at $700 per share and brings a Rule 10b–5 lawsuit against Gale and Haslem. Can Gale and Haslem argue that there is no reliance on their failure to disclose the $700 trading price among non-members?

In the next case (previously seen in Chapter 3) the Supreme Court addresses the question of reliance in the context of affirmative statements made to the market generally. What is left of the reliance requirement after *Basic*?

Basic Inc. v. Levinson

485 U.S. 224 (1988).

■ JUSTICE BLACKMUN delivered the opinion of the Court.

This case requires us to ... determine whether a person who traded a corporation's shares on a securities exchange after the issuance of a materially misleading statement by the corporation may invoke a rebuttable presumption that, in trading, he relied on the integrity of the price set by the market.

I.

[Combustion Engineering sought to purchase Basic, Inc. (a publicly-traded manufacturer of chemical refractories for the steel industry). Combustion entered into negotiations with Basic in 9/76. Basic made statements on 10/21/77, 9/25/78, and 11/6/78 that no merger negotiations were taking place and there were no other developments to explain the high volume of trading in Basic stock as well as large price fluctuations. Then on 12/18/78 Basic asked the NYSE to suspend trading and the next day announced the pending merger with Combustion Engineering. Investors filed a class action under § 10(b) and Rule 10b–5 (with a class period from 10/21/77 to 12/18/78), alleging "they were injured by selling Basic shares at artificially depressed prices in a market affected by petitioners' misleading statements and in reliance thereon."]

* * *

We granted certiorari ... to determine whether the courts below properly applied a presumption of reliance in certifying the class, rather than requiring each class member to show direct reliance on Basic's statements.

* * *

IV.

We turn to the question of reliance and the fraud-on-the-market theory. Succinctly put:

> The fraud on the market theory is based on the hypothesis that, in an open and developed securities market, the price of a company's stock is determined by the available material information regarding the company and its business.... Misleading statements will therefore defraud purchasers of stock even if the purchasers do not directly rely on the misstatements.... The causal connection between the defendants' fraud and the plaintiffs' purchase of stock in such a case is no less significant than in a case of direct reliance on misrepresentations.

Our task, of course, is not to assess the general validity of the theory, but to consider whether it was proper for the courts below to apply a rebuttable presumption of reliance, supported in part by the fraud-on-the-market theory.

This case required resolution of several common questions of law and fact concerning the falsity or misleading nature of the three public statements made by Basic, the presence or absence of scienter, and the materiality of the misrepresentations, if any. In their amended complaint, the named plaintiffs alleged that in reliance on Basic's statements they sold their shares of Basic stock in the depressed market created by petitioners. Requiring proof of individualized reliance from each member of the proposed plaintiff class effectively would have prevented respondents from proceeding with a class action, since individual issues then would have overwhelmed the common ones. The District Court found that the presumption of reliance created by the fraud-on-the-market theory provided "a practical resolution to the problem of balancing the substantive requirement of proof of reliance in securities cases against the procedural requisites of [Fed. Rule Civ. Proc.] 23." The District Court thus concluded that with reference to each public statement and its impact upon the open market for Basic shares, common questions predominated over individual questions, as required by Fed. Rule Civ. Proc. 23(a)(2) and (b)(3).

Petitioners and their amici complain that the fraud-on-the-market theory effectively eliminates the requirement that a plaintiff asserting a claim under Rule 10b–5 prove reliance. They note that reliance is and long has been an element of common-law fraud and argue that because the analogous express right of action includes a reliance requirement, so too must an action implied under § 10(b).

We agree that reliance is an element of a Rule 10b–5 cause of action. There is, however, more than one way to demonstrate the causal connection. Indeed, we previously have dispensed with a requirement of positive proof of reliance, where a duty to disclose material information had been breached, concluding that the necessary nexus between the plaintiffs' injury and the defendant's wrongful conduct had been established. . . .

The modern securities markets, literally involving millions of shares changing hands daily, differ from the face-to-face transactions contemplated by early fraud cases, and our understanding of Rule 10b–5's reliance requirement must encompass these differences.

> In face-to-face transactions, the inquiry into an investor's reliance upon information is into the subjective pricing of that information by that investor. With the presence of a market, the market is interposed between seller and buyer and, ideally, transmits information to the investor in the processed form of a market price. Thus the market is performing a substantial part of the valuation process performed by the investor in a face-to-face transaction. . . .

Presumptions typically serve to assist courts in managing circumstances in which direct proof, for one reason or another, is rendered difficult. The courts below accepted a presumption, created by the fraud-on-the-market theory and subject to rebuttal by petitioners, that persons who had traded Basic shares had done so in reliance on the integrity of the price set by the market, but because of petitioners' material misrepresentations that price had been fraudulently depressed. Requiring a plaintiff to show a speculative state of facts, i.e., how he would have acted if omitted material information had been disclosed, or if the misrepresentation had not been made, would place an unnecessarily unrealistic evidentiary burden on the Rule 10b–5 plaintiff who has traded on an impersonal market.

Arising out of considerations of fairness, public policy, and probability, as well as judicial economy, presumptions are also useful devices for allocating the burdens of proof between parties. The presumption of reliance employed in this case is consistent with, and, by facilitating Rule 10b–5 litigation, supports the congressional policy embodied in the 1934 Act. In drafting that Act, Congress expressly relied on the premise that securities markets are affected by information, and enacted legislation to facilitate an investor's reliance on the integrity of those markets:

> . . . The idea of a free and open public market is built upon the theory that competing judgments of buyers and sellers as to the fair price of a security brings [sic] about a situation where the market price reflects as nearly as possible a just price. Just as artificial manipulation tends to upset the true function of an open market, so the hiding and secreting of important information obstructs the operation of the markets as indices of real value.

The presumption is also supported by common sense and probability. Recent empirical studies have tended to confirm Congress' premise that the market price of shares traded on well-developed markets reflects all publicly available information, and, hence, any material misrepresentations. It has been noted that "it is hard to imagine that there ever is a buyer or seller who does not rely on market integrity. Who would knowingly roll the dice in a crooked crap game?" . . . An investor who buys or sells stock at the price set by the market does so in reliance on the integrity of that price.

Because most publicly available information is reflected in market price, an investor's reliance on any public material misrepresentations, therefore, may be presumed for purposes of a Rule 10b–5 action....[27]

Any showing that severs the link between the alleged misrepresentation and either the price received (or paid) by the plaintiff, or his decision to trade at a fair market price, will be sufficient to rebut the presumption of reliance. For example, if petitioners could show that the "market makers" were privy to the truth about the merger discussions here with Combustion, and thus that the market price would not have been affected by their misrepresentations, the causal connection could be broken: the basis for finding that the fraud had been transmitted through market price would be gone.[28] Similarly, if ... news of the merger discussions credibly entered the market and dissipated the effects of the misstatements, those who traded Basic shares after the corrective statements would have no direct or indirect connection with the fraud.[29] Petitioners also could rebut the presumption of reliance as to plaintiffs who would have divested themselves of their Basic shares without relying on the integrity of the market. For example, a plaintiff who believed that Basic's statements were false and that Basic was indeed engaged in merger discussions, and who consequently believed that Basic stock was artificially underpriced, but sold his shares nevertheless because of other unrelated concerns, e.g., potential antitrust problems, or political pressures to divest from shares of certain businesses, could not be said to have relied on the integrity of a price he knew had been manipulated.

■ JUSTICE WHITE, with whom JUSTICE O'CONNOR joins, concurring in part and dissenting in part.

I dissent from the Court's holding because I do not agree that the "fraud-on-the-market" theory should be applied in this case.

I

Even when compared to the relatively youthful private cause-of-action under § 10(b), the fraud-on-the-market theory is a mere babe. Yet today,

27. ... [T]o invoke the presumption a plaintiff must allege and prove: (1) that the defendant made public misrepresentations; (2) that the misrepresentations were material; (3) that the shares were traded on an efficient market; ... and (5) that the plaintiff traded the shares between the time the misrepresentations were made and the time the truth was revealed....

28. By accepting this rebuttable presumption, we do not intend conclusively to adopt any particular theory of how quickly and completely publicly available information is reflected in market price. Furthermore, our decision today is not to be interpreted as addressing the proper measure of damages in litigation of this kind.

29. We note there may be a certain incongruity between the assumption that Basic shares are traded on a well-developed, efficient, and information-hungry market, and the allegation that such a market could remain misinformed, and its valuation of Basic shares depressed, for 14 months, on the basis of the three public statements. Proof of that sort is a matter for trial, throughout which the District Court retains the authority to amend the certification order as may be appropriate. Thus, we see no need to engage in the kind of factual analysis the dissent suggests that manifests the "oddities" of applying a rebuttable presumption of reliance in this case.

the Court embraces this theory with the sweeping confidence usually reserved for more mature legal doctrines. In so doing, I fear that the Court's decision may have many adverse, unintended effects as it is applied and interpreted in the years to come.

At the outset, I note that there are portions of the Court's fraud-on-the-market holding with which I am in agreement. Most importantly, the Court rejects the version of that theory, heretofore adopted by some courts, which equates "causation" with "reliance," and permits recovery by a plaintiff who claims merely to have been harmed by a material misrepresentation which altered a market price, notwithstanding proof that the plaintiff did not in any way rely on that price. I agree with the Court that if Rule 10b–5's reliance requirement is to be left with any content at all, the fraud-on-the-market presumption must be capable of being rebutted by a showing that a plaintiff did not "rely" on the market price. For example, a plaintiff who decides, months in advance of an alleged misrepresentation, to purchase a stock; one who buys or sells a stock for reasons unrelated to its price; one who actually sells a stock "short" days before the misrepresentation is made—surely none of these people can state a valid claim under Rule 10b–5. . . .

* * *

Even if I agreed with the Court that "modern securities markets . . . involving millions of shares changing hands daily" require that the "understanding of Rule 10b–5's reliance requirement" be changed, I prefer that such changes come from Congress in amending § 10(b). The Congress, with its superior resources and expertise, is far better equipped than the federal courts for the task of determining how modern economic theory and global financial markets require that established legal notions of fraud be modified. In choosing to make these decisions itself, the Court, I fear, embarks on a course that it does not genuinely understand, giving rise to consequences it cannot foresee.[5]

* * *

C

At the bottom of the Court's conclusion that the fraud-on-the-market theory sustains a presumption of reliance is the assumption that individuals rely "on the integrity of the market price" when buying or selling stock in "impersonal, well-developed market[s] for securities." Even if I was

---

5. For example, Judge Posner in his Economic Analysis of Law § 15.8, pp. 423–424 (3d ed. 1986), submits that the fraud-on-the-market theory produces the "economically correct result" in Rule 10b–5 cases but observes that the question of damages under the theory is quite problematic. Notwithstanding the fact that "at first blush it might seem obvious," the proper calculation of damages when the fraud-on-the-market theo-ry is applied must rest on several "assumptions" about "social costs" which are "difficult to quantify." Of course, answers to the question of the proper measure of damages in a fraud-on-the-market case are essential for proper implementation of the fraud-on-the-market presumption. Not surprisingly, the difficult damages question is one the Court expressly declines to address today.

prepared to accept (as a matter of common sense or general understanding) the assumption that most persons buying or selling stock do so in response to the market price, the fraud-on-the-market theory goes further. For in adopting a "presumption of reliance," the Court also assumes that buyers and sellers rely—not just on the market price—but on the "integrity" of that price. It is this aspect of the fraud-on-the-market hypothesis which most mystifies me.

To define the term "integrity of the market price," the majority quotes approvingly from cases which suggest that investors are entitled to " 'rely on the price of a stock as a reflection of its value.' " But the meaning of this phrase eludes me, for it implicitly suggests that stocks have some "true value" that is measurable by a standard other than their market price. While the Scholastics of Medieval times professed a means to make such a valuation of a commodity's "worth," I doubt that the federal courts of our day are similarly equipped.

Even if securities had some "value"—knowable and distinct from the market price of a stock—investors do not always share the Court's presumption that a stock's price is a "reflection of [this] value." Indeed, "many investors purchase or sell stock because they believe the price inaccurately reflects the corporation's worth." If investors really believed that stock prices reflected a stock's "value," many sellers would never sell, and many buyers never buy (given the time and cost associated with executing a stock transaction). As we recognized just a few years ago: "Investors act on inevitably incomplete or inaccurate information, [consequently] there are always winners and losers; but those who have 'lost' have not necessarily been defrauded." Yet today, the Court allows investors to recover who can show little more than that they sold stock at a lower price than what might have been.[7]

I do not propose that the law retreat from the many protections that § 10(b) and Rule 10b–5, as interpreted in our prior cases, provide to investors. But any extension of these laws, to approach something closer to an investor insurance scheme, should come from Congress, and not from the courts.

* * *

NOTES

1. *Reliance in class actions.* The combination of *Affiliated Ute* and *Basic* greatly eases the plaintiffs' burden in pleading the reliance element in a class

---

7. This is what the Court's rule boils down to in practical terms. For while, in theory, the Court allows for rebuttal of its "presumption of reliance"—a proviso with which I agree—in practice the Court must realize, as other courts applying the fraud-on-the-market theory have, that such rebuttal is virtually impossible in all but the most extraordinary case.

Consequently, while the Court considers it significant that the fraud-on-the-market presumption it endorses is a rebuttable one, the majority's implicit rejection of the "pure causation" fraud-on-the-market theory rings hollow. In most cases, the Court's theory will operate just as the causation theory would, creating a non-rebuttable presumption of "reliance" in future 10b–5 actions.

action. For omissions in breach of a fiduciary duty (one type of insider trading, which we will cover in greater detail in Chapter 6), *Affiliated Ute* holds that reliance is presumed if the omitted fact is material. For omissions that render statements misleading (''half-truths''), the result is less clear, with some courts requiring proof of reliance on the half-truth, see *Abell v. Potomac Insurance Co.*, 858 F.2d 1104 (5th Cir. 1988), and others applying the *Affiliated Ute* presumption. See *Chris-Craft Indus., Inc. v. Piper Aircraft Corp.*, 480 F.2d 341 (2d Cir. 1973). Under *Basic*, both affirmative misstatements and half truths are also presumed to have induced reliance if they have been disseminated into ''efficient'' markets under the fraud-on-the-market theory. As a result, the reliance element, which historically has made class action treatment inappropriate for common law fraud, is not a substantial barrier for Rule 10b–5 suits against companies whose securities are traded in efficient markets. The presumption does not apply, however, in markets lacking in informational efficiency, thereby excluding smaller companies in thinly-traded markets from substantial exposure to securities fraud class actions. See *Binder v. Gillespie*, 184 F.3d 1059 (9th Cir. 1999) (*Basic* presumption does not apply to issuer whose stock was traded in the ''pink sheets'').

2. *What does the* Basic *presumption mean?* Does the *Basic* presumption require that the plaintiff-investor have relied on the integrity of the market price being unaffected by fraud, or does it require that the investor have relied on the price as an accurate assessment of the value of the security? Justice Blackmun had this to say in response to an inquiry from Justice Brennan on a draft of the opinion:

> My intention in this opinion was to set out the simple proposition that because market price generally reflects all publicly available information (including misrepresentations), an investor's reliance on market price to reflect the true value of the security (or at least the average of the estimates of the value that many different traders placed on the stock) becomes reliance on the misrepresentation. When, because of a material misrepresentation, the price does not reflect the normal evaluation of the security, those who relied on the price to be accurate have been defrauded. That presumption, however, is limited by its own terms. If the material misrepresentation did not affect the price, then those who traded at market price were not affect by the misrepresentation. Similarly, if there exists such a person who did not rely on the integrity of the market price to be accurate, that person was not <u>defrauded</u> by the misrepresentation (although he did receive less money for his shares than he would have received absent the misrepresentation).

Letter from Justice Harry A. Blackmun to Justice Brennan. (January 25, 1988) (on file at the Library of Congress). Blackmun's explanation suggests that investors who are not relying on the accuracy of the market price, such as short sellers (who believe the market price is overvalued), should not be entitled to the presumption. *See Zlotnick v. TIE Communications*, 836 F.2d 818 (3d Cir. 1988) (rejecting presumption for a short seller).

In the real world, the meaning of the presumption seldom makes a difference because defendants find it impractical to invoke the rebuttal option, as the justices suspected would be the case. Consider Justice Brennan's response to Justice Blackmun:

> In my view, the market relies on the defendant's misstatement, and plaintiffs are defrauded because they are forced to act through the market.

Your view requires that in addition plaintiffs specifically depend on the integrity of the market, that is, that the market is fair. This difference of opinion, I must agree, will have little, if any, effect on the outcome of section 10(b) cases. If, as I suspect, defendants find it impractical to utilize the rebuttal option, and if the measure of damages is ultimately resolved as the difference between the price actually received and the price that would have been received had the market been fair, my view and your view will lead to identical results, although by somewhat different routes.

Letter from Justice William F. Brennan Jr. to Justice Blackmun (January 27, 1988) (on file at the Library of Congress). How would a defendant faced with a class of hundreds, perhaps thousands, of investors go about rebutting the presumption of reliance for each investor?

QUESTIONS

1. What is the empirical basis for the fraud-on-the-market theory?

2. Investors suffer from well-documented behavioral biases, including a tendency to trade too often, hold on to losing stocks too long, and to pay too much attention to more recent, salient information. These biases affect the trading markets for both small and large companies. Should these behavioral biases affect *Basic*'s reliance presumption?

3. Is the *Basic* Court correct when it observes that: "It has been noted that 'it is hard to imagine that there ever is a buyer or seller who does not rely on market integrity. Who would knowingly roll the dice in a crooked crap game?' "

4. After *Affiliated Ute* and *Basic* what remains of the reliance requirement for the plaintiff's cause of action?

HYPOTHETICAL SEVEN

Recall that DigitalBase's common stock is traded on Nasdaq/NMS. Suppose DigitalBase decides to conduct a seasoned offering of its common stock. Several months after the offering, Jill, an outside investor, buys DigitalBase stock (that may or may not have come from the seasoned offering) on the secondary market without reading the prospectus, based solely on the secondary market price. It turns out that the prospectus contained misleading revenue numbers that overstated earnings. Can Jill recover?

1. *Scenario One*: What if Jill had bought DigitalBase stock as above, but now let's also assume that both Goldman and Fidelity know about the misstatements as a result of rumors being passed around among Wall Street insiders?

2. *Scenario Two*: Suppose Jill buys DigitalBase stock, but she does so even though she knows about the misleading financial statements because she feels the stock is undervalued despite the misstatement. Can Jill recover?

3. *Scenario Three*: What if Jill buys the DigitalBase stock because she believes it is undervalued but doesn't know about the misstatements?

D. LOSS CAUSATION

Congress codified the loss causation rule developed by the courts in 1995 in § 21D(b)(4). That provision stipulates: "In any private action arising under [the Exchange Act], the plaintiff shall have the burden of proving that the act or omission of the defendant alleged to violate [the Act] caused the loss for which the plaintiff seeks to recover damages." The Supreme Court explains the loss causation requirement in the following case. How does proof of loss causation differ from proof of transaction causation and proof of damages?

Dura Pharmaceuticals, Inc. v. Broudo

544 U.S. __ (2005).

■ BREYER, J.

A private plaintiff who claims securities fraud must prove that the defendant's fraud caused an economic loss. Exchange Act § 21D(b)(4). We consider a Ninth Circuit holding that a plaintiff can satisfy this requirement—a requirement that courts call "loss causation"—simply by alleging in the complaint and subsequently establishing that "the price" of the security *"on the date of purchase* was inflated because of the misrepresentation." In our view, the Ninth Circuit is wrong, both in respect to what a plaintiff must prove and in respect to what the plaintiffs' complaint here must allege.

I

Respondents are individuals who bought stock in Dura Pharmaceuticals, Inc., on the public securities market between April 15, 1997, and February 24, 1998. They have brought this securities fraud class action against Dura and some of its managers and directors (hereinafter Dura) in federal court. In respect to the question before us, their detailed amended . . . complaint makes substantially the following allegations:

(1) Before and during the purchase period, Dura (or its officials) made false statements concerning both Dura's drug profits and future Food and Drug Administration (FDA) approval of a new asthmatic spray device.

(2) In respect to drug profits, Dura falsely claimed that it expected that its drug sales would prove profitable.

(3) In respect to the asthmatic spray device, Dura falsely claimed that it expected the FDA would soon grant its approval.

(4) On the last day of the purchase period [of the Respondent's class action], February 24, 1998, Dura announced that its earnings would be lower than expected, principally due to slow drug sales.

(5) The next day Dura's shares lost almost half their value (falling from about $39 per share to about $21).

(6) About eight months later (in November 1998), Dura announced that the FDA would not approve Dura's new asthmatic spray device.

(7) The next day Dura's share price temporarily fell but almost fully recovered within one week.

Most importantly, the complaint says the following (and nothing significantly more than the following) about economic losses attributable to the spray device misstatement: *"In reliance on the integrity of the market, [the plaintiffs] ... paid artificially inflated prices for Dura securities"* and the plaintiffs suffered *"damage[s]"* thereby. (emphasis added).

* * *

The Court of Appeals for the Ninth Circuit ... held that the complaint adequately alleged "loss causation." The Circuit wrote that "plaintiffs establish loss causation if they have shown that the price *on the date of purchase* was inflated because of the misrepresentation." (emphasis in original). It added that "the injury occurs at the time of the transaction." Since the complaint pleaded "that the price at the time of purchase was overstated," and it sufficiently identified the cause, its allegations were legally sufficient.

* * *

II

* * *

A

We begin with the Ninth Circuit's basic reason for finding the complaint adequate, namely, that at the end of the day plaintiffs need only "establish," *i.e.,* prove, that "the price *on the date of purchase* was inflated because of the misrepresentation." In our view, this statement of the law is wrong. Normally, in cases such as this one (*i.e.,* fraud-on-the-market cases), an inflated purchase price will not itself constitute or proximately cause the relevant economic loss.

For one thing, as a matter of pure logic, at the moment the transaction takes place, the plaintiff has suffered no loss; the inflated purchase payment is offset by ownership of a share that *at that instant* possesses equivalent value. Moreover, the logical link between the inflated share purchase price and any later economic loss is not invariably strong. Shares are normally purchased with an eye toward a later sale. But if, say, the purchaser sells the shares quickly before the relevant truth begins to leak out, the misrepresentation will not have led to any loss. If the purchaser sells later after the truth makes its way into the market place, an initially inflated purchase price *might* mean a later loss. But that is far from inevitably so. When the purchaser subsequently resells such shares, even at a lower price, that lower price may reflect, not the earlier misrepresentation, but changed economic circumstances, changed investor expectations, new industry-specific or firm-specific facts, conditions, or other events, which taken separately or together account for some or all of that lower price. (The same is true in respect to a claim that a share's higher price is lower than it would otherwise have been—a claim we do not consider here.) Other things being equal, the longer the time between purchase and sale, the more likely that this is so, *i.e.*, the more likely that other factors caused the loss.

Given the tangle of factors affecting price, the most logic alone permits us to say is that the higher purchase price will *sometimes* play a role in bringing about a future loss. It may prove to be a necessary condition of any such loss, and in that sense one might say that the inflated purchase price suggests that the misrepresentation (using language the Ninth Circuit used) "touches upon" a later economic loss. But, even if that is so, it is insufficient. To "touch upon" a loss is not to *cause* a loss, and it is the latter that the law requires.

For another thing, the Ninth Circuit's holding lacks support in precedent. Judicially implied private securities-fraud actions resemble in many (but not all) respects common-law deceit and misrepresentation actions. The common law of deceit subjects a person who "fraudulently" makes a "misrepresentation" to liability "for pecuniary loss caused" to one who justifiably relies upon that misrepresentation. And the common law has long insisted that a plaintiff in such a case show not only that had he known the truth he would not have acted but also that he suffered actual economic loss.

Given the common-law roots of the securities fraud action (and the common-law requirement that a plaintiff show actual damages), it is not surprising that other courts of appeals have rejected the Ninth Circuit's "inflated purchase price" approach to proving causation and loss. Indeed, the Restatement of Torts, in setting forth the judicial consensus, says that a person who "misrepresents the financial condition of a corporation in order to sell its stock" becomes liable to a relying purchaser "for the loss" the purchaser sustains "when the facts ... become generally known" and "as a result" share value "depreciate[s]." § 548A, Comment *b*, at 107. . . .

We cannot reconcile the Ninth Circuit's "inflated purchase price" approach with these views of other courts. And the uniqueness of its perspective argues against the validity of its approach in a case like this one where we consider the contours of a judicially implied cause of action with roots in the common law.

Finally, the Ninth Circuit's approach overlooks an important securities law objective. The securities statutes seek to maintain public confidence in the marketplace. They do so by deterring fraud, in part, through the availability of private securities fraud actions. But the statutes make these latter actions available, not to provide investors with broad insurance against market losses, but to protect them against those economic losses that misrepresentations actually cause.

The statutory provision at issue here and the paragraphs that precede it emphasize this last mentioned objective. The statute insists that securities fraud complaints "specify" each misleading statement; that they set forth the facts "on which [a] belief" that a statement is misleading was "formed"; and that they "state with particularity facts giving rise to a strong inference that the defendant acted with the required state of mind."

Exchange Act § 21D(b)(1),(2). And the statute expressly imposes on plaintiffs "the burden of proving" that the defendant's misrepresentations "caused the loss for which the plaintiff seeks to recover." Exchange Act § 21D (b)(4).

The statute thereby makes clear Congress' intent to permit private securities fraud actions for recovery where, but only where, plaintiffs adequately allege and prove the traditional elements of causation and loss. By way of contrast, the Ninth Circuit's approach would allow recovery where a misrepresentation leads to an inflated purchase price but nonetheless does not proximately cause any economic loss. That is to say, it would permit recovery where these two traditional elements in fact are missing.

In sum, we find the Ninth Circuit's approach inconsistent with the law's requirement that a plaintiff prove that the defendant's misrepresentation (or other fraudulent conduct) proximately caused the plaintiff's economic loss. We need not, and do not, consider other proximate cause or loss-related questions.

B

Our holding about plaintiffs' need to *prove* proximate causation and economic loss leads us also to conclude that the plaintiffs' complaint here failed adequately to *allege* these requirements. We concede that the Federal Rules of Civil Procedure require only "a short and plain statement of the claim showing that the pleader is entitled to relief." Fed. Rule Civ. Proc. 8(a)(2). And we assume, at least for argument's sake, that neither the Rules nor the securities statutes impose any special further requirement in respect to the pleading of proximate causation or economic loss. But, even so, the "short and plain statement" must provide the defendant with "fair notice of what the plaintiff's claim is and the grounds upon which it rests." The complaint before us fails this simple test.

As we have pointed out, the plaintiffs' lengthy complaint contains only one statement that we can fairly read as describing the loss caused by the defendants' "spray device" misrepresentations. That statement says that the plaintiffs "paid artificially inflated prices for Dura's securities" and suffered "damage[s]." The statement implies that the plaintiffs' loss consisted of the "artificially inflated" purchase "prices." The complaint's failure to claim that Dura's share price fell significantly after the truth became known suggests that the plaintiffs considered the allegation of purchase price inflation alone sufficient. The complaint contains nothing that suggests otherwise.

For reasons set forth in Part II–A, however, the "artificially inflated purchase price" is not itself a relevant economic loss. And the complaint nowhere else provides the defendants with notice of what the relevant economic loss might be or of what the causal connection might be between that loss and the misrepresentation concerning Dura's "spray device."

We concede that ordinary pleading rules are not meant to impose a great burden upon a plaintiff. But it should not prove burdensome for a plaintiff who has suffered an economic loss to provide a defendant with some indication of the loss and the causal connection that the plaintiff has in mind. At the same time, allowing a plaintiff to forgo giving any indication of the economic loss and proximate cause that the plaintiff has in mind would bring about harm of the very sort the statutes seek to avoid. It would permit a plaintiff "with a largely groundless claim to simply take up the time of a number of other people, with the right to do so representing an *in terrorem* increment of the settlement value, rather than a reasonably founded hope that the [discovery] process will reveal relevant evidence." Such a rule would tend to transform a private securities action into a partial downside insurance policy.

For these reasons, we find the plaintiffs' complaint legally insufficient. We reverse the judgment of the Ninth Circuit, and we remand the case for further proceedings consistent with this opinion.

* * *

QUESTIONS

1. What purpose does the loss causation requirement serve? Would that purpose be undermined by not requiring plaintiffs to plead loss causation in their complaint?

2. In discussing the loss causation requirement, the Seventh Circuit has said that: "No social purpose would be served by encouraging everyone who suffers an investment loss because of an unanticipated change in market conditions to pick through offering memoranda with a fine-tooth comb in the hope of uncovering a misrepresentation." *Bastian v. Petren Resources Corporation*, 892 F.2d 680 (7th Cir. 1990). Why not? Wouldn't this help "crush out" fraud?

3. How does the Court define the "value" of a security?

4. Why would it be wrong "to transform a private securities action into a partial downside insurance policy"?

5. The Court says that "it should not prove burdensome for a plaintiff who has suffered an economic loss to provide a defendant with some indication of the loss and the causal connection that the plaintiff has in mind." Do you agree? What are the potential obstacles to pleading loss causation?

IV.   RULE 10b–5 DEFENDANTS

As an implied private cause of action, Rule 10b–5 provides no laundry list of potential defendants. Instead, "any person" who makes a material misstatement and meets the other requirements of the Rule 10b–5 cause of action is potentially a defendant. Even if a person does not directly make the material misstatement, should she nonetheless still face Rule 10b–5 liability?

Put more concretely, when DigitalBase's CEO, Hillary, puts out overly optimistic statements on its new GigaBase product, should DigitalBase's attorneys, auditors, past underwriters, suppliers, or customers also find themselves liable under Rule 10b–5 for the statements? What distinguishes some third parties from others in terms of Rule 10b–5 liability?

A. SECONDARY LIABILITY

The misstatement element of the Rule 10b–5 cause of action has important consequences for who can be held responsible for securities fraud. What is the misstatement in the following case? Who made the misstatement? Who should be responsible for it?

Central Bank of Denver v. First Interstate Bank of Denver

511 U.S. 164 (1994).

■ JUSTICE KENNEDY delivered the opinion of the Court.

As we have interpreted it, § 10(b) of the Securities Exchange Act of 1934 imposes private civil liability on those who commit a manipulative or deceptive act in connection with the purchase or sale of securities. In this case, we must answer a question reserved in two earlier decisions: whether private civil liability under § 10(b) extends as well to those who do not engage in the manipulative or deceptive practice, but who aid and abet the violation.

I

In 1986 and 1988, the Colorado Springs–Stetson Hills Public Building Authority (Authority) issued a total of $26 million in bonds to finance public improvements at Stetson Hills, a planned residential and commercial development in Colorado Springs. Petitioner Central Bank of Denver served as indenture trustee for the bond issues.

The bonds were secured by landowner assessment liens, which covered about 250 acres for the 1986 bond issue and about 272 acres for the 1988 bond issue. The bond covenants required that the land subject to the liens be worth at least 160% of the bonds' outstanding principal and interest. The covenants required AmWest Development, the developer of Stetson Hills, to give Central Bank an annual report containing evidence that the 160% test was met.

In January 1988, AmWest provided Central Bank with an updated appraisal of the land securing the 1986 bonds and of the land proposed to secure the 1988 bonds. The 1988 appraisal showed land values almost unchanged from the 1986 appraisal. Soon afterwards, Central Bank received a letter from the senior underwriter for the 1986 bonds. Noting that property values were declining in Colorado Springs and that Central Bank was operating on an appraisal over 16 months old, the underwriter expressed concern that the 160% test was not being met.

Central Bank asked its in-house appraiser to review the updated 1988 appraisal. The in-house appraiser decided that the values listed in the appraisal appeared optimistic considering the local real estate market. He suggested that Central Bank retain an outside appraiser to conduct an independent review of the 1988 appraisal. After an exchange of letters between Central Bank and AmWest in early 1988, Central Bank agreed to delay independent review of the appraisal until the end of the year, six months after the June 1988 closing on the bond issue. Before the independent review was complete, however, the Authority defaulted on the 1988 bonds.

Respondents First Interstate Bank of Denver and Jack K. Naber had purchased $2.1 million of the 1988 bonds. After the default, respondents sued the Authority, the 1988 underwriter, a junior underwriter, an AmWest director, and Central Bank for violations of § 10(b) of the Securities Exchange Act of 1934. The complaint alleged that the Authority, the underwriter defendants, and the AmWest director had violated § 10(b). The complaint also alleged that Central Bank was "secondarily liable under § 10(b) for its conduct in aiding and abetting the fraud."

* * *

Like the Court of Appeals in this case, other federal courts have allowed private aiding and abetting actions under § 10(b).... We granted certiorari to resolve the continuing confusion over the existence and scope of the § 10(b) aiding and abetting action.

II

* * *

In § 10(b), Congress prohibited manipulative or deceptive acts in connection with the purchase or sale of securities. It envisioned that the SEC would enforce the statutory prohibition through administrative and injunctive actions. Of course, a private plaintiff now may bring suit against violators of § 10(b). But the private plaintiff may not bring a 10b–5 suit against a defendant for acts not prohibited by the text of § 10(b). To the contrary, our cases considering the scope of conduct prohibited by § 10(b) in private suits have emphasized adherence to the statutory language, " 'the starting point in every case involving construction of a statute.' "
. . .

* * *

Our consideration of statutory duties, especially in cases interpreting § 10(b), establishes that the statutory text controls the definition of conduct covered by § 10(b). That bodes ill for respondents, for "the language of Section 10(b) does not in terms mention aiding and abetting." To overcome this problem, respondents and the SEC suggest (or hint at) the novel argument that the use of the phrase "directly or indirectly" in the text of § 10(b) covers aiding and abetting.

The federal courts have not relied on the "directly or indirectly" language when imposing aiding and abetting liability under § 10(b), and with good reason. There is a basic flaw with this interpretation. According to respondents and the SEC, the "directly or indirectly" language shows that "Congress ... intended to reach all persons who engage, even if only indirectly, in proscribed activities connected with securities transactions." The problem, of course, is that aiding and abetting liability extends beyond persons who engage, even indirectly, in a proscribed activity; aiding and abetting liability reaches persons who do not engage in the proscribed activities at all, but who give a degree of aid to those who do. A further problem with respondents' interpretation of the "directly or indirectly" language is posed by the numerous provisions of the 1934 Act that use the term in a way that does not impose aiding and abetting liability.

Congress knew how to impose aiding and abetting liability when it chose to do so. If, as respondents seem to say, Congress intended to impose aiding and abetting liability, we presume it would have used the words "aid" and "abet" in the statutory text. But it did not.

We reach the uncontroversial conclusion, accepted even by those courts recognizing a § 10(b) aiding and abetting cause of action, that the text of the 1934 Act does not itself reach those who aid and abet a § 10(b) violation. Unlike those courts, however, we think that conclusion resolves the case.... The issue ... is not whether imposing private civil liability on aiders and abettors is good policy but whether aiding and abetting is covered by the statute.

As in earlier cases considering conduct prohibited by § 10(b), we again conclude that the statute prohibits only the making of a material misstatement (or omission) or the commission of a manipulative act. The proscription does not include giving aid to a person who commits a manipulative or deceptive act....

III

Because this case concerns the conduct prohibited by § 10(b), the statute itself resolves the case, but even if it did not, we would reach the same result. When the text of § 10(b) does not resolve a particular issue, we attempt to infer "how the 1934 Congress would have addressed the issue had the 10b–5 action been included as an express provision in the 1934 Act." For that inquiry, we use the express causes of action in the securities Acts as the primary model for the § 10(b) action. The reason is evident: Had the 73d Congress enacted a private § 10(b) right of action, it likely would have designed it in a manner similar to the other private rights of action in the securities Acts....

Following that analysis here, we look to the express private causes of action in the 1933 and 1934 Acts. In the 1933 Act, § 11 prohibits false statements or omissions of material fact in registration statements; it identifies the various categories of defendants subject to liability for a violation, but that list does not include aiders and abettors. Section 12 prohibits the sale of unregistered, nonexempt securities as well as the sale of securities by means of a material misstatement or omission; and it limits liability to those who offer or sell the security. In the 1934 Act, § 9 prohibits any person from engaging in manipulative practices such as wash sales, matched orders, and the like. Section 16 regulates short-swing trading by owners, directors, and officers. Section 18 prohibits any person from making misleading statements in reports filed with the SEC. And § 20A, added in 1988, prohibits any person from engaging in insider trading.

This survey of the express causes of action in the securities Acts reveals that each (like § 10(b)) specifies the conduct for which defendants may be held liable. Some of the express causes of action specify categories of defendants who may be liable; others (like § 10(b)) state only that "any person" who commits one of the prohibited acts may be held liable. The important point for present purposes, however, is that none of the express causes of action in the 1934 Act further imposes liability on one who aids or abets a violation.

From the fact that Congress did not attach private aiding and abetting liability to any of the express causes of action in the securities Acts, we can infer that Congress likely would not have attached aiding and abetting liability to § 10(b) had it provided a private § 10(b) cause of action. . . . In *Blue Chip Stamps*, we noted that it would be "anomalous to impute to Congress an intention to expand the plaintiff class for a judicially implied cause of action beyond the bounds it delineated for comparable express causes of action." . . .

Our reasoning is confirmed by the fact that respondents' argument would impose 10b–5 aiding and abetting liability when at least one element critical for recovery under 10b–5 is absent: reliance. A plaintiff must show reliance on the defendant's misstatement or omission to recover under 10b–5. Were we to allow the aiding and abetting action proposed in this case, the defendant could be liable without any showing that the plaintiff relied upon the aider and abettor's statements or actions. Allowing plaintiffs to circumvent the reliance requirement would disregard the careful limits on 10b–5 recovery mandated by our earlier cases.

IV

* * *

Congress did not overlook secondary liability when it created the private rights of action in the 1934 Act. Section 20 of the 1934 Act imposes liability on "controlling person[s]"—persons who "control any person liable under any provision of this chapter or of any rule or regulation thereunder." This suggests that "when Congress wished to create such [secondary] liability, it had little trouble doing so." Aiding and abetting is "a method by which courts create secondary liability" in persons other than the violator of the statute. The fact that Congress chose to impose some forms of secondary liability, but not others, indicates a deliberate congressional choice with which the courts should not interfere.

* * *

The SEC points to various policy arguments in support of the 10b–5 aiding and abetting cause of action. It argues, for example, that the aiding and abetting cause of action deters secondary actors from contributing to fraudulent activities and ensures that defrauded plaintiffs are made whole.

Policy considerations cannot override our interpretation of the text and structure of the Act, except to the extent that they may help to show that adherence to the text and structure would lead to a result "so bizarre" that Congress could not have intended it. That is not the case here.

Extending the 10b–5 cause of action to aiders and abettors no doubt makes the civil remedy more far reaching, but it does not follow that the objectives of the statute are better served. Secondary liability for aiders and abettors exacts costs that may disserve the goals of fair dealing and efficiency in the securities markets.

As an initial matter, the rules for determining aiding and abetting liability are unclear, in "an area that demands certainty and predictability." That leads to the undesirable result of decisions "made on an ad hoc basis, offering little predictive value" to those who provide services to participants in the securities business. "Such a shifting and highly fact-oriented disposition of the issue of who may [be liable for] a damages claim for violation of Rule 10b–5" is not a "satisfactory basis for a rule of liability imposed on the conduct of business transactions." Because of the uncertainty of the governing rules, entities subject to secondary liability as aiders and abettors may find it prudent and necessary, as a business judgment, to abandon substantial defenses and to pay settlements in order to avoid the expense and risk of going to trial.

In addition, "litigation under Rule 10b–5 presents a danger of vexatiousness different in degree and in kind from that which accompanies litigation in general." Litigation under 10b–5 thus requires secondary actors to expend large sums even for pretrial defense and the negotiation of settlements.

This uncertainty and excessive litigation can have ripple effects. For example, newer and smaller companies may find it difficult to obtain advice from professionals. A professional may fear that a newer or smaller company may not survive and that business failure would generate securities litigation against the professional, among others. In addition, the increased costs incurred by professionals because of the litigation and settlement costs under 10b–5 may be passed on to their client companies, and in turn incurred by the company's investors, the intended beneficiaries of the statute.

We hasten to add that competing policy arguments in favor of aiding and abetting liability can also be advanced. The point here, however, is that it is far from clear that Congress in 1934 would have decided that the statutory purposes would be furthered by the imposition of private aider and abettor liability.

* * *

Because the text of § 10(b) does not prohibit aiding and abetting, we hold that a private plaintiff may not maintain an aiding and abetting suit under § 10(b). The absence of § 10(b) aiding and abetting liability does not mean that secondary actors in the securities markets are always free from liability under the securities Acts. Any person or entity, including a lawyer, accountant, or bank, who employs a manipulative device or makes a material misstatement (or omission) on which a purchaser or seller of securities relies may be liable as a primary violator under 10b–5, assuming *all* of the requirements for primary liability under Rule 10b–5 are met. In any complex securities fraud, moreover, there are likely to be multiple violators; in this case, for example, respondents named four defendants as primary violators.

* * *

NOTES

1. *The SEC. Central Bank* raised doubts as to whether the SEC could pursue "aiders and abettors" in its enforcement actions. Congress eliminated any uncertainty on this score, however, by adding § 20(e) to the Exchange Act as part of the PSLRA, which allows the SEC to pursue actions against "any person that knowingly provides substantial assistance to another person in violation of a provision of this title." This amendment reflects a political compromise: the SEC had its "aiding-and-abetting" enforcement authority restored, but with a more stringent requirement of a "knowing" state of mind.

QUESTIONS

1. Why isn't the decision by Central Bank to delay an independent appraisal indirect participation in the fraudulent activity? What does "indirectly" mean?

2. The Court talks of the reliance requirement of Rule 10b–5 and the fear that imposing aiding and abetting liability will allow plaintiffs to "circumvent the reliance requirement." Is this a real concern?

3. Is the Court correct in its assertion that §§ 11 and 12, among other explicit liability provisions, do not provide for aiding and abetting liability?

B.   WHO IS A PRIMARY VIOLATOR?

The lower courts have disagreed over the proper interpretation of *Central Bank*. Some courts have adopted a "bright line" test that requires that the defendant's misstatement be directly attributable to him. *See, e.g., Shapiro v. Cantor*, 123 F.3d 717, 720 (2d Cir. 1997) ("if *Central Bank* is to have any real meaning, a defendant must actually make a false or misleading statement in order to be held liable under Section 10(b). Anything short of such conduct is merely aiding and abetting, and no matter how substantial that aid may be, it is not enough to trigger liability under Section 10(b).").

The Ninth Circuit follows a more lenient "substantial participant" test that allows for primary violator liability if the defendants had a significant role in preparing the document alleged to have been misleading. *See, e.g., In re Software Toolworks*, 50 F.3d 615 (9th Cir. 1994). There is general agreement, however, that corporations continue to be liable for misstatements made by their officers and employees. *See Suez Equity Investors, L.P. v. The Toronto–Dominion Bank*, 250 F.3d 87 (2d Cir. 2001) (*"Central Bank* did not eliminate primary liability for business entities.*"*).

Wright v. Ernst & Young LLP

152 F.3d 169 (2d Cir. 1998).

■ MESKILL, CIRCUIT JUDGE.

Plaintiff-appellant Irene Wright appeals from a final judgment rendered in the United States District Court for the Southern District of New York. . . . The question we must answer is whether, under the Act, persons who purchase stock in a company that issued a press release containing false and misleading financial information, with a notation that the information is unaudited and without mention of its outside auditor, can recover from the auditor for its private approval of the information contained in the press release. We conclude that under these circumstances, primary liability is foreclosed by *Central Bank of Denver v. First Interstate Bank of Denver*, 511 U.S. 164 (1994), and by our recent decision in *Shapiro v. Cantor*, 123 F.3d 717 (2d Cir. 1997). Accordingly, we affirm the judgment of the district court dismissing the amended complaint.

BACKGROUND

The appellee, Ernst & Young LLP, is a firm engaged in the business of providing various accounting services, including auditing and financial analysis. At all relevant times, Ernst & Young was the outside auditor for BT Office Products, Inc., a corporation engaged in the distribution and sale of office products. The gravamen of the amended complaint is that Ernst & Young violated the antifraud provisions of the Act by orally approving BT's materially false and misleading financial statements that BT in turn disseminated to the public in a January 30, 1996 press release. Plaintiff-appellant Irene Wright (Wright) represents a class of investors who purchased BT common stock during the period between BT's January 30, 1996 press release and BT's public statement on March 28, 1996 disavowing the financial statements contained in that release. Wright claims that because "the market knew and relied on the fact that these financial statements were approved by [Ernst & Young]," Ernst & Young is liable for losses suffered once BT's true financial picture emerged. . . .

As set forth in the amended complaint against Ernst & Young, BT embarked on a series of acquisitions in 1987, including the purchase of a stationer known as Summit Office Supply (BT–Summit). As BT expanded, its management decided to engage Ernst & Young to audit its year-end financial statements. Ernst & Young issued audit opinions certifying the accuracy of BT's financial statements for the years ending December 31, 1993 and December 31, 1994. Later, in July 1995, the firm updated and re-

released the December 31, 1994 audit opinion as a "Report of Independent Auditors" for use in BT's initial public offering prospectus, which included a statement of BT's first quarter earnings for 1995. The audit upon which that report was based included a "full-scope" audit of several BT subsidiaries, but only a "limited review" of BT–Summit's accounts.

In the fall of 1995, the firm began a new "full-scope" audit of BT–Summit. Pursuant to this effort, it discovered an under-accrual of BT–Summit's accounts payable and alerted BT management. Upon consideration, however, Ernst & Young concluded that the under-accrual was not material and advised BT that it was probably a carryover of a similar under-accrual from the year before. Accordingly, the amended complaint avers that "on January 22, 1996 [Ernst & Young] signed off on BT Office Products' 1995 financial statements ... and authorized [BT] to release its 1995 year end results with full knowledge of the fact that the market would and did interpret the release of these figures as having been approved by [Ernst & Young]." The amended complaint further states that based on Ernst & Young's oral assurances, BT issued a press release on January 30, 1996 that set forth BT's 1995 financial results and indicated strong growth during 1995. The press release also stated, however, that the figures were "unaudited" and it made no mention of Ernst & Young.

In late February and March of 1996, it became apparent to both BT and Ernst & Young that the under-accrual problem at BT–Summit was more serious than previously believed. A further investigation revealed not only that BT–Summit employees used improper accounting techniques, but substantial company funds had been embezzled. In light of these discoveries, BT announced on March 28, 1996 that it was restating its 1995 financial results from a previously announced profit of $1.5 million to a loss of $200,000. With that announcement, BT's stock lost more than 25% of its value, injuring Wright and the other class members.

The amended complaint alleges that "due to [the firm's] recklessness and failure to follow Generally Accepted Auditing Standards ('GAAS') [Ernst & Young, by electing to perform only a limited review of BT–Summit,] did not uncover the massive 'accounting and financial reporting irregularities' at BT–Summit." Allegedly because of this recklessness, Wright and other class members purchased stock at an artificially inflated price and later suffered injury once BT's true financial picture emerged. . . .

DISCUSSION

On appeal, Wright argues that the district court (1) erred in holding that the amended complaint failed to allege that Ernst & Young made an actionable misstatement within the meaning of the Act; (2) erred in crediting the "unaudited" disclaimer in BT's press release and thus erred in rejecting her allegation that the market understood the press release as an implied statement by Ernst & Young that the financial information contained therein was accurate. . . .

* * *

1. Actionable Statements and § 10(b)

Wright first argues that because a defendant can incur primary liability under the Act for false statements that are not directly communicated to the public, there is no requirement that the false statement be attributed to the defendant at the time of its dissemination. Thus, Wright maintains that although BT's press release attributes no statement to Ernst & Young, the amended complaint nevertheless alleges a false statement within the meaning of § 10(b) because it alleges that Ernst & Young "assured" BT of the accuracy of its 1995 financial results, knowing that BT would, in turn, promptly disseminate those results to investors in the press release.

Further, Wright argues that even if the amended complaint does not allege conduct amounting to a false statement, it does state a § 10(b) cause of action under post-*Central Bank* authority because Ernst & Young is alleged to have "substantially participated" in the fraud.... We disagree on both counts.

We conclude that Wright's arguments are foreclosed by *Central Bank*.... In *Central Bank*, the Supreme Court addressed the legitimacy of secondary liability claims in private actions brought pursuant to § 10(b). The Court concluded from the text of the Act that Congress never intended to impose secondary liability under § 10(b) and thus the Act "does not itself reach those who aid and abet ... [but] prohibits only the making of a material misstatement (or omission) or the commission of a manipulative act." The Court further observed that authorizing a § 10(b) cause of action based on aiding and abetting would circumvent the "reliance" requirement of Rule 10b–5 by allowing a plaintiff to prevail "without any showing that the plaintiff relied upon the aider and abettor's statements or actions." However, the Court did not hold that secondary actors are always free from liability under the Act. Rather, secondary actors like accountants may be held liable as primary violators if *all* the requirements for primary liability are met, including "a material misstatement (or omission) on which a purchaser or seller of securities relies."

In the wake of *Central Bank,* federal courts have differed over the threshold required for a secondary actor's conduct to implicate primary liability. As Judge Gleeson of the Eastern District of New York observed,

> [s]ome courts have held that a third party's review and approval of documents containing fraudulent statements is not actionable under Section 10(b) because one must *make* the material misstatement or omission in order to be a primary violator....
>
> Other [courts] have held that third parties may be primarily liable for statements made by others in which the defendant had significant participation. *See, e.g., In re Software Toolworks,* 50 F.3d 615, 628 n. 3 (9th Cir. 1994) (accountant may be primarily liable based on its "significant role in drafting and editing" a letter sent by the issuer to the SEC)....

These two differing approaches have been characterized respectively as the "bright line" test and the "substantial[] participat[ion]" test.

In *Shapiro,* we followed the "bright line" test after observing that " '[i]f *Central Bank* is to have any real meaning, a defendant must actually make a false or misleading statement in order to be held liable under Section 10(b). Anything short of such conduct is merely aiding and abetting.... ' " [C]ontrary to Wright's argument, a secondary actor cannot incur primary liability under the Act for a statement not attributed to that actor at the time of its dissemination. Such a holding would circumvent the reliance requirements of the Act, as "[r]eliance only on representations made by others cannot itself form the basis of liability." Thus, the misrepresentation must be attributed to that specific actor at the time of public dissemination, that is, in advance of the investment decision....

In this case, BT's press release did not attribute any assurances to Ernst & Young and, in fact, did not mention Ernst & Young at all. Thus, Ernst & Young neither directly nor indirectly communicated misrepresentations to investors. Therefore, the amended complaint failed to allege that Ernst & Young made "a material misstatement (or omission) on which a purchaser or seller of securities relie[d]." *Central Bank,* 511 U.S. at 191. Moreover, as the district court aptly recognized, because the press release contained a clear and express warning that no audit had yet been completed, there is no basis for Wright to claim that Ernst & Young had endorsed the accuracy of those results.

* * *

2. The "Unaudited" Disclaimer

Wright next argues that the district court erred in giving effect to BT's disclaimer in the press release which stated that the financial results were "unaudited." ...

Wright cannot prevail regardless of how we treat the disclaimer. As noted, Ernst & Young's assurances were never communicated to the public either directly or indirectly. BT issued the press release without a whisper of Ernst & Young's involvement. Thus, in order to resurrect Wright's claim that Ernst & Young made an actionable statement within the meaning of § 10(b), we would have to do more than just refuse to give effect to the "unaudited" disclaimer. We would also have to ignore the absence of any mention of Ernst & Young in BT's press release and focus instead on what the market might have implicitly "understood" about Ernst & Young's involvement in that press release. In other words, we would have to grant Wright an exception to the rule established by the Supreme Court that secondary actors such as accountants may not be held primarily liable unless they themselves have made "a material misstatement (or omission) on which a purchaser or seller of securities relies." We find no justification for granting such an exception.

* * *

QUESTIONS

1. Suppose that it was common knowledge that Ernst & Young audited BT's books. Assume that BT's press release containing the materially misleading financial results did not mention Ernst & Young, but failed to denote specifically that the press release results were "unaudited." Do you agree with the court that the presence or absence of the "unaudited" disclaimer is irrelevant?

2. One of the justifications in *Central Bank* behind eliminating aiding and abetting liability is the fear that aiding and abetting does away with the reliance requirement for such defendants. Why isn't there reliance if it is common knowledge among investors that Ernst & Young is BT's auditor and the firm has verified all of BT's financial statements, audited and unaudited?

HYPOTHETICAL EIGHT

Recall the restatement of DigitalBase's revenues, required because the company booked as revenue contracts that were still contingent. The plaintiffs in the DigitalBase class action have named DigitalBase's top distributor, ComputerMart, as a defendant. According to the complaint, ComputerMart entered into a purchase agreement subject to a secret right of return with DigitalBase. ComputerMart agreed to this arrangement after DigitalBase's sales representative told ComputerMart that he "needed to make this quarter's sales quota or I am going to be looking for work." ComputerMart has filed a motion to dismiss. What would the result be under *Central Bank*?

C.   CONTROL PERSON LIABILITY

Central Bank's rejection of aiding-and-abetting liability for Rule 10b–5 has put new emphasis on the Exchange Act's provision explicitly creating vicarious liability. Who can be subjected to liability as a "control person" under § 20(a)?

Arthur Children's Trust v. Keim

994 F.2d 1390 (9th Cir. 1993).

■ NOONAN, CIRCUIT JUDGE.

In these consolidated appeals Arthur Children's Trust et al. (the Investors) appeal summary judgment in favor of Howard Keim (Keim).... The underlying action against Keim is for securities fraud in violation of the Securities and Exchange Act of 1934 and Rule 10b–5. He is alleged to have been a control person as defined by § 20(a) of an issuer of fraudulent securities.... We reverse the summary judgment in favor of Keim....

FACTS

In January 1985 an agreement for a joint venture called Los Caballos Development Associates (the Venture) was entered into by Los Caballos de Santa Fe, Inc., a New Mexico corporation (the Santa Fe Company) and Parkland Development Corporation, an Arizona corporation (Parkland). [The parties agreed to establish a management committee to manage the business affairs of the Venture, including incurring any obligation on behalf of Venture in excess of $20,000. The management committee also had the power to require the venturers to contribute additional funds equally to the Venture.]

* * *

The Management Committee was to consist of eight members, with each venturer nominating four and Parkland having the right to designate the chairman, whose vote in case of a tie would be decisive and who was to be responsible for "the day-to-day business decisions and operations." Parkland nominated John Hill, Michael Smith, Timothy Sprague and Larry LaPrade, with LaPrade designated as chairman. The Santa Fe company nominated its chairman, Burton Melton; its president, Don Burt; and two of its directors, Mark Conkling and Keim.

The purpose of the Venture was a real estate development south of Santa Fe which, when completed, would include private residences, retail shops, a hotel and—as a centerpiece—a stadium and accompanying facilities to constitute a major equestrian convention center—hence the project's appealing name, "The Horses," in Spanish.

LaPrade and Smith began the task of money-raising, using as a vehicle Incor, a corporation controlled by them. As a result of Incor's solicitation the Investors, mostly pension plans for doctors, were led to purchase the Venture's notes. All the representations made to the Investors were made by Incor, LaPrade or Smith. The Venture put no restrictions on their methods. No representations to the Investors were made by Keim.

On March 1, 1985 the Venture issued a promissory note for $3,760,000 payable to the holders listed on Exhibit A attached to the note....

Soon after this financing had been accomplished, the Venture was in difficult straits. According to a memorandum of July 3, 1985 from Peter Webb, controller of the Santa Fe company, to the members of the Management Committee of the Venture, including Keim, the committee on June 17, 1985 discussed the "precarious situation regarding our financial capabilities to meet our obligations to the Incor investors and our other contractual obligations." The Venture's current deposits were "adequate to cover our Incor interest obligations," but if "we continue to pay our development obligations we could be out of money as soon as October." Michael Smith had stated that if construction financing were not in place by October he "would address the problem." In light of this statement, "it was agreed" that Webb "should continue to pay our obligations as they are incurred or due using all available funds including those previously earmarked for interest payments to Incor's investors." ...

According to the minutes of the Management Committee for July 10, 1985, at which Keim was present, a large number of topics were discussed. Among other things:

> ... Financing package was discussed. Sprague stated that we had to raise from three to five million dollars worth of equity.... He said that there were tax considerations to think of, perhaps potential pension fund money. Three and one half million dollars raised by ourselves, the

rest banks. Great tax shelters for prospective investors. Keim felt tax benefits would be there. Pension Plan money is easier to tap.

Following a discussion of "the appraisal," Larry LaPrade raised the possibility of a bridge loan, "starting in August." Keim said "he was prepared to give all out whatever it takes. Pension Plan 15%."

In addition to being a member of the Management Committee of the Venture, Keim was chairman of its Development Committee. He had a 10 percent equity interest in the enterprise. He was also owed a $100,000 "development fee" by the Santa Fe company, a fee which he asserted in a letter to Larry LaPrade of November 27, 1985 had been assumed by LaPrade, apparently meaning that the Venture had assumed it. A budget of the Venture reflects only one fee for development—$100,000 owed Keim.

According to the affidavit of Timothy Sprague:

> Various discussions were had between members of the management committee, including Howard Keim, with respect to the raising of seed capital for the project. As time progressed throughout 1985, the project having continued to incur significant development expenses and no construction or permanent financing having been obtained for the project, these discussions among the members of the management committee included "rolling over" previous loans secured for the project by Michael Smith and Larry LaPrade, together with the raising of new monies through additional loans.

> Mr. Keim—who was constantly pressing the venture for payment of his own fees—was generally an advocate of Smith and LaPrade's lending activities, his comments essentially being to get it done.

Sprague further swore that at the July 1985 meeting or prior thereto, Smith advised the members of the Management Committee that "he was borrowing monies for the project from doctor pension plans by offering to secure their loans by the project's real property, on a 50% loan to value ratio. Previously, at the time of the original loan, it was discussed that it would also be secured by the personal guarantees of all the Los Caballos venturers, excluding defendant Keim, who I understand refused to provide one." On a flight from Albuquerque to Phoenix in July 1985 Sprague also described to Keim "Smith and LaPrade's manner of raising funds."

On March 1, 1986 the Venture again executed a promissory note, secured by a mortgage on its real estate, in the amount of $5,400,000....

All of the foregoing facts are not disputed, with one large exception. According to Keim's deposition, he had no knowledge of how LaPrade and Smith were raising the money and no knowledge of who was providing it.

The Venture was a financial disaster. LaPrade and Smith entered bankruptcy. The Investors lost their money.

PROCEEDINGS

On December 21, 1988 the Investors filed suit under the Securities and Exchange Act of 1934 against six of the members of the Management

Committee, including Keim. . . . The third claim for relief asserted that the defendants who had been members of the Management Committee of the Venture were controlling persons in the sense that section 20(a) of the Securities and Exchange Act of 1934 defines "controlling persons." They were alleged to have known the dire financial straits of the Venture and, knowing it, to have also known that no one would have invested in it unless provided incentives which no defendant had reason to believe were being promised or unless there were false representations. In this situation, knowing that millions of dollars were being raised for their project from private investors, the control persons allegedly undertook no action to implement controls on LaPrade, Smith and Sprague; they allegedly exercised no "internal control or supervision" to prevent violation of the securities law; they allegedly either did not inquire as to the representations made to induce the loans or knew that the loans were induced by fraudulent representations.

After discovery had been conducted . . . Keim on January 21, 1991 moved for summary judgment. . . .

. . . [T]he district court found that Keim had no control over the financing and was therefore not a control person. Moreover, the court found "nothing to indicate that Keim knew anything about 'false representations.' Therefore, he is not liable as a controlling person." The court did not discuss the Venture's role as issuer of the notes. The court granted Keim's motion for summary judgment and denied the Investors' cross-motion.

* * *

ANALYSIS

The Case Against Keim

* * *

The Issuer's Scienter. If the representations made by LaPrade were false, the issuer had the scienter that *Ernst & Ernst v. Hochfelder,* 425 U.S. 185 (1976) requires for Rule 10b–5 liability. The issuer is chargeable with the knowledge of LaPrade, the head of its Management Committee, acting to market the issuer's securities. That LaPrade acted through Incor cannot insulate the issuer from his knowledge. The issuer is equally possessed of scienter if the providing of the appraisal reports to Incor for fund-raising is found to have been the providing of information not fraudulently but recklessly. Such recklessness would be established by showing that knowing of Incor's fund-raising, the issuer provided the reports to be read by laypersons in " 'an extreme departure from the standards of ordinary care' " and with the danger of misleading the purchasers of the securities " 'so obvious' " that the issuer must have been aware of it.

The Controlling Persons of the Issuer. In general, the determination of who is a controlling person . . . is an intensely factual question. A director is not automatically liable as a controlling person. *Burgess v. Premier*

Corp., 727 F.2d 826, 832 (9th Cir. 1984) (a director who was uninvolved in the company's day-to-day cattle business and was without experience in the business and had nothing to do with the prospectuses issued to the doctor investors was not a controlling person, nor was a director who had minimal interaction with the company, due partly to ill health).... "Accordingly, although a person's being an officer or director does not create any *presumption* of control, it is a sort of red light." It is not uncommon for control "to rest with a group of persons, such as the members of the corporation's management."

Here the persons controlling the issuer in every material respect were the Management Committee, whose decisions, as the Joint Venture Agreement specifies, were "binding on the Venturers." The "major or significant business decisions affecting the Venture" were to be made by the Management Committee. Every decision which might "materially affect the Venture" was the Management Committee's to make. A line was drawn by the agreement between decisions of this kind which were confided to the committee and "day-to-day business decisions and operations."

The terms and representations on which the Venture's financing were obtained were not a day-to-day affair. They were "major" or "significant." They materially affected the Venture. They had to be determined by the Management Committee....

The members of this committee were "a narrowly defined group" charged with the task of making these decisions, hence "it is reasonable to presume that [they] had the power to control."

Webb's memorandum of July 3, 1985 shows that the Management Committee on June 17, 1985 specifically discussed the "precarious situation regarding our financial capabilities to meet our obligations to the Incor investors." According to that memorandum, the members of the Management Committee, including Keim, were informed that the Venture would run out of money as soon as October 1985. The Management Committee then decided to use for current obligations funds "previously earmarked for interest payments to Incor's investors."

According to the minutes of the Management Committee for July 10, 1985, which Keim attended, there was explicit discussion of the "financing package"—necessarily a reference to the package to be put together by Incor, the company doing the financing.... The amount to be raised was discussed. Keim specifically addressed the tapping of pension plan money. Keim also took the lead in stating what rate of interest should be paid.

Webb's memorandum of the June 17, 1985 meeting and the minutes of the meeting of July 10, 1985 show the Management Committee acting by consensus, not by vote. The committee does not appear to have been dominated by LaPrade or by the Parkland members as a whole. Keim appears as a vocal and active participant in the management of the Venture.

Keim states that in fact he had no control over LaPrade, Smith and Incor and argues that this undisputed fact should relieve him of liability as a controlling person. Keim misunderstands the basis on which his liability is alleged. He is sued not because he controlled those marketing the investment contracts but because he was one of the persons controlling the issuer of the investment contracts.

The Controlling Person's Scienter. To establish the liability of a controlling person, the plaintiff does not have the burden of establishing that person's scienter distinct from the controlled corporation's scienter. If the plaintiff had this obligation, the controlling person provision "would hardly make anyone liable who would not be so otherwise." But a defendant who is a controlling person of an issuer with scienter has the burden of proving his absence of scienter. Under the controlling person statute that means that Keim, as a person controlling the issuer, was subject to liability unless he establishes that he "acted in good faith and did not directly or indirectly induce the act or acts constituting the violation or cause of action."

Some of our earlier cases took the position that in proving the liability of a controlling person, the plaintiff has the burden of showing that the defendant does not come within the good faith exception. But it has now been established that this burden falls upon the controlling person. . . . Those controlling an issuer of securities are liable for the conduct of the issuer and so are liable if an issuer intentionally or recklessly permitted the fraudulent marketing of its securities.

Consequently, Keim has the burden of proving his good faith. His own declaration of innocence does not meet that burden when the Investors have offered evidence disputing his ignorance of the financing; when Webb's memo of July 3, 1985 shows Keim was aware that Incor had recruited the Investors and that the interest payments to them were in jeopardy; when the minutes of the Management Committee for July 10, 1985 show him as a participant in the discussion of financing; when his letter to LaPrade of November 27, 1985 and the affidavit of Sprague show him pressing for his $100,000 developer's fee; when Sprague's affidavit shows him influential enough to avoid giving the personal guarantee extracted from the others; when Sprague has deposed that Keim was told that the loans from the Investors were to be secured on the basis that they would be half the value of the property; and when his responsibilities as a member of the Management Committee necessarily made him familiar with the cash needs and cash resources of the Venture. In the face of these proffered facts, Keim's alleged good faith and his not having directly or indirectly induced the allegedly fraudulent marketing of the Venture's notes could not be determined by summary judgment. Accordingly, summary judgment in his favor is reversed.

* * *

NOTES

1. *Culpable participation.* The Ninth Circuit follows the majority rule requiring that the plaintiff only needs to prove that the defendant actually participated in the operations of the corporation and had the ability to exercise control over the transaction in question. The Second and Third Circuits, however, require a showing of "culpable participation" in the fraud by the alleged controlling person. *See, e.g., Boguslavsky v. Kaplan*, 159 F.3d 715 (2d Cir. 1998). Courts following the majority rule applied in *Arthur Children's Trust* believe that the culpability of the alleged controlling person is more appropriately addressed by the "good faith" defense provided by the statute.

QUESTIONS

1. Could the defendant Keim have pushed the Venture into new business directions or new sources of financing if the rest of the management committee was opposed? Does Keim need to have this power to be a control person?

2. Status as a director by itself is not enough to trigger control person liability according to *Keim*. What more is required? Is it enough that a director (or member of the management committee as in *Keim*) appreciates the facts underlying the alleged fraud yet remains passive?

V. DAMAGES

A. OPEN MARKET DAMAGES

The rule in class actions for fraud in connection with an actively traded security is the out-of-pocket measure traditionally used by tort law, that is, the difference between price paid and the value of the security at the time of the purchase. From an economic perspective, overall sanctions (i.e., damages in private actions plus fines imposed by the SEC plus reputational harm), multiplied by the probability that sanctions will be imposed on wrongdoers, should equal the social costs of the harm caused by fraud. Because the probability of sanctions is less than 100%—some fraudsters will get away with it—the sanction imposed needs to be greater than the harm caused by fraud.

The measure of damages in securities cases is not, however, social harm with a multiplier to reflect the probability of detection. Instead, a compensatory measure is used based on the out-of-pocket measure of damages. The resulting enormous damages that would be required to compensate the victims of fraud raises the question of whether the overall level of sanctions for fraud is appropriate to the level of harm caused by the fraud.

Compensation through the out-of-pocket measure of damages makes sense in cases in which the corporation has been selling securities through fraud. Compensation corrects the distortion caused by fraud in two ways. First, requiring compensation to the victim discourages the corporation from committing the fraud. If the corporation has committed fraud to sell its securities its gain is likely to be roughly equivalent to the plaintiff's loss. Second, compensation discourages investors from expending resources trying to avoid fraud, termed precaution costs. Expenditures by both the perpetrator and the victim due to fraud are a social waste, so compensation makes sense in that context. The federal securities laws encourage such fraud suits by providing a very generous standard for recovery for fraud in public offerings under §§ 11 and 12 of the Securities Act, which we will study in Chapter 8. Despite that encouragement, claims asserting a misrepresentation made by a company in connection with an offering of securities make up only a small percentage of securities class actions.

The overwhelming majority of securities fraud class actions do not involve corporations selling securities. As you have seen in the cases in this chapter, the typical securities fraud class action plaintiffs' attorneys sue the corporation and its officers under Rule 10b–5 of the Securities Exchange Act for alleged misrepresentations regarding the company's operations, financial performance, or future prospects that inflate the price of the company's stock in secondary trading markets such as the NYSE and the Nasdaq. Because the corporation has not sold securities (and thereby transferred wealth to itself), it has no institutional incentive to spend real resources in executing the fraud.

This type of fraud, commonly referred to as fraud on the market, also differs from what we typically consider fraud in that there is no net wealth transfer away from investors, at least in the aggregate. Instead, the wealth transfers caused by fraud on the market overwhelmingly occur between equally innocent investors. For every shareholder who *bought* at a fraudulently inflated price, another shareholder has *sold*: The buyer's individual loss is offset by the seller's gain. Assuming all traders are ignorant of the fraud, over time they will come out winners as often as losers from fraudulently distorted prices. Therefore, shareholders as a group should have no expected loss from fraud on the market, so they would have no incentive to take precautions against the fraud (even if such precautions were feasible).

Despite the fact that the corporation being sued has not gained from fraud on the market, the out-of-pocket measure affords full compensation to investors who come out on the losing end of a trade at a price distorted by misrepresentation. Those investors are entitled to recover their losses from the corporation based on its managers' misstatements. Depending on the trading volume in secondary markets, the potential recoverable damages in such suits can be a substantial percentage of the corporation's total capitalization, easily reaching hundreds of millions of dollars. With potential damages in this range, class actions are a big stick to wield against fraud. Given the somewhat arbitrary quality of these damages, based on trading volume, what is the probability of Rule 10b–5 for secondary market fraud providing the optimal level of deterrence against fraud? Or perhaps overwhelming damages are needed given the barriers to recovery in a Rule 10b-5 suit?

HYPOTHETICAL NINE

Consider DigitalBase's past accounting practices that led to its recent restatement. Assume that during the period when the misleading information affected the secondary market, 10 million shares of DigitalBase changed hands.

Recall that the share price dropped from $15 to $10 when the restatement was announced.

1. Assume that private plaintiffs' attorneys are successful in winning a Rule 10b–5 judgment at trial based on DigitalBase's past overstatement of revenues. What is the proper out-of-pocket measure of damages? What information would you need to determine this?

2. Who was harmed by DigitalBase's overstatement of revenues in prior years?

3. Who benefited from DigitalBase's overstatement of revenues in prior years? How much did DigitalBase itself benefit? Does the out-of-pocket damages measure do a good job of approximating this benefit?

B.   FACE-TO-FACE DAMAGES

In face-to-face transactions, the court is not limited to the out-of-pocket measure. The damages measure can vary according to the circumstances of the situation, as illustrated by the case below.

Pidcock v. Sunnyland America, Inc.

854 F.2d 443 (11th Cir. 1988).

■ VANCE, CIRCUIT JUDGE.

* * *

Appellant John Pidcock and L.B. "Dude" Harvard, Sr. each owned fifty percent of Sunnyland America, Inc., a holding company for the ownership and operation of several meat packing plants. Dude Harvard served as president of the corporation and was actively involved in the daily operations of the meat packing companies. Pidcock served as chairman of the board, and although he attended the quarterly board meetings regularly he did not participate in the daily operations of the business.

Dude Harvard had two sons, Joe and Bryant, who both began working for Sunnyland at an early age and gradually worked their way up to management positions. In 1981 Joe was promoted from vice president in charge of sales and marketing to president of the corporation. Bryant was vice president in charge of operations. The Harvard sons' growing control over Sunnyland's operations was consistent with the desire of Dude Harvard and Pidcock that one day Joe and Bryant would take over the business.

Eventually Dude Harvard and Pidcock began to explore the possibility of selling Sunnyland. Joe Harvard took responsibility for conducting all sale negotiations, including the coordination of all information relating to potential purchasers. Pidcock trusted and relied on his longtime partner's son to provide him with all material information.

After one serious prospective purchaser of Sunnyland failed to follow through with an offer, the three Harvards decided to buy out Pidcock. On October 22, 1982 Joe and Bryant met with Pidcock and formally offered to purchase Pidcock's half of the company for $2.2 million. The Harvards painted a gloomy forecast for the possibility of any third party interest in buying Sunnyland. On October 26 Pidcock wrote Joe Harvard to accept the offer. Pidcock made this decision for several reasons, including the Harvards' assurances that sale of the company to a third party was doubtful.[2] On December 21 Pidcock signed a contract for the redemption of his stock.

There were numerous conversations between Pidcock and the Harvards between the October 22 offer and the December 21 signing. Joe represented the Harvards during the negotiations. There was little direct communication between Pidcock and Dude Harvard. Pidcock made it clear that he knew he was selling his interest in Sunnyland at a bargain price. He also informed the Harvards that a possibility of selling Sunnyland to a third party would cause him to reconsider his decision to sell out, and that a likelihood of selling the company to a third party would cause him to change his decision to sell altogether. Pidcock questioned Joe Harvard repeatedly regarding the existence of an interested third party. With one minor exception, Joe made no mention of any interested third parties.

Joe Harvard, however, was not telling the truth. . . . In November John Sherman, a real estate broker with the Richard Tift Company, had learned of Joe Harvard's interest in selling Sunnyland. On December 10 Sherman had called Harvard and obtained permission to list Sunnyland for sale at $16 million. Six days later Sherman had called Harvard again and revealed that the Field Packing Company had an interest in Sunnyland. . . .

On the morning of December 21 Sherman and his senior business associate Richard Tift had met with Dude and Joe Harvard in Sunnyland's offices. After the meeting, Dude Harvard had spoken privately with Tift and asked him, as a personal favor, not to mention to Pidcock anything about the Harvards' efforts to sell Sunnyland. That afternoon, Pidcock executed the redemption agreement.

After the signing of the redemption agreement, Sherman continued to work towards the sale of Sunnyland to Field Packing. On March 30, 1983 Sunnyland and Pidcock closed on the redemption of Pidcock's shares. After the redemption the Harvards instituted a program of operational changes and improvements to Sunnyland facilities at a cost of over $1 million. Eventually Soparind Meat Packing Corporation purchased Sunnyland in January 1985 for a total of $7.3 million. In the summer of 1986 Pidcock learned from Richard Tift of Tift's December 1982 meeting with Joe Harvard.

Pidcock filed this action under Rule 10b–5 on October 1, 1986 seeking to recover the difference between the true fair market value of his stock and the $2.2 million he received.[4] Following a bench trial the district court

---

2. Pidcock also was concerned about his failing health, his desire to safeguard his wife's financial future and his faltering trust in the Harvard sons' ability to manage Sunnyland.

4. Pidcock calculated this amount to be as much as $3,602,395.

found that had Pidcock known of the brokerage arrangement between the Harvards and the Tift Company and of Field Packing's interest in Sunnyland, Pidcock would have postponed the December 21 execution of the redemption agreement. The district court noted that Dude Harvard's request that Richard Tift not tell Pidcock about the Harvards' efforts to sell Sunnyland implied that the Harvards themselves believed that Pidcock would have reconsidered had he known of the Harvard–Tift relationship. The district court thus held that the misrepresentation or omission of this information was material under Rule 10b–5. The district court also held that the Harvards made the material false representations or omissions with scienter, and that Pidcock justifiably relied on them.

The district court, however, ruled that because Soparind was not a viable purchasing prospect prior to January 1984, Soparind's purchase of Sunnyland was beyond the causal chain of events flowing from the Harvards' fraudulent conduct. The district court viewed Soparind as "a completely different purchaser, unrelated to the information withheld from Pidcock when he entered the redemption agreement." The court therefore held that Pidcock had failed to prove proximate causation of damages. The court denied recovery under Rule 10b–5.

II.

*   *   *

Pidcock argues on appeal that the district court erred in granting judgment for defendants on the sole ground that Pidcock failed to establish that the Harvards' deception proximately caused him any damages. Pidcock specifically argues that the district court failed to consider a line of securities cases providing that where a defrauding purchaser obtains a profit, the defrauded seller may be able to recover that profit as damages. Where this disgorgement remedy applies, Pidcock contends, the plaintiff is entitled to a presumption on the issue of proximate causation.

The traditional rule for measuring damages proximately caused by a defendant's fraud in 10b–5 actions is the difference between the value of the securities at the time of the fraudulent transaction and the price received. The Supreme Court has held that the general measure of damages for defrauded sellers is the difference between what the seller received and what the seller would have received had there been no fraudulent conduct. *Affiliated Ute Citizens of Utah v. United States*, 406 U.S. 128, 155 (1972). Where the defrauding purchaser receives more than the seller's actual loss, however, the damages are the purchaser's profits. *Affiliated Ute*, 406 U.S. at 155.

The origin of the rule that a defrauding purchaser's profits must be disgorged is *Janigan v. Taylor*, 344 F.2d 781 (1st Cir. 1965), which was cited with approval in *Affiliated Ute*. The *Janigan* court held that once it has been determined that a purchaser acquired property by fraud, any profit subsequently realized by the defrauding purchaser should be deemed the proximate consequence of the fraud. The court's holding applied whether or not the profit was foreseeable. In an oft-quoted passage the *Janigan* court explained:

> If the property is not bought from, but sold to the fraudulent party, future accretions not foreseeable at the time of the transfer even on the true facts, and hence speculative, are subject to another factor, viz., that they accrued to the fraudulent party. It may, as in the case at bar, be entirely speculative whether, had plaintiffs not sold, the series of fortunate occurrences would have happened in the same way, and to their same profit. However, there can be no speculation but that the defendant actually made the profit and, once it is found that he acquired the property by fraud, that the profit was the proximate consequence of the fraud, whether foreseeable or not. It is more appropriate to give the defrauded party the benefit even of windfalls than to let the fraudulent party keep them.

344 F.2d at 786. The reason for this rule is simple fairness: "it is simple equity that a wrongdoer should disgorge his fraudulent enrichment."

The *Janigan* court noted, however, that there are limits to this disgorgement principle. As the Fifth Circuit explained: "A significant limitation on the disgorgement doctrine is that a plaintiff may not recover any portion of the profits attributable to the defendant's 'special or unique efforts ... other than those for which he is duly compensated.' "

Certain actions taken by defrauding purchasers after the fraudulent transaction will limit the plaintiff's recovery of subsequent profits under the *Janigan* disgorgement principle. Aggressive and enterprising management activities may break the causal chain between the fraud and the profits. Extending personal guaranties on bank loans for working capital and introducing new lines of business may also preclude disgorgement. Modernization also may qualify as a special effort or contribution, depending on whether or not the defendants were acting in their compensated corporate capacities. The mere passage of time, if long enough, may limit the amount of profits recoverable by a previously defrauded seller.[10]

Certain events, however, are insufficient by themselves to prevent disgorgement. The *Janigan* court held that gains in the company's affairs attributable to the defendant's efforts, however extraordinary, were still subject to disgorgement if performed as part of the defendant's regular salaried responsibilities. Thus price rises, increased efficiency and an improvement in the business cycle are not the kinds of events that will allow a defrauding purchaser to keep resulting profits.

Even more important for this case, the ending of divided control is not a valid reason for limiting the plaintiff's recovery of the defendant's profits.

---

10. Another limit on the availability of disgorgement, not applicable in this case, involves publicly traded securities. "When a seller of publicly traded securities has learned of previously undisclosed material facts, and decides nevertheless not to replace the sold securities, he cannot later claim that his failure to obtain subsequent stock appreciation was a proximate consequence of his prior ignorance."

This is particularly true when the defendants, like the Harvards, obtained undivided control of the company by the fraudulent non-disclosure.

In this case we hold that the district court erred in not considering the disgorgement remedy under *Janigan* and its progeny. We further hold that Pidcock is entitled to a presumption that the damages he suffered as a result of the fraud are equal to the profits the Harvards realized upon the sale of Sunnyland to Soparind. Pidcock retains the burden of proof on the issue of damages. He is entitled to the benefit of a presumption, however, because the Harvards are in the better position to explain how the profit came about. Thus, the presumption operates so as to require the Harvards to come forward with evidence showing that the profit is attributable to causes other than their fraudulent purchase of Pidcock's interest. If they fail to come forward with such evidence, Pidcock will prevail on the strength of the presumption. If, on the other hand, they do carry their burden of going forward, Pidcock will not prevail unless he persuades the trier of fact that the explanation should not be accepted.

* * *

QUESTIONS

1. Do plaintiffs in a Rule 10b–5 action get to force disgorgement of all of the defendant's profits?

2. Who bears the burden of proof of showing whether any of the profits were due to the unique or special efforts of the defendants?

3. Why are sellers of securities traded in the public capital markets not entitled to price gains subsequent to the disclosure of the truth?

Garnatz v. Stifel, Nicolaus & Co., Inc.

559 F.2d 1357 (8th Cir. 1977).

■ MATTHES, SENIOR CIRCUIT JUDGE.

Stifel, Nicolaus & Co., a brokerage firm, and Kingsley O. Wright, a vice-president of that firm, appeal from a judgment entered against them on a jury verdict awarding Milton W. Garnatz damages of $45,000 with interest and costs.... [P]laintiff's complaint was based on defendants' alleged violations of § 10(b) of the Securities Exchange Act of 1934; Rule 10b–5 promulgated thereunder; and § 17 of the Securities Act of 1933.

I

Garnatz is a man of limited education and modest means. His familiarity with the securities markets is characteristically that of the average, individual investor, not the sophisticated trader.

In November of 1972, plaintiff attended a series of investment seminars sponsored by Stifel, Nicolaus. On the basis of representations made at those seminars and at two personal meetings with Kingsley Wright, plaintiff agreed to participate in a special bond margin account program which was purportedly designed to maximize his income while preserving his capital. The representations plaintiff specifically relied on in deciding to join in the program were: (1) that all purchases had to be approved by the board of directors of Stifel, Nicolaus; (2) that the use of a margin account entailed no risk to plaintiff's capital; (3) that the bonds purchased would not decrease more than one percent in value; (4) that the interest rate on the margin account would never exceed eight percent; and (5) that defendants' recommended purchases would be without risk. Defendants do not seriously challenge the allegation that these representations were both false and material.

Plaintiff insisted on avoiding speculation, yet most of the bonds purchased for him were either low-rated or non-rated by Standard & Poors. Although safety was a key feature of defendants' sales pitch, in order to pay the interest rate on the margin account and still provide a sufficiently attractive return, it was apparently necessary to purchase high-yield, and consequently highly-speculative bonds. At no time was any bond purchase approved by the board of directors of Stifel, Nicolaus.

Plaintiff entered into the program in late 1972. By April of 1973, the market value of Garnatz' account had declined over one percent. As a result, plaintiff was forced to relinquish all income from the bonds to pay increased margin calls. During this period, Wright repeatedly reassured Garnatz that the drop was only temporary and strongly recommended that plaintiff stay with the program, which he did. In August of 1974, the interest rate on the margin account jumped from eight percent to thirteen percent, as permitted by a change in Missouri's usury law. Garnatz does not dispute the fact that by that time he was, or should have been, on notice of the fraud.

II

The implication of a private damage remedy for violations of the federal securities laws is based partly on the notion that the abrogation of a statutorily imposed duty is tortious. Following the model of the common law tort of deceit, in § 10(b) and Rule 10b–5 actions "the defendant is liable to respond in such damages as naturally and proximately result from the fraud. . . . " Normally, federal courts measure those damages according to the out-of-pocket rule. As applied to a fraudulently induced purchase of securities, that rule provides for the recovery of the difference between the actual value of the securities and their purchase price. Recovery is also allowed for any consequential damages proximately resulting from the fraud. The rule was designed to provide plaintiffs with a compensatory recovery rather than allowing damages for a lost expectancy. It works best in the typical situation where the defendant's fraud conceals the actual value of the item purchased, yet does not affect the overall market value of that item.

Of course, the out-of-pocket rule is not a talisman. Indeed, this court has shown no hesitation in varying that measure when necessary on the facts of a given case. Our function is to fashion the remedy best suited to the harm.

In the present case, defendants urge strict application of the out-of-pocket rule. They would deny plaintiff any recovery at all, since the value of the bonds equaled their purchase price. But the fact that plaintiff got what he paid for does not mean he did not suffer any legally cognizable injury from defendants' fraud. It merely indicates that the fraud did not relate to the price of the bonds. . . .

[T]he gravamen of the present action was not whether Garnatz bought the bonds for a fair price, but that he bought at all. Absent defendants' representations regarding the safety of the program, plaintiff's express disdain for speculation undoubtedly would have precluded his participation; but the fraudulent promise of a low-cost, income-maximizing, and risk-free investment package overcame plaintiff's caution. Under these circumstances, we believe that a rescissory damage measure . . . is appropriate. Such a measure seeks to return the parties to the status quo ante the sale. In effect, the plaintiff is refunded his purchase price, reduced by any value received as a result of the fraudulent transaction. As applied to the case at bar, plaintiff can recover the decline in value of his bonds until his actual or constructive notice of the fraud, as well as any other losses properly attributable to defendants' wrongdoing. That decline in value is determined by the losses taken on bond sales plus the losses sustained on bonds held, as long as all such losses were incurred prior to the date that plaintiff knew, or should have known, of the fraud.

Some would argue, as defendants have here, that a rescissory measure of damages allows recovery of losses due to market forces rather than the defendants' conduct. We recognize that neither Stifel, Nicolaus nor Kingsley Wright caused plaintiff's bonds to decline in value. But plaintiff's purchase of these low-rated and non-rated bonds was induced by defendants' wrongful concealment of the risks normally attendant to such transactions. Those risks should therefore rightly be borne by defendants. Moreover, since plaintiff's losses were natural, proximate, and foreseeable consequences of defendants' fraud, the causative connection is sufficient. Of course, the responsibility for losses incurred after actual or constructive notice of the fraud must fall to plaintiff.

* * *

NOTES

1. *Punitive damages.* Exchange Act § 28(a) limits the amount of damages in a Rule 10b–5 claim to "actual damages," thereby excluding punitive damages. Punitive damages may be recoverable for pendent state claims of common law fraud. In the typical 10b–5 class action, however, state claims will ordinarily be preempted by the Securities Litigation Uniform Standards Act.

QUESTIONS

1. Why was Garnatz not entitled to the disgorgement of profits measure of damages?

2.   How can investors be harmed if they got what they paid for?

3.   The fraud in *Garnatz* is sometimes called "fraud in the inducement." How does the characterization of the fraud affect the damages measure? Was there loss causation in *Garnatz*?

4.   Courts generally enjoy wide discretion in selecting among available Rule 10b–5 damage measurements. What principles do you think should guide this discretion? Should courts systematically choose the measure that provides the plaintiffs the largest recovery?

C.   PROPORTIONATE LIABILITY

The traditional rule in Rule 10b–5 actions was joint-and-several liability. Accountants won an important victory in the PSLRA with the adoption of a proportionate liability provision. See Exchange Act § 21D(f). Under this provision, defendants who are found to be only reckless are required to pay only their proportionate share of the damages caused. The jury (or finder of fact) must determine the percentage of responsibility (based on conduct and causal relationship to damages) as well as whether the defendant's actions were knowing.

There are two exceptions to the general rule of proportionality, however: (1) Defendants are jointly and severally liable to a plaintiff who is entitled to damages exceeding 10% of his net worth, if the plaintiff's net worth is less than $200,000; and (2) Defendants also must make up any shortfall due to a codefendant's insolvency, which comprises up to 50% of their own liability. The far larger exception is that knowing violators continue to be jointly and severally liable for the entire judgment. The provision also makes explicit defendants' right to seek contribution from other violators, whether or not they have been named as defendants.

HYPOTHETICAL TEN

Return to DigitalBase's reluctant disclosure in its 10–Q that the introduction of the GigaBase product will be delayed at least two years and its subsequent restatement of revenues of the prior year. Suppose that prior to these disclosures, Hillary (the CEO) engaged in insider trading, selling off ten million DigitalBase shares into the market at the pre-disclosure market price. Suppose that the out-of-pocket measure of damages for the nondisclosure is equal to $100 million. Moreover, assume that the defendants at trial are DigitalBase, Hillary, and Arthur & Young, the auditor.

1.   If you were a member of the jury, how would you go about assigning relative culpability among DigitalBase, Hillary, and Arthur & Young?

2.   Assume that DigitalBase has gone bankrupt (with no remaining assets) by the time plaintiffs obtain a judgment. Hillary has long since left the country for an untraceable Caribbean locale, leaving Arthur & Young as the lone remaining solvent defendant. Given your assignment of culpability above, how much money can the plaintiffs recover from Arthur & Young?

3.   Suppose that you, a juror, know about DigitalBase's bankrupt status and the absence of Hillary while making relative culpability assessments. How does this change your decision? See Exchange Act § 21D(f)(6).

CHAPTER 6

Insider Trading

Rules and Statutes

—*Sections 10(b), 16, 20, 20A and 21A of the Exchange Act*

—*Rules 10b–5, 10b5–1, 10b5–2, 10b–18, 14e–3, 16a–1, 16a–2, 16a–3, 16a–4, 16b–3, 16b–6 of the Exchange Act*

MOTIVATING HYPOTHETICAL

Merritt is a broker at Sparrow Securities. Sparrow Securities' standard client agreement requires Sparrow to keep client's account information confidential. One of Merritt's best customers is Jack, CEO of InClone Pharmaceuticals. One morning, Jack calls Merritt and tells Merritt to sell half of Jack's two million InClone shares, then trading at $65, because Jack "needs to diversify his holdings." Apparently part of Jack's diversification strategy is speculating in other biotechnology firms—Jack also tells Merritt to purchase call options on BioGen shares for his account. Without asking questions, Merritt sells the InClone shares and buys the BioGen options.

Later that morning, Merritt calls another of his customers, Martha, CEO of Martha Media Inc. (Merritt was introduced to Martha at a party by her good friend, Jack). Martha is out of the office when Merritt calls, but her secretary takes a message: "Merritt says InClone is headed south—Jack is dumping his shares. Sell?" Martha calls in for her messages later that day. She returns Merritt's call, but he is out to lunch, so she leaves instructions with Merritt's assistant to sell her 10,000 shares of InClone stock if the price falls to $60 "according to our plan." By the time Merritt gets back to the office from his two-hour, two-martini lunch, the price on InClone stock has hit $59.25 and he immediately dumps Martha's shares. (His superiors at Sparrow have made it clear that Merritt is to keep Martha happy!)

Jack and Martha's investment moves pay off in a big way—before the markets open the next day, InClone announces a tender offer for BioGen's stock at a 50% premium over BioGen's closing price from the day before. Jack's BioGen options, for which he paid $100,000, are now worth $1.3 million, as the market price surges in response to the news of InClone's tender offer. The market is less kind to InClone's shares—analysts are worried that InClone is badly overpaying for BioGen. InClone shares drop to $55. Martha avoids a $42,500 loss.

I. ECONOMICS OF INSIDER TRADING

"Insider" trading is something of a misnomer. The modern law of insider trading addresses not only trading by conventional insiders—corporate officers and directors—but also outsiders who have been given access to confidential information affecting the value of a corporation's securities. The most conspicuous members of this group include accountants, consultants, investment bankers, and lawyers. More controversially, prohibitions against insider trading now reach trading on confidential information not only in the securities of one's employer or principal, but also the securities of other companies. For example, an executive of Coca–Cola who uses secret information about a new Coke product to sell short Pepsi–Cola stock, anticipating that Pepsi would be at a competitive disadvantage in the face of Coke's blockbuster new product, would be guilty of insider trading (unless he disclosed to Coca–Cola's board his intention to trade Pepsi stock). We can therefore view modern insider trading doctrine as more generally governing which trading advantages are permissible in the securities markets.

Why prohibit insider trading? As we learned in Chapter 1, information is the lifeblood of securities markets. Insider trading is the starkest example of the profit opportunities afforded by information. Access to material information that other investors lack is the path to (relatively) risk-free profits. This fact, however, merely tells us that some investors will do better than others, that is, that insider trading will lead to transfers of wealth among investors. Why should society spend its resources deterring such transfers? Don't we have better things to worry about?

The traditional justification offered for prohibitions against insider trading is fairness: rules against insider trading protect the integrity of, and public confidence in, the stock market. There will inevitably be some information that is withheld from outsiders because companies have a variety of reasons for keeping information confidential, such as not tipping their hands to competitors. Insiders, of course, will have access to this information in the course of doing their jobs.

How does informed insider trading in the secondary markets influence outsiders? Investors view trading advantages for insiders as unfair. In a world without insider trading prohibitions, outsiders do not know whether the share price accurately reflects the company's future prospects, but they do know that they are going to be net losers when they trade with insiders. Insider traders will only buy when they know that the stock price is too low, and they will only sell when they know the stock price is too high. Therefore, anytime an outsider trades with an insider, the outsider knows that the insider trader is taking advantage of him/her. To avoid trading losses, uninformed traders would prefer to trade only with other (equally ignorant) uninformed traders. Mispricing is inevitable (absent a requirement that the firm disclose all material information instantly), but gains and losses should average out when trading occurs between equally igno-rant outsiders. In an impersonal market, however, outsiders do not know when they are trading with an insider, so insider trading imposes a transaction cost on all trading. The level of insider trading, moreover, is not fixed. Where insider trading is not prohibited, the amount of insider trading as a fraction of total trading volume is likely greater than in markets where it is prohibited.

Even if an outsider is lucky enough to avoid trading with a better-informed outsider, they cannot avoid the greater transaction costs created by insider trading. The transaction cost of insider trading is incorporated in the price of *all* trading. Market makers, like outsiders, know that they are at a disadvantage when trading with insiders, and like outsiders, they cannot know when they are trading with an insider. In order to compensate for the losses suffered by trading with an insider, market makers will increase the bid-ask spread. For example, instead of buying at $10.05 and selling at $10.10, market makers buy at $10.00 and sell at $10.15. Alterna-tively, they may reduce the number of shares ("depth") that they are willing to buy or sell at a quoted price. This increase in the bid-ask spread and decline in depth increases transaction costs for investors, who are therefore less likely to buy and sell. The risk of dealing with insider traders is magnified in the options market, a favorite haven for insider traders because of the leverage it provides to the value of their information. Insider trading makes options more expensive to buy and sell, thereby further impairing liquidity.

How does insider trading affect corporate issuers? Investors are reluc-tant to play in what they perceive to be a rigged game. At a minimum, they must be compensated for bearing the risk that the game is fixed. Because insider trading reduces the returns from investing in the stock market, investors will discount the amount that they are willing to pay for shares to reflect the risk of insider trading. Corporations pay the price for this discounting because they receive less when they sell shares to the public. Insider trading prohibitions—if effective—reduce the discount demanded by investors and the cost of capital for issuers.

Should we care about the loss in liquidity, greater bid-ask spread, and greater stock price discounts that stem from insider trading? The public confidence argument flies in the face of very high levels of investor participation in the U.S. markets even before insider trading became the subject of vigorous enforcement, starting in the 1960s. Moreover, even if insiders are prohibited from trading, the informational playing field is far from level. Not all outside investors are the same. Sophisticated, institu-tional investors enjoy an information advantage over most individual investors. Any informational advantage, such as one produced by astute research or the fortuitous discovery of a confidential document carelessly left on the subway, can produce a trading advantage for the holder of the information and the resulting impairment of liquidity outlined above. The securities markets are treacherous waters for uninformed investors even without the presence of insider traders.

As you read the materials in this chapter, consider the relative costs of insider trading and informed outsider trading. Are both forms of informational advantages in the secondary markets problematic? Advantages that society should prohibit? With civil sanctions? With criminal sanctions? Also consider how well the insider trading doctrine, as developed by the courts and the SEC, matches the problem of information asymmetry in the securities markets. As you will discover in reading the cases, the path of the law is seldom driven by economic analysis, and insider trading doctrine is no exception.

II. INSIDER TRADING AT COMMON LAW

Prior to the passage of the securities laws, the primary legal remedy for insider trading was common law fraud. As you read the pre-Exchange Act case below, think about the limits of the common law rule identified by the Supreme Court. What sort of informational asymmetries are not covered by the rule? Is the law of deceit the right place to look for a prohibition against insider trading? What are the alternatives?

Strong v. Repide

213 U.S. 419 (1909).

■ PECKHAM, J.

This action . . . was brought by the plaintiff Mrs. Strong, as the owner of 800 shares of the capital stock of the Philippine Sugar Estates Development Company, Limited . . . , to recover such shares from defendant (who was already the owner of 30,400 of the 42,030 shares issued by the company) on the ground that . . . defendant fraudulently concealed from plaintiff's agent, one F. Stuart Jones, facts affecting the value of the stock. . . .

In addition to his ownership of almost three fourths of the shares of the stock of the company, the defendant was one of the five directors of the company, and was elected by the board the agent and administrator general of such company, "with exclusive intervention in the management" of its general business.

* * *

[The Philippine Sugar Estates Development Company owned property in the Philippines known as the Dominican lands, and they comprised nearly one half the value of all the "friar" lands. The governor of the Philippine Islands, on behalf of the Philippine government made an offer to buy all of the friar lands for approximately $6 million in gold. After some negotiation with the various owners of the friar lands, the offer was increased to approximately $7.5 million.]

All the owners of all these friar lands, with the exception of the *D didn't want* defendant, who represented his company, were willing and anxious to accept this offer and to convey the lands to the government at that price. He alone held out for a better offer while all the other owners were endeavoring to persuade him to accept the offer of the government. . . . [T]he contract for the sale was finally signed by the defendant as attorney in fact for his company, December 21, 1903. The defendant, of course, as the negotiations progressed, knew that the decision of the question lay with him, and that if he should decide to accept the last offer of the government, *3/4 li → Ds decision* his decision would be the decision of his company, as he owned three fourths of its shares, and the negotiations would then go through as all the owners of the balance of the land desired it. If the sale should not be consummated, and things should remain as they were, the defendant also *all or nothing deal* knew that the value of the lands and of the shares in the company would be almost nothing. . . .

While this state of things existed, and before the final offer had been made by the governor, the defendant, although still holding out for a higher price for the lands, took steps, about the middle or latter part of September, 1903, to purchase the 800 shares of stock in his company owned by Mrs. Strong, which he knew were in the possession of F. Stuart Jones, as her agent. The defendant, having decided to obtain these shares, instead of seeing Jones, who had an office next door, employed one Kauffman . . . and Kauffman employed a Mr. Sloan, a broker, who had an office some distance away, to purchase the stock for him, and told Sloan that the stock was for a member of his wife's family. Sloan communicated with the husband of Mrs. Strong, and asked if she desired to sell her stock. The husband referred him to Mr. Jones for consultation, who had the stock in his possession. Sloan did not know who wanted to buy the shares, nor did Jones when he was spoken to. Jones would not have sold at the price he did had he known it was the defendant who was purchasing, because, as he said, it would show increased value, as the defendant would not be likely to purchase more stock unless the price was going up. As the articles of incorporation, by subdivision 20, required a resolution of the general meeting of stockholders for the purpose of selling more than one hacienda, and as no such general meeting had been called at the time of the sale of the stock, Mr. Jones might well have supposed there was no immediate prospect of a sale of the lands being made, while, at the same time, defendant had knowledge of the probabilities thereof, which he had acquired by his conduct of the negotiations for their sale, as agent of all the shareholders, and while acting specially for them and himself.

The result of the negotiations was that Jones, on or about October 10, 1903, . . . sold the 800 shares of stock for $16,000, Mexican currency, . . . *1/10 worth.* about one tenth of the amount they became worth by the sale of the lands between two and three months thereafter. In all the negotiations in regard to the purchase of the stock from Mrs. Strong, through her agent Jones, not one word of the facts affecting the value of this stock was made known to plaintiff's agent by defendant, but, on the contrary, perfect silence was kept.

* * *

If the purchase of the stock by the defendant was obtained by reason of his fraud or deceit, . . . the sale cannot stand.

* * *

The question in this case . . . is whether, under the circumstances above set forth, it was the duty of the defendant, acting in good faith, to disclose to the agent of the plaintiff the facts bearing upon or which might affect the value of the stock.

If it were conceded, for the purpose of the argument, that the ordinary relations between directors and shareholders in a business corporation are not of such a fiduciary nature as to make it the duty of a director to disclose to a shareholder the general knowledge which he may possess regarding the value of the shares of the company before he purchases any from a shareholder, yet there are cases where, by reason of the special facts, such duty exists. . . . The case before us is of the same general character. On the other hand, there [are cases holding] that no relationship of a fiduciary nature exists between a director and a shareholder in a business corporation. . . . These cases involved only the bare relationship between director and shareholder. It is here sought to make defendant responsible for his actions, not alone and simply in his character as a director, but because, in consideration of all the existing circumstances above detailed, it became the duty of the defendant, acting in good faith, to state the facts before making the purchase. That the defendant was a director of the corporation is but one of the facts upon which the liability is asserted, the existence of all the others in addition making such a combination as rendered it the plain duty of the defendant to speak. He was not only a director, but he owned three fourths of the shares of its stock, and was, at the time of the purchase of the stock, administrator general of the company, with large powers, and engaged in the negotiations which finally led to the sale of the company's lands (together with all the other friar lands) to the government at a price which very greatly enhanced the value of the stock. . . . No one knew as well as he the probability of the sale of the lands to the government. No one knew as well as he the probable price that might be obtained on such sale. The lands were the only valuable asset owned by the company. Under these circumstances, and before the negotiations for the sale were completed, the defendant employs an agent to purchase the stock, and conceals from the plaintiff's agent his own identity and his knowledge of the state of the negotiations and their probable result, with which he was familiar as the agent of the shareholders, and much of which knowledge he obtained while acting as such agent, and by reason thereof. . . . Concealing his identity when procuring the purchase of the stock, by his agent, was in itself strong evidence of fraud on the part of the defendant. Why did he not ask Jones, who occupied an adjoining office, if he would sell? But, by concealing his identity, he could, by such means, the

[margin note: There are cases where by reason of special facts relations between D and SH require disclosure by D to SH general knowledge that can affect price before D purchases shares from SH.]

more easily avoid any questions relative to the negotiations for the sale of the lands and their probable result, and could also avoid any actual misrepresentations on that subject, which he evidently thought were necessary in his case to constitute a fraud. . . . The whole transaction gives conclusive evidence of the overwhelming influence defendant had in the course of the negotiations as owner of a majority of the stock and as agent for the other owners, and it is clear that the final consummation was in his hands at all times. If, under all these facts, he purchased the stock from the plaintiff, the law would indeed be impotent if the sale could not be set aside or the defendant cast in damages for his fraud. . . .

[U]nder the circumstances detailed, there was a legal obligation on the part of the defendant to make these disclosures.

* * *

NOTES

In *Strong v. Repide*, the Supreme Court follows those courts adopting the "special facts" doctrine. The "special facts" found by the Court in *Strong* amount to active concealment of the defendant's identity, thereby depriving the plaintiff-shareholder of a basis for inquiring about the transaction and the company's prospects. The Court notes, however, that the courts were not unanimous in finding a duty under such circumstances.

There was a consensus at common law, however, that a corporate insider who traded in an impersonal market on the basis of confidential information did not defraud the shareholder with whom he had traded. In the leading case of *Goodwin v. Agassiz*, 283 Mass. 358, 186 N.E. 659 (1933), the Supreme Judicial Court of Massachusetts rejected a claim that an insider commits fraud when trading over a stock exchange on the basis of confidential information. In *Goodwin*, the plaintiff-shareholder sold his shares in a mining company to two of the company's insiders, its president and general manager (who were also directors). The insiders were aware of a geologist's theory that the land owned by the company might contain valuable copper deposits. They kept this information secret, however, in order to obtain options on surrounding land that might also contain copper. Knowing that the company's stock price would rise if the theory panned out, the insiders bought heavily in the company's shares. These purchases, done over the Boston Stock Exchange, were completely anonymous—the shareholders had no idea to whom they had sold.

The court rejected the plaintiff's claim of fraud. Although the court recognized that the directors of a corporation "stand in a relation of trust to the corporation and are bound to exercise the strictest good faith in respect to its property and business," it held that directors do not "occupy the position of trustee toward individual stockholders." Thus, there was "no fiduciary relation between them and the plaintiff in the matter of the sale of his stock." The court acknowledged that the result may have been different in a face-to-face transaction, but concluded that any such duty to shareholders did not carry over to an anonymous exchange transaction.

QUESTIONS

1. Reliance is an element of common law deceit, as well as private actions under Rule 10b–5. Do you think that there was reliance by Mrs. Strong or her agent, Jones? What if the transaction had taken place over the Manila Stock Exchange?

2. How would knowledge of the identity of the purchaser (Repide) have benefited Mrs. Strong in making her decision to sell or hold?

3. How would the result change in *Strong v. Repide* if Repide, as a director and managing agent, were aware that the company was unlikely to be able to sell the friar lands, but withheld the information from Mrs. Strong (an existing shareholder) when selling her additional shares (while actively concealing his identity)? What if an unrelated third party purchased shares from Repide?

HYPOTHETICAL ONE

Consider how the law of insider trading under state common law (as represented by *Strong v. Repide* and *Goodwin v. Agassiz*) would apply to the InClone hypothetical. Recall that Jack, the CEO of InClone, instructed Merritt, his broker, to sell 50% of his InClone holdings (assume the sales were in the open secondary market). He also has his broker purchase BioGen options with the proceeds. Martha receives a tip from the same broker about Jack's trades and she also sells InClone shares.

1. Has Jack violated the "special facts" doctrine by purchasing BioGen options or by selling his InClone shares?

2. Has Martha violated the "special facts" doctrine with her sale of InClone shares?

3. Suppose that Jeffrey is an outside director on BioGen's board. Jeffrey had no other business relationship with BioGen. Jeffrey also knows of InClone's impending acquisition offer for BioGen and buys a large number of BioGen shares over the New York Stock Exchange prior to the announcement of the offer. Has Jeffrey violated the "special facts" doctrine?

III. RULE 10b–5 AND THE CLASSICAL THEORY OF INSIDER TRADING

Fast forward to the 1930s: Congress adopted the Exchange Act in 1934, largely ignoring the topic of insider trading (with the limited exception of § 16, discussed below). The SEC, after also ignoring insider trading for the first twenty-five years of its history after the enactment of the Exchange Act, eventually stepped into the void, arguing that insider trading violates the antifraud prohibition of Rule 10b–5.

As you go through the cases, consider the SEC's interest in prohibiting insider trading. Is it the source of information (i.e., coming from inside or outside the traded firms) that seems important? Or is it the identity of the person engaged in the trades (an insider versus an outsider)? Or are both the source and the identity of the trader irrelevant—should maintaining a "parity" of information across all traders in the market be the central goal? The following table captures the possibilities, based on the type of trader and the source of information:

	Insider Trader	Outsider Trader
Corporate (inside) Information	Core insider	?
Outside Information	?	?

"Insider trading" typically evokes situations involving corporate insiders trading on inside corporate information. When Jack attempts to sell shares in his company, InClone, based on inside information of InClone's upcoming acquisition of BioGen, Jack is trading as a "core insider." But what about other forms of informational advantages in the market, including trades based on so-called outside information (information not obtained from the company whose securities are being traded—the "traded firm")? When Jack trades Biogen options, he is capitalizing on outside information from the perspective of Biogen share and option holders. And what if a non-insider, say a tippee of an insider, trades based on inside corporate information? Should outsiders be liable as well? Should the tipping insider share that liability?

A.   CORE INSIDERS

The SEC first pursued its insider trading theory in administrative proceedings against securities professionals, beginning with *Cady, Roberts & Co.*, 40 S.E.C. 907 (1961), before pressing the theory in the courts against corporate executives, most notably in *SEC v. Texas Gulf Sulphur Co.*, 401 F.2d 833 (2d Cir. 1968) (en banc), cert. denied, 394 U.S. 976 (1969). The SEC and the Justice Department had little trouble persuading the activist Second Circuit to find an insider trading prohibition in § 10(b). *Texas Gulf Sulphur* sets forth the "equal access" theory of insider trading:

Equal Access theory of Insider trading

> The essence of the Rule is that anyone who, trading for his own account in the securities of a corporation has "access, directly or indirectly, to information intended to be available only for a corporate purpose and not for the personal benefit of anyone" may not take "advantage of such information knowing it is unavailable to those with whom he is dealing," i.e., the investing public. . . . Insiders, as directors or management officers are, of course, by this Rule, precluded from so unfairly dealing, but the Rule is also applicable to one possessing the information who may not be strictly termed an "insider." . . .

Rule.

> The core of Rule 10b–5 is the implementation of the Congressional purpose that all investors should have equal access to the rewards of participation in securities transactions. It was the intent of Congress that all members of the investing public should be subject to identical market risks, which market risks include, of course the risk that one's evaluative capacity or one's capital available to put at risk may exceed another's capacity or capital. The insiders here were not trading on an equal footing with the outside investors.

On its face, *Texas Gulf Sulphur* prohibits not only core insiders, but also outsiders, from trading based on non-public, material corporate information.

[handwritten: Texas Gulf.]

[handwritten: Corp. Inside: - core insider } prohibited - outsider]

	Insider Trader	Outsider Trader
Corporate (inside) Information	Core insider prohibited (*Texas Gulf Sulphur*)	Outsider prohibited (*Texas Gulf Sulphur*)
Outside Information	?	?

After their successes in the Second Circuit, the SEC turned its eye toward trades based on outside information. After all, unequal access and the trading advantages it confers can come from either inside or outside the firm. Non-public information that a state regulator is about to adopt a particular video poker machine for deployment throughout the state, for example, confers a large trading advantage for purchasers of the video poker machine company's stock even though this information comes from "outside" the company. By the time of the case below, the SEC was arguing for a general theory of equality of access to information, whether or not there was a duty owed to the person on the other side of the transaction or to the source of the information.

The SEC's efforts met with more skepticism in the Supreme Court than in the Second Circuit. Where does Justice Powell find the insider trading prohibition that he incorporates into Rule 10b–5 in *Chiarella*? How does Powell's theory differ from the SEC's? And how does *Chiarella* affect *Texas Gulf Sulphur*'s prohibition against outsiders trading on corporate inside information?

[handwritten: Duty to Disclose + Silence = fraud 10b]

Chiarella v. United States *[handwritten: —NO]*

445 U.S. 222 (1980).

■ POWELL, J.

[handwritten: Facts: Printer → got confid. information from announcements. traded secs, earned. Issue: whether he had duty to disclose that he is trading with info? No. No duty to disclose, if there is no duty to speak.]

[handwritten: Issue] The question in this case is whether a person who learns from the confidential documents of one corporation that it is planning an attempt to secure control of a second corporation violates § 10(b) of the Securities Exchange Act of 1934 if he fails to disclose the impending takeover before trading in the target company's securities.

[handwritten: No duty to speak, unless special relationship. Printer → complete stranger.]

Petitioner is a printer by trade. In 1975 and 1976, he worked as a "markup man" in the New York composing room of Pandick Press, a financial printer. Among documents that petitioner handled were five announcements of corporate takeover bids. When these documents were delivered to the printer, the identities of the acquiring and target corporations were concealed by blank spaces or false names. The true names were sent to the printer on the night of the final printing.

[handwritten: identities were concealed]

The petitioner, however, was able to deduce the names of the target companies before the final printing from other information contained in the documents. Without disclosing his knowledge, petitioner purchased stock in the target companies and sold the shares immediately after the takeover attempts were made public. By this method, petitioner realized a gain of slightly more than $30,000.... Subsequently, the Securities and Exchange Commission began an investigation of his trading activities. In May 1977, petitioner entered into a consent decree with the Commission in which he agreed to return his profits to the sellers of the shares. On the same day, he was discharged by Pandick Press.

In January 1978, petitioner was indicted on 17 counts of violating § 10(b) ... and SEC Rule 10b–5.... [H]e was brought to trial and convicted on all counts.

The Court of Appeals for the Second Circuit affirmed petitioner's conviction. We granted certiorari and we now reverse.

II

* * *

This case concerns the legal effect of the petitioner's silence. The District Court's charge permitted the jury to convict the petitioner if it found that he willfully failed to inform sellers of target company securities that he knew of a forthcoming takeover bid that would make their shares more valuable....

Although the starting point of our inquiry is the language of the statute, § 10(b) does not state whether silence may constitute a manipulative or deceptive device. Section 10(b) was designed as a catch-all clause to prevent fraudulent practices. But neither the legislative history nor the statute itself affords specific guidance for the resolution of this case. When Rule 10b–5 was promulgated in 1942, the SEC did not discuss the possibility that failure to provide information might run afoul of § 10(b).

The SEC took an important step in the development of § 10(b) when it held that a broker-dealer and his firm violated that section by selling securities on the basis of undisclosed information obtained from a director of the issuer corporation who was also a registered representative of the brokerage firm. In *Cady, Roberts & Co.*, 40 S.E.C. 907 (1961), the Commission decided that a corporate insider must abstain from trading in the shares of his corporation unless he has first disclosed all material inside information known to him. The obligation to disclose or abstain derives from—

> [a]n affirmative duty to disclose material information[, which] has been traditionally imposed on corporate 'insiders', particular officers, directors, or controlling stockholders. We, and the courts have consistently held that insiders must disclose material facts which are known to them by virtue of their position but which are not known to persons with whom they deal and which, if known, would affect their investment judgment.

The Commission emphasized that the duty arose from (i) the existence of a relationship affording access to inside information intended to be available only for a corporate purpose, and (ii) the unfairness of allowing a corporate insider to take advantage of that information by trading without disclosure.[8]

That the relationship between a corporate insider and the stockholders of his corporation gives rise to a disclosure obligation is not a novel twist of the law. At common law, misrepresentation made for the purpose of inducing reliance upon the false statement is fraudulent. But one who fails to disclose material information prior to the consummation of a transaction commits fraud only when he is under a duty to do so. And the duty to disclose arises when one party has information "that the other [party] is entitled to know because of a fiduciary or other similar relation of trust and confidence between them."[9]

* * *

Thus, administrative and judicial interpretations have established that silence in connection with the purchase or sale of securities may operate as a fraud actionable under § 10(b) despite the absence of statutory language or legislative history specifically addressing the legality of nondisclosure. But such liability is premised upon a duty to disclose arising from a relationship of trust and confidence between parties to a transaction. Application of a duty to disclose prior to trading guarantees that corporate insiders, who have an obligation to place the shareholder's welfare before their own, will not benefit personally through fraudulent use of material, nonpublic information.

III

In this case, the petitioner was convicted of violating § 10(b) although he was not a corporate insider and he received no confidential information from the target company. Moreover, the "market information" upon which he relied did not concern the earning power or operations of the target company, but only the plans of the acquiring company. Petitioner's use of that information was not a fraud under § 10(b) unless he was subject to an affirmative duty to disclose it before trading. In this case, the jury instructions failed to specify any such duty. In effect, the trial court instructed the jury that petitioner owed a duty to everyone; to all sellers, indeed, to the

---

8. In *Cady, Roberts*, the broker-dealer was liable under § 10(b) because it received nonpublic information from a corporate insider of the issuer. Since the insider could not use the information, neither could the partners in the brokerage firm with which he was associated. The transaction in *Cady, Roberts* involved sale of stock to persons who previously may not have been shareholders in the corporation. The Commission embraced the reasoning of Judge Learned Hand that "the director or officer assumed a fiduciary relation to the buyer by the very sale; for it would be a sorry distinction to allow him to use the advantage of his position to induce the buyer into the position of a beneficiary although he was forbidden to do so once the buyer had become one." *Id.*, at 914, n. 23, quoting *Gratz v. Claughton*, 187 F.2d 46, 49 (CA2), cert. denied, 341 U.S. 920 (1951).

9. Restatement (Second) of Torts § 551(2)(a) (1976).

market as a whole. The jury simply was told to decide whether petitioner used material, nonpublic information at a time when "he knew other people trading in the securities market did not have access to the same information."

* * *

This reasoning suffers from two defects. First not every instance of financial unfairness constitutes fraudulent activity under § 10(b). Second, the element required to make silence fraudulent—a duty to disclose—is absent in this case. No duty could arise from petitioner's relationship with the sellers of the target company's securities, for petitioner had no prior dealings with them. He was not their agent, he was not a fiduciary, he was not a person in whom the sellers had placed their trust and confidence. He was, in fact, a complete stranger who dealt with the sellers only through impersonal market transactions.

[handwritten margin note: No duty to disclose ↳ complete stranger]

We cannot affirm petitioner's conviction without recognizing a general duty between all participants in market transactions to forgo actions based on material, nonpublic information. Formulation of such a broad duty, which departs radically from the established doctrine that duty arises from a specific relationship between two parties, should not be undertaken absent some explicit evidence of congressional intent. . . .

[handwritten margin note: Duty arises from special relationship between the parties. • agent • fiduciary • prior dealings]

[N]o such evidence emerges from the language or legislative history of § 10(b). Moreover, neither the Congress nor the Commission ever has adopted a parity-of-information rule. Instead the problems caused by misuse of market information have been addressed by detailed and sophisticated regulation that recognizes when use of market information may not harm operation of the securities markets. For example, the Williams Act limits but does not completely prohibit a tender offeror's purchases of target corporation stock before public announcement of the offer. Congress' careful action in this and other areas contrasts, and is in some tension, with the broad rule of liability we are asked to adopt in this case.

* * *

We see no basis for applying such a new and different theory of liability in this case. . . . Section 10(b) is aptly described as a catchall provision, but what it catches must be fraud. When an allegation of fraud is based upon nondisclosure, there can be no fraud absent a duty to speak. We hold that a duty to disclose under § 10(b) does not arise from the mere possession of nonpublic market information. The contrary result is without support in the legislative history of § 10(b) and would be inconsistent with the careful plan that Congress has enacted for regulation of the securities markets.

[handwritten margin note: Sec. 10(b) - catch all fraud. Duty to speak → → nondisclosure → → Fraud]

IV

* * *

[T]he United States offers an alternative theory to support petitioner's conviction. It argues that petitioner breached a duty to the acquiring corporation when he acted upon information that he obtained by virtue of his position as an employee of a printer employed by the corporation. The breach of this duty is said to support a conviction under § 10(b) for fraud perpetrated upon both the acquiring corporation and the sellers.

We need not decide whether this theory has merit for it was not submitted to the jury.... the jury was instructed that the petitioner employed a scheme to defraud if he "did not disclose ... material non-public information in connection with the purchases of the stock."

* * *

The judgment of the Court of Appeals is *Reversed.*

STEVENS, J., concurring.

* * *

I agree with the Court's determination that petitioner owed no duty of disclosure to the sellers, that his conviction rested on the erroneous premise that he did owe them such a duty, and that the judgment of the Court of Appeals must therefore be reversed.

The Court correctly does not address ... whether the petitioner's breach of his duty of silence—a duty he unquestionably owed to his employer and to his employer's customers—could give rise to criminal liability under Rule 10b–5. Respectable arguments could be made in support of either position. On the one hand, if we assume that petitioner breached a duty to the acquiring companies that had entrusted confidential information to his employers, a legitimate argument could be made that his actions constituted "a fraud or a deceit" upon those companies "in connection with the purchase or sale of any security." On the other hand, inasmuch as those companies would not be able to recover damages from petitioner for violating Rule 10b–5 because they were neither purchasers nor sellers of target company securities, it could also be argued that no actionable violation of Rule 10b–5 had occurred. I think the Court wisely leaves the resolution of this issue for another day.

* * *

NOTES

Classical theory

1. *The "classical" and "misappropriation" theories.* The theory outlined by Justice Powell in *Chiarella*, under which an insider violates Rule 10b–5 by trading in the shares of his own company without disclosing confidential information, has come to be known as the "classical" theory of insider trading.

Alternative theory

The alternative theory advanced by the government, that Chiarella had defrauded Pandick Press and its clients by using their confidential information to trade in securities, has come to be known as the "misappropriation" theory. We will return to the misappropriation theory in the *Carpenter* and *O'Hagan* cases below.

2. *Rule 14e–3.* Shortly after the *Chiarella* decision, the SEC promulgated Rule 14e–3 of the Exchange Act to address the problem of non-public, material informational advantages in the context of tender offers. When any person initiates a tender offer for an Exchange Act reporting company's stock, Rule

14e–3 restricts the use of non-public, material information relating to that offer. Once a tender offer is initiated, Rule 14e–3 prohibits any person (other than the potential acquirer) from trading in the target company's stock based on non-public, material information obtained from the target company, the acquirer, or an officer or director of either, among others. Unlike theories under Rule 10b–5, the prohibition of Rule 14e–3 is not tied to the presence of deception or the breach of a fiduciary duty.

3. *Rule 10b–18.* Although the SEC is concerned with manipulation and its adverse effects on the capital markets, there are certain necessary corporate actions that the SEC has accommodated, such as share buyback programs. The main concern with a share buyback is that the corporation may be creating an exaggerated appearance of market interest in its stock, thus "manipulating" the market. To address this concern, the SEC promulgated Rule 10b–18, which provides a safe harbor for corporations and their affiliates and/or agents from liability for manipulation under § 9(a)(2) and § 10(b). The safe harbor applies when an issuer bids for or purchases shares of its common stock and complies with the safe harbor's requirements.

There are four elements to Rule 10b–18:

- An issuer and its affiliated purchasers must use only one broker or dealer to solicit purchasers or to make bids on a single day. An issuer, however, may use more than one broker or dealer if the transaction has *not* been solicited by or for the issuer.

- An issuer bid or purchase should not constitute the day's opening transaction. In addition, no issuer purchases should be made within one-half hour of the close of trading on the national exchange.

- The bid or price paid by an issuer or its affiliate cannot exceed the current independently published bid or the last reported independent sale price.

- Excluding any block purchases, an issuer's purchases should not exceed the higher of one round lot or the number of round lots closest to 25% of the trading volume for that security.

Like with other safe harbors, the Rule 10b–18 safe harbor is not the exclusive means by which an issuer can purchase its common stock. The safe harbor does, however, enable an issuer to purchase its shares while ensuring that it is not violating the manipulation prohibitions. It does not, however, protect the issuer from Rule 10b–5 claims if it has repurchased shares while in possession of material, non-public information.

QUESTIONS

1. How does the theory outlined by Justice Powell differ from the common law "special facts" doctrine of *Strong v. Repide*?

2. How does Powell's theory differ from that of the Second Circuit in *Texas Gulf Sulphur*?

3. Could Pandick Press or its clients state a Rule 10b–5 cause of action against Chiarella?

4. What happened to Chiarella's relationship with Pandick Press? Does this tell us anything about the need to use Rule 10b–5 to protect Pandick Press?

HYPOTHETICAL TWO

Recall that Jack, the CEO of InClone, ordered his broker Merritt to sell half of Jack's two million InClone shares shortly before InClone announced its pending acquisition of BioGen. Jack also ordered Merritt to purchase call options in BioGen making a huge profit after the announcement of the acquisition.

1. Has Jack violated the classical theory by purchasing BioGen options? By selling his InClone shares?

2. Would Jack have violated the classical theory if he had purchased InClone put options? (Put options allow their holder to sell stock at a specified price.) See § 20(d). What if he had sold highly-leveraged InClone "junk" bonds?

3. Suppose InClone was selling preferred stock in a private placement while it was contemplating the BioGen tender offer. Assuming nondisclosure of the tender offer, would the company have violated the classical theory? Could InClone have purchased call options of BioGen stock?

4. Suppose that Jack leaves a detailed notebook containing information on the impending acquisition on the roof of his Jaguar. The notebook falls off as Jack is pulling away. Katharina finds the notebook in the street (emblazoned with InClone's official seal). She proceeds to sell InClone shares short and buy call options on BioGen. Has Katharina run afoul of 10b–5?

B. TIPPER/TIPPEE LIABILITY

Justice Powell adverted to the problem of individuals receiving confidential information from insiders in a footnote of *Chiarella*: " 'Tippees' of corporate insiders have been held liable under § 10(b) because they have a duty not to profit from the use of inside information that they know is confidential and know or should know came from a corporate insider. The tippee's obligation has been viewed as arising from his role as a participant after the fact in the insider's breach of a fiduciary duty." How far does tippee liability extend to non-insider traders? After *Chiarella*, the insider trading doctrine can be summarized as follows:

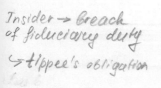

Insider → Breach of fiduciary duty ↳ tippee's obligation

	Insider Trader	Outsider Trader
Corporate (inside) Information	*Chiarella* Classical Insider Trading Theory	Tippee Liability?
Outside Information	?	?

The Supreme Court grappled with the question of when tippees would be liable for their trading in the case below, which features a rather unusual set of facts. Does the standard Justice Powell crafted in *Dirks* unduly constrain the SEC and the Justice Department? What policy interest is Powell protecting by adopting a standard narrower than the one urged by the SEC?

Dirks v. Securities and Exchange Commission

463 U.S. 646 (1983).

■ POWELL, J.

Petitioner Raymond Dirks received material nonpublic information from "insiders" of a corporation with which he had no connection. He disclosed this information to investors who relied on it in trading in the shares of the corporation. The question is whether Dirks violated the antifraud provisions of the federal securities laws by this disclosure.

I

In 1973, Dirks was an officer of a New York broker-dealer firm who specialized in providing investment analysis of insurance company securities to institutional investors. On March 6, Dirks received information from Ronald Secrist, a former officer of Equity Funding of America. Secrist alleged that the assets of Equity Funding, a diversified corporation primarily engaged in selling life insurance and mutual funds, were vastly overstated as the result of fraudulent corporate practices. Secrist also stated that various regulatory agencies had failed to act on similar charges made by Equity Funding employees. He urged Dirks to verify the fraud and disclose it publicly.

Dirks decided to investigate the allegations. He visited Equity Funding's headquarters in Los Angeles and interviewed several officers and employees of the corporation. The senior management denied any wrongdoing, but certain corporation employees corroborated the charges of fraud. Neither Dirks nor his firm owned or traded any Equity Funding stock, but throughout his investigation he openly discussed the information he had obtained with a number of clients and investors. Some of these persons sold their holdings of Equity Funding securities, including five investment advisers who liquidated holdings of more than $16 million.

* * *

During the two-week period in which Dirks pursued his investigation and spread word of Secrist's charges, the price of Equity Funding stock fell from $26 per share to less than $15 per share. This led the New York Stock Exchange to halt trading on March 27. Shortly thereafter California insurance authorities impounded Equity Funding's records and uncovered evidence of the fraud. Only then did the Securities and Exchange Commission (SEC) file a complaint against Equity Funding[3] and only then, on April 2, did the *Wall Street Journal* publish a front-page story based largely on information assembled by Dirks. Equity Funding immediately went into receivership.

The SEC began an investigation into Dirks' role in the exposure of the fraud. After a hearing by an administrative law judge, the SEC found that Dirks had aided and abetted violations of § 17(a) of the Securities Act of 1933, § 10(b) of the Securities Exchange Act of 1934, and SEC Rule 10b–5,

---

3. As early as 1971, the SEC had received allegations of fraudulent accounting practices at Equity Funding. Moreover, on March 9, 1973, an official of the California Insurance Department informed the SEC's regional office in Los Angeles of Secrist's charges of fraud. Dirks himself voluntarily presented his information at the SEC's regional office beginning on March 27.

by repeating the allegations of fraud to members of the investment community who later sold their Equity Funding stock. The SEC concluded: "Where 'tippees'—regardless of their motivation or occupation—come into possession of material 'information that they know is confidential and know or should know came from a corporate insider,' they must either publicly disclose that information or refrain from trading." Recognizing, however, that Dirks "played an important role in bringing [Equity Funding's] massive fraud to light," the SEC only censured him. [The D.C. Circuit upheld the censure imposed by the SEC.]

In view of the importance to the SEC and to the securities industry of the question presented by this case, we granted a writ of certiorari. We now reverse.

II

* * *

In examining whether Chiarella had an obligation to disclose or abstain, the Court found that there is no general duty to disclose before trading on material nonpublic information, and held that "a duty to disclose under § 10(b) does not arise from the mere possession of nonpublic market information." Such a duty arises rather from the existence of a fiduciary relationship.

* * *

III

We were explicit in *Chiarella* in saying that there can be no duty to disclose where the person who has traded on inside information "was not [the corporation's] agent, . . . was not a fiduciary, [or] was not a person in whom the sellers [of the securities] had placed their trust and confidence." Not to require such a fiduciary relationship, we recognized, would "depar[t] radically from the established doctrine that duty arises from a specific relationship between two parties" and would amount to "recognizing a general duty between all participants in market transactions to forgo actions based on material, nonpublic information." This requirement of a specific relationship between the shareholders and the individual trading on inside information has created analytical difficulties for the SEC and courts in policing tippees who trade on inside information. Unlike insiders who have independent fiduciary duties to both the corporation and its shareholders, the typical tippee has no such relationships.[14] In view of this

---

14. Under certain circumstances, such as where corporate information is revealed legitimately to an underwriter, accountant, lawyer, or consultant working for the corporation, these outsiders may become fiduciaries of the shareholders. The basis for recognizing this fiduciary duty is not simply that such persons acquired nonpublic corporate information, but rather that they have entered into a special confidential relationship in the conduct of the business of the enterprise and are given access to information solely for corporate purposes. When such a person breaches his fiduciary relationship, he may be treated more properly as a tipper than a tippee. For such a duty to be imposed,

absence, it has been unclear how a tippee acquires the *Cady, Roberts* duty to refrain from trading on inside information.

A

The SEC's position, as stated in its opinion in this case, is that a tippee "inherits" the *Cady, Roberts* obligation to shareholders whenever he receives inside information from an insider:

> In tipping potential traders, Dirks breached a duty which he had assumed as a result of knowingly receiving confidential information from [Equity Funding] insiders. Tippees such as Dirks who receive non-public material information from insiders become subject to the same duty as [the] insiders. Such a tippee breaches the fiduciary duty which he assumes from the insider when the tippee knowingly transmits the information to someone who will probably trade on the basis thereof ... Presumably, Dirks' informants were entitled to disclose the [Equity Funding] fraud in order to bring it to light and its perpetrators to justice. However, Dirks–standing in their shoes–committed a breach of the fiduciary duty which he had assumed in dealing with them, when he passed the information on to traders.

This view differs little from the view that we rejected as inconsistent with congressional intent in *Chiarella*.... Here, the SEC maintains that anyone who knowingly receives nonpublic material information from an insider has a fiduciary duty to disclose before trading.[15]

In effect, the SEC's theory of tippee liability ... appears rooted in the idea that the antifraud provisions require equal information among all traders. This conflicts with the principle set forth in *Chiarella* that only some persons, under some circumstances, will be barred from trading while in possession of material nonpublic information ... We reaffirm today that "[a] duty [to disclose] arises from the relationship between parties ... and not merely from one's ability to acquire information because of his position in the market."

Imposing a duty to disclose or abstain solely because a person knowingly receives material nonpublic information from an insider and trades on it could have an inhibiting influence on the role of market analysts, which the SEC itself recognizes is necessary to the preservation of a healthy market.[17]

[handwritten margin note: Rule / Duty to disclose arises from relationship between the parties and no merely from ability to acquire information]

however, the corporation must expect the outsider to keep the disclosed nonpublic information confidential, and the relationship at least m t imply such a duty.

15.   Apparently, the SEC believes this case differs from *Chiarella* in that Dirks' receipt of inside information from Secrist, an insider, carried Secrist's duties with it, while Chiarella received the information without the direct involvement of an insider and thus inherited no duty to disclose or abstain. The SEC fails to explain, however, why the receipt of nonpublic information from an insid-

er automatically carries with it the fiduciary duty of the insider. As we emphasized in *Chiarella*, mere possession of nonpublic information does not give rise to a duty to disclose or abstain; only a specific relationship does that. And we do not believe that the mere receipt of information from an insider creates such a special relationship between the tippee and the corporation's shareholders....

17.   The SEC expressly recognized that "[t]he value to the entire market of [analysts'] efforts cannot be gainsaid; market effi-

It is commonplace for analysts to "ferret out and analyze information,"[18] and this often is done by meeting with and questioning corporate officers and others who are insiders. And information that the analysts obtain normally may be the basis for judgments as to the market worth of a corporation's securities. The analyst's judgment in this respect is made available in market letters or otherwise to clients of the firm. It is the nature of this type of information, and indeed of the markets themselves, that such information cannot be made simultaneously available to all of the corporation's stockholders or the public generally.

B

The conclusion that recipients of inside information do not invariably acquire a duty to disclose or abstain does not mean that such tippees always are free to trade on the information. The need for a ban on some tippee trading is clear. Not only are insiders forbidden by their fiduciary relationship from personally using undisclosed corporate information to their advantage, but they may not give such information to an outsider for the same improper purpose of exploiting the information for their personal gain. Similarly, the transactions of those who knowingly participate with the fiduciary in such a breach are "as forbidden" as transactions "on behalf of the trustee himself." *Mosser v. Darrow,* 341 U.S. 267, 272 (1951). As the Court explained in *Mosser,* a contrary rule "would open up opportunities for devious dealings in the name of the others that the trustee could not conduct in his own." Thus, the tippee's duty to disclose or abstain is derivative from that of the insider's duty. As we noted in *Chiarella,* "[t]he tippee's obligation has been viewed as arising from his role as a participant after the fact in the insider's breach of a fiduciary duty."

Thus, some tippees must assume an insider's duty to the shareholders not because they receive inside information, but rather because it has been

---

ciency in pricing is significantly enhanced by [their] initiatives to ferret out and analyze information, and thus the analyst's work redounds to the benefit of all investors." The SEC asserts that analysts remain free to obtain from management corporate information for purposes of "filling in the 'interstices in analysis'...." But this rule is inherently imprecise, and imprecision prevents parties from ordering their actions in accord with legal requirements. Unless the parties have some guidance as to where the line is between permissible and impermissible disclosures and uses, neither corporate insiders nor analysts can be sure when the line is crossed.

18. On its facts, this case is the unusual one. Dirks is an analyst in a broker-dealer firm, and he did interview management in the course of his investigation. He uncovered, however, startling information that required no analysis or exercise of judgment as to its market relevance. Nonetheless, the principle at issue here extends beyond these facts. The SEC's rule—applicable without regard to any breach by an insider—could have serious ramifications on reporting by analysts of investment views.

Despite the unusualness of Dirks' "find," the central role that he played in uncovering the fraud at Equity Funding, and that analysts in general can play in revealing information that corporations may have reason to withhold from the public, is an important one. Dirks' careful investigation brought to light a massive fraud at the corporation. And until the Equity Funding fraud was exposed, the information in the trading market was grossly inaccurate. But for Dirks' efforts, the fraud might well have gone undetected longer.

Insider → fid. Duty to corp → disclosure → breach to tippee
Tippee → knows/should have known → breach

III RULE 10B–5 AND THE CLASSICAL THEORY OF INSIDER TRADING   377

made available to them *improperly*.... Thus, a tippee assumes a fiduciary duty to the shareholders of a corporation not to trade on material nonpublic information only when the insider has breached his fiduciary duty to the shareholders by disclosing the information to the tippee and the tippee knows or should know that there has been a breach.... Tipping thus properly is viewed only as a means of indirectly violating the *Cady, Roberts* disclose-or-abstain rule.

Tippee assumes fiduciary duty to SHs not to trade on material nonpublic info only when insider breached his fiduciary duty to SHs.

C

In determining whether a tippee is under an obligation to disclose or abstain, it thus is necessary to determine whether the insider's "tip" constituted a breach of the insider's fiduciary duty. All disclosures of confidential corporate information are not inconsistent with the duty insiders owe to shareholders. In contrast to the extraordinary facts of this case, the more typical situation in which there will be a question whether disclosure violates the insider's *Cady, Roberts* duty is when insiders disclose information to analysts. In some situations, the insider will act consistently with his fiduciary duty to shareholders, and yet release of the information may affect the market. For example, it may not be clear—either to the corporate insider or to the recipient analyst—whether the information will be viewed as material nonpublic information. Corporate officials may mistakenly think the information already has been disclosed or that it is not material enough to affect the market. Whether disclosure is a breach of duty therefore depends in large part on the purpose of the disclosure. This standard was identified by the SEC itself in *Cady, Roberts:* a purpose of the securities laws was to eliminate "use of inside information for personal advantage." Thus, the test is whether the insider personally will benefit, directly or indirectly, from his disclosure. Absent some personal gain, there has been no breach of duty to stockholders. And absent a breach by the insider, there is no derivative breach.[22] ...

whether disclosure is in breach depends on a purpose.

purpose of sec. laws is to eliminate use on inside info for personal advantage

Tippee:
No breach to SHs if:
• absence of personal gain
• absence of breach by insider (no derivative breach)

The SEC argues that, if inside-trading liability does not exist when the information is transmitted for a proper purpose but is used for trading, it would be a rare situation when the parties could not fabricate some ostensibly legitimate business justification for transmitting the information. We think the SEC is unduly concerned. [Determining whether there has been a breach of duty] requires courts to focus on objective criteria, *i.e.,* whether the insider receives a direct or indirect personal benefit from the

---

22. An example of a case turning on the court's determination that the disclosure did not impose any fiduciary duties on the recipient of the inside information is *Walton v. Morgan Stanley & Co.,* 623 F.2d 796 (CA2 1980). There, the defendant investment banking firm, representing one of its own corporate clients, investigated another corporation that was a possible target of a takeover bid by its client. In the course of negotiations the investment banking firm was given, on a confidential basis, unpublished material information. Subsequently, after the proposed takeover was abandoned, the firm was charged with relying on the information when it traded in the target corporation's stock. For purposes of the decision, it was assumed that the firm knew the information was confidential, but that it had been received in arm's-length negotiations. In the absence of any fiduciary relationship, the Court of Appeals found no basis for imposing tippee liability on the investment firm.

disclosure, such as a pecuniary gain or a reputational benefit that will translate into future earnings. There are objective facts and circumstances that often justify such an inference. For example, there may be a relationship between the insider and the recipient that suggests a *quid pro quo* from the latter, or an intention to benefit the particular recipient. The elements of fiduciary duty and exploitation of nonpublic information also exist when an insider makes a gift of confidential information to a trading relative or friend. The tip and trade resemble trading by the insider himself followed by a gift of the profits to the recipient.

Determining whether an insider personally benefits from a particular disclosure, a question of fact, will not always be easy for courts. But it is essential, we think, to have a guiding principle for those whose daily activities must be limited and instructed by the SEC's inside-trading rules, and we believe that there must be a breach of the insider's fiduciary duty before the tippee inherits the duty to disclose or abstain. In contrast, the rule adopted by the SEC in this case would have no limiting principle.[24]

IV

Under the inside-trading and tipping rules set forth above, we find that there was no actionable violation by Dirks. It is undisputed that Dirks himself was a stranger to Equity Funding, with no pre-existing fiduciary duty to its shareholders. He took no action, directly or indirectly, that induced the shareholders or officers of Equity Funding to repose trust or confidence in him. There was no expectation by Dirks' sources that he would keep their information in confidence. Nor did Dirks misappropriate or illegally obtain the information about Equity Funding. Unless the insiders breached their *Cady, Roberts* duty to shareholders in disclosing the nonpublic information to Dirks, he breached no duty when he passed it on to investors. . . .

It is clear that neither Secrist nor the other Equity Funding employees violated their *Cady, Roberts* duty to the corporation's shareholders by providing information to Dirks.[27] The tippers received no monetary or

24. Without legal limitations, market participants are forced to rely on the reasonableness of the SEC's litigation strategy, but that can be hazardous, as the facts of this case make plain. . . .

27. In this Court, the SEC appears to contend that an insider invariably violates a fiduciary duty to the corporation's shareholders by transmitting nonpublic corporate information to an outsider when he has reason to believe that the outsider may use it to the disadvantage of the shareholders. "Thus, regardless of any ultimate motive to bring to public attention the derelictions at Equity Funding, Secrist breached his duty to Equity Funding shareholders." This perceived "duty" differs markedly from the one that

the SEC identified in *Cady, Roberts* and that has been the basis for federal tippee-trading rules to date. In fact, the SEC did not charge Secrist with any wrongdoing, and we do not understand the SEC to have relied on any theory of a breach of duty by Secrist in finding that Dirks breached his duty to Equity Funding's shareholders.

[T]o constitute a violation of Rule 10b–5, there must be fraud. There is no evidence that Secrist's disclosure was intended to or did in fact "deceive or defraud" anyone. Secrist certainly intended to convey relevant information that management was unlawfully concealing, and–so far as the record shows–he believed that persuading Dirks to investigate was the best way to disclose the fraud. Other

personal benefit for revealing Equity Funding's secrets, nor was their purpose to make a gift of valuable information to Dirks. As the facts of this case clearly indicate, the tippers were motivated by a desire to expose the fraud. In the absence of a breach of duty to shareholders by the insiders, there was no derivative breach by Dirks. Dirks therefore could not have been "a participant after the fact in [an] insider's breach of a fiduciary duty."

* * *

NOTES

Rule

1. *Joint and several liability.* Under the *Dirks* theory, both the tipper and tippee violate Rule 10b–5 if the insider gives the outsider information for the purpose of trading. Consequently, the tipper is jointly-and-severally liable with the tippee for the tippee's profits.

2. *Temporary insiders.* In Footnote 14 of *Dirks*, the Supreme Court explains that underwriters, accountants, lawyers, or consultants may enter into a "special confidential relationship" whereby they come under a fiduciary duty similar to insiders with respect to non-public, material information obtained through the relationship.

3. *The Supreme Court and securities law.* The Supreme Court granted certiorari in *Dirks* because of the case's "importance to the SEC and the securities industry." There was no split among the circuits (the usual basis for certiorari) at the time of the grant. The grant reflects Justice Powell's influence in bringing securities cases to the Court's docket. The Court's average number of securities cases per term during his tenure was *twice* that of the periods before or since.

QUESTIONS

1. Why is "[t]he need for a ban on some tippee trading [] clear"?

2. The Court in *Dirks* seems particularly concerned with preserving the flow of corporate information to outside financial analysts. What kind of investors are likely to benefit from such tips to analysts? Who (if anyone) is harmed?

3. Today, if a senior officer at Equity Funding were to pass on information about fraud at the company to a broker-dealer employee like Dirks without simultaneously disclosing the information to the public at large, he would be violating Regulation FD (covered in Chapter 4). Section 102 of Regulation FD, however, states: "No failure to make a public disclosure required solely [by Regulation FD] shall be deemed to be a violation of Rule 10b–5." Why not? What would Justice Powell have thought of Regulation FD?

HYPOTHETICAL THREE

Return to the Martha Media hypothetical and consider various possible "chains" of information transmission.

efforts had proved fruitless. Under any objective standard, Secrist received no direct or indirect personal benefit from the disclosure.

1. *Scenario One*: Recall the path of information involved when Martha sells her InClone stock:

Jack (CEO of InClone) → Merritt (the broker) → Martha (who then sells)

What if Jack tells Merritt to "make sure Martha knows that I'm dumping my stock in InClone ASAP"? Merritt gives the information to Martha, telling her that Jack "wants you to have a heads-up." Is Martha liable for insider trading?

2. *Scenario Two*: Assume Jack has made an impermissible tip under *Dirks* to Martha. Suppose Martha telephones her best friend Curtis and tells him that Merritt told her Jack was dumping his InClone shares. "Merritt is so well connected," Martha tells Curtis.

Jack → Merritt (the broker) → Martha → (via phone call from Martha) Curtis

Curtis then sells InClone shares short. Has Curtis run afoul of *Dirks*?

3. *Scenario Three*: Suppose Martha writes that "Merritt says sell sell sell InClone" on a piece of paper that is later thrown out in the trash. Joel, a street person rummaging through Martha's trash (known for its excellent finds) finds the note signed by "Martha" and decides to sell InClone short. Has Joel run afoul of *Dirks*?

Jack → Merritt (the broker) → Martha → (via trash) Joel

4. *Scenario Four*: Suppose that Martha simply overheard the information about InClone's acquisition of BioGen while in an elevator with Jack. Jack, unfortunately, has a loud voice and was talking about the deal on his cell phone. (Practice tip for future lawyers: shut up on elevators.)

Jack → Martha

Has Martha run afoul of the *Dirks* anti-tipping rule?

IV. THE MISAPPROPRIATION THEORY

The classical insider trading theory after *Dirks* focuses on information obtained from inside the corporation whose stocks are traded. The contours of the doctrine can be summarized as follows:

	Insider Trader	Outsider Trader
Corporate (inside) Information	*Chiarella* classical theory *Dirks* temporary insiders	*Dirks* tipper-tippee liability
Outside Information	?	?

Left undecided after *Chiarella* and *Dirks*, however, was the question of information generated outside the traded firm. Not all informational advantages in the market come from the issuer; there are many other potential sources of information. Imagine that you are an individual investor considering whether to buy InClone stock. Who are the other outsider traders in the market? Do you think you are at a relative informational disadvantage or advantage relative to these other traders?

A wide range of outsiders trade in the secondary market. Large institutional investors—including pension funds and mutual funds—spend large sums of money engaged in "buy-side" securities research. Institutional investors may also obtain information through close relationships with investment banks engaged in "sell-side" research. Although investment banks often will provide public research reports for all investors, favored institutional investors have greater access to the analysts, allowing them to ask questions and learn information about companies not otherwise available to the public. Other companies may also have material nonpublic information on a particular traded firm. Suppose Microsoft is about to enter the biotechnology business. The potential for added competition from Microsoft is likely material information for InClone and other biotechnology companies. To the extent Microsoft (or its officers) trade on this information (selling InClone stock short, for example), Microsoft and its officers enjoy a large trading advantage. Warren Buffett, a highly successful investor from Omaha, Nebraska, is likely to be at a trading advantage compared to almost any individual outside investor; some investors are simply more talented than others at picking stocks.

Given the range of trading advantages among outsiders, which trading advantages should society prohibit and what should be allowed? Here are some possibilities:

- prohibit all non-public material informational advantages
- prohibit all advantages obtained through an unequal access advantage giving investors an "unerodable" informational advantage
- prohibit only advantages obtained through a breach of a fiduciary duty
- allow only those informational advantages obtained through the "hard work" of the trading investor
- allow all outside informational advantages

Given the harm to uninformed investors (in the form of reduced liquidity and market depth) when trading with the more informed, why not simply adopt the first alternative and ban all nonpublic material informational advantages? Why tolerate any informational advantages? Some argue that giving profits to those with an informational advantage gives investors an incentive to research and uncover useful information about a company. Granting such investors a "property" right to their information will generate a greater amount of information in the securities markets. Others focus on the "unfairness" of allowing the abuse of an "unerodable" informational advantage over uninformed investors. Advantages created by skill or effort are not deemed "unfair."

Under Rule 10b–5, deciding which outside informational advantages to allow is resolved by the misappropriation theory. Remember that the Court reserved the question of the validity of the misappropriation theory in *Chiarella* because it was not presented to the jury. The SEC and the Justice Department continued to press the theory, which led to its eventual return to the Supreme Court. It took two cases, however, before the Court would pass on the validity of the misappropriation theory. As you read the following cases, compare the limits of the misappropriation theory with those of the classical theory. Note that the author of the following draft opinion, Justice Lewis F. Powell, Jr., also wrote the Court's opinions in *Chiarella* and *Dirks*. Do you agree with his view or the position adopted in *O'Hagan*? Which better serves the policy interests of insider trading prohibitions? Which is more faithful to the text of § 10(b) and Congress's intention in adopting that provision?

Carpenter v. United States (1st Draft)

(Circulated: Dec. 10, 1986).

■ POWELL, J., dissenting from denial of certiorari.

A divided panel of the Court of Appeals for the Second Circuit has resolved an important question of securities law in a way that appears to conflict with recent opinions of this Court. As this decision—particularly by this Court of Appeals—could have substantial precedential effect, I would grant the petition for certiorari. . . .

I

In this case, the Court of Appeals affirmed petitioners' convictions for wire fraud, mail fraud, and securities fraud. . . . [T]he petition challenges the securities fraud convictions. The convictions rest on a conspiracy involving petitioner Winans, a reporter for the Wall Street Journal, and petitioners Felis and Brant, stockbrokers with the firm of Kidder Peabody. The final party to the conspiracy was petitioner Carpenter, an employee of the Wall Street Journal who carried messages from Winans to Felis and Brant. Winans informed Brant and Felis of the dates on which the Wall Street Journal would publish columns discussing particular securities. Advance knowledge of the dates on which certain columns would appear enabled Brant and Felis to profit by trading in anticipation of price changes that would follow publication of the columns. The columns themselves consisted of public information. The only nonpublic information provided by Winans was the publication schedule for the columns.

[handwritten margin note: Reporter disclosed dates when articles would appear in Wall Street Journal]

The petitioners were charged with wire fraud, mail fraud, and securities fraud. After a bench trial, the District Court convicted petitioners. On appeal, the Court of Appeals for the Second Circuit affirmed. In the Court of Appeals' view, petitioners were guilty of criminal securities fraud under the "misappropriation" theory of securities fraud under § 10(b) of the Securities Exchange Act of 1934, and Rule 10b–5. Under this theory, a person is liable under Rule 10b–5 if he misappropriates material nonpublic information and then uses the information in connection with the purchase or sale of securities. The Court of Appeals noted that we left open the question of the legitimacy of the misappropriation theory in *Chiarella*. But the court noted that its Circuit has adopted that theory since our decision in *Chiarella*. . . .

II

A comparison of the Court of Appeals' opinion in this case with our recent precedents demonstrates the need for examination by this Court of

classical theory.

the misappropriation theory. In *Chiarella,* we began our analysis of Rule 10b–5 with the proposition that parties to a business transaction generally do not have an affirmative duty to disclose information about the transaction. The Court noted, however, that a failure to disclose material information could be fraudulent in certain circumstances. "But such liability is premised upon a duty to disclose arising from a relationship of trust and confidence between parties to a transaction." Such a duty applied when corporate insiders traded in the securities of their corporation. In such a case, "the duty arose from (1) the existence of a relationship affording access to inside information intended to be available only for a corporate purpose, and (2) the unfairness of allowing a corporate insider to take advantage of that information by trading without disclosure."

Chiarella Rules
Insiders

duty to disclose from special relationship

In *Dirks,* we examined the circumstances under which outsiders could be held liable under Rule 10b–5. We noted:

Dirks outsiders

> [U]nder certain circumstances, such as where corporate information is revealed legitimately to an underwriter, accountant, lawyer, or consultant working for the corporation, these outsiders may become fiduciaries of the shareholders. The basis for recognizing this fiduciary duty is not simply that such persons acquired nonpublic corporate information, but that they have entered into a special confidential relationship in the conduct of the business of the enterprise and are given access to information solely for corporate purposes.

Improper Info
information from insider who breached special relationship + knowledge of outsider (tippee)

Thus, *Dirks* established that when outsiders have a fiduciary duty to the shareholders, they cannot purchase securities from those shareholders without first informing them of material information that might influence the decision to purchase or sell the securities.

proper info
+ when info revealed legit. to lawyer, accou → they become fiduciaries

The Court also noted that even if a particular outsider were not under a fiduciary duty to the corporation's shareholders, he could not trade on information that corporate insiders had disclosed to him improperly. As the Court explained, "[T]ippee responsibility must be related back to insider responsibility by a necessary finding that the tippee knew the information was given to him in breach of a duty by a person having a special relationship to the issuer not to disclose the information. . . . "

Applying these principles to this case, it is difficult to understand how any of the petitioners were guilty of criminal securities fraud. The Court of Appeals found no fiduciary relationship between any of the petitioners and the parties from whom they purchased securities. The only fiduciary duty discussed by the court is petitioner Winans' duty to the Wall Street Journal. But our previous decisions establish that the duty of an individual to his employer, alone, is insufficient to support an action under Rule 10b–5. The inquiry under that section must focus on "petitioner's relationship with the sellers of the . . . securities. . . . " What we said in *Chiarella* is true here: "[Petitioner] was not their agent, he was not a fiduciary, he was not a person in whom the sellers had placed their trust and confidence. He was, in fact, a complete stranger who dealt with the sellers only through impersonal market transactions." As the petitioners in this case had no fiduciary obligation to disclose the information before dealing in the securi-

chiarella's position: duty of employee to employer is not enough to establish a claim under 10(b)(5).
↓
time for misappropriation theory.

ties, their convictions under § 10(b) and Rule 10b–5 are without support in any prior decision of this Court.

III

In *Chiarella*, the Court had no occasion to address the merits of the misappropriation theory. The question is important, because the theory broadens substantially the ambit of criminal liability under the securities laws. There appears to be little or no support for the decision below in the language or history of the Securities Act of 1934.

The Court of Appeals has had three occasions to address the misappropriation theory since we left this question open in *Chiarella*.... In my view, this case presents "an important question of federal law which has not been, but should be, settled by this Court." The time has come for this Court to resolve that question. I dissent from the Court's denial of certiorari in this case.

NOTES

1. *Powell's draft*. The Court initially voted to deny certiorari in *Carpenter*. Powell prepared the draft opinion above in response to that denial. After Powell circulated his draft, Justice O'Connor and Chief Justice Rehnquist joined his dissent. The dissent was never published, however, because Justices Brennan and Scalia changed their votes to grant certiorari.

Before *Carpenter* was argued, Justice Powell retired. His successor, Anthony Kennedy, was not confirmed until after the argument. The Court split 4–4 on the misappropriation theory under the securities laws and it therefore issued no opinion on the validity of the theory (but affirmed the Second Circuit's decision judgment upholding Winans' conviction based on the misappropriation theory).

Given Powell's rejection of the misappropriation theory in his draft dissent, it is reasonable to conclude that if Justice Powell had not retired when he did, the Supreme Court would have rejected the misappropriation theory in 1987. The 4–4 split, however, left the question open. In the case that follows, the Court finally resolved the question of the validity of the misappropriation theory. The case also addresses the validity of Rule 14e–3, a rule adopted by the SEC (in the wake of its defeat in *Chiarella*) to combat insider trading in connection with tender offers. As you read *O'Hagan* consider what role is left (if any) for the classical theory developed by Powell.

2. *Mail and wire fraud*. Carpenter also came up on appeal from a Second Circuit decision affirming the convictions of Winans based on the federal mail and wire fraud statutes. A unanimous Court affirmed the Second Circuit's judgment with respect to the mail and wire fraud convictions. The distinction between securities fraud and mail and wire fraud is important because the SEC does not have authority to enforce the mail and wire fraud statutes. Only the Justice Department can enforce those provisions, and only in a criminal prosecution.

QUESTIONS

1. According to Justice Powell, what sort of relationship is required to give rise to Rule 10b–5 liability?

2. One argument supporting the misappropriation theory is that without such liability, investors would lack the incentive to invest in securities research (often termed the "property rights" approach to insider trading). Absent the misappropriation theory, do outside sources of information (such as the *Wall Street Journal*) have any tools with which to protect their valuable interest in information?

Rule: Person who trades securities for personal profit using confidential information in breach of fiduciary duty to the source of information, is guilty of violation of 10(b) / 10b-5

United States v. O'Hagan

521 U.S. 642 (1997).

rule 14e-3 → is OK (proscribes trading on undisclosed information in tender offers).

■ GINSBURG, J.

This case concerns the interpretation and enforcement of § 10(b) and § 14(e) of the Securities Exchange Act of 1934, and rules made by the Securities and Exchange Commission pursuant to these provisions, Rule 10b–5 and Rule 14e–3(a).... In particular, we address and resolve these issues: (1) Is a person who trades in securities for personal profit, using confidential information misappropriated in breach of a fiduciary duty to the source of the information, guilty of violating § 10(b) and Rule 10b–5? (2) Did the Commission exceed its rulemaking authority by adopting Rule 14e–3(a), which proscribes trading on undisclosed information in the tender offer setting, even in the absence of a duty to disclose? Our answer to the first question is yes, and to the second question, viewed in the context of this case, no.

10b-5
10e-3(a)

I

Respondent James Herman O'Hagan was a partner in the law firm of Dorsey & Whitney in Minneapolis, Minnesota. In July 1988, Grand Metropolitan PLC, a company based in London, England, retained Dorsey & Whitney as local counsel to represent Grand Met regarding a potential tender offer for the common stock of the Pillsbury Company, headquartered in Minneapolis. Both Grand Met and Dorsey & Whitney took precautions to protect the confidentiality of Grand Met's tender offer plans.... [O]n October 4, 1988, Grand Met publicly announced its tender offer for Pillsbury stock.

O'Hagan partner in the law firm

bought call options of client with potential tender offer

On August 18, 1988, while Dorsey & Whitney was ... representing Grand Met, O'Hagan began purchasing call options for Pillsbury stock.... By the end of September, he owned 2,500 unexpired Pillsbury options, apparently more than any other individual investor. O'Hagan also purchased, in September 1988, some 5,000 shares of Pillsbury common stock, at a price just under $39 per share. When Grand Met announced its tender offer in October, the price of Pillsbury stock rose to nearly $60 per share. O'Hagan then sold his Pillsbury call options and common stock, making a profit of more than $4.3 million.

bought → 39$
sold → 60$
4.3 m. profit.

The Securities and Exchange Commission initiated an investigation into O'Hagan's transactions, culminating in a 57–count indictment. The indictment alleged that O'Hagan defrauded his law firm and its client, Grand Met, by using for his own trading purposes material, nonpublic

information regarding Grand Met's planned tender offer . . . A jury convicted O'Hagan on all 57 counts, and he was sentenced to a 41–month term of imprisonment.

A divided panel of the Court of Appeals for the Eighth Circuit reversed all of O'Hagan's convictions.

* * *

II

We address first the Court of Appeals' reversal of O'Hagan's convictions under § 10(b) and Rule 10b–5.... We hold that criminal liability under § 10(b) may be predicated on the misappropriation theory.

A

* * *

Classical theory of insider trading.

Under the "traditional" or "classical theory" of insider trading liability, § 10(b) and Rule 10b–5 are violated when a corporate insider trades in the securities of his corporation on the basis of material, nonpublic information. Trading on such information qualifies as a "deceptive device" under § 10(b), we have affirmed, because "a relationship of trust and confidence [exists] between the shareholders of a corporation and those insiders who have obtained confidential information by reason of their position with that corporation." That relationship, we recognized, "gives rise to a duty to disclose [or to abstain from trading] because of the 'necessity of preventing a corporate insider from . . . tak[ing] unfair advantage of . . . uninformed . . . stockholders.' " The classical theory applies not only to officers, directors, and other permanent insiders of a corporation, but also to attorneys, accountants, consultants, and others who temporarily become fiduciaries of a corporation.

Insiders + outsiders

The "misappropriation theory" holds that a person commits fraud "in connection with" a securities transaction, and thereby violates § 10(b) and Rule 10b–5, when he misappropriates confidential information for securities trading purposes, in breach of a duty owed to the source of the information. Under this theory, a fiduciary's undisclosed, self-serving use of a principal's information to purchase or sell securities, in breach of a duty of loyalty and confidentiality, defrauds the principal of the exclusive use of that information. In lieu of premising liability on a fiduciary relationship between company insider and purchaser or seller of the company's stock, the misappropriation theory premises liability on a fiduciary-turned-trader's deception of those who entrusted him with access to confidential information.

The two theories are complementary, each addressing efforts to capitalize on nonpublic information through the purchase or sale of securities. The classical theory targets a corporate insider's breach of duty to shareholders with whom the insider transacts; the misappropriation theory outlaws trading on the basis of nonpublic information by a corporate "outsider" in breach of a duty owed not to a trading party, but to the

• outlaws trading on the basis of nonpublic info. by
outsider in breach of duty owed to source of inform.

O'Hagan → owed duty to client (as lawyer), re tender offer.

IV THE MISAPPROPRIATION THEORY 387

source of the information. The misappropriation theory is thus designed to "protec[t] the integrity of the securities markets against abuses by 'outsiders' to a corporation who have access to confidential information that will affect th[e] corporation's security price when revealed, but who owe no fiduciary or other duty to that corporation's shareholders." ... [5]

B

Misappropriation → deceptive practice

We agree with the Government that misappropriation ... satisfies § 10(b)'s requirement that chargeable conduct involve a "deceptive device or contrivance" used "in connection with" the purchase or sale of securities. We observe, first, that misappropriators, as the Government describes them, deal in deception. A fiduciary who "[pretends] loyalty to the principal while secretly converting the principal's information for personal gain," "dupes" or defrauds the principal....

Misappropriation is deal in deception

A company's confidential information ... qualifies as property to which the company has a right of exclusive use. The undisclosed misappropriation of such information, in violation of a fiduciary duty ... constitutes fraud akin to embezzlement—"the fraudulent appropriation to one's own use of the money or goods entrusted to one's care by another." ...

Company's confid. Info → is a property for exclusive use (embezzlement)

Deception through nondisclosure is central to the theory of liability for which the Government seeks recognition.... As counsel for the Government stated in explanation of the theory at oral argument: "To satisfy the common law rule that a trustee may not use the property that [has] been entrusted [to] him, there would have to be consent. To satisfy the requirement of the Securities Act that there be no deception, there would only have to be disclosure." See generally Restatement (Second) of Agency §§ 390, 395 (1958) (agent's disclosure obligation regarding use of confidential information).

The misappropriation theory advanced by the Government is consistent with *Santa Fe Industries, Inc. v. Green,* 430 U.S. 462 (1977), a decision underscoring that § 10(b) is not an all-purpose breach of fiduciary duty ban; rather, it trains on conduct involving manipulation or deception.... Full disclosure forecloses liability under the misappropriation theory: Because the deception essential to the misappropriation theory involves feigning fidelity to the source of information, if the fiduciary discloses to the source that he plans to trade on the nonpublic information, there is no "deceptive device" and thus no § 10(b) violation—although the fiduciary-turned-trader may remain liable under state law for breach of a duty of loyalty.

safe harbor ↓ disclosure to the source

5. The Government could not have prosecuted O'Hagan under the classical theory, for O'Hagan was not an "insider" of Pillsbury, the corporation in whose stock he traded. Although an "outsider" with respect to Pillsbury, O'Hagan had an intimate association with, and was found to have traded on confidential information from, Dorsey & Whitney, counsel to tender offeror Grand Met. Under the misappropriation theory, O'Hagan's securities trading does not escape Exchange Act sanction ... simply because he was associated with, and gained nonpublic information from, the bidder, rather than the target.

IN connection with purchase or sale of securities.   10(b)

the element is not consumated when fiduciary gains confid. info but when w/o disclosure uses info for purchase or sell securities

We turn next to the § 10(b) requirement that the misappropriator's deceptive use of information be "in connection with the purchase or sale of [a] security." This element is satisfied because the fiduciary's fraud is consummated, not when the fiduciary gains the confidential information, but when, without disclosure to his principal, he uses the information to purchase or sell securities. The securities transaction and the breach of duty thus coincide. This is so even though the person or entity defrauded is not the other party to the trade, but is, instead, the source of the nonpublic information. A misappropriator who trades on the basis of material, nonpublic information, in short, gains his advantageous market position through deception; he deceives the source of the information and simultaneously harms members of the investing public.

The misappropriation theory targets information of a sort that misappropriators ordinarily capitalize upon to gain no-risk profits through the purchase or sale of securities. Should a misappropriator put such information to other use, the statute's prohibition would not be implicated. The theory does not catch all conceivable forms of fraud involving confidential information; rather, it catches fraudulent means of capitalizing on such information through securities transactions.

* * *

The misappropriation theory comports with § 10(b)'s language, which requires deception "in connection with the purchase or sale of any security," not deception of an identifiable purchaser or seller. The theory is also well tuned to an animating purpose of the Exchange Act: to insure honest securities markets and thereby promote investor confidence. Although informational disparity is inevitable in the securities markets, investors likely would hesitate to venture their capital in a market where trading based on misappropriated nonpublic information is unchecked by law. An investor's informational disadvantage vis-à-vis a misappropriator with material, nonpublic information stems from contrivance, not luck; it is a disadvantage that cannot be overcome with research or skill.

In sum, considering the inhibiting impact on market participation of trading on misappropriated information, and the congressional purposes underlying § 10(b), it makes scant sense to hold a lawyer like O'Hagan a § 10(b) violator if he works for a law firm representing the target of a tender offer, but not if he works for a law firm representing the bidder. The text of the statute requires no such result.[9] The misappropriation at issue

---

9. As noted earlier, however, the textual requirement of deception precludes § 10(b) liability when a person trading on the basis of nonpublic information has disclosed his trading plans to, or obtained authorization from, the principal—even though such conduct may affect the securities markets in the same manner as the conduct reached by the misappropriation theory.... [T]he fact that § 10(b) is only a partial antidote to the problems it was designed to alleviate does not call into question its prohibition of conduct that falls within its textual proscription. Moreover, once a disloyal agent discloses his imminent breach of duty, his principal may seek appropriate equitable relief under state law. Furthermore, in the context of a tender offer, the principal who authorizes an agent's trading on confidential information may, in the

here was properly made the subject of a § 10(b) charge because it meets the statutory requirement that there be "deceptive" conduct "in connection with" securities transactions.

Tender Offer * *
disclose or abstain!!!   III   *14(e)* → *one doesn't need to breach fiduciary duty*

We consider next the ground on which the Court of Appeals reversed O'Hagan's convictions for fraudulent trading in connection with a tender offer, in violation of § 14(e) of the Exchange Act and SEC Rule 14e–3(a). A sole question is before us as to these convictions: Did the Commission ... exceed its rulemaking authority under § 14(e) when it adopted Rule 14e–3(a) without requiring a showing that the trading at issue entailed a breach of fiduciary duty? We hold that the Commission, in this regard and to the extent relevant to this case, did not exceed its authority.

* * *

Through § 14(e) and other provisions on disclosure in the Williams Act, Congress sought to ensure that shareholders "confronted by a cash tender offer for their stock [would] not be required to respond without adequate information." ...

* * *

As characterized by the Commission, Rule 14e–3(a) is a "disclose or abstain from trading" requirement. The Second Circuit concisely described the Rule's thrust:

> One violates Rule 14e–3(a) if he trades on the basis of material   *Disclose*
> nonpublic information concerning a pending tender offer that he
> knows or has reason to know has been acquired 'directly or indirectly'
> from an insider of the offeror or issuer, or someone working on their
> behalf. Rule 14e–3(a) is a disclosure provision. It creates a duty in
> those traders who fall within its ambit to abstain or disclose, *without*
> *regard to whether the trader owes a pre-existing fiduciary duty* to
> respect the confidentiality of the information.

In the Eighth Circuit's view, because Rule 14e–3(a) applies whether or not the trading in question breaches a fiduciary duty, the regulation exceeds the SEC's § 14(e) rulemaking authority.

* * *

The United States urges that the Eighth Circuit's reading of § 14(e) misapprehends both the Commission's authority to define fraudulent acts and the Commission's power to prevent them. "The 'defining' power," the United States submits, "would be a virtual nullity were the SEC not permitted to go beyond common law fraud (which is separately prohibited in the first [self-operative] sentence of Section 14(e))."

* * *

Commission's view, incur liability for an Ex-   change Act violation under Rule 14e–3(a).

We need not resolve in this case whether the Commission's authority under § 14(e) to "define ... such acts and practices as are fraudulent" is broader than the Commission's fraud-defining authority under § 10(b), for we agree with the United States that Rule 14e–3(a), as applied to cases of this genre, qualifies under § 14(e) as a "means reasonably designed to prevent" fraudulent trading on material, nonpublic information in the tender offer context.[17] A prophylactic measure, because its mission is to prevent, typically encompasses more than the core activity prohibited ... § 14(e)'s rulemaking authorization gives the Commission "latitude," even in the context of a term of art like "manipulative," "to regulate nondeceptive activities as a 'reasonably designed' means of preventing manipulative acts, without suggesting any change in the meaning of the term 'manipulative' itself." We hold, accordingly, that under § 14(e), the Commission may prohibit acts not themselves fraudulent under the common law or § 10(b), if the prohibition is "reasonably designed to prevent ... acts and practices [that] are fraudulent."[18]

Because Congress has authorized the Commission, in § 14(e), to prescribe legislative rules, we owe the Commission's judgment "more than mere deference or weight." Therefore, in determining whether Rule 14e–3(a)'s "disclose or abstain from trading" requirement is reasonably designed to prevent fraudulent acts, we must accord the Commission's assessment "controlling weight unless [it is] arbitrary, capricious, or manifestly contrary to the statute." In this case, we conclude, the Commission's assessment is none of these.

standard of analysis

* * *

The United States emphasizes that Rule 14e–3(a) reaches trading in which "a breach of duty is likely but difficult to prove." "Particularly in the context of a tender offer," as the Tenth Circuit recognized, "there is a fairly wide circle of people with confidential information," notably, the attorneys, investment bankers, and accountants involved in structuring the transaction. The availability of that information may lead to abuse, for "even a hint of an upcoming tender offer may send the price of the target company's stock soaring." Individuals entrusted with nonpublic information, particularly if they have no long-term loyalty to the issuer, may find the temptation to trade on that information hard to resist in view of "the very large short-term profits potentially available [to them]."

17. We leave for another day, when the issue requires decision, the legitimacy of Rule 14e–3(a) as applied to "warehousing," which the Government describes as "the practice by which bidders leak advance information of a tender offer to allies and encourage them to purchase the target company's stock before the bid is announced." As we observed in *Chiarella*, one of the Commission's purposes in proposing Rule 14e–3(a) was "to bar warehousing under its authority to regulate tender offers." The Government acknowledges that trading authorized by a principal breaches no fiduciary duty. The instant case, however, does not involve trading authorized by a principal; therefore, we need not here decide whether the Commission's proscription of warehousing falls within its § 14(e) authority to define or prevent fraud.

18. The Commission's power under § 10(b) is more limited.

Reasoning

"[I]t may be possible to prove circumstantially that a person [traded on the basis of material, nonpublic information], but almost impossible to prove that the trader obtained such information in breach of a fiduciary duty owed either by the trader or by the ultimate insider source of the information." The example of a "tippee" who trades on information received from an insider illustrates the problem. Under Rule 10b–5, "a tippee assumes a fiduciary duty to the shareholders of a corporation not to trade on material nonpublic information only when the insider has breached his fiduciary duty to the shareholders by disclosing the information to the tippee and the tippee knows or should know that there has been a breach." [quoting from *Dirks*, 463 U.S., at 660]. To show that a tippee who traded on nonpublic information about a tender offer had breached a fiduciary duty would require proof not only that the insider source breached a fiduciary duty, but that the tippee knew or should have known of that breach. "Yet, in most cases, the only parties to the [information transfer] will be the insider and the alleged tippee."

In sum, it is a fair assumption that trading on the basis of material, nonpublic information will often involve a breach of a duty of confidentiality to the bidder or target company or their representatives. The SEC, cognizant of the proof problem that could enable sophisticated traders to escape responsibility, placed in Rule 14e–3(a) a "disclose or abstain from trading" command that does not require specific proof of a breach of fiduciary duty. That prescription, we are satisfied, applied to this case, is a "means reasonably designed to prevent" fraudulent trading on material, nonpublic information in the tender offer context. Therefore, insofar as it serves to prevent the type of misappropriation charged against O'Hagan, Rule 14e–3(a) is a proper exercise of the Commission's prophylactic power under § 14(e).

* * *

NOTES

1. *Splitting the elements.* Consider the "classic" case of insider trading in which a corporate officer, who owes a fiduciary duty to the corporation's shareholders, purchases shares from these shareholders without informing them of non-public, material information that the corporation has found a large gold deposit on its lands. In this case, the deception and breach of fiduciary duty are linked directly with the purchase transaction. The misappropriation theory breaks apart the Rule 10b–5 elements of deception and breach of a fiduciary duty. Under the misappropriation theory, neither the deception nor the breach of fiduciary duty must occur against the party trading opposite to the violator. Instead, a third party is introduced—the source of the information. If the violator breaches her fiduciary duty to the source by trading on this information to trade—without disclosure to the source—with another party then this satisfies the "in connection with" requirement. The Court's holding in *O'Hagan* validates the separation of those elements.

QUESTIONS

1. Why did the Justice Department choose not to pursue O'Hagan under the classical theory of insider trading set forth in *Chiarella* and *Dirks*?

2. What if O'Hagan had brazenly told Grand Met and his law firm before the acquisition was announced that he planned to buy Pillsbury options?

3. What happened to the "in connection with the purchase or sale" requirement of Rule 10b–5? If the fiduciary duty breach is to the source of information rather than to investors in the market who lose from the insider trades, how is the fraud in connection with the purchase or sale of securities?

To strengthen the prohibitions against insider trading (and following a wave of insider trading scandals in the mid-1980s), Congress enacted the Insider Trading and Securities Fraud Enforcement Act of 1988. The Act provides, among other things, the following major provisions:

- A controlling person of someone who is found liable for insider trading or tipping can be held liable for a civil penalty not exceeding the greater of $1 million or three times the profits made or losses avoided by the controlled person, if the controlling person knew, or should have known, about the violation and failed to prevent such a violation (codified in § 21A of the Exchange Act)

- The Act authorizes the SEC to pay bounties to persons who provide information that eventually leads to imposition of a civil penalty on the alleged violator of insider trading law. The informant can receive up to 10% of the penalty collected (codified in § 21A of the Exchange Act)

- The Act clarifies who has standing to bring a private cause of action based on insider trading (codified in § 20A of the Exchange Act). Section 20A authorizes contemporaneous traders to bring an action against the person who unlawfully traded on material, nonpublic information. The measure of damages in a private cause of action is the profits gained or losses avoided by the defendant

HYPOTHETICAL FOUR

Return to the InClone hypothetical. Recall that the following transactions took place:

- Jack, the CEO of InClone, ordered his broker Merritt to sell 50% of his two million InClone shares

- Jack ordered Merritt to purchase call options for BioGen shares

- Martha, acting on a tip from Merritt that Jack was selling InClone shares, sells 10,000 of her own InClone shares

1. Has Jack violated the misappropriation theory by purchasing BioGen options? By selling his InClone shares? Has Merritt? Has Martha? See Rule 10b5–2. Would it make a difference if the InClone board of directors had approved Jack's transactions in advance?

2. What liability would Jack or Martha face in an action brought by the SEC? See § 21A. Would Merritt and Sparrow Securities face any liability?

3. What if Merritt announces to Sparrow Securities his intention to trade on the information obtained from Jack (despite Sparrow Securities' protests)? Can Merritt do so under the misappropriation theory?

4. If any of these transactions violated the misappropriation theory, who has standing to bring a private right of action? See § 20A.

5. Did Jack violate Rule 14e–3 by purchasing BioGen options? By selling his InClone shares? Did Martha?

6. Suppose Harvey, a professional thief, breaks into InClone's offices prior to public announcement of the acquisition and uncovers information on the tender offer for BioGen. Harvey then purchases BioGen options the next day, eventually making $10 million from these trades. Has Harvey violated Rule 10b–5? Rule 14e–3?

7. Suppose InClone was selling preferred stock in a private placement at the time it was contemplating the BioGen tender offer. Assuming nondisclosure of the tender offer, would it have violated the misappropriation theory?

After *O'Hagan* we are left with the following doctrinal matrix for Rule 10b–5 liability. Keep in mind that other rules interact with Rule 10b–5 to regulate informational advantages. Most important of these are Regulation FD (selective disclosures) and Rule 14e–3 (tender offer related information).

	Insider Trader	Outsider Trader
Corporate (inside) Information	*Chiarella* classical theory *Dirks* temporary insiders	*Dirks* tipper-tippee liability
Outside Information	?	*O'Hagan* misappropriation theory

HYPOTHETICAL FIVE

Suppose that Jack, the CEO of InClone, learns at his bridge club that Amgenics (a competing biotechnology company) is planning to file for bankruptcy. Assume that this is non-public, material information but also highly relevant to the stock price of InClone. An officer of Amgenics carelessly happens to mention this information at the bridge club and Jack simply overheard. Can Jack sell InClone stock while in possession of this non-public, material information? Does he violate his fiduciary duty to InClone's shareholders by trading?

V.   SECTION 16

Insider trading was a focal point for criticisms during the hearings that led to the adoption of the Exchange Act. Notwithstanding this attention, § 16 is the only section in which the 1934 Congress explicitly addressed the subject of insider trading. Section 16 takes a three-pronged approach to trading by insiders of companies with an equity security registered with the SEC. Section 16(a) requires statutory insiders (officers, defined in Rule

Statutory Insiders

Form 3 –
initial statements
of ownership

Form 4 – changes
in ownership.

Form 5 – annual st.

16a–1, directors and 10% shareholders) to report transactions in their company's equity securities within two business days of the trade (see Exchange Act Rule 16a–3). Statutory insiders report by filing Form 3, for initial statements of ownership, or Form 4, for changes in ownership, with the SEC's EDGAR electronic filing system. Statutory insiders must also file an annual statement of their ownership position using Form 5 or, at their discretion, an earlier filed Form 4. The availability of Form 4 on the EDGAR system allows interested observers to track the trading patterns of statutory insiders. The availability of Form 4 filings allows plaintiffs' attorneys to demonstrate the presence of abnormally high volumes of insider transactions as a means of meeting the pleading scienter with particularity requirement discussed in Chapter 5.

Short-swing profits
– profits gained or
losses avoided from
a purchase followed
by sale within 6 months
or sale followed by
purchase within 6 months

SHs are authorized
to bring derivative
actions on behalf of
corporation

Section 16(b) requires the disgorgement of "short-swing" profits to the corporation by those same statutory insiders. "Short-swing" profits are defined as profits gained (or losses avoided) from a purchase followed by a sale within six months or a sale followed by a purchase within the same period. The corporation is authorized to bring suit under § 16(b) to recover an insider's short-swing profits. What is the likelihood of the statutory insiders authorizing the corporation to bring suit against themselves? Rare indeed, unless one set of statutory insiders has the corporation bring suit against another set of insiders or former insiders. To remedy this potential problem of underenforcement, § 16(b) also authorizes shareholders to bring derivative actions on behalf of the corporation. Not surprisingly, a segment of the plaintiffs' attorney bar specializes in monitoring Form 4 filings to ferret out § 16(b) violations and bring a derivative suit to recover short swing profits. The bright-line rule nature of § 16(b) violations makes litigating such cases relatively easy for plaintiffs' attorneys.

Section 16(c) bans all short sales of the company's equity securities by the statutory insiders. Insiders are not allowed to bet against their company, a practice that the 1934 Congress found particularly galling. One of the justifications for prohibiting insider trading under Rule 10b–5 is that corporate insiders may find it easier to bet against the company through short sales and then sabotage the company. With the prohibition on short sales, does the argument for prohibiting insider trading become weaker?

A.   SECTION 16 AND EMPLOYEE COMPENSATION

Transactions by officers and directors are relatively straightforward. The only major controversy regarding the transactions of officers and directors involves the exercise of stock options. The SEC broadened § 16 in 1991 to include options, convertible securities, and other rights relating to equity securities as "equity securities of such issuer." The expansion of the definition of "equity security" to include forms of derivative securities not only implicated reporting requirements for options, but also short-swing profits liability under § 16(b). The SEC takes the position that any acquisition or disposition of a derivative security, e.g., an option, involves either a purchase or sale.

Rules 16b–3(d)(3) and 16b–6(b), however, exempt most subsequent exercises and conversions of those derivative securities. This exemption helps reduce potential short-swing profit liability when an insider exercises options, because such a transaction is exempt and therefore does not constitute a "purchase or sale." As a result, these exemptions have eased the administration of employee benefit plans involving derivative securities. Rule 16b–3 exempts transactions between the issuer and its officers or directors in most circumstances. Tax-conditioned plans (these include a "Qualified Plan," "Excess Benefit Plan" or "Stock Purchase Plan") are exempted almost across the board; other transactions with the issuer are exempted if they are approved by the board, a committee of independent directors, or the shareholders.

One nuance regarding the application of § 16 to officers and directors is timing: Rule 16a–2 exempts transactions occurring within the six months *before* becoming an officer or a director. Transactions occurring during the six months *after* ceasing to be an officer or director are not similarly exempt.

Congress added another trading restriction for officers and directors in § 306 of the Sarbanes–Oxley Act. Section 306 prohibits officers and directors from trading in the company's securities during any blackout period of more than three days during which the employees of the corporation are barred from trading the company's securities held in employee benefit plans (a "blackout period"). Any profits from prohibited trading can be recovered by the company, either directly or through a derivative action by any of the company's security holders.

B.   WHAT IS A SALE?

Transactions by 10% shareholders pose considerably greater analytical difficulties, as demonstrated by the following two cases. What counts as a sale within the meaning of § 16?

Kern County Land Co. v. Occidental Petroleum Corp.

411 U.S. 582 (1973).

■ WHITE, J.

Section 16(b) of the Securities Exchange Act of 1934 provides that officers, directors, and holders of more than 10% of the listed stock of any company shall be liable to the company for any profits realized from any purchase and sale or sale and purchase of such stock occurring within a period of six months. Unquestionably, one or more statutory purchases occur when one company, seeking to gain control of another, acquires more than 10% of the stock of the latter through a tender offer made to its shareholders. But is it a § 16(b) "sale" when the target of the tender offer defends itself by merging into a third company and the tender offeror then exchanges his stock for the stock of the surviving company and also grants an option to purchase the latter stock that is not exercisable within the statutory six-month period? This is the question before us in this case.

I

On May 8, 1967, after unsuccessfully seeking to merge with Kern County Land Co. (Old Kern), Occidental Petroleum Corp. (Occidental) announced an offer, to expire on June 8, 1967, to purchase on a first-come, first-served basis 500,000 shares of Old Kern common stock at a price of $83.50 per share.... By May 10, 1967, 500,000 shares, more than 10% of the outstanding shares of Old Kern, had been tendered. On May 11, Occidental extended its offer to encompass an additional 500,000 shares. At the close of the tender offer, on June 8, 1967, Occidental owned 887,549 shares of Old Kern.

Immediately upon the announcement of Occidental's tender offer, the Old Kern management undertook to frustrate Occidental's takeover attempt.... Old Kern undertook merger discussions with Tenneco, Inc., and, on May 19, 1967, the Board of Directors of Old Kern announced that it had approved a merger proposal advanced by Tenneco. Under the terms of the merger, Tenneco would acquire the assets, property, and goodwill of Old Kern, subject to its liabilities, through "Kern County Land Co." (New Kern), a new corporation to be formed by Tenneco to receive the assets and carry on the business of Old Kern. The shareholders of Old Kern would receive a share of Tenneco cumulative convertible preference stock in exchange for each share of Old Kern common stock which they owned....

Realizing that, if the Old Kern–Tenneco merger were approved and successfully closed, Occidental would have to exchange its Old Kern shares for Tenneco stock and would be locked into a minority position in Tenneco, Occidental took other steps to protect itself. Between May 30 and June 2, it negotiated an arrangement with Tenneco whereby Occidental granted Tenneco Corp., a subsidiary of Tenneco, an option to purchase at $105 per share all of the Tenneco preference stock to which Occidental would be entitled in exchange for its Old Kern stock when and if the Old Kern–Tenneco merger was closed. The premium to secure the option at $10 per share, totaled $8,866,230 and was to be paid immediately upon the signing of the option agreement. If the option were exercised, the premium was to be applied to the purchase price. By the terms of the option agreement, the option could not be exercised prior to December 9, 1967, a date six months and one day after expiration of Occidental's tender offer. On June 2, 1967, within six months of the acquisition by Occidental of more than 10% ownership of Old Kern, Occidental and Tenneco Corp. executed the option....

The Old Kern–Tenneco merger plan was presented to and approved by Old Kern shareholders at their meeting on July 17, 1967. Occidental refrained from voting its Old Kern shares, but in a letter read at the meeting Occidental stated that it had determined prior to June 2 not to oppose the merger and that it did not consider the plan unfair or inequitable. Indeed, Occidental indicated that, had it been voting, it would have voted in favor of the merger.

Meanwhile, the Securities and Exchange Commission had refused Occidental's request to exempt from possible § 16(b) liability Occidental's exchange of its Old Kern stock for the Tenneco preference shares that would take place when and if the merger transaction were closed....

The Old Kern–Tenneco merger transaction was closed on August 30. Old Kern shareholders thereupon became irrevocably entitled to receive Tenneco preference stock, share for share in exchange for their Old Kern stock. Old Kern was dissolved and all of its assets, including all claims, demands, rights and choses in action accrued or to accrue under and by virtue of the Securities Exchange Act of 1934 ... were transferred to New Kern.

The option granted by Occidental on June 2, 1967, was exercised on December 11, 1967. Occidental, not having previously availed itself of its right, exchanged certificates representing 887,549 shares of Old Kern stock for a certificate representing a like number of shares of Tenneco preference stock. The certificate was then endorsed over to the optionee-purchaser, and in return $84,229,185 was credited to Occidental's accounts at various banks. Adding to this amount the $8,886,230 premium paid in June, Occidental received $93,905,415 for its Old Kern stock (including the 1,900 shares acquired prior to issuance of its tender offer). In addition, Occidental received dividends totaling $1,793,439.22. Occidental's total profit was $19,506,419.22 on the shares obtained through its tender offer.

On October 17, 1967, New Kern instituted a suit under § 16(b) against Occidental to recover the profits which Occidental had realized as a result of its dealings in Old Kern stock....

The Court [of Appeals] held that neither the option nor the exchange constituted a "sale" within the purview of § 16(b).... We affirm.

II

Section 16(b) provides, inter alia, that a statutory insider must surrender to the issuing corporation "any profit realized by him from any purchase and sale, or any sale and purchase, of any equity security of such issuer ... within any period of less than six months." As specified in its introductory clause, § 16(b) was enacted "(f)or the purpose of preventing the unfair use of information which may have been obtained by (a statutory insider) ... by reason of his relationship to the issuer." Congress recognized that shortswing speculation by stockholders with advance, inside information would threaten the goal of the Securities Exchange Act to "insure the maintenance of fair and honest markets." Insiders could exploit information not generally available to others to secure quick profits. As we have noted, "the only method Congress deemed effective to curb the evils of insider trading was a flat rule taking the profits out of a class of transactions in which the possibility of abuse was believed to be intolerably great." ...

Although traditional cash-for-stock transactions that result in a purchase and sale or a sale and purchase within the six-month, statutory period are clearly within the purview of § 16(b), the courts have wrestled with the question of inclusion or exclusion of certain "unorthodox" transactions.[24] The statutory definitions of "purchase" and "sale" are broad and, at least arguably, reach many transactions not ordinarily deemed a sale or purchase. In deciding whether borderline transactions are within the reach of the statute, the courts have come to inquire whether the transaction may serve as a vehicle for the evil which Congress sought to prevent–the realization of short-swing profits based upon access to inside information–thereby endeavoring to implement congressional objectives without extending the reach of the statute beyond its intended limits. The statute requires the inside, short-swing trader to disgorge all profits realized on all "purchases" and "sales" within the specified time period, without proof of actual abuse of insider information, and without proof of intent to profit on the basis of such information. Under these strict terms, the prevailing view is to apply the statute only when its application would serve its goals.

In the present case, it is undisputed that Occidental became a "beneficial owner" within the terms of § 16(b) when, pursuant to its tender offer, it "purchased" more than 10% of the outstanding shares of Old Kern. We must decide, however, whether a "sale" within the ambit of the statute took place either when Occidental became irrevocably bound to exchange its shares of Old Kern for shares of Tenneco pursuant to the terms of the merger agreement between Old Kern and Tenneco or when Occidental gave an option to Tenneco to purchase from Occidental the Tenneco shares so acquired.[28]

III

On August 30, 1967, the Old Kern–Tenneco merger agreement was signed, and Occidental became irrevocably entitled to exchange its shares of Old Kern stock for shares of Tenneco preference stock. Concededly, the transaction must be viewed as though Occidental had made the exchange on that day. But, even so, did the exchange involve a "sale" of Old Kern shares within the meaning of § 16(b)? We agree with the Court of Appeals that it did not, for we think it totally unrealistic to assume or infer from the facts before us that Occidental either had or was likely to have access to inside information, by reason of its ownership of more than 10% of the outstanding shares of Old Kern, so as to afford it an opportunity to reap

---

24. The term has been applied to stock conversions, exchanges pursuant to mergers and other corporate reorganizations, stock reclassifications, and dealings in options, rights, and warrants.

28. Both events occurred within six months of Occidental's first acquisition of Old Kern shares pursuant to its tender offer. Although Occidental did not exchange its Old Kern shares until December 11, 1967, it is not contended that that date, rather than the date on which Occidental became irrevocably bound to do so, should control. Similarly, although the option was not exercised until December 11, 1967, no liability is asserted with respect to that event, because it occurred more than six months after Occidental's last acquisition of Old Kern stock.

speculative, short-swing profits from its disposition within six months of its tender-offer purchases.

It cannot be contended that Occidental was an insider when, on May 8, 1967, it made an irrevocable offer to purchase 500,000 shares of Old Kern stock at a price substantially above market. At that time, it owned only 1,900 shares of Old Kern stock, far fewer than the 432,000 shares needed to constitute the 10% ownership required by the statute. There is no basis for finding that, at the time the tender offer was commenced, Occidental enjoyed an insider's opportunity to acquire information about Old Kern's affairs.

* * *

By May 10, 1967, Occidental had acquired more than 10% of the outstanding shares of Old Kern. It was thus a statutory insider when, on May 11, it extended its tender offer to include another 500,000 shares. We are quite unconvinced, however, that the situation had changed materially with respect to the possibilities of speculative abuse of inside information by Occidental. Perhaps Occidental anticipated that extending its offer would increase the likelihood of the ultimate success of its takeover attempt or the occurrence of a defensive merger. But, again, the expectation of such benefits was unrelated of the use of information unavailable to other stockholders or members of the public with sufficient funds and the intention to make the purchases Occidental had offered to make before June 8, 1967.

The possibility that Occidental had, or had the opportunity to have, any confidential information about Old Kern before or after May 11, 1967, seems extremely remote. Occidental was, after all, a tender offeror, threatening to seize control of Old Kern, displace its management, and use the company for its own ends. The Old Kern management vigorously and immediately opposed Occidental's efforts.... Old Kern's management refused to discuss with Occidental officials the subject of an Old Kern–Occidental merger. Instead, it undertook negotiations with Tenneco and forthwith concluded an agreement, announcing the merger terms on May 19. Requests by Occidental for inspection of Old Kern records were sufficiently frustrated by Old Kern's management to force Occidental to litigate to secure the information it desired.

There is, therefore, nothing in connection with Occidental's acquisition of Old Kern sought to be classified a "sale" under § 16(b) to indicate either the possibility of inside information being available to Occidental by virtue of its stock ownership or the potential for speculative abuse of such inside information by Occidental. Much the same can be said of the events leading to the exchange of Occidental's Old Kern stock for Tenneco preferred, which is one of the transactions that is sought to be classified a 'sale' under § 16(b). The critical fact is that the exchange took place and was required pursuant to a merger between Old Kern and Tenneco. That merger was not engineered by Occidental but was sought by Old Kern to frustrate the attempts of Occidental to gain control of Old Kern. Occidental obviously did not participate in or control the negotiations or the agreement between Old Kern and Tenneco. Once agreement between those two companies crystallized, the course of subsequent events was out of Occidental's hands. Old Kern needed the consent of its stockholders, but as it turned out, Old Kern's management had the necessary votes without the affirmative vote of Occidental.... Once the merger and exchange were approved, Occidental was left with no real choice with respect to the future of its shares of Old Kern.... Occidental could, of course, have disposed of its shares of Old Kern for cash before the merger was closed. Such an act would have been a § 16(b) sale and would have left Occidental with a prima facie § 16(b) liability. It was not, therefore, a realistic alternative for Occidental as long as it felt that it could successfully defend a suit like the present one. We do not suggest that an exchange of stock pursuant to a merger may never result in § 16(b) liability. But the involuntary nature of Occidental's exchange, when coupled with the absence of the possibility of speculative abuse of inside information, convinces us that § 16(b) should not apply to transactions such as this one.

IV

Petitioner also claims that the Occidental–Tenneco option agreement should itself be considered a sale, either because it was the kind of transaction the statute was designed to prevent or because the agreement was an option in form but a sale in fact. But the mere execution of an option to sell is not generally regarded as a "sale." And we do not find in the execution of the Occidental–Tenneco option agreement a sufficient possibility for the speculative abuse of inside information with respect to Old Kern's affairs to warrant holding that the option agreement was itself a "sale" within the meaning of § 16(b).... Occidental wanted to avoid the position of a minority stockholder with a huge investment in a company over which it had no control and in which it had not chosen to invest. On the other hand, Tenneco did not want a potentially troublesome minority stockholder that had just been vanquished in a fight for the control of Old Kern. Motivations like these do not smack of insider trading; and it is not clear to us ... how the negotiation and execution of the option agreement gave Occidental any possible opportunity to trade on inside information it might have obtained from its position as a major stockholder of Old Kern.... In any event, Occidental was dealing with the putative new owners of Old Kern, who undoubtedly knew more about Old Kern and Tenneco's affairs than did Occidental....

Neither does it appear that the option agreement, as drafted and executed by the parties, offered measurable possibilities for speculative abuse....

The option ... covered Tenneco preference stock, a stock as yet unissued, unregistered, and untraded. It was the value of this stock that underlay the option and that determined whether the option would be exercised, whether Occidental would be able to profit from the exercise, and whether there was any real likelihood of the exploitation of inside information. If Occidental had inside information when it negotiated and signed the option agreement, it was inside information with respect to Old Kern. Whatever it may have known or expected as to the future value of Old Kern stock, Occidental had no ownership position in Tenneco giving it any actual or presumed insights into the future value of Tenneco stock. . . .

* * *

QUESTIONS

1. What if Occidental had sold for cash the Old Kern shares it obtained from its tender offer prior to the Tenneco merger closing in order to divest the Old Kern shares as quickly as possible? How does the Court's focus on the "speculative abuse of inside information" apply to this situation?

2. Suppose Occidental had negotiated with Old Kern immediately after purchasing Old Kern shares in the tender offer. Through the negotiations, Occidental obtained confidential and material information concerning Old Kern. After failing to acquire Old Kern, Occidental sold the shares previously purchased in the tender offer into the open secondary market six months and a day after the close of the tender offer. Does § 16(b) require the disgorgement of Occidental's profits?

———————

The Court, in *Reliance Electric Co. v. Emerson Electric Co.*, 404 U.S. 418 (1972), had previously held that when a 10% shareholder reduces its holdings below 10% in two transactions, with the first bringing its holdings below the 10% threshold, that a second transaction further liquidating its holdings is not within the reach of § 16(b). When does an investor become a 10% holder for purposes of § 16? The *Foremost–McKesson* case below considers two possibilities: (a) immediately at the time the holder initially acquires a block of 10% or (b) only after the initial acquisition of a 10% block. Taking the position that a shareholder becomes a 10% holder right at the time of the initial acquisition would expand the scope of § 16's short-swing profit prohibition. Is that broader reach necessary necessary to protect against trades based on non-public, material inside information?

Foremost–McKesson, Inc. v. Provident Securities Co.

423 U.S. 232 (1976).

■ POWELL, J.

This case presents an unresolved issue under § 16(b) of the Securities Exchange Act of 1934. . . . Section 16(b)'s last sentence . . . provides that it "shall not be construed to cover any transaction where such beneficial owner was not such both at the time of the purchase and sale, or the sale and purchase, of the security involved. . . . " The question presented here is whether a person purchasing securities that put his holdings above the 10% level is a beneficial owner "at the time of the purchase" so that he must account for profits realized on a sale of those securities within six months. . . .

The corporate "insiders" whose trading is regulated by § 16(b) are defined in § 16(a), as "(e)very person who is directly or indirectly the beneficial owner of more than 10 per centum of any class of any equity security (other than an exempted security) which is registered pursuant to ... of this title, or who is a director or an officer of the issuer of such security."

I

Provident Securities Co., was a personal holding company. In 1968 Provident decided tentatively to liquidate and dissolve, and it engaged an agent to find a purchaser for its assets. Foremost–McKesson, Inc., emerged as a potential purchaser, but extensive negotiations were required to resolve a disagreement over the nature of the consideration Foremost would pay. Provident wanted cash in order to facilitate its dissolution, while Foremost wanted to pay with its own securities.

Eventually a compromise was reached, and Provident and Foremost executed a purchase agreement embodying their deal on September 25, 1969. The agreement provided that Foremost would buy two-thirds of Provident's assets for $4.25 million in cash and $49.75 million in Foremost convertible subordinated debentures.... Foremost delivered four debentures totalling $49.75 million to Provident with principal amounts of $25 million, $15 million, $7.25 million, and $2.5 million respectively. These debentures were immediately convertible into more than 10% of Foremost's outstanding common stock.

On October 21 Provident, Foremost, and a group of underwriters executed an underwriting agreement to be closed on October 28. The agreement provided for sale to the underwriters of the $25 million debenture. On October 24 Provident distributed the $15 million and $7.25 million debentures to its stockholders, reducing the amount of Foremost common into which the company's holdings were convertible to less than 10%. On October 28 the closing under the underwriting agreement was accomplished. Provident thereafter distributed the cash proceeds of the debenture sale to its stockholders and dissolved.

Provident's holdings in Foremost debentures as of October 20 were large enough to make it a beneficial owner of Foremost within the meaning of § 16. Having acquired and disposed of these securities within six months, Provident faced the prospect of a suit by Foremost to recover any profits realized on the sale of the debenture to the underwriters. Provident therefore sued for a declaration that it was not liable to Foremost under § 16(b). The District Court granted summary judgment for Provident, and the Court of Appeals affirmed.

* * *

The Court of Appeals ... held that in a purchase-sale sequence the phrase "at the time of the purchase," "must be construed to mean prior to the time when the decision to purchase is made." Thus, although Provident became a beneficial owner of Foremost by acquiring the debentures, it was not a beneficial owner "at the time of the purchase." Accordingly, the exemptive provision prevented any § 16(b) liability on Provident's part.

II

The meaning of the exemptive provision has been disputed since § 16(b) was first enacted. The discussion has focused on the application of the provision to a purchase-sale sequence, the principal disagreement being whether "at the time of the purchase" means "before the purchase" or "immediately after the purchase." The difference in construction is determinative of a beneficial owner's liability in cases such as Provident's where such owner sells within six months of purchase the securities the acquisition of which made him a beneficial owner. . . .

The Court of Appeals . . . found unpersuasive the rationales offered . . . for the "immediately after the purchase" construction. It noted that construing the provision to require that beneficial-ownership status exist before the purchase in a purchase-sale sequence would not foreclose an "immediately after the purchase" construction in a sale-repurchase sequence. More significantly, the Court of Appeals challenged directly the premise of the earlier cases that a "before the purchase" construction in a purchase-sale sequence would allow abuses Congress intended to abate. The court reasoned that in § 16(b) Congress intended to reach only those beneficial owners who both bought and sold on the basis of inside information, which was available to them only after they became statutory "insiders."

III

A

* * *

Foremost invokes the observation in *Reliance Electric Co.* that "where alternative constructions of the terms of § 16(b) are possible, those terms are to be given the construction that best serves the congressional purpose of curbing short-swing speculation by corporate insiders." From these premises Foremost argues that the Court of Appeals' construction of the exemptive provision must be rejected because it makes § 16(b) inapplicable to some possible abuses of inside information that the statute would reach under the ["immediately after the purchase"] construction. We find this approach unsatisfactory in its focus on situations that § 16(b) may not reach rather than on the language and purpose of the exemptive provision itself. Foremost's approach also invites an imposition of § 16(b)'s liability without fault that is not consistent with the premises upon which Congress enacted the section.

B

The exemptive provision, which applies only to beneficial owners and not to other statutory insiders, must have been included in § 16(b) for a purpose.

* * *

[After an extensive review of the legislative history, the Court concluded]: The legislative record thus reveals that the drafters focused directly on the fact that S. 2693 covered a short-term purchase-sale sequence by a beneficial owner only if his status existed before the purchase, and no concern was expressed about the wisdom of this requirement. But the explicit requirement was omitted from the operative language of the section when it was restructured to cover sale-repurchase sequences. In the same draft, however, the exemptive provision was added to the section. On this record we are persuaded that the exemptive provision was intended to preserve the requirement of beneficial ownership before the purchase. Later discussions of the present § 16(b) in the hearings are consistent with this interpretation. We hold that, in a purchase-sale sequence, a beneficial owner must account for profits only if he was a beneficial owner "before the purchase."

* * *

But even if the legislative record were more ambiguous, we would hesitate to adopt Foremost's construction. It is inappropriate to reach the harsh result of imposing § 16(b)'s liability without fault on the basis of unclear language. If Congress wishes to impose such liability, we must assume it will do so expressly or by unmistakable inference.

* * *

B

Our construction of § 16(b) also is supported by the distinction Congress recognized between short-term trading by mere stockholders and such trading by directors and officers. The legislative discourse revealed that Congress thought that all short-swing trading by directors and officers was vulnerable to abuse because of their intimate involvement in corporate affairs. But trading by mere stockholders was viewed as being subject to abuse only when the size of their holdings afforded the potential for access to corporate information. These different perceptions simply reflect the realities of corporate life.

It would not be consistent with this perceived distinction to impose liability on the basis of a purchase made when the percentage of stock ownership requisite to insider status had not been acquired. To be sure, the possibility does exist that one who becomes a beneficial owner by a purchase will sell on the basis of information attained by virtue of his newly acquired holdings. But the purchase itself was not one posing dangers that Congress considered intolerable, since it was made when the purchaser owned no shares or less than the percentage deemed necessary to make one an insider. Such a stockholder is more analogous to the stockholder who never owns more than 10% and thereby is excluded entirely from the operation of § 16(b), than to a director or officer whose every purchase and sale is covered by the statute. While this reasoning might not compel our construction of the exemptive provision, it explains why Congress may have seen fit to draw the line it did.

C

Section 16(b)'s scope, of course, is not affected by whether alternative sanctions might inhibit the abuse of inside information. Congress, however, has left some problems of the abuse of inside information to other remedies. These sanctions alleviate concern that ordinary investors are unprotected against actual abuses of inside information in transactions not covered by § 16(b).... Today an investor who can show harm from the misuse of material inside information may have recourse, in particular, to § 10(b) and Rule 10b–5.[29]

* * *

QUESTIONS

1. Why do purchasers attempt to collect "toehold" holdings of 10% or more if it does not (as the Court says) create an informational advantage?

2. Compare two situations:

(A) Purchaser, a long-time 10% block holder, buys an additional 10% block—five months later the purchaser sells the block for a profit.

(B) Purchaser, with no prior share ownership, buys a 20% block—five months later the purchaser sells the block for a profit.

For those investors who eventually buy the shares in the block, is there any difference between (A) and (B)?

3. Why are 10% holders exempted both before and after attaining that status, but not corporate officers and directors? Is the risk of "speculative abuses" greater for officers and directors?

C. CALCULATING SECTION 16(b) DAMAGES

Cases involving novel fact situations aside, § 16(b) provides for strict liability for officers, directors, and 10% beneficial owners who purchase-sell or sell-purchase within any six month period. If insiders make only two transactions—e.g., a purchase followed by a sale of the same amount of stock—calculating profits is straightforward. But what if an insider has

29. Rule 10b–5 has been held to embrace evils that Foremost urges its construction of § 16(b) is necessary to prevent. The Rule has been applied to trading by one who acquired inside information in the course of negotiations with a corporation, such as the negotiations for Provident's purchase of the Foremost debentures. And a stockholder trading on information not generally known has been held subject to the sanctions of the Rule. The liability of insiders who improperly "tip" others, may reduce the threat that beneficial owners not themselves represented on the board of directors will be able to acquire inside information from officers and directors. We cite these cases for illustrative purposes without necessarily implying approval.

multiple purchases and sales during the six month period? Consider the following pattern of trades:

Date	Shares Purchased	Purchase Price	Shares Sold	Sale Price
1/1	1,000	$10		
2/1			1,000	$ 8
3/1	1,000	$12		
4/1			1,000	$13
5/1	1,000	$14		
5/15			1,000	$14.50

Looking at this pattern, one might think that the insider lost a net $500 on her trades during the six month period. After the first buy-sell transaction (completed on 2/1), the insider has lost a net $2,000. After the second buy-sell transaction (completed on 4/1), the insider has lost a net $1,000. And after the third buy-sell transaction (completed on 5/15) the insider has lost a net $500.

However, courts calculate damages under § 16(b) to generate the maximum possible profits possible. In *Smolowe v. Delendo Corp.*, 136 F.2d 231, 239 (2d Cir.), cert. denied, 320 U.S. 751 (1943), the Second Circuit explained:

> The statute is broadly remedial. Recovery runs not to the stockholder, but to the corporation. We must suppose that the statute was intended to be thoroughgoing, to squeeze all possible profits out of stock transactions, and thus to establish a standard so high as to prevent any conflict between the selfish interest of a fiduciary officer, director, or stockholder and the faithful performance of his duty.... The only rule whereby all possible profits can be surely recovered is that of lowest price in, highest price out—within six months—as applied by the district court.

Following the "lowest price in, highest price out" methodology, the trades in the table are matched as follows:

1/1 purchase of 1,000 at $10 → 5/15 sale of 1,000 at $14.50

(Profit = $4,500)

3/1 purchase of 1,000 at $12 → 4/1 sale of 1,000 at $13

(Profit = $1,000)

The total profit for § 16(b) purposes is therefore $5,500.

No other matches are then made if they would result in zero or negative profits. The 5/1 purchase of 1,000 shares at $14 is not matched with the 2/1 sale of 1,000 shares at $8, which would generate a loss of $6,000, giving a net profit of -$500. The "lowest price in, highest price out" methodology therefore does not consider the insider's net investment performance during the six month statutory window, but instead focuses solely on the pairs of transactions generating the greatest profit calculation, and thus, the largest damages award.

QUESTION

1. Although the "lowest price in, highest price out" formula maximizes profits, it is hard to see how an insider who is an overall loser during the statutory six month period has been exploiting an informational advantage. If the § 16(b) profit calculation is arbitrary, why not simply impose an arbitrary damage amount (e.g., a flat $100,000 penalty)?

*

CHAPTER 7

PUBLIC OFFERINGS

Rules and Statutes

—*Sections 2(a)(3), 2(a)(4), 2(a)(7), 2(a)(10), 2(a)(11), 4(1), 4(3), 4(4), 5, 7(a), 8, 10 of the Securities Act*

—*Rules 134, 135, 137, 138, 139, 153, 163, 163A, 164, 168, 169, 172, 173, 174, 405, 408(b), 409, 412, 413, 415, 420, 421, 424, 430, 430A, 430B, 430C, 433, 460, 461, 462 of the Securities Act*

—*Forms S–1, S–3*

—*Regulation S–K, Item 512(a)*

—*Rule 15c2–8 of the Exchange Act*

—*Regulation M, Rules 100–105*

MOTIVATING HYPOTHETICAL

Sherry is the CEO of Smartway, Inc., an Internet company providing an on-line market for unsold airline tickets. Smartway's primary customers are last-minute travelers willing to fly on a moment's notice for heavily discounted tickets. Established in 2000, Smartway now sells over $10 million in tickets per month and has a growing base of customers, many of whom provide Smartway with repeat business. Smartway has contracts with several of the major airlines to sell last-minute tickets. Many of these contracts, however, are due to expire in the next couple of years. Afraid that the airlines may attempt to set up their own last-minute air travel service, Sherry believes that Smartway must expand rapidly to become the dominant player in the last-minute travel market. Once Smartway achieves a "monopolist" position, Sherry believes that the airlines will have no choice but to sell their last-minute tickets through Smartway. To fund the expansion, Sherry is considering various financing options, including an initial public offering (IPO) of Smartway common stock. Smartway common is not currently publicly traded.

I.   ECONOMICS OF PUBLIC OFFERINGS

Businesses exist to make a profit. To create those profits, businesses sell both goods and services to customers in return for money. Revenues translate into profits, however, only after businesses pay for the inputs required to produce those goods and services. Costs may include expenses for employees, electricity, supplies, leases, and so on. Certain expenses go to items that provide value in the immediate future (e.g., the wages for an employee to work for the next month). Other expenses, termed capital expenses, reflect purchases of tangible assets that can be used for production for an extended period of time (e.g., a computer network).

Some businesses require relatively few capital assets. Consider a photography business run by a sole proprietor. The sole proprietor may purchase a camera and some developing equipment. By far the greatest expense of the photographer is her own time and effort (commonly referred to as the photographer's "human capital," although not by accountants). At the other end of the spectrum are businesses requiring significant amounts of more traditional capital assets. General Motors makes automobiles and trucks. To produce those vehicles, General Motors owns a number of factories. In addition, it purchases large amounts of steel and other raw materials.

Capital-intensive businesses may have a timing problem. Products will eventually generate revenue when sold, but businesses often must make expenditures well before the time of sale. General Motors needs to spend considerable amounts of money up front either constructing or purchasing factories (say $200 million). The expenditure on a factory, characterized by accountants as a capital expense, will generate revenue when output is sold, not only in the year the factory is built but also for many years after (say $10 million per year). Although the stream of revenues over time may eventually exceed the initial capital costs, a capital-intensive business initially spends far more cash than it receives (in the case of GM, a $190 million deficit after one year).

Companies have a number of options to cover such a cash flow shortfall. Many smaller businesses find investment funds through either internally generated funds, such as the prior year's profits, or through contributions of money from the founder-owners of the business. A photographer in a sole proprietorship will often put up her own money into buying a camera and development equipment. As the business grows, the photographer may use some of the earnings to purchase additional gear.

Larger businesses often face capital expenditures that dwarf the resources of most individuals. Few individuals are able to finance the purchase of an entire automobile factory (and even if they could, they may not wish to put such a substantial portion of their wealth into one particular investment). Some larger businesses may finance a large capital expenditure out of internally generated funds. Microsoft, for example, sits on an enormous cash hoard that it can draw upon to purchase other businesses without relying on outside sources of financing. Businesses lacking the tremendous cash flow of Microsoft have a range of external solutions to the timing problem.

Banks lend considerable sums to businesses. As part of the loan, banks will typically demand a security interest in the assets of the debtor-business and possibly a personal guarantee from the owners of the business. Bank debt, however, is not without problems. As a loan, bank debt typically requires businesses to make regular interest and principal payments. For some types of investments, the expected stream of revenues may be uncertain and only available far into the future, if at all. In the late 1990s, entrepreneurs started a flurry of new Internet-based businesses. These startups, including Amazon.com for example, promised potentially high returns, but only in the distant future and with great risk. (Most of these startups did, in fact, fail.) Such companies simply will not generate adequate revenue to make interest and principal payments in the first few years after the loan is made. Banks will also often impose numerous covenants designed to protect their debt investment, including minimum debt-equity ratios and limitations on the ability of a company to spend their money.

Many businesses will seek additional capital in the form of equity. Equity capital affords the flexibility of not requiring any fixed monetary payoff, such as an interest payment for a loan. As the saying goes, "Equity is soft; debt is hard." Companies that only expect to be profitable in the distant future may find equity financing better suited to their needs. Equity, however, has a downside. From the perspective of the companies' pre-existing owners, bringing in more equity owners dilutes the potential upside return from the business. Common stock, for example, provides holders the "residual" return of all profits after everyone else is paid, including creditors. If the company sells more common stock, the pre-existing common stock holders (e.g., the founders of the company) are left with a smaller proportionate share of the profits. This effect is commonly called "dilution."

Bringing outside investors into a business also poses another problem: How will the outside investors know that the business will be operated to benefit *all* the equity owners, rather than have its profits and assets diverted to the founders or managers of the firm? Businesses seeking to expand their ownership base typically will take advantage of one of the off-the-shelf organizational forms provided under state law (e.g., limited partnership, LLC, or corporation). Those forms carry with them restrictions on self-dealing by managers, which are intended to ease the concerns of potential investors. If effective, these restrictions increase the amount investors are willing to pay for an ownership stake in the business.

In summary, a business project requiring large initial amounts of money and promising to provide even more money in the future is typically at the heart of the desire for more capital. Moreover, the process of raising capital is not one-size-fits-all because businesses face choices. Companies may self-finance through retained earnings or seek a loan from a bank. Companies may turn to their existing shareholders for more capital contributions. Or companies may turn to the broader capital markets for financing. In this chapter we discuss the application of the federal securities laws to one avenue for raising capital—the decision on the part of companies to raise capital through a public offering of securities into the U.S. capital markets. Later in Chapter 9, we discuss a different option—the private placement of securities to more sophisticated investors.

A.   A BRIEF DESCRIPTION OF THE PUBLIC OFFERING PROCESS

Suppose that Sherry and the board of directors of Smartway, Inc. make the decision to pursue an initial public offering of the common stock of Smartway. How do they proceed? The first step is talking to an investment bank, typically located in Wall Street. Among the large investment banks are household names such as Goldman Sachs and Morgan Stanley.

If Smartway has a visible public presence and the market for IPOs is "hot," investment bankers already may have approached Sherry about a potential public offering. The market for IPOs ebbs and flows and the number of offerings rises dramatically during hot periods. In a slower market, or if Smartway is less prominent, Sherry may need to seek out the Wall Street investment banks herself, either directly or through an intermediary such as Smartway's attorneys (who may in turn have contacts with Wall Street law firms and investment banks).

Underwriters
- advice on structure, price
*   offering amount*

What role do investment banks play in a public offering? In their capacity as underwriters, investment banks perform several critical tasks. First, for companies going public for the first time (and to a lesser extent for more seasoned issuers), underwriters provide advice on the structure of the corporation, the offered securities, and the offering amount and price. The goal of this process is to depict the firm and the offering in the best light possible for public investors. Many startup companies develop complex capital structures and control relationships to accommodate the interests of various early-stage investors. The public capital market, in contrast, prefers simplified capital structures. For example, IPO companies will typically have only one class of common stock. Among other things, a simplified capital structure makes it easier to value the stock of a corporation. Certain corporate governance features are also favored in the public capital markets (such as an independent board and a separate chairman and CEO), so companies going public will typically adjust their board structure to appeal to public owners.

Second, investment banks help guide companies through the SEC's registration process. As you will discover in this chapter, the securities laws require companies making a public offering to file and distribute mandatory disclosure documents containing information on the company, its management, and financials as well as information related to the offering (e.g., the security being offered, the underwriters, the discount for the underwriters, the number of securities offered, and the offering price). The securities laws also restrict the ability of companies to discuss the offering and disseminate information that may influence or otherwise condition the market for the upcoming public offering.

Finally, investment banks will take on a marketing role, assisting the company in selling the securities to the public. As repeat players in the capital markets, investment banks bring with them a wealth of contacts with institutional investors and securities dealers. As we discuss below, the role of the investment bank turns on the form of offering employed.

1. DIFFERENT TYPES OF OFFERINGS

Issuers can access the public capital markets in a number of ways. The securities laws do not mandate any particular means of sale to the public. Indeed, recent years have witnessed the rise of Internet-based offerings and auction offerings. The most common type of offering by far, however, is the firm commitment. Below we describe briefly the firm commitment as well as three lesser-used alternatives—best efforts, direct public offerings, and the Dutch auction.

Firm Commitment. In a firm commitment, the underwriter guarantees the sale of the offering. Technically, the underwriter (or a group of underwriters forming a "syndicate") will purchase the entire offering from the issuer before turning around and reselling the securities to investors. From the issuer's standpoint, the underwriter's purchase ensures that the issuer will receive a certain amount of proceeds from the offering. The underwriter purchases the securities from the issuer at a discount to the price at which they subsequently will be offered to the public. The underwriter receives the discount for both helping to sell the offering and taking on the risk that the offering may not sell.

Consider the following example. If Smartway plans on selling 10 million shares at $20 per share, the underwriter may purchase the shares from Smartway at $18.60 per share, for a $1.40 underwriter's discount—often referred to as the "gross spread." Typically, the gross spread accounts for 7% of the public offering price for an initial public offering. The underwriter earns its return when it resells the shares to the public at $20 per share.

The certainty enjoyed by the issuer by way of a firm commitment offering may help ensure the value of the offering. Consider a company that needs to raise $100 million to develop a new product. A firm commitment offering ensures all investors that the company will in fact obtain the full $100 million. Knowing that the company will receive the financing it needs to launch the new product may reassure investors that the offering will be a profitable investment for them.

Best Efforts. An investment bank assisting in a best efforts offering agrees only to use its "best efforts" to sell the offering. Unlike a firm commitment, the investment bank does not purchase the securities. Instead, the investment bank acts purely as a selling agent, receiving a commission on each security sold. Compared to the firm commitment offering, the investment bank assumes less risk and the issuer retains more risk. If the securities do not sell, the issuer will receive smaller proceeds. The underwriter will only bear the opportunity cost of commissions unearned; it will not be stuck holding unattractive securities. Typically smaller, more speculative companies that cannot attract a firm commitment underwriting from an investment bank raise capital through best efforts public offerings.

Investors face greater risks in a best efforts offering. First, because the investment bank is not putting its own money on the line, the investors have less confidence in the securities' valuation. Investment banks in a firm commitment offering, by contrast, have a strong incentive to ensure that the offering is priced correctly, or even underpriced, lest they be left holding the securities.

Second, the issuer may not sell out the entire issue in a best efforts offering. If the offering is intended to fund the development of a new product, or the entry into a new market, obtaining only a fraction of the expected offering proceeds may jeopardize the business plan. How can a company launch a new product that will require $100 million if it only raised $25 million in a best efforts offering? To combat such fears, a variant of the best efforts offerings is the conditional best efforts offering under which the underwriters and issuer promise to rescind all sales if the offering is not sold out ("all or nothing").

Direct Public Offering. Issuers can sell securities directly to the investing public without an underwriter. The most common form of direct public offering involves an offering by a company to its existing public shareholders (referred to as a "rights" offering), but it is also possible for a company to sell to the public at large. Direct public offerings to the public at large are rare. First, many issuers lack the necessary expertise to complete a public offering (pricing, marketing, etc.). Issuers also lack a pre-existing network among securities dealers and large institutional investors. Second, investment banks play a gatekeeping role. Investors look to the investment bank to screen out poor or fraudulent offerings. With no investment bank to vouch for the offering, investors are likely to discount substantially the price they are willing to pay for the offered securities.

Dutch Auction Offering. A recent innovation in public offerings is the Dutch auction. In a Dutch auction, the issuer and underwriters do not fix a price for the offering. Instead, investors place bids for a desired number of shares at a specified price. After all the bids are placed, the issuer then chooses the highest price that will (given the range of bids) result in the offering completely selling out. So for example, imagine that Smartway wants to sell 1 million shares. The following bids are made:

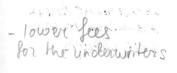

> Bid 1: 200,000 shares for $50 per share
>
> Bid 2: 150,000 shares for $45 per share
>
> Bid 3: 500,000 shares for $40 per share
>
> Bid 4: 150,000 shares for $35 per share
>
> Bid 5: 300,000 shares for $30 per share
>
> Bid 6: 400,000 shares for $20 per share

In this case, the market-clearing price for 1 million shares is $35 per share. At the offering price of $35 per share, the issuer will be able to sell the full 1 million shares. Put another way, the Dutch auction procedure allows the issuer to set the highest single price that will still allow it to sell all the desired shares. It also tends to result in substantially lower fees for the underwriters.

2. THE UNDERWRITERS

An important hierarchy exists among underwriters. Some well-known underwriters stand at the top of the hierarchy (such as Goldman Sachs and Morgan Stanley, among others). This group is often referred to as the "bulge bracket." Typically, after a successful issuance of securities, the underwriters involved will publish an advertisement known as a "tombstone" providing details of the offering. The tombstone will list all of the underwriters in a series of brackets, with the bulge bracket at the top. Placement in the different brackets depends on the reputation of the particular underwriter and the amount of the offering underwritten by the underwriter (the two concepts are linked, with bulge bracket underwriters typically underwriting the largest portions of the offering and receiving greater selling concessions relative to the other, lower-ranking underwriters participating in the offering). Higher-reputation underwriters generally participate only in offerings of more established, well-known companies.

In recent years, many new firms have joined the ranks of underwriters. For example, Wit Capital Group Inc. was established in the late 1990s to assist companies engaged in offerings over the Internet. Having more investment banks competing for underwriting business may reduce the cost to issuers. Competition, on the other hand, may lead individual investment bankers eager to drum up more business to sacrifice the long-term reputation of the underwriter to land the big deal at hand, even if the issuer is of questionable quality. Doing so may result in a large bonus for the specific investment banker for bringing in more business, while the reputational hit the underwriter will eventually receive once the market learns of the issuer's problems is spread across the entire firm.

In the red hot public offering market of the late 1990s, investment banks competing with one another would often bring in-house analysts along for a sales pitch to an issuer's management (a practice known as a "bake-off"). Allegedly, the investment banks would attempt to win the issuer's business by promising, among other things, that the analyst would provide very positive analyst reports, whatever the merits, on the company. The positive reports would help elevate the public offering price and sustain the secondary market price of the company, allowing the company's insiders to eventually sell their own holdings at a higher price. The New York State Attorney General, Eliot Spitzer, investigated such practices at Merrill Lynch and other investment banks, eventually resulting in a joint settlement with the SEC and ten major Wall Street investment banks for over $1.4 billion in 2002. NASD and NYSE rules now limit such bake-offs.

3. THE UNDERWRITING PROCESS

Most public offerings are conducted as firm commitment offerings. Although in theory a single investment bank could take on the entire firm commitment offering, typically a syndicate of underwriters will share the offering. Spreading the offering out among multiple underwriters reduces the risk to any one underwriter of purchasing the securities from the issuer. Although this reduces the potential profit for any one underwriter, it also reduces the risk of an unsold offering.

In the syndicate, typically one to three underwriters will take on the role of the managing underwriter. Even if an offering has more than one managing underwriter, one investment bank will still take the primary role in the offering (often referred to as the lead or book-running manager). The managing underwriter in charge of the "book" is responsible for allocating the offered shares to investors. The managing underwriter will take charge for getting the issuer ready for the public offering, ensuring that the registration statement is filed and becomes effective, pricing the offering, performing due diligence for the registration statement, negotiating with the issuer on behalf of the syndicate, and managing the ultimate distribution of the securities to the public. For these extra services, the lead managing underwriter will typically take 20% or so of the gross spread. So if Smartway sells shares to the underwriters at $18.60 and the IPO price is $20.00, the lead managing underwriter will receive from the underwriters $0.28 per share (20% of the $1.40 gross spread) as compensation for its role as lead manager.

Initially the managing underwriter and the issuer will sign only a non-binding letter of intent to do the public offering. The letter of intent will specify the role of the managing underwriter in the registration process and the size of the underwriting discount (i.e., the gross spread). The letter of intent often will also specify an overallotment option for the underwriters (referred to as the "Green Shoe option," after the first company to use the technique) under which underwriters, at their discretion, may expand the number of shares in the offering up to 15%. The letter of intent will not specify one critical term: the price of the offering. Pricing is left until later—just before sales commence. Only at that point will the issuer and the underwriters enter into a binding underwriting agreement.

After the registration statement is filed, the managing underwriter(s) will invite other underwriters to participate in the syndicate for the firm commitment offering. To govern their relationship with each other, the members of the syndicate will sign an agreement among themselves. The agreement among underwriters will grant to the lead underwriter the authority to act on behalf of the syndicate. The agreement among underwriters will also specify each underwriter's liability for the offering, which will typically be proportionate to the amount of shares they underwrite.

Members of the syndicate are compensated out of the gross spread through a "selling concession." Typically, the selling concession is about 60% of the gross spread. For the Smartway gross spread of $1.40 per share, the selling concession is equal to $0.84 per share. Each underwriter receives a selling concession in proportion to the number of shares that the underwriter purchases from the issuer (the underwriter's "allocation" of shares). If any of the allocated shares are sold by another underwriter or a dealer, the selling concession goes to them.

The remaining 20% of the gross spread (equal to $0.28 per share in the Smartway offering) then goes to paying various expenses involved with underwriting the offering. These expenses include the fees of the counsel for the underwriters, expenses relating to the "road show," and the costs of stabilization (covered below). The road show involves representatives from the issuer and lead underwriter traveling from city to city promoting the offering to institutional investors.

Road show

Costs of stabilization

Just before the offering is made to the public, the issuer and the lead underwriter, acting on behalf of the underwriter syndicate, will finally sign a formal underwriting agreement. The underwriting agreement will set forth the terms of the offering including the number of shares to be sold (by the issuer to the underwriters), the public offering price, the gross spread, and the overallotment option. The terms of the agreement are determined by bargaining and regulations. The NASD requires that underwriting fees be "reasonable." Moreover, the SEC will not declare a registration statement effective (i.e., ready for public sale) until the NASD approves the underwriting arrangement. See Rule 461 of the Securities Act. The underwriting agreement will also contain representations and warranties by the company to the underwriters, relating to, among other things, the completeness and accuracy of the information contained in the registration statement. In addition, the underwriting agreement frequently will include a provision requiring the issuer to indemnify the underwriters for certain securities law liabilities arising from the offering. (The enforceability of this provision, however, is open to question, as discussed below.)

formal agreement

All terms.

SEC will not declare regist. st. effective until NASD approves underw. agreement

4. UNDERPRICING

One of the most curious aspects of the IPO market is underpricing. Companies going public for the first time on average experience a large first-day jump in their stock price from the initial public offering price. During the late 1990s, some Internet companies experienced a first-day increase of over 100%. For example, theglobe.com, an Internet website hosting company, went public at $9 per share and ended its first-day of trading at $63½ per share, trading as high as $97 on that first day. Underpricing of this sort suggests that issuers are leaving money on the table when they negotiate with the underwriters over the offering price. Issuers could price their offerings higher and obtain greater offering proceeds; rather than obtaining $9 per share for its offering, theglobe.com could have received up to $60 or so per share. Instead, the difference between the offering price and the secondary market price on the first day of trading goes to those investors lucky enough to purchase at the $9 offering price. What explains the underpricing phenomenon?

jump on 1st day

money on the table

difference goes to secondary market sellers

Underpricing is even more puzzling given the fact that offerings that are substantially underpriced, and experience a correspondingly large first-day "pop" upwards in the stock price, perform relatively poorly over the first three years of the offering. (Query: Where is theglobe.com today?) Why are investors paying steep secondary market prices to buy shares that are likely to perform poorly? Underpricing is greater during "hot" issues markets when large numbers of IPOs are sold into the public capital markets. One of the central advantages claimed for the Dutch auction

Dutch auction is mar. market is willing to pay

process, described above, is the elimination of underpricing, which means that the issuer is able to capture greater proceeds from the offering. Recall that in a Dutch auction, the issuer obtains information on the market's willingness to pay for its securities from individual bids for specific quantities of securities at certain prices. Using the information from the pool of bids, an issuer can select the highest price that produces sufficient bids to sell out the offering. The issuer through a Dutch auction obtains the maximum the market is willing to pay, leaving no money on the table.

The Dutch auction process, while beneficial for the issuer, is less clearly good for the investing public. If underpricing results from the irrational exuberance of investors artificially driving up stock prices on the first-day of the IPO above fundamental values, the Dutch auction process may not eliminate the underlying irrational exuberance. The exuberant will simply put in an inflated bid in the auction. The winners in a traditional offering—at the expense of the exuberant investors—are the initial IPO purchasers (often institutional investors), who purchase underpriced shares and profit by reselling these shares in the secondary market. In a Dutch auction, the issuer profits instead of institutional investors. Although the issuer may gain higher offering proceeds, the offering price produced by the auction will still reflect any irrational frenzy in the market, leading to an offering price far in excess of the company's fundamental value. As the market cools, the secondary market price may decline just as it would under a more traditional public offering.

5.   CAPITAL STRUCTURE

A common misperception is that companies going public sell their entire capital stock to the public as part of that initial offering. Suppose that Smartway seeks to sell 10 million shares at $20 per share in its IPO. After a successful offering, Smartway will have $200 million in gross proceeds (ignoring, for now, the gross spread and other expenses) and 10 million shares of publicly traded common stock. As depicted in the table below, the 10 million shares *could* represent the entire amount of outstanding Smartway common stock. For example, a company could engage in a public offering creating the *initial* capital stock of the corporation as depicted below:

	Assets	**Liabilities (Equity)**
Pre–Offering	$0	$0 (from 0 shares of common stock)
Post–Offering	$200 million	$200 million (from 10 million shares of common stock sold in the public offering)

Such offerings are not common. A company is unlikely to succeed with such an offering. Investors will be dubious of an offering by a company with no assets, no prior owners and no operating history. A company without any operating history is simply too great a risk. Even if the initial managers of the corporation have a strong business background, investors will wonder why the initial managers have not invested any of their own money prior to the offering.

Companies typically come to an initial public offering with at least some, and often extensive, operating and financial history. With this history come assets and a pre-existing ownership base. Consider the example of Smartway as depicted in the table below.

	Assets	Liabilities (Equity)
Pre–Offering	$25 million	$25 million (from 15 million outstanding shares of common stock primarily in the hands of Sherry, the CEO, and other insiders)
Post–Offering	$225 million	$225 million (from 25 million outstanding shares of common stock after 10 million are sold in the public offering)

Things could get even more complicated. Suppose that in the past, the Smartway business needed a quick injection of capital to overcome a short-term liquidity problem. Jack, a wealthy outside investor, provided the capital in return for preferred stock in Smartway.

	Assets	Liabilities (Equity)
Pre–Offering	$25 million	$10 million of preferred stock in the hands of Jack (convertible into 5 million shares of common stock) $25 million (from 15 million outstanding shares of common stock primarily in the hands of Sherry, the CEO, and other insiders)
Post–Offering	$235 million	$225 million (from 30 million outstanding shares of common stock after 10 million are sold in the public offering—with Jack converting his preferred into 5 million shares of common stock)

Moreover, not all businesses are structured as corporations. Not only do businesses have a choice in the form of external financing they pursue, but they also have a choice of the organizational form under state law (including sole proprietorships, partnerships, limited liability companies and corporations). Prior to its initial public offering, for example, suppose Smartway conducts its business through two separate (and interrelated) organizational forms: the limited partnership (Smartway Partnership) and the corporation (Smartway Management Corp.).

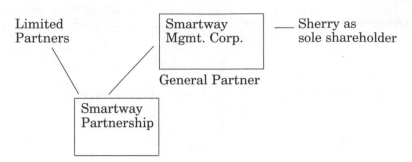

[handwritten margin note: Limited partnership if one partner → unlimited liability]

The limited partnership form allows outside investors (pre-public offering) to invest in Smartway while enjoying limited liability and favorable tax treatment. Limited partnerships require one general partner to face unlimited liability. To avoid unlimited liability, a corporation, Smartway Management Corp, takes on the role of general partner. Sherry then receives her return as the shareholder of Smartway Management Corp.

Although this moderately complicated structure may work for a small number of outside investors, investors in the public capital markets typically prefer a simple corporate structure, with the entire business held by one formally incorporated entity, and a simple capital structure, e.g., only common stock for equity. The simple corporate and capital structure makes it easier for outside investors to determine precisely what they will receive from the investment and what the pre-existing investors of the corporation will receive. Prior to going public, the business, the lead underwriter, and attorneys will reconfigure the various ownership interests and state law entities into a single corporate form with common stock ownership.

Further changes may be necessary. Investors typically prefer companies incorporated in Delaware, the choice of most large public companies. As part of the process of reorganizing for the initial public offering, businesses incorporated in other states will typically reincorporate in Delaware.

B. PUBLIC OFFERING DISCLOSURE

The primary problem facing investors in a public offering is valuing the offered securities. Issuers and their insiders enjoy an informational advantage over outside investors. The risk for outside investors is that issuers may use this advantage to sell overvalued shares. More sophisticated investors compensate by demanding a lower price to purchase shares. The result is that issuers are forced to accept less for their securities than they would otherwise receive if investors had full information, which raises the cost of capital for issuers.

The securities laws respond to the problem of informational advantages by requiring disclosure. The two primary disclosure documents are the registration statement and the statutory prospectus, which consists of Part I of the registration statement. The two documents give rise to two different levels of liability exposure (a topic covered in considerably more detail in Chapter 8):

Document	Use	Special Antifraud Provision
Registration Statement *Part I– statutory prospec.*	Filed with SEC	Section 11 Liability —Due diligence defense for non-issuer participants
Statutory Prospectus	Distributed to Investors	Section 12(a)(2) Liability —Reasonable care defense for sellers

Defense for non-issuer

Defense for non-seller

For domestic companies engaged in a public offering, the two basic forms for the registration statement are Forms S–1 and S–3. Information on these registration forms can be divided into three categories: (a) transaction-related information (e.g., the offering amount, use of proceeds, underwriters, etc.), (b) company information, and (c) exhibits and undertakings. The forms differ both in what they require and in their eligibility requirements as follows:

- Form S–1 is available to all issuers. Form S–1 is the most comprehensive of the disclosure documents and contains all three categories of information disclosure. The prospectus under Form S–1 contains both company information and transaction-related information. Form S–1 issuers that are Exchange Act reporting issuers and current in their filings for the past twelve months, among other requirements, may incorporate company-related information by reference from prior SEC filings. *by reference*

- Form S–3 is available to issuers, that have, among other situations, been a reporting company for one year and have over $75 million capitalization in the hands of non-affiliates. Form S–3 companies may incorporate by reference company-related information contained in documents already filed with the SEC and are not required to give investors an annual report. *–75 m/one year* *–not req. to give annual report*

Forms S–1 (for certain Exchange Act reporting issuers) and S–3 reflect the SEC's choice to allow incorporation-by-reference of certain information. Under incorporation-by-reference, issuers are able to refer to similar information disclosed in the past in another SEC filing—e.g., Forms 10–K, 10–Q, and 8–K (discussed in Chapter 4).

Facilitating incorporation-by-reference is the SEC's streamlined integrated disclosure system (also covered in Chapter 4), which provides a consistent set of disclosure requirements in Regulations S–K and S–X for both the Securities and Exchange Acts. Incorporation-by-reference relies on both integrated disclosure and an assumption about how the capital markets process information. Investors for companies trading in a relatively efficient market can rely on publicly available information being reflected in the stock market price. Alternatively, for well-known companies, brokers and others who filter information on behalf of retail investors may canvass the entire array of SEC filings for a company, providing a unified assessment. *Integrated disclosure system*

The Internet also makes it easier for investors to get information from multiple documents. Indeed, the notion of "a" document is somewhat amorphous on the Internet. If a document on the Internet hyperlinks to disclosure contained in another document, should this be treated as one or two documents? Does it matter from the perspective of an investor if the investor has to "click" through a link to obtain more information on a potential investment, as opposed to scrolling down within the same document?

1. PLAIN ENGLISH DISCLOSURES

In the late 1990s, the SEC reformed the statutory prospectus to make it more accessible to everyday investors. Instead of turgid prose containing jargon and terms comprehensible only to financial professionals, the SEC mandated that the prospectus contain language drafted in a "clear, concise and understandable manner." Consider the following Securities Act rules governing how information is presented in the statutory prospectus:

> Rule 420—Legibility of Prospectus—Includes, among other requirements, that the prospectus must be in Roman type "at least as large and as legible as 10–point modern type."

> Rule 421—Presentation of Information in Prospectuses—Issuers can vary the order of information provided in the prospectus but must ensure that the order does not "obscure any of the required information." Information in the prospectus must be presented in a "clear, concise, and understandable manner" and follow "plain English" principles. Issuers must use "short sentences," "active voice," and avoid "legal and highly technical business terminology."

Despite the admirable goal of more readable prose, were the SEC's plain English reforms worth the cost? Consider the audience for the registration statement and prospectus in a public offering. If retail investors (including individual day traders, retirees, etc.) are the primary audience for the offering documents, plain English disclosure may make those documents more comprehensible. That assumption, however, is undercut by the fact that sophisticated institutional investors make up by far the largest segment of investors participating in public offerings. Even among those individual investors who attempt to purchase in an IPO, how many actually read the disclosure documents rather than relying on the advice of sophisticated intermediaries (such as a broker) or their own "gut" instinct? The SEC has forced issuers to write more clearly—but has anyone noticed?

Jargon is not always bad. Some forms of highly technical phrases provide a quick and certain form of communication among those familiar with the jargon. Consider the phrase "cash flow needs will become significant in the second quarter of the upcoming fiscal year." Is "cash flow" jargon? What if we force firms to replace this language with something more understandable, but somewhat less precise such as: "We're spending more than we're taking in." Although a larger segment of investors may understand such a phrase, more sophisticated investors may glean less information if "cash flow" has a commonly understood meaning. Has plain language disclosure sacrificed depth for breadth in disclosure?

2. SMALL BUSINESS ISSUERS

The public offering process is expensive, particularly for companies going public for the first time. Their direct costs include hiring an attorney and an independent auditor, reorganizing the company, and paying the underwriters' commission. Companies doing an initial public offering also face a several month delay from the time they start drafting the registration statement to the time the securities are sold. For smaller issuers raising only a modest amount of capital, the high costs of a full-blown public offering may cause the issuers to look elsewhere for their capital needs. For example, issuers may sell to a restricted set of more sophisticated investors in a private placement (covered in Chapter 9).

To encourage small businesses to raise capital, the SEC provides two additional registration statement forms: Forms SB–1 and SB–2. "Small business issuers"—defined as issuers with revenues of under $25 million for their most recent fiscal year (subject to some exclusions)—are eligible to use Form SB–2. Unlike the other registration forms, Form SB–2 references Regulation S–B, a simplified version of Regulation S–K. Regulation S–B provides "plain language" instructions. Issuers must provide only two fiscal years' worth of audited income statements and an audited balance sheet for the past year. Financial information must comport with Generally Accepted Accounting Principles but does not have to follow Regulation S–X. Form S–1, in contrast, requires three fiscal years of audited financial statements comporting with Regulation S–X. Additionally, Form SB–2 requires less extensive disclosure of the non-financial information.

Form SB–1 is available to small business issuers for offerings up to $10 million in any twelve-month period. Form SB–1 also draws on Regulation S–B. Form SB–1 is even more streamlined than Form SB–2, with issuers providing disclosure in a simple question and answer format. Form SB–1 requires the same audited financial statements as Form SB–2.

Although reducing offering costs may stimulate the growth of small businesses, does it come at the cost of investor welfare? Consider the risks of fraud. On the one hand, larger issuers with active secondary markets for their stock have the potential, because they offer greater amounts of securities, to defraud larger numbers of investors than smaller companies. On the other hand, greater numbers of securities analysts follow larger companies and few or none follow small business issuers, increasing the opportunities for a smaller company to mislead investors.

II. THE GUN–JUMPING RULES

The federal securities laws tightly regulate public offerings under a regime often referred to as the gun-jumping rules. The gun-jumping rules have at least three broad goals. First, the registration process revolves around the generation of two mandatory disclosure documents: a formal registration statement and a statutory prospectus. Second, the gun-jumping

*3 period structure
of gun-jumping rules*

2.   rules require the distribution of the statutory prospectus in connection with the offering to the investing public and for a specified period of time thereafter. Third, the gun-jumping rules restrict information about the

3.   offering if it is not part of the registration statement or prospectus.

The public offering process is divided into three periods: the Pre–Filing Period, the Waiting Period, and the Post–Effective Period. The Pre–Filing Period ends and the Waiting Period begins when the issuer files the registration statement with the SEC. The Waiting Period gives way to the Post–Effective Period when the SEC declares the registration statement "effective."

Pre–Filing Period ◆ Waiting Period ◆ Post–Effective Period
Filing of the   Registration
Registration   Statement
Statement   Effective

The three period structure of the gun-jumping rules dates back to the enactment of the Securities Act in 1933. Since then, the SEC has modified repeatedly the actual public offering process. In 2005, the SEC adopted a broad ranging series of reforms ("2005 Public Offering Reforms") to take into account the needs of large, well-followed issuers and the changing technological environment through which investors obtain information. We discuss the impact of the 2005 Public Offering Reforms on the gun-jumping rules throughout this chapter. The reforms categorized issuers into four groups:

Non-Reporting Issuer—issuer that is not required to file reports pursuant to § 13 or § 15(d) of the Exchange Act and is not filing such reports voluntarily.

Unseasoned Issuer—issuer that is required to file reports pursuant to § 13 or § 15(d) of the Exchange Act, but it does not satisfy the requirements of Form S–3 or Form F–3 for a primary offering of its securities.

Seasoned Issuer—issuer that is eligible to use Form S–3 or Form F–3 to register primary offerings of securities. Primary offerings includes securities to be sold by the issuer or on its behalf, on behalf of its subsidiary, or on behalf of a person of which it is the subsidiary.

Well-Known Seasoned Issuers (WKSI)—More popularly known as "wick sees," they are defined in Rule 405. WKSI status depends on meeting several requirements with respect to a specified "determination date." The determination date is the date the issuer's most recent shelf registration statement was filed, or its most recent § 10(a)(3) amendment to a shelf registration statement, whichever is later. If the issuer has not filed a shelf registration statement then the determination date is the date of the filing of the most recent annual report on Form 10–K. The principal issuers eligible for WKSI status are:

- the issuer is eligible to register a primary offering of its securities on Form S–3 or Form F–3; or

- the issuer, as of a date within 60 days of the determination date, has either:

  - a minimum $700 million of common equity worldwide market value held by non-affiliates; or

  - issued $1 billion aggregate principal amount of non-convertible securities in registered offerings during the past three years and either will register only "non-convertible securities, other than common equity, and full and unconditional guarantees." If such an issuer has a public float of $75 million in common equity at the determination date, it can also issue common equity as a WKSI.

Not all of these issuers are eligible for WKSI status. Issuers are disqualified if they:

- are not current in their Exchange Act filings or late in satisfying those obligations for the preceding twelve months;

- an ineligible issuer or asset-backed issuer; or

- an investment company or business development company.

Ineligible issuers under Rule 405 include, among others, those issuers that within the past three years were a blank check or shell company or issued a registered penny stock offering are ineligible. Issuers that filed a bankruptcy petition within the past three years also fall into the ineligible issuer category, unless they have filed an annual report with audited financial statements subsequent to their emergence from bankruptcy. Also ineligible are issuers that have violated the anti-fraud provisions of the federal securities laws during the last three years and issuers that filed a registration statement that is the subject of any pending proceeding under § 8 of the Securities Act, or has been the subject of any refusal or stop order under § 8 in the past three years. (We discuss § 8 refusal and stop orders later in the chapter.) Issuers subject to a pending proceeding under § 8A in connection with an offering are also ineligible.

What kind of company qualifies as a WKSI? Clearly, the SEC has in mind relatively large market capitalization companies with equity trading in a liquid secondary market (and a corresponding following of research analysts). Companies such as Microsoft, IBM, and McDonald's will clearly qualify for WKSI status, absent any prior securities law violations, but many medium-size companies will also qualify. WKSI-eligible issuers represented approximately 30% of listed issuers, and accounted for about 95% of U.S. market capitalization in 2004.

A. PRE-FILING PERIOD

The Pre–Filing Period runs until the registration statement is filed with the SEC. Two key provisions of § 5 of the Securities Act govern this period. Section 5(a) prohibits all sales until the registration statement becomes effective. Section 5(c) bans all offers prior to the filing of the

[handwritten margin notes:]
60 days w/ determ date
• 700m common equity w/wide
• 1 bill aggregate securities (3 years)
• 75m in common equity

Ineligible issuers
- w/ past 3 years were blank check or shell co.
- filed bankrupt. petition (w/3 years) unless audit that recovered.
- SEC proceedings now or 3/years.

- Large com with equity trading in a liquid second. market.

Pre-filing [until RS is filed]
5a - prohibits sales
5c - prohibits offers

registration statement. Once the Waiting Period commences, § 5(c) no longer applies:

quiet period   *offer*   *sales*

Pre–Filing Period | Waiting Period | Post–Effective Period

§ 5(a) *prohibits sales* ————————→

§ 5(c) *prohibits offers.* —→

1. WHAT IS AN "OFFER"

Key to understanding the Pre–Filing Period is § 5(c). Section 5(c) restricts all "offers" until a registration statement is filed with the SEC. The quiet period imposed on companies is a direct consequence of the broad definition the securities laws give to the term "offer." Section 2(a)(3) of the Securities Act defines "offer," but much of the meaning of what constitutes an "offer" is found in SEC administrative rulings and a series of SEC Securities Act Releases.

The SEC has long held the view that the term "offer" is broader than communication including an explicit offer of securities for sale. In the SEC's view "offer" encompasses all communications that may "condition" the market for the securities. The SEC in, *In the Matter of Carl M. Loeb, Rhoades & Co.* (February 9, 1959) wrote:

The broad sweep of [the definition of an offer under § 2(a)(3)] is necessary to accomplish the statutory purposes in the light of the process of securities distribution as it exists in the United States. Securities are distributed in this country by a complex and sensitive machinery geared to accomplish nationwide distribution of large quantities of securities with great speed. Multi-million dollar issues are often oversubscribed on the day the securities are made available for sale. This result is accomplished by a network of prior informal indications of interest or offers to buy between underwriters and dealers and between dealers and investors based upon mutual expectations that, at the moment when sales may legally be made, many prior indications will immediately materialize as purchases. It is wholly unrealistic to assume in this context that "offers" must take any particular legal form. Legal formalities come at the end to record prior understandings, but it is the procedures by which these prior understandings, embodying investment decisions, are obtained or generated which the Securities Act was intended to reform....

[W]e have made clear our position that the statute prohibits issuers, underwriters and dealers from initiating a public sales campaign prior to the filing of a registration statement by means of publicity efforts which, even though not couched in terms of an express offer, condition the public mind or arouse public interest in the particular securities....

We accordingly conclude that publicity, prior to the filing of a registration statement by means of public media of communication, with respect to an issuer or it securities, emanating from broker dealer

OFFER under 2(a)(3)

firms who as underwriters or prospective underwriters have negotiated or are negotiating for a public offering of the securities of such issuer, must be presumed to set in motion or to be a part of the distribution process and therefore to involve an offer to sell or a solicitation of an offer to buy such securities prohibited by Section 5(c) ....

publicity by public media from broken/dealer, underwriter

– is presumed to be part of distribution → Involves offer.

Brokers and dealers properly and commendably provide their customers with a substantial amount of information concerning business and financial developments of interest to investors, including information with respect to particular securities and issuers. Section 5, nevertheless, prohibits selling efforts in connection with a proposed public distribution of securities prior to the filing of a registration statement and, as we have indicated, this prohibition includes any publicity which is in fact a part of a selling effort. Indeed, the danger to investors from publicity amounting to a selling effort may be greater in cases where an issue has "news value" since it may be easier to whip up a "speculative frenzy" concerning the offering by incomplete or misleading publicity and thus facilitate the distribution of an unsound security at inflated prices. This is precisely the evil which the Securities Act seeks to prevent.

QUESTIONS

1. What counts as an offer?

2. If investors eventually will receive (or have access to) a final statutory prospectus, why does it matter that they earlier obtain information that "conditions" the market?

Securities Act Release No. 3844

Securities and Exchange Commission (Oct. 8, 1957).

* * *

A basic purpose of the Securities Act of 1933 [and] the Securities Exchange Act of 1934 ... is to require the dissemination of adequate and accurate information concerning issuers and their securities in connection with the offer and sale of securities to the public, and the publication periodically of material business and financial facts, knowledge of which is essential to an informed trading market in such securities.

There has been an increasing tendency ... to give publicity through many media concerning corporate affairs which goes beyond the statutory requirements. This practice reflects a commendable and growing recognition on the part of industry and the investment community of the importance of informing security holders and the public generally with respect to important business and financial developments.

This trend should be encouraged. It is necessary, however, that corporate management, counsel, underwriters, dealers and public relations firms recognize that the Securities Acts impose certain responsibilities and limitations upon persons engaged in the sale of securities and that publicity and public relations activities under certain circumstances may involve violations of the securities laws and cause serious embarrassment to issuers and underwriters in connection with the timing and marketing of an issue of securities. These violations not only pose enforcement and administrative problems for the Commission, they may also give rise to civil liabilities by the seller of securities to the purchaser....

The terms "sale," "sell," "offer to sell" and "offer for sale" are broadly defined in Section 2[a](3) of the Act and these definitions have been liberally construed by the Commission and the courts.

It follows from the express language and the legislative history of the Securities Act that an issuer, underwriter or dealer may not legally begin a public offering or initiate a public sales campaign prior to the filing of a registration statement. It apparently is not generally understood, however, that the publication of information and statements, and publicity efforts, generally, made in advance of a proposed financing, although not couched in terms of an express offer, may in fact contribute to conditioning the public mind or arousing public interest in the issuer or in the securities of an issuer in a manner which raises a serious question whether the publicity is not in fact part of the selling effort....

Example #1

An underwriter-promoter is engaged in arranging for the public financing of a mining venture to explore for a mineral which has certain possible potentialities for use in atomic research and power. While preparing a registration statement for a public offering, the underwriter-promoter distributed several thousand copies of a brochure which described in glowing generalities the future possibilities for use of the mineral and the profit potential to investors who would share in the growth prospects of a new industry. The brochure made no reference to any issuer or any security nor to any particular financing. It was sent out, however, bearing the name of the underwriting firm and obviously was designed to awaken an interest which later would be focused on the specific financing to be presented in the prospectus shortly to be sent to the same mailing list.

The distribution of the brochure under these circumstances clearly was the first step in a sales campaign to effect a public sale of the securities and as such, in the view of the Commission, violated Section 5 of the Securities Act.

Example #2

An issuer in the promotional stage intended to offer for public sale an issue of securities the proceeds of which were to be employed to explore for and develop a mineralized area. The promoters and prospective underwriter prior to the filing of the required registration statement ... arranged for a series of press releases describing the activities of the company, its proposed program of development of its properties, estimates of ore reserves and plans for a processing plant. This publicity campaign continued after the filing of a registration statement and during the period of the offering. The press releases, which could be easily reproduced and employed by dealers and salesmen engaged in the sales effort, contained representations, forecasts and quotations which could not have been supported as reliable data for inclusion in a prospectus or offering circular under the sanctions of the Act.

It is the Commission's view that issuing information of this character to the public by an issuer or underwriter through the device of the press release and the press interview is an evasion of the requirements of the Act governing selling procedures, a violation of Sections 5 and 17(a) of the Act, and that such activity subjects the seller to the risk of civil and penal sanctions and liabilities of the Act.

* * *

Example #6

* * *

The president of a company accepted, in August, an invitation to address a meeting of a security analysts' society to be held in February of the following year for the purpose of informing the membership concerning the company, its plans, its record and problems. By January a speech had been prepared together with supplemental information and data, all of which was designed to give a fairly comprehensive picture of the company, the industry in which it operates and various factors affecting its future growth. Projections of demand, operations and profits for future periods were included. The speech and the other data had been printed and it was intended that several hundred copies would be available for distribution at the meeting. In addition, since it was believed that stockholders, creditors, and perhaps customers might be interested in the talk, it was intended to mail to such persons and to a list of other selected firms and institutions copies of the material to be used at the analysts' meeting.

Later in January, a public financing by the company was authorized, preparation of a registration statement was begun and negotiation with underwriters was commenced. It soon appeared that the coming meeting of analysts, scheduled many months earlier, would be or about the time the registration statement was to be filed. This presented the question whether, in the circumstances, delivery and distribution of the speech and the supporting data to the various persons mentioned above would contravene provisions of the Securities Act.

It seemed clear that the scheduling of the speech had not been arranged in contemplation of a public offering by the issuer at or about the time of its delivery. In the circumstances, no objection was raised to the delivery of the speech at the analysts' meeting. However, since printed copies of the speech might be received by a wider audience, it was suggested that printed copies of the speech and the supporting data not be made available at the meeting nor be transmitted to other persons.

* * *

Securities Act Release No. 5180

Securities and Exchange Commission (Oct. 16, 1971).

The Commission today took note of situations when issuers whose securities are "in registration" may have [to] refuse to answer legitimate inquiries from stockholders, financial analysts, the press, or other persons concerning the company or some aspect of its business. The Commission hereby emphasizes that there is no basis in the securities acts or in any policy of the Commission which would justify the practice of non-disclosure of factual information by a publicly held company on the grounds that it has securities in registration under the Securities Act of 1933. Neither a company in registration nor its representatives should instigate publicity for the purpose of facilitating the sale of securities in a proposed offering. Further, any publication of information by a company in registration other than by means of a statutory prospectus should be limited to factual information and should not include such things as predictions, projections, forecasts or opinions with respect to value.

GUIDELINES

The Commission strongly suggests that all issuers establish internal procedures designed to avoid problems relating to the release of corporate information when in registration. As stated above, issuers and their representatives should not initiate publicity when in registration, but should nevertheless respond to legitimate inquiries for factual information about the company's financial condition and business operations. Further, care should be exercised so that, for example, predictions, projections, forecasts, estimates and opinions concerning value are not given with respect to such things, among other, as sales and earnings and value of the issuer's securities.

It has been suggested that the Commission promulgate an all inclusive list of permissible and prohibited activities in this area. This is not feasible for the reason that determinations are based upon the particular facts of each case. However, the Commission as a matter of policy encourages the flow of factual information to shareholders and the investing public. Issuers in this regard should:

1. Continue to advertise products and services.

2. Continue to send out customary quarterly, annual and other periodic reports to stockholders.

3. Continue to publish proxy statements and send out dividend notices.

4. Continue to make announcements to the press with respect to factual business and financial development; i.e., receipt of a contract, the settlement of a strike, the opening of a plant, or similar events of interest to the community in which the business operates.

5. Answer unsolicited telephone inquiries from stockholders, financial analysts, the press and others concerning factual information.

6. Observe an 'open door' policy in responding to unsolicited inquiries concerning factual matters from securities analysts, financial analysts, security holders, and participants in the communications field who have a legitimate interest in the corporation's affairs.

7. Continue to hold stockholder meetings as scheduled and to answer sharcholders' inquiries at stockholder meetings relating to factual matters.

In order to curtail problems in this area, issuers in this regard should avoid:

1. Issuance of forecasts, projections, or predictions relating but not limited to revenues, income or earnings per share.

2. Publishing opinions concerning values.

* * *

NOTES

1. *"Conditioning" the market.* The SEC actively polices efforts that may condition the market prior to the effective date of the registration statement. Leading up to the initial public offering of Salesforce.com, a provider of customer relationship management software, the CEO of Salesforce.com told a reporter that "the S.E.C. prohibits me from making any statements that would hype my I.P.O.," and the statement was subsequently released in a *New York Times* article. The CEO also discussed "the software business and his competitors" in the article. The SEC deemed these communications as conditioning the market and forced Salesforce.com to delay its initial public offering. See Laurie J. Flynn and Andrew Ross Sorkin, *Salesforce.com Is Said To Delay Its Public Offering*, New York Times, May 19, 2004. Why is delaying the offer the usual remedy for § 5(c) violations? The SEC believes that delay will allow any conditioning of the market to subside.

2. *The Pre–Filing Period.* When does the Pre–Filing Period begin? This question is important because companies in the Pre–Filing Period enter into a quiet period during which a company and others associated with the offering may communicate about the offering or the company's future prospects only at their own peril. The SEC in Release No. 5180 notes that the Pre–Filing Period begins once the company is "in registration." But when does this occur?

Rule 163A provides a safe harbor for the issuer clarifying when the Pre–Filing Period begins. Communications made by the issuer, or those working on behalf of an issuer (other than an underwriter or dealer participating in the offering), prior to 30 days before the filing of the registration statement with the SEC are excluded from the definition of an "offer" for purposes of § 5(c). To be eligible for the safe harbor, the communication may not refer to the offering. In addition, the issuer must "take reasonable steps within its control to prevent further distribution or publication of the information during the 30–day period immediately before the issuer files the registration statement." Regulation FD's prohibition on selective disclosures (discussed in Chapter 4) applies to communications under the safe harbor. The safe harbor is not available for certain issuers, such as blank check and shell companies and penny stock issuers, and for certain types of offerings, such as business combination transactions.

3. *The Internet.* The growth of the Internet has provided issuers with a new medium through which to communicate with investors, posing new challenges for both the SEC and issuers. Information provided through the worldwide web is unique because different websites are interconnected through "hyperlinks." An investor accessing finance.yahoo.com, for example, may learn about a particular issuer and then click on a link to go to that issuer's homepage to continue the research. Such hyperlinks make obtaining relevant information quick and easy for investors, but do hyperlinks run afoul of the gun-jumping rules?

As part of the 2005 Public Offering Reforms, the SEC mandated the treatment of all non-real time electronic communication offering securities for sale as "graphic communications" and, thus, a written offer for purposes of the Securities Act. See Rule 405. Thus, emails, videotapes, CD–ROMs, and recorded electronic version of roadshow presentations that offer securities for sale are all written offers. (Roadshows and other communications distributed electronically on a "real time" basis, however, are treated as oral communications.)

[handwritten margin note: Roadshows → oral commun.]

The SEC also clarified the treatment of hyperlinks from one web page to another. Rule 433 provides that written offers includes offers of the issuer's securities that are "contained on an issuer's Web site or hyperlinked by the issuer from the issuer's Web site to a third party's Web site." Rule 433(e)(1). For example, hyperlinks included within a written communication offering the issuer's securities that connect to another web site or to other information are considered part of that written communication. Rule 433 excludes "historical issuer information" contained in a separate section on the issuer's Web site from the definition of written offers unless the information was incorporated by reference, included in a prospectus of the issuer used in the offering, or otherwise used or referred to in the offering. Rule 433(e)(2).

[handwritten margin note: pure factual info → ok. soft info → predictions]

A common theme throughout the SEC releases is the distinction between "purely factual" disclosure of information and disclosures that refer to the offering directly or make forecasts, projections, or predictions (so-called "soft" information). Although avoiding disclosures that refer to the offering is relatively straightforward, how are issuers to determine which disclosures are purely factual? Exchange Act reporting issuers face both periodic disclosure requirements and a constant stream of questions from analysts and the investing public. How can such an issuer balance these demands for information with the imposition of a quiet period for disclosures that do not meet the purely factual standard? Achieving such a balance turns on how clearly the releases define such purely factual disclosures.

The SEC clarified what counts as an offer under the gun-jumping rules with several new safe harbors in its 2005 Public Offering Reforms. In addition to the Rule 163A safe harbor for communications occurring prior to 30 days before the filing of the registration statement, the SEC provided two additional safe harbors for regularly released business and forward-looking information as described below.

Reporting Issuer Safe Harbor—Rule 168 of the Securities Act allows most Exchange Act reporting issuers (and those working on their behalf, other than underwriters and dealers participating in the offering) to continue the regular release of "factual business information" and "forward-looking information." Information in periodic reports (e.g., a 10–K) and other materials filed with the SEC are included within the safe harbor. Rule 168 provides an exemption from § 5(c)'s prohibition on offers in the Pre–Filing period. By excluding communications from the definition of an offer, the Rule also exempts communications from § 2(a)(10)'s definition of "prospectus" and thereby excludes the communications from the application of § 5(b)(1) in the Waiting and Post–Effective periods.

Factual business information includes, among other things, factual information about the issuer and its business, advertisements of the issuer's products or services, and factual information contained in the issuer's periodic Exchange Act reports. Forward-looking information that is permitted includes financial projections, statements about the issuer management's plans and the issuer's future economic performance, and any underlying assumptions. Allowing reporting issuers the ability to publish or disseminate certain forward-looking information during a public offering is a dramatic change from the SEC's hostile attitude toward forward-looking information set forth in the Releases above. As a condition to use Rule 168, the issuer must have "previously released or disseminated" the same type of information in the "ordinary course of its business" and the information must be "materially consistent in timing, manner and form" with the issuer's similar past releases or disseminations of such information. Rule 168(d). The safe harbor does not cover information relating to the offering itself.

Non-Reporting Issuer Safe Harbor—Analogous to the safe harbor under Rule 168 for reporting issuers, Rule 169 of the Securities Act allows for the continuing disclosure of "factual business information" by or on behalf of non-Exchange Act reporting issuers (i.e., most IPO issuers). Underwriters and dealers participating in the offering may not make use of Rule 169. As with Rule 168, Rule 169 provides an exemption from § 5(c)'s prohibition on offers in the Pre–Filing Period. By excluding communications from the definition of an offer, the Rule also exempts communications from § 2(a)(10)'s definition of "prospectus" for purposes of § 5(b)(1) in the Waiting and Post–Effective periods.

Unlike Rule 168, however, Rule 169 does not exempt forward-looking information from the definition of an offer. (Information relating to the offering is also ineligible). Rule 169 tracks Rule 168's requirements that the issuer have previously released or disseminated information of the same type in the ordinary course of business and in the same "timing, manner, and form." Rule 169 also requires that the information must have been disseminated previously to "persons, such as customers and suppliers, other than in their capacities as investors or potential investors in the issuer's securities, by the issuer's employees or agents who regularly and historically have provided such information to such persons." Rule 169(d)(3).

(thereby reducing their risk). The investment banks acting as dealers will earn no more than the standard dealer's commission from their sales. Harold, on behalf of Sparrow Securities, readily agrees to this arrangement from the prospective dealers' counter-proposal.

4.   Sparrow Securities sends Omri, a recent business school graduate working for Harold, to get Smartway ready for the public offering. Omri goes over Smartway's books, corporate records, board minutes and other records. He also has extensive discussions with Smartway's auditors, Ernst & Arthur. After some thought, Omri recommends that Smartway reincorporate in Delaware, adopt anti-takeover protections (including a classified board of directors), and convert all existing preferred shares into common stock. Are Omri's discussions with Ernst & Arthur okay?

To reduce the tension between timely disclosure and the impact of gun-jumping rules, the SEC has promulgated a number of safe harbor rules. Rule 135, for example, provides a safe harbor for short, factual notices of a proposed registered offering.

Consider the structure of the Rule 135 safe harbor. First, Rule 135 applies only for the issuer, any other security holder selling in the offering (e.g., if the insiders are selling some of their shares in the public offering), and those working on behalf of either of these parties. Second, Rule 135 excludes notices meeting its requirements from the definition of "offer" for purposes of § 5. What legal conclusions are avoided by escaping the definition of "offer"? During the Pre–Filing Period, § 5(c) prohibits all offers. Thus, communications meeting the requirements of Rule 135 do not run afoul of § 5(c)'s prohibition. The more general ban on sales in § 5(a), however, continues in force. As we will see when we cover the Waiting Period, § 5(b) continues with a prohibition on most written offers (included within the definition of a "prospectus"). Because Rule 135 generally excludes the communications it requires from the scope of an "offer," Rule 135 also exempts them from the definition of a prospectus for purposes of § 5(b).

Rule 135 places tight limits on the information that may be disclosed. The communication may, among other things, identify the issuer, the amount and basic terms of the offered securities, the purpose of the offering, and the anticipated timing of the offering. Outside of these narrow areas, communication is not protected under Rule 135. Notably, the underwriter cannot be identified by name (which makes it difficult for the underwriter to rely on Rule 135). On the other hand, failure to meet the terms of Rule 135 does not necessarily mean that § 5(c) has been violated. Instead, the absence of the Rule 135 safe harbor means only that issuers (and others) must contend with the uncertain question of whether their communications fall within the definition of "offer."

Given the SEC's adoption of new safe harbors as part of the 2005 Public Offering Reforms under Rules 163 (for well-known seasoned issuers), 163A (prior to the 30 day period before filing of the registration statement), 168 (factual and forward-looking statements by a reporting issuer) and 169 (factual statements by a non-reporting issuer), what function does Rule 135 continue to play? Consider the situation of a non-WKSI issuing a factual notice related to the offering prior to the filing of the registration statement.

HYPOTHETICAL THREE

Excited by the prospect of Smartway's upcoming public offering, Sherry puts out a press release on Smartway's plans for the IPO. The press release mentions that Smartway expects to raise $200 million for the offering and that the proceeds will be used to expand Smartway's business through a nationwide advertising campaign. The press release does not mention Sparrow Securities by name, instead only stating "a well-known, national investment bank has agreed in principle to act as our managing underwriter." Any problems?

B. WAITING PERIOD

After filing its registration statement with the SEC, the issuer enters into the "Waiting Period." This refers to waiting for the SEC's Division of Corporation Finance to declare the registration statement effective. Two important and separate tasks take place during the Waiting Period. First, the issuer and underwriters attempt to gauge market interest in the offering. Second, the SEC may review the registration statement before declaring it effective.

In this section, we consider (1) the mechanism for gauging market sentiment, and (2) the process of becoming effective and the SEC enforcement powers relating to registration. During the Waiting Period, the gun-jumping rules continue to restrict issuers and their affiliates from conditioning the market (albeit in a less intrusive fashion). For companies with an active secondary trading market prior to the offering, however, it is nonetheless important to allow information to flow out to investors. We also consider here safe harbors for analyst communications of opinions on investments to investors, which apply throughout the public offering process.

1. GAUGING MARKET SENTIMENT

Issuers and underwriters typically promote their offering and obtain feedback from the market during the Waiting Period. Underwriters doing a firm commitment offering are particularly keen to learn about the market's reaction to the prospective offering. Recall that in a firm commitment offering, both the underwriter's own money and (indirectly) its reputation for bringing quality, well-priced offerings to the market are on the line. Underwriters that price an offering too high will end up holding unsold allotments of the offered securities. Those who price the offering too low may leave the issuer with smaller proceeds.

During the Pre–Filing Period, § 5(c) leaves little room to gauge market sentiment. Section 5(c) restricts all offers prior to the filing of the registration statement. As we saw above, this restriction on offers, combined with the broad definition of offers under § 2(a)(3), leads to an almost complete prohibition on communications relating to the offering in the Pre–Filing Period for non-well known seasoned issuers. (Recall though that Rule 163 dramatically expands the ability of well-known seasoned issuers to discuss the offering in the Pre–Filing Period.) With the filing of the registration statement, however, § 5(c) no longer applies, but § 5(b)(1) steps in during the Waiting Period to restrict the transmission, through interstate commerce, of any "prospectus" not meeting the requirements of the statutory prospectus as set forth in § 10 of the Securities Act. Note also that § 5(a) still prohibits sales during the Waiting Period.

[Handwritten margin note: During PRE-Filing → almost complete prohibition on non-well known seasoned issuers]

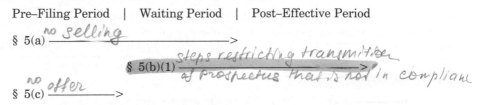

Pre–Filing Period | Waiting Period | Post–Effective Period

§ 5(a) —— *no selling* ——————>

§ 5(b)(1) *steps restricting transmitter of prospectus that is not in compliance* ——>

§ 5(c) —— *no offer* ——>

Section 5(b)(1) prohibits the transmission of prospectuses not meeting the requirements of § 10, but permits both preliminary and final prospectuses. The definition of a prospectus under § 2(a)(10) of the Securities Act is key to understanding the extent of § 5(b)(1)'s prohibition. Although generally defining a prospectus to include all "prospectuses," § 2(a)(10) also includes any "notice, circular, advertisement, letter, or communication, written or by radio or television, which offers any security for sale or confirms the sale of any security" in the definition of a prospectus. Note two things about this definition: (a) the breadth of the types of communication included and (b) the requirement that communication must either offer the security or confirm the sale of the security to qualify as a "prospectus." What types of communications "offer" the security for sale? Section 2(a)(3)'s definition of an offer continues to provide the answer.

Thus, § 2(a)(10)'s prospectus definition sweeps in all written and broadcast communications offering the security; § 5(b) then prohibits such communications if they do not comply with § 10. Section 10(b) authorizes a preliminary prospectus that can be used to satisfy § 5(b)(1) in the Waiting Period. Section 10(a) defines the final prospectus that must be distributed to investors in the Post–Effective Period. To understand how this works, consider the following relationships within the Securities Act:

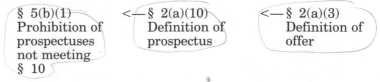

§ 5(b)(1)   <— § 2(a)(10)   <— § 2(a)(3)
Prohibition of   Definition of   Definition of
prospectuses   prospectus   offer
not meeting
§ 10

In practice, § 5(b)(1) reintroduces the general prohibition on offers placed on all communications in the Pre–Filing Period, but because the prohibition is now limited to offers by means of a prospectus not complying with § 10, the restriction is not as broad as in the § 5(c) prohibition on all offers during the Pre–Filing Period. Written offers in the form of a preliminary prospectus under § 10(b) are explicitly permitted and only written and broadcast communications are restricted in the Waiting Period. By negative implication, oral communications not involving a broadcast medium are permitted during the Waiting Period. In addition, the SEC has provided issuers with additional latitude for gauging market sentiment through a number of safe harbors. Consider the following forms of available communication in the Waiting Period.

a. The Preliminary Prospectus

Under Securities Act Rule 430, the preliminary prospectus must contain essentially the same information as the final statutory prospectus, with the exception of price-related information. Typically, the issuer and the managing underwriter will set the price just before the registration statement is declared effective. (Setting the price earlier imposes large risks on the underwriters in a firm commitment offering—what happens if the prevailing market price turns out to be different from the price set?) The final prospectus may reflect changes in the offering or revisions based on the SEC's comments on the preliminary prospectus. Reporting issuers may also use a Rule 431 summary prospectus during the Waiting Period, but few do.

b. The Roadshow

Underwriters and issuers rely on their ability to make oral offers to conduct "roadshows" across the country to pitch their offered securities to potential investors. Typically conducted over a two-week period, the road-show allows the issuer's top management and representatives from the managing underwriter the chance to sell the offering in face-to-face discussions with institutional investors across the country.

c. The Free Writing Prospectus

Rule 164 allows issuers more freedom to distribute prospectuses that do not meet the requirements of a formal § 10(b) preliminary prospectus in the Waiting Period (termed "free writing prospectuses"). Free writing prospectuses (discussed in greater detail below) complying with the requirements of Rule 433 used after the filing of the registration statement by an issuer and other offering participants, including underwriters and dealers, are treated as a § 10(b) prospectus. Once categorized as a § 10(b) prospectus, a free writing prospectus satisfies § 5(b)(1)'s requirement that all prospectuses in the Waiting Period meet the requirements of § 10.

d. "Tombstone" advertisements

Even for prospectuses that fail to meet the requirements of § 10, the SEC provides other safe harbors. Although Rule 135 continues to apply in the Waiting Period, the SEC provides broader safe harbors for communications during the Waiting Period. Securities Act Rule 134 provides far more leeway for issuers seeking to disclose information on the offering and on their own business to the investing public. Moreover, not only the issuer, but also the underwriters, can use Rule 134.

What protection is afforded by coming within Rule 134's safe harbor for "tombstone" advertisements? When it applies, Rule 134 excludes communications from the definition of a prospectus under § 2(a)(10). (Note that the last clause of § 2(a)(10) allows the SEC to exclude written offers to sell from the definition of a prospectus.) Recall that § 5(b)(1) prohibits transmission of a prospectus that does not meet the requirements of § 10 (the formal statutory prospectus). By excluding written notices from the broad definition of a prospectus contained in § 2(a)(10), Rule 134 excludes those notices from the prohibition of § 5(b)(1). As long as no sales take place (still prohibited by § 5(a)), notices complying with Rule 134 are exempted from the gun-jumping rules. Communications under Rule 134 are also excluded from the definition of a "free writing prospectus" under Rule 405.

Rule 134 offers no protection, however, in the Pre–Filing Period. Why? Recall that § 5(c) prohibits all offers in the Pre–Filing Period. Rule 134, which only excludes communications from the definitions of a prospectus and a free writing prospectus, does not limit the reach of § 5(c), which forbids all "offers," written or oral.

What kind of information is permitted under Rule 134? Among other things, Rule 134 allows the disclosure of the issuer's legal identity and business location, the amount and type of security to be offered, the business of the issuer, and the price of the security are all permitted. Other information about the issuer permitted includes "the address, phone number and e-mail address of the issuer's principal offices" as well as the "geographic areas in which it conducts business." Rule 134(a)(1). The names of all the underwriters, not just the managing underwriters, and their roles in the offering as well as a description of the marketing events, such as roadshow presentations, and a description of the procedures through which the underwriters will conduct the offering are permissible under Rule 134(a)(10), (11) and (12). Rule 134 also provides for disclosure of the identity of any selling security holders if included in the registration statement, the names of securities exchanges or other securities markets where the securities will be listed, and the ticker symbol. Rule 134(a)(18), (19), (20).

In addition to allowing these categories of information, Rule 134(b) mandates the disclosure of certain information, including a boilerplate legend indicating that securities may not be sold prior to the registration statement becoming effective. Rule 134(b) also requires the disclosure of the name and address of a person from whom an investor may obtain a § 10 statutory prospectus. These mandatory disclosures are not required if the communication is accompanied (or preceded) by a § 10 statutory prospectus (other than a free writing prospectus) or if the Rule 134 notice "does no more than state from whom a written prospectus meeting the requirements of § 10 of the Act may be obtained, identify the security, state the price thereof and state by whom orders will be executed.'' Rule 134(c).

Rule 134 does not allow the disclosure of a detailed description of the offered securities, such as a term sheet. Issuers may, nonetheless, transmit written details about the terms of the offering through other means in the Waiting Period, such as a free writing prospectus.

e. Solicitations of interest

Rule 134 also enables issuers to obtain indications of interest from investors. Under Rule 134(d), if a § 10 statutory prospectus (other than a free writing prospectus) accompanies or precedes a Rule 134 communication, the communication may solicit an offer to buy or some other indication of interest. Rule 134(d) provides for a mandatory boilerplate legend advising the investor of his or her right to revoke the offer to buy prior to acceptance by the underwriter and that indications of interest involve no legal obligation. (Expressions of interest that are not followed by actual orders, however, may lead the underwriters to exclude the investor from subsequent offerings.)

No legal obligation to buy.

The requirement that a § 10 prospectus precede or accompany a communication under Rules 134(c) and 134(d) is satisfied if the communication is electronic and contains an active hyperlink to the § 10 prospectus. Communications relating to an investment company or business development company are excluded from Rule 134's safe harbor.

HYPOTHETICAL FOUR

Sherry, working closely with Harold and Sparrow Securities, filed a registration statement for Smartway's offering with the SEC. Sherry is eager to take Smartway's story to investors and persuade them to purchase stock in the upcoming IPO. Do any of the following scenarios (all during the Waiting Period) violate the gun-jumping rules?

1. *Scenario One*: Sherry and Harold hold a series of meetings with large institutional investors interested in investing in high-growth, initial public offering stock. They fly to Boston, New York, Miami, Chicago, Los Angeles, and other cities over a couple of weeks. In each city, they make a presentation to a group of investors and answer questions.

2. *Scenario Two*: Larissa, a broker working for Sparrow Securities, learns of the upcoming Smartway offering through internal communications within Sparrow. She immediately calls her list of "favored" investor-clients consisting of all recent college graduates from her alma mater which she obtains from her school's alumni web site. For each potential investor who takes her call (a distressingly low percentage!), she spends about five minutes touting Smartway's great growth prospects, the strength of the management team, and the tendency of IPO stocks to rise quickly in price after the offering.

3. *Scenario Three*: Sherry has Smartway's investor relations staff put together an advertisement touting the upcoming offering for placement in the *Wall Street Journal*. Among other things, the advertisement is directed at "investors who want a high return" and states Smartway's intent to sell $200 million in common stock within the next year. The ad also includes a detailed five–year projection of future profits. The advertisement does not, however, mention Sparrow Securities.

4.   *Scenario Four*: Sherry has the investor relations people at Smartway put together a "tombstone" announcement of the offering that is carried in the *Wall Street Journal*. The tombstone mentions Sparrow Securities and Smartway and has a brief description of Smartway's business. In addition, the tombstone provides a summary table of the past three years audited income statements of Smartway (including revenues, costs, and earnings). Finally, the advertisement includes the standard legend indicating that no sales can be made before the effective date.

5.   *Scenario Five*: Larissa mails out a copy of the preliminary prospectus (omitting, among other things, the pricing information on the offering) to all the members of her college graduating class. She includes with the preliminary prospectus a letter stating, "I think this is a good investment that might interest you. Please call me if you want to talk further about Smartway's upcoming public offering. Go Bears!"

2.   FREE WRITING PROSPECTUSES

Written and broadcast communications that offer to purchase or solicit an offer to buy securities are traditionally prohibited in the Waiting Period through the interaction of § 2(a)(10) (providing for a broad definition of prospectus) and § 5(b)(1) (§ 10 prospectus delivery requirement). Perhaps the biggest change in the 2005 Public Offering Reforms is the SEC's decision to allow free writing prior to the effective date of the registration statement under the concept of "free writing prospectus." The new "free writing prospectus" expands the ability of issuers to distribute prospectuses not meeting the requirements of a formal § 10 prospectus. Under Rule 164, a free writing prospectus that meets the requirements of Rule 433 is treated as § 10(b) prospectus for purposes of § 5(b)(1). Once categorized as a § 10(b) prospectus, a free writing prospectus satisfies § 5(b)(1)'s requirement that prospectuses meet the requirements of § 10. As a consequence, issuers and other offering participants, including underwriters and dealers, may send out a wide range of written (including broadcast and electronic) communications in the Waiting Period that raise interest in the offering.

a.   *Definition of a Free Writing Prospectus*

A free writing prospectus includes any written communication that offers to sell or solicits an offer to buy a security that is or will be subject to a registration statement and that does not meet the requirements of a § 10 statutory final or preliminary prospectus or a § 2(a)(10)(a) form of traditional free writing. Rule 405. Rule 405 goes on to define written communication to include written, printed, broadcast and graphic communications. Graphic communications, in turn, are defined to include "all forms of electronic media," such as e-mails, Web sites, CD–ROMS, videotapes, and "substantially similar messages widely distributed" over a variety of electronic communication networks. Significantly, the SEC excluded real-time electronic communication from the definition of graphic communication, leaving real-time electronic transmissions within the "oral" category of communication. Included in the definition of a free writing prospectus, however, are indirect communications from the issuer to the marketplace through media sources, including interviews given by corporate officers that could be construed as offering a security.

real-time electronic communications → oral categorys

b. Issuer Requirements

For Rule 164 to apply, the issuer or other offering participant must meet the conditions set forth in Rule 433. Rule 433 provides for different requirements depending on the type of issuer as set forth below. (Rules 164 and 433 exclude certain ineligible issuers and transactions.)

Non–Reporting and Unseasoned Issuers—Use of free writing prospectuses is permitted only after the filing of the registration statement, so non-reporting and unseasoned issuers cannot use Rule 433 to communicate free writing prospectuses in the Pre–Filing Period. For free writing prospectuses made by the issuer or on behalf of the issuer, including any paid advertisement or publication, the free writing prospectus must be accompanied or preceded by the most recent statutory prospectus that satisfies the requirements of § 10, including a price range if required. If an electronic free writing prospectus is used, Rule 433 provides that issuers may meet the statutory prospectus delivery requirement by simply including a hyperlink to the issuer's most recent preliminary prospectus. For a free writing prospectus from a media source not affiliated with nor paid by the issuer or other offering participant, the statutory prospectus is not required to precede or accompany the media free writing prospectus. Rule 433(b)(2)(i).

Rule 433 - only after filing regist. st. ↳ free writing Pr + preliminary prospectus

If FWP is not affiliated and not paid → no prelim. pros. is required

Issuers that have already sent a statutory prospectus to an investor may send subsequent free writing prospectuses without any additional information so long as there have been no material changes in the information in the previously sent statutory prospectus. After the effective date of the registration statement, issuers must send a § 10(a) final prospectus either preceding or together with the free writing prospectus, even if an earlier preliminary prospectus was sent to the recipient. Rule 433(b)(2)(i).

Prelim + FWP ↳ Final prospec.

Seasoned Issuers and Well–Known Seasoned Issuers—Seasoned and well-known seasoned issuers, as well as other offering participants, may use a free writing prospectus at any time after the filing of the registration statement. As with non-reporting and unseasoned issuers, the exemption under Rules 164 and 433 applies only after the filing of a registration statement. The filed registration statement must contain a statutory prospectus that satisfies § 10 (including a "base prospectus" under Rule 430B for shelf registrations as discussed at the end of the chapter). Unlike non-reporting and unseasoned issuers, seasoned and WKSI issuers do not have to deliver the statutory prospectus to recipients of a free writing prospectus.

Recall that under Rule 163, a well-known seasoned issuer may also use a free writing prospectus or make oral offers prior to the filing of the registration statement. A WKSI and related offering participants do not have to deliver a statutory prospectus with the free writing prospectus and, instead, must only provide a legend indicating where to access or hyperlink to the preliminary or base prospectus. A WSKI may therefore distribute free writing prospectuses freely throughout the public offering process, using Rule 163 in the Pre–Filing Period and Rules 164 and 433 thereafter.

c.   *Disclosure, filing and retention requirements*

Rule 433 imposes two disclosure requirements. First, the free writing prospectus may not contain information that is inconsistent with information contained in either a filed statutory prospectus or a periodic or current report incorporated by reference into the registration statement. Rule 433(c)(1). Second, the free writing prospectus must include a specified legend indicating that the issuer has filed a registration statement with the SEC and where the recipient may obtain the preliminary or base prospectus. Rule 433(c)(2).

Rule 433 requires that certain free writing prospectuses be filed with the SEC. Once filed, the information is made available to the public through the SEC's EDGAR system. The issuer must file a free writing prospectus on or before the date of first use in two situations:

- Any "issuer free writing prospectus" used by any person;

- Any "issuer information" that is contained in a free writing prospectus prepared by any other person (but not information prepared by a person other than the issuer on the basis of issuer information).

Rule 433(d)(1). The issuer must also file "a description of the final terms of the issuer's securities in an offering or of the offering contained in a free writing prospectus or portion thereof prepared by or on behalf of the issuer or any offering participant, after such terms have been established." Rule 433(d)(1)(i)(C). The issuer does not need to file free writing prospectuses that contain terms that do not reflect the final terms. The issuer has until two days of the "later of the date such final terms have been established for all classes of the offering and the date of first use" to file the final terms. Rule 433(d)(5).

The application of the Rule 433 filing requirement is straightforward for "issuer free writing prospectuses" which are defined to encompass all information distributed by the issuer, on behalf of the issuer, or used or referred to by the issuer. Rule 433(h)(1). Such issuer free writing prospectuses must be filed with the SEC without exception. Less clear are the filing obligations resulting from free writing prospectuses of other persons, i.e., the underwriters. Rule 433(d)(1)(i)(B) requires the issuer to file free writing prospectuses prepared by other persons that contain "issuer information." Rule 433(h)(2) defines "issuer information" as "material information about the issuer or its securities that has been provided by or on behalf of the issuer." Issuers do not need to file the free writing prospectus of other persons if the prospectus is based on issuer information, but does not directly include such information. According to the SEC, "[e]xamples of this information would include information prepared by underwriters that could be, but would not be limited to, information that is proprietary to an underwriter." Securities Act Release No. 8501.

Rule 433 imposes filing obligations on persons other than the issuer. Other participants in the offering, including underwriters, must file free writing prospectuses that are distributed in "a manner that was reasonably designed to achieve broad unrestricted dissemination" unless previously filed with the SEC. Rule 433(d)(1)(ii). What is "broad unrestricted dissemination"? The SEC tells us that "[f]ree writing prospectuses sent directly to customers of an offering participant, without regard to number, would not be broadly disseminated." Securities Act Release No. 8501.

There are exceptions to the filing requirement. Issuers and other participants may avoid the filing requirement of Rule 433(d)(1) if the free writing prospectus does not contain "substantive changes from or additions to a free writing prospectus previously filed with the Commission." Rule 433(d)(3). Issuers do not need to file the free writing prospectus of other persons if the issuer information was already included in a previously filed prospectus or free writing prospectus. Rule 433(d)(4). Issuers transmitting pre-recorded versions of an electronic roadshow (considered a graphic communication) may qualify for free writing prospectus treatment under Rule 433 even if they do not file the roadshow with the SEC. Non-reporting issuers registering common equity or convertible equity securities, however, must file roadshows that qualify as written communications with the SEC unless the issuer makes a "bona fide" version of the roadshow available without restriction to any person. Rule 433(d)(8). To be "bona fide," one or more of an issuer's officers or other management personnel must make a presentation in the roadshow, among other requirements. Rule 433(h)(5).

Media sources, in the business of disseminating written communication, that publish or distribute a free writing prospectus containing information on the offering provided by the issuer or any person participating in the offering (e.g., an interview of the CEO of Smartway about the upcoming IPO) and who are not compensated by the issuer or other participants in the offering are exempt from the filing and information requirements under Rule 433. The issuer or other offering participant, however, must file the media communication with the required Rule 433 legend within four business days of becoming aware of the media communication. Rule 433(f)(1). Alternatively, the issuer or offering participant may file a copy of the all the materials provided to the media including "transcripts of interviews or similar materials." Rule 433(f)(2)(iii). The issuer or other offering participant may avoid filing the media communication if the substance of the communication was already filed with the SEC. Rule 433(f)(2)(i). The issuer or other offering participant may include additional information if the issuer or other offering participant believes it is needed to correct information included in the communication. Rule 433(f)(2(ii).

One concern with the greatly expanded filing requirements under the free writing prospectus rules is the possibility that an issuer may inadvertently fail to file by the required deadline (on or before the date of first use in the case of an issuer free writing prospectus). If that happens, the issuer risks a § 5 violation, exposing the issuer to potentially ruinous § 12(a)(1) liability (discussed in Chapter 8) if the issuer goes forward with the offering. To address this concern, the SEC allows issuers and other participants that immaterially or unintentionally miss the filing deadline for a free writing prospectus to cure the violation. Rule 164(b). The cure provision is only available if the issuer has acted in good faith and with reasonable care and issuer must cure the mistake by filing the free writing prospectus as soon as practicable after discovering the failure to file. Rule 164(c) also allows the issuer to cure an omission of the required legend in the free writing prospectus so long as the omission was made in good faith and after reasonable effort to comply with the requirement, the free writing prospectus is amended as soon as practicable to include the legend, and any recipients of the free writing prospectus without the legend are sent the version with the legend.

Finally, Rule 433(g) requires issuers and offering participants to retain any free writing prospectus that they have used for three years after the date of the initial bona fide offering of the securities. Immaterial or unintentional failure to follow the record retention requirement will not result in a violation of § 5(b)(1) so long as the issuer made a "good faith and reasonable effort" to comply with the requirement. Rule 164(d).

d.   Antifraud Liability and Regulation FD Implications

The free writing prospectus is not considered part of the formal registration statement and thus is not subject to potential § 11 antifraud liability. Nonetheless, free writing prospectuses are considered "public" communications under Rule 433(a) for purposes of § 12(a)(2) antifraud liability (as the term "public" is used by the Supreme Court in *Gustafson v. Alloyd Holdings*, covered in Chapter 8).

Regulation FD provides an exception for communications relating to a registered public offering. For the Pre–Filing Period safe harbors contained in Rules 163 (well-known seasoned issuer Pre–Filing offers) and 163A (greater than 30 days prior to filing exclusion) described above, the SEC provided an explicit exception to this Regulation FD exception (meaning that Regulation FD *does* apply to such communications). The SEC failed to provide a similar exception to the exception for free writing prospectuses under Rules 164 and 433. Why not? The exclusion from Regulation FD may not make much practical difference. Free writing prospectuses that include new information from the issuer must be filed with the SEC on or before their first day of use. The agency posts such filings on EDGAR, thus resulting in the board public dissemination of the information even without the application of Regulation FD.

HYPOTHETICAL FIVE

Sherry, the CEO of Smartway, working closely with Harold and Sparrow Securities, has filed a registration statement for Smartway's offering with the

SEC. Do any of the following scenarios (all during the Waiting Period) violate § 5?

1. *Scenario One*: Smartway mails out a glossy pamphlet containing a photograph of Sherry and detailed information on the offering and how the offering will be "rocket fuel" propelling Smartway's growth. The pamphlets are mailed to, among others, all the doctors and lawyers located in California and New York.

2. *Scenario Two*: Sherry decides to give an interview to *Business 2.0* magazine. In the interview, Sherry discusses the offering and her hope that Smartway's business will rapidly expand due to the capital provided by the offering. The *Business 2.0* article quotes the entire interview.

3. *Scenario Three*: Harold of Sparrow Securities sends out an information packet on the Smartway offering, including the basic terms and its own analysis of the valuation of the company, together with the preliminary prospectus to potential dealers in the offering and a select group of institutional investors that have participated in prior IPOs with Sparrow Securities. In constructing its valuation analysis, Sparrow relied on detailed financial information obtained from Smartway as well as discussions with Smartway's chief financial officer, Kumar. Sparrow Securities fails to file the information packet with the SEC.

4. *Scenario Four*: To help drum up more interest in Sparrow's upcoming IPO, Harold has Sparrow's brokerage department mail out the same information packet from Scenario Three to all the individual investor-clients with accounts at Sparrow.

5. *Scenario Five*: Recall that Sherry and Harold embarked on a "road show" across the country to pitch the offering to institutional investors. Suppose that Sherry has one of the road show presentations recorded and posted as a media file on the investor relations section of Smartway's website.

6. *Scenario Six*: Sparrow Securities sends an email to its investor clients containing a hyperlink to a PDF version of its preliminary prospectus. The email also contains hyperlinks to various press stories (in the *Wall Street Journal*, *Fortune*, etc.) discussing Smartway's upcoming offering.

———————

To summarize, the Waiting Period increases the available means of communicating "offers" through four broad avenues not generally available during the Pre–Filing Period:

(1) oral communications;

(2) statutory prospectuses under § 10(b) (see Rules 430, 431);

(3) tombstone and safe harbor statements (Rule 134, § 2(a)(10)(b)); and

(4) free writing prospectuses (Rules 164 and 433).

3. THE PROCESS OF GOING EFFECTIVE

While the issuer and managing underwriter busily encourage market interest during the Waiting Period, the registration statement sits with the SEC. The issuer must wait for the registration statement to become

[handwritten margin note: 20th day Effective]

"effective" before selling any securities to the public. Under § 8(a) of the Securities Act, a registration statement is supposed to become effective the "twentieth day" after the filing thereof." In practice, no issuer allows its registration statement to become effective automatically after twenty days. Instead, issuers commonly file a delaying amendment under Rule 473, waiting for the SEC to declare the registration statement effective. The SEC has the power under § 8(a) to accelerate the effective date of a registration statement. Typically, the issuer and the underwriters will file an acceleration request with the SEC at least two days prior to the offering's desired effective date.

[handwritten margin note: 461 – acceleration of Effective date]

Rule 461 outlines the factors the SEC weighs in deciding whether to grant a request for acceleration of the effective date. Among the factors that may result in a denial of acceleration include inaccurate or inadequate information in a material respect within the preliminary prospectus, failure to make a bona fide effort to conform the prospectus to the plain English requirements of Rule 421(d), a current SEC investigation of the issuer, a controlling person of the issuer, or one of the underwriters, and an objection by the NASD to the compensation to be paid to the underwriters and other broker-dealers participating in the offering. Rule 461 also stresses the importance of the "adequacy of information respecting the registrant . . . available to the public." Rule 460, in turn, states that one of the considerations in determining the adequacy of information is the distribution of the preliminary prospectus a reasonable time in advance of the anticipated effective date to each underwriter and dealer "reasonably anticipated" to be invited to participate in the offering. A sufficient number of copies of the preliminary prospectus should be provided to ensure "adequate distribution."

Why file a delaying amendment and wait for the SEC's approval? Why not just start selling twenty days after filing? First, under § 8(a), *any* amendment to the registration statement resets the filing date for purposes of determining when the registration statement becomes effective. Thus, issuers who intend to rely on the twenty day effective period instead of waiting for the SEC's approval must file a complete and final registration statement twenty days prior to making their first sale. The price, of course, is one of the items that must be disclosed in the registration statement.

[handwritten margin note: Filing complete RS would require fixing price 20 days before sale (before solicitation)]

Filing a complete registration statement would therefore require fixing the price twenty days before sale. Consider why an issuer would not want to fix the price of the offering twenty days before commencing any sales. If the price is fixed at $20, what if the price the market is willing to pay goes up to $25? What if the price the market is willing to pay goes down to $15? Recall that the underwriter is using the Waiting Period to assess investor sentiment through the roadshow. Note, however, that under Rule 430A, the issuer may, under certain circumstances, file a form of the prospectus that omits price-related information as part of the registration statement.

Second, as we will cover in Chapter 8, stringent antifraud provisions apply to misstatements and omissions in the registration statement and prospectus. Rather than face potentially crippling antifraud lawsuits, the issuer can obtain comments from the SEC identifying deficiencies and correct them before selling to the public.

Third, issuers that fail to afford the SEC the time the agency deems necessary risk a formal SEC refusal or stop order. The SEC has a number of formal powers with which to stop a registration statement's effectiveness. Section 8(b) of the Securities Act gives the SEC the authority to issue a refusal order preventing a registration statement from going effective if the registration statement is "on its face incomplete or inaccurate in any material respect." To issue a refusal order, the SEC must give the issuer notice within ten days of the filing of the registration statement. Moreover, the SEC must hold a hearing within ten days of the giving of notice. The wheels of government do not spin so fast, so the refusal authority is a largely empty threat.

A more potent threat is found in § 8(d), which authorizes the SEC to issue a stop order suspending the effectiveness of a registration statement. Under § 8(d), the SEC may issue a stop order if the registration statement contains "any untrue statement of a material fact or omits to state any material fact required to be stated therein or necessary to make the statements therein not misleading." As with the refusal order under § 8(b), the § 8(d) stop order requires both notice and a hearing within fifteen days of the giving of notice. To assist the SEC in determining whether to issue a stop order, § 8(e) authorizes the SEC to investigate the issuer and underwriters.

Stop order suspending Effectiveness of Reg. St.

The SEC review process is relatively informal. If the SEC finds the registration statement wanting during the comment period, it will typically send the issuer a comment letter. Issuers, of course, do not have to respond to the comment letter. But the SEC may refuse to accelerate effectiveness or, more drastically, initiate a formal investigation leading to a refusal or stop order. Suffice it to say that either of these events would put the issuer in a very bad light with investors.

comment letter ↓ stop ↓ investigation

The SEC's Division of Corporation Finance reviews some, but not all, registration statements. In 1980 the SEC adopted a policy of selective review. The SEC reviews all IPO registration statements, but only selected registration statements for seasoned offerings. On average, the review process takes a little over 40 days for IPOs. Seasoned offerings are reviewed far less frequently and for a shorter time. Non-shelf registrations on Form S–3 are reviewed less than 15% of the time and spend on average less than ten days with the SEC. See S.E.C., *Report of the Advisory Committee on Capital Formation and Regulatory Processes*, app. A. (1996).

Review – IPO

4. ANALYSTS

The gun-jumping rules restrict "offers" of securities. For non-public companies doing an IPO, the gun-jumping rules are only an inconvenience. Such companies typically have no audience of public investors prior to the

non-public IPO – inconvenience

offering. On the other hand, for companies whose shares are trading in the secondary market, the gun-jumping rules may chill the flow of information to secondary market investors. Although investors cannot buy the registered shares until the effective date, investors can purchase economically similar (and often identical) shares on the secondary market.

The issuer is not the only source of information on companies traded in the market. Securities analysts—whether independent or associated with a brokerage firm—provide a constant stream of information on many publicly-traded companies. When a company such as Microsoft—with an active secondary market and many analysts covering the company's stock—does a seasoned offering, should the securities laws restrict the disclosure to the secondary market of these analysts' recommendations? The SEC's definition of an "offer" is surely broad enough to capture such recommendations, which would put analysts and their employers at risk of violating § 5.

To avoid that conclusion, the SEC provides for various safe harbors for the publication or distribution of "research reports" under Rules 137, 138, and 139. Research reports are defined as a written communication that "includes information, opinions, or recommendations with respect to securities of an issuer or an analysis of a security of an issuer, whether or not it provides information reasonably sufficient upon which to base an investment decision." Rules 137(e), 138(d), 139(d). Rule 405 defines written communication to include broadcast and graphic communications (including e-mails and websites, among other forms of communication).

Rule 137 provides a safe harbor for broker-dealers not participating in the offering. If Rule 137 applies, the broker-dealer providing a research report on a security has not made an "offer" or "participated in an offering" within the definition of "underwriter" in § 2(a)(11). Note that Rule 137 does not exclude broker-dealers from the definition of a dealer, so broker-dealers excluded from the definition of an underwriter under Rule 137 still cannot take advantage of § 4(1). Section 4(1), recall, exempts transactions not involving any issuer, underwriter, or dealer. Broker-dealers fall within the definition of a "dealer" in § 2(a)(12) of the Securities Act, and therefore cannot rely on the § 4(1) exemption. Rule 137, instead allows unaffiliated broker-dealers making recommendations in their regular course of business to take advantage of § 4(3) (as interpreted by Rule 174, discussed below). The following diagram depicts the operation of Rule 137.

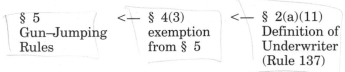

| § 5
Gun–Jumping
Rules | <— | § 4(3)
exemption
from § 5 | <— | § 2(a)(11)
Definition of
Underwriter
(Rule 137) |

The availability of a § 4(3) exemption from § 5 does not flow automatically from the application of Rule 137. Dealers can rely on § 4(3) if two conditions apply: (a) the dealer is not an underwriter and (b) the publication or distribution of research does not take place during the prospectus delivery requirement period as defined in § 4(3) in conjunction with Rule

174. Rule 137 only removes the dealer from the definition of an underwriter. Even with Rule 137, a non-participating broker-dealer must take care not to publish or distribute research that may condition the market during the prospectus delivery period. Fortunately, this is not a great constraint for non-participating broker-dealers providing research for Exchange Act reporting companies. Rule 174 reduces the prospectus delivery period for a previously reporting company to zero days.

How does a non-participating broker-dealer qualify for the protections of Rule 137? Rule 137 applies only to research reports that a broker-dealer publishes or distributes "in the regular course of its business." Rule 137 explicitly excludes from its coverage all broker-dealers who receive compensation from the issuer, selling security holder, other participants in the offering, or "any other person interested in the securities." (Regular subscription fees for research are allowed under Rule 137.) Rule 137 also does not apply for securities of issuers who, during the past three years, were a blank check company, shell company, or issuer in a penny stock offering.

[handwritten margin note: Broker-Dealer Research Reports in Regular course of Business — not an underwr. no compensation]

The SEC provides two alternative means in Rules 138 and 139 for broker-dealers participating in the distribution to provide opinions on companies during the registration process. (As with Rule 137, not all companies are eligible: blank check companies, shell companies, and penny stock issuers are excluded.) First, Rule 138 provides a limited safe harbor, exempting research reports of participating broker-dealers from the definition of an "offer for sale" or "offer to sell" for purposes of § 2(a)(10) (definition of prospectus) and 5(c) (prohibition on offers in the Pre–Filing Period). The issuer must be required to file Exchange Act periodic reports and have filed all required reports under Forms 10–K, 10–KSB, 10–Q, 10–QSB, and 20–F. Rule 138 divides securities into two groups: (a) common stock and debt and preferred securities convertible into common stock; and (b) debt and preferred securities not convertible into common stock. Rule 138 gives broker-dealers a safe harbor to provide opinions on one group of securities even though the issuer is offering securities belonging to the *other* group. In order to police attempted circumventions of § 5, any broker or dealer seeking to use Rule 138 to publish research reports on a specific type of securities must have previously published or distributed research on the same types of securities in the "regular course of business." Rule 138(a)(3).

Second, Rule 139 provides a more general safe harbor for participating broker-dealers publishing research reports on Exchange Act reporting issuers. If the requirements of Rule 139 are met, the research reports are deemed not to constitute an "offer for sale" or "offer to sell" for purposes of §§ 2(a)(10) and 5(c). Rule 139 therefore directly protects broker-dealer opinions (that otherwise may be viewed as conditioning the market) from the reach of both § 5(b) and (c).

Rule 139 imposes differing requirements based on whether the research report is issuer-specific or covers an industry generally. For issuer-specific research reports, the SEC limits the type of issuers that may qualify for a Rule 139 exemption from §§ 2(a)(10) and 5(c). Only issuers eligible for Form S–3 or F–3 pursuant to the $75 million minimum public float or investment grade securities provisions of the Forms are eligible. Rule 139(a)(1)(i). A broker-dealer must (1) publish or distribute research reports in the "regular course of its business" and (2) not be initiating (or re-initiating after a lapse) coverage of the issuer or its securities. Rule 139(a)(1)(iii). The research reports need not, however, have been published for any minimum period of time, nor do they need to have covered the same securities being sold in the offering.

For "industry reports," the SEC allows a broker-dealer to publish or disseminate research on a broader range of issuers. Eligible issuers include all reporting issuers. However, greater requirements are placed on the research itself. Rule 139(a)(2)(i). An industry report must include "similar information with respect to a substantial number of issuers in the issuer's industry or sub-industry, or . . . a comprehensive list of securities currently recommended by the broker or dealer." Rule 139(a)(2)(iii). The broker-dealer may not devote any "materially greater space or prominence" to the issuer compared with any other securities or companies. Rule 139(a)(2)(iv). Finally, the broker or dealer must (1) publish or distribute research reports in "the regular course of its business" and (2) "at the time of the publication or distribution of the research report, is including similar information about the issuer or its securities in similar reports." Rule 139a(2)(v).

Note that broker-dealers who are participating in an offering have one additional avenue to avoid the strictures of the gun-jumping rules. Rather than look to Rules 138 or 139, the broker-dealer who is participating may attempt to treat their research report as a free writing prospectus under Rules 164 and 433. Assuming the various information, prospectus delivery (if any), filing, legending, and record retention requirements are met, participating broker-dealers may avoid the requirements of Rules 138 or 139, such as the "regular course of its business" and the "at the time of publication or distribution" requirements of Rule 139.

HYPOTHETICAL SIX

Smartway shares are not currently publicly traded, so there are no analysts following its securities. The news of its impending public offering, however, has caused some members of the investment community to take notice of Smartway. Consider whether any of these discussions of Smartway's initial public offering run afoul of the gun-jumping rules.

1. *Scenario One*: Lan is a reporter for the *Wall Street Journal*. She heard of Smartway's public offering from a friend who saw Smartway's Rule 135 notice. After researching Smartway's business, Lan writes a story on the offering as part of a general report on the high-flying IPO market. The story is published on page C1 of the *Journal* (the market page) and includes projections on Smartway's future profitability.

2. *Scenario Two*: Lavina is a research analyst at Silverman Brothers. Silverman regularly publishes analyst opinions on companies in various sectors.

Silverman is not participating in the offering. Nonetheless, Lavina writes an analyst report on Smartway, giving the company a "neutral" recommendation for the IPO. Silverman publishes the analyst report, distributing it to brokers within the company as well as to its many retail and institutional investor clients. This is, however, Silverman's first analyst report on Smartway.

3. *Scenario Three*: Grace is a research analyst at Sparrow Securities, the managing underwriter for Smartway's offering. In preparation for the IPO, Grace writes a research report for Smartway, giving the company a "buy" recommendation for the IPO. Sparrow publishes a summary of the report (with the buy recommendation) in its monthly newsletter sent out prior to the effective date of the offering. Smartway has previously not been covered in the regular newsletter.

4. *Scenario Four*: Grace is a research analyst at Sparrow Securities. Suppose that in the past, Smartway had sold a large number of non-convertible bonds in private placements to a group of insurance companies. The insurance companies eventually resold the bonds, creating a liquid secondary market for the bonds among institutional investors well before Smartway's decision to do an initial public offering of its common stock. Sparrow Securities decides to publish a special report covering the traded bonds. Published prior to the IPO's effective date, the report summarizes Grace's research into the bonds and her opinion that the bonds are a "good buy."

C. POST-EFFECTIVE PERIOD

Just before the registration statement goes effective, the underwriters and the issuer will typically sign a formal underwriting agreement, specifying, among other things, the offering price to the public and the discount at which shares are sold to the underwriters in a firm commitment offering. After the registration statement becomes effective, § 5(a) no longer applies and the issuer and those participating in the offering can begin selling their shares. In a firm commitment offering, the underwriters then purchase the discounted securities and begin sales to investors. For many public offerings, the entire offering process is completed within the first day of the offering. The public offering may commence at 10 A.M. and underwriters may complete the sale of all firm commitment shares by the end of the trading day, if not earlier. For particularly "hot" IPO issues, the demand for the shares may outstrip the number of offered shares. The managing underwriter, or "book-running" underwriter, may have latitude in deciding to whom to allocate shares. Typically, larger institutional investors with repeat relationships with specific investment banks will be given preference in obtaining offered shares.

Despite the freedom to make sales in the Post–Effective Period, the issuer and others continue to face restrictions, most critically § 5(b). Section 5(b)(2) prohibits the transmission of securities "for the purpose of sale or for delivery after sale" unless accompanied or preceded by a statutory prospectus. In the Post–Effective Period, only a prospectus meeting the requirements of § 10(a) constitutes a valid statutory prospectus. The § 10(b) preliminary prospectus authorized by Rule 430 no longer meets the requirements of § 5(b).

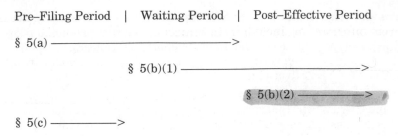

For most purchases of securities, no actual stock certificate is transmitted, making § 5(b)(2) somewhat anachronistic. The real bite of § 5(b) lies in § 5(b)(1). Section 5(b)(1) continues to restrict written materials and broadcasts offering a security for sale unless such materials qualify as a § 10 prospectus. Can the prohibition of § 5(b)(1) be avoided by simply eschewing all written or broadcast communication offering the security? No, the definition of a prospectus in § 2(a)(10) includes written confirmations of sale. Consequently, underwriters sending confirmations fall within the prospectus delivery requirement. At the latest, a final prospectus must be sent with the confirmation of sales thereby bringing the confirmation within the § 2(a)(10)(a) "free writing" exception. (Perhaps realizing that the final prospectus does little good to an investor with the confirmation of sale, if the issuer is not already a reporting company, the SEC in Rule 15c2–8(b) requires that participating brokers must send a copy of the preliminary prospectus at least 48 hours prior to the sending of the confirmation.)

Section 2(a)(10)(a) removes "free writing" from the definition of a prospectus in the Post–Effective Period. In addition to confirmations of sales, "free writing" potentially includes all offering materials which would otherwise be a prospectus not complying with § 10(a). The free writing exception in § 2(a)(10)(a) excludes such communications from the definition of a prospectus if a formal § 10(a) statutory prospectus either accompanies or precedes the free writing after the effective date of the registration statement. Issuers and broker-dealers can therefore send confirmations and other selling documents to potential investors after the effective date as long as they also include the final statutory prospectus. The concept of "free writing" under § 2(a)(10)(a) pre-dates and is distinct from the exemption for "free writing prospectuses" under Rules 164 and 433. Post-effective communications that fit under the traditional free writing exception contained in § 2(a)(10)(a) are not treated as free writing prospectuses.

In this section we discuss: (1) the form of the statutory prospectus, (2) the prospectus delivery requirement, and (3) the updating of information contained in the statutory prospectus and registration statement.

1. FORMS OF THE FINAL PROSPECTUS

The final statutory prospectus adds price-related information (e.g., the offering price, the underwriters' discount, etc.) to the information contained in the preliminary prospectus. Part I of the relevant registration statement form (e.g., Form S–1 or S–3 for most domestic issuers) details the required information, including information on the business, properties, management, capital stock, and audited financial statements.

As originally conceived, the final prospectus contained all the required information in one physical document. Investors would receive the entire document through the mail or directly from their broker or a dealer. Over time, the definition of a final prospectus was relaxed. Printing a physical document takes time, but issuers and underwriters, typically want to set the price immediately before selling securities to the public. If the issuers and underwriters set the offering price too high, few investors will buy the securities. If the offering price is set too low, the issuer (and to a lesser extent the underwriters) leave money on the table, foregoing possibly higher proceeds.

Rule 430A of the Securities Act alleviates these timing concerns. Under Rule 430A, the final prospectus filed as part of the registration statement may omit price-related information. Rule 430A is available only for all-cash, firm commitment offerings, so offerings for non-cash consideration (e.g., an exchange offer for stock) and best efforts offerings cannot use Rule 430A. (Recall that underwriters bear less risk in a best efforts offering because the underwriters are not left holding any unwanted securities if the price is set too high.) Rule 430A also applies to registration statements that are immediately effective upon filing with the SEC pursuant to Rule 462(e) and (f). Rule 462(e) deals with automatic shelf registration statements filed by a well-known seasoned issuer (we cover shelf registration later in the chapter).

Issuers using Rule 430A must eventually file price-related information with the SEC. If the filing occurs within fifteen business days after the effective date of the registration statement, then no post-effective amendment is necessary. Instead, issuers must file a prospectus containing the pricing information under Rule 424(b). After fifteen business days, the price-related information must be filed as a post-effective amendment to the registration statement.

Issuers relying on Rule 430A must also agree to the undertaking in Item 512(i) of Regulation S–K. Item 512(i) provides that for antifraud purposes (e.g., § 11 liability) price-related information filed after the effective date of the registration statement shall be deemed to be part of the registration statement as of the date the registration statement was originally declared effective. If the price-related information were instead filed as a post-effective amendment, then Item 512(i) provides for liability purposes that "each post-effective amendment that contains a form of prospectus shall be deemed to be a new registration statement relating to the securities offered therein, and the offering of such securities at that time shall be deemed to be the initial bona fide offering thereof."

2. PROSPECTUS DELIVERY REQUIREMENT

One of the primary goals of the public offering process is the creation of the mandatory disclosure documents: the registration statement and the statutory prospectus. Creation of the documents, however, can only address issuers' underlying informational advantage over investors if investors receive, whether directly or indirectly, the information in the document. To whom, and more critically, for how long after the offering begins, must the statutory prospectus be sent?

a.   The Traditional Delivery Requirement

Section 5(b) provides the cornerstone of the prospectus delivery requirement time. Under § 5(b)(1), recall that all persons bear an obligation to send the statutory prospectus in the Post–Effective Period either with or preceding the written confirmations. Rule 15c2–8(h), in turn, requires the managing underwriter to ensure that all broker-dealers "participating in the distribution or trading in the registered security" are provided with sufficient copies of the final prospectus in order to comply with the prospectus delivery requirement.

How long does the prospectus delivery requirement last? Section 5(b) provides no limit. Consider the cost an indefinite delivery requirement would place on secondary market transactions. Because § 5 applies to "any person," even individual investors selling securities in the secondary market (and their brokers) would have an obligation to send a statutory prospectus to purchasing investors. How would an individual investor obtain the statutory prospectus to send with the confirmation? What if the sale takes place many years after the original public offering?

Fortunately, the prospectus delivery requirement has a more reasonable duration. Two important exemptions from § 5 limit the reach of § 5(b). First, § 4(1) exempts transactions not involving any "issuer, underwriter, or dealer" from § 5. Congress enacted § 4(1) specifically to exempt individuals selling in ordinary secondary market transactions from the gun-jumping requirements. Section 4(1) exempts the vast majority of secondary market transactions. Brokers' roles in those transactions in the secondary market, if unsolicited, are exempted by § 4(4).

Note that § 4(1) does not exempt transactions for securities dealers; they have to find their own exemption. Section 5(b) applies broadly to all persons, so even securities dealers who did not participate in the public offering must deliver a statutory prospectus with the confirmation during the prospectus delivery period. Section 4(3) provides an exemption specifically for dealers, but its availability is limited. Dealers still acting as underwriters for the offering are not allowed to use the § 4(3) exemption for securities that are part of an unsold allotment, so they must comply with § 5(b)'s prospectus delivery requirements. For dealers not acting as an underwriter (either because they are not participating in the offering or because they have sold all of their allotment), § 4(3)—in conjunction with Rule 174—establishes time limits for § 5(b)'s delivery requirements. The time periods are as follows:

0 days—Exchange Act reporting issuer prior to the offering (i.e., an issuer subject to the reporting requirements of § 13 or 15(d) of the Exchange Act)

25 days—Issuer whose securities will be listed on a national securities exchange or Nasdaq

40 days—Issuer that does not fit any of the above categories *not* doing an initial public offering

90 days—Issuer that does not fit any of the above categories doing an initial public offering

b. *Access Equals Delivery*

When the Securities Act was enacted in 1933, paper documents were the primary means of communication. Although the telegraph and telephone did exist, neither instrument provided a convenient medium to transmit a large amount of information. Investors interested in learning directly about a particular public offering had to read the paper version of the statutory prospectus.

Even in the 1930s, however, the benefit to the investors from the prospectus delivery requirement was less than clear. The SEC can mandate that the prospectus be delivered to the door of many individual investors, but it cannot make them read it. (And recycling was less prevalent in the 1930s than it is today!) Why would an investor ignore the prospectus? For individual investors making only a small investment, the cost of reading and deciphering the prospectus—shrouded in legalese and dense with accounting figures—outweighs the potential benefit of doing so.

Even with a readership well below 100%, mandatory disclosure nonetheless may protect retail investors in one of three ways. First, the mere drafting of a disclosure document that the SEC may review encourages issuers to be truthful in their disclosures. That incentive is bolstered by the possibility of an antifraud suit under the generous standards of §§ 11 and 12(a)(2).

Second, retail investors may obtain information indirectly. Retail investors may never read the prospectus, but they may read analyst reports on the company and/or obtain advice from their brokers before investing. Both of these sources may be enlightened by the disclosures in the prospectus. To be sure, recent scandals in the United States involving analyst opinions from many prominent investment banks call into question the value of analyst and broker recommendations. This problem seems most acute when the analyst and broker are associated with a brokerage firm that also provides investment banking advice and underwriting services to issuers.

Finally, even if the retail investors make no effort to digest the information, disclosure may influence the market for the offering. Most public offerings are purchased primarily by institutional investors. If these investors are not willing to purchase the securities (at least at the price range initially contemplated), the issuer and underwriters may need to reduce the price to sell out the entire offering.

What is the best way to distribute the mandatory disclosure? As part of the SEC's 2005 Public Offering Reforms, the SEC promulgated Rule 172, under which "access equals delivery" for the prospectus delivery requirement. (Certain issuers and transactions are excluded.) Rule 172(c) imposes several conditions to qualify for an exemption. Most importantly, the issuer must file a final § 10(a) statutory prospectus with the SEC (with the possible omission of certain information as provided by Rule 430A) or "make a good faith and reasonable effort to file such prospectus within the time required under Rule 424 and in the event that the issuer fails to file timely such a prospectus, the issuer files the prospectus as soon as practicable thereafter." Rule 172(c)(3). The filing condition is not required for dealers to take advantage of Rule 172 who would otherwise face a prospectus delivery requirement due to the operation of §§ 5 and 4(3). Rule 172(c)(4). If Rule 172(c) is satisfied, Rule 172(a) exempts written confirmations of sales from the reach of § 5(b)(1), obviating the need for broker-dealers to mail out a final prospectus together with the confirmation of sales. Similarly, Rule 172(b) deems the requirement that a prospectus precede or accompany a security transmitted for sale as met for purposes of § 5(b)(2). General free writing other than the written confirmation of sales is not covered under Rule 172 and therefore falls under the traditional prospectus delivery requirement discussed above (although a seasoned issuer or WKSI may avoid prospectus delivery if they instead comply with the free writing prospectus requirements under Rule 164 and 433).

Underwriters, brokers and dealers are not completely freed from the requirement to transmit additional information along with the confirmation of sales. Rule 173 requires that for transactions in which the final prospectus delivery requirement applies under Rule 174 and § 4(3), participating underwriters, brokers, and dealers (or issuer if sold directly by the issuer) must send to each purchasing investor, who purchased directly from the respective underwriter, broker, dealer, or issuer, notice that the sale took place under an effective registration statement or a final prospectus pursuant to an effective registration statement, thereby informing the purchaser that they may have rights under §§ 11 and 12(a)(2). The notice must be provided not later than two business days following the completion of the sale. Purchasers may request a copy of the final prospectus from the person sending out the notice. After the effective date of the registration statement, notices mailed under Rule 173 are exempt from § 5(b)(1) (and thus avoid the prospectus delivery requirement). Compliance with Rule 173's notice requirement is not a prerequisite for the application of the Rule 172 access-as-delivery safe harbor from the prospectus delivery requirement.

HYPOTHETICAL SEVEN

Suppose Smartway and Sparrow Securities commence sales of the initial public offering on June 1st. Among the underwriters in the offering are Sparrow Securities (with the largest allotment of shares) and Villagebank, a large investment bank based in New York City. Villagebank was allocated 400,000 Smartway shares for sale. Assume that by June 3rd, Villagebank has sold 300,000 shares from its allotment leaving 100,000 more shares to sell. Do any of the following run afoul of § 5?

1. *Scenario One*: Villagebank sells shares out of its remaining allotment to Kevin, an investor based in New York City. Together with the confirmation of sales, Villagebank mails out a copy of the final prospectus.

2. *Scenario Two*: Simultaneously with the commencement of the offering, Smartway's shares are listed on Nasdaq. Secondary market trading quickly follows. Marx Securities, a securities dealer not participating in Smartway's offering decides to sell some of its Smartway common stock inventory into the market one week after the start of Smartway's IPO. Marx Securities mails the stock certificates for the shares it sells to purchasing investors but does not send a statutory prospectus to the investors.

3. *Scenario Three*: Suppose instead that Marx Securities simply pitches Smartway securities through cold calls to retail investors who then purchase Smartway shares. Marx Securities acts as their broker in placing the investors' orders with a market maker in Sparrow stock. Marx Securities sends each purchasing investor a written confirmation, but not the statutory prospectus.

4. *Scenario Four*: Suppose that Villagebank issues an analyst report on Smartway on June 10. At that time, Villagebank still holds 50,000 shares from its allotment. The report covers a number of high-growth companies, including Smartway. The report recommends Smartway as a "buy" and talks glowingly about Smartway's future growth prospects. The analyst report is sent to all of Villagebank's customers.

5. *Scenario Five*: Suppose that Jack, a coffee importer from Brazil, decides to purchase some Smartway stock on the secondary market. He contacts his broker, Joel, at Villagebank and instructs him to purchase 1,000 shares at the prevailing market price. Joel executes the order for Jack on June 10, sending him a written confirmation two days later, but does not include the statutory prospectus.

4. UPDATING THE PROSPECTUS AND REGISTRATION STATEMENT

Not all public offerings sell out on the first day of the offering. Less desirable offerings may take some time to sell. As we discuss below, issuers may also register an offering to take place over an extended period of time (a "shelf registration"). Even after the offering is initially sold, we saw in the prospectus delivery section above that under certain circumstances § 5(b) imposes a continuing obligation on dealers to send the final prospectus along with any written confirmation of sales (or afford access through filing under Rule 172).

Information about the issuer may change after the effective date of the registration statement. The CEO of the issuer may resign. The issuer may decide to shift into a different line of business. The issuer may terminate its auditor and hire a new independent accountant. A company may become the target of a new lawsuit that, while unrelated to the public offering, may pose a significant contingent financial liability. For investors contemplating whether to buy the issuer's offered securities, either directly from the underwriters or through later secondary market trading, should it matter that the final prospectus and registration statement have become outdated?

The concept of materiality helps answer this question. Recall that materiality is defined by reference to the "total mix of information." Information that in isolation may seem important to reasonable investors loses its materiality if the market already has the information. For companies whose securities trade in an informationally efficient capital market, "new" information on the company may already be incorporated in the stock market price, making updating the prospectus and registration statement unnecessary. Indeed, most investors would never read an updated prospectus. As a practical matter, the market price is the *only* way such new information will (indirectly) reach the investors. Consider the extent to which the efficient capital market hypothesis informs the requirements for updating the prospectus and registration statement.

a. *Updating the Prospectus*

Depending on the type of issuer, the prospectus delivery requirement may extend up to 90 days after the start of the public offering for securities dealers who are not part of the underwriting syndicate. Underwriters selling their allotment are required to deliver a prospectus until their allotment is entirely sold. Most updates to the prospectus take place through a process known as "stickering" under which new information is added to the relevant page of the prospectus. Rule 424(b)(3)–(5) sets forth the procedure for stickering.

Three basic duties require updating of the final prospectus:

Section 10(a)(3) of the Securities Act. Under § 10(a)(3), if a prospectus is used more than nine months after the effective date of the registration statement, the information used in the prospectus may not be more than sixteen months old to the extent that the information is known to the "user of the prospectus" or can be provided without unreasonable effort or expense.

Antifraud Liability. No explicit updating duty is specified in § 12(a)(2) or Rule 10b–5 antifraud liability. Instead, the prospect of antifraud liability indirectly imposes an incentive for issuers to update the prospectus. If the information in a prospectus is no longer accurate, the issuer and others involved with the prospectus are potentially liable for both § 12(a)(2) and Rule 10b–5 liability.

Shelf Registration. Issuers doing a shelf registration under Rule 415 must update the prospectus to reflect any "fundamental" change to the information set forth in the registration statement pursuant to Item 512(a) of Regulation S–K. As we discuss below, Item 512(a) also requires the filing of a post-effective amendment to the registration statement.

For non-shelf registration offerings, does § 10(a)(3) provide an adequate incentive for issuers to update the prospectus? Since the prospectus delivery requirement for non-shelf public offerings may continue at most for 90 days after the commencement of the offering, § 10(a)(3)'s nine-month updating requirement has little effect. Only underwriters still selling an unsold allotment of securities are subject to the updating requirement. (The SEC takes a dim view of a non-shelf registration that continues for an extended period after the effective date of the registration statement.) Thus, § 10(a)(3) is generally important only for shelf registration offerings.

Instead, antifraud liability provides the major incentive for updating the prospectus. Antifraud liability, however, may impose a number of different requirements on investor-plaintiffs as well as provide possible defenses for the defendants. Rule 10b–5, for example, requires plaintiffs to demonstrate that the defendants had scienter (whether intentional or reckless) with respect to the fraud. Section 12(a)(2) has no scienter requirement, but defendants can avoid antifraud liability so long as they did not know (nor could have known with "reasonable care") about the materially misleading misstatement or omission.

Another potential source of liability is § 12(a)(1). In *SEC v. Manor Nursing Centers, Inc.*, 458 F.2d 1082 (2d Cir. 1972), the Second Circuit held that a grossly misleading prospectus would violate the prospectus delivery violations of § 5, thus potentially giving rise to a cause of action under § 12(a)(1).

The Second Circuit's opinion in *Manor Nursing* has not attracted broad support. The Fifth Circuit in *SEC v. Southwest Coal & Energy Co.*, 624 F.2d 1312, 1318–19 (5th Cir. 1980), wrote:

> The *Manor Nursing* thesis of fraud as a basis for § 5 violations has been roundly criticized ... § 12[a](1) provides strict liability for one who offers or sells a security in violation of § 5. Sections 11 and 12[a](2) similarly provide liability for offers or sales of securities upon misrepresentation or misleading nondisclosure of material facts, but only if the offeror cannot demonstrate that he did not know, and could

not reasonably have been expected to know, of the untruth or omission. Under the *Manor Nursing* construct, however, one who proves a misrepresentation actionable under § 11 or § 12[a](2) has also proved a violation of § 5, thus automatically establishing liability per se under § 12[a](1). Not only does this interpretation render § 11 and 12[a](2) essentially superfluous as remedial mechanisms, but it also obliterates the due diligence defense contained in these sections, plainly intended to be available to defendants in actions under the 1933 Act based on such misrepresentations or nondisclosures. Such a result could not possibly have been intended by the drafters of these provisions.

b.   Updating the Registration Statement

The registration statement must be accurate as of its effective date because antifraud liability under § 11 and Rule 10b–5 is measured as of that time. In addition, the SEC may issue a stop order pursuant to § 8(d), as discussed above, if the registration statement contains misrepresentations. The SEC's authority under § 8(d), however, only reaches registration statements that contain a material misstatement at the time of the effective date. See *Charles A. Howard*, 1 S.E.C. 6 (1933). Although issuers (and other associated parties) may have a duty to correct materially false or misleading information in the registration statement at the time of the effective date, no duty exists to update previously accurate information. Thus, there is no general duty to update the registration statement.

There are two major exceptions to the general rule that there is no duty to update the registration statement. First, issuers using a Rule 415 shelf registration, as we will see below, must include an Item 512(a) undertaking pursuant to Regulation S–K. The Item 512(a) undertaking requires the issuer to make a post-effective amendment to the registration statement for certain events, including any § 10(a)(3) change to the prospectus, any "fundamental" change to the information set forth in the registration statement, or any material change to the plan of distribution. Rule 412 allows issuers to use incorporation-by-reference of Exchange Act filings instead of a post-effective amendment to meet the updating requirement of Item 512(a).

Second, in certain circumstances, if the issuer updates the prospectus, the issuer also must file that updated prospectus as a post-effective amendment to the registration statement. Recall that the statutory prospectus is Part I of the registration statement. Rule 424(a) requires that "substantive changes from or additions to" a previously filed prospectus must be filed as part of the registration statement (technically as an amendment to the registration statement). Non-substantive changes may be made by "stickering" the prospectus without a new filing.

What counts as a "substantive" change or addition is unclear. The SEC felt it necessary to require shelf registration issuers to include an undertaking under Item 512(a) for "fundamental" changes to the registration statement, implying that a *mere* "fundamental" change would normally not warrant an amendment to the registration statement without the undertaking. On the other hand, the SEC has expressed the view that even without an Item 512(a) undertaking for non-shelf registration offerings, "the staff generally requires that post-effective amendments be filed to reflect material changes." See Securities Act Release No. 6276 (Dec. 23, 1980).

Updating the registration statement (through an amendment) has far greater negative consequences than does stickering the prospectus for developments occurring during Post–Effective Period. A post-effective amendment to the registration statement under § 8(c) of the Securities Act becomes effective only at the discretion of the SEC. When the amendment becomes effective, all the information in the registration statement is assessed at the new effective date for purposes of § 11 antifraud liability. Issuers filing a post-effective amendment to the registration statement therefore open themselves up to additional possible antifraud liability if they have not updated all of the information in the registration statement.

HYPOTHETICAL EIGHT

Smartway's IPO registration statement has been declared effective by the SEC. In the registration statement and final prospectus, Smartway disclosed that it is in the midst of negotiating a contract with the Law Professors Association of America, Inc. (LPAA) to obtain rights to use the likenesses of well-known law professors as a marketing tool to help sell more airline tickets. (Sherry believes, perhaps wrongly, that law students are a great target customer base because they have a great respect and regard for their professors.) The registration statement did not include a risk factor mentioning the possibility that the LPAA contract may not come through. Two weeks after the effective date of the registration statement, the LPAA has gone bankrupt and, consequently, all of the contract talks with LPAA have fallen through. Moreover, all the big-name law professors have broken ranks and signed with Smartway's major competitors. Is there any duty to update either the final prospectus or the registration statement and why?

III. PUBLIC OFFERING TRADING PRACTICES

During and immediately after a public offering, underwriters have a lot at stake in maintaining (or better yet, increasing) the market price of the offered securities. If the securities price drops precipitously during an offering, the underwriter may have trouble selling unsold allotments of securities. In a firm commitment offering, the underwriter bears the risk of selling the securities and thus suffers in the case of any unsold allotment. In addition, most public offerings include an overallotment option for underwriters to expand the size of the offering. This "Green Shoe" option allows the underwriters to purchase up to an additional 15% of the offered securities at the discounted price for resale to investors at the offering price. If the price holds up, the overallotment option can mean additional profits for the underwriters.

A price drop after an offering commences may harm underwriters indirectly as well. Part of the service underwriters offer to issuers (and a principal justification for the large underwriter's discount) derives from the relationships the underwriters enjoy with large institutional investors. These investors depend on the underwriters to bring them fairly priced—or better still, underpriced—securities. If the price drops, the institutional investors that purchased initially in the offering will lose money and the underwriters will lose face (and, potentially, customers for future offerings).

Underwriters may attempt to affect artificially the secondary market price of a security through fraud. For example, the underwriters may disclose false information after the start of the offering that the company's profits are projected to climb sharply. Antifraud liability limits such shenanigans.

Left unregulated, underwriters might purchase shares in the market in an attempt to inflate secondary market price. Large volume purchases may push the market price higher for at least two possible reasons. First, increased demand could exhaust the supply of securities that investors are willing to sell at a particular price. Investors may have a range of beliefs on the value of the security or, alternatively, face different tax consequences from the sale of securities. To induce more investors to sell in the face of increased demand, the market price must increase. Second, the presence of a large volume of purchase orders may signal to the market that informed investors have non-public information that the company is undervalued (and are acting on this information by purchasing securities). This signal will also cause the market price to rise.

Regulation M supplements the general antifraud and anti-manipulation provisions of the securities laws, such as §§ 9(a), 10(b), and 15(c) of the Exchange Act, focusing in particular on manipulation that may take place in connection with securities offerings. The SEC explains the purpose of Regulation M:

> As a prophylactic, anti-manipulation measure, Regulation M is designed to prohibit activities that could artificially influence the market for the offered security, including, for example, supporting the offering price by creating the exaggerated perception of scarcity of the offered security or creating the misleading appearance of active trading in the market for the security.

Securities Act Release No. 8511 (Dec. 9, 2004). No explicit private cause of action exists for Regulaton M violations. Instead, the SEC may bring an enforcement action for a violation.

A.   IPO ALLOCATIONS

On December 6, 2000 the *Wall Street Journal* ran a front-page story exposing abuses in the market for initial public offerings. See Susan Pulliam & Randall Smith, *Seeking IPO Shares, Investors Offer to Buy More in After–Market*, Wall St. J. A1 (Dec. 6, 2000). The story revealed "tie-in" agreements between investment banks and initial investors seeking to participate in "hot" offerings. Under those agreements, initial investors would commit to buy additional shares of the offering company's stock in secondary market trading in return for allocations of shares in the IPO. As the *Wall Street Journal* related, those "[c]ommitments to buy in the aftermarket lock in demand for additional stock at levels above the IPO price. As such, they provide the rocket fuel that sometimes boosts IPO prices into orbit on the first trading day." This process of encouraging purchases in the aftermarket at ever-higher prices has come to be known as "laddering." The *Journal*'s account of the practice essentially lays out a conspiracy between underwriters and their favored investor-customers to engage in a scheme of market manipulation. Retail investors—who end up purchasing the stock after the IPO at inflated prices—systematically lose from the manipulation.

What benefits do underwriters receive from boosting the aftermarket price? At first glance, the clear winners from a hot IPO are those initial investors who purchase at the IPO offering price, typically large institutional investors. Underwriters may then benefit in a number of indirect ways. First, underwriters in a firm commitment offerings (under which the underwriters bear the risk of failing to sell out the offering) reduce their risk. Investors are more willing to purchase IPO shares if they expect immediate gains in the stock price in the secondary market. Second, underwriters gain a reputational benefit. By elevating the aftermarket price above the IPO price, underwriters allow their customers—the institutional IPO investors—to sell their overvalued stock to retail investors in the aftermarket. A drop in stock price before the institutional investors sell their IPO allotments into the secondary market would damage the underwriters' IPO reputation among the institutional investors. Among the services underwriters provide to issuers is their ability, which is based on the underwriters' reputation, to bring investors willing to buy the IPO stock. Laddering therefore may enhance the underwriters' reputation with future issuers as well. Third—and less benign from the issuer's perspective—underwriters may obtain under-the-table commissions from favored investor-clients. In a follow-up story on the laddering scheme, the *Journal* reported a joint investigation into the allegations by the SEC and the U.S. Attorney for the Southern District of New York. That story pointed to underwriters demanding commissions from investors favored with hot IPO allocations: "Wall Street dealers may have sought and obtained larger-than-typical trading commissions in return for giving coveted allocations of IPOs to certain investors." See Randall Smith & Susan Pulliam, *U.S. Probes Inflated Commissions for Hot IPOs*, Wall St. J. C1 (Dec. 7, 2000).

Not surprisingly, the fallout from these revelations has been severe for the investment banking industry. The SEC's investigation into the practice has led to substantial settlements with many of the best known investment banks. For example, CS First Boston settled for $100 million with the SEC and, as is customary, neither admitted nor denied guilt in the matter. The magnitude of these fines suggests that the SEC was able to uncover hard evidence of the laddering scheme. The NASD has proposed rules to try and dampen the frothy IPO aftermarket that makes such abuses possible. The rules would, among other things, ban market orders on the first day of trading after the IPO.

If market purchases on behalf of underwriters artificially raise the price of securities, these purchases distort the true value of the securities, causing investors purchasing the securities to pay too much. One possible regulatory response to the problem of underwriter trading practices designed to maintain or increase the secondary market price of an offered security would be a flat ban. The SEC, however, did not take such an approach. Instead, the SEC adopted a more nuanced approach in Regulation M under the Exchange Act to regulate trading practices surrounding a distribution of securities.

Regulation M balances three disparate considerations. First, not all purchases (or bids) on the part of underwriters and others associated with an offering are intended to manipulate the secondary market price. Investment banks acting as underwriters may also act as market makers for the stock. (To serve as market makers, the banks must have the ability to purchase the stock at prevailing market prices to maintain market liquidity.) In addition, investment banks acting as underwriters may also have a brokerage division that purchases securities on behalf of clients in unsolicited transactions.

Second, attempts to affect artificially the market price through purchases are much less likely to work for companies with a "deep" secondary market with large volumes of unrelated, independent trades. An underwriter purchasing 100,000 shares is much more likely to affect the market price for a company with an average daily trading volume of 200,000 shares than a company with an average daily trading volume of 10 million shares.

Regulation M also distinguishes between efforts to raise the market price above its current level (banned market manipulation) and efforts simply to maintain the market price at the offering price (regulated stabilization). Although both distort the market price, the potential for distortion is greater with efforts to raise the market price. For example, consider where the market price for Smartway immediately after the public offering is $20 per share. Information then reaches that market that the true value of Smartway is only $17 per share. Efforts to manipulate the price upwards (if successful) can result in a price of above $20 (say $25 per share)—resulting in an overvaluation of $8 per share. With stabilization, the maximum price permitted is $20 per share (the public offering price). Thus, the potential overvaluation is only $3 per share.

B.   MARKET MANIPULATION

Regulation M regulates efforts to manipulate the market price of a company's securities during a public offering of "covered" securities. Covered securities include "any security that is the subject of a distribution, or any reference security." Regulation M defines a reference security as "a security into which a security that is the subject of a distribution . . . may be converted, exchanged, or exercised or which, under the terms of the subject security, may in whole or in significant part determine the value of the subject security." Rule 100, Regulation M. Thus, if a company is issuing convertible bonds then the reference security is the class of common shares into which the bonds could be converted. The common shares, as reference securities, would also come under the restrictions of Regulation M as covered securities.

example

In order to curb market manipulation, Rules 101 and 102 limit certain types of trading during the "restricted period." The restricted period is defined under Rule 100 and depends in part on the worldwide average daily trading volume (the "ADTV") for the two months, among other possible time periods, preceding the filing of the registration statement. The different possible restricted periods are as follows:

2 months

1. For any security with an ADTV value of $100,000 or more of an issuer whose common equity securities have a public float value of $25 million or more, the period beginning on the later of one business day prior to the determination of the offering price or such time that a person becomes a distribution participant, and ending upon such person's completion of participation in the distribution; and

2. For all other securities, the period beginning on the later of five business days prior to the determination of the offering price or such time that a person becomes a distribution participant, and ending upon such person's completion of participation in the distribution.

3. In the case of a distribution involving a merger, acquisition, or exchange offer, the period beginning on the day proxy solicitation or offering materials are first disseminated to security holders, and ending upon the completion of the distribution.

"Distribution participant" is defined to include an "underwriter, prospective underwriter, broker, dealer, or other person who has agreed to participate or is participating in a distribution." Rule 100.

Rule 101(a) prohibits the underwriters and their affiliated purchasers from bidding for, purchasing, or inducing another to bid for or purchase a covered security during the restricted period. Exceptions are provided, however, including offers to sell or solicitations of offers to buy the securities being distributed. Rule 101(b)(9). The underwriters must be able to sell the offering, even if Rule 101 prohibits them from purchasing shares or inducing others to purchase covered securities other than the actual securities being distributed. Other notable exceptions include:

Exceptions:
- Research under 138/139

- Research falling under the safe harbors of Rule 138 or 139, even if considered an "attempt to induce any person to bid or purchase." Rule 101(b)(1).

- Stabilization transactions under Rule 104. Rule 101(b)(2).

- Stabilization

[handwritten margin note: Bids and purchases from issuers to underwriters — in firm commitment]

- Bids and purchases relating to transactions in connection with the distribution not effected on a securities exchange, inter-dealer quotation system, or electronic communications network (i.e., when the underwriters purchase directly from the issuer in a firm commitment offering). Rule 101(b)(8).

[handwritten margin note: De minimis transactions < 2%]

- De minimis transactions, defined as purchases "during the restricted period, other than by a passive market maker, that total less than 2% of the ADTV of the security being purchased, or unaccepted bids." Persons relying on the de minimis exception must maintain and enforce "written policies and procedures reasonably designed to achieve compliance with the other provisions of this section." Rule 101(b)(7).

[handwritten margin note: Exception: Actively traded securities: daily → 1m. ↓ comm. eq. → 150m. ↓]

Rule 101(c)(1) provides that the restrictions of Rule 101 do not apply to certain "actively-traded securities," defined as securities with an average daily trading volume at least $1 million, issued by a company with a public float of common equity of at least $150 million. Rule 101(c)(1) reflects the view that market manipulation in a distribution of securities is less effective (and less likely) if the securities already enjoy a liquid secondary market prior to the offering.

Rule 102 provides similar bid and purchase restrictions for issuers (and selling security holders) and purchasers affiliated with them. Rule 102 parallels Rule 101 in prohibiting bids, purchases, or inducements of bids or purchases by another person of covered securities during the restricted period. Rule 102, however, provides fewer exceptions to issuers than Rule 101 affords distribution participants. Most importantly, issuers and their affiliates are not permitted to engage in stabilization transactions under Rule 104.

As part of an overhaul of Regulation M proposed in late 2004, the SEC proposed a new Rule 106. Proposed Rule 106 would prohibit the issuer and other distribution participants from, among other things, accepting additional consideration from investors to participate in the offering. The SEC takes a broad view of "consideration," intending Rule 106 to focus on abuses where the underwriters required or induced "customers to pay excessive commissions on transactions in other securities, to purchase 'cold' IPO shares, and to make purchases in the aftermarket of the offered security." Securities Act Release No. 8511 (Dec. 9, 2004). The proposed prohibition on investors offering to purchase shares in the aftermarket in return for an allocation of shares in a public offering goes directly to the heart of the IPO laddering scandal described above.

HYPOTHETICAL NINE

Smartway and its underwriter Sparrow Securities have commenced the initial public offering of 10 million shares at $20 per share. The IPO is a firm commitment underwriting with Sparrow Securities and the other underwriters purchasing the securities from Smartway at a 7% underwriters' discount. In addition, the underwriters enjoy an overallotment option of 1 million shares.

The underwriters agree to purchase the firm commitment shares from Smartway on the day the registration statement becomes effective. The price of the offering initially jumps up to $30 per share but then starts falling down to $25 per share on the first day of trading. Consider whether the following market activities run afoul of Regulation M.

1. *Scenario One*: During the course of the public offering, Sparrow Securities initiates market research for Smartway, issuing a "buy" recommendation for Smartway securities.

2. *Scenario Two*: Suppose that Sparrow Securities promises to allocate 100,-000 additional shares of Smartway's IPO to the Million Dollar Hedge Fund. Million Dollar, in turn, promises to purchase 10,000 shares of Smartway in the secondary market at prices above the offering price in the first day of trading.

3. *Scenario Three*: Sparrow Securities completes its sales of allotted Smartway IPO shares two days after the offering. The shares of Smartway start to sag in the secondary market to a price below the offering price. On day three, Sparrow starts buying shares in a successful attempt to raise the market price back to a level above the offering price. On day four, Sparrow exercises its overallotment option and then sells additional quantities of IPO shares to the market.

C. STABILIZATION

Rule 104 of Regulation M regulates efforts on the part of any person (including the issuer, underwriters, and others) to stabilize the market price. Stabilization is defined to include bids and purchases with the "purpose of pegging, fixing, or maintaining the price of a security" (Rule 100). Rule 104 stabilization is the principal exception to the prohibition of Rule 101.

What types of stabilization in connection with a public offering of a security qualify under Rule 104? First, stabilization is only permitted to prevent or retard a drop in the secondary market price of a security. Purchases intended to increase the market price are not permitted under Rule 104(b).

Second, Rule 104 requires that stabilization bids must give way to "any independent bid" at the same price regardless of the size of the independent bid at the time it is entered (Rule 104(c)).

Third, Rule 104 requires notice to the market of stabilization. Those seeking to stabilize must give prior notice to the market and disclose the purpose of the bid to the person with whom the bid is entered. In addition, the prospectus must contain a statement notifying investors of the stabilization. To facilitate monitoring of stabilization, a group attempting stabilization may also only have one stabilizing bid in a market at any one time (Rule 104(d)).

Finally, the stabilization price cannot be greater than the offering price (Rule 104(f)). In addition, stabilization is not allowed for "at-the-market" offerings where the price is not fixed. Rule 104 then distinguishes between initiating and maintaining stabilization. Initiation of stabilization that occurs when the principal market for the securities is open must take place at a price no higher than the last independent transaction price if the security has traded in the principal market on that day. Similar formulations apply if the security has not traded on that day; the rule looks instead at the previous day's transaction price and the last current asking price for the stock. Persons seeking to continue with stabilization after initiation may maintain the initial stabilization price in the principal and other markets. Persons may also reduce the stabilizing price at any time regardless of changes to the independent bids and transaction prices for the security. Persons may increase the stabilization price—while staying below the offering price—only to the extent of the highest current independent bid for the security in the principal market (if the market is open).

HYPOTHETICAL TEN

Sparrow Securities decides that maintaining the market price at near the offering price ($20 per share) after the start of the public offering would assist the efforts of the underwriters to sell out the entire offering and provide an orderly secondary market for investors. Assume that Smartway securities are listed for trading on the Nasdaq after the offering (and thus Nasdaq is the "principal" market for Smartway shares). Are any of the following permissible under the federal securities laws?

1. *Scenario One*: After the Smartway IPO commences, the market price sinks immediately to $15 per share (the last transaction price on Nasdaq). Sparrow Securities commences stabilization, putting in a bid to purchase 1,000 shares of Smartway at $20 per share, the IPO offering price.

2. *Scenario Two*: After the Smartway IPO commences, the market price increases dramatically to $50 per share (the last transaction price on Nasdaq). Happy, but worried that this price will not last, Sparrow Securities puts in a stabilization bid for 1,000 shares at $50 per share.

IV. SHELF REGISTRATION

The public offering process imposes both large costs and significant delays on issuers. Issuers must not only pay the direct expense of drafting the registration statement and submitting it for SEC review, but also worry that their communications may run afoul of the quiet period imposed through the gun-jumping rules.

How can issuers reduce the cost of the registration process? Suppose Smartway registers an enormous number of shares at the time of the initial public offering. May Smartway then draw from this reserve of registered shares indefinitely into the future to sell additional securities into the market while avoiding the expense of a new registration? If the registration statement and prospectus are kept current, investors may already have adequate information to assess any newly-offered securities.

There are barriers, however, standing in the way of continuous registration for Smartway. Section 6(a) of the Securities Act states that a "registration statement shall be deemed effective only as to the securities specified therein as proposed to be offered." The SEC in *Shawnee Chiles*

Syndicate, 10 S.E.C. 109, 113 (1941), interpreted § 6(a) as prohibiting issuers from registering securities not intended to be offered immediately or in the near future. Although the precise time limit on sale is not clear, sales continuing for over a month after the effective date pose a problem.

[handwritten margin note: 6(a) – immediate offer in near future – over 1 month – problem]

For little-known issuers seeking to sell stock indefinitely into the future, the SEC's prohibition of indefinite registration of securities protects investors from unwise purchases of securities. Investors also enjoy other legal protections. If an issuer sells securities using an out-of-date or otherwise misleading prospectus, the issuer and those soliciting purchases on its behalf potentially face § 12(a)(2) antifraud liability.

Consider the following situations. Why should these issuers face a time limit on the effectiveness of their registration statement?

Situation 1

Smartway sells 1 million convertible bonds for a total of $100 million. Each bond is convertible at any time, at the option of the bondholder, into one share of Smartway common stock. At the time the bonds are sold they are priced at $100 per bond while Smartway's common stock trades at $80 per share. No rational bondholder would convert at these prices. Should Smartway's business take off, however, the conversion feature of the bond allows the bondholder to take advantage of the upside. For example, if Smartway's common stock rises to $120 per share (assume that the bond price remains constant), the bondholder will convert to obtain the higher priced shares.

The offering of convertible bonds involves two securities: (a) the bond and (b) the security into which the bonds may be converted (common stock in the case of Smartway). Section 2(a)(3) of the Securities Act states (emphasis supplied):

> The issue or transfer of a right or privilege, when originally issued or transferred with a security, giving the holder of such security the right to convert such security into another security of the same issuer or of another person, or giving a right to subscribe to another security of the same issuer or of another person, which right cannot be exercised until some future date, *shall not be deemed to be an offer or sale of such other security; but the issue or transfer of such other security upon the exercise of such right of conversion or subscription shall be deemed a sale of such other security.*

[handwritten margin note: time when converted]

Smartway's sale of convertible bonds implicates the offer and sale of the bonds as well as the common stock into which they can be converted. It is a current offer for purposes of § 5 of the Securities Act because it can be exercised immediately even though it would be economically irrational to do so. But because the conversion is likely to occur on a delayed basis (if at all), the information in the registration statement is likely to be stale when the "sale" actually takes place.

[handwritten margin note: conversion on delayed basis]

Situation 2

Consider seasoned and well-known seasoned issuers. For many (but perhaps not all) Form S–3 issuers, large numbers of analysts and investors follow the stock of the company. Over ten different analysts, for example, provide ongoing opinions and recommendations for Yahoo! Inc., a likely WKSI. By definition, seasoned issuers and WKSIs also must comply with the Exchange Act reporting requirements (and remain current in their filings), providing a periodic flow of company-specific information to the capital markets. The informational benefit to investors of forcing such issuers to go through the registration process for any one issuance of securities is therefore reduced. If a large supply of information relevant to investors (both from mandatory periodic filings and outside analyst reports) already exists in the market, additional mandatory disclosure contained in the registration statement is unlikely to provide investors with much additional protection. Indeed, under the integrated disclosure system, much of the information contained in the registration statement will simply be incorporated by reference from the existing periodic disclosure filings (i.e., Forms 10–K, 10–Q and 8–K filings).

To address these situations, among others, the SEC promulgated Rule 415 of the Securities Act to allow for shelf registration. Under shelf registration, issuers (and others) are able to sell registered securities for an extended period of time after the initial effective date of the registration statement, avoiding the time limitation imposed by the SEC's interpretation of § 6(a).

Rule 415 provides that offerings meeting its requirements may be offered on a "continuous or delayed basis in the future." Rule 415 imposes five basic requirements. First, only certain types of offerings may qualify. These include:

- Securities which are to be offered or sold solely by or on behalf of a person or persons *other than the registrant,* a subsidiary of the registrant or a person of which the registrant is a subsidiary (Rule 415(a)(1)(i))

- Securities which are to be issued upon *conversion* of other outstanding securities (Rule 415(a)(1)(iv))

- Securities the offering of which will be *commenced promptly*, will be made on a continuous basis and may continue for a period in excess of 30 days from the date of initial effectiveness (Rule 415(a)(1)(ix))

- Securities registered (or qualified to be registered) on *Form S–3* or Form F–3 which are to be offered and sold on an immediate, continuous or delayed basis by or on behalf of the registrant, a subsidiary of the registrant or a person of which the registrant is a subsidiary (Rule 415(a)(1)(x))

Second, for non-S–3 issuers, Rule 415(a)(2) imposes a two-year time limit for shelf registration offerings falling under Rules 415(a)(1)(viii) (business combinations) and (ix) (continuous offerings to be commenced promptly). The rule leaves some wiggle room; securities for such offerings must be "reasonably expected to be offered and sold" within two years from the effective date of the registration statement. Note that offerings on behalf of persons other than the registrant (e.g., a large pre-existing shareholder of the registrant) or issued upon conversion are not subject to this two-year time limit. Nor are securities sold by Form S–3 issuers under Rule 415(a)(1)(ix) or (x) subject to the two-year limitation.

Third, Rule 415 requires updating of the prospectus and registration statement. Rule 415(a)(3) requires that the issuer "furnish the undertakings required by Item 512(a) of Regulation S–K" for all shelf registration offerings. Item 512(a)(1)(i) of Regulation S–K provides that the issuer will file any prospectus required under § 10(a)(3) as a post-effective amendment. Thus, if an issuer updates a prospectus used more than nine months after the effective date of the registration statement with more current information under § 10(a)(3), the issuer pursuant to Item 512(a) must file the prospectus as an amendment to the registration statement.

[handwritten margin note: 3. updating of prospectus / Reg. S. 512(a) Reg. S-K → undertaking to update]

Item 512(a)(1)(ii) also requires an issuer to reflect in the prospectus any "fundamental" changes in the registration statement. The issuer must file the new prospectus with the "fundamental" changes as an amendment to the registration statement. In addition, Item 512(a)(1)(iii) requires that issuers file a post-effective amendment containing any "material" change to the plan for distribution of the offering (e.g., the number of shares). For Form S–3 issuers, however, Item 512(a) excuses companies from making a post-effective amendment if the information is contained in any Exchange Act filing that is incorporated by reference into the registration statement or the information is included in a filed prospectus supplement under Rule 424(b).

[handwritten margin note: fundamental changes. material change. Form S-3 - excuses (reference.)]

The filing of a post-effective amendment to the registration statement includes the information in the registration statement for purposes of § 11 antifraud liability. Moreover, the amendment resets the effective date of the registration statement. As we discuss in Chapter 8, § 11 measures the accuracy of information in the registration statement as of the effective date, so all of the information in the registration statement must be accurate as of that date.

Can the issuer avoid the additional exposure to § 11 liability created by an amendment by opting instead for a prospectus supplement or incorporation-by-reference of the required Item 512(a) information? No—regardless of the method with which an issuer chooses to satisfy the Item 512(a) updating requirements, the issuer will still face potential § 11 liability for that information. "Information included in a base prospectus or in an Exchange Act periodic report incorporated into a prospectus is included in the registration statement." Securities Act Release No. 8591 (July 19, 2005). Item 512(a)(5) makes clear that the prospectus supplements authorized by Rule 430B and 430C (discussed below) are also deemed to be part of the registration statement and therefore subject to § 11 liability. Only the Rule 430B prospectus supplement (for shelf registration), however, resets the registration date for the entire registration statement, and even then,

[handwritten margin note: face See 11. Liability for amendments ↑ Prospectus is included in registration statement]

only for the issuer and underwriters (thereby excluding the officers, directors and experts from new liability exposure). Rule 430B(f)(2).

Fourth, Rule 415(a)(4) provides that in an "at the market" equity offering by or on behalf of the issuer, the issuer may only make use of Rule 415(a)(1)(x) to qualify for a shelf registration. Rule 415(a)(4) defines an "at the market" equity offering as "an offering of equity securities into an existing trading market for outstanding shares of the same class at other than a fixed price."

Fifth, Rule 415(a)(5) imposes a three-year limit to shelf offerings registered under Rules 415(a)(1)(vii), (ix) (if registered on Form S–3 or F–3), and (x). Although issuers falling under Rule 415(a)(5) must re-register every three years, the SEC eased the burden of doing so. The issuer must file a new registration statement for those offerings, but securities registered under a prior shelf registration statement may continue to be sold until the "earlier of the effective date of the new registration statement or 180 days after the third anniversary of the initial effective date of the prior registration statement." Rule 415(a)(5)(ii)(A). In the case of a continuous offering of securities, the issuer may continue selling the securities until the effective date of the new registration statement. Rule 415(a)(5)(ii)(B). Under Rule 415(a)(6), issuers may include in a new registration statement any unsold securities covered in an earlier shelf registration statement falling under Rule 415(a)(5). Rule 415(a)(6) also allows the issuer to roll over any previously paid and unused filing fees with regard to the unsold securities to offset filing fees for the new registration statement.

In addition to the basic requirements for a Rule 415 shelf registration, the SEC provides special rules for (A) automatic shelf registrations and (B) the use of a minimal "base" prospectus.

A. AUTOMATIC SHELF REGISTRATION   WKSI

The SEC eases the restrictions on shelf offerings for well-known seasoned issuers. Well-known seasoned issuers can file an automatic shelf registration for most types of offerings filed on Form S–3. See Rule 405. Rule 462 treats an automatic shelf registration statement, as well as any post-effective amendment, as becoming effective upon filing with the SEC, even without the opportunity for SEC review. Rule 401(g)(2) provides that an automatic shelf registration statement and any post-effective amendment are "deemed filed on the proper registration form unless and until the Commission notifies the issuer of its objection." The presumption of proper form allows an issuer certainty that it is using the proper form in filing an automatic shelf registration statement unless it hears otherwise from the SEC. Well-known seasoned issuers may register an unspecified amount of securities on an automatic shelf registration statement. The automatic shelf registration need only indicate the name or class of the securities. Rule 430B(a).

Well-known seasoned issuers using an automatic shelf registration statement can also add additional classes of securities to the offering without filing a new registration statement. (Rule 413 requires the filing of a new registration statement to cover additional securities for most other types of offerings.) Under Rule 413(b), additional classes of securities may be added to an automatic shelf registration statement through a post-effective amendment. Drafting a post-effective amendment is a much simpler task than drafting an entire new registration statement. The ability to add an additional class of securities at a later time gives WKSIs "significant latitude" to determine the precise types and amount of securities to register, including securities of their eligible subsidiaries and secondary offerings of their securities (in the hands of insiders, for example).

[margin note: can add addit. class of secur. by post effective amendment.]

Rather than pay filing fees based on the amount of securities registered up front, a WKSI can "pay-as-you-go," paying filing fees only when the securities are actually sold. Rule 456(b). The SEC also allows WKSIs using the automatic shelf registration process to exclude more information from the base prospectus filed with the registration statement, as discussed below. WKSIs may then include the omitted information with the prospectus supplement.

[margin note: WKSI can pay-as-you-go. allowed to exclude more info from Reg. St]

Rule 415(a)(5) imposes a time limit of three years from the initial effective date for automatic shelf registration statements. In the case of an automatic shelf registration statement, the three-year re-registration requirement serves primarily a house-keeping purpose (aggregating all updates into one document) for WKSIs. A WKSI using an automatic shelf registration statement may simply file a new registration statement that becomes effective immediately upon filing under Rule 462(e). Under Rule 415(a)(6), any unsold securities and filing fees paid in connection with the unsold securities are transferred to the new automatic shelf registration statement. The three-year time limit therefore does not limit delay the ability of a WKSI to sell securities under an initial shelf registration statement. The ability to register an unspecified amount of a class of securities for, essentially, an unlimited time combined with the ability to add on new classes of securities under Rule 413(b) means that WKSIs may seemlessly sell any amount of securities off the shelf without delay after the filing the initial shelf registration statement.

[margin note: house-keeping purpose]
[margin note: 3year → doesn't limit.]

B. The Base Prospectus

A shelf registration issuer could simply file a complete prospectus, including price-related information, with the initial registration statement. The issuer's only obligation would then be to update the registration statement pursuant to Item 512(a) as well as to file any required prospectus supplements, such as under § 10(a)(3) of the Securities Act. In practice, issuers will often file only a minimal "base" prospectus with the initial registration statement in a shelf offering. The base prospectus omits information related to the public offering price and the underwriters, among other information. Instead, the issuer will include any omitted information from the base prospectus as part of a prospectus supplement. Rule 424(b)(2) requires that the issuer file such a prospectus supplement with the SEC "no later than the second business day following the earlier of the date of the determination of the offering price or the date it is first used after effectiveness in connection with a public offering or sales." The prospectus supplement that is filed under Rule 424(b)(2) may disclose "public offering price, description of securities, specific method of distribution or similar matters."

In the 2005 Public Offering Reforms, the SEC adopted Rule 430B, bringing much needed clarity to what information an issuer may omit from the base prospectus. Rule 430B represents a shelf registration corollary to Rule 430A. (Rule 430C provides a "catch all" prospectus supplement provision for offerings not covered by Rules 430A and B). Rule 430B provides that the following information may be omitted from the base prospectus filed with a registration statement at the initial effective date.

[margin note: Info that can be omitted in base Prospectus]

1. • Shelf offerings pursuant to Rule 415(a)(1)(vii) (mortgage-related securities) or (x) may omit "information that is unknown or not reasonably available to the issuer pursuant to Rule 409." Rule 430B(a). What exactly constitutes information that is "unknown" or "not reasonably available"? Information omitted generally includes the public offering price and other price-related information, such as the underwriting discount. In addition, to the extent the issuer does not know the specific characteristics of securities to be offered on the shelf at the time of the initial filing of the registration statement, the issuer may omit such information, providing only general terms. The issuer may then include more specific details for offered securities later as part of a prospectus supplement. Other information may also qualify for omission, such as the identities of the underwriters for future takedowns off the shelf, if unknown at the time of filing of the initial registration statement.

2. • Shelf offerings under an automatic shelf registration statement and pursuant to Rule 415(a)(1), other than Rule 415(a)(1)(vii) or (viii), may omit "whether the offering is a primary offering or an offering on behalf of persons other than the issuer or a combination thereof, the plan of distribution for the securities, a description of the securities registered other than an identification of the name or class of such securities, and the identification of other issuers." Rule 430B(a). Thus, a WKSI making use of an automatic shelf registration statement may omit information on the plan of distribution and on whether the shelf is a primary or secondary offering even if the issuer knows the information or the information is otherwise reasonably available. The issuer may not know in advance which of its investors in a private placement, for example, will want to take advantage of a registered offering to resell their securities.

3. • Shelf offerings pursuant to Rule 415(a)(1)(i) conducted by an issuer eligible for Form S-3 or F-3 may omit the information specified in Rule 430B(a) as well as "the identities of selling security holders and amounts of securities to be registered on their behalf." This exclusion applies only for (1) an automatic shelf registration statement or (2) situations where "(i) The initial offering transaction of the

securities . . . the resale of which are being registered on behalf of each of the selling security holders, was completed; (ii) The securities . . . were issued and outstanding prior to the original date of filing the registration statement covering the resale of the securities; (iii) The registration statement refers to any unnamed selling security holders in a generic manner by identifying the initial offering transaction in which the securities were sold." A fourth requirement (iv), is that the issuer cannot have been, in the past three years, a blank check or shell company or an issuer in a penny stock offering. Rule 430(b)(2).

Under Rule 430B, a base prospectus omitting information pursuant to the Rule would meet the requirements of § 10 for purposes of § 5(b)(1) of the Securities Act. Rule 430B does not, however, allow the omission of such information for a prospectus to satisfy § 10(a) for purposes of § 5(b)(2) or for the free writing exception contained in § 2(a)(10)(a). Thus, the issuer must eventually include the omitted information to transmit securities for sale (under § 5(b)(2)) or to engage in traditional free writing under § 2(a)(10)(a).

omitted info filled eater

What is the mechanism for later including the omitted information in the prospectus? Rule 430B gives issuers flexibility in how to file the additional information through either a prospectus supplement, Exchange Act report (incorporated by reference), or a post-effective amendment. Rule 430B(d). Item 512(A)(5) and Rule 430B(e) and (f) make clear that any additional information filed later, regardless of whether through incorporation-by-reference, a prospectus supplement, or a post-effective amendment, is deemed part of the registration statement. For the issuer and the underwriters, this creates a new effective date for the registration statement for § 11 antifraud liability purposes. For certain other defendants, including officers, directors, and experts, the effective date is unchanged for the other portions of the registration statement.

NOTES

1. *Underwriters.* Rule 415 creates a dilemma for underwriters. On the one hand, the shelf registration process is designed to allow issuers to sell securities quickly by incorporating by reference their prior Exchange Act filings. Speed, however, undercuts the ability of underwriters to perform adequate due diligence on the offering, necessary if they are to avoid § 11 liability for any misstatements in the registration statement. The problems created for underwriters by this accelerated pace are explored in the *WorldCom* case, excerpted in Chapter 8.

speed undercuts ability of underw to DD.

2. *Overhang.* When a company registers securities for sale through a shelf registration, the stock price of the company typically drops. The price drop is known as the shelf registration overhang. One explanation for shelf overhang is that the presence of a large supply hanging over the market results in a fear of substantial dilution among present stockholders, lowering the stock price. The potential sale of securities in and of itself, however, will not necessarily dilute pre-existing security holders. If a company sells common stock at a premium to

price drop - fear of dilusion

the market price, the sale should increase the per share value of the pre-existing common stock. (But who would buy at a premium to the market price?) Dilution will occur only where the shares are sold at a price *lower* than the market price. But why would managers ever choose to sell for less than the market price? Only a company with serious cash flow problems would dilute shareholders this way.

An alternative explanation for market overhang is that managers can time stock sales to coincide with market overvaluation of the stock. Imagine that pre-existing shareholders cannot tell whether the market under or overvalues the stock (but managers do know this). First, consider when the stock is overvalued. Those who own pre-existing stock will be less likely to obtain the benefit from selling overvalued stock (as the company will flood the market with new stock in this case). Second, consider when the stock is undervalued. The owners of pre-existing stock will then bear the entire cost of selling undervalued stock. Pre-existing shareholders, therefore, will systematically bear the cost of selling undervalued stock but miss out on selling overvalued stock—reducing their expected returns and therefore lowering the price of stock in the marketplace.

HYPOTHETICAL ELEVEN

Two years have passed since Smartway's initial public offering (in which Smartway issued eleven million shares of common at $20 per share). Smartway's shares now trade on Nasdaq at around $80 per share. Assume that no affiliates of Smartway own any of the publicly traded shares and that Smartway has been current in its Exchange Act filings over the past two years. Smartway has occasional cash flow problems and wants to be able to raise additional funds quickly to cover its cash shortfalls. Consider the following options for raising more capital.

1. *Scenario One*: Smartway will issue $500 million of non-convertible bonds. Sherry does not know when Smartway will need this capital, but she hopes to be able to sell the bonds over the next six years as dictated by Smartway's cash flow needs. Can Smartway structure its bond offering to achieve Sherry's goal?

2. *Scenario Two*: Suppose that six months after the initial effective date of the shelf registration described in Scenario One, Sherry is indicted for insider trading and jailed; she is replaced with a new CEO. If this were not a shelf registration and Smartway had not yet completed its offering, what updating would Smartway have to do? What about with Rule 415(a)(3)? What difference does it make?

3. *Scenario Three*: Can Smartway issue $500 million of voting common stock through sales directly into Nasdaq over the next two years? Smartway would prefer not to pay an underwriter's commission for the offering.

4. *Scenario Four*: Smartway moves forward with its shelf registration offering of common stock through Nasdaq with the assistance of Sparrow Securities as an advisor. On February 1, Smartway files a Form S–3 registration statement, including a "base prospectus." The base prospectus excludes information on the offering price, underwriters, underwriting discount, and on the securities offered (referring only to an "unspecified" amount of "common stock"). Later, on June 1, Smartway sells $200 million of common off the shelf. The common stock is sold at the prevailing market price of $80 per share and sold through the assistance of Sparrow Securities as underwriter. On June 2, Smartway files a prospectus supplement containing the previously omitted information with the SEC. Has Smartway complied with Rule 415?

5. *Scenario Five*: Smartway will issue $250 million of convertible bonds on a delayed basis over the next two years. Each bond (principal amount of $100) can be converted at any time into one share of voting common (assume that if all the bonds were converted into common today they would result in $100 million of common). The bonds' term is ten years; the conversion therefore may take place up to ten years after the bonds are sold.

6. *Scenario Six*: Many Smartway officers purchased shares prior to Smartway's initial public offering. These shares are "restricted" in the sense that the securities laws prohibit the officers from freely reselling the shares into the public markets absent a registration statement. (We explain why in Chapter 10.) May the officers use a shelf registration for these shares covering a ten-year period?

CHAPTER 8

CIVIL LIABILITY UNDER THE SECURITIES ACT

Rules and Statutes

—*Sections 2(a)(3), 2(a)(10), 2(a)(11), 6(a), 10–13, 15, 27, 27A of the Securities Act*

—*Rules 158, 159, 159A, 176 of the Securities Act*

MOTIVATING HYPOTHETICAL

InterPhone, Inc. was founded three years ago by two siblings, Zoe (InterPhone's CEO and chair of its board) and Elmo (InterPhone's Chief Technology Officer or "CTO"). InterPhone specializes in providing equipment to businesses providing phone service over the Internet. To start InterPhone, Zoe and Elmo each put in $100,000 of their own money, hard work and ideas. Zoe and Elmo's initial capital carried InterPhone through its first year. By year two, InterPhone needed more capital to continue research and development. Zoe and Elmo put together their first formal business plan. That document outlined InterPhone's business, its plans for growth, its key personnel, its need and use for funds, as well as financials. After shopping their plan around to various venture capital firms, Zoe and Elmo eventually got VenRisk LLC to invest $10 million in InterPhone. In return, VenRisk demanded half the seats on InterPhone's board of directors as well as 40 percent of InterPhone's common stock. Now, at the end of year three, InterPhone again requires more capital. InterPhone enlists Sparrow Securities to be its managing underwriter for its initial public offering. The IPO distributed 10 million shares of InterPhone common stock at $20 per share. Unfortunately, InterPhone's registration statement and prospectus omitted Elmo's prior criminal conviction for commodities fraud and overstated InterPhone's earnings for the past two years.

I. PUBLIC OFFERINGS, UNCERTAINTY AND INFORMATION ASYMMETRY

Companies need capital if they wish to expand into new businesses, develop new products, or launch new marketing campaigns. Not all companies turn to outside sources of funding for these projects. Some companies have mature, cash-producing lines of business. For example, Microsoft generates significant amounts of cash from its operating system and software each year. Other companies cannot look to their current business for cash. Startup companies hold out the promise of large profits in the (hopefully not too distant) future. To get these later profits, startups must spend large amounts of cash hiring employees, engaging in research and development, and producing and marketing their products, among other expenses.

If later profits were certain, startups would have no problem in raising funds. Who wouldn't want to invest in a sure thing? Unfortunately, the amount of future profits is often difficult to forecast. This is the problem of uncertainty. Moreover, issuers (and their insiders) often have better information than outside investors on the true risks facing a company. This is the problem of information asymmetry.

The public capital markets provide one source of capital. Through a securities offering, a company is able to sell securities to a broad segment of the investing public. Most public investors prefer to remain passive and take very small positions in a large number of firms. Through diversification, investors are able to reduce the risk of investing in the securities of a particular company. This advantage of the public capital markets, however, also heightens the potential downside for investors. Dispersed and passive investors are at the greatest risk of getting defrauded. Such investors often have the least leverage and incentive to learn about and monitor the company in which they invest, thus creating a recipe for potential opportunism by insiders.

The registration process that we covered in Chapter 7 attempts to reduce uncertainty and information asymmetry through mandatory disclosure of information deemed important to investors. Companies raising capital in a public offering must persuade investors of the high value of the offered securities. Although many companies disclose information honestly, some issuers may misrepresent themselves to raise more capital. The civil liability provisions of the Securities Act that we will cover in this chapter are intended to ensure that the disclosures mandated by the registration process actually provide investors with accurate information. Section 12(a)(1) guards against circumvention of the rules of the registration process. Section 11 of the Securities Act targets fraud in the registration statement. Section 12(a)(2) of the Act similarly provides a civil antifraud provision for the public offering prospectus and statements relating to that prospectus.

II. Section 11 Liability

Section 11 of the Securities Act provides a civil antifraud provision for misstatements and omissions in the registration statement. As you learned in Chapter 5, plaintiffs seeking to file a securities fraud suit against an issuer and other participating parties can file a Rule 10b–5 action which mirrors in many respects the common law cause of action for deceit.

Section 11 relaxes or eliminates a number of the common law requirements for fraud in an effort to deter fraud by corporate issuers and make it easier for investors to obtain compensation. As you read through the following materials, consider what plaintiffs gain from including a § 11 antifraud claim in their complaint.

A. STANDING

Not all investors can bring suit under § 11. Companies making a public offering register particular securities with the SEC. The registration statement filed with the SEC covers only those securities sold as part of that specific public offering. In InterPhone's initial public offering, the company filed a registration statement covering 10 million shares of common stock at $20 per share. Because § 11 targets misstatements in the registration statement, courts have interpreted § 11 as imposing a stringent "tracing requirement." Plaintiffs seeking to bring a § 11 claim must show that the specific shares they purchased were included in the public offering under the registration statement that contained the alleged misstatement.

Even for companies, such as InterPhone, doing an initial public offering, § 11's tracing requirement may stymie some plaintiffs. IPO companies typically will have other shares outstanding of the same class as those sold in the initial public offering. The founders of InterPhone, for example, obtained common stock when they initially capitalized the company. Similarly, VenRisk LLC, the venture capital investor in InterPhone, purchased InterPhone common stock prior to InterPhone's initial public offering. These early investors may use Rule 144 (discussed in Chapter 10) to sell non-registered securities into the public market after the required holding period. Such sales are relatively rare, however, prior to the company making a public offering for the first time. Instead, insiders and venture capitalists that wish to sell their shares will often have the shares registered as a secondary offering pursuant to the registration statement for the company's IPO. The insiders and venture capitalists that do not sell in the IPO will typically sign lock-up agreements under which they agree not to sell their non-registered shares for a certain period of time (usually six months). During this lock-up period, investors purchasing stock in the secondary market may argue that the only shares trading in the secondary markets are those registered for the IPO.

For more seasoned companies raising additional capital in a subsequent "seasoned" public offering (sometimes years after the initial public offering), § 11's tracing requirement erects a far greater hurdle. Consider how an investor of a company such as IBM would go about showing that the shares purchased in the secondary market in fact are the same shares IBM sold in its most recent public offering, rather than one of its several prior public offerings. Enterprising plaintiffs' attorneys have attempted to maneuver around the tracing requirement of § 11 with creative theories. The following case is a good example of such an attempt, as well as an illustration of the problems that modern clearing procedures create for

§ 11 plaintiffs. Do you agree with the plaintiff's tracing theory? Does the tracing requirement create an unreasonable hurdle to recovery under § 11?

Abbey v. Computer Memories, Inc.

634 F.Supp. 870 (N.D. Cal. 1986).

■ Lynch, District Judge.

I. Background

Defendants in this case have brought a motion for summary judgment on Count I of plaintiff Abbey's complaint. Count I asserts a claim under section 11 of the Securities Act of 1933. Defendants argue that they are entitled to summary judgment on Count I because, among other reasons, Abbey cannot possibly trace his shares to the offering upon which section 11 liability would be based....

On August 23, 1983, defendant Computer Memories, Inc. ("CMI") made a public offering of approximately 2,000,000 shares of common stock pursuant to a registration statement and prospectus also dated August 23, 1983. It is the August 23, 1983 registration statement upon which plaintiff bases his section 11 claim.

Abbey purchased a total of 10,000 shares of CMI stock. One thousand of these shares were purchased before the August 23, 1983 offering and therefore clearly cannot form a basis for a damages claim under section 11.... The remaining 9,000 shares were purchased on August 29, 1983, approximately one week after the effective date of the registration statement. These shares were not purchased pursuant to the offering or from any of the participants in the offering, but were purchased in the open market at a price higher than the offering's price.

Abbey purchased his shares through Fidelity Brokerage Services, Inc., a stock broker. However, Fidelity did not actually execute the stock purchase. Instead, Fidelity placed a purchase order through its subsidiary, National Financial Services Corporation, Inc., with the Pershing division of Donaldson Lufkin & Jenrette Securities Corporation. Pershing then executed two purchases of CMI stock, totaling 9,000 shares, from Mayer & Schweitzer, Inc., a stock brokerage firm which serves as a market-maker for CMI's common stock.

The purchase of Abbey's CMI stock was effected between Pershing and Mayer & Schweitzer through the continuous net settlement system of the National Securities Clearing Corporation. Under the continuous net settlement system used by NSCC, the CMI stock sold by Mayer & Schweitzer did not physically trade hands on the date it was purchased by Pershing. Rather, the trade was merely recorded as a part of the net adjustment made to the CMI accounts of Mayer & Schweitzer and of Pershing to reflect all of the two firms' respective trades for that day.

On September 6, 1983, the settlement date for the August 29, 1983 trade, the transfer of Abbey's CMI stock was effected between Pershing and Mayer & Schweitzer through an electronic bookkeeping entry made by the Depository Trust Company. The DTC maintains deposits of large quantities of various stocks for the benefit of its broker-participants. These deposits minimize the need for the physical transfer of shares when the participants engage in stock transactions among one another. Thus, all of the CMI shares purchased by Abbey were a part of the common pool of CMI shares held in DTC's vault on the day of the transfer. There is no evidence before the Court concerning whether Abbey ever took physical possession of his shares or whether they remained in DTC's vault. However, the important point for purposes of this motion is that it is undisputed that Abbey's CMI shares were at one time part of the CMI shares commingled in DTC's vault.

Defendants have submitted affidavits indicating that it is impossible for Abbey to show that his stock came from the offering. These affidavits state that the stock kept in DTC's vault was completely fungible and that it would therefore be impossible to determine the origin of Abbey's stock. Defendants argue that because it is impossible for Abbey to directly trace any of his shares to the offering, the defendants are entitled to summary judgment on Abbey's section 11 claim.

Abbey has not submitted any evidence refuting the defendants' claim that it is impossible for Abbey to directly trace any of his shares to the offering. Rather, Abbey makes the following three arguments against granting summary judgment: (1) that section 11 does not require "direct tracing" and that Abbey can fulfill the tracing requirement by producing circumstantial evidence showing that it is more probable than not that a certain percentage of his shares were issued in the offering; (2) that because Abbey's shares were comingled with other shares held in DTC's vault, Abbey must be considered as having held a proportionate interest in all the stock held by DTC, thereby creating an issue of fact as to whether any of the comingled shares can be traced to the offering; (3) that defendants are not entitled to summary judgment because they have not shown that none of Abbey's shares came from the offering. For the reasons described below, the Court rejects each of Abbey's arguments and grants the defendants' motion.

II.   Tracing Based on the Timing and Circumstances of the Trade

Abbey purchased 9,000 shares of CMI common stock approximately one week after the offering. The offering added 2 million shares of common stock to the 9 million shares previously outstanding. Abbey argues that the timing of his purchase combined with the fact that 18 percent of the shares then outstanding were new shares (2 million of the 11 million then outstanding) make it highly probable that at least some of his shares were from the offering. He contends that nothing in the language of section 11 precludes him from fulfilling the tracing requirement by simply showing by circumstantial evidence that a portion of his shares probably came from the offering.

Abbey's argument is inconsistent with the existing precedent. Although the language of section 11 does not clearly require direct tracing, courts have uniformly interpreted section 11 as requiring more than a showing that a plaintiff's stock "might" have come from the relevant offering....

Relaxing the tracing requirement such that a plaintiff may fulfill it by showing even a high probability that some of his shares were from the relevant offering would be inconsistent with the narrow scope of potential liability envisioned by section 11. Section 11 limits its conclusive presumption of reliance to persons acquiring any securities issued pursuant to the registration statement, notwithstanding the obvious fact that a false or misleading statement in or an omission from a registration statement could easily affect the price of stock issued prior to the offering.... Section 11 simply was not intended to provide a remedy to every person who might have been harmed by a defective registration statement. The Court believes that the language of section 11 and the existing case law indicate that a plaintiff who can only show that his or her shares might have been issued in the relevant offering should not be given the benefit of section 11's conclusive presumption of reliance; such a person should be treated the same as individuals whose shares clearly were not issued in the offering.

It is important to note that section 11's direct tracing requirement does not leave individuals who have been harmed by a defective registration statement completely without a remedy. Abbey, for example, may still pursue his lawsuit under his 10b–5 claim. The "direct tracing" requirement simply precludes a shareholder from taking advantage of section 11's relaxed liability requirements when the shareholder's connection to the relevant offering is so attenuated that he or she cannot directly trace his or her shares to the offering. In such cases, requiring a shareholder to pursue other remedies, which may require a showing of reliance, seems imminently reasonable.

III. Tracing Based on the Fungible Mass Theory

There is no dispute that Abbey's shares were comingled with the other CMI shares held in DTC's vault. Abbey argues that because his shares were comingled he must be considered as having owned a fractional interest in each of the CMI shares then held as a "fungible mass" by DTC. Abbey notes that "[s]uch comingled ownership has long been recognized in several areas of commerce, including grain storage, investment certificate bailment, priority allocation in bankruptcy, and even money or coinage." Abbey argues that because he must be deemed as having owned a fractional share of all the stock held by DTC when his shares were purchased, an issue of fact exists as to whether any of DTC's shares then in its inventory were issued pursuant to the offering.

If the Court were to accept Abbey's fungible mass theory of tracing, an issue of fact would exist. Defendants have neither shown that none of the stock held by DTC was issued in the offering nor that it is impossible to trace the origin of any of that stock. Moreover, the Court concedes that, in plaintiff's words, it is a "virtual certainty" that some of the DTC stock was issued pursuant to the offering. However, the Court rejects the fungible mass theory as a method for tracing.

The purpose of section 11's tracing requirement is to limit standing to sue to those individuals who actually purchased shares issued pursuant to a defective registration statement. . . . If the Court accepted Abbey's fungible mass argument, any purchaser of stock that had been part of a fungible mass containing new shares would have standing to sue. In essence, the tracing requirement would be transformed from a standing requirement into a means of allocating damages, because standing would seldom be lacking. This result would circumvent section 11's intended narrow application. . . .

Admittedly, the fungible mass theory adds an additional wrinkle to the "might-have-been-issued" argument by asserting that the shareholder actually owned a fractional interest in at least one stock that is directly traceable to the relevant offering. However, the Court finds that while comingled ownership theories serve useful purposes in other areas of the law, they have no place in the section 11 standing context because the result would be circumvention of the intent of section 11. . . .

The Court is satisfied that no genuine issue of fact exists as to the tracing issue because plaintiff is undisputably unable to directly trace his shares to the offering. Therefore, defendants are granted summary judgment on Count I of Abbey's complaint. . . .

* * *

QUESTIONS

1. Section 11 does not require plaintiffs to demonstrate any reliance on the registration statement. Does the lack of a reliance requirement justify imposing a strict tracing requirement for § 11?

2. In one of the earliest cases to impose a tracing requirement on Section 11 plaintiffs, *Barnes v. Osofsky*, 373 F.2d 269 (2d Cir. 1967), Judge Henry Friendly justified the requirement by pointing to § 11(g)'s limit on damages:

> [T]he over-all limitation of § 11(g) that "In no case shall the amount recoverable under this section exceed the price at which the security was offered to the public," and the provision of § 11(e) whereby, with qualifications not here material, an underwriter's liability shall not exceed "the total price at which the securities underwritten by him and distributed to the public were offered to the public," point in the direction of limiting § 11 to purchasers of the registered shares, since otherwise their recovery would be greatly diluted when the new issue was small in relation to the trading in previously outstanding shares. . . .

Do you agree with the *Barnes* court's reading of § 11(g)? Does the *Barnes* court prevent dilution of recovery at the expense of another policy goal of § 11?

HYPOTHETICAL ONE

Suppose that Bird purchases 10,000 shares at $20 per share directly from Sparrow Securities, the managing underwriter in InterPhone's initial public offering. Bird's shares are purchased on the day of the IPO. Recall that the registration statement and prospectus omitted Elmo's (InterPhone's CTO) prior criminal conviction for commodities fraud and overstated InterPhone's earnings for the past two years.

1. *Scenario One*: Will Bird have standing to bring a § 11 fraud suit based on the misleading statements in InterPhone's registration statement?

2. *Scenario Two*: What if Bird purchases additional InterPhone shares two weeks later through her broker? Assume that the trades are executed on Nasdaq with one of several marketmakers quoting InterPhone's shares.

3. *Scenario Three*: Suppose that one-year prior to the IPO, InterPhone's biggest shareholder, VenRisk LLC, had sold 100,000 shares into the public market under Rule 144. After the IPO, the shares previously sold by VenRisk account for 1% of the outstanding shares trading in Nasdaq. Does this change your answer to Question 2?

B. STATUTORY DEFENDANTS

Unlike the other civil antifraud provisions of the securities laws, § 11 defines the range of potential defendants. The list includes:

(1) those who signed the registration statement (§ 11(a)(1)) including the issuer, the chief executive officer, and the chief financial officer among others (§ 6(a));

(2) directors (§ 11(a)(2), (3));

(3) various experts who prepared or certified a part of the registration statement (§ 11(a)(4));

(4) underwriters (§ 11(a)(5)); and

(5) controlling persons of any of the above (§ 15)

To consider the scope of § 11's delineated list of defendants, consider *Escott v. BarChris Construction Corp.*, 283 F.Supp. 643 (S.D.N.Y. 1968). *Escott,* the seminal case on § 11's due diligence requirement, is excerpted later in the chapter. BarChris Construction Co. was involved in the business of constructing bowling alleys. BarChris raised capital in a debenture offering to help finance the construction of more bowling alleys. The BarChris offering involved a number of players including the following insiders:

Name	Position
Russo	Chief Executive Officer and BarChris Director
Vitolo and Pugliese	Founders, Executive Officers and BarChris Directors
Kircher	Treasurer, Chief Financial Officer, and BarChris Director
Birnbaum	Secretary and BarChris Director

In addition, a number of outside participants might have played a role in making (or approving) the misstatements in BarChris's registration statement, including:

Name	Position
Auslander	BarChris Director
Grant	Outside Counsel and BarChris Director
Drexel Burnham	Managing Underwriter
Coleman	Partner at Drexel and BarChris Director
Casperson	Associate at Drexel
Drinker, Biddle & Reath	Drexel Burnham's Attorneys
Ballard	Partner at Drinker, Biddle & Reath
Stanton	Associate at Drinker, Biddle & Reath
Peat Marwick	Auditor (certified BarChris's financial statements only)
Berardi	Senior Accountant

QUESTIONS

1. Among the list of insider and outsider participants in the BarChris public debenture offering, which participants may plaintiffs potentially sue under § 11 and why?

2. BarChris itself is not in the list of insider and outsider participants. Can a plaintiff contemplating suing for fraud in the BarChris public debenture offering's registration statement also sue BarChris under § 11?

3. Can we sue Peat Marwick, the auditors for BarChris, for misstatements relating to future competitive threats contained in the risk factor section of the registration statement?

4. Suppose that MegaCorp Inc. owns 70% of BarChris's common stock. Is MegaCorp a potential § 11 defendant?

5. What purpose do you think placing liability on Peat Marwick (the auditors) and Drexel Burnham (the managing underwriter) serves? Given this purpose, does the treatment of Drinker, Biddle & Reath (the attorneys for the managing underwriter) make sense?

C.   ELEMENTS OF THE CAUSE OF ACTION

One way to understand the power of § 11 liability is to compare § 11 with Rule 10b–5 and state common law fraud. Section 11, Rule 10b–5, and state common law fraud all require a showing of a material misstatement. In the securities context, as discussed in Chapter 2, materiality depends on what a reasonable investor would view as significant given the "total mix" of information available to the investor.

Other than materiality, however, the elements of a § 11 cause of action are considerably easier to satisfy than the requirements for Rule 10b–5 and common law fraud. Plaintiffs in a Rule 10b–5 or state common law fraud suit bear the burden of showing that the defendant acted with scienter. Plaintiffs must also show that the defendant's fraud caused their loss and that they relied on the misstatement (or omission where a duty to disclose exists). Section 11, on the other hand, imposes no additional burdens on the plaintiff beyond a misstatement and materiality.

Elements	Section 11	Rule 10b–5 and State Common Law Fraud
Misstatement (or omission where duty to disclose exists)	√	√
Materiality	√	√
Scienter		√
Reliance		√
Loss Causation	Defense	√

The lack of a scienter, reliance, or causation requirement on § 11 plaintiffs does not necessarily mean plaintiffs may ignore these elements completely. If the issuer makes public an earnings statement covering a period of at least twelve months beginning after the effective date of the registration statement, § 11(a) provides that plaintiffs then bear the burden of demonstrating reliance.

Misstatements in the registration statement for § 11 purposes are determined as of the effective date, i.e., the information in the registration statement must be accurate on the date the SEC declares it effective. One consideration in amending the registration statement (which results in a new effective date as of the time of the amendment) is increased antifraud liability exposure. The filing of a post-effective amendment does two things. First, the information is included in the registration statement and thereby comes under the coverage of § 11. Second, the filing of a post-effective amendment resets the effective date. Information that was accurate at an earlier effective date may face § 11 liability if no longer accurate as of the new effective date.

Issuers must amend the registration statement in certain instances. We saw in Chapter 7 that issuers doing a Rule 415 shelf registration must furnish an undertaking pursuant to Item 512(a) to file a post-effective amendment to the registration statement if, among other things, a "fundamental" change has occurred. Issuers that qualify for Form S–3, among others, may avoid a post-effective amendment to a shelf registration statement otherwise required under Item 512(a)(1)(i) (prospectuses required under § 10(a)(3)) or Item 512(a)(1)(ii) (fundamental changes) through incorporation of the information by reference to an Exchange Act reporting filing or a prospectus supplement.

Consider how incorporation-by-reference differs for purposes of § 11 from a post-effective amendment. The information incorporated by reference is considered part of the registration statement and, as with a post-effective amendment, becomes subject to § 11 liability. It is unclear, however, what happens to the effective date. Does incorporation-by-reference reset the effective date, in which case there is no difference compared with a post-effective amendment from the perspective of § 11 liability? Or is the effective date left unchanged, and only liability for the specific information incorporated by reference measured at the time it was included into the registration statement?

The SEC's 2005 Public Offering Reforms shed some light on this issue. Under those reforms, a prospectus supplement containing information omitted in the earlier base shelf registration prospectus under Rule 430B would both (a) be considered part of the registration statement and (b) reset the effective date for the entire registration statement for the issuer and underwriters. Rule 430B(f); Item 512(a)(5)(ii). The SEC, however, did not provide for a similar resetting of the effective date for Item 512(a)(1)(i), (ii), and (iii) information included through incorporation-by-reference (or, as allowed under the SEC's proposal, a prospectus supplement) into the shelf registration prospectus. Such information is part of the registration statement and faces potential § 11 liability, but it does not generate a new effective date for the entire registration statement.

HYPOTHETICAL TWO

Put yourself in the shoes of a plaintiff's class action attorney. You observe InterPhone's initial public offering at $20 per share. One month after the offering, InterPhone's share price has dropped to $10 per share amid rumors that InterPhone improperly added $10 million to its earnings by shifting certain expenses to a subsidiary.

1. What information would you need to collect in order to file a Rule 10b–5 fraud action against InterPhone? What information would you need to collect to file a § 11 cause of action?

2. If you were the general counsel of InterPhone evaluating the firm's litigation options, how does § 11 exposure change your settlement calculus?

D.   DEFENSES

Section 11 defendants have a number of possible defenses. A defendant who, among other things, resigns from her position and notifies the SEC of her actions may obtain a defense under § 11(b). Alternatively, defendants may attempt to show actual knowledge on the part of plaintiffs of the alleged fraud in the registration statement at the time the plaintiffs purchased their securities. In a situation where one specific plaintiff makes a § 11 allegation, how are defendants supposed to show actual knowledge on the part of a plaintiff? Where will they obtain evidence of the plaintiff's knowledge? Expand this problem to a class action. How will defendants ascertain what knowledge each member of the class had at the time of purchase?

The most important use of the actual knowledge defense as a defense does not require proof of the knowledge on the part of specific plaintiffs. Instead, the defense typically is employed after the issuer (or other party) makes a public announcement detailing and correcting the fraud. After such an announcement, defendants may argue the entire market "knew" of the fraud, thereby eliminating any subsequent § 11 liability. Alternatively, one could argue that once the correcting information is in the "total mix" of information in the market, the prior fraud is no longer material. This defense provides a strong impetus for potential § 11 defendants to correct misstatements as soon as possible through public disclosure.

Section 11 lawsuits are barred after a one/three year statute of limitations imposed by § 13 of the Securities Act. Plaintiffs must file the § 11 lawsuit within one year after they find out about the fraud or should have found out about the fraud through the exercise of reasonable care (a "discovery" statute). In no case may plaintiffs bring the § 11 lawsuit more than three years after the securities were offered to the public (a "repose" statute).

1. DUE DILIGENCE DEFENSE

By far the most important defense for § 11 defendants is the due diligence defense contained in § 11(b)(3). Issuers are excluded from the due diligence defense. Section 11 divides all other defendants into two categories: experts and non-experts. The requirement placed on each then turns on whether the alleged fraud is found in a non-expertised or expertised section of the registration statement. The most obvious example of an expertised section would be the audited financials of the issuer; the auditor serves as the expert for this portion of the registration statement. Are there other examples of experts and expertised sections?

Due Diligence Defense Requirements

(Measured at time of effective date of the registration statement)

	Non–Expertised	Expertised
Expert	No Liability—§ 11(a)(4)	Reasonable Investigation, Reasonable Ground to Believe and Did Believe of Truth—§ 11(b)(3)(B)
Non–Expert	Reasonable Investigation, Reasonable Ground to Believe and Did Believe of Truth—§ 11(b)(3)(A)	Reasonable Ground to Believe and Did Believe of Truth—§ 11(b)(3)(C)

The coarse two-by-two framework of due diligence embodied within § 11 may not completely capture the range of § 11 defendants and situations in which the defendants may find themselves during the registration process. Among the class of non-experts are top executive officers of the issuer, underwriters, outside directors of the issuer with some specific role in the offering (such as an attorney-director or underwriter-director), and outside directors with no other role. To what extent should the due diligence defense vary based on the position and role a particular non-expert defendant plays in the offering process and, more generally, in relation to the issuer?

Escott v. BarChris Construction Corp.

283 F. Supp. 643 (S.D.N.Y. 1968).

■ McLean, District Judge.

This is an action by purchasers of 5 1/2 per cent convertible subordinated fifteen year debentures of BarChris Construction Corporation (BarChris)....

The action is brought under § 11 of the Securities Act of 1933. Plaintiffs allege that the registration statement with respect to these debentures filed with the Securities and Exchange Commission, which became effective on May 16, 1961, contained material false statements and material omissions. . . .

At the time relevant here, BarChris was engaged primarily in the construction of bowling alleys. . . . The introduction of automatic pin setting machines in 1952 gave a marked stimulus to bowling. It rapidly became a popular sport, with the result that "bowling centers" began to appear throughout the country in rapidly increasing numbers. BarChris benefited from this increased interest in bowling. Its construction operations expanded rapidly. It is estimated that in 1960 BarChris installed approximately three per cent of all lanes built in the United States. . . .

BarChris's sales increased dramatically from 1956 to 1960. According to the prospectus, net sales, in round figures, in 1956 were some $800,000, in 1957 $1,300,000, in 1958 $1,700,000. In 1959 they increased to over $3,300,000, and by 1960 they had leaped to over $9,165,000. . . .

In general, BarChris's method of operation was to enter into a contract with a customer, receive from him at that time a comparatively small down payment on the purchase price, and proceed to construct and equip the bowling alley. When the work was finished and the building delivered, the customer paid the balance of the contract price in notes, payable in installments over a period of years. BarChris discounted these notes with a factor and received part of their face amount in cash. The factor held back part as a reserve. . . . [The factor, James Talcott Inc., would purchase the notes at a discount for cash and then require BarChris to guarantee a percentage of the notes sold. Initially BarChris guaranteed 25% of the notes. But under a revised "alternative" financing arrangement, BarChris eventually guaranteed 100% of the notes].

BarChris was compelled to expend considerable sums in defraying the cost of construction before it received reimbursement. As a consequence, BarChris was in constant need of cash to finance its operations, a need which grew more pressing as operations expanded. . . . By early 1961, BarChris needed additional working capital. The proceeds of the sale of the debentures involved in this action were to be devoted, in part at least, to fill that need. . . .

The registration statement became effective on May 16. The closing of the financing took place on May 24. On that day BarChris received the net proceeds of the financing. . . .

[The court then analyzed the materiality of errors in the debenture registration statement finding, among others: (1) exaggerated 1960 sales figures in the audited financials due to the inclusion of sales of completed alleys not yet in fact sold by BarChris (and now operated by BarChris as wholly-owned subsidiaries); (2) misrepresentation that BarChris guaranteed 25% of the notes transferred to Talcott when in fact the guarantee was for 100% for most of the notes; (3) misrepresentation that all loans by corporate officers to BarChris had been repaid; (4) misrepresentation that the offering proceeds would be used to construct a new plant, develop a new equipment line, and provide working capital when in fact the proceeds were used to pay existing debt.]

The "Due Diligence" Defenses

* * *

Every defendant, except BarChris itself, to whom, as the issuer, these defenses are not available, and except Peat, Marwick, whose position rests on a different statutory provision, has pleaded these affirmative defenses.... As to each defendant, the question is whether he has sustained the burden of proving these defenses. Surprising enough, there is little or no judicial authority on this question. No decisions directly in point under § 11 have been found.

Before considering the evidence, a preliminary matter should be disposed of. The defendants do not agree among themselves as to who the "experts" were or as to the parts of the registration statement which were expertised. Some defendants say that Peat, Marwick was the expert, others say that BarChris's attorneys, Perkins, Daniels, McCormack & Collins, and the underwriters' attorneys, Drinker, Biddle & Reath, were also the experts. On the first view, only those portions of the registration statement purporting to be made on Peat, Marwick's authority were expertised portions. On the other view, everything in the registration statement was within this category, because the two law firms were responsible for the entire document.

The first view is the correct one. To say that the entire registration statement is expertised because some lawyer prepared it would be an unreasonable construction of the statute. Neither the lawyer for the company nor the lawyer for the underwriters is an expert within the meaning of § 11. The only expert, in the statutory sense, was Peat, Marwick, and the only parts of the registration statement which purported to be made upon the authority of an expert were the portions which purported to be made on Peat, Marwick's authority....

I turn now to the question of whether defendants have proved their due diligence defenses. The position of each defendant will be separately considered.

Russo

Russo was, to all intents and purposes, the chief executive officer of BarChris. He was a member of the executive committee. He was familiar with all aspects of the business. He was personally in charge of dealings with the factors. He acted on BarChris's behalf in making the financing agreements with Talcott and he handled the negotiations with Talcott in the spring of 1961. He talked with customers about their delinquencies.

In short, Russo knew all the relevant facts. He could not have believed that there were no untrue statements or material omissions in the prospectus. Russo has no due diligence defenses.

Vitolo and Pugliese

They were the founders of the business who stuck with it to the end. Vitolo was president and Pugliese was vice president. Despite their titles, their field of responsibility in the administration of BarChris's affairs during the period in question seems to have been less all embracing then Russo's. Pugliese in particular appears to have limited his activities to supervising the actual construction work.

Vitolo and Pugliese are each men of limited education. It is not hard to believe that for them the prospectus was difficult reading, if indeed they read it at all.

But whether it was or not is irrelevant. The liability of a director who signs a registration statement does not depend upon whether or not he read it or, if he did, whether or not he understood what he was reading.

And in any case, Vitolo and Pugliese were not as naive as they claim to be. They were members of BarChris's executive committee. At meetings of that committee BarChris's affairs were discussed at length. They must have known what was going on. Certainly they knew of the inadequacy of cash in 1961. They knew of their own large advances to the company which remained unpaid. They knew that they had agreed not to deposit their checks until the financing proceeds were received. They knew and intended that part of the proceeds were to be used to pay their own loans.

All in all, the position of Vitolo and Pugliese is not significantly different, for present purposes, from Russo's. They could not have believed that the registration statement was wholly true and that no material facts had been omitted. And in any case, there is nothing to show that they made any investigation of anything which they may not have known about or understood. They have not proved their due diligence defenses.

Kircher

Kircher was treasurer of BarChris and its chief financial officer. He is a certified public accountant and an intelligent man. He was thoroughly familiar with BarChris's financial affairs. He knew the terms of BarChris's agreements with Talcott. He knew of the customers' delinquency problem. He participated actively with Russo in May 1961 in the successful effort to hold Talcott off until the financing proceeds came in. He knew how the financing proceeds were to be applied and he saw to it that they were so applied. He arranged the officers' loans and he knew all the facts concerning them.

Moreover, as a member of the executive committee, Kircher was kept informed as to those branches of the business of which he did not have direct charge. He knew about the operation of alleys, present and prospective.... In brief, Kircher knew all the relevant facts.

Kircher worked on the preparation of the registration statement. He conferred with Grant and on occasion with Ballard. He supplied information to them about the company's business. He read the prospectus and understood it. He knew what it said and what it did not say.

Kircher's contention is that he had never before dealt with a registration statement, that he did not know what it should contain, and that he relied wholly on Grant, Ballard and Peat, Marwick to guide him. He claims that it was their fault, not his, if there was anything wrong with it. He says that all the facts were recorded in BarChris's books where these "experts" could have seen them if they had looked. He says that he truthfully answered all their questions. In effect, he says that if they did not know enough to ask the right questions and to give him the proper instructions, that is not his responsibility.

There is an issue of credibility here. In fact, Kircher was not frank in dealing with Grant and Ballard. He withheld information from them. But even if he had told them all the facts, this would not have constituted the due diligence contemplated by the statute. Knowing the facts, Kircher had reason to believe that the expertised portion of the prospectus, i.e., the 1960 figures, was in part incorrect. He could not shut his eyes to the facts and rely on Peat, Marwick for that portion.

As to the rest of the prospectus, knowing the facts, he did not have a reasonable ground to believe it to be true. On the contrary, he must have known that in part it was untrue. Under these circumstances, he was not entitled to sit back and place the blame on the lawyers for not advising him about it.

Kircher has not proved his due diligence defenses....

Birnbaum

Birnbaum was a young lawyer, admitted to the bar in 1957, who, after brief periods of employment by two different law firms and an equally brief period of practicing in his own firm, was employed by BarChris as house counsel and assistant secretary in October 1960. Unfortunately for him, he became secretary and a director of BarChris on April 17, 1961, after the first version of the registration statement had been filed with the Securities and Exchange Commission. He signed the later amendments, thereby becoming responsible for the accuracy of the prospectus in its final form.

Although the prospectus, in its description of "management," lists Birnbaum among the "executive officers" and devotes several sentences to a recital of his career, the fact seems to be that he was not an executive officer in any real sense. He did not participate in the management of the company. As house counsel, he attended to legal matters of a routine nature. Among other things, he incorporated subsidiaries, with which BarChris was plentifully supplied.... He was thus aware of that aspect of the business.

Birnbaum examined contracts.... One of Birnbaum's more important duties, first as assistant secretary and later as full-fledged secretary, was to keep the corporate minutes of BarChris and its subsidiaries. This necessarily informed him to a considerable extent about the company's affairs....

It seems probable that Birnbaum did not know of many of the inaccuracies in the prospectus. He must, however, have appreciated some of them. In any case, he made no investigation and relied on the others to get it right.... [H]e was entitled to rely upon Peat, Marwick for the 1960 figures, for as far as appears, he had no personal knowledge of the company's books of account or financial transactions. But he was not entitled to rely upon Kircher, Grant and Ballard for the other portions of the prospectus. As a lawyer, he should have known his obligations under the statute. He should have known that he was required to make a reasonable investigation of the truth of all the statements in the unexpertised portion of the document which he signed. Having failed to make such an investigation, he did not have reasonable ground to believe that all these statements were true. Birnbaum has not established his due diligence defenses except as to the audited 1960 figures.

Auslander

Auslander was an "outside" director, i.e., one who was not an officer of BarChris. He was chairman of the board of Valley Stream National Bank in Valley Stream, Long Island. In February 1961 Vitolo asked him to become a director of BarChris. Vitolo gave him an enthusiastic account of BarChris's progress and prospects. As an inducement, Vitolo said that when BarChris received the proceeds of a forthcoming issue of securities, it would deposit $1,000,000 in Auslander's bank.

In February and early March 1961, before accepting Vitolo's invitation, Auslander made some investigation of BarChris. He obtained Dun & Bradstreet reports which contained sales and earnings figures for periods earlier than December 31, 1960. He caused inquiry to be made of certain of BarChris's banks and was advised that they regarded BarChris favorably. He was informed that inquiry of Talcott had also produced a favorable response.

On March 3, 1961, Auslander indicated his willingness to accept a place on the board. Shortly thereafter, on March 14, Kircher sent him a copy of BarChris's annual report for 1960. Auslander observed that BarChris's auditors were Peat, Marwick. They were also the auditors for the Valley Stream National Bank. He thought well of them.

Auslander was elected a director on April 17, 1961. The registration statement in its original form had already been filed, of course without his signature. On May 10, 1961, he signed a signature page for the first amendment to the registration statement which was filed on May 11, 1961. This was a separate sheet without any document attached. Auslander did not know that it was a signature page for a registration statement. He vaguely understood that it was something "for the SEC."

Auslander attended a meeting of BarChris's directors on May 15, 1961. At that meeting he, along with the other directors, signed the signature sheet for the second amendment which constituted the registration statement in its final form. Again, this was only a separate sheet without any document attached. Auslander never saw a copy of the registration statement in its final form.

At the May 15 directors' meeting, however, Auslander did realize that what he was signing was a signature sheet to a registration statement. This was the first time that he had appreciated that fact. A copy of the registration statement in its earlier form as amended on May 11, 1961 was passed around at the meeting. Auslander glanced at it briefly. He did not read it thoroughly.

At the May 15 meeting, Russo and Vitolo stated that everything was in order and that the prospectus was correct. Auslander believed this statement.

In considering Auslander's due diligence defenses, a distinction is to be drawn between the expertised and non-expertised portions of the prospectus. As to the former, Auslander knew that Peat, Marwick had audited the 1960 figures. He believed them to be correct because he had confidence in Peat, Marwick. He had no reasonable ground to believe otherwise.

As to the non-expertised portions, however, Auslander is in a different position. He seems to have been under the impression that Peat, Marwick was responsible for all the figures. This impression was not correct, as he would have realized if he had read the prospectus carefully. Auslander made no investigation of the accuracy of the prospectus. He relied on the assurance of Vitolo and Russo, and upon the information he had received in answer to his inquiries back in February and early March. These inquiries were general ones, in the nature of a credit check. The information which he received in answer to them was also general, without specific reference to the statements in the prospectus, which was not prepared until some time thereafter.

It is true that Auslander became a director on the eve of the financing. He had little opportunity to familiarize himself with the company's affairs. The question is whether, under such circumstances, Auslander did enough to establish his due diligence defense with respect to the non-expertised portions of the prospectus. . . .

Section 11 imposes liability in the first instance upon a director, no matter how new he is. He is presumed to know his responsibility when he becomes a director. He can escape liability only by using that reasonable care to investigate the facts which a prudent man would employ in the management of his own property. In my opinion, a prudent man would not act in an important matter without any knowledge of the relevant facts, in sole reliance upon representations of persons who are comparative strangers and upon general information which does not purport to cover the particular case. To say that such minimal conduct measures up to the statutory standard would, to all intents and purposes, absolve new directors from responsibility merely because they are new. This is not a sensible construction of Section 11, when one bears in mind its fundamental purpose of requiring full and truthful disclosure for the protection of investors.

I find and conclude that Auslander has not established his due diligence defense with respect to the misstatements and omissions in those portions of the prospectus other than the audited 1960 figures. . . .

Grant

Grant became a director of BarChris in October 1960. His law firm was counsel to BarChris in matters pertaining to the registration of securities. Grant drafted the registration statement for the stock issue in 1959 and for the warrants in January 1961. IIe also drafted the registration statement for the debentures. In the preliminary division of work between him and Ballard, the underwriters' counsel, Grant took initial responsibility for preparing the registration statement, while Ballard devoted his efforts in the first instance to preparing the indenture.

Grant is sued as a director and as a signer of the registration statement. This is not an action against him for malpractice in his capacity as a lawyer. Nevertheless, in considering Grant's due diligence defenses, the unique position which he occupied cannot be disregarded. As the director most directly concerned with writing the registration statement and assuring its accuracy, more was required of him in the way of reasonable investigation than could fairly be expected of a director who had no connection with this work.

There is no valid basis for plaintiffs' accusation that Grant knew that the prospectus was false in some respects and incomplete and misleading in others. Having seen him testify at length, I am satisfied as to his integrity. I find that Grant honestly believed that the registration statement was true and that no material facts had been omitted from it.

In this belief he was mistaken, and the fact is that for all his work, he never discovered any of the errors or omissions which have been recounted at length in this opinion, with the single exception of Capitol Lanes. He knew that BarChris had not sold this alley and intended to operate it, but he appears to have been under the erroneous impression that Peat, Marwick had knowingly sanctioned its inclusion in sales because of the allegedly temporary nature of the operation.

Grant contends that a finding that he did not make a reasonable investigation would be equivalent to a holding that a lawyer for an issuing company, in order to show due diligence, must make an independent audit of the figures supplied to him by his client. I do not consider this to be a realistic statement of the issue. There were errors and omissions here which could have been detected without an audit. The question is whether, despite his failure to detect them, Grant made a reasonable effort to that end.

Much of this registration statement is a scissors and paste-pot job. Grant lifted large portions from the earlier prospectuses, modifying them in some instances to the extent that he considered necessary. But BarChris's affairs had changed for the worse by May 1961. Statements that were accurate in January were no longer accurate in May. Grant never discovered this. He accepted the assurances of Kircher and Russo that any change which might have occurred had been for the better, rather than the contrary.

It is claimed that a lawyer is entitled to rely on the statements of his client and that to require him to verify their accuracy would set an unreasonably high standard. This is too broad a generalization. It is all a matter of degree. To require an audit would obviously be unreasonable. On the other hand, to require a check of matters easily verifiable is not unreasonable. Even honest clients can make mistakes. The statute imposes liability for untrue statements regardless of whether they are intentionally untrue. The way to prevent mistakes is to test oral information by examining the original written record.

There were things which Grant could readily have checked which he did not check. For example, he was unaware of the provisions of the agreements between BarChris and Talcott. He never read them. Thus, he did not know, although he readily could have ascertained, that BarChris's contingent liability on Type B leaseback arrangements was 100 per cent, not 25 per cent. He did not appreciate that if BarChris defaulted in repurchasing delinquent customers' notes upon Talcott's demand, Talcott could accelerate all the customer paper in its hands, which amounted to over $3,000,000.

As to the backlog figure, Grant appreciated that scheduled unfilled orders on the company's books meant firm commitments, but he never asked to see the contracts which, according to the prospectus, added up to $6,905,000. Thus, he did not know that this figure was overstated by some $4,490,000 . . . .

On the subject of minutes, Grant knew that minutes of certain meetings of the BarChris executive committee held in 1961 had not been written up. Kircher, who had acted as secretary at those meetings, had complete notes of them. Kircher told Grant that there was no point in writing up the minutes because the matters discussed at those meetings were purely routine. Grant did not insist that the minutes be written up, nor did he look at Kircher's notes. If he had, he would have learned that on February 27, 1961 there was an extended discussion in the executive committee meeting about customers' delinquencies, that on March 8, 1961 the committee had discussed the pros and cons of alley operation by BarChris, that on March 18, 1961 the committee was informed that BarChris was constructing or about to begin constructing twelve alleys for which it had no contracts, and that on May 13, 1961 Dreyfuss, one of the worst delinquents, had filed a [bankruptcy] petition . . . .

As far as customers' delinquencies is concerned, although Grant discussed this with Kircher, he again accepted the assurances of Kircher and

Russo that no serious problem existed. He did not examine the records as to delinquencies, although BarChris maintained such a record. Any inquiry on his part of Talcott or an examination of BarChris's correspondence with Talcott in April and May 1961 would have apprised him of the true facts. . . .

Grant was entitled to rely on Peat, Marwick for the 1960 figures. He had no reasonable ground to believe them to be inaccurate. But the matters which I have mentioned were not within the expertised portion of the prospectus. As to this, Grant, was obliged to make a reasonable investigation. I am forced to find that he did not make one. . . .

The Underwriters and Coleman

The underwriters other than Drexel made no investigation of the accuracy of the prospectus. . . . They all relied upon Drexel as the "lead" underwriter.

Drexel did make an investigation. The work was in charge of Coleman, a partner of the firm, assisted by Casperson, an associate. Drexel's attorneys acted as attorneys for the entire group of underwriters. Ballard did the work, assisted by Stanton.

* * *

Like Grant, Ballard, without checking, relied on the information which he got from Kircher. He also relied on Grant who, as company counsel, presumably was familiar with its affairs. . . .

In any event, it is clear that no effectual attempt at verification was made. The question is whether due diligence required that it be made. Stated another way, is it sufficient to ask questions, to obtain answers which, if true, would be thought satisfactory, and to let it go at that, without seeking to ascertain from the records whether the answers in fact are true and complete?

I have already held that this procedure is not sufficient in Grant's case. Are underwriters in a different position, as far as due diligence is concerned?

The underwriters say that the prospectus is the company's prospectus, not theirs. Doubtless this is the way they customarily regard it. But the Securities Act makes no such distinction. The underwriters are just as responsible as the company if the prospectus is false. And prospective investors rely upon the reputation of the underwriters in deciding whether to purchase the securities. . . .

The purpose of Section 11 is to protect investors. To that end the underwriters are made responsible for the truth of the prospectus. If they may escape that responsibility by taking at face value representations made to them by the company's management, then the inclusion of underwriters among those liable under Section 11 affords the investors no additional protection. To effectuate the statute's purpose, the phrase "reasonable investigation" must be construed to require more effort on the part of the underwriters than the mere accurate reporting in the prospectus of "data presented" to them by the company. It should make no difference that this data is elicited by questions addressed to the company officers by the underwriters, or that the underwriters at the time believe that the company's officers are truthful and reliable. In order to make the underwriters' participation in this enterprise of any value to the investors, the underwriters must make some reasonable attempt to verify the data submitted to them. They may not rely solely on the company's officers or on the company's counsel. A prudent man in the management of his own property would not rely on them.

It is impossible to lay down a rigid rule suitable for every case defining the extent to which such verification must go. It is a question of degree, a matter of judgment in each case. In the present case, the underwriters' counsel made almost no attempt to verify management's representations. I hold that that was insufficient.

On the evidence in this case, I find that the underwriters' counsel did not make a reasonable investigation of the truth of those portions of the prospectus which were not made on the authority of Peat, Marwick as an expert. Drexel is bound by their failure. It is not a matter of relying upon counsel for legal advice. Here the attorneys were dealing with matters of fact. Drexel delegated to them, as its agent, the business of examining the corporate minutes and contracts. It must bear the consequences of their failure to make an adequate examination.

The other underwriters, who did nothing and relied solely on Drexel and on the lawyers, are also bound by it. It follows that although Drexel and the other underwriters believed that those portions of the prospectus were true, they had no reasonable ground for that belief, within the meaning of the statute. Hence, they have not established their due diligence defense, except as to the 1960 audited figures.[26]

* * *

Peat, Marwick

* * *

[With regard to Peat, Marwick, the court found that the auditor failed to follow generally accepted accounting standards in performing its audit. The court held that this failure to meet industry standards meant that Peat, Marwick had failed to show due diligence.]

NOTES

The SEC has provided some guidance on the issue of what constitutes due diligence through Rule 176. Rule 176 varies the level of required due diligence

---

26. In view of this conclusion, it becomes unnecessary to decide whether the underwriters other than Drexel would have been protected if Drexel had established that as lead underwriter, it made a reasonable investigation.

based on the type of issuer, the type of security, the presence of another relationship to the issuer when the person is a director, and the type of underwriting arrangement for underwriters, among other factors. Unfortunately, Rule 176 gives little guidance on how these factors should be weighed in considering the due diligence requirement.

QUESTIONS

1. Section 11 imposes different due diligence standards for non-experts depending on whether the alleged fraud is in an expertised or non-expertised portion of the registration statement. Great importance is placed on who qualifies as an expert and what sections of the registration statement are considered expertised. Do you think attorneys drafting the registration statement should be deemed experts for the entire registration statement? Why do you think the *Escott* court rejected this approach?

2. The *Escott* court focuses on the fact that a number of defendants simply relied on the representations of BarChris insiders. What more should the defendants have done in addition to listening to insiders?

3. What would you have done if you were in Birnbaum's shoes? Recall that Birnbaum was the "young attorney" who had recently obtained employment as BarChris's house counsel, secretary, and member of the board of directors.

4. Why does the *Escott* court not require each defendant to undertake a "complete audit" of BarChris to meet his/her due diligence requirement? Wouldn't doing so encourage third parties to get involved in ferreting out fraud in the registration statement?

2. DUE DILIGENCE, UNDERWRITERS, AND THE FORM S–3 ISSUER

Companies that qualify for Form S–3 in their offerings may incorporate, by reference, previously filed SEC documents. Incorporating documents by reference is quicker than drafting new ones, so one advantage for Form S–3 issuers is speed. Information incorporated-by-reference, however, becomes part of the registration statement and therefore comes under the scope of § 11 liability. Should underwriters, directors, auditors and other potential § 11 defendants bear the same due diligence responsibility on past-filed documents incorporated by reference in the registration statement? Suppose a Form S–3 issuer sells securities through a shelf registration. How should underwriters balance the time pressure of the shelf registration process and the need to conduct a thorough due diligence investigation of the issuer?

In re WorldCom, Inc. Securities Litigation

346 F. Supp. 2d 628 (S.D.N.Y. 2004).

■ COTE, J.

This Opinion addresses issues related to an underwriter's due diligence obligations. Following the conclusion of fact discovery, several of the parties in this consolidated securities class action arising from the collapse of WorldCom, Inc. ("WorldCom") have filed for summary judgment....

It is undisputed that at least as of early 2001 WorldCom executives engaged in a secretive scheme to manipulate WorldCom's public filings concerning WorldCom's financial condition....

* * *

WorldCom announced a massive restatement of its financials on June 25, 2002. It reported its intention to restate its financial statements for 2001 and the first quarter of 2002. According to that announcement, "[a]s a result of an internal audit of the company's capital expenditure accounting, it was determined that certain transfers from line cost expenses to capital accounts during this period were not made in accordance with generally accepted accounting principles (GAAP)." The amount of transfers was then estimated to be over $3.8 billion. Without the improper transfers, the company estimated that it would have reported a net loss for 2001 and the first quarter of 2002....

* * *

WorldCom's Accounting Strategies

* * *

Andersen [Worldcom's auditor] was unaware of the manipulation of line costs through this capitalization scheme.... The improper capitalization of line costs continued through the first quarter of 2002. WorldCom's internal audit department had completed its last audit of WorldCom's capital expenditures in approximately January of 2002, and had not uncovered any evidence of fraud. In May of 2002, it began another audit of the company's capital expenditures.... and was able to uncover the transfer of line costs to capital accounts....

* * *

[Prior to the public disclosure of WorldCom's accounting fraud, WorldCom sold two bond offerings in 2000 and 2001. WorldCom sold the bonds through Form S–3 shelf registration statements in both offerings. The Form S–3 statements in the two offerings incorporated audited financials by reference to the most recent Form 10–K (the 1999 and 2000 Form 10–Ks). Andersen provided "comfort letters," as described by the court below, for the underwriters in both offerings on the accuracy of the unaudited interim financials used in the Form S–3. Eds.—The issues in the two offerings are similar; for the sake of brevity, we provide details on only the 2001 Offering.]

In February 2001 [prior to the 2001 Offering], several of the Underwriter Defendants downgraded WorldCom's credit rating due to their assessment of WorldCom's deteriorating financial condition. Then, during the weeks that followed, several of the Underwriter Defendants made a commitment to WorldCom to help it restructure its massive credit facility. In doing so, there is evidence that at least some of the Underwriter

Defendants internally expressed concern again about WorldCom's financial health. WorldCom had required the banks to participate in the restructuring of the credit facility if a bank wished to play a significant role in its next bond offering, the 2001 Offering. That offering turned out to be the largest public debt offering in American history. The Lead Plaintiff contends that the evidence of the Underwriter Defendants' concerns about WorldCom's financial condition in the months immediately preceding the 2001 Offering undercuts their contention that the due diligence that they performed in connection with the 2001 Offering was reasonable.

* * *

There is evidence that several of the Underwriter Defendants decided to make a commitment to the restructuring of the credit facility and to attempt to win the right to underwrite the 2001 Offering, while at the same time reducing their own exposure to risk from holding WorldCom debt by engaging in hedging strategies, such as credit default swaps.

* * *

2000 Form 10–K

* * *

With respect to long-distance services, the document reported that revenue fell in 2000 in absolute terms and as a percentage of total WorldCom revenues. In its description of operations, line costs were shown as a decreasing percentage of revenues for each year from 1998 to 2000, beginning with 45.3% in 1998, and ending at 39.6% in 2000. The Form 10–K explained that the improvement was a result of increased data and dedicated Internet traffic.

2001 Offering

Through the 2001 Offering WorldCom issued $11.9 billion worth of notes. The May 9, 2001 registration statement and May 14, 2001 prospectus supplement for the 2001 Offering incorporated WorldCom's 2000 10–K. . . .

J.P. Morgan and [Salomon Smith Barney ("SSB")] served as co-book runners. Each of the Underwriter Defendants for the 2001 Offering have stated that they relied on the due diligence performed by SSB and J.P. Morgan. [Cravath, Swaine & Moore] represented the Underwriter Defendants.

A May 16, 2001 memorandum prepared by Cravath describes the due diligence conducted from April 19 through May 16, 2001 in connection with the 2001 Offering. On April 23, the Underwriter Defendants forwarded due diligence questions to WorldCom. The due diligence for the 2001 Offering included telephone calls with WorldCom on April 30 and May 9, and a May 9 telephone call with Andersen and WorldCom. The due diligence inquiry also included a review of WorldCom's board minutes, 1998 revolving credit agreement, SEC filings, and press releases from April 19 to May 16, 2001.

* * *

On May 9, a banker from J.P. Morgan and two Cravath attorneys spoke by telephone with Sullivan [WorldCom's CFO] ... and with representatives of Andersen. Andersen indicated that it had not issued any management letters to WorldCom and that there were no accounting concerns. WorldCom and Andersen assured J.P. Morgan that there was nothing else material to discuss. In neither the April 30 due diligence telephone call nor the May 9 call did Sullivan disclose the ... capitalization of line costs.

On May 9 and 16, Andersen issued comfort letters for the WorldCom first quarter 2001 financial statement. The 2001 comfort letters stand in contrast to the 2000 comfort letter [used in a WorldCom 2000 debt offering], which expressed that nothing had come to Andersen's attention to cause it to believe that "[a]ny material modifications should be made to the unaudited condensed consolidated financial statements ... , incorporated by reference in the Registration Statement, for them to be in conformity with generally accepted accounting principles" or that "[t]he unaudited condensed consolidated financial statements ... do not comply as to form in all material respects with the applicable accounting requirements of the Act and the related published rules and regulations." In 2001, by comparison, the letters indicated that nothing had come to Andersen's attention that caused it to believe that the financial statements "were not determined on a basis substantially consistent with that of the corresponding amounts in the audited consolidated balance sheets of WorldCom as of December 31, 2000 and 1999, and the consolidated statements of operations, shareholders' investment and cash flows for each of the three years in the period ended December 31, 2000.... " A J.P. Morgan banker and a Cravath attorney noticed the absence of the "negative GAAP assurance" in the 2001 comfort letter. An SSB banker noted that the issue was important to understand but advised against getting "too vocal" about it since "WorldCom's a bear to deal with on that subject."

* * *

III. *The Underwriter Defendants' Motion for Summary Judgment; The Financial Statements*

The Underwriter Defendants move for summary judgment with respect to the financial statements that were incorporated into the Registration Statements. They assert that there is no dispute that they acted reasonably in relying on Andersen's audits and comfort letters. The Underwriter Defendants contend that they were entitled to rely on WorldCom's audited financial statements and had no duty to investigate their reliability so long as they had "no reasonable ground to believe" that such financial statements contained a false statement. They also assert that they were entitled to rely in the same way on Andersen's comfort letters for the unaudited quarterly financial statements incorporated into the Registration Statements.

* * *

A.   *Role of the Underwriter*

[I]n enacting Section 11, "Congress recognized that underwriters occupied a unique position that enabled them to discover and compel disclosure of essential facts about the offering. Congress believed that subjecting underwriters to the liability provisions would provide the necessary incentive to ensure their careful investigation of the offering." At the same time, Congress specifically rejected the notion of underwriters as insurers. Rather, it imposed upon underwriters the obligation to "exercise diligence of a type commensurate with the confidence, both as to integrity and competence," placed in them by those purchasing securities.

Underwriters must "exercise a high degree of care in investigation and independent verification of the company's representations." Overall, "[n]o greater reliance in our self-regulatory system is placed on any single participant in the issuance of securities than upon the underwriter." Underwriters function as "the first line of defense" with respect to material misrepresentations and omissions in registration statements. . . .

B.   *The "Due Diligence" Defenses*

* * *

Although the requirements of due diligence vary depending on whether the registration statement has been made in part or in whole on the authority of an expert, the standard for determining what constitutes a reasonable investigation and reasonable ground for belief is the same: "[T]he standard of reasonableness shall be that required of a prudent man in the management of his own property."

Courts have distinguished between these two standards by labeling them the due diligence defense and the reliance defense, referring in the latter case to the reliance permitted by the statute on an expert's statement.

* * *

C.   *Accountants as Experts*

[W]hile Section 11(b) does not define the term expert or explain what sort of documents and/or work constitutes that "made on an expert's authority," it is settled that an accountant qualifies as an expert, and audited financial statements are considered expertised portions of a registration statement.

Not every auditor's opinion, however, qualifies as an expert's opinion for purposes of the Section 11 reliance defense. To distinguish among auditor's opinions, some background is in order. While financial statements are prepared by the management of a company, an accountant serving as the company's auditor may give an opinion as to whether the financial statements have been presented in conformity with GAAP. This opinion is given after the accountant has performed an audit of the company's books and records. Audits are generally completed once a year, in connection with a company's year-end financial statements. There are ten audit standards with which an auditor must comply in performing its annual audit. They are known as Generally Accepted Auditing Standards ("GAAS"). If an auditor signs a consent to have its opinion on financial statements incorporated into a company's public filings, the opinion may be shared with the public through incorporation.

Public companies are also required under the Exchange Act to file quarterly financial statements, which are referred to as interim financial statements. While not subject to an audit, interim financial statements included in Form 10–Q quarterly reports are reviewed by an independent public accountant using professional standards and procedures for conducting such reviews, as established by GAAS. The standards for the review of interim financial statements are set forth in Statement of Auditing Standards No. 71, Interim Financial Information ("SAS 71"). When a public company files a registration statement for a sale of securities, the auditor is customarily asked by underwriters to provide a comfort letter. The comfort letter will contain representations about the auditor's review of the interim financial statements. There is frequently more than one comfort letter for a transaction: an initial comfort letter, and a second or "bringdown" comfort letter issued closer to the time of closing. . . .

In an effort to encourage auditor reviews of interim financial statements, the SEC acted in 1979 to assure auditors that their review of unaudited interim financial information would not subject them to liability under Section 11. . . .

The objective of an audit is to provide a reasonable basis for expressing an opinion regarding the financial statements taken as a whole. A review of interim financial information does not provide a basis for the expression of such an opinion, because the review does not contemplate a study and evaluation of internal accounting control; tests of accounting records and of responses to inquiries by obtaining corroborating evidential matter through inspection, observation, or confirmation; and certain other procedures ordinarily performed during an audit. A review may bring to the accountant's attention significant matters affecting the interim financial information, but it does not provide assurance that the accountant will become aware of all significant matters that would be disclosed in an audit.

* * *

Underwriters may not rely on an accountant's comfort letters for interim financial statements in presenting such a defense. Comfort letters do not "expertise any portion of the registration statement that is otherwise non-expertised."

D. *Integrated Disclosure, Shelf Registration, and Rule 176*

* * *

Together, the mechanism of incorporation by reference and the expansion of shelf registration significantly reduced the time and expense necessary to prepare public offerings, thus enabling more "rapid access to today's capital markets." As the SEC recognized, these changes affected the time in which underwriters could perform their investigations of an issuer. Underwriters had weeks to perform due diligence for traditional registration statements. By contrast, under a short-form registration regime, "[p]reparation time is reduced sharply" thanks to the ability to incorporate by reference prior disclosures.

These two innovations triggered concern among underwriters. Members of the financial community worried about their ability "to undertake a reasonable investigation with respect to the adequacy of the information incorporated by reference from periodic reports filed under the Exchange Act into the short form registration statements utilized in an integrated disclosure system." . . .

Because an underwriter could select among competing underwriters when offering securities through a shelf registration, some questioned whether an underwriter could "afford to devote the time and expense necessary to conduct a due diligence review before knowing whether it will handle an offering and that there may not be sufficient time to do so once it is selected." Others doubted whether they would have the chance "to apply their independent scrutiny and judgment to documents prepared by registrants many months before an offering."

[T]he SEC introduced Rule 176 in 1981 "to make explicit what circumstances may bear upon the determination of what constitutes a reasonable investigation and reasonable ground for belief as these terms are used in Section 11(b)." . . . At the time Rule 176 was finalized, the SEC took care to explain that integrated disclosure was intended to "simplify disclosure and reduce unnecessary repetition and redelivery of information," not to "modify the responsibility of underwriters and others to make a reasonable investigation." [T]he SEC advised underwriters concerned about the time pressures created by integrated disclosure to "arrange [their] due diligence procedures over time for the purpose of avoiding last minute delays in an offering environment characterized by rapid market changes." It also reminded them that an underwriter is "never compelled to proceed with an offering *until he has accomplished his due diligence.*" (emphasis supplied). . . .

The SEC's intent to maintain high standards for underwriter due diligence is confirmed by its many discussions of appropriate due diligence techniques in the integrated disclosure system. In proposing Rule 176, the SEC acknowledged that different investigatory methods would be needed "in view of the compressed preparation time and the volatile nature of the capital markets." Nonetheless, it emphasized that such techniques must be *"equally thorough."* (emphasis supplied). Among the strategies recommended by the SEC were the development of a "reservoir of knowledge about the companies that may select the underwriter to distribute their securities registered on short form registration statements" through a "careful review of [periodic Exchange Act] filings on an ongoing basis," consultation of analysts' reports, and active participation in the issuer's investor relations program, especially analysts and brokers meetings.

At the time the SEC finalized the shelf registration rule two years later, it again recognized that "the techniques of conducting due diligence investigations of registrants qualified to use short form registration ... would differ from due diligence investigations under other circumstances." Nonetheless, it stressed the use of "anticipatory and continuous due diligence programs" to augment underwriters' fulfillment of their due diligence obligations. Among other practices, the SEC approvingly noted the increased designation of one law firm to act as underwriters' counsel, which "facilitates continuous due diligence by ensuring on-going access to the registrant on the underwriters' behalf"; the holding of "Exchange Act report 'drafting sessions,' " which allow underwriters "to participate in the drafting and review of periodic disclosure documents before they are filed"; and "periodic due diligence sessions," such as meetings between prospective underwriters, their counsel, and management shortly after the release of quarterly earnings.

* * *

E.   *Case Law: Reliance Defense*

* * *

[U]nderwriters' reliance on audited financial statements may not be blind. Rather, where "red flags" regarding the reliability of an audited financial statement emerge, mere reliance on an audit will not be sufficient to ward off liability....

[T]he phrase "red flags" can be used to describe ... those facts which come to a defendant's attention that would place a reasonable party in defendant's position "on notice that the audited company was engaged in wrongdoing to the detriment of its investors." ... Any information that strips a defendant of his confidence in the accuracy of those portions of a registration statement premised on audited financial statements is a red flag, whether or not it relates to accounting fraud or an audit failure....

* * *

1.   *Audited Financial Statements*

The Underwriter Defendants contend that they were entitled to rely on Andersen's unqualified "clean" audit opinions for WorldCom's 1999 and 2000 Form 10–Ks as expertised statements under Section 11(b)(3)(C). Their motion for summary judgment on their reliance defense is denied.

a. *2000 Registration Statement*

The Lead Plaintiff points to one issue that it contends gave the Underwriter Defendants a reasonable ground to question the reliability of WorldCom's 1999 Form 10–K. According to the computations presented by the Lead Plaintiff, WorldCom's reported E/R ratio [Eds.—defined as the ratio of line cost expenses to revenues] was significantly lower than that of the equivalent numbers of its two closest competitors, Sprint and AT & T.[47] The Lead Plaintiff argues that, in the extremely competitive market in which WorldCom operated, that discrepancy triggered a duty to investigate such a crucial measurement of the company's health. The Lead Plaintiff has shown that there are issues of fact as to whether the Underwriter Defendants had reasonable grounds to believe that the 1999 Form 10–K was inaccurate in the lines related to the E/R ratio reflected in that filing.

The Underwriter Defendants argue that the difference in the E/R ratios was insufficient as a matter of law to put the Underwriter Defendants on notice of any accounting irregularity. In support of this, they point to the fact that this difference was publicly available information and no one else announced a belief that it suggested the existence of an accounting fraud at WorldCom.

The fact that the difference was publicly available information does not absolve the Underwriter Defendants of their duty to bring their expertise to bear on the issue.... If a "prudent man in the management of his own property," upon reading the 1999 Form 10–K and being familiar with the other relevant information about the issuer's competitors would have questioned the accuracy of the figures, then those figures constituted a red flag and imposed a duty of investigation on the Underwriter Defendants. A jury would be entitled to find that this difference was of sufficient importance to have triggered a duty to investigate the reliability of the figures on which the ratio was based even though the figures had been audited.

The Underwriter Defendants contend that an audited figure can never constitute a red flag and impose a duty of investigation. This argument mischaracterizes the Lead Plaintiff's position. The Lead Plaintiff has pointed to facts extraneous to WorldCom's audited figures to argue that a reasonable person would have inquired further about the discrepancy between the audited figures and the comparable information from competitors....

The Underwriter Defendants argue that the standard that should apply is whether they had "clear and direct notice" of an "accounting" problem. They argue that case law establishes that "ordinary business events" do not constitute red flags. They are wrong. There is no basis in law to find a requirement that a red flag arises only when there is "clear and direct" notice of an accounting issue. The standard under Section 11 is whether a defendant has proven that it had "no reasonable ground to believe and did not believe" that a registration statement contained materi-

---

47. WorldCom's E/R ratio was 43%. The expert for the Lead Plaintiff calculates that AT & T's equivalent ratio was 46.8% and Sprint's was 53.2%.

al misstatements, a standard given meaning by what a "prudent man" would do in the management of his own property. Nor is the bar lowered because there is an expert's opinion on which an underwriter is entitled to rely. . . . There is no category of information which can always be ignored by an underwriter on the ground that it constitutes an ordinary business event. What is ordinary in one context may be sufficiently unusual in another to create a duty of investigation by a "prudent man."

* * *

2. *Interim Financial Statements*

The Underwriter Defendants contend that, pursuant to Sections 11(b)(3)(A) and 12(a)(2), they were entitled to rely on Andersen's comfort letters for WorldCom's unaudited interim financial statements for the first quarter of 2000 and 2001 so long as the Lead Plaintiff is unable to show that the Underwriter Defendants were on notice of any accounting red flags. They argue that this statement of the due diligence defense is particularly appropriate because WorldCom was a seasoned issuer and the Registration Statements were part of the integrated disclosure system that allowed the Exchange Act periodic reports to be incorporated by reference. . . . They argue that in the context of integrated disclosure for shelf registrations, and as a result of SEC Rule 176, the focus is on an underwriter's continuous learning about an "industry" and reasonable reliance on other professionals, such as an issuer's auditor. As a consequence, they contend that there is no difference from the point of view of the underwriter between audited and unaudited financial statements so long as the underwriter receives an auditor's comfort letter. According to the Underwriter Defendants, so long as there are no red flags that bring the auditor's assessment into question, the receipt of a comfort letter "goes a long way to establish" due diligence with respect to all matters of accounting. . . . Finally, they argue that it is material that no amount of reasonable diligence could have uncovered the capitalization of line costs since the WorldCom management deliberately concealed it from Andersen and every other outsider and would never have given them any documents or information that would have revealed the fraud. . . .

In connection with the [2001] Offering, the Underwriter Defendants emphasize that J.P. Morgan and SSB had recently had occasion to work closely with WorldCom on other projects. The two firms had participated in the two tracking stock realignment of WorldCom announced in November 2000, and J.P. Morgan had acted as a lead manager and sole book-runner for WorldCom's $2 billion private placement in December 2000. They point to these activities as part of their continuous due diligence for WorldCom. . . .

In judging [the due diligence reasonable investigation], a jury will have to consider the non-exclusive list of factors enumerated in Rule 176. Insofar as Rule 176 is concerned, there does not appear to be any dispute that WorldCom was a "well-established" issuer, that the notes at issue were investment-grade debt securities, that SSB and J.P. Morgan assigned experienced personnel to the due diligence teams, that they spoke to the issuer's CFO and in 2001 also spoke to Andersen, that the underwriting was a firm commitment underwriting, that the underwriting was through a shelf registration, that many analysts and credit reporting agencies followed and reported on WorldCom, that the issuer and not the Underwriter Defendants had responsibility for preparing the interim financial statements, and that Andersen and not the Underwriter Defendants had responsibility for reviewing the interim financial statements.

The Lead Plaintiff has shown that there are questions of fact, however, as to whether the Underwriter Defendants conducted a reasonable investigation in either 2000 or 2001. It points to what it contends is evidence of the limited number of conversations with the issuer or its auditor, the cursory nature of the inquiries, the failure to go behind any of the almost formulaic answers given to questions, and the failure to inquire into issues of particular prominence in the Underwriter Defendants' own internal evaluations of the financial condition of the issuer or in the financial press. It argues in particular with respect to 2001, that having internally downgraded WorldCom's credit rating and having taken steps to limit their exposure as WorldCom creditors, the Underwriter Defendants were well aware that WorldCom was in a deteriorating financial position in a troubled industry, and that a reasonable investigation would have entailed a more searching inquiry than that undertaken by the Underwriter Defendants. Given the enormity of these two bond offerings, and the general deterioration in WorldCom's financial situation, at least as of the time of the 2001 Offering, they argue that a particularly probing inquiry by a prudent underwriter was warranted. These issues of fact require a jury trial.

The Underwriter Defendants have framed their summary judgment motion in a way that is incompatible with their burden of proving their due diligence defense under Section 11. They seek to restrict the inquiry on their due diligence solely to the work undertaken with respect to the interim financial statements and therefore to restrict it to a determination of whether any red flags existed that would put them on notice of a duty to make an inquiry of the interim financial statements. This formulation converts the due diligence defense into the reliance defense and balkanizes the task of due diligence.

In order to succeed with a due diligence defense, the Underwriter Defendants will have to show that they conducted a reasonable investigation of the non-expertised portions of the Registration Statements and thereafter had reasonable ground to believe that the interim financial statements were true. In assessing the reasonableness of the investigation, their receipt of the comfort letters will be important evidence, but it is insufficient by itself to establish the defense.

[A]n underwriter must conduct a reasonable investigation to prevail on the due diligence defense, even if it appears that such an investigation would have proven futile in uncovering the fraud. Without a reasonable investigation, of course, it can never be known what would have been uncovered or what additional disclosures would have been demanded.

The Underwriter Defendants argue that if they are not entitled to rely on a comfort letter, the costs of capital formation in the United States will be substantially increased since underwriters will have to hire their own accounting firms to rehash the work of the issuer's auditor. Nothing in this Opinion should be read as imposing that obligation on underwriters or the underwriting process. The term "reasonable investigation" encompasses many modes of inquiry between obtaining comfort letters from an auditor and doing little more, on one hand, and having to re-audit a company's books on the other. Nonetheless, if aggressive or unusual accounting strategies regarding significant issues come to light in the course of a reasonable investigation, a prudent underwriter may choose to consult with accounting experts to confirm that the accounting treatment is appropriate and that additional disclosure is unnecessary.

Underwriters perform a different function from auditors. They have special access to information about an issuer at a critical time in the issuer's corporate life, at a time it is seeking to raise capital. The public relies on the underwriter to obtain and verify relevant information and then make sure that essential facts are disclosed.... They are not being asked to duplicate the work of auditors, but to conduct a reasonable investigation. If their initial investigation leads them to question the accuracy of financial reporting, then the existence of an audit or a comfort letter will not excuse the failure to follow through with a subsequent investigation of the matter. If red flags arise from a reasonable investigation, underwriters will have to make sufficient inquiry to satisfy themselves as to the accuracy of the financial statements, and if unsatisfied, they must demand disclosure, withdraw from the underwriting process, or bear the risk of liability.

* * *

QUESTIONS

1. What is the difference, for due diligence purposes, between an audited financial statement and an unaudited financial statement accompanied by a "comfort letter" from the auditor?

2. How does a "red flag" affect the ability of a non-expert defendant to rely on the auditor for the accuracy of the audited financials?

3. What do underwriters have to do to satisfy the due diligence defense for non-expertised sections of the registration statement?

4. The court discusses the dilemma facing underwriters involved in shelf registration offerings incorporating information by reference from prior Exchange Act reporting filings. The court supports the SEC's position that issuers and underwriters may accommodate the need to do due diligence even for previously filed documents incorporated-by-reference in a registration statement by simply taking more time prior to the commencement of the offering. How would such accommodations affect the advantages afforded by filing a Form S–3?

5. The court notes that the SEC suggests that one solution to the compressed time frame for offerings allowed by integrated disclosure is to have the issuer maintain an ongoing relationship with a primary investment bank. What are the pros and cons of having underwriters (and other professionals) develop repeat and ongoing relationships with large public companies?

HYPOTHETICAL THREE

InterPhone has now been sued in a § 11 class action. The lawsuit alleges that the registration statement for its offering was materially misleading because it failed to disclose Elmo's (InterPhone's CTO) prior criminal conviction for commodities fraud and overstated InterPhone's earnings for the last two years. In addition to InterPhone, the following players, all involved with InterPhone's initial public offering, have been named in the § 11 suit:

- Zoe, the CEO and a director
- Oscar, an outside director
- Sparrow Securities, the managing underwriter
- Arthur & Young, the auditor
- VenRisk, a substantial shareholder

1. Why was Elmo not named in the § 11 suit?

2. Zoe, of course, knew about her brother Elmo's prior criminal conviction, but she and Elmo agreed that it did not need to be disclosed because it happened four years ago, before Zoe and Elmo even started InterPhone. Besides, Elmo got probation, so how big a deal could it have been? In her deposition, Zoe testified that she had no idea that InterPhone's financial statements were inaccurate; she relied completely on InterPhone's CFO, the Count, who told her that he would "make sure the numbers would support a public offering." Will Zoe be able to show due diligence for the non-expertised portion? The expertised portion?

3. Oscar is a former commissioner of the Federal Communications Commission. Zoe invited him to join the board because he has great contacts in Washington. He attends board meetings only sporadically. Oscar did not have much involvement with the registration process; he skimmed the narrative portion of the registration statement and told InterPhone's lawyers that the details in his biography were all correct. He did not review the financial statements at all. In his deposition, Oscar testifies that he had no idea about Elmo's conviction and that he believed that InterPhone's financial statements were accurate because Arthur & Young certified them. Will Oscar be able to show due diligence for the non-expertised portion? The expertised portion?

4. Sparrow Securities, as the managing underwriter for the offering, performed the due diligence for the underwriting syndicate. Sparrow's lawyers reviewed the registration statement prepared by InterPhone's lawyers and made a number of comments on the draft. They also submitted a series of questions to Zoe, the Count, and Elmo. Among the questions posed was, "Is there any information omitted from the biographies of the officers and directors that might be material to investors?" Zoe, the Count, and Elmo all answered this question, "No." With respect to the financial statements, Sparrow had one of its analysts review the statements; the analyst said that there was nothing in the statements that raised any concerns. Will Sparrow Securities be able to show due diligence for the non-expertised portion? The expertised portion?

5. Arthur & Young's lead partner for the InterPhone account testifies that he was duped by the Count. It turns out that the Count reduced InterPhone's expenses by establishing a company, InterSub, to conduct InterPhone's research and development. InterSub (owned by the Count) funded the R & D by borrowing, securing the loan with the Count's InterPhone shares. Because the Count's shares were restricted, the bank insisted that InterPhone guarantee the loan. Arthur & Young's lead partner testifies that the Count assured him that InterSub was an independent entity and he took the Count's word for it. Moreover, Arthur & Young's audit team checked only a sample of InterPhone's contracts and the contract with InterSub was not one of the contracts selected for review. The Arthur & Young lead partner testifies that he knew nothing about InterPhone's guarantee of InterSub's loan. He also testifies that he reviewed the entire registration statement, but that he knew nothing about Elmo's prior criminal conviction. The plaintiffs' accounting expert testifies in her deposition that the guarantee of InterSub's loan should have been disclosed as a contingency in InterPhone's financial statements. Will Arthur & Young be liable for the non-expertised portion? The expertised portion?

6. VenRisk owned 40% of InterPhone's shares prior to the offering and InterPhone's nominees held half of InterPhone's board seats. One of VenRisk's partners, Telly, sat on InterPhone's board and the board's audit committee. Telly testifies that he had no clue that Elmo had a prior run-in with the law. With respect to InterPhone's financial statements, Telly said that he carefully reviewed the reports prepared by Arthur & Young each year for the audit committee and was satisfied that InterPhone's statements complied with GAAP. Telly also testifies that he and the other board members approved the contract with InterSub and that he accepted the Count's assurance that InterPhone's guarantee of the InterSub loan did not need to be disclosed in InterPhone's financial statements. Is VenRisk potentially liable? Does it have any defense available to it?

E. Damages

Unlike Rule 10b–5, § 11 clearly specifies the damages measure. For each share traceable to the registered offering, § 11 damages equal the difference between what the plaintiff paid for their shares (but not exceeding the offering price) and one of three possibilities depending on whether, and if so when, the plaintiff sold their shares:

1) If the plaintiff sold her shares prior to the filing of suit, then the price at which the plaintiff disposed of the shares;

2) If the plaintiff still owns her shares at the end of the suit, then the value of the shares at the time of the filing of the § 11 lawsuit; and

3) If the plaintiff sold her shares after the filing of the suit (but before judgment), the price at which the plaintiff disposed of the shares if greater than their value at the time of the filing of the suit.

Section 11(e) also provides an affirmative loss causation defense that allows defendants to reduce their liability if they can prove that the depreciation of the stock's value resulted from factors other than the misstatement in the registration statement.

HYPOTHETICAL FOUR

Consider the case where Bird purchased 100 shares from InterPhone's initial public offering at $20 per share. Assume that InterPhone's registration statement was materially misleading. Plaintiffs' attorneys filed suit against InterPhone (and other participants in the offering) six months after the IPO. At that time, InterPhone's price on Nasdaq has fallen to $10 per share. Assume that the $10 per share market price represents the "value" of InterPhone at the time of the filing of suit. What are Bird's damages in the following scenarios?

1. *Scenario One*: Bird chooses to hold onto her 100 InterPhone shares until the end of the lawsuit, at which point judgment is returned against InterPhone.

2. *Scenario Two*: Two months after the IPO (and before the filing of suit), Bird sells her shares at the then prevailing market price of $30 per share to Rosita who holds on to her shares until judgment at trial.

3. *Scenario Three*: Same as in Scenario Two, except that Bird sells to Rosita for a price of $15 per share?

4. *Scenario Four*: Now suppose that Bird sells 100 shares of InterPhone to Rosita for a price of $15 per share eight months after the IPO (i.e., two months after the filing of suit)? What if Bird had sold at a price of $5 per share?

1.   MEASURING § 11 DAMAGES

Section 11's use of the word "value" in its damages measure allows for litigants in a § 11 action to invoke a wide variety of alternatives to the market price at the time of the filing of suit. Does the court do a good job in measuring value in the case that follows?

Beecher v. Able

435 F. Supp. 397 (S.D.N.Y. 1975).

■ MOTLEY, DISTRICT JUDGE.

INTRODUCTION

In its Findings of Fact and Conclusions of Law ... the court found that defendant Douglas Aircraft Company, Inc. (Douglas) had on July 12, 1966 sold $75 million of its 4 3/4 convertible debentures due July 1, 1991 under a materially false prospectus. In particular, the court found that the break-even prediction ... rendered the prospectus misleading....

[T]he parties are in disagreement regarding the content to be given several significant terms used in § 11(e).

* * *

VALUE AS OF THE TIME OF SUIT

[T]he value of the securities at the time of suit was sharply contested at trial. To establish "value", plaintiff asks the court first to look to the trading price on the day of suit and then to reduce that price by a sum which reflects the undisclosed financial crisis of defendant. At trial, plaintiff characterized the market for these debentures as free, open and sophisticated, marked by a heavy volume of trading on national exchanges. Plaintiffs relied on trading data from July to mid-October 1966 and the testimony of their expert . . . , in reaching the conclusion that market price was the best evidence of maximum fair value. The reason plaintiffs urge that market price reflects maximum fair value, as opposed to value, is because the buying public was unaware of the financial crisis gripping defendant in mid-October 1966. Thus, according to plaintiff, had the buying public been aware of the crisis they would have paid less for the security.

[The plaintiffs presented a number of points to support their argument that Douglas Aircraft Co's debentures would have been lower in price had the investing public known of the full extent of the "crisis" within Douglas including: (1) mounting losses; (2) "cash tightness" within Douglas; (3) the demand on the part of eight banks which had previously extended credit to Douglas for a greater interest rate as well as an infusion of equity capital among other things; (4) discussion among the banks to the effect that the management of Douglas needed "strengthening".]

* * *

In sum, plaintiff's claim that the market price of the debentures reflects a sophisticated assessment of the security's value, but that insofar as the financial plight summarized above was undisclosed, market price should be lowered to arrive at fair value. That is, had investors known of the crisis, they would simply have paid less.

The defendant urges the court to adopt a somewhat different approach from plaintiffs' in establishing "value" of the security at time of suit. Defendant contends that the market action of this offering was volatile and often unrelated to fair value. In particular defendant claims that on the date suit was filed the market price of the debenture was temporarily depressed by panic selling in response to the release of the defendant's disappointing third quarter earnings results. Thus, according to defendant, the market price of the debenture on the date of suit was not a reliable indicator of fair value. Defendant would have the court look to the optimistic long-range prospects of the defendant company and set a value which would not only off-set panic selling but which would reflect defendant's anticipated future gains, or the investment feature of the offering. . . .

[Defendants presented a number of points in support of their "panic selling" theory of value including that (1) the price of the debentures fell from well above 80 in September, 1966 to 75 1/2 at the time of the filing of suit only to rebound back to their initial levels by November 1966 and to above 100 throughout 1967; (2) Douglas enjoyed a substantial backlog of unfilled orders which would translate into higher profits in the future; and (3) banks continued to extend Douglas credit (although on stricter terms)]

* * *

As the above arguments indicate both parties for different reasons are dissatisfied with market price as conclusive evidence of value. The court is urged to look to market price and then either add or subtract a certain amount, depending on which party's claims proves more convincing. Plaintiffs through their expert conclude that fair value on the date of suit was 41. In contrast, defendant through its expert concludes that the value of the debentures on the date of suit was between 80 and 82 1/2. As noted elsewhere, closing market price on the date of suit was 75 1/2.

Case law, commentators and the parties agree that realistic value may be something other than market price, where the public is either misinformed or uninformed about important factors relating to the defendant-offeror's well being. . . . The court has previously indicated that in its view market price is merely some evidence of value. Moreover, the conclusion that "value" is not synonymous with "market price" seems clearly dictated by the plain language of Section 11(e) in which both "price" (sometimes "amount paid") and "value" are used, apparently deliberately, to connote different concepts.

After considering the above evidence offered by the parties with respect to "value" at the time of suit, the court makes the following observations and findings and reaches the following conclusions. Although the plaintiffs produced considerable evidence tending to show the unfavorable financial situation of defendant at the time of suit, the evidence does not convince the court that the situation was as desperate or life-threatening as it has been characterized by plaintiffs. More importantly, the court does not agree with plaintiffs that had investors known of the defendant's financial situation they would invariably have paid less for the debentures and that the court should set a value considerably below market price.

As the parties seem to agree, the market for these debentures was, in the main, a sophisticated market. As such, it no doubt was most interested in the long range investment and speculative features of this particular offering. The defendant's immediate financial troubles would likely be viewed as temporary rather than terminal by such a market. . . .

As defendant urged, notwithstanding the then current financial difficulties, the future of Douglas was hopeful. In particular, the substantial backlog of unfilled orders as well as the banks' continued extension of credit suggested a reasonable basis for belief in recovery. The court relies heavily on these factors in reaching the conclusion that at the time of suit the fair value of the debentures should reflect the reasonably anticipated future recovery of defendant. . . .

Defendant also argued that the value of the debentures at the time of suit was higher than market price because on that date the market price was artificially lowered due to panic selling in response to the revelation of the third quarter earnings. The evidence strongly supports the conclusion that the market price on the day of suit was characterized by panic selling. The court relies heavily on the trading data in reaching this conclusion. In particular, these data show that following the announcement of the third quarter results the market price dropped off and continued to decline at a rate in excess of the pre-revelation rate. The sharp and continued increase in volume between revelation and mid-October suggests a market reacting to news, here presumably news of the third quarter earnings. In addition to these trading data, there was convincing expert testimony which tends to confirm the conclusion that panic selling was affecting the market price at the time of suit. . . .

The court notes that, notwithstanding the fact that the market for these debentures was normally sophisticated, elements of the buying public were apparently given to irrational investment behavior and the prices during the several weeks following the revelation were substantially affected by that behavior. In the court's view, there is nothing inherently contradictory in concluding both that the market for these debentures was normally intelligent and paid a price which fairly reflects value, and that the market was occasionally irrational and paid a price below fair value.

Based on the foregoing factual findings the court concludes that market price is some evidence of fair value. Using the market price as a starting point, the court further concludes that whatever amount might rightly be subtracted to account for the temporary financial crisis of defendant at time of suit, should be off-set by adding a like amount to account for the reasonable likelihood of defendant's recovery. That is, in the court's view, with respect to value at the time of suit the defendant's financial difficulties were balanced by the defendant's probable recovery.

Finally, the court concludes that there was convincing evidence that the market price of the debentures on the day of suit was influenced by panic selling. Hence the price was somewhat below where it might have been, even in a falling market. To correct for this aberration, the court adds 9 1/2 points to the market price of 75 1/2 to establish a figure of 85 as fair value on the date of suit. It is expected that the figure of 85 as value represents a fair value of these debentures unaffected by the panic selling which along with other factors depressed the market price from 88 on September 26, 1966 to 75 1/2 on October 14, 1966.

In reaching this figure the court notes that the market fell 12 points between July 12 and September 26, 1966 at an average rate of .22 per day for 54 trading days. Had that rate continued for the 14 trading days September 27 to October 14, 1966 the price of the debentures would have been at approximately 84.92. Thus, 85 seems a fair value as of October 14, 1966. The 85 figure may well have obtained in a falling market, unaffected by panic selling. . . .

QUESTIONS

1. Is the court correct in dismissing the plaintiff's argument that the market would have reduced the price of Douglas had it known of the negative nonpublic information? Among other things, the *Beecher* court notes, "the defendant's financial difficulties were balanced off by the defendant's probable recovery." But why, even if the court were correct, wouldn't negative information at least increase the *probability* of poorer financial performance and therefore warrant a reduced price for the Douglas debentures?

2. Does the analysis in *Beecher* give you much confidence in the ability of courts to determine the fair value of a security? Although the market price may not capture true value with one hundred percent accuracy, would the market price nonetheless tend to be more accurate than a court's determination?

3. The *Beecher* court finds persuasive the notion that panic selling may have artificially depressed the price for Douglas debentures at the time of the filing of suit. Do you think that panic selling is probable in an actively-traded securities market with sophisticated investors?

2.   LOSS CAUSATION DEFENSE

Section 11(e) tells us that the damage measure depends (at least under certain circumstances) on the difference between the offering price and the value at the time of the filing of suit. As *Beecher* discusses, courts may look at a range of factors in determining this value. Once a value has been determined, Section 11(e) allows defendants to argue that the difference between the offering price and value is not due to fraud in the registration statement but instead results from exogenous causes. This is a switch from Rule 10b–5, under which the plaintiff bears the burden of showing loss causation. In the case below, has the court properly applied this affirmative defense?

Akerman v. Oryx Communications, Inc.

810 F.2d 336 (2d Cir. 1987).

■ MESKILL, CIRCUIT JUDGE.

Plaintiffs Morris and Susan Akerman and Dr. Lawrence Kuhn appeal from an order . . . granting summary judgment disposing of their claims under section 11 of the Securities Act of 1933 against defendants. . . .

We affirm the judgment on the plaintiffs' section 11 claims . . . and remand to the district court for further proceedings.

BACKGROUND

This case arises out of a June 30, 1981, initial public offering of securities by Oryx, a company planning to enter the business of manufacturing and marketing abroad video cassettes and video discs of feature films for home entertainment. Oryx filed a registration statement and an accompanying prospectus dated June 30, 1981, with the Securities and Exchange Commission (SEC) for a firm commitment offering of 700,000 units. Each unit sold for $4.75 and consisted of one share of common stock and one warrant to purchase an additional share of stock for $5.75 at a later date.

The prospectus contained an erroneous pro forma unaudited financial statement relating to the eight month period ending March 31, 1981. It reported net sales of $931,301, net income of $211,815, and earnings of seven cents per share. Oryx, however, had incorrectly posted a substantial transaction by its subsidiary to March instead of April when Oryx actually received the subject sale's revenues. The prospectus, therefore, overstated earnings for the eight month period. Net sales in that period actually totaled $766,301, net income $94,529, and earnings per share three cents.

Oryx's price had declined to four dollars per unit by October 12, 1981, the day before Oryx revealed the prospectus misstatement to the SEC. The unit price had further declined to $3.25 by November 9, 1981, the day before Oryx disclosed the misstatement to the public. After public disclosure, the price of Oryx rose and reached $3.50 by November 25, 1981, the day this suit commenced.

Plaintiffs allege that the prospectus error rendered Oryx liable for the stock price decline pursuant to sections 11.... In July 1982, Oryx moved for summary judgment on the grounds, inter alia, that the misstatement was not material for purposes of establishing liability under section 11 and that the misstatement had not actually caused the price decline for purposes of damages under section 11....

The Akermans' section 11(a) claim survived an initial summary judgment attack when the court concluded that the prospectus misstatement was material. We note, however, that the district court held that the misstatement was material only "as a theoretical matter." As described below, this conclusion weighs heavily in our judgment that the district court correctly decided that the defendants had carried their burden of showing that the misstatement did not cause the stock price to decline.

The misstatement resulted from an innocent bookkeeping error whereby Oryx misposted a sale by its subsidiary to March instead of April. Oryx received the sale's proceeds less than one month after the reported date. The prospectus, moreover, expressly stated that Oryx "expect[ed] that [the subsidiary's] sales will decline." Indeed, Morris Akerman conceded that he understood this disclaimer to warn that Oryx expected the subsidiary's business to decline....

Thus, although the misstatement may have been "theoretically material," when it is considered in the context of the prospectus' pessimistic forecast of the performance of Oryx's subsidiary, the misstatement was not likely to cause a stock price decline.... Indeed, the public not only did not react adversely to disclosure of the misstatement, Oryx's price actually rose somewhat after public disclosure of the error.

The applicable section 11(e) formula for calculating damages is "the difference between the amount paid for the security (not exceeding the price at which the security was offered to the public) and ... the value thereof as of the time such suit was brought." The relevant events and stock prices are:

Date	Event	Oryx Stock Price
June 30, 1981	Initial public offering	$4.75
October 15, 1981	Disclosure of error to SEC	$4.00
November 10, 1981	Disclosure of error to public	$3.25
November 25, 1981	Date of suit	$3.50

The price decline before disclosure may not be charged to defendants.... At first blush, damages would appear to be zero because there was no depreciation in Oryx's value between the time of public disclosure and the time of suit.

The Akermans contended at trial, however, that the relevant disclosure date was the date of disclosure to the SEC and not to the public. Under plaintiffs' theory, damages would equal the price decline subsequent to October 15, 1981, which amounted to fifty cents per share. Plaintiffs attempted to support this theory by alleging that insiders privy to the SEC disclosure—Oryx's officers, attorneys and accountants, and underwriters and SEC officials—sold Oryx shares and thereby deflated its price before public disclosure. The district court attributed "at least possible theoretical validity" to this argument. After extensive discovery, however, plaintiffs produced absolutely no evidence of insider trading....

The district court invited statistical studies from both sides to clarify the causation issue. Defendants produced a statistical analysis of the stocks of the one hundred companies that went public contemporaneously with Oryx. The study tracked the stocks' performances for the period between June 30, 1981 (initial public offering date) and November 25, 1981 (date of suit). The study indicated that Oryx performed at the exact statistical median of these stocks and that several issues suffered equal or greater losses than did Oryx during this period. Defendants produced an additional study which indicated that Oryx stock "behaved over the entire period ... consistent[ly] with its own inherent variation."

Plaintiffs offered the following rebuttal evidence. During the period between SEC disclosure and public disclosure, Oryx stock decreased nineteen percent while the over-the-counter (OTC) composite index rose five percent (the first study). During this period, therefore, the OTC composite index outperformed Oryx by twenty-four percentage points. Plaintiffs also produced a study indicating that for the time period between SEC disclosure and one week after public disclosure, eighty-two of the one hundred new issues analyzed in the defendants' study outperformed Oryx's stock....

The parties' conflicting comparisons, however, lack credibility because they fail to reflect any of the countless variables that might affect the stock price performance of a single company.... Statistical analyses must control for relevant variables to permit reliable inferences....

The studies comparing Oryx's performance to the other one hundred companies that went public in May and June of 1981 are similarly flawed. The studies do not evaluate the performance of Oryx stock in relation to the stock of companies possessing any characteristic in common with Oryx, e.g., product, technology, profitability, assets or countless other variables which influence stock prices, except the contemporaneous initial offering dates.

Perhaps more important, the Akermans' study of the one hundred new issues focuses on a time frame which controverts one of their own theories explaining the public's failure to react adversely to disclosure. The Akermans argue that the thin market in Oryx stock prevented immediate public reaction to disclosure of the prospectus error. Their study, however, measures Oryx's performance from SEC disclosure to one week after public disclosure. A thin market, according to the Akermans' own explanation, would not reflect the impact of bad news in such a short time period (one week). This internal inconsistency seriously undercuts the probative value of the Akermans' study.

Finally, we note that this time period drew its relevance from the Akermans' theory that insider trading deflated Oryx's price during this period. As previously stated, this theory has no support even after extensive discovery and is not pressed on appeal.

Granting the Akermans every reasonable, favorable inference, the battle of the studies is at best equivocal; the studies do not meaningfully point in one direction or the other. . . .

Defendants met their burden, as set forth in section 11(e), by establishing that the misstatement was barely material and that the public failed to react adversely to its disclosure. . . . Despite extensive discovery, plaintiffs completely failed to produce any evidence, other than unreliable and sometimes inconsistent statistical studies and theories, suggesting that Oryx's price decline actually resulted from the misstatement. . . .

QUESTIONS

1. Is the accounting error in *Akerman* really material only as a "theoretical matter"? If you were an investor, would you care about an error that more than doubled reported earnings? If the error is material, does the fact that the error is "innocent" matter under § 11?

2. The *Akerman* court places considerable weight on the lack of a substantial price decline right after the announcement of the accounting error—saying that "at first blush" the damages appear to equal zero. Why might the date of announcement by the firm not coincide with the date at which the market learns of the fraud?

3. How does "theoretical materiality" relate to the defendant's burden of showing loss causation? Do you think the plaintiff in *Akerman* benefited much from defendants bearing the burden of proof on loss causation?

4. What is the importance of the procedural posture of the case?

HYPOTHETICAL FIVE

InterPhone's initial public offering for 10 million shares at $20 per share took place on January 1. InterPhone omitted information about Elmo, the

CTO, from the registration statement, failing to mention Elmo's prior criminal conviction for commodities fraud. Assume that this omission is material.

Rumors started circulating soon after the offering about Elmo's true background. However, InterPhone waited until February 1 to make a corrective disclosure. On the same date, *Telecom World* magazine released a story on the rapidly shrinking market for Internet phone gear (InterPhone's primary source of revenue). Also on February 1, the Federal Reserve Chairman testified before Congress that the economy was doing better than expected. On February 5, several prominent plaintiffs' attorneys filed class action lawsuits under § 11 against InterPhone.

Assume that InterPhone's shares, although listed on Nasdaq, have a relatively low trading volume. In addition, only one analyst (from Sparrow Securities) covers InterPhone. InterPhone's share price displays the following pattern:

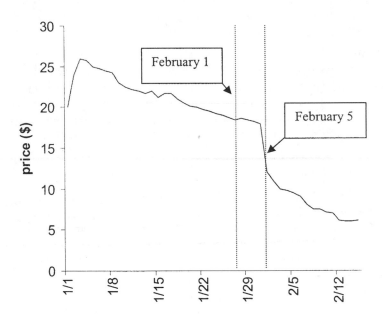

If you are the plaintiff, what arguments do you make regarding loss causation? If you are the defendant what can you argue about loss causation? What additional information would you like to know?

3.   INDEMNIFICATION, CONTRIBUTIONS, AND JOINT AND SEVERAL LIABILITY

Section 11 starts with the presumption that all defendants are jointly and severally liable for § 11 damages, with two statutory exceptions. First, § 11(e) limits the liability of underwriters to "the total price at which the securities underwritten by him and distributed to the public were offered to the public." Second, § 11(f)(2)(A) limits the liability of outside directors to their proportionate liability (based on their degree of wrongdoing relative to that of other defendants). Section 11(f)(2)(A) is just one of many reforms to private securities fraud litigation enacted in the Private Securities Litigation Reform Act of 1995 discussed in Chapter 5.

Outside of the statutory modifications to joint and several liability, parties may attempt to adjust their relative exposure to liability through both contract as well as implied contribution rights under § 11. Underwriters will commonly seek an agreement on the part of the issuer to indemnify the underwriters for any securities fraud liability. Should courts enforce such agreements?

attempt to adjust U-rs

Eichensholtz v. Brennan

52 F.3d 478 (3d Cir. 1995).

■ SEITZ, CIRCUIT JUDGE.

I. FACTS

International Thoroughbred Breeders is a Delaware corporation in the business of buying, selling, and leasing interests in thoroughbred horses for breeding. In 1977, Garden State Racetrack burned down. In 1983, ITB proposed a plan to purchase the Garden State grounds, construct a new facility, and operate a thoroughbred and harness racing facility. ITB raised money for this undertaking through the sale of securities....

Plaintiffs alleged violations of section 10(b) of the Securities and Exchange Act of 1934; Rule 10b–5; sections 11, 12[a](2), and 17(a) of the Securities Act of 1933....

claim

[A settlement agreement was reached between the plaintiffs and a subset of the defendants, including ITB. The non-settling defendants, including the underwriter for the public offerings, First Jersey, sought both contribution rights as well as enforcement of their indemnification agreement for securities liability with ITB.]

Indemn Agreement

The court agrees with the non-settling defendants that under section 11 of the Securities Act of 1933, they have an express right to seek contribution for liability under that section....

express right to seek contribution for liability

However, there is no express right to indemnification under the 1933 or 1934 Acts. Further, those courts that have addressed the issue have concluded that there is no implied right to indemnification under the federal securities laws.... This circuit has not yet addressed this issue.

- No express right for indemn-n.
- No implied right for Ind-n.

As will be explained below, indemnification runs counter to the policies underlying the 1933 and 1934 Acts. In addition, there is no indication that Congress intended that indemnification be available under the Acts.... In drafting the Acts, Congress was not concerned with protecting the underwriters, but rather it sought to protect investors. Here, it is the underwriters, not the victims, who seek indemnification. We agree with those courts that have held that there is no implied right to seek indemnification under the federal securities laws.

In addition, in support of its right to seek indemnification from ITB, First Jersey relies on its underwriting agreements with ITB. . . .

Each of four separate underwriting agreements between ITB and First Jersey contains provisions for indemnification. In these provisions, ITB agreed to indemnify First Jersey from any and all loss, liability, claims, damage, and expense arising from any material misstatement, untrue statement, or omission in the public offering.

Generally, federal courts disallow claims for indemnification because such claims run counter to the policies underlying the federal securities acts. . . . The underlying goal of securities legislation is encouraging diligence and discouraging negligence in securities transactions. These goals are accomplished "by exposing issuers and underwriters to the substantial hazard of liability for compensatory damages."

The non-settling defendants argue that the policy of not enforcing indemnification provisions should not apply in cases, as here, where an underwriter was merely negligent, played a "de minimis" role in the public offering at issue, or was being held derivatively or vicariously liable. We disagree. . . .

As stated, the federal securities laws seek, inter alia, to encourage underwriters to conduct thorough independent investigations. Unlike contribution, contractual indemnification allows an underwriter to shift its entire liability to the issuer before any allegation of wrongdoing or a determination of fault. . . . If the court enforced an underwriter indemnification provision, it would effectively eliminate the underwriter's incentive to fulfill its investigative obligation. . . .

In addition, if the court were to allow the non-settling defendants to avoid secondary or derivative liability "merely by showing ignorance[, it] would contravene the congressional intent to protect the public, particularly unsophisticated investors, from fraudulent practices." . . . The public depends upon an underwriter's investigation and opinion, and it relies on such opinions when investing. Denying claims for indemnification would encourage underwriters to exhibit the degree of reasonable care required by the 1933 and 1934 Acts. . . .

We turn now to whether the bar order impermissibly impinges on the non-settling defendants' right to contribution. . . .

In general, the settlement of complex litigation before trial is favored by the federal courts. However, in multi-party litigation, settlement may be difficult. Defendants, who are willing to settle, "buy little peace through settlement unless they are assured that they will be protected against co-defendants' efforts to shift their losses through cross-claims for indemnity, contribution, and other causes related to the underlying litigation." . . . In cases involving multiple defendants, a right to contribution inhibits partial settlement.

Therefore, in order to encourage settlement in these cases, modern settlements increasingly incorporate settlement bar orders into partial settlements. "In essence, a bar order constitutes a final discharge of all obligations of the settling defendants and bars any further litigation of claims made by non-settling defendants." . . .

In the present case, the district court adopted the proportionate judgment reduction rule. It concluded that the proportionate judgment reduction is the fairest method, and the non-settling defendants will not be prejudiced by a proportionate fault reduction. We agree with the determination of the district court.

Under the proportionate judgment reduction method, the jury, in the non-settling defendants' trial, will assess the relative culpability of both settling and non-settling defendants, and the non-settling defendants will pay a commensurate percentage of the judgment. The risk of a "bad" settlement falls on the plaintiffs, who have a financial incentive to make certain that each defendant bears its share of the damages. . . . As pointed out by the Ninth Circuit, the proportionate fault rule satisfies the statutory contribution goals of equity, deterrence, and the policy goal of encouraging settlement. The proportionate fault rule is the equivalent of a contribution claim; the non-settling defendants are only responsible for their portion of the liability.

Proportionate judgment reduction method

Proportionate fault rule — equivalent of a contribution claim

We conclude that the district court did not abuse its discretion in imposing the bar order with the proportionate judgment reduction provision. . . .

QUESTIONS

1. Underwriters who demonstrate due diligence escape § 11 liability completely. Is indemnification only a concern for underwriters who fail to meet due diligence?

2. Who bears the risk under the proportionate judgment reduction method? Do the settling defendants or the plaintiffs make up the difference when the non-settling defendants' judgment is reduced?

3. Should underwriters be allowed to purchase insurance against potential § 11 liability?

HYPOTHETICAL SIX

The registration statement for InterPhone's initial public offering contained a number of misstatements, including a failure to disclose Elmo's prior criminal conviction and misstatements in the audited financial statements. Assume that the following players are involved with InterPhone's initial public offering and all face the specter of § 11 liability:

- Zoe, the CEO and a director
- Oscar, an outside director
- Sparrow Securities, the managing underwriter

- Arthur & Young, the auditor

1. If Sparrow Securities had an enforceable indemnification contract clause with InterPhone, would the underwriter still investigate and research to verify the accuracy of disclosures in the registration statement? Or would underwriters entitled to full indemnification shirk on their certification role in a public offering?

2. Suppose that Zoe and Oscar are considering settlement while Sparrow Securities and Arthur & Young are not. Why would Zoe and Oscar worry about potential liability for contribution to Sparrow Securities and Arthur & Young?

3. Suppose that Zoe and Oscar settle for only a small fraction of what they might owe at trial. The plaintiffs' attorneys agree to the settlement to allow them to focus their attention on the real deep pockets, Arthur & Young and Sparrow Securities. If you were a member of a jury considering contribution among the various defendants, how would you go about determining how much responsibility to assign to Arthur & Young and Sparrow Securities for the misrepresentations involving Elmo's criminal conviction and the audited financials? What information would you want to know? Is it likely such information would be available at trial?

4. Assume that, in addition to the other misstatements in the InterPhone registration statement, the filing also failed to disclose certain compensation received by Sparrow Securities in connection with the offering. Specifically, Sparrow received "bonus" commission payments from some of its customers in exchange for receiving an allocation of InterPhone IPO shares from Sparrow. InterPhone was unaware of this practice. Will InterPhone be liable for this omission in a § 11 suit? Can it recover any damages it has to pay from Sparrow Securities?

III.   SECTION 12(a)(1)

Unlike the other liability provisions that we have studied, § 12(a)(1) of the Securities Act is not an antifraud provision. Instead, § 12(a)(1) provides a private cause of action for violations of § 5's gun-jumping rule requirements. Violations of § 5 can occur at a number of different points in the public offering process. A company may release information during the pre-filing period that "conditions" the market. During the waiting period, an underwriter may send out free writing together with the preliminary prospectus. After the SEC declares the registration statement effective, underwriters may fail to deliver the prospectus during the required prospectus delivery period.

As you go through the materials on § 12(a)(1), consider how the various aspects of a § 12(a)(1) lawsuit differ from an antifraud suit under either § 11 of the Securities Act or Rule 10b–5 of the Exchange Act.

A.   STANDING AND DEFENDANTS

The questions "Who has standing to sue?" and "Who are potential defendants?" are interconnected under § 12(a)(1). Section 12(a)(1) provides that:

> Any person who . . . offers or sells a security in violation of section 5 . . . shall be liable . . . to the person purchasing such security from him. . . .

Standing and Ds.

A person who purchases a security offered or sold in violation of § 5 therefore has standing to sue under § 12(a)(1). The class of potential defendants includes those who offer or sell to the purchasing person. In the case below, the Supreme Court defines the precise scope of who is engaged in offers and sales.

Class of potential Ds → those who offer to sell to purchasing person

Pinter v. Dahl

486 U.S. 622 (1988).

■ JUSTICE BLACKMUN delivered the opinion of the Court.

* * *

The controversy arises out of the sale prior to 1982 of unregistered securities (fractional undivided interests in oil and gas leases) by petitioner Billy J. "B.J." Pinter to respondents Maurice Dahl and Dahl's friends, family, and business associates. Pinter is an oil and gas producer in Texas and Oklahoma, and a registered securities dealer in Texas. Dahl is a California real estate broker and investor, who, at the time of his dealings with Pinter, was a veteran of two unsuccessful oil and gas ventures. In pursuit of further investment opportunities, Dahl employed an oil field expert to locate and acquire oil and gas leases. This expert introduced Dahl to Pinter. Dahl advanced $20,000 to Pinter to acquire leases, with the understanding that they would be held in the name of Pinter's Black Gold Oil Company and that Dahl would have a right of first refusal to drill certain wells on the leasehold properties. Pinter located leases in Oklahoma, and Dahl toured the properties, often without Pinter, in order to talk to others and "get a feel for the properties." Upon examining the geology, drilling logs, and production history assembled by Pinter, Dahl concluded, in the words of the District Court, that "there was no way to lose."

understanding

After investing approximately $310,000 in the properties, Dahl told the other respondents about the venture. Except for Dahl and respondent Grantham, none of the respondents spoke to or met Pinter or toured the properties. Because of Dahl's involvement in the venture, each of the other respondents decided to invest about $7,500.

Dahl assisted his fellow investors in completing the subscription-agreement form prepared by Pinter. Each letter-contract signed by the purchaser stated that the participating interests were being sold without the benefit of registration under the Securities Act. . . . Dahl received no commission from Pinter in connection with the other respondents' purchases.

no commission

When the venture failed and their interests proved to be worthless, respondents brought suit against Pinter . . . seeking rescission under

§ 12[a](1) of the Securities Act for the unlawful sale of unregistered securities. . . .

The District Court, after a bench trial, granted judgment for respondent-investors. . . . A divided panel of the Court of Appeals for the Fifth Circuit affirmed. . . . [In affirming, the Court of Appeals considered whether Dahl could be considered a statutory seller under § 12(a)(1) and therefore potentially liable in contribution to Pinter, ultimately finding the Dahl was not such a statutory seller].

In determining whether Dahl may be deemed a "seller" for purposes of § 12[a](1), such that he may be held liable for the sale of unregistered securities to the other investor-respondents, we look first at the language of § 12[a](1). . . . That statute provides, in pertinent part: "Any person who . . . offers or sells a security" in violation of the registration requirement of the Securities Act "shall be liable to the person purchasing such security from him." This provision defines the class of defendants who may be subject to liability as those who offer or sell unregistered securities. But the Securities Act nowhere delineates who may be regarded as a statutory seller, and the sparse legislative history sheds no light on the issue. The courts, on their part, have not defined the term uniformly.

At the very least, however, the language of § 12[a](1) contemplates a buyer-seller relationship not unlike traditional contractual privity. Thus, it is settled that § 12[a](1) imposes liability on the owner who passed title, or other interest in the security, to the buyer for value. . . . Dahl, of course, was not a seller in this conventional sense, and therefore may be held liable only if § 12[a](1) liability extends to persons other than the person who passes title.

A

In common parlance, a person may offer or sell property without necessarily being the person who transfers title to, or other interest in, that property. We need not rely entirely on ordinary understanding of the statutory language, however, for the Securities Act defines the operative terms of § 12[a](1). Section 2[a](3) defines "sale" or "sell" to include "every contract of sale or disposition of a security or interest in a security, for value," and the terms "offer to sell," "offer for sale," or "offer" to include "every attempt or offer to dispose of, or solicitation of an offer to buy, a security or interest in a security, for value." Under these definitions, the range of persons potentially liable under § 12[a](1) is not limited to persons who pass title. The inclusion of the phrase "solicitation of an offer to buy" within the definition of "offer" brings an individual who engages in solicitation, an activity not inherently confined to the actual owner, within the scope of § 12. . . .

Determining that the activity in question falls within the definition of "offer" or "sell" in § 2[a](3), however, is only half of the analysis. The second clause of § 12[a](1), which provides that only a defendant "from" whom the plaintiff "purchased" securities may be liable, narrows the field of potential sellers. Several courts and commentators have stated that the purchase requirement necessarily restricts § 12 primary liability to the owner of the security.... In effect, these authorities interpret the term "purchase" as complementary to only the term "sell" defined in § 2[a](3). Thus, an offeror, as defined by § 2[a](3), may incur § 12 liability only if the offeror also "sells" the security to the plaintiff, in the sense of transferring title for value....

We do not read § 12[a](1) so restrictively. The purchase requirement clearly confines § 12 liability to those situations in which a sale has taken place. Thus, a prospective buyer has no recourse against a person who touts unregistered securities to him if he does not purchase the securities.... The requirement, however, does not exclude solicitation from the category of activities that may render a person liable when a sale has taken place. A natural reading of the statutory language would include in the statutory seller status at least some persons who urged the buyer to purchase. For example, a securities vendor's agent who solicited the purchase would commonly be said, and would be thought by the buyer, to be among those "from" whom the buyer "purchased," even though the agent himself did not pass title....

Doesn't exclude solicitation

An interpretation of statutory seller that includes brokers and others who solicit offers to purchase securities furthers the purposes of the Securities Act—to promote full and fair disclosure of information to the public in the sales of securities. In order to effectuate Congress' intent that § 12[a](1) civil liability be *in terrorem* ... the risk of its invocation should be felt by solicitors of purchases. The solicitation of a buyer is perhaps the most critical stage of the selling transaction. It is the first stage of a traditional securities sale to involve the buyer, and it is directed at producing the sale. In addition, brokers and other solicitors are well positioned to control the flow of information to a potential purchaser, and, in fact, such persons are the participants in the selling transaction who most often disseminate material information to investors. Thus, solicitation is the stage at which an investor is most likely to be injured, that is, by being persuaded to purchase securities without full and fair information. Given Congress' overriding goal of preventing this injury, we may infer that Congress intended solicitation to fall under the mantle of § 12[a](1).

solicitation – 1 stage of selling

solicitation is offer to buy for value

Although we conclude that Congress intended § 12[a](1) liability to extend to those who solicit securities purchases, ... Congress did not intend to impose rescission based on strict liability on a person who urges the purchase but whose motivation is solely to benefit the buyer. When a person who urges another to make a securities purchase acts merely to assist the buyer, not only is it uncommon to say that the buyer "purchased" from him, but it is also strained to describe the giving of gratuitous advice, even strongly or enthusiastically, as "soliciting." Section 2[a](3) defines an offer as a "solicitation of an offer to buy ... for value." The person who gratuitously urges another to make a particular investment decision is not, in any meaningful sense, requesting value in exchange for his suggestion or seeking the value the titleholder will obtain in exchange for the ultimate sale. The language and purpose of § 12[a](1) suggest that

If not → gratuitous advice

the person who gratuitously urges another to make investment is not requesting value

*12(a)(1) →
includes successful
solicitors who serves
his own financial
interest*

liability extends only to the person who successfully solicits the purchase, motivated at least in part by a desire to serve his own financial interests or those of the securities owner. If he had such a motivation, it is fair to say that the buyer "purchased" the security from him and to align him with the owner in a rescission action.

B

Petitioner is not satisfied with extending § 12[a](1) primary liability to one who solicits securities sales for financial gain. Pinter assumes, without explication, that liability is not limited to the person who actually parts title with the securities, and urges us to validate, as the standard by which additional defendant-sellers are identified, that version of the "substantial factor" test utilized by the Fifth Circuit before the refinement espoused in this case. Under that approach, grounded in tort doctrine, a nontransferor § 12[a](1) seller is defined as one "whose participation in the buy-sell transaction is a substantial factor in causing the transaction to take place." The Court of Appeals acknowledged that Dahl would be liable as a statutory seller under this test. . . .

The deficiency of the substantial-factor test is that it divorces the analysis of seller status from any reference to the applicable statutory language and from any examination of § 12 in the context of the total statutory scheme. Those courts that have adopted the approach have not attempted to ground their analysis in the statutory language. Instead, they substitute the concept of substantial participation in the sales transaction, or proximate causation of the plaintiff's purchase, for the words "offers or sells" in § 12. The "purchase from" requirement of § 12 focuses on the defendant's relationship with the plaintiff-purchaser. The substantial-factor test, on the other hand, focuses on the defendant's degree of involvement in the securities transaction and its surrounding circumstances. Thus, although the substantial-factor test undoubtedly embraces persons who pass title and who solicit the purchase of unregistered securities as statutory sellers, the test also would extend § 12[a](1) liability to participants only remotely related to the relevant aspects of the sales transaction. Indeed, it might expose securities professionals, such as accountants and lawyers, whose involvement is only the performance of their professional services, to § 12[a](1) strict liability for rescission. The buyer does not, in any meaningful sense, "purchas[e] the security from" such a person. . . .

*Rejection of
substantial factor
test
– do not include*

[T]he substantial-factor test introduces an element of uncertainty into an area that demands certainty and predictability. As the Fifth Circuit has conceded, the test affords no guidelines for distinguishing between the defendant whose conduct rises to a level of significance sufficient to trigger seller status, and the defendant whose conduct is not sufficiently integral to the sale. None of the courts employing the approach has articulated what measure of participation qualifies a person for seller status, and logically sound limitations would be difficult to develop. As a result, decisions are made on an ad hoc basis, offering little predictive value to participants in securities transactions. . . . We find it particularly unlikely that Congress would have ordained *sub silentio* the imposition of strict liability on such an unpredictably defined class of defendants....

C

We are unable to determine whether Dahl may be held liable as a statutory seller under § 12[a](1). The District Court explicitly found that "Dahl solicited each of the other plaintiffs (save perhaps Grantham) in connection with the offer, purchase, and receipt of their oil and gas interests." We cannot conclude that this finding was clearly erroneous. It is not clear, however, that Dahl had the kind of interest in the sales that make him liable as a statutory seller. We do know that he received no commission from Pinter in connection with the other sales, but this is not conclusive. Typically, a person who solicits the purchase will have sought or received a personal financial benefit from the sale, such as where he "anticipat[es] a share of the profits," or receives a brokerage commission. But a person who solicits the buyer's purchase in order to serve the financial interests of the owner may properly be liable under § 12[a](1) without showing that he expects to participate in the benefits the owner enjoys.

The Court of Appeals apparently concluded that Dahl was motivated entirely by a gratuitous desire to share an attractive investment opportunity with his friends and associates. This conclusion, in our view, was premature. The District Court made no findings that focused on whether Dahl urged the other purchases in order to further some financial interest of his own or of Pinter. Accordingly, further findings are necessary to assess Dahl's liability....

NOTES

Section 12(a)(1) (and § 12(a)(2) discussed below) provides one more formulation on which third parties should face liability for violations of the securities laws. Private liability under Rule 10b–5 depends on the notion of who is a "primary" violator. Liability under § 11, in contrast, extends to those persons and entities listed in § 11(a) as statutory defendants.

Section 12's approach differs from both Rule 10b–5 and § 11 in focusing on the relationship of the participating party and the investor purchasing securities. The *Pinter* Court stresses the importance of the person making contact with investors: "The solicitation of a buyer is perhaps the most critical stage of the selling transaction. It is the first stage of a traditional securities sale to involve the buyer, and it is directed at producing the sale."

Why do the approaches to secondary liability vary for the different causes of action provided in private securities laws? If solicitation is the key step in dealing with investors, why not make § 11 and Rule 10b–5 liability turn on whether a defendant engages in solicitation? If other, non-soliciting participants in an offering may still deter fraud (perhaps through their ability to monitor the issuer and influence the issuer's decision-making), why not make these other participants also liable under § 12?

QUESTIONS

1.   How sophisticated an investor do you think Dahl is? Dahl was the veteran of several "unsuccessful" oil and gas ventures. Can poor investment choices make an investor sophisticated?

2.   The *Pinter* court rejects including "substantial participants" as potential § 12(a)(1) defendants in part because this class of defendants is "unpredictably defined." Is the class of defendants who help "solicit" the offers more definite?

3.   Try to apply the *Pinter* standard for determining potential defendants in a § 11 lawsuit. Which § 11 defendants would (and would not) meet the requirements of *Pinter*?

HYPOTHETICAL SEVEN

Two years after InterPhone's initial public offering, Zoe decides that InterPhone needs to raise additional capital to fund a new marketing campaign. She estimates that InterPhone needs about $50 million to launch the campaign, which will focus on a large number of TV ads in which she plans to star. InterPhone will conduct the offering as a private placement exempt from § 5 pursuant to Rule 506 of Regulation D. (We cover Regulation D in Chapter 10.) Unfortunately, InterPhone's selling agent, Grover Securities, made an impermissible general solicitation in finding investors for the private placement. Assume that InterPhone does not qualify for any other exemption from § 5's registration requirements and is liable under § 12(a)(1).

1.   *Scenario One*: Suppose that two friends, Bert and Ernie, are investors in the InterPhone private placement. Bert learned of the private placement from Ernie. Ernie routinely passes on investment tips to Bert at their weekly tennis game. Assume that no money ever changes hands between the two (aside from Bert having to pay for lunch when he loses the tennis match *again*). Can InterPhone sue Ernie under § 12(a)(1) for contribution as a statutory seller?

2.   *Scenario Two*: Suppose that InterPhone's attorneys, Snuffle & Gus LLP, administered the physical mailing of InterPhone's offering memorandum to all offerees. Can InterPhone sue Snuffle & Gus under § 12(a)(1) for contribution as another statutory seller? What if Snuffle & Gus included with the offering memorandum a cover letter with Snuffle & Gus's name prominently displayed at the top of the letter?

3.   *Scenario Three*: What happens if the U.S. economy goes into a recession right after the investors purchase the stock from InterPhone's private placement? InterPhone's stock falls in value due to the recession; its failure to adhere to the registration requirements has nothing to do with the stock's decline. Can InterPhone argue that the § 12(a)(1) rescission remedy and damages should be reduced?

4.   *Scenario Four*: Suppose that instead of holding onto his InterPhone securities purchased from the private placement at $20 per share, Bert had sold the shares at $10 per share to Kermit. Who may Kermit sue? Who may Bert sue?

B.   ELEMENTS OF THE CAUSE OF ACTION

Section 12(a)(1) works to crush out § 5 violations. Plaintiffs need only show a § 5 violation involving a security that they purchased. No further requirement of scienter (or even negligence), causation, reliance, or a showing of damages is required. Plaintiffs who demonstrate a § 5 violation then are entitled to rescission (getting their money back in exchange for the securities). Plaintiffs who already have sold the securities may seek damages.

C.   Damages and Defenses

We saw that defendants in a § 11 antifraud action enjoyed a number of defenses. Defendants could attempt to show due diligence or that the loss in the issuer's shares was due to other exogenous causes. Should defendants in a § 12(a)(1) rescission action for a violation of § 5 enjoy similar defenses? What if an underwriter made an innocent mistake in sending out "free writing" during the waiting period? What if the stock price dropped after the offering but due to clearly unrelated reasons (e.g., a sharp spike in the price of oil)?

[handwritten margin note: Defense: - due diligence - lack of causation (loss was caused by other reason).]

The short answer for § 12(a)(1) is that defendants enjoy no defenses. As with other Securities Act civil liability provisions, however, § 13 imposes a statute of limitations of one year from discovery and three years from sale.

[handwritten margin note: 12(a)(1) → No defense]

HYPOTHETICAL EIGHT

1. Consider Bird, an investor in the InterPhone initial public offering who bought 100 shares at $20 per share. Assume that InterPhone's underwriters failed to send a final prospectus to Bird with her confirmation. If InterPhone's share price rises to $30, will she exercise her right under § 12(a)(1) to obtain rescission? If InterPhone's shares drop to $10 per share, will Bird pursue her § 12(a)(1) remedy?

2. Suppose that Rosita is another investor in the InterPhone IPO. She did receive a final prospectus with her confirmation of sale. Can she bring suit for § 12(a)(1) recession for InterPhone's failure to send Bird a final prospectus with the confirmation of sale?

3. Recall that Sparrow Securities is the managing underwriter for InterPhone's initial public offering. Consider the following chain of transactions:

    a.   InterPhone sells to Sparrow Securities at $18.60 per share

    b.   Sparrow Securities sells to Bird at $20 per share

    c.   Bird sells to Kermit at $10 per share

Suppose that a § 5 violation occurred during the Waiting Period (impermissible free writing was mailed out to prospective investors). What damages may Bird and Kermit obtain under § 12(a)(1)?

IV.   Section 12(a)(2) Liability

Section 11 focused on misstatements in the registration statement; § 12(a)(2) provides a private cause of action for misstatements in the prospectus. Section 12(a)(2) provides in part that:

> Any person who ... offers or sells a security ... by the use of any means or instruments of transportation or communication in interstate commerce ... by means of a prospectus or oral communication, which includes an untrue statement of a material fact or omits to state a material fact necessary in order to make the statements, in the light of the circumstances under which they were made, not misleading ... shall be liable ... to the person purchasing such security from him....

Like Rule 10b–5 and § 11, § 12(a)(2) requires a material misstatement or omission as well as the use of an instrumentality of interstate commerce. Section 12(a)(2) also shares many features with its sibling, § 12(a)(1). Like § 12(a)(1), only those purchasing securities have standing to sue under § 12(a)(2). Potential defendants are those who offer or sell the securities. Courts have applied the Supreme Court's § 12(a)(1) analysis in *Pinter* to determine which participating parties in an offering are involved with offering (including soliciting) and selling the securities for purposes of § 12(a)(2).

A.   The Scope of § 12(a)(2)

Although § 12(a)(2) shares similarities with other antifraud provisions and § 12(a)(1), it does differ in one important respect: Section 12(a)(2) only reaches fraud committed "by means of a prospectus or oral communication." Unfortunately, the Securities Act leaves some ambiguity in defining a prospectus. Section 2(a)(10) provides that a "prospectus" means "any prospectus, notice, circular, advertisement, letter, or communication, written or by radio or television, which offers any security for sale or confirms the sale of security...." Defining prospectus to mean "any prospectus" has a certain circularity to it. The SEC has, instead, traditionally focused on the term "communication" in defining the scope of the "gun-jumping" rules that govern the Pre–Filing and Waiting Periods during the registration process. The agency's focus on "communication" leads to a broad interpretation of "prospectus," sweeping in virtually any written statement that could be seen as "arousing" the interest of investors in an issuer or its securities.

Complicating the matter further is § 10 of the Securities Act. Section 10 does not define a prospectus, but instead sets forth the information required for prospectuses that satisfies the requirements of § 5(b)'s prospectus delivery requirement. In short, a § 10 prospectus forms Part I of the formal registration statement and contains information on the biographies of management, the composition of the board of directors, and a description of the company's business and assets, among other information.

Section 12(a)(2) thus leaves courts to puzzle over at least two possible alternatives for the scope of its application:

1. Any prospectus meeting the SEC's broad interpretation of the definition contained in § 2(a)(10)

2. Only prospectuses forming Part I of the registration statement which satisfy § 10 of the Securities Act

The Supreme Court interpreted "prospectus" for purposes of § 12 in the case below. Did the Court select one of these two alternatives, or did it choose yet another interpretation for the term "prospectus"?

Gustafson v. Alloyd

513 U.S. 561 (1995).

■ JUSTICE KENNEDY delivered the opinion of the Court.

Under § 12[a](2) of the Securities Act of 1933 buyers have an express cause of action for rescission against sellers who make material misstatements or omissions "by means of a prospectus." The question presented is whether this right of rescission extends to a private, secondary transaction, on the theory that recitations in the purchase agreement are part of a "prospectus."

I

Petitioners Gustafson, McLean, and Butler (collectively Gustafson) were in 1989 the sole shareholders of Alloyd, Inc., a manufacturer of plastic packaging and automatic heat sealing equipment. Alloyd was formed, and its stock was issued, in 1961. In 1989, Gustafson decided to sell Alloyd and engaged KPMG Peat Marwick to find a buyer. In response to information distributed by KPMG, Wind Point Partners II, L.P., agreed to buy substantially all of the issued and outstanding stock through Alloyd Holdings, Inc., a new corporation formed to effect the sale of Alloyd's stock. The shareholders of Alloyd Holdings were Wind Point and a number of individual investors.

In preparation for negotiating the contract with Gustafson, Wind Point undertook an extensive analysis of the company, relying in part on a formal business review prepared by KPMG. Alloyd's practice was to take inventory at year's end, so Wind Point and KPMG considered taking an earlier inventory to use in determining the purchase price. In the end they did not do so, relying instead on certain estimates and including provisions for adjustments after the transaction closed.

On December 20, 1989, Gustafson and Alloyd Holdings executed a contract of sale. Alloyd Holdings agreed to pay Gustafson and his coshareholders $18,709,000 for the sale of the stock plus a payment of $2,122,219, which reflected the estimated increase in Alloyd's net worth from the end of the previous year, the last period for which hard financial data were available. Article IV of the purchase agreement, entitled "Representations and Warranties of the Sellers," included assurances that the company's financial statements "present fairly ... the Company's financial condition" and that between the date of the latest balance sheet and the date the agreement was executed "there ha[d] been no material adverse change in ... [Alloyd's] financial condition." The contract also provided that if the year-end audit and financial statements revealed a variance between esti-mated and actual increased value, the disappointed party would receive an adjustment.

The year-end audit of Alloyd revealed that Alloyd's actual earnings for 1989 were lower than the estimates relied upon by the parties in negotiat-ing the adjustment amount of $2,122,219. Under the contract, the buyers had a right to recover an adjustment amount of $815,000 from the sellers. Nevertheless, on February 11, 1991, the newly formed company (now called Alloyd Co., the same as the original company) and Wind Point brought suit . . . seeking outright rescission of the contract under § 12[a](2). Alloyd (the new company) claimed that statements made by Gustafson and his coshare-holders regarding the financial data of their company were inaccurate, rendering untrue the representations and warranties contained in the contract. The buyers further alleged that the contract of sale was a "prospectus," so that any misstatements contained in the agreement gave rise to liability under § 12[a](2). Pursuant to the adjustment clause, the defendants remitted to the purchasers $815,000 plus interest, but the adjustment did not cause the purchasers to drop the lawsuit. . . .

II

* * *

As this case reaches us, we must assume that the stock purchase agreement contained material misstatements of fact made by the sellers and that Gustafson would not sustain its burden of proving due care. On these assumptions, Alloyd would have a right to obtain rescission if those misstatements were made "by means of a prospectus or oral communica-tion." The Courts of Appeals agree that the phrase "oral communication" is restricted to oral communications that relate to a prospectus. The determinative question, then, is whether the contract between Alloyd and Gustafson is a "prospectus" as the term is used in the 1933 Act.

Alloyd argues that "prospectus" is defined in a broad manner, broad enough to encompass the contract between the parties. This argument is echoed by the dissents. . . . Gustafson, by contrast, maintains that prospec-tus in the 1933 Act means a communication soliciting the public to purchase securities from the issuer. . . .

Three sections of the 1933 Act are critical in resolving the definitional question on which the case turns: § 2[a](10), which defines a prospectus; § 10, which sets forth the information that must be contained in a prospectus; and § 12, which imposes liability based on misstatements in a prospectus. In seeking to interpret the term "prospectus," we adopt the premise that the term should be construed, if possible, to give it a consistent meaning throughout the Act. That principle follows from our duty to construe statutes, not isolated provisions. . . .

A

We begin with § 10. . . . An examination of § 10 reveals that, whatever else "prospectus" may mean, the term is confined to a document that, absent an overriding exemption, must include the "information contained in the registration statement." By and large, only public offerings by an issuer of a security, or by controlling shareholders of an issuer, require the preparation and filing of registration statements. It follows, we conclude, that a prospectus under § 10 is confined to documents related to public offerings by an issuer or its controlling shareholders.

This much (the meaning of prospectus in § 10) seems not to be in dispute. Where the courts are in disagreement is with the implications of this proposition for the entirety of the Act, and for § 12 in particular.... We conclude that the term "prospectus" must have the same meaning under §§ 10 and 12. In so holding, we do not, as the dissent by Justice Ginsburg suggests, make the mistake of treating § 10 as a definitional section.... Instead, we find in § 10 guidance and instruction for giving the term a consistent meaning throughout the Act.

The 1933 Act, like every Act of Congress, should not be read as a series of unrelated and isolated provisions.... That principle applies here. If the contract before us is not a prospectus for purposes of § 10—as all must and do concede—it is not a prospectus for purposes of § 12 either.

The conclusion that prospectus has the same meaning, and refers to the same types of communications (public offers by an issuer or its controlling shareholders), in both §§ 10 and 12 is reinforced by an examination of the structure of the 1933 Act. Sections 4 and 5 of the Act together require a seller to file a registration statement and to issue a prospectus for certain defined types of sales (public offerings by an issuer, through an underwriter). Sections 7 and 10 of the Act set forth the information required in the registration statement and the prospectus. Section 11 provides for liability on account of false registration statements; § 12[a](2) for liability based on misstatements in prospectuses. Following the most natural and symmetrical reading, just as the liability imposed by § 11 flows from the requirements imposed by §§ 5 and 7 providing for the filing and content of registration statements, the liability imposed by § 12[a](2) cannot attach unless there is an obligation to distribute the prospectus in the first place (or unless there is an exemption)....

The primary innovation of the 1933 Act was the creation of federal duties—for the most part, registration and disclosure obligations—in connection with public offerings.... We are reluctant to conclude that § 12[a](2) creates vast additional liabilities that are quite independent of the new substantive obligations the Act imposes. It is more reasonable to interpret the liability provisions of the 1933 Act as designed for the primary purpose of providing remedies for violations of the obligations it had created. Indeed, §§ 11 and 12[a](1)—the statutory neighbors of § 12[a](2)—afford remedies for violations of those obligations.... Under our interpretation of "prospectus," § 12[a](2) in similar manner is linked to the new duties created by the Act.

On the other hand, accepting Alloyd's argument that any written offer is a prospectus under § 12 would require us to hold that the word "prospectus" in § 2 refers to a broader set of communications than the same term in § 10.... In the name of a plain meaning approach to statutory interpretation, the dissents discover in the Act two different species of prospectuses: formal (also called § 10) prospectuses, subject to both §§ 10 and 12, and informal prospectuses, subject only to § 12 but not to § 10.... Nowhere in the statute, however, do the terms "formal prospectus" or "informal prospectus" appear. Instead, the Act uses one term—"prospectus"—throughout. In disagreement with the Court of Appeals and the dissenting opinions, we cannot accept the conclusion that this single operative word means one thing in one section of the Act and something quite different in another....

B

Alloyd's contrary argument rests to a significant extent on § 2[a](10), or, to be more precise, on one word of that section. Section 2[a](10) provides that "[t]he term 'prospectus' means any prospectus, notice, circular, advertisement, letter, or communication, written or by radio or television, which offers any security for sale or confirms the sale of any security." Concentrating on the word "communication," Alloyd argues that any written communication that offers a security for sale is a "prospectus." Inserting its definition into § 12[a](2), Alloyd insists that a material misstatement in any communication offering a security for sale gives rise to an action for rescission, without proof of fraud by seller or reliance by the purchaser. In Alloyd's view, § 2[a](10) gives the term "prospectus" a capacious definition that, although incompatible with § 10, nevertheless governs in § 12....

The word "communication," however, on which Alloyd's entire argument rests, is but one word in a list, a word Alloyd reads altogether out of context.

The relevant phrase in the definitional part of the statute must be read in its entirety, a reading which yields the interpretation that the term "prospectus" refers to a document soliciting the public to acquire securities. We find that definition controlling. Alloyd's argument that the phrase "communication, written or by radio or television," transforms any written communication offering a security for sale into a prospectus cannot consist with at least two rather sensible rules of statutory construction. First, the Court will avoid a reading which renders some words altogether redundant.... If "communication" included every written communication, it would render "notice, circular, advertisement, [and] letter" redundant, since each of these are forms of written communication as well....

The constructional problem is resolved by the second principle Alloyd overlooks, which is that a word is known by the company it keeps (the doctrine of *noscitur a sociis*).... From the terms "prospectus, notice, circular, advertisement, [or] letter," it is apparent that the list refers to documents of wide dissemination. In a similar manner, the list includes communications "by radio or television," but not face-to-face or telephonic conversations. Inclusion of the term "communication" in that list suggests that it too refers to a public communication.

When the 1933 Act was drawn and adopted, the term "prospectus" was well understood to refer to a document soliciting the public to acquire securities from the issuer.... In this respect, the word "prospectus" is a term of art, which accounts for congressional confidence in employing what might otherwise be regarded as a partial circularity in the formal, statutory definition.... The use of the term "prospectus" to refer to public solicitations explains as well Congress' decision in § 12[a](2) to grant buyers a right to rescind without proof of reliance. See H.R.Rep. No. 85, 73d Cong., 1st Sess., 10 (1933) ("The statements for which [liable persons] are responsible, although they may never actually have been seen by the prospective purchaser, because of their wide dissemination, determine the market price of the security ... ").

The list of terms in § 2[a](10) prevents a seller of stock from avoiding liability by calling a soliciting document something other than a prospectus, but it does not compel the conclusion that Alloyd urges us to reach and that the dissenting opinions adopt. Instead, the term "written communication" must be read in context to refer to writings that, from a functional standpoint, are similar to the terms "notice, circular, [and] advertisement." The term includes communications held out to the public at large but that might have been thought to be outside the other words in the definitional section....

D

It is understandable that Congress would provide buyers with a right to rescind, without proof of fraud or reliance, as to misstatements contained in a document prepared with care, following well-established procedures relating to investigations with due diligence and in the context of a public offering by an issuer or its controlling shareholders. It is not plausible to infer that Congress created this extensive liability for every casual communication between buyer and seller in the secondary market. It is often difficult, if not altogether impractical, for those engaged in casual communications not to omit some fact that would, if included, qualify the accuracy of a statement. Under Alloyd's view any casual communication between buyer and seller in the aftermarket could give rise to an action for rescission, with no evidence of fraud on the part of the seller or reliance on the part of the buyer. In many instances buyers in practical effect would have an option to rescind, impairing the stability of past transactions where neither fraud nor detrimental reliance on misstatements or omissions occurred. We find no basis for interpreting the statute to reach so far.

III

* * *

The legislative history of the Act concerning the precise question presented supports our interpretation with much clarity and force. Congress contemplated that § 12[a](2) would apply only to public offerings by an issuer (or a controlling shareholder). The House Report stated: "The bill affects only new offerings of securities.... It does not affect the ordinary redistribution of securities unless such redistribution takes on the characteristics of a new offering." The observation extended to § 12[a](2) as well. Part II, § 6 of the House Report is entitled "Civil Liabilities." It begins: "Sections 11 and 12 create and define the civil liabilities imposed by the act.... Fundamentally, these sections entitle the buyer of securities sold upon a registration statement ... to sue for recovery of his purchase price." It will be recalled that as to private transactions, such as the Alloyd purchase, there will never have been a registration statement. If § 12[a](2) liability were imposed here, it would cover transactions not within the contemplated reach of the statute....

Alloyd's transaction is private.

* * *

In sum, the word "prospectus" is a term of art referring to a document that describes a public offering of securities by an issuer or controlling shareholder. The contract of sale, and its recitations, were not held out to the public and were not a prospectus as the term is used in the 1933 Act.

Prospectus is a term of art → document that describes public offering of securities by an issuer or controlling SH.

Contract for private parties is not

The judgment of the Court of Appeals is reversed, and the case is remanded for further proceedings consistent with this opinion.

It is so ordered.

* * *

■ JUSTICE GINSBURG, with whom JUSTICE BREYER joins, dissenting.

A seller's misrepresentation made "by means of a prospectus or oral communication" is actionable under § 12[a](2) of the Securities Act of 1933. To limit the scope of this civil liability provision, the Court maintains that a communication qualifies as a prospectus only if made during a public offering.[1] Communications during either secondary trading or a private placement are not "prospectuses," the Court declares, and thus are not covered by § 12[a](2)....

To construe a legislatively defined term, courts usually start with the defining section. Section 2[a](10) defines prospectus capaciously as "any prospectus, notice, circular, advertisement, letter, or communication, written or by radio or television, which offers any security for sale or confirms the sale of any security." The items listed in the defining provision, notably "letters" and "communications," are common in private and secondary sales, as well as in public offerings. The § 2[a](10) definition thus does not confine the § 12[a](2) term "prospectus" to public offerings.

Dissent: 2a(10) prospectus was confined to public offerings

The Court bypasses § 2[a](10), and the solid support it gives the Court of Appeals' disposition. Instead of beginning at the beginning, by first attending to the definition section, the Court starts with § 10, a substantive provision. The Court correctly observes that the term "prospectus" has a circumscribed meaning in that context. A prospectus within the contemplation of § 10 is a formal document, typically a document composing part

---

1. I understand the Court's definition of a public offering to encompass both transactions that must be registered under § 5 and transactions that would have been registered had the securities involved not qualified for exemption under § 3.

of a registration statement; a § 10 prospectus, all agree, appears only in public offerings. The Court then proceeds backward; it reads into the literally and logically prior definition section, § 2[a](10), the meaning "prospectus" has in § 10.

To justify its backward reading—proceeding from § 10 to § 2[a](10) and not the other way round—the Court states that it "cannot accept the conclusion that [the operative word 'prospectus'] means one thing in one section of the Act and something quite different in another." Our decisions, however, constantly recognize that "a characterization fitting in certain contexts may be unsuitable in others." . . .

According "prospectus" discrete meanings in § 10 and § 12[a](2) is consistent with Congress' specific instruction in § 2 that definitions apply "unless the context otherwise requires". . . . As the Court of Appeals construed the Act, § 2[a](10)'s definition of "prospectus" governs § 12[a](2), which accommodates without strain the definition's broad reach; by contrast, the specific context of § 10 requires a correspondingly specific reading of "prospectus". . . .

QUESTIONS

1. After *Gustafson,* Alloyd Holdings cannot rely on § 12(a)(2) to recover for alleged fraud in the sales contract it signed with Gustafson. What other causes of action does Alloyd Holdings have available to it? How do these causes differ?

2. Recall that § 5(b)(1) of the Securities Act makes it unlawful for any person to use the instrumentalities of interstate commerce to "carry or transmit any prospectus relating to any security with respect to which a registration statement has been filed under this Act, unless such prospectus meets the requirements of Section 10." If the word "prospectus" has one consistent meaning in the Securities Act, why is § 5(b) necessary?

3. Suppose that InterPhone engages in a private placement under Rule 506 for the sale of $50 million of its common stock. During the selling effort, InterPhone's representatives tell potential investors orally that InterPhone expects its new ad campaign will "increase revenues by 50%." Assuming such oral representations are materially misleading, can investors in the private placement bring suit under § 12(a)(2)?

4. Consider an offering by a small business issuer under Regulation A of the Securities Act. (Regulation A provides an exemption from § 5 and is discussed more fully in Chapter 9.) Regulation A does not require the distribution of a prospectus that meets the requirements of § 10. Instead, Regulation A only requires that offerees receive an offering circular. A Regulation A offering is public in the sense that broad-based selling efforts may take place and investors may engage in immediate resales, allowing the creation of a public secondary market. After *Gustafson,* may an investor in a Regulation A offering sue under § 12(a)(2) for fraud in a Regulation A offering circular?

B. IMPLICATIONS OF *GUSTAFSON*

Gustafson confines § 12(a)(2) liability to public offerings. Questions remain, however, as to who may bring suit for fraud involved in the public offering. Information disclosed in the prospectus and registration statement, for example, affects not only those investors who purchase directly from the issuer and its underwriters but also other investors in the market.

Immediately after sales of securities in a public offering commence, secondary market trading will typically begin even before all of the offered shares have been distributed. Both primary transactions (involving sales by the issuer) and secondary transactions (involving sales by other investors) will often occur simultaneously following the start of a public offering. When one investor sells shares to another in an unsolicited broker's transaction, we have seen that §§ 4(1) and 4(4) of the Securities Act exempt the transaction from the prospectus delivery requirement. Nonetheless, the disclosures made in the prospectus are likely to influence the price in secondary market trading. Should investors who purchase in secondary market transactions at the time of a public offering have the ability to bring a § 12(a)(2) lawsuit for fraud in the public offering prospectus?

In Re Valence Technology Securities Litigation

1996 WL 37788 (N.D. Cal.).

■ WARE, DISTRICT JUDGE.

[*Valence* involved a securities class action brought on behalf of those who purchased stock from May 7, 1992, the date of Valence Technology's initial public offering, to August 10, 1994. Among other claims, the plaintiffs alleged a violation of § 12(a)(2) of the Securities Act. Addressing the issue of whether purchasers in the secondary market are eligible to bring a § 12(a)(2) claim, the court wrote:]

As the allegations on their face demonstrate that Plaintiff did not purchase in the Valence public offering, Plaintiffs appear to be claiming that a nexus exists between this aftermarket purchase and the public offering on December 22, 1993. However, Plaintiffs cite no authority for their proposition that § 12[a](2) supports liability for transactions "traceable" to a public offering. The Supreme Court has stated that "the liability imposed by § 12[a](2) [ ] cannot attach unless there is an obligation to distribute the prospectus in the first place (or unless there is an exemption)." Gustafson v. Alloyd Co., 513 U.S. 561 (1995). The purchase at issue in this case required no prospectus and no exemption applies. The Court also held that "[t]he intent of Congress and the design of the statute require that § 12(2) liability be limited to public offerings." ... The Court is persuaded that § 12[a](2) applies only to a transaction which requires a prospectus to be delivered. The language in *Gustafson* makes irrelevant whether the transaction is "traceable" to a public offering. Accordingly, the Court hereby dismisses with prejudice Plaintiffs' § 12[a](2) claims as to Plaintiff Bergelson for failure to state a claim.

How does *Gustafson*'s interpretation of § 12(a)(2) interact with § 11's standing requirement? As seen in *Valence Technology*, courts are unwilling to extend § 12(a)(2) liability to those who purchase in secondary market transactions which do not require prospectus delivery. Does parallel reasoning mean § 11 liability only covers purchases of shares (traceable to the registration statement) during the required prospectus delivery period?

Hertzberg v. Dignity Partners, Inc.

191 F.3d 1076 (9th Cir. 1999).

Who can bring a suit

■ Fletcher, Circuit Judge.

[Dignity Partners sold common stock in an initial public offering. Investors purchased Dignity common stock in the open market more than 25 days after the IPO (after the prospectus delivery requirement had expired). The investors brought a class action against Dignity under § 11 of the Securities Act. Judge William Fletcher reversed the district court's holding that the investors lacked standing because they did not purchase in the IPO or within 25 days of the offering:]

Section 11(a) provides that where a material fact is misstated or omitted from a registration statement accompanying a stock filing with the Securities and Exchange Commission, "any person acquiring such security" may bring an action for losses caused by the misstatement or omission. The district court read this phrase as if it had been written, "any person acquiring such security on the first day of an initial public offering or in the twenty-five day period thereafter."[3] This reading adds a significant limitation not found in the original text....

Dignity believes that its reading of Section 11 is supported by the Supreme Court's decision in *Gustafson*. We believe that Dignity is mistaken. In *Gustafson*, the Supreme Court interpreted Section 12 of the Security Act rather than Section 11, and limited its decision to determining what was a "prospectus" under Section 12. Dicta in *Gustafson* indicate that a suit under Section 12 may only be maintained by a person who purchased the stock in the offering under the prospectus, but the Court gave no indication that it intended this restriction to apply to Section 11.

Dignity relies on the Supreme Court's statements in *Gustafson* that Section 12 is a companion to Section 11 for its claim that Section 11 applies only to people who purchased their stock in the initial offering. However, while Section 11 and Section 12 are indeed parallel statutes, their wording is significantly different as to who can bring a suit. As already noted,

---

3. The district court ruled from the bench and did not issue a written decision, so we are not certain where it got the 25–day period. Such a 25–day period was most likely borrowed from the 25–day after-market period of [Rule 174]. However, this section pertains to false statements in prospectuses (a Section 12 violation), not registration statements (a Section 11 violation). We note that defendant does not seriously argue in support of the 25–day period. Rather, it argues that any after-market purchase is excluded from the protection of Section 11, whether made one day or 26 days after the initial public offering.

[handwritten margin note: 12: suit is permitted only by person purchasing from person who issued prospectus.]

Section 11 permits suit without restriction by "any person acquiring such security." Section 12, by contrast, permits suit against a seller of a security by prospectus only by "the person purchasing such security from him," thus specifying that a plaintiff must have purchased the security directly from the issuer of the prospectus.

Congress's decision to use "from him" in Section 12 but not in Section 11 must mean that Congress intended a different meaning in the two sections.... Further, there is nothing in the reasoning or underlying logic of *Gustafson* that indicates that we should read into Section 11 the express privity requirement of Section 12.

* * *

HYPOTHETICAL NINE

Assume that InterPhone does a seasoned public offering two years after its IPO for an additional 1 million shares of common stock at $30 per share. InterPhone makes a number of misleading and material misstatements in the management discussion and analysis section of the prospectus and registration statement. Consider the following purchasers of InterPhone's stock:

1. *Scenario One*: Bird buys directly from the seasoned public offering after reading the final prospectus. Can she bring a § 11 antifraud lawsuit against the issuer and its underwriters? Can she bring a § 12(a)(2) lawsuit?

2. *Scenario Two*: Ernie buys directly from the seasoned public offering and he receives a copy of the final prospectus with his confirmation of sale, but he does not read it. Can he bring a § 11 antifraud lawsuit against the issuer and its underwriters? Can he bring a § 12(a)(2) lawsuit?

3. *Scenario Three*: After the offering, Rosita buys shares of InterPhone two months after reading a copy of the prospectus she obtained from her friend, Ernie. Assume that Rosita purchases directly from Bird. Bird had earlier purchased her shares solely from the seasoned public offering. Can Rosita bring a § 11 antifraud lawsuit against the issuer and its underwriters? Can she bring a § 12(a)(2) lawsuit?

C. ELEMENTS OF THE CAUSE OF ACTION

[handwritten margin note: 12(a)(2) - misstatement / omission - in prospectus or or com - causal connection]

Section 12(a)(2) requires plaintiffs to prove a material misstatement or omission contained in a prospectus or related oral communication. Plaintiffs must also show the use of an instrumentality of interstate commerce.

Section 12(a)(2) does not require a showing of either scienter or reliance. Although § 12(a)(2) does not explicitly mention causation, courts have treated the "by means of" phrase as requiring some limited showing of a causal connection between the prospectus and the purchaser's decision to buy the issuer's securities.

Consider the interpretation in *Sanders v. John Nuveen & Co.* of "by means of." Note that *Sanders* is a pre-*Gustafson* case: Would *Sanders* state a valid § 12(a)(2) case after *Gustafson*?

Sanders v. John Nuveen & Co. *Yes.*

619 F.2d 1222 (7th Cir. 1980).

■ TONE, CIRCUIT JUDGE.

The issue we decide on this appeal is whether plaintiff class members *Issue* have established their claims under § 12[a](2) of the Securities Act of 1933. Holding that they have, we affirm the district court's judgment in their favor.

* * *

Plaintiff class consists of forty-two purchasers of unsecured short term *42 purchasers of* promissory notes aggregating $1,612,500 issued by Winter & Hirsch, Inc. *unsecured short-term* (WH), a consumer finance company. The purchases were made from John *promissory notes.* Nuveen & Co., Inc. during a seven-month period immediately preceding WH's default on the notes in February 1970. . . .

Nuveen was the exclusive underwriter of the WH notes, which were *Nuveen-exclusive* sold, like other commercial paper, through its branch offices throughout *underwriter of WH* the United States. . . . *notes, which were sold like other commercial paper reports*

Nuveen prepared and circulated to prospective customers "commercial paper reports" on the WH commercial paper that it held for sale. Three members of the plaintiff class testified to having received copies of these reports before they bought WH notes. Two other members testified to having received commercial paper reports, but could not swear to having received them before making their purchases. Nine class members, including the three who had received reports before purchasing, testified that, when they bought their WH notes, Nuveen salesmen made oral statements *oral statements* about the quality of the notes. There was no evidence of oral communications to any other class members. All class members received the usual written confirmations advising them that they had purchased certain described notes and that Nuveen had sold the notes as principal.

WH's default was the product of a fraud it perpetrated with the *WH - Fraud* connivance of the certified public accountants who audited its financial statements and rendered opinions thereon. . . . Nuveen was not aware of *N - was honestly* the fraud and held "the mistaken but honest belief that financial state- *not aware* ments (of WH) prepared by certified public accountants correctly represent- ed the condition of" WH. It accordingly proceeded to sell the WH notes and also to issue commercial paper reports thereon that reflected the false WH financial statements.

* * *

Defendants admit that the reports were prospectuses and that they *Reports were prospectuses* were false and misleading. The reports repeated the false financial informa- tion contained in the WH financial statements. Also, they stated that the figures were from a detailed audit when in fact the auditors' opinions stated that no detailed audit had been made.

Defendants' only response to this argument is that, except as to the three members proved to have received copies of reports before their purchases, the reports had no "causal relationship" with the sales of the WH notes.

Although the "by means of" language in the statute requires some causal connection between the misleading representation or omission and plaintiff's purchase, defendants' interpretation of that standard is much too stringent. It is well settled that § 12[a](2) imposes liability without regard to whether the buyer relied on the misrepresentation or omission.... To require a plaintiff to have received a commercial paper report before purchasing, as defendants would have us do, would tend toward erroneously imposing a reliance requirement.

The statutory language, as amplified by the legislative history, indicates that a plaintiff need not prove that he ever received the misleading prospectus. The statute imposes liability in favor of a purchaser on any person who "(o)ffers or sells a security .. by means of a prospectus or oral communication" that is misleading. Although the statute explicitly requires privity between plaintiff-purchaser and defendant-seller, its terms do not require that the particular sale to an individual plaintiff be directly by means of the prospectus alleged to be misleading. The causal connection contemplated by the statute is revealed in the House Report on the bill that, after changes not relevant here, became the Securities Act of 1933.... Referring to §§ 11 and 12, the two sections imposing civil liabilities, the report declared that statements issued in connection with the sale of securities,

> although they may never actually have been seen by the prospective purchaser, because of their wide dissemination, determine the market price of the security which in the last analysis reflects those manifold causes that are the impelling motive of the particular purchase. The connection between the statements made and the purchase of the security is clear, and, for this reason, it is the essence of fairness to insist upon the assumption of responsibility for the making of these statements.

Defendants argue that this is not "an open market trading case where dissemination of information to some buyers or sellers can have an impact upon the market price and thus affect transactions by people who never saw the documents." The attempted distinction lacks substance. Even though short term commercial paper is not ordinarily traded in the same way as stock and instruments of indebtedness of publicly held companies, the price it will bring depends upon the financial condition of the issuer relative to that of other issuers and the going interest rates in the money market. In that sense there is a market price. A prospectus that reports on the issuer's financial condition affects that price. In the case at bar, publication of WH's true financial condition would have caused a total collapse of the market for its notes....

The false and misleading WH commercial paper reports issued by Nuveen therefore satisfy the statute's requirement of a false or misleading prospectus "by means of" which the security was sold, regardless of whether all plaintiff class members received copies of those reports....

NOTES

Compared with Rule 10b–5, § 12(a)(2) offers a much more generous cause of action for plaintiffs. Under § 12(a)(2), plaintiffs do not need to show reliance or scienter. Although some causation must be shown, *Sanders* illustrates that causation can be quite attenuated—the focus is not on individual investors, but instead on the market as a whole.

some causation must be shown

Perhaps *Gustafson* can be better understood in light of the relative ease with which plaintiffs may pursue a § 12(a)(2) claim. The *Gustafson* Court itself mentioned a concern that every "casual communication" in the secondary market might fall under § 12(a)(2) liability if the definition of prospectus were not limited. By constraining what is a prospectus to documents used in a public offering (or, perhaps, to § 10 prospectuses), *Gustafson* limits the scope of § 12(a)(2). Arguably, this limitation allows persons to talk more freely without the fear of antifraud liability.

QUESTIONS

1. *Sanders* says that: "A prospectus that reports on the issuer's financial condition affects that price. In the case at bar, publication of WH's true financial condition would have caused a total collapse of the market for its notes." Is it true that a prospectus containing the truth would have caused a "total collapse" of the market? If so, then not revealing the truth may in fact have caused the investors to purchase the notes. How could such a total collapse occur?

D. DEFENSES

As with §§ 11 and 12(a)(1), § 13's one-three year statute of limitations applies. Unlike § 12(a)(1), however, defendants in a § 12(a)(2) action may assert additional defenses. To avoid liability, defendants may attempt to demonstrate that the plaintiffs in fact knew about the untruth or omission in the prospectus. Defendants may also attempt to show an absence of loss causation under § 12(b), providing evidence that the drop in the issuer's stock price is due to factors unrelated to the fraud.

1/3 S of L.

drop → unrelated to fraud.

The most important difference between the two sections is that § 12(a)(2) provides that defendants who meet their burden of proof by showing that they "did not know, and in the exercise of reasonable care could not have known, of such untruth or omission" may escape liability.

D's who meet burden of proof by showing that they didn't know had no reason to know may escape liability

Antifraud lawsuits related to a public offering often assert claims under both § 11 and 12(a)(2) because most misstatements in the registration statement will carry over to the prospectus. A question that often arises during such suits is whether the "reasonable care" requirement is equivalent to the care required by § 11's due diligence defense. Recall that § 11 has two levels of due diligence requirement depending on whether the untruth or omission is in an expertised or non-expertised portion of the registration statement. If § 12(a)(2) tracks § 11's care requirement, which version of the due diligence test—the expertised or non-expertised form— does it follow?

Section 12(a)(2) has a defense of reasonable care that is less demanding than the duty of due diligence imposed under Section 11. Section 12(a)(2) provides that a defendant shall not be liable if he "sustain[s] the burden of proof that he did not know, and in the exercise of reasonable care could not have known, of such untruth or omission" which is "necessary in order to make the statements, in the light of the circumstances under which they were made, not misleading."

Thus, while Section 11 imposes a duty to conduct a reasonable investigation as to any portion of a registration statement not made on the authority of an expert, Section 12(a)(2) does not make any distinction based upon "expertised" statements and only requires the defendant to show that it used reasonable care. This difference is attributable to the emphasis placed on the importance of registration statements and the underwriter's vital role in assuring their accuracy. *See John Nuveen & Co. v. Sanders,* 450 U.S. 1005, 1009 (1981) (Powell, J., dissenting from denial of cert.). Because Section 11 imposes a more exacting standard, this Opinion principally addresses the law that applies to Section 11.

In Re Worldcom, Inc. Securities Litigation, 346 F. Supp. 2d 628, 663–664 (S.D.N.Y. 2004).

QUESTIONS

1. How does the § 12(a)(2) defense apply to "expertised" portions of the prospectus?

2. Is there any reason to impose different standards of care under §§ 11 and 12(a)(2) for third-party gatekeepers?

E. Damages

Section 12(a)(2) provides the same remedies as those available under § 12(a)(1): rescission, if the plaintiff still holds the security, or damages, if the plaintiff has sold the security. Damages, if the security has been sold, are measured by the difference between the plaintiff's purchase price and his/her sales price.

CHAPTER 9

EXEMPT OFFERINGS

Rules and Statutes

—*Sections 3(a)(11), 3(b), 4(2) of the Securities Act*
—*Rules 135c, 147, 152, 155 of the Securities Act*
—*Regulation A, Rules 251–263*
—*Regulation S, Rules 901–905*
—*Regulation D, Rules 501–508*

MOTIVATING HYPOTHETICAL

Trendy, Inc. is a manufacturer of trendy fruit juice drinks. One of Trendy's most popular products is a low calorie lime-flavored drink known as Lean Green. Lean Green has enjoyed wild success in Trendy's home region of the Pacific Northwest. Trendy hopes to expand the campaign for Lean Green into several cities outside the Pacific Northwest (including Chicago and Iowa City). Such a campaign, however, is costly, involving both advertising costs as well as expenses related to expanding Trendy's distribution network. Privately held, Trendy does not have the cash on hand to finance the expansion. Kim, the CEO of Trendy, does not feel the time is right for a large-scale public offering. Nor does she want to obtain the required funds (upwards of $10 million) through bank financing.

I. INTRODUCTION

Companies that seek to raise capital have a variety of choices. They may turn to bank financing. Bank loans, however, typically require steady payments of interest. Many banks will also impose operating restrictions on the company such as maximum debt-equity ratios as well as covenants against certain forms of investments on the part of the company. At the other extreme, companies may go directly to the public and offer securities broadly. As we saw in Chapters 7 and 8, public offerings face stringent and costly regulations under of the Securities Act. Issuers engaged in a public offering must comply with mandatory disclosure requirements (in the form of the registration statement and statutory prospectus), the gun-jumping rules of § 5, and heightened antifraud liability under §§ 11 and 12(a)(2) of the Securities Act.

Notwithstanding these requirements, the public offering process is not "one size fits all." Smaller business issuers can do a public offering with reduced disclosure through Forms SB–1 and SB–2. Foreign issuers also face less disclosure burden when filing Forms F–1 or F–3. Nonetheless, the gun-jumping rules and antifraud liability provisions of the public offering process remain for these issuers along with the corresponding costs and delays from these rules. Although Form S–3 issuers get some relief from the burden of the gun-jumping rules through shelf registration, shelf offerings are typically permitted only for an expected maximum period of two years. (The SEC's 2005 Public Offering Reforms, covered in Chapter 7 allow certain, larger issuers to offer securities through a shelf registration for up to three years without requiring a new registration statement.)

Should issuers be allowed to sell securities to investors with reduced securities regulatory protections? Regulation is not free. The rigorous protection afforded to investors in the public registration process results in some issuers simply choosing not to sell securities to investors, instead turning to alternative forms of financing or eschewing an otherwise profitable business venture. Public investors then lose the opportunity to invest in such companies.

Moreover, not all investors require the same level of protection. Investors may benefit from the mandatory disclosures of the public offering process if the investors are unable or unwilling to negotiate for information disclosure on their own. If many investors stand in a similar position, collective action problems may undermine efforts to obtain information. Similarly, the gun-jumping rules benefit less sophisticated investors the most, as they are presumably more vulnerable to over-optimism and other biases that may lead them to focus on company advertising materials at the expense of hard financial facts. Sophisticated institutional investors purchasing securities through negotiated transactions with issuers require less protection. Such investors can demand information from the issuer and have the expertise to evaluate the company based on this information.

The securities laws recognize the high costs of public offerings and that the benefits may vary depending on the issuer's and investors' situations. Issuers selling securities are afforded a number of exemptions from § 5. In this chapter we discuss exempt offerings under the following provisions of the Securities Act:

- Section 4(2)
- Regulation D
- Regulation A
- Section 3(a)(11) and Rule 147
- Regulation S

As we go through each type of exempt offering, assess the balance taken between the cost of securities regulation and the need for regulatory protection. Given the array of exempt offering possibilities, also consider whether any one type of offering dominates from the issuer's perspective. Or do the exempt offerings vary in costs and benefits depending on the situation? Also consider whether the presence of so many exempt offerings undermines the public offering process. Why would an issuer choose to endure the public offering process if it can raise capital less expensively through one of the exempt offerings?

II. SECTION 4(2) OFFERINGS

Section 4(2) of the Securities Act exempts "transactions by an issuer not involving any public offering" from § 5. While the term "issuer" is relatively straightforward (defined under § 2(a)(4) of the Securities Act) and the effect of receiving an exemption from § 5 is also clear (i.e., the issuer does not have to follow the gun-jumping or prospectus delivery rules), the term "public offering" is less clear. How narrowly targeted must an offering be to be "non-public"?

[handwritten margin note: transaction by issuer not involving any public offering]

[handwritten margin note: Public offering:]

The Supreme Court and the SEC have generally eschewed a plain meaning approach to defining "public" under § 4(2). Instead, the definition has turned on the more fundamental question of the purposes of the securities laws and whether the costs of the regulations are outweighed by its benefits. The question of what constitutes a "public" offering therefore involves many of the same issues with which we wrestled earlier in defining "security."

[handwritten margin note: Issue: what constitutes public?]

In 1935, the SEC's General Counsel issued an opinion enumerating factors relevant to the determination of whether an offering is "public." Those factors include:

- the number of offerees
- the relationship of the offerees to each other and to the issuer
- the number of units offered
- the size of the offering
- the manner of the offering

Securities Act Release No. 285 (Jan. 24, 1935). Consider the status of the SEC's General Counsel's test after the following Supreme Court opinion.

SEC v. Ralston Purina Co.

346 U.S. 119 (1953).

■ MR. JUSTICE CLARK, delivered the opinion of the Court.

Section [4(2)] of the Securities Act of 1933 exempts "transactions by an issuer not involving any public offering" from the registration requirements of § 5. We must decide whether Ralston Purina's offerings of treasury stock to its "key employees" are within this exemption. . . .

Ralston Purina manufactures and distributes various feed and cereal products. Its processing and distribution facilities are scattered throughout the United States and Canada, staffed by some 7,000 employees. At least since 1911 the company has had a policy of encouraging stock ownership among its employees; more particularly, since 1942 it has made authorized but unissued common shares available to some of them. Between 1947 and 1951, the period covered by the record in this case, Ralston Purina sold nearly $2,000,000 of stock to employees without registration and in so doing made use of the mails.

In each of these years, a corporate resolution authorized the sale of common stock "to employees * * * who shall, without any solicitation by the Company or its officers or employees, inquire of any of them as to how to purchase common stock of Ralston Purina Company." A memorandum sent to branch and store managers after the resolution was adopted, advised that "The only employees to whom this stock will be available will be those who take the initiative and are interested in buying stock at present market prices." Among those responding to these offers were employees with the duties of artist, bakeshop foreman, chow loading foreman, clerical assistant, copywriter, electrician, stock clerk, mill office clerk, order credit trainee, production trainee, stenographer, and veterinarian.... No records were kept of those to whom the offers were made; the estimated number in 1951 was 500.

The company bottoms its exemption claim on the classification of all offerees as "key employees" in its organization. Its position on trial was that "A key employee * * * is not confined to an organization chart. It would include an individual who is eligible for promotion, an individual who especially influences others or who advises others, a person whom the employees look to in some special way, an individual, of course, who carries some special responsibility, who is sympathetic to management and who is ambitious and who the management feels is likely to be promoted to a greater responsibility." That an offering to all of its employees would be public is conceded.

The Securities Act nowhere defines the scope of [§ 4(2)'s] private offering exemption. Nor is the legislative history of much help in staking out its boundaries....

Decisions under comparable exemptions in the English Companies Acts and state "blue sky" laws, the statutory antecedents of federal securities legislation have made one thing clear–to be public, an offer need not be open to the whole world....

Exemption from the registration requirements of the Securities Act is the question. The design of the statute is to protect investors by promoting full disclosure of information thought necessary to informed investment decisions. The natural way to interpret the private offering exemption is in light of the statutory purpose. Since exempt transactions are those as to which "there is no practical need for * * * (the bill's) application," the applicability of § [4(2)] should turn on whether the particular class of persons affected need the protection of the Act. An offering to those who are shown to be able to fend for themselves is a transaction "not involving any public offering."

The Commission would have us go one step further and hold that "an offering to a substantial number of the public" is not exempt under § [4(2)]. We are advised that "whatever the special circumstances, the Commission has consistently interpreted the exemption as being inapplicable when a large number of offerees is involved." But the statute would seem to apply to a "public offering" whether to few or many. It may well be that offerings to a substantial number of persons would rarely be exempt. Indeed nothing prevents the commission, in enforcing the statute, from using some kind of numerical test in deciding when to investigate particular exemption claims. But there is no warrant for superimposing a quantity limit on private offerings as a matter of statutory interpretation.

large number

The exemption, as we construe it, does not deprive corporate employees, as a class, of the safeguards of the Act. We agree that some employee offerings may come within § [4(2)], e.g., one made to executive personnel who because of their position have access to the same kind of information that the act would make available in the form of a registration statement.[12] Absent such a showing of special circumstances, employees are just as much members of the investing "public" as any of their neighbors in the community. . . .

employees as a class are not deprived of protection of an Act → executive personell that has acess to Registr. statemenc

Keeping in mind the broadly remedial purposes of federal securities legislation, imposition of the burden of proof on an issuer who would plead the exemption seems to us fair and reasonable. . . . [O]nce it is seen that the exemption question turns on the knowledge of the offerees, the issuer's motives, laudable though they may be, fade into irrelevance. The focus of inquiry should be on the need of the offerees for the protections afforded by registration. The employees here were not shown to have access to the kind of information which registration would disclose. The obvious opportunities for pressure and imposition make it advisable that they be entitled to compliance with § 5.

Focus on need of offerees for protections.

Reversed.

QUESTIONS

1. Why did Ralston Purina concede that a general offering of its stock to all its employees would be public?

2. Why would Ralston Purina want to sell stock to its own employees? Why did it define its "key employees" as it did?

3. Under the Court's interpretation, can we say definitively that an offering to ten is private? Or that an offering to 1,000 is public?

---

12. This was one of the factors stressed in an advisory opinion rendered by the Commission's General Counsel in 1935. 'I also regard as significant the relationship between the issuer and the offerees. Thus, an offering to the members of a class who should have special knowledge of the issuer is less likely to be a public offering than is an offering to the members of a class of the same size who do not have this advantage. This factor would be particularly important in offerings to employees, where a class of high executive officers would have a special relationship to the issuer which subordinate employees would not enjoy.'

4. What types of investors can "fend for themselves"?

5. Who bears the burden of proof to show whether an exemption from § 5 applies?

Doran v. Petroleum Management Corp.

545 F.2d 893 (5th Cir. 1977).

■ GOLDBERG, CIRCUIT JUDGE.

In this case a sophisticated investor who purchased a limited partnership interest in an oil drilling venture seeks to rescind. The question raised is whether the sale was part of a private offering exempted by § 4(2) of the Securities Act of 1933 from the registration requirements of that Act. We hold that in the absence of findings of fact that each offeree had been furnished information about the issuer that a registration statement would have disclosed or that each offeree had effective access to such information, the district court erred in concluding that the offering was a private placement. Accordingly, we reverse and remand.

I.   Facts

Prior to July 1970, Petroleum Management Corporation (PMC) organized a California limited partnership for the purpose of drilling and operating four wells in Wyoming. . . .

As found by the district court, PMC contacted only four other persons with respect to possible participation in the partnership. All but the plaintiff declined.

During the late summer of 1970, plaintiff William H. Doran, Jr., received a telephone call from a California securities broker previously known to him. The broker, Phillip Kendrick, advised Doran of the opportunity to become a "special participant" in the partnership. PMC then sent Doran the drilling logs and technical maps of the proposed drilling area. PMC informed Doran that two of the proposed four wells had already been completed. Doran agreed to become a "special participant" in the Wyoming drilling program. In consideration for his partnership share, Doran agreed to contribute $125,000 toward the partnership. . . .

[The Wyoming Oil and Gas Conservation Commission ordered PMC's wells sealed for almost year as punishment for PMC's deliberate overproduction of oil in violation of the Commission's production allowances. Even after the wells were re-opened, they produced less income. As a result, Doran obtained less from his investment than expected, leading him to default on a note taken out to finance his purchase of special participant interests in PMC.]

* * *

II.   The Private Offering Exemption

No registration statement was filed with any federal or state regulatory body in connection with the defendants' offering of securities. Along with two other factors that we may take as established that the defendants sold or offered to sell these securities, and that the defendants used interstate transportation or communication in connection with the sale or offer of sale the plaintiff thus states a prima facie case for a violation of the federal securities laws.

The defendants do not contest the existence of the elements of plaintiff's prima facie case but raise an affirmative defense that the relevant transactions came within the exemption from registration found in § 4(2). Specifically, they contend that the offering of securities was not a public offering. The defendants, who of course bear the burden of proving this affirmative defense, must therefore show that the offering was private.

This court has in the past identified four factors relevant to whether an offering qualifies for the exemption. The consideration of these factors, along with the policies embodied in the 1933 Act, structure the inquiry. The relevant factors include the number of offerees and their relationship to each other and the issuer, the number of units offered, the size of the offering, and the manner of the offering. Consideration of these factors need not exhaust the inquiry, nor is one factor's weighing heavily in favor of the private status of the offering sufficient to ensure the availability of the exemption. Rather, these factors serve as guideposts to the court in attempting to determine whether subjecting the offering to registration requirements would further the purposes of the 1933 Act.

The term "private offering" is not defined in the Securities Act of 1933. The scope of the § 4(2) private offering exemption must therefore be determined by reference to the legislative purposes of the Act. In *SEC v. Ralston Purina Co.*, the SEC had sought to enjoin a corporation's offer of unregistered stock to its employees, and the Court grappled with the corporation's defense that the offering came within the private placement exemption. The Court began by looking to the statutory purpose:

> Since exempt transactions are those as to which "there is no practical need for . . . (the bill's) application," the applicability of (§ 4(2)) should turn on whether the particular class of persons affected need the protection of the Act. An offering to those who are shown to be able to fend for themselves is a transaction "not involving any public offering."

According to the Court, the purpose of the Act was "to protect investors by promoting full disclosure of information thought necessary to informed investment decisions." It therefore followed that "the exemption question turns on the knowledge of the offerees." That formulation remains the touchstone of the inquiry into the scope of the private offering exemption. It is most nearly reflected in the first of the four factors: the number of offerees and their relationship to each other and to the issuer.

In the case at bar, the defendants may have demonstrated the presence of the latter three factors. A small number of units offered, relatively modest financial stakes, and an offering characterized by personal contact between the issuer and offerees free of public advertising or intermediaries such as investment bankers or securities exchanges these aspects of the instant transaction aid the defendants' search for a § 4(2) exemption.

Nevertheless, with respect to the first, most critical, and conceptually most problematic factor, the record does not permit us to agree that the defendants have proved that they are entitled to the limited sanctuary afforded by § 4(2). We must examine more closely the importance of demonstrating both the number of offerees and their relationship to the issuer in order to see why the defendants have not yet gained the § 4(2) exemption.

A.   The Number of Offerees

Establishing the number of persons involved in an offering is important both in order to ascertain the magnitude of the offering and in order to determine the characteristics and knowledge of the persons thus identified.

The number of offerees, not the number of purchasers, is the relevant figure in considering the number of persons involved in an offering. A private placement claimant's failure to adduce any evidence regarding the number of offerees will be fatal to the claim. The number of offerees is not itself a decisive factor in determining the availability of the private offering exemption. Just as an offering to few may be public, so an offering to many may be private.... In the case at bar, the record indicates that eight investors were offered limited partnership shares in the drilling program a total that would be entirely consistent with a finding that the offering was private.

* * *

[I]n considering the need of the offerees for the protection that registration would have afforded we must look beyond Doran's interests to those of all his fellow offerees. Even the offeree-plaintiff's 20–20 vision with respect to the facts underlying the security would not save the exemption if any one of his fellow offerees was in a blind.

B.   The Offerees' Relationship to the Issuer

Since *SEC v. Ralston*, courts have sought to determine the need of offerees for the protections afforded by registration by focusing on the relationship between offerees and issuer and more particularly on the information available to the offerees by virtue of that relationship. Once the offerees have been identified, it is possible to investigate their relationship to the issuer.

1.   The role of investment sophistication

The lower court's finding that Doran was a sophisticated investor is amply supported by the record, as is the sophistication of the other offerees. Doran holds a petroleum engineering degree from Texas A & M University. His net worth is in excess of $1,000,000. His holdings of approximately twenty-six oil and gas properties are valued at $850,000.

Nevertheless, evidence of a high degree of business or legal sophistication on the part of all offerees does not suffice to bring the offering within the private placement exemption ... "if the plaintiffs did not possess the information requisite for a registration statement, they could not bring their sophisticated knowledge of business affairs to bear in deciding whether or not to invest.... " Sophistication is not a substitute for access to the information that registration would disclose.... although the evidence of the offerees' expertise "is certainly favorable to the defendants, the level of sophistication will not carry the point. In this context, the relationship between the promoters and the purchasers and the 'access to the kind of information which registration would disclose' become highly relevant factors."[10]

In short, there must be sufficient basis of accurate information upon which the sophisticated investor may exercise his skills. Just as a scientist cannot be without his specimens, so the shrewdest investor's acuity will be blunted without specifications about the issuer. For an investor to be invested with exemptive status he must have the required data for judgment.

2. The requirement of available information

The interplay between two factors, the relationship between offerees and issuer and the offerees' access to information that registration would disclose, has been a matter of some conceptual and terminological difficulty. For purposes of this discussion, we shall adopt the following conventions: We shall refer to offerees who have not been furnished registration information directly, but who are in a position relative to the issuer to obtain the information registration would provide, as having "access" to such information. By a position of access we mean a relationship based on factors such as employment, family, or economic bargaining power that enables the offeree effectively to obtain such information. When offerees, regardless of whether they occupy a position of access, have been furnished with the information a registration statement would provide, we shall say merely that such information has been disclosed. When the offerees have access to or there has been disclosure of the information registration would provide, we shall say that such information was available.

The requirement that all offerees have available the information registration would provide has been firmly established by this court as a necessary condition of gaining the private offering exemption. Our decisions have been predicated upon *Ralston Purina*, where the Supreme Court held that in the absence of a showing that the "key employees" to whom a corporation offered its common stock had knowledge obviating the need for registration, the offering did not qualify for the private offering exemption. The Court said that an employee offering would come within the exemption if it were shown that the employees were "executive personnel who because

---

10. We do not intimate that evidence of the offerees' sophistication is required in all cases to establish a private offering exemption under § 4(2)....

of their position have access to the same kind of information that the act would make available in the form of a registration statement."

... Because the district court ... inferred from evidence of Doran's sophistication that his purchase of a partnership share was incident to a private offering, we must remand so that the lower court may determine the extent of the information available to each offeree.

More specifically, we shall require on remand that the defendants demonstrate that all offerees, whatever their expertise, had available the information a registration statement would have afforded a prospective investor in a public offering. Such a showing is not independently sufficient to establish that the offering qualified for the private placement exemption, but it is necessary to gain the exemption and is to be weighed along with the sophistication and number of the offerees, the number of units offered, and the size and manner of the offering. Because in this case these latter factors weigh heavily in favor of the private offering exemption, satisfaction of the necessary condition regarding the availability of relevant information to the offerees would compel the conclusion that this offering fell within the exemption....

C.   On Remand: The Issuer–Offeree Relationship

In determining on remand the extent of the information available to the offerees, the district court must keep in mind that the "availability" of information means either disclosure of or effective access to the relevant information. The relationship between issuer and offeree is most critical when the issuer relies on the latter route.

To begin with, if the defendants could prove that all offerees were actually furnished the information a registration statement would have provided, whether the offerees occupied a position of access pre-existing such disclosure would not be dispositive of the status of the offering. If disclosure were proved and if, as here, the remaining factors such as the manner of the offering and the investment sophistication of the offerees weigh heavily in favor of the private status of the offering, the absence of a privileged relationship between offeree and issuer would not preclude a finding that the offering was private. Any other conclusion ... would conflict with the policies of the [§ 4(2)] exemption.

Alternatively it might be shown that the offeree had access to the files and record of the company that contained the relevant information. Such access might be afforded merely by the position of the offeree or by the issuer's promise to open appropriate files and records to the offeree as well as to answer inquiries regarding material information. In either case, the relationship between offeree and issuer now becomes critical, for it must be shown that the offeree could realistically have been expected to take advantage of his access to ascertain the relevant information.[12] Similarly

---

12.   For example, the offeree's ability to compel the issuer to make good his promise may depend on the offeree's bargaining power or on his family or employment relationship to the issuer.

the investment sophistication of the offeree assumes added importance, for it is important that he could have been expected to ask the right questions and seek out the relevant information.

In sum, both the relationship between issuer and offeree and the latter's investment sophistication are critical when the issuer or another relies on the offeree's "access" rather than the issuer's "disclosure" to come within the exemption. . .

* * *

Once the alternative means of coming within the private placement exemption are clearly separated, we can appreciate the proper role to be accorded the requirement that the offerees occupy a privileged or "insider" status relative to the issuer. That is to say, when the issuer relies on "access" absent actual disclosure, he must show that the offerees occupied a privileged position relative to the issuer that afforded them an opportunity for effective access to the information registration would otherwise provide.[18] When the issuer relies on actual disclosure to come within the exemption, he need not demonstrate that the offerees held such a privileged position. Although mere disclosure is not a sufficient condition for establishing the availability of the private offering exemption, and a court will weigh other factors such as the manner of the offering and the investment sophistication of the offerees, the "insider" status of the offerees is not a necessary condition of obtaining the exemption.

* * *

QUESTIONS

1. How does the *Doran* court tie *Ralston Purina* together with the 1935 SEC General Counsel Opinion's factors?

2. What test does the *Doran* court use to determine whether an offering qualifies for § 4(2)?

3. Would the *Doran* court treat an outside investor that had considerable financial resources and represented the only possible source of financing for the issuer as having "access" to information similar to that in a registration statement?

4. What happens to the offering if Doran is sophisticated and he is given full access to information, but one of the offerees (who did not eventually purchase) was not given the same information or was not sophisticated?

---

18. That all offerees are in certain respects "insiders" does not ensure that the issuer will gain the private placement exemption. An insider may be an insider with respect to fiscal matters of the company, but an outsider with respect to a particular issue of securities. He may know much about the financial structure of the company but his position may nonetheless not allow him access to a few vital facts pertaining to the transaction at issue. If Doran had effective access to all information that registration would provide, he would be a transactional insider. That is all we require regarding the availability of information. If, on the other hand, his inside knowledge was incomplete or his access ineffective, he would be a transactional outsider despite the fact that we might consider him an "insider" for other purposes.

5. How important is sophistication to the court? Would a completely unsophisticated offeree qualify for the exemption?

HYPOTHETICAL ONE

1. *Scenario One*: Trendy decides to move forward with a private placement offering structured to meet the requirements of § 4(2). Trendy identifies all the retirees from Grist, a local toothpaste factory and has invitations to invest hand delivered to the 300 retirees (following up each hand delivery with a phone call). All the offerees are given the opportunity to go hiking with Kim, the CEO of Trendy, and discuss the offering. Ten (relatively-fit) retirees take the hike, each spending about two hours discussing Trendy's business and future prospects. All ten hikers decide to purchase (sending their checks in the mail) and Trendy raises $10 million from the offering (selling 10,000 shares of common stock to the ten investors in aggregate). Does Trendy's offering comply with § 4(2)?

2. *Scenario Two*: What if Trendy instead offers and sells securities through an unregistered offering to 30 members of the "Rich Inheritors" club? All members of the club are over 21 and have a net worth of over $100 million inherited entirely from their parents. The 30 club members are each afforded the same opportunity to go hiking with Kim to discuss the offering and all 30 (indolent and rich, but fit) investors each spend two hours hiking with Kim. All 30 purchase shares of the offering.

3. *Scenario Three*: Same as Scenario Two, except Trendy offers and sells to 30 members of the "Poor Professors" club. Each member is a tenured finance professor with a net worth of under $100,000. None of the professors are fit enough to hike, so Kim spends two hours drinking lattés with them.

III. REGULATION D

Although some offerings clearly fall within § 4(2), substantial areas of uncertainty remain. Founders setting up a corporation and putting in cash in exchange for the corporation's initial capital stock are certainly within the scope of § 4(2). When the corporation accepts first-round investments from venture capitalists, do these transactions also fall within the ambit of § 4(2)? If the venture capitalists can "fend for themselves" and have access to information equivalent to that provided in the registration statement then § 4(2) applies to protect the transaction from the registration requirements of § 5. Suppose, however, that the growing corporation then turns to other groups of investors including: (a) family and friends; (b) wealthy individuals; and (c) smaller institutional investors. Will the offering to these investors also fall under § 4(2)?

The penalty for guessing incorrectly stings. If § 4(2) does not apply, § 5 applies (absent another exemption). If the issuer is not exempt from § 5, then the issuer will face possible § 12(a)(1) liability. Recall that § 12(a)(1) does not require a showing of scienter, causation, reliance or even a material misstatement or omission. Instead, § 12(a)(1) imposes strict liability for violations of § 5. The harshness of the § 12(a)(1) remedy deters issuers from making a private placement unless they are confident of their exemption from § 5.

To provide issuers greater certainty in private placements, the SEC promulgated Regulation D of the Securities Act (Rules 501–508). Rule 506 provides a safe harbor for the § 4(2) exemption. Although Regulation D does not eliminate all uncertainty, it is far more predictable than § 4(2). Consider the interaction of Regulation D and § 4(2). Assuming that Regulation D is somewhat narrower than § 4(2), how does the safe harbor rule affect the structuring of private placements? If you were the CEO of a corporation contemplating a private placement, under what circumstances would you step outside the boundaries of Regulation D and "push the envelope" of what the law allows under § 4(2)?

The starting point to understanding Regulation D is Rules 504, 505, and 506. These rules set forth the requirements for the three basic exemptions under Regulation D. Although we started our discussion with § 4(2), only Rule 506 is a § 4(2) exemption. Offerings under Rules 504 and 505 fall under § 3(b) of the Securities Act, which allows the SEC to exempt from § 5 offerings up to $5 million. Two other provisions are important to keep in mind in understanding Regulation D. Rule 501 provides definitions used throughout Regulation D. Rule 502 sets forth the various requirements referenced by the three types of offerings found in Rules 504–506.

[handwritten margin note: Exemption under 5 mil]

The three types of Regulation D offerings differ in the eligibility of certain issuers to use the exemptions. Rule 506 is open to all issuers. Rule 505 excludes investment companies. Rule 505 also disqualifies certain issuers that, among other things, were involved in a past securities laws violation. Rule 504 prohibits not only investment companies and "blank check" companies, but also Exchange Act reporting issuers. The exclusion of Exchange Act reporting issuers limits Rule 504 offerings to smaller companies without a liquid secondary trading market. Excluding blank check companies prevents smaller, development stage companies without a specific business plan or purpose from using Rule 504. The following table summarizes the exclusions from Regulation D.

[handwritten margin notes: 506 - open to all Issuers; 505 - disqualifies certain issuers: - ex. invest. companies - ex. past sec. violaters; 504: prohibits - invest. companies - blank check comp. - Exch. Act report. issuers]

	Rule 504 (§ 3(b))	Rule 505 (§ 3(b))	Rule 506 (§ 4(2))
Excluded Issuers	Not '34 Act Co. Not Investment Co. Not Blank Check Co.	Not Investment Co. Disqualification (505(b)(2)(iii))	None

Regulation D offerings under Rules 504–506 also differ with respect to the following categories:

- aggregate offering price
- purchasers
- general solicitation
- information disclosure
- resale restrictions

We examine each criterion in turn. As you read the materials, do any of the three types of Regulation D offerings dominate the others from the issuer perspective?

A.   AGGREGATE OFFERING PRICE

The most conspicuous difference among the various Regulation D exemptions is the allowable offering amount, i.e., "aggregate offering price." Under Rule 504, issuers may sell up to $1 million of securities, under Rule 505, issuers may sell up to $5 million of securities, and under Rule 506, issuers may sell an unlimited amount.

Constraining the aggregate offering price limits the potential scope of a Regulation D offering. Smaller offerings are less likely to involve widespread public selling efforts. Individual retail investors are therefore also unlikely to invest in such smaller offerings.

Given the aggregate offering price limitations, two questions exist. Why might an issuer prefer a Rule 504 or 505 offering over a Rule 506 offering, which does not limit the offering amount? The answer, of course, is that the requirements for a Rule 506 private placement are more restrictive.

Second, what stops an issuer from simply doing repeated Rule 504 or 505 offerings to evade the offering price limitation? (For example, a corporation could sell $5 million on May 1, $5 million on June 1, $5 million on June 15, etc.) Both Rules 504 and 505 with an aggregation rule that determines the aggregate offering price. Under both Rules, issuers must reduce the offering price ceiling—$1 million for Rule 504 and $5 million for Rule 505—by the amount of securities sold in the twelve months preceding the offering pursuant to either (1) an offering under § 3(b) of the Securities Act (which includes both Rule 504 and 505 offerings), or (2) an offering made in violation of § 5. Thus, a corporation that sold $5 million of securities on May 1 under Rule 505 would have its aggregate offering price ceiling Rule 504 and 505 offerings limited to $0 until May 1 of the next year.

HYPOTHETICAL TWO

Trendy decides to do a Regulation D offering to raise capital for its contemplated expansion of the marketing and distribution of Trendy's Lean Green drink.

1. *Scenario One*: Suppose that Trendy raises $1 million per month over a five-month period from January 2005 to May 2005. Sales are made to 25 unsophisticated purchasers. Do any of the three Regulation D offering types exempt Trendy from § 5?

2. *Scenario Two*: After raising $5 million from January 2005 to May 2005, suppose that on February 1, 2006, Trendy decides to engage in a new round of financing. Trendy seeks to raise an additional $5 million quickly in an exempt offering to twenty unsophisticated purchasers. Can Trendy sell securities under any of the Regulation D exemptions?

3. *Scenario Three*: Suppose that earlier in June 2004, Trendy sold $10 million of common stock attempting to use § 4(2). Trendy made the mistake of selling to 25 investors without providing either information or access. How does this 2004 offering affect Trendy's January to May, 2005 sale of securities in Scenario One?

B. PURCHASERS

The SEC's central concern with unregistered offerings is the broad-based sales of securities to the general public. Many public investors lack investment sophistication, leading them to purchase overvalued securities. In addition, public investors may feed off of each other's over-optimism, driving the price of overvalued securities still higher. Regulation D addresses this concern in part by restricting purchasers.

First, Regulation D limits the number of purchasers. Rules 505 and 506 limit offerings to a maximum of 35 purchasers. Rule 504, however, does not limit the number of purchasers. Instead, the $1 million aggregate offering price limitation indirectly constrains the size of the offering.

The 35 purchaser ceiling under Rules 505 and 506 has an enormous loophole in determining the number of purchasers. Rule 501(e) determines the number of purchasers, but does not count all investors as purchasers. *35* For example, under Rule 501(e)(1)(i) any "relative, spouse or relative of the spouse of a purchaser who has the same principal residence as the purchaser" is not counted as a separate purchaser. More importantly, Rule 501(e)(1)(iv) excludes "accredited investors" from the purchaser tally. *accredited Investors are not purchasers.*

Who counts as an accredited investor? Many of the categories involve large entities and institutions, including banks, insurance companies, trusts, partnerships, and corporations (all with a minimum of $5 million total assets among other requirements). In addition, Rule 501(a) defines three additional categories of accredited investors:

- Rule 501(a)(4): Any director, executive officer, or general partner of the issuer of the securities.

- Rule 501(a)(5): Any natural person whose individual net worth, or joint net worth with that person's spouse, at the time of his purchase exceeds $1,000,000.

- Rule 501(a)(6): Any natural person whose individual income exceeded $200,000 in each of the two most recent years or whose joint income with his/her spouse exceeded $300,000 in each of those years and has a reasonable expectation of reaching the same income level in the current year.

The concept of accredited investors is central to Regulation D. Because accredited investors are excluded from the calculation of the number of purchasers, issuers may sell to an unlimited number of accredited investors under Rules 505 and 506. Although Rule 505's separate aggregate offering price limit of $5 million works independently to constrain such offerings, Rule 506 has no such limit. In theory, therefore, an issuer may sell an *Issuer can sell to an unlimited number of accredited investors* unlimited amount of securities under Rule 506 (i.e., into the billions of dollars) to an unlimited number of accredited investors.

Issuers typically rely on placement agents to provide access to pre-screened pools of accredited investors. Placement agents maintain databases of potential accredited investors, typically determining accredited status through self-reported information contained on suitability questionnaires filled out by the investors. But what if an investor lies or makes a mistake on the questionnaire? Rule 501(a) provides that the issuer need only "reasonably" believe that an investor falls in one of the specified categories of accredited investors.

[handwritten margin note: reasonable believe by issuer]

In practice, even accredited investors have a limited appetite for privately placed securities. The chief constraint on that appetite is that securities sold through Regulation D are "restricted": resales are limited from the date of investment unless the securities are registered under § 5 or the selling investor finds an exemption from § 5. Rule 144, covered in Chapter 10, provides such an exemption, allowing resales of restricted securities after a specified holding period of one year, if other conditions of the Rule are met, or two years without restriction. If the accredited investors decide to rebalance their portfolios, or need to raise cash for some other reason, the investors will be unable to sell the restricted securities for the first year after their purchase.

[handwritten margin note: Rule 144 resale - allows resale + conditions 1 year w/o Limit - 2 years]

HYPOTHETICAL THREE

Trendy decides to do a Regulation D offering under Rule 505 to raise capital for its contemplated expansion of the marketing and distribution of Trendy's Lean Green drink. Suppose that Trendy raises $1 million per month over a five-month period from January 2005 to May 2005. Sales are made to 35 unsophisticated purchasers. Trendy also makes sales to the following investors. Do these additional sales create any problems under Regulation D?

1. *Scenario One*: Trendy sells securities in the offering to all of its executive vice presidents, including to Alan, the VP for drink research and Laura, the VP for human resources.

2. *Scenario Two*: Trendy sells securities in the offering to Dale. Dale is a retiree who has a stock portfolio of $1.1 million; the entire portfolio is invested in index funds and Dale has no other significant assets or debts. Dale lives off the dividends from the portfolio (along with limited sales of capital) to pay for monthly expenses. (Dale lives in San Francisco where rents can run up to $3,000 per month for a one-bedroom apartment.) Dale has no other source of money, but enjoys golfing.

3. *Scenario Three*: Trendy sells securities to Beth. Beth has a Ph.D. in financial economics from the University of California, Berkeley. Beth worked only one year for Morgan Stanley before being fired for insider trading. During that year, however, Beth made $2,000,000 from her trading efforts and has a net worth today of $700,000 (after paying stiff civil penalties to the SEC). Beth now froths milk for cappuccinos and makes $7.00 an hour.

4. *Scenario Four*: What if Beth shares an apartment with Andrei, one of the 35 unsophisticated purchasers in the offering. If Beth and Andrei are simply good friends (but nothing more), does Beth count as a purchaser, thereby increasing the total to 36 purchasers?

5. *Scenario Five*: Trendy sells securities to the Trendy Investment Partnership. TIP was formed a month prior to Trendy's offering and has 50 partners. None of the partners, individually, is an accredited investor. TIP's total net assets are $1 million.

In comparing the three Regulation D offerings, a clear tradeoff exists between the restrictions on the aggregate offering price and the number of purchasers. Rule 504 imposes no limit on purchasers but restricts offerings to $1 million. Rule 505, in contrast, restricts the number of purchasers to 35 and allows offerings of up to $5 million.

What of Rule 506? At first glance, Rule 506 dominates Rule 505 from the issuers' perspective. Under Rule 506, an issuer may sell to up to 35 purchasers with no aggregate offering price limit. But Rule 506 offerings face an additional regulatory constraint not present for Rule 504 or 505 offerings: Rule 506 purchasers who are not accredited investors must also meet a sophistication requirement. Under Rule 506(b)(2)(ii):

> Each purchaser who is not an accredited investor either alone or with his purchaser representative(s) has such knowledge and experience in financial and business matters that he is capable of evaluating the merits and risks of the prospective investment, or the issuer reasonably believes immediately prior to making any sale that such purchase comes within this description.

How are issuers supposed to determine whether an investor (alone or with a purchaser representative) is able to evaluate the merits and risks of an investment? One could imagine issuers looking to factors such as:

- Wealth and income (much like for accredited investor status for individuals)

- Experience (general business or more specific to securities investment?)

- Education

- Present investment status (well-diversified or not)

- Performance on an investment test (much like a driver's license)

Among these factors, which ones are mostly likely to correlate with the ability to assess the merits and risks of investments? How expensive would it be for an issuer to administer such a screen for sophistication? What risk would the issuer run that a court or the SEC may later question the accuracy and reasonableness of the screen? In practice, because Rule 506's sophistication requirement is somewhat vague, many Rule 506 offerings exclude non-accredited investors altogether and sell only to accredited investors.

The following table summarizes the tradeoff between aggregate offering price and purchaser restrictions for the three types of Regulation D offerings:

	Rule 504 (§ 3(b))	**Rule 505 (§ 3(b))**	**Rule 506 (§ 4(2))**
Aggregate Offering Price	≤ $1 million (Rules 504(b)(2), 501(c)) Prior 12 mo. and during offering aggregation with § 3(b) offerings and § 5(a) violations	≤ $5 million (Rules 505(b)(2)(i), 501(c)) Prior 12 mo. and during offering aggregation with § 3(b) offerings and § 5(a) violations	Unlimited
Number of Purchasers	No limit on purchasers	≤ 35 purchasers (Rules 505(b)(2)(ii), 501(a), 501(e))	≤ 35 purchasers (Rules 506(b)(2)(i), 501(a), 501(e)) Sophistication requirement (Rules 506(b)(2)(ii), 501(h))

HYPOTHETICAL FOUR

1. *Scenario One*: Trendy decides to raise $20 million through a common stock offering under Rule 506 of Regulation D. Among purchasers who buy the stock is Howard, who is not an accredited investor. Howard spent a year and a half in business school studying the financial markets, before dropping out. Howard presently sells cool drinks from a street side vending stand in Washington Square Park in New York City. Do Howard's purchases jeopardize the Rule 506 exemption?

2. *Scenario Two*: Suppose that Howard turns to his friend Nicole, an investment banker, to help him with his investment decisions. Do Howard's purchases jeopardize the Rule 506 exemption?

3. *Scenario Three*: What if Nicole, Howard's potential purchaser representative, is also a director of Trendy, Inc.?

C. GENERAL SOLICITATION

Regulation D's restrictions on the number and sophistication of *purchasers* do not necessarily address the concern embodied in § 4(2) for *offerees*. Broad-based offerings to the general public may lead the public into a "frenzy," overwhelming even the good instincts of more sophisticated investors.

To address this concern, Regulation D addresses "offerees" separately from purchasers. Rule 502(c) bans general solicitations:

[N]either the issuer nor any person acting on its behalf shall offer or sell securities by any form of general solicitation or general advertising. . . .

This ban applies to both Rule 505 and 506 offerings. Rule 504 exempts issuers from Rule 502(c) if the issuer meets certain state law offering requirements as outlined in Rule 504(b)(1)(i)-(iii). Rule 504 issuers may avoid the general solicitation ban of Rule 502(c) if the issuer sells exclusively in a state that provides for the registration of the securities under state law and also requires the public filing and delivery to investors of a "substantive disclosure document" prior to sale.

In certain areas, the application of Rule 502(c) is clear. Suppose an issuer decides to take to the airwaves, broadcasting an upcoming private placement under Rule 506. This clearly would count as general advertising. Including a disclaimer in the advertisement restricting the solicitation to an arbitrary subset of the general public will not change this result. Suppose the placement agent for the issuer (typically an investment bank assisting with the private placement) creates a glossy offering pamphlet for the private placement and mails the pamphlet out to the following groups:

- all redheads in the United States
- all residents of Ann Arbor, Michigan
- all students taking civil procedure at NYU Law School

Although these groups are restricted, they do not create any meaningful restriction in the sense of culling out investors based on sophistication or ability to "fend for themselves."

The harder question arises with respect to investors who are selected at least somewhat based on their financial sophistication or wealth (from which sophistication perhaps can be assumed?). Consider the following groups:

- all executive officers of the *Fortune 500* companies
- all finance professors in the United States
- the 50 wealthiest people in the United States as identified in *Forbes*

Would an unsolicited mailing of an offering pamphlet to these investors run afoul of the prohibition on general solicitations?

In the Matter of Kenman Corp.

S.E.C., [1984–1985 Transfer Binder] Fed. Sec. L. Rep. (CCH) ¶ 83,767 (Apr. 19, 1985).

* * *

During certain times from on or about August 29, 1983 through May 15, 1984, Kenman Securities and Kenman [the parent corporation of Kenman Securities] participated in two limited partnerships offerings. Missiondale Palms Associates ("Missiondale") is a Utah limited partnership organized in August 1983 to acquire an apartment complex in Tucson, Arizona. Kenman is the general partner of Missiondale. From on or about August 29, 1983, Kenman through Kenman Securities sold limited partnership interests in Missiondale to 39 investors who invested a total of $875,000. No registration statement under the Securities Act was filed with the Commission or is in effect concerning the Missiondale limited partnership interests.

Orem Dairy Queen Associates ("Orem Associates") is a Utah limited partnership organized in January 1984 to acquire land and a franchise for a Dairy Queen restaurant and to construct and operate the restaurant in Orem, Utah. Kenman is the general partner of Orem Associates. From on or about January 13, 1984, Kenman through Kenman Securities sold limited partnership interests in Orem Associates to 25 investors who invested a total of $280,000. No registration statement was filed with the

Commission or is in effect concerning the Orem Associates limited partnership interests. A Form D was filed with the Commission with respect to the Orem Associates offering, on or about March 2, 1984, which offering was made pursuant to Rule 506 of Regulation D.

In early 1983, Kenman and Kenman Securities mailed information concerning Missiondale to an unknown number of persons. This information included a one page cover letter, a four page promotional document and a reply card to request a personal sales meeting with Kenman's president. Kenman and Kenman Securities also mailed similar information concerning Orem Associates to an unknown number of persons in early 1984.

Persons to whom Kenman and Kenman Securities sent materials were chosen from six sources. First, they utilized a list of persons who had participated in prior offerings by them. Second, they reviewed the annual reports of fifty "Fortune 500" companies and obtained the names of executive officers. The third source was a list of names of persons who had previously invested $10,000 or more in real estate offerings by issuers other than Kenman. This list was purchased by Kenman from a third party. The fourth source was a list of physicians in the State of California. The fifth source was a list of managerial engineers employed by Hughes Aircraft Company or by similar companies. Sixth, Kenman obtained a copy of the Morris County, New Jersey Industrial Directory and selected names of the presidents of certain listed companies.

Kenman and Kenman Securities did not keep sufficiently detailed records to identify the specific persons or the actual number of persons to whom information was sent concerning the Missiondale and the Orem Associates offerings. However, information concerning the offerings were sent to a number of persons on a list of names compiled from these sources....

No registration statement was filed with the Commission or is in effect with respect to either offering.

* * *

Based on the foregoing, the Commission finds that Kenman and Kenman Securities willfully violated Sections 5(a) and 5(c) of the Securities Act in that they offered and sold limited partnership interests in Missiondale and Orem Associates when no registration statement was filed with the Commission or was in effect and no exemption from registration was available.

The materials mailed to potential investors in connection with the Missiondale and Orem Associates limited partnership offerings constituted "offers" to sell securities within the meaning of Section 5 of the Securities Act, and therefore were "prospectuses" within the meaning of Section 2[a](10) of the Securities Act. Section 5(c) of the Securities Act makes it unlawful to use the mails to offer to sell a security by the use of any prospectus or otherwise, unless a registration statement has been filed with the Commission or an exemption is applicable. Section 5(a) of the Securities

Act prohibits the use of the mails in the sale of a security unless a registration statement is in effect for such security or an exemption is applicable.

Kenman and Kenman Securities relied on the exemption from registration under Section 4(2) of the Securities Act with respect to the Missiondale and Orem Associates offerings. In addition, the Orem Associates offering was structured to qualify under the "safe harbor" provided by Rule 506 of Regulation D.

[handwritten margin note: 4(2) + safe harbor under 506]

An offering pursuant to Rule 506 must comply with Rules 501 through 503 of Regulation D. Rule 502(c) precludes the offer and sale of securities "by any form of general solicitation or general advertisement ... " Section 4(2) of the Securities Act provides an exemption from registration for "transactions by an issuer not involving any public offering." The exemption from registration under Section 4(2) is not available to an issuer that is engaged in a general solicitation or general advertising.

[handwritten margin note: 502(c) → general solicitation is prohibited]

[handwritten margin note: 4(2) → is not avail if gen. solicitate.]

The Commission concludes that Kenman and Kenman Securities engaged in general solicitations[6] and therefore the exemptions from registration under Section 4(2) with respect to the Missiondale and Orem Associates offerings and the safe harbor of Rule 506 of Regulation D with respect to the Orem Associates offering were not available.

* * *

QUESTIONS

1. If you applied a plain language-dictionary meaning to the phrase "general solicitation or general advertising," would Kenman's offers fall within the definition?

2. What result if Kenman had only sold to those investors that had purchased before from Kenman?

3. The *Kenman* court wrote: "The exemption from registration under Section 4(2) is not available to an issuer that is engaged in a general solicitation or general advertising." Is this consistent with *Ralston Purina* and *Doran*?

---

6. In determining what constitutes a general solicitation, the Commission's Division of Corporation Finance has underscored the existence and substance of pre-existing relationships between the issuer and those being solicited. Kenman admits that persons who received the Orem Associates mailings had no pre-existing relationship with Kenman. These persons were selected only because their names were on lists that were purchased or created by Kenman. Although the make-up of the lists may indicate that the persons themselves have some degree of investment sophistication or financial well-being, utilization of lists of thousands of persons with no pre-existing relationship to the offeror clearly does not comply with the limitation of Rule 502(c) on the manner of solicitation. Here, Kenman mailed information concerning Orem Associates not only to previous Kenman investors, but to an unknown number of persons with whom Kenman had no prior contact or relationship.

[handwritten note: unknown persons with no previous contact or relationship.]

[handwritten note: Key of the cnL.]

SEC NO–ACTION LETTER
MINERAL LANDS RESEARCH & MARKETING CORPORATION

Publicly Available December 4, 1985

LETTER TO SEC

March 21, 1985

Office of Chief Counsel
Division of Corporation Finance
Securities and Exchange Commission
450 Fifth Street, N.W.
Washington, D.C. 20549

Gentlemen:

We are writing on behalf of our client Mineral Lands Research & Marketing Corporation for your advice concerning a proposed offering of the Company's securities without registration under the Securities Act of 1933 in reliance on the exemption contained in Rule 504 of Regulation D promulgated under the Act.

BACKGROUND

The Company was formed for the purpose of locating, identifying and acquiring mineral properties with a view to selling, developing or joint venturing the properties. The Company proposes to raise up to $500,000 through the sale of its equity securities in reliance upon the exemption from registration contained in Rule 504. The Company does not intend to rely on the exemption from the application of the provisions of Rule 502(c) and (d) contained in Rule 504(b)(1). Potential investors will be provided with a disclosure document containing substantially the same information as would be included in a Registration Statement on Form S–18 under the Act. All sales will be effected through the officers and directors of the Company who will not receive any commissions or any other additional remuneration in connection with the sales. It is anticipated that most of the offers and sales will be made through one officer and director of the Company to individuals with whom he has a prior existing business relationship, although a limited number of offers and sales are anticipated to be made through other officers and directors. This officer and director is a licensed insurance broker and is the owner of a sole proprietorship through which he sells a variety of insurance and financial products. He proposes to offer the Company's securities to up to 600 of his existing clientele and anticipates that each investor will purchase between $500 and $2,000 of the Company's securities. It is likely that most of the investors will neither qualify as "accredited investors" within the meaning of Rule 501(a) of Regulation D nor be sophisticated investors.

DISCUSSION

Rule 502(c) of Regulation D provides as a condition to the availability of the Rule 504 exemption that "neither the issuer nor any person acting on its behalf shall offer or sell the securities by any form of general solicitation or general advertising." Although there is no limitation on the number of offerees or purchasers involved in offerings pursuant to Rule 504 as there is with offerings pursuant to Rules 505 and 506, the Commission has indicated "that depending on the actual circumstances, offerings made to such large numbers of purchasers may involve a violation of the prohibitions against general solicitation and general advertising."

The Staff of the Commission has taken the position that the mailing of a written offer by an issuer to up to 330 persons having a pre-existing relationship with the general partner of the issuer would not exceed the terms of Rule 502(c). The Staff also noted, however, that the general partner had determined that the investment was suitable for the proposed investors and that they had the requisite sophistication. Although this latter condition will most likely not be satisfied as to a majority, if not all, of the investors in the Company's proposed offering, we nonetheless believe that the proposed manner of offering by the Company would not constitute general advertising or general solicitation because most of the offerees are a limited group with whom an officer and director of the issuer has a pre-existing business relationship and Rule 504 does not require that the investment be suitable for the purchaser or that the purchaser be sophisticated.

REQUEST

We respectfully request that the Division concur with our opinion and advise us that it would not recommend any action to the Commission if the Company proceeds with the offering of securities described above. We understand that such a position would be based upon the facts and circumstances described in this letter and that any different facts or conditions might require a different response.

Very truly yours,

Mark J. Sather

For the Firm

[Eds—In the typical no-action letter, the SEC staff's response follows immediately after the requesting letter as set forth below:]

SEC LETTER

* * *

You have requested that the Division take a no-action position with respect to the availability of an exemption from Regulation D. As the Commission stated in its adopting release for Regulation D, the staff will not issue no-action letters with respect to transactions under Regulation D. Your letter does, however, present an interpretive issue to which we will respond. That question concerns the application of Rule 502(c) to the Company's proposal to offer securities to persons with whom officers and directors of the Company have prior business relationships.

class of offerees - 600 pre-exist.

The class of offerees includes 600 persons who are existing clients of an officer who is an insurance broker. It is your view that the proposed manner of offering would not constitute general advertising or solicitation because most of the offerees consist of a limited group with whom an officer and director of the issuer has pre-existing business relationships.

The Division agrees with your view that the existence of relationships between an issuer and offerees is an important factor in determining whether offers violate Rule 502(c). The types of relationships with offerees that may be important in establishing that a general solicitation has not taken place are those that would enable the issuer (or a person acting on its behalf) to be aware of the financial circumstances or sophistication of the persons with whom the relationship exists or that otherwise are of some substance and duration. As your letter does not include sufficient facts to enable us to make a determination whether the type of relationship contemplated is present, the Division is unable to express a view on this matter.

? Issue!! Do you need pre-exist. relat. or you need sophistication

Sincerely,

— and pre-ex. R. helps to access sophistication.

J.M. Aalbregtse

Special Counsel
Securities and Exchange Commission

———

Assess sophistication!!

How do brokerage firms acting as placement agents in a private placement obtain the requisite pre-existing relationships with investors? The SEC in a series of no-action letters has indicated that brokerage firms may actively solicit investors with a general interest in investing in private placements. See EF Hutton, SEC No–Action Letter (Dec. 3, 1985); Bateman Eichler, Hill Richards, SEC No–Action Letter (Dec. 3, 1985). The solicitation may not mention any particular private placement offering. Moreover, the solicitations must take place a sufficient amount of time prior to any contemplated offering to enable the brokerage firm to assess the sophistication of the investors. Recent SEC no-action letters have indicated that on-line offeree questionnaires followed by screening on the part of brokerage firms are acceptable. See IPOnet, SEC No–Action Letter (July 26, 1996).

HYPOTHETICAL FIVE

Trendy moves forward with a Rule 506 offering to raise $10 million for its expansion campaign for the Lean Green drink. Eager to find investors for the offering, Kim, the CEO of Trendy, employs West Securities to help sell the offering. Mark, the managing partner of West Securities, is working to sell the securities. Are these sales practices permissible under Rule 502(c)?

1. *Scenario One*: Mark walks up and down his alma mater's health club locker room, the Yale Club in New York, telling everyone about his offering, passing out offering circulars, and collecting purchase requests. Assume that Mark knows everyone in the health club on a first-name basis.

2. *Scenario Two*: Suppose Trendy tells West Securities that it will reduce its offering down to $5 million in order to fit within Rule 505. Mark again goes to solicit interest from among his friends at the health club.

3. *Scenario Three*: Mark goes to the financial district in Boston and drops in unannounced at the offices of large mutual fund managers for Fidelity, Scudder, Dreyfus, and other prominent mutual funds (all very sophisticated investors). Mark again passes out offering circulars and collects purchase requests. Assume that Mark only knows of the mutual fund managers by reputation, having seen their names repeatedly in the *Wall Street Journal*.

4. *Scenario Four*: Trendy completes a Rule 506 offering on January 1 for $10 million in common stock, selling to ten accredited investors and twenty sophisticated purchasers. Later in the year, Trendy makes a Rule 505 offering for $4 million of common stock from July 1 to July 30, selling to 30 unsophisticated purchasers. Trendy makes another Rule 505 offering for $1 million of common stock from December 1 to December 15 of the same year, selling to five unsophisticated purchasers. If Trendy engaged in general solicitation in its January Rule 506 offering, but not in the later two Rule 505 offerings, does that affect the other two offerings? (Assume no integration of the offerings.)

D. DISCLOSURE

The public offering process focuses on the creation of the registration statement and statutory prospectus. Through mandatory disclosure, the gun-jumping rules seek to reduce the informational advantage that issuers have over public investors. Of course, no one forces an investor to purchase securities in an offering. Investors can always simply walk away if an issuer does not provide information. Nonetheless, in the public offering context, mandatory disclosure may be justified if some investors lack the sophistication to recognize the importance of disclosure. Similarly, if a large number of investors invest in an offering, no one investor may expend the resources to bargain with the issuer to obtain disclosure. If the issuer is the least cost provider of information—e.g., on firm-specific information relating to the issuer itself—then forcing the issuer to make such disclosure may benefit all investors.

Do these same arguments apply for a private placement to a small number of sophisticated investors? Instead of a large number of retail investors clamoring for the latest IPO stock, picture instead ten or so of your favorite mutual funds, the occasional hedge fund and insurance company considering whether to purchase securities in a private placement. Part of the rationale behind the *Ralston Purina*'s "fend for themselves" formulation is that for some types of investors, the stringent protections of the securities laws are unnecessary (or at least not cost-justified).

Private placements under Regulation D do not entirely eliminate disclosure. Rule 502(b) divides Regulation D along two dimensions: (1) the type of investor (accredited or not) and (2) the type of offering (Rule 504 v. Rule 505 or 506). Based on this division, the following disclosure is mandated:

	Non-Accredited Investor	**Accredited Investor**
Rule 504 Offering	No specific disclosure required	No specific disclosure required
Rule 505 or 506 Offering	Specific disclosure required by Rule 502(b)(2)	No specific information disclosure required

Issuers do not need to provide any disclosure to accredited investors pursuant to Rule 502(b)(1). Issuers making a Rule 504 offering, as well, face no mandatory information disclosure requirements, at least under the federal securities laws (recall though that such offerings may face state securities registration requirements) (see Rule 502(b)(1)). For Rule 505 or 506 offerings to a non-accredited investor, the type of disclosure mandated under Rule 502(b)(2) then varies based on: (1) the type of issuer and (2) the size of the offering.

	Non-Exchange Act Reporting Company	**Exchange Act Reporting Company**
Offerings up to $2 million	Non-financial info under Rule 502(b)(2)(i)(A) Financial info under Rule 502(b)(2)(i)(B)(1)	Rule 502(b)(2)(ii)
Offerings up to $7.5 million	Non-financial info under Rule 502(b)(2)(i)(A) Financial info under Rule 502(b)(2)(i)(B)(2)	Same as above
Offerings over $7.5 million	Non-financial info under Rule 502(b)(2)(i)(A) Financial info under Rule 502(b)(2)(i)(B)(3)	Same as above

The information disclosure for Exchange Act reporting issuers does not vary by offering amount. Instead, Exchange Act reporting issuers have a choice. They may either provide a combination of the most recent annual report, the definitive proxy statement, and (only if requested by the purchaser in writing) the most recent Form 10–K (Rule 502(b)(2)(ii)(A)) or just the most recent Form 10–K if it contains the information found in the annual report (Rule 502(b)(2)(ii)(B)). In either case, issuers must also disclose any more recent Exchange Act filings made since the information provided under Rule 502(b)(2)(ii)(A) or (B). Also, issuers must provide "a brief description of the securities being offered, the use of the proceeds from the offering, and any material changes in the issuer's affairs that are not disclosed in the documents furnished." (Rule 502(b)(2)(ii)(C)).

For non-Exchange Act reporting issuers, Rule 502(b)(2)(i)(A) provides for the same non-financial information disclosure regardless of offering amount. Rule 502(b)(2)(i)(A) makes reference to the "same kind" of information contained in Part I of the registration statement used in a public offering. For those issuers eligible for a Regulation A offering (discussed below), slightly less disclosure is required. Regulation A eligible issuers must include the "same kind" of information as required under Part II of Form 1–A.

The offering amount becomes important only with respect to the disclosure of financial information for non-Exchange Act reporting issuers. Rules 502(b)(2)(i)(B)(1) through (3) provide for the different levels of financial disclosure. Generally, as the offering amount increases, the level of financial disclosure increases (with a greater audit requirement). Students can trace the exact requirements provided for in Rules 502(b)(2)(i)(B)(1) to (3) through the following referenced forms:

- Up to $2 million: Item 310 of Regulation S–B (except only the issuer's balance sheet must be audited).

- Up to $7.5 million: Financial statement information contained in Form SB–2 (except only the audited balance sheet is required if obtaining audited financial statements takes "unreasonable effort or expense").

- Over $7.5 million: Financial statement information contained in the public offering registration statement (except only the audited balance sheet is required if obtaining audited financial statements takes "unreasonable effort or expense").

In addition, Rule 502(b) provides a catchall provision to ensure that non-accredited investors receive notice of information given to accredited investors. Under Rule 502(b)(2)(iv), the issuer must give non-accredited investors a brief written description of "any material written information concerning the offering that has been provided by the issuer to any accredited investor" not already given to the non-accredited investors. Also, if the non-accredited investor provides a written request for the information, the issuer must furnish the information to the non-accredited investor within a reasonable time prior to the purchase.

Note also that Rule 502(b)(2)(v) requires the issuer to give each purchaser the "opportunity to ask questions and receive answers" relating to the offering. The issuer must also supply any additional information necessary to verify the accuracy of the specific mandatory disclosure items in Rules 502(b)(2)(i) and (ii) upon the request of any purchaser provided the "issuer possesses or can acquire without unreasonable effort or expense" the information.

HYPOTHETICAL SIX

Kim, the CEO for Trendy Inc., has come to you for advice about what information to distribute as part of Trendy's upcoming Rule 506 private placement for $10 million in common stock. She has the following questions.

1. If Trendy sells only to accredited investors (mostly large financial institutions), what information must Trendy disclose?

2. What is your advice on the information Trendy should disclose voluntarily to the accredited investors?

E.   RESALE RESTRICTIONS

Securities sold through Regulation D generally cannot be freely resold with one major exception. Investors that purchase securities sold through a Rule 504 offering that complies with the state law registration requirement specified by Rule 504(b)(1) may freely resell the securities. A liquid public secondary market is possible immediately after a Rule 504 offering. The small size of the Rule 504 offering (limited to $1 million) and state law restrictions may, however, limit the development of any secondary market in the Rule 504 securities.

For Rule 505 and 506 offerings, Rule 502(d) explicitly restricts resales. Rule 502(d) provides that:

> [S]ecurities acquired in a transaction under Regulation D shall have the status of securities acquired in a transaction under section 4(2) of the Act and cannot be resold without registration under the Act or an exemption therefrom.

Not only are the securities sold through Regulation D so-called "restricted securities," but Rule 502(d) imposes a requirement that the *issuer* take reasonable care to discourage investors from reselling the securities (at least under circumstances in which the purchasers would be deemed "underwriters" under § 2(a)(11)). Among other things, the issuer must disclose in writing the unregistered status of the securities and place a legend on the securities indicating that they have not been registered under the Securities Act.

One difficulty created by Regulation D's "restricted" securities is that the Securities Act does not regulate securities, but instead focuses on transactions. Consider the application of § 4(1)'s exemption from § 5. As long as the *transaction* does not involve an issuer, underwriter, or dealer, investors may freely resell even a restricted security even though the security has never been registered for a public offering. As we will see in Chapter 10, the key concept for resales is whether the investor is acting as an underwriter for the dealer. If the investor has underwriter status, the § 4(1) exemption is unavailable, thereby rendering any resale subject to § 5.

What is the downside of owning a restricted security? Investors hope for a positive future return when they purchase a security. Securities provide a return directly through dividends. In addition, a security holder may also benefit through capital appreciation. Many companies, however, do not pay dividends—particularly high growth companies—because earnings are plowed back into growing the business. As the future profitability of the company grows, so does the company's stock price. Investors can exploit this capital appreciation by selling their securities. Restrictions on resale, therefore, severely impinge the ability of investors to realize their capital appreciation. Investors interested in diversifying their portfolio are also unable to do so when faced with restrictions on resale. As we will see in Chapter 10, investors can resell even restricted securities, but those avenues are limited. Consequently, private placement investors typically require an illiquidity discount to induce them to purchase securities in a private placement.

HYPOTHETICAL SEVEN

What would be wrong with simply labeling securities as "restricted" and then never allowing resales without registration by the issuer? Consider the effect of an indefinite ban on resales in the following two scenarios.

1. *Scenario One*: Trendy, Inc. issues $10 million of common stock in a private placement. Trendy is not listed on an exchange nor does its stock trade on Nasdaq. Few investors know much about Trendy's business or finances.

2. *Scenario Two*: Megasoft, Inc. issues $10 million of common stock in a private placement. Megasoft's common stock trades on the NYSE and Megasoft has a market capitalization of $200 billion. Several analysts follow Megasoft and regularly issue opinions evaluating Megasoft common stock.

F. RULE 504

Rule 504 stands apart from the other two Regulation D offerings in that Rule 504 allows issuers to avoid the general solicitation (Rule 502(c)), disclosure (Rule 502(b)), and resale restriction (Rule 502(d)) requirements. An issuer complying with Rule 504 may solicit offers broadly without disclosing any information. Investors purchasing through a Rule 504 offering, moreover, may immediately resell the securities into the public secondary markets. Issuers complying with Rule 504 can essentially engage in a mini-public offering.

There are two caveats, however, to this observation. First, Rule 504 is limited in its aggregate offering price to $1 million and applies only to certain types of issuers (excluding Exchange Act reporting issuers). The mini-public offering allowable under Rule 504 therefore is primarily of use for small, less well-followed issuers that need to raise a small amount of capital. The ability to engage in general solicitation and avoid disclosure may not matter if only more sophisticated investors participate in the market for such offerings. Sophisticated investors will presumably demand disclosure and will have the wherewithal to fend for themselves despite receiving a general solicitation.

Second, issuers seeking to use Rule 504 to avoid the general solicitation and resale restrictions of Regulation D must comply with state law registration requirements. Indeed, issuers engaged in such small offerings governed under state law may seek another exemption from the § 5 registration process: the intrastate offering exemption. We discuss the intrastate offering exemption and state law registration requirements later in the chapter.

G.   INTEGRATION

Issuers must account for prior offerings under § 3(b) and in violation of § 5 when calculating the aggregate offering price ceiling for Rule 504 and Rule 505 offerings. The reduction in the aggregate offering price ceiling prevents issuers from easily avoiding the offering amount limitation through multiple, separate offerings closely spaced in time.

In addition to aggregation under Rules 504 and 505, issuers may also seek to divide offerings artificially to evade other Regulation D requirements. For example, both Rule 505 and Rule 506 offerings impose a limit of 35 purchasers. An issuer may divide an offering for $10 million to 60 purchasers into two parts—selling $5 million to 30 purchasers in two "separate" offerings to avoid the 35–purchaser limit.

Similarly, suppose an issuer seeks to sell $9 million of securities to 40 accredited investors (with whom the issuer has a pre-existing relationship) and $1 million to twenty individual investors where no pre-existing relationship exists. Such an offering would violate Rule 502(c)'s prohibition on general solicitation due to the presence of the individual investors. Nonetheless, the issuer could seek to characterize the offering as two separate offerings: one offering of $9 million to the 40 accredited investors with the preexisting relationship under Rule 506; and a second offering of $1 million to the twenty individual investors under Rule 504, to which the general solicitation ban does not apply (assuming state law registration requirements are met). Left unconstrained, the ability of issuers to break apart transactions would allow an end run around many of the Regulation D limitations.

The integration doctrine restrains the ability of issuers to recharacterize offerings strategically. Several factors are relevant in determining whether seemingly separate offers and sales should be treated as one transaction (integrated). These factors are as follows:

- whether the sales are part of a single plan of financing
- whether the sales involve issuance of the same class of securities
- whether the sales have been made at or about the same time
- whether the same type of consideration is received
- whether the sales are made for the same general purpose

Securities Act Release No. 4552 (November 6, 1962)

To provide greater certainty for issuers, the SEC in Regulation D provides a safe harbor from integration under Rule 502(a). Rule 502(a) applies six months prior to the start of the offering and six months after the *end* of the offering. To illustrate, imagine that a Regulation D private placement occurs from 7/1/06 to 8/1/06 as depicted below:

<--------------------			-------------------->
Minus	Start	End	Plus
6 months	Offering	Offering	6 months
1/1/06	7/1/06	8/1/06	2/1/07

Two time periods are important for the Rule 502(a) safe harbor: (a) *the safe harbor window* stretching from the beginning of the pre-offering six month period to the end of the post-offering six month period (1/1/06 to 2/1/07 in the diagram above) and (b) the *six-month periods window* consisting of the pre-offering and post-offering six month periods but not the time period of the offering itself (1/1/06 to 7/1/06 and 8/1/06 to 2/1/07 in the diagram above).

Sales outside the *safe harbor window* are deemed separate from the Regulation D offering, with one exception. During the *six-month periods window*, if the issuer offers or sells securities that "are of the same or similar class as those offered or sold under Regulation D," then the issuer loses the safe harbor entirely.

HYPOTHETICAL EIGHT

1. *Scenario One*: Trendy is contemplating a private placement offering to raise $10 million to fund its Lean Green drink expansion campaign. Trendy wants to raise this money through sales using a broker-dealer that has contacts with 70 individual investors (non-accredited but sophisticated) who want in the aggregate to purchase about $9 million of common stock. Trendy also plans on making cold calls to two wealthy individual investors (assume accredited) to sell the remaining $1 million of common stock. If there were no integration doctrine, how could Trendy structure its transactions within Regulation D, allowing it to raise all this money in the next month?

2. *Scenario Two*: Suppose Trendy instead decides to do the following two offerings:

On January 1, Trendy conducts a Rule 505 offering of preferred stock sold through its brokers to investors with whom the company has a pre-existing relationship. The offering raises $5 million and the proceeds are used to expand its Lean Green production facilities. Thirty purchasers (non-accredited) are involved in the offering.

Exactly two years later, Trendy decides to hire a new marketing consultant and engage in a new marketing campaign for Lean Green. To fund the campaign, Trendy conducts a private placement under Rule 506 for $10 million of bonds to ten purchasers (non-accredited) in return for the purchasers' marketing efforts.

3. *Scenario Three*: Suppose Trendy reads Rule 502(a) and decides to structure the following series of transactions:

On 1/1 Trendy makes a Rule 504 offering for $1 million of common stock selling to ten individual purchasers (non-accredited and unsophisticated) through broker-dealers who have pre-existing relationships with the purchasers. The offer closes on 1/1 and is all cash. The proceeds are used to expand the Lean Green production facilities.

On 3/1 Trendy makes a Rule 506 offering for $10 million of common stock, selling to 35 individual purchasers (non-accredited) through broker-dealers with pre-existing relationships with the purchasers. The offer closes on 3/1 and is all cash. The proceeds are also used to expand the Lean Green production facilities.

Trendy on 11/1 decides to conduct a Rule 505 offering, selling $4 million of common stock to 25 former law students with whom the CEO has pre-existing relationships (all took the CEO's securities regulation class a few years ago but alas remain unsophisticated). The offering is all in cash and the proceeds are used to fund a new office building for Trendy's executive officers.

Any problems with these offerings?

H.   INNOCENT AND INSIGNIFICANT MISTAKES

To err is human; fortunately Regulation D forgives (some) mistakes. Under Rule 508, failure to comply with a requirement for a Rule 504, 505, or 506 offering will not necessarily result in a loss of exemptions for an offer or sale to a particular individual or entity.

Recall that in our study of the gun-jumping rules for registered public offerings, we did not see an explicit "insignificant and innocent" defense for issuers. Issuers that inadvertently condition the market in the Pre–Filing Period or innocently include additional free writing with the preliminary prospectus in the Waiting Period violate § 5. Moreover, a defect in the offer or sale of securities to *one* investor would taint the offering for all investors, with the consequence that the entire transaction would violate § 5. Section 12(a)(1) then provides a strict liability private cause of action for all those who purchased securities sold in the offering. Despite the innocuousness or innocence of the mistake, investors can rescind their purchases, typically after the issuer's price has dropped, recovering their full purchase price under § 12(a)(1).

Given the SEC's hard stance with regard to registered offerings, why does Regulation D excuse insignificant and innocent mistakes? Indeed, in some ways, mistakes are harder to justify in a Regulation D offering. Because Regulation D is relatively bright-line (at least when compared with the rest of the securities laws), issuers have an easier time complying. Does Rule 508 result in issuers taking a lax approach to complying with Regulation D requirements?

One possible justification for Rule 508 is that the investors in a Regulation D offering are more sophisticated (at least on average) compared with investors in a public offering. Presumably such sophisticated investors are able to "fend for themselves" and thus do not necessarily need the full gamut of securities law protections. But if this is the case, why not make § 5 optional for sophisticated investors?

Although more generous than the gun-jumping rules, Rule 508's forgiveness is limited in several respects. First, Rule 508 does not shield the issuer from SEC enforcement actions. The SEC may bring an enforcement action against the issuer for violation of § 5 given the authority granted to the SEC under § 20 of the Securities Act. Rule 508 only shields the issuer from private actions under § 12(a)(1) for a § 5 violation.

Second, Rule 508 limits excuse to those situations where "failure to comply did not pertain to a term, condition or requirement directly intended to protect that particular individual or entity." Thus, if the issuer failed to deliver the required information disclosure under Rule 502(b) to a particular investor and that investor sues for violation of § 5, the issuer cannot rely on Rule 508 to cure the defect in its use of Regulation D. If *other* investors (who did receive the information under Rule 502(b)) complain about the lack of information given to a particular investor, however, the issuer may then invoke Rule 508 to bar the claim of these other investors.

Third, even if the failure to comply was not related to a requirement directly intended to protect the particular investor suing, Rule 508 will also be unavailable to the issuer unless the failure to comply was "insignificant with respect to the offering as a whole." This exclusion has real teeth; certain types of failures to comply are defined by the SEC as significant, thereby making Rule 508 inapplicable. The failures relate to the following (as listed in Rule 508(a)(2)):

- the general solicitation prohibition (Rule 502(c))
- the aggregate offering price limitation (Rules 504(b)(2), 505(b)(2)(i))
- the limit on the number of purchasers (Rules 505(b)(2)(ii) and 506(b)(2)(i))

Finally, Rule 508(a)(3) requires that "[a] good faith and reasonable attempt was made to comply with all applicable terms, conditions, and requirements of Rule 504, 505 or 506."

HYPOTHETICAL NINE

Trendy conducts a private placement for $10 million of common stock under Rule 506, selling to five large hedge funds (all accredited investors with pre-existing relationships with Trendy and the placement agent for the offering) and 36 sophisticated, non-accredited purchasers (all lower-level Trendy employees). Two of the non-accredited purchasers tell Trendy that they are cousins and live in the same house. Consider how Rule 508 may apply to the following circumstances.

1. *Scenario One*: It turns out that the cousins are not in fact cousins, but just friends (and they lied on their offeree questionnaire about their status). The large hedge funds seek to sue under § 12(a)(1) to rescind their purchases.

2. *Scenario Two*: Suppose instead that Trendy simply forgot to mail the required disclosures under Rule 502(b) to the cousins. The cousins eventually get the information after they make their purchases. The large hedge funds seek to sue under § 12(a)(1) to rescind their purchases.

3. *Scenario Three*: Suppose that one of the non-accredited investors was not an employee and had no pre-existing relationship with Trendy. The large hedge funds seek to sue under § 12(a)(1) to rescind their purchases.

I. OTHER ASPECTS OF REGULATION D

1. FORM D

Rule 503 requires that issuers engaged in a Rule 504, 505, or 506 offering file a Form D with the SEC. The issuer has until the fifteenth day after the start of the offering to file Form D. No immediate penalty results if an issuer fails to file Form D. Rule 507, however, provides that an issuer may not use Regulation D if it is subject to an order, judgment, or decree by any court enjoining it from violating Rule 503.

Form D contains basic identification data (including information on the promoters of the offering, 10% beneficial owners, and the executive officers and directors of the issuer), information on the offering (including broker-dealers assisting with the offering and their commission, the minimum investment required of an investor, etc.) and information on the offering price, the number of investors, expenses, and use of proceeds, among other things.

2.   EXCHANGE ACT FILING

Exchange Act reporting issuers of equity securities in an unregistered offering must also file a Form 8–K with the SEC. Item 3.02(a) of Form 8–K provides that the issuer must report the information specified in Item 701 of Regulation S–K, including information on the securities sold, the underwriters and other purchasers, the consideration received for the securities, the use of proceeds, and the exemption claimed from § 5. If the equity securities sold in the unregistered offering account for less than 1% of the outstanding equity securities of the same class, Item 3.02(b) exempts the issuer from the Form 8–K filing requirement (an even more generous exemption applies for small business issuers). All Exchange Act reporting issuers, including those exempt under Form 8–K, must provide similar information on unregistered sales of securities in their periodic Form 10–K and 10–Q filings unless already reported in a prior filing. Because the Form 8–K filing requirement applies to all unregistered sales, issuers must file a Form 8–K not only for Regulation D offerings, but also for § 4(2), Regulation A, intrastate, and Regulation S offerings exempt from § 5.

3.   DISQUALIFICATION

In addition to the general disqualification of Rule 507, Rule 505 (but not Rule 504 or 506) provides for disqualification in certain circumstances. Rule 505(b)(2)(iii) references the disqualifiers contained in Rule 262 of Regulation A (covered later in this chapter). Absent a reprieve from the SEC, if "the issuer, any of its predecessors or any affiliated issuer," "any director, officer or general partner of the issuer, beneficial owner of 10 percent or more of any class of its equity securities," or any "underwriter" (including placement agents) were involved in specified prior conduct in violation of the securities law, then the issuer is disqualified from using Rule 505.

J.   THE PRIVATE PLACEMENT PROCESS

Although the legal requirements for a private placement are complicated, many issuers successfully sell securities through a private placement under § 4(2) or Regulation D. How does the typical private placement work in practice? This depends on the size of the offering. If a company sells securities to its top officers, the offering will typically take place under § 4(2) without much formality.

If the company is offering securities to outside investors, the issuer will hire a placement agent to assist in the offering. Examples of private placement agents include Thomas Capital Group and WR Hambrecht & Co. Most private placements are done as best efforts offerings under which the placement agent is compensated through a commission for each security sold in the offering and reimbursed for expenses.

The placement agent, much like an underwriter in a registered public offering, will first review the business and finances of the issuer. One goal of this initial review is to give the placement agent the opportunity to develop a "due diligence" package to give later to investors who are considering the offering. The review will also result in a recommended plan of financing. This plan may include recommended timing, types of securities, and amounts to be raised through a private placement. In some cases, a third party rating agency may then rate the issuer and the offered securities (particularly for debt securities).

Once a plan of financing is agreed upon and the issuer moves forward with a private placement, the placement agent will also help write up a private placement memorandum. No specific SEC form dictates the exact contents of the private placement memorandum, although Rule 502(b) specifies what information must be included. The memorandum typically contains similar information to a public offering statutory prospectus, detailing the issuer's business, properties, management, and financials. The requirements of the securities laws aside, most sophisticated investors in the private placement market will simply avoid offerings that lack a private placement memorandum containing this standardized package of information.

Once the private placement memorandum is ready, the placement agent will begin marketing the offering. This involves contacting investors with whom the agent has a pre-existing relationship (complying with the general solicitation prohibition in Regulation D). For issuers unfamiliar with the private placement market, the placement agent will guide the issuer toward investors most likely to participate in the offering and provide advice on how best to sell the offering. The placement agent may also set up roadshow meetings between the issuers and investors. Investors, for their part, may look to the placement agent to screen issuers, recommending only viable, worthwhile investments. The due diligence package created by the placement agent will also assist investors in valuing the private placement.

Investors wishing to participate in the offering may then negotiate terms with the issuer. In a bond offering, for example, investors will focus particular attention on the bond covenant protections contained in the bond indenture. Such terms may include maximum debt-equity ratios, restrictions on dividends, and so on. Once investors make the decision to purchase, the private placement agent will assist with the execution of the subscription agreements and the transfer of money and securities.

Regulation D and § 4(2) provide only one set of exemptions from § 5's registration requirement. Other exemptions, particularly § 4(1)'s exemption covering most secondary market transactions, are also important. We finish our coverage of exemptions with three additional exemptions from registration: Regulation A, the intrastate offering exemption under § 3(a)(11) and Rule 147 of the Securities Act, and Regulation S.

Given the availability of § 4(2) and Regulation D, why have Congress and the SEC provided these additional exemptions? Section 4(2) and Regulation D focus primarily on the needs of the investors (i.e., are the investors able to fend for themselves), the relatively small scope of the offering, and the selling efforts. What additional factors may lead Congress and the SEC to exempt offerings from § 5? Paramount are: (1) the needs of small business issuers; (2) the presence of an alternative regulatory regime (state-based securities regulation); and (3) the importance of national boundaries and the need to respect the authority of other countries.

IV. REGULATION A

Small business issuers enjoy a number of routes to raise capital in the securities markets that impose fewer disclosure requirements and regulations. For small businesses that seek to engage in a full-blown public offering, Form SB–1 and SB–2, as discussed in Chapter 7 (Public Offerings), require less disclosure particularly with respect to the financial statements. Although small business issuers doing a registered public offering must comply with § 5's gun-jumping regime, less stringent disclosure reduces both the cost of preparing the registration statement and the potential for antifraud liability requirements.

Non–Exchange Act reporting companies (typically smaller business issuers with fewer than 500 shareholders or less than $10 million in assets) may also take advantage of Rule 504 to engage in a broad public offering of freely resalable securities. Rule 504, however, imposes a $1 million limit on the aggregate offering price and requires issuers to comply with state law registration requirements in order to avoid the general solicitation (Rule 502(c)) and resale limitations (Rule 502(d)) of Regulation D.

Standing in between public offerings using Form SB–1 or SB–2 on the one hand, and Rule 504 on the other hand, is Regulation A. Regulation A allows smaller issuers to raise more capital than a Rule 504 offering with fewer gun-jumping restrictions than public offerings under Form SB–1 or SB–2. Securities sold through Regulation A enjoy unrestricted status, allowing secondary market trading to commence immediately after the shares are sold to the public. Thus, shares offered under Regulation A do not suffer from the illiquidity discount imposed on most Regulation D offerings.

A.   TYPE OF ISSUER

Only certain issuers can take advantage of the mini-public offering process of Regulation A (see Rule 251(a)). Issuers must be, among other things, organized under the laws of the United States or Canada and have their principal place of business in the U.S. or Canada. Exchange Act reporting companies are also excluded from Regulation A.

As with Rule 505 of Regulation D, Regulation A has a disqualifying provision. Rule 262 prevents issuers involved in bad acts from using Regulation A. Rule 262's disqualification is based on the presence of specified bad acts on the part of three groups of potential participants in a Regulation A offering:

- The issuer, including any predecessors or any affiliated issuer
- Key individuals and entities connected with the issuer or the offering (including any director or officer of the issuer, beneficial owner of 10 percent or more of any class of its equity securities, any promoter of the issuer presently connected with it in any capacity, and any underwriter of the securities to be offered, among others)
- Underwriter of the securities

For issuers, the specified bad acts leading to disqualification include (among others):

- The issuer is currently a subject of an SEC proceeding or examination under § 8 of the Securities Act or was the subject of a stop or refusal order within five years of filing the Regulation A offering statement.
- The issuer was convicted within five years prior to the filing of the offering statement of any felony or misdemeanor in connection with the purchase or sale of any security or involving a "false filing" with the SEC.

For key individuals and entities connected with the issuer or the offering, the list of bad acts focus on past securities-related wrongdoings including (among others):

- The individual or entity has been convicted of any felony or misdemeanor related to the purchase or sale of securities in the ten years prior to the filing of the offering statement for the Regulation A offering. The conviction must relate to a false filing with the SEC or involve the "conduct of the business of an underwriter, broker, dealer, municipal securities dealer, or investment adviser."
- The individual or entity is subject to a court order, judgment, or decree entered within five years of the filing of the Regulation A offering statement enjoining the individual or entity from engaging in prohibited conduct related to the purchase or sale of any security.

The conviction must relate to a false filing with the SEC or involve the "conduct of the business of an underwriter, broker, dealer, municipal securities dealer, or investment adviser."

Underwriters (who are included in the above list of key individuals and entities connected with the issuer or offering) also face a specific list of bad acts relating to their past activities as underwriters. This list includes (among others):

- Underwriters who underwrote securities in a registered offering that is subject to any pending proceeding or examination, refusal order, or stop order under § 8 of the Securities Act entered into within five years prior to the filing of the Regulation A offering statement.

Rule 262 gives discretion to the SEC to waive the disqualification.

In comparing Regulation A with a registered public offering or a Rule 504 offering, note that Rule 504, like Regulation A, is limited to non-Exchange Act reporting companies. Rule 504, however, does not contain a disqualification provision. Registered public offerings, by contrast, allow all issuers regardless of Exchange Act reporting status and without any disqualification. The following table summarizes these differences.

	Public Offering	**Regulation A**	**Rule 504**
Excluded Issuers	None	–Not '34 Act Rep. Co. –Not Investment Co. –Not Blank Check Co. –Rule 262 Disqualification	–Not '34 Act Rep. Co. –Not Investment Co. –Not Blank Check Co.

HYPOTHETICAL TEN

Imagine that Frauds–R–Us, Inc., a non-Exchange Act reporting issuer, seeks capital to expand its short-term loan business located in New Jersey. Frauds–R–Us had previously attempted to make a registered initial public offering a year ago. After the filing of the registration statement for the IPO, the SEC had recommended that the company provide more detailed biographical descriptions for the directors and top officers of the company. Frauds–R–Us steadfastly refused and chose instead to wait out the twenty-day period for its registration statement to become effective. Thereafter, the SEC gave notice, held a hearing, and issued a stop order pursuant to § 8(d) suspending the effectiveness of the registration statement. Now, a year later, Frauds–R–Us is attempting to raise capital once more from the public capital markets, this time armed with the full biography of its directors and officers.

1. Can Frauds–R–Us engage in a Regulation A offering for $5 million?

2. Can Frauds–R–Us go back and register for an initial public offering for $50 million?

B.   AGGREGATE OFFERING PRICE

Regulation A, like Rules 504 and 505, is a § 3(b) exemption, which limits offerings to a maximum of $5 million. Accordingly, Rule 251(b) of Regulation A restricts the aggregate offering price to $5 million. Unlike

Regulation D, Regulation A contemplates allowing insiders and other pre-existing shareholders to use a Regulation A offering to sell their own shares in a secondary offering. Regulation A aggregate offering price limit specifically includes a limit for secondary offering shares of $1.5 million (taken out of the $5 million overall limit).

The following table compares Regulation A against both registered public offerings (for which there is no aggregate offering price limit) and Rule 504.

	Public Offering	**Regulation A**	**Rule 504**
Aggregate Offering Price Limitation	None	≤ $5 million (of which no more than $1.5 million from selling security holders) –Prior 12–month aggregation with Reg. A offerings only (Rule 251(b))	≤ $1 million (504(b)(2), 501(c)) (not available for non-issuers) –Prior 12–month aggregation with § 3(b) offerings and § 5(a) violations

As with Regulation D, the $5 million aggregate offering price limit is reduced based on all securities within a twelve-month look-back window before the start of the offering and during the offering itself. Unlike Regulation D, however, only securities sold pursuant to Regulation A are counted against the aggregate offering price. Compare this with the aggregate offering price for Rule 504 and 505 offerings; under those Regulation D exemptions, the aggregate offering price limit is reduced by securities sold under § 3(b) as well as violations of § 5. Regulation A is therefore far more lenient in allowing issuers to engage in multiple prior § 3(b) (but not Regulation A) offerings, without reducing the maximum amount of proceeds that can be derived from a Regulation A offering.

HYPOTHETICAL ELEVEN

Trendy Inc. decides to make the following series of offerings (each taking place in one day). Assume that the offerings are for distinct and separate purposes (e.g., research and development, construction of Lean Green factory, advertising) and will not be integrated:

January 1—Sale of $3 million of securities under Rule 506 to 30 accredited individual investors (all making more than $200,000 per year)

November 1—Sale of $5 million of securities under Regulation A

December 1—Sale of $2 million of securities under Rule 505 of Regulation D to 30 accredited investors

The January 1st offering under Rule 506 was done using broad-based solicitations to accredited investors. Neither Trendy nor its placement agent had any prior contact with the accredited investors. Are any of the offers exempt?

C. DISCLOSURE

Regulation A imposes mandatory disclosure requirements on issuers. The mandatory disclosure includes two types of documents: the offering statement and offering circular, roughly analogous to the registration statement and statutory prospectus, respectively:

- Offering Statement—Securities Act Form 1–A sets forth the contents of the Regulation A offering statement. Rule 252(a) also provides that issuers must include additional material information "necessary to make the required statements, in the light of the circumstances under which they are made, not misleading."

- Offering Circular—Rule 253(a) states that the offering circular "shall include the narrative and financial information required by Form 1–A."

Part I of Form 1–A contains information specific to Regulation A, including whether any significant participating parties in the offering are subject to the disqualification provision of Rule 262. Form 1–A also requires the disclosure of any unregistered securities sold by the issuer (or any of its predecessors or affiliated issuers) within one year prior to the filing of the Form 1–A. In addition, the issuer (and its affiliates) must disclose any current or proposed offerings in addition to the Regulation A offering. If the issuer uses any "testing-the-waters" related documents pursuant to Rule 254 (discussed below), the issuer must disclose the dates the documents were used and the last communication with the offerees.

The information contained in the offering circular (contained in Part II of Form 1–A) resembles that of the statutory prospectus used in a registered public offering. Form 1–A provides different disclosures under "Model A" (for corporate issuers) and "Model B" (for all other sellers and for corporate issuers that so choose). Under both models, the required categories of information include, among others:

- The Company
- Risk Factor
- Business and Properties
- Use of Proceeds
- Description of Securities Being Offered
- Plan of Distribution
- Dividends, Distributions and Redemptions
- Directors, Executive Officers and Significant Employees
- Principal Stockholders
- Management Relationships, Transactions and Remuneration

While non-financial information disclosed in the Form 1–A offering circular is similar to the § 10 statutory prospectus, the required financial disclosure is less demanding. Among other financial information, issuers are required to file a current balance sheet dated within 90 days prior to the filing of the offering statement (or earlier if permitted by the SEC). The issuer must also file an income statement and statement of cash flows and other stockholder equity "for each of the 2 fiscal years preceding the date of the most recent balance sheet being filed, and for any interim period between the end of the most recent of such fiscal years and the date of the most recent balance sheet being filed, or for the period of the issuer's existence if less than the period above." Financial statements must be prepared according to U.S. GAAP accounting rules, but they do not need to be audited. Issuers that have prepared audited financial statements for other purposes are required, however, to provide the audited financials.

HYPOTHETICAL TWELVE

After consulting with her attorneys and reading through Form 1–A, Kim, the CEO of Trendy, has concluded that Trendy does not need to have the company's financials audited in preparation for a Regulation A offering. Nonetheless, Kim ultimately agrees with Trendy's investment bank (acting as the placement agent for the offering), that obtaining audited financials for Trendy's past three years would be a good idea for the offering. Why did the investment bank recommend this?

D. REGULATION A GUN-JUMPING

The gun-jumping rules of Regulation A focus on two key events: (1) the filing of the offering statement with the SEC and (2) the "qualification" of the offering statement (roughly corresponding to the effective date for a registered public offering), after which sales may commence to the general public. Using these two events, we can divide the time periods for a Regulation A offering into three time periods (corresponding to the public offering process): (1) the Pre–Filing Period; (2) Waiting Period; and (3) Post–Qualification period.

	Filing		Qualification	
Pre–Filing Period	|	Waiting Period	|	Post–Qualification Period

As we go through each Regulation A offering period, consider how the restrictions on offers differ from those contained in § 5's gun-jumping rules.

1. PRE–FILING PERIOD

At first glance, the rules governing the Pre–Filing Period for a Regulation A offering seem analogous to the Pre–Filing Period under § 5. Under Rule 251(d)(1)(i), "no offers of securities shall be made unless a Form 1–A offering statement has been filed with the Commission." Rule 251(d)(1)(i), however, has a major exception contained within Rule 254. Rule 254 lifts the prohibition on offers in certain situations, allowing issuers to "test the waters" in the Pre–Filing period and determine the appetite of investors for the offering.

Under Rule 254(a), an issuer may provide prospective purchasers "a written document or make scripted radio or television broadcasts to determine whether there is any interest in a contemplated securities offering." After the issuer submits the documents or broadcast script to the SEC pursuant to Rule 254(b), the issuer may also commence with oral communications and other broadcasts in the Pre–Filing Period even if such communications might condition the market (see Rule 254(a)). Thus, the testing-the-waters provision embodied within Rule 254 allows investors to obtain a wealth of information on the company well before ever receiving either a preliminary offering circular or final offering circular.

Rule 254(b) requires the issuer to file with the SEC the document or broadcast script used in the testing the waters solicitation prior to or at the time it is first used. Rule 254(b), among other things, also requires disclaimers that "no money or other consideration is being solicited" and any "indication of interest made by a prospective investor involves no obligation or commitment of any kind." Rule 254(b) prohibits any solicitations of interest under Rule 254 after the filing of the offering circular.

Rule 254(b) starts with the statement: "While not a condition to any exemption pursuant to this section...." What is the purpose of this statement? The requirements of Rule 254(b) are not phrased in a voluntary manner. Although Rule 254(b) provides that issuers that violate its terms may still obtain the exemption in Rule 254(a) (and thus do not violate § 5), the issuers are still open to a possible SEC enforcement action for violation of the terms of Rule 254(b) itself. Among other things, the SEC may seek to suspend the Regulation A exemption for the issuer.

One fear of the SEC in implementing testing the waters under Rule 254 was the possibility of opportunistic testing of the waters. Issuers could abuse testing the waters to drive investors considering a Regulation A offering into a "frenzy," leading to poor investment choices. Alternatively, consider the follow possible sequence of events. An issuer could (a) initiate a Regulation A offering; (b) test the waters, thereby priming the market for the company's securities; (c) withdraw the Regulation A offering; and finally, (d) commence a full-blown public offering. To the extent investors are in fact misled by the initial, non-regulated disclosures, Regulation A could provide a backdoor way for issuers to condition the market for a § 5 public offering.

To check these opportunistic behaviors, testing the waters is strictly limited to the Pre–Filing Period only (see Rule 254(b)(3)). Rule 254(b)(4) furthermore requires that sales may not be made until twenty calendar days after the last communication testing the waters. The twenty–day period provides a buffer between the decision on the part of investors to actually purchase and any testing the waters solicitation, giving investors a cooling off period. Is this cooling off period sufficient? And if the cooling off period is sufficient, why not allow testing the waters for registered public offerings? The SEC's 2005 Public Offering Reforms, discussed in Chapter 7, allow certain issuers in a registered public offering to communicate more freely during the public offering Pre–Filing Period. Well-known seasoned issuers may test the waters with oral and written offers in the public offering Pre–Filing Period. For non-Exchange Act reporting issuers, however, the SEC's reforms do not provide for any Pre–Filing Period communication relating to the public offering itself. Non–Exchange Act reporting issuers must still turn to Regulation A if they want to test the waters.

Issuers also face possible integration of any Regulation A testing the waters solicitations with an eventual registered public offering. If testing-the-waters solicitations made in an aborted Regulation A offering are integrated with a later registered public offering, the non-Exchange Act reporting issuer may violate § 5(c) and face possible § 12(a)(1) liability.

Of course, some issuers may innocently decide after commencing a Regulation A offering that the issuers' interests are better served by a larger (i.e., greater then $5 million) registered public offering. To protect such issuers, the SEC provides a separate integration safe harbor separating testing-the-waters solicitations under Rule 254 and any subsequent registered public offering. Rule 254(d) states that integration will not occur if "at least 30 calendar days have elapsed between the last solicitation of interest and the filing of the registration statement" with the SEC. Note that this 30–day period is more favorable to the issuer than the normal six-month safe harbor period for offerings subsequent to the Regulation A offering contained in the general integration safe harbor under Rule 251(c) (discussed below).

HYPOTHETICAL THIRTEEN

1. Suppose Kim, the CEO of Trendy, decides to have Trendy do a Regulation A offering. Kim is not sure about the potential market for Trendy's stock nor is she sure about the possible offering price the market will bear. Prior to the filing of the offering statement, she decides to survey the market through newspaper ads and scripted radio commercials. The ads tout the bright prospects for Trendy and the good potential for new investors. Is there anything wrong with Trendy's initial advertising campaign for the offering?

2. Assume that Kim intended all along to do a registered public offering. To find a backdoor way to use testing the waters for the public offering, she first had Trendy initiate a Regulation A offering (with full-blown testing the waters in newspaper and scripted radio ads). Trendy then withdrew its Regulation A offering. After 35 days, Trendy then commenced its registered public offering. Have Trendy and Kim violated § 5?

2. WAITING PERIOD

After the offering statement is filed with the SEC, the issuer enters into the Waiting Period for the Regulation A offering. During the Waiting Period, Rule 254's provision for testing the waters is no longer applicable. As a result, the information flow from the issuer is considerably reduced. In the Waiting Period, the following types of communications are permissible (analogous to the Waiting Period in a registered offering):

- Oral offers (Rule 251(d)(1)(ii)(A))
- Written offers pursuant to Rule 255 (Rule 251(d)(1)(ii)(B))

- Tombstone type statements (Rule 251(d)(1)(ii)(C))

Rule 255 provides for a "preliminary" offering circular containing the same information as the final offering circular but excluding price-related information (e.g., the offering price, underwriting discounts and commissions, etc.). Free writing is not allowed during the Waiting Period. The SEC's 2005 Public Offering Reforms allow free writing prospectuses in the Waiting Period for a registered public offering as discussed in Chapter 7. The SEC did not, however, provide for similar free writing prospectuses in a Regulation A offering.

HYPOTHETICAL FOURTEEN

Suppose that Trendy continues with its Regulation A offering. It files an offering circular and continues with its newspaper and radio advertising campaign. Is this permitted?

3. POST–QUALIFICATION PERIOD

Like § 6(a)'s twenty-calendar day delay from filing to the effective date for registered public offerings, Rule 252(g) provides that qualification of the offering statement will occur twenty calendar days after the filing. Issuers may voluntarily delay qualification until the SEC gives its approval by using a delaying notation in the offering statement as specified in Rule 252(g)(2).

Once in the Post–Qualification Period, sales may commence (Rule 254(d)(2)(i)). More disclosure is now permitted. Issuers may engage in free writing. Free writing may be sent out either together with or after the prospective purchaser has been sent a final offering circular (Rule 254(d)(1)(iii)).

Regulation A requires that an offering circular be delivered in the Post–Qualification Period. First, purchasers must be sent either a preliminary or final offering circular 48 hours before the mailing of the confirmation of sales (Rule 251(d)(2)(i)(B)). Second, the final offering circular (if not delivered earlier) must be delivered with the confirmation of sales (Rule 251(d)(2)(i)(C)). Dealers no longer acting as (or not otherwise) an underwriter for the offering must supply investors with the most current offering circular either before or together with the confirmation of sales for a period of 90 days from the qualification of the Regulation A offering statement (Rule 251(d)(2)(ii)). The SEC in the 2005 Public Offering Reforms provide that the filing of the final § 10(a) statutory prospectus with the SEC counts as "delivery" for purposes of the prospectus delivery requirement of § 5(b) under certain conditions (see Rule 172). The SEC, however, did not extend the "access equals delivery" rule to Regulation A.

As with a registered public offering, Regulation A requires updating of the offering circular. The Regulation A updating requirement, however, is broader. Rule 253(e) requires issuers to revise the offering circular anytime during the course of the offering when: (1) information in the offering circular becomes false or misleading given existing circumstances, (2) material developments have occurred, or (3) a fundamental change in the information initially presented in the offering circular has occurred. Rule 10b–5 antifraud liability (and potentially § 12(a)(2)) also provides an incentive for the issuer to update the offering circular whenever it becomes materially misleading. In addition, Rule 253(e)(2) mandates that issuers must update the offering circular used in a continuous offering (in particular the financial statements) twelve months after the qualification date.

Unlike a registered public offering, Regulation A requires issuers to file every revised or updated offering circular as an amendment to the offering statement. Such a filing then results in a re-qualification (with a new qualification date) for the entire offering statement. In the registered public offering context, amending the registration statement resets the clock for purposes of § 11 liability. Regulation A, however, has no comparable, heightened antifraud provision. Thus, although the offering statement is updated along with the offering circular, it does not create additional liability exposure.

HYPOTHETICAL FIFTEEN

1. *Scenario One*: Suppose Trendy's offering statement is now qualified. Twenty days after qualification, Jones Securities, a securities dealer, not connected in any way to Trendy's Regulation A offering, decides to purchase some Trendy stock on the secondary market. Two days later, Jones Securities sells these shares into the open market to several individual investors and mails a confirmation of sales (and nothing else). Any problem with this?

2. *Scenario Two*: Jones Securities sends the final offering circular to investors with the confirmation of sales. Jones also includes a packet of written glossy brochures touting Trendy's great growth prospects together with the final offering circular. Assume that most, but not all, of the investors who purchased the securities from Jones Securities received the preliminary offering circular a month earlier. Any problem?

3. *Scenario Three*: Two weeks into the Regulation A offering, Trendy's financial officer, Jake Jones discovers an accounting error that overstates Trendy's prior year revenue by 15%. Must Trendy amend the offering circular?

E. INTEGRATION

Regulation A follows the integration factors used in other exemptions. Recall that these factors are whether the sales:

> (1) are part of a single plan of financing; (2) involve issuance of the same class of securities; (3) have been made at or about the same time; (4) are made for the same general purpose; and (5) involve the same type of consideration.

Securities Act Release No. 4552 (November 6, 1962).

Regulation A provides its own, unique safe harbor from integration. Regulation A provides a "two-sided" integration safe harbor. If the terms of Rule 251(c) of Regulation A are met, then the Regulation A offering will not be integrated into another offering. Symmetrically, the other offering will also not have the Regulation A offering integrated into it. Thus, the Regulation A protects both offerings from integration.

How do we get this result? Rule 251(c) states that: "Offers and sales made in reliance on this Regulation A will not be integrated with.... " This language implies that no integration will take place between the Regulation A offering and the other offers and sales. In contrast, note that Rule 502(a) of Regulation D states that if its terms are met, then the other offers and sales simply "will not be considered part of that Regulation D offering." Rule 502(a) does not say that the Regulation D offering will not be integrated into the other offering. Thus, while Regulation A provides a two-sided anti-integration safe harbor, Regulation D's safe harbor protects only one side.

Among the offerings covered under Rule 251(c), note that two in particular are protected from integration under a current Regulation A offering:

- Prior offers or sales of securities
- Subsequent offers or sales of securities that are made more than six months after the completion of the Regulation A offering

Compared with the safe harbor afforded under Rule 502(a) of Regulation D, Regulation A therefore provides a much narrower time frame during which the integration safe harbor does not apply (and hence, a broader integration safe harbor).

HYPOTHETICAL SIXTEEN

1. *Scenario One*: Trendy engages in the following series of offerings:

    1/1 to 1/30—Sale of $5 million of common stock pursuant to Rule 505 to 25 unsophisticated purchasers to fund expansion of the Lean Green product.

    2/1 to 2/28—Testing the waters offers for a $5 million offering of common stock pursuant to Regulation A. On 3/1, the offering statement is filed with the SEC. On 4/1, sales commence and by 4/15 all $5 million of common stock has been sold. Proceeds will be used to fund expansion of the Lean Green product.

2. *Scenario Two*: Same as in Scenario One above and Trendy engages in the following additional offering:

    11/1 to 11/30—Sale of $5 million of common stock to investors all located in California pursuant to an intrastate offering exemption under § 3(a)(11) of the Securities Act (discussed later in the chapter). Proceeds will be used to expand distribution of Lean Green.

3. *Scenario Three*: What if Trendy had tested the waters as part of a Regulation A offering during the Pre–Filing Period and then decided that it should do a Rule 506 offering for $10 million? It waits 40 days and then commences its Rule 506 offering. Do the advertising and other promotional disclosures for the earlier Regulation A offering constitute a "general solicitation" for purposes of Rule 502(c)?

F. INSIGNIFICANT DEVIATIONS

Not all failures to comply with the terms of Regulation A will result in a loss of the exemption. Rule 260 provides that failures to comply are excused if the person relying on the Regulation A exemption to engage in offers or sales to a particular individual or entity does so under the following circumstances:

1. The failure to comply did not relate to a provision of Regulation A directly intended to protect that particular individual or entity.

2. The failure to comply with Regulation A was "insignificant with respect to the offering as a whole." Failure to follow Rules 251(a) (issuer qualification), 251(b) (aggregate offering price), 251(d)(1) (restriction on offers) and 251(d)(3) (continuous or delayed offerings) are defined as significant to the offering as a whole; thus failure to comply with these provisions cannot be excused.

3. A good faith and reasonable attempt was made to comply with Regulation A (Rule 260(a)(3)).

As with Regulation D's Rule 508, Rule 260 does not shield persons failing to comply with Regulation A from the possibility of an SEC enforcement action under § 20 of the Securities Act.

HYPOTHETICAL SEVENTEEN

Consider the following errors in Trendy's Regulation A offering and whether they might potentially be treated as insignificant deviations under Rule 260.

1. Trendy sends out free writing with its preliminary offering circular in the Waiting Period.

2. Trendy's attorneys made a mistake. It turns out that Trendy in fact is required to make periodic disclosures as an Exchange Act reporting company because it has over $10 million in net assets and more than 500 shareholders.

3. Trendy's placement agents make a mistake and Trendy sells $5.1 million through its Regulation A offering.

4. Trendy fails to send a copy of the preliminary offering circular to Emma, a prospective investor in the Waiting Period. Later, in the Post–Qualification Period, Trendy finally mails her a copy of the final offering circular with the confirmation of sales.

G. ANTIFRAUD LIABILITY

An important consideration for issuers considering a Regulation A offering is antifraud liability. Rule 10b–5 applies to fraud in connection with the purchase or sale of securities and therefore applies to misleading statements and omissions (where there is a duty to disclose) in the offering circular, offering statement, and other documents used in the Regulation A offering.

From Chapter 8, we saw that § 11 (registration statement) and § 12(a)(2) (prospectus) provided heightened antifraud liability for documents used in a public offering under § 5. Because Regulation A involves an offering statement and not a registration statement, § 11 does not apply.

The application of § 12(a)(2) is less clear. Although the offering circular is analogous to the prospectus and is widely distributed in a Regulation A-style public offering, § 12(a)(2) may not apply to Regulation A because the offering circular is not termed a "prospectus." On the other hand, the Supreme Court in *Gustafson v. Alloyd*, 513 U.S. 561 (1995), indicated that prospectus refers to documents used in a public offering. In her dissent, Justice Ginsburg wrote:

> I understand the Court's definition of a public offering to encompass both transactions that must be registered under § 5, and transactions that would have been registered had the securities involved not qualified for exemption under § 3.

Recall that the SEC's authority to establish the Regulation A mini-public offering exemption is found in § 3. Moreover, Regulation A does not restrict the type of investors to whom securities can be offered. At least under Justice Ginsburg's reading of the scope of the majority opinion in *Gustafson* (unrefuted by the majority), § 12(a)(2) would apply to the publicly-distributed documents in a Regulation A offering.

H.   INTERNET OFFERINGS

In the mid–1990s, issuers took advantage of the Internet to facilitate Regulation A offerings. Andrew Klein, a former associate at a Wall Street law firm, decided that his calling lay more in beer than in securities work. He left the law to form Spring Street Brewing Co. Needing capital and relying on his expertise in securities law, Klein made a public offering of Spring Street stock in 1995 exclusively over the Internet and without the assistance of underwriters. Klein set up a website where investors could obtain the prospectus for the offering and indicate their interest in purchasing shares. Klein relied on Regulation A to exempt his direct public offering from § 5 of the Securities Act. Regulation A, unlike a private placement exemption under Rules 505 or 506 of Regulation D, allowed Klein to sell his offering through a general solicitation.

Although Spring Street failed to meet its goal of $5 million (it only sold about $1.6 million of stock), the offering caught the attention of entrepreneurs, Wall Street, and the SEC. Entrepreneurs were intrigued with the idea of bypassing the underwriters (and their high commissions) while still reaching a wide audience of investors through the Internet and avoiding many of the stringent gun-jumping prohibitions under § 5. Conversely, Wall Street was concerned about the potential lost revenues if Internet direct public offerings took off. The SEC worried about the risks Regulation A offerings posed for unsophisticated investors trolling the Internet for "good buys." Fortunately (or unfortunately depending on your point of view), the promise of Internet offerings through Regulation A has yet to take off. Although a number succeeded with direct public offerings over the Internet after Spring Street, the collapse of the "Internet bubble" in the early 2000s effectively dried up demand for such offerings. The SEC has since provided guidance on how Internet-based communications would be treated for purposes of registered public offerings, with their latest guidance coming as part of the SEC's 2005 Public Offering Reforms described in Chapter 7.

V. INTRASTATE OFFERINGS

Section 5 of the Securities Act reaches broadly to regulate all offers and sales of securities involving interstate commerce. Even for a securities offering that takes place exclusively in one state, issuers and those working on the issuers' behalf implicate § 5 if they use a telephone, the mail, or other instruments of interstate commerce.

Despite the reach of § 5 to offerings essentially intrastate in character, reasons exist to exempt such offerings from the registration requirements. Offerings that take place solely within one state may have less effect on the confidence of investors in the national securities marketplace. Often intrastate offerings are smaller in scope and are sold to investors that have a general knowledge of the typically local companies offering the securities, reducing the need for the broad-based securities protections of § 5. Finally, state-based securities regulators provide a substitute for federal securities regulation. Particularly if the offering is sold in only one state, state regulators have both a greater incentive to police the offering (all the investors are within their jurisdiction) and a greater ability to do so.

Long before the enactment of the Securities Act of 1933 and the Securities Exchange Act of 1934, states imposed "Blue Sky" regulations, starting with Kansas in 1911.* Today states vary widely in their methods of regulation. Some states, such as New York, impose only antifraud liability. Other states, including California, Texas, and Wisconsin, require issuers to meet a merit test, prohibiting issuers from offering or selling securities that failed to meet certain substantive criteria (and thus are deemed "unfair" for investors). Most states combine disclosure with limited merit review. Although the predominant number of states model their Blue Sky laws

---

* Justice McKenna defined "Blue Sky" in *Hall v. Geiger–Jones Co.*, 242 U.S. 539 (1917):

> The name that is given to the law indicates the evil at which it is aimed, that is, to use the language of a cited case, "speculative schemes which have no more basis than so many feet of 'blue sky'"; or, as stated by counsel in another case, "to stop the sale of stock in fly-by-night concerns, visionary oil wells, distant gold mines and other like fraudulent exploitations." Even if the descriptions be regarded as rhetorical, the existence of evil is indicated, and a belief of its detriment; and we shall not pause to do more than state that the prevention of deception is within the competency of government and that the appreciation of the consequences of it is not open for our review.

after the Uniform Securities Act of 1957 and the Revised Uniform Securities Act of 1985, with variations across different states, the model codes do not specify a single method of securities regulation. Instead, the "uniform" acts allow states to pick and choose from among antifraud liability, disclosure, and merit-regulation options.

The diversity of regulatory approaches among the states forced issuers selling securities in multiple states to spend time and resources to comply with each states' securities registration requirements. In 1996, Congress narrowed the scope of state securities regulation with the National Securities Markets Improvement Act of 1996 ("NSMIA"). Certain "covered securities," including securities listed or approved for listing on the NYSE, AMEX and the Nasdaq/National Market system are exempted from state securities registration requirements. Covered securities also include securities issued in an exempt offering under Rule 506 of Regulation D, if the issuer has securities listed on one of the above markets. Covered securities, however, do not include securities exempt from registration pursuant to Rules 504 or 505 of Regulation D or under § 3(a)(11) of the intrastate offering exemption. Although NSMIA bars state registration of certain securities, states can continue to investigate and enforce their antifraud laws.

We start with a discussion of the intrastate offering exemption under § 3(a)(11). We then discuss the safe harbor for intrastate offerings provided under Rule 147.

A. SECTION 3(a)(11) OFFERINGS

Section 3(a)(11) of the Securities Act exempts from § 5:

Any security which is a part of an issue offered and sold only to persons resident within a single State or Territory, where the issuer of such security is a person resident and doing business within or, if a corporation, incorporated by and doing business within, such State or Territory.

Consider the SEC's own view of the scope of § 3(a)(11) in the following release. Despite the presence of possible state securities regulation, the SEC has generally construed § 3(a)(11) narrowly. Why do you think the SEC has taken this attitude toward the intrastate exemption?

Securities Act Release No. 4434

Securities and Exchange Commission (Dec. 6, 1961).

* * *

The legislative history of the Securities Act clearly shows that [the § 3(a)(11)] exemption was designed to apply only to local financing that may practicably be consummated in its entirety within the State or Territory in which the issuer is both incorporated and doing business. . . .

'Issue' Concept

A basic condition of the exemption is that the entire issue of securities be offered and sold exclusively to residents of the state in question. Consequently, an offer to a non-resident which is considered a part of the intrastate issue will render the exemption unavailable to the entire offering.

Whether an offering is "a part of an issue", that is, whether it is an integrated part of an offering previously made or proposed to be made, is a question of fact and depends essentially upon whether the offerings are a related part of a plan or program. Thus, the exemption should not be relied upon in combination with another exemption for the different parts of a single issue where a part is offered or sold to non-residents....

[S]ince the exemption is designed to cover only those security distributions, which, as a whole, are essentially local in character, it is clear that the phrase "sold only to persons resident" as used in Section 3(a)(11) cannot refer merely to the initial sales by the issuing corporation to its underwriters, or even the subsequent resales by the underwriters to distributing dealers. To give effect to the fundamental purpose of the exemption, it is necessary that the entire issue of securities shall be offered and sold to, and come to rest only in the hands of residents within the state. If any part of the issue is offered or sold to a non-resident, the exemption is unavailable not only for the securities so sold, but for all securities forming a part of the issue, including those sold to residents. It is incumbent upon the issuer, underwriter, dealers and other persons connected with the offering to make sure that it does not become an interstate distribution through resales. It is understood to be customary for such persons to obtain assurances that purchases are not made with a view to resale to non-residents.

Doing Business Within the State

In view of the local character of the Section 3(a)(11) exemption, the requirement that the issuer be doing business in the state can only be satisfied by the performance of substantial operational activities in the state of incorporation. The doing business requirement is not met by functions in the particular state such as bookkeeping, stock record and similar activities or by offering securities in the state. Thus, the exemption would be unavailable to an offering by a company made in the state of its incorporation of undivided fractional oil and gas interests located in other states even though the company conducted other business in the state of its incorporation. While the person creating the fractional interests is technically the "issuer" as defined in Section 2[a](4) of the Act, the purchaser of such security obtains no interest in the issuer's separate business within the state. Similarly, an intrastate exemption would not be available to a "local" mortgage company offering interests in out-of-state mortgages which are sold under circumstances to constitute them investment contracts....

If the proceeds of the offering are to be used primarily for the purpose of a new business conducted outside of the state of incorporation and unrelated to some incidental business locally conducted, the exemption should not be relied upon. So also, a Section 3(a)(11) exemption should not be relied upon for each of a series of corporations organized in different states where there is in fact and purpose a single business enterprise or financial venture whether or not it is planned to merge or consolidate the various corporations at a later date.

Residence Within the State

Section 3(a)(11) requires that the entire issue be confined to a single state in which the issuer, the offerees and the purchasers are residents. Mere presence in the state is not sufficient to constitute residence as in the case of military personnel at a military post. The mere obtaining of formal representations of residence and agreements not to resell to non-residents or agreements that sales are void if the purchaser is a non-resident should not be relied upon without more as establishing the availability of the exemption.

An offering may be so large that its success as a local offering appears doubtful from the outset. Also, reliance should not be placed on the exemption for an issue which includes warrants for the purchase of another security unless there can be assurance that the warrants will be exercised only by residents. With respect to convertible securities, a Section 3(a)(9) exemption may be available for the conversion.

A secondary offering by a controlling person in the issuer's state of incorporation may be made in reliance on a Section 3(a)(11) exemption provided the exemption would be available to the issuer for a primary offering in that state. It is not essential that the controlling person be a resident of the issuer's state of incorporation.

Resales

From these general principles it follows that if during the course of distribution any underwriter, any distributing dealer (whether or not a member of the formal selling or distributing group), or any dealer or other person purchasing securities from a distributing dealer for resale were to offer or sell such securities to a non-resident, the exemption would be defeated. In other words, Section 3(a)(11) contemplates that the exemption is applicable only if the entire issue is distributed pursuant to the statutory conditions. Consequently, any offers or sales to a non-resident in connection with the distribution of the issue would destroy the exemption as to all securities which are a part of that issue, including those sold to residents regardless of whether such sales are made directly to non-residents or indirectly through residents who as part of the distribution thereafter sell to non-residents. . . .

This is not to suggest, however, that securities which have actually come to rest in the hands of resident investors, such as persons purchasing without a view to further distribution or resale to non-residents, may not in due course be resold by such persons, whether directly or through dealers or brokers, to non-residents without in any way affecting the exemption. The relevance of any such resales consists only of the evidentiary light which they might cast upon the factual question whether the securities had in fact come to rest in the hands of resident investors. If the securities are resold but a short time after their acquisition to a non-resident this fact, although not conclusive, might support an inference that the original offering had not come to rest in the state, and that the resale therefore constituted a part of the process of primary distribution; a stronger inference would arise if the purchaser involved were a security dealer. It may be noted that the non-residence of the underwriter or dealer is not pertinent as long as the ultimate distribution is solely to residents of the state. . . .

Conclusion

In conclusion, the fact should be stressed that Section 3(a)(11) is designed to apply only to distributions genuinely local in character. From a practical point of view, the provisions of that section can exempt only issues which in reality represent local financing by local industries, carried out through local investment. Any distribution not of this type raises a serious question as to the availability of Section 3(a)(11). Consequently, any dealer proposing to participate in the distribution of an issue claimed to be exempt under Section 3(a)(11) should examine the character of the transaction and the proposed or actual manner of its execution by all persons concerned with it with the greatest care to satisfy himself that the distribution will not, or did not, exceed the limitations of the exemption. Otherwise the dealer, even though his own sales may be carefully confined to resident purchasers, may subject himself to serious risk of civil liability under Section 12[a](1) of the Act for selling without prior registration a security not in fact entitled to exemption from registration. In Release No. 4386, we noted that the quick commencement of trading and prompt resale of portions of the issue to non-residents raises a serious question whether the entire issue has, in fact, come to rest in the hands of investors resident in the state of the initial offering.

Busch v. Carpenter

827 F.2d 653 (10th Cir. 1987).

■ Seymour, Circuit Judge.

Paul and Linda Busch brought this action under [§ 12 of the Securities Act] against Craig Carpenter, George Jensen, and Ronald Burnett to recover the purchase price of shares of stock in Sonic Petroleum, Inc. Plaintiffs alleged that the stock had not been registered as required by [§ 5(a) of the Securities Act], and that the stock did not qualify for the intrastate offering exemption set out in [§ 3(a)(11) of the Securities Act].[1]

---

1. Plaintiffs also alleged that defendants had violated Rule 147, which is a "safe harbor" provision establishing the circumstances in which the SEC will not challenge

... The parties filed cross motions for summary judgment, and the district court granted judgment for defendants. We affirm in part, reverse in part, and remand for further proceedings.

I.

BACKGROUND

The undisputed facts are briefly as follows. Sonic was incorporated in Utah on October 2, 1980. The three defendants were officers and directors of Sonic at its inception. Carpenter was president until May 1981, and a director and officer through June 26, 1981, the date on which plaintiffs bought their shares. Jensen was vice president and a director through June 26. Burnett was secretary and a director until May 1981. During October and November of 1980, Sonic publicly offered and sold shares of Sonic stock to Utah residents through Olsen & Company, Inc. Although Sonic complied with Utah state registration requirements, it did not file a registration statement under federal securities law, relying on the exemption from registration provided for intrastate offerings. Sonic, which had no prior operating history at the time of this offering, was incorporated in Utah and purportedly organized to acquire, extract, and market natural resources such as oil, gas, and coal. Although the company had not undertaken this activity in Utah or anywhere else, it maintained its corporate office, books, and records in Utah at the time of the initial offering. It is not disputed that the offering of 25,000,000 shares of Sonic was sold for $500,000 entirely to Utah residents.

In late March or early April of 1981, Carpenter was contacted by William Mason, an Illinois oil and gas promoter, about a merger of Sonic with Mason's operations in Illinois. Sonic and Mason reached an agreement, effective May 25, 1981, under which Sonic issued Mason a controlling block of stock and acquired an Illinois drilling corporation privately owned by Mason. Carpenter, Jensen, Mason, Mason's wife, and their son were officers and directors of the new company, which was renamed Mason Oil Co., Inc. Burnett had resigned his positions with Sonic at the shareholders meeting on the proposed merger, and he took no part in the operation of Mason Oil. Shortly after Mason Oil was formed, William Mason drew $351,126 from the remainder of the $435,000 net proceeds of the original Sonic offering and deposited it in Illinois. This money was not used in Utah.

In May 1981, Mason and Carpenter set up Norbil Investments, a brokerage account in Utah, so that Mason and his friends could buy shares of the company's stock. Plaintiffs, who are California residents, bought their stock through Norbil. Plaintiffs also presented evidence of purchases

the applicability of the intrastate offering exemption. The district court held that defendants' failure to comply with Rule 147 did not preclude them from establishing that they were nonetheless entitled to the exemption. Plaintiffs do not raise this ruling as error on appeal.

through Norbil of stock by other non-residents between May and August 1981.

II.
THE INTRASTATE OFFERING EXEMPTION

* * *

Congress ... recognized that the protections of the 1933 Act were not essential for those securities that could be supervised effectively by the states. Section 3(a)(11) therefore exempts from the Act's registration requirements "[a]ny security which is a part of an issue offered and *sold only to persons resident within a single State* or Territory, *where the issuer of such security is* a person resident and doing business within or, if a corporation, *incorporated by and doing business within, such State* or Territory." (emphasis added).

In light of the 1933 Act's broad remedial purpose, its exemption provisions are to be narrowly construed. Once a plaintiff makes out a prima facie case that the securities offered or sold were not registered, the defendant bears the burden of demonstrating its entitlement to an exemption.

A.   Coming to Rest

The district court ruled that the resale of stock to non-residents occurred after the issued securities had come to rest in Utah and concluded that the public offering was therefore consummated in Utah within the meaning of section 3(a)(11). On appeal, plaintiffs contend that the court's ruling was erroneous and that the circumstances of the resale defeated the intrastate exemption.

In order to fall within the intrastate exemption, initial sales to state residents must be bona fide. The intrastate exemption becomes unavailable whenever sales or purchases by an issuer, an intermediary, or a subsequent purchaser circumvent the federal securities laws. The SEC has consistently maintained that a distribution of securities must have "actually come to rest in the hands of resident investors—persons purchasing for investment and not with a view to further distribution or for purposes of resale." We agree.

During the proceedings below, plaintiffs contended that the resale to non-residents within seven months of the initial offering in and of itself precluded the application of the intrastate offering exemption. The Amicus [the SEC] raises a new argument on appeal, contending that because defendants had the burden to show their right to the exemption, they had the burden below to present evidence that the original buyers bought with investment intent. The [SEC] argues that without such a showing, summary judgment for defendants was improper. Plaintiffs have abandoned their claim that resale alone was enough to defeat the exemption. They now join in the [SEC's] argument, and rely on that argument to assert that they are entitled to summary judgment.

We reject the [SEC's] argument. The intrastate offering exemption requires that the issue be "offered and sold only to persons resident within a single State." In our view, a seller seeking summary judgment makes a prima facie showing that the offering was consummated within a state by showing that the stock was sold only to residents of that state. We disagree with [the SEC] that, in order to be entitled to summary judgment, the issuer should be required to disprove all the possible circumstances that might establish the stock has not come to rest. It seems more logical to us to impose on the other party the burden of producing some contrary evidence on this issue when the seller claiming the exemption has satisfied the facial requirement of the statute. In the face of defendants' undisputed showing that all of the original buyers were Utah residents, plaintiffs were therefore required to produce evidence that the stock had not come to rest but had been sold to people who intended to resell it out of state.

The evidence fails to suggest that any of Sonic's publicly offered shares were issued under questionable circumstances. Carpenter and Mason did not know each other until their initial conversation in the spring of 1981.... Moreover, the interstate purchases by Mason and others of freely trading shares several months after the completion of the intrastate offering do not, without more, impugn the investment intent of the original buyers or otherwise imply an effort to evade the federal securities laws. Norbil served as a conduit for over-the-counter purchases made by Olsen & Company on behalf of Mason and various acquaintances. Although Carpenter did collect from buyers, pay Olsen, and transfer the stock certificates to their new owners, there is simply no indication that those who sold through Norbil had not originally purchased their stock for investment purposes.... Accordingly, the trial court did not err in concluding that no genuine question of fact was raised on whether the issue had come to rest in the hands of Utah residents.

B.   Doing Business

Plaintiffs alternatively contend that defendants were not entitled to the intrastate offering exemption because the corporate issuer was not doing business in Utah as required by section 3(a)(11). There is no dispute that the newly formed company, not yet operational, maintained its offices, books, and records in Salt Lake City. The decisive issue concerns whether, under the circumstances of this case, Sonic's failure to invest a portion of the proceeds from its initial public offering in Utah could defeat the intrastate exemption.

Although neither the statute nor its legislative history defines the doing business requirement, courts have uniformly held that it refers to activity that actually generates revenue within an issuer's home state. The leading case is *Chapman v. Dunn*, 414 F.2d 153 (6th Cir.1969), which involved a company that maintained its offices and issued stock in Michigan while operating its sole productive venture, an oil and gas business, in Ohio. The *Chapman* court reasoned that "doing business" in the context of securities regulation connotes substantially more activity than that which would warrant exercising personal jurisdiction in ordinary civil suits. Effective supervision of stock offerings, the court added, can entail on-site inspections, familiarity with local economic conditions, and sometimes reliance upon judicial process. State oversight of business operations located elsewhere could often prove cumbersome, costly, and ineffective. The *Chapman* court therefore approved the SEC's view that the intrastate exemption applies only in cases of local financing for local industries. The court held that "doing business" refers to income-producing activity, and that an issuer must conduct a "predominant amount" of that activity within its home state.

* * *

[A]n issuer cannot claim the exemption simply by opening an office in a particular state. Conducting substantially all income-producing operations elsewhere defeats the exemption, as do the plans of recently organized companies to invest the net proceeds of initial public offerings only in other states. Doing business under the 1933 Act means more than maintaining an office, books, and records in one state.

Viewing the evidence and drawing reasonable inferences most favorably to plaintiffs, a fact issue exists regarding . . . Sonic's plans for the use of proceeds. . . . Here the corporation never did more than maintain its office, books, and records in Utah. This was not sufficient to make a prima facie showing of compliance with the intrastate offering exemption. While its prospectus stated that no more than twenty percent of all proceeds would be used outside of Utah, Sonic nonetheless transferred essentially all of its assets to Mason in Illinois. The record contains no evidence, moreover, of any prior efforts whatever at locating investment opportunities within Utah. These considerations support a reasonable inference that Sonic may have been intending all along to invest its assets outside the state. Although Carpenter and Mason may have been strangers to one another, this fact alone fails to dispel the possibility that Sonic had been seeking and perhaps investigating other business operations out of state. If so, and we intimate no view on this unresolved fact question, the intrastate exemption would be unavailable.

We are not persuaded by defendants' argument that Sonic did business in Utah when its public offering was consummated, that its stated purpose was to do business within that state, and that the company should not be penalized for reorganizing its operations at a later date. We have already noted that under the Act, doing business means more than opening an office at the time of a public offering. The issue is not whether a newly formed company performs such minimal corporate functions within a state, but whether subsequent proceeds are to be employed in that same state. A newly formed company may not claim the exemption while planning covertly to invest the proceeds of a local offering in other states. . . . Accordingly, we conclude that a genuine issue of material fact exists precluding summary judgment in favor of all defendants.

* * *

IV.

CONCLUSION

In view of our conclusion that fact questions exist on whether the company was doing business in Utah within the ambit of the intrastate exemption and as to Carpenter's liability for any violation of the Act, we reverse in part and remand for further proceedings....

QUESTIONS

1. Who bears the burden of demonstrating that all the purchasers of securities under § 3(a)(11) are residents of the same state?

2. Sonic was initially incorporated in Utah and had its office, corporate books, etc. in Utah. Why didn't this establish that Sonic was resident and doing business in Utah?

3. What if Sonic had substantial income producing activities in Utah but intended all along to use the proceeds from the offering to drill for gas in Nevada?

Although the motivations behind § 3(a)(11) are straightforward (exempting local financing for local businesses from federal securities registration requirements), the application of § 3(a)(11) is more ambiguous. Consider the following concepts important in determining the application of § 3(a)(11):

- Issuer Resident and Doing Business in a State
- Investors Resident in a State
  - —When are sales to investors outside the states integrated?
  - —When do sales to investors within the state "come to rest"?

Section 3(a)(11) defines none of these items with precision. Instead, we are left with somewhat vague standards. The SEC in Securities Act Release 4552, for example, put forth a multi-prong test for integration. We are told that two offerings may be integrated and treated as one to the extent the two offerings have the same general purpose, plan of financing, consideration, and are close in time to one another. Release 4552 does not tell us, however, how to balance these factors if they do not all point in the same direction.

Similarly, if investors within the state resell their securities to out-of-state investors, does this result in a loss of the exemption? The answer depends on whether the in-state investors had "investment intent." Although the passage of time (in particular over two years) before a resale suggests initial investment intent, the SEC does not favor reliance upon the mere passage of time as evidence of investment intent (see Preliminary Notes to Rule 144). Consider how you would resolve these ambiguities in the following hypothetical.

HYPOTHETICAL EIGHTEEN

Assume that Trendy is based in San Francisco, CA. On January 1 it sold $50 million worth of common stock through a private placement to 30 sophisticated purchasers and accredited investors across the United States pursuant to Rule 506 of Regulation D. Trendy used the $50 million to construct a soft drink manufacturing plant in Los Angeles, CA. On August 1, Trendy then sold an additional $20 million of common stock solely to California investors. Trendy used the proceeds from the offering to finish construction of the manufacturing plant.

1. If Trendy's January 1 and August 1 offerings are integrated, what effect does that have on the § 3(a)(11) offering?

2. Will the two offerings be integrated? Do any safe harbors protect against integration?

3. Assume that on July 31, Trendy had $20 million in cash that it could use either to finish construction of the factory or invest in a new research and development facility located in Arizona. Rather than make this choice, Trendy conducts an intrastate offering of common stock to California residents, raising an additional $20 million in cash. Trendy directs the proceeds from the intrastate offering to finance the construction of the factory. Trendy simultaneously directs the $20 million in cash it had on hand prior to the intrastate offering to build the R & D facility in Arizona. Does this jeopardize the § 3(a)(11) exemption?

B. RULE 147

To bring certainty to issuers seeking to raise capital through an intrastate offering, the SEC promulgated Rule 147 in 1974. Like Rule 506, Rule 147 is not exclusive. Issuers that fail to meet the terms of Rule 147 may still seek to use § 3(a)(11). Given the relative certainty of Rule 147, however, few issuers would purposely seek to test the limits of § 3(a)(11). Consider the following SEC Release announcing the adoption of Rule 147.

Exchange Act Release No. 5450

Securities and Exchange Commission (Jan. 7, 1974).

The Securities and Exchange Commission today adopted Rule 147 which defines certain terms in, and clarified certain conditions of, Section 3(a)(11) of the Securities Act of 1933. . . .

Background and Purpose

* * *

Section 3(a)(11) was intended to allow issuers with localized operations to sell securities as part of a plan of local financing. Congress apparently believed that a company whose operations are restricted to one area should be able to raise money from investors in the immediate vicinity without having to register the securities with a federal agency. In theory, the investors would be protected both by their proximity to the issuer and by state regulation. Rule 147 reflects this Congressional intent and is limited in its application to transactions where state regulation will be most effective. The Commission has consistently taken the position that the exemption applies only to local financing provided by local investors for local companies. To satisfy the exemption, the entire issue must be offered and sold exclusively to residents of the state in which the issuer is resident and doing business. An offer or sale of part of the issue to a single non-resident will destroy the exemption for the entire issue.

The Transaction Concept

Although the intrastate offering exemption is contained in Section 3 of the Act, which Section is phrased in terms of exempt "securities" rather than "transactions", the legislative history and Commission and judicial interpretations indicate that the exemption covers only specific transactions and not the securities themselves. Rule 147 reflects this interpretation.

The "Part of an Issue" Concept

The determination of what constitutes "part of an issue" for purposes of the exemption, i.e. what should be "integrated", has traditionally been dependent on the facts involved in each case. The Commission notes in Securities Act Release 4434 that "any one or more of the following factors may be determinative of the question of integration:

1. are the offerings part of a single plan of financing;

2. do the offerings involve issuance of the same class of security;

3. are the offerings made at or about the same time;

4. is the same type of consideration to be received; and

5. are the offerings made for the same general purpose."

In this connection, the Commission generally has deemed intrastate offerings to be "integrated" with those registered or private offerings of the same class of securities made by the issuer at or about the same time....

As adopted, the rule provides in Subparagraph (b)(2) that, for purposes of the rule only, certain offers and sales of securities, discussed below, will be deemed not to be part of an issue and therefore not be integrated, but the rule does not otherwise define "part of an issue." Accordingly, as to offers and sales not within (b)(2), issuers who want to rely on Rule 147 will have to determine whether their offers and sales are part of an issue by applying the five factors cited above.

The "Person Resident Within" Concept

The object of the Section 3(a)(11) exemption, i.e., to restrict the offering to persons within the same locality as the issuer who are, by reason of their proximity, likely to be familiar with the issuer and protected by the state law governing the issuer, is best served by interpreting the residence requirement narrowly. In addition, the determination of whether all parts of the issue have been sold only to residents can be made only after the securities have "come to rest" within the state or territory. Rule 147 retains these concepts, but provides more objective standards for determining when a person is considered a resident within a state for purposes of the rule and when securities have come to rest within a state.

The "Doing Business Within" Requirement

Because the primary purpose of the intrastate exemption was to allow an essentially local business to raise money within the state where the investors would be likely to be familiar with the business and with the management, the doing business requirement has traditionally been viewed strictly. First, not only should the business be located within the state, but the principal or predominant business must be carried on there. Second, substantially all of the proceeds of the offering must be put to use within the local area.

Rule 147 reinforces these requirements by providing specific percentage amounts of business that must be conducted within the state, and of proceeds from the offering that must be spent in connection with such business. In addition, the rule requires that the principal office of the issuer be within the state.

Synopsis of Rule 147

1. Preliminary Notes

The first preliminary note to the rule indicates that the rule does not raise any presumption that the Section 3(a)(11) exemption would not be available for transactions which do not satisfy all of the provisions of the rule. The second note reminds issuers that the rule does not affect compliance with state law. The third preliminary note to the rule briefly explains that rule's purpose and provisions.

As initially proposed, the rule was intended not to be available for secondary transactions. In order to make this clear, the fourth preliminary note indicates that the rule is available only for transactions by an issuer and that the rule is not available for secondary transactions. However, in accordance with long standing administrative interpretations of Section 3(a)(11), the intrastate offering exemption may be available for secondary offers and sales by controlling persons of the issuer, if the exemption would have been available to the issuer.

2. Transactions Covered—Rule 147(a)

Paragraph (a) of the rule provides that offers, offers to sell, offers for sale and sales of securities that meet all the conditions of the rule will be deemed to come within the exemption provided by Section 3(a)(11). Those conditions are: (1) the issuer must be resident and doing business within the state or territory in which the securities are offered and sold (Rule 147(c)); (2) the offerees and purchasers must be resident within such state or territory (Rule 147(d)); (3) resales for a period of 9 months after the last sale which is part of an issue must be limited as provided (Rule 147(e) and (f)). In addition, the revised rule provides that certain offers and sales of securities by or for the issuers will be deemed not "part of an issue" for purposes of the rule only (Rule 147(b)).

3.   "Part of an Issue"—Rule 147(b)

Subparagraph (b)(1) of the rule provides that all securities of the issuer which are part of an issue must be offered, offered for sale or sold only in accordance with all of the terms of the rule. For the purposes of the rule only, subparagraph (b)(2) provides that all securities of the issuer offered, offered for sale or sold pursuant to the exemptions provided under Section 3 or 4(2) of the Act or registered pursuant to the Act, prior to or subsequent to the six month period immediately preceding or subsequent to any offer, offer to sell, offer for sale or sale pursuant to Rule 147 will be deemed not part of an issue provided that there are no offers, offers to sell or sales of securities of the same or similar class by or for the issuer during either of these six month periods. If there have been offers or sales during the six months, then in order to determine what constitutes part of an issue, reference should be made to the five traditional integration factors discussed above....

4.   Nature of the Issuer—Rule 147(c)—"Person Resident Within"—Rule 147(c)(1)

Subparagraph (c)(1) of the rule defines the situation in which issuers would be deemed to be "resident within" a state or territory. A corporation, limited partnership or business trust must be incorporated or organized pursuant to the laws of such state or territory. Section 3(a)(11) provides specifically that a corporate issuer must be incorporated in the state....

5.   Nature of the Issuer—Rule 147(c)—Doing Business Within—Rule 147(c)(2)

Subparagraph (c)(2) of the rule provides that the issuer will be deemed to be "doing business within" a state or territory in which the offers and sales are to be made if: (1) at least 80 percent of its gross revenues and those of its subsidiaries on a consolidated basis (a) for its most recent fiscal year (if the first offer of any part of the issue is made during the first six months of the issuer's current fiscal year) or (b) for the subsequent six month period, or for the twelve months ended with that period (if the first offer of any part of the issue is made during the last six months of the issuer's current fiscal year) were derived from the operation of a business or property located in or rendering of services within the state or territory; (2) at least 80 percent of the issuer's assets and those of its subsidiaries on a consolidated basis at the end of the most recent fiscal semi-annual period prior to the first offer of any part of the issue are located within such state or territory; (3) at least 80 percent of the net proceeds to the issuer from the sales made pursuant to the rule are intended to be and are used in connection with the operation of a business or property or the rendering of services within such state or territory; and (4) the issuer's principal office is located in the state or territory.

* * *

Finally, subparagraph (c)(2) of the rule provides that an issuer which has not had gross revenues from the operation of its business in excess of $5,000 during its most recent twelve month period need not satisfy the revenue test of subsection (c)(2)(i). The provisions of paragraph (c) are intended to assure that the issuer is primarily a local business. Many comments were received requesting more elaboration with respect to the above standards. The following examples demonstrate the manner in which these standards would be interpreted:

Example 1. X corporation is incorporated in State A and has its only warehouse, only manufacturing plant and only office in that state. X's only business is selling products throughout the United States and Canada through mail order catalogs. X annually mails catalogs and order forms from its office to residents of most states and several provinces of Canada. All orders are filled at and products shipped from X's warehouse to customers throughout the United States and Canada. All the products shipped are manufactured by X at its plant in State A. These activities are X's sole source of revenues.

Question. Is X deriving more than 80 percent of its gross revenues from the "operation of a business or . . . rendering of services" within State A?

Interpretive Response. Yes, this aspect of the "doing business within" standard is satisfied.

Example 2. Assume the same facts as Example 1, except that X has no manufacturing plant and purchases the products it sells from corporations located in other states.

Question. Is X deriving more than 80 percent of its gross revenues from the "operation of a business or . . . rendering of services" within State A?

Interpretive Response. Yes, this aspect of the "doing business within" standard is satisfied.

* * *

6.   Offerees and Purchasers: Persons Resident—Rule 147(d)

Paragraph (d) of the rule provides that offers and sales may be made only to persons resident within the state or territory. An individual offeree or purchaser of any part of an issue would be deemed to be a person resident within the state or territory if such person has his principal residence in the state or territory. Temporary residence, such as that of many persons in the military service, would not satisfy the provisions of paragraph (d). In addition, if a person purchases securities on behalf of other persons, the residence of those persons must satisfy paragraph (d). If the offeree or purchaser is a business organization its residence will be deemed the state or territory in which it has its principal office, unless it is an entity organized for the specific purpose of acquiring securities in the offering, in which case it will be deemed to be a resident of a state only if all of the beneficial owners of interests in such entity are residents of the state.

As initially proposed, subparagraph (d)(2) provided that an individual, in order to be deemed a resident, must have his principal residence in the state and must not have any present intention of moving his principal residence to another state. The Commission believes that it would be difficult to determine a person's intentions, and accordingly, has deleted the latter requirement. In addition, as initially proposed, the rule would have deemed the residence of a business organization to be the state in which it was incorporated or otherwise organized. The Commission believes that the location of a company's principal office is more of an indication of its local character for purposes of the offeree residence provision of the rule than is its state of incorporation. Section 3(a)(11) requires that an issuer corporation be incorporated within the state, but there is no similar requirement in the statute for a corporation that is an offeree or purchaser.

7. Limitations on Resales—Rule 147(e)

Paragraph (e) of the rule provides that during the period in which securities that are part of an issue are being offered and sold and for a period of nine months from the date of the last sale by the issuer of any part of the issue, resales of any part of the issue by any person shall be made only to persons resident within the same state or territory. This provides objective standards for determining when an issue "comes to rest." The rule as initially proposed limited both reoffers and resales during a twelve month period after the last sale by the issuer of any part of the issue. However, the Commission believes that it would be difficult for an issuer to prohibit or even learn of reoffers. Thus, the limitation on reoffers would be impractical because, if any purchaser made a reoffer outside of such state or territory, the issuer would lose the exemption provided by the rule. In addition, the Commission determined that a shorter period would satisfy the coming to rest test for purposes of the rule. Thus, the twelve month period has been reduced to nine months.

Persons who acquire securities from issuers in transactions complying with the rule would acquire unregistered securities that could only be reoffered and resold pursuant to an exemption from the registration provisions of the Act. . . .

8. Precautions Against Interstate Offers and Sales—Rule 147(f)

Paragraph (f) of the rule requires issuers to take steps to preserve the exemption provided by the rule, since any resale of any part of the issue before it comes to rest within the state to persons resident in another state or territory will, under the Act, be in violation of Section 5. The required steps are: (i) placing a legend on the certificate or other document evidencing the security stating that the securities have not been registered under the Act and setting forth the limitations on resale contained in paragraph (e); (ii) issuing stop transfer instructions to the issuer's transfer agent, if any, with respect to the securities, or, if the issuer transfers its own securities, making a notation in the appropriate records of the issuer; and (iii) obtaining a written representation from each purchaser as to his residence. Where persons other than the issuer are reselling securities of the issuer during the time period specified in paragraph (e) of the rule, the issuer would, if the securities are presented for transfer, be required to take steps (i) and (ii). In addition, the rule requires that the issuer disclose in writing the limitations on resale imposed by paragraph (e) and the provisions of subsections (f)(1)(i) and (ii) and subparagraph (f)(2).

Operation of Rule 147

Rule 147 will operate prospectively only. The staff will issue interpretative letters to assist persons in complying with the rule, but will consider requests for "no action" letters on transactions in reliance on Section 3(a)(11) outside the rule only on an infrequent basis and in the most compelling circumstances.

The rule is a nonexclusive rule. However, persons who choose to rely on Section 3(a)(11) without complying with all the conditions of the rule would have the burden of establishing that they have complied with the judicial and administrative interpretations of Section 3(a)(11) in effect at the time of the offering. The Commission also emphasizes that the exemption provided by Section 3(a)(11) is not an exemption from the civil liability provisions of Section 12[a](2) or the anti-fraud provisions of Section 17 of the Act or of Section 10(b) of the Securities Exchange Act of 1934. The Commission further emphasizes that Rule 147 is available only for transactions by issuers and is not available for secondary offerings.

In view of the objectives and policies underlying the Act, the rule would not be available to any person with respect to any offering which, although in technical compliance with the provisions of the rule, is part of a plan or scheme by such person to make interstate offers or sales of securities. In such cases, registration would be required. In addition, any plan or scheme that involves a series of offerings by affiliated organizations in various states, even if in technical compliance with the rule, may be outside the parameters of the rule and of Section 3(a)(11) if what is being financed is in effect a single business enterprise.

* * *

HYPOTHETICAL NINETEEN

1.   Trendy sells $20 million of common stock in an intrastate offering solely to California residents. Incorporated and headquartered in California, Trendy plans to use the proceeds to finance additional drink-related research and development at its lab located in Berkeley, CA. Research expenditures typically include purchasing a large amount of raw materials from around the globe (e.g., exotic plant roots, etc. to use in formulating new drinks). Assume that at least

50% of the proceeds will be used to purchase these raw materials for use in the Berkeley lab. Does the offering comply with Rule 147?

2. What if Trendy, in conducting the $20 million intrastate offering, circulates an offering memorandum rife with inaccuracies relating to the background of Trendy's officers and directors?

3. Kim, the CEO of Trendy, is also its largest shareholder. Kim decides to cash out some of her holdings. If Kim were simply to sell her securities through a broker into the national securities markets, she would run afoul of § 5. Instead, Kim seeks to sell her securities in a broad-based offering solely to residents of California using ads placed in the *Los Angeles Times*. Would this offering be covered by Rule 147?

4. George, a purchaser of the securities in Trendy's California intrastate offering, suddenly finds out that he needs a new car three months after making his investment. George liquidates his Trendy holdings (his only liquid asset) to purchase the car, selling the securities to his brother-in-law in New York.

5. In conducting an intrastate offering under Rule 147, Trendy makes a mistake. It fails to check for the residency of one out of 500 investors in its offerings. As it turns out, the one investor recently moved to Arizona. Does Trendy's offering still qualify under Rule 147?

VI. REGULATION S

Up to now, we have focused on domestic issuers and investors. The United States, of course, is only one among over a hundred countries with an organized securities market. Securities transactions may take place across a number of different countries. Imagine a German investor purchasing the securities of a Japanese corporation through a transaction on the New York Stock Exchange. Or, alternatively, investors located in Iowa may go onto the Internet and purchase shares in an Italian corporation on the London Stock Exchange.

When a securities transaction cuts across national borders, which country should regulate that transaction? Presently, each country decides for itself whether to apply its securities laws to a transaction. Germany may choose to regulate in order to protect investors residing in Germany. Similarly, the United States may intervene to protect the integrity of the U.S. capital markets. If multiple countries intervene to regulate the same transaction, problems may arise. Issuers and others participating in the offering face potentially duplicative regulation, raising costs without increasing the level of protections for investors. Worse yet, some regulations may conflict. One country may require issuers to disclose certain types of information while another country may impose a "quiet period."

For primary offerings of securities, the United States follows a largely territorial approach to regulation. Section 5 covers all transactions involving an offer or sale of securities through interstate commerce. Arguably, a transaction completely outside the United States, and therefore not involving interstate commerce, will not implicate § 5. But the reach of the definition of interstate commerce is broad. Suppose an issuer in France selling securities to investors located in Paris advertises the offering in a French newspaper. The French newspaper is distributed in France, but is also sold in the United States. The distribution of the ad through the circulation of the French newspaper into the United States implicates interstate commerce and therefore § 5.

Even if § 5 does apply to a transaction taking place outside the United States, the SEC provides an exemption under Regulation S of the Securities Act (Rules 901 to 905). Consider the merits of taking an expansive (or narrow) view of the reach of U.S. securities laws. What would be wrong with applying the U.S. regime to securities transactions taking place in France, Japan, and Brazil if investors in the U.S. are affected by such transactions?

A.   BASIC REGULATION S REQUIREMENTS   *Rule 901 S - outside the US.*

Regulation S exempts certain "offshore" offers and sales from § 5. Exemption from § 5 does not exempt issuers or securities transactions from the entire scope of U.S. securities regulation. An exemption from § 5 frees the issuers from the gun-jumping rules and the heightened public offering antifraud provisions of §§ 11 and 12(a)(2), but it does not exempt the issuer from, among other regulations, Rule 10b–5 antifraud liability.* Whether Rule 10b–5 applies to transactions occurring outside the United States depends on the application of the judicially created conduct and effects doctrine. Under the conduct test, the extraterritorial application of Rule 10b–5 turns on whether the defendants engaged in significant conduct related to the fraud inside the United States. The effects test focuses on the presence of a substantial impact from the fraud on U.S. markets and investors.

[Margin notes: Exempt - frees the issuers from the gun-jumping rules - heightened public offering antifraud 11/12(a)(2). Does not exempt 10b-5. Conduct Test: extraterritorial application of 10b-5 turns on whether D's engaged in significant conduct related to fraud inside U. Effect test: Presence of a substantial impact from fraud on U.S markets and investors.]

Rule 901 of Regulation S provides the actual exemption from § 5, exempting offers and sales to the extent they are "outside the United States." Whether a securities transaction is considered as outside the United States depends on whether the transaction falls under one of the three categories of exempt offerings provided under Regulation S, termed Category 1, 2, and 3 offerings. The SEC explains its approach:

> The Regulation adopted today is based on a territorial approach to Section 5 of the Securities Act. The registration of securities is intended to protect the U.S. capital markets and investors purchasing in the U.S. market. Principles of comity and the reasonable expectations of participants in the global markets justify reliance on laws applicable in jurisdictions outside the United States to define requirements for transactions effected offshore. The territorial approach recognizes the primacy of the laws in which a market is located. As investors choose

[Margin note: Territorial Approach]

---

* Arguably, under *Gustafson v. Alloyd Holding*, 513 U.S. 561 (1995), § 12(a)(2) also applies to an unregistered public offering. If so, then Regulation S does not protect issuers engaged in public offerings abroad from § 12(a)(2) liability.

their markets, they choose the laws and regulations applicable in such markets.

Offshore Offers and Sales, Securities Act Release No. 6863 (1990).

As with many of the other provisions contained in the Securities Act, many of the nuances of Regulation S are found in its definitional provisions, Rule 902. We list key defined terms and their associated Rule 902 provision below:

Designated Offshore Securities Market—Rule 902(b)

Directed Selling Efforts—Rule 902(c)

Distributor—Rule 902(d)

Distribution Compliance Period—Rule 902(f)

Offering Restrictions—Rule 902(g)

Offshore Transaction—Rule 902(h)

Substantial U.S. Market Interest—Rule 902(j)

U.S. Person—Rule 902(k)

Two basic requirements are imposed on all three offering categories. All offerings must take place through an "offshore transaction" and involve no "directed selling efforts" into the U.S. Consider each requirement in turn.

1. OFFSHORE TRANSACTION

Offshore transactions involve transactions where offers are not made to a "person in the United States" (see Rule 902(h)). Geography is key to an offshore transaction. A person may be a U.S. citizen or resident, but if she receives an offer while on vacation in Bangalore, this qualifies as an offer outside the United States. Not only must offers take place outside the United States, the actual purchase transaction must occur offshore as well. Rule 902(h) provides two alternative means for the purchase transaction to qualify as an offshore transaction. First, the buyer is "outside the United States or the seller and any person acting on its behalf reasonably believe that the buyer is outside the United States" at the time of origination of the buy order. Alternatively, the transaction is executed in a "designated offshore securities market," and neither the seller nor anyone acting on behalf of the seller knows that the transaction was prearranged with a U.S. buyer.

The offshore transaction requirement embodies the focus of Regulation S on territoriality. As a necessary (but not sufficient) condition of obtaining the Regulation S exemption, either specific evidence must exist that the buyer is actually outside the U.S. at the time of the buy order or the transaction is executed in a designated offshore securities market. The SEC explains the emphasis on the buyer's location:

[T]he location of the buyer overseas clearly and objectively provides evidence of the offshore nature of the transaction. The requirement that the buyer itself, rather than its agent, be outside the United States reduces evidentiary difficulties and problems in administering the Regulation, both for regulators and private parties attempting to ensure compliance with the conditions of the safe harbor. Second, the buyer's location outside the United States supports the expectation that the buyer is or should be aware that the transaction is not subject to registration under the Securities Act.

Securities Act Release No. 6863 (April 24, 1990).

Under Rule 902(b), the SEC may label a foreign securities market (exchange or non-exchange market) as a designated offshore securities market. Designated offshore securities markets include the London Stock Exchange, the Frankfurt Stock Exchange, and the Tokyo Stock Exchange, among many others. The SEC frequently adds new securities exchanges to the list of designated offshore securities market. In 2003, for example, the SEC labeled the Cairo and Alexandria Stock Exchanges of Egypt as designated offshore securities markets. Among factors the SEC considers in providing such a designation are: foreign law, the "community" of brokers, dealers, and other securities professionals and their operating history within the country, government and self-regulatory oversight, and the presence of an organized clearance and settlement system.

The SEC explains its rationale for using the execution of a trade on a designated offshore securities market as a proxy for an offshore transaction by stating:

> Such execution of a transaction in a foreign marketplace provides objective evidence of the foreign locus of the transaction. Moreover, buyers in such markets may be presumed to rely on the regulatory protections afforded by local law and not U.S. registration requirements.

Securities Act Release No. 6863 (April 24, 1990).

HYPOTHETICAL TWENTY

Suppose that Trendy Inc. (a U.S.-incorporated issuer) is still searching for new sources of capital. Trendy has already engaged in a series of private placements as well as an intrastate offering. The prior financing has helped launch Trendy's marketing campaign for the Lean Green drink. Now, Trendy wants to expand Lean Green internationally (first throughout North America and then into Europe and Asia). Kim, the CEO of Trendy, worries that Trendy may have exhausted the supply of potential private placement and intrastate offering investors in the United States. Instead, Kim wants to sell Trendy common stock in a series of public offerings in Germany and France. Kim hopes to conduct the offerings pursuant to Regulation S. Which of the following are "offshore" transactions?

1. *Scenario One*: Trendy, Inc. offers and sells securities to investors in Topeka, Kansas.

2. *Scenario Two*: Trendy makes all offers and sales to German citizens in Germany.

3. *Scenario Three*: Trendy attempts to make all offers and sales to German citizens in Germany. United States citizens from Kansas vacationing in Hamburg, Germany, however, happen to obtain and read some of the offering documents. The Kansas investors purchase securities directly from German distributors working on behalf of Trendy while they are still in Germany.

4. *Scenario Four*: Investors in Kansas decide to purchase securities in Trendy, Inc. after tasting the Lean Green drink. They instruct their broker to purchase common shares. The broker, unknown to the investors, executes the orders through the Frankfurt Stock Exchange. Among the Trendy securities purchased are securities recently sold by Trendy into the German market pursuant to Regulation S.

5. *Scenario Five*: Same facts as Scenario Four, but the order is executed on the Korea Stock Exchange.

2.   NO DIRECTED SELLING EFFORTS

For securities sold through Regulation S, Rule 902(c) defines "directed selling efforts" as "any activity undertaken for the purpose of, or that could reasonably be expected to have the effect of conditioning the market." Rule 902(c) provides that conditioning the market includes "placing an advertisement in a publication 'with a general circulation in the United States' that refers to the offering of securities being made in reliance upon this Regulation S." Publications with general circulation include "any publication that is printed primarily for distribution in the United States" or had an average circulation in the U.S. of 15,000 or more copies per issue for the preceding twelve months.

In considering the scope of Rule 902(c), recall the broad definition given to "conditioning the market" in the gun-jumping rules (see Chapter 7). Efforts designed to raise investor interest in the issuer, even if they do not mention the issuer or offering explicitly (but instead discuss the general industry and mention the underwriter for example) may be considered as conditioning the market. In addition, the SEC takes a dim view of references to forward-looking information, including earnings projections, treating such non-"factual" disclosures as likely to condition the market. Although the SEC's 2005 Public Offering Reforms provide various exemptions and safe harbors for communications from treatment as an "offer" or "prospectus" during the public offering process, the SEC continues to maintain a broad view of "conditioning the market."

Several forms of communications are excluded from the definition of directed selling efforts. Among the excluded communications are advertisements required to be published under U.S. or foreign law (or pursuant to the rules of a self-regulatory organization such as the NYSE), provided that the advertisements include no more information than legally required and provide a boilerplate statement that the securities may not be offered or sold in the U.S. (or to a U.S. person, if the offering is under Category 2 or 3). Rule 902(c)(3)(ii) also provides that a tombstone advertisement of the offering (with very limited information disclosure) in a publication with general circulation in the U.S. will not count as a directed selling effort.

The SEC provides the following guidance for companies on disclosure directed into the U.S. during a Regulation S offering:

> An isolated, limited contact with the United States generally will not constitute directed selling efforts that result in a loss of the safe harbor for the entire offering. The Regulation likewise is not intended to inhibit routine activities conducted in the United States for purposes other than inducing the purchase or sale of the securities being distributed abroad, such as routine advertising and corporate communications. The dissemination of routine information of the character and content normally published by a company, and unrelated to a securities selling effort, generally would not be directed selling efforts under the Regulation. For example, press releases regarding the financial results of the issuer or the occurrence of material events with respect to the issuer generally will not be deemed to be "directed selling efforts."

> Similarly, the Regulation is not intended to limit or interfere with news stories or other bona fide journalistic activities, or otherwise hinder the flow of normal corporate news regarding foreign issuers. Access by journalists for publications with a general circulation in the United States to offshore press conferences, press releases and meetings with company press spokespersons in which an offshore offering or tender offer is discussed need not be limited where the information is made available to the foreign and U.S. press generally and is not intended to induce purchases of securities by persons in the United States or tenders of securities by U.S. holders in the case of exchange offers.

Securities Act Release No. 6863 (April 24, 1990).

HYPOTHETICAL TWENTY-ONE

Trendy is moving forward with a Regulation S offering of its common stock in Germany. Consider the following communications from Trendy and whether they may be considered as directed selling efforts into the United States.

1. Trendy takes out an advertisement in the *Wall Street Journal* that has the following statement:

> Trendy is a worldwide leader in the alternative drink market. Trendy's Lean Green drink both refreshes the soul and helps line the pockets of Trendy's investors. We project increasing long-term profits (at over a 25% annual rate of growth) for Trendy's investors over the next ten years. To be a Trendy investor is to be a well-satisfied investor.

2. Trendy advertises the offering in the European edition of the *Investor Times*. The U.S. edition of the *Investor Times* does not include the Trendy advertisement. Some copies of the European edition, however (representing less than 1% of the circulation of the European edition) inevitably make their way into the United States in the hands of business travelers flying into the U.S. from Europe.

3.   Trendy advertises the offering on a German-based Internet site devoted to providing investors in Germany with information on offerings in Germany. The Internet site is in German. Investors in the U.S. can find the website (and translate the contents badly into English using an Internet-based auto-translation service).

B.   CATEGORIES OF REGULATION S OFFERINGS

Whether an offering is considered as outside the United States depends on whether the offering falls under one of the three categories of exempt offerings provided in Regulation S. In broad terms, the three categories are divided based on the risk that an offering will (a) catch the initial interest of investors in the U.S. and (b) result in eventual flowback of the securities into the U.S. securities markets.

1.   CATEGORY 1 (RULE 903(b)(1))

Category 1 offerings face the fewest restrictions under Regulation S. Issuers eligible for a Category 1 offering only need to meet the basic offshore transaction and no directed selling efforts requirements to qualify for the exemption. The SEC believes that Category 1 offerings pose the least risk of generating U.S. interest in the offering or flowback of securities into the U.S.

Several types of offerings qualify as Category 1 offerings. Consider the two most important types of Category 1 offerings. First, offerings involving *foreign* issuers that reasonably believe at the start of the offering that "no substantial U.S. market interest" exists in the class of securities offered or sold qualify as Category 1 offerings.

Rule 902(j) defines the term "substantial U.S. market interest." For equity securities, a substantial U.S. market interest exists if the securities exchanges and inter-dealer quotation systems in the U.S. in aggregate represent the single largest market for the class of securities measured for a period defined as "the shorter of the issuer's prior fiscal year or the period since the issuer's incorporation." Substantial U.S. market interest also exists if 20% or more of all trading in the class of equity securities took place in the United States (in a securities exchange or inter-dealer quotation systems) and less than 55% of trading took place in a securities market of a single foreign country for the same period of time.

Second, securities sold through an "overseas directed offering" may also qualify as a Category 1 offering. Among other types of offerings, overseas-directed offerings include offerings by a *foreign* issuer into a single foreign country to the residents of that country. Domestic issuers may qualify for a Category 1 offering only if they sell non-convertible debt securities, denominated in a foreign currency, through an overseas directed offering. The direct offering must comply with local laws, customary practices, and document requirements of the single foreign country (see Rule 903(b)(1)(ii)).

(margin handwritten notes)
2 prons.
category I
off shore
US residents
foreigners
US

1. No substantial US. market Interest

substan market interest for equity

2. Overseas directed offering

A common feature of these two offerings is the low likelihood that securities will flow from their initial overseas marketplace back into the United States. If no substantial interest exists in the U.S. for the securities, investors seeking to sell securities into the U.S. will face low liquidity and large price discounts from those few investors willing to purchase the securities. Thus, flowback is likely to be minimal. Similarly, if the securities are sold in a directed manner into one market to foreign residents, an active trading market will likely arise (or may already exist) in that foreign market. Liquidity begets liquidity; because investors seek liquidity for their trades, investors will gravitate toward this foreign marketplace.

HYPOTHETICAL TWENTY-TWO

1. Trendy is incorporated in the U.S. and conducts most of its business in the U.S. Assume nonetheless that the secondary market with the highest volume for Trendy's common stock is the Frankfurt Stock Exchange. Over 90% of the secondary market transactions in Trendy common stock take place in the Frankfurt Stock Exchange. Trendy seeks to raise additional capital through a Regulation S offering in Europe of common stock. Does Trendy qualify for Category 1?

2. What if Bland, Inc., Trendy's major European competitor based in London, makes an offering of common stock entirely in Japan conforming to Japanese securities laws? Bland's major secondary market is the NYSE with over 80% of stock trading taking place there. Does Bland qualify for Category 1?

2. CATEGORY 2 OFFERINGS (RULE 903(b)(2))   *Substantial Market Interest*

For companies with a substantial U.S. market interest that want to sell their securities in more than one country, most offerings of domestic and foreign issuers fall into Category 2 or 3. Whether an offering is eligible for Category 2 depends on three factors: (a) foreign or domestic U.S. issuer; (b) Exchange Act reporting issuer or not; and (c) debt or equity offering.

Foreign issuers present less risk that an offering of securities outside the United States will flow back to the U.S. or otherwise affect U.S. capital markets or investors. More information is generally available on an Exchange Act reporting issuer, reducing the harm to investors if flowback to the U.S. does occur. On the other hand, Exchange Act reporting status means that a secondary market for the issuer's shares exists in the U.S., heightening the risk of flowback into the U.S. and the impact from any fraud in the offering on U.S. markets, even if the fraud occurs overseas. Finally, debt securities pose less risk to investors. Because the returns from debt investments are more predictable than equity, the harm to investors from the lack of information provided by registration, even for securities that eventually flow back into the U.S., is diminished.

Foreign - less risk

Ex Act. reporting issuer - good.

Debt better than equity

Combining these three factors, the following table details the eligibility for Category 2 status for those offerings that cannot qualify under Category 1. Category 3 acts as a catchall. Offerings that fail to meet either Category 1 or 2 are automatically considered Category 3 offerings:

	Exchange Act reporting issuer	Non–Exchange Act reporting issuer
Foreign issuer	Equity—Category 2	Equity—Category 3
	Debt—Category 2	Debt—Category 2
Domestic issuer	Equity—Category 3	Equity—Category 3
	Debt—Category 2	Debt—Category 3

Note that domestic issuers are only eligible for Category 2 if they are an Exchange Act reporting issuer *and* making a debt offering abroad.

Category 2 issuers must meet several requirements. Key to the duration of these requirements is the "distribution compliance period." Rule 902(f) defines the distribution compliance period as commencing from the *later* of: (a) when securities are first offered pursuant to Regulation S to persons other than distributors; or (b) the date the offering closes. All offers and sales by a distributor of securities from an unsold allotment or subscription are also deemed, regardless of timing, as occurring during the distribution compliance period.

As with Category 1 offerings, Category 2 offerings must comply with the basic offshore offering and no directed selling efforts requirements. In addition to the basic requirements, Category 2 offerings must also comply with "transactional restrictions" for a 40–day distribution compliance period. Under the transactional restrictions, offers and sales may not be made to a U.S. person or for the account or benefit of a U.S. person. Distributors are excluded from this prohibition, allowing sales to U.S.-based distributors. Rule 902(d) defines a distributor as:

> any underwriter, dealer, or other person who participates, pursuant to a contractual arrangement, in the distribution of the securities offered or sold in reliance on this Regulation S

If a distributor sells securities to another distributor, dealer, or person receiving a selling concession, the distributor must send notice to the purchaser that the purchaser is under the same restrictions on offers that apply to the selling distributor.

"U.S. Person" is defined in Rule 902(k). Consider the interaction of the "U.S. Person" definition with the definition of an offshore transaction discussed above. The offshore transaction definition focuses on, among other things, offers "not made to a person in the United States." See Rule 902(h). Whether a person is "in the United States" for purposes of an offshore transaction is defined by a person's actions (i.e., whether they physically leave the U.S.). A U.S. Person by contrast, is defined by status (i.e., whether a person is a resident of the United States). Thus, an issuer (or distributor) making a Category 2 offering could not offer or sell securities to an investor resident in Kansas who happens to be in Germany. Although the investor would not be in the United States, the investor would still be a U.S. Person.

Transactional Restrictions

- *Offers and sales May not be made to a U.S. person.*
- *Distributors (underwriter, dealer) are excluded*

category 2. foreigners US resident US resident or a citizen

To enhance compliance with the transactional restrictions, Category 2 offerings must also comply with "offering restrictions." Rule 902(g) defines the required offering restrictions. First, the offering restrictions apply for the duration of the 40–day distribution compliance period.

offering Restrictions
1. 40 days distribution compliance period
2. Restrictions on distributors

Second, the offering restrictions require that distributors agree in writing that all offers and sales during the distribution compliance period will occur through exempt transactions under Regulation S, some other exemption from registration, or through a registered offering under § 5. Distributors must also agree not to engage in hedging transactions for the duration of the distribution compliance period. Hedging transactions are contemporaneous transactions designed to shift the economic risk of owner-ship of Regulation S offered securities into the United States while formally keeping ownership outside the United States. For example, U.S. investors could engage in an equity swap with foreign holders of a Regulation S-offered security. Under the swap, the foreign investors would maintain formal ownership of the Regulation S security but receive a return based on some other security (or basket of securities such as the S & P 500 index). The U.S. investor, in turn, would receive the return from ownership of the Regulation S security and owe the foreign investors the return on the other security or basket of securities. If allowed, such hedging transac-tions would result in the flowback of the economic risk of ownership of Regulation S securities into the United States.

Third, the offering restrictions require that a disclaimer on various offering documents state that the securities are unregistered and may not be offered or sold in the United States or to a U.S. person except through an exemption from registration, such as Regulation S, or registration under § 5. Among documents that must include the required statement are the offering prospectus (cover or inside cover page) and advertisements for the offering.

3. Disclaimers

HYPOTHETICAL TWENTY-THREE

Bland, Inc. (Trendy's London-based competitor) is an Exchange Act report-ing company whose major secondary market is the New York Stock Exchange. Bland hires Morimoto Securities located in Tokyo as its placement agent. Under their agreement, Morimoto Securities will first purchase the shares from Bland at a discount and resell the shares to investors in a firm commitment offering. Morimoto plans to offer the stock throughout Asia, selling to both securities dealers and to a few select institutional investors. Suppose that the offering commences on June 1 when Morimoto purchases 10 million shares of Bland common stock. Morimoto begins offers to investors on June 2, selling the shares over a period of three weeks.

1. *Scenario One*: Morimoto Securities offers and sells common stock to inves-tors throughout Asia. For which category of Regulation S offering do the offers and sales qualify?

2. *Scenario Two*: Morimoto Securities sells securities in Bland's offering to the fabulously wealthy Mr. Gates (a resident of Seattle and former chairman of a major U.S. investment bank) who happens to be visiting in Japan during the offering and purchases Bland stock while still in Japan.

3. *Scenario Three*: Bland instead sells securities through Morimoto Securities to a Japanese incorporated entity, Bland Investor Ltd. Bland Investor was incorporated a month prior to the offering. Bland Investor has only one shareholder, the fabulously wealthy Mr. Gates.

3.   CATEGORY 3 OFFERINGS (RULE 903(b)(3))

Category 3 offerings provide a catchall form of Regulation S offering for issuers unable to qualify for the other two categories of offerings. U.S. issuers seeking to sell equity fall under Category 3 regardless of their Exchange Act reporting status. Non–Exchange Act reporting foreign issuers selling equity securities also fall under Category 3 if they cannot qualify under Category 1.

Category 3 securities represent the greatest risk of flowback into the United States. Flowback risk derives from securities that (a) are more likely to gravitate to the U.S. market (due, for example, to the predominance of U.S. issuers in Category 3) and/or (b) pose greater potential harm to investors (due to the lack of information on non-Exchange Act reporting issuers). Accordingly, Regulation S places greater restrictions on Category 3 offerings.

As with Category 1 and 2 offerings, issuers eligible for a Category 3 offering must comply with the offshore offering and no directed selling efforts basic requirements. In addition to the two basic requirements, Regulation S imposes on Category 3 offerings the same offering restrictions as Category 2. The distribution compliance period differs, however. For offerings of debt securities, the offering restrictions extend for the same 40–day distribution compliance period as Category 2, but for equity offerings, the offering restrictions apply for a one-year distribution compliance period.

Category 3 offerings then face additional requirements depending on whether the offering involves debt or equity securities. Debt securities face fewer restrictions for a shorter period because the risk of flowback is lower for the primarily institutional debt market. Three transactional restrictions apply to debt securities during the 40–day distribution compliance period. First, offers and sales must not be made to a U.S. person or for the account or benefit of a U.S. person. Second, in transactions where a distributor sells securities to another distributor, dealer, or person receiving a selling concession, the distributor must send notice to the purchaser that the purchaser is under the same restrictions and offers that apply to the selling distributor. Lastly, the debt securities must be in the form of a temporary global security. The issuer may not exchange the temporary global security for definitive securities until after the expiration of the 40–day compliance period. The issuer is also prohibited from making the exchange for a definitive security unless the requesting investor (excluding distributors) certifies that he/she is either not a U.S. person or that he/she purchased the securities through a transaction exempt from the registration requirements of § 5.

In the case of equity securities, several transactional restrictions apply during the one-year distribution compliance period. First, offers and sales may not be made to a U.S. person or for the account or benefit of a U.S. person. Second, in transactions in which a distributor sells securities to another distributor, dealer, or person receiving a selling concession, the distributor must send notice to the purchaser that the purchaser is under the same restrictions and offers that apply to the selling distributor. Finally, offers and sales made prior to the expiration of the distribution compliance period must meet several additional requirements:

Purchaser Certification (Rule 903(b)(3)(iii)(B)(1)). The purchaser of the Regulation S securities (excluding a distributor) must make a certification that the purchaser is not a U.S. person and is not acquiring the securities for the account of a U.S. person. Alternatively, the purchaser may certify that the purchase occurred through a transaction exempt from the registration requirements.

Purchaser Contract Obligations (Rule 903(b)(3)(iii)(B)(2)). The issuer is required to obtain the purchaser's contractual consent to various purchaser restrictions. Purchasers must agree to resell any purchased Category 3 securities only in accordance with Regulation S, some other exemption from registration, or through registration under § 5. Purchasers also must agree not to engage in any hedging transactions with the Regulation S securities unless in compliance with the Securities Act.

Legend (Rule 903(b)(3)(iii)(B)(3)). The issuers must place a legend on the securities stating that the securities may be transferred only under the resale provisions of Regulation S, some other exemption from registration, or registration under § 5. The legend must also state that hedging transactions may not take place unless in compliance with the Securities Act. Many foreign stock exchanges will not allow listing of securities with a legend restricting the transferability of such securities.

Transfer Restrictions (Rule 903(b)(3)(iii)(B)(4)). Issuers must agree (either by contract or within the corporate charter or bylaws) to not register the transfer of securities that take place outside the scope of Regulation S, some other exemption to registration, or a registered offering under § 5. If foreign law prohibits issuers from refusing to register a transfer of securities, among other situations, issuers may opt instead to implement alternative procedures to protect against prohibited resales (including the legend as detailed in Rule 903(b)(3)(iii)(B)(3)).

HYPOTHETICAL TWENTY-FOUR

For the following problems, assume that Trendy is an Exchange Act reporting company whose major secondary market is the New York Stock

Exchange. Trendy hires Sprout Securities located in Brussels as its placement agent. Under their agreement, Sprout Securities will not purchase the shares from Trendy but instead act as a selling agent using its best efforts (and taking a hefty commission). Sprout plans on offering the stock throughout Europe through sales to both securities dealers and to a few select institutional investors. Suppose that the offering commences on June 1 for 10 million shares of Trendy Inc. Sprout Securities immediately places 5 million of the shares. The other 5 million, however, are more difficult to place. The offering finally closes (with all the shares sold) on July 1.

1. Sprout offers and sells common stock to investors throughout Europe. For which category of Regulation S does this offering qualify?

2. Lexa, an investor living in Germany, purchased shares directly from Sprout Securities on June 1. Lexa holds the securities only for a week and then sells them back to Sprout (acting as a market maker for Trendy's common stock). Sprout Securities then turns around and sells the securities to Kon Sik, an investor living in Korea on July 10.

3. As part of Trendy's offering of common stock in Brussels, Sprout Securities advertises the offering throughout Belgium. Sales are made to all manner of investors, including mailroom clerks, chow delivery foremen and secretaries. Trendy raises $20 million from the offering. Assuming Regulation S applies, is this legal under the federal securities laws?

C.   INTEGRATION

Despite the availability of Regulation S, U.S. issuers face substantial costs when raising capital abroad. Not only are the transaction costs (such as international travel and communication) higher, but the issuer also faces a new array of laws for each country where securities are offered and sold. U.S. issuers will therefore be selective in raising capital abroad. For example, a U.S. issuer with a significant business presence in another country may offer and sell securities in that country to build loyalty among investor-customers and to gain greater influence over government regulators.

U.S. issuers may also sell securities abroad when the size of the offering exceeds the ability of the U.S. capital market to absorb easily the size of the offering. In such cases, the issuer may have a U.S. tranche (typically under Regulation D) and a series of other tranches of securities for different countries under Regulation S. Typically, the different tranches are offered at the same time.

When an issuer offers the same securities, for the same consideration (usually cash), at about the same period of time, with the same general purpose and plan of financing, the issuer must worry about the possibility that the different tranches will be integrated. Integration of the Regulation D offering (consisting of sales to U.S. investors) with the Regulation S tranches will result in a loss of the Regulation S exemption. Likewise, the presence of unsophisticated investors (and possibly general solicitation) in the offshore tranche will destroy the Regulation D exemption.

The SEC provides comfort to issuers worried about the integration problem. Rather than establish a safe harbor against integration, the SEC went one step further. The SEC simply stated that integration would not occur:

> Offshore transactions made in compliance with Regulation S will not be integrated with registered domestic offerings or domestic offerings that satisfy the requirements for an exemption from registration under the Securities Act, even if undertaken contemporaneously. Resales of securities offered and sold in offshore transactions pursuant to Rule 144A [discussed in Chapter 10] are consistent with Rule 904. Of course, the securities sold pursuant to Rule 144A would be restricted securities.

Further than a safe-harbor

Securities Act Release No. 6863 (April 24, 1990).

D.   RESALES

As we will discuss in Chapter 10, resales after an exempt transaction are not necessarily exempt from § 5. Investors reselling soon after the exempt offering run the risk of being classified as underwriters. Investors who are deemed "underwriters" are considered part of the issuer's primary transaction and therefore cannot qualify for the § 4(1) exemption from § 5.

Rule 905 of the Securities Act makes clear that equity securities of domestic U.S. issuers acquired from the issuer, a distributor in the offering or an affiliate in a transaction covered under Rule 901 or 903 are "restricted securities" as provided for in Rule 144. Rule 905 further specifies that the securities remain restricted securities even if acquired through an exempt resale pursuant to Rule 901 or Rule 904. Because of the restricted status of Regulation S securities, investors cannot resell equity securities of domestic issuers without an exemption from § 5 (such as Rule 144) or registration under § 5.

901/903 restricted sec.

Restriction on resale

Promulgated in 1998, Rule 905 closed off an interpretation of Regulation S commonly held in the securities industry. Many believed that purchasers of securities sold in a Regulation S offering could freely resell the securities back into the U.S. after the distribution compliance period. Prior to the reforms in 1998, the distribution compliance period for equity securities (even those of domestic issuers) was only 40 days. The combination of a short distribution compliance period combined with a belief that resales could commence after the expiration of the period led to rapid resales of Regulation S securities back into the U.S. The SEC ultimately adopted Rule 905 to stop such resales, at least for equity securities of domestic issuers. What is less clear is what happens for resales of securities sold by foreign issuers and debt securities of domestic issuers. After the distribution compliance period, may investors resell these securities into the United States? Even after a 40–day distribution compliance period, as in the case of an Exchange Act reporting foreign issuer selling equity securities?

An important point of debate surrounding the promulgation of Rule 905 was whether restricted status should extend to the equity securities of foreign issuers:

> The commenters also noted that if equity securities issued by these foreign companies are deemed restricted securities, the issuers in essence would be applying to their offshore offerings many of the standard practices used in U.S. private placements. The certification and purchaser agreement requirements would impose a significant burden on foreign issuers that wish to conduct public offerings in their home jurisdictions. In addition, many foreign stock exchanges will not permit trading of legended securities. The commenters asserted that the legending and stop transfer restrictions, as well as to a lesser extent the disclosure and certification requirements that would be imposed by the rule, would impede both public offerings and trading in those securities on offshore public markets that do not accept legended stock for trading. As a result, the classification of foreign equity securities as "restricted" could create a strong disincentive for foreign companies to list their securities on U.S. markets.

Securities Act Release No. 7505 (February 17, 1998).

Rule 904 provides a special resale provision for Regulation S securities. First, Rule 904 specifies a class of person who may use Rule 904's resale exemption. This class includes "any person other than the issuer, a distributor, any of their respective affiliates ... or any person acting on behalf of any of the foregoing." Affiliates, however, do not include any officer or director of the issuer who is an affiliate solely from his or her position as an officer or director.

Second, Rule 904 imposes a number of requirements to qualify the resale for an exemption from § 5. Exempt resales involve the same basic requirements as the issuer exemptions under Regulation S. The offer or sale must take place through an "offshore transaction." No "directed selling efforts" may be made inside the United States by the selling investor, the selling investor's affiliates or agents.

Additional requirements apply if the selling investors are securities dealers or persons otherwise receiving selling concessions (i.e., the persons either receive a commission or purchased the securities at a discount from the issuer, a distributor or an affiliate of either) and the distribution compliance period has not expired. For such resales, the selling investor (or any person acting on behalf of the selling investor) must not be aware that the offeree or buyer is a U.S. person. If the purchaser is a dealer or a person who will receive a selling concession when he or she resells the securities, the selling investor must send a notice informing the purchaser that "the securities may be offered and sold during the distribution compliance period only in accordance with the provisions of this Regulation S" or some other exemption from § 5's registration requirements or through a registered offering.

Additional requirements are also placed on officers or directors (deemed affiliates by virtue of their position as an officer or director) who engage in resales of Regulation S securities. No selling concession may be paid by the officer or director other than the usual and customary broker's commission.

Although Rule 904 provides a special resale provision for Regulation S securities and Regulation S securities are "restricted," there are alternative avenues for resale. As discussed in the next chapter, investors holding unregistered securities may still be able to resell the securities if the investors are not deemed "underwriters" (enabling the investors to take advantage of § 4(1)'s exemption from § 5).

E. GLOBAL REGULATION S OFFERINGS

Many large securities offerings now are offered and sold concurrently in several securities markets around the world. A German automobile company may seek to raise $1 billion to finance the manufacture of sport-utility vehicles. To do so, the German company may decide to offer senior secured notes in the following amounts: $400 million in the United States, $200 million in South America, and the remaining $400 million in Europe. Spreading an offering across different countries in separate "tranches" helps ensure adequate investor appetite for large offerings of securities. Often, large global offerings consist of debt securities. Debt provides investors less upside but also more protection from loss compared with equity. Investors may particularly value the downside protection of debt when purchasing securities of foreign issuers.

Issuers will typically offer and sell the U.S. tranche of securities pursuant to Rule 144A (covered in Chapter 10). Technically such an offering involves an initial sale by the issuer on a firm commitment basis to a broker-dealer under a § 4(2) or Regulation D exemption from § 5. The placement agent will then turn around and resell the securities to "qualified institutional buyers," primarily large institutional investors, pursuant to the resale exemption in Rule 144A. Issuers will use Regulation S to offer and sell the non-U.S. tranches of securities. The anti-integration position of the SEC with respect to Regulation S allows the issuer to make concurrent Rule 144A/Regulation S offerings. See Securities Act Release No. 6863 (April 24, 1990). Although securities sold abroad under Regulation S escape the registration requirements of § 5, issuers and other participants must still comply with the applicable securities laws of the markets in which they offer and sell securities.

CHAPTER 10

SECONDARY MARKET TRANSACTIONS

Rules and Statutes

—*Sections 2(a)(11), 2(a)(12), 4(1), 4(2), 4(3), 4(4) of the Securities Act*

—*Rules 144, 144A, 405 of the Securities Act*

—*Regulation S–K, Item 405*

—*Rules 12g3–2, 15c2–11 of the Exchange Act*

MOTIVATING HYPOTHETICAL

Skipper is the CEO of Island Tours, Inc. The company, based in Hawaii, provides tourists with short boat tours of the Hawaiian Islands. Formed ten years ago, Island Tours has raised capital through a series of private placements of common stock to its own officers (including Skipper) as well as three "angel investors" based in California (including Howell, the heir to the Howell Oil empire). Currently, Skipper owns 40% of Island Tours outstanding common stock and Howell owns 2% of the common stock. Both purchased all of their stock in Island Tours' earlier private placements. Three years ago, Island Tours went public with an offering of $100 million of common stock. Island Tours stock is publicly traded on Nasdaq. Due to better-than-expected popularity of its tours, Island Tours common stock price has been increasing rapidly. Eager to take advantage of the recent price increase and diversify their holdings, both Skipper and Howell would like to sell some of their common stock into the public markets.

I. INTRODUCTION

Why do investors purchase securities? For most people, securities are simply a means of storing and building wealth. Investors are willing to part with money today to buy securities in the hope of receiving even more money in the future. Securities can provide a return, in the form of dividends in the case of stock, or interest payments in the case of bonds. For years, AT & T's common stock was favored by those seeking a steady return and a relatively predictable stream of dividends. Not all common stock pays dividends. Amazon.com has never paid a dividend to its common shareholders, but it has not had difficulty attracting investors who seek return in the form of capital gains. Even some shareholders holding dividend-paying stocks may need to cash out quickly and, therefore, prefer a more immediate way of getting a return from their investment. Investors interested in cashing out may turn to the secondary securities markets.

The secondary securities markets provide investors liquidity, matching prospective sellers with potential buyers. The securities markets, however, differ from other markets. In most markets, buyers deal directly with sellers or the sellers' agents. So a student purchasing a book typically deals with a bookstore (working as the consignment agent for the book publisher). One could imagine a similar structure for the securities markets, with purchasers interacting directly with sellers. And for some transactions, typically involving large block trades, purchasers do in fact negotiate directly with sellers. But, for most secondary market transactions, direct negotiations between purchasers and sellers are simply impractical. The capital markets provide a mechanism to bring together potential sellers and purchasers of securities quickly and at low cost. With a large number of potential buyers and sellers, any particular investor will have confidence that he or she can transact at the prevailing market price quickly and at a minimal cost.

What are the market mechanisms of liquidity? Some markets, including the NYSE, rely on direct interpersonal communications to facilitate transactions. An organized securities exchange, the NYSE provides a physical market space (the trading floor) where brokers interact with one another. On the trading floor, brokers literally shout out orders to one another to buy and sell securities. Although somewhat chaotic, this "open outcry system" allows the market price to adjust rapidly to new information. To ensure the liquidity of its listed securities, the NYSE also provides for "specialists." Specialists facilitate the matching of brokers seeking to buy and sell securities on behalf of their customer. The specialists also stand ready as dealers to buy or sell the stock when no one else will.

Most markets today, however, do not rely on brokers interacting at one centralized physical location. Instead, computers and electronic communication allow traders to be brought together, in a virtual sense, from all over the world. In the largest of these computerized markets, Nasdaq, securities dealers hold themselves out to the public as being willing, continuously during the trading day, to buy and sell securities for their own account at particular prices. Such dealers are known as market makers. The price at which the market maker buys securities (the bid price) is always set below the price at which the market maker is willing to sell securities (the ask price). For example, Sparrow Securities may act as a market maker for Island Tours, Inc. Suppose Sparrow Securities, in its capacity as a market maker, makes known through the Nasdaq quotation system that it is willing to sell 100 shares of Island Tours for $100 and buy 100 shares for $99.75. Sparrow Securities then makes money on the "spread" of a quarter per share between the selling price of $100 and the buying price of $99.75. (For actively traded securities, the spread is usually much narrower than this.) On the Nasdaq, any single security may have multiple market makers all competing with one another based on the spread. This competition reduces transaction costs for investors seeking to buy or sell securities on Nasdaq.

Not all securities may enter into the public secondary capital market in the United States. Section 5 of the Securities Act applies not only to any "person" but also to all transactions. Thus, no transactions may occur even after the effective date of a registration statement without complying with § 5. Section 5 continues to apply indefinitely–e.g., years after the public offering. If securities are sold using a means of interstate commerce without a current registration statement and a formal statutory prospectus either preceding or accompanying the communication, there is a § 5 violation. Section 5 applies, by its terms, even if both the buyer and seller of the securities are outside investors with no affiliation with the corporation and no ability to force registration or generate an up-to-date statutory prospectus.

But of course the story does not end here. Applying § 5 indefinitely to secondary transactions would dry up liquidity in the U.S. capital markets. Secondary market transactions are made possible through the exemptions from § 5, namely §§ 4(1) and 4(4). Section 4(1) exempts transactions from § 5 so long as no "issuer, underwriter, or dealer" is present in the transaction. Section 4(4) exempts unsolicited broker's transactions. Sections 4(1) and 4(4) create the necessary breathing space for the vast majority of secondary market transactions in the United States to take place. Determining the scope of secondary market trading therefore requires an examination of §§ 4(1) and 4(4).

II.   WHO IS AN UNDERWRITER?

Critical to the application of § 4(1) is the definition of "underwriter" under the securities laws. If an underwriter is present, § 4(1) no longer exempts the transaction from § 5. Section 2(a)(11) of the Securities Act defines the term "underwriter." Under § 2(a)(11) any person who does the following is an underwriter:

- purchases from an issuer with a view to, or offers or sells for an issuer in connection with, the distribution of any security
- participates or has a direct or indirect participation in any such undertaking
- participates or has a participation in the direct or indirect underwriting of any such undertaking

Obviously, Wall Street investment banks assisting an issuer in a public offering of securities fall within the underwriter definition. Both firm commitment (in which an investment bank purchases the securities at a discount with the intent of reselling them) and best efforts (in which the investment bank acts as an agent selling the securities on behalf of the issuer) are common methods by which the underwriter brings a public offering onto the market. Both types of offering are covered by the definition of underwriter. Section 2(a)(11), however, captures far more than Wall Street investment banks.

Gilligan, Will & Co. v. S.E.C.

267 F.2d 461 (2d Cir. 1959).

■ Lumbard, Circuit Judge.

The question for decision is whether Gilligan, Will & Co. and its partners, James Gilligan and William Will, were underwriters with respect to the distribution of Crowell–Collier Publishing Company securities and as such willfully violated the Securities Act of 1933 by acquiring and distributing debentures and common stock which were not registered. For reasons which are discussed below, this question turns on whether the issue was a "public offering" as those words are used in the Act.

* * *

We hold that there was substantial evidence to justify the findings and conclusions of the Commission that the issue was a public offering and that petitioners were underwriters....

The principal and essential purpose of the 1933 Act is to protect investors by requiring registration with the Commission of certain information concerning securities offered for sale. For reasons which will be developed, the crucial provisions of law in this case are § 5 of the 1933 Act which makes it unlawful for anyone, by any interstate communication or use of the mails, to sell or deliver any security unless a registration statement is in effect; and § 4(1) which exempts from this prohibition "transactions by any person other than issuer, underwriter, or dealer" and § 4(2) which exempts "transactions by an issuer not involving any public offering."

* * *

On July 6, 1955, Elliott & Company agreed with Crowell–Collier to try to sell privately, without registration, $3,000,000 of Crowell–Collier 5% debentures, convertible at any time into common stock at $5 a share, and [the] Elliott firm received an option on an additional $1,000,000 of debentures. Edward L. Elliott, a partner in Elliott & Company, advised Gilligan [of Gilligan, Will & Co.] of this agreement. He told Gilligan that Gilligan could purchase, but only for investment, as much of the $3,000,000 as he wished.... Gilligan was told by Elliott that Crowell–Collier had "turned the corner" and was then operating on a profitable basis.... Gilligan agreed to purchase $100,000 of debentures for his own account....

On August 10, 1955 the $100,000 debentures were delivered to Gilligan, Will & Co., which sent a letter to Crowell–Collier stating: "that said debentures are being purchased for investment and that the undersigned has no present intention of distributing the same."

In May 1956, after Gilligan noticed that the advertising in Crowell–Collier magazines was not increasing, he decided to convert his debentures into common stock and to sell the stock. Later in May [Gilligan and others] sold the stock at a profit on the American Stock Exchange. . . .

Petitioners assert that they were not "underwriters" within the meaning of the exemption provided by . . . § 4(1). Since § 2[a](11) defines an "underwriter" as "any person who has purchased from an issuer with a view to * * * the distribution of any security" and since a "distribution" requires a "public offering," the question is whether there was a "public offering." Petitioners . . . assert that whether there was a "distribution" must be judged solely by their own acts and intention, and not by the acts or intention of the issuer or others. In other words they claim that whether the total offering was in fact public, their purchases and resales may be found to be exempt on the ground that they were not underwriters if their own resales did not amount to a public offering.

In the view we take of this case we need not decide whether, if the petitioners had purchased with a view to only such resales as would not amount to a distribution or public offering, their acts would be exempt even though the issue was in fact a public offering. We find that the resales contemplated and executed by petitioners were themselves a distribution or public offering as the latter term has been defined by the Supreme Court, and we therefore find that petitioners were underwriters and that their transactions were not exempt under § 4(1).

In *S.E.C. v. Ralston Purina Co.*, 1953, 346 U.S. 119, the Supreme Court considered the exemptions provided by § [4(2)]. Two of its holdings are significant here. First, it held that an issuer who claims the benefit of an exemption from § 5 for the sale of an unregistered security has the burden of proving entitlement to it. . . .

The Court also defined the standard to be applied in determining whether an issue is a public offering. It held that the governing fact is whether the persons to whom the offering is made are in such a position with respect to the issuer that they either actually have such information as a registration would have disclosed, or have access to such information. The stipulation of facts here expressly states that the purchasers "were not supplied with material information of the scope and character contemplated by the Securities Act nor were the purchasers in such a relation to the issuer as to have access to such information concerning the company and its affairs."

* * *

The Commission also found that "The sales by Gilligan and registrant of the underlying common stock on the American Stock Exchange in May 1956, clearly constituted a public distribution." Petitioners contest this conclusion on the ground that since the conversion and sales occurred more than ten months after the purchase of the debentures the Commission was bound to find that the debentures so converted had been held for investment, and that the sales were therefore exempt under § 4(1) since made by a person other than an issuer, underwriter or dealer. Petitioners concede that if such sales were intended at the time of purchase, the debentures would not then have been held as investments; but it argues that the stipulation reveals that the sales were undertaken only after a change of the issuer's circumstances as a result of which petitioners, acting as prudent investors, thought it wise to sell. The catalytic circumstances were the failure, noted by Gilligan, of Crowell–Collier to increase its advertising space as he had anticipated that it would. We agree with the Commission that in the circumstances here presented the intention to retain the debentures only if Crowell–Collier continued to operate profitably was equivalent to a "purchased * * * with a view to * * * distribution" within the statutory definition of underwriters in § 2[a](11). To hold otherwise would be to permit a dealer who speculatively purchases an unregistered security in the hope that the financially weak issuer had, as is stipulated here, "turned the corner," to unload on the unadvised public what he later determines to be an unsound investment without the disclosure sought by the securities laws, although it is in precisely such circumstances that disclosure is most necessary and desirable. The Commission was within its discretion in finding on this stipulation that petitioners bought "with a view to distribution" despite the ten months of holding.

* * *

NOTES

1.   Gilligan's status as an affiliated person of a broker-dealer is irrelevant to the court's holding that he was an underwriter. It is clear that anyone who purchases securities from an issuer with a view to their distribution is an "underwriter," even if he or she is not employed in the financial services industry.

QUESTIONS

1.   If the issuer's changed circumstances (such as a downturn in profits) do not qualify as enough of a change to exclude the investor from status as an underwriter, what sort of changed circumstance would be consistent with having "investment intent" at the time the securities were initially purchased?

2.   In affirming the SEC's decision, the court worried that "To hold otherwise would be to permit a dealer who speculatively purchases an unregistered security in the hope that the financially weak issuer had, as is stipulated here, 'turned the corner,' to unload on the unadvised public what he later determines to be an unsound investment without the disclosure sought by the securities laws, although it is in precisely such circumstances that disclosure is most necessary and desirable." Should the degree of "speculation" influence the determination of whether there has been a public offering?

3.   Suppose Gilligan resold his shares to Goldbucks Brothers, a Wall Street investment bank, within days of purchasing them from Crowell–Collier. Goldbucks Brothers signs a letter stipulating that "said debentures are being purchased for investment and the undersigned has no present intention of distributing the same." Has Gilligan violated § 5?

Gilligan, Will makes two important points. First, *Gilligan, Will* provides guidance on the "changed circumstances" that will allow an investor to make the claim that she did not purchase securities with a "view to" the resale of such securities. Investors who did not purchase with a "view to" resale are not underwriters under § 2(a)(11), thus making § 4(1)'s exemption from § 5 potentially available. A change in the circumstances of the issuer (e.g., a downturn in the issuer's business) will not allow the investor to resell without being deemed an underwriter. Instead, courts focus instead on the reselling investor's changed circumstances.

What type of changed circumstances are consistent with "investment intent"? The passage of time may indicate that the investor initially held with investment intent, but has now changed her mind. As discussed in the *Ackerberg v. Johnson* case below, courts use a two-year holding period rule of thumb in determining whether the "securities have come to rest," and therefore the initial purchaser did not initially purchase with a "view to" the securities resale. After a three-year holding period the presumption of investment intent becomes "conclusive." Alternatively, even without the passage of time, an investor may provide evidence of her initial investment intent by showing an unexpected change in circumstances that led her to change her investment plans. An investor, for example, could argue that an unexpected need to purchase a new car, for example, required her to liquidate her portfolio of restricted securities.

Second, *Gilligan, Will* draws a connection between the term "distribution" in the definition of an underwriter in § 2(a)(11) and the term "public offering" in § 4(2) as defined by *Ralston Purina*. If the term "distribution" is equivalent to a "public offering," can a reselling investor sell to investors able to "fend for themselves" without becoming an underwriter? The ABA Committee on Federal Regulation of Securities has referred to such a resale as a "secondary private placement." We consider this connection in greater depth later in the chapter when we discuss the § 4 (1 ½) exemption for control person resales.

Consider the "view to" aspect of the definition of an underwriter and the investment intent test in the following hypothetical.

HYPOTHETICAL ONE

Suppose that Desert Tours Inc., a competitor of Island Tours, has yet to go public. Instead, Desert Tours has raised capital exclusively through private placements of common stock to accredited investors. Consider the following resales by those accredited investors.

1. *Scenario One*: Gilligan purchased 2,000 shares of Desert Tours for a total of $200,000 in one of the private placements. At the time of the offering, Gilligan believed that Desert Tours was a highly speculative investment. Over the first few months after the private placement, Desert Tours made far greater profits than expected. (It turns out that people were clamoring to ride through the desert on a horse with no name). Six months after his purchase, Gilligan is sure his stock is now worth a lot more than what he paid for it. Can he cash in by reselling his shares to retail investors in the secondary market?

2.   *Scenario Two*: Suppose that Gilligan purchased $200,000 in a Desert Tours private placement a week ago. A hurricane two days ago has badly eroded the foundation of Gilligan's beachfront cottage; his contractor estimates that rebuilding the foundation will cost $200,000. The contractor insists on payment up front in cash. (Gilligan has been somewhat slow with payment in the past.) Can Gilligan sell his Desert Tours stock to pay his contractor?

3.   *Scenario Three*: Mary Ann purchased 2,000 shares of Desert Tours for a total of $200,000. Assume that she obtained an offering circular at the time of the private placement giving detailed information on Desert Tour's business and finances. Three years have passed since Mary Ann purchased shares in the private placement. She would now like to resell her shares in the secondary market. Desert Tours—a highly secretive company—has made no disclosures since the private placement. Can Mary Ann sell?

Section 2(a)(11)'s definition of underwriter extends beyond those who purchase from the issuer with a view to reselling the securities; it also includes those who offer or sell for the issuer and those who otherwise "participate" in the offering. The *Chinese Consolidated* case below demonstrates the breadth of this definition. It also demonstrates the Securities Act's focus on transactions rather than issuers, investors, and securities. What does this transactional focus mean for the operation of §§ 5 and 4(1)?

S.E.C. v. Chinese Consolidated Benevolent Ass'n, Inc.

120 F.2d 738 (2d Cir. 1941).

■ HAND, CIRCUIT JUDGE.

The Securities and Exchange Commission seeks to enjoin the defendant from the use of any instruments of interstate commerce or of the mails in disposing, or attempting to dispose, of Chinese Government bonds for which no registration statements has ever been made.

The defendant is a New York corporation organized for benevolent purposes having a membership of 25,000 Chinese. On September 1, 1937, the Republic of China authorized the issuance of $500,000,000 in 5% bonds. In October, 1937, the defendant set up a committee which has had no official or contractual relation with the Chinese government for the purpose of:

(a) Uniting the Chinese in aiding the Chinese people and government in their difficulties.

(b) Soliciting and receiving funds from members of Chinese communities in New York, New Jersey and Connecticut, as well as from the general public in those states, for transmission to China for general relief.

All the members of the committee were Chinese and resided in New York City. Through mass meetings, advertising in newspapers distributed through the mails, and personal appeals, the committee urged the members of Chinese communities in New York, New Jersey and Connecticut to purchase the Chinese government bonds referred to and offered to accept funds from prospective purchasers for delivery to the Bank of China in New York as agent for the purchasers. At the request of individual purchasers and for their convenience the committee received some $600,000 to be used for acquiring the bonds, and delivered the moneys to the New York agency of the Bank of China, together with written applications by the respective purchasers for the bonds which they desired to buy. The New York agency transmitted the funds to its branch in Hong Kong with instructions to make the purchases for the account of the various customers. The Hong Kong bank returned the bonds by mail to the New York branch which in turn forwarded them by mail to the purchasers at their mailing addresses, which, in some cases, were in care of the defendant at its headquarters in New York. Neither the committee, nor any of its members, has ever made a charge for their activities or received any compensation from any source. The Bank of China has acted as an agent in the transactions and has not solicited the purchase of bonds or the business involved in transmitting the funds for that purpose.

No registration statement under the Securities Act has ever been made covering any of the Chinese bonds advertised for sale. Nevertheless the defendant has been a medium through which over $600,000 has been collected from would-be purchasers and through which bonds in that amount have been sold to residents of New York, New Jersey and Connecticut.

* * *

We think that the defendant has violated Section 5(a) of the Securities Act when read in connection with Section 2[a](3) because it engaged in selling unregistered securities issued by the Chinese government when it solicited offers to buy the securities "for value." The solicitation of offers to buy the unregistered bonds, either with or without compensation, brought defendant's activities literally within the prohibition of the statute. The Chinese government as issuer authorized the solicitation, or merely availed itself of gratuitous and even unknown acts on the part of the defendant whereby written offers to buy, and the funds collected for payment, were transmitted to the Chinese banks does not affect the meaning of the statutory provisions which are quite explicit. In either case the solicitation was equal for the benefit of the Chinese government and broadly speaking was for the issuer in connection with the distribution of the bonds.

* * *

Under Section 4(1) the defendant is not exempt from registration requirements if it is "an underwriter." ... Though the defendant solicited the orders, obtained the cash from the purchasers and caused both to be forwarded so as to procure the bonds, it is nevertheless contended that its acts could not have been for the Chinese government because it had no contractual arrangement or even understanding with the latter. But the aim of the Securities Act is to have information available for investors. This objective will be defeated if buying orders can be solicited which result in uninformed and improvident purchases. It can make no difference as regards the policy of the act whether an issuer has solicited orders through an agent, or has merely taken advantage of the services of a person interested for patriotic reasons in securing offers to buy. The aim of the issuer is to promote the distribution of the securities, and of the Securities Act is to protect the public by requiring that it be furnished with adequate information upon which to make investments. Accordingly the words "(sell) for an issuer in connection with the distribution of any security" ought to be read as covering continual solicitations, such as the defendant was engaged in, which normally would result in a distribution of issues of unregistered securities within the United States. Here a series of events were set in motion by the solicitation of offers to buy which culminated in a distribution to buy which culminated in a distribution that was initiated by the defendant. We hold that the defendant acted as an underwriter....

Section 4(1) was intended to exempt only trading transactions between individual investors with relation to securities already issued and not to exempt distributions by issuers. The words of the exemption in Section 4(1) are: "Transaction by any person other than an issuer, underwriter, or dealer; * * *". The issuer in this case was the Republic of China. The complete transaction included not only solicitation by the defendant of offers to buy, but the offers themselves, the transmission of the offers and the purchase money through the banks to the Chinese government, the acceptance by that government of the offers and the delivery of the bonds to the purchaser or the defendant as his agent. Even if the defendant is not itself "an issuer, underwriter, or dealer" it was participating in a transaction with an issuer, to wit, the Chinese Government. The argument on behalf of the defendant incorrectly assumes that Section 4(1) applies to the component parts of the entire transaction we have mentioned and thus exempts defendant unless it is an underwriter for the Chinese Republic. Section 5(a)(1), however, broadly prohibits sales of securities irrespective of the character of the person making them. The exemption is limited to "transactions" by persons other than "issuers, underwriters or dealers". It does not in terms or by fair implication protect those who are engaged in steps necessary to the distribution of security issues. To give Section 4(1) the construction urged by the defendant would afford a ready method of thwarting the policy of the law and evading its provisions....

It is unreasonable to conjure up all the difficulties that might arise if every attempt to suggest investment in a foreign bond issue were to be treated as a sale requiring a registration statement under the Act. This is a case where there was systematic continuous solicitation, followed by collection and remission of funds to purchase the securities, and ultimate distribution of the bonds in the United States through defendant's aid. We do not think results should be determined by the mere passage of title to the securities in China....

* * *

QUESTIONS

1. The Association did not accept any money from the Chinese government for its actions, nor was it considered an agent for the government. Nonetheless, the court held that the Association was acting "for the issuer." Is this a sensible reading of § 2(a)(11)'s definition of an underwriter?

2. Would the result change if the Association had not collected or transmitted any money, but simply urged people to send money directly to the Bank of China?

3. What if the *Wall Street Journal*'s editorial page opines that the bonds are not only a good investment but also a good way of showing America's support for China? Would the editorial page be part of the issuer's distribution?

III.   CONTROL PERSONS' RESALES

"Control persons" of issuers face greater regulation than other investors. Control persons can be liable for the actions of those under their control (see Securities Act § 15). And as we saw in Chapter 6, insiders (a broader set of individuals that may include control persons under certain circumstances) face various prohibitions on insider trading.

In addition to insider trading prohibitions, control persons, absent an exemption, must register their sale of securities under the Securities Act. Why? Recall that § 5 by its terms applies to *all* offers and sales of securities. Without anything more, ordinary secondary market transactions would become subject to § 5's registration requirements. But, § 4(1) exempts most ordinary secondary market transactions from § 5. Control persons, however, do not qualify for § 4(1) if they sell securities with the assistance of an intermediary because § 2(a)(11) makes the intermediary an underwriter. The presence of an underwriter in the transaction destroys the § 4(1) exemption for the entire transaction and all those participating in the transaction, including control persons. Thus, without an exemption, the control person must register its offer and sales of securities pursuant to § 5.

A.   UNDERWRITERS FOR CONTROL PERSONS

What is the statutory basis for this conclusion? The definition of underwriter under § 2(a)(11) primarily focuses on the relationship with the issuer. The last sentence of § 2(a)(11) deals with the control persons:

> As used in this paragraph the term "issuer" shall include, in addition to an issuer, any person directly or indirectly controlling or controlled by the issuer, or any person under direct or indirect common control with the issuer.

Thus, for purposes of § 2(a)(11) the term "issuer" includes control persons. In determining whether a person is acting as an underwriter, we need to consider whether the person is selling or offering securities for a control person (or otherwise participating in such sales). Control persons are not deemed, however, to be issuers for other provisions, including most critically § 4(1).

Why subject control persons to the registration requirements imposed on issuers if the control person relies on an underwriter? Consider the following hypothetical.

HYPOTHETICAL TWO

Skipper is the CEO of Island Tours and owns 40% of the outstanding common stock. Skipper rules Island Tours with an iron hand, making all major policy decisions and dominating the nominees he has put on the board of directors. Skipper, of course, is also the Chairman of the board of directors.

1. Suppose that Skipper decides to resell 1 million of his own Island Tours shares on the Nasdaq. Skipper plans to sell the shares in many transactions over time to reduce the negative impact on the stock price from such a large amount of shares entering the market. Do Skipper's sales raise concerns for public investors?

2. Recall that Howell is the other major shareholder of Island Tours, with 2% of the outstanding common stock. Suppose that Howell sits on the board of directors of Island Tours. Howell's board position affords him access to many internal details about Island Tours. Howell decides to sell 10,000 shares of Island Tours on the Nasdaq. Do Howell's sales raise any concerns?

Section 2(a)(11)'s definition of "underwriter" recognizes the informational advantages enjoyed by control persons. How does this definitional twist affect the ability of control persons to resell their securities?

U.S. v. Wolfson

405 F.2d 779 (2d Cir. 1968).

■ WOODBURY, SENIOR CIRCUIT JUDGE.

It was stipulated at the trial that at all relevant times there were 2,510,000 shares of Continental Enterprises, Inc., issued and outstanding. The evidence is clear, indeed is not disputed, that of these the appellant Louis E. Wolfson himself with members of his immediate family and his right hand man and first lieutenant, the appellant Elkin B. Gerbert, owned 1,149,775 or in excess of 40%. The balance of the stock was in the hands of approximately 5,000 outside shareholders. The government's undisputed evidence at the trial was that between August 1, 1960, and January 31, 1962, Wolfson himself sold 404,150 shares of Continental through six brokerage houses. . . .

[T]here is ample evidence that . . . as the largest individual shareholder [Wolfson] was Continental's guiding spirit in that the officers of the corporation were subject to his direction and control and that no corporate policy decisions were made without his knowledge and consent. Indeed

Wolfson admitted as much on the stand. No registration statement was in effect as to Continental; its stock was traded over-the-counter.

The appellants do not dispute the foregoing basic facts. They took the position at the trial that they had no idea ... that there was any provision of law requiring registration of a security before its distribution by a controlling person to the public. On the stand in their defense they took the position that they operated at a level of corporate finance far above such "details" as the securities laws; as to whether a particular stock must be registered. They asserted and their counsel argued to the jury that they were much too busy with large affairs to concern themselves with such minor matters and attributed the fault of failure to register to subordinates in the Wolfson organization and to failure of the brokers to give notice of the need. Obviously in finding the appellants guilty the jury rejected this defense, if indeed, it is any defense at all.

* * *

The appellants argue that they come within [the § 4(1)] exemption for they are not issuers, underwriters or dealers. At first blush there would appear to be some merit in this argument. The immediate difficulty with it, however, is that § 4(1) by its terms exempts only "transactions," not classes of persons and ignores § 2[a](11) of the Act which defines an "underwriter".....

In short, the brokers provided outlets for the stock of issuers and thus were underwriters. Wherefore the stock was sold in "transactions by underwriters" which are not within the exemption of § 4(1)....

But the appellants contend that the brokers in this case cannot be classified as underwriters because their part in the sales transactions came within § 4(4), which exempts "brokers' transactions executed upon customers' orders on any exchange or in the over-the-counter market but not the solicitation of such orders."[1] The answer to this contention is that § 4(4) was designed only to exempt the brokers' part in security transactions. Control persons must find their own exemptions.

There is nothing inherently unreasonable for a broker to claim the exemption of § 4(4) when he is unaware that his customer's part in the transaction is not exempt.... It will hardly do for the appellants to say that because they kept the true facts from the brokers they can take advantage of the exemption the brokers gained thereby.

* * *

QUESTIONS

1. What do you think about the defense's argument that Wolfson "operated at a level of corporate finance far above such 'details' as the securities laws"?

---

1. It is undisputed that the brokers in-   the appellants.
volved in this case did not solicit orders from

What if Wolfson had said instead that he "acted in good faith and did not realize that he was violating any securities laws"?

2. What if Wolfson had simply sold 400,000 shares in a negotiated transaction with Warren Buffett, a sophisticated (and extremely successful) investor from Omaha, Nebraska? Assume that the negotiation and sale is all done without the assistance of a third party.

3. Wolfson sold his shares through brokerage firms. Are the brokerage firms "dealers" under the Securities Act? Even if the court held that no underwriter assisted Wolfson in the sales, what problem does the presence of a "dealer" create for the § 4(1) exemption?

4. Section 4(1) is considered a "transaction" exemption. If the transaction meets the requirements of § 4(1), then all involved are exempt from § 5 registration requirements. Does the court take the same approach with § 4(4)'s exemption from § 5?

5. In discussing § 4(4)'s exemption for unsolicited broker's transactions, the court implies that a broker may have difficulty in relying on the exemption if the broker his customer does not qualify for an exemption. How does this interpretation fit the language of § 4(4)?

B. SECTION 4 (1 ½) EXEMPTION

The operation of § 2(a)(11) in combination with §§ 4(1) and 5 places a registration obligation on control persons seeking to resell their securities. As we saw in Chapter 7, registration for a public offering can be time-consuming and expensive. Not all control persons may have the power to force registration because the definition of control person found in Rule 405 is not based on the power to force registration but can be read more broadly.

Certain transactions may not require the protections afforded by the public registration process. We can draw an analogy between issuer private placements to investors able to "fend for themselves" and control person resales to investors also able to fend for themselves. Although the private placement exemption under § 4(2) is available only to issuers, the same rationale (that investors do not need the protection of the public registration process) applies to control person resales to sophisticated investors.

In response to the need of control persons to resell securities and the ability of certain investors to protect themselves (reducing the need for registration), courts have recognized the so-called § 4 (1 ½) exemption. As the case below discusses in footnote six, there technically is no § 4 (1 ½) exemption. Instead, the § 4 (1 ½) exemption is a § 4(1) exemption (with its emphasis on the definition of an underwriter) informed by § 4(2)'s distinction between public and private offerings.

Ackerberg v. Johnson, Jr.

892 F.2d 1328 (8th Cir. 1989).

■ BEAM, CIRCUIT JUDGE.

This appeal arises out of the sale of 16,500 unregistered shares of Vertimag Systems Corporation stock for $99,000. Norman J. Ackerberg brought suit against Piper, Jaffray & Hopwood and several of its employees (the PJH defendants), as well as against Clark E. Johnson, Jr., the chairman of the board of Vertimag, from whom Ackerberg bought most of his shares.

* * *

I.   BACKGROUND

Ackerberg bought the Vertimag shares in March of 1984. Ackerberg bought 12,500 shares from Johnson, who, in addition to being the chairman of the board, was one of the founders of Vertimag and its largest individual stockholder. . . .

On March 17, 1984, Ackerberg signed a subscription agreement, prepared by counsel for Vertimag. Ackerberg testified by deposition that he read and understood this document. Vertimag's counsel stressed to Ackerberg that no sale could be made without the subscription agreement, which agreement informed Ackerberg that the Vertimag securities were unregistered and not readily transferable. . . .

Ackerberg also represented in the subscription agreement that his yearly income was in excess of $200,000, that his net worth was over $1,000,000, and that his liquid assets exceeded $500,000. Indeed, Ackerberg's account at PJH alone totaled around $500,000.

* * *

Johnson['s] position [was not] the same as that of the PJH defendants for purposes of federal securities law.[4] On appeal, then, Johnson argues that the district court erred . . . by concluding that Johnson was not entitled to an exemption under § 4(1) of the 1933 Act. We agree with Johnson that he is entitled, as a matter of law, to an exemption under § 4(1), because Johnson is not an issuer, underwriter or dealer.

Johnson argues that he is entitled to an exemption under § 4(1) of the 1933 Act, which provides that the registration requirements of the 1933 Act shall not apply to "transactions by any person other than an issuer,

---

4. While Ackerberg acknowledges that Johnson's position is not the same as that of the PJH defendants, Ackerberg suggests that the merit of Johnson's claim to an exemption under § 4(1), is determined by the actions of the PJH defendants. Ackerberg argues that because of the involvement of PJH, a broker and, therefore, a dealer within § 4(1), the § 4(1) exemption cannot be available for Johnson, even if Johnson is not an issuer, underwriter or dealer. We disagree. While it is true that § 4(1) exempts transactions and not individuals, the mere involvement of a broker, qua broker, in a secondary transaction by persons other than an issuer, underwriter or dealer, is insufficient to vitiate the exemption. . . . Were its involvement enough to deny the § 4(1) exemption to persons not issuers, underwriters or dealers, few secondary transactions involving the resale of restricted securities would be exempt under § 4(1). Ackerberg has cited no persuasive authority that such is the law, and given that the purpose of the § 4(1) exemption is to exempt trading as opposed to distributions, we cannot agree with Ackerberg's contention. . . .

underwriter, or dealer."[6] We agree with the district court that the burden of proving entitlement to an exemption is on the party claiming entitlement. We disagree, however, that Johnson has failed to meet his burden. In the absence of any finding that this transaction involved a distribution, Johnson has shown that he is not an issuer, underwriter or dealer within the meaning of § 4(1)....

The parties do not seriously argue that Johnson was an issuer or a dealer. Clearly he is neither. Rather, Ackerberg contends that Johnson is an underwriter within § 4(1).

When considering whether Johnson is an underwriter, it is helpful to consider that the § 4(1) exemption is meant to distinguish "between distribution of securities and trading in securities."

The statutory definition of "underwriter" is found in § 2[a](11).... The congressional intent in defining "underwriter" was to cover all persons who might operate as conduits for the transfer of securities to the public. Thus, "underwriter" is generally defined in close connection with the definition and meaning of "distribution." ... Given the statutory definition of "underwriter," the exemption should be available if: (1) the acquisition of the securities was not made "with a view to" distribution; or (2) the sale was not made "for an issuer in connection with" a distribution. Relevant to both inquiries are whether the securities have come to rest in the hands of the security holder and whether the sale involves a public offering.

We begin by considering whether the securities were acquired by Johnson with a view to their distribution. The inquiry depends on the distinction between a distribution and mere trading; so long as Johnson initially acquired his shares from the issuer with an investment purpose and not for the purpose of reselling them, the acquisition was not made "with a view to" distribution. While this determination would at first seem to be a fact-specific inquiry into the security holder's subjective intent at the time of acquisition, the courts have considered the more objective criterion of whether the securities have come to rest. That is, the courts look to whether the security holder has held the securities long enough to negate any inference that his intention at the time of acquisition was to distribute them to the public. Many courts have accepted a two-year rule of thumb to determine whether the securities have come to rest.... [A] three-

---

6. It is clear that the applicable and appropriate exemption to be applied in this case is § 4(1). To the extent that Ackerberg argues that both Johnson and the PJH defendants rely on a "§ 4(1 1/2)" exemption, he misunderstands the nature of a § 4(1) exemption. While the term "§ 4(1 1/2) exemption" has been used in the secondary literature the term does not properly refer to an exemption other than § 4(1). Rather, the term merely expresses the statutory relationship between § 4(1) and § 4(2). That is, the definition of underwriter, found in § 2[a](11) depends on the existence of a distribution, which in turn is considered the equivalent of a public offering. Section 4(2) contains the exemption for transactions not involving a public offering. Any analysis of whether a party is an underwriter for purposes of § 4(1) necessarily entails an inquiry into whether the transaction involves a public offering. While the term "4(1 1/2) exemption" adequately expresses this relationship, it is clear that the exemption for private resales of restricted securities is § 4(1). We need not go beyond the statute to reach this conclusion.

year holding period is "well nigh conclusive" that securities were acquired without a view to distribution.

Johnson purchased his securities in 1979 or 1980, when Vertimag Systems was incorporated in California. He did not sell any of these shares to Ackerberg until 1984.... Thus, Johnson held his shares for at least four years before selling them to Ackerberg, a period well in excess of the usual two years required to find that the securities have come to rest.

Our second inquiry is whether the resale was made "for an issuer in connection with" a distribution. Whether the sale was "for an issuer" can also be determined by whether the shares have come to rest. That is the best objective evidence of whether a sale is "for an issuer" is whether the shares have come to rest.

To determine whether the sale was made "in connection with" a distribution, however, requires that we consider directly the meaning of "distribution," and thus whether the resale involved a public offering. The definition of "distribution" as used in § 2[a](11) is generally considered to be synonymous with a public offering....

The case law is equally clear that a public offering is defined not in quantitative terms, but in terms of whether the offerees are in need of the protection which the Securities Act affords through registration. Thus, the Supreme Court held in *SEC v. Ralston Purina*, 346 U.S. 119 (1953) that the proper focus is on the need of the offerees for information.

Since exempt transactions are those as to which "there is no practical need for [§ 5's] application," the applicability of [the private placement exemption] should turn on whether the particular class of persons affected needs the protection of the Act. An offering to those who are shown to be able to fend for themselves is a transaction "not involving any public offering." This circuit has followed *Ralston Purina* by finding that a public offering "turns on the need of the offerees for the protections afforded by registration.... If the offerees have access to such information, registration is unnecessary, and the section 4(2) exemption should apply."

That "distribution" should be read in terms of "public offering," and the need of the offerees for information, makes sense in light of the purpose of the 1933 Act.... Moreover, the parties in this case do not dispute that Ackerberg is a sophisticated investor, not in need of the protections afforded by registration under the 1933 Act. As earlier stated, Ackerberg read and signed a subscription agreement in which he represented that: he had the knowledge and experience in investing to properly evaluate the merits and risks of his purchase of Vertimag securities; he was able to bear the economic risk of the investment in Vertimag securities; he was given full and complete information regarding Vertimag Systems Corporation; he knew that the securities were not registered under the 1933 Act, and were being sold pursuant to exemptions from the 1933 Act; and he knew that the sale was being made in reliance on his representations in the subscription agreement. Ackerberg further represented that his net worth was substantial, and the record clearly shows that Ackerberg is, if not a conscientious investor, at least a prolific one. We, therefore, have no trouble finding that Ackerberg is a sophisticated investor and not in need of the protections afforded by registration under the 1933 Act. Hence, this case involves no public offering, and thus no distribution. Absent a distribution, Johnson cannot be an underwriter within § 4(1), and is, therefore, entitled to that exemption.

* * *

QUESTIONS

1. What would happen if Johnson had sold shares of Vertimag to Mary Ann, an unsophisticated retail investor, one month after purchasing the securities from Vertimag and without any disclosure of information?

2. What is the purpose of the court's "second inquiry" into "whether the resale was made 'for an issuer in connection with' a distribution" after determining in its presumably first inquiry that Johnson did not purchase with a view to resell the securities? Who is the "issuer" here?

3. The court concludes its "second inquiry" with the statement that "Johnson cannot be an underwriter within § 4(1), and is, therefore, entitled to that exemption." Is there another step necessary to conclude § 4(1) applies to protect Johnson's sale of Vertimag shares to Ackerberg?

Whenever a control person resells shares, we must undertake two separate analyses. First, as we do with non-control persons, we ask whether the control person is acting as an underwriter for the issuer. Section 4(1) is not available if the control person is acting as an underwriter for the issuer. So control persons must avoid acting as an underwriter purchasing with a view to distribution for their resales. For investors who are not control persons, this is the only inquiry.

A second inquiry is required, however, for control persons. We must ask whether an intermediary assisting the control person in the resale (e.g., a brokerage firm) is acting as an underwriter for the control person. Even if the control person is reselling securities years after purchasing them from the issuer in a private placement (or alternatively, securities purchased through a registered public offering or in the secondary markets), the control person potentially faces registration requirements under § 5. If the intermediary assisting the control person is not an underwriter (under the § 4 (1 ½) doctrine, for example), then the control person may then take advantage of § 4(1).

The following hypothetical lays out the difference between these two inquiries.

HYPOTHETICAL THREE

Suppose that Skipper, the CEO and majority shareholder of Island Tours, purchases 100,000 additional shares of Island Tours directly from the company at a price of $10 per share as part of a broader Rule 506 private placement. Skipper himself is an accredited investor. In the Rule 506 offering, Island Tours sold to ten other accredited investors and 35 sophisticated non-accredited purchasers. Consider how the securities laws apply to the following transactions.

1. *Scenario One*: One month after purchasing his shares in the private placement Skipper—ignoring the advice of Island Tours' general counsel that it is too soon to resell—wants to resell the 100,000 shares to five individual investors. Each investor has a Ph.D. in finance (specializing in the valuation of Island tour companies - a fairly narrow niche), Skipper provides each investor with detailed information on Island Tours. None of the five individual investors, however, qualifies as an accredited investor under Regulation D. Skipper takes care to ensure that no third party assists him in the sales.

2. *Scenario Two*: Suppose after holding onto the 100,000 shares for four years, Skipper decides to sell the stock to a large number of retail investors using unsolicited brokers' transactions through his broker, Sparrow Securities.

3. *Scenario Three*: Suppose that Skipper holds on to the shares he purchased in the private placement. He also buys 50,000 more shares in the open secondary market (assume these shares can be traced back to Island Tour's initial public offering). A week after the secondary market purchase, Skipper has a change of heart and decides to resell those shares through Sparrow Securities on the Nasdaq.

IV.   RULE 144

Investors face considerable uncertainty in attempting to determine whether they fall under the definition of underwriter. Although the investment intent test provides some guidance on whether the investors purchased the securities with a "view to" the resale of the securities, the application of the test is far from clear, particularly for resales occurring less than two years from their initial purchase. Moreover, the SEC has long disfavored the focus of the investment intent test on the circumstances of the investor seeking to resell unregistered securities. Instead, the SEC argues that the permissibility of resales should focus more on the amount of information on the issuer available in the secondary market.

Investors may also seek to escape underwriter status through sales not involving a "distribution" of the securities. In determining whether the seller is an underwriter, courts equate "distribution" with "public offering" and look to *Ralston Purina* in determining whether the purchasers of the securities are able to "fend for themselves." As with the investment test, the scope of what constitutes a public offering is somewhat amorphous.

To provide greater clarity and to shift the focus of resales onto the availability of information about the issuer, in 1972 the SEC promulgated Rule 144 as a safe harbor for resales from § 5's registration requirements. The following excerpt comes from the SEC release promulgating Rule 144:

[T]he rule as adopted is not exclusive. However, persons who offer or sell restricted securities without complying with Rule 144 are hereby put on notice by the Commission that in view of the broad remedial purposes of the Act and of public policy which strongly supports registration, they will have a substantial burden of proof in establishing that an exemption from registration is available for such offers or sales. . . .

Moreover, with respect to restricted securities acquired after the effective date of the rule, the staff will not issue "no-action" letters relating to resales of such securities. Further, in connection with such resales the Commission hereby puts all persons including brokers and attorneys on notice that the "change in circumstances" concept should no longer be considered as one of the factors in determining whether a person is an underwriter. . . . [T]he "change in circumstances" concept in the Commission's opinion fails to meet the objectives of the Act, since the circumstances of the seller are unrelated to the need of investors for the protections afforded by the registration and other provisions of the Act.

Further . . . the Commission hereby gives notice that in deciding whether a person is an underwriter, the length of time the securities have been held will be considered but the fact that securities have been held for a particular period of time does not by itself establish the availability of an exemption from registration. . . .

Securities Act Release No. 5223 (Jan. 11, 1972).

Complying with Rule 144 exempts the party in question from taking part in a "distribution" of securities and thus from being deemed an underwriter under § 2(a)(11). Why does this matter? Recall that § 4(1) exempts transaction from § 5's registration requirements but only if an "underwriter" is not present. By excluding certain parties from underwriter status, Rule 144 makes § 4(1) (potentially) available.

Rule 144's application varies based on two factors: (1) the presence of an "affiliate" and (2) the presence of "restricted" or "unrestricted" securities. Rule 144(a)(1) defines an "affiliate" as "a person that directly, or indirectly through one or more intermediaries, controls, or is controlled by, or is under common control with, such issuer." Note the relationship of this language with the last sentence of § 2(a)(11). Rule 144(a)(3) includes in its definition of "restricted" security a security "acquired directly or indirectly from the issuer, or from an affiliate of the issuer, in a transaction or chain of transactions not involving any public offering," or acquired in a transaction in which Section 502(d) applies (e.g., Rule 505 or Rule 506 offerings). Given these two factors, the following questions must be addressed in applying Rule 144:

	Affiliates	Non–Affiliates
Restricted Securities	Is the affiliate an underwriter for the issuer? Is the non-affiliate an underwriter for the issuer?	Is a third party an underwriter for the affiliate?
Unrestricted Securities	Is a third party an underwriter for the affiliate?	Section 4(1) generally exempts this transaction from § 5 without Rule 144

For resales involving either (1) a non-affiliate selling restricted securities or (2) an affiliate selling either restricted or unrestricted securities, Rule 144 may provide relief from underwriter status, both for the reselling party and for those working on behalf of the reselling party. Consider the following two situations.

1. *Any person who sells restricted securities for their own account.* If the person who resells restricted securities is considered an underwriter for the issuer, then the entire transaction collapses into the issuer's transaction, as we saw in *Gilligan, Will*. Moreover, § 4(1) does not apply to exempt the transaction from § 5 due to the presence of the issuer and underwriter in the transaction. On the other hand, if Rule 144 applies, the reselling party is deemed not to be an underwriter and the resale transaction is deemed separate from the issuer's original private placement, thereby avoiding integration with the issuer's offering. Because the separate resale transaction does not involve an issuer, underwriter, or dealer, the reselling party may take advantage of § 4(1)'s exemption from § 5.

2. *Any person who sells restricted or unrestricted securities for the account of an affiliate.* If a person sells restricted or even unrestricted (i.e., securities that were registered for a public offering in the past) for an affiliate, the person may be considered an underwriter under § 2(a)(11) to the extent the affiliate is a "control person" of the issuer. Once the person is an underwriter, § 4(1)'s exemption no longer is available, exposing the transaction to § 5, as we saw in *Wolfson*. Complying with Rule 144 allows the person selling on behalf of the affiliate to escape status as an underwriter. If the transaction does not otherwise involve an issuer, underwriter, or dealer, then § 4(1) exempts the entire transaction from § 5.

Rule 144 applies both for general resales of restricted securities and for affiliate resales of both restricted and unrestricted securities.

To qualify for Rule 144's exemption from underwriter status, those seeking to use Rule 144 must meet a number of requirements considered below. As we go through the requirements, consider whether investors in the secondary market are sufficiently protected if Rule 144's conditions are met. Does your opinion differ based on the type of issuer? For example, Exchange Act reporting issuers already must comply with periodic disclosure requirements (i.e., Forms 10–K, 10–Q, and 8–K). Exchange Act reporting issuers also tend to be larger with a more active secondary market. Such issuers enjoy greater third-party sources of information, including analysts and other securities market professionals. More than ten securities analysts cover Microsoft, for example, providing a steady stream of investment reports and recommendations on Microsoft's stock. For a company that recently went public, or indeed may not even have gone public yet, no analysts may cover the company's stock.

The basic requirements of Rule 144 fall into the following categories:

- Current Public Information (Rule 144(c))
- Holding Period for Restricted Securities (Rule 144(d))
- Limitation on Amount of Securities Sold (Rule 144(e))
- Manner of Sale (Rule 144(f))
- Notice of Proposed Sale (Rule 144(h))

Despite these extensive requirements, Rule 144 makes a major exception. Rule 144(k) allows for resales of restricted securities by persons other than affiliates that take place at least two years after "the later of the date the securities were acquired from the issuer or from an affiliate of the issuer." For such sales none of Rule 144's other requirements apply. (Technically, Rule 144(d)'s one-year holding period requirement has already elapsed if the two-year holding period requirement of Rule 144(k) is met.) The basic requirements of Rule 144 therefore only apply for securities sold on behalf of affiliates and for resales of restricted securities by non-affiliates who have held the securities for less than two years. After the two-year holding period, non-affiliates may freely resell restricted securities without regard to the availability of current public information, the manner of sale, or the amount of securities sold.

A.   CURRENT PUBLIC INFORMATION

Rule 144(c) requires that adequate current public information regarding the issuer be available to investors. Information is deemed available for Exchange Act reporting issuers if: (1) the issuers have had reporting status for at least 90 days immediately preceding the sale of the securities; and (2) the issuer is current in its Exchange Act periodic disclosure filings for the past twelve months.

How will an investor attempting to resell securities know whether an Exchange Act reporting issuer has met its disclosure obligations? Rule 144(c) provides that the investor may "rely upon a written statement from the issuer that it has complied with such reporting requirements unless he knows or has reason to believe that the issuer has not complied with such requirements."

Non–Exchange Act reporting issuers must make available the information specified in Rule 15c2–11(a)(5)(i)-(xiv) and (xvi) of the Exchange Act. Rule 15c2–11 refers to the information broker-dealers must keep on hand (and reasonably current) with respect to companies on which the broker-dealers publish a quotation or submit a price quotation in "any quotation medium." The information includes, among other things, the name of the corporation, the state of incorporation, the number of shares or total amount of securities outstanding as of the end of the issuer's most recent fiscal year, the most recent balance sheet, profit and loss, and retained earning statements, and similar financial information is required for the two preceding fiscal years as well, assuming the issuer or its predecessor has been in existence. Non–Exchange Act reporting issuers that wish to encourage a liquid secondary market for their shares in the over-the-counter market will voluntarily supply the required Rule 15c2 11 information to broker-dealers acting as market makers in the stock. (Recall that market makers continuously publish bid and ask quotations for stocks in which they make a market).

B.   HOLDING PERIOD FOR RESTRICTED SECURITIES

Rule 144(d) imposes a holding period before an investor can use Rule 144 to sell restricted securities. The holding period runs from the later of the acquisition of the securities from (1) the issuer or (2) an affiliate of the issuer. The SEC provides the following rationale behind the holding period requirement:

> [A] holding period prior to resale is essential, among other reasons, to assure that those persons who buy under a claim of a section 4(2) exemption have assumed the economic risks of investment, and therefore, are not acting as conduits for sale to the public of unregistered securities, directly or indirectly, on behalf of an issuer. It should be noted that there is nothing in section 2[a](11) which places a time limit on a person's status as an underwriter. The public has the same need for protection afforded by registration whether the securities are distributed shortly after their purchase or after a considerable length of time.

Securities Act Release 5223 (Jan. 11, 1972).

Note two important features of the holding period requirement. First, Rule 144(d) states that a "minimum of one year must elapse between the later of the date of the acquisition of the securities from the issuer or from an affiliate of the issuer, and any resale of such securities. . . ." The focus of Rule 144(d) on the "date of the acquisition for the securities from the issuer or from an affiliate of the issuer" implicitly allows subsequent non-affiliate holders to "tack" on the holding period of the initial acquirer. For example, the holding period for securities acquired through a gift is calculated from their initial acquisition by the donor (Rule 144(d)(3)(v)). Second, the holding period only applies to restricted securities. For unrestricted securities—e.g., securities sold through a prior public offering—there is no holding period requirement for use of Rule 144.

But wait a second. If the securities are unrestricted, why do we need Rule 144 at all? Why not go directly to § 4(1), which exempts most secondary market transactions after a public offering? The answer lies in the treatment of affiliates under Rule 144. If someone assists the control person in the distribution of securities, even if unrestricted, the assisting person is considered an underwriter under § 2(a)(11). With the presence of an underwriter in the transaction, the control person is unable to rely on § 4(1) to avoid § 5's registration requirements—control persons always need to be worried about the possibility of a distribution. The control person must therefore turn to either the § 4 (1 ½) exemption or Rule 144 to avoid a distribution. Holding periods are not relevant for sales by controlling persons of securities that were previously publicly traded. Rule 144, therefore, does not require any additional holding period for sales by affiliates. Affiliates must comply with the holding period requirement, however, if they acquired their shares from the issuer pursuant to § 4(2) or another exemption.

HYPOTHETICAL FOUR

Island Tours has been an Exchange Act reporting company since going public three years ago. To raise additional capital, Island Tours sold an additional $2 million of common stock through a Regulation D private placement to several accredited investors six months after its public offering. In the private placement, Skipper, the CEO, purchased 100,000 shares at $10 per share and Mary Ann, an outside investor with no other affiliation with Island Tours, also purchased 100,000 shares. Does Rule 144 permit the following resales?

1. *Scenario One*: Suppose Mary Ann wants to resell on Nasdaq the 100,000 shares three months after the private placement. Can she do this?

2. *Scenario Two*: Mary Ann wants to resell her 100,000 shares thirteen months after the private placement. Assume that Island Tours has been late in filing its latest Form 10–K with the SEC.

3. *Scenario Three*: Assume Mary Ann purchased her 100,000 shares from the private placement thirteen months ago. Six months after the purchase, Mary Ann pledged the shares as collateral for a full-recourse loan she obtained from Bank of Michigan. Mary Ann has recently failed to make her loan payments. The Bank takes possession of the 100,000 shares and seeks to sell the shares immediately to pay down the loan. Assume that Island Tours is current in all its Exchange Act reporting filings.

4. *Scenario Four*: What if Mary Ann waits to sell 25 months after the private placement, but Island Tours has not filed its latest Form 10–K on time?

5. *Scenario Five*: What if Skipper waits to sell 25 months after the private placement through unsolicited broker's transactions (using Sparrow Securities), but Island Tours has not filed its latest Form 10–K on time?

6. *Scenario Six*: Skipper purchases 1,000 shares of Island Tours on Nasdaq. One week later, Skipper has second thoughts about the purchase and resells them through an unsolicited broker's transaction back into the secondary market. Assume that Island Tours is current in all its Exchange Act reporting filings.

C. LIMITATION ON AMOUNT OF SECURITIES SOLD

Rule 144(e) restricts the amount of resales of restricted securities (and unrestricted securities in the case of affiliate sales) that may occur in a three-month period. The limit is the greater of:

(i)   one percent of the outstanding shares or units of the same class of securities,

(ii)   the average weekly reported trading volume of the same class of securities on all national securities exchanges and/or an inter-dealer quotation system (e.g., Nasdaq) during the four calendar weeks preceding the filing of notice of the sale with the SEC, or

(iii) the average weekly trading volume in the same class of securities for the four calendar weeks preceding the filing of the notice of sale with the SEC as reported through the consolidated transaction reporting system contemplated by Rule 11Aa3-1 of the Exchange Act. Also known as the consolidated tape system, the consolidated transaction reporting system aggregates transactions for a particular security on the national securities exchanges (e.g., NYSE and AMEX) and the over-the-counter market (e.g., Nasdaq) and reports them on a consolidated tape.

Note that the volume limit is determined through reference to the entire secondary market trading volume of a particular company. Thus an investor can sell a larger number of securities for larger, more liquid issuers.

Why limit volume? Consider the following excerpt from the SEC release promulgating Rule 144:

It is consistent with the rationale of the Act that Section 4(1) be interpreted to permit only routine trading transactions as distinguished from distributions. Therefore, a person reselling securities under Section 4(1) of the Act must sell the securities in such limited quantities and in such a manner so as not to disrupt the trading markets. The larger the amount of securities involved, the more likely it is that such resales may involve methods of offering and amounts of compensation usually associated with a distribution rather than routine trading transactions. Thus, solicitation of buy orders or the payment of extra compensation are not permitted by the rule.

Securities Act Release No 33–5223 (Jan. 11, 1972).

The SEC's first justification for the volume limit in Rule 144 is a fear that a large number of securities entering the market at once will disrupt the market. A large sale of securities may cause the stock price, at least temporarily, to drop. Rule 144's volume limitation may help avoid such a shock to the market. This rationale is not without problems. Large block sales of previously registered securities are not restricted by Rule 144. Non-affiliates may sell an unlimited amount of unrestricted securities into the public securities markets. Moreover, the risk of a large stock price drop from a large block sale is unclear. Sellers of stock have a natural incentive not to cause the stock price to drop precipitously as they sell their shares because it will reduce the proceeds from their sales. They will therefore try to disguise their sales by breaking them up among a number of brokers or spacing them out over time.

The second rationale is that the sale of a large amount of securities at once increases the likelihood that the reselling investors may use tactics associated with public offerings—including offering brokers greater commissions and attempting to condition the market with overly positive information on the company. The size of an offering can therefore be viewed as a proxy for public offering tactics.

HYPOTHETICAL FIVE

To raise additional capital, Island Tours sold an additional $2 million of common stock through a Regulation D private placement to several accredited investors six months after its public offering. Island Tours now has 10 million shares of common stock outstanding. Assume that the average weekly trading volume of Island Tours has consistently been around 125,000 shares at about $10 per share. Mary Ann, an outside investor with no other affiliation with Island Tours, purchased 150,000 shares in the private placement.

1. *Scenario One*: Thirteen months after the private placement, Mary Ann decides to sell the 150,000 shares she purchased in Island Tours' recent private placement.

2. *Scenario Two*: Mary Ann, after some thought, decides to reduce her planned sale to 100,000 shares. Suppose that the Professor and Lovey also purchased 100,000 shares in the private placement. Both separately decide to sell their 100,000 shares at about the same time as Mary Ann, for a total of 300,000 shares resold into the market. Assume that Mary Ann, the Professor and Lovey are all outside investors of Island Tours.

3. *Scenario Three*: Skipper also purchased 100,000 shares in Island Tours' recent private placement. Suppose that along with the shares in the private placement, Skipper also purchased 100,000 unrestricted shares in the public capital markets. Skipper now proposes reselling all 200,000 into the market.

4. *Scenario Four*: Same facts as Scenario Three, except now Skipper decides to resell only his 100,000 restricted shares through unsolicited brokers' transactions on the Nasdaq. At about the same time, he resells the 100,000 unrestricted shares. The sale of the unrestricted shares is negotiated and solicited, with the assistance of Sparrow Securities, with Howell, a member of the board of directors and 2% shareholder of Island Tours.

D. MANNER OF SALE

Rule 144(f) carefully limits the means by which resales into the secondary market take place. Sellers may either engage in unsolicited "brokers' transactions" as provided for in § 4(4) or directly with a "market maker" as defined in § 3(a)(38) of the Exchange Act. Market makers are dealers who continuously offer quotations in specific securities, holding themselves out to the general secondary market as being willing to buy or sell the securities at specified buy and sell prices.

Rule 144(g) defines what constitutes an unsolicited "brokers' transaction" in § 4(4). Brokers may not solicit orders. Moreover, the broker may do "no more than execute the order or orders to sell the securities as agent for the person for whose account the securities are sold; and receives no more than the usual and customary broker's commission...." (Rule 144(g)(1)). Rule 144(g) provides some exceptions to the general prohibition on solicitations. Among other things, brokers may inquire of customers who have indicated an "unsolicited bona fide interest in the specific securities within the preceding 10 business days...."

Merely engaging in an unsolicited transaction (or one of the exempted solicited types of transactions) is not sufficient to qualify the trade as an unsolicited brokers' transaction under Rule 144(g). Rule 144(g) also affirmatively requires brokers to make a reasonable inquiry into the circumstances of the sale transaction. The purpose of the inquiry is to determine whether the seller is acting as an underwriter taking part in the distribution of securities for the issuer. The reasonable inquiry includes (but is not limited to) looking at the Form 144 filing required of some sellers (described below) indicating the expected amount of securities to be sold under Rule 144. In addition, the broker needs to determine the length of time the seller has held the securities, how the seller acquired the securities, whether the sellers intend to sell additional securities of the same class, and if the seller has made any solicitations.

HYPOTHETICAL SIX

Imagine that you are a broker working for Sparrow Securities. You receive a large flow of orders from many different investors. You receive an order from Skipper, the CEO of Island Tours, to sell unregistered securities previously sold through Island Tours' private placement of thirteen months ago. The securities all bear a Rule 502(d) legend indicating their restricted status.

1. As the broker, how do you go about making the various inquiries required by Rule 144(g)?

2. Suppose that Sparrow Securities maintains a list of customers that have indicated to brokers at Sparrow Securities within the past ten days a desire that they would like to purchase the stock of "high growth-high risk startup companies." Sparrow Securities records the names of only those customers who have purchased similar securities in the past from Sparrow Securities. As the broker receiving the sale order from Skipper, can you contact the customers on the list and sell them the Island Tours restricted securities?

E.   NOTICE OF PROPOSED SALE

Sellers proposing to use Rule 144 to resell their securities must normally file a Form 144 with the SEC. Form 144 requires sellers to disclose their identity, their relationship with the issuer, the date and nature of the acquisition transactions through which the selling shareholder acquired the securities to be sold, information on all securities of the issuer that the investor sold during the past three months, the name and address of each broker and market maker through whom securities are to be sold, and the proposed amounts of securities to be sold through each broker and market maker.

A small sale exception exists for the Form 144 filing requirement. Sellers need not file if, for any given three month period, they do not exceed 500 shares for an aggregate sale price less than or equal to $10,000.

Sellers must file the Form 144 no later than the placing of the first sale order with a broker or with the execution of the trade directly with a market maker (pursuant to Rule 144(f)). Because the disclosure is for prospective trades and may be filed prior to actual execution of the trade, the Form 144 may indicate more shares than the actual amount sold. Sellers filing a Form 144 must have a bona fide intention to sell the securities within a reasonable time after filing the form.

The SEC makes Form 144 available to the public. Those interested in viewing the Form 144 filings for the securities of a particular company may easily do so on Internet finance sites. For example, Yahoo.com provides information on insider "planned sales" obtained from Form 144 filings.

Why is Form 144 required to be filed ahead of the actual trade transactions? Perhaps disclosure in advance of trades helps inform the market about insiders' informational advantages. If insiders know that the stock market is overvaluing the company, for example, they may dump their stock holdings. Pre-trading disclosure that insiders are about to sell stock may alert the market to this inside information, reducing the ability of insiders to exploit informational advantages. Insiders (at least the top officers) are likely to be deemed control persons of the issuer, and thus, affiliates for purposes of Rule 144. Resales by insiders of both restricted and unrestricted securities, therefore, often will need Rule 144—with its notice requirement—to escape the regulatory reach of § 5. Moreover, Rule 144(k)'s exemption after two years from the Rule 144(h) disclosure requirement does not apply to affiliates.

On the other hand, Rule 144(h) has serious limitations as a pre-trading disclosure mechanism. First, insiders can file the Form 144 concurrently with placing a trade with a market maker, leaving the market with no time to react to a Form 144 disclosure. Second, because Form 144 discloses only *proposed* sales, the actual sales may differ, limiting the value of the signal to the market. Insiders must disclose their actual sales on Form 4. A Form 4 is required to be filed no later than the end of the second business day following the day of the transaction, a bit late to provide the market with pre-trading disclosure. Finally, insiders do not necessarily need to rely on Rule 144 to resell securities; they may also take advantage of § 4 (1 ½).

F.   OTHER CONSIDERATIONS

The SEC in its notes to Rule 144 makes clear that the Rule, working through the definition of an underwriter and § 4(1), provides an exemption only from § 5's registration requirements. There is no exemption from antifraud liability. Of course, antifraud liability geared to specific public offering documents (§ 11 for the registration statement and § 12(a)(2) for the prospectus) does not apply. Rule 10b–5, however, continues to apply to any materially misleading disclosures in communications relating to the sale of securities under Rule 144.

V.   RULE 144A

Rule 144 is not the exclusive means by which investors can resell restricted securities. Investors may always fall back on the "changed circumstance" exception to the investment intent test (although disfavored by the SEC) or the definition of a "distribution" for purposes of determining if an underwriter is present in the transaction. Either avenue may allow the investor to use § 4(1) to exempt the transaction from § 5.

In 1990, the SEC promulgated another means for investors to resell securities—to a restricted set of investors—under Rule 144A. The SEC intended Rule 144A to provide greater access to the U.S. private placement market for foreign issuers. Through a combination of Regulation D and Rule 144A, foreign issuers can sell a large amount of securities into the United States while both avoiding the registration requirements of § 5 and allowing for immediate resales. The rule has proved equally useful, however, to domestic issuers.

Rule 144A exempts resales by two types of sellers. First, Rule 144A(b) covers offers and sales by a person other than an issuer or dealer. If the conditions of Rule 144A(d) are met, then Rule 144A(b) provides that the offers or sales do not constitute a "distribution" of securities. Consequently, the person offering the securities is not an underwriter. As with Rule 144, excluding the seller from the definition of underwriter makes § 4(1) available.

Rule 144A(c) exempts securities dealers. To the extent the terms of Rule 144A are met, securities dealers are not deemed as "participants in a distribution of securities within the meaning of section 4(3)(C) of the Act." In addition, the dealers are excluded from the definition of underwriter. Finally, the securities are also not deemed to be "offered to the public" under § 4(3)(A). The combination of these provisions allows the dealer to rely on the § 4(3) exemption.

Why do issuers, investment banks, and securities lawyers commonly refer to a Rule 144A "offering"? Technically, Rule 144A exempts only resales. Issuers cannot rely on Rule 144A to protect primary transactions from the reach of § 5. How does the Rule 144A resale exemption facilitate primary sale of securities by issuers?

Here's how it works in practice:

- The issuer sells the securities under § 4(2) or Rule 506 of Regulation D to an investment bank (a dealer);
- The investment bank—relying on Rule 144A(c)—then resells the securities to a broad range of large institutional investors.

Combining Rule 144A with an initial private placement allows issuers to sell enormous amounts of securities through an investment bank to many sophisticated institutional investors. Unlike an offering solely under § 4(2) or Rule 506, combining a private placement with Rule 144A allows the initial investors in the offering to resell the securities, as long as the purchasers are institutional investors.

Since Rule 144A was adopted, the amount of securities sold through the safe harbor provision has grown exponentially. In 1990, issuers made eight placements totaling $916.0 million. Today, Rule 144A offerings total hundreds of billions annually, with a particular emphasis on debt and convertible debt securities.

Rule 144A(d) sets forth four basic requirements:

(A) Offers and sales must be to a "qualified institutional buyer" (QIB)

(B) Purchasers must be notified of the exemption

(C) Non-fungibility

(D) Disclosure

We consider each of the requirements in turn.

A. OFFERS AND SALES TO A QUALIFIED INSTITUTIONAL BUYER

Rule 144A(d)(1) requires that all offers and sales be made only to qualified institutional buyers or those the seller reasonably believes to be qualified institutional buyers. Qualified institutional buyers are defined to include an entity (investing for their own account or for the accounts of other QIBs) that in the aggregate owns and invests on a discretionary basis $100 million or more in securities of companies unaffiliated with the QIB (see Rule 144A(a)(1)). Insurance companies, investment companies, corporations, and partnerships, among others, are included as entities that qualify as a QIB. The $100 million threshold represents a presumption on the part of the SEC that institutions with such a large portfolio will have extensive sophistication and experience in dealing with the financial markets.

Additional requirements are imposed on banks, which must not only meet the $100 million requirement, but also have an audited net worth of $25 million to be considered qualified institutional buyers. According to the SEC:

> As federally-insured depository institutions, domestic banks and savings and loans are able to purchase securities with funds representing deposits of their customers. These deposits are backed by federal insurance funds administered by the Federal Deposit Insurance Corporation. In light of this government support, these financial institutions are able to purchase securities without placing themselves at risk to the same extent as other types of institutions. In this respect, banks and savings and loans effectively are able to purchase securities using public funds. Therefore, the amount of securities owned by a bank or savings and loan institution may not, on its own, be a sufficient

measure of such institution's size and investment sophistication, and Rule 144A is intended to cover only resales to institutions that are sophisticated securities investors.

Securities Act Release No. 6862 (April 23, 1990).

Although banks face more stringent requirements for QIB status, Rule 144A gives greater latitude to securities dealers. In order to qualify as QIBs, securities dealers registered under § 15 of the Exchange Act need only own or invest on a discretionary basis $10 million in the aggregate of securities. (The issuers of the $10 million in securities must not be affiliated with the dealer.) Securities dealers are presumed to have at least a modicum of financial sophistication.

In addition, securities dealers acting in a "riskless principal" transaction for a QIB also qualify for QIB status. In a riskless principal transaction, the broker-dealer is simultaneously acquiring a security from one entity and selling the same security to another entity. Although title to the security does momentarily lie with the broker-dealer, the broker-dealer is essentially acting as an agent for the two parties ultimately selling and buying the security. Securities dealers that bear no risk are hardly in need of regulatory protection. Dealers acting as intermediaries in a riskless principal transaction "grease the wheels" to bring together potential buyers and sellers.

B.   PURCHASER AWARENESS OF EXEMPTION

Rule 144A(d)(2) requires that the seller and those working on its behalf take reasonable steps to ensure that the purchaser knows that the sale is made in reliance on Rule 144A. Such steps include placing a legend on the securities indicating (1) their restricted status; and (2) that resales may only take place through registration or an exemption from § 5. Issuers will also obtain a restricted CUSIP identifier for the securities. A CUSIP is assigned to financial instruments, providing a unique identifier for any particular stock, bond, etc. Issuers will also include a similar statement in the private placement memorandum used in a Regulation D/Rule 144A offering.

Straightforward on its face, Rule 144A(d)(2) is noteworthy for what it does not require. Unlike Regulation D, which bans general solicitations, Rule 144A(d) does not restrict selling efforts on the part of sellers seeking to find prospective purchasers. Only *purchases* must be made by qualified institutional buyers, who must be made aware of the Rule 144A exemption and receive certain specified information (or rights to information) as discussed below.

Consider the following possible transaction. An issuer sells securities to an investment bank under Rule 506 of Regulation D. The investment bank shortly thereafter freely solicits QIBs. Normally, the second step of solicitations combined with sales to QIBs would be included in the issuer's initial sale (e.g., the investment bank would be acting as an underwriter and the ultimate purchasers would be the QIBs) and potentially run afoul of

Regulation D's ban on general solicitations and general advertising under Rule 502(c). Particularly if there is no pre-existing relationship with the ultimate purchasers and broad based selling tactics (such as the widespread dissemination of offering circulars) are used, issuers would face a decided risk under Rule 502(c). With Rule 144A, however, the issuer and the investment bank may solicit QIBs without jeopardizing the initial Rule 506 exemption.

C. FUNGIBILITY

Rule 144A(d)(3) restricts the exemption to only certain types of securities. Issuers cannot offer or sell securities of the same class as securities listed on a national securities exchange or trading on a U.S. automated inter-dealer quotation system (i.e., Nasdaq). So Microsoft, whose common stock trades on Nasdaq, cannot use Rule 144A(d)(3) to offer common stock.

Microsoft could then respond in a number of ways. As one possibility, Microsoft may issue a new series of preferred stock through a Rule 144A offering. More commonly, Microsoft may issue a class of debt securities convertible into the Nasdaq-traded common stock. Consider the problem if Microsoft allowed investors to convert the value of their bonds into common stock at a conversion price equal to the market price of the common stock at the time of the Rule 144A offering. As investors converted, Microsoft would be issuing common stock. Rule 144A(d)(3), however, specifically excludes convertible securities that allow investors to convert into securities listed on a national securities exchange or quoted on Nasdaq unless the effective conversion premium is at least ten percent. The conversion premium greatly reduces the chance of rapid conversion into the underlying listed or quoted stock. The conversion premium ensures that conversion will only take place (if at all) in the future if the price of the listed or quoted securities rises by more than ten percent.

D. DISCLOSURE

Rule 144A(d)(4) imposes disclosure requirements. Exchange Act reporting issuers, however, as well as certain foreign private issuers (as specified in Rule 12g3–2(b) of the Exchange Act), are exempt from the information requirements. For other issuers, Rule 144A(d)(4) requires that the holder of the securities as well as any prospective purchaser have the right, on their request, to obtain specified information from the issuer.

The specified information under Rule 144A(d)(4) must be "reasonably current" and include "a very brief statement of the nature of the business of the issuer and the products and services it offers; and the issuer's most recent balance sheet and profit and loss and retained earnings statements, and similar financial statements for such part of the two preceding fiscal years as the issuer has been in operation (the financial statements should be audited to the extent reasonably available)." On its face, Rule 144A(d)(4)'s information requirement is unusual in the duration of the obligation. Sellers seeking to use Rule 144A must ensure that the issuer is willing to provide the specified information for trades well into the resale market. The SEC emphasized the relatively low cost nature of the continuing disclosure requirement:

> The Commission does not believe that the limited information requirement should impose a significant burden on those issuers subject to the requirement. Many foreign issuers that will be subject to the requirement, which were the focus of the commenters' concern, will have securities traded in established offshore markets, and already will have made the required information publicly available in such markets. Even for domestic issuers, the required information represents only a portion of that which would be necessary before a U.S. broker or dealer could submit for publication a quotation for the securities of such an issuer in a quotation medium in the United States. The Commission expects that the kinds of information commonly furnished under Rule 12g3–2(b) by foreign private issuers almost invariably would satisfy the information requirement and that foreign private issuers who wish their securities to be Rule 144A-eligible will simply obtain a Rule 12g3–2(b) exemption on a voluntary basis. Financial statements meeting the timing requirements of the issuer's home country or principal trading markets would be considered sufficiently current for purposes of the information requirement of the Rule.

Securities Act Release No. 6862 (April 23, 1990).

Even if the cost were not high, why would an issuer agree to continue to provide such reasonably current information well after the initial sale of the securities? Consider what happens to an issuer that refuses to provide such information to subsequent purchasers in the resale market. The initial purchaser will then be unable to use Rule 144A to subsequently resell, thereby chilling the secondary market. The initial investors, in turn, will then ratchet downward the amount they are willing to pay the issuer for the securities, reflecting an illiquidity premium. The issuer's own best interests, therefore, will lead the issuer to contract with investors to provide for an on-going right to obtain reasonably current information.

Indeed, despite the relatively narrow reach of Rule 144A(d)(4)'s disclosure requirement, most issuers engaged in a Rule 144A offering will voluntarily disclose in an offering circular. The offering circular will not only advise investors of the use of the Rule 144A exemption from § 5, but will also provide information disclosure similar to that of the registration statement, including audited financial statements and a description of the business, properties, management, and shareholders. Issuers disclose not because of any legal mandate, but because the market requires the information. Issuers failing to disclose will face a large discount on the offering price or, in the extreme, find their securities unmarketable.

E.   RESALES

Securities resold through Rule 144A continue to be classified as restricted securities. Liquidity is important to investors. Even qualified institutional buyers may hesitate (or demand at the very least a large discount) unless the securities can be resold eventually in the public markets. QIBs may also resell to other QIBs immediately under Rule 144A. The ability to resell to other QIBs creates a "super"-secondary market of only QIBs for unregistered securities sold through Rule 144A.

The fact that Rule 144A allows resales to other QIBs does not ensure that a secondary market will arise. Bringing together potential buyers and sellers in an organized market setting is costly. Moreover, because of the limited number of QIBs, such a market is necessarily not as deep as the public capital markets. The SEC originally envisioned that Rule 144A resales would take place through electronic trading systems and, in particular, through the NASD's automated PORTAL trading system ("Private Offerings, Resale and Trading through Automated Linkages"). Clearance and settlement of trade on the PORTAL system take place through the Depository Trust Company. In practice, relatively few Rule 144A securities are actually traded using the automated PORTAL system.

Rule 144A is not an exclusive safe harbor. Despite the focus in Rule 144A on the type of security (i.e., whether the security is non-fungible with one traded on a national securities exchange or on Nasdaq), ultimately the Securities Act focuses on transactions. Purchasers of securities under Rule 144A can eventually resell the securities freely through Rule 144 after meeting either the one or two year holding period requirement. Once resold through Rule 144, the Rule 144A securities may then be freely resold in the public secondary market among all investors. Regulation S also allows QIBs to resell securities purchased in a Rule 144A transaction offshore to persons outside the United States.

HYPOTHETICAL SEVEN

Island Tours wants to raise additional capital to expand its operations internationally to provide tours in Aruba and the Maldives. Island Tours' common stock has traded on Nasdaq since its IPO three years ago. Skipper, the CEO of Island Tours, does not want to expose the company (or himself) to potential § 11 liability from the offering. Island Tours turns to you for advice. Consider the following possible scenarios:

1. *Scenario One*: Island Tours proposes to sell $50 million of a new class of preferred stock to about ten large mutual funds. Island Tours cold calls 100 mutual funds (assume that these are QIBs) as potential purchasers and provides each mutual fund with some basic information on Island Tours and three years worth of audited financials. Can Island Tours sell to the mutual funds under Rule 144A?

2. *Scenario Two*: Island Tours hires Goldbucks Brothers to act as its selling agent. Through Goldbucks Brothers, Island Tours sells $50 million of a new class of preferred shares to 10 accredited purchasers under Rule 506. Lovey, one of the accredited purchasers, bought $1 million in the offering (assume Lovey has a net worth of $5 million). Two days after the offering, Lovey cold calls Fidelity (a qualified institutional buyer) and Fidelity agrees to purchase all of her preferred shares in Island Tours. Is this okay?

3. *Scenario Three*: Lovey sells to Fidelity three months after she purchases the securities from Island Tours (assume that Fidelity gets the required information package under Rule 144A(d)(4) from Island Tours). Fidelity in turn sells the securities to Vanguard (also a QIB) the next week. Any problem? What if Fidelity sells the securities to the Professor, an academic with a net worth of $900,000, the next day?

4. *Scenario Four*: Suppose Island Tours goes ahead instead with a Rule 506 offering of $10 million of its common stock to ten accredited investors (including Lovey). Can Lovey sell $1 million of the common stock purchased in the Rule 506 offering to Fidelity (a QID) under Rule 144A?

F. RULE 144A AND REGISTRATION UNDER THE SECURITIES ACT

Despite the possibility of different resale exemptions from § 5 that allow qualified institutional buyers to resell securities eventually into the broader secondary market, QIBs often demand registration rights from issuers. Registration rights allow QIBs to force the issuer to register the Rule 144A shares for immediate resale to the general public through a secondary public offering.

What are the benefits of providing registration rights? Restricted securities, as we have seen above, are illiquid. Despite the availability of the PORTAL system, most QIBs prefer to resell into the broader secondary markets. Securities sold without an accompanying registration rights agreement receive a correspondingly large discount from investors. Mutual funds and insurance companies are also limited in their ability to invest in illiquid securities. Open-end mutual fund, for example, may hold up to a maximum of 15 percent of the fund's assets in illiquid securities. The SEC has made clear, nonetheless, that Rule 144A securities are not necessarily considered illiquid for purposes of determining the 15 percent ceiling for mutual funds. See Securities Act Release No. 6862 (April 23, 1990). Providing for registration rights allows such potential QIBs to invest in a Regulation D/Rule 144A offering.

One method for issuers to register securities initially sold through a Rule 144A offering is through shelf registration. Rule 415(a)(1)(i) allows for the shelf registration of secondary offerings of shares. Typically, the issuer will agree as part of the primary offering to QIBs to maintain the shelf registration for two years, after which QIBs may turn to Rule 144 to resell the restricted securities. A more common method for issuers to give effect to a registration rights agreement is through a public exchange offer. In the exchange offer, identical registered securities are exchanged for the restricted Rule 144A securities. The SEC has, however, confined the use of such exchange offers for U.S. issuers to non-convertible debt securities and investment grade preferred stock. See, e.g., SEC No–Action Letter, Exxon Capital Holding Corp. (available May 13, 1988).

If issuers are willing to grant QIBs registration rights, why not simply sell the securities through a public offering in the first place rather than through Rule 144A? First, registration rights are often limited. Issuers may, for example, provide for a delayed effective date to give themselves time before investors may exercise the registration rights. Second, courts have held that the initial Rule 144A offering and any subsequent public exchange offering are considered separate, non-integrated transaction. See *American High–Income Trust v. AlliedSignal*, 329 F. Supp. 2d 534 (S.D.N.Y.2004). The offering memorandum used in the Rule 144A transaction is thus not a "prospectus" for purposes of § 12(a)(2) liability. Neither the issuer nor any of the placement agents will face §§ 11 or 12(a)(2) liability for misstatements relating to the initial Rule 144 private placement, although Rule 10b–5 continues to apply. Although issuers may face Securities Act liability for a subsequent public exchange offering (when and if such an offering occurs), placement agents are not liable if they do not participate in the exchange.

CHAPTER 11

FEDERAL REGULATION OF SHAREHOLDER VOTING

Rules and Statutes

—*Sections 14(a), 27 of the Exchange Act*

—*Rule 14a–1 through Rule 14a–15 of the Exchange Act*

—*Schedule 14A of the Exchange Act*

MOTIVATING HYPOTHETICAL

FoodNow provides grocery delivery services in a number of major metropolitan areas. Since its founding six years ago in Alaska, FoodNow has enjoyed phenomenal growth, increasing its revenues by over 100% each year. Unfortunately, the company has yet to earn a profit. Two years ago, FoodNow went public with an offering of its common stock. FoodNow shares trade on the New York Stock Exchange and FoodNow presently has a market capitalization of $10 billion and over 2,000 shareholders. Nathan, the CEO and Chairman of FoodNow, owns 3% of the outstanding stock. The board of FoodNow consists of seven directors including Nathan, two other executive officers, and four outside directors. Lisa, an individual investor in Chicago, owns 100 shares of FoodNow as part of her portfolio of equity investments.

I. INTRODUCTION

Corporations range from small businesses with one shareholder to large multi-national conglomerates with thousands of shareholders. In theory, shareholders are the residual "owners" of the corporation. After all other claimants, including employees, suppliers, and creditors, are paid what they are owed under contract, shareholders receive the residual profits (or bear the residual loss, but only to the extent of their investment). Although residual, the profits can be significant. Consider how well the equity holders of Microsoft have done since the company's IPO in 1986.

Although corporations enjoy considerable freedom under state corporate law to allocate voting power among their equity holders, generally the most residual class of securities in a corporation (i.e., common stock) retains voting power. Through their votes, shareholders typically elect the board of directors of a corporation. The board controls the operation of the corporation, including the choice of the top executive officers of the corporation.

In the past, most directors of large, public corporations were elected annually at the shareholders meeting. During the early 1990s, many corporations adopted so-called "staggered" boards. With a staggered board, shareholders elect one-third of the directors annually for three-year terms. As we will discuss in Chapter 12, staggered boards make it more difficult for insurgent shareholders to displace the incumbent board. Even shareholders with a majority of the voting power must wait for two annual meetings to obtain two-thirds control over the board. In the context of a hostile takeover, control over the board is important to remove any defenses a corporation may have adopted.

Shareholders also vote to approve certain major transactions, such as a statutory merger with another corporation. Corporate officers and directors may also have shareholder votes to ratify certain transactions in which the officers and directors have a conflict of interest. In certain jurisdictions, shareholders also vote to ratify the company's choice of outside auditor.

Although shareholders are entitled to cast their votes at the annual shareholder meeting, most shareholders do not attend the meeting. If you owned only 100 shares of FoodNow, would you fly out to the company's headquarters in Alaska to attend the annual meeting? Instead, most shareholders vote by proxy, completing a proxy card (referred to as a "form of proxy") and allowing a proxy (typically the incumbent board of directors) to vote their shares at the shareholder meeting.

How does a typical proxy vote take place? First, the issuer identifies shareholders eligible to vote. Not all shareholders of a corporation are allowed to vote; shareholders must be shareholders as of the "record date" in order to vote. The board of directors usually sets the record date up to a couple of months before the meeting date. Complicating matters, most investors who own shares through brokerage accounts are not the owners of record. Instead, the shares are held in "street name" with the brokerage firms listed as the legal owners of the shares. Brokerage firms are required to send the proxy card to the shareholders who own shares in street name so the shareholders can vote their shares. Not all shareholders return the proxy card. If a shareholder fails to vote, the brokerage firm can vote the street name shares for routine matters, including the uncontested election of directors, but not on non-routine matters, such as shareholder issue proposals. Broker votes are almost always cast in support of the incumbent board. Tabulation companies, such as Mellon Investor Services, collect the proxies. Once collected, the tabulation company will certify the proxies and tabulate results.

Shareholder voting is not cheap. Those seeking shareholders' votes must bring the issue to the shareholders' attention. The officers and directors of a corporation enjoy privileges of incumbency in capturing the shareholders' attention. They have immediate access to the shareholders of record of the corporation (through the corporate transfer agent). This allows managers to identify those shareholders not holding their shares in street name, typically larger, institutional owners who carry more weight in determining a vote. More importantly, the officers and directors can send out a proxy statement to the shareholders at the corporation's expense. Outsiders nominating an opposing slate of candidates for the board of directors (or some other voting issue for shareholders) must bear the cost of mailing out separate proxy solicitations. Outsiders must also often engage in more direct lobbying such as "wining and dining" shareholders holding a large number of votes to persuade them to vote for the alternate slate of directors. State corporate law allows reimbursement of such expenses incurred by outsiders only if the outsiders win control of the board *and* obtain a shareholder vote approving such reimbursement. Moreover, those "soliciting" a proxy vote face both disclosure requirements and antifraud liability, further raising the cost to insurgent outsiders.

Compounding the high costs of getting shareholders to vote on a particular issue is the rational apathy of many shareholders. Suppose Lisa, the shareholder with 100 shares of FoodNow, must choose between Food-Now's slate of directors and some competing slate. Reading disclosures and deciding how to vote takes time and effort. Even if Lisa does vote, her vote is unlikely to matter. What are the chances that her 100 shares, out of a total of say 100 million shares, will be pivotal in the vote? From Lisa's perspective, her 100 share investment may not justify her time and attention. Lisa, if she is like many individual investors, may simply throw proxy solicitations in the trash.

In this chapter we discuss the basic federal securities regulatory framework governing the solicitation of proxies used in shareholder voting. We focus particularly on the election of directors involving a potential corporate change of control. We then examine the present scope of shareholder voting power. If shareholders are the residual owners of the firm, should they have more voting power? And who should decide the allocation of power within a corporation? As part of this discussion, we assess the ability of shareholders to insert their own proposals on the company's proxy statement under Rule 14a–8 of the Exchange Act.

II.   SOLICITATION OF PROXIES

State corporate law allocates power between shareholders and the board of directors. As noted above, shareholders of large public corporations typically have the right only to elect the board of directors and to ratify certain major corporate transactions. A corporation may also turn to shareholders to ratify transactions in which a director or officer has a conflict of interest, thereby insulating the transaction from greater judicial scrutiny. Outside of these episodic voting events, shareholders generally have no say in the management of the corporation.

When outsiders seek to use shareholder proxies to elect a competing slate of nominees to the board of directors, we call that a "proxy contest." During the 1950s, insurgents turned to proxy contests as a device to replace the directors and thereby take control of the corporation. Although typically roundly defeated, insurgents occasionally succeeded. Robert Young, for example, wrested control of the New York Central Railroad from the Vanderbilt family through a proxy contest in 1954. By the 1970s, however, proxy contests fell into disuse, displaced by tender offers, which allowed a bidder to purchase shares outright from public investors rather than simply obtaining their votes. Among other advantages of the tender offer, investors are much more likely to tender their shares to an unknown bidder (particularly if offered cash) than they are to vote for an unknown insurgent's nominees in a proxy contest. If an unknown insurgent wins a proxy contest, investors who still own shares will have to live with the consequences on share value. At least the prior incumbent managers are something of a known quantity to investors.

In recent years, increasing use of defensive tactics aimed at fending off hostile tender offers has resulted in a resurgence in the use of proxy contests. As we discuss later in Chapter 12, companies often employ "poison pills" that dilute the interest of a hostile bidder if the bidder crosses a certain threshold of share ownership. For a hostile bidder to succeed in a tender offer, the bidder must first obtain board approval to redeem the poison pill. The Delaware Chancery Court explains the strategy:

> When poison pills became prevalent, would-be acquirors resorted to proxy contests as a method of obtaining indirectly that which they could no longer get through a tender offer. By taking out the target company's board through a proxy fight or a consent solicitation, the acquiror could obtain control of the board room, redeem the pill, and open the way for consummation of its tender offer.

In re Gaylord Container Corp. Shareholders Litigation, 753 A.2d 462, 482 (Del. Ch. 2000).

The federal securities regulatory scheme only applies to proxy solicitations that occur for companies required to register their securities under Exchange Act § 12. Recall from Chapter 4 that this section requires companies to register if they have securities listed on a national securities exchange (§ 12(a)) or a specified minimum amount of total assets and shareholders (§ 12(g) and Rule 12g–1). Throughout the proxy rules, companies with securities registered under § 12 with respect to which proxies are solicited are referred to as the "registrant." Companies required to make Exchange Act reporting filings pursuant to § 15(d) are not subject to the proxy rules.

For registrants, § 14(a) of the Exchange Act and its accompanying rules regulate the proxy solicitation process. Section 14(a) focuses on when a person acts "to solicit or to permit the use of his name to solicit any proxy." If no solicitation occurs, the federal securities requirements for proxies do not apply. If a solicitation has occurred then the proxy rules contained in Rule 14a–3 through Rule 14a–15 apply, absent an exemption. We start by examining what is a "solicitation."

A. WHAT IS A "SOLICITATION"?

When does a solicitation for a proxy occur? Consider Gary, the head of the fictitious state of Berkeley's Public Employee Retirement System (BEPERS), a large shareholder of FoodNow. Gary has nominated a competing slate of candidates for election to FoodNow's board of directors. Gary calls up dozens of institutional investors holding FoodNow stock and asks them for their proxy to vote for his candidates. Gary's communications clearly constitute a solicitation of a proxy under the definition of a solicitation in Rule 14a–1(*l*).

The definition of solicitation is much broader than explicit communications intended to obtain an actual proxy for voting purposes. Rule 14a–1(*l*) of the Exchange Act treats any communication "under circumstances reasonably calculated to result in the procurement, withholding or revocation of a proxy" as a solicitation. Rule 14a–1(f) defines "proxy" to include not only "every proxy" but also "consent or authorization" where "consent or authorization may take the form of failure to object or to dissent." The Rule 14a–1(*l*) definition of a "solicitation" of a proxy therefore extends to communications by third parties who are not seeking the power to vote proxies on a particular voting issue. For example, investors discussing how to vote, presumably influencing the views of other investors, may be engaged in a proxy solicitation.

Once a communication is considered a proxy solicitation, the communicating party faces a number of requirements. Absent an exemption, the soliciting party may need to file a preliminary proxy statement with the SEC, wait for SEC approval, and then mail a formal proxy statement to those privy to the communications. Aside from imposing direct mailing and filing costs as well as delays, this regime discourages communications by investors wishing to remain anonymous. Because proxy statements are required to be filed with the SEC, the registrant and other shareholders are able to determine not only the identity of communicating parties but also the substance of such communications. Moreover, because Rule 14a–9's antifraud prohibitions apply to all proxy solicitations, investors also face the specter of potential antifraud liability. Incumbent management, for example, may bring a suit for violation of the proxy rules as part of its defense against a proxy contest. Such a suit may impose costs on insurgents and stir up doubt among shareholders about the insurgent. Rule 14a–9 suits are a two-way street. Insurgent shareholders may also bring a Rule 14a–9 action against the incumbent board of directors for fraud in the incumbent's proxy statement.

The SEC narrows the broad definition of a solicitation under Rule 14a–1(*l*) through a number of exemptions. There are two basic categories of exemptions. The first category, contained in Rule 14a–1(*l*)(2), removes the communication completely from the definition of a proxy solicitation. Rule 14a–1(*l*)(2)(iv), for example, excludes from the definition of a proxy solicitation public announcements by shareholders on how they intend to vote, including public speeches, press releases, and newspaper advertisements. Because of the exclusion, communicating parties are shielded from Rule

14a–9's antifraud prohibitions as well as the other proxy requirements. If Gary can convince Fidelity Investments to vote in favor of BEPERS' candidates, Fidelity can announce its intentions through a newspaper advertisement, helping to convince other shareholders to join Gary's cause. Because such an announcement is excluded from the definition of a solicitation under Rule 14a–1(*l*)(2)(iv), Fidelity does not face any proxy rule-related costs or potential liability.

The second category of exemptions, found in Rule 14a–2, does not remove communication from the definition of a solicitation but instead exempts the solicitation from the application of a subset of the proxy rules. Rule 14a–2(a)(6) allows "tombstone"-like advertisements about a proxy solicitation. Under Rule 14a–2(a)(6), solicitations made through "a newspaper advertisement which informs security holders of a source from which they may obtain copies of a proxy statement, form of proxy and any other soliciting material" and that do no more than: (i) name the registrant, (ii) state the reason for the advertisement, and (iii) identify the proposal or proposals are not required to comply with Rules 14a–3 through 14a–15.

Similarly, Rule 14a–2(b) exempts certain solicitations from some, but not all, of the proxy rules. An exemption under Rule 14a–2(b) relieves soliciting parties from the information disclosure requirements of the proxy rules, among other requirements. The exemption is not all-inclusive. In particular, Rule 14a–9's antifraud prohibition continues to apply. Rule 14a–2(b)(1) exempts solicitations by a person who does not seek "the power to act as proxy for a security holder and does not furnish or otherwise request, or act on behalf of a person who furnishes or requests, a form of revocation, abstention, consent or authorization." Rule 14a–2(b)(1), however, excludes from the exemption certain persons such as an officer or director of the registrant and nominees to the board of directors "for whose election as a director proxies are solicited." Also excluded is any person who, "because of a substantial interest in the subject matter of the solicitation, is likely to receive a benefit from a successful solicitation that would not be shared pro rata by all other holders of the same class of securities." Rule 14a–2(b)(2) similarly exempts solicitations not made on behalf of the registrant "where the total number of persons solicited is not more than ten."

HYPOTHETICAL ONE

Gary, who heads the fictitious state of Berkeley's Public Employee Retirement System (BEPERS), is contemplating a proxy control contest, putting up his own competing slate of nominees for election to FoodNow's board of directors. The following communications occur. Consider whether any (or all) of these communications constitute a proxy solicitation.

1. Gary telephones nine institutional investors. In the phone calls, he discusses at length the reasons that the institutional investors should give him their proxy to vote for his nominees to the board.

2. Goldbucks Brothers, one of the institutional investors that received a phone call from Gary, telephones Milberg Investments to confer regarding the proxy contest. Both Goldbucks Brothers and Milberg are large shareholders of FoodNow.

3. After some consideration, Goldbucks Brothers decides to support Gary's slate of nominees. To give Gary an added boost, Goldbucks Brothers posts its decision on its web page.

4. The *Wall Street Journal* publishes an editorial extolling the virtues of Gary and his slate of board nominees which is published at the same time shareholders receive proxy solicitations from Gary and from FoodNow's incumbent management.

B.   PROXY DISCLOSURE

As with the rest of the federal securities regime, the regulation of proxy solicitations focuses on disclosure. We discuss two aspects of the proxy disclosure regime: (1) the disclosure and filing requirements for the "proxy statement" sent to shareholders whose proxy is being solicited and (2) the ability of parties to engage in proxy solicitations before the furnishing of the proxy statement, "testing the waters" before launching a full-blown proxy contest.

1.   DISCLOSURE AND FILING REQUIREMENTS

Rule 14a–3(a) prohibits solicitations before a formal proxy statement containing information specified by the SEC is delivered to the solicited shareholder, either concurrently with or prior to the solicitation. For those seeking to obtain the actual proxy from shareholders to make votes, shareholders must receive a "form of the proxy" as specified in Rule 14a–4. The form of the proxy must set forth in bold-face whether the proxy solicitation is on behalf of the board of directors or some other party and must specify separately each voting item as well as boxes for approval, disapproval, or abstention.

The formal proxy disclosure document comes in two flavors: the preliminary and definitive proxy statements, as defined in Schedule 14A. For certain routine voting issues, only a definitive proxy statement is required of the registrant. If the registrant is soliciting proxies for an annual meeting and the only voting issues involve the election of directors, the election, approval, or ratification of accountants, or other routine matters, the registrant needs only to file a definitive proxy statement with the SEC no later than the first date such materials are sent to shareholders (Rule 14a–6(b)).

For all other voting issues, the registrant and other parties soliciting proxies must first file a preliminary proxy statement with the SEC at least ten calendar days prior to the date the definitive proxy statement is first sent or given to security holders. Even for more routine matters, such as the election of directors, if the "registrant comments upon or refers to a solicitation in opposition in connection with the meeting in its proxy material" then the registrant must also meet the preliminary proxy statement filing requirement (Rule 14a–6(a)).

The preliminary proxy statements must clearly indicate that they are "preliminary copies" (Rule 14a–6(e)). The preliminary proxy statements must also indicate when the definitive proxy statement is expected to be released to security holders (Rule 14a–6(d)). The soliciting party is able to designate certain information contained in the preliminary proxy statement as "confidential." Unless marked as confidential, information in the preliminary proxy statement is available online through the EDGAR system at www.sec.gov.

Although parties may solicit proxies once a preliminary proxy statement has been delivered, parties may not deliver a form of proxy, consent or authorization to any security holder "unless the security holder concurrently receives, or has previously received, a definitive proxy statement that has been filed with the Commission pursuant to Rule 14a–6(b)." Those seeking to obtain proxy votes must wait until the definitive proxy statement is filed with the SEC.

In theory, soliciting parties may begin using a definitive proxy ten days after filing the preliminary proxy statement with the SEC. The soliciting party does not need to wait for SEC approval before moving forward with the use of a definitive proxy statement for solicitations. The soliciting party must nonetheless file the definitive proxy statement with the SEC under Rule 14a–6(b). In practice, the registrant and other soliciting parties will typically wait for SEC approval of the preliminary proxy before proceeding with the definitive proxy statement. For certain voting issues, particularly mergers, the soliciting parties will give the SEC considerably more than ten days to review the proxy statement.

Why wait for SEC approval? The SEC staff often provides comments on the preliminary proxy statement, which can take much longer than the ten calendar-day waiting period, extending six to eight weeks. Waiting for SEC approval provides soliciting parties some degree of comfort that their proxy statement is valid and does not violate Rule 14a–9. SEC approval, however, will not shield the soliciting party from a later Rule 14a–9 action. Similarly, those who choose to ignore the SEC's comments run the risk of a possible SEC enforcement action. Note the similarity here with the practice of delaying the effective date for a registration statement during the waiting period to allow for SEC review in the public offering process discussed in Chapter 7.

Schedule 14A requires a number of disclosures. For registrants seeking proxies relating to the election of directors at the annual meeting, Schedule 14A requires that the proxy statement include, among other things, information on:

- date, time, and place of the meeting of shareholders (Item 1)
- the persons making the solicitation (Item 4)
- voting securities (Item 6)
- ownership of certain beneficial owners holding more than 5% of any class of the registrant's voting securities (Item 6)

- director nominees and officers of the registrant (Item 7)

- audit, nominating and compensation committees of the board of directors, including whether the members of the audit and nominating committees are independent (Item 7)

- compensation of directors and officers (Item 8)

Schedule 14A, like other mandatory disclosure documents in the federal securities regime, incorporates by reference a number of items in Regulations S-K and S-X. Item 8 of Schedule 14A, for example, deals with the compensation of directors and executive officers and makes explicit reference to Item 402 of Regulation S-K. Item 11(l) of Form S-1, dealing with executive compensation (see Chapter 7 on public offerings), likewise references Item 402 of Regulation S-K.

Schedule 14A reduces the amount of information required for insurgents putting forth a competing slate of nominees for election to the board of directors. Such insurgents do not need to present information on the directors and officers of the registrant or board committees of the registrant. Insurgents need not provide details on compensation of directors and officers of the registrant. Shareholders already receive that information in the management's own proxy statement. Only information on the insurgent's own nominees to the board is required.

For registrants seeking a shareholder vote for certain major corporate events and transactions other than election of directors, Schedule 14A requires additional disclosure, including:

- Authorization or Issuance of Securities Otherwise than for Exchange (Item 11)

- Modification or Exchange of Securities (Item 12)

- Mergers, Consolidations, Acquisitions and Similar Matters (Item 14)

- Acquisition or Disposition of Property (Item 15)

Information contained in the proxy statement must be "clearly presented" (see Rule 14a–5). Rule 14a–5 also specifies minimum legibility requirements. The information in the proxy statement, however, need not follow the order presented in Schedule 14A.

Together with the required proxy statement, solicitations on behalf of the registrant relating to an annual meeting at which directors are to be elected must be accompanied or preceded by an annual report to security holders. Rule 14a–3(b) mandates specific information that must be included in the annual report, including audited financial statements.

For communications relating to a proxy vote not excluded under the definitional provision for a solicitation in Rule 14a–1(l) or otherwise exempt under Rule 14a–2, Rule 14a–3 provides a special exemption from the proxy statement delivery requirement. Rule 14a–3(f) excludes from the proxy statement delivery requirement any "communication made by means of speeches in public forums, press releases, published or broadcast opinions, statements, or advertisements appearing in a broadcast media, newspaper, magazine or other bona fide publication disseminated on a regular basis." Rule 14a–3(f)'s exemption has two prerequisites. First, no form of proxy may be provided to the security holder in connection with the communication. Second, at the time the communication is made, a definitive proxy statement relating to the solicitation must have been filed with the SEC under Rule 14a–6(b).

Consider the purpose of Rule 14a–3(f). Imagine that an insurgent wishes to advertise her views on a proxy contest in the *Wall Street Journal*, thereby maximizing the distribution of her views. Because the insurgent is soliciting a proxy (with large institutional investors for example), the insurgent will not qualify for the Rule 14a–1(*l*)(2)(iv) exclusion for public communications on the vote. The insurgent will, absent anything else, have to distribute a copy of the proxy statement either together with the *Wall Street Journal* or prior to the delivery of the newspaper to every recipient under Rule 14a–3. The prohibitive cost of the proxy statement delivery requirement would likely eliminate all public communication by the insurgent. Company officials would face a similar requirement, but they can use corporate funds to pay the cost of distributing the proxy statement. Rule 14a–3(f) eliminates the otherwise prohibitive cost to insurgents of delivering the proxy statement to all those receiving a public solicitation. Rule 14a–9's antifraud prohibition, however, continues to apply.

2. TESTING THE WATERS

For activist shareholders seeking to dislodge an incumbent board through a proxy contest, the cost and delay associated with drafting a proxy statement and awaiting SEC clearance for the definitive proxy statement may deter many from launching a contest in the first place. Consider the position of a potential insurgent weighing whether to launch a contest without knowing how shareholders might react to such a contest. If shareholders are receptive, a proxy contest may have a decent chance of dislodging the incumbent directors (or at least putting pressure on the incumbent managers to institute some change in their policies). On the other hand, if shareholders are not receptive then the insurgent will waste both its time and resources on a futile proxy contest.

Assessing shareholders' interest in a proxy contest (or other proxy issue), therefore, is important in reducing the risk facing insurgents. The proxy rules provide several avenues for insurgents to "test the waters." In order to be useful, "testing the waters" must be available before the insurgent undertakes the expense of drafting and filing the proxy statement. As we discussed above, Rule 14a–2(b)(2) exempts solicitations of ten or fewer shareholders from most of the proxy rules (but not antifraud liability). For many public companies, the top ten institutional investors own a sizeable fraction of the outstanding shares. Getting the opinion of just the top ten institutions, therefore, may provide potential insurgents with vital information on their likelihood of success.

In 2000, the SEC promulgated Rule 14a–12, significantly expanding the ability of the registrant, potential insurgents, and shareholders to "test the waters" through communications prior to the furnishing of a preliminary or definitive proxy statement to investors. Testing the waters allows an insurgent to avoid initiating a costly proxy contest that is unlikely to succeed. The SEC provided this justification:

> We recognize the many recent developments in technology that have enabled companies to communicate more frequently with security holders at a significantly reduced cost. In addition, security holders and the markets are demanding more information from public companies about new developments and proposed transactions. In light of the rapid pace of change in the securities markets and developments in technology, we believe the time has come to update the proxy rules to permit security holder communications to flow more freely and to facilitate a more informed security holder base.

Securities Act Release No. 7760 (October 26, 1999).

Solicitations under Rule 14a–12 may be either oral or written. In the case of written communications, the soliciting parties must identify participants in the solicitation (e.g., the insurgent) as well as describe "their direct or indirect interests, by security holdings or otherwise" in the registrant or, in the alternative, provide a "prominent legend in clear, plain language advising security holders where they can obtain that information" (Rule 14a–12(a)(1)(i)). Soliciting parties must also include with written solicitations a "prominent legend in clear, plain language advising security holders to read the proxy statement when it is available because it contains important information" (Rule 14a–12(a)(1)(ii)).

Oral solicitations no longer face any proxy statement delivery requirement pursuant to Rule 14a–12. This opens up the possibility that soliciting parties may shift from written to oral communications, particularly to communicate confidential information to a select number of shareholders. The SEC has made clear, however, that telephone scripts, presentation materials, and electronic communications are written communications for purposes of Rule 14a–12. Moreover, Regulation FD (prohibiting selective disclosure of non-public, material information by an Exchange Act reporting issuer) may prohibit the use of oral communications, even if permitted under Rule 14a–12, that result in the selective dissemination of information by a registrant to its shareholders.

Any soliciting materials "published, sent or given to security holders" pursuant to Rule 14a–12(a) must be filed with the SEC no later than the first date on which the information is disseminated to the security holders (Rule 14a–12(b)). Whether solicitations under Rule 14a–12 take place through oral or written communications, a form of proxy (i.e., a proxy voting card) may not be given to any shareholder receiving a solicitation under Rule 14a–12 until the shareholder has also received a definitive proxy statement under Rule 14a–3(a). In theory, a shareholder will not be able to vote until he or she receives a definitive proxy statement. How closely will a shareholder look at the definitive proxy statement after communicating directly with an insurgent under Rule 14a–12?

Rule 14a–12 has opened up the proxy solicitation process to communication prior to the furnishing of a proxy statement. At the same time, electronic communication over the Internet (including web sites, message boards, and emails) has drastically reduced the cost of communication. Lower costs combined with a more relaxed regulatory attitude toward proxy-related communication under Rule 14a–12 have given rise to increased communication regarding proxy contests and barriers for insurgents seeking to wage a proxy contest. In 2001, for example, Travis Street Partners LLC, an investment fund, used the Internet in a proxy contest to elect three directors to the ICO Inc. board of directors. Travis Street used its web page and message board to keep interested parties informed of its proxy campaign. Not only did Travis Street keep investors informed about the contest, the Internet provided Travis Street with valuable information on potential supporters who registered their email addresses and other contact information on Travis Street's web page.

Until recently, proxy control contests were exceedingly rare. Insurgents faced high costs in identifying large shareholders. Even when large shareholders were identified, insurgents faced SEC review of all communication with the shareholders as potential proxy solicitations. In addition, almost all such contests failed, with incumbent directors retaining their seats. Today, an insurgent putting forth a competing slate of director nominees may make oral and written solicitations even before filing a preliminary proxy statement with the SEC under Rule 14a–12. Incumbents receive no formal notice of the outsider's efforts to drum up support for a proxy contest until the outsider files the preliminary proxy statement with the SEC. Insurgents may also persuade large institutional investors to join their efforts to displace the incumbents. Large institutional investors can publicly announce their intentions on the proxy contest vote pursuant to Rule 14a–1(l) without triggering the proxy rules. The insurgent may also take out newspaper ads and make other forms of public communication under Rule 14a–3(f) without distributing a proxy statement. A couple of barriers remain. Insurgents who individually or together with a group beneficially own more than 5% of the target company's stock must comply with disclosure requirements under § 13(d) of the Exchange Act (covered in Chapter 12). Rule 14a–9 antifraud liability also applies to all proxy solicitation communications.

HYPOTHETICAL TWO

Gary of the BEPERS fund has not yet filed a definitive proxy statement with the SEC. Nonetheless, the financial markets are awash with rumors of Gary's impending proxy contest for control of FoodNow's board of directors. Which proxy solicitation requirements apply to the following communications?

1. *Scenario One*: Gary sends out a short letter to all the major institutional investor shareholders of FoodNow. The letter describes at length the perceived problems with FoodNow and the incompetence of Nathan, the CEO and Chairman. Gary does not mention the identities of his competing slate of directors, but does state: "I am presently assembling a team of highly respected nominees to FoodNow's board and will provide more information later with the definitive proxy statement.''

2. *Scenario Two*: What if Gary also mails out a detailed proposal for how he would turn FoodNow's business around to FoodNow's ten largest outside shareholders? The mailing contains confidential information about Gary's proposed business strategy should he obtain control of FoodNow.

3. *Scenario Three*: What if Gary, instead of sending out the letter selectively to large institutional investors, publishes it in the *Wall Street Journal*?

C. RULE 14a–9 ANTIFRAUD LIABILITY

As with the other areas of the securities laws, the proxy rules provide for antifraud liability to ensure the veracity of disclosed information. Rule 14a–9 provides:

> No solicitation subject to this regulation shall be made by means of any proxy statement, form of proxy, notice of meeting or other communication, written or oral, containing any statement which, at the time and in the light of the circumstances under which it is made, is false or misleading with respect to any material fact, or which omits to state any material fact necessary in order to make the statements therein not false or misleading or necessary to correct any statement in any earlier communication with respect to the solicitation of a proxy for the same meeting or subject matter which has become false or misleading.

Rule 14a–9 and § 14(a) do not explicitly provide for private causes of action to enforce the antifraud prohibition. Should private parties be able to bring a cause of action under § 14(a) and Rule 14a–9?

J.I. Case Co. v. Borak
377 U.S. 426 (1964).

■ MR. JUSTICE CLARK delivered the opinion of the Court.

This is a civil action brought by respondent, a stockholder of petitioner J. I. Case Company, charging deprivation of the pre-emptive rights of respondent and other shareholders by reason by a merger between Case and the American Tractor Corporation. It is alleged that the merger was effected through the circulation of a false and misleading proxy statement by those proposing the˙ merger.... We consider only the question of whether § 27 of the [Exchange] Act authorizes a federal cause of action for rescission or damages to a corporate stockholder with respect to a consummated merger which was authorized pursuant to the use of a proxy statement alleged to contain false and misleading statements violative of § 14(a) of the Act....

I.

Respondent, the owner of 2,000 shares of common stock of Case acquired prior to the merger, brought this suit ... seeking to enjoin a proposed merger between Case and the American Tractor Corporation

(ATC) on various grounds, including ... misrepresentations contained in the material circulated to obtain proxies.... They alleged: that petitioners, or their predecessors, solicited or permitted their names to be used in the solicitation of proxies of Case stockholders for use at a special stockholders' meeting at which the proposed merger with ATC was to be voted upon; that the proxy solicitation material so circulated was false and misleading in violation of § 14(a) of the Act and Rule 14a–9 which the Commission had promulgated thereunder; that the merger was approved at the meeting by a small margin of votes and was thereafter consummated; that the merger would not have been approved but for the false and misleading statements in the proxy solicitation material; and that Case stockholders were damaged thereby. The respondent sought judgment holding the merger void and damages for himself and all other stockholders similarly situated, as well as such further relief "as equity shall require."

* * *

II.

It appears clear that private parties have a right under § 27 to bring suit for violation of § 14(a) of the Act. Indeed, this section specifically grants the appropriate District Courts jurisdiction over "all suits in equity and actions at law brought to enforce any liability or duty created" under the Act. The petitioners make no concessions, however, emphasizing that Congress made no specific reference to a private right of action in § 14(a); that, in any event, the right ... should be limited to prospective relief only....

III.

* * *

The purpose of § 14(a) is to prevent management or others from obtaining authorization for corporate action by means of deceptive or inadequate disclosure in proxy solicitation. The section stemmed from the congressional belief that "(f)air corporate suffrage is an important right that should attach to every equity security bought on a public exchange." It was intended to "control the conditions under which proxies may be solicited with a view to preventing the recurrence of abuses which * * * (had) frustrated the free exercise of the voting rights of stockholders." "Too often proxies are solicited without explanation to the stockholder of the real nature of the questions for which authority to cast his vote is sought." These broad remedial purposes are evidenced in the language of the section which makes it "unlawful for any person * * * to solicit or to permit the use of his name to solicit any proxy or consent or authorization in respect of any security * * * registered on any national securities exchange in contravention of such rules and regulations as the Commission may prescribe as necessary or appropriate in the public interest or for the protection of investors." While this language makes no specific reference to a private right of action, among its chief purposes is "the protection of investors," which certainly implies the availability of judicial relief where necessary to achieve that result. . . .

. . . [T]he possibility of civil damages or injunctive relief serves as a most effective weapon in the enforcement of the proxy requirements. The Commission advises that it examines over 2,000 proxy statements annually and each of them must necessarily be expedited. Time does not permit an independent examination of the facts set out in the proxy material and this results in the Commission's acceptance of the representations contained therein at their face value, unless contrary to other material on file with it. Indeed, on the allegations of respondent's complaint, the proxy material failed to disclose alleged unlawful market manipulation of the stock of ATC, and this unlawful manipulation would not have been apparent to the Commission until after the merger.

We, therefore, believe that under the circumstances here it is the duty of the courts to be alert to provide such remedies as are necessary to make effective the congressional purpose. . . .

It is for the federal courts "to adjust their remedies so as to grant the necessary relief" where federally secured rights are invaded. "And it is also well settled that where legal rights have been invaded, and a federal statute provides for a general right to sue for such invasion, federal courts may use any available remedy to make good the wrong done." Section 27 grants the District Courts jurisdiction "of all suits in equity and actions at law brought to enforce any liability or duty created by this title * * *.".

Nor do we find merit in the contention that such remedies are limited to prospective relief. . . . [I]f federal jurisdiction were limited to the granting of declaratory relief, victims of deceptive proxy statements would be obliged to go into state courts for remedial relief. And if the law of the State happened to attach no responsibility to the use of misleading proxy statements, the whole purpose of the section might be frustrated. Furthermore, the hurdles that the victim might face (such as separate suits, . . . security for expenses statutes, bringing in all parties necessary for complete relief, etc.) might well prove insuperable to effective relief.

IV.

Our finding that federal courts have the power to grant all necessary remedial relief is not to be construed as any indication of what we believe to be the necessary and appropriate relief in this case. We are concerned here only with a determination that federal jurisdiction for this purpose does exist. Whatever remedy is necessary must await the trial on the merits. . . .

* * *

QUESTIONS

1. The Court points to the goal of "protection of investors" as implying "the availability of judicial relief where necessary to achieve that result." Is this rationale too broad? Do the securities laws have goals other than investor protection?

2. Instead of a private cause of action, why not simply provide more funding for SEC review of proxy statements and after-the-fact enforcement actions?

3. Why would it be costly for shareholders to go to state court to seek damages and other relief for fraud in the proxy statement?

4. Is *Borak* consistent with Court's concern in *Blue Chip*, *Virginia Bankshares*, *Gustafson*, and *Central Bank of Denver* over speculative and frivolous lawsuits?

The *Borak* Court dealt with the ability of a shareholder to bring a private cause of action under Rule 14a–9. What about the registrant itself? May the incumbent board of directors authorize the corporation to sue insurgent shareholders for violating Rule 14a–9? What about for a violation of the other proxy rules? Courts have generally held that the registrant can bring suit to obtain equitable remedies for violations of the proxy rules. See *Studebaker Corp. v. Gittlin*, 360 F.2d 692, 695 (2d Cir. 1966); *Greater Iowa Corp. v. McLendon*, 378 F.2d 783, 794 (8th Cir. 1967). By contrast, at least one court has denied standing for corporations seeking damages and expressed skepticism as to the availability of equitable remedies. See *Diceon Electronics, Inc. v. Calvary Partners, L.P.*, 772 F.Supp. 859 (D.Del. 1991). Allowing the registrant to sue to enforce the proxy rules reduces the burden on the SEC to police proxies. Moreover, the registrant will have better information than the SEC as to the use of proxies relating to the registrant's own securities. The incumbent board of directors, however, may use corporate funds to harass insurgents and other outside shareholders to raise the cost of a proxy contest, thereby further entrenching the incumbents.

Left undecided by *Borak* is the state of mind plaintiffs need to show to bring a Rule 14a–9 cause of action. Should there be strict liability for false proxy solicitations under Rule 14a–9? Or should liability require a showing of negligence, recklessness, or actual knowledge of the falsehood on the part of the communicating party? As with our discussion of scienter under Rule 10b–5 in Chapter 5, tradeoffs must be made in selecting an appropriate state of mind requirement. Requiring actual intent to deceive may result in many cases of actual fraud escaping liability due to evidentiary problems. On the other hand, too lenient a state of mind requirement, such as negligence or strict liability, will capture innocent mistakes. Imposing liability on innocent mistakes will not increase deterrence and may result in more frivolous lawsuits. Consider how the Third Circuit in *Gould* dealt with the state of mind question in a Rule 14a–9 cause of action.

Gould v. American–Hawaiian S. S. Co.

535 F.2d 761 (3d Cir. 1976).

■ MARIS, CIRCUIT JUDGE.

[McLean Industries merged into Reynolds. Under the merger agreement, Reynolds would swap for each McLean Industries common share one share of a new Reynolds preferred stock with an annual dividend of $2.25, a liquidation and redemption price of $50 and a conversion privilege into one and one-half shares of common stock upon payment of $22. McLean Industries sent a proxy to its shareholders to obtain approval for the merger. Lazard Freres & Co. was McLean Industries' financial advisor. Prior to the merger, Litton, National Bulk and the McLean family were major shareholders of McLean Industries. Litton and National Bulk had separately negotiated financing agreements that effectively gave them a veto power over the merger. Litton and National Bulk refused to accept Reynolds securities as part of the merger and negotiated to receive $50 in cash for each of their McLean shares. Certain shareholders who received Reynolds securities as part of the merger brought suit against Litton, National Bulk, and others alleging, among other things, that the proxy statement sent in the merger was materially misleading in failing to explain why certain shareholders received cash and others received Reynolds securities.]

The proxy statement, 74 pages in length, was issued on April 10, 1969 and mailed to the McLean Industries shareholders on April 15th, accompanied by a two-page covering letter by Malcolm McLean [Eds—also a defendant and holder of 33.9% of McLean stock prior to the merger]. The statement and letter described the proposal for the merger, stating that the Litton and National Bulk interests were to receive $50 per share in cash and that those interests as well as the McLean family interests all together representing 64% of the McLean Industries common stock outstanding (slightly less than the necessary two-thirds) had agreed to vote for the merger. The statement included market prices of Reynolds and McLean Industries stock from 1964 through the first quarter of 1969 and other relevant information. Attached to the statement was the Plan and Agreement of Merger.

The market price of Reynolds common stock had declined to $40.125 by April 8, 1969. On May 12th Lazard issued an updated opinion to McLean Industries valuing, as of that date, the new Reynolds preferred stock at $45 per share, but also stating that Lazard continued to consider the terms of the merger fair. This updated Lazard report was reviewed by the board of directors of McLean Industries at a special meeting . . . on May 13th immediately prior to the shareholders' meeting. The seven directors present voted to reaffirm their approval of the merger. At the meeting which followed, the merger was approved by the shareholders. . . .

* * *

[The appellate court upheld the district court summary judgment determination that the proxy statement was false or misleading with respect to a material fact within the meaning of Rule 14a–9(a) and, therefore, violated § 14(a) of the Act. The court then turned to the issue of the defendants' liability, focusing particularly on the issue of the required state of mind.]

Defendant ... strongly argues that the proper standard of liability to be applied ... is a lack of good faith or, at least, scienter rather than negligence. As we have seen, the district court held negligence to be the appropriate standard under section 14(a) and we agree. The defendant urged in the district court that section 10(b) of the Act provides an analogy and that under that section the courts have held that scienter must be shown. That section and Rule 10b–5 ... which implements it make unlawful manipulative and deceptive devices or practices in connection with the purchase and sale of securities. It would seem clearly more appropriate to apply the standard of actual knowledge in determining liability for such fraudulent practices many of which might well appear innocent on their face.

We agree with the district court that section 14(a) and Rule 14a–9(a) may be more closely analogized to section 11 of the Securities Act of 1933 which deals with civil liability for false registration statements. Each section (section 14(a) as implemented by Rule 14a–9(a) and section 11) proscribes a type of disclosure or lack of it, i.e., false or misleading statements or omissions of material facts, and each enumerates specific classes of individuals who bear liability for failure to meet the required standard of disclosure. Moreover, each involves single specific documents which are of primary importance in two fundamental areas of securities regulation, sales of securities and the exercise of the shareholders' voting power. Since section 11 of the Securities Act clearly establishes negligence as the test for determining liability, the parallel between the two sections would strongly support adoption of negligence as the standard under section 14(a).

All of the courts which have discussed the question, so far as the reported decisions indicate, have favored applying the rule of negligence as the criterion for determining liability under section 14(a). The language of section 14(a) and Rule 14a–9(a) contains no suggestion of a scienter requirement.... The importance of the proxy provisions to informed voting by shareholders has been stressed by the Supreme Court, which has emphasized the broad remedial purpose of the section, implying the need to impose a high standard of care on the individuals involved. And, unlike sections 10(b) and 18 of the Act, which encompass activity in numerous and diverse areas of securities markets and corporate management, section 14(a) is specially limited to materials used in soliciting proxies. Given all of these factors the imposition of a standard of due diligence as opposed to actual knowledge or gross negligence is quite appropriate.

* * *

QUESTIONS

1. The court states that "[t]he language of section 14(a) and Rule 14a–9(a) contains no suggestion of a scienter requirement." Does the language of § 14(a) and Rule 14a–9(a) suggest a negligence standard?

2. Why not apply a scienter standard for antifraud liability under § 14(a)? Aren't we imposing liability for innocent mistakes (even if negligent)? Why should it matter that § 14(a) and Rule 14a–9(a) are "specially limited to materials used in soliciting proxies" (much like § 11 focuses on the registration statement)?

3. If we take the Supreme Court's "broad remedial" purpose for § 14(a) seriously, why not eliminate the state of mind requirement altogether? Section 11 provides for a due diligence negligence-like *defense,* and even that only for non-issuer defendants.

———

The Supreme Court in *Borak* did not decide what causal connection between fraud in a proxy solicitation and harm to shareholders engaged in a vote was required to establish liability. Should plaintiffs have to establish that each shareholder read the fraudulent proxy solicitation and changed their vote in reliance on the solicitation? Note the similarities between the Supreme Court's approach in the *Electric Auto–Lite* case below and in the *Basic v. Levinson* case discussed in Chapter 5. Without the fraud-on-the-market presumption of reliance for Rule 10b–5 provided for in *Basic v. Levinson*, individualized determinations of reliance would make class actions impracticable. What does the Court say about causation in *Electric Auto–Lite*?

Mills v. Electric Auto–Lite Co.

396 U.S. 375 (1970).

■ MR. JUSTICE HARLAN delivered the opinion of the Court.

This case requires us to consider a basic aspect of the implied private right of action for violation of § 14(a) of the Securities Exchange Act of 1934 recognized by this Court in *J. I. Case Co. v. Borak*, 377 U.S. 426 (1964). As in *Borak* the asserted wrong is that a corporate merger was accomplished through the use of a proxy statement that was materially false or misleading. The question with which we deal is what causal relationship must be shown between such a statement and the merger to establish a cause of action based on the violation of the Act.

I

Petitioners were shareholders of the Electric Auto–Lite Company until 1963, when it was merged into Mergenthaler Linotype Company. They brought suit on the day before the shareholders' meeting at which the vote was to take place on the merger against Auto–Lite, Mergenthaler, and a third company, American Manufacturing Company, Inc. The complaint sought an injunction against the voting by Auto–Lite's management of all proxies obtained by means of an allegedly misleading proxy solicitation; however, it did not seek a temporary restraining order, and the voting went ahead as scheduled the following day. Several months later petitioners filed an amended complaint, seeking to have the merger set aside and to obtain such other relief as might be proper.

[Petitioners] alleged that the proxy statement sent out by the Auto–Lite management to solicit shareholders' votes in favor of the merger was misleading, in violation of § 14(a) of the Act and SEC Rule 14a–9 thereunder. Petitioners recited that before the merger Mergenthaler owned over 50% of the outstanding shares of Auto–Lite common stock, and had been in control of Auto–Lite for two years. American Manufacturing in turn owned about one-third of the outstanding shares of Mergenthaler, and for two years had been in voting control of Mergenthaler and, through it, of Auto–Lite. Petitioners charged that in light of these circumstances the proxy statement was misleading in that it told Auto–Lite shareholders that their board of directors recommended approval of the merger without also informing them that all 11 of Auto–Lite's directors were nominees of Mergenthaler and were under the "control and domination of Mergenthaler." ...

On petitioners' motion for summary judgment ... the District Court for the Northern District of Illinois ruled as a matter of law that the claimed defect in the proxy statement was, in light of the circumstances in which the statement was made, a material omission. The District Court concluded, from its reading of the *Borak* opinion, that it had to hold a hearing on the issue whether there was "a causal connection between the finding that there has been a violation of the disclosure requirements of § 14(a) and the alleged injury to the plaintiffs" before it could consider what remedies would be appropriate.

After holding such a hearing, the court found that under the terms of the merger agreement, an affirmative vote of two-thirds of the Auto–Lite shares was required for approval of the merger, and that the respondent companies owned and controlled about 54% of the outstanding shares. Therefore, to obtain authorization of the merger, respondents had to secure the approval of a substantial number of the minority shareholders. At the stockholders' meeting, approximately 950,000 shares, out of 1,160,000 shares outstanding, were voted in favor of the merger. This included 317,000 votes obtained by proxy from the minority shareholders, votes that were "necessary and indispensable to the approval of the merger." The District Court concluded that a causal relationship had thus been shown....

[R]espondents took an interlocutory appeal to the Court of Appeals for the Seventh Circuit. That court affirmed the District Court's conclusion that the proxy statement was materially deficient, but reversed on the question of causation. The court acknowledged that, if an injunction had been sought a sufficient time before the stockholders' meeting, "corrective measures would have been appropriate." However, since this suit was brought too late for preventive action, the courts had to determine "whether the misleading statement and omission caused the submission of sufficient proxies," as a prerequisite to a determination of liability under the Act. If the respondents could show, "by a preponderance of probabilities, that the merger would have received a sufficient vote even if the proxy statement had not been misleading in the respect found," petitioners would be entitled to no relief of any kind.

The Court of Appeals acknowledged that this test corresponds to the common-law fraud test of whether the injured party relied on the misrepresentation. However, rightly concluding that "(r)eliance by thousands of individuals, as here, can scarcely be inquired into," the court ruled that the issue was to be determined by proof of the fairness of the terms of the merger. If respondents could show that the merger had merit and was fair to the minority shareholders, the trial court would be justified in concluding that a sufficient number of shareholders would have approved the merger had there been no deficiency in the proxy statement. In that case respondents would be entitled to a judgment in their favor.

* * *

II

As we stressed in *Borak*, § 14(a) stemmed from a congressional belief that "(f)air corporate suffrage is an important right that should attach to every equity security bought on a public exchange." The provision was intended to promote "the free exercise of the voting rights of stockholders" by ensuring that proxies would be solicited with "explanation to the stockholder of the real nature of the questions for which authority to cast his vote is sought." The decision below, by permitting all liability to be foreclosed on the basis of a finding that the merger was fair, would allow the stockholders to be by-passed, at least where the only legal challenge to the merger is a suit for retrospective relief after the meeting has been held. A judicial appraisal of the merger's merits could be substituted for the actual and informed vote of the stockholders.

The result would be to insulate from private redress an entire category of proxy violations—those relating to matters other than the terms of the merger. Even outrageous misrepresentations in a proxy solicitation, if they did not relate to the terms of the transaction, would give rise to no cause of action under § 14(a). Particularly if carried over to enforcement actions by the Securities and Exchange Commission itself, such a result would subvert the congressional purpose of ensuring full and fair disclosure to shareholders.

Further, recognition of the fairness of the merger as a complete defense would confront small shareholders with an additional obstacle to making a successful challenge to a proposal recommended through a defective proxy statement. The risk that they would be unable to rebut the corporation's evidence of the fairness of the proposal, and thus to establish their cause of action, would be bound to discourage such shareholders from the private enforcement of the proxy rules that "provides a necessary supplement to Commission action."

Such a frustration of the congressional policy is not required by anything in the wording of the statute or in our opinion in the *Borak* case. . . . Use of a solicitation that is materially misleading is itself a violation of law, as the Court of Appeals recognized in stating that injunctive relief would be available to remedy such a defect if sought prior to the stockholders' meeting. In *Borak*, which came to this Court on a dismissal of the complaint, the Court limited its inquiry to whether a violation of § 14(a) gives rise to "a federal cause of action for rescission or damages." . . . In the present case there has been a hearing specifically directed to the causation problem. The question before the Court is whether the facts found on the basis of that hearing are sufficient in law to establish petitioners' cause of action, and we conclude that they are.

Where the misstatement or omission in a proxy statement has been shown to be "material," as it was found to be here, that determination itself indubitably embodies a conclusion that the defect was of such a character that it might have been considered important by a reasonable shareholder who was in the process of deciding how to vote. This requirement that the defect have a significant propensity to affect the voting process is found in the express terms of Rule 14a–9, and it adequately serves the purpose of ensuring that a cause of action cannot be established by proof of a defect so trivial, or so unrelated to the transaction for which approval is sought, that correction of the defect or imposition of liability would not further the interests protected by § 14(a).

In this case, where the misleading aspect of the solicitation involved failure to reveal a serious conflict of interest on the part of the directors, the Court of Appeals concluded that the crucial question in determining materiality was "whether the minority shareholders were sufficiently alerted to the board's relationship to their adversary to be on their guard." An adequate disclosure of this relationship would have warned the stockholders to give more careful scrutiny to the terms of the merger than they might to one recommended by an entirely disinterested board. Thus, the failure to make such a disclosure was found to be a material defect "as a matter of law," thwarting the informed decision at which the statute aims, regardless of whether the terms of the merger were such that a reasonable stockholder would have approved the transaction after more careful analysis.

There is no need to supplement this requirement, as did the Court of Appeals, with a requirement of proof of whether the defect actually had a decisive effect on the voting. Where there has been a finding of materiality, a shareholder has made a sufficient showing of causal relationship between the violation and the injury for which he seeks redress if, as here, he proves that the proxy solicitation itself, rather than the particular defect in the solicitation materials, was an essential link in the accomplishment of the transaction. This objective test will avoid the impracticalities of determining how many votes were affected, and, by resolving doubts in favor of those the statute is designed to protect, will effectuate the congressional policy of ensuring that the shareholders are able to make an informed choice when they are consulted on corporate transactions.[7]

* * *

7. We need not decide in this case whether causation could be shown where the management controls a sufficient number of shares to approve the transaction without any votes from the minority. . . .

QUESTIONS

1. If a court determines that the terms of a merger are "fair," why should shareholders have an antifraud claim? What is the loss to shareholders from any misstatement or omission in the proxy solicitation materials if they received "fair" terms?

2. What, in addition to materiality, is required to show causation?

3. What sort of "impracticalities" are avoided through the Court's use of materiality in determining whether causation exists for purposes of a § 14(a) and Rule 14a–9 violation?

———————

The Supreme Court in the 1990s moved generally toward restricting implied private causes of action under Rule 10b–5. The Court did not spare Rule 14a–9 from this trend. How would the *Virginia Bankshares* Court have ruled on whether Rule 14a–9 and § 14(a) provide an implied private cause of action if not bound by the precedents in *Borak* and *Mills*?

Virginia Bankshares, Inc. v. Sandberg

501 U.S. 1083 (1991).

■ JUSTICE SOUTER delivered the opinion of the Court.

[FABI, a bank holding company, conducted a merger in which the First American Bank of Virginia (Bank) was merged into Virginia Bankshares (VBI), a subsidiary of FABI. Prior to the merger, VBI already owned 85% of the Bank's shares. FABI hired an outside investment bank to give an opinion on the value of the Bank's minority shares and the investment bank came back with a valuation of $42 per share. The Bank's board of directors approved the merger at that price. Virginia law required that the shareholders of the Bank vote on the merger, and the directors of the Bank sent out a proxy statement to the shareholders for the vote. Even though minority shareholders could vote, their vote was not necessary to approve the merger. VBI's 85% ownership interest alone was sufficient to approve the merger.

The proxy disclosed that the directors had approved the merger because of "the opportunity for the minority shareholders to achieve a 'high' value." Moreover, the directors disclosed that that the merger was at a "fair" price for the stock. Plaintiff brought a securities fraud suit under § 14(a) as implemented by SEC Rule 14a–9 alleging that the directors did not believe the statements of "high" value or "fair price."]

* * *

[The] issue before us, left open in *Mills v. Electric Auto–Lite Co.*, is whether causation of damages compensable through the implied private right of action under § 14(a) can be demonstrated by a member of a class of minority shareholders whose votes are not required by law or corporate bylaw to authorize the transaction giving rise to the claim . . . .

Although a majority stockholder in *Mills* controlled just over half the corporation's shares, a two-thirds vote was needed to approve the merger proposal. After proxies had been obtained, and the merger had carried, minority shareholders brought a *Borak* action. The question arose whether the plaintiffs' burden to demonstrate causation of their damages traceable to the § 14(a) violation required proof that the defect in the proxy solicitation had had "a decisive effect on the voting." The *Mills* Court avoided the evidentiary morass that would have followed from requiring individualized proof that enough minority shareholders had relied upon the misstatements to swing the vote. Instead, it held that causation of damages by a material proxy misstatement could be established by showing that minority proxies necessary and sufficient to authorize the corporate acts had been given in accordance with the tenor of the solicitation, and the Court described such a causal relationship by calling the proxy solicitation an "essential link in the accomplishment of the transaction." In the case before it, the Court found the solicitation essential, as contrasted with one addressed to a class of minority shareholders without votes required by law or by law to authorize the action proposed, and left it for another day to decide whether such a minority shareholder could demonstrate causation.

In this case, respondents address Mills' open question by proffering two theories that the proxy solicitation addressed to them was an "essential link" under the *Mills* causation test. They argue, first, that a link existed and was essential simply because VBI and FABI would have been unwilling to proceed with the merger without the approval manifested by the minority sharcholders' proxies, which would not have been obtained without the solicitation's express misstatements and misleading omissions. On this reasoning, the causal connection would depend on a desire to avoid bad shareholder or public relations, and the essential character of the causal link would stem not from the enforceable terms of the parties' corporate relationship, but from one party's apprehension of the ill will of the other.

In the alternative, respondents argue that the proxy statement was an essential link between the directors' proposal and the merger because it was the means to satisfy a state statutory requirement of minority share-holder approval, as a condition for saving the merger from voidability resulting from a conflict of interest on the part of one of the Bank's directors, Jack Beddow, who voted in favor of the merger while also serving as a director of FABI. Under the [Virginia Corporate Code], minority approval after disclosure of the material facts about the transaction and the director's interest was one of three avenues to insulate the merger from later attack for conflict, the two others being ratification by the Bank's directors after like disclosure and proof that the merger was fair to the corporation. On this theory, causation would depend on the use of the proxy statement for the purpose of obtaining votes sufficient to bar a minority shareholder from commencing proceedings to declare the merger void.

Although respondents have proffered each of these theories as establishing a chain of causal connection in which the proxy statement is claimed to have been an "essential link," neither theory presents the proxy solicitation as essential in the sense of *Mills'* causal sequence, in which the solicitation links a directors' proposal with the votes legally required to authorize the action proposed. As a consequence, each theory would, if adopted, extend the scope of *Borak* actions beyond the ambit of *Mills* and expand the class of plaintiffs entitled to bring *Borak* actions to include shareholders whose initial authorization of the transaction prompting the proxy solicitation is unnecessary.

Assessing the legitimacy of any such extension or expansion calls for the application of some fundamental principles governing recognition of a right of action implied by a federal statute, the first of which was not, in fact, the considered focus of the *Borak* opinion. The rule that has emerged in the years since *Borak* and *Mills* came down is that recognition of any private right of action for violating a federal statute must ultimately rest on congressional intent to provide a private remedy. From this the corollary follows that the breadth of the right once recognized should not, as a general matter, grow beyond the scope congressionally intended.

This rule and corollary present respondents with a serious obstacle, for we can find no manifestation of intent to recognize a cause of action (or class of plaintiffs) as broad as respondents' theory of causation would entail. At first blush, it might seem otherwise, for the *Borak* Court certainly did not ignore the matter of intent. Its opinion adverted to the statutory object of "protection of investors" as animating Congress' intent to provide judicial relief where "necessary," and it quoted evidence for that intent from House and Senate Committee Reports.... *Borak*'s probe of the congressional mind, however, never focused squarely on private rights of action, as distinct from the substantive objects of the legislation....

Looking to the Act's text and legislative history mindful of this heightened concern reveals little that would help toward understanding the intended scope of any private right. According to the House Report, Congress meant to promote the "free exercise" of stockholders' voting rights, and protect "[f]air corporate suffrage," from abuses exemplified by proxy solicitations that concealed what the Senate Report called the "real nature" of the issues to be settled by the subsequent votes. While it is true that these Reports, like the language of the Act itself, carry the clear message that Congress meant to protect investors from misinformation that rendered them unwitting agents of self-inflicted damage, it is just as true that Congress was reticent with indications of how far this protection might depend on self-help by private action. The response to this reticence may be, of course, to claim that § 14(a) cannot be enforced effectively for the sake of its intended beneficiaries without their participation as private litigants. But the force of this argument for inferred congressional intent depends on the degree of need perceived by Congress, and we would have trouble inferring any congressional urgency to depend on implied private actions to deter violations of § 14(a), when Congress expressly provided private rights of action in §§ 9(e), 16(b), and 18(a) of the same Act.[11]

The congressional silence that is thus a serious obstacle to the expansion of cognizable *Borak* causation is not, however, a necessarily insurmountable barrier. This is not the first effort in recent years to expand the scope of an action originally inferred from the Act without "conclusive guidance" from Congress, see *Blue Chip Stamps v. Manor Drug Stores*, 421 U.S., at 737, and we may look to that earlier case for the proper response to such a plea for expansion. There, we accepted the proposition that where a legal structure of private statutory rights has developed without clear indications of congressional intent, the contours of that structure need not be frozen absolutely when the result would be demonstrably inequitable to a class of would-be plaintiffs with claims comparable to those previously recognized. Faced in that case with such a claim for equality in rounding out the scope of an implied private statutory right of action, we looked to policy reasons for deciding where the outer limits of the right should lie. We may do no less here, in the face of respondents' pleas for a private remedy to place them on the same footing as shareholders with votes necessary for initial corporate action.

A

Blue Chip Stamps set an example worth recalling as a preface to specific policy analysis of the consequences of recognizing respondents' first theory, that a desire to avoid minority shareholders' ill will should suffice to justify recognizing the requisite causality of a proxy statement needed to garner that minority support. It will be recalled that in *Blue Chip Stamps* we raised concerns about the practical consequences of allowing recovery, under § 10(b) of the Act and Rule 10b–5, on evidence of what a merely hypothetical buyer or seller might have done on a set of facts that never occurred, and foresaw that any such expanded liability would turn on "hazy" issues inviting self-serving testimony, strike suits, and protracted discovery, with little chance of reasonable resolution by pretrial process. These were good reasons to deny recognition to such claims in the absence of any apparent contrary congressional intent.

The same threats of speculative claims and procedural intractability are inherent in respondents' theory of causation linked through the directors' desire for a cosmetic vote. Causation would turn on inferences about what the corporate directors would have thought and done without the minority shareholder approval unneeded to authorize action. A subsequently dissatisfied minority shareholder would have virtual license to

---

11. The object of our enquiry does not extend further to question the holding of either *J.I. Case Co. v. Borak*, 377 U.S. 426 (1964), or *Mills v. Electric Auto–Lite Co.*, 396 U.S. 375 (1970), at this date.... Our point is simply to recognize the hurdle facing any litigant who urges us to enlarge the scope of the action beyond the point reached in Mills.

allege that managerial timidity would have doomed corporate action but for the ostensible approval induced by a misleading statement, and opposing claims of hypothetical diffidence and hypothetical boldness on the part of directors would probably provide enough depositions in the usual case to preclude any judicial resolution short of the credibility judgments that can only come after trial. Reliable evidence would seldom exist. Directors would understand the prudence of making a few statements about plans to proceed even without minority endorsement, and discovery would be a quest for recollections of oral conversations at odds with the official pronouncements, in hopes of finding support for or post facto guesses about how much heat the directors would have stood in the absence of minority approval. The issues would be hazy, their litigation protracted, and their resolution unreliable. Given a choice, we would reject any theory of causation that raised such prospects, and we reject this one.

B

The theory of causal necessity derived from the requirements of Virginia law dealing with postmerger ratification seeks to identify the essential character of the proxy solicitation from its function in obtaining the minority approval that would preclude a minority suit attacking the merger. Since the link is said to be a step in the process of barring a class of shareholders from resort to a state remedy otherwise available, this theory of causation rests upon the proposition of policy that § 14(a) should provide a federal remedy whenever a false or misleading proxy statement results in the loss under state law of a shareholder plaintiff's state remedy for the enforcement of a state right. Respondents agree with the suggestions of counsel for the SEC and FDIC that causation be recognized, for example, when a minority shareholder has been induced by a misleading proxy statement to forfeit a state-law right to an appraisal remedy by voting to approve a transaction or when such a shareholder has been deterred from obtaining an order enjoining a damaging transaction by a proxy solicitation that misrepresents the facts on which an injunction could properly have been issued. Respondents claim that in this case a predicate for recognizing just such a causal link exists in [the Virginia Corporate Code], which sets the conditions under which the merger may be insulated from suit by a minority shareholder seeking to void it on account of Beddow's conflict.

This case does not, however, require us to decide whether § 14(a) provides a cause of action for lost state remedies, since there is no indication in the law or facts before us that the proxy solicitation resulted in any such loss. The contrary appears to be the case. Assuming the soundness of respondents' characterization of the proxy statement as materially misleading, the very terms of the Virginia statute indicate that a favorable minority vote induced by the solicitation would not suffice to render the merger invulnerable to later attack on the ground of the conflict. The statute bars a shareholder from seeking to avoid a transaction tainted by a director's conflict if, *inter alia*, the minority shareholders ratified the transaction following disclosure of the material facts of the transaction and the conflict. . . .

* * *

QUESTIONS

1. Why is the Court concerned with expanding the acceptable causal link between a shareholder vote and a merger to include what the board might have done in a "hypothetical" situation?

2. Is the Court arguing that under state law the plaintiffs would still have the ability to void the merger if the proxy solicitation was materially misleading and, thus, there is no need for Rule 14a–9 to provide a cause of action for "lost state remedies"?

D. MANAGING THE COSTS OF PROXY SOLICITATIONS

The goal of the federal proxy regime is to ensure that all shareholders have equal and fair access to vote; the tools used to accomplish this goal, however, have their costs. Insurgents who nominate a competing slate for the board of directors or who seek to influence the shareholder vote on whether to ratify a merger, for example, face mandatory disclosure requirements under Schedule 14A as well as potential antifraud liability under § 14(a) and Rule 14a–9. Even those who are not active insurgents, but instead merely want to discuss an upcoming proxy vote with other shareholders, may potentially fall under the definition of a proxy solicitation under Rule 14a–1(*l*) and thereby become subject to mandatory disclosure and antifraud liability. Although there are exceptions, understanding these exceptions may require the assistance of an attorney, who most likely will not work for free.

The costs for an insurgent are not limited to the costs of complying with the federal securities regime. Consider what other costs might affect an insurgent seeking to engage in a proxy contest to change the board of directors. At a minimum, insurgents must communicate with shareholders. Although broad based communications to all the shareholders may have some effect, insurgents often will focus their efforts on convincing those shareholders with the greatest shareholdings.

HYPOTHETICAL THREE

Gary, the head of the fictional state of Berkeley's Public Employee Retirement Fund (BEPERS), has decided to move forward with a proxy contest to nominate a competing slate of nominees to FoodNow's board. Gary has filed the required Schedule 14A and now seeks to communicate directly with FoodNow's shareholders. You are Gary's advisor, and he asks you what he should do next.

1. COMMUNICATING WITH SHAREHOLDERS

One of the major costs facing shareholders attempting to solicit proxies during a vote is the cost of identifying and communicating with shareholders eligible to vote. The securities laws require a corporation to provide information on its principal shareholders in several areas:

- Section 16(a) of the Exchange Act—Beneficial owners of more than 10 percent of any class of any equity security of companies that are required to register under § 12 and must file any changes in ownership on Form 4.

- Beneficial owners of "more than five percent of any class of the registrant's voting securities" (as defined in Item 403 of Regulation S–K) must be identified in multiple securities filing documents, including the annual Form 10–K, the proxy statement under Schedule 14A, and the registration statement under Form S–1.

- Williams Act—Under § 13(d) of the Exchange Act, shareholders that hold more than 5 percent of any class of equity (either individually or working in concert with a group) must file a Schedule 13D, publicly disclosing their share ownership.

Thus, insurgents may easily identify shareholders with over 5 percent beneficial ownership interest in the corporation. Most public corporations, however, have few shareholders holding more than 5 percent of the shares. Even when there is such a shareholder, the shareholder may already have close ties with management and hold seats on the board of directors, making the shareholder unlikely to support any insurgent proxy contest. Identifying smaller shareholders will not be so easy, but may nonetheless be crucial to an insurgent. For an insurgent to have a chance at dislodging incumbent board members, the insurgent must obtain the support of a wide range of medium-sized institutional investor shareholders.

Consider the top three beneficial owners of Yahoo! Inc. as disclosed in the company's 2004 proxy statement:

Name and Address of Beneficial Ownership	Amount and Nature of Beneficial Ownership	Percent of Class
FMR Corp	48,603,799	7.30%
David Filo	45,801,563	6.90%
Jerry Yang	37,127,580	5.60%

As reported in the 2004 proxy statement, two of the three large block shareholders, David Filo and Jerry Yang, are both founders and employees of Yahoo! (both held the position of "Chief Yahoo"). Yang also sits on the board of directors of the corporation. Neither, therefore, would be likely to vote for any insurgent. The other large shareholder, FMR Corp., has no reported ties with Yahoo! other than its share ownership. To overcome the votes in the hands of Filo and Yang as well as the tendency of most public shareholders to side with management, an insurgent would have to find more shareholders than just FMR Corp. to change the Yahoo! board of directors.

The corporation itself is the lowest cost source for identifying the corporation's shareholders of record. Rule 14a–7 of the Exchange Act requires the corporation to assist the security holder in communicating with the other shareholders in certain circumstances, including when the corporation is seeking to make a proxy solicitation in connection with a security holder meeting. Upon a request by a security holder under Rule 14a–7, the corporation must either mail the security holder's soliciting materials or provide a security holder with a list consisting of all the shareholders of record including "banks, brokers and similar entities holding securities in the same class or classes as holders which have been or are to be solicited on management's behalf." The requesting security holder does not get a free ride, however; the corporation is entitled to "reasonable expenses" from the requesting security holder. For a typical public company, the expenses can total close to $20,000.

A corporation that chooses to mail out an insurgent's materials to shareholders under Rule 14a–7 can thereby avoid providing the identity of its shareholders to the insurgent. If an insurgent hopes to rely on individual communications with larger shareholders, obtaining the shareholders' names is critical to the success of a contest. Insurgents have other means of uncovering shareholder identity. Institutional investment managers who exercise investment discretion over accounts holding certain specified § 13(f) equity securities with an aggregate fair market value of $100 million are required under § 13(f) of the Exchange Act to file a Form 13–F detailing their holdings of these § 13(f) securities. The SEC publishes an update to the list of § 13(f) securities on a quarterly basis. Form 13–F filings do not cover all shareholders, however, disclosing only institutional investment managers. Private data sources, such as Thomson Financial, also provide ownership and contact information for institutional shareholders of public corporations.

Even when insurgents know the identities of the major shareholders, communicating with them can be quite costly. Insurgents that use Rule 14a–7 may have the corporation mail packets of written materials to shareholders. Written materials, however, are rarely effective in convincing a shareholder to take sides with an insurgent against management. If you were a busy investment manager and received a written package from an unknown shareholder about a possible proxy contest involving one of the companies in your portfolio, what would you do? Would you even bother to read the materials? Insurgents typically focus instead on more targeted communication with certain larger institutional investors, including public pension funds and socially responsible funds that often are more willing to oppose incumbent managers. Even after identifying important institutional investors, an insurgent must then identify who makes decisions with respect to proxy votes. Although some institutions decide internally how to vote their shares, many institutions obtain advice on how to vote from proxy voting services such as Institutional Shareholder Services Inc. (ISS). In 2002, Hewlett Packard sought shareholder approval for a merger with Compaq against the opposition of prominent Hewlett Packard shareholder Walter Hewlett (a former board member of HP). Both HP company officials and Walter Hewlett lobbied ISS intensively. In the end, ISS recommended that its clients vote in favor of the merger, helping lead to its eventual shareholder approval.

Establishing communication with influential shareholders is only the first step toward obtaining votes. Insurgents, particularly if unknown to shareholders, must convince often skeptical shareholders to side with them. To do so, insurgents must expend considerable resources communicating with a handful of shareholders. Obtaining the public support of some of these large shareholders as well as positive press reports may sway other shareholders to support the insurgents.

2. MANAGEMENT DEFENSIVE TACTICS

Incumbent managers are unlikely to remain passive when confronted with a proxy contest or merger opposition; managers will also lobby major shareholders. Under state law, these lobbying efforts are typically reimbursed by the company.

Managers may also adopt additional defensive tactics to stymie insurgents in a proxy contest. The first and more common countermeasure is the implementation of the so called "classified" or "staggered" Board. Directors in a staggered board are typically elected for staggered three-year terms. At any one annual meeting, shareholders may only elect one-third of the board. Those seeking to engage in a proxy contest to change the control of a corporation must therefore conduct two such consecutive campaigns to win control. Adopting a classified board, however, requires shareholder approval, which is unlikely to be forthcoming in the midst of a proxy contest. Thus, this defensive measure must have been adopted well in advance of the proxy contest.

Second, managers may attempt to change the date of the annual meeting, delaying the meeting to forestall a change of control through a proxy contest. Changing the meeting date after the establishment of a record date may invalidate proxies already collected by the insurgents. The insurgent must then re-solicit shareholders to obtain a new set of proxies for the later meeting date. State corporate law, however, limits the ability of managers to change the meeting date if the change is intended to entrench incumbents.

Third, managers may inflict legal costs on insurgents. Section 14(a) and Rule 14a–9 provide antifraud liability for material misstatements and half-truths in proxy solicitations. In theory, antifraud liability works to ensure that investors receive accurate information and, using this information, make informed voting decisions. In practice, antifraud liability may have a more pernicious impact on those seeking to bring a proxy contest. As a defensive tactic, management may bring a lawsuit against an insurgent for providing a materially misleading proxy statement. Even if the proxy statement is not deficient, the prospect of having to defend a lawsuit raises the costs and imposes potential delay on an insurgent.

3. REIMBURSEMENT OF EXPENSES

Proxy contests are costly. An insurgent who brings a contest to replace the directors out of a desire to increase the value of the corporation is acting on behalf of all the shareholders. State corporate law, however, generally does not provide for mandatory reimbursement of insurgents. Instead, insurgents are reimbursed only if they win control over the board of directors and thereby are able to obtain board approval for reimbursement. Reimbursement must also be ratified by the other shareholders.

Shareholder activists, who bring a proxy contest and fail to win control, but obtain corporate governance reforms, are not reimbursed by the corporation for their expenses under state corporate law. Similarly, activists who solicit proxies opposing a management-sponsored proposal (e.g., a merger) are not reimbursed by the corporation even if their opposition benefits all shareholders.

Why should the corporation reimburse expenses? Payments from the corporation represent a pro rata reduction in value for all shareholders. So the real issue is whether the group of all shareholders should pay for the activists' efforts. If the activist in fact is acting on behalf of the group of all shareholders in bringing a contest (e.g., to replace underperforming managers and thereby raising the overall value of the corporation), then reimbursement makes sense.

Why not force reimbursement for all activist proxy solicitations, whether or not there is a change in control? Certainly the lack of reimbursement deters activists from soliciting proxies that may benefit all shareholders. Without reimbursement, such activists bear all the costs of engaging in proxy solicitations, but capture only part of the benefit. Not all activists, however, will act in the best interests of all the shareholders. Should corporate money be used to subsidize activists engaged in self-interested solicitations?

Although state corporate law generally does not treat insurgents very generously, the SEC has forced corporations to support shareholder activists indirectly through the proxy rules. We discuss this support next as part of the broader discussion of how much power over the corporation should the securities law mandate be given to shareholders.

4. BROKER VOTES

The odds are stacked against an insurgent bringing a proxy contest to change the control of the board. Proxy contests, as a result, are relatively rare. In the absence of a proxy contest, incumbent directors enjoy a large "leg up" in obtaining a high favorable vote because of the broker vote rule. Under New York Stock Exchange rules, brokers can vote shares held in street name if the beneficial owner fails to provide voting instructions for routine matters, such as an uncontested director election. Brokers as a matter of course vote these shares in favor of incumbent directors. Because of the large fraction of shares held in street name, combined with the tendency of smaller shareholders to ignore proxy voting, broker votes for incumbent managers can be a large portion of the overall favorable vote. Even for companies that perform relatively poorly, it is not uncommon for incumbent directors to receive strong majorities.

What is the consequence of a guaranteed high vote total for incumbent directors where the election is uncontested? In recent years, many shareholder activists have conducted "just vote no" campaigns, withholding votes from directors of underperforming companies. Technically, most shareholders never get the chance to vote no. Instead, the form of the proxy received from the company only gives the shareholder the choice either to give the incumbent board the proxy to vote for the incumbent board's candidates or to withhold such authority. Roy Disney, the grandson of Walt Disney and former board member of Walt Disney Company, waged a "just vote no" campaign seeking to withhold votes for the re-election of Michael Eisner, the CEO of Disney, to the board of directors in 2004. Roy Disney was aided in his efforts by a recommendation on the part of Institutional Shareholder Services, an influential proxy voting advisory firm, to withhold votes for Eisner. Shareholders in 2004 withheld over 40% of the votes from Eisner for re-election to the board. Eisner was re-elected anyhow because, running unopposed, he obtained a plurality of the votes cast at the meeting.

Directors may be embarrassed if they receive large numbers of withheld votes in a "just vote no" campaign. A high "no" vote count is also a public signal of shareholder disapproval with the CEO, making it more likely that the board may oust the CEO. In Eisner's case, the board removed him from the chairman's position on the board. Eisner later announced his retirement as CEO effective in 2005. Disney, however, may have been an aberration given the large amount of publicity surrounding Roy Disney's fight with Michael Eisner.

For companies further removed from the public limelight, the broker vote rule makes it difficult for activities on the part of shareholders, short of a full-blown proxy contest, to voice their displeasure with management through "just vote no" campaigns. The broker vote rule also favors incumbent managers in areas outside of the uncontested election of directors. Broker votes, for example, are also cast in favor of stock option plans presented for approval to shareholders.

III. SHAREHOLDER DEMOCRACY

Shareholders of publicly-held corporations have little ability to influence corporate policy. Shareholders have the right to vote in elections for the board of directors and the ratification of certain major transactions such as a merger. For everyday business decisions, decisionmaking authority is vested under state corporate law with the board of directors.

This separation between ownership and control brings many benefits for investors. Dispersed investors in the public markets typically do not want to expend time or effort monitoring managers or setting corporate policy. Giving investors greater say in the corporation will not change corporate policy very much if investors are rationally apathetic. More perniciously, some shareholders may use additional power to hold the company hostage, extracting side payments at the expense of the other shareholders. Keeping shareholders out of the day-to-day operation of the corporation may better serve the interests of passive shareholders as a group.

Separating ownership and control, however, leads to the possibility that the managers may pursue their own agenda at the expense of outside shareholders. State corporate law tries to keep management in check by giving shareholders the power to elect the board of directors. Agency costs within the corporation are also limited by court review of business decisions (within the limits of the business judgment rule) and the possibility of a hostile takeover.

Shareholder voting has the potential to play an important role in controlling corporate agency costs. Shareholders (particularly those with only small ownership interests) are, however, unlikely to expend much energy in deciding how to vote. Shareholders with small interests will view their vote as unlikely to be pivotal, making it even less likely that they will spend time or energy on deciding how to vote.

In thinking about shareholder voting, two issues are paramount. First, which issues should be put to a shareholder vote? Rational apathy among shareholders leaves open the risk that a small group of shareholders may use the shareholder voting process for their own narrow self-interest. A shareholder may gain from the publicity surrounding a shareholder vote, even if it does not benefit other shareholders. Managers may also pay off a more active shareholder to ward off a possible shareholder vote, again at the expense of the group of all shareholders. Many potential shareholder issue proposals, discussed below, never reach an actual vote. Instead, the shareholder sponsor will negotiate an informal settlement with the corporation's management. Should we ban such settlements? If we do, we will also be banning value-increasing corporate governance changes adopted voluntarily by managers as part of such a settlement.

Second, what role should the SEC play in reducing the costs of shareholder voting? The SEC's primary regulatory tool is disclosure. Is disclosure enough? Should the SEC intervene more actively to reduce the agency costs in firms facing dispersed shareholders?

A.   Shareholder Issue Proposals

In response to the high cost of shareholder voting, the SEC promulgated Rule 14a–8 to promote shareholder "democracy." Rule 14a–8 allows shareholders to piggyback certain types of proposals onto the management's annual proxy statement for the election of directors. If the shareholder proposal and its sponsor meet all of Rule 14a–8's requirements, companies must include the proposal in the company's own proxy statement and identify the proposal on the company's form of proxy. Shareholders cannot, however, use Rule 14a–8 to nominate their own slate of directors or propose a merger. Insurgents waging a proxy contest must find their own means to communicate with shareholders.

Proxy issue proposals typically deal with matters involving far smaller sums of money. Examples of proxy issue proposals include proposals to:

- Remove a corporation's poison pill takeover defensive device
- Include more diversity on the board of directors
- Expand the company's equal employment policies
- Report on or improve the corporation's labor standards

At first glance, the proxy rules appear generous to shareholder-sponsored issue proposals. Unlike other SEC rules we have examined in this casebook, Rule 14a–8 is written in "plain language." (Query: Would drafting the rest of the securities laws in the same format make them more comprehensible?) Rule 14a–8(a), for example, describes shareholder proposals as follows: "A shareholder proposal is your recommendation or requirement that the company and/or its board of directors take action, which you intend to present at a meeting of the company's shareholders. Your proposal should state as clearly as possible the course of action that you believe the company should follow."

Rule 14a–8 imposes both eligibility and procedural requirements on sponsors of shareholder proposals. The Rule also excludes certain types of proposals altogether. Dropping out of the coverage of Rule 14a–8 does not necessarily mean the end of the road for a proposal. The shareholder sponsor can always mail out its own separate proxy solicitation containing the proposal. Doing so, however, will require the sponsor to incur the cost of printing documents and mailing them out. Although the Internet drastically reduces such costs, few shareholders to date have made issue proposals in proxy solicitations separate from the company's proxy statement pursuant to Rule 14a–8.

1. ELIGIBILITY AND PROCEDURAL REQUIREMENTS

Rule 14a–8 allows only certain shareholders to include a shareholder proposal in the company's proxy statement. Sponsors must be the record or beneficial owner of at least 1% or $2,000 of the outstanding securities entitled to vote, and they must have held that amount continuously for at least one year prior to the date the proposal is submitted to the company. Sponsors must continue to hold onto these securities through the date of the shareholders' meeting (Rule 14a–8(b)). For most publicly-held corporations, the relevant constraint will be the $2,000 in share holding. For example, Best Buy Co. Inc., a retail consumer electronics chain, had a market capitalization of around $18 billion in 2004. Shareholders attempting to meet the 1% requirement would need to hold $180 million of Best Buy common shares. The $2,000 threshold is considerably easier to meet.

Eligible sponsors of a shareholder proposal must then meet several procedural requirements:

- Sponsors may make only one proposal per shareholders' meeting (Rule 14a–8(c)).

- The proposal must not exceed 500 words (Rule 14a–8(d)).

- Sponsors must, with some exceptions, submit the proposal to the company no later than 120 days prior to the calendar date corresponding to when the company sent out its proxy statement for the previous year's annual meeting (Rule 14a–8(e)).

- Sponsors (or their representatives) must appear at the annual shareholder meeting (Rule 14a–8(h)).

The company bears the burden of proof if it rejects a shareholder proposal (Rule 14a–8(g)). If the company believes that a proposal or its sponsor violates any of the eligibility or procedural requirements, the company generally must notify the sponsor of the deficiency and allow the sponsor to correct the deficiency (Rule 14a–8(f)). If the deficiency cannot be remedied (e.g., if the proposal was submitted after the 120 days deadline specified in Rule 14a–8(e)) then the company does not need to give notice to the sponsor before rejecting the proposal.

Companies that intend to include a statement opposing the shareholder proposal in the company proxy statement must send the opposing statement to the sponsor of the proposal no later than 30 calendar days before they file the definitive proxy statement (Rule 14a–8(m)). Rule 14a–8(m) tells shareholder sponsors that "if you believe that the company's opposition to your proposal contains materially false or misleading statements that may violate our anti-fraud rule, Rule 14a–9, you should promptly send to the Commission staff and the company a letter explaining the reasons for your view."

2. SUBSTANTIVE EXCLUSIONS

Rule 14a–8 limits the type of proposal that must be included in the company's proxy. Recall that Rule 14a–8 is designed to reduce the cost to shareholders of communicating with other shareholders over issues of importance to all shareholders. Allowing proposals furthering a personal grievance would be unlikely to advance this goal. Suppose a shareholder is unhappy with the lack of imported brie cheese in FoodNow's inventory because the shareholder really likes brie. Allowing that shareholder to vent his unhappiness in the company's own proxy statement would probably not increase overall shareholder welfare.

Rule 14a–8(i) accordingly allows the company to exclude the following proposals that are unlikely to appeal to most shareholders:

- Personal grievance, special interest proposals (Rule 14a–8(i)(4)).

- Irrelevant proposals—"If the proposal relates to operations which account for less than 5 percent of the company's total assets at the end of its most recent fiscal year, and for less than 5 percent of its net earnings and gross sales for its most recent fiscal year, and is not otherwise significantly related to the company's business" (Rule 14a–8(i)(5)).

- Proposals where the corporation lacks the power or authority to implement the proposal (Rule 14a–8(i)(6)).

Rule 14a–8 also screens out proposals unlikely to add to overall shareholder welfare because they have already been proposed or are in the process of being dealt with as follows:

- Proposals that have been substantially implemented (Rule 14a–8(i)(10)).

- Proposals that substantially duplicate another proposal already on the company's proxy statement (Rule 14a–8(i)(11)).

- Resubmitted proposals that were submitted in the past and received little support (Rule 14a–8(i)(12)).

Rule 14a–8(i)(12) provides a numerical standard for excluding previously-submitted proposals. If more than three calendar years have passed since the last time a proposal dealing with "substantially the same subject matter" as a prior proposal was included in the company's proxy then the resubmitted proposal is not excludable under Rule 14a–8(i)(12). If three calendar years or less have passed, then Rule 14a–8(i)(12) blocks the resubmitted proposal if the proposal received less than the following thresholds:

3% of the vote if proposed once within the preceding five calendar years;

6% of the vote on its last submission to shareholders if proposed twice previously within the preceding five calendar years; or

10% of the vote on its last submission to shareholders if proposed three times or more previously within the preceding five calendar years.

Proposals that deal with specific corporate policy decisions (and have not already been submitted or otherwise dealt with), on the other hand, are likely to affect the welfare of all shareholders and thus capture the interest of shareholders as a group. One could imagine a regime in which shareholders have more direct voting control over day-to-day corporate policy decisions. State corporate law, however, has generally avoided this course, instead vesting management control of the corporation in the board of directors. This separation of ownership (in the shareholders) and control (in the officers and directors) allows shareholders to remain passive. The separation of ownership and control therefore appeals to investors seeking a return without having to expend time or resources in determining corporate policy.

Rule 14a–8 recognizes the desire of shareholders to remain passive and the allocation of authority to the officers and directors by generally blocking proposals that may undermine this division of power under state corporate law. In particular, Rule 14a–8 blocks:

- Proposals that are improper under state law (Rule 14a–8(i)(1)).

Proposals that mandate that the board of directors take a specific policy direction (e.g., entering a new market for FoodNow) would be prohibited under state corporate law. Shareholders avoid the Rule 14a–8(i)(1) prohibition for proposals improper under state law by framing their proposals as recommendations. The SEC provides the following advice in the note to Rule 14a–8(i)(1): "In our experience, most proposals that are cast as recommendations or requests that the board of directors take specified action are proper under state law." For example, sponsors will simply *suggest* that a corporation remove its poison pill, rather than demanding its removal.

What impact do precatory proposals have on corporate managers? If a proposal is couched as a suggestion, why should managers pay it any heed? Managers may implement voluntarily a proposal that receives a lot of votes to avoid damaging publicity. Outside directors may also feel obliged to support a proposal that obtains a majority of shareholder votes even if it is only a recommendation. Outside directors interested in their own reputations may not care for the spotlight of media attention surrounding a proxy issue proposal. If the proposal is renewed, more opportunities are created to establish communication links and relationships between shareholders that may encourage more action by the shareholders. A takeover proposal or proxy control contest, for example, may become easier after an issue proposal garners substantial support. Finally, managers seeking to maximize shareholder welfare may be unaware of how popular a proposal is until shareholders vote in its favor. Once made aware of the popularity, managers may voluntarily adopt the proposal.

Rule 14a–8 also blocks:

- Proposals that deal with "ordinary business operations" (Rule 14a–8(i)(7)).

- Proposals relating to the amount of dividends (Rule 14a–8(i)(13)).

- Proposals relating to the election to the board of directors (Rule 14a–8(i)(8)).

- Proposals that otherwise conflict with a voting proposal put forward by the company (Rule 14a–8(i)(9)).

A sponsor may attempt to craft a proposal outside of the scope of ordinary business operations. For example, a sponsor may propose that the corporation establish a committee to examine the human rights policies of countries in which the corporation does business. Proposals that do not involve "ordinary business operations" may nonetheless be deemed irrelevant from the corporate perspective under Rule 14a–8(i)(5).

Finally, some proposals are excluded as violations of law generally or the proxy rules specifically:

- Proposal if implemented would violate "any state, federal, or foreign law to which it is subject" (Rule 14a–8(i)(9))

- Proposal conflicts with any of the proxy rules, including Rule 14a–9's antifraud prohibition (Rule 14a–8(i)(9))

HYPOTHETICAL FOUR

Ivan, who has held over $2,000 of FoodNow stock for several years, is considering submitting an issue proposal for inclusion in FoodNow's proxy statement. He is unhappy with FoodNow's performance and even more unhappy with its management. Consider the following scenarios.

1. *Scenario One*: Ivan submits a proposal mandating that the corporation deliver not only groceries, but also prescription drugs. Ivan believes doing so will dramatically enhance FoodNow's profits.

2. *Scenario Two*: Ivan submits a proposal that FoodNow should make a special payment of $1 million to Ivan for all the anguish Ivan has suffered watching FoodNow's stock price drop.

3. *Scenario Three*: Ivan submits a proposal recommending that the board of directors study its nomination procedures for directors and assess how "economic" diversity can be increased among nominees to the board. Two years ago, Roberta (unrelated to Ivan) submitted a proposal requesting FoodNow's board study increasing minority representation on the board. The proposal received only 2% of the vote.

4. *Scenario Four*: Ivan submits the following proposal: "FoodNow makes too much profit at the expense of hard, working class people who need to buy groceries. We request that FoodNow commission a study on the impact of its high prices on the cost of living of middle and lower income Americans."

What is left after excluding this list of prohibited subject matters? Shareholders are caught in a bind between the requirements that proposals not be irrelevant (Rule 14a–8(i)(5)) and be within the scope of the corporation's authority (Rule 14a–8(i)(6)) on the one hand, and the requirements that the proposal not deal with "ordinary business operations" (Rule 14a–8(i)(7)) and not otherwise be improper under state law (Rule 14a–8(i)(1)). Most relevant proposals within the corporation's authority are also likely to be proposals that are improper under state law and deal with "ordinary business operations."

The *Lovenheim* case addresses whether a proposal is relevant to a corporation. Rule 14a–8(i)(5) provides both a bright-line numerical cutoff and also a looser standard to determine whether the proposal is "not otherwise significantly related to the company's business." Does the cutoff or the standard control?

Lovenheim v. Iroquois Brands Ltd.

618 F. Supp. 554 (D.D.C. 1985).

■ GASCH, DISTRICT JUDGE.

I.   BACKGROUND

This matter is now before the Court on plaintiff's motion for preliminary injunction. Plaintiff Peter C. Lovenheim, owner of two hundred shares of common stock in Iroquois Brands, Ltd. (hereinafter "Iroquois/Delaware"), seeks to bar Iroquois/Delaware from excluding from the proxy materials being sent to all shareholders in preparation for an upcoming shareholder meeting information concerning a proposed resolution he intends to offer at the meeting. Mr. Lovenheim's proposed resolution relates to the procedure used to force-feed geese for production of paté de foie gras in France,[2] a type of paté imported by Iroquois/Delaware. Specifically, his resolution calls upon the Directors of Iroquois/Delaware to:

> form a committee to study the methods by which its French supplier produces paté de foie gras, and report to the shareholders its findings and opinions, based on expert consultation, on whether this production method causes undue distress, pain or suffering to the animals involved and, if so, whether further distribution of this product should be discontinued until a more humane production method is developed.

Attachment to Affidavit of Peter C. Lovenheim.

Mr. Lovenheim's right to compel Iroquois/Delaware to insert information concerning his proposal in the proxy materials turns on the applicability of section 14(a) of the Securities Exchange Act of 1934 and the shareholder proposal rule promulgated by the Securities and Exchange Commission Rule 14a–8. . . .

Iroquois/Delaware has refused to allow information concerning Mr. Lovenheim's proposal to be included in proxy materials being sent in connection with the next annual shareholders meeting. In doing so, Iroquois/Delaware relies on an exception to the general requirement of Rule 14a–8, Rule 14a–8[i](5). That exception provides that an issuer of securities "may omit a proposal and any statement in support thereof" from its proxy statement and form of proxy:

> if the proposal relates to operations which account for less than 5 percent of the issuer's total assets at the end of its most recent fiscal year, and for less than 5 percent of its net earnings and gross sales for its most recent fiscal year, and is not otherwise significantly related to the issuer's business.

Rule 14a–8[i](5).

* * *

2. Paté de foie gras is made from the liver of geese. According to Mr. Lovenheim's affidavit, force-feeding is frequently used in order to expand the liver and thereby produce a larger quantity of paté. Mr. Lovenheim's affidavit also contains a description of the force-feeding process:

> Force-feeding usually begins when the geese are four months old. On some farms where feeding is mechanized, the bird's body and wings are placed in a metal brace and its neck is stretched. Through a funnel inserted 10–12 inches down the throat of the goose, a machine pumps up to 400 grams of corn-based mash into its stomach. An elastic band around the goose's throat prevents regurgitation. When feeding is manual, a handler uses a funnel and stick to force the mash down.

Plaintiff contends that such force-feeding is a form of cruelty to animals.

II. LIKELIHOOD OF PLAINTIFF PREVAILING ON MERITS

* * *

Iroquois/Delaware's reliance on the argument that this exception applies is based on the following information contained in the affidavit of its president: Iroquois/Delaware has annual revenues of $141 million with $6 million in annual profits and $78 million in assets. In contrast, its paté de foie gras sales were just $79,000 last year, representing a net loss on paté sales of $3,121. Iroquois/Delaware has only $34,000 in assets related to paté. Thus none of the company's net earnings and less than .05 percent of its assets are implicated by plaintiff's proposal. These levels are obviously far below the five percent threshold set forth in the first portion of the exception claimed by Iroquois/Delaware.

Plaintiff does not contest that his proposed resolution relates to a matter of little economic significance to Iroquois/Delaware. Nevertheless he contends that the Rule 14a–8[i](5) exception is not applicable as it cannot be said that his proposal "is not otherwise significantly related to the issuer's business" as is required by the final portion of that exception. In other words, plaintiff's argument that Rule 14a–8 does not permit omission of his proposal rests on the assertion that the rule and statute on which it is based do not permit omission merely because a proposal is not economically significant where a proposal has "ethical or social significance."[8]

Iroquois/Delaware challenges plaintiff's view that ethical and social proposals cannot be excluded even if they do not meet the economic or five percent test. Instead, Iroquois/Delaware views the exception solely in economic terms as permitting omission of any proposals relating to a de minimis share of assets and profits. Iroquois/Delaware asserts that since corporations are economic entities, only an economic test is appropriate.

The Court would note that the applicability of the Rule 14a–8[i](5) exception to Mr. Lovenheim's proposal represents a close question given the lack of clarity in the exception itself. In effect, plaintiff relies on the word "otherwise," suggesting that it indicates the drafters of the rule intended that other noneconomic tests of significance be used. Iroquois/Delaware relies on the fact that the rule examines other significance in relation to the issuer's business. Because of the apparent ambiguity of the rule, the Court considers the history of the shareholder proposal rule in

---

8. The assertion that the proposal is significant in an ethical and social sense relies on plaintiff's argument that "the very availability of a market for products that may be obtained through the inhumane force-feeding of geese cannot help but contribute to the continuation of such treatment." Plaintiff's brief characterizes the humane treatment of animals as among the foundations of western culture and cites in support of this view the Seven Laws of Noah, an animal protection statute enacted by the Massachu-setts Bay Colony in 1641, numerous federal statutes enacted since 1877, and animal protection laws existing in all fifty states and the District of Columbia. An additional indication of the significance of plaintiff's proposal is the support of such leading organizations in the field of animal care as the American Society for the Prevention of Cruelty to Animals and The Humane Society of the United States for measures aimed at discontinuing use of force-feeding.

determining the proper interpretation of the most recent version of that rule.

Prior to 1983, paragraph 14a–8[i](5) excluded proposals "not significantly related to the issuer's business" but did not contain an objective economic significance test such as the five percent of sales, assets, and earnings specified in the first part of the current version. Although a series of SEC decisions through 1976 allowing issuers to exclude proposals challenging compliance with the Arab economic boycott of Israel allowed exclusion if the issuer did less than one percent of their business with Arab countries or Israel, the Commission stated later in 1976 that it did "not believe that subparagraph [i](5) should be hinged solely on the economic relativity of a proposal." Thus the Commission required inclusion "in many situations in which the related business comprised less than one percent" of the company's revenues, profits or assets "where the proposal has raised *policy questions* important enough to be considered 'significantly related' to the issuer's business."

As indicated above, the 1983 revision adopted the five percent test of economic significance in an effort to create a more objective standard. Nevertheless, in adopting this standard, the Commission stated that proposals will be includable notwithstanding their "failure to reach the specified economic thresholds if a significant relationship to the issuer's business is demonstrated on the face of the resolution or supporting statement." Thus it seems clear based on the history of the rule that "the meaning of 'significantly related' is not *limited* to economic significance."

* * *

[T]he Court cannot ignore the history of the rule which reveals no decision by the Commission to limit the determination to the economic criteria relied on by Iroquois/Delaware. The Court therefore holds that in light of the ethical and social significance of plaintiff's proposal and the fact that it implicates significant levels of sales, plaintiff has shown a likelihood of prevailing on the merits with regard to the issue of whether his proposal is "otherwise significantly related" to Iroquois/Delaware's business.[16]

* * *

QUESTIONS

1. If a proposal deals with an aspect of a company that accounts for less than 5% of the business, is it still possible for such a proposal to have economic significance to the company and its shareholders?

2. What limit is there on the phrase "otherwise significant" in Rule 14a–8(i)(5) if it includes items of non-economic significance?

---

16. The result would, of course, be different if plaintiff's proposal was ethically significant in the abstract but had no meaningful relationship to the business of Iroquois/Delaware as Iroquois/Delaware was not engaged in the business of importing paté de foie gras.

3. What if the plaintiff in *Lovenheim* also is a shareholder in Microsoft Corporation (which is not in the foie gras business) and the plaintiff seeks to include the same proposal on the Microsoft proxy statement?

New York City Employees' Retirement System v. Dole Food Co., Inc.

795 F. Supp. 95 (S.D.N.Y. 1992).

■ CONBOY, DISTRICT JUDGE.

Proceeding by an order to show cause, the New York City Employees' Retirement System ("NYCERS") brings this action for a preliminary injunction that would enjoin defendant Dole Food Company, Inc. from the solicitation of shareholder proxies for Dole's upcoming annual meeting without informing shareholders of NYCERS' shareholder proposal. In the alternative, NYCERS seeks inclusion of the proposal on a supplemental mailing prior to the annual meeting.

I. Background

NYCERS is a public pension fund that owns approximately 164,841 shares of common stock in Dole Food Company, Inc. On December 12, 1991, New York City Comptroller Elizabeth Holtzman, in her capacity as the custodian of NYCERS' assets, wrote to the executive vice president of Dole, requesting Dole to include the following proposal ("the NYCERS proposal") in its proxy statement prior to its annual meeting:

NEW YORK CITY EMPLOYEE'S [sic.] RETIREMENT SYSTEM

SHAREHOLDER RESOLUTION ON HEALTH CARE

TO DOLE FOOD COMPANY, INC.

WHEREAS: The Dole Food Company is concerned with remaining competitive in the domestic and world marketplace, acknowledging the positive relationship between the health and well being of its employees and productivity, and the resulting effect on corporate growth and financial stability; and

WHEREAS: Sustained double-digit increases in health care costs have put severe financial pressure on a company attempting to continue to provide adequate health care for its employees and their dependents; and

WHEREAS: The company has a societal obligation to conduct its affairs in a way which promotes the health and well being of all;

BE IT THEREFORE RESOLVED: That the shareholders request the Board of Directors to establish a committee of the Board consisting of outside and independent directors for the purpose of evaluating the impact of a representative cross section of the various health care reform proposals being considered by national policy makers on the company and their [sic.] competitive standing in domestic and international markets. These various proposals can be grouped in three generic categories; the single payor model (as in the Canadian plan), the limited payor (as in the Pepper Commission Report) and the employer mandated (as in the Kennedy–Waxman legislation).

Further, the aforementioned committee should be directed to prepare a report of its findings. The report should be prepared in a reasonable time, at a reasonable cost and should be made available to any shareholder upon written request.

SUPPORTING STATEMENT

Our nation is now at a crossroads on health care. Because of cutbacks in public programs, jobs that offer no benefits and efforts by employers to shift health care costs to workers, 50 million Americans have health care coverage that is inadequate to meet their needs and another 37 million have no protection at all.

The United States spends $2 billion a day, or eleven percent of its gross national product, on health care. As insurance premiums increase 18 to 30 percent a year, basic health care has moved well beyond the reach of a growing number of working families. This increase also places heavy pressure on employer labor costs. There is no end in sight to this trend.

As a result and because of the significant social and public policy issues attendant to operations involving health care, we urge shareholders to SUPPORT the resolution.

On January 16, 1992, J. Brett Tibbitts, deputy general counsel of Dole Food Company, Inc., wrote to the office of chief counsel of the Securities & Exchange Commission's division of corporation finance and stated Dole's position that Dole could exclude the NYCERS proposal from its proxy statement because the proposal concerned employee benefits, an assertedly "ordinary business operation," and both SEC regulations and the law of the Dole's state of incorporation relegate such ordinary business operations to management, not shareholder, control.

On February 10, 1992, John Brousseau, special counsel to the SEC's division of corporation finance, responded to Tibbitts' letter with the following written statement:

> ... There appears to be some basis for your view that the proposal may be excluded pursuant to rule 14a–8[i](7) because the proposal is directed at involving the Company in the political or legislative process relating to an aspect of the Company's operations. Accordingly, we will not recommend enforcement action to the Commission if the proposal is omitted from the Company's proxy materials....

In conjunction with NYCERS' request for an order to show cause, NYCERS submitted an affidavit of Theodore R. Marmor, a professor of political science and public policy at Yale University. In his affidavit, Professor Marmor averred, inter alia, that (1) at least 37 million Americans have no health insurance; (2) the United States spends more on health per capita than any other developed nation; (3) health care expenditures in 1989 represented 56 percent of pre-tax company profits in 1989, as compared to 8 percent in 1985; and (4) the national average cost for health care per employee is $3,200, and some large companies pay $5,000 or more per employee. Professor Marmor also defined and explained the three major categories of national health care proposals pending in Congress:

* * *

II.   Discussion

* * *

Rule 14(a)–8[i] allows a corporation to omit a shareholder proposal from its proxy statement because of certain enumerated circumstances. In substance, Dole argues that the instant matter fits within the "ordinary business operations," "insignificant relation," and "beyond power to effectuate" exceptions enumerated in Rule 14(a)–8[i].[1]

The corporation has the burden to show that a proposal fits within an exception to Rule 14(a)–8(a). Our determination on this matter also takes into account NYCERS' own burden, as discussed above, of demonstrating a "substantial" likelihood of success on the merits.

On April 16, this Court held a hearing pursuant to NYCERS' request for a mandatory injunction. At the hearing, counsel for both parties elaborated on the legal arguments that they had submitted in their papers, but neither party produced any witnesses, or any proof by affidavit of the nature of Dole's employee health care programs, coverage, costs, union agreements or insurance contracts. Indeed, the argument and the parties' briefs were largely abstract in nature. Nevertheless, for the reasons stated below, we find that NYCERS has met its burden of showing that it is substantially likely that Dole would fail to show on the merits that the proposal falls within one of the enumerated exceptions.

1.   Rule 14a–8[i](7): "Ordinary Business Operations"

* * *

The term "ordinary business operations" is neither self-explanatory nor easy to explain. The exception does not elaborate on whether "business operations" encompass merely certain routine internal functions or whether they can extend to cost-benefit analyses or profit-making activity. The SEC's commentary on the current version of the "ordinary business operations" exception states, "[W]here proposals involve business matters that are mundane in nature and do not involve any substantial policy or other considerations, the sub-paragraph may be relied upon to omit them." This commentary indicates that even if the proposal touches on the way

---

1. In its letter of January 16, 1992 to the SEC, Dole objected to NYCERS' proposal in part on the ground that the proposal violated the provision of Hawaii law that states that a company's board of directors has exclusive control over the establishment of committees and the choice of which directors will serve on committees. The SEC staff "no-action" letter did not address this argument, and Dole did not raise this argument in its papers or at the hearing before the Court; accordingly, we do not consider it.

daily business matters are conducted, the statement may not be excluded if it involves a significant strategic decision as to those daily business matters, i.e., one that will significantly affect the manner in which a company does business. One Court has held that the purpose of the "ordinary business exception" is to prevent shareholders from seeking to "assert the power to dictate the minutiae of daily business decisions."

While we give due deference to the SEC staff opinion letter in this case and other similar cases, we find that NYCERS has shown under that the proposal does not relate to "ordinary business operations." If one aspect of "ordinary business operations" is certain, it is that the outcome of close cases such as the instant one are largely fact-dependent. Nevertheless, Dole has not provided the Court with any information on (1) whether Dole has a health insurance program; (2) if such a program exists at Dole, how it operates; and (3) the amount of corporate financial resources that Dole devotes to health insurance. Instead, Dole argues, "To the extent [the NYCER proposal] relates to Dole's business at all, it relates to its employee relations and health care benefits, a matter traditionally within the 'ordinary business' category". In support of its position, Dole cites several SEC "No–Action" letters relating to proposals similar to the instant one. However, the SEC "No–Action" letters contain scarcely any analysis, and, while they are entitled to deference, they do not bind this Court. We note that the SEC itself has changed its reasoning as to why proposals relating to national employee health insurance relate to "ordinary business relations." The SEC has shifted rationales for rejecting proposals such as this one, initially stressing the "employee relations" aspect of national health insurance and then emphasizing its "political [and] legislative" dimensions. . . .

As Professor Marmor's affidavit demonstrates . . . the proposals in the instant case relate to a strategic policy choice as to the prospect of a major outlay to the federal treasury, as well as possible internal changes that may affect the entire scope of Dole's employee health insurance policy. The question of which plan, if any, that Dole should support, and how Dole would choose to function under the plans (e.g., "pay or play") could have large financial consequences on Dole. . . . [T]he proposal in the instant case does not seek to involve the corporation in making abstract political proposals but rather requests the corporation to study existing, concrete plans before Congress that affect the scope of Dole's health insurance operations.

The proposed report primarily relates to Dole's policy making on an issue of social significance that, while not relating to a specific health care policy at Dole, nevertheless relates to a distinct type of operations that Dole has undoubtedly grappled with in the past. Accordingly, we do not find that the instant proposal relates to "ordinary business operations."

2. Rule 14a–8[i](5): "Insignificant Relationship" Exception

* * *

Dole does not dispute that the clear language of the NYCERS proposal in large part relates to national health insurance's impact on Dole. Without specific reference to Rule 14a–8(c)(5), Dole argues that the NYCERS proposal lacked a discrete nexus to Dole's distinct line of business, presumably the manufacture of food products. Dole's argument is essentially made under the exception referred to in the last phrase of Rule 14a–8[i](5), i.e., that the proposal is "not otherwise significantly related to the registrant's business."

We need not address Dole's "nexus" argument because we find the activity addressed by the NYCERS proposal relates to activities that likely occupy outlays more than five percent of Dole's income. It is substantially likely that Dole's health insurance outlays constitute more than five percent of its income. Dole has offered no information on the percentage of its income that it devotes to employee health insurance. In his affidavit, Professor Marmor stated that nationwide, 1989 health care expenditures represented 56 percent of pre-tax company profits. We find it substantially likely that this figure applies to Dole to a greater or lesser extent. Because the subject of the proposed study likely relates to a significant aspect of Dole's business, we find that the proposal does not fall within the exception stated in Rule 14(a)–8[i](5).

3.   Rule 14(a)–8[i](6): "Beyond Power to Effectuate" Exception

* * *

Dole argues, "The NYCERS proposal requests the analysis of, and implicitly suggests that Dole should attempt to influence the selection of, national health care reform proposals." However, Dole does not point to any language that suggests that a necessary consequence of the proposal is political lobbying. While couched in language that clearly supports a national solution to the problems of growing health insurance costs, the NYCERS proposal merely calls for the commission of a research report on national health insurance proposals and their impact on Dole's competitive standing. Moreover, we fail to see why such a study necessarily "deals with a matter beyond the registrant's power to effectuate." For example, a decision that Dole's interests mandate a choice to "pay" rather than "play" under two of the three major proposals would clearly be within Dole's power to effectuate if these proposals are enacted. Moreover, Dole might conceivably find that it is in its interests to draft such a proposal and lobby for its enactment. For the reasons stated above, we disagree with Dole's argument that the political aspect of this proposal means that it does not relate to Dole's business in a substantial way.

* * *

Having found that the required showing has been met, this Court directs Dole to include in its proxy materials for its June 4, 1992 annual meeting NYCERS' shareholder proposal submitted to Dole by letter dated December 12, 1991.

SO ORDERED.

QUESTIONS

1. Is the court correct in holding that because health care reform if enacted would have large financial consequences on Dole, the proposal is therefore significant for purposes of Rule 14a–8(i)(5)?

2. Consider the interaction of Rule 14a–8(i)(5) (irrelevant proposals) and Rule 14a–8(i)(7) (ordinary business proposals). The *Dole Food* court states that even though the NYCERS proposal deals with "employee relations," an aspect of ordinary business operations, it nevertheless implicates large "financial consequences" for Dole Food and thus does not fall under Rule 14a–8(i)(7). How does this interpretation of Rule 14a–8(i)(7) affect the scope of Rule 14a–8(i)(5)?

3. The corporation has the power to commission a study. In some cases, for example, the study may concern the impact of global warming on the environment, or the impact of a potential asteroid strike on corporate profitability. Is the ability to commission a study all the *Dole Food* court requires to avoid exclusion under Rule 14a–8(i)(6)?

4. What is wrong with allowing an issue proposal under Rule 14a–8 that is not significantly related to a company's business and is beyond the power of a business to effectuate? Shouldn't shareholders have the ability to use their own corporation as a medium of communication?

On appeal, the Second Circuit vacated the district court's holding in *Dole Food* as moot. Dole Foods had already included the NYCERS health care reform proposal on the corporate proxy; the proposal was defeated, gaining a little over six percent of the total votes cast. The Second Circuit wrote: "Since the relief sought by NYCERS was secured by the mailing of the proxy, and the mailing and the contents of the proxy cannot now be changed or halted by any action we might take, the controversy is no longer alive." Once vacated, the district court's holding lost its precedential value in order to "avoid giving preclusive effect to a judgment never reviewed by an appellate court." See *New York City Employees' Retirement System v. Dole Food Co., Inc.*, 969 F.2d 1430 (2d Cir. 1992).

The issue of whether a shareholder activist could avoid the exclusion in Rule 14a–8(i)(7) for proposals that deal with "ordinary business" matters by linking the proposal to greater social and ethical issues continues to be an important topic of concern. In 1991, Cracker Barrel Old Country Stores, a restaurant chain, fired a number of workers for violating the company's policy banning the employment of those "whose sexual preferences fail to demonstrate normal heterosexual values which have been the foundation of families in our society." In 1992, the New York City Employees Retirement System (NYCERS) submitted a proposal under Rule 14a–8 to Cracker Barrel requesting that the company "implement non-discriminatory policies relating to sexual orientation and to add explicit prohibitions against such discrimination to their corporate employment policy statement." Cracker Barrel sought to exclude the proposal under Rule 14a–8(i)(7) as dealing with employee relations, an aspect of the "ordinary business" of the corporation. Cracker Barrel asked the SEC for a no-action letter that the SEC's staff would not recommend any action by the SEC against Cracker Barrel if the company used Rule 14a–8(i)(7) to exclude the proposal. The SEC not only granted the no-action letter but stated:

> [I]n recent years ... the line between includable and excludable employment-related proposals based on social policy considerations has become increasingly difficult to draw. The distinctions recognized by the staff are characterized by many as tenuous, without substance and effectively nullifying the application of the ordinary business exclusion to employment related proposals. The Division has reconsidered the application of Rule 14a–8[i](7) to employment-related proposals in light of these concerns and the staff's experience with these proposals in recent years. As a result, the Division has determined that the fact that a shareholder proposal concerning a company's employment policies and practices for the general workforce is tied to a social issue will no longer be viewed as removing the proposal from the realm of ordinary business operations of the registrant. Rather, determinations with respect to any such proposals are properly governed by the employment-based nature of the proposal.

Cracker Barrel Old Country Stores, Inc., 1992 SEC No–Act. LEXIS 984 (Oct. 13, 1992). The SEC staff made clear that proposals aimed at the compensation of senior executives and directors were "inherently outside the scope of normal or routine practices in the running of the company's operations." The SEC's *Cracker Barrel* policy excluding all employment-related proposals even if implicating important social and ethical policy issues under Rule 14a–8(i)(7) remained in place until 1998 when the SEC revisited the issue in the following SEC Release.

Amendments to Rules on Shareholder Proposals

Exchange Act Release No. 34–40018 (SEC 1998).

* * *

We proposed to reverse the position announced in the 1992 *Cracker Barrel* no-action letter concerning the Division's approach to employment-related shareholder proposals raising social policy issues. In that letter, the Division announced that

> The fact that a shareholder proposal concerning a company's employment policies and practices for the general workforce is tied to a social issue will no longer be viewed as removing the proposal from the realm of ordinary business operations of the registrant. Rather, determinations with respect to any such proposals are properly governed by the employment-based nature of the proposal.

We are adopting our proposal to reverse the *Cracker Barrel* position, which provided that all employment-related shareholder proposals raising social policy issues would be excludable under the "ordinary business" exclusion.

The Division will return to its case-by-case approach that prevailed prior to the *Cracker Barrel* no-action letter.

In applying the "ordinary business" exclusion to proposals that raise social policy issues, the Division seeks to use the most well-reasoned and consistent standards possible, given the inherent complexity of the task. From time to time, in light of experience dealing with proposals in specific subject areas, and reflecting changing societal views, the Division adjusts its view with respect to "social policy" proposals involving ordinary business. . . .

We believe that reversal of the Division's *Cracker Barrel* no-action letter, which the Commission had subsequently affirmed, is warranted. Since 1992, the relative importance of certain social issues relating to employment matters has reemerged as a consistent topic of widespread public debate. In addition, as a result of the extensive policy discussions that the *Cracker Barrel* position engendered, and through the rulemaking notice and comment process, we have gained a better understanding of the depth of interest among shareholders in having an opportunity to express their views to company management on employment-related proposals that raise sufficiently significant social policy issues.

Reversal of the *Cracker Barrel* no-action position will result in a return to a case-by-case analytical approach. In making distinctions in this area, the Division and the Commission will continue to apply the applicable standard for determining when a proposal relates to "ordinary business." The standard . . . provided an exception for certain proposals that raise significant social policy issues.

While we acknowledge that there is no bright-line test to determine when employment-related shareholder proposals raising social issues fall within the scope of the "ordinary business" exclusion, the staff will make reasoned distinctions in deciding whether to furnish "no-action" relief. Although a few of the distinctions made in those cases may be somewhat tenuous, we believe that on the whole the benefit to shareholders and companies in providing guidance and informal resolutions will outweigh the problematic aspects of the few decisions in the middle ground.

Nearly all commenters from the shareholder community who addressed the matter supported the reversal of this position. Most commenters from the corporate community did not favor the proposal to reverse *Cracker Barrel*, though many indicated that the change would be acceptable as part of a broader set of reforms.

Going forward, companies and shareholders should bear in mind that the *Cracker Barrel* position related only to employment-related proposals raising certain social policy issues. Reversal of the position does not affect the Division's analysis of any other category of proposals under the exclusion, such as proposals on general business operations.

Finally, we believe that it would be useful to summarize the principal considerations in the Division's application, under the Commission's oversight, of the "ordinary business" exclusion. The general underlying policy of this exclusion is consistent with the policy of most state corporate laws: to confine the resolution of ordinary business problems to management and the board of directors, since it is impracticable for shareholders to decide how to solve such problems at an annual shareholders meeting.

The policy underlying the ordinary business exclusion rests on two central considerations. The first relates to the subject matter of the proposal. Certain tasks are so fundamental to management's ability to run a company on a day-to-day basis that they could not, as a practical matter, be subject to direct shareholder oversight. Examples include the management of the workforce, such as the hiring, promotion, and termination of employees, decisions on production quality and quantity, and the retention of suppliers. However, proposals relating to such matters but focusing on sufficiently significant social policy issues (e.g., significant discrimination matters) generally would not be considered to be excludable, because the proposals would transcend the day-to-day business matters and raise policy issues so significant that it would be appropriate for a shareholder vote.[43]

The second consideration relates to the degree to which the proposal seeks to "micro-manage" the company by probing too deeply into matters of a complex nature upon which shareholders, as a group, would not be in a position to make an informed judgment. This consideration may come into play in a number of circumstances, such as where the proposal involves intricate detail, or seeks to impose specific time-frames or methods for implementing complex policies....

[I]n the Proposing Release we explained that one of the considerations in making the ordinary business determination was the degree to which the proposal seeks to micro-manage the company. We cited examples such as where the proposal seeks intricate detail, or seeks to impose specific time-frames or to impose specific methods for implementing complex policies. Some commenters thought that the examples cited seemed to imply that all proposals seeking detail, or seeking to promote time-frames or methods, necessarily amount to "ordinary business." We did not intend such an implication. Timing questions, for instance, could involve significant policy where large differences are at stake, and proposals may seek a reasonable level of detail without running afoul of these considerations.

Further, in a footnote to the same sentence citing examples of "micro-management," we included a citation to *Capital Cities/ABC, Inc.*, (Apr. 4, 1991) involving a proposal on the company's affirmative action policies and practices. Some commenters were concerned that the citation might imply that proposals similar to the *Capital Cities* proposal today would automatically be excludable under "ordinary business" on grounds that they seek excessive detail. Such a position, in their view, might offset the impact of reversing the *Cracker Barrel* position. However, we cited *Capital Cities/ABC, Inc.* only to support the general proposition that some proposals may intrude unduly on a company's "ordinary business" operations by

---

43. See, e.g., Reebok Int'l Ltd. (Mar. 16, 1992) (noting that a proposal concerning senior executive compensation could not be excluded pursuant to rule 14a–8(c)(7)).

virtue of the level of detail that they seek. We did not intend to imply that the proposal addressed in *Capital Cities*, or similar proposals, would automatically amount to "ordinary business." Those determinations will be made on a case-by-case basis, taking into account factors such as the nature of the proposal and the circumstances of the company to which it is directed.

* * *

HYPOTHETICAL FIVE

Ivan, who has held over $2,000 of FoodNow common stock for several years, has some proposals that he thinks FoodNow should establish a board committee to study. Consider the likelihood that FoodNow will successfully obtain a SEC no-action letter if it excludes from the company's annual proxy statement the following proposals.

1. *Proposal One*: RESOLVED: "The committee should examine the negative impact of the public's perception of the company's inhumane policies toward livestock used in FoodNow's butcher shops."

2. *Proposal Two*: RESOLVED: "The committee should study the feasibility of changes in FoodNow's salary scale. In particular we request the committee to study increasing salaries for workers making less than $100,000 per year by 10%. All other workers should take a 5% pay cut. A more equitable wage scale will not only increase employee morale but also reduce greater societal unrest, thereby strengthening the moral fabric of this nation."

B. SEC AUTHORITY OVER VOTING POWERS

A key concern in the shareholder issue proposal process under Rule 14a–8 is the need to reconcile federal disclosure requirements with state corporate law. Rule 14a–8(i)(1) prohibits proposals that are not valid under applicable state law. Traditionally the division of power and authority within a corporation is at the core of state corporate law. The SEC, nonetheless, has required corporations to include a number of shareholders proposals that deal with the incumbent directors' control over the corporation. These include proposals (couched as recommendations) to declassify a staggered board of directors, include more diversity on the board, and remove a poison pill, among others.

Should the SEC get more involved in dictating the corporate governance of publicly-held firms? A key determinant of shareholder power is whether all shares have equal voting rights. For most corporations, votes are closely tied to rights to residual cash flows from the firm (i.e., dividends and rights to assets in liquidation). Because shareholders enjoy the upside if a firm does well and the downside if the firm does poorly, they are given the right to vote to elect the board of directors. Giving voting power to the residual owners of a firm puts control in the hands of those with the interest in maximizing the value of the firm as a whole.

One could imagine giving voting power to a non-residual claimant of the firm, such as a bank that made a loan to the corporation. How would you vote if you were a non-residual claimant such as a bank? Non-residual claimants typically care most about preserving capital and will generally not be interested in maximizing the overall value of the firm, but instead will seek to minimize risk (e.g., by putting all the corporate money in an extremely safe bank vault). Generally, parties negotiating for allocation of control will do so in a way that maximizes the firm's value, leaving more value to divide among all the various claimants in the firm.

If voting power and rights to cash flows diverge, the potential for mischief on the part of those in control increases substantially. Imagine a manager who owns 1% of the residual cashflow but has managed to capture 50% of the votes, thereby insulating herself from possible hostile takeovers or proxy control contests. Such a manager would face only the relatively weak constraint of state court review to constrain actions that increase the manager's private benefits of control at the expense of the other shareholders. As you read *The Business Roundtable* case below, consider the wisdom of allowing the SEC to intervene directly to force alignment of voting power and rights to residual cash flows within the firm.

The Business Roundtable v. S.E.C.

905 F.2d 406 (D.C. Cir. 1990).

■ WILLIAMS, CIRCUIT JUDGE.

In 1984 General Motors announced a plan to issue a second class of common stock with one-half vote per share. The proposal collided with a longstanding rule of the New York Stock Exchange that required listed companies to provide one vote per share of common stock. The NYSE balked at enforcement, and after two years filed a proposal with the Securities and Exchange Commission to relax its own rule. The SEC did not approve the rule change but responded with one of its own. On July 7, 1988, it adopted Rule 19c–4, barring national securities exchanges and national securities associations, together known as self-regulatory organizations (SROs), from listing stock of a corporation that takes any corporate action "with the effect of nullifying, restricting or disparately reducing the per share voting rights of [existing common stockholders]." The rule prohibits such "disenfranchisement" even where approved by a shareholder vote conducted on one share/one vote principles. Because the rule directly controls the substantive allocation of powers among classes of shareholders, we find it in excess of the Commission's authority under § 19 of the Securities Exchange Act of 1934. Neither the wisdom of the requirement, nor of its being imposed at the federal level, is here in question.

* * *

Two components of § 19 give the Commission authority over the rules of self-regulatory organizations. First, § 19(b) requires them to file with the Commission any proposed change in their rules. The Commission is to approve the change if it finds it "consistent with the requirements of [the Exchange Act] and the rules and regulations thereunder applicable" to the self-regulatory organization. § 19(b)(2). This provision is not directly at issue here, but, as we shall see, both the procedure and the terms guiding Commission approval are important in understanding the scope of the authority the Commission has sought to exercise. That is found in § 19(c), which allows the Commission on its own initiative to amend the rules of a self-regulatory organization as it deems necessary or appropriate [1] to insure the fair administration of the self-regulatory organization, [2] to conform its rules to requirements of [the Exchange Act] and the rules and regulations thereunder applicable to such organization, or [3] otherwise in furtherance of the purposes of [the Exchange Act]. As no one suggests that either of the first two purposes justifies Rule 19c–4, the issue before us is the scope of the third, catch-all provision.

* * *

What then are the "purposes" of the Exchange Act? The Commission supports Rule 19c–4 as advancing the purposes of a variety of sections ... but we first take its strongest–§ 14's grant of power to regulate the proxy process. The Commission finds a purpose "to ensure fair shareholder suffrage." Indeed, it points to the House Report's declarations that "[f]air corporate suffrage is an important right," and that "use of the exchanges should involve a corresponding duty of according to shareholders fair suffrage".... The formulation is true in the sense that Congress's decision can be located under that broad umbrella.

But unless the legislative purpose is defined by reference to the means Congress selected, it can be framed at any level of generality–to improve the operation of capital markets, for instance. In fact, although § 14(a) broadly bars use of the mails (and other means) "to solicit ... any proxy" in contravention of Commission rules and regulations, it is not seriously disputed that Congress's central concern was with disclosure.

While the House Report indeed speaks of fair corporate suffrage, it also plainly identifies Congress's target—the solicitation of proxies by well informed insiders "without fairly informing the stockholders of the purposes for which the proxies are to be used." The Senate Report contains no vague language about "corporate suffrage," but rather explains the purpose of the proxy protections as ensuring that stockholders have "adequate knowledge" about the "financial condition of the corporation ... [and] the major questions of policy, which are decided at stockholders' meetings." Finally, both reports agree on the power that the proxy sections gave the Commission—"power to control the conditions under which proxies may be solicited."

That proxy regulation bears almost exclusively on disclosure stems as a matter of necessity from the nature of proxies. Proxy solicitations are, after all, only communications with potential absentee voters. The goal of federal proxy regulation was to improve those communications and thereby to enable proxy voters to control the corporation as effectively as they might have by attending a shareholder meeting.

We do not mean to be taken as saying that disclosure is necessarily the sole subject of § 14. But . . . Rule 19c–4 much more directly interferes with the substance of what the shareholders may enact. It prohibits certain reallocations of voting power and certain capital structures, even if approved by a shareholder vote subject to full disclosure and the most exacting procedural rules.

The Commission noted in the preamble to the Proposed Rule its conviction that collective action problems could cause even a properly conducted shareholder vote (with ample disclosure and sound procedures) to bring about results injurious to the shareholders. We do not question these findings. But we think the Commission's reliance on them is a clue to its stretch of the congressional purposes. As the Commission itself observed, "[s]ection 14(a) contains an implicit assumption that shareholders will be able to make use of the information provided in proxy solicitations in order to vote in corporate elections." In 1934 Congress acted on the premise that shareholder voting could work, so long as investors secured enough information and, perhaps, the benefit of other procedural protections. It did not seek to regulate the stockholders' choices. If the Commission believes that premise misguided, it must turn to Congress.

With its step beyond control of voting procedure and into the distribution of voting power, the Commission would assume an authority that the Exchange Act's proponents disclaimed any intent to grant. Noting that opponents expressed alarm that the bill would give the Commission "power to interfere in the management of corporations," the Senate Committee on Banking and Currency said it had "no such intention" and that the bill "furnish[ed] no justification for such an interpretation."

There are, of course, shadings within the notion of "management." With the present rule the Commission does not tell any corporation where to locate its next plant. But neither does state corporate law; it regulates the distribution of powers among the various players in the process of corporate governance, and the Commission's present leap beyond disclosure is just that sort of regulation. . . .

Surprisingly, the Commission does not concede a lack of jurisdiction over such issues. When questioned at oral argument as to what state corporation rules are not related to "fair corporate suffrage," SEC counsel conceded only that further intrusions into state corporate governance "would present more difficult situations." In fact the Commission's apparent perception of its § 19 powers has been immensely broad, unbounded even by any pretense of a connection to § 14. In reviewing the previous SRO rule changes on issues of independent directors and independent audit committees, it grounded its review in a supposed mandate to "protect investors and the public interest." The Commission made no attempt to limit the concept by reference to the concrete purposes of any section. Rather, it reasoned that the rule changes protected investors by "creat[ing] uniformity that helps to assure investors that all the companies traded in those markets have the fundamental safeguards they have come to expect of major companies." If Rule 19c–4 were validated on such broad grounds, the Commission would be able to establish a federal corporate law by using access to national capital markets as its enforcement mechanism. This would resolve a longstanding controversy over the wisdom of such a move in the face of disclaimers from Congress and with no substantive restraints on the power. It would, moreover, overturn or at least impinge severely on the tradition of state regulation of corporate law. As the Supreme Court has said, "[c]orporations are creatures of state law, and investors commit their funds to corporate directors on the understanding that, except where federal law expressly requires certain responsibilities of directors with respect to stockholders, state law will govern the internal affairs of the corporation." At least one Commissioner shared this view, stating "[s]ection 19(c) does not provide the Commission carte blanche to adopt federal corporate governance standards through the back door by mandating uniform listing standards." (Grundfest, Comm'r, concurring). We read the Act as reflecting a clear congressional determination not to make any such broad delegation of power to the Commission. . . .

[The court went on to address and dispose of the SEC's arguments that Rule 19c–4 is authorized under the SEC's powers pursuant to § 6(b)(5) (registering an exchange), § 15A(b)(6) (registering an association of brokers and dealers) and § 11A (giving the SEC power to "facilitate the establishment of a national market system for securities"). In each instance the court found that the SEC failed to show a Congressional purpose to allow the SEC to regulate corporate governance].

* * *

QUESTIONS

1.   Why would varying from one share-one vote disenfranchise shareholders? What if shareholders know before they purchase their securities about the presence of multiple classes of common shares with varying voting power?

2.   Why is the court concerned about the SEC's reliance on the purpose under § 14(a) of ensuring "fair shareholder suffrage" or the broader purpose to "protect investors and the public interest"?

3.   How does the court limit the use of "fair shareholder suffrage" as a justification for regulation? At what "means" does the court look?

C.   EXPANDING THE SEC'S ROLE IN CORPORATE GOVERNANCE

Despite the setback in *The Business Roundtable*, the SEC's role in determining how corporations should allocate power among managers and shareholders has grown significantly with the enactment of the Sarbanes–Oxley Act in 2002. Sarbanes–Oxley intrudes directly on a publicly-held firm's corporate governance in a variety of ways. We canvassed the major provisions of the Act relating to corporate governance in Chapter 4. The bottom line is that federal law now dictates many characteristics of the board of directors for public companies, including independence and committee structure.

Perhaps emboldened by the Sarbanes–Oxley Act, the SEC in 2003 proposed a radical new method of electing members to the board of directors. See Exchange Act Release No. 48626 (October 14, 2003). Historically, outside insurgents could launch a full blown contest to elect a competing slate to a company's board of directors, but as discussed above, such contests are quite costly and correspondingly rare.

The SEC proposal builds on the shareholder issue proposal process under Rule 14a–8. The SEC proposed allowing certain shareholders to nominate directors directly on the company's proxy statement. Under the proposal, not all shareholders can nominate candidates on the company's proxy statement. Nominations would be restricted in three ways:

1. The proposal allows shareholder nomination of directors only if a "triggering event" has occurred, such as a greater than majority shareholder vote on an issue proposal to allow shareholder nomination of directors on the company's proxy.

2. The SEC would allow only relatively large shareholders (with 5% or more of a class of voting securities) to propose nominees to the board.

3. The proposal imposes independence requirements on the nominees and limits on the number of shareholder nominees permitted on the company proxy (ensuring only minority representation on the board of directors).

The SEC proposal met with stiff resistance and, to date, the SEC has not moved forward toward adoption. Was the SEC too ambitious? Should the SEC have limited further (or, conversely, expanded) the ability of shareholders to nominate candidates to the board through proposed Rule 14a–11? Or was the proposal simply a bad idea? Old proposals have a way of reappearing. The SEC's "Aircraft Carrier" proposal to reform the public offering process in the late 1990s met a seemingly similar demise only to come back to life in modified form as part of the SEC's 2005 Public Offering Reforms.

QUESTIONS

1. The SEC's proposal requires a "triggering event" before shareholders may nominate directors using the company proxy statement. Should the triggering event include more direct indicia of problems in the company, such as poor economic performance, an earnings restatement, or sanctions by the SEC?

2. The SEC proposed allowing only certain shareholders to nominate directors on the company's proxy statement. The SEC's proposal used 5% ownership of voting securities as the threshold for eligibility. Why not use a 10% or 20% threshold or a 1% or 2% threshold?

3. The SEC proposed allowing eligible shareholders to nominate only a limited number of directors (one if the board of directors consists of eight or fewer directors). Why limit the number of nominations by shareholders?

4. Under the SEC proposal, corporations would be able to opt out of the Rule in the corporate charter, assuming state law allows such opt-out. Should this ability to opt-out be extended to Rule 14a–8 shareholder issue proposals?

CHAPTER 12

TAKEOVER REGULATION

Rules and Statutes

—*Rules 165, 425 of the Securities Act*

—*Sections 13(d), 13(e)(1), 13(g), 14(d), 14(e), 14(f) of the Exchange Act*

—*Rules 13d–1, 13d–2, 13d–3, 13d–5, 13d–7, 13e–1, 13e–3, 13e–4, 14d–1 through 14d–11, 14e–1 through 14e–5, 14e–8 of the Exchange Act*

—*Schedule 13D, Schedule 13G, Schedule TO, Schedule 14D–9*

MOTIVATING HYPOTHETICAL

Liza is the managing partner of Slash/Burn Fund LLP, a leveraged buyout firm that specializes in identifying underperforming companies and buying out their public shareholders. Slash/Burn then improves the operating performance of the firms that it acquires by rationalizing their operations (i.e., firing the deadwood) and selling off underperforming divisions. After making these changes, Slash/Burn sells the company off, either to other firms in the target's industry sector or back to the public through an IPO.

The latest target in Liza's sights is Sleeping Bear Inc. Sleeping Bear's stock is traded over the Nasdaq–Small Cap market. Sleeping Bear manufactures and sells a line of pajamas and clothing for children, all of which carry the distinctive logo of a sleeping bear. All of Sleeping Bear's clothes are produced in its factory in the Upper Peninsula of Michigan. Ben, the founder and CEO of Sleeping Bear, takes pride in the quality products sold by Sleeping Bear as well as the "family values" that the company promotes. Ben and his family hold a 15% stake in the company. Sleeping Bear is a major employer in the Upper Peninsula. The company provides its employees with salaries that are generous for the area, as well as good medical, dental and retirement plans. Sleeping Bear makes its contribution to its employees' retirement plan in the form of company stock. As a result, Sleeping Bear's employees hold 30% of the company's outstanding shares. Sleeping Bear's generous treatment of its employees has made them intensely loyal. The labor pool in the Upper Peninsula is somewhat thin, however, and this has limited Sleeping Bear's ability to expand production and extend distribution of its products overseas. This has reduced the company's growth and kept its stock price in the $12 to $13 range.

Liza thinks Sleeping Bear could reduce its costs by outsourcing production of its clothing to plants in China. She estimates such a move could reduce Sleeping Bear's production costs by 25%. The vast labor supply there would also allow Sleeping Bear to expand production and extend distribution of its product line into Asia. (Liza is confident that the Sleeping Bear logo will be as popular with children in Asia as it is with children in the United States.) Of course, moving production to China would entail shutting down Sleeping Bear's factory in the Upper Peninsula.

I.   THE MARKET FOR CORPORATE CONTROL

Acquirors seek to obtain control of a target corporation for a variety of reasons. An acquiror, often another corporation but not always, may believe that the target corporation is run poorly and that, under the guidance of the acquiror, the target's businesses could generate far greater profit. An acquiror may desire to expand into a new line of business, a new geographical market, or obtain particular expertise or intellectual property. Although expanding or developing expertise could be done in-house, purchasing a target corporation may be a faster and/or cheaper means by which to achieve these goals. Alternatively, an acquiror may believe that combining with a target corporation may offer cost synergies or, through reduced competition, allow the combined company to raise prices resulting in greater profits.

Once the acquiror decides to seek control of a target corporation, the acquiror can choose among a variety of transactional forms to achieve this goal. The acquiror may purchase the assets of the business from the target corporation. The acquiror, or a subsidiary of the acquiror, may execute a statutory merger with the target company. Or the acquiror may simply buy the shares of the target company through a tender offer and keep the target as a subsidiary corporation (or, alternatively, merge the target company either into the acquiror or a subsidiary of the acquiror). If the board of directors of the target corporation acquiesces to the change in control, the choice between these different forms turns on various factors, such as tax consequences, administrative ease, and liability concerns.

If the target's board of directors decides to resist the overtures of the acquiror, however, the acquiror's only realistic option will be to proceed through a tender offer, appealing directly to the target's shareholders. The federal securities regulation of tender offers was enacted in the Williams Act (codified in the Exchange Act) in response to hostile tender offers. Consequently, understanding hostile takeovers is critical to understanding the Williams Act's regulation of tender offers.

Hostile takeovers present a potentially important mechanism to constrain managers of corporations who may be tempted to deviate from the best interests of the shareholders. Managers who expropriate too much value for themselves may face a hostile takeover attempt. The prospect of a hostile takeover, in turn, may deter managers from overreaching in the first place. Managers of the target company (or more accurately, the directors) are not, however, defenseless in the face of a hostile takeover. The board of the target may adopt a "poison pill" or other defensive tactics against the takeover attempt, seeking to entrench itself. Much of the state corporate law regulation of takeovers deals with the compatibility of defensive measures with the target board's fiduciary duties to the shareholders.

Although we cover briefly the state corporate law aspects of hostile takeover regulation, our primary concern is how the federal securities laws deal with takeovers. As with the federal regulation of proxy solicitations, the federal securities laws intersect with the domain of state corporate law in regulating takeovers. Consequently, federal securities regulation affects the number of hostile takeovers and their impact on agency costs within public corporations. Is the balance struck by the Williams Act appropriate? Or should Congress give the SEC more (or less) authority to regulate hostile takeovers?

A. HOSTILE TAKEOVERS

The market for corporate control most recently became a subject of intense popular and academic debate during the 1980s. That decade saw a wave of takeovers that brought the hostile tender offer back into public view.

The archetypal sequence for a 1980s-style hostile tender offer went something like this. A potential acquiror would make overtures to the management of the "target" company about a possible sale or merger of the company, which management would promptly rebuff. The acquiror would then go over the head of the target management to the shareholders, announcing a hostile bid for the target in the form of a tender offer for at least a majority of the target company's shares. As we will explore later in the chapter, the definition of a tender offer is not precise, but it would certainly include a broad based, limited time offer at a fixed price to purchase sufficient shares to obtain control.

The acquiror would generally set the tender offer price at a substantial premium above the prevailing market price for those shares. Some target corporations are quite large. Famously Kohlberg Kravis Roberts took over R.J. Reynolds, the cigarette company, in the 1990s. Reynolds' market capitalization at the time was in the billions of dollars. To finance a premium tender offer price, many acquirors use debt financing, borrowing a substantial amount of cash to use in the bid. The debt load incurred by the target to pay for a tender offer would include, not infrequently, highly-leveraged "junk bonds," so called because of their high risk of default. (That epithet, of course, tends to downplay the bonds' correspondingly high interest rates.) Other acquirors may simply use their own stock or debt securities as consideration for the tender offer. Cash, however, is more attractive to many target shareholders; an acquiror's securities are not as easily valued as cold hard cash.

Once faced with a hostile tender offer bid, target management would then—notwithstanding the substantial premium above the market price for the target company's stock—denounce the offer as a "low-ball bid" that did not reflect the target company's "intrinsic value." Management's denunciation would be backed up by the analysis of an investment bank (paid for by the target company) purporting to show that the company's "fair" value greatly exceeded the amount offered by the hostile bidder.

The announcement of the hostile bid would put the target company "in play" and "risk arbitrageurs" would buy up large blocks of the target company's stock in the hope that a more generous offer would be forthcoming, either because the acquiror would be forced to raise its bid to buy target management's acquiescence or a rival bidder would emerge. Management would then seek out a "white knight" bidder (preferably one that would allow the managers to retain their jobs or, at the very least, obtain lucrative consulting jobs after the acquisition) or hunker down to fight off the assault by buying back shares or selling off assets and distributing the proceeds as an extraordinary dividend.

Often, management would succeed in its efforts to keep the acquiror at bay. On occasion, however, the acquiror (or a rival bidder) would succeed in persuading a majority of the shareholders to tender into the offer, perhaps after raising its bid once or twice. With ownership of a majority of shares, the acquiror would then replace the incumbent directors with the acquiror's own hand-picked directors, thereby obtaining direct control over the target company. Typically, a short time later, the remaining public shareholders would be "frozen out" in a follow-on merger between the target and an acquisition subsidiary set up by the acquiror. The acquiror would use the assets of the target company to secure the debt used to finance the tender offer. The acquiror would also attempt to wring cost savings out of the target company and sell off "non-strategic" assets. If these efforts succeeded, the debt would be paid down and the acquiror's investment richly rewarded. If they failed, the company would descend into bankruptcy, where the equity holders would be wiped out and the bondholders converted into stockholders of the reorganized company.

All of this is great drama (memorialized in Hollywood classics such as Oliver Stone's *Wall Street*), but does it matter for anyone not directly caught up in the struggle? Politicians and pundits certainly thought that it did. Where was the wealth coming from to fund those enormous takeover premiums? Hostile takeovers were denounced as expropriating wealth from workers, bondholders and the communities that provided a home to target companies. Hostile acquirors—in order to enrich themselves and target company shareholders—were causing the companies that they took over to renege on implicit bargains that the target companies had made with these stakeholders.

Alternatively, perhaps the takeover premiums were not high enough. Short-sighted shareholders may sell out their shares at a premium to the market price. The market price, so the argument goes, may not reflect the real value of the company. If managers only are given enough time to execute their plans, the company may realize far greater value for its shareholders. Moreover, much of the information about the plans is confidential, making it impossible for the managers simply to disclose the information to the market without ruining the value of their long-term plans.

Others, however, defended the hostile takeover wave as bringing much needed accountability to corporate managers. Dispersed public shareholders, beset by collective action problems, had little sway over the company managers who were supposed to be working in the shareholders' interests. Outside directors—typically selected by the incumbent CEO—lacked either the will or the clout to bring managers to heel. This pervasive agency problem, the proponents of hostile takeovers argued, could only be ameliorated by the threat of hostile takeover. Mismanaged firms were the ones that could be profitably taken over via the tender offer mechanism; the premium paid in the tender offer reflected the expected gains that would accrue from eliminating managerial shirking. Moreover, the *in terrorem* effect of the threat of a takeover would have a salutary effect on other managers, who would be encouraged to work harder, take on more risk, and pay out more of the company's cash flows to shareholders.

B. STATE CORPORATE LAW REGULATION

Before addressing the federal securities regulation of tender offers under the Williams Act, we briefly summarize the state corporate law regime governing takeovers. By far the most developed state takeover law is found in Delaware, which not coincidentally is also the state of incorporation of a majority of America's largest public companies.

Consider an acquiror seeking to obtain control over the business of a target corporation. When the target firm's board does not want to cede control to the acquiror, a hostile acquiror cannot purchase the corporate assets or do a statutory merger with the target firm. What is left to the persistent acquiror? The acquiror may seek to purchase the shares of the target company directly. Under Delaware (and other) state corporate law, the board of directors is given the ultimate authority to make corporate decisions. An acquiror with sufficient shares will obtain the power to elect the board of directors. Once in control of the board, the acquiror may then vote to sell all the target company's assets or do a statutory merger. Alternatively, the acquiror may simply leave the target corporation as a subsidiary of the acquiror.

Faced with a hostile tender offer for the shares of the target firm, the target board of directors is not powerless. The board enjoys several avenues to block a hostile takeover attempt. Consider the following (non-exhaustive) possibilities:

- *Greenmail*—The target company may pay off a potential acquiror using corporate funds. Under such greenmail agreements, the target company either purchases the acquiror's target company shares outright or, alternatively, simply pays the acquiror not to purchase any additional shares (a "standstill" agreement).

- *White Knight defense*—The target board may seek to find another buyer for the target corporation who will give more favorable terms

(The more favorable terms are often to the incumbent managers and board members in the form of a lucrative post-merger consulting contract.)

- *Lockup Option*—The target board may attempt to tilt a bidding contest toward a White Knight by agreeing to sell certain high value corporate assets (the "crown jewels") at a discount price. Alternatively, the company may provide the favored bidder an option on the company's stock at a favorable price. Both strategies transfer value to the White Knight (and arguably may induce the White Knight to get into the bidding contest in the first place) while reducing the value of the target to the hostile bidder.

- *"Too big to purchase" defense*—The target board may attempt to purchase another corporation to make itself too big to take over. Alternatively, the target may launch a bid for the hostile acquiror, the "Pac Man" defense.

- *Lawsuit*—The target board may file lawsuits against the acquiring corporation alleging violations of the Williams Act, antitrust laws, and other legal wrongs. Even if unsuccessful, a lawsuit may slow down a hostile bid, giving the incumbent target managers time to fashion a sturdier defense (such as finding a White Knight).

- *Charter Amendments*—Companies amended their corporate charters to require supermajority voting to approve any transaction (such as a merger) with a shareholder holding above a certain minimum threshold of shares (15% for example).

- *Poison Pill*—By far the most important hostile defensive tactic today is the poison pill. There are different kinds of poison pills. A "flip-in" poison pill plan, if triggered, inflicts massive dilution on any acquiror of a substantial percentage of a company's stock (typically defined as somewhere in the 10–20% range) that purchases its stake without the incumbent board's consent. If the poison pill is triggered, shareholders of the target company *other than the acquiror* are entitled to purchase additional shares from the target company at a steep discount from the market price. This fire sale on the company's shares substantially reduces the value of existing shares because of the enormous increase in the number of shares having claims to the corporation's cash flow. Suppose you owned 100,000 shares of Microsoft's common stock. Imagine what would happen to the value of your shares if all other shareholders (excluding you) could suddenly buy one share for every one they owned at 50% of the market price. The target board typically retains the power to redeem the poison pill, giving the board the ability to acquiesce to a friendly merger.

Two important issues under state corporate law are (1) when a target board's fiduciary duty requires it to redeem a poison pill; and (2) whether a target board can protect the poison pill from redemption by a successor board (so-called "no hand" and "dead hand" poison pills). Delaware forbids no hand poison pills, which cannot be redeemed, and dead hand poison pills, which only incumbent directors may redeem. See *Quickturn Design Sys., Inc. v. Mentor Graphics Corp.*, 721 A.2d 1281 (Del. 1998); *Carmody v. Toll Bros.*, 723 A.2d 1180 (Del. Ch. 1998). The possibility of redeeming a pill has led acquirors to launch a tender offer for a majority of shares combined with a proxy contest to replace the incumbent directors. Once new directors are in place, they may redeem the poison pill, clearing the way for a successful tender offer.

- *Classified Board*—A classified board slows the ability of a successful acquiror of a majority of a target company's shares to take control over the board of directors. Most classified boards are divided into three groups, with each group of directors facing election once every three years. Thus a hostile acquiror who wished to obtain control over a target board using a proxy solicitation to replace incumbent directors must wait until the second annual meeting after acquiring a majority of shares to obtain majority control over the board. This delay is particularly costly when combined with a poison pill. Unable to obtain control over the board, the acquiror cannot force a redemption of the pill, which would allow it to purchase a majority of the shares. A company with both a classified board and poison pill is effectively invulnerable to a hostile takeover.

Much of state corporate law deals with whether the board meets its fiduciary obligations to the shareholders when it employs a defensive tactic to discourage a hostile takeover. The incumbent managers and board members do not have free rein to entrench themselves against all hostile bidders. Unlike ordinary, everyday business decisions, which largely avoid court review under the "business judgment rule," a decision to employ a defensive tactic in the face of a hostile bid faces more intrusive court review. The degree of court review depends on whether the target company has decided to put itself up for auction (fairly strict scrutiny) or maintain its ongoing plans (highly deferential in practice). See *Revlon, Inc. v. MacAndrews & Forbes Holdings, Inc.*, 506 A.2d 173, 179 (Del. 1985); *Unocal Corp. v. Mesa Petroleum Co.*, 493 A.2d 946 (Del. 1985).

Finally, state corporate law provides explicit statutes authorizing particular defensive tactics against a hostile takeover. After the Supreme Court validated state anti-takeover statutes in *CTS Corp. v. Dynamics Corp.*, 481 U.S. 69 (1987), state legislatures were free to protect incumbent management and workers from the threat of takeover. Many states responded to the opportunity presented by the *CTS Corp.* decision by adopting antitakeover statutes. One type of statute permits managers to take into consideration "other constituencies" (including employees, the local community, and so on) in determining how to respond to a hostile tender offer. Another type of statute deals with control share acquisitions. Under a control share acquisition statute, a shareholder who crosses a predefined threshold of ownership (i.e., 50%) is stripped of the voting rights on these shares unless a majority of the remaining disinterested shareholders votes to restore the acquiror's voting rights.

Although the debate over whether hostile takeovers benefit shareholders and/or society was never definitely resolved as a matter of theory, it was resolved as a matter of practical politics. State antitakeover statutes and the poison pill make acquiring a controlling block of shares in a company prohibitively expensive—absent the incumbent board's consent. The effectiveness of the poison pill as an anti-takeover device is testified to by the fact that no one has ever dared to trigger a pill and face the dilution that it would cause. The only way around the pill is to stage a proxy fight in conjunction with a tender offer, replace the incumbent board with a slate of the acquiror's nominees, and have the new board redeem the poison pill. Even this path is effectively foreclosed if the target company has a classified board, which limits turnover on the board to a third of the directors each year. The result has been that the number of hostile takeovers has shrunk to a trivial percentage of overall merger and acquisition activity.

So why study the market for corporate control at all? There are still a handful of hostile takeovers and they may be economically significant. Oracle Inc. waged a $10 billion hostile takeover attempt for PeopleSoft beginning in 2003. After much legal wrangling, Oracle finally completed a successful tender offer for PeopleSoft's shares in December 2004. Moreover, the theoretical question of whether lawmakers should encourage or discourage hostile takeovers remains open. The part of the federal securities laws that governs takeovers, the Williams Act, is still germane to the many tender offers that take place as part of negotiated acquisitions. Some acquirors prefer the tender offer over the primary transactional alternative, the statutory merger, because it allows them to take over the target company relatively quickly. The tender offer eliminates the need for a shareholder meeting before taking control. This allows the acquiror to assume operational control more quickly and may discourage the entry of rival bidders for the company, which could result in a greater acquisition cost or losing out on the target altogether.

C. GENESIS OF THE WILLIAMS ACT

Many of the takeovers of the 1980s targeted companies that were products of an earlier takeover wave during the 1960s. That earlier takeover wave provided the impetus for Congress's adoption of the Williams Act. The Williams Act, adopted in 1968 as an amendment to the Exchange Act, intervenes in that market in three ways. First, it requires disclosure by anyone purchasing 5% or more of a public company's stock. Second, it requires disclosure by anyone making a tender offer for 5% or more of a public company's stock. Third, it regulates the tender offer process to enhance the bargaining position of target company shareholders.

The Supreme Court has described Congress's motivation for enacting the Williams Act:

[T]he Williams Act ... was adopted in 1968 in response to the growing use of cash tender offers as a means for achieving corporate takeovers. Prior to the 1960's, corporate takeover attempts had typically involved either proxy solicitations, regulated under § 14 of the Securities Exchange Act, or exchange offers of securities, subject to the registration requirements of the 1933 Act. The proliferation of cash tender offers, in which publicized requests are made and intensive campaigns conducted for tenders of shares of stock at a fixed price, removed a substantial number of corporate control contests from the reach of existing disclosure requirements of the federal securities laws.

Piper v. Chris–Craft Industries, Inc., 430 U.S. 1, 22 (1977).

The regulatory "gap" that Congress intended to fill with the Williams Act is summarized by the case below. Why do you think that acquirors placed such importance on maintaining confidentiality?

General Time Corp. v. Talley Industries, Inc.

403 F.2d 159 (2d Cir. 1968).

■ FRIENDLY, CIRCUIT JUDGE:

These appeals are two more chapters in a controversy arising from the efforts of Talley Industries, Inc. to displace the management of General Time Corporation and ultimately to acquire or merge with it.

* * *

General Time ... brought an action in the Southern District of New York ... [which] alleged violation of Rule 10b–5 ... in that [Talley and its affiliates] had purchased General Time stock without disclosing the extent of their associations or their full intentions with respect to merger and the like; stockholders had thereby been induced to part with stock at less than they could ultimately have obtained.

* * *

As indicated above, the gist of the complaint under Rule 10b–5 was that defendants went about the acquisition of General Time stock ... without disclosing their association or [Talley's] plan for a merger whose terms might be more favorable than the price paid for the stock being acquired. We know of no rule of law, applicable at the time, that a purchaser of stock, who was not an 'insider' and had no fiduciary relation to a prospective seller, had any obligation to reveal circumstances that might raise a seller's demands and thus abort the sale. Indeed, secrecy had long been the hallmark of most stock acquisition programs, at least in their initial stages. The very fact that Congress has recently thought it desirable to pass new legislation amending §§ 13 and 14 of the Securities Exchange Act to require disclosure under certain circumstances is an indication that no such obligation previously existed....

* * *

QUESTIONS

1. In *General Time*, Judge Friendly applies the common law rule (as incorporated by Rule 10b–5) that purchasers who are not fiduciaries of the seller are not obliged to disclose their reasons for purchasing. Why do you think that was the common law rule? Do you agree with the rule? If not, under what circumstances would you require disclosure?

2. Why should it matter if the target company shareholders do not receive the "full" value for their shares due to the acquiror's silence? If assets go to a higher value use through a takeover (or wayward managers are removed) then isn't this a good result?

HYPOTHETICAL ONE

The year is 1967 (i.e., pre-Williams Act). Liza, the managing partner at the leveraged buyout firm Slash/Burn Fund LLP, comes to you seeking advice on launching Slash/Burn's tender offer for Sleeping Bear. She wants advice on how to structure the tender offer and disclosure of that offer so that she maximizes her chances of successfully taking over Sleeping Bear. At the same time, she wants to pay as little as possible to obtain control. And of course, she wants to stay within the letter of the law.

Here is what Liza proposes: a tender offer for 51% of the Sleeping Bear common stock at $20 per share, to be followed by a squeeze-out merger to eliminate the remaining 49% of the shares at $15. (Recall that Sleeping Bear's stock has been trading in the $12 to $13 range.) She plans to announce Slash/Burn's offer Friday afternoon after the markets close with the offer to remain open until close of business on Monday. Shares tendered into the offer will be taken up on a "first come, first served" basis. Once tendered the shares cannot be withdrawn. She knows that Ben, the CEO and founder of Sleeping Bear, will be a harder sell given his emotional commitment to Sleeping Bear, so she plans to call him privately and offer him $22 for his shares. Can Liza structure Slash/Burn's offer in this way? And what does she need to disclose about her offer and her plans for Sleeping Bear? Is this a good deal for Sleeping Bear's shareholders?

The Williams Act regulates tender offers in four ways: first, by requiring disclosure of holdings of 5% or more of any class of equity securities for a reporting company (§ 13(d)); second, by requiring disclosures from anyone who makes a tender offer for more than 5% of a reporting company's equity securities (§ 14(d)); third, by imposing certain substantive rules on the timing and procedures for tender offers for such securities; and fourth, by prohibiting fraud in connection with tender offers. We cover each of these topics in turn.

II.   THE "EARLY WARNING" PROVISION OF § 13(d)

A typical strategy for potential bidders contemplating a tender offer is to acquire a "toehold" stake in the target company's stock through secondary market transactions before announcing the tender offer. The toehold serves two primary purposes: (1) it may enhance the acquiror's prospects of acquiring 51% of the shares; and (2) if the acquiror is outbid for the target, selling the toehold to a rival acquiror may provide a profitable consolation prize. Assembling the toehold stake is a delicate task—acquiring too much at one time will create an imbalance between "buy" and "sell" orders for the stock, thereby tipping off other traders in the market that something is afoot and driving the price higher. On the other hand, Wall Street is a tight-knit community, so the longer the orders for the stock are spaced out, the greater the risk of rumors spreading during the buying period. The combination of these risks means that a potential acquiror will have difficulty acquiring more than 10% to 20% of a company's stock before news of the acquisition is likely to spread, with a predictable spike in the company's stock price. So even without a legal duty to disclose, news of the acquisition will reach the market eventually.

For the CEO confronted by a surprise offer for his company, however, "eventually" may be too late. If a hostile acquiror already has 20% of the stock locked up, getting the last 31% is not a very daunting challenge. Worse yet, the CEO confronted by the surprise offer has little time in which to maneuver to repurchase stock, find a "white knight," or adopt defensive measures. In a hostile takeover situation, delay is the ally of the defense.

Congress felt the pain of the CEO confronted by the surprise tender offer and adopted § 13(d) of the Exchange Act, the "early warning" provision of the Williams Act. The § 13(d) notification requirement is triggered when any person (or group of persons) acquires beneficial owner-ship of 5% or more of an equity security registered under § 12 of the Exchange Act. Within ten days of passing the 5% threshold, the acquiror must notify the issuer, the exchange where the security is traded, and the SEC. Note that "toehold" acquisitions are not foreclosed entirely; not only can the acquiror purchase 5% before giving notice, it can accumulate additional shares without disclosure during the ten-day window following the date it reaches the 5% trigger.

The notice required goes beyond disclosing the existence of the stake. The acquiror must disclose, in a Schedule 13D:

(1) the identity and background of the acquiror, or the members of the group making the acquisition;

(2) the source and amount of funds used in the acquisition;

(3) the purpose of the transaction;

(4) the number of securities held;

(5) any "contracts, arrangements, understandings or relationships" concerning the issuer's securities.

If there are any material changes to any of the facts disclosed in the Schedule 13D, the acquiror must amend its Schedule 13D. The acquisition or disposition of 1% or more of the subject securities is deemed material; smaller transactions "may be material, depending upon the facts and circumstances."

A frequently amended item relates to the purpose of the transaction. A common response to this item is that the securities have been acquired for "investment purposes," i.e., with no current intention of attempting to take control of the issuer. Certain "passive" investors—e.g., banks, broker-dealers, mutual funds—can file a less-extensive Schedule 13G instead of the 13D, if they disclaim interest in exercising control. If their purpose changes, however, they must file a Schedule 13D within ten days of that change of heart. Schedule 13D requires disclosure of "any plans or proposals" that involve changes in control and changes to be made after control has been acquired:

(1) to acquire or dispose of the securities of the issuer;

(2) any extraordinary transaction involving the issuer, including a merger, reorganization or liquidation;

(3) to sell or transfer material amounts of the issuer's assets;

(4) to change the makeup of the issuer's board or management;

(5) to materially change the issuer's capitalization or dividend policy;

(6) "Any other material change in the issuer's business or corporate structure";

(7) to change the issuer's charter or by-laws, or "other actions which may impede the acquisition of control of the issuer by any person";

(8) to delist any of the issuer's securities;

(9) to terminate the issuer's registration as a reporting company;

(10) "Any action similar to any of those enumerated above."

Clearly the intention to acquire control has to be disclosed in the Schedule 13D. More intrusively, however, § 13(d) requires a potential acquiror to reveal up-front almost any change that an acquiror intends to make after the acquisition is completed. This disclosure allows management and rival bidders to know the principal sources of value that the acquiror sees in making the acquisition; management and rival bidders are then free to implement these strategic changes themselves. It also sheds a good deal of light on what the bidder's reservation price may be, information of particular interest to the shareholders of the target company. How high a price can they extract from the bidder? The Williams Act regime is a substantial departure from the common law and Rule 10b–5 doctrine we saw in *General Time*.

What happens if a potential acquiror attempts to avoid the early warning system under § 13(d) by keeping its own holdings underneath the 5% threshold while having others, working in agreement with the acquiror, purchase significant quantities of shares? The Williams Act requires a "group" to report under § 13(d) if the aggregate ownership crosses the 5% threshold. How do we determine the existence of a "group"? How do we know when a "group" has formed? Rule 13d–5(b)(1) tells us that a group is formed (and filing is therefore required) "[w]hen two or more persons agree to act together for purpose of acquiring, holding, voting or disposing of equity securities of an issuer, the group formed thereby shall be deemed to have acquired beneficial ownership . . ." The case below further explores these issues. It also addresses an important question for litigation strategy: Who has standing (other than the SEC) to object to a failure to file a Schedule 13D?

Hallwood Realty Partners, L.P. v. Gotham Partners, L.P.

286 F.3d 613 (2d Cir. 2002).

■ CALABRESI, CIRCUIT JUDGE.

Appellant Hallwood Realty Partners, L.P. brought this action asserting a violation of § 13(d) of the Securities and Exchange Act. Specifically, Hallwood alleged that the defendants formed a group to purchase and amass Hallwood units for the purpose of effecting a take-over of Hallwood and substantially altering its business and operations, without disclosing their group, its activities, or its intentions in public filings, as required under § 13(d). Hallwood sought (i) various forms of injunctive relief; (ii) a declaratory judgment that the defendants, by forming a § 13(d) group, had become an "Acquiring Person" under the terms of Hallwood's "poison pill";[1] and (iii) an award of monetary damages. Hallwood also requested a jury trial.

The district court struck Hallwood's demand for a jury trial after holding that § 13(d) provides no cause of action for money damages and that Hallwood was not entitled to a jury trial on its injunctive and declaratory claims. Following a bench trial, the district court dismissed these equitable claims because it concluded that Hallwood had not proved the existence of a group of investors under § 13(d).

Hallwood appeals both decisions, arguing (1) that the district court improperly rejected circumstantial evidence in determining whether a § 13(d) group existed, and (2) that the court erred in denying Hallwood's jury demand. We affirm the judgment and order of the district court.

BACKGROUND

Hallwood is a limited partnership that acquires, owns, and operates commercial real estate. Hallwood units are traded on the American Stock Exchange. The various defendants in this case were purchasers of Hallwood units.

The defendants began acquiring Hallwood units in the early to mid 1990s. Each individual defendant claims to have made an independent decision to purchase units, based on due diligence and a common under-

---

1. Hallwood has a rights plan, or "poison pill," that is triggered if any one unit-holder, or group acting in concert, acquires beneficial ownership of more than fifteen per-cent of Hallwood units. When the rights plan is triggered, the value of the units is significantly diluted.

standing among knowledgeable investors that Hallwood units were undervalued.

Defendants Gotham Partners, L.P., Gotham Partners III, L.P., and Gotham Holdings II, L.L.C. started buying Hallwood units in 1994. In December 1995, Gotham filed a Schedule 13D with the Securities and Exchange Commission in which it stated that it had acquired 5.05% of the outstanding Hallwood units "for investment purposes." It continued purchasing units (and updating its Schedule 13D) over the following ten months, amassing 14.82% of the units by October 1996. In June 1997, Gotham amended its filing to say that it was seeking to remove Hallwood's general partner. Soon after, Gotham sued Hallwood and certain of its affiliates, officers, and directors in the Delaware Chancery Court, alleging, inter alia, breaches of fiduciary duty and of Hallwood's partnership agreement.

Defendant Interstate began buying Hallwood units in mid 1995. In November 1998, Interstate filed a Schedule 13D disclosing that it had acquired 5.7% of the outstanding Hallwood units. Interstate filed amendments to its Schedule 13D on March 25, 1999 (7.0%), August 30, 1999 (8.0%), and July 28, 2000 (9.0%). At no time did it disclose any plan to act in concert with other unitholders to change or influence the control of Hallwood.

Defendant PMG started acquiring Hallwood units in 1992. By January 2000, PMG had amended its Schedule 13G[4] to disclose an aggregate holding of 6.5%. PMG consistently reported that it acquired these units "in the ordinary course of business and . . . not . . . for the purpose of . . . changing or influencing the control of the issuer . . . and . . . not . . . in connection with or as a participant in any transaction having such purpose or effect." Defendant EFO allegedly bought at least 2% of Hallwood's units. EFO filed no 13D or 13G schedules.

At trial, Hallwood put forward direct and circumstantial evidence supporting its allegations. It provided evidence of meetings and other communications among the defendants beginning in 1994–95 and continuing through 2000, as well as evidence that Hallwood was discussed in these communications. It demonstrated that the defendants each had purchased Hallwood units during the relevant period, and it emphasized in particular a "burst of purchases" by Gotham and Interstate starting in the same week. Hallwood submitted a magazine article that described similar tactics used by Gotham to take over another company.

Hallwood also had hired a private investigator who, disguised as a potential investor, had met with certain defendants and was allegedly told by them of a coordinated plan to gain control of Hallwood. Specifically, the investigator testified that Dennis Reiland, a representative of PMG, conveyed to him the existence of a Gotham-led group designed to take over

---

4. A Schedule 13G is similar to a Schedule 13D, but it may be filed only by certain classes of purchasers and only if the purchasers have no intent to change or influence the issuer or to act in concert with others who so intend.

Hallwood. The investigator submitted an audiotape of a conversation he had with Christopher Mahowald, a representative of EFO, and a copy of EFO'S "Investment Recommendation" with respect to Hallwood, which Mahowald had given him. The "Investment Recommendation," Hallwood argued, could be read to imply that EFO was part of a Gotham-led attempt (involving the Delaware litigation mentioned above), to take over Hallwood and to "realize value" (i.e., to liquidate, sell, or recapitalize the company). According to Hallwood, the recommendation could also be taken to indicate the involvement of both Interstate and [its general partner] in the plan.

These allegations were contested at trial by the defendants. On February 23, 2001, the district court rendered an oral decision, concluding that Hallwood had failed to prove that a group, as contemplated by § 13(d), existed, and entering judgment, dismissing the plaintiff's claims.

DISCUSSION

I.

Hallwood first argues that the district court refused to credit circumstantial evidence in its determination that Hallwood had not proved the existence of a group for purposes of § 13(d). Hallwood contends that this was a legal error subject to de novo review.

In response to hostile corporate take-overs in the 1960s, Congress, in 1968, passed the Williams Act, of which § 13(d) is a part. Among other things, § 13(d) requires a group that has acquired, directly or indirectly, beneficial ownership of more than five percent of a class of registered equity securities, to file a 13D Schedule with the issuer, with the exchanges on which the security is traded, and with the SEC, disclosing, among other things, the identity of its members and the purpose of its acquisition. Section 13(d) applies to a group of persons or entities who "act . . . for the purpose of acquiring, holding or disposing of securities. . . . " The agreement among these entities may be formal or informal, and need not be expressed in writing. Under § 13(d), a court evaluating an allegation of the existence of a group must "determine whether there is sufficient direct or circumstantial evidence to support the inference of a formal or informal understanding between [the defendants]" for the purpose of acquiring, holding, or disposing of securities. Whether the requisite agreement exists is a question of fact.

Hallwood claims that the district court's decision that there was insufficient evidence to establish the existence of a § 13(d) group was faulty because of the court's "rejection of using circumstantial evidence to show a § 13(d) group and its insistence on having direct 'smoking gun' evidence that plainly is not required by law." Hallwood cites cases in which this court has held that the existence of a group may be proved through direct or circumstantial evidence, as well as cases establishing the variety of circumstantial indicia that support an inference of group activity for purposes of § 13(d). Hallwood asserts that the court below refused to credit such circumstantial "factors," and that we therefore should vacate its decision and remand for new proceedings.

This claim is meritless. Nothing in the district court's oral ruling suggests that it failed to consider circumstantial evidence or that it refused to give weight to the factors listed by appellant and mentioned in prior caselaw. Indeed, Judge Kaplan expressly noted that prior relationships and trading patterns were relevant to a decision regarding the existence of a § 13(d) group. The court also specifically referenced most of the circumstantial evidence presented by Hallwood. Thus, in its oral ruling, the court mentioned evidence of discussions between the defendants, evidence of a viable exit strategy for the investment, and evidence regarding whether Gotham had a particular modus operandi. It observed in conclusion that "[t]he fact that I haven't referred to each and every tidbit [of the proof offered] shouldn't be taken as evidencing a failure to pay attention to it."

The district court demanded more than "simply ticking off factors, each of which ... may well be relevant." It noted: "What one has to do instead or in addition, rather, is to draw back or focus on whether the inference of collusion really is justified in light of all the circumstances." The court did not, therefore, reject the use of circumstantial evidence; rather, it properly pointed out that a complex factual finding such as that required here cannot be reduced to a checklist.

II.

* * *

Hallwood contends that [the district court's ruling denying Hallwood a jury trial based on its claim for damages under § 13(d)] was in error, because a private cause of action for damages to issuers is implied under § 13(d). This question is one of first impression for our court.

Over the years, the Supreme Court has come to view the implication of private remedies in regulatory statutes with increasing disfavor. In 1964, in *J.I. Case Co. v. Borak*, 377 U.S. 426, 433, (1964), the Court held that the broad remedial purpose of § 14(a) of the Securities Exchange Act was sufficient to give rise to a private right of action for damages. This approach was narrowed a decade later in *Cort v. Ash*, 422 U.S. 66 (1975), in which the Court set forth four factors to be considered in determining whether a private right of action is implicit in any given statute: (1) legislative intent, (2) the consistency of the remedy with the underlying purposes of the legislative scheme, (3) whether the plaintiff was a member of the class for whose benefit the statute was enacted, and (4) whether the cause of action is one traditionally relegated to state law. Later, in cases such as *Transamerica Mortgage Advisors, Inc. v. Lewis*, 444 U.S. 11, 15–16 (1979) and *Touche Ross & Co. v. Redington*, 442 U.S. 560, 575 (1979), the Court focused the analysis on the single question of whether congressional intent to create a private cause of action can be found in the relevant statute.

Courts in this circuit have consistently declined to imply a cause of action for shareholders under § 13(d). Courts have identified various reasons for denying shareholders a private cause of action under § 13(d).

First, the relevant legislative history reveals "an absence of legislative intent to imply a right of action under § 13(d)," particularly for money damages. Second, § 13(d) does not contain rights-creating language; it simply requires investors to file certain statements and "[s]tatutes that focus on the person regulated rather than the individuals protected create 'no implication of an intent to confer rights on a particular class of persons.'" Finally, courts have found significant the existence of an express remedy under § 18(a) ... available to those shareholders who can prove reliance on misleading filings.

Hallwood attempts to distinguish these cases by noting, first, that they all involve damages claims by shareholders, not issuers, and, as such, can be viewed as having been premised on the existence of § 18(a), an explicit damages remedy that is available to shareholders but not to issuers. Second, and more significantly, Hallwood stresses that this circuit has expressly held that issuers have a private cause of action under § 13(d) for injunctive relief. Hallwood then highlights the Supreme Court's statement that once an implied right of action is found, "we presume the availability of all appropriate remedies unless Congress has expressly indicated otherwise." According to Hallwood, the holdings of [these cases] taken together require that, absent clear congressional indications to the contrary, there must be a damages remedy for issuers under § 13(d).

We hold today that there are sufficient congressional indications to the contrary, and that, therefore, there is no private damages remedy for issuers under § 13(d). [W]e find those indications in the purpose for which the relevant statute was enacted.

The aim of § 13(d) is to ensure that investors will be informed about purchases of large blocks of shares. In *GAF Corp.*, we found that this congressional purpose was furthered by providing issuers with the right to sue "to enforce [the] duties created by [the] statute," as the issuer "unquestionably is in the best position to enforce section 13(d). The statute requires a copy of the statement to be sent by registered mail to the issuer ... and the issuer, in the course of constantly monitoring transactions in its stock, better than anyone else will know when there has been a failure to file." 453 F.2d at 719. This court, however, expressly distinguished money damages from such injunctive relief, which furthers the object of § 13(d) by increasing honest disclosure for the benefit of investors without placing incumbent management in a stronger position than aspiring control groups. We noted that we were recognizing the rights of issuers "seeking equitable or prophylactic relief—not monetary damages—to take the necessary steps to effectuate the purposes of section 13(d)." In other words, in *GAF Corp.* we recognized that issuers have a private cause of action and standing to sue for injunctive relief because, inter alia, such relief increases the accurate information available to investors, while at the same time recognizing, in dicta, that monetary damages for issuers would not similarly benefit investors.

Moreover, an implied cause of action for damages not only does not serve the same aim as a cause of action for injunctive relief, but it also may actually frustrate congressional purposes. The legislative history of the Williams Act, of which § 13(d) is a part, makes clear that the Act was intended to assist shareholders while at the same time remaining "even-handed" in any struggle between the issuer and entity purchasing large quantities of stock. We think it manifest that a damages remedy granted to issuers is likely to "tip the balance" between the two sides, while the issuer's ability to sue for injunctive relief does not do anything of the kind.

... Accordingly, we affirm the district court's striking of Hallwood's jury demand.

* * *

QUESTIONS

1. What more did Hallwood need to show to establish the existence of a "group"?

2. How would you know if you were part of a "group"?

3. Should shareholders have the right to sue for damages for a violation of § 13(d)? Should target companies? What alternative causes of action are available?

4. Why not tip the balance in tender offers toward incumbent managers of the target by providing for monetary damages? Hasn't the Williams Act already tipped the balance between an acquiror and the target corporation?

HYPOTHETICAL TWO

Return now to the present day (i.e., post-Williams Act enactment). Liza of Slash/Burn LLP has hired Sparrow Securities to assist her in her effort to take over Sleeping Bear. She has directed Sparrow to buy up quietly 4.9% of Sleeping Bear's common stock. She also instructs Sparrow to contact institutional investors with stakes in Sleeping Bear to sound out their receptiveness to a potential takeover. Sparrow contacts Berkeley's Public Employee Retirement System (BEPERS) and Milberg Investments, a hedge fund. BEPERS and Milberg hold 6% and 8%, respectively, of Sleeping Bear's common stock. Both have previously filed Schedule 13Gs disclosing their holdings in Sleeping Bear. BEPERS acknowledges that Sleeping Bear has "underperformed," but is happy with Sleeping Bear's "commitment to the community." At the right price, however, BEPERS says it could be persuaded to support a tender offer. Milberg is less equivocal—it says that Ben "has got to go" and that it has been contemplating a proxy contest to oust him and replace him with someone possessing "more hard-nosed business sense." Milberg says that a tender offer might be an attractive alternative to a proxy contest—at the right price. Does a Schedule 13D need to be filed? By whom?

III. TENDER OFFERS

Section 14(d) of the Exchange Act imposes both disclosure obligations and substantive requirements on persons making a tender offer for more than 5% of an issuer's equity securities. Section 14(e) of the Exchange Act imposes antifraud and anti-manipulation obligations on all forms of tender offers. We will discuss those requirements in detail below. In order for those requirements to apply, however, we first need to address a threshold question: What is a "tender offer"?

A.   WHAT IS A "TENDER OFFER"?

Not all offers to purchase shares fall into the definition of a tender offer. If a potential acquiror simply negotiates to purchase a control block of shares from the owner of the shares, this one-on-one transaction is not a tender offer. Similarly, if an investor places a market order to purchases 100 shares of a particular public company, this relatively small order is also not a tender offer. What exactly should count as a tender offer (and therefore trigger the regulatory requirements of the Williams Act)?

Hanson Trust PLC v. SCM Corporation

774 F.2d 47 (2d Cir. 1985).

■ MANSFIELD, CIRCUIT JUDGE.

Hanson Trust PLC appeal[s] from an order of the Southern District of New York granting SCM Corporation's motion for a preliminary injunction restraining them, their officers, agents, employees and any persons acting in concert with them, from acquiring any shares of SCM and from exercising any voting rights with respect to 3.1 million SCM shares acquired by them on September 11, 1985. The injunction was granted on the ground that Hanson's September 11 acquisition of the SCM stock through five private and one open market purchases amounted to a "tender offer" for more than 5% of SCM's outstanding shares, which violated §§ 14(d)(1) and (6) of the Williams Act and rules promulgated by the Securities and Exchange Commission thereunder. We reverse.

The setting is the familiar one of a fast-moving bidding contest for control of a large public corporation: first, a cash tender offer of $60 per share by Hanson, an outsider, addressed to SCM stockholders [commencing on August 21, 1985].... [Hanson's initial tender offer provided, among other things, that after the tender offer Hanson may purchase additional shares through "privately negotiated transactions" or "another tender offer"]. [N]ext, a counterproposal by an "insider" group consisting of certain SCM managers and their "White Knight," Merrill Lynch Capital Markets (Merrill), for a "leveraged buyout" at a higher price ($70 per share); then an increase by Hanson of its cash offer to $72 per share, followed by a revised SCM–Merrill leveraged buyout offer of $74 per share with a "crown jewel" irrevocable lock-up option to Merrill designed to discourage Hanson from seeking control by providing that if any other party (in this case Hanson) should acquire more than one-third of SCM's outstanding shares (66 2/3% being needed under N.Y.Bus.L. § 903(a)(2) to effectuate a merger) Merrill would have the right to buy SCM's two most profitable businesses (consumer foods and pigments) at prices characterized by some as "bargain basement." The final act in this scenario was the decision of Hanson, having been deterred by the SCM–Merrill option (colloquially described in the market as a "poison pill"), to terminate its cash tender offer [on September 11] and then to make private purchases, amounting to 25% of SCM's outstanding shares, leading SCM to seek and obtain the preliminary injunction from which this appeal is taken. . . .

* * *

If Hanson could acquire slightly less than one-third of SCM's outstanding shares it would be able to block the $74 per share SCM–Merrill offer of a leveraged buyout. This might induce the latter to work out an agreement with Hanson, something Hanson had unsuccessfully sought on several occasions since its first cash tender offer.

Within a period of two hours on the afternoon of September 11 Hanson made five privately-negotiated cash purchases of SCM stock and one open-market purchase, acquiring 3.1 million shares or 25% of SCM's outstanding stock. The price of SCM stock on the NYSE on September 11 ranged from a high of $73.50 per share to a low of $72.50 per share. Hanson's initial private purchase, 387,700 shares from Mutual Shares, was not solicited by Hanson but by a Mutual Shares official, Michael Price, who, in a conversation with Robert Pirie of Rothschild, Inc., Hanson's financial advisor, on the morning of September 11 (before Hanson had decided to make any private cash purchases), had stated that he was interested in selling Mutual's Shares' SCM stock to Hanson. Once Hanson's decision to buy privately had been made, Pirie took Price up on his offer. The parties negotiated a sale at $73.50 per share after Pirie refused Price's asking prices, first of $75 per share and, later, of $74.50 per share. This transaction, but not the identity of the parties, was automatically reported pursuant to NYSE rules on the NYSE ticker at 3:11 P.M. and reported on the Dow Jones Broad Tape at 3:29 P.M.

Pirie then telephoned Ivan Boesky, an arbitrageur who had a few weeks earlier disclosed in a Schedule 13D statement filed with the SEC that he owned approximately 12.7% of SCM's outstanding shares. Pirie negotiated a Hanson purchase of these shares at $73.50 per share after rejecting Boesky's initial demand of $74 per share. At the same time Rothschild purchased for Hanson's account 600,000 SCM shares in the open market at $73.50 per share. . . .

Following the NYSE ticker and Broad Tape reports of the first two large anonymous transactions in SCM stock, some professional investors surmised that the buyer might be Hanson. Rothschild then received telephone calls from (1) Mr. Mulhearn of Jamie & Co. offering to sell between 200,000 and 350,000 shares at $73.50 per share, (2) David Gottesman, an arbitrageur at Oppenheimer & Co. offering 89,000 shares at $73.50, and (3) Boyd Jeffries of Jeffries & Co., offering approximately 700,000 to 800,000 shares at $74.00. Pirie purchased the three blocks for Hanson at $73.50 per share. The last of Hanson's cash purchases was completed by 4:35 P.M. on September 11, 1985.

In the early evening of September 11 SCM successfully applied to Judge Kram in the present lawsuit for a restraining order barring Hanson from acquiring more SCM stock for 24 hours.... Judge Kram held an evidentiary hearing on September 12–13, at which various witnesses testified, including Sir Gordon White, Hanson's United States Chairman, two Rothschild representatives (Pirie and Gerald Goldsmith).... Sir Gordon White testified that on September 11, 1985, after learning of the $74 per share SCM–Merrill leveraged buyout tender offer with its "crown jewel" irrevocable "lock-up" option to Merrill, he instructed Pirie to terminate Hanson's $72 per share tender offer, and that only thereafter did he discuss the possibility of Hanson making market purchases of SCM stock. Pirie testified that the question of buying stock may have been discussed in the late forenoon of September 11 and that he had told White that he was having Hanson's New York counsel look into whether such cash purchases were legally permissible.

SCM argued before Judge Kram (and argues here) that Hanson's cash purchases immediately following its termination of its $72 per share tender offer amounted to a de facto continuation of Hanson's tender offer, designed to avoid the strictures of § 14(d) of the Williams Act, and that unless a preliminary injunction issued SCM and its shareholders would be irreparably injured because Hanson would acquire enough shares to defeat the SCM–Merrill offer.... The district court, characterizing Hanson's stock purchases as "a deliberate attempt to do an 'end run' around the requirements of the Williams Act," made no finding on the question of whether Hanson had decided to make the purchases of SCM before or after it dropped its tender offer but concluded that even if the decision had been made after it terminated its offer preliminary injunctive relief should issue. From this decision Hanson appeals.

DISCUSSION

* * *

[T]his appeal turns on whether the district court erred as a matter of law in holding that when Hanson terminated its offer and immediately thereafter made private purchases of a substantial share of the target company's outstanding stock, the purchases became a "tender offer" within the meaning of § 14(d) of the Williams Act. Absent any express definition of "tender offer" in the Act, the answer requires a brief review of the background and purposes of § 14(d).

Congress adopted § 14(d) in 1968 "in response to the growing use of cash tender offers as a means of achieving corporate takeovers ... which ... removed a substantial number of corporate control contests from the reach of existing disclosure requirements of the federal securities laws."

The typical tender offer, as described in the Congressional debates, hearings and reports on the Williams Act, consisted of a general, publicized bid by an individual or group to buy shares of a publicly-owned company, the shares of which were traded on a national securities exchange, at a price substantially above the current market price. The offer was usually accompanied by newspaper and other publicity, a time limit for tender of shares in response to it, and a provision fixing a quantity limit on the total number of shares of the target company that would be purchased.

Prior to the Williams Act a tender offeror had no obligation to disclose any information to shareholders when making a bid. The Report of the Senate Committee on Banking and Currency aptly described the situation: "by using a cash tender offer the person seeking control can operate in almost complete secrecy. At present, the law does not even require that he disclose his identity, the source of his funds, who his associates are, or what he intends to do if he gains control of the corporation." The average shareholder, pressured by the fact that the tender offer would be available for only a short time and restricted to a limited number of shares, was forced "with severely limited information, [to] decide what course of action he should take." . . .

The purpose of the Williams Act was, accordingly, to protect the shareholders from that dilemma by insuring "that public shareholders who are confronted by a cash tender offer for their stock will not be required to respond without adequate information."

Congress took "extreme care," however, when protecting shareholders, to avoid "tipping the balance of regulation either in favor of management or in favor of the person making the takeover bid." Indeed, the initial draft of the bill, proposed in 1965, had been designed to prevent "proud old companies [from being] reduced to corporate shells after white-collar pirates have seized control." Williams withdrew that draft following claims that it was too biased in favor of incumbent management. In the end, Congress considered it crucial that the act be neutral and place " 'investors on an equal footing with the takeover bidder' . . . without favoring either the tender offeror or existing management."

Congress finally settled upon a statute requiring a tender offer solicitor seeking beneficial ownership of more than 5% of the outstanding shares of any class of any equity security registered on a national securities exchange first to file with the SEC a statement containing certain information specified in § 13(d)(1) of the Act, as amplified by SEC rules and regulations. Congress' failure to define "tender offer" was deliberate. Aware of "the almost infinite variety in the terms of most tender offers" and concerned that a rigid definition would be evaded, Congress left to the court and the SEC the flexibility to define the term.

Although § 14(d)(1) clearly applies to "classic" tender offers of the type described above, courts soon recognized that in the case of privately negotiated transactions or solicitations for private purchases of stock many of the conditions leading to the enactment of § 14(d) for the most part do not exist. The number and percentage of stockholders are usually far less than those involved in public offers. The solicitation involves less publicity than a public tender offer or none. The solicitees, who are frequently directors, officers or substantial stockholders of the target, are more apt to be sophisticated, inquiring or knowledgeable concerning the target's business, the solicitor's objectives, and the impact of the solicitation on the target's business prospects. In short, the solicitee in the private transaction is less likely to be pressured, confused, or ill-informed regarding the businesses and decisions at stake than solicitees who are the subjects of a public tender offer.

These differences between public and private securities transactions have led most courts to rule that private transactions or open market purchases do not qualify as a "tender offer" requiring the purchaser to meet the pre-filing strictures of § 14(d). The borderline between public solicitations and privately negotiated stock purchases is not bright and it is frequently difficult to determine whether transactions falling close to the line or in a type of "no man's land" are "tender offers" or private deals. This has led some to advocate a broader interpretation of the term "tender offer" ... and to adopt the eight-factor "test" of what is a tender offer, which was recommended by the SEC:

(1) active and widespread solicitation of public shareholders for the shares of an issuer;

(2) solicitation made for a substantial percentage of the issuer's stock;

(3) offer to purchase made at a premium over the prevailing market price;

(4) terms of the offer are firm rather than negotiable;

(5) offer contingent on the tender of a fixed number of shares, often subject to a fixed maximum number to be purchased;

(6) offer open only for a limited period of time;

(7) offeree subjected to pressure to sell his stock;

(8) public announcements of a purchasing program concerning the target company precede or accompany rapid accumulation of large amounts of the target company's securities.

Although many of the above-listed factors are relevant for purposes of determining whether a given solicitation amounts to a tender offer, the elevation of such a list to a mandatory "litmus test" appears to be both unwise and unnecessary. As even the advocates of the proposed test recognize, in any given case a solicitation may constitute a tender offer even though some of the eight factors are absent or, when many factors are present, the solicitation may nevertheless not amount to a tender offer because the missing factors outweigh those present....

[S]ince the purpose of § 14(d) is to protect the ill-informed solicitee, the question of whether a solicitation constitutes a "tender offer" within the meaning of § 14(d) turns on whether, viewing the transaction in the light of the totality of circumstances, there appears to be a likelihood that unless the pre-acquisition filing strictures of that statute are followed there will be a substantial risk that solicitees will lack information needed to make a carefully considered appraisal of the proposal put before them.

Applying this standard, we are persuaded on the undisputed facts that Hanson's September 11 negotiation of five private purchases and one open market purchase of SCM shares, totalling 25% of SCM's outstanding stock, did not under the circumstances constitute a "tender offer" within the meaning of the Williams Act. Putting aside for the moment the events preceding the purchases, there can be little doubt that the privately negotiated purchases would not, standing alone, qualify as a tender offer, for the following reasons:

(1) In a market of 22,800 SCM shareholders the number of SCM sellers here involved, six in all, was miniscule compared with the numbers involved in public solicitations of the type against which the Act was directed.

(2) At least five of the sellers were highly sophisticated professionals, knowledgeable in the market place and well aware of the essential facts needed to exercise their professional skills and to appraise Hanson's offer. . . .

(3) The sellers were not "pressured" to sell their shares by any conduct that the Williams Act was designed to alleviate, but by the forces of the market place. Indeed, in the case of Mutual Shares there was no initial solicitation by Hanson; the offer to sell was initiated by Mr. Price of Mutual Shares. Although each of the Hanson purchases was made for $73.50 per share, in most instances this price was the result of private negotiations after the sellers sought higher prices and in one case price protection, demands which were refused. The $73.50 price was not fixed in advance by Hanson. Moreover, the sellers remained free to accept the $74 per share tender offer made by the SCM–Merrill group.

(4) There was no active or widespread advance publicity or public solicitation, which is one of the earmarks of a conventional tender offer. Arbitrageurs might conclude from ticker tape reports of two large anonymous transactions that Hanson must be the buyer. However, liability for solicitation may not be predicated upon disclosures mandated by Stock Exchange Rules.

(5) The price received by the six sellers, $73.50 per share, unlike that appearing in most tender offers, can scarcely be dignified with the label "premium." The stock market price on September 11 ranged from $72.50 to $73.50 per share. Although risk arbitrageurs sitting on large holdings might reap sizeable profits from sales to Hanson at $73.50, depending on their own purchase costs, they stood to gain even more if the SCM–Merrill offer of $74 should succeed, as it apparently would if they tendered their shares to it. Indeed, the $73.50 price, being at most $1 over market or 1.4% higher than the market price, did not meet the SEC's proposed definition of a premium, which is $2.00 per share or 5% above market price, whichever is greater.

(6) Unlike most tender offers, the purchases were not made contingent upon Hanson's acquiring a fixed minimum number or percentage of SCM's outstanding shares. Once an agreement with each individual seller was

reached, Hanson was obligated to buy, regardless what total percentage of stock it might acquire. Indeed, it does not appear that Hanson had fixed in its mind a firm limit on the amount of SCM shares it was willing to buy.

(7) Unlike most tender offers, there was no general time limit within which Hanson would make purchases of SCM stock. Concededly, cash transactions are normally immediate but, assuming an inability on the part of a seller and Hanson to agree at once on a price, nothing prevented a resumption of negotiations by each of the parties except the arbitrageurs' speculation that once Hanson acquired 33 1/3% or an amount just short of that figure it would stop buying.

In short, the totality of circumstances that existed on September 11 did not evidence any likelihood that unless Hanson was required to comply with § 14(d)(1)'s pre-acquisition filing and waiting-period requirements there would be a substantial risk of ill-considered sales of SCM stock by ill-informed shareholders.

There remains the question whether Hanson's private purchases take on a different hue, requiring them to be treated as a "de facto" continuation of its earlier tender offer, when considered in the context of Hanson's earlier acknowledged tender offer, the competing offer of SCM–Merrill and Hanson's termination of its tender offer. After reviewing all of the undisputed facts we conclude that the district court erred in so holding.

In the first place, we find no record support for the contention by SCM that Hanson's September 11 termination of its outstanding tender offer was false, fraudulent or ineffective. Hanson's termination notice was clear, unequivocal and straightforward. Directions were given, and presumably are being followed, to return all of the tendered shares to the SCM shareholders who tendered them. Hanson also filed with the SEC a statement pursuant to § 14(d)(1) of the Williams Act terminating its tender offer. As a result, at the time when Hanson made its September 11 private purchases of SCM stock it owned no SCM stock other than those shares revealed in its § 14(d) pre-acquisition report filed with the SEC on August 26, 1985.

The reason for Hanson's termination of its tender offer is not disputed: in view of SCM's grant of what Hanson conceived to be a "poison pill" lock-up option to Merrill, Hanson, if it acquired control of SCM, would have a company denuded as the result of its sale of its consumer food and pigment businesses to Merrill at what Hanson believed to be bargain prices. Thus, Hanson's termination of its tender offer was final; there was no tender offer to be "continued." Hanson was unlikely to "shoot itself in the foot" by triggering what it believed to be a "poison pill". . . .

Nor does the record support SCM's contention that Hanson had decided, before terminating its tender offer, to engage in cash purchases. Judge Kram referred only to evidence that "Hanson had considered open market purchases before it announced that the tender offer was dropped" (emphasis added) but made no finding to that effect. Absent evidence or a finding that Hanson had decided to seek control of SCM through purchases of its stock, no duty of disclosure existed under the federal securities laws.

Second, Hanson had expressly reserved the right in its August 26, 1985, pre-acquisition tender offer filing papers, whether or not tendered shares were purchased, "thereafter ... to purchase additional Shares in the open market, in privately negotiated transactions, through another tender offer or otherwise." Thus, Hanson's privately negotiated purchases could hardly have taken the market by surprise. Indeed, professional arbitrageurs and market experts rapidly concluded that it was Hanson which was making the post-termination purchases.

Last, Hanson's prior disclosures of essential facts about itself and SCM in the pre-acquisition papers it filed on August 26, 1985, with the SEC pursuant to § 14(d)(1), are wholly inconsistent with the district court's characterization of Hanson's later private purchases as "a deliberate attempt to do an 'end run' around the requirements of the Williams Act." On the contrary, the record shows that Hanson had already filed with the SEC and made public substantially the same information as SCM contends that Hanson should have filed before making the cash purchases. The term "tender offer," although left somewhat flexible by Congress' decision not to define it, nevertheless remains a word of art. Section 14(d)(1) was never intended to apply to every acquisition of more than 5% of a public company's stock. If that were the case there would be no need for § 13(d)(1), which requires a person, after acquiring more than 5%, to furnish the issuer, stock exchange and the SEC with certain pertinent information. Yet the expansive definition of "tender offer" advocated by SCM, and to some extent by the SEC as amicus, would go far toward rendering § 13(d)(1) a dead letter. In the present case, we were advised by Hanson's counsel upon argument on September 23 that on that date it was filing with the SEC the information required by § 13(d)(1) of the Williams Act with respect to its private purchases of SCM stock. In our view this is all that is required by the Act in the present circumstances.

It may well be that Hanson's private acquisition of 25% of SCM's shares after termination of Hanson's tender offer was designed to block the SCM–Merrill leveraged buyout group from acquiring the 66 2/3% of SCM's stock needed to effectuate a merger. It may be speculated that such a blocking move might induce SCM to buy Hanson's 25% at a premium or lead to negotiations between the parties designed to resolve their differences. But we know of no provision in the federal securities laws or elsewhere that prohibits such tactics in "hardball" market battles of the type encountered here.

Thus the full disclosure purposes of the Williams Act as it now stands appear to have been fully satisfied by Hanson's furnishing to the public, both before and after termination of its tender offer, all of the essential relevant facts it was required by law to supply.

SCM further contends, and in this respect it is supported by the SEC as an amicus, that upon termination of a tender offer the solicitor should be subject to a waiting or cooling-off period (10 days is suggested) before it may purchase any of the target company's outstanding shares. However, neither the Act nor any SEC rule promulgated thereunder prohibits a former tender offeror from purchasing stock of a target through privately negotiated transactions immediately after a tender offer has been terminated. Indeed, it is significant that the SEC's formal proposal for the adoption of such a rule (Proposed Rule 14e–5) has never been implemented.... Thus, the existing law does not support the prohibition urged by SCM and the SEC. We believe it would be unwise for courts judicially to usurp what is a legislative or regulatory function by substituting our judgment for that of Congress or the SEC.

In recognition of Congress' desire in enacting the Williams Act to avoid favoring either existing corporate management or outsiders seeking control through tender offers the role of the courts in construing and applying the Act must likewise be one of strict neutrality. Although we should not hesitate to enforce the Act's disclosure provisions through appropriate relief, we must also guard against improvident or precipitous use of remedies that may have the effect of favoring one side or the other in a takeover battle when allegations of violation of the Act, often made in the heat of the contest, may not be substantiated. In this context the preliminary injunction, which is one of the most drastic tools in the arsenal of judicial remedies, must be used with great care, lest the forces of the free market place, which in the end should determine the merits of takeover disputes, are nullified.

* * *

QUESTIONS

1. The court says that "since the purpose of § 14(d) is to protect the ill-informed solicitee, the question of whether a solicitation constitutes a 'tender offer' within the meaning of § 14(d) turns on whether [there is] a likelihood that unless the pre-acquisition filing strictures of that statute are followed there will be a substantial risk that solicitees will lack information needed to make a carefully considered appraisal of the proposal put before them." Does the court only need to worry about the welfare of those being solicited? Are there other parties who might be affected by the solicitees' decision to sell to the bidder? Does tender offer regulation have the same goals as the regulation of securities offerings?

2. Why does the SEC favor the eight-factor test for a "tender offer"?

3. Would the court have reached a different result if Hanson had announced a new tender offer after its purchases of shares from Ivan Boesky and others?

4. Should there be a "cooling off" period during which purchases are banned after abandoning a tender offer? Alternatively, if a bidder makes a new tender offer after abandoning a prior one, should any purchases between the two offers be deemed to be part of the second offer?

HYPOTHETICAL THREE

Slash/Burn, with the assistance of Sparrow Securities, has assembled a 7.9% block of shares in Sleeping Bear. Liza, the managing partner of Slash/

Burn, has now filed Slash/Burn's Schedule 13D. The 13D discloses that Slash/Burn has purchased the 7.9% block for "investment purposes," but it reserves the right to switch to a tender offer or proxy contest in the future. The 13D also says that Slash/Burn may purchase additional Sleeping Bear shares if they can be acquired on "favorable terms." The market responds to the filing of Slash/Burn's 13D (and Liza's reputation) by pushing the price of Sleeping Bear stock from $12.75 to $15.00 on heavy trading volume.

Liza puts Sparrow Securities to work acquiring Sleeping Bear shares on favorable terms. She has Sparrow contact institutional investors with stakes in Sleeping Bear to offer to purchase their shares. Sparrow is instructed to buy up to 25% of Sleeping Bear's shares (which would give Slash/Burn a total of 32.9%). Sparrow is also instructed not to pay more than $18 per share. On Friday morning, Sparrow calls up Berkeley's Public Employee Retirement System (BEPERS), Milberg Investments, and six other institutional investors holding Sleeping Bear's stock. In the aggregate these institutions hold 35% of Sleeping Bear's stock. Sparrow offers each of them $17.50 for their shares. Sparrow tells them that Slash/Burn will not pay more than that. Moreover, the offer is only good until the markets close or "until we get what we need." BEPERS and four of the other institutions agree to sell their shares to Slash/Burn. Milberg asks, however, whether Slash/Burn is planning to do a tender offer. Sparrow refuses to answer the question. In the face of Sparrow's stonewalling, Milberg refuses to sell at less than $20.00 per share. The two other institutions also refuse to sell at $17.50. As result, Sparrow is only able to acquire 18% of the shares. Sleeping Bear stock closes at $17.00 on Friday amid rumors that Slash/Burn will be launching a tender offer.

After the markets close on Friday, Sparrow calls Gordon, managing partner of the Gekko Fund, a prominent "risk arbitrageur" that is rumored to have been buying up Sleeping Bear stock. After some haggling, Gordon agrees to sell Gekko's 5% stake in Sleeping Bear to Slash/Burn at $18.50 per share (bringing Slash/Burn's total ownership up to 30.9% of Sleeping Bear's stock). Have Slash/Burn and Sparrow Securities made a tender offer for Sleeping Bear? What result if Slash/Burn immediately announces a formal tender offer for Sleeping Bear shares after it completes these transactions?

B. TENDER OFFER REGULATION

In this part, we discuss the disclosure requirements and substantive regulation that apply to tender offers. The SEC's regulatory authority over tender offers under § 14(d), and therefore many of the rules the agency has promulgated governing tender offers, only apply to tender offers seeking 5% or more of a company's *equity* securities. (A parallel set of rules has been adopted by the SEC to deal with tender offers by the issuer for its own equity securities under § 13(e), termed a "repurchase tender offer." A more restrictive set of rules applies under Rule 13e–3 if the purchases by the issuer or its affiliates will result in the issuer's delisting.)

The SEC's rulemaking authority sweeps more broadly under § 14(e), which proscribes fraud in connection with tender offers. The rules that the SEC has promulgated pursuant to § 14(e) apply to tender offers generally, no matter the percentage of securities sought. It also reaches tender offers for debt, another hole in § 14(d). The difference between these rules pushes the SEC to fit its rules under § 14(e) to give them the broadest possible scope. It also pushes sharp operators to make tender offers for less than the 5% threshold, a loophole exploited by bidders in "mini-tender offers."

1.   DISCLOSURE REQUIREMENTS

The tender offer formally begins when "the bidder has first published, sent or given the means to tender to security holders." Rule 14d–2. The bidder can communicate information about the tender offer without formally beginning the offer as long as shareholders are not provided with the means to tender their shares and any written communications are filed with the SEC on the date of the communication.

The principal disclosure document required in connection with tender offers is the Schedule TO. The bidder must file Schedule TO with the SEC upon commencement of the tender offer. Filing the Schedule TO with the SEC is just the beginning. The bidder must also give notice to the target company, the market where the target company's shares are traded (Rule 14d–3), and most importantly, the shareholders of the target company (Rule 14d–6). As discussed in the SEC release below, the bidder has several options under Rule 14d–4 for notifying the target shareholders of the terms of its offer. Most commonly used is a summary advertisement in a national newspaper (the *Wall Street Journal* is a popular choice), followed up by direct mailing of the materials to the shareholders of the target company. The target company is obliged to cooperate in the mailing by Rule 14d–5.

Schedule TO requires information about the bidder and its plans similar to that found in the Schedule 13D. Schedule TO also requires, however, disclosure relating to the terms of the offer, e.g., consideration to be paid (i.e., cash, securities, or a blend of the two), what percentage of the shares are being sought, and any negotiations between the bidder and the target. If securities are to be offered as consideration for the tender offer, the offer is called an exchange offer. The securities being used as consideration must be registered under the Securities Act. Rules 165 and 425 exempt offers of this sort from most of the gun-jumping rules that we studied in Chapter 7.

The target company is required to tell its shareholders the company's view of the tender offer. Rule 14e–2 requires target management to disclose whether it: (1) recommends acceptance or rejection of the tender offer; (2) expresses no opinion and is remaining neutral; or (3) is unable to take a position. This disclosure must be made within ten days of the commencement of the bid and is accomplished through Schedule 14D–9. Rule 14d–9. Any material changes in management's position require updating of the Schedule 14D–9. Finally, Rule 13e–1 requires the target company to file notice with the SEC before purchasing its own equity securities—in open market transactions or otherwise—while a tender offer is pending. Repurchasing securities is a fairly common tender offer defensive tactic. The prospect of such repurchases (if at a premium) will cause shareholders to eschew tendering with a hostile bidder. Reducing the number of shares in the hands of outside investors may also concentrate ownership among incumbent managers and others supportive of the managers.

2. REGULATION OF THE TERMS OF THE OFFER

Unlike other areas of the securities laws, tender offer regulation goes beyond imposing disclosure requirements to specifying the terms of the transaction. The Supreme Court has characterized the impetus behind the adoption of the Williams Act as: "plac[ing] investors on an equal footing with the takeover bidder . . . without favoring either the tender offeror or existing management." *Piper v. Chris–Craft Industries, Inc.*, 430 U.S. 1, 30 (1977).

Disclosure was not deemed sufficient to level the playing field. Simply mitigating information asymmetries was not enough; Congress sought to constrain bidding procedures as well. The Williams Act endeavors to put shareholder-offerees on an equal bargaining position with tender offerors. Particularly as interpreted by the SEC in its rulemaking, the Williams Act also seeks to minimize distinctions among the shareholders who are being solicited. The table below summarizes those rules:

Description	Rule	Effect
Duration	14e–1	Tender offer must be open for at least twenty business days If price paid or percentage changes, the offer must remain open for an additional ten business days after the change
Withdrawal Rights	14d–7	Shareholders can withdraw their tendered shares anytime before the offer closes
Best Price	14d–10	Each shareholder must be paid the highest price paid to any shareholder in the tender offer
All Holders	14d–10	Tender offer must be open to *all* shareholders of the same class
Pro Rata	14d–8	If an offer for less than all of the shares is oversubscribed, the offeror must take up the shares pro rata from those shares tendered
Exclusivity	14e–5	Bidder cannot purchases shares outside the tender offer during the pendency of the offer
Subsequent Offering Period	14d–11	Bidder can purchase shares not tendered during the offering period for an additional three to twenty business days as long as it pays the same consideration paid in the tender offer

These rules enhance the bargaining position of shareholders confronted by a tender offer by increasing the potential for competition. The twenty business day minimum offering period under Rule 14e–1 provides an opportunity for competing bidders to throw their hats in the ring. Management is also provided with an opportunity to come up with its own alternative to the tender offer through a recapitalization or by seeking a "white knight." It is this specter of competition that drives the premiums that ordinarily accompany tender offers. It also means that target company shareholders are likely to extract most of the gains available from the transaction. That's the good news for shareholders. The bad news for shareholders is that tender offers are less likely to be made if acquiring control is more expensive for bidders. The tradeoff for shareholders: fewer bids, but at higher premia.

The minimum twenty day offer period is reinforced by withdrawal rights in Rule 14d–7. If a more generous bid comes along, the shareholder can withdraw her shares from the first offer and tender them to the higher bidder. Of course, the arrival of a higher bidder may induce the first bidder to raise its bid. If the first bidder ups the ante to induce more shareholders to tender, the shareholder who has already tendered also gets the benefit of the higher price. The smart money, however, just waits until right before the close of the tender offer period. The All Holders provision in Rule14d–10(a)(1) ensures that shareholders will be allowed to tender at any time. Moreover, the bidder cannot encourage earlier tendering by taking up the shares on a "first come, first served" basis; if the offer is oversubscribed, the shares must be taken up pro rata from among all those tendered pursuant to Rule 14d–8. The shares not purchased are returned to the shareholders.

Equal treatment of shareholders is also fostered by the SEC's rules. Bidders cannot favor institutional investors (who have more shares to tender) or management (who can make things difficult for the bidder if the tender offer threatens their employment) with a higher price, and they must make their offer available to all shareholders. In addition to the All Holders provision in Rule 14d–10(a)(1), Rule 14d–10(a)(2) ensures that each shareholder receives the best price for tendering her shares. Moreover, Rule 14e–5 prohibits the bidder from going outside the tender offer, during the pendency of the offer, to strike a separate deal with institutional investors, management, or any other shareholder.

The final rule in our table, Rule 14d–11, is a recent innovation, allowing the bidder to purchase shares after the formal tender offer on the same terms as the offer. Unlike the other rules, which attempt to influence the substance of the offer, Rule 14d–11 is more of a housekeeping measure. Its primary purpose is to allow the bidder that has succeeded in obtaining a majority of the shares—making control a *fait accompli*—to "clean up" the remaining minority shares held by the public. Getting 100% of the shares through this process is unlikely, but a bidder may well get to 90% of the shares. Reaching the 90% threshold allows the bidder to use the "short form" merger statute under state corporate law, allowing the bidder to "freeze out" the remaining minority shareholders without the formality (and attendant expense) of a shareholder vote on the merger.

HYPOTHETICAL FOUR

Recall Slash/Burn's 1967 tender offer from Hypothetical One (i.e., pre-Williams Act). The key terms of that offer were the following: Slash/Burn proposed to purchase 51% of the Sleeping Bear common stock at $20 per share, to be followed by a squeeze-out merger to eliminate the remaining 49% of the shares at $15. Liza planned to announce Slash/Burn's offer Friday afternoon after the markets close with the offer to remain open until close of business on Monday. The shares tendered into the offer were to be taken up on a "first come, first served" basis. Once tendered the shares could not be withdrawn. Liza planned to offer Ben, the CEO of Sleeping Bear, $22 for his shares. Which rules would this offer violate if it were made today? What does she need to disclose about her offer and her plans for Sleeping Bear? Are Sleeping Bear's shareholders better off with these protections in place?

3. ANTIFRAUD RULES

As with most of the disclosure requirements under the securities laws, the tender offer rules are bolstered by an antifraud prohibition. Section 14(e) tracks § 10(b) in prohibiting the familiar trilogy:

(1) making "any untrue statement of a material fact";

(2) omitting "to state any material fact necessary in order to make the statements made . . . not misleading"; and

(3) engaging "in any fraudulent, deceptive or manipulative acts or practices."

Like § 10(b), § 14(e) requires misrepresentation or nondisclosure. *Schreiber v. Burlington Northern, Inc.*, 472 U.S. 1 (1985). Also like § 10(b), the plaintiff must show scienter. *Connecticut Nat. Bank v. Fluor Corp.*, 808 F.2d 957 (2d Cir. 1987). Section 14(e) differs from § 10(b), however, in its transactional nexus: "in connection with any tender offer or request or invitation for tenders, or any solicitation of security holders in opposition to or in favor of any such offer, request, or invitation." This transactional nexus has two important implications. First, no purchase or sale is required, so non-tendering shareholders may have standing to assert a violation (although they may have difficulty in showing loss causation). Second, the provision reaches not only misstatements and omissions made by the bidder, but also the target company (or others, such as large blockholders) that may be responding to the offer. Not surprisingly, the broad reach of this antifraud rule has been an invitation to suits and countersuits by bidders and target company management, each alleging that the other side is playing fast and loose with the facts. Courts have reacted to the opportunities for abusive litigation in this context by denying both the bidder and the target standing to pursue money damages; only injunctive relief is available. *See, e.g., Piper v. Chris–Craft Industries, Inc.*, 430 U.S. 1 (1977). This restriction does not extend to target company shareholders, who can obtain monetary damages under § 14(e).

The SEC has bolstered § 14(e) with a number of rules intended to curb particular fraudulent practices. Rule 14e–3 (which we covered in Chapter 6) prohibits insider trading in connection with tender offers. Rule 14e–4 targets fraudulent practices by shareholders. It prohibits short tendering, i.e., borrowing shares to tender into a tender offer. Short tendering is mainly a concern with partial tender offers, in which shareholders may attempt to circumvent the pro rata requirement by tendering more shares than they own. For example, imagine that an acquiror has made a bid for only 50,000 of a total of 100,000 outstanding shares of a target company. Suppose that, with nothing more, 70,000 shares would be tendered, resulting in the purchase of 5/7th of each shareholder's tendered shares. Consider a particular shareholder who desires to have 1,000 shares purchased in the tender offer. The shareholder then borrows 400 shares and tenders 1,400. Assuming for simplicity that the pro rata share remains 5/7th, the shareholder will have 1,000 of his shares purchased in the tender offer (and the shareholder may then return the 400 borrowed shares).

Two other rules are aimed at bidders. Rule 14e–8 prohibits announcing a tender offer without the means to complete it. Announcing a tender offer is a particularly effective way to manipulate a company's stock price upward, allowing the person making the announcement to cash out his holdings when the market price jumps at the announcement. Rule 14e–1 requires prompt payment for the securities purchased in the tender offer. The opportunities for abuse presented by delayed payment are discussed in the SEC release below.

4.   SLIPPING IN UNDER THE RADAR SCREEN: "MINI-TENDER OFFERS"

"Mini-tender offers" are so-called because they seek to purchase less than 5% of a company's equity securities. Why limit an offer to such a small percentage? Because the rules under § 14(e) leave bidders considerably greater latitude than those promulgated under § 14(d), which only apply to offers for more than 5% of the equity securities of an Exchange Act reporting company.

Mini-tender offers became something of a cottage-industry in the 1990s. They offer a fascinating example of investor ignorance. Most mini-tender offers were made at *less* than the prevailing market price for the subject security. The bidder making the offer could purchase the shares and promptly resell them into the market, profiting from the difference between the tender offer price and the market price. Why would anyone tender into a below-market tender offer? Apparently at least some investors receiving a mini-tender offer automatically assumed that any tender offer would be at a premium above the market price and reflexively tendered without any investigation into the merits of the offer.

Lacking the statutory authority to proscribe such offers altogether, the SEC nonetheless felt compelled to crack down on mini-tender offers in the interest of investor protection, bringing a number of actions against bidders making such offers for violation of the anti-fraud rules. In 1999, for example, the SEC brought action against IG Holdings Inc. for engaging in over 200 mini-tender offers at prices below prevailing market prices.

The SEC also issued the interpretive release below, which discusses the basic structure of the tender offer regulatory regime and explains the purposes that the SEC believes are furthered by that regime. Does investor behavior in response to mini-tender offers tell us anything about the need for a regulatory regime for tender offers generally?

Commission Guidance on Mini–Tender Offers and Limited Partnership Tender Offers

Release No. 34–43069 (SEC 2000).

* * *

I.   Tender Offer Regulatory Scheme

* * *

Federal tender offer regulation is based on three statutory sections of the Exchange Act and our regulations adopted under those sections. The applicability of each section and its underlying regulations depends on: (i) the party conducting the offers, (ii) the nature of the subject security, (iii) whether the security is registered under Section 12 of the Exchange Act, and (iv) whether or not the bidder would own more than five percent of the securities after the tender offer.

A.   Section 14(d) and Regulation 14D

Section 14(d) of the Exchange Act and Regulation 14D apply to all tender offers for Exchange Act registered equity securities made by parties other than the target (or affiliates of the target), so long as upon consummation of the tender offer the bidder would beneficially own more than five percent of the class of securities subject to the offer. A bidder must include any shares it owns before the commencement of the tender offer in calculating the five percent amount. For example, if a bidder owns four percent of the target's securities before it commences the tender offer, it could not make an offer for more than one percent of the target's securities without triggering Section 14(d) and Regulation 14D requirements.

Regulation 14D requires the bidder to make specific disclosures to security holders and mandates certain procedural protections. The disclosure focuses on the terms of the offer and information about the bidder. The procedural protections include the right to withdraw tendered securities while the offer remains open, the right to have tendered securities accepted on a pro rata basis throughout the term of the offer if the offer is for less than all of the securities, and the requirement that all security holders of the subject class of securities be treated equally.[13] Also, Regulation 14D requires the bidder to file its offering documents and other information with the Commission and hand deliver a copy to the target and any competing bidders.

Regulation 14D also requires the target to send to security holders specific disclosure about its recommendation, file a Schedule 14D–9 containing that disclosure, and send the Schedule 14D–9 to the bidder.

B.   Rule 13e–4

Rule 13e–4 . . . applies to all tender offers by the issuer for its equity securities when the issuer has a class of equity securities registered under

---

13. This rule requires that the tender offer be made to all security holders and that the highest consideration paid to any security holder be paid to all security holders.

Section 12 or when the issuer files periodic reports under Section 15(d) of the Exchange Act. Rule 13e–4 also applies to a tender offer by an affiliate of the issuer for the issuer's securities where the tender offer is not subject to Section 14(d). Rule 13e–4 is different from Regulation 14D because it applies even if the class of securities sought in the offer is not registered under Section 12. Also, Rule 13e–4 applies regardless of the amount of securities sought in the offer. Rule 13e–4 provides for disclosure, filing and procedural safeguards that generally mirror those provided under Section 14(d) and Regulation 14D.

C.   Section 14(e) and Regulation 14E

Section 14(e) of the Exchange Act is the antifraud provision for all tender offers, including mini-tender offers and tender offers under Regulation 14D and Rule 13e–4. Section 14(e) prohibits fraudulent, deceptive, and manipulative acts in connection with a tender offer. Regulation 14E provides the basic procedural protections for all tender offers, including mini-tender offers and tender offers under Regulation 14D and Rule 13e–4.

Section 14(e) and Regulation 14E apply to all tender offers, even where the offer is for less than five percent of the outstanding securities and offers where the bidder would not own more than five percent after the consummation of the offer. Section 14(e) and Regulation 14E apply to tender offers for any type of security (including debt). These provisions apply both to registered and unregistered securities (including securities issued by a private company), except exempt securities under the Exchange Act, such as municipal bonds.

Regulation 14E requires that a tender offer be open for at least 20 business days, that the offer remain open for 10 business days following a change in the offering price or the percentage of securities being sought, and that the bidder promptly pay for or return securities when the tender offer expires. Regulation 14E also requires the target company to state its position about the offer within 10 business days after the offer begins. The target must state either that it recommends that its security holders accept or reject the offer; that it expresses no opinion and remains neutral toward the offer; or that it is unable to take a position on the offer. With a tender offer not subject to Regulation 14D, however, the bidder is not required to send its offer to the target. Therefore, the target may not know about the tender offer. The target should take all steps to comply with its obligations under Regulation 14E within 10 business days or as soon as possible upon becoming aware of the offer.

II.   Mini–Tender Offers

A.   Background

We have observed an increase in tender offers that would result in the bidder holding not more than five percent of a company's securities. These so-called "mini-tender offers" are generally structured to avoid the filing, disclosure and procedural requirements of Section 14(d) and Regulation

14D. These offers are subject only to the provisions of Section 14(e) and Regulation 14E. . . .

We are concerned that the substance of the disclosure in many of these offers is not adequate under Section 14(e) and Regulation 14E. We also are concerned that bidders are not adequately disseminating the disclosure to security holders. Further, we are concerned that many bidders are not paying for securities promptly at the expiration of the tender offer, as required by Regulation 14E. Recently, we have brought enforcement actions that address some concerns we have with mini-tender offers.

The offering documents in mini-tender offers frequently are very brief and contain very little information. Often, these mini-tender offers are made at a price below the current market price. However, frequently there is no disclosure of this fact in the offering documents or in any disclosure that the security holders ultimately receive. This lack of disclosure can mislead security holders because most tender offers, especially third-party offers, historically have been made at prices that are at a premium to the current market price. Many investors could reasonably assume that a mini-tender offer also involves a premium to market price. However, because of the lack of disclosure given to shareholders, it is often difficult for shareholders to determine the actual price that will be paid in the offer and whether it is below the market price.

* * *

B. Disclosure Guidelines

As discussed above, we believe security holders need better and clearer disclosure in mini-tender offers. To avoid "fraudulent, deceptive or manipulative practices" within the meaning of Section 14(e), we recommend that bidders in mini-tender offers consider the following issues in crafting disclosures in the tender offer documents that are provided to security holders.

• **Offer Price**: Price information is material to security holders. Because tender offers typically are made at prices that are at a premium to market, investors could reasonably assume that a mini-tender offer also includes a premium. Bidders should disclose clearly if the offer price is below the market price.

If the price offered is below the market price when the offer commences, the disclosure should clearly explain this prominently in the document. Also, the explanation should include the market price (or the bid and ask prices) on the day of commencement, or the most recent practicable date. . . .

Some mini-tender offers have been made at, or slightly above, the market price of the security. The offer is then repeatedly extended until the market price rises above the offer price. These offers generally do not have withdrawal rights. The bidder then purchases the shares below the market price. If the bidder intended never to purchase the shares unless the market price rose above the offer price, and did not disclose this intent, we believe that this would be a "fraudulent, deceptive or manipulative practice" within the meaning of Section 14(e).

- **Price Changes**: We believe that a bidder's intent to reduce the offering price based on distributions made to security holders by the target company and fees imposed by the bidder is material information. In describing the offer price, the bidder should disclose, if applicable, that the price may be reduced by any distributions or fees and the amount, if known. If the bidder changes the price, the tender offer would need to be extended for 10 business days as provided by Rule 14e–1(b).

- **Withdrawal Rights**: The ability to withdraw a tender while the offer is open can influence an investor's decision whether to tender. The bidder should disclose clearly whether security holders have the right to withdraw the shares they tendered during the offer. If no withdrawal rights exist, the disclosure should indicate that security holders who tender their shares cannot withdraw their shares. The disclosure should also clearly state, if applicable, that if the bidder extends the offer, the shares tendered before the extension still cannot be withdrawn and may be held through the end of the offer until payment. If withdrawal rights do exist, the disclosure should explain fully the procedures for withdrawing tendered shares.

- **Pro Rata Acceptance**: A pro rata provision has a direct bearing on the amount of time available for an investment decision. If no pro rata provision exists, the offer can, in effect, be open for less than 20 business days because shares will be purchased on a first come, first served basis. The bidder should disclose clearly whether tendered securities will be accepted on a pro rata basis if the offer is oversubscribed. If shares will not be accepted on a pro rata basis, the disclosure should describe the effect on security holders.

- **Target Recommendation**: Security holders should be advised, before an investment decision is made, that additional, material information will come from management of the target company. This disclosure is especially important in instances where withdrawal rights do not exist. The bidder should disclose that if the target is aware of the offer, the target is required to make a recommendation to security holders regarding the offer within 10 business days of commencement. We encourage the bidder to send the offering document to the target at the commencement of the tender offer so the target can comply with its obligation under Rule 14e–2 to make a recommendation regarding the tender offer.

- **Identity of Bidder**: Identification of the bidder provides security holders with insight regarding financial resources, capacity to pay for tendered securities, and historic business practices. The bidder should completely and accurately disclose its identity, including control persons of the bidder and promoters. For example, it may be meaningful to disclose the controlling security holders, executive officers and directors of a corporate bidder, or the general partner (and its control persons) of a partnership bidder. The bidder also should disclose any affiliation between the target and the bidder.

- **Plans or Proposals**: In deciding whether to tender, it may be material to know whether the bidder intends to continue the acquisition program at some future point. The bidder should disclose its plans or proposals regarding future tender offers of the securities of the same target.

- **Ability to Finance Offer**: Security holders need to know whether the bidder has the ability to buy the securities. The bidder should disclose whether it has the funds necessary to consummate the offer. If the bidder does not have the financing for the offer (e.g., cash or a commitment letter from a bank) at the commencement of the offer, the bidder should clearly state it cannot buy the securities until it obtains financing

Bidders in mini-tender offers often do not have the financing necessary to purchase the shares in the offer. In many cases they merely accept the shares in the offer and then attempt to sell those shares in the market and use the proceeds to pay the security holders who tendered. When the offer is made at a premium, bidders sometimes improperly hold the shares and wait for the market price to rise above the offer price before they attempt to sell the shares in the market. This plan is not disclosed to security holders. We believe this method of financing tender offers is inappropriate and may be a "fraudulent, deceptive or manipulative practice" within the meaning of Section 14(e). Rule 14e–8(c) expressly prohibits a person from publicly announcing a tender offer if that person "does not have the reasonable belief that the person will have the means to purchase the securities to complete the offer." Furthermore, this method of financing does not comply with prompt payment as required by Rule 14e–1(c).

- **Conditions to the Offer**: It is important for security holders to be able to evaluate the genuineness of the offer. We believe therefore that a tender offer can be subject to conditions only where the conditions are based on objective criteria, and the conditions are not within the bidder's control. If the conditions are not objective and are within the bidder's control (e.g., the offer may be terminated for any reason or may be extended indefinitely), we believe the offer would be illusory and may constitute a "fraudulent, deceptive or manipulative" practice within the meaning of Section 14(e). We believe the bidder should disclose all material conditions to the offer.

- **Extensions of the Offer**: We believe that a bidder's ability and intent to extend the offer period is material information. This information is particularly important when there are no withdrawal rights. Security holders will be unable to withdraw shares tendered even if the offer is extended and shares are locked up for an unexpectedly long time. The initial disclosure materials should state whether the offer could be extended, whether the bidder intends to extend the offer, under what circumstances the bidder would extend, and, if the bidder intends to extend, the anticipated length of any extension. If the offer is extended after the initial disclosure materials are provided to security holders, the bidder should publicly announce this fact.

C. Dissemination Guidelines

In enacting the Williams Act, Congress stressed the importance of not merely specifying disclosure requirements but also ensuring that information is communicated to security holders. The bidder in a tender offer must make reasonable efforts to disseminate material information about the tender offer to security holders. The failure to disseminate the disclosure frustrates the purpose of the tender offer rules.

Rule 14e–1(a) states that a tender offer must be held open for 20 business days from the date the offer is first "published or sent to security holders." Section 14(e) and Regulation 14E do not state how tender offers should be "published or sent to security holders." However, Rule 14d–4, which applies only to tender offers subject to Section 14(d) and Regulation 14D, provides guidance in this area: Rule 14d–4 sets out three alternative methods of dissemination for cash tender offers. The purpose of Rule 14d–4 is to add content and clarity to the term "published or sent or given" in Section 14(d)(1). Dissemination under Rule 14d–4 is deemed "published or sent or given to security holders" for purposes of Section 14(d)(1). These dissemination methods are as follows:

1. publishing the offering document in a newspaper;
2. publishing a summary advertisement containing certain information in a newspaper and mailing to security holders a copy of the full offering document upon request; or
3. mailing the offering document to security holders using a security holder list.

Rule 14d–4 also provides that these methods of dissemination are not exclusive or mandatory.

Depending on the facts and circumstances, adequate publication of a tender offer under Rule 14d–4 may require publication of the offering document in a newspaper with a national circulation or may only require publication in a newspaper with metropolitan or regional circulation. Publication in all editions of a daily newspaper with a national circulation will always constitute adequate publication for purposes of Rule 14d–4.

We believe that dissemination of material information using mechanisms the bidder knows or is reckless in not knowing are inadequate would be a "fraudulent, deceptive or manipulative" practice within the meaning of Section 14(e) and Rule 14e–1. For example, we believe that merely sending the offering documents to DTC is not an adequate means of communicating the information to security holders. DTC is not in business to, and in fact does not disseminate the tender offer materials to security holders. DTC sends only limited notice information to its participants about tender offers. Broker-dealers and banks have taken a variety of approaches in dealing with mini-tender offer materials. As a result, the bidder has no reasonable assurance that dissemination to DTC and then through broker-dealers or banks will satisfy the requirements of Section 14(e). Further, many bidders have refused to pay broker-dealers and banks the costs of forwarding information to security holders. Consequently, the tender offer document is not consistently reaching security holders to whom the offer is made. It is the bidder's obligation to assure that security holders get material information about the tender offer. If a bidder adequately disseminates the information to security holders through another method, such as one of the methods provided in Rule 14d–4, the bidder also may send the information to DTC for forwarding to its participants.

Also, we believe that only posting the information on a web site would not be adequate dissemination. Not all security holders have access to the Internet. By merely posting a tender offer on a web site, the bidder does not adequately publish the offer, nor is the offer deemed sent to security holders.

If a bidder makes a material change to the tender offer, the bidder must disseminate the changes in a manner reasonably likely to inform security holders of the change. The bidder generally should disseminate the change in the same manner as it disseminated the original offer.

D. Prompt Payment

Rule 14e–1(c) requires the bidder to pay the consideration offered or return the tendered securities promptly after the termination or withdrawal of the tender offer. The rule does not define "promptly." However, we have stated that this standard may be determined by the practices of the financial community, including current settlement practices. In most cases, the current settlement practice is for the payment of funds and delivery of securities no later than the third business day after the date of the transaction. We view payment within these time periods as "prompt" under Rule 14e–1(c). We understand that some bidders have waited up to 30 days to pay tendering security holders. We believe that this delay in payment is inconsistent with the prompt payment requirements of Rule 14e–1(c).

* * *

QUESTIONS

1. Is non-disclosure of the market price of a security that is sought in a tender offer a material omission?

2. Is additional disclosure likely to protect investors who tender into mini-tender offers at below market prices?

3. Is any useful purpose served by leaving tender offers for less than 5% partially unregulated? Should Congress expand the SEC's § 14(d) authority to include *all* tender offers?

4. Are the rules promulgated by the SEC under § 14(e) all necessary to prevent "such acts and practices as are fraudulent, deceptive or manipulative"? Is some other purpose being served?

HYPOTHETICAL FIVE

Slash/Burn has acquired 30.9% of Sleeping Bear's stock, and the most recent market price for Sleeping Bear stock is $17.00 per share. Liza, the managing partner of Slash/Burn, is now ready to make the big push to obtain control of Sleeping Bear. She files her Schedule TO with the SEC and delivers it to Sleeping Bear's headquarters and the Nasdaq. The tender offer is for up to 20% of Sleeping Bear's stock and the offering price is $20. Sleeping Bear promptly files its Schedule 14D–9 recommending shareholders not tender into the offer, which Ben, the CEO of Sleeping Bear, denounces as "lowball." Unfortunately for Ben, Sleeping Bear has a provision in its corporate charter barring it from adopting a poison pill. Sleeping Bear does have a $25 million line of credit with the Bank of Michigan, however, which Ben announces he will use to buy back Sleeping Bear shares in open market transactions. After filing the required notice under Rule 13e–1, Sleeping Bear begins buying up shares, succeeding in buying up 10% of the outstanding shares. Sleeping Bear's purchases also have the effect of driving the market price of its stock to $19.50.

Meanwhile, the response to Slash/Burn's tender offer has been tepid. When the offering period expired, Slash/Burn has managed to purchase only 10% of Sleeping Bear's shares. (Sleeping Bear employees hold 33% of the company's stock in their retirement plans and *none* of them are tendering.) Slash/Burn promptly announces that it has closed on the 10% of shares that were tendered, and that with the repurchases by Sleeping Bear, it now holds over 45% of Sleeping Bear's shares. Slash/Burn also announces that it is willing to pay the same $20 consideration for any and all shares tendered within the next ten business days. Slash/Burn does not have the financing to pay for the remaining 55% of the shares, but it figures that nowhere near that many shareholders will tender into the offer at this point, given the anemic response to the initial tender offer and the large percentage of stock held by Ben and the Sleeping Bear employees. Is this subsequent offer permitted?

5.   THE SCOPE OF THE TENDER OFFER

The complicated rules applying to the substance of tender offers create ample opportunity for interference with the other agreements typically entered into as part of an acquisition. Management compensation is an area subject to extensive negotiation in most acquisition contexts. Do the tender offer rules extend to deals struck between the acquiror and the target company's management?

Gerber v. Computer Associates International, Inc.

303 F.3d 126 (2d Cir. 2002).

■ PARKER, CIRCUIT JUDGE.

This appeal concerns a transaction in which defendant Computer Associates International, Inc., a computer software company, acquired On–Line Software International, Inc., another computer software company, by means of a tender offer and follow-up merger. Plaintiff Joel Gerber, an On–Line shareholder, commenced a class action in 1991 on behalf of On–Line shareholders who tendered their stock in CA's tender offer. Gerber alleged that, in acquiring On–Line, CA paid more money per share to Jack Berdy, On–Line's chairman and chief executive officer, than it paid to other On–Line shareholders, in violation of various provisions of the Williams Act and regulations promulgated thereunder.

... [A] jury returned a $5.7 million verdict for the plaintiff class. Judgment was entered on the verdict, and the District Court denied CA's motion for judgment as a matter of law or, in the alternative, for a new trial. CA ... appeal[s] and we affirm.

BACKGROUND

CA is in the business of designing and marketing computer software products. In July 1991, CA's chairman, Charles Wang, approached the chairman and chief executive officer of On–Line, Jack Berdy, to discuss the possibility of CA's acquiring On Line. On–Line, which Berdy founded in 1969, was also in the software business. Berdy owned 1.5 million shares of On–Line stock, representing approximately 25% of the company's outstanding shares. Berdy and Wang, as well as Sanjay Kumar, the chief operating officer of CA, negotiated extensively over the price that CA would pay for On–Line's stock.

Negotiations over the terms of a non-compete agreement proceeded concurrently with negotiations over the purchase price. CA insisted that Berdy and other On–Line executives, who would be leaving the company following the acquisition, agree not to compete with CA for a specified period of time, but Berdy initially resisted entering into a non-compete agreement. At one point in the negotiations, CA offered to purchase On–Line's stock (which was then trading at approximately $10 per share on the New York Stock Exchange) for $14 per share and to pay Berdy $9 million for a seven-year non-compete agreement. On–Line's Board of Directors felt that CA's offer of $14 per share was too low and that the $9 million offered to Berdy for his agreement not to compete was too high. The On–Line Board sought $16 per share, and the negotiations continued. Negotiations stalled when CA offered $15.50 per share and On–Line insisted on $16. CA and On–Line ultimately agreed that CA would offer to purchase On–Line's stock for $15.75 per share, and that CA would pay Berdy $5 million for a five-year non-compete agreement. The central issue in this litigation is whether the $5 million was compensation for Berdy's non-compete agreement or unlawful additional compensation for his On–Line stock.

On August 15 and 16, 1991, there was an unusually large amount of trading in On–Line stock. On August 15, the stock price rose $1, and the NYSE asked On–Line about the unusual trading activity. On the morning of August 16, when the stock price rose another dollar, On–Line told the NYSE that it was in discussions with CA and that a press release might be issued shortly. Berdy told CA that On–Line was under pressure from the NYSE to issue a press release. Around noon on August 16, On Line and CA reached their agreement at $15.75 per share, On–Line told the NYSE that it would issue a press release, and trading in On–Line stock was halted. Later that day, each company issued a press release announcing that it had reached an agreement with the other. CA's press release stated in relevant part that CA—

has reached an agreement in principle with the management of [On–Line] whereby CA will acquire all of the outstanding common stock of

On–Line for $15–3/4 per share in cash. The transaction is subject to the approval of the Boards of Directors of On–Line and CA, the execution of definitive agreements and regulatory approval.

On–Line's press release was very similar to CA's, except it also noted that "no assurance can be given that a transaction between On–Line and Computer Associates of any sort will occur."

After issuing their August 16 press releases, CA and On–Line continued to negotiate the terms and conditions of their agreement. They agreed that the transaction would take the form of a tender offer and a follow-up merger. On August 20, CA's Board of Directors approved a Merger Agreement, a Stock Purchase and Non Competition Agreement (the "Berdy Agreement"), and several related agreements. The CA Board also authorized the requisite Securities and Exchange Commission filings and the dissemination to On–Line shareholders of an Offer to Purchase. On August 21, On–Line's Board unanimously approved the Merger Agreement, recommended the transaction to On–Line shareholders, and authorized the necessary filings with the SEC.

Pursuant to the Berdy Agreement, which was executed by CA ... and Berdy, [CA's merger subsidiary] purchased Berdy's On–Line stock for $15.75 per share, the same price that CA offered to all other On–Line shareholders. The Berdy Agreement also provided that he could not tender his shares in the tender offer, and that, if another bidder made a better offer, [CA's merger subsidiary] retained an option to purchase Berdy's shares for $15.75 per share. The Berdy Agreement contained a provision prohibiting him from "engag[ing] in any business activities which are competitive with the computer software business activities of CA, [... or On–Line]" for a period of five years, in consideration for which CA agreed to pay Berdy $5 million. Berdy, who in addition to being On–Line's Chairman had been a medical student since 1989, was not restricted from "engag[ing] in the design, development, marketing, licensing or sale of computer software designed for use in the medical industry, in the biological sciences or as a teaching aid for educational purposes." Gerber argues that, because Berdy was disengaging from the business to pursue his medical studies, CA was not genuinely concerned about the possibility of his competing and that the $5 million payment to him—or part of it—was actually additional compensation to ensure that CA acquired Berdy's large block of On–Line shares. CA, on the other hand, insists that it genuinely feared potential competition from Berdy and that the entire $5 million was consideration for Berdy's agreement not to compete.

On August 21, 1991, CA and On–Line executed the Merger Agreement, obligating CA to commence the tender offer "as promptly as practicable," and CA ... and Berdy executed the Berdy Agreement. On August 22, CA and On–Line issued a joint press release announcing that the two companies had entered into an agreement and that CA "will make a tender offer today" and conduct a follow-up merger. The same day, August 22, CA filed with the SEC and disseminated to On–Line shareholders the Offer to Purchase, offering to purchase all shares of On–Line stock not owned by

Berdy for $15.75 per share. The Offer to Purchase stated that it would remain open until September 20, 1991. A majority of On–Line shareholders tendered their shares to CA, and CA ... completed the acquisition of On–Line with the follow-up merger.

Gerber is an On–Line shareholder who tendered his stock in response to CA's tender offer. He brought this action individually and on behalf of a class of On–Line shareholders ... who tendered On–Line stock to CA in the tender offer. The complaint alleged that several defendants had violated Section 14(d)(7) of the Securities Exchange Act of 1934 and SEC Rule 14d–10, as well as various other provisions of the federal securities laws, by offering and paying more consideration to Berdy for his On–Line shares than it offered or paid to other On–Line shareholders.

The gravamen of Gerber's Williams Act claims is that the $5 million that CA paid to Berdy, while nominally consideration for Berdy's five-year non-compete agreement, was actually additional consideration for Berdy's On–Line stock.

DISCUSSION

* * *

I.   Sufficiency of Williams Act Claims

Defendants challenge the legal sufficiency of Gerber's Williams Act claims. Section 14(d)(7) provides:

> Where any person varies the terms of a tender offer or request or invitation for tenders before the expiration thereof by increasing the consideration offered to holders of such securities, such person shall pay the increased consideration to each security holder whose securities are taken up and paid for pursuant to the tender offer or request or invitation for tenders whether or not such securities have been taken up by such person before the variation of the tender offer or request or invitation.

Rule 14d–10 provides in relevant part:

(a) No bidder shall make a tender offer unless:

>   (1) The tender offer is open to all security holders of the class of securities subject to the tender offer; and

>   (2) The consideration paid to any security holder pursuant to the tender offer is the highest consideration paid to any other security holder during such tender offer.

Section 14(d)(7) and Rule 14d–10 collectively are commonly referred to as the All Holders/Best Price Rule. Rule 14d–10(a)(1) codifies the All Holders Requirement, and Rule 14d–10(a)(2) codifies the Best Price Rule.

A.   Whether the Berdy Agreement Was Executed During the Tender Offer

Defendants' arguments regarding the legal sufficiency of the Williams Act claims focus primarily on timing. First, defendants argue that CA's $5 million payment to Berdy could not have violated the Best Price Rule because the Berdy Agreement was executed prior to the commencement of CA's tender offer, and the Best Price Rule is not triggered until a tender offer has begun. According to defendants, the tender offer did not begin until August 22, 1991, when CA disseminated the Offer to Purchase and issued a joint press release with On–Line explicitly announcing a tender offer. Gerber argues that the Best Price Rule was triggered on August 16, 1991, when CA and On Line issued press releases announcing that they had reached an agreement in principle. If defendants are correct, and the tender offer did not commence until August 22, then the Berdy Agreement preceded the tender offer and is not subject to the Best Price Rule. If Gerber is correct, and the tender offer commenced on August 16, then the Berdy Agreement was executed during the tender offer and must satisfy the Best Price Rule.

In order to determine when the tender offer commenced, we turn to SEC Rule 14d–2. In 1991, Rule 14d–2(b) provided:[2]

> A public announcement by a bidder through a press release, newspaper advertisement or public statement which includes the information in paragraph (c) of this section with respect to a tender offer in which the consideration consists solely of cash and/or securities exempt from registration under section 3 of the Securities Act of 1933 shall be deemed to constitute the commencement of a tender offer. . . .

Rule 14d–2(c) provided:

> The information referred to in paragraph (b) of this section is as follows:
>
> (1) The identity of the bidder;
>
> (2) The identity of the subject company; and
>
> (3) The amount and class of securities being sought and the price or range of prices being offered therefor.

Under Rule 14d–2(b), if CA's August 16 press release "include[d] the information in [Rule 14d–2(c)]," then the August 16 press release "shall be deemed to constitute the commencement of [the] tender offer." CA's August 16 press release states:

> Computer Associates International, Inc. ("CA") announced today that it has reached an agreement in principle with the management of On–Line Software International, Inc. whereby CA will acquire all of the outstanding common stock of On–Line for $15–3/4 per share in cash. The transaction is subject to the approval of the Boards of Directors of On–Line and CA, the execution of definitive agreements and regulatory approval.

This press release includes all the information listed in Rule 14d–2(c): (1) it identifies CA as the bidder; (2) it identifies On–Line as the subject

---

2. Rule 14d–2 was amended subsequent to the events giving rise to this litigation, but the parties do not urge us to apply the amendment retroactively.

company; and (3) it identifies "all ... outstanding common stock" as the amount and class of securities being sought, and "$15–3/4 per share in cash" as the offer price. CA nonetheless contends that its August 16 press release should not be deemed to have commenced a tender offer because the press release was not made "with respect to a tender offer," because the press release states that the transaction is subject to future conditions, and because CA issued the press release to fulfill certain disclosure obligations. For the reasons discussed below, we reject each of these contentions.

In arguing that its August 16 press release was not made "with respect to a tender offer," CA confuses the test for whether a tender offer has occurred with the test for when a tender offer commences. CA argues that, under the "totality of the circumstances" test of *Hanson Trust PLC v. SCM Corp.*, 774 F.2d 47 (2d Cir. 1985), and the eight-factor test of *Wellman v. Dickinson*, 475 F.Supp. 783 (S.D.N.Y. 1979), the tender offer began on August 22, not August 16, because those tests were not satisfied until August 22. As the District Court correctly found, however, *Hanson* and *Wellman* both involve the issue of whether a tender offer has occurred, not when a tender offer starts, and the parties here do not dispute that a tender offer occurred. Rather, the only question is when the tender offer commenced, a question which is answered by Rule 14d–2(c), not by *Hanson* or *Wellman* . . . . Here, however, it is undisputed that a tender offer occurred, and CA's August 16 press release announced a transaction that undisputedly was a tender offer. Thus, we have no trouble concluding that CA's August 16, 1991 press release was made "with respect to a tender offer."

CA also argues that its August 16 press release was not made "with respect to a tender offer" because the press release does not contain the words "tender offer." While the August 16 press release does not contain the words "tender offer," Rule 14d–2(c) imposes no such requirement. Because the entire purpose of that rule is to prescribe the information that a public announcement must contain in order to commence a tender offer, we deem it dispositive that the words "tender offer" are not among the Rule's prescriptions. To the extent CA asks us to graft an additional requirement onto Rule 14d–2(c), we decline to do so. "Were the label used by the acquiror determinative, virtually all of the provisions of the Williams Act, including the filing and disclosure requirements[,] could be evaded simply by an offeror's announcement that offers to purchase [ ] stock were private purchases."

We also reject CA's argument that the press release did not commence a tender offer because it stated that the transaction was subject to future conditions—i.e., the approval of On–Line's and CA's Boards of Directors, the execution of definitive agreements, and regulatory approval. Nothing in Rule 14d–2 or Rule 14d–10 renders them inapplicable to tender offers that are subject to conditions. Indeed, CA's ultimate Offer to Purchase, which CA contends commenced the tender offer, also states that the transaction is subject to certain conditions. . . . CA's August 16 press release did not announce mere "negotiations looking toward an offer"; rather, the release stated that CA and On Line had "reached an agreement in principle." Accordingly, whatever conditions remained after CA's August 16 press release do not prevent that release from marking the commencement of the tender offer.

* * *

B. Whether Berdy Was Paid During the Tender Offer

Next, CA argues that, regardless of when the tender offer commenced, the $5 million payment to Berdy cannot violate the Best Price Rule because Berdy was paid after, and not during, the tender offer. CA relies on Rule 14d–10(a)(2), which requires a bidder to pay to any security holder pursuant to a tender offer "the highest consideration paid to any other security holder during such tender offer." While Rule 14d–2 governs the determination of when a tender offer commences, no pertinent rule or statute addresses when a tender offer concludes. CA would have us create a rigid rule equating the duration of a tender offer, for purposes of Rule 14d–10(a)(2), with the offer's self-prescribed expiration date. Such a rule would benefit CA, as its tender offer "closed" on September 20, 1991, and Berdy was not paid until September 25, 1991. We believe that the phrase "during the tender offer," however, is flexible enough to include CA's payment to Berdy, which occurred after the shares had been tendered but before any other On–Line shareholder was paid. We deem it significant that Berdy was paid before all other On–Line shareholders, so that, if Berdy was not paid "during the tender offer," then neither was any other On–Line shareholder.

More fundamentally, equating the termination of a tender offer with the offer's self-imposed expiration date, as CA would have us do, would make it all too easy to contract around the Best Price Rule. For example, the Berdy Agreement required CA to pay Berdy for his On–Line stock at a closing which was to occur "as soon as practicable after the expiration of the [tender offer].... " If this agreement removed Berdy's $5 million payment from the ambit of the Best Price Rule, then the Best Price Rule would be rendered toothless. Rule 14d–10 "cannot be so easily circumvented."

In concluding that Berdy was paid during the tender offer, we draw upon our decision in *Field*, 850 F.2d 938, where we looked past the labels that the parties had attached to their transactions. In *Field*, defendants Julius and Eddie Trump commenced a tender offer at a price of $22.50 per share for the stock of Pay'n Save Corporation, withdrew the tender offer four days later, acquired an option to purchase the shares of certain Pay'n Save directors for $25.00 per share ($23.50 per share plus a $900,000 premium for so-called "fees and expenses"), then announced a new tender offer at $23.50 per share. The plaintiffs argued that the arrangement violated the Best Price Rule, as the Pay'n Save directors received $1.50 more per share than other Pay'n Save shareholders. The defendants argued that their agreement with the directors was not executed during a tender offer, as the agreement was executed after the original tender offer was withdrawn and before the second tender offer commenced. We refused to give effect to the defendants' use of the labels "withdrawal" and "new" tender offer. Instead, we focused on the Trumps' intent. Because the Trumps never abandoned the goal of their original tender offer, we concluded that the second tender offer was a continuation of the first, and that the Trumps had entered into the agreement to purchase the Pay'n Save directors' stock during the tender offer.

Like the defendants in *Field*, CA continuously pursued the goal of its tender offer, the acquisition of On–Line. We have already determined that the Berdy Agreement was executed during the tender offer, and a properly instructed jury determined that CA paid part of the $5 million to Berdy as compensation for his On–Line shares. Far from having abandoned its intent to acquire On–Line, CA paid Berdy in support of its tender offer. In assessing CA's intent, it is significant that Berdy was paid before all other On–Line shareholders. In purchasing a majority of the outstanding common stock of On Line, and in paying the On–Line shareholders for that stock, CA clearly intended to acquire On–Line. Thus, when CA paid Berdy in support of its continuous goal of acquiring On–Line, it did so during the tender offer. We noted in *Field* that "giving effect to every purported withdrawal that allows a discriminatory premium to be paid to large shareholders would completely undermine the 'best-price rule.' " Finding that Berdy was paid after, and not during, the tender offer would have the same effect.

In summary, the tender offer commenced on August 16, 1991, the date that CA issued its press release announcing its agreement in principle with On–Line and Berdy was paid "during such tender offer." Accordingly, we conclude that Gerber's Williams Act claims are sufficient as a matter of law.

* * *

NOTES

1. *Damages.* The remedy for violation of the best price rule is to bring non-favored shareholders *up* to the level enjoyed by the favored shareholder. Note that the damages in *Gerber* were more than double the amount by which the jury concluded that Computer Associates had overpaid Berdy. In cases where the executive being compensated holds a smaller percentage of the shares, the ratio of damages to overpayment can potentially be much greater.

2. *Defining the limits of a tender offer.* The Ninth Circuit applied a similarly flexible standard in defining the contours of a tender offer when confronted by a similar Rule 14d–10 claim. *Epstein v. MCA Corp.*, 50 F.3d 644 (9th Cir. 1995), vacated on other grounds, 516 U.S. 367 (1996). The Seventh Circuit, however, in the course of rejecting a Rule 14d–10 claim, emphasized the risk inherent in such a flexible approach:

> With millions or even billions of dollars at stake, precise definition of the blackout period is essential, and the SEC has accordingly consistently differentiated actions "during" an offer from those close to the offer's

beginning or end. The line is arbitrary, to be sure; it invites transactions that use the rules for personal advantage ("tax planning" is a respected specialty of the bar, while "tax evasion" is a felony); but some line is essential, and it had best be a bright one.

* * *

Accepting plaintiffs' request to treat the tender offer and the merger as a single step would imperil countless ordinary transactions—from two-tier tender offer and merger sequences (with different prices, or different forms of securities, offered in the two tiers) to simple employment agreements under which the surviving entity promises to employ managers for stated terms or give severance pay.

Lerro v. Quaker Oats Co., 84 F.3d 239, 243 (7th Cir. 1996).

QUESTIONS

1. Why would a bidder want to pay management more than other shareholders in a tender offer?

2. What is the danger of an amorphous definition of when a tender offer occurs and what is the benefit of the *Lerro* court's emphasis on predictability?

3. Does the Seventh Circuit's emphasis on predictability in *Lerro* allow clever corporate lawyers to evade the Best Price Rule?

4. How does the current Rule 14d–2 affect the ability of acquirors and target managers to contract outside the reach of the tender offer rules?

HYPOTHETICAL SIX

Recall that Slash/Burn's tender offer failed to obtain over 50% of the shares of Sleeping Bear (obtaining only 45% of the outstanding shares in total). Liza, the managing partner of Slash/Burn, has decided that it is time to make peace with Ben, the CEO of Sleeping Bear. (More importantly, Slash/Burn is not getting much of a response to its subsequent offer to purchase more Sleeping Bear shares.) Although the subsequent offer is still pending, Liza calls Ben and offers him $22 per share for his Sleeping Bear stock. Ben counter-offers to sell Liza his stock at $20, *if* she will agree to retain him as CEO for the next ten years (with an annual pay increase of $50,000 per year) and sign a new ten-year contract with Sleeping Bear's union, giving the workers annual 5% increases over the ten years and protection against layoffs. This deal will not allow Liza to achieve the cost savings she wants, but it will allow her to expand production in Asia, so Liza reluctantly agrees. Ben and Liza agree not to put their deal in writing until after the subsequent offer expires. Have Ben and Liza violated the SEC's rules under the Williams Act? Which ones?

*

INDEX

References are to Pages.

†